Peterson's®

Master the™ GED® Test 2020

PETERSON'S

PETERSON'S

About Peterson's

Peterson's® has been your trusted educational publisher for over 50 years. It's a milestone we're quite proud of, as we continue to offer the most accurate, dependable, high-quality educational content in the field, providing you with everything you need to succeed. No matter where you are on your academic or professional path, you can rely on Peterson's for its books, online information, expert test-prep tools, the most up-to-date education exploration data, and the highest quality career success resources—everything you need to achieve your education goals. For our complete line of products, visit **www.petersons.com.**

For more information about Peterson's range of educational products, contact Peterson's, 8740 Lucent Blvd., Suite 400, Highlands Ranch, CO 80129, or find us online at **www.petersons.com**.

ISBN-13: 978-0-7689-4369-6

Printed in the United States of America

10 9 8 7 6 5 4 3 2 1 22 21 20

Thirty-first Edition

Peterson's Updates

Check out our website at **www.petersonspublishing.com/publishingupdates** to see if there is any new information regarding the test and any revisions or corrections to the content of this book. We've made sure the information in this book is accurate and up to date; however, the test format or content may have changed since the time of publication.

Contents

PART III REASONING THROUGH LANGUAGE ARTS

PART IV THE SOCIAL STUDIES TEST

Credits

Excerpts from *The Fortieth Door*, by Mary Hastings Bradley

Obesity and Cancer Risk, National Cancer Institute website (www.cancer.gov)

Mystery of the Missing Waves on Titan, Science@NASA website (science.nasa.gov)

Adam's Needle, U.S. Department of Agriculture website (www.usda.gov)

Lead in the Environment, U.S. Environmental Protection Agency, Office of Superfund Remediation and Technology Innovation website (www.epa.gov)

Passage about "Migrant Mother" excerpted from *No Caption Needed: Iconic Photographs, Public Culture, and Liberal Democracy*, "Migrant Mother," by Robert Hariman and John Louis Lucaites; University of Chicago Press website (http://www.press.uchicago.edu/Misc/Chicago/316062.html).

Excerpts from *The Game*, by Jack London

Excerpts from *Journey to the Center of the Earth*, by Jules Verne

Excerpts from *The Story of a Pioneer*, by Anna Howard Shaw, D.D. M.D.

Excerpt from *An Autobiography by Theodore Roosevelt*, by Theodore Roosevelt

Excerpt from "The Yellow Wallpaper," by Charlotte Perkins Gilman

"How 3D Printers Work," U.S. Department of Energy website (www.energy.gov)

Excerpt from *Life on the Mississippi*, by Mark Twain

"Responding to Climate Change," NASA website (climate.nasa.gov)

Excerpt from "How Individuals Make Choices Based on Their Budget Constraint," *Principles of Macroeconomics, 2e*, by Open Stax, licensed under Creative Commons Attribution License v4.0 (https://open.umn.edu/opentextbooks/textbooks/192)

Before You Begin

You've decided to get your high school diploma by preparing to take the GED test. This is a great step! By now, you know that a high school diploma is a very important document to possess. With your diploma, you will be able to take advantage of training and educational opportunities beyond the high school level and increase your earning potential.

You want to do your best on the GED test, and that's why you purchased this book. Used correctly, this self-tutor will show you what to expect while giving you the most effective practice with subjects you can expect to see on the actual exam. Peterson's *Master the™ GED® Test* provides you with the necessary tools to make the most of the study time you have, including:

- **Top 10 GED® Test-Taking Tips** lists the 10 most important tips to help you score high on the GED test.
- **Part I** is essential reading if you are preparing to take the GED test. You'll find out about the overall structure of the GED test, what each section of the test covers, the scoring and passing requirements, scheduling and testing procedures, and what you need to do to get ready to take the exam.
- **Part II** allows you to dip your toes into the GED test waters by taking a Diagnostic Practice Test. Use the results of this Diagnostic Test to determine where you need to focus your GED test preparation.
- **Parts III–VI** review the subject matter for each test area of the GED test—Reasoning Through Language Arts, Social Studies, Science, and Mathematical Reasoning—and offer you powerful strategies for attacking every question type you'll encounter in the actual exam.
- **Part VII** consists of two full-length Practice Tests, with answer explanations for each question. Each test contains a number and mix of question types similar to what you'll encounter on the actual exam. To accurately measure your performance on these Practice Tests, be sure to adhere strictly to the stated time limits for each section.
- **The Appendixes** include a Word List to help boost your vocabulary for ALL of the sections of the GED test and the Mathematics Formula Guide.

THE DIAGNOSTIC PRACTICE TEST AND PROCESS

The diagnostic practice test does more than give you testing experience. It helps you recognize your strengths and pinpoint areas that need improvement. By understanding your "testing profile," you can immediately address your weak areas by working through the relevant review chapters, learning the pertinent test-taking tips, and studying the numerous examples and explanations provided.

The Review Sections

The Reasoning Through Language Arts section provides an opportunity to improve your language skills, which are necessary for good performance in reading, writing, and in all other academic areas. The reading selections consist of a wide range of reading matter, from nonfiction to a scene from a novel to business memos and emails. Writing questions will examine usage, organization, and mechanics skills in a variety of situations.

The Social Studies section covers history, civics and government, economics, and geography. The review will help you sharpen your comprehension, analysis, evaluation, and application skills for the actual exam.

The Science section reviews those subjects that will appear on the actual GED exam: life science (biology), Earth science (geology and oceanography), space science (astronomy), and physical science (chemistry and physics). The review will help you with your ability to recall and understand information, draw inferences and conclusions, evaluate data, and apply concepts and ideas to other situations.

The Mathematical Reasoning section provides user-friendly explanations of math processes in recognition of the particular difficulty that many students have in this area. The review, examples, and answer explanations will help you better comprehend the difficult concepts in the tested areas of numbers, number sense, and operations; data, statistics, and probability; algebra, functions, and patterns; and geometry and measurement.

THE PRACTICE TESTS

When you have completed your reviews, take the practice tests under simulated test conditions to sharpen your skills. Find a quiet place where you won't be distracted or interrupted, set a timer for the required time, and work through each test as though it were test day.

SPECIAL STUDY FEATURES

Overview

Each chapter begins with a bulleted overview listing the topics that will be covered in the chapter. You know immediately where to look for a topic that you need to work on.

Summing It Up

Each review chapter ends with a point-by-point summary that captures the most important items. The summaries are a convenient way to review the content of the chapters.

Notes, Tips, and Alerts

As you work your way through the book, keep your eye on the margins to find notes, tips, and alerts that will draw your attention to valuable concepts, advice, and shortcuts.

Access Two Timed, Full-Length GED® Tests Online

Peterson's provides you with access to two additional practice tests for the GED test. The testing content of these two practice tests was created by the test-prep experts at Peterson's. The Peterson's online testing experience resembles the testing experience you will find on the GED test. You can access two practice tests at **/www.petersons.com/testprep/product/ged-practice-tests/**. Enter the code **GED2020** at checkout.

Print or Online? You Decide!

In addition to the two online tests that are included with the purchase of this book, Peterson's now gives you the option to take the diagnostic and practice tests in Peterson's *Master the™ GED® Test* either on paper or online. Choose how you want to take them: on paper for a more traditional study approach, or online to simulate the actual GED test-taking experience, with automated timing, instant feedback, and scoring results. Take all the tests on paper, all online, or in a combination of the two. The choice is yours.

To access all your free online tests, go to **www.petersons.com/testprep/product/ged-practice-tests/** and select *Master the™ GED® Test*. Enter the coupon code **GED2020** at check out. *

* Coupon code is intended only for the original purchaser of the book and is valid for 18 months after the initial book print date.

WORD LIST

Vocabulary *as such* is not tested on the GED test; however, there are plenty of indirect and hidden vocabulary questions throughout the exam. The broader, more varied, and more accurate your vocabulary knowledge, the better your chances of answering questions quickly and correctly. To help you with this task, we've put together a list of about 500 commonly used words on the GED test, including hundreds of related words—words that are variants of the primary words or words that share a common word root. You'll find the Word List in the Appendix section. Use it to enhance your vocabulary study for all parts of the GED test.

YOU'RE WELL ON YOUR WAY TO SUCCESS

Knowledge is power. By using Peterson's *Master the™ GED® Test*, you will be studying the most comprehensive test-preparation guide available for the GED test, and you will become extremely knowledgeable about the new GED test. We look forward to helping you pass the GED test and obtain your GED test certificate or diploma. Good luck!

GIVE US YOUR FEEDBACK

Peterson's publishes a full line of resources to help guide you. Peterson's publications can be found at high school guidance offices, college libraries and career centers, your local bookstore or library, and online at **www.petersons.com**.

We welcome any comments or suggestions you may have about this publication.

Peterson's
8740 Lucent Blvd., Suite 400
Highlands Ranch, CO 80129
Email: custsvc@petersons.com

PART I

THE GED® TEST—THE BASICS

All About the GED® Test

Chapter 1

OVERVIEW

- **The GED® Test**
- **What is the GED® Test?**
- **The Four GED® Tests—At a Glance**
- **GED® Test Scoring and Passing Requirements**
- **GED® Test Availability, Scheduling, and Fees**
- **Retaking All or Part of the GED® Test**
- **Score Transcripts and Your GED® Test Certificate**
- **Getting Ready for the GED® Tests**
- **Obtaining More Information About the GED® Test**
- **Top 10 GED® Test-Taking Tips**
- **Summing It Up**

Congratulations on taking the first step to advancing your academic career. Whether you are taking the GED test to prepare for college entrance or looking for the career opportunities that become available after completing the GED test, you are not alone. Since 1943, more than 18 million people have earned their GED credential. It is estimated that in the United States today, 1 out of every 7 high school students will complete their education by taking the GED exams.

This book was designed to assist you in successfully passing all four of the individual tests in the GED test. The lessons in this book will help you develop skills essential to passing each test, and the individual subject reviews will help you become comfortable with the knowledge areas covered on the tests. The example questions provided throughout the lessons, along with the book's Diagnostic and Practice Tests (including access to two online tests), afford you plenty of practice with just the types of questions you will encounter on the actual GED test.

THE GED® TEST

According to the GED test makers, the GED test "measures the college- and career-readiness skills students need, and [it] prepares them with a basic level of computer literacy to compete in today's job market." The GED test is given entirely on the computer at official GED test centers. You'll learn more about this later in the chapter.

The GED test is aligned with Common Core Standards, a national set of standards designed to help students attain their highest potential. Many of the questions on the GED test require you to show *how* you got the answer—not just filling in a correct multiple-choice bubble. On the GED test, you will need to type, click on graphs, use a "drag-and-drop" feature, and more. But don't worry—Peterson's *Master the GED® Test* has just what you need to help you succeed on this important test.

WHAT IS THE GED® TEST?

The GED test is actually a battery of four standardized tests that measure skills required of high school graduates in the United States and Canada. The ultimate goal in passing these exams is a certificate that is equivalent to a high school diploma. A GED certificate can be useful for gaining admission to college, for obtaining certain vocational licenses, or for finding employment in the many types of jobs that require a high school diploma or its equivalent.

The battery of four GED tests are designed and administered by the GED Testing Service® of the American Council on Education® in partnership with Pearson. This new organization formed in 2011 to represent a public-private partnership. These tests (referred to as tests of General Education Development, or GED) were originally developed to help veterans returning from service in World War II regain academic skills and complete an education that had been interrupted by the war. Many returning veterans used this additional education to obtain civilian jobs. Since the 1940s, the emphasis of the GED tests has gradually shifted from knowledge required for industrial jobs to the kinds of knowledge and skills needed for today's information-driven world. In 2014, the test was revised to not only provide adults with a diploma equivalency, but also measure career- and college-readiness skills. This test is fully computer-based and includes "technology-enhanced items" in addition to traditional multiple-choice and extended-response essay questions. One thing has not changed, though: millions of motivated students like you have earned their high school credential by completing the GED battery of tests.

THE FOUR GED® TESTS—AT A GLANCE

In order to pass the GED tests and earn a GED certificate, for each subject area, you must demonstrate a mastery of skills and knowledge at least equal to 40 percent of high school graduates. The test measures a foundational core of knowledge and skills, ensuring that adults are prepared for college and careers. Each of the four tests is designed to gauge the same four broad skills:

1. Comprehension (understanding and interpreting information)
2. Analysis (drawing specific inferences and conclusions from information)
3. Synthesis and evaluation (characterizing, generalizing from, and making judgments about information)
4. Application (using information in ways other than those presented)

Of course, each of the four tests measures these skills in its own unique way. And to be successful on the GED tests, in addition to exercising this skill set, you must apply your common knowledge and your common sense, both of which are acquired through everyday experiences and observations, as well as through rudimentary education.

The GED® Test Structure

The GED test consists of four individual tests, all of which must now be taken on a computer-based testing platform, which allows for richer interactive test items. Each test covers a different component of standard high school curriculum, and it is aligned to GED Assessment Targets derived from the Common Core State Standards and similar standards in Texas and Virginia. The following table shows the various areas that each test covers, along with the number of questions available and the time limit for each test.

Test	Content Areas	Number and Types of Questions	Time Limit

Reasoning Through Language Arts	• Reading comprehension
	  ○ Informational (75%)
	  ○ Literature (25%)
	• Writing
	• Editing
		• 45–50 questions
		  ○ multiple-choice
		  ○ drop-down
		  ○ select-an-area
		  ○ drag-and-drop
		  ○ extended response
			150 minutes

Social Studies	• US history (20%)
	• Civics and government (50%)
	• Economics (15%)
	• Geography and the world (15%)
		• 30–35 questions
		  ○ multiple-choice
		  ○ drop-down
		  ○ fill-in-the-blank
		  ○ drag-and-drop
		  ○ select-an-area
			70 minutes

Science	• Life science (40%)
	• Earth and space science (20%)
	• Physical science (40%)
		• 30–35 questions
		  ○ multiple-choice
		  ○ drop-down
		  ○ fill-in-the-blank
		  ○ drag-and-drop
		  ○ select-an-area
			90 minutes

Mathematical Reasoning	• Quantitative problem solving (45%)
	• Algebraic problem solving (55%)
		• 46 questions
		  ○ multiple-choice
		  ○ drop-down
		  ○ fill-in-the-blank
		  ○ drag-and-drop
		  ○ select-an-area
			115 minutes

The GED test includes six question types—multiple-choice and five technology-enhanced items: drop-down, drag-and-drop, fill-in-the-blank, select-an-area, and extended response. Let's take a closer look at the question types.

Multiple-choice items have four answer choices consisting of one correct answer and three incorrect answers (known as distractors):

Multiple-Choice Example

Which of these animals is a reptile?

- ❍ A. Condor
- ❍ B. Komodo dragon
- ❍ C. Lemur
- ❍ D. Salamander

NOTE

For your convenience in answering questions and checking answers, this book uses letter designations (A, B, C, etc.) for answer choices. Although the letters will not appear on the actual GED test, having these letters to refer to will make it easier for you to check your answers against the answer key and explanation sections.

To answer the question, you will click on the radio button next to the answer you want to select:

Multiple-Choice Example

Which of these animals is a reptile?

- ❍ A. Condor
- ● B. Komodo dragon
- ❍ C. Lemur
- ❍ D. Salamander

If you want to change your answer, simply click on another choice. Since there is only one correct answer for multiple-choice questions, your selection will be updated to the last answer you clicked.

Drop-down questions feature answer choices to be chosen from a drop-down menu embedded into the question. They will appear on screen as a box that says "Select."

Drop-Down Example

Cameron plays tennis every day after school. He is [Select ▼] to make the team this year. The coach has noticed his [Select ▼].

To answer the question, select your answer from the menu by clicking directly on the answer choice. Although you may encounter questions with multiple drop-down menus on the GED test, remember that there is only one correct answer per drop-down menu.

Drop-Down Example

Cameron plays tennis every day after school. He is [committed ▼] to make the team this year. The coach has noticed his [Select ▼].

Select
comitment
commitment
commentmint
committment

To change an answer, click on the drop-down menu and select the answer you wish to submit.

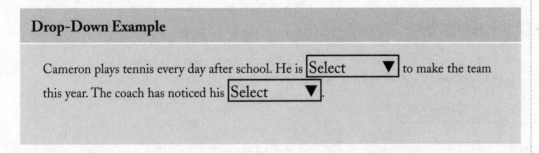

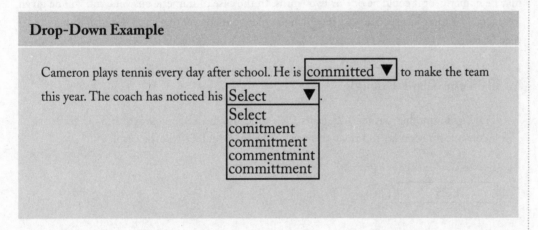

Fill-in-the-blank questions require you to type an answer. This question type will display an empty answer box.

Fill-in-the-Blank Example

Tilly's grandmother pays her 25 cents each time she feeds the goldfish. If Tilly feeds the goldfish from Monday to Friday this week, how many dollars will she earn?

Express your answer as a decimal.

[ ] dollars

To answer a fill-in-the-blank question, click inside the answer box and type your answer. The answer may be numeric, or it could be one or two words. In the case of numeric answers, you will be given instructions if there is a specific way in which to enter your answer (e.g., as a decimal, rounded to a specific unit).

Fill-in-the-Blank Example

Tilly's grandmother pays her 25 cents each time she feeds the goldfish. If Tilly feeds the goldfish from Monday to Friday this week, how many dollars will she earn?

Express your answer as a decimal.

[**1.25**] dollars

To change an answer you have entered, first use the Backspace key to delete what you have typed and then type a new answer.

Drag-and-drop questions are interactive tasks that will require you to use your mouse to move items (such as pictures, words, or numbers) to a new location on the computer screen.

Drag-and-Drop Example

Place the times of day in order (from earliest to latest) from left to right.

Times:

1:00 a.m.

8:45 p.m. **9:30 a.m.**

12:00 p.m.

To answer a drag-and-drop question, you will click on an answer and then drag it to the location of your choice and drop (release the mouse) it there. Repeat the drag-and-drop steps for each answer you wish to move.

Drag-and-Drop Example

Place the times of day in order (from earliest to latest) from left to right.

Times:

1:00 a.m.	**9:30 a.m.**	**12:00 p.m.**	**8:45 p.m.**

Once you have moved the item to its desired location, its original position usually will be empty. However, sometimes a copy of the answer choice will remain in its original position. When this occurs, it means you can choose the answer again to drop in another location.

To change an answer, click and drag an answer to another location or back to its original position.

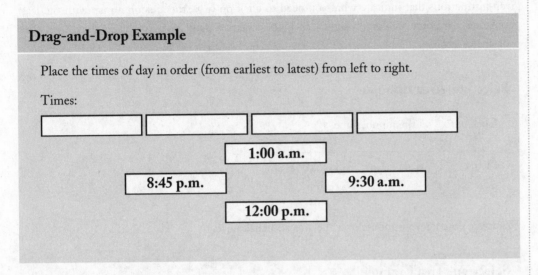

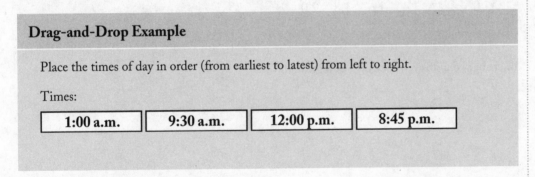

Select-an-area questions (formerly known as hot spot questions) require you to answer by clicking on an image. The image could be a graph, chart, coordinate grid, number line, or text. You will be given instructions that indicate what you need to click on (e.g., the area on a map with the least population, the point on a graph signifying highest sales, a point on a graph identified by its two coordinates, etc.).

Select-an-Area Example

Click on 1.8 on the number line.

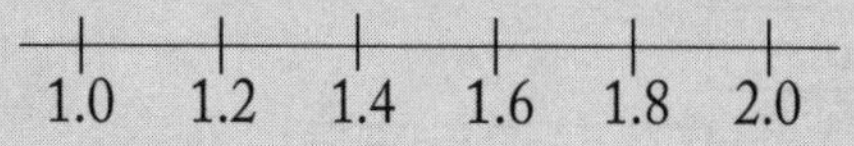

To answer, position your mouse over the area and click once.

Select-an-Area Example

Click on 1.8 on the number line.

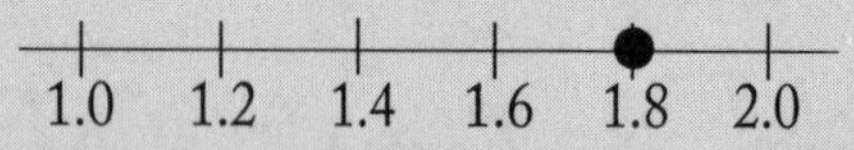

To change your answer, click on a new location.

Finally, there is one **extended response** item, located in the Reasoning Through Language Arts Test. The question requires you to analyze two source texts and produce a writing sample that meets the criteria in a set rubric. The interface for this question type was redesigned for the 2019 GED to make the instructions more accessible for test takers, to provide a larger writing space, and to allow for scrolling when reading the source texts.

To answer the extended response question will require you to type your analysis in the space provided. The interface is a simple text editor that includes a few word processing tools, such as cut, copy, and paste. The emphasis on this portion of the test is not on formatting; it is on presenting a sound, evidence-based analysis. For more information about extended response questions, refer to Chapter 5, "Mastering Extended Response" beginning on page 211.

The Reasoning Through Language Arts Test

The Reasoning Through Language Arts Test consists of 45–50 questions. There are three parts of the Reading Through Language Arts Test: parts one and three are made up of multiple-choice and technology-enhanced questions, while part two consists of an extended response essay. The technology-enhanced items for this test include select-an-area, drop-down, and drag-and-drop. Some questions are presented in groups—each group based on the same selection of text. The reading selections vary in length (400–900 words for reading comprehension, 350–450 for language comprehension, and 550–650 for extended-response passages) and are drawn from a wide variety of sources, including fiction and nonfiction, such as informational articles and workplace documents.

The reading comprehension portion of the Reasoning Through Language Arts Test does *not* test your knowledge of literature or other factual information. Rather, the test is designed to gauge your ability to understand, analyze, and draw reasonable inferences from reading material, as well as to apply what you've read. So everything you will need to know in order to answer the questions correctly will be provided in the selections of text. The language comprehension portion of the Reasoning Through Language Arts Test will test your knowledge and understanding of English language conventions and usage. The extended-response item will require you to produce a writing sample based on paired source passages. Your writing sample will be scored based on how well you analyze arguments, provide evidence, organize thoughts, and write fluently.

The Social Studies Test

The Social Studies Test consists of 30–35 questions. The majority of these are multiple-choice questions, but there are also technology-enhanced items. The technology-enhanced items for this test include drop-down, fill-in-the-blank, drag-and-drop, and select-an-area. Each question is based on a brief passage of text, a visual depiction, or both. As many as 20 of the questions may be accompanied by a visual (a diagram, table, graph, chart, cartoon, or other illustration). In some cases, the same visual applies to two or more questions.

The Social Studies Test is designed to measure your ability to understand, analyze, synthesize, evaluate, and apply a variety of social studies concepts in three main skill areas: Reading and Writing in Social Studies, Social Studies Concepts, and Mathematical Reasoning in Social Studies. These skills are applied to real-world social and historical situations in four content areas: civics and government (50%), US history (20%), geography and the world (15%), and economics (15%). (The version of the GED test administered in Canada covers Canadian history and government instead of US history and government.) The Social Studies Test requires that you apply your critical-thinking skills and knowledge in the context of social studies material, both written and visual. To succeed on the test, you need not memorize dates, names, events, geographical data, or other trivia. All the information you'll need to respond to the questions successfully will be provided.

The Science Test

The Science Test consists of 30–35 questions. The majority of these are multiple-choice questions, but there are also technology-enhanced items. The technology-enhanced items for this test include drop-down, fill-in-the-blank, drag-and-drop, and select-an-area. Each question is based on a brief passage of text, a visual depiction, or both. Many of the questions are accompanied by visuals (diagrams, tables, graphs, charts, and illustrations). In some cases, the same visual applies to two or more questions.

The Science Test is designed to gauge your ability to understand, analyze, synthesize, evaluate, and apply basic high school science concepts. The content areas covered on the test include life science, earth and space science, and physical science. The Science Test is primarily a critical-thinking skills test rather than a knowledge test. Most of what you need to know to respond successfully to the questions will be provided. However, the test does presuppose the basic level of science knowledge that most people have acquired through their everyday observations and experiences.

The Mathematical Reasoning Test

The Mathematical Reasoning Test consists of 46 questions. The majority of these are multiple-choice questions, but there are also technology-enhanced items. The technology-enhanced items for this test include drop-down, fill-in-the-blank, drag-and-drop, and select-an-area.

Mathematical Reasoning Test questions cover two areas: quantitative problem solving and algebraic problem solving. Some questions are based on visuals such as geometry figures and data presented in graphical format (tables, charts, and graphs).

An on-screen calculator (shown at right) is provided for two areas: quantitative problem solving and algebraic problem solving, but there will be five items that you need to answer without the use of a calculator. The items that allow use of the calculator emphasize number operations and calculations, while the items that do not allow calculator use place greater emphasis on math concepts, estimation, and "mental math."

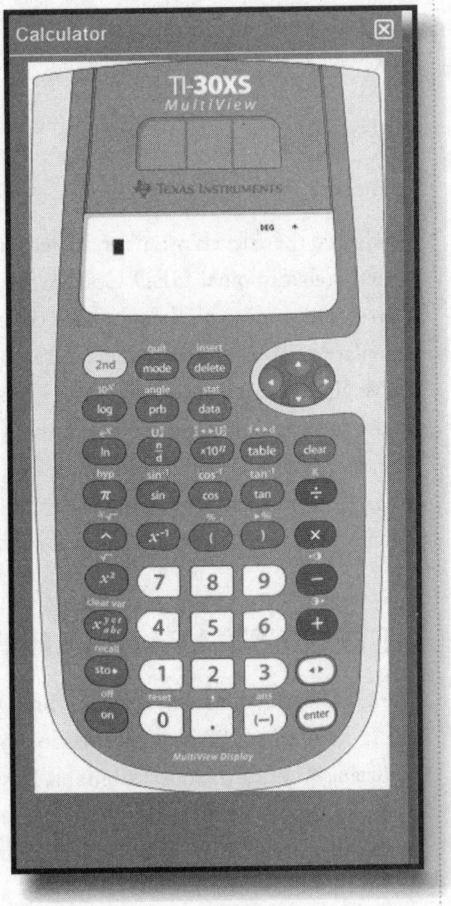

GED® TEST SCORING AND PASSING REQUIREMENTS

For each GED test, the more questions you answer correctly, the higher your score. No penalties are assessed for incorrect responses. Your extended-response answer will be scored based on a three-trait rubric by an automated scoring engine that replicates human scoring. These traits identify the qualities of the writing being evaluated. Your response is scored on a six-point scale, and each trait is worth up to two points, so the final raw score is 12 points. Your score for the extended response will be combined with your score for the rest of the scoring module for Reasoning Through Language Arts.

Each GED test section is scored separately, with a minimum score of 145 needed to pass each of the tests. This passing score has been set to reflect the abilities of current high school graduates. Test takers get individual score reports for each of the four tests (Reasoning Through Language Arts, Social Studies, Science, and Mathematical Reasoning).

These subject test score levels indicate the test taker's readiness for college, as shown below:

Score	Level Description
0–144	Level 1: Below Passing
145*–164	Level 2: GED Passing Score/High School Equivalency
165–174	Level 3: GED College Ready
175–200	Level 4: GED College Ready + Credit

*The passing score in New Jersey is 150.

So what do these levels mean for the test taker? GED Passing Score means what it always has—you've earned your diploma! GED College Ready means that you likely have the skills to take college courses. Depending on the school or college program for which you're applying, you may be able to skip placement testing, remedial classes, or non-credit classes. GED College Ready + Credit means you've already mastered some of the skills taught in introductory-level college courses. Depending on the school or program for which you're applying, you might be eligible for up to 3 Math credits, 3 Science credits, 3 Social Studies credits, and 1 English credit. If you earn GED College Ready or GED College Ready + Credit scores, be sure to check with your future school to see what their policies are. It can save you time and money once you start working on your program or degree.

ALERT

Beware of online programs that offer high school equivalency tests for a fee. GED tests are administered only at certified GED testing centers.

GED® TEST AVAILABILITY, SCHEDULING, AND FEES

The GED battery of tests is offered throughout most of the United States, every Canadian province, and in more than 100 international locations. The GED is not currently offered in Indiana, Iowa, Louisiana, Maine, Missouri, Montana, New Hampshire, New York, Tennessee, or West Virginia—but if you live in one of these states, you can register to take the test in a neighboring state that allows nonresidents to take the exam. The tests are offered in English, French, Spanish, large print, Braille, and even audio format. Special testing accommodations may be available for test takers with a diagnosed learning disability, Attention Deficit/Hyperactivity Disorder, emotional/mental health conditions, physical/chronic health disabilities, or any other condition that may interfere with a test taker's ability to fully demonstrate what he or she knows under standard testing conditions. For more information about the GED test and accommodations for disabilities, visit www.ged.com/about_test/accommodations/.

Testing centers are typically located at adult-education and community-education facilities. Some centers are located at military installations. Finding a convenient testing center should not be difficult if you live in a populous state. California, for example, boasts more than 200 testing centers altogether, across every county in the state.

You can find local testing centers by visting **www.pearsonvue.com/ged/locate/**. GED testing is scheduled through MyGED™ (**ged.com**). Each of the four GED tests can be taken separately, at any time, based on the test taker's preferences, scheduling, and readiness. (The total GED testingtime is more than 7 hours, not including breaks between tests—far too long for a single testing day.)

The number of times the GED tests are administered each year varies from one testing center to another. Each center establishes its own schedule. Centers in urban areas may offer testing every day, whereas centers in remote, rural areas may offer testing only once or twice a year. The GED Testing Service charges testing jurisdictions $40 per module, making it $160 for the complete test. Testing jurisdictions will set their own price for test takers, and the overall price will vary from state to state.

It is important to note that while the GED tests are taken on the computer, they cannot be taken online outside a certified testing center. Test officials strongly warn of fraudulent online programs that offer high school equivalencies for a fee.

RETAKING ALL OR PART OF THE GED® TEST

Once you receive your GED test transcript (see "Score Transcripts and Your GED Test Certificate"), you will be eligible to retake any or all of the individual GED tests for which you did not meet the minimum passing score. Most testing centers charge an additional fee for retaking all or part of the GED test. You may retake the same test no more than three times during the same calendar year.

At the time of retesting, you will be given a different version of the exam, which means that you will not be tested on the same questions you worked with previously. Multiple scores for the same test (for example, the Mathematical Reasoning Test) are *not* averaged. Only your highest score for each test is considered in determining whether you have attained the minimum passing score for that test.

SCORE TRANSCRIPTS AND YOUR GED® TEST CERTIFICATE

You will be able to access your scores online within 24 hours after your test is completed. Official and unofficial transcripts provide scaled scores, but they do not provide the number of correct or incorrect answers for any of the four tests. However, you will receive a comprehensive assessment of strengths and weaknesses along with a college- and career-readiness evaluation. Once you receive your scores, you may present it to a college admissions office or as proof for employment purposes that you have met all GED test requirements.

The GED test certificate is a separate document issued by the state where you took the GED tests. (Some states refer to this document as a diploma.) GED test certificates are generally mailed. However, most states require that you reach a minimum age before the certificate is issued to you. It is important to keep your certificate in a safe place because some states will issue only one to you.

NOTE

Some states allow you to obtain a digital copy of your transcript and diploma. To find out if your state participates in online credentialing, log in to your MyGED™ account and go to **www.ged.com/life_after_ged/**.

GETTING READY FOR THE GED® TESTS

Be sure to give yourself plenty of time to prepare for all four of the GED tests. Many GED test candidates find that taking a course with an instructor gives them the needed structure to accomplish their goal. Others have the self-discipline to study on a regular basis without the structure of a class. Regardless of which method you use, GED test counselors often recommend spreading out GED testing—rather than taking all the GED tests in a short period of time—to allow plenty of time to prepare adequately for each test.

Setting and Sticking to a Study Schedule

Let's look at potential GED test study plans. Pick the one that works best for you, depending on how much time you have before the test.

If you have six months or more before you take the GED:

- Review this chapter carefully to make sure you understand what the GED tests are like, and what's expected.
- Consider taking a GED prep class along with your solo prep. MyGED **(ged.com)** can help you find a course near you.
- Take the diagnostic test to figure out what you do well, what you need to work on, and how the test works.
- Read each strategy and content review chapter, and work through the examples and practice sections.
- Read all answer explanations.
- Take the two full-length practice tests at the end of this book, plus the online practice tests.
- Based on your practice test scores, review the chapters where you still need some work.

If you have three months or less before you take the GED:

- Review this chapter carefully to make sure you understand what the GED tests are like, and what's expected.
- Take the diagnostic test to figure out what you do well, what you need to work on, and how the test works.
- Read each strategy and content review chapter, and work through the examples and practice sections.
- Read all answer explanations.
- Take the two full-length practice tests at the end of this book, plus the online practice tests.
- Based on your practice test scores, go back to the chapters where you still need some work.

If you have only a month or less to prepare for the GED:

- Review this chapter carefully to make sure you understand what the GED tests are like, and what's expected.
- Take the diagnostic test to figure out what you do well, what you need to work on, and how the test works.

- Once you know your problem areas, read the chapters that focus on that material. Make sure you work through all examples and practice sections in these chapters.
- Read all answer explanations carefully.
- Take as many practice exams as you can in the weeks or days leading up to the test.

Getting ready for the GED tests is a bit like training for an athletic event. The more you practice under exam-like conditions, the better you'll perform during the actual exam. So be sure to take your practice tests under simulated testing conditions. Avoid interruptions and distractions, sit at a desk in a quiet spot, and adhere strictly to the time limit imposed during the actual test. Try to take each practice test from beginning to end in one sitting, just as you will during the actual test. Do not underestimate the role that endurance can play at the test center. Be sure to thoroughly review each test after taking it, so you can identify your weaknesses and focus on them in further study.

Using Other Resources to Prepare for the Tests

Tap online and offline sources of local, national, and international news. Read articles from reputable magazines and websites focusing on current topics in science, economics, and politics. As you read, try to distinguish main ideas from supporting details, fact from opinion, and well-supported conclusions from poorly supported ones.

Examine charts, tables, and graphs provided in newspapers and magazines. Read a good daily newspaper and analyze its editorial cartoons (you'll see editorial cartoons on the GED Social Studies Test). Ask yourself what ideas these various types of graphics are attempting to convey, what conclusions you can draw from them, and whether they are presenting information in an objective manner or from a certain slant or perspective.

Don't forget about textbooks and subject-review books, whether written for high school students or for a more general audience. At your library, you'll find basic introductory books on math, biology, physics, chemistry, earth science, astronomy, economics, history, civics, and geography. Multi-volume works such as the Time-Life book series contain easy-to-understand information relevant to the GED Social Studies and Science tests.

In short, spending time between now and test day to sharpen your reading and critical-thinking skills will serve you well during all of the GED tests.

The Day Before the Test and the Day of the Test

The day before your actual test, avoid studying or practicing for it. In fact, try to avoid even thinking about the test. Consider this day your day off to relax by seeing a movie or spending time with friends. Take some pressure off yourself, and your mind will be fresher on exam day. The night before the test, eat a good dinner and get a good night's rest. On the morning of the test, eat a good breakfast and arrive at the testing center early so that you have time to unwind a bit before the exam. Chat with other test takers about anything other than the test itself.

As you enter the testing room, try not to be nervous about taking the test. Remind yourself that the GED tests are practical measures of knowledge that you have gained through study and your life experiences. In addition, find reassurance in the hard work and hours of preparation you have invested in this endeavor. As the testing clock starts to run, tackle your test with confidence and enthusiasm—knowing that you have done your best to prepare for it.

OBTAINING MORE INFORMATION ABOUT THE GED® TEST

For locations and dates for GED testing in your area, contact your state's GED Testing Service® or a nearby GED Testing Center®. For general information about the GED tests, including information about future test changes, visit the official GED test website:

GED Testing Service
help@ged.com
1-877-EXAM-GED (877-392-6433)
ged.com

If you're interested in enrolling in a GED test-prep course, try contacting the adult education or continuing education department at your local community college or university. For additional self-study, you can utilize a variety of other GED test-prep books and GED test websites.

TOP 10 GED® TEST-TAKING TIPS

The general strategies and tips provided here apply to all four of the GED tests (except for the extended response portion of the Reasoning Through Language Arts Test). Be sure to look over this Top 10 list again just before exam day—you'll be glad you did.

1. **Use your erasable white board to make notes.**

   Erasable white boards are available for use as an alternative to scratch paper for organizing and planning during each of the four GED test subjects. They can help you organize your thoughts, keep key ideas straight in your mind, and prevent careless errors. When reading a passage of text, consider jotting down words and phrases that are essential to understanding the passage's ideas. For lengthy or confusing text passages, write notes or make brief outlines on your erasable white board (which will be provided). During the portion of the Mathematical Reasoning Test for which a calculator is not allowed, perform all but the simplest computations on your erasable white board.

2. **When answering a question based on visual information, size up the visual first.**

   Many questions on the Mathematical Reasoning, Science, and Social Studies tests contain visual information (graphs, charts, illustrations, diagrams, and so forth). Inspect any such "visual" carefully. Try to understand what the visual involves and what its overall intent and meaning is. Be sure to read any title or caption, which may provide clues for answering the question at hand.

3. **Make sure you understand the question.**

   Read each question carefully so you know exactly what it is asking. Pay attention to key words such as *true, accurate, supports, probably, best, least likely*, and *most likely*. These words tell you the features to look for in the correct answer choice. (Note that these and other keywords may also appear in **boldface**.) Also look for words in capital letters such as NOT, EXCEPT, and CANNOT. These capitalized words tell you that the question is being asked in the negative. If a question is based on a passage of text, read the question stem (the question itself, apart from the answer choices) before you read the passage so you have an idea of what to look for in the passage.

4. **Attempt to answer the question in your own words before reading the answer choices.**

   If you can formulate your own answer to a question, by all means do so. Then you can simply look for the answer choice that best matches what you already know is correct. What's more, you'll waste less time trying to understand the other choices, which can often be confusing and even nonsensical.

5. **Read all the answer possibilities carefully.**

   The first answer choice you read might appear to provide a good answer, but by reading further you may discover that there is a better choice. Never select a final answer before reading and carefully considering all choices. For drop-down items, be sure to read each option as it fits into the sentence, and do not just read it on its own.

6. **Select an answer choice that answers the question being asked.**

   This may seem obvious, but you should be careful not to choose an answer merely because it provides accurate information or a true statement, or because it is supported by information given in a passage of text or a visual. If the answer does not respond to the question, eliminate it.

7. **Try to eliminate as many incorrect answer choices as possible.**

   Many questions will come with answer choices that are wrong because they provide the opposite of what the question asks for. For instance, a question that asks which statement is best supported by the text will probably come with at least two choices that are *contradicted* by the text. Some incorrect answer choices might be *off topic,* meaning that they convey ideas that are not relevant to the specific topic or the question. If you're paying attention, you can easily spot these sorts of answer choices and eliminate them to improve your odds of answering the questions correctly.

8. **Apply common sense and common knowledge to your advantage.**

   Many questions may involve concepts and topics that are unfamiliar to you. You can use your real-life, practical knowledge and common sense to help you answer many such questions—or at least to narrow the number of possible answer choices.

9. **Answer every question, even if you need to guess.**

   Your score on each of the four tests is determined by the number of questions you answer correctly. You won't be penalized for incorrect answers, so you should never leave a question unanswered. If you don't know the answer, just guess—you have nothing to lose and everything to gain.

10. **Pace yourself to leave enough time for reviewing your answers.**

    Don't be a constant clock watcher, but do check the time every so often to make sure you are on pace to read and answer all questions within the time allowed. Try to maintain a pace that leaves you at least five minutes to return to those questions you were unsure about and reconsider them.

SUMMING IT UP

- The GED test is actually a battery of **four standardized tests** that measure skills required of high school graduates in the United States and Canada. The ultimate goal in passing these exams is a certificate that is equivalent to a high school diploma.
- The tests that make up the GED test battery are **Reasoning Through Language Arts, Social Studies, Science**, and **Mathematical Reasoning**.
- There are six question types on the GED tests—**multiple-choice** and five technology-enhanced items: **drag-and-drop, drop-down, fill-in-the-blank, select-an-area**, and one **extended response** item (included in the Reasoning Through Language Arts test).
- For each GED test, the more questions you answer correctly, the higher your score. No penalties are assessed for incorrect responses. The extended response item is evaluated by an automated scoring engine that replicates human scoring, and this score is combined with your score for the remainder of the test.
- The GED test is delivered solely on the computer at official testing centers. The test offers same-day scoring on all four parts—including the score report for reporting and remediation. The score levels indicate the test taker's readiness for college:
  - 0–144 points: Below Passing
  - 145–164 points: GED Passing Score/High School Equivalency
  - 165–174 points: GED College Ready
  - 175–200 points: GED College Ready + Credit
- In order to earn your GED certificate, you must attain a minimum score of 145 (150 in New Jersey) on each separate test.
- The four GED tests can be taken in any order, separately, and at any time, based on the test taker's preferences.
- For general information about the GED test, visit the official GED test website at **ged.com**.
- Getting ready for the GED tests is like training for an athletic event. The more you practice under exam-like conditions, the better you'll perform during the actual exam. Be sure to review each practice test after taking it so you can identify your weaknesses and focus on them in further study.

PART II

DETERMINING STRENGTHS AND WEAKNESSES

Practice Test 1: Diagnostic Test

OVERVIEW

- **Introduction to the Diagnostic Test**
- **Answer Sheet—Practice Test 1: Diagnostic Test**
- **Reasoning Through Language Arts**
- **Mathematical Reasoning**
- **Science**
- **Social Studies**
- **Answer Keys and Explanations**
- **Are You Ready to Take the GED® Test?**

INTRODUCTION TO THE DIAGNOSTIC TEST

Before you start your preparation and review for the GED test, it's important for you to understand your strengths and weaknesses. That way, you can tailor your studying to focus on the areas where you need the most work.

The key to creating a study plan that gets results is to not waste precious time—that's where this Diagnostic Test comes in. The test that follows mirrors the actual GED test. As you take it, make a note of which sections give you trouble and which, if any, you are able to complete with some ease. After completing the test and calculating your score, you will have a better sense of where you should focus your studying.

Preparing to Take the Diagnostic Test

Aim to take this Diagnostic Test as you would the real GED test. As with the actual test, you will most likely want to take it in sections, as the combined time of the four tests—Reasoning Through Language Arts, Mathematical Reasoning, Science, and Social Studies—lasts more than seven hours.

Technology-Enhanced Questions

Although the GED test is delivered on computer, this paper-and-pencil diagnostic test is a useful tool to help you focus on concepts rather than method of delivery. Throughout the diagnostic test you will see questions that are formatted to represent the technology-enhanced question types you will encounter on the actual GED test:

- Drag-and-drop, which will appear with a diagram; for example, a Venn diagram, flow chart, or series of boxes
- Drop-down, which will appear with a drop-down menu icon: Select ▼
- Select-an-area, which will appear with an image that you are instructed to "Click" on or "Select," such as a map or number line
- Fill-in-the-blank, which appear with an empty box: [ ]
- Extended response, which will appear only in the Reasoning Through Language Arts Test and is presented with its own set of instructions

These simulations are included to familiarize you with how the questions are presented and the number of questions of each type you may encounter. Simply answer these questions in the spaces provided on your answer sheet.

Before you begin, gather all the things you will need to take the test. These include:

- No. 2 pencils (at least three)
- A calculator with fresh batteries (Note: A calculator is incorporated into the test interface; if a student chooses to bring a personal calculator, only the TI-30XS Multiview Scientific calculator is approved for use during testing.)
- A timer

Find a quiet room, set aside a block of time, and minimize all distractions. Have a snack, turn off your phone, and get to work! Don't forget to set your timer for the time specified for each section, which is noted at the top of the first page of each test section. Stick to that time to simulate the real test.

When you're done with the test, turn to page 101 for extensive answer explanations for every test question and to calculate your final score.

It may seem like overkill to plan a practice test so strictly, but you really will want to get a sense of how long you can spend on each question in each section. Then you can begin to work out a pacing schedule for yourself.

Remember to check the "Are You Ready to Take the GED Test?" section to gauge how close you are to mastering the GED test.

Good luck!

ANSWER SHEET: PRACTICE TEST 1: DIAGNOSTIC TEST

Reasoning Through Language Arts

Part I

1. Ⓐ Ⓑ Ⓒ Ⓓ
2. ______________
3. Ⓐ Ⓑ Ⓒ Ⓓ
4. ______________
5. Ⓐ Ⓑ Ⓒ Ⓓ
6. Ⓐ Ⓑ Ⓒ Ⓓ
7. Ⓐ Ⓑ Ⓒ Ⓓ
8. Ⓐ Ⓑ Ⓒ Ⓓ
9. Ⓐ Ⓑ Ⓒ Ⓓ
10. Ⓐ Ⓑ Ⓒ Ⓓ
11. Ⓐ Ⓑ Ⓒ Ⓓ
12. ______________
13. Ⓐ Ⓑ Ⓒ Ⓓ
14. ______________
15. Ⓐ Ⓑ Ⓒ Ⓓ
16. ______________
17. Ⓐ Ⓑ Ⓒ Ⓓ

Part II
Write your response using the pages provided after this answer sheet.

Part III

18. Ⓐ Ⓑ Ⓒ Ⓓ
19. Ⓐ Ⓑ Ⓒ Ⓓ
20. Ⓐ Ⓑ Ⓒ Ⓓ
21. Ⓐ Ⓑ Ⓒ Ⓓ
22. Ⓐ Ⓑ Ⓒ Ⓓ
23. Ⓐ Ⓑ Ⓒ Ⓓ
24. Ⓐ Ⓑ Ⓒ Ⓓ
25. Ⓐ Ⓑ Ⓒ Ⓓ
26. Ⓐ Ⓑ Ⓒ Ⓓ
27. Ⓐ Ⓑ Ⓒ Ⓓ
28. Use diagram below.
29. Ⓐ Ⓑ Ⓒ Ⓓ
30. Ⓐ Ⓑ Ⓒ Ⓓ
31. Ⓐ Ⓑ Ⓒ Ⓓ
32. Ⓐ Ⓑ Ⓒ Ⓓ
33. ______________
34. Use diagram below.
35. Ⓐ Ⓑ Ⓒ Ⓓ
36. Ⓐ Ⓑ Ⓒ Ⓓ
37. ______________
38. ______________
39. ______________
40. ______________
41. ______________
42. ______________
43. ______________
44. ______________
45. ______________
46. ______________
47. ______________
48. ______________
____
____

28.

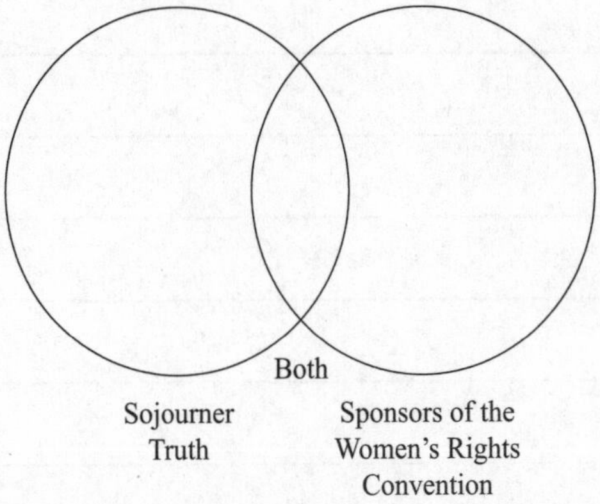

34.

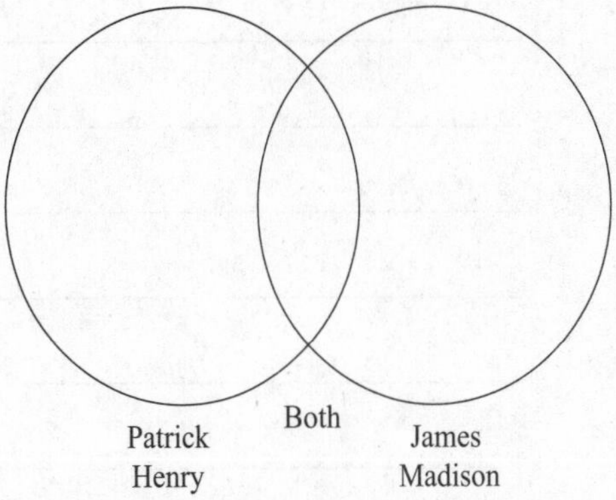

Extended Response

answer sheet

Mathematical Reasoning

1. ____________
2. Ⓐ Ⓑ Ⓒ Ⓓ
3. Ⓐ Ⓑ Ⓒ Ⓓ
4. Ⓐ Ⓑ Ⓒ Ⓓ
5. Ⓐ Ⓑ Ⓒ Ⓓ
6. Ⓐ Ⓑ Ⓒ Ⓓ
7. Ⓐ Ⓑ Ⓒ Ⓓ
8. Ⓐ Ⓑ Ⓒ Ⓓ
9. Ⓐ Ⓑ Ⓒ Ⓓ
10. Ⓐ Ⓑ Ⓒ Ⓓ
11. Ⓐ Ⓑ Ⓒ Ⓓ
12. Ⓐ Ⓑ Ⓒ Ⓓ
13. Ⓐ Ⓑ Ⓒ Ⓓ
14. Ⓐ Ⓑ Ⓒ Ⓓ
15. ____________
16. ____________
17. Ⓐ Ⓑ Ⓒ Ⓓ
18. ____________
19. Ⓐ Ⓑ Ⓒ Ⓓ
20. Ⓐ Ⓑ Ⓒ Ⓓ
21. ____________
22. ____________
23. Ⓐ Ⓑ Ⓒ Ⓓ
24. Ⓐ Ⓑ Ⓒ Ⓓ
25. Use diagram below.
26. Ⓐ Ⓑ Ⓒ Ⓓ
27. Ⓐ Ⓑ Ⓒ Ⓓ
28. Ⓐ Ⓑ Ⓒ Ⓓ
29. Ⓐ Ⓑ Ⓒ Ⓓ
30. Use diagram below.
31. ____________
32. Ⓐ Ⓑ Ⓒ Ⓓ
33. Ⓐ Ⓑ Ⓒ Ⓓ
34. Ⓐ Ⓑ Ⓒ Ⓓ
35. ____________

    ____
36. Ⓐ Ⓑ Ⓒ Ⓓ
37. Ⓐ Ⓑ Ⓒ Ⓓ
38. Ⓐ Ⓑ Ⓒ Ⓓ
39. Ⓐ Ⓑ Ⓒ Ⓓ
40. Ⓐ Ⓑ Ⓒ Ⓓ
41. Ⓐ Ⓑ Ⓒ Ⓓ
42. Ⓐ Ⓑ Ⓒ Ⓓ
43. Ⓐ Ⓑ Ⓒ Ⓓ
44. Ⓐ Ⓑ Ⓒ Ⓓ
45. Ⓐ Ⓑ Ⓒ Ⓓ
46. ____________

    ____

25.

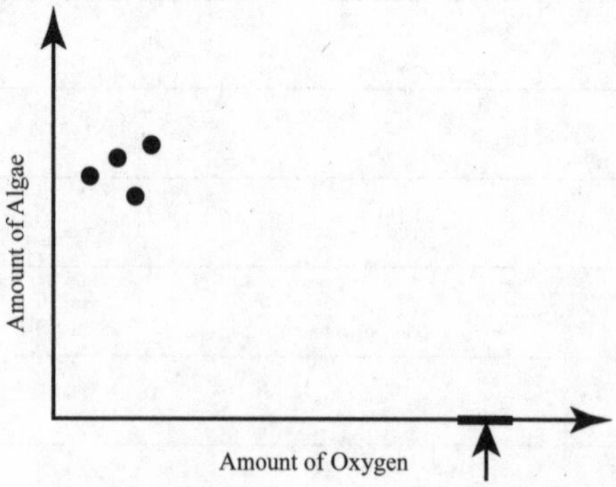

30.

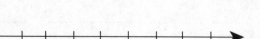

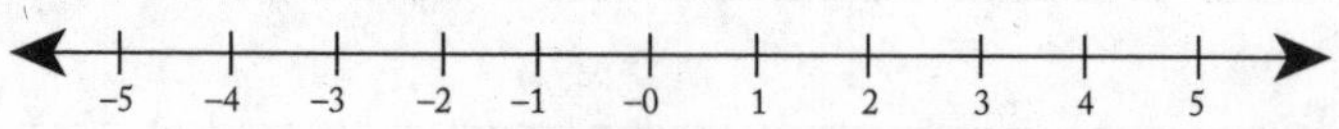

Science

1. Ⓐ Ⓑ Ⓒ Ⓓ
2. Ⓐ Ⓑ Ⓒ Ⓓ
3. Ⓐ Ⓑ Ⓒ Ⓓ
4. Ⓐ Ⓑ Ⓒ Ⓓ
5. Ⓐ Ⓑ Ⓒ Ⓓ
6. ____________
7. Ⓐ Ⓑ Ⓒ Ⓓ
8. ____________
9. Ⓐ Ⓑ Ⓒ Ⓓ
10. Ⓐ Ⓑ Ⓒ Ⓓ
11. Ⓐ Ⓑ Ⓒ Ⓓ
12. Ⓐ Ⓑ Ⓒ Ⓓ
13. Ⓐ Ⓑ Ⓒ Ⓓ
14. Ⓐ Ⓑ Ⓒ Ⓓ
15. Ⓐ Ⓑ Ⓒ Ⓓ
16. Ⓐ Ⓑ Ⓒ Ⓓ
17. Ⓐ Ⓑ Ⓒ Ⓓ
18. Ⓐ Ⓑ Ⓒ Ⓓ
19. ____________
20. Ⓐ Ⓑ Ⓒ Ⓓ
21. ____________
22. Ⓐ Ⓑ Ⓒ Ⓓ
23. Ⓐ Ⓑ Ⓒ Ⓓ
24. Ⓐ Ⓑ Ⓒ Ⓓ
25. Ⓐ Ⓑ Ⓒ Ⓓ
26. Ⓐ Ⓑ Ⓒ Ⓓ
27. ____________
28. ____________
29. Ⓐ Ⓑ Ⓒ Ⓓ
30. Ⓐ Ⓑ Ⓒ Ⓓ
31. Ⓐ Ⓑ Ⓒ Ⓓ
32. ____________
    ____
33. Ⓐ Ⓑ Ⓒ Ⓓ
34. Ⓐ Ⓑ Ⓒ Ⓓ
35. Ⓐ Ⓑ Ⓒ Ⓓ

Social Studies

1. Ⓐ Ⓑ Ⓒ Ⓓ	**13.** Ⓐ Ⓑ Ⓒ Ⓓ	**25.** Ⓐ Ⓑ Ⓒ Ⓓ
2. Ⓐ Ⓑ Ⓒ Ⓓ	**14.** Ⓐ Ⓑ Ⓒ Ⓓ	**26.** Ⓐ Ⓑ Ⓒ Ⓓ
3. Ⓐ Ⓑ Ⓒ Ⓓ	**15.** ____________	**27.** ____________
4. Ⓐ Ⓑ Ⓒ Ⓓ	**16.** ____________	**28.** Ⓐ Ⓑ Ⓒ Ⓓ
5. Ⓐ Ⓑ Ⓒ Ⓓ	**17.** Ⓐ Ⓑ Ⓒ Ⓓ	**29.** ____________
6. Ⓐ Ⓑ Ⓒ Ⓓ	**18.** Ⓐ Ⓑ Ⓒ Ⓓ	**30.** Ⓐ Ⓑ Ⓒ Ⓓ
7. Ⓐ Ⓑ Ⓒ Ⓓ	**19.** Ⓐ Ⓑ Ⓒ Ⓓ	**31.** Ⓐ Ⓑ Ⓒ Ⓓ
8. Ⓐ Ⓑ Ⓒ Ⓓ	**20.** Ⓐ Ⓑ Ⓒ Ⓓ	**32.** Ⓐ Ⓑ Ⓒ Ⓓ
9. Ⓐ Ⓑ Ⓒ Ⓓ	**21.** Ⓐ Ⓑ Ⓒ Ⓓ	**33.** Ⓐ Ⓑ Ⓒ Ⓓ
10. ____________	**22.** Ⓐ Ⓑ Ⓒ Ⓓ	**34.** Ⓐ Ⓑ Ⓒ Ⓓ
11. ____________	**23.** Ⓐ Ⓑ Ⓒ Ⓓ	**35.** Ⓐ Ⓑ Ⓒ Ⓓ
12. Ⓐ Ⓑ Ⓒ Ⓓ	**24.** Ⓐ Ⓑ Ⓒ Ⓓ	

REASONING THROUGH LANGUAGE ARTS

150 Minutes • 49 Questions

Directions: The Reasoning Through Language Arts Test consists of passages of fiction and nonfiction reading material. After you read a passage, answer the questions that follow it, referring back to the passage as needed. Answer all questions based on what is stated and implied in the passage.

Most questions are in multiple-choice format. Others are meant to prepare you for the technology-enhanced questions that you will find on the test, such as fill-in-the-blanks and drag-and-drops. There is also an extended response question that requires you to read a paired passage that represents two views on a topic and write a well-organized essay supporting one of the viewpoints. Record your answers on the Reasoning Through Language Arts section of the answer sheet provided. To review how to answer these questions on your answer sheet, please refer to "Technology-Enhanced Questions" on page 24.

Part I

Questions 1–6 refer to the following passage.

He didn't want to go. He loathed the very thought of it. Every flinching nerve in him protested.

A masked ball—a masked ball at a Cairo hotel! Grimacing through peep-holes, self-conscious advances, flirtations ending in giggles! Tourists as nuns, tourists as Turks, tourists as God-knows-what, all preening and peacocking!

Unhappily he gazed upon the girl who was proposing this horror as a bright delight. She was a very engaging girl—that was the mischief of it. She stood smiling there in the bright, Egyptian sunshine, gay confidence in her gray eyes. He hated to shatter that confidence.

And he had done little enough for her during her stay in Cairo. One tea at the Gezireh Palace Hotel, one trip to the Sultan al Hassan Mosque, one excursion through the bazaars—not exactly an orgy of entertainment for a girl from home!

He had evaded climbing the Pyramids and fled from the ostrich farm. He had withheld from inviting her to the camp on the edge of the Libyan desert where he was excavating, although her party had shown unmistakable signs of a willingness to be diverted from the beaten path of its travel.

And he was not calling on her now. He had come to Cairo for supplies and she had encountered him by chance upon a corner of the crowded Mograby [western section], and there promptly she had invited him to to-night's ball.

"But it's not my line, you know, Jinny," he was protesting. "I'm so fearfully out of dancing—"

"More reason to come, Jack. You need a change from digging up ruins all the time—it must be frightfully lonely out there on the desert. I can't think how you stand it."

Jack Ryder smiled. There was no mortal use in explaining to Jinny Jeffries that his life on the desert was the only life in the world, that his ruins held more thrills than all the fevers of her tourist crowds, and that he would rather gaze upon the mummied effigy of any lady of the dynasty of Amenhotep than upon the freshest and fairest of the damsels of the present day.

It would only tax Jinny's credulity and hurt her feelings. And he liked Jinny—though not as he liked Queen Hatasu or the little nameless creature he had dug out of a king's ante-room.

Jinny was an interfering modern. She was the incarnation of impossible demands.

But of course there was no real reason why he should not stop over and go to the dance.

—from *The Fortieth Door*, by Mary Hastings Bradley

1. Which of the following lines from the passage reveals where the upcoming event Jack does not want to attend will be held?

A. "a masked ball at the Cairo hotel!"

B. "One tea at the Gezireh Palace Hotel"

C. "one excursion through the bazaars"

D. "He had evaded climbing the Pyramids"

2. Based on the passage, which word **best** describes Jinny's personality? Choose your answer from the drop-down menu.

Select ▼

A. Daring

B. Fun-loving

C. Tiresome

D. Demanding

3. How does Jack feel about attending the ball?

A. He hates parties and refuses to go.

B. He hates the idea, but he likes Jinny and wants to please her.

C. He doesn't like parties, but he is glad Jinny invited him anyway.

D. He doesn't like to dance and doesn't like Jinny, but he feels obligated to be nice to her.

4. Jack's thoughts about Jinny reveal that he Select ▼.

A. thinks people are interfering

B. likes the dead mummies better than he likes Jinny

C. is glad that he ran into Jinny and gladly shows her around the city

D. likes Jinny and thinks that it might not be so bad to be with people after all

5. What clues in the text illustrate that Jack is well suited to his work?

A. He likes to travel.

B. He likes living in the desert.

C. He is fascinated by the ruins and what they hold.

D. He lives in the desert area but also feels at home with colleagues in Cairo.

6. Where did Jack and Jinny first encounter each other in Egypt?

A. Gezireh

B. The Libyan Desert

C. Mograby

D. The Sultan al Hassan Mosque

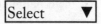

Questions 7–11 refer to the following passage.

John Dewey and Education

John Dewey, an American educator and philosopher of education, was a prolific writer on the subject. He was particularly interested in the place of education in a democratic republic.

The place of public education within a democratic society has been widely discussed and debated through the years. Perhaps no one has written more widely on the subject in the United States than John Dewey, sometimes called "the father of public education," whose theories of education have a large social component, that is, an emphasis on education as a social act and the classroom or learning environment as a replica of society.

Dewey defined various aspects or characteristics of education. First, it was a necessity of life inasmuch as living beings needed to maintain themselves through a process of renewal. Therefore, just as humans needed sleep, food, water, and shelter for physiological renewal, they also needed education to renew their minds, assuring that their socialization kept pace with physiological growth.

A second aspect of education was its social component, which was to be accomplished by providing the young with an environment that would provide a nurturing atmosphere to encourage the growth of their as yet undeveloped social customs.

A third aspect of public education was the provision of direction to youngsters, who might otherwise be left in uncontrolled situations without the steadying and organizing influences of school. Direction was not to be of an overt nature, but rather indirect through the selection of the school situations in which the youngster participated.

Finally, Dewey saw public education as a catalyst for growth. Since the young came to school capable of growth, it was the role of education to provide opportunities for that growth to occur. The successful school environment is one in which a desire for continued growth is created—a desire that extends throughout one's life beyond the end of formal education. In Dewey's model, the role of education in a democratic society is not seen as a preparation for some later stage in life, such as adulthood. Rather, education is seen as a process of growth that never ends, with human beings continuously expanding their capacity for growth. Neither did Dewey's model see education as a means by which the past was recapitulated. Instead, education was a continuous reconstruction of experiences, grounded very much in the present environment.

Since Dewey's model places a heavy emphasis on the social component, the nature of the larger society that supports the educational system is of paramount importance. The ideal larger society, according to Dewey, is one in which the interests of a group are all shared by all of its members and in which interactions with other groups are free and full. According to Dewey, education in such a society should provide members of the group a stake or interest in social relationships and the ability to negotiate change without compromising the order and stability of the society.

Thus, Dewey's basic concept of education in a democratic society is based on the notion that education contains a large social component designed to provide direction and assure children's development through their participation in the group to which they belong.

7. In the context of the passage, the **best** synonym for *paramount* is

A. difficult.

B. supreme.

C. minor.

D. curious.

8. Based on the passage, which is the **most** reasonable inference about John Dewey's primary goal for public education?

A. Teaching children how to behave

B. Making the United States a strong military power

C. Creating a strong and stable society

D. Teaching children how to make friends

9. In the context of the passage, what does the word *compromising* mean?

A. Making vulnerable

B. Strongly supporting

C. Rendering nonsensical

D. Clarifying carefully

10. Which of the following is NOT something Dewey believes is a problem in education?

A. Focusing on preparing students for adulthood

B. A lack of steadying influences for students

C. Recapitulating the past

D. A lack of overt direction for students

11. What, according to Dewey, is the primary characteristic of the ideal society?

A. One in which all citizens have adequate sleep, food, water, and shelter

B. One in which group interests are shared by all members and in which all members may interact with other groups freely

C. One in which human beings continuously expand their capacity for growth in an unending process

D. A democratic society wherein education is seen as a preparation for some later stage in life, such as adulthood

Questions 12–17 refer to the following passage.

John Adams was an active participant in the movement toward independence, one of the writers of the Declaration of Independence, and after the Revolution, the country's first vice president and second president. During his time in Philadelphia meeting with other delegates to the Constitutional Convention, he and his wife Abigail continually wrote letters to one another. Their correspondence left a legacy of history and a glimpse of their relationship. The following is a letter John Adams wrote to Abigail just a few weeks after the Battle of Bunker Hill, the first battle of the Revolution.

Philadelphia, 7 July, 1775.

I have received your very agreeable favors of June 22 and 25. They contain more particulars than any letters I had before received from anybody.

It is not at all surprising to me, that the wanton, cruel, and infamous conflagration of Charlestown [the site of the Battle of Bunker Hill], the place of your father's nativity, should afflict him.

Let him know that I sincerely condole with him on that melancholy event. It is a method of conducting war long since become disreputable among civilized nations. But every year brings us fresh evidence that we have nothing to hope for from our loving mother country, but cruelties more abominable than those which are practiced by the savage Indians.

The account you give me of the numbers slain on the side of our enemies is afflicting to humanity, although it is a glorious proof of the bravery of our worthy countrymen. Considering all the disadvantages under which they fought, they really exhibited prodigies of valor. Your description of the distresses of the worthy inhabitants of Boston and the other seaport towns is enough to melt a heart of stone. Our consolation must be this, my dear, that cities may be rebuilt, and a people reduced to poverty may acquire fresh property. But a constitution of government, once changed from freedom, can never be restored. Liberty, once lost, is lost forever. When the people once surrender their share in the legislature, and their right of defending the limitations upon the Government, and of resisting every encroachment upon them, they can never regain it.

The loss of Mr. Mather's library, which was a collection of books and manuscripts made by himself, his father, his grandfather, and great-grandfather, and was really very curious and valuable, is irreparable. The family picture you draw is charming indeed. My dear Abby, Johnny, Charley, and Tommy, I long to see you, and to share with your mamma the pleasures of your conversation. I feel myself much obliged to Mr. Bowdoin, Mr. Wibird, and the two families you mention, for their civilities to you. My compliments to them. Does Mr. Wibird preach against oppression and the other cardinal vices of the times? Tell him the clergy here of every denomination, not excepting the Episcopalian, thunder and lighten every Sabbath. They pray for Boston and the Massachusetts. They thank God most explicitly and fervently for our remarkable successes. They pray for the American army. They seem to feel as if they were among you.

You ask if every member feels for us? Every member says he does, and most of them really do. But most of them feel more for themselves. In every society of men, in every club I ever yet saw, you find some who are timid, their fears hurry them away upon every alarm; some who are selfish and avaricious, on whose callous hearts nothing but interest and money can make impression. There are some persons in New York and Philadelphia to whom a ship is dearer than a city, and a few barrels of flour than a thousand lives—other men's lives, I mean.

You ask, Can they realize what we suffer? I answer, No. They can't. They don't. And, to excuse them as well as I can, I must confess, I should not be able to do it myself, if I was not more acquainted with it by experience than they are.

I am grieved for Dr. Tufts's ill-health, but rejoiced exceedingly at his virtuous exertions in the cause of his country. I am happy to hear that my brothers were at Grape Island, and behaved well. My love to them, and duty to my mother.

It gives me more pleasure than I can express, to learn that you sustain with so much fortitude the shocks and terrors of the times. You are really brave, my dear. You are a heroine, and you have reason to be. For the worst that can happen can do you no harm. A soul as pure, as benevolent, as virtuous and pious as yours, has nothing to fear, but everything to hope and expect from the last of human evils. I am glad you have secured an asylum, though I hope you will not have occasion for it. …

I am forever yours.

12. Which of the following quotes from the letter shows that Adams believed the Revolution was necessary for the colonists to get their freedom? Choose your answer from the drop-down menu. Select ▼

A. "Liberty, once lost, is lost forever."

B. "For the worst that can happen can do you no harm."

C. "They seem to feel as if they were among you."

D. "a glorious proof of the bravery of our worthy countrymen"

13. Which words in the text confirm that this letter is one of many that John and Abigail wrote to one another while they were separated?

A. "They seem to feel as if they were among you."

B. "Our consolation must be this, my dear"

C. "I long to see you."

D. "I am glad you have secured an asylum."

14. Abigail knows Select ▼, which John does not know.

A. the number of British troops who were killed

B. about the disadvantages of the colonial army

C. about the fight in Charlestown

D. where Abgail and the children will take refuge if fighting breaks out nearby

15. What can you conclude about war from this letter?

A. Wars are destructive.

B. The Adams were patriotic people.

C. People's lives are disrupted during war.

D. People continue their normal lives during wartime.

16. When John says Abigail's description "is enough to melt a heart of stone," he means Select ▼.

A. her description is tough

B. her description is endearing

C. her letters show she is clever with words

D. her letters are heartwarming

17. What is Abigail's father particularly upset about?

A. The conflagration of Charlestown

B. The Battle of Bunker Hill

C. The loss of Mr. Mather's Library

D. Oppression and other cardinal vices

Part II

The following passages represent two views of the value of arts education in society. Analyze both viewpoints and determine which one is best supported. Use specific and relevant evidence from the passages to support your response. Use reasons and examples to support your position. Take 45 minutes to plan, draft, and edit your response.

Debating the Importance of Arts Education

Passage 1

Allowing arts education to fall by the wayside will be detrimental for our students and their futures as a part of society. Teaching the arts to young students can change the way they learn and help them to develop life-long skills. Motor skills can be developed through arts and crafts participation: drawing with crayons, holding paintbrushes, and cutting with scissors all help to develop dexterity—which is necessary for writing. Making art can also provide young students a simpler way to learn colors, shapes, and various actions, while also teaching them the importance of visual learning, an important aspect of interpreting and analyzing information. Although it seems obvious that learning the arts aids in creativity, it is sometimes misunderstood as to why this is so important if a student is going to pursue a degree not focused on one of these creative aspects. The arts, however, can teach students how to aptly express themselves and take risks, even encouraging students to seek alternative directions and other ways to conceptualize their thoughts. Furthermore, the arts give students a way to grasp their cultural surroundings. By teaching young students to understand artistic concepts—texture, shape, colors, etc.—a teacher can properly describe the characteristics of reality, and the student is more likely to accurately interpret these representations. Last, but certainly not least, there are several studies that show a strong correlation between art and overall achievement. Americans for the Arts states that youth who participate in the arts for at least three hours a day, three days a week for a full year, are *four* times more likely to have their academic achievements recognized, to participate in a math or science fair, or even to win an award for writing an essay or poem than those students who do not participate in the arts. By teaching the arts, we can ensure that students will understand the place creative skills have in education, the workplace, and society.

Passage 2

With the increased dependency on technology and the never-faltering importance of math and sciences, focusing on the arts in schools is becoming less and less relevant. It is crucial to give our students an education that can best help them get into colleges upon graduating high school, and well-paying jobs upon graduating college. By adding more focus on art, we are taking away from other subjects that aid in college and job preparation. These days, many students graduate high school without any experience writing cover letters, formatting resumes, or overall real-world experience. If any subject should be added to our core curriculums, it should be job preparedness. Although the arts hone creativity and may help students inclined to work in fields where liberal arts are the main focus, they still need to know how to market themselves and know how to break into the job market. Most students who will end up in a creative field are born with these inclinations, finding themselves with an inherent attraction to these subjects. We should focus more on developing interview skills, salary negotiation, e-mail etiquette, and adapting in the workplace. These skills will make the biggest difference in the success of our students and ensure that they will be contributing members of our society.

Part III

Questions 18–22 refer to the following passage.

Martin Luther King's Push for Civil Rights

The following speech was delivered on the steps of the Lincoln Memorial at the height of the 1960s civil rights movement by Dr. Martin Luther King Jr., head of the Southern Christian Leadership Conference and the movement's most eloquent spokesperson.

We have…come to this hallowed spot to remind America of the fierce urgency of Now. This is no time to engage in the luxury of cooling off or to take the tranquilizing drug of gradualism. Now is the time to make real the promises of democracy. Now is the time to rise from the dark and desolate valley of segregation to the sunlit path of racial justice. Now is the time to lift our nation from the quicksands of racial injustice to the solid rock of brotherhood. Now is the time to make justice a reality for all of God's children.

It would be fatal for the nation to overlook the urgency of the moment. This sweltering summer of the Negro's legitimate discontent will not pass until there is an invigorating autumn of freedom and equality . . .Those who hope that the Negro needed to blow off steam and will now be content will have a rude awakening if the nation returns to business as usual. And there will be neither rest nor tranquility in America until the Negro is granted his citizenship rights. The whirlwinds of revolt will continue to shake the foundations of our nation until the bright day of justice emerges.

But there is something that I must say to my people, who stand on the warm threshold which leads into the palace of justice: In the process of gaining our rightful place, we must not be guilty of wrongful deeds. Let us not seek to satisfy our thirst for freedom by drinking from the cup of bitterness and hatred. We must forever conduct our struggle on the high plane of dignity and discipline. We must not allow our creative protest to degenerate into physical violence. Again and again, we must rise to the majestic heights of meeting physical force with soul force. The marvelous new militancy which has engulfed the Negro community must not lead us to a distrust of all white people, for many of our white brothers, as evidenced by their presence here today, have come to realize that their destiny is tied up with our destiny. And they have come to realize that their freedom is inextricably bound to our freedom. We cannot walk alone.

And as we walk, we must make the pledge that we shall always march ahead. We cannot turn back. There are those who are asking the devotees of civil rights, "When will you be satisfied?" We can never be satisfied as long as the Negro is the victim of the unspeakable horrors of police brutality . . .We cannot be satisfied as long as the Negro's basic mobility is from a smaller ghetto to a larger one. We can never be satisfied as long as our children are stripped of their selfhood and robbed of their dignity by signs stating "For Whites Only." We cannot be satisfied as long as a Negro in Mississippi cannot vote and a Negro in New York believes he has nothing for which to vote. No, no, we are not satisfied, and we will not be satisfied until "justice rolls down like waters and righteousness like a mighty stream."

I am not unmindful that some of you have come out of great trials and tribulations. Some of you have come fresh from narrow jail cells. And some of you have come from areas where your quest—quest for freedom—left you battered by the storms of persecution and staggered by the winds of police brutality. You have been the veterans of creative suffering. Continue to work with the faith that unearned suffering is redemptive. Go back to Mississippi, go back to Alabama, go back to South Carolina, go back to Louisiana, go back to the slums and ghettos of our northern cities, knowing that somehow this situation can and will be changed. Let us not wallow in the valley of despair, I say to you today, my friends.

18. In the context of the passage, what is the definition of *militancy*?

A. Forceful violence

B. Disciplined structure

C. Extreme patriotism

D. Vigorous activeness

19. Which of the following is NOT something that King indicates is unproductive to securing civil rights?

A. Bitterness

B. Violence

C. Dissatisfaction

D. Hatred

20. According to King in lines 15 and 16, for what or whom would overlooking the urgency of the moment be fatal?

A. Martin Luther King, Jr.

B. The Civil Rights Movement

C. The Southern Christian Leadership Conference

D. The United States

21. King's main argument in the third paragraph is that

A. gradual change is not adequate.

B. white people are part of the Civil Rights Movement.

C. all protest must remain peaceful.

D. now that summer is over, autumn will bring freedom and equality.

22. In the context of the passage, what is the **best** definition for *trials*?

A. Hearings

B. Experiments

C. Ordeals

D. Examinations

Questions 23–28 refer to the following passages.

Liberating Women

In 1848, a Woman's Rights Convention was held at Seneca Falls, New York. Sponsored by Lucretia Mott, Martha Wright, Elizabeth Cady Stanton, and Mary Ann McClintock, the convention featured the creation of a "Declaration of Sentiments," a document based on America's Declaration of Independence, in which men's unfair dominion over women was described. Crusader for the rights of African Americans and women, Sojourner Truth was born a slave on a Dutch estate around 1797 and named Isabella. The first edition of her biography was written by Olive Gilbert, a white friend of hers, and published in 1850.

Passage 1—Declaration of Sentiments

The history of mankind is a history of repeated injuries and usurpations on the part of man toward woman, having in direct object the establishment of an absolute tyranny over her. To prove this, let facts be submitted to a candid world.

He has never permitted her to exercise her inalienable right to the elective franchise.

He has compelled her to submit to laws, in the formation of which she had no voice. He has withheld from her rights which are given to the most ignorant and degraded men—both natives and foreigners.

Having deprived her of this first right of a citizen, the elective franchise, thereby leaving her without representation in the halls of legislation, he has oppressed her on all sides.

He has made her, if married, in the eye of the law, civilly dead.

He has taken from her all right in property, even to the wages she earns.

He has made her, morally, an irresponsible being, as she can commit many crimes with impunity, provided they be done in the presence of her husband. In the covenant of marriage, she is compelled to promise obedience to her husband, he becoming, to all intents and purposes, her master—the law giving him power to deprive her of her liberty, and to administer chastisement.

He has so framed the laws of divorce, as to what shall be the proper causes, and in the case of separation, to whom the guardianship of the children shall be given, as to be wholly regardless of the happiness of women—the law, in all cases, going upon a false supposition of the supremacy of man, and giving all power into his hands.

After depriving her of all rights as a married woman, if single, and the owner of property, he has taxed her to support a government which recognizes her only when her property can be made profitable to it.

He has endeavored, in every way that he could, to destroy her confidence in her own powers, to lessen her self-respect, and to make her willing to lead a dependent and abject life.

Passage 2—Sojourner Truth

After emancipation had been decreed by the State, some years before the time fixed for its consummation, Isabella's master told her if she would do well, and be faithful, he would give her "free papers," one year before she was legally free by statute. In the year 1826, she had a badly diseased hand, which greatly diminished her usefulness; but on the arrival of July 4, 1827, the time specified for her receiving her "free papers," she claimed the fulfillment of her master's promise; but he refused granting it, on account (as he alleged) of the loss he had sustained by her hand. She plead that she had worked all the time, and done many things she was not wholly able to do, although she knew she had been less useful than formerly; but her master remained inflexible. Her very faithfulness probably operated against her now, and he found it less easy than he thought to give up the profits of his faithful Bell, who had so long done him efficient service.

But Isabella inwardly determined that she would remain quietly with him only until she had spun his wool—about one hundred pounds—and then she would leave him, taking the rest of the time to herself. "Ah!" she says, with emphasis that cannot be written, "the slaveholders are TERRIBLE for promising to give you this or that, or such and such a privilege, if you will do thus and so; and when the time of fulfillment comes, and one claims the promise, they, forsooth, recollect nothing of the kind; and you are, like as not, taunted with being a LIAR; or, at best, the slave is accused of not having performed *his* part or condition of the contract." "Oh!" said she, "I have felt as if I could not live through the *operation sometimes.* Just think of us! *So* eager for our pleasures, and just foolish enough to keep feeding and feeding ourselves up with the idea that we should get what had been thus fairly promised; and when we think it is almost in our hands, find ourselves flatly denied! Just think! how *could* we bear it?"

23. According to the first passage, under what circumstances does the government tax a woman unfairly?

A. If she is married
B. If she is not moral
C. If she owns property
D. If she wants to get divorced

24. In the context of the first passage, what is the definition of *tyranny*?

A. Horrible violence
B. Guiding care
C. Oppressive control
D. Brutish behavior

25. From whose point of view is the second passage written?

A. Elizabeth Cady Stanton
B. Olive Gilbert
C. Isabella
D. Mary Ann McClintock

26. Under what circumstances would Isabella leave her master in the second passage?

A. As soon as she received her "free papers"
B. When her master allowed her to leave
C. After she had spun one hundred pounds of wool
D. After she had made him a considerable profit

27. Which of the following is a likely reason the writers patterned the Declaration of Sentiments after the Declaration of Independence?

A. To explain their own complaints against English rule

B. To explain why they disapproved of Sojourner Truth's treatment at the hands of her master

C. To demonstrate that women had complaints similar to those of the Founding Fathers

D. To demonstrate that women could write well

28. Drag the characteristics that fit the descriptions of Sojourner Truth or the sponsors of the Woman's Rights Convention to the correct space in the Venn diagram. If there is a common characteristic, drag it into the center of the diagram. (Enter the answers on the answer sheet diagram.)

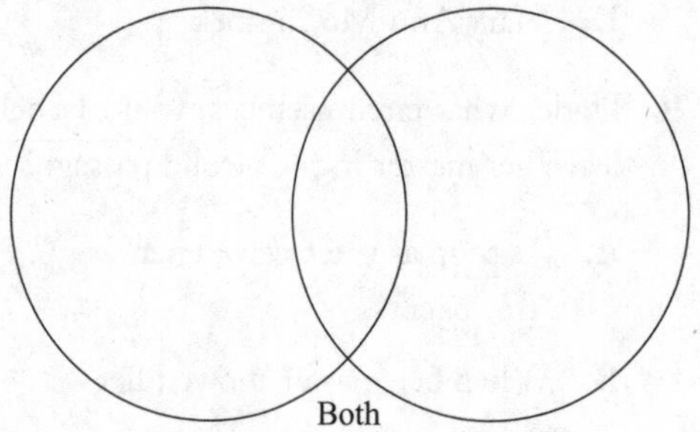

A. Spent a life in slavery

B. Legally able to vote after 1848

C. Not treated as citizens of the United States

D. Legally able to obtain a divorce

Questions 29–34 refer to the following passages.

Debating the Constitution

The following two passages represent two views of the Constitution.

Passage 1

We are descended from a people whose Government was founded on liberty. Our glorious forefathers of Great-Britain, made liberty the foundation of every thing. That country is become a great, mighty, and splendid nation; not because their Government is strong and energetic; but, Sir, because liberty is its direct end and foundation. We drew the spirit of liberty from our British ancestors; by that spirit we have triumphed over every difficulty. But now, Sir, the American spirit, assisted by the ropes and chains of consolidation, is about to convert this country to a powerful and mighty empire. If you make the citizens of this country agree to become the subjects of one great consolidated empire of America, your Government will not have sufficient energy to keep them together.

Such a Government is incompatible with the genius of republicanism. There will be no checks, no real balances, in this Government. What can avail your specious imaginary balances, your rope-dancing, chain-rattling, ridiculous ideal checks and contrivances? But, Sir, We are not feared by foreigners. We do not make nations tremble. Would this, Sir, constitute happiness, or secure liberty? I trust, Sir, our political hemisphere will ever direct their operations to the security of those objects. Consider our situation, Sir. Go to the poor man, ask him what he does; he will inform you, that he enjoys the fruits of his labour, under his own fig-tree, with his wife and children around him, in peace and security. Go to every other member of the society, you will find the same tranquil ease and content; you will find no alarms or disturbances. Why then tell us of dangers to terrify us into an adoption of this new Government? and yet who knows the dangers that this new system may produce; they are out of the sight of the common people. They cannot foresee latent consequences. I dread the operation of it on the middling and lower class of people. It is for them I fear the adoption of this system.

—Patrick Henry, The Virginia Ratifying Convention, June 5, 1788

Passage 2

In order to lay a due foundation for that separate and distinct exercise of the different powers of government, which to a certain extent is admitted on all hands to be essential to the preservation of liberty, it is evident that each department should have a will of its own; and consequently should be so constituted that the members of each should have as little agency as possible in the appointment of the members of the others. Were this principle rigorously adhered to, it would require that all the appointments for the supreme executive, legislative, and judiciary magistracies should be drawn from the same fountain of authority, the people, through channels having no communication whatever with one another. Perhaps such a plan of constructing the several departments would be less difficult in practice than it may in contemplation appear. Some difficulties, however, and some additional expense would attend the execution of it. Some deviations, therefore, from the principle must be admitted. In the constitution of the judiciary department in particular, it might be inexpedient to insist rigorously on the principle: first, because peculiar qualifications being essential in the members, the primary consideration ought to be to select that mode of choice which best secures these qualifications; secondly, because the permanent tenure by which the appointments are held in that department, must soon destroy all sense of dependence on the authority conferring them.

It is equally evident, that the members of each department should be as little dependent as possible on those of the others, for the emoluments annexed to their offices. Were the executive magistrate, or the judges, not independent of the legislature in this particular, their independence in every other would be merely nominal.

—James Madison, *The Federalist*, No. 51

29. What is Madison's point in the second passage?

A. Separation of powers is impossible to achieve.

B. Separation of powers is both necessary and achievable.

C. Centralized government will be detrimental to ordinary citizens.

D. Judges need to be independent of the legislature.

30. What is Henry's point in stating, "There will be no checks, no real balances, in this Government"?

A. He thinks that the Federalists are lying.

B. He does not believe in the principle of checks and balances.

C. Since Great Britain does not have them, he thinks the United States does not need them.

D. He thinks the government will lack the ability to enforce a separation of powers.

31. What is a possible synonym for *tenure* as it appears in the second passage?

A. Requirements

B. Term

C. Duties

D. Descriptions

32. Why is Madison arguing that the branches of government should be as separate as possible?

A. To prevent oversight of departments by other departments

B. To avoid having a government like Great Britain

C. So that the members of one branch have little influence over the members of the others

D. So that the citizens have more power

33. Henry's primary motivation for opposing a centralized government, according to the passage, is that he Select ▼.

A. is concerned that bureaucracy will take over the government

B. believes that other countries fear the United States

C. wants the United States to be an empire like Great Britain

D. fears that ordinary citizens will suffer under a centralized government

34. Drag the statements into the provided Venn diagram above the name of the politician who the statements support, according to the passage. If there is one that applies to both, place it in the center. (Enter the answers on the answer sheet diagram.)

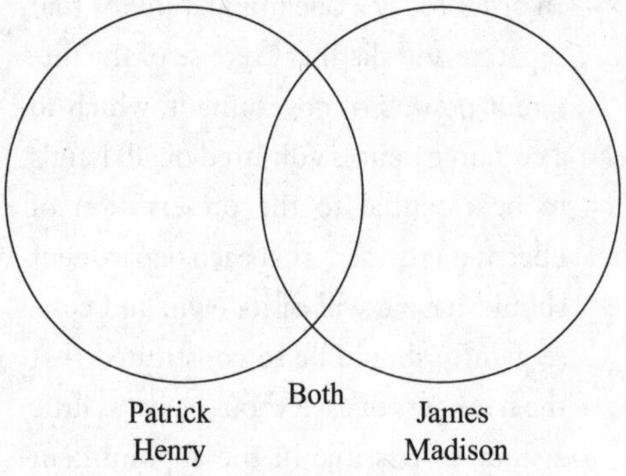

A. Limiting the power of the government is necessary to preserve liberty.

B. The government will corrupt the successes of the middle and lower class people.

C. It will be difficult for the government to maintain separation of powers.

D. The judiciary should be dependent on the legislature.

Questions 35 and 36 refer to the following passage.

Patriotism and Oratory

Frances Wright was a reformer, author, and orator, unusual occupations for a woman in the early nineteenth century. Born in Scotland, she became an American citizen in 1825. The following is from a speech she gave in New Harmony, Indiana, on July 4, 1828.

In continental Europe, of late years, the words patriotism and patriot have been used in a more enlarged sense than it is usual here to attribute to them, or than is attached to them in Great Britain. Since the political struggles of France, Italy, Spain, and Greece, the word patriotism has been employed, throughout continental Europe, to express a love of the public good; a preference for the interests of the many to those of the few; a desire for the emancipation of the human race from the thrall of despotism, religious and civil: in short, patriotism there is used rather to express the interest felt in the human race in general than that felt for any country, or inhabitants of a country, in particular. And patriot, in like manner, is employed to signify a lover of human liberty and human improvement rather than a mere lover of the country in which he lives, or the tribe to which he belongs. Used in this sense, patriotism is a virtue, and a patriot is a virtuous man. With such an interpretation, a patriot is a useful member of society capable of enlarging all minds and bettering all hearts with which he comes in contact; a useful member of the human family, capable of establishing fundamental principles and of merging his own interests, those of his associates, and those of his nation in the interests of the human race. Laurels and statues are vain things, and mischievous as they are childish; but could we imagine them of use, on such a patriot alone could they be with any reason bestowed. . . .

If such a patriotism as we have last considered should seem likely to obtain in any country, it should be certainly in this. In this, which is truly the home of all nations, and in the veins of whose citizens flows the blood of every people on the globe. Patriotism, in the exclusive meaning, is surely not made for America. Mischievous every where, it were here both mischievous and absurd. The very origin of the people is opposed to it. The institutions, in their principle, militate against it. This day we are celebrating protests against it. It is for Americans, more especially to nourish a nobler sentiment; one more consistent with their origin, and more conducive to their future improvement. It is for them more especially to know why they love their country, not because it is their country, but because it is the palladium of human liberty—the favoured scene of human improvement. It is for them more especially, to know why they honour their institutions, and feel that they honour them because they are based on just principles. It is for them, more especially, to examine their institutions, because they have the means of improving them; to examine their laws, because at will they can alter them.

diagnostic test—Language Arts

35. Based on the passage, what is Wright's opinion on the reason for being patriotic as an American citizen?

A. Patriotism should be based in national pride.

B. Patriotism is a virtue, and a patriot is a virtuous man.

C. Patriotism is the love of country because of the principles on which it is founded, not on residency.

D. Patriotism is mischievous.

36. When Wright states that America "is truly the home of all nations," to what is she likely referring?

A. America is made up of immigrants from all over the world.

B. America has not been declared a country yet.

C. Every nation claims to own America.

D. People from all over the world like to visit America.

Questions 37–48 refer to the following document.

The following is a document you might find in the workplace. The passage contains errors in grammar, spelling, and punctuation.

Memorandum

To: All Staff Members

From: John Smith, CEO

Date: August 28, 2019

Subject: Workplace Etiquette

(1) Employees thrive in friendly, focused [Select ▼] overall success of the company. (2) In order to be the best [Select ▼] workplace etiquette should be acknowledged.

(3) Your attire [Select ▼] (4) Women should avoid thin-strapped tops, never wear halter tops, and [Select ▼] appropriate coverage. (5) We allow [Select ▼] (6) However, the dress code is still *business* casual, not just casual. (7) Do not wear open-toed shoes or tennis shoes, and don't wear sandals at any time.

(8) Cell phones can be distracting during the day, so please keep them silenced. (9) If [Select ▼] step into one of the break rooms and shut the door. (10) [Select ▼] the time you spend making these calls or save them for your lunch hour.

(11) Remember that emails are still important conversations with your supervisors or coworkers, and they will not be taken lightly. (12) Try and match the tone of whomever you are emailing. (13) If they use your first name, it's okay to use theirs. (14) Respond to all emails, even if the response is as simple as a sentence saying it was received.

(15) We are an open office, meaning that we share communal spaces and have limited closed offices. (16) Although this is a positive environment [Select ▼] (17) When you visit a coworker's desk, [Select ▼] (18) If you are visiting an office, knock before entering. (19) We still want to promote an open office culture, so don't be afraid to visit others!

(20) Last but not least, the communal spaces—break room, copy room and kitchen—are open to all employees. (21) [Select ▼] (22) Feel free to use the refrigerator, coffee maker, and microwave. (23) Please clean up [Select ▼] yourself—we want a safe, clean, and welcoming environment for everyone. (24) If you have any questions or concerns regarding this memo, please don't hesitate to email me at johnsmith@gmail.com re: Workplace Etiquette.

(24) If you have any questions or concerns regarding this memo, please don't hesitate to email me at johnsmith@gmail.com re: Workplace Etiquette.

(25) Genuinely,
John Smith, CEO

37. Sentence 1: Employees thrive in friendly, focused [Select ▼] overall success of the company.

A. environments leading to the

B. environments; leading to the

C. environments: leading to the

D. environments, leading to the

38. Sentence 2: In order to be the best [Select ▼] workplace etiquette should be acknowledged.

A. coworkers he can be, some

B. coworkers we can be, some

C. coworkers we can be some

D. coworkers she can be, some

diagnostic test — Language Arts

39. Sentence 3: Your attire [Select ▼]

A. should be business-appropriate because we follow professional guidelines so men should wear slacks and button-down shirts with a tie (jacket not required) and women should wear slacks, skirts, or dresses (at least knee length).

B. should be business-appropriate. We follow professional guidelines, so men should wear slacks and button-down shirts with a tie; (jacket not required), and women should wear slacks, skirts, or dresses (at least knee length).

C. should be business-appropriate. We follow professional guidelines: men should wear slacks and button-down shirts with a tie (jacket not required), and women should wear slacks, skirts, or dresses (at least knee length).

D. should be business-appropriate, because we follow professional guidelines, so men should wear slacks and button-down shirts with a tie (jacket not required), and women should wear slacks, skirts, or dresses (at least knee length).

40. Sentence 4: Women should avoid thin-strapped tops, never wear halter tops, and [Select ▼] appropriate coverage.

A. should be maintaining

B. should, maintain

C. she should be maintaining

D. maintain

41. Sentence 5: We allow [Select ▼]

A. Business Casual attire on fridays: jeans are permitted.

B. business casual attire on friday's: jeans are permitted.

C. Business Casual attire on Fridays: jeans are permitted.

D. business casual attire on Fridays: jeans are permitted.

42. Sentence 9: If [Select ▼] step into one of the break rooms and shut the door.

A. you need to make a personal call, please

B. you need to make a personal call please

C. you need to makes a personal call, please

D. need to make a personal call, please

43. Sentence 10: [Select ▼] the time you spend making these calls or save them for your lunch hour.

A. Miniaturize

B. Minimize

C. Minimal

D. Miniature

44. Sentence 16: Although this is a positive environment [Select ▼]

A. for discussing project details, and makes it easier to get to know one another: it can sometimes lead to more distractions.

B. for discussing project details and makes it easier to get to know one another, it can sometimes lead to more distractions.

C. for discussing project details and makes it easier to get to know one another? It can sometimes lead to more distractions.

D. for discussing project details, and makes it easier to get to know one another, it can sometimes lead to more distractions.

45. Sentence 17: When you visit a coworker's desk, [Select ▼]

A. wait for them to acknowledge you before diving in to your request.

B. weight for them to acknowledge you before diving into your request.

C. wait for them to acknowledge you before diving into your request.

D. weight for them to acknowledge you, before diving in to your request.

46. Sentence 21: [Select ▼]

A. Feel free to use office supplies and help yourself to the complimentary snacks in the cupboards marked as shared food.

B. Feel free to use office supplies, complimentary snacks in the cupboards, and shared food.

C. Feel free to use office supplies and help yourself to the complimentary snacks in the cupboards designated for shared food.

D. Shared food can be found; so help yourself in the cupboard, and feel free to use office supplies.

47. Sentence 23: Please clean up [Select ▼] yourself—we want a safe, clean, and welcoming environment for everyone.

A. after

B. for

C. with

D. as

diagnostic test — Language Arts

48. Which answers **best** describe proper etiquette in the workplace? Drag and drop the correct answers into the chart. (Enter the correct answers in the spaces provided on the answer sheet.)

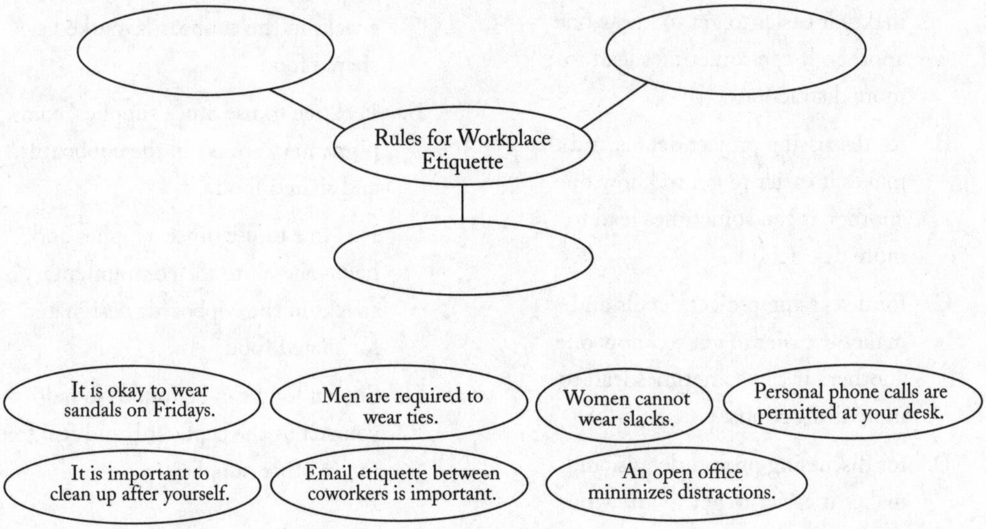

A. It is okay to wear sandals on Fridays.

B. Men are required to wear ties.

C. Women cannot wear slacks.

D. Personal phone calls are permitted at your desk.

E. It is important to clean up after yourself.

F. Email etiquette between coworkers is important.

G. An open office minimizes distractions.

STOP! DO NOT GO ON UNTIL TIME IS UP.

MATHEMATICAL REASONING

115 Minutes • 46 Questions

Directions: The Mathematical Reasoning Test will have calculator-allowed questions mixed with calculator-prohibited questions, with the calculator tool available to use when it is an option. However, for this test, the calculator-prohibited questions are grouped together as the first five questions.

Most questions are multiple-choice, but to answer some questions, you will be required to fill an answer in a blank, drag and drop correct answers, and select answers on a given graphic. Record your answers on the Mathematical Reasoning section of the answer sheet provided. To review how to answer these questions on your answer sheet, please refer to "Technology-Enhanced Questions" on page 24.

The test contains some questions where you will need to apply one or more mathematics formulas. The formulas provided on the following page will help you to answer those questions. Other questions will refer to charts, graphs, and figures. Unless otherwise noted, charts, graphs, and figures are drawn to scale.

Mathematics Formula Sheet

The GED Mathematical Reasoning Test contains a formula sheet, which displays formulas relating to geometric measurement and certain algebra concepts. Formulas are provided to test takers so that they may focus on *application*, rather than the *memorization*, of formulas.

Area of a:

parallelogram	$A = bh$	
trapezoid	$A = \frac{1}{2}h(b_1 + b_2)$	

Surface Area and Volume of a:

rectangular/right prism	$SA = ph + 2B$	$V = Bh$
cylinder	$SA = 2\pi rh + 2\pi r^2$	$V = \pi r^2 h$
pyramid	$SA = \frac{1}{2}ps + B$	$V = \frac{1}{3}Bh$
cone	$SA = \pi rs + \pi r^2$	$V = \frac{1}{3}\pi r^2 h$
sphere	$SA = 4\pi r^2$	$V = \frac{4}{3}\pi r^3$

(p = perimeter of base B; $\pi \approx 3.14$)

Algebra

slope of a line	$m = \frac{y_2 - y_1}{x_2 - x_1}$
slope-intercept form of the equation of a line	$y = mx + b$
point-slope form of the equation of a line	$y - y_1 = m(x - x_1)$
standard form of a quadratic equation	$y = ax^2 + bx + c$
quadratic formula	$x = \frac{-b \pm \sqrt{b^2 - 4ac}}{2a}$
Pythagorean theorem	$a^2 + b^2 = c^2$
simple interest	$I = prt$

(I = interest, p = principal, r = rate, t = time)

The use of a calculator is prohibited for questions 1–5.

SHOW YOUR WORK HERE

1. There are 78 sophomores at a school. Each is required to take at least one year of either chemistry or physics, but they may take both. 15 are enrolled in both chemistry and physics, and 47 are enrolled only in chemistry. How many students are enrolled only in physics? ______

2. Dividing the sum of $3\frac{7}{8}$ and $2\frac{11}{16}$ by $\frac{5}{8}$ yields which value?

   A. $\frac{15}{32}$

   B. $1\frac{1}{5}$

   C. $4\frac{1}{4}$

   D. $10\frac{1}{2}$

3. The perimeter of the hexagon shown is 240 centimeters. What is the length of each side?

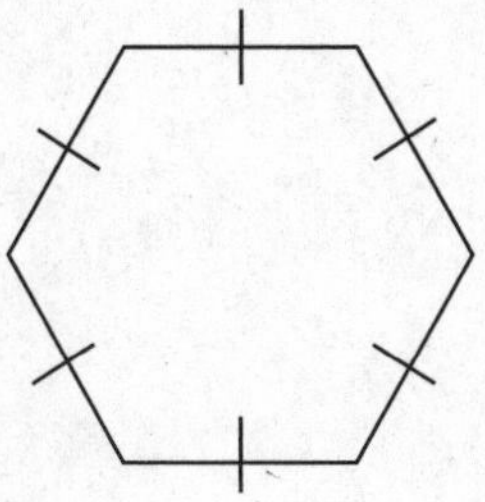

   A. 40 cm

   B. 48 cm

   C. 80 cm

   D. 120 cm

SHOW YOUR WORK HERE

4. If $x = -\frac{3}{4}$, compute $\dfrac{\frac{1}{x} - x}{\frac{1}{x} + x}$.

A. $-\frac{1}{7}$

B. $\frac{7}{25}$

C. 1

D. $\frac{175}{144}$

5. The average team score for the first 5 basketball games of the season is 45 points. The scores of the first 5 games are 54, 60, 28, 42, and

A. 31.

B. 36.

C. 41.

D. 46.

The use of a calculator is allowed for questions 6–46.

6. If an isosceles triangle has two angles that each measure 34°, what is the measure of its third angle?

A. 34°

B. 90°

C. 112°

D. 147°

7. Compute $-2^3|3-9|$.

A. –48

B. –36

C. 48

D. 96

8. A rectangular box with a surface area of 248 square inches is 4 inches high and 10 inches long. What is its width?

A. 6 inches

B. 10 inches

C. 40 inches

D. 60 inches

SHOW YOUR WORK HERE

9. A farmer wants to construct a fence to create a square horse corral with an area of 10,000 square feet. Fence posts along each side will be 10 feet apart at their center.

Including the four corner posts, how many posts are needed to construct the fence?

A. 36

B. 40

C. 44

D. 100

10. If $g(x) = x^3 - 16x$, what are the x-values at which the graph of $g(x)$ crosses the x-axis?

A. 0 only

B. −16, 0, and 16

C. −4, 0, and 4

D. −2, 0, and 2

11. A botanist observing the growth rate of a climbing vine records growth of 0.36 meters over one 24-day period. What was the vine's growth rate, per day, expressed in centimeters? [1 meter = 100 centimeters]

A. 0.015 cm/day

B. 1.5 cm/day

C. 8.64 cm/day

D. 864 cm/day

SHOW YOUR WORK HERE

12. The figure shows two line segments connecting a circle's center to its circumference. What is the value of y in terms of x ?

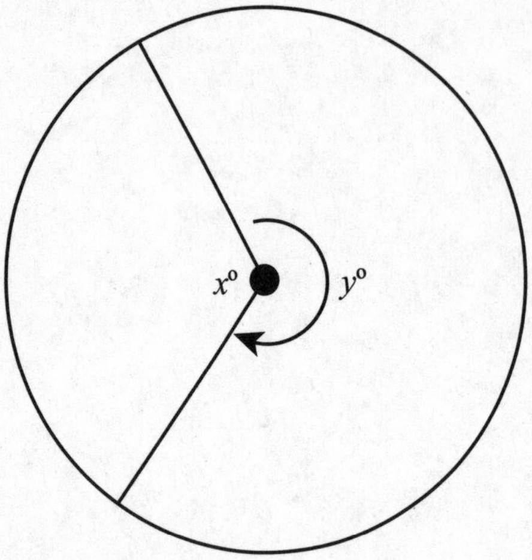

A. $\frac{360}{x}$

B. $\frac{x}{180}$

C. $360 - x$

D. $\frac{x}{360}$

13. If $x^2 + 4x = 0$, how many values of x are possible?

A. None

B. One

C. Two

D. Infinitely many

14. Suppose a and b are nonzero real numbers. If $bx - a = y$ and $ay - b = x$, what is the value of x?

A. $-(a + 1)$

B. $\frac{a^2 + b}{ab + 1}$

C. $\frac{a + b}{ab - 1}$

D. $\frac{a^2 + b}{ab - 1}$

15. In the number line shown, the vertical marks are equally spaced.

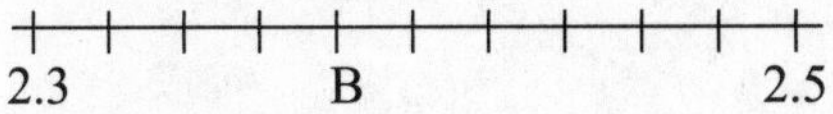

What is the value of B?

16. Quadrilateral *ABCD* is a square. The coordinates of point *A* are (3, 2), the coordinates of point *B* are (–3, 2), and the coordinates of point *C* are (–3, –4).

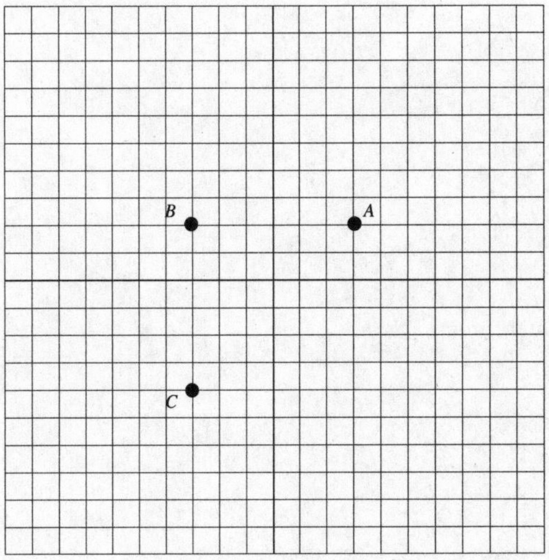

Click on the coordinate grid to show the location of point *D*. (Enter the coordinates of point *D* on the answer sheet.)

17. How many different ways can you add four positive, odd integers together for a sum of 10? The integers may be used more than once, and the sequence of the integers should not be considered.

A. One

B. Two

C. Three

D. Four

SHOW YOUR WORK HERE

18. The length of Cassie's family room is exactly half the length of her bedroom. Both rooms are rectangular, and the area of the two rooms is the same. If Cassie's family room has a length of L and a width of W, write an expression that represents the width of her bedroom.

19. The average of three consecutive odd integers is 39. Which equation can be used to determine these integers?

A. $\frac{N+(N+2)+(N+4)}{3}=39$

B. $\frac{N+(N+1)+(N+2)}{3}=39$

C. $\frac{N+(N+1)+(N+3)}{3}=39$

D. $\frac{N+3N+5N}{3}=39$

Questions 20 and 21 refer to the following graph.

Imports and Exports For Country X and Country Y, 2013–2018

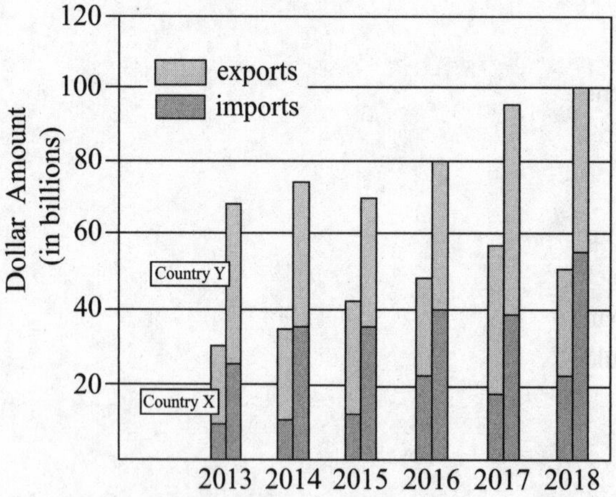

Note: *For each year, the combined height of two bar segments shows total imports and exports of a country.*

SHOW YOUR WORK HERE

20. In which of the following years did Country Y's imports exceed Country X's imports by the smallest percentage?

A. 2014

B. 2015

C. 2016

D. 2018

21. Which **best** describes Country Y's overall import and export trend over the six-year period shown? Choose your answer from the drop-down menu.

Select ▼

A. Imports decreased; exports decreased.

B. Imports increased; exports exhibited no clear trend.

C. Imports exhibited no clear trend; exports increased.

D. Neither imports nor exports exhibited a clear trend.

SHOW YOUR WORK HERE

SHOW YOUR WORK HERE

22. A group of travelers has assembled a tepee that has a circular base. As shown in the figure, the side of the tepee measures 17 meters from the ground to the tepee's peak, and the height of the tepee is 15 meters. What is the diameter of the tepee's circular base?

[   ] meters

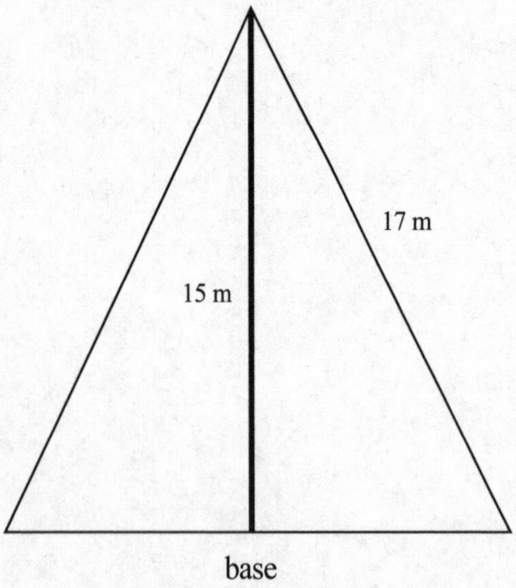

23. What value should be placed in the box to make this true?

$$\frac{8^2 \times \left(2^4\right)^3}{16} = 2^{\square}$$

A. $\frac{9}{2}$

B. 14

C. 18

D. 69

24. A restaurant kitchen stores large cans of peas, as shown below. Each can has a volume of $2{,}880\pi$ cm^3 and a height of 20 cm. A cook is trying to figure out how many cans of peas he can fit side by side on one shelf. What is the diameter of the can of peas?

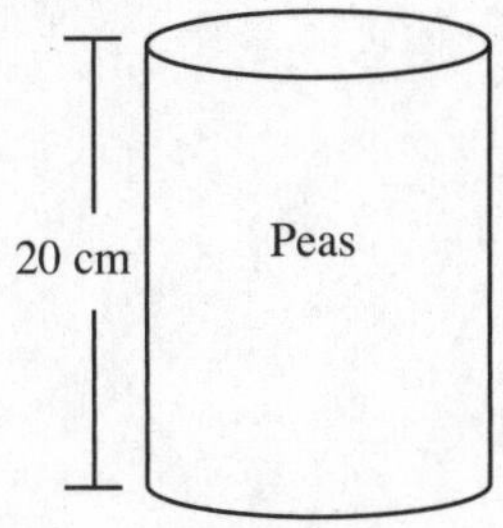

A. 12 cm

B. 24 cm

C. 20 cm

D. 144 cm

25. A scientist performs an experiment and determines a very high negative correlation between the amount of oxygen and the amount of a certain type of algae in a tank. He uses the graph shown to plot the data. The first data points he collected are already plotted. Use your mouse to click a possible last data point above the arrow on the *x*-axis that would show the high negative correlation determined by the scientist. (Enter the answer on the answer sheet diagram.)

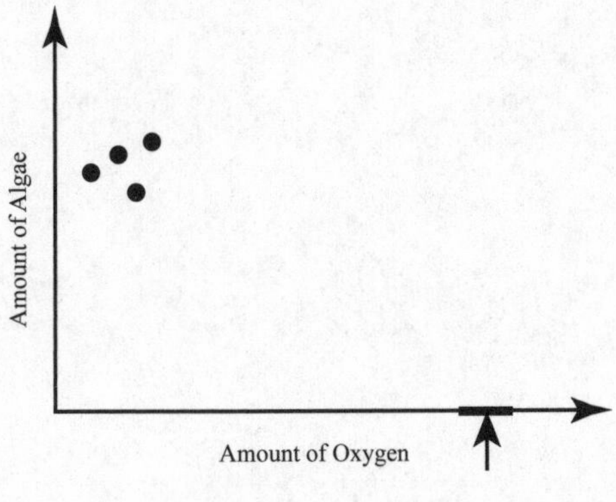

SHOW YOUR WORK HERE

26. Suppose a is a nonzero real number. Which of these expressions is equivalent to $\frac{3x}{a^2} - \frac{x}{3a}$?

A. $\frac{(9-a)x}{3a^2}$

B. $\frac{8x}{3a^2}$

C. $\frac{2x}{a^2 - 3a}$

D. $\frac{(9-a)x}{6a^2}$

27. Factor $16x^2 - 8x + 1$.

A. $(16x - 1)(x - 1)$

B. $(8x - 1)(2x - 1)$

C. $(4x - 1)(4x + 1)$

D. $(4x - 1)^2$

28. Herman is covering 20 square tiles with cloth. In order to calculate how much cloth he needs, he must square the length in centimeters, c, of each side of a tile and then add x extra centimeters to account for error. Which equation should Herman use to calculate how much total cloth he will need to cover the 20 tiles?

A. $20c^2 + x$

B. $20c^2 + 20x$

C. $20 + c^2 \times x$

D. $20c^2 + x^2$

29. Solve for y_1: $\frac{x - x_1}{y - y_1} = m$

A. $y_1 = \frac{x - y - x_1}{m}$

B. $y_1 = y + \frac{x_1 - x}{m}$

C. $y_1 = x + y - x_1$

D. $y_1 = my - x + x_1$

SHOW YOUR WORK HERE

30. Click on a point on the number line below that satisfies the inequality $-2x - 3 > -1$. (Enter the answer on the answer sheet diagram.)

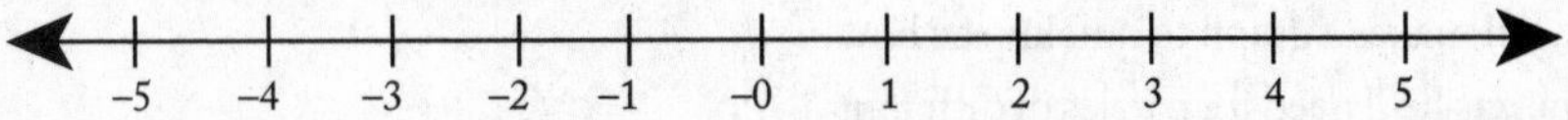

31. The cost to build sign posts in Everytown is a fee of $60 per hour for the labor plus $240 per sign post. Each sign post takes 1.5 hours to build. The retainer fee for the contractor who supplies the labor is $1,200. Drag and drop the variables, numbers, and signs below to create an inequality that will determine how many sign posts, *p*, can be built in Everytown with a budget of $8,000. Not all numbers may be used. (Enter the inequality on the answer sheet.)

Number choices: 60 90 240 300 330 1,200 8,000 1.5*p* 240*p* 330*p*

Signs: + – × ÷ ≤ ≥ < >

32. A computer company is trying to figure out what its sales in dollars will be for its new line of tablets. It has figured out that unit sales will follow the demand curve 45,000 – 160*p*, where *p* is the selling price of the tablet. If this is how many tablets it will sell, which equation will yield the total sales in dollars?

A. $45{,}000 + 160p^2 = \text{total sales}$

B. $45{,}000 + 160p + p = \text{total sales}$

C. $45{,}000p - 160p^2 = \text{total sales}$

D. $160p^2 + p = \text{total sales}$

SHOW YOUR WORK HERE

33. Sal's Pizza hosts pizza parties for children's birthdays. Sal has determined that it's best to have 3 pizzas for every group of 8 children at a party. Sal makes a graph to quickly see how many pizzas he'll need for parties of different sizes. What is the slope of the line in Sal's graph?

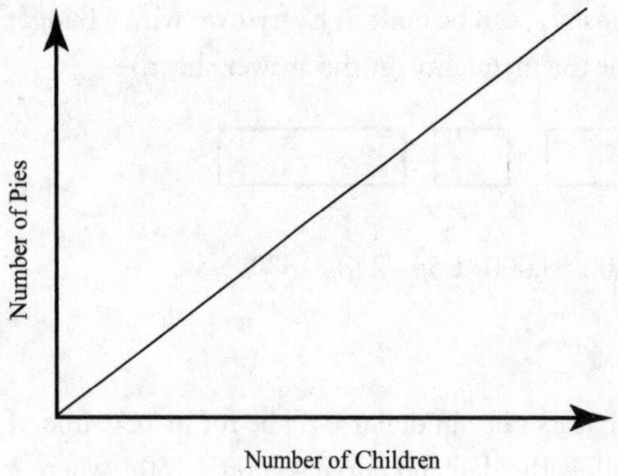

A. $\frac{8}{3}$

B. $\frac{3}{8}$

C. $\frac{1}{3}$

D. $\frac{1}{8}$

34. What is the equation of the line with slope $-\frac{3}{2}$ and x-intercept (–4, 0)?

A. $y = -\frac{3}{2}x - 6$

B. $x = -\frac{3}{2}y - 6$

C. $x = -\frac{2}{3}y$

D. $y = -\frac{3}{2}x - 4$

35. Drag and drop numbers or variables to make the following statement true. The function graphed below is decreasing on the interval [   ] $\leq x \leq$ [   ]. (Enter the answers on the spaces provided on the answer sheet.)

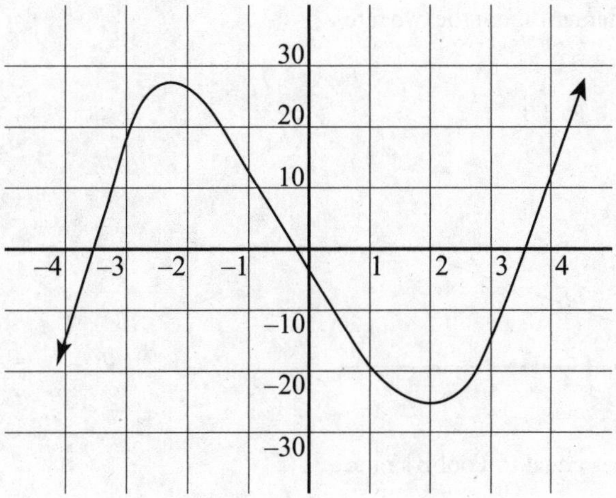

–4, –2, –1, 0, 1, 2, 4, x

36. What is the equation of a line passing through the points (–4, 5) and (2, 2)?

SHOW YOUR WORK HERE

A. $y=-\frac{1}{2}x-\frac{3}{2}$

B. $y=-\frac{1}{2}x-3$

C. $y=\frac{1}{2}x+3$

D. $y=-\frac{1}{2}x+3$

37. Two pools are being filled at a day camp. Pool A is being filled at a rate of 12 gallons per hour. Pool B's fill rate is shown in the graph. Which statement about the two rates is true?

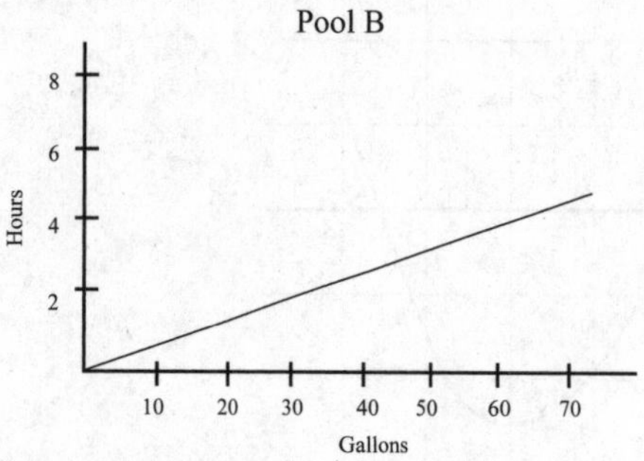

A. Pool A's rate is equal to Pool B's rate.

B. Pool B is filling at a rate that is 3 gallons per hour faster than Pool A's rate.

C. Pool A is filling at a rate that is 3 gallons per hour faster than Pool B's rate.

D. Pool A is filling at a rate that is half as fast as Pool B's rate.

38. Pamela has \$4.30 in dimes and quarters. The number of dimes is one fewer than three times the number of quarters. If q is the number of quarters and d is the number of dimes, which system can be solved to determine the values of q and d?

SHOW YOUR WORK HERE

A. $\begin{cases} d = 3(q-1) \\ 10d + 25q = 430 \end{cases}$

B. $\begin{cases} d = 3q-1 \\ 10d + 25q = 4.30 \end{cases}$

C. $\begin{cases} d = 3q-1 \\ 0.10d + 0.25q = 4.30 \end{cases}$

D. $\begin{cases} q = 3d-1 \\ 0.10d + 0.25q = 4.30 \end{cases}$

39. Consider the line $y = -\frac{2}{3}x + 5$. Which of the following is a correct interpretation of the quantity $-\frac{2}{3}$?

A. The y-value on the graph decreases by 3 units for every 2 units increase in x.

B. The y-value on the graph decreases by 2 units for every 3 units increase in x.

C. The y-value on the graph increases by 2 units for every 3 units increase in x.

D. The graph of the line crosses the y-axis at $\left(0, -\frac{2}{3}\right)$.

diagnostic test—Mathematical Reasoning

40. Rick left home driving down a country road at 35 miles per hour. His sister realized he forgot his laptop at home and set out to catch him, following the same route, at 45 miles per hour. By the time she left, he was 6 miles ahead of her. Which equation can be used to determine the time t, in hours, it takes for her to catch Rick?

A. $35t = 45t$

B. $35t = 45(t + 6)$

C. $35t = 6 + 45t$

D. $35t + 6 = 45t$

SHOW YOUR WORK HERE

41. Monthly electricity charges in a township are calculated using a unit rate per kilowatt hour consumed by a household plus a $20 fixed delivery fee. Using the table shown, find the linear equation that **best** represents y, the total monthly electricity charges, as a function of x, the number of kilowatt hours consumed per month.

Kilowatt Hours Consumed Per Month (x)	Monthly Service Delivery Fee	Total Electricity Charges Per Month (y)
400 kwh	$20	$36.80
900 kwh	$20	$57.80
1100 kwh	$20	$66.20

A. $x = 0.42y - 20$

B. $x = 0.042y + 20$

C. $y = 0.42x - 20$

D. $y = 0.042x + 20$

42. A father and son decide to participate in a half-marathon. The father is given a 0.75-mile head start and jogs at a pace of 5 miles per hour for t hours. The son jogs at a pace of 6.5 miles per hour for t hours. Which of the following is an accurate description of the distance d (in miles) between the father and son at any time t (in hours)?

A. $d = 6.5t - 5t$

B. $d = 0.75 + 5t$

C. $d = 6.5t$

D. $d = 0.75 - 1.5t$

43. The number of complete turns that a small gear makes is related to the number of turns made by a larger gear to which it is connected. The linear function $c = 3.5t$ describes this relationship, where c represents the number of complete turns that the small gear makes for each complete turn of the larger gear, and t represents the number of complete turns made by the larger gear. Which of the following is an equivalent representation of this linear function?

A.

t	c
3	21
6	42
9	63

B.

t	c
1	3
2	6
5	15

C. For every 7 turns the smaller gear makes, the larger gear makes 2 turns.

D. For every 3.5 complete turns of the larger gear, the smaller gear makes one complete turn.

SHOW YOUR WORK HERE

diagnostic test—Mathematical Reasoning

44. Which statements regarding the graph of the function $y = -2x - 5$ is true?

SHOW YOUR WORK HERE

A. The graph is a line passing through the point (0, −5) with slope of −2.

B. The graph contains the points (−3, −11) and (3, 1).

C. The graph crosses the y-axis at −5 and when the value of x decreases by 1 unit, the y-value decreases by 2 units.

D. The graph is a line that does not cross the x-axis.

45. If $f(x) = -x^2(2 + 3x)$ what is $f(-4)$?

A. −320

B. −80

C. 80

D. 160

46. Consider the graph of the following line:

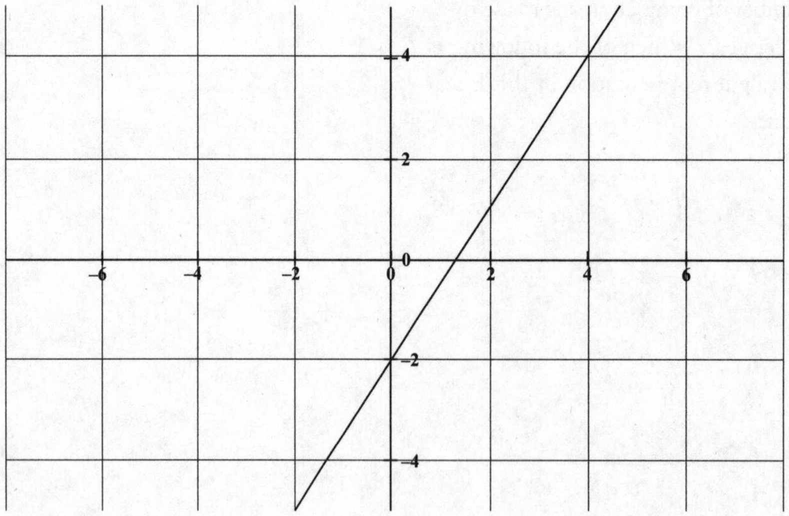

What is the equation of this line? Fill in the boxes to express it in slope-intercept form:

$$y = \square x + \square$$

STOP! DO NOT GO ON UNTIL TIME IS UP.

SCIENCE

90 Minutes • 35 Questions

Directions: The Science Test consists of questions in several formats designed to measure your knowledge of general science concepts. The questions are based on brief passages of text and visual information (charts, graphs, diagrams, and other figures). Some questions are based on both text and visual information. Study the information provided, and answer the question(s) that follow, referring back to the information as needed.

Most questions are multiple-choice, but to answer some questions, you will be required to select from a drop-down menu, fill an answer in a blank, drag and drop correct answers, and select answers on a given graphic. Record your answers on the Science section of the answer sheet provided. To review how to answer these questions on your answer sheet, please refer to "Technology-Enhanced Questions" on page 24.

Question 1 refers to the following information.

If one side of a stemmed plant receives more sunlight than the other side, the growth hormone auxin, which stimulates vertical growth of the elongated stem, will concentrate on the shady side of the stem in order to stimulate more growth there.

1. What will be the result of this stimulation?

   A. The plant will grow beyond its ability to nourish itself.

   B. The plant will bend toward the light.

   C. The plant will wither where auxin is absent.

   D. The plant will bend toward the ground.

Question 2 refers to the following diagram.

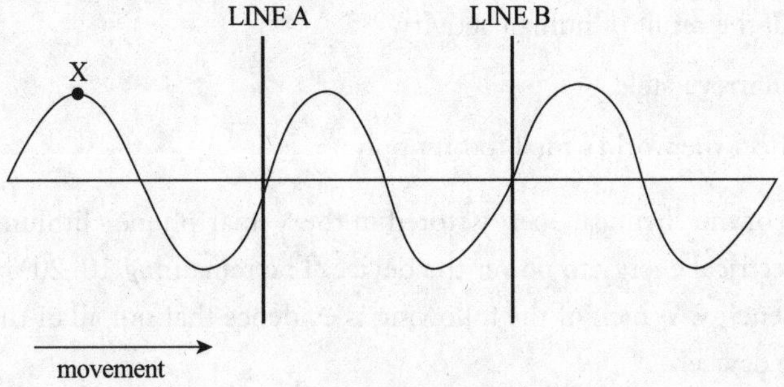

2. The wave crest shown as point X will reach line A in 3 seconds. In how many seconds will the same wave crest reach line B?

   A. 7 seconds

   B. 9 seconds

   C. 10 seconds

   D. 11 seconds

Question 3 refers to the following information.

Most stomach ulcers, which can cause stomach pain and vomiting, are caused by bacteria called *Helicobacter pylori*. Before the discovery of these bacteria, ulcers were thought to be caused by stress. The standard treatment for ulcers today is antibiotics, which kill the bacteria. Two Australian doctors, Barry Marshall and Robin Warren, won the Nobel Prize for this discovery. Dr. Marshall proved that *H. pylori* caused ulcers by drinking broth that was infected with the bacteria.

3. Which of the following was a probable outcome of Dr. Marshall's experiment?

A. Dr. Marshall's illness could not be successfully treated with antibiotics.

B. Dr. Marshall's illness could be successfully treated with anti-stress techniques.

C. Dr. Marshall became ill with stomach pains after drinking the infected broth.

D. Dr. Marshall became ill with skin rashes after drinking the infected broth.

Question 4 is based on the following information.

The biosphere encompasses all life-sustaining regions of the earth, its atmosphere, and its oceans. The following significant changes have been observed and documented during the last century.

- Wilderness areas have been deforested by the clear-cutting of trees to make wood products.
- Rivers and oceans have been polluted by fertilizer and sewage runoff.
- The protective ozone layer of the earth's atmosphere has been depleted by the overuse of certain air pollutants.
- Livestock overgrazing has led to the desertification of grasslands, reducing agricultural output and available habitats for native plant and animal species.

4. How can all these findings be reconciled as having one common cause or characteristic?

A. They are all caused by global climate change.

B. They are all the result of human activity.

C. They are all irreversible.

D. They all affect the world's total food supply.

5. About 80–90% of the chemical energy stored in the a smartphone's lithium-ion battery is converted to electrical energy to power the device. The remaining 10–20% is converted to other forms of energy. Which of the following is evidence that not all of the battery's energy is powering the device?

A. The device becomes hotter the longer it is used.

B. The device is able to receive and send voice calls.

C. The device's display lights up when the screen is touched.

D. The device is able to take photographs and videos.

Question 6 refers to the following illustration.

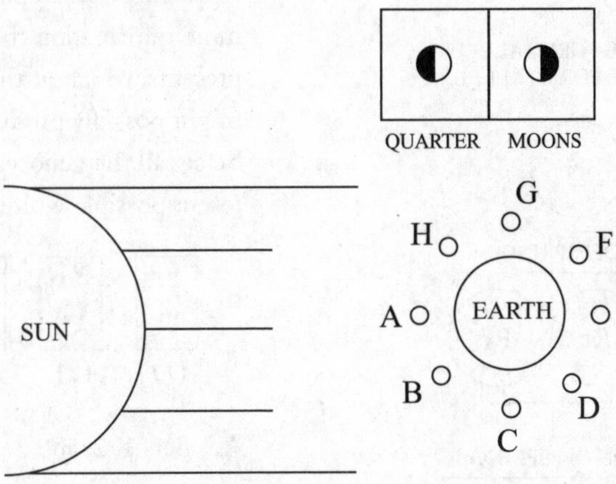

6. Referring to the illustration, at which moon positions would someone on Earth directly below the moon see a quarter moon in the sky? Images are not drawn to scale. Choose the accurate positions by clicking on the images of the moon. More than one may be correct. (Enter the correct position(s) letters in the space provided on the answer sheet.)

Question 7 refers to the following diagram.

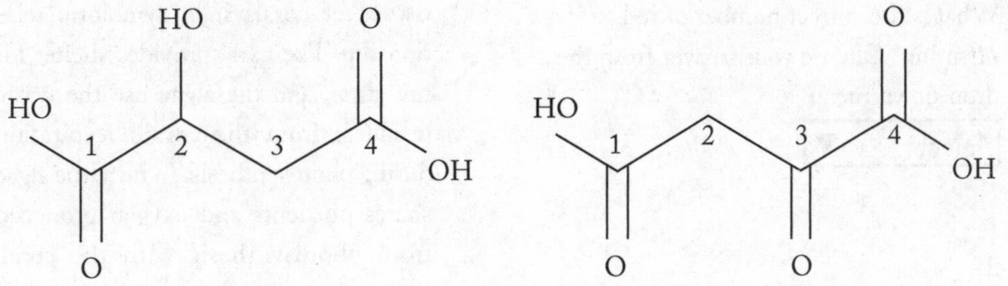

Malate Oxaloacetate

Note: *The carbon atoms have been numbered in each molecule.*

7. One of the steps of the citric acid cycle involves the conversion of malate to oxaloacetate. Which of the following transformations occurs when malate is converted to oxaloacetate?

A. The OH group on carbon 2 is moved to carbon 3.

B. The OH group on carbon 2 is moved to carbon 3 and transformed into a double-bonded oxygen.

C. The double-bonded oxygen on carbon 3 is moved to carbon 2 and transformed into an OH group.

D. The double-bonded oxygen on carbon 4 is moved to carbon 3.

Questions 8 and 9 refer to the following diagram.

R= DOMINANT GENE FORM (ALLELE)
r= RECESSIVE GENE FORM (ALLELE)

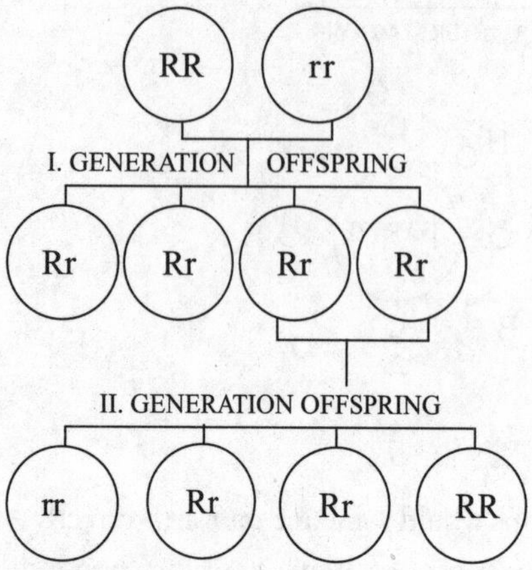

GENOTYPE	TRAIT FORM
RR	RED COLOR
Rr	RED COLOR
rr	WHITE COLOR

8. What is the correct number of red offspring? Choose your answer from the drop-down menu.

Select ▼

1

2

3

4

5

6

7

8

9. Each genotype pair in the illustration represents a set of parents. Without any more information than what the diagram presents, which of the four sets of parents might possibly produce a white offspring? Select all the genotype pairs that represent possible white offspring.

rr rr	RR rr	Rr Rr	rr Rr
(1)	**(2)**	**(3)**	**(4)**

A. Sets 1, 2, and 3

B. Sets 1, 2, and 4

C. Sets 1, 3, and 4

D. Sets 2, 3, and 4

Question 10 refers to the following information.

Photosynthetic algae live inside the tissues of corals in a symbiotic relationship. The coral provides shelter for the algae, and the algae use the waste products from the coral's respiration during photosynthesis. In turn, the algae shares nutrients and oxygen produced from photosynthesis with the coral. Rising ocean temperatures have caused the algae in many coral reefs to die, which causes the coral to turn white. This process is called coral bleaching and usually results in the death of the coral.

10. Which of the following can be concluded from the information provided?

A. Algae need coral to survive.

B. Coral need algae to survive.

C. If ocean warming continues, less coral will die.

D. If ocean temperatures cool, more algae will die.

Question 11 refers to the following illustration.

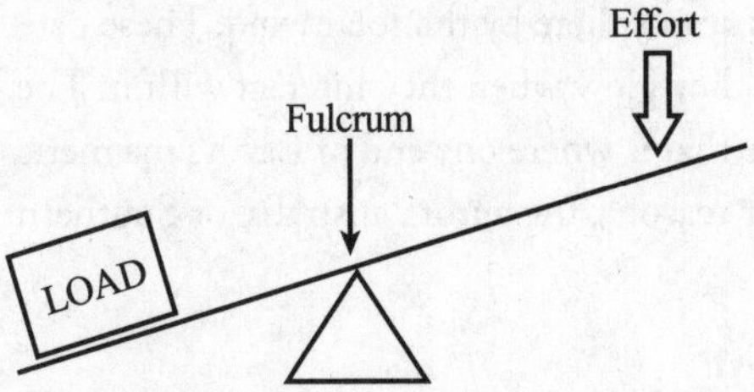

11. The simple machine shown here has a measurable mechanical advantage. A student wants to design an experiment to demonstrate and measure the mechanical advantage for this type of simple machine. Which of these tools should the student use as an example of the machine?

A. A crowbar

B. A wedge

C. A wheelbarrow

D. A nutcracker

12. In modern whales, the front limbs have been modified into large flippers, and the hind limbs have been lost. However, whales retain remnants of the bones of the pelvis, even though they have no hind limb (leg) bones. What does this suggest about the evolution of whales?

A. Whales evolved from animals that did not have pelvis bones.

B. Whales evolved from animals that did not have front limbs.

C. Whales evolved from animals that had complete hind limbs.

D. Whales will evolve hind limbs in the future.

Question 13 refers to the following diagram.

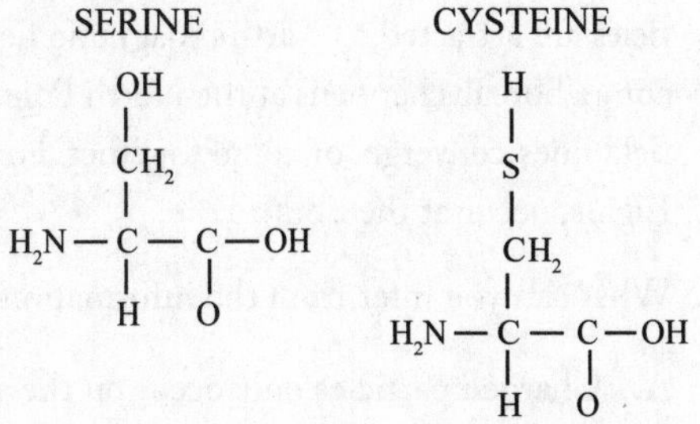

13. How does a serine molecule differ from a cysteine molecule?

A serine molecule contains a different number of

A. oxygen atoms.

B. carbon atoms.

C. nitrogen atoms.

D. hydrogen atoms.

Question 14 refers to the following information.

Turkeys have 80 chromosomes in each cell that is not a gamete. This is also known as their diploid number ($2n$). In sexually reproducing organisms, gametes (reproductive cells) contain a haploid number (n) of chromosomes.

14. How many chromosomes does a turkey egg or sperm cell contain?

A. 23

B. 40

C. 80

D. 160

Question 15 refers to the following information.

The aurora borealis, or Northern Lights, is an atmospheric phenomenon caused by charged particles from the sun that are blown into Earth's atmosphere by the solar wind. These particles are attracted to Earth's magnetic field, and they glow when they interact with it. The aurora borealis happens at the North Pole because that is where one end of Earth's magnetic field lines converge, or come together. For similar reasons, the aurora australis, or Southern Lights, occur at the South Pole.

15. What can you infer from the information provided?

A. Charged particles only occur on the sun.

B. An aurora equatorius must occur at the equator as well.

C. Auroras happen only in cold climates like the North and South Poles.

D. The other end of Earth's magnetic field lines converges at the South Pole.

Question 16 refers to the following chart.

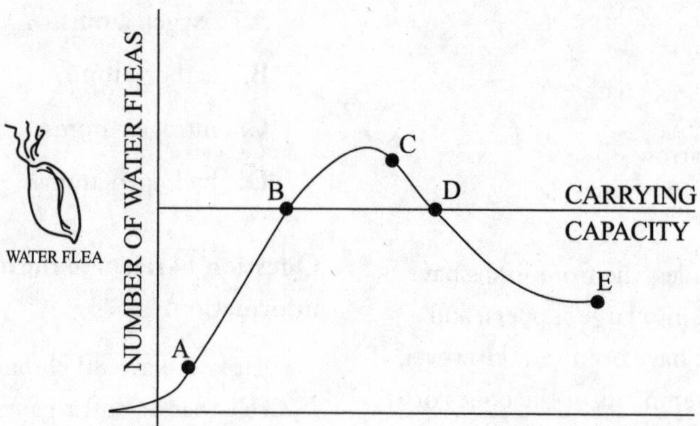

Note: *When a population reaches carrying capacity, just enough resources are available to support the existing population.*

16. According to the chart, at what point does the water flea population exceed the environment's ability to support them?

A. Point A

B. Point B

C. Point C

D. Point E

Questions 17 and 18 refer to the following information.

The Hertzsprung-Russell Diagram plots stars according to luminosity (brightness), surface temperature, and spectral class (color).

***Note:** Absolute magnitude is a measure of luminosity (brightness) that uses an inverted scale.*

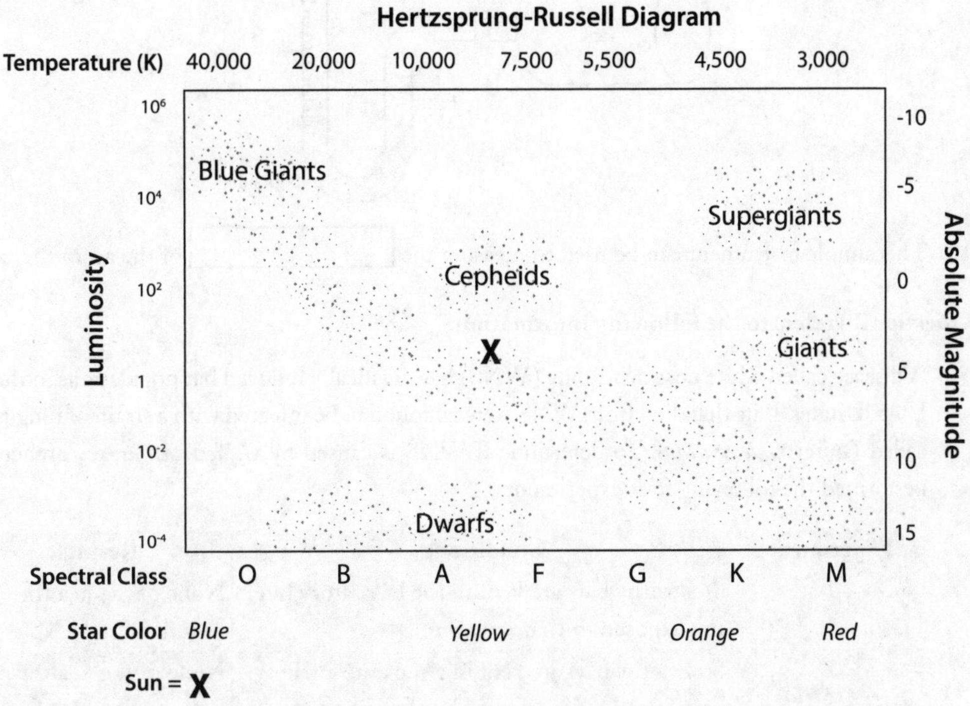

17. Which statement does the Hertzsprung-Russell Diagram **best** support?

A. Red stars are hotter than blue stars.

B. Giants are among the coldest stars.

C. Dwarfs are more luminous than cepheids.

D. Orange stars are more luminous than red stars.

18. What conclusion can you draw from the Hertzsprung-Russell Diagram?

A. Our sun is typical in terms of brightness and surface temperature.

B. Our sun is old compared to most other stars.

C. The stars in the universe appear in broad bands and in clusters.

D. The number of stars in the universe is expanding.

Question 19 refers to the following illustration.

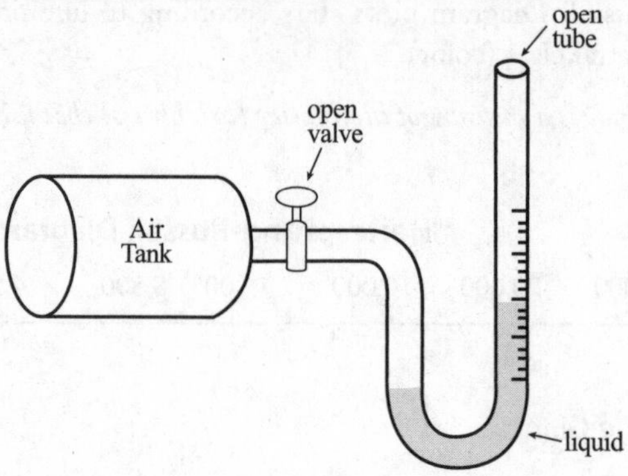

19. This simple instrument can be used to measure the ________ of the air in the tank.

Question 20 refers to the following information.

A disease called white nose syndrome (WNS) has drastically reduced bat populations in the United States. Bats that died from WNS were all found to be infected with a strain of fungus called *Geomyces destructans*. To determine if WNS is caused by *G. destructans*, researchers performed the following four experiments:

Experiment	Conditions	Results
1	34 healthy bats are kept in the laboratory but not exposed to *G. destructans*	None of the healthy bats develop WNS
2	36 healthy bats are kept in a separate enclosure from WNS-infected bats in the same laboratory room; healthy and sick bats share the same air but do not touch	None of the healthy bats develop WNS
3	18 healthy bats are placed in the same enclosure as WNS-infected bats; healthy and sick bats share the same air and can touch	16 of the healthy bats develop WNS
4	29 healthy bats had *G. destructans* applied to their wings and are placed in their own enclosure in the laboratory	All 29 of the healthy bats develop WNS

20. Based on the information given, which of the following is a valid conclusion to draw from these experiments?

A. WNS is spread through the air.

B. WNS is not caused by *G. destructans*.

C. WNS is spread through direct contact with *G. destructans*.

D. Bats housed in the same enclosure do not touch.

Question 21 refers to the following illustration and information.

TYPES OF EPITHELIAL TISSUE

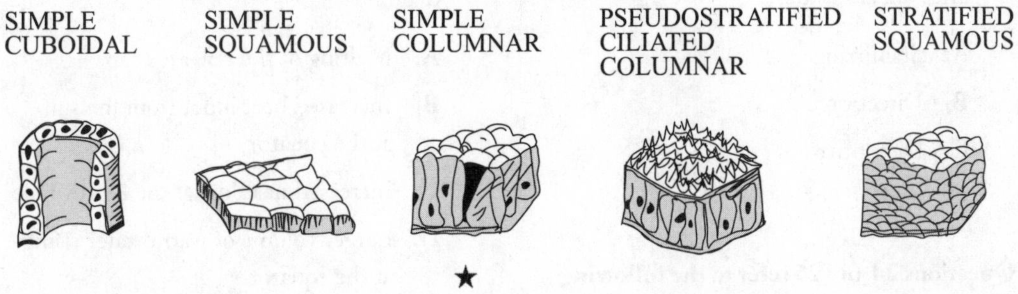

The illustrations show five types of tightly packed epithelial tissues, which form the thin membranes lining most internal and external surfaces of an animal's body. Thinner tissues allow for the exchange of particles through the membrane, whereas thicker tissues serve largely as barriers.

21. Which type of epithelial tissue lines a lung's air sacs, which must freely pass oxygen to blood vessels in exchange for carbon dioxide? Drag and drop the star onto the type of epithelial tissue that lines a lung's air sac. (Enter the correct type of epithelial tissue on the answer sheet.)

Questions 22 and 23 refer to the following information.

There are four types of natural selection: stabilizing selection, directional selection, disruptive selection, and kin selection. In stabilizing selection, traits that are the average condition for a population are selected. In directional selection, traits that tend toward one extreme for a population are selected. In disruptive selection, both extremes of a trait are selected. In kin selection, traits that benefit related members of a group are selected. The graph below shows the frequency of the extreme and average conditions of a trait in a typical population.

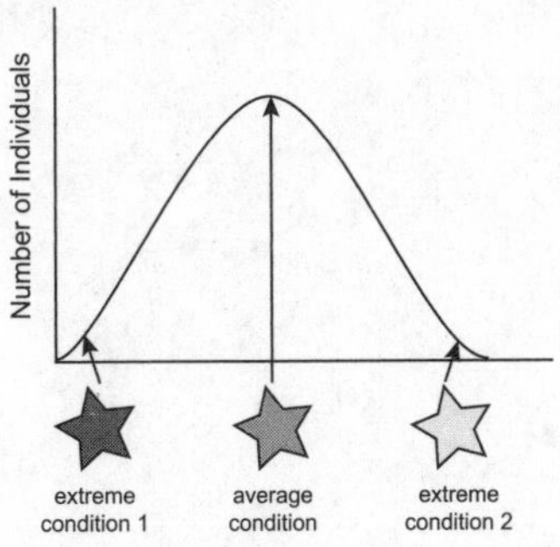

22. A population of black, dark brown, and light brown lizards live on a hillside. Dark brown lizards are the most common, and black and light brown lizards are rare. After a landslide of light-colored rocks changes the state of the hillside, the lizards are selected for changes. Which of the following is **most likely** to happen?

A. Dark brown lizards will continue to be the most common lizard in the population because they are most likely to survive on a light-colored hillside.

B. Black lizards will become the most common lizard because they are most likely to survive on a light-colored hillside.

C. Light brown lizards will become the most common lizard because they are most likely to survive on a light-colored hillside.

D. Black and light brown lizards will be equally common in the population because they have an equal likelihood of survival on a light-colored hillside.

23. Based on the likely outcome of the lizard population, what type of selection occurs after the landslide?

- **A.** Stabilizing
- **B.** Directional
- **C.** Disruptive
- **D.** Kin

Questions 24 and 25 refer to the following illustration.

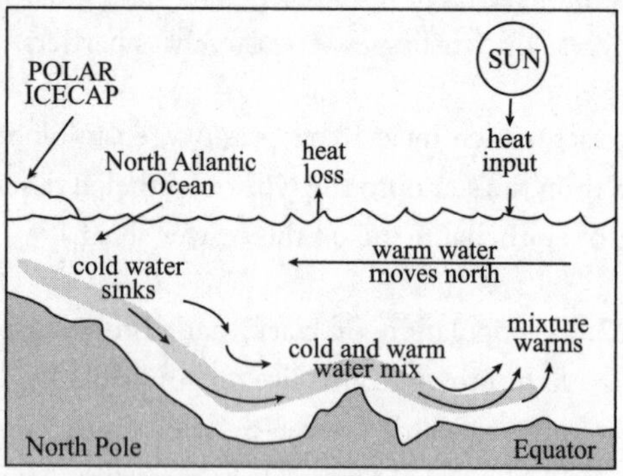

24. What overall idea does the diagram convey?

- **A.** The Atlantic Ocean's depth is greatest near the equator.
- **B.** Ocean water circulates between the equator and the North Atlantic Ocean.
- **C.** Warm ocean water rises, while colder ocean water sinks.
- **D.** Unusually warm air can disturb the normal currents of the Atlantic Ocean.

25. Which of the following changes is **most likely** to stop the process shown in the diagram?

- **A.** Melting of the polar ice cap
- **B.** Increased heat input from the sun at the equator
- **C.** Increased heat loss at the North Pole
- **D.** Larger volume of warm water rising at the equator

26. The white-tailed ptarmigan has evolved coloration that changes with the seasons. In the winter, it is totally white, while in the summer, it is speckled gray and brown. This changing coloration is an effective camouflage against predators. Which of the following describes the **most likely** habitat of this bird?

- **A.** African grassland
- **B.** Canadian prairie
- **C.** Tropical rain forest
- **D.** Equatorial wetland

Question 27 refers to the following graph.

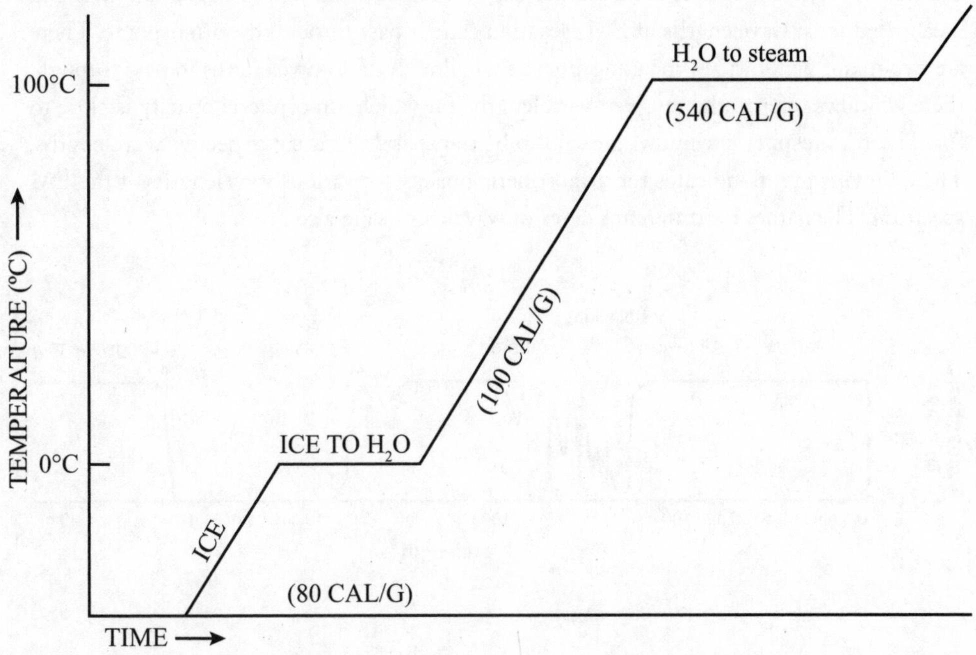

27. At a minimum, how much heat energy is required to change 1 gram of ice into steam?

[ ]

28. Like light matter, dark matter attracts all other matter gravitationally, and so it sustains a gravitational field. As astronomers study a galaxy, they can infer the presence of dark matter if the galaxy's motion is different from that predicted by the mass of observable light matter alone. Therefore, the theoretical existence of dark matter is based on the application of an understanding of the force of [ ].

diagnostic test — Science

Questions 29 and 30 refer to the following information.

Earth's atmosphere is opaque to most wavelengths of electromagnetic (EM) radiation, which means that most wavelengths of EM radiation cannot pass through the atmosphere. There are two main "windows" in the atmosphere that allow certain wavelengths to pass through; these windows refer to the range of wavelengths for which atmospheric opacity is close to 0%. These atmospheric windows are said to be transparent to their respective wavelengths. The following graph indicates the atmospheric opacity for various wavelengths of the EM spectrum. The names for different ranges of wavelengths are also given.

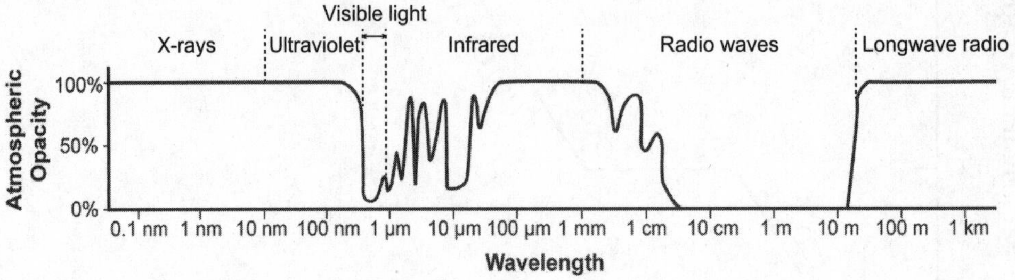

29. Without atmospheric windows, Earth would be perpetually dark. Which atmospheric window allows Earth's surface to be illuminated during the day and, thus, life on Earth to exist?

A. Ultraviolet

B. Visible light

C. Infrared

D. Radio wave

30. Which of the following is a process that can occur because of an atmospheric window?

A. Infrared radiation being reflected back to Earth's surface by the atmosphere and creating the greenhouse effect

B. Ozone in the upper atmosphere blocking most ultraviolet radiation from reaching the earth's surface

C. Scientists using dish-shaped telescopes to collect radio waves from outer space to study astronomical objects

D. Airplanes being able to fly from one spot to another on Earth through the upper atmosphere

31. Sediment sorting is the process that causes similar-sized sediment particles to be deposited in the same place. Sediments that have traveled farther from where they are created tend to be better sorted than sediments that have only traveled a short distance. What is the **best** explanation for this observation?

A. Sediment particles have more time to settle out by size the farther they travel.

B. More sediment particles can be added to the mixture the farther they travel.

C. Sediment particles become more rounded the farther they travel.

D. Sediment particles become harder the farther they travel.

Questions 32 and 33 refer to the following information.

The diagram below represents a coiled spring about to push a cart (panel A) and then the same spring uncoiling and shoving the cart forward (panel B). The large arrows in panel B represent the direction of motion.

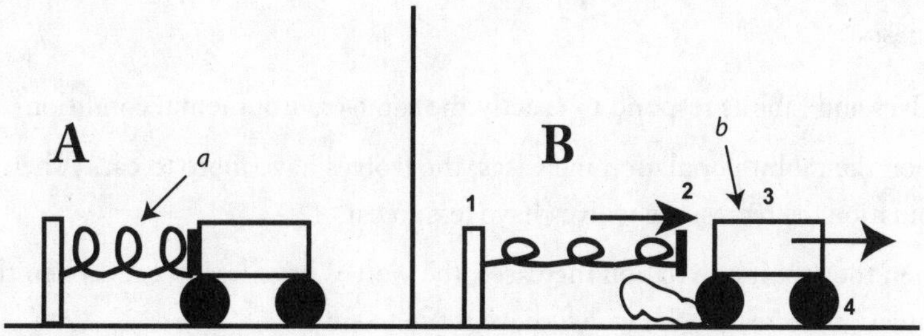

32. The spring indicated by arrow *a* has [ ] energy and the cart indicated by arrow *b* has [ ] energy.

33. In panel B, which number indicates the location where work is done?

A. 1

B. 2

C. 3

D. 4

Question 34 refers to the following graph.

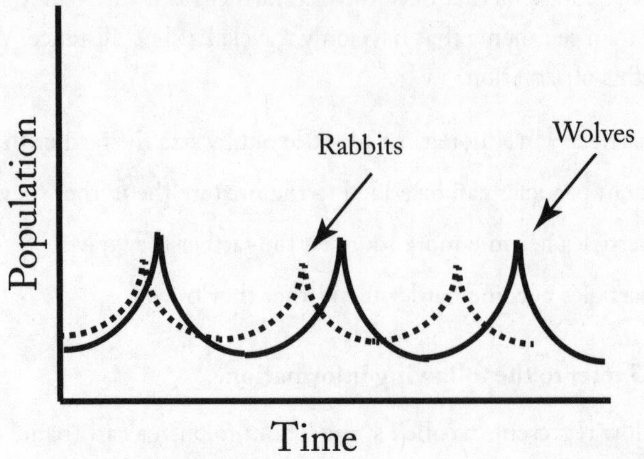

34. The graph shows the changes in the populations of rabbits and wolves on a small, isolated island. Which provides the **best** explanation for the pattern in the population changes of the two species?

A. Wolves and rabbits respond to exactly the same environmental conditions.

B. When the rabbit population increases, the wolves have more to eat. When the rabbit population decreases, the wolves have less to eat.

C. When the rabbit population increases, the wolves have less to eat. When the rabbit population decreases, the wolves have more to eat.

D. When the wolves need more to eat, they move to a new area.

35. A plant is growing near a window in a classroom. The teacher forgets to water the plant and raise the shade over the window before leaving for the weekend. When the teacher returns on Monday, the plant is wilting and some leaves have fallen off. The teacher concludes that the lack of water has caused the damage to the plant. Is this a valid conclusion?

A. Yes, because the teacher forgot to water the plant.

B. Yes, because the only reason plants wilt is because they lack water.

C. No, because the teacher watered the plant on Monday.

D. No, because the teacher also forgot to give the plant light.

STOP! DO NOT GO ON UNTIL TIME IS UP.

SOCIAL STUDIES

70 Minutes • 35 Questions

Directions: The Social Studies Test consists of a series of questions involving general social studies concepts. The questions are based on brief passages of text and visual information (graphs, charts maps, cartoons, and other figures). Some questions are based on both text and visual information. Study the information provided, and answer the question(s) that follow it, referring back to the information as needed.

Most questions are in multiple-choice format. Others are meant to prepare you for the technology-enhanced questions that you will find on the test, such as drop-down, select-an-area, and fill-in-the-blank questions. Record your answers on the Social Studies section of the answer sheet provided. To review how to answer these questions on your answer sheet, please refer to "Technology-Enhanced Questions" on page 24.

Question 1 refers to the following information.

In geography, *regions* are used to divide the world into units of study. All the common land and human characteristics define a region. For example, the British Isles is a region located in Western Europe. On the other hand, *place* is used to define specific points within a region and how humans interact with and perceive those points. Everything within a specific area makes up place, such as natural objects, artifacts, and culture. The British Isles consists of the Republic of Ireland, the United Kingdom, and the numerous islands around their coasts. Ireland is a predominantly Catholic country, while Great Britain is a predominantly Protestant country. Although considered part of the same region, the citizens of these two countries have come to develop cultural differences.

1. According to the passage, which of the following statements is true about the Irish and British experience of region and place?

   A. Irish and British people live in the same place.

   B. In general, the Irish and British practice different traditions.

   C. The British Isles is a region that only recently recognized the religions of both British and Irish citizens.

   D. The Republic of Ireland and the United Kingdom reject their inclusion in the British Isles.

Question 2 refers to the following information.

The Native American nations of the Pacific Northwest lived primarily in what is now Oregon and Washington. They enjoyed access to abundant food sources, owing to their proximity to freshwater fishing and fertile farmland. Unlike their counterparts in the east, the Native Americans in this region built and lived primarily in longhouses.

These structures were made of cedar trees. They recorded stories on elaborate totem poles. The nations of the Eastern Woodland Native Americans also lived in longhouses, as well as wigwams. Food sources primarily came from fruits, nuts, and berries; squash, corn, and beans; and meat from small animals.

2. Based on information in the passage, which statement correctly compares the Native Americans of the Eastern Woodlands to those of the Northwest Coast?

A. Native Americans of both the Eastern Woodlands and the Northwest farmed.

B. Only the Native Americans of the Northwest lived in longhouses.

C. The Eastern Woodlands Native Americans had a greater variety of totem poles than the those of the Northwest Coast.

D. The Native Americans of the Northwest Coast were more advanced than those of the Eastern Woodlands.

Questions 3–5 are based on the following information.

James Madison is sometimes known as the "father of the Constitution." He was a leading influence at the Constitutional Convention and wrote articles in support of the adoption of the Constitution. Here are some quotations from those articles:

"The accumulation of all powers—legislative, executive, and judiciary—in the same hands…is the very definition of tyranny."

—James Madison, *Federalist 47*

"In order to lay a due foundation for that separate and distinct exercise of the different powers of government… it is evident that each [branch of government] should have a will of its own…"

—James Madison, *Federalist 51*

3. Which of the following had the greatest influence on the formation of Madison's arguments in both *Federalist* articles?

A. Previous experience with Great Britain

B. Failure of the Articles of Confederation

C. Anti-Federalist opposition to the creation of a Constitution

D. Selection of George Washington as President of the United States

4. Which of the following would be a power granted to the branches of government consistent with Madison's arguments?

A. Taxation

B. Declaration of war

C. Veto

D. Regulation of interstate commerce

5. What evidence could **best** be used to support the arguments presented by Madison in the *Federalist* articles?

A. Failure of the political system in Great Britain

B. Failure of the Articles of Confederation

C. Anti-Federalist insistence on creation of a Bill of Rights

D. Uprisings such as Shay's Rebellion

Questions 6 and 7 are based on the following cartoon.

This cartoon was drawn in 1874 during the Reconstruction, an era of rebuilding after the US Civil War.

6. What idea is the artist who created the image trying to convey?

A. Southern government after the Civil War was dominated by powerful whites.

B. Newly freed slaves struggled to obtain the equality promised to them after the Civil War.

C. The uncertainty of life following the removal of protections for African Americans after the Civil War.

D. The Ku Klux Klan were the most powerful group in Southern society.

7. Which of the following Southern responses to the Thirteenth, Fourteenth, and Fifteenth Amendments is NOT consistent with the image?

A. Practice of lynching

B. Creation of black codes

C. Creation of Jim Crow laws

D. Exodus of blacks to the North

Question 8 is based on the following information.

The founders of the United States government deliberately created a system in which no one person or group could assume a majority of power. After gaining independence from Great Britain, the framers of the Constitution paid close attention to the operations of the central government. The first three of seven Articles called for a separation of federal powers into three segments. The executive branch, administered by the President, enforces laws and holds veto power over bills. Congress presides over the legislative branch, which writes, debates, and passes bills into law. The nine justices of the US Supreme Court oversee the judicial branch, interpreting law and intervening in conflicts among the branches of the government. The result is a system of checks and balances, although the executive branch should have more influence than the judicial and legislative branches. Each of the 50 states has a government modeled on the federal system, while cities and towns within each state have a local government.

8. Which statement expresses an opinion or a value judgment rather than a fact?

A. Each of the 50 states has a government modeled on the federal system, while cities and towns within each state have a local government.

B. The first three of seven Articles called for a separation of federal powers into three segments.

C. The founders of the United States government deliberately created a system in which no one person or group could assume a majority of power.

D. The result is a system of checks and balances, although the executive branch should have more influence than the judicial and legislative branches.

Question 9 is based upon the following passage.

By the beginning of the seventeenth century, New World exploration excited the imaginations of poets and adventurers alike. The reality of life in the new land, however, was quite different. Read the following view of life in the Virginia colony.

"A True Relation of Such Occurrences and Accidents of Noate as Hath Happened in Virginia . . ." (excerpts)

About the tenth of September there was about 46 of our men dead, at which time Captaine Wingefield having ordred the affaires in such sort that he was generally hated of all, in which respect with one consent he was deposed from his presidencie, and Captaine Ratcliffe according to his course was elected.

Our provision now being within twentie dayes spent, the Indians brought us great store both of Corne and bread ready made: and also there came such aboundance of Fowles into the Rivers, as greatly refreshed our weake estates, where uppon many of our weake men were presently able to goe abroad.

As yet we had no houses to cover us, our tents were rotten and our Cabbins worse than nought: our best commodities was Yron which we made into little chissels.

The president, and Captaine Martins sicknes, me to be Cape Marchant, and yet to spare no paines in making houses for the company, who notwithstanding our misery, little ceased their mallice, grudging and muttering.

As at this time were most of our chiefest men either sicke or discontented, the rest being in such dispaire, as they would rather starve and rot with idleness, then be persuaded to do any thing for their owne reliefe without constraint: our victualles being now within eighteene dayes spent, and the Indians trade decreasing, I was sent to the mouth of the river to Kegquohtan an Indian Towne, to trade for Corne, and try the river for Fish, but our fishing we could not effect by reason of the stormy weather. The Indians thinking us neare famished, with carelesse kindnes, offered us little pieces of bread and small handfulls of beanes or wheat, for a hatchet or a piece of copper: In like maner I entertained their kindnes, and in like scorne offered them like commodities, but the Children, or any that shewe extraordinary kundnes, I liberally confronted with free gifte such trifles as wel contented them.

—John Smith

9. The passage directly contradicts which of the following?

A. Natives were savages that held no culture, intelligence, or value to Europeans.

B. Jamestown settlers were unprepared for colonization of the land.

C. Europeans struggled with harsh conditions due to weather and sickness.

D. Natives helped the Jamestown settlers survive the difficult settlement process.

Questions 10 and 11 refer to the following graph.

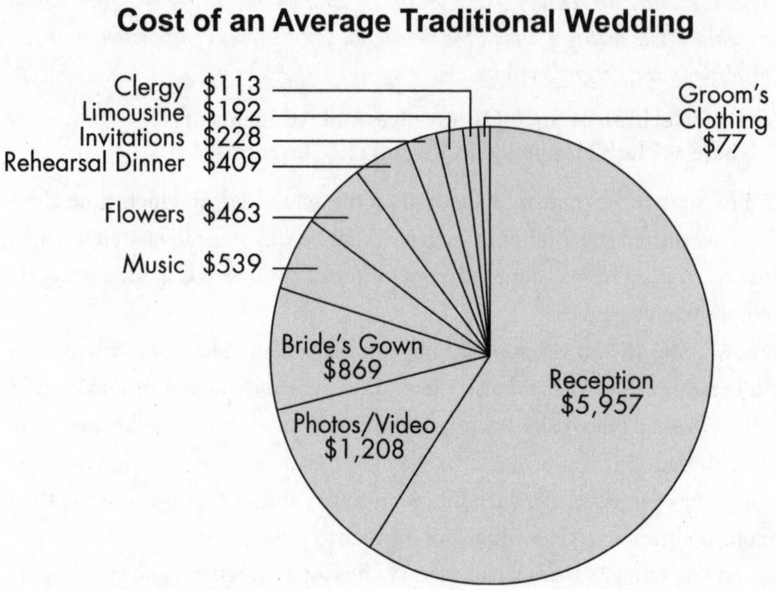

★ $

10. Drag and drop the star next to the category in the graph that costs less than the limousine, but more than the groom's clothing. (Enter the category in the space provided on the answer sheet.)

11. Drag and drop the dollar sign next to the category that would save the **most** money for a couple on a limited budget. (Enter the category in the space provided on the answer sheet.)

Question 12 is based on the following passage.

Now, therefore I, Abraham Lincoln, President of the United States, by virtue of the power in me vested as Commander-in-Chief, of the Army and Navy of the United States in time of actual armed rebellion against the authority and government of the United States, and as a fit and necessary war measure for suppressing said rebellion, do, on this first day of January, in the year of our Lord one thousand eight hundred and sixty-three, and in accordance with my purpose so to do publicly proclaimed for the full period of one hundred days, from the day first above mentioned, order and designate as the States and parts of States wherein the people thereof respectively, are this day in rebellion against the United States, the following, to wit:

Arkansas, Texas, Louisiana (except the Parishes of St. Bernard, Plaquemines, Jefferson, St. John, St. Charles, St. James Ascension, Assumption, Terrebonne, Lafourche, St. Mary, St. Martin, and Orleans, including the City of New Orleans), Mississippi, Alabama, Florida, Georgia, South Carolina, North Carolina, and Virginia, (except the forty-eight counties designated as West Virginia, and also the counties of Berkley, Accomac, Northampton, Elizabeth City, York, Princess Ann, and Norfolk, including the cities of Norfolk and Portsmouth[)], and which excepted parts, are for the present, left precisely as if this proclamation were not issued.

And by virtue of the power, and for the purpose aforesaid, I do order and declare that all persons held as slaves within said designated States, and parts of States, are, and henceforward shall be free; and that the Executive government of the United States, including the military and naval authorities thereof, will recognize and maintain the freedom of said persons.

—Excerpt from The Emancipation Proclamation, Abraham Lincoln

12. For what purpose was the Emancipation Proclamation worded so carefully?

A. The strategic value of the Border States was so vital that Lincoln was sure not to upset them with his position on slavery.

B. Lincoln wanted slaves in the South to hear about the Proclamation and attempt to escape or rebel against their masters in order to create a numerical advantage.

C. The divisiveness over slavery was so high in the Senate between North and South that Lincoln had to be mindful of how he handled emancipation.

D. Lincoln was unsupportive of emancipation but understood the political and military value of freeing the slaves for the North.

Question 13 is based on the following information.

A court of original jurisdiction has the authority to conduct the original trial of a case. This court is called the trial court. A court with appellate jurisdiction has the authority to hear an appeal of a case decided by a trial court. This court is called the appeals court. An appeals court does not conduct a new trial; instead it reviews the record of the trial and rules on whether or not the trial was conducted fairly and the law applied correctly.

US FEDERAL COURT SYSTEM

Court	Original Jurisdiction	Appellate Jurisdiction
US Supreme Court	Lawsuits between two state governments	Cases appealed from US Court of Appeals and cases appealed from state supreme courts
US Courts of Appeals	None	Cases appealed from US District Courts
US District Courts	Cases involving federal law or the US Constitution	None

13. What court would conduct the trial in a case in which the federal government charges a company with violating federal pollution regulations?

A. A state trial court in the state in which the violation occurred

B. The US Supreme Court

C. A state supreme court

D. A US District Court

14. Prior to the Pendleton Civil Service Reform Act of 1883, presidential and other federal government appointments were often made under an informal "spoils system," by which government jobs were given to loyal supporters rather than awarded on the basis of merit. The Act mandated that jobs would henceforth be awarded on the basis of merit and prohibited the firing of any employee for political reasons.

Which of the following resulted from the demise of the spoils system?

A. Political lobbying

B. Civilian jury duty

C. Term limits for elected officials

D. Civil service exams

Questions 15 and 16 refer to the following information.

MILITARY CAMPAIGNS—US REVOLUTIONARY WAR

Battle of Brandywine

On September 11, 1777, British General Sir William Howe sailed from New York City and landed near Elkton, Maryland in northern Chesapeake Bay. Howe engaged American General George Washington's army near Brandywine Creek. Howe sent the majority of his forces across the Brandywine and attacked Washington's rear flank.

Due to poor scouting, the Americans did not detect Howe's approaching forces until it was too late. Once discovered, they sent three divisions in an attempt to block Howe's advances.

Washington brought in General Nathaniel Greene to hold off Howe's forces long enough for the bulk of the American forces to retreat northeast, ultimately encamping at Valley Forge for the winter. The retreat of Washington's army resulted in Philadelphia being taken by the British on September 23. It remained under British control until June 1778.

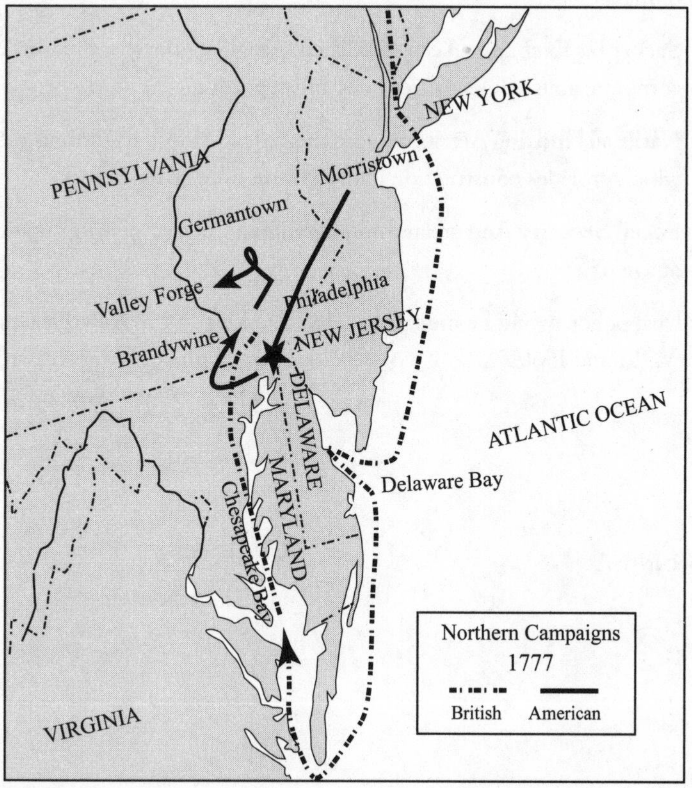

15. Click on the map to identify the location to which Washington's army retreated from Howe's forces. (Enter the location in the space provided on the answer sheet.)

16. Click on the map to identify which city was left vulnerable by General Washington's retreat. (Enter the location in the space provided on the answer sheet.)

Questions 17 and 18 are based on the following information.

President Franklin Roosevelt's New Deal (1933–1936) included a variety of programs that were introduced to relieve Americans from the economic fallout of the Great Depression.

1933	**Civilian Conservation Corps:** provided immediate work in reforestation, road construction, and national park development on government land to 250,000 men
	Securities Act of 1933: designed to provide oversight and regulation to stocks and bonds trading
	Banking Act of 1933: established the Federal Deposit Insurance Corporation (FDIC), which provided insurance to people with accounts in the case of bank failure
1934	**Farm Mortgage Refinancing Act:** provided farmers with assistance in mortgage refinance
	Securities Exchange Act: established to regulate the stock market and prevent corporate abuse of securities sales and reporting
	National Housing Act: introduced the Federal Housing Administration (FHA), which provides construction and renovation loans for homes
1935	**Social Security Act:** created to guarantee retirees a pension upon retirement at age 65

17. Which New Deal policy would be **most** similar to the WPA and PWA?

A. CCC

B. FDIC

C. FHA

D. Social Security Act

18. Looking at the New Deal policies, FDR seemed **most** concerned with regulation of which of the following?

A. Housing

B. Farming

C. Banking

D. Conservation

Questions 19 and 20 refer to the following passage and illustration.

The United States has seen steady, incremental monetary inflation going back to 1950. During a period of general monetary inflation, the price of goods and services increases (or "inflates") in terms of a specific currency (form of money), such as the US dollar. At the same time, the value of that currency can decline relative to other currencies, depending on inflation rates in countries that use other currencies. The following illustration tells the story of the value of the US dollar in selected years.

Purchasing Power of the Dollar

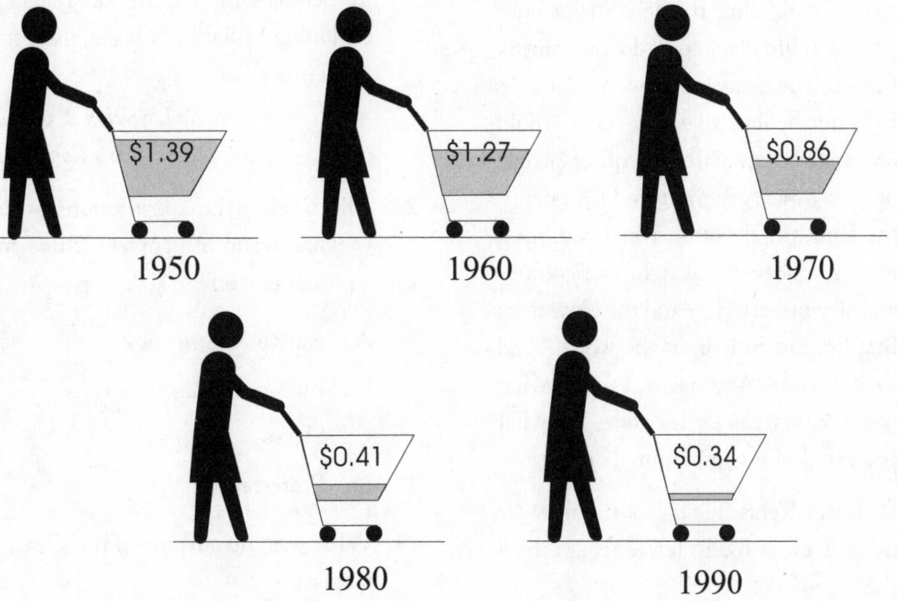

19. Referring to the illustration, which could be the base year, in which one dollar could buy one dollar's worth of goods?

A. 2001

B. 1976

C. 1967

D. 1983

20. During the first decade of this century, the euro appreciated in value in relation to the US dollar. How might a resident of a European country whose currency is the euro be expected to respond to this relationship?

A. By taking vacations in the United States instead of Europe

B. By saving more money

C. By investing in European real estate

D. By exchanging their euros for gold and silver

Question 21 is based on the following information.

At the height of the Cold War struggle between the United States and the Soviet Union, President Kennedy stated in his inaugural address (January 20, 1961):

"In the long history of the world, only a few generations have been granted the role of defending freedom in its hour of maximum danger. I do not shrink from this responsibility—I welcome it. I do not believe that any of us would exchange places with any other people or any other generation. The energy, the faith, the devotion which we bring to this endeavor will light our country and all who serve it—and the glow from that fire can truly light the world. And so, my fellow Americans: ask not what your country can do for you—ask what you can do for your country."

21. President Kennedy's use of the term "freedom" is **most likely** referencing which of the following?

A. Democracy

B. Communism

C. The US Constitution

D. Immigration

Questions 22 and 23 are based on the following information.

Representatives and direct Taxes shall be apportioned among the several States which may be included within this Union, according to their respective Numbers, which shall be determined by adding to the whole Number of free Persons, including those bound to Service for a Term of Years, and excluding Indians not taxed, three fifths of all other Persons.

—*Article I, Section 2, Clause 3, US Constitution*

22. This article of the Constitution was referring to what group of people as three-fifths of all other persons?

A. Native Americans

B. Immigrants

C. Slaves

D. Protestants

23. What was the purpose of the Three-Fifths Clause?

A. To provide population equality for Congressional representation in both the North and the South

B. An attempt to halt the future use of slavery in the South

C. To provide greater Congressional representation for the South

D. To provide greater Congressional representation for the North

Questions 24 and 25 are based on the following information.

The act to establish the judicial courts of the United States authorizes the supreme court "to issue writs of mandamus, in cases warranted by the principles and usages of law, to any courts appointed, or persons holding office, under the authority of the United States." The secretary of state, being a person, holding an office under the authority of the United States, is precisely within the letter of the description; and if this court is not authorized to issue a writ of mandamus to such an officer, it must be because the law is unconstitutional....

The constitution vests the whole judicial power of the United States in one supreme court, and such inferior courts as congress shall, from time to time, ordain and establish...In the distribution of this power it is declared that "the supreme court shall have original jurisdiction in all cases affecting ambassadors, other public ministers and consuls, and those in which a state shall be a party. In all other cases, the supreme court shall have appellate jurisdiction...."

—Justice John Marshall,
Marbury v. Madison (1803)

24. The ruling in *Marbury v. Madison* established which of the following?

A. Checks and balances between the three branches of government

B. Democratic Republican control of the judicial branch

C. Limits to the ability of the judicial branch to rule on federal matters

D. Uncontrolled power of the judicial branch to rule on federal matters

25. According to the passage, what kind of judicial order was authorized by the Supreme Court in *Marbury v. Madison*?

A. Writ of habeas corpus

B. Writ of mandamus

C. Judicial review

D. Warrant for arrest

Question 26 is based on the following information.

After the passage of the Stamp Act in 1765, a piece of English legislation that required American colonists to pay taxes on materials printed on special paper that bore the stamp of British manufacture, a series of secret societies sprang up in the colonies. The term "Sons of Liberty" became associated with these groups. Their members included artisans, merchants, and others concerned with what was perceived as the growing hostility of the British government towards the American colonies. While groups designating themselves as the Sons of Liberty were found in major American cities, they were not part of a larger, organized group. All groups shared a common motto, "No taxation without representation."

26. What role did the passage of the Stamp Act have on creating the "Sons of Liberty"?

A. It created a unifying ideology that connected members of colonial society.

B. It created small pockets of resistance that failed to find a common goal.

C. It divided the "Sons of Liberty" into pro- and anti-British groups.

D. It helped to organize a large military resistance to Great Britain.

27. If neither candidate for President of the United States obtains the required number of electoral votes, the decision will be determined by the [ ].

28. In 1977, Frank Collins, a leader of a neo-Nazi party in the United States, announced he would march with his following through a predominately Jewish neighborhood in Skokie, Illinois. Skokie was home to many Holocaust survivors and their relatives. The American Civil Liberties Union tried to stop the march and sued, but the Supreme Court ruled Collins and his following able to proceed. What amendment did the Supreme Court cite allowing the neo-Nazis to march?

A. Second Amendment

B. First Amendment

C. Eighteenth Amendment

D. Twelfth Amendment

Question 29 is based on the following passage.

As the population of the United States grew rapidly during the early nineteenth century, settlers began pushing further southeast to claim new land. Five nations—Cherokee, Creek, Choctaw, Chicasaw, and Seminole—lived in this region. Settlers pressured the US government to aid in removing the Native Americans from this land. Initially, Indian migration was voluntary, with some nations agreeing to the terms of treaties that relocated them to new lands west of the Mississippi River. Other Indian nations remained, refusing to negotiate for land that they considered home. While the Cherokee appealed to the Supreme Court to maintain their territory, the Creeks and Seminoles resisted with force. Eventually, most Native Americans relocated to western territorial allotments. The Cherokee were the last to leave. In the winter of 1838, during what became known as the Trail of Tears, 4,000 Cherokee people died of exposure, disease, and hunger. In the end, 46,000 Native Americans were relocated west. The result was 25 million acres of land comprising present-day Alabama, Florida, Georgia, Tennessee, Mississippi, Kentucky, and North Carolina became available to settlers.

29. Which term **best** represents the ideology behind *why* Native Americans were relocated, as described in the passage? Choose the correct answer from the drop-down menu. [Select ▼]

A. Trail of Tears

B. Manifest Destiny

C. Southern Manifesto

D. Emancipation Proclamation

Questions 30 and 31 are based upon the following passage.

Jose and Taurabia Paivo emigrated from Portugal in 1933 and settled in Fall River, Massachusetts. Jose had been trained as a bookkeeper but was unable to find work. One day, as he stopped to rest and eat a sandwich his wife had packed for him, a stranger asked what he was eating. Jose explained that it was a cured fish that his wife had prepared according to an old family recipe. He tore off a piece and offered it to the stranger, who devoured it with relish. "You should sell this," the stranger remarked.

That night, Jose discussed the incident with his wife. They both mused that it would be fun and maybe profitable to open a restaurant, but they lacked the funds to start. Then Taurabia remembered that a small bodega up the street might possibly offer them space if they agreed to split the profits. As added incentive, Jose offered to help the owner maintain his books. Their delicacies caught on, and, within a few years, Jose and Taurabia had enough cash flow to rent a space of their own. As the 1930s turned into the 1940s, and the city's factories thrived with the need for wartime supplies like blankets, shoes, and uniforms, business expanded and Jose and Taurabia opened a second establishment. After the war, when their children were old enough to help out, the Paivos opened still more restaurants, now in other cities and towns in New England.

But by the 1970s, things changed. Fast food chains began to lure business away, and economic conditions in many New England cities drove residents elsewhere, even as property taxes rose. One by one, the restaurants closed. By 1981, both of the senior Paivos had passed away, and their children closed the last eatery.

30. The success of the original business enterprise was due in large part to the Paivos' ability to

A. barter.

B. advertise.

C. economize.

D. wait.

31. A significant factor in the business's ultimate demise was

A. property reassessment.

B. unionization.

C. poor management.

D. inventory unavailability.

Questions 32 and 33 refer to the following information.

The Constitution provides for changing times with a process for amendment, or change. Today, the Constitution includes 27 amendments. The first 10 amendments, called the Bill of Rights, are outlined here.

BILL OF RIGHTS

First Amendment: Religious and political freedom

Second Amendment: The right to bear arms

Third Amendment: The right to refuse to house soldiers in peacetime

Fourth Amendment: Protection against unreasonable search and seizure

Fifth Amendment: The right of accused persons to due process of the law

Sixth Amendment: The right to a speedy and public trial

Seventh Amendment: The right to a jury trial in civil cases

Eighth Amendment: Protection against cruel and unusual punishment

Ninth Amendment: The rights of the people to powers that may not be spelled out in the Constitution

Tenth Amendment: The rights of the people and the states to powers not otherwise given to the federal government, states, or people

32. Which of the following does NOT explain a reason for inclusion of a Bill of Rights into the US Constitution?

A. Fears of abuse of power being concentrated in a central government

B. Anti-Federalist opposition to the Constitution

C. Support for individual rights not directly addressed by the Constitution

D. Desire to limit individual freedoms by specifically addressing them in the first 10 amendments

33. A family that was forced by the US Army to provide housing and food for a group of soldiers could appeal to the courts based on which amendment to the Constitution?

A. The Second Amendment

B. The Third Amendment

C. The Ninth Amendment

D. The Tenth Amendment

Questions 34 and 35 are based on the following information.

Japan's unique culture is the result of centuries of influence, as well as its geographic characteristics. The closest point to it is in mainland Asia, 115 miles away. This geographic isolation resulted in diminished threats of foreign invasion. Peoples from various Asian countries migrated to Japan, chief among them Mongolians. During 250 BCE to 300 CE, the Yayoi, a matriarchal society, introduced rice cultivation, iron- and bronze-making, and weaving. During the third century, cultural shifts that are presumed to be the result of Korean influence introduced into Japanese culture advanced weaponry and the use of horses in combat. As Japan became an increasingly powerful nation, it became more open to Chinese cultural influence. The introduction of Confucianism signaled a significant shift in Japanese culture. By stressing adherence to hierarchical relationships and emphasizing education as a means to advance in government, Confucian values disrupted the hereditary Japanese nobility.

34. Why does the passage indicate there are diminished threats of foreign invasion to Japan?

A. Japan is an internationally neutral country.

B. Japan is geographically isolated.

C. Japan is a country of immigrants.

D. Japan is an isolationist nation.

35. The migration of people from other Asian countries resulted in

A. ethnic wars in Japan.

B. a class system based on country of origin.

C. a blending of Asian cultures and influence.

D. primitive weaponry.

STOP! DO NOT GO ON UNTIL TIME IS UP.

ANSWER KEYS AND EXPLANATIONS

Reasoning Through Language Arts

Part I

1. A
2. Fun-loving (B)
3. B
4. likes the dead mummies better than he likes Jinny (B)
5. C
6. C
7. B
8. C
9. A
10. D
11. B
12. "Liberty, once lost, is lost forever" (A).
13. D
14. the number of British troops who were killed (A)
15. D
16. her letters are heartwarming (D)
17. A

Part II

See Extended Response Samples

Part III

18. D
19. C
20. D
21. C
22. C
23. C
24. C
25. B
26. C
27. C
28. See explanation.
29. B
30. D
31. B
32. C
33. fears that ordinary citizens will suffer under a centralized government (D)
34. See explanation.
35. C
36. A
37. environments, leading to the (D)
38. coworkers we can be, some (B)
39. should be business-appropriate. We follow professional guidelines: men should wear slacks and button-down shirts with a tie (jacket not required), and women should wear slacks, skirts, or dresses (at least knee length). (C)
40. maintain (D).
41. business casual attire on Fridays: jeans are permitted. (D)
42. you need to make a personal call, please (A)
43. Minimize (B)
44. for discussing project details and makes it easier to get to know one another, it can sometimes lead to more distractions. (B)
45. wait for them to acknowledge you before diving into your request. (C)
46. Feel free to use office supplies and help yourself to the complimentary snacks in the cupboards designated for shared food. (C)
47. after (A)
48. See explanation.

Part I

1. **The correct answer is A.** The masked ball is the event that Jack does not want to attend. While the author implies that he did not want to have tea at the Gezireh Palace Hotel (choice B), have an excursion through the bazaars (choice C), or climb the Pyramids (choice D), these are past events, not upcoming ones.

2. **The correct answer is *Fun-loving* (B).** Jinny enjoys doing things she thinks are fun, like going for tea, shopping in bazaars, and going to parties. None of Jinny's amusements are particularly dangerous, so choice A is not the best answer. While Jack seems to find some of Jinny's suggestions tiresome, he still finds her engaging, so choice C is not the best answer. Jinny wants to do things Jack does not want to do, but she doesn't really demand that he does these things, so choice D is also incorrect.

3. **The correct answer is B.** Jack is conflicted by the invitation. He hates the idea of any party, particularly a costume ball (lines 1–5). On the other hand, he finds Jinny attractive (she's "a bright delight" and "very engaging") and therefore decides that he will go. Choice A is only partly correct; Jack does hate parties, but he ultimately decides to go. Choice C is also partly correct—again, Jack doesn't like parties, but he is not especially glad to be invited. Choice D doesn't work because it's clear in the passage that Jack does like Jinny.

4. **The correct answer is *likes the dead mummies better than he likes Jinny* (B).** Jack is comfortable away from crowds and people. He prefers to be with the ancient mummies than with others, including Jinny, even though he likes her. In lines 58–61, the passage specifically compares Jack's feelings for Queen Hatasu and Jinny, suggesting that he will never like Jinny quite as much as he likes the mummies.

5. **The correct answer is C.** Jack prefers being in the presence of the ancient mummies to being with "modern" people. There is not enough information in the passage to support the idea that Jack enjoys traveling for his work, so choice A doesn't quite fit. Choice B is a possibility, but the work he does seems more important to him than being in the desert overall. Choice D doesn't work because Jack clearly does not feel at home with his colleagues or other people.

6. **The correct answer is C.** According to the passage, Jack "had come to Cairo for supplies and Jinny had encountered him by chance upon a corner of the crowded Mograby." Gezireh (choice A) and the Sultan al Hassan Mosque (choice D) are places Jack and Jinny visited together after first encountering each other in Mograby. The edge of the Libyan desert (choice B) is where Jack's camp is, not where he first encountered Jinny in Egypt.

7. **The correct answer is B.** In this sentence, *paramount* means "supreme" because society is very important in supporting its educational system. The words *difficult* (choice A) and *curious* (choice D) would not make sense in this context. The word *minor* (choice C) means the opposite of the correct answer.

8. **The correct answer is C.** Much of the passage discusses the characteristics of a stable and strong, or an ideal society, and how Dewey felt public education could best maintain such a society. The passage focuses on education and never mentions the military, so you can eliminate choice B right away. There is also nothing in the passage that teaches specific skills to children; instead, the passage talks about Dewey's larger ideas for education, so choices A and D don't fit either.

9. **The correct answer is A.** In this sentence, *compromising* means "making vulnerable." The phrases *strongly supporting* (choice B), *rendering nonsensical* (choice C), and *clarifying carefully* (choice D) would not make as much sense in this context.

10. **The correct answer is D.** According to the passage, Dewey's education model emphasizes a lack of overt direction for students. However, he believes that a focus on preparing students for adulthood (choice A), a lack of steadying influences for students (choice B), and a focus on recapitulating the past (choice C) are problems that should be avoided when educating.

11. **The correct answer is B.** The passage specifically says, "the ideal larger society, according to Dewey, is one in which the interests of a group are all shared by all of its members and in which interactions with other groups are free and full."

12. **The correct answer is *"Liberty, once lost, is lost forever"* (A).** Adams explains that some things can be replaced, but that once the government takes away people's freedom, liberty can't be replaced. "For the worst that can happen can do you no harm" is about Abigail's bravery, not a reason to get involved in the Revolution. "They seem to feel as if they were among you" is about the kinship felt by the clergy and the Revolutionaries. "A glorious proof of the bravery of our worthy countrymen" is Adams's description of the number of kills made by the Revolutionary army, but does not suggest that the war is necessary.

13. **The correct answer is D.** John responds to Abigail's news in a previous letter by commenting about her taking precaution in finding a secure place to stay should it become unsafe for her to stay in their home. This is the only option that suggests that there has been a dialogue between the two people. The other choicess are very vague, and do not mention any kind of relationship or previous conversation.

14. **The correct answer is *the number of British troops who were killed* (A).** John comments that Abigail has given him an account of the "numbers slain on the side of our enemies," implying that he had not known this detail. John offers details about each of the other options, suggesting that he knows about them.

15. **The correct answer is D.** Although there are changes during war, the letter is also full of information about their family, and people that John and Abigail know. At the end of the letter, John explicitly says that "it gives me more pleasure than I can express, to learn that you sustain with so much fortitude the shocks and terrors of the times." This suggests that although the times are difficult, Abigail is consistent.

16. **The correct answer is *her letters are heartwarming* (D).** John is emotionally touched by Abigail's descriptions of the people affected by war. That rules out *tough*, and although her words may be clever, John doesn't mention that specifically. *Endearing* is close, but *heartwarming* is a more specific emotion, and is a better answer.

17. **The correct answer is A.** In the second paragraph, Adams writes at length about how upset Abigail's father is about the conflagration of Charlestown. Adams mentions only that Charlestown is the site of the Battle of Bunker Hill, not that the battle, itself, upset Abigail's father, so choice B is incorrect. While Mr. Mather's library was likely lost in the conflagration, it is the conflagration as a whole rather than the specific loss of this one building that has upset Abigail's father, so choice C is not the best answer. While Adams speaks of "oppression" and the other cardinal vices" (choice D) as problems, he does not imply that such things are particularly upsetting to Abigail's father.

Part II

Extended response. Answers will vary. You will find two sample analyses on pages 109–110.

Part III

18. **The correct answer is D.** In the passage, King praises his fellow Americans for how active they have become in the civil rights movement, so *vigorous activeness* is the best definition of *militancy* in this context. King speaks out against physical violence, so choice A is incorrect. *Disciplined structure* (choice B) may describe life in the military, but it does not define the word *militancy* in this context. King never describes civil rights as an issue of patriotism, so choice C does not make sense.

19. **The correct answer is C.** King indicates that civil rights activists are dissatisfied and does not indicate they have no right to feel that way. He specifically warns against succumbing to bitterness (choice A), the urge to commit physical violence (choice B), and hatred (choice D) as unproductive to securing civil rights.

20. **The correct answer is D.** The second paragraph states that it "would be fatal for the nation to overlook the urgency of the moment." King is urging his listeners to continue working for civil rights and justice instead of just waiting for change to come, and he clarifies that the nation he's referring to is America, which he says would have "neither rest nor tranquility... until the Negro is granted his citizenship rights."

21. **The correct answer is C.** The main point of the third paragraph is that protests must remain peaceful. King specifically states, "We must not allow our creative protest to degenerate into physical violence." Uniting with white supporters is a secondary point.

22. **The correct answer is C.** In the context of line 79, the word *trials* means "ordeals." While trials could be used to mean *hearings* (choice A), *experiments* (choice B), or *examinations* (choice D) in a different context, none of these synonyms make sense in this particular context.

23. **The correct answer is C.** According to the ninth paragraph, "After depriving her of all rights as a married woman, if single, and the owner of property, he has taxed her to support a government which recognizes her only when her property can be made profitable to it." The passage specifies that married women are not taxed, which eliminates choices A and D. While the author speaks out against ways that men have made women morally irresponsible, this is not discussed in relation to taxes, so choice B is incorrect.

24. **The correct answer is C.** The entire passage describes how men subject women to oppressive control. Violence is not mentioned in the passage, so choice A is not a logical conclusion. Guiding care (choice B) is the opposite of tyranny. While tyranny may seem similar to brutish behavior, choice D fails to include the key aspect of control.

25. The correct answer is B. Olive Gilbert is the author of the passage and offers her own opinion on events throughout. Without any information to suggest otherwise, you can assume that the writer of the passage is also the speaker and provides the main point of view.

26. The correct answer is C. According to the second paragraph of passage 2, "But Isabella inwardly determined that she would remain quietly with him only until she had spun his wool—about one hundred pounds—and then she would leave him." She had already received her "free papers," so choice A is incorrect. Her master was determined to not allow her to leave, so choice B is incorrect as well. Whether or not spinning one hundred pounds of wool would make her master "a considerable profit" is not indicated in the passage, so choice D is not the best answer.

27. The correct answer is C. The writers of the Declaration of Sentiments used the Declaration of Independence as a pattern to describe their dissatisfaction with their rights as citizens in comparison with those of men. The first passage never mentions women's issues with English rule, so choice A is not supported by the passage. Although the second passage is thematically related (women losing rights at the hands of men), there is no indication that Sojourner Truth (choice B) was a factor in the Declaration of Sentiments. There is also not enough information in the passage to support the idea that the women were just trying to demonstrate that they could write well (choice D).

28. Choice A should be placed in Sojourner Truth's section of the diagram (she is the only one described as a slave in either passage), **choices B and D** should be placed in the sponsors of the Woman's Rights Convention's section of the diagram (slaves were not necessarily able to legally vote after 1848 or obtain a divorce), and **choice C** should be placed in the center (neither Sojourner Truth nor the Women's Rights Convention sponsors were considered full citizens at the time).

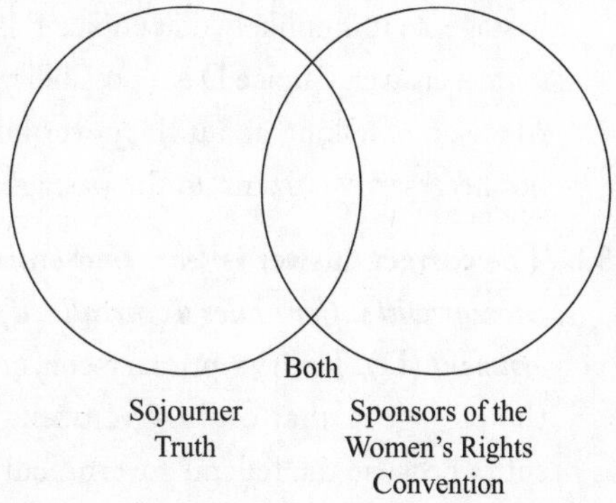

29. The correct answer is B. Madison is arguing that the principle of separation of powers will be difficult to implement, but not as difficult as some people think. In lines 22–26, Madison states that it would be less difficult than it appears, and spends the rest of the passage outlining ways in which powers could stay separate. Choices A and C are the opposite of Madison's points throughout the passage. The independence of judges from the legislature (choice D) is an example of the separation of powers Adams advocates, but it is not the main point.

30. The correct answer is D. Henry says that the government will lack "sufficient energy" to keep the states united, and this argument applies to the checks and balances issue.

31. **The correct answer is B.** In the context of line 34 of passage 2, the word *tenure* means "term." The words *requirements* (choice A), *duties* (choice C), and *descriptions* (choice D) would not make as much sense if used in place of *tenure* in this particular context.

32. **The correct answer is C.** Madison is arguing for a separation of powers in order to prevent one branch or person having undue influence over others. Choice A is the opposite of what Madison is arguing. Great Britain is never mentioned by name in the passage, so it is unlikely that choice B is the correct answer. Choice D is a possibility, but Madison is talking about the government, not necessarily citizens, in the passage.

33. **The correct answer is *fears that ordinary citizens will suffer under a centralized government* (D).** Henry's primary concern in the passage is that ordinary citizens will suffer because the federal government will not work. There is no information in the passage to support the idea that Henry is worried about a bureaucracy taking over (choice A), whether other countries are afraid of the United States (choice B), or whether the United States can be an empire like Great Britain (choice C).

34. **Choice A** should be placed in the center, as both supported this idea. **Choice B** should be placed in Henry's section of the diagram, and **choices C and D** should be placed in Madison's section of the diagram.

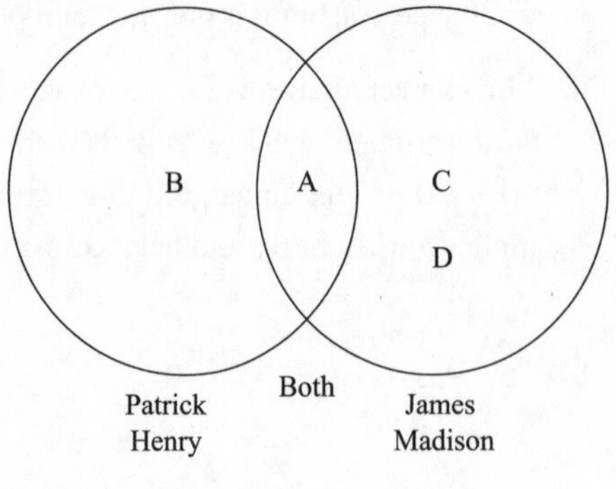

35. **The correct answer is C.** In lines 57–62, Wright explains from where a citizen's love of county should stem: "It is for them more especially to know why they love their country, not because it is their country, but because it is the palladium of human liberty—the favoured scene of human improvement." Wright goes on to say that the citizens should love their country because they have control over its destiny.

36. **The correct answer is A.** In lines 43–45, Francis Wright writes that American is made up of people in whose "veins … flows the blood of every people on the globe," meaning that it is a melting pot of nationalities.

37. **The correct answer is *environments, leading to the* (D).** In choice A, the sentence is missing a comma to separate the independent clause from the adverbial phrase *leading to the overall success of the company*, and choice D corrects that error. Neither a semicolon (choice B) nor a colon (choice C) are used to separate a complete clause from a phrase that modifies it.

38. **The correct answer is *coworkers we can be, some* (B).** Edit to correct errors in pronoun usage, including pronoun–antecedent agreement, unclear pronoun references, and pronoun case and number. *Coworkers* is plural, so the pronoun should match in number: use *we* instead of *he*. Choice A does not change the pronoun reference. Choice C makes the sentence a run-on, and choice D just changes the gender of the pronoun but doesn't fix the number agreement error.

39. The correct answer is *should be business-appropriate. We follow professional guidelines: men should wear slacks and button-down shirts with a tie (jacket not required), and women should wear slacks, skirts, or dresses (at least knee length)* (C). Edit to eliminate run-on sentences, fused sentences, or sentence fragments. Choice C breaks up the sentences appropriately and punctuates them correctly using a colon and commas. Choice A leaves the original sentence as is and is a run-on lacking punctuation. Choice B introduces an incorrectly used semicolon. Choice D keeps the long sentence structure and inserts unnecessary commas, which makes it confusing.

40. The correct answer is *maintain* (D). Edit to ensure parallelism. Choice A lacks parallelism since the first two clauses in the sentence are written in the present tense while this one is written in the present continuous tense. Choice B introduces an unnecessary comma. Choice C changes the pronoun to the singular, which introduces a lack of pronoun-antecedent agreement in addition to the lack of parallelism. Choice D is the only answer choice that corrects the parallelism issue without introducing any new errors.

41. The correct answer is *business casual attire on Fridays: jeans are permitted* (D). Edit to ensure correct use of capitalization. Choice A includes two capitalization errors. Choice B fixes only one of the capitalization problems but introduces incorrect use of an apostrophe. Choice C corrects only one capitalization error. Only choice D fixes both instances of improper capitalization without introducing other errors.

42. The correct answer is *you need to make a personal call, please* (A). Edit to correct errors in straightforward subject–verb agreement. In choice A, the sentence has the correct subject-verb agreement, with the plural verb *need* paired with the pronoun *you*. Choice B is incorrect, as removing the comma after *call* would create a run-on sentence. Choice C uses the correct verb *need* but changes *make* to the singular form pointlessly. Choice D introduces an additional error, depriving the sentence of its subject.

43. The correct answer is *Minimize* (B). Edit to correct errors involving frequently confused words. The correct word for this context is the verb *minimize*. In choice A, the word *miniaturize* is used incorrectly, since *miniaturize* refers to literally shrinking an object. Therefore, choice A is incorrect. The sentence requires a verb, not an adjective such as *minimal* (choice C) or *miniature* (choice D).

44. The correct answer is *for discussing project details and makes it easier to get to know one another, it can sometimes lead to more distractions* (B). Edit to ensure correct use of punctuation (e.g., commas in a series or in appositives and other nonessential elements, end marks, and appropriate punctuation for clause separation). Choice B uses only one comma, making the sentence simple and clear without breaking it up awkwardly. Choice A contains an unnecessary comma after *details* and introduces a colon incorrectly. Choice C inserts a question mark after the dependent clause making it an interrogative fragment. Choice D inserts an unnecessary comma that divides the compound predicate (is … *makes*) for the subject pronoun *this*.

45. **The correct answer is *wait for them to acknowledge you before diving into your request* (C).** Edit to correct errors involving homonyms (*wait* and *weight*) and frequently confused words (*in to* and *into*). Choice A, contains erroneous word selections. Choices B and D each fix only half of the problem, while choice C fixes both.

46. **The correct answer is *Feel free to use office supplies and help yourself to the complimentary snacks in the cupboards designated for shared food* (C).** Edit to eliminate dangling or misplaced modifiers or illogical word order. By replacing *marked as shared food* with *designated for shared food*, the message is clear—the cupboards, not the snacks themselves—are designated for shared food. In choice A, it is unclear if it is the snacks or the cupboards that are marked as shared food. Choice B may be grammatically correct, but it changes the intended meaning of the sentence. Choice D makes the structure more confusing.

47. **The correct answer is *after* (A).** Edit to eliminate nonstandard or informal usage. Choice A correctly uses the commonly standard phrase *clean up after yourself* instead of the nonstandard *clean up for yourself*, which is also used in choice B. Choices C and D are both nonstandard and nonsensical.

48. **The correct answers are B** ("Men are required to wear ties"), **E** ("It is important to clean up after yourself"), and **F** ("Email etiquette between coworkers is important.").

Extended Response: Sample Essays

High-Scoring Analysis

Art should be defended from attacks on its importance in education. In educating our youth, the arts should continue to be taught for the important skills of dexterity and creativity. Many real-world problems require creative approaches to solving them and the arts teach students to think and act creatively. Indeed, reality is multi-faceted and the arts aid students in understanding and interpreting various representations of reality. Teaching students the arts is an important aspect of their education that should not be dismissed.

Teaching the arts encourages creativity in application to problem solving. Very few problems have one path to a solution; often many paths can lead to the correct solution. Encouraging students to think outside the box will help lead them to the correct answer. Individual students learn best in different ways and have skills that are stronger in one area than another. By encouraging different approaches to the same problem, students are more likely to be able to rely on their strengths rather than their weaknesses. Creativity allows students to apply different skills to the same problem.

The arts develop dexterity and motor-skills that are often overlooked in schools. Much teaching and learning is done with technology that requires little manual dexterity, but the arts require and teach fine motor skills. While it may be argued that technology encourages different motor skills rather than none at all, it is certain that the motor skills needed for the fine arts are finer than those required for a typist or for other devices. This craftsmanship can prepare students for vocations other than office-jobs and may have health benefits for being relaxing.

Finally, reality is multi-faceted and complex, and the arts teach students to think about complex issues in diverse ways. As the essay "The Importance of Art in Child Development" states, "A teacher can properly describe the characteristics of reality, and the student is more likely to accurately interpret these representations." In philosophy, this describing is especially important when encountering complex problems. In real life, too, for example in marketing, the ability to describe and interpret descriptions plays an important role, and the arts foster these skills.

It is no wonder, then, that according to the essay "The Importance of Art in Child Development," students who participated in the arts in school were more likely to have achievements in other fields such as science or literature. The arts are related to all fields in their usefulness and in the skills they teach.

Explanation

This analysis is high-scoring because it generates logical text-based arguments or explanations and cites relevant, specific, and sufficient evidence from source texts to support them. It contains ideas that are thoroughly and logically developed, with full elaboration of main ideas; contains purposeful, logical progression of ideas with details closely tied to their main points; establishes an effective organizational structure; applies transitional devices strategically and effectively; chooses words purposefully and carefully; applies advanced vocabulary and strategically applies awareness of audience and purpose of the task to enhance meaning throughout the response. It demonstrates competent and fluent application of conventions; demonstrates effectively varied sentence structure and an overall fluency that enhances clarity.

Specifically, the analysis argues that the arts are still useful in education for their fostering of unique skills that are suitable to the real world and the abstract. It develops these ideas progressively with details closely tied to their main points (e.g., the motor skills acquired by the arts could be used in a variety of vocations); and it presents arguments against its case in order to respond to them (e.g., that technology encourages different motor skills). The composition uses advanced vocabulary.

Low-Scoring Analysis

There are many reasons why we should continue to teach art in school. Art is not just beautiful it is also useful. Art teaches skills we would not otherwise learn. There are some things technology cannot impart. I think all students should be required to study the arts.

The arts are important to our cultural heritage. You have to know a lot about art history to enjoy a visit to the museum. The different styles and artists have evolved over the centuries. Studying art history can teach students an appreciation for the art their culture has produced. It can also teach students an appreciation for other cultures' arts.

Technology is more useful than art, but it does not provide the same lessons. Technology helps to get things done; art is more beautiful to admire. Technology helps prepare students for office work as in computer skills. Art on the other hand prepares the student for work at a museum. Both are important for society but one is more useful than the other.

There are concepts that can only be learned in an art class, such as color, shape, texture. These visual concepts can help people learn to interpret visual information in a variety of ways. Art history is also important to know for conversation, which can help getting a job.

When it comes to getting a job, that's one thing art history won't help you with. You might impress your employer if you know art in depth, but he or she will not hire you for that reason. It is much more important to have a well-written resume and cover letter. These are skills that you can learn in school instead of art. But that does not mean art should not be taught in school. Art should still be taught for its cultural value and beauty.

Explanation

This low-scoring analysis does not attempt to create an argument; it cites minimal to no evidence from source texts. An attempt to analyze the issue and assess the validity of the arguments in source texts is present, but minimal or no understanding of the given arguments. The composition contains ideas that are insufficiently or illogically developed, with little elaboration on main ideas; contains an unclear progression of ideas; and establishes no discernible organizational structure. It demonstrates minimal control of basic conventions; and demonstrates consistently flawed sentence structure.

Specifically, this composition tries to develop the claim that "we should continue to teach art in school," but goes off in a variety of directions, not all of which are connected to the thesis, i.e., there is no discernible argument. It does not use the source texts and does not analyze the given arguments. There is no organizational structure and no progression of ideas; if anything, the piece of writing contradicts itself and forms a conclusion unrelated to the given arguments.

Mathematical Reasoning

1. 16	**18.** $\frac{W}{2}$	**32.** C
2. D	**19.** A	**33.** B
3. A	**20.** C	**34.** A
4. B	**21.** Imports increased; exports exhibited no clear trend. (B)	**35.** –2; 2
5. C	**22.** 16	**36.** D
6. C	**23.** 14 (B)	**37.** B
7. A	**24.** B	**38.** C
8. A	**25.** close to the x-axis	**39.** B
9. B	**26.** A	**40.** C
10. C	**27.** D	**41.** D
11. B	**28.** B	**42.** D
12. C	**29.** B	**43.** C
13. C	**30.** any point to the left of –1 on the number line	**44.** A
14. D	**31.** $330p + 1{,}200 \leq 8{,}000$	**45.** D
15. 2.38		**46.** $\frac{3}{2}, -2$
16. (3, –4)		
17. C		

1. **The correct answer is 16.** Let C = the number of students enrolled in chemistry only. Let P = the number of students in physics only. Let B = the number of students in both chemistry and physics:

   $C + P + B = 78$, so $47 + P + 15 = 78$.

   $P = 16$

2. **The correct answer is D.** Convert the mixed numbers to improper fractions with the least common denominator 16: $3\frac{7}{8} = \frac{31}{8} = \frac{62}{16}$ and $2\frac{11}{16} = \frac{43}{16}$. The sum is $\frac{105}{16}$. Now, the desired quotient is

   $\frac{105}{16} \div \frac{5}{8} = \frac{105}{16} \times \frac{8}{5} = \frac{21}{2} = 10\frac{1}{2}$.

   Choice A is incorrect because you added mixed numbers incorrectly; you must first find a common denominator when adding fractions. Choice B is incorrect because you multiplied instead of dividing, and you added mixed numbers incorrectly; you must first find a common denominator when adding fractions. Choice C is incorrect because you multiplied instead of dividing.

3. **The correct answer is A.** The diagram shows that all sides of the hexagon are congruent. Therefore, $240 \div 6 = 40$. Each of the other choices is the result of using the wrong number of sides when computing the length of one side. Choice B uses 5, choice C uses 3, and choice D uses 2.

4. **The correct answer is B.** Substitute in the given x-value and simplify, as follows:

$$\frac{\frac{1}{-\frac{3}{4}}-\left(-\frac{3}{4}\right)}{\frac{1}{-\frac{3}{4}}+\left(-\frac{3}{4}\right)}=\frac{-\frac{4}{3}+\frac{3}{4}}{-\frac{4}{3}-\frac{3}{4}}=\frac{\frac{-16+9}{12}}{\frac{-16-9}{12}}=\frac{-7}{-25}=\frac{7}{25}$$

Choice A is incorrect because you must first find a common denominator when adding or subtracting fractions. Choice C is the result of incorrectly canceling terms, not factors, in the numerator and denominator. Choice D is incorrect because when dividing the top expression by the bottom one, you forgot to replace the fraction after the division sign by its reciprocal when converting to a product.

5. **The correct answer is C.** If the average of the 5 games is 45, the sum of the 5 games must be equal to $45 \times 5 = 225$. Add the scores given: $54 + 60 + 28 + 42 = 184$, and then subtract this from 225: $225 - 184 = 41$. The other choices arise from various arithmetic errors.

6. **The correct answer is C.** Let x represent the missing angle. Using the triangle sum rule, the sum of the three angles must be 180°. Solve the equation $34° + 34° + x = 180°$ to get $x = 112°$. Choice A is incorrect because all three angles cannot be 34° since they would not sum to 180°. Choice B is incorrect because if the triangle contained a 90° angle, it would be an isosceles right triangle; the only isosceles right triangle is one for which there are two 45° angles. Choice D is incorrect because only one of the 34° angles was used when finding the sum of the angles.

7. **The correct answer is A.** Use the order of operations:

$$-2^3\,|\,3-9\,| = -8|-6| = -8(6) = -48$$

Choice B is incorrect because $-2^3 \neq -6$. Choice C is incorrect because $-2^3 = -8$, not 8. Choice D is incorrect because $|\,3-9\,| \neq |\,3\,|+|\,9\,|$.

8. **The correct answer is A.** The surface area formula for a rectangular box is $SA = 2(lw + lh + wh)$. Substitute $SA = 248$, $l = 10$, and $h = 4$ and then, solve for w:

$$248 = 2(10w + (10)(4) + 4w)$$
$$248 = 2(14w + 40)$$
$$248 = 28w + 80$$
$$168 = 28w$$
$$6 = w$$

Choice B is the length, and choices C and D are areas of faces of the box.

9. **The correct answer is B.** The corral is to be square, and so the length of any side equals $\sqrt{10{,}000} = 100$. Constructing one complete side, including both end posts, requires 11 posts (not 10) spaced 10 feet apart. Constructing two of the other three sides requires only 10 posts, while the fourth side requires only 9 posts since its end posts are already in place. The total number of posts needed is $11 + (2)(10) + 9 = 40$. Choice A is the number you get if you under-counted the number of posts needed by one per side, while choice C is the number you get if you over-counted the number of posts needed by one per side. Choice D is the length of a side of the corral.

10. **The correct answer is C.** The y-coordinate of points on the x-axis is 0. Solve the equation $x^3 - 16x = 0$:

$$x^3 - 16x = 0$$
$$x\left(x^2 - 16\right) = 0$$
$$x(x-4)(x+4) = 0$$
$$x = -4, 0, 4$$

Choice A is incorrect because two solutions are missing. Choice B is incorrect because the x-values that make $x^2 - 16$ equal to 0 are not −16 and 16. Choice D is incorrect because the x-values that make $x^2 - 16$ equal to 0 are not −2 and 2.

11. The correct answer is B. In order to find the growth rate per day, first divide by 24 (the number of days):

0.36 meters ÷ 24 = 0.015 meters per day

To convert to centimeters, shift the decimal point to the right by two places:

0.015 meters per day = 1.5 cm per day. Choice A is the result of not converting meters to centimeters. Choices C and D are the results of multiplying by 24, instead of dividing by it, and making a conversion error.

12. The correct answer is C. The central angle for an entire circle is 360°. So, $y° + x° = 360°$. Solving for y yields $y = 360 - x$. The other choices result from a misunderstanding of central angles of a circle.

13. The correct answer is C. Factor out x on the left side of the equation: $x(x + 4) = 0$. There are two possible x-values, or roots: $x = 0$; $x = -4$.

14. The correct answer is D. Use the substitution. Plug the expression for y given by the first equation into the second one, and solve the resulting equation for x:

$$\begin{aligned} a(bx - a) - b &= x \\ abx - a^2 - b &= x \\ abx - x &= a^2 + b \\ x(ab - 1) &= a^2 + b \\ x &= \frac{a^2 + b}{ab - 1} \end{aligned}$$

Choice A is incorrect because you cannot cancel terms in the numerator and denominator of a fraction; you can only cancel like factors. Choice B is incorrect because when solving a linear equation of the form $cz + d = e$, you subtract d from both sides instead of adding it to both sides. Choice C is the result of not using the distributive property when simplifying.

15. The correct answer is 2.38. The region of the number line from 2.3 to 2.5 has been divided into 10 congruent regions. The distance from 2.3 to 2.5 is 0.2. Thus, the vertical marks are spaced at intervals of 0.02. Accordingly, B = 2.38.

16. The correct answer is (3, –4). When point A (3, 2), and point B (–3, 2) are connected, they form a horizontal line segment of length 6. Each side of the square must have a length of 6. The missing corner is 6 units below (3, 2), which puts it at (3, –4).

17. The correct answer is C. Determine the answer systematically, beginning with the largest possible integer:

$$7 + 1 + 1 + 1 = 10$$

$$5 + 3 + 1 + 1 = 10$$

$$3 + 3 + 3 + 1 = 10$$

As you can see, there are three different ways.

18. The correct answer is $\frac{W}{2}$. The length of the bedroom (the longer room) is $2L$. Since the two areas both equal $L \times W$, the width of the bedroom must be $\frac{W}{2}$ because $(\not{2}L) \cdot \left(\frac{W}{\not{2}}\right) = LW$.

19. The correct answer is A. Let N be the smallest of the three integers. The other two consecutive odd integers are then $N + 2$ and $N + 4$. The average of the three integers is the sum of them divided by 3. Since this is assumed to equal 39, we get

$$\frac{N + (N + 2) + (N + 4)}{3} = 39.$$

Choice B is incorrect because this uses three consecutive integers, not consecutive odd integers. Choice C is incorrect because these three integers are not consecutive odd integers because one of N and $N + 1$ must be even. Choice D is incorrect because N, $3N$, and $5N$ are not consecutive odd integers even though 1, 3, and 5 are.

20. The correct answer is C. For each year, compare the heights of the two dark bars. The year 2016 was the only one among the four choices for which Country Y's imports (about \$39 billion) were less than twice Country X's imports (about \$21 billion).

21. The correct answer is Imports increased; exports exhibited no clear trend (B). To answer this question, examine the right bar for each of the six years shown. The size of the dark portion (Country Y's imports) increases through the second year shown, then remains about the same for the third year, then increases, slightly decreases, and increases for the last three years shown. So the general trend over the six-year period was for the value of imports to increase. The size of the bar's light portion (Country Y's exports) decreases for the first three years shown, then increases for two years, and then decreases. So there is no clear export trend for the six-year period as a whole.

22. The correct answer is 16. Assuming the tepee is symmetrical and level, it is an isosceles triangle. Any isosceles triangle can be divided into two congruent right triangles by dropping the top vertex down to the base perpendicularly; so, we can use the Pythagorean theorem to determine the unknown measurement. Side *A* is 15 meters. $A^2 = 225$ meters. Side *C* is 17 meters. $C^2 = 289$ meters.

$$\begin{aligned} 225 + B^2 &= 289 \\ B^2 &= 289 - 225 \\ B^2 &= 64 \\ B &= 8 \end{aligned}$$

This is the radius, not the diameter, so we need to multiply it by 2.

The diameter is 16 meters.

23. The correct answer is 14 (B). Use the exponent rules, as follows:

$$\begin{aligned} \frac{8\times\left(2^4\right)^3}{16} &= \frac{\left(2^3\right)^2\times\left(2^4\right)^3}{2^4} \\ &= \frac{2^6\times 2^{12}}{2^4} \\ &= \frac{2^{18}}{2^4} \\ &= 2^{\boxed{14}} \end{aligned}$$

Choice A is incorrect because $\frac{x^a}{x^b} \neq x^{\frac{a}{b}}$. Choice C is incorrect because $\frac{x^a}{x^b} \neq x^{\frac{a}{b}}$ and $x^a \bullet x^b \neq x^{a \bullet b}$ Choice D is incorrect because $\left(x^a\right)^b \neq x^{a^b}$.

24. The correct answer is B. The volume of a cylinder is $\pi r^2 h$, where *r* is the radius and *h* is the height. The height is 20 cm, and the volume is $2{,}880\pi$ cm³. Substitute these values into the formula for the volume to calculate the radius:

$$\begin{aligned} \pi r^2 20 &= 2{,}880\pi \\ r^2 \bullet 20 &= 2{,}880 \\ r^2 &= 144 \\ r &= 12 \end{aligned}$$

The radius is 12, so the diameter is 2 times the radius, or 24. Choice A is the radius, not the diameter, choice C is the height, and choice D is the square of the radius.

25. The correct answer is anywhere very close to the *x*-axis. A high negative correlation means that the data slants down to the right as shown below. The last data point would be very close to the horizontal *x*-axis above the arrow.

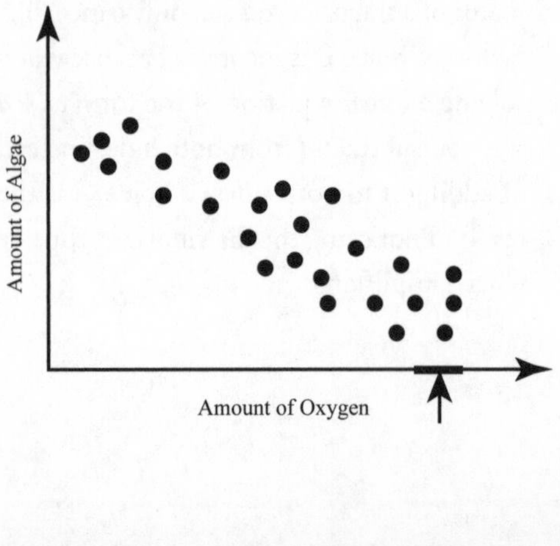

26. The correct answer is A. Convert both fractions to equivalent ones with the common denominator $3a^2$: $\frac{3x}{a^2} = \frac{9x}{3a^2}$ and $\frac{x}{3a} = \frac{ax}{3a^2}$.

Hence,

$$\frac{3x}{a^2} - \frac{x}{3a} = \frac{9x}{3a^2} - \frac{ax}{3a^2} = \frac{9x - ax}{3a^2} = \frac{(9-a)x}{3a^2}.$$

Choice B is incorrect because you did not convert $\frac{x}{3a}$ to one with the common denominator $3a^2$. Choice C is incorrect because you do not add or subtract fractions by simply adding or subtracting the numerators and denominators; you must first get a common denominator. Choice D is incorrect because you do not add the denominators of fractions when adding or subtracting them; you simply add or subtract the numerators and put the resulting sum or difference over the least common denominator.

27. The correct answer is D. The only product that yields $16x^2 - 8x + 1$ when expanded is $(4x - 1)^2$. All others have the correct squared and constant terms, but the wrong middle term.

28. The correct answer is B. For each tile, Herman needs $c^2 + x$ centimeters of cloth. He needs this much cloth for each of 20 tiles, so he must multiply this expression by 20. $20(c^2 + x) = 20c^2 + 20x$. Choice A is incorrect because the x should be multiplied by 20 as well (by the distributive property). Choice C has the addition and multiplication signs interchanged. Choice D squares the x instad of multiplying by 20. Choice D squares the x instead of multiplying by 20.

29. The correct answer is B. Cross-multiply, simplify, and isolate the term with y_1 on one side. Then, divide both sides by its coefficient:

$$\frac{x - x_1}{y - y_1} = m$$
$$x - x_1 = m(y - y_1)$$
$$x - x_1 = my - my_1$$
$$x - x_1 - my = -my_1$$
$$\frac{x - x_1 - my}{-m} = y_1$$
$$y_1 = y + \frac{x_1 - x}{m}$$

Choice A is incorrect because there is a sign error. Choice C is incorrect because you cannot cancel terms in the numerator and denominator of a fraction; you can only cancel like factors. Choice D is incorrect because you did not use the distributive property.

30. The correct answer is any point to the left of –1 on the number line. Simplify the inequality by adding 3 to both sides: $-2x > 2$ and then dividing by -2:

$$\frac{-2x}{-2} > \frac{2}{-2}$$
$$x < -1$$

(Remember to change the inequality sign when dividing by a negative.)

31. The correct answer is $330p + 1{,}200 \le 8{,}000$. First calculate the cost for a single sign post. It is \$240 plus \$60 multiplied by 1.5: $240 + (60)(1.5) = 240 + 90 = 330$. Each sign post costs \$330, so p sign posts cost $330p$. Add the retainer fee of \$1,200: $330p + 1{,}200$ to calculate the total cost of p sign posts. This number must be less than or equal to, $\le$, 8,000.

32. The correct answer is C. The number of units sold is given as $45{,}000 - 160p$. Multiply this expression by the selling price of each unit, p:

$(45{,}000 - 160p)(p) = 45{,}000p - 160p^2 =$ total sales. The other choices are the result incorrectly using the demand curve to compute sales.

33. The correct answer is B. The line Sal draws to represent the demand for pizza must go up, or rise, 3 units for every 8 unit increase in the number of children, which is the horizontal run on this graph. The slope of a line is the rise over the run, or $\frac{\text{rise}}{\text{run}} = \frac{3}{8}$. Choice A is the reciprocal of the current slope; remember, slope is rise over run, not run over rise. Choices C and D are incorrect because they do not use both pieces of information given when computing the slope.

34. The correct answer is A. Using the form $y = mx + b$, you have $m = -\frac{3}{2}$. You need the y-intercept b. To find it, substitute the point (–4, 0) and slope into the equation and solve for b:

$$0 = -\frac{3}{2}(-4) + b$$
$$0 = 6 + b$$
$$-6 = b$$

The equation of the line is $y = -\frac{3}{2}x - 6$.

Choice B is incorrect because you need to interchange the x and y in the equation. Choice C is incorrect because the y-intercept is (0, 0). Choice D is incorrect because you mistakenly used the x-intercept as though it were the y-intercept.

35. The correct answers are –2 and 2. This is the graph of a positive cubic function. However, it is decreasing with a negative slope in the interval $-2 \leq x \leq 2$.

36. The correct answer is D. First calculate the slope by finding the difference in the y-values divided by the difference in the x-values: $\frac{5-2}{-4-2} = \frac{3}{-6} = -\frac{1}{2}$. Insert a pair of (x, y)-values and the slope into the slope-intercept form of a line: $2 = -\frac{1}{2}(2) + b$ to find the value of b: $2 = -1 + b$, $b = 3$. The equation is $y = -\frac{1}{2}x + 3$. Choices A and B have the wrong y-intercept. Choice C has the wrong sign on the slope.

37. The correct answer is B. To calculate the rate for Pool B, determine the slope of the line in the graph. Take 2 points to calculate slope: (0, 0) and (30, 2). Find the difference in the y-values divided by the difference in the x-values: $\frac{2-0}{30-0} = \frac{2}{30} = \frac{1}{15}$. This is interpreted as Pool B being filled 15 gallons every 1 hour, which is 3 gallons per hour faster than Pool A's rate.

38. The correct answer is C. The number of dimes expressed in terms of the number of quarters is given by $d = 3q - 1$. The portion of the total amount contributed by d dimes is $0.10d$ and the portion of the total contributed by q quarters is $0.25q$. Since the sum is \$4.30, we get the equation $0.10d + 0.25q = 4.30$. So the system shown in choice C is correct. Choice A is incorrect because the parentheses in the first equation should be removed to yield the correct expression for the number of dimes. Choice B is incorrect because the right-side of the second equation should be multiplied by 100. Choice D is incorrect because d and q should be interchanged in the first equation.

39. The correct answer is B. The slope of a line is the change in the y-values divided by the change in the x-values. If the slope is negative, then the y-values are decreasing as the x-values increase. For the given line, the slope is $-\frac{2}{3}$. This means that the y-value on the graph decreases by 2 units for every 3 units increase in x, which is choice B. Choice A is incorrect because the 3 and 2 are interchanged. Choice C does not account for the negative sign on the slope. Choice D is incorrect because the slope and the y-intercept are switched.

40. The correct answer is C. Using distance equals rate times time, Rick travels $35t$ miles and his sister travels $(6 + 45t)$ miles at the moment she catches him. Equating these two expressions yields $35t = 6 + 45t$. Choice A is incorrect because 6 should be added to the right-side. Choice B is incorrect because the parentheses should be removed on the right-side. Choice D is incorrect because the 6 should be on the right side, not the left.

41. The correct answer is D. The total electricity charges per month equal a \$20 fixed delivery fee plus the product of the number of kilowatt hours consumed times the cost per kilowatt hour. So the equation has the general form $y = m \times x + 20$. In this equation, y equals the electricity charge per month, m equals the rate per kilowatt hour, and x is the number of kilowatt hours consumed during the month. You must determine the value of m based on the information provided in the table. Since the equation is assumed to be linear, you can do this by taking the values for any one of the total charges per month and substituting them into the general equation.

For example, use the first row in the table by substituting $x = 400$ and $y = 36.80$ and solve for m:

$$y = m \times x + 20$$
$$36.60 = m(400) + 20$$
$$16.80 = 400m$$
$$m = 0.042$$

So the equation is $y = 0.042x + 20$. Choices A and B are incorrect because you are asked to find the equation that best represents y as a function of x, the number of kilowatt hours consumed per month. Thus, x is the independent variable, and y is the dependent variable. Choice C is incorrect because you subtracted the \$20 monthly fixed delivery fee rather than adding it.

42. The correct answer is D. Recall that *distance equals rate times time*. The distance the father has traveled at time t equals the sum of the head start and the rate at which he jogs times the number of hours he has been jogging. Symbolically, this is given by the expression $0.75 + 5t$. Likewise, the distance the son has traveled at time t is the rate at which he jogs times the time he has been jogging; this is described by the expression $6.5t$. The distance, d, between them is the difference between the two expressions: $d = 0.75 + 5t - 6.5t = 0.75 - 1.5t$. So, choice D is the correct answer. Choice A does not account for the head start that the father is given. Choice B is the number of miles the father has jogged in t hours, but does not account for the relative position to his son. Choice C is the number of miles the son has jogged in t hours, but does not account for the relative position to his father.

43. The correct answer is C. Because 3.5 is equivalent to $c = \frac{7}{2}t$, the slope of this function is $\frac{7}{2}$, which means for every 2 turns of the larger gear, the smaller gear turns 7 times. Choice A is incorrect because while this represents a linear function; the slope is 7, not $\frac{7}{2}$. Choice B is incorrect because while this represents a linear function, the slope is 3, not 3.5. Choice D is incorrect because you interchanged the meaning of *c* and *t*.

44. The correct answer is A. The function is expressed in slope-intercept form $y = mx + b$, where *m* is a slope and *b* is the *y*-intercept. Here, the slope is indeed –2 and the *y*-intercept is –5. Choice B is incorrect because substituting these points into the equation does not yield a correct statement in either case. Choice C is incorrect because while it does cross the *y*-axis at –5, the interpretation of the slope implies that it is 2, not –2. Choice D is incorrect because the slope of a linear function would need to be zero for the graph not to cross the *x*-axis; here, the slope is –2, not 0.

45. The correct answer is D. Substitute in –4 for *x* and simplify using the order of operations:

$$\begin{aligned} f(-4) &= -(-4)^2(2 + 3(-4)) \\ &= -16(2 - 12) \\ &= -16(110) \\ &= 160 \end{aligned}$$

Choice A is incorrect because you did not use the order of operations. Choices B and C are incorrect because $-(-4)^2 \neq 8$.

46. The correct answer is $y = \frac{3}{2}x + -2$. The line crosses the *y*-axis at –2. So in the slope-intercept form $y = mx + b$, the value of *b* is –2. To compute the slope, use two of the points that are clearly on the line, say (0, –2) and (4, 4). The slope is $m = \frac{4-(-2)}{4-0} = \frac{3}{2}$. So the equation is $y = \frac{3}{2}x - 2$.

Science

1. B	**13.** A	**25.** A
2. A	**14.** B	**26.** B
3. C	**15.** D	**27.** 720 calories
4. B	**16.** C	**28.** gravity
5. A	**17.** B	**29.** B
6. positions G and C	**18.** A	**30.** C
7. B	**19.** pressure	**31.** A
8. 7	**20.** C	**32.** potential, kinetic
9. boxes A, C, D	**21.** simple squamous	**33.** B
10. B	**22.** C	**34.** B
11. A	**23.** B	**35.** D
12. C	**24.** B	

1. **The correct answer is B.** With added growth stimulation, the stem's shady side will grow vertically at a faster rate than the stem's sunny side. As a result, the stem will bend toward the light. If auxin concentrated on the sunny side of the stem, rather than on the shady side, then the plant would bend toward the ground (choice D). Choices A and C will not occur.

2. **The correct answer is A.** The time it takes for crest X to reach line A is three-fourths the wave's period (the time it would take for crest X to reach the point of the next crest in the figure). Hence the wave's period is 4 seconds. Line B is located one full wavelength plus three-fourths of a second wavelength to the right of point X. Multiply that distance by the wave's period:

$$1\frac{3}{4} \times 4 = 7 \text{ seconds}$$

3. **The correct answer is C.** Dr. Marshall proved that *H. pylori* causes ulcers, so he must have become sick with ulcer-like symptoms after drinking the infected broth. His illness would have been successfully treated with antibiotics, so choice A is incorrect. Since stress does not cause ulcers, they cannot be cured with anti-stress techniques (choice B). *H. pylori* causes stomach pain and vomiting, not skin rashes, so choice D is incorrect.

4. **The correct answer is B.** All four changes described in the passage are the result of human activity: clear-cutting forests, channeling fertilizer and sewage into rivers and oceans, overusing air pollutants, and allowing livestock to overgraze grasslands. None of these findings are caused by global climate change (choice A), although clear-cutting forests and overgrazing can lead to climate change because they remove plants that absorb carbon dioxide. Since all of these changes are caused by human activity, they are all reversible, not irreversible (choice C). The depletion of the ozone layer does not affect the world's food supply (choice D).

5. **The correct answer is A.** When one form of energy is converted to another, some is inevitably lost as heat (thermal energy). This is evidenced by how hot a smartphone gets

when it is in continuous use. The other answer choices all describe functions of the device that are powered by electrical energy, so these are all useful conversions of chemical energy.

6. **Positions G and C are correct.** When the moon is at either position C or G, a person directly below the moon would observe that half of the moon's facing surface is lit by the sun. Position A shows the new moon phase (none of the facing surface is lit). Position E shows the full moon phase (unless a lunar eclipse is occurring). Positions B and H show crescent moon phases (most of the facing surface is unlit). Positions D and F show autumn moon phases (most of the facing surface is lit).

7. **The correct answer is B.** In a simplified diagram of an organic molecule, carbon atoms exist at the intersection points of straight lines. In the diagram given, the carbon atoms have also been numbered so that we can easily refer to them. The ends of both molecules are the same: both carbon 1 and carbon 4 are each bonded to one OH group and double-bonded to an oxygen. In oxaloacetate, there are three double-bonded oxygen atoms on the main carbon chain, while in malate there are only two. So the OH group on carbon 2 in malate must have been moved to carbon 3 and transformed to a double-bonded oxygen in oxaloacetate. None of the transformations in the other answer choices have occurred in the conversion of malate to oxaloacetate.

8. **The correct answer is 7.** Genotypes RR and Rr are expressed as red. All but one of the eight offspring shown in the diagram are red.

9. **The correct answer is C.** The diagram shows that the pairing in Set 3, *Rr* and *Rr*, produced one *rr* (white) offspring. Although the diagram does not show either pairing provided in Sets 1 or 4, we can see that each parent in both pairings can contribute at least one *r* allele to an offspring. Therefore, each of these pairings can produce *rr* (white) offspring. The diagram shows that the pairing in Set 2 produced only *Rr* (red) offspring.

10. **The correct answer is B.** When the algae die and coral bleaching occurs, the coral usually dies, which shows that it relies on the algae to survive. We are not given enough information in the passage to determine if the opposite is also true since we are only told what happens if the algae dies first, not if the coral dies first. Thus, we cannot conclude that choice A is true from the passage. Choice C is incorrect because the passage tells us that algae die because of rising ocean temperatures, so if ocean warming continues, more algae and thus more coral will die, not less. Similarly, if ocean temperatures cool, then less algae will die, not more, so choice D is incorrect.

11. **The correct answer is A.** By using a lever of the sort shown in the illustration, you can increase the output force (moving the load) while applying the same amount of, or possibly less, input force (effort). A crowbar would be the best example of the choices given. Wedges (choice B) and wheelbarrows (choice C) are not levers, so they are not the same type of simple machine shown. A nutcracker (choice D) is a different type of lever than the one shown in the illustration.

12. **The correct answer is C.** Since whales retain remnants of the pelvic bones, they must have inherited these bones from an ancestor that had complete, typical pelvic bones that supported complete, typical hind limbs. In addition, the question stem states that whales lost their hind limbs, so they must have evolved from animals with hind limbs. The question stem says that whales have remnants of pelvis bones, so they did not evolve

their unusual pelvis bones from scratch; that is, they did not evolve from animals that did not have pelvis bones (choice A). Although whales have unusual front limbs that have been modified into flippers, they still have front limbs, so they must have evolved from animals that had front limbs. Thus, choice B is incorrect. Whales live in the ocean and have no need for hind limbs, so there is no reason to expect that they will re-evolve the hind limbs that they have lost (choice D).

13. **The correct answer is A.** Serine contains 3 oxygen atoms, while cysteine contains only 2. Both molecules contain 3 carbon atoms, 1 nitrogen atom, and 7 hydrogen atoms.

14. **The correct answer is B.** As the passage states, gametes are the reproductive cells of a sexually reproducing organism. Thus, eggs and sperm are gametes that contain a haploid number of chromosomes. The haploid number (n) is half of the diploid number ($2n$), so a turkey gamete contains $80 \div 2 = 40$ chromosomes. Choice A (23) is the number of chromosomes in a human gamete, not a turkey gamete. Choice C (80) is the diploid number, or the number of chromosomes in any non-gamete cell. Choice D (160) is two times the diploid number, not half.

15. **The correct answer is D.** The passage states that the Southern Lights happen for similar reasons to why the Northern Lights happen at the North Pole. We know that the Northern Lights happen at the North Pole because this is one place where Earth's magnetic field lines converge. Logically, the South Pole—the opposite of the North Pole—must be the place where the other end of Earth's magnetic field lines converge. You may also remember that magnets have north and south poles and that the poles are where magnetic field lines converge. The passage says that the charged particles that cause auroras come from the sun, but it does not say that only the sun contains charged particles (choice A). You should recall that all atoms contain charged particles (protons and electrons), so charged particles are certainly present on Earth and everywhere else in the universe. There is no discussion of the magnetic field lines of the equator, so it is not reasonable to infer that auroras happen at the equator as well (in fact, they do not). Thus, choice B is not a valid inference. There is also no discussion of how temperature or climate affects auroras, so choice C is not a valid inference.

16. **The correct answer is C.** At point C, the water flea population has gone over the carrying capacity for the environment. The carrying capacity is the maximum population that can be supported by the resources in the environment. Once the population goes over the carrying capacity, the environment can no longer support it. Point A (choice A) and point E (choice D) are both below the carrying capacity, so the environment can support the population at these points. Point B (choice B) is at the carrying capacity, so the environment has exactly enough resources to support the population at this point.

17. **The correct answer is B.** The temperature scale is given across the top of the diagram. Temperatures decrease from left to right, so that stars with the lowest surface temperatures are plotted at the right end of the diagram. Giant stars are clustered near the diagram's right side, which means that they are among the coldest stars. Blue stars are the hottest stars. Luminosity is given on the left side of the diagram and increases as you move up. Dwarfs are at the bottom of the diagram, which means they are less luminous than cepheids, which are in the middle. Orange stars come in a variety of luminosities, as do red stars, so you cannot say

that orange stars in general are more luminous than red stars; you can only compare specific orange stars to specific red stars.

18. **The correct answer is A.** Our solar system's sun (denoted by the X on the diagram) is located near the center of the diagram. The other plotted points are distributed fairly equally above and below X, as well as to the left and to the right of X. This distribution tells you that the sun is about average, or typical, in both its brightness (measured on the vertical scale) and its surface temperature (measured on the horizontal scale). You cannot determine the age of our sun (choice B) or how the number of stars in the universe is changing (choice D) from the diagram. Choice C is incorrect because the way that the stars are plotted in bands and clusters on the diagram is not how they are physically arranged in the universe; the diagram is just plotting their characteristics.

19. **The correct answer is *pressure*.** If the tube were open at both ends (instead of being connected to the air tank on one end), the level of the liquid would be the same on both sides of the *U* in the tube, since the atmospheric air would be exerting equal pressure on both ends. But the higher level on the right side of the *U* indicates that the pressure from the air tank is greater than the atmospheric pressure. (The various level marks up and down the tube provide a quantitative measure of that pressure.)

20. **The correct answer is C.** Healthy bats that came into direct contact with the fungus *Geomyces destructans* developed WNS, so WNS is spread through direct contact with the fungus. In Experiment 3, healthy bats came into direct contact with *G. destructans* through other bats; they were in the same enclosure as WNS-infected bats and were able to touch them. A few bats were lucky enough to not come into direct contact with the fungus, as 2 out of the 18 healthy bats escaped infection. In Experiment 4, the researchers directly applied *G. destructans* to the healthy bats' wings, and they all became infected with WNS. WNS is not spread through the air (choice A) because healthy bats that shared the same air as infected bats did not get sick if they did not touch the sick bats (Experiment 2). It has been explained how we can conclude that WNS is caused by *G. destructans*, so choice B is incorrect. In the description for Experiment 3, it is explained that bats in the same enclosure can touch and, as most of the healthy bats developed WNS, it is clear that they did touch infected bats. Thus, choice D is incorrect.

21. **The correct answer is simple squamous.** An air sac within a lung takes in oxygen, which it passes through its lining to blood vessels, which then pass carbon dioxide back through the lining to the air sac to be expelled into the air. To accomplish the exchange, the lining must be single-layered, thin, and leaky (diffuse). The tissue shown as simple squamous best serves this purpose. The other tissue types are all thicker than the simple squamous tissue and would not as easily permit the passage of oxygen and carbon dioxide.

22. **The correct answer is C.** The lizards that have the best chance at becoming the most common in the population will be the ones that are most likely to survive to reproduce in their environment. After the landslide, the hillside is covered in light-colored rocks. The light brown lizards will be hardest to see in these rocks and will the most likely to survive to reproduce. Black and dark brown lizards would be easier to see against a light-colored hillside and would be less likely to survive, so the remaining choices are incorrect.

23. **The correct answer is B.** Light brown lizards are being selected because they are most likely to survive to reproduce after the land-

slide. This is an example of directional selection because a trait that was an extreme condition (light brown lizards were rare) is being selected. Dark brown lizards were the average and most common condition, so if they were selected, this would be an example of stabilizing (choice A) selection. If both black and light brown lizards were being selected, this would be an example of disruptive selection (choice C) selection. Kin selection (choice D) would favor the reproductive success of the relatives of the light brown lizards, even at the cost of their own survival.

24. **The correct answer is B.** Following the arrows in the illustration shows that cold water in the North Atlantic Ocean (near the North Pole) sinks and then travels south toward the equator, warming and mixing with warmer water along the way. Once warmer, that water rises to the surface and moves northward to where it started in the North Atlantic. While choice A appears to be true based on the diagram, this is a minor detail that is not the overall idea conveyed by the diagram. This is a generalized diagram that does not show every point in the Atlantic Ocean, and since it does not accurately represent water depth, choice C is not the best answer. Choice D is true, but this is not shown by the diagram; it is something that can be concluded after understanding the overall idea of the diagram.

25. **The correct answer is A.** Any change that is in the opposite direction of what is occurring in the diagram is most likely to stop it. Melting of the polar ice cap will send an enormous amount of fresh water into the ocean at the North Pole. Fresh water is less dense than salt water, so it is unlikely to sink. In addition, the loss of ice at the North Pole will cause the temperature of the ocean water there to get warmer, making it even less likely to sink. This will shut down the circulation pattern shown in the diagram. The other choices all describe amplifying the conditions shown in the diagram, which will just strengthen the circulation shown in the diagram. Increased heat input from the sun at the equator (choice B) will make water there warmer and more likely to move north, increased heat loss at the North Pole (choice C) will make water there colder and more likely to sink, and a larger volume of warm water rising at the equator (choice D) will drive a larger volume of warm water northward.

26. **The correct answer is B.** The ptarmigan is white in the winter, which means it must live somewhere cold enough to snow in the winter. The only choice given where it is cold enough to snow in the winter is the Canadian prairie. The range of the white-tailed ptarmigan stretches from the Cascade Mountains in Washington State to the tundra of Alaska and northern Canada.

27. **The correct answer is *720 calories*.** It takes 80 calories to change the state from ice to water (the lower plateau); 100 calories are needed to raise the temperature from 0°C to 100°C, and an additional 540 calories are needed to change the water into steam. The total amount of heat energy required is 720 calories.

28. **The correct answer is *gravity*.** Scientists infer the existence of dark matter from how gravity operates on light matter. Thus, their understanding of dark matter is theoretical. Because dark matter produces gravity, it can affect the gravity produced by light matter. This causes a change in the motion of light matter, such as in the galaxy described in the question.

29. **The correct answer is B.** According to the graph, atmospheric opacity is close to 0% for visible light, with wavelengths of around 400–800 nm. This is the visible light window, which allows the wavelengths necessary to illuminate the world to pass through the

atmosphere to the earth's surface—without the visible light window, we would always live in the dark. Visible light is what it sounds like: it consists of the wavelengths that humans (and many other organisms) can see. Visible light includes the wavelengths necessary for photosynthesis to occur. Photosynthesis is the basis of all food chains and thus for life on Earth. The atmosphere is opaque to ultraviolet (choice A) and most infrared (choice C) radiation; these wavelengths are also invisible to the human eye. While there is an atmospheric window for radio waves (choice D), these wavelengths are also invisible to the human eye.

30. **The correct answer is C.** Scientists take advantage of the atmospheric window for radio waves (wavelengths from about 5 cm to 20 m as shown on the graph) to study the Universe. Radio waves from distant astronomical objects can be focused and collected by huge dish-shaped radio telescopes. Radio waves can be used to study objects that cannot be seen in visible light. The greenhouse effect is caused by the atmosphere being opaque to infrared radiation, not transparent, so choice A is incorrect. Ozone causes the atmosphere to be opaque to ultraviolet radiation, not transparent, so choice B is incorrect. Electromagnetic radiation does not affect the ability of airplanes to fly, so choice D is incorrect.

31. **The correct answer is A.** Sediment particles settle out by size as they travel, generally as they are carried by moving water or wind. The farther the particles travel, the more time there is for the heavier and larger particles to settle out first, followed by the lighter and smaller particles. If sediments are dumped quickly in one place, they will not have time to be sorted. More sediment particles can be added to a mixture of sediments as it travels, but that will only make deposits less well-sorted. Sediments do become more rounded the farther they travel, but this does not affect how well they are sorted (the weight of the particles does). Sediment particles become more broken up, not harder, the farther they travel.

32. **The correct answers are *potential* and *kinetic*, in that order.** The coiled spring has energy based on internal stress caused by its compressed position; until the spring is released, the energy is potential energy as no force has actually been applied to anything. In panel B, the potential energy in the spring has been transformed into kinetic energy (the energy of motion) in the now-moving cart.

33. **The correct answer is B.** Position 2 is where force is applied to the cart, converting the potential energy in the spring to kinetic energy in the moving cart. Work is also applied as the spring moves from its coiled to its uncoiled state, but Position 1 (choice A) is indicating the base of the spring, which does not move when the spring uncoils. Position 3 (choice C) is indicating the kinetic energy in the cart, not the force applied to create that kinetic energy. Position 4 (choice D) indicating the motion of the wheels, is also kinetic energy, not work.

34. **The correct answer is B.** A close look at the graph shows that the rabbit population increases before the wolf population does and decreases before the wolf population decreases. The pattern suggests that the wolf population is responding to changes in the rabbit population. More rabbits means more favorable conditions for wolves; the wolves multiply and eat more rabbits, leading the rabbit population to crash. Deprived of their food source, the wolf population declines

soon afterward. Then the cycle repeats. Choice A cannot be true since the populations rise and fall at slightly different times. Choice C is the opposite of the pattern that is present, and choice D is not possible since the question states that this dynamic is occurring on an isolated island, so there is nowhere to go.

35. **The correct answer is D.** Plants need both water and light to stay healthy, and the teacher forgot to give both of these things to the plant over the weekend. To draw a valid conclusion, only one variable can be changed at the same time, and in this case, two variables are changing: the amount of water and light. Plants can wilt for many reasons, and there is no indication that the teacher watered the plant on Monday.

Social Studies

1. B	**13.** D	**25.** B
2. A	**14.** D	**26.** A
3. A	**15.** Valley Forge	**27.** House of Representatives
4. C	**16.** Philadelphia	**28.** B
5. B	**17.** A	**29.** Manifest Destiny (B)
6. B	**18.** C	**30.** A
7. D	**19.** C	**31.** A
8. D	**20.** A	**32.** D
9. A	**21.** A	**33.** B
10. Clergy	**22.** C	**34.** B
11. Reception	**23.** A	**35.** C
12. A	**24.** A	

1. **The correct answer is B.** Although they live in the same region, the people of Great Britain generally subscribe to Protestantism, while the majority of Irish are Catholic. The other statements are untrue conclusions about the Irish and British experience of region and place.

2. **The correct answer is A.** While Native Americans of the Northwest Coast relied heavily on fishing as their food source, both they and the Native Americans of the Eastern Woodlands farmed. Both the nations of the Eastern Woodlands and Pacific Northwest lived in longhouses, so choice B is incorrect. Since the Pacific Northwest nations carved totem poles, choice C is incorrect. From the information given, it's impossible to tell which group of Native Americans was more advanced—a term that is very subjective and depends on how a person defines it—so choice D is incorrect.

3. **The correct answer is A.** The fear of tyranny created by a concentration of power that colonists had experienced with Great Britain had the greatest influence on Madison's writing. While the failure of the Articles did influence Madison, his specific positions in the passages are about abuse and division of power to protect against said abuses, making choice B incorrect. Choice C is incorrect because Madison's opinion was not shaped by the opposition even if he was writing to persuade them. Choice D is incorrect because Washington had yet to be selected.

4. **The correct answer is C.** The ability of each branch of government to "check and balance" one another is supported by the use of a veto. Taxation (choice A), declaration of war (choice B), and regulation of interstate commerce (choice D) are not examples of balancing power between the branches.

5. **The correct answer is B.** The failure of the Articles of Confederation proved the need for a government that divided power equally between the branches. Choice A is incorrect because Great Britain's political system did not fail and the Constitution was modeled after it in many ways. Choice C is incorrect because Madison was arguing that

the Constitution did not need these protections (although he ultimately included them). Choice D would support the need for revision of the Articles but not support the ideas presented by Madison about checks and balances.

6. **The correct answer is B.** The image is expressing the burden that African Americans still carry following the Civil War and the power whites hold over them. Choice A is incorrect because while powerful whites did dominate the Southern government, the cartoon is more focused on the struggle that African Americans face than a specific commentary on political power. Choice C is incorrect because there were few protections in place for African Americans prior to or after the war to be removed. Choice D is incorrect because the focus of the image is on the African Americans and their struggle, not the one member of the KKK.

7. **The correct answer is D.** The movement of African Americans (the second Great Migration) to the North was an African American reaction to the Southern responses. Choices A, B, and C are all examples of Southern resistance to the Reconstruction Amendments.

8. **The correct answer is D.** The use of the word *should* in the statement in choice D indicates it is not a fact, but rather a judgment or opinion. All the other answer choices are statements of facts broadly accepted as true.

9. **The correct answer is A.** Europeans believed that Natives were primitive beings, but the passage supports the opposite, as their ability to adapt to their surroundings and growing techniques saved the colonizers from certain death. Choices B, C, and D are all true statements that are supported in the passage.

10. **The correct answer is Clergy.** According to the graph, the clergy costs $113, which is between the cost of the limousine ($192) and the cost of the groom's clothing ($77).

11. **The correct answer is Reception.** Since the reception is by far the greatest single expense, the most savings probably could be made there.

12. **The correct answer is A.** Lincoln needed to retain the Border States during the war and their views on slavery would be in conflict with total emancipation during this period of the war. Choice B is incorrect because the North already had a large numerical advantage. Choice C is incorrect because Southern states were not part of the Senate during the Civil War. Choice D is incorrect because Lincoln was supportive of Emancipation.

13. **The correct answer is D.** The US District Courts (of which there are 94) have original jurisdiction and conduct trials in cases involving federal laws and regulations. State trial courts (choice A) generally take cases involving state laws, not federal laws. The Supreme Court (choice B) has original jurisdiction only in special cases. State supreme courts (choice C) do not have original jurisdiction and cannot conduct trials.

14. **The correct answer is D**. Appointment based on "merit" means that a position is given to the person most qualified to perform it. One way to determine which applicants are best qualified for a job is by administering an appropriate exam. (In fact, civil service exams were established by the Pendleton Civil Service Reform Act.) Political lobbying (choice A), civilian jury duty (choice B), and term limits for elected officials (choice C) were not established by the Pendleton Civil Service Act.

15. **The correct answer is Valley Forge.** The map shows the American forces stopping at Valley Forge after retreating from Howe's forces.

16. **The correct answer is Philadelphia.** The map indicates the path of Washington's retreat, away from Philadelphia, which was left open to British attack. The city was under British occupation for nearly a year.

17. **The correct answer is A.** The Civilian Conservation Corps provided employment to many unemployed workers, just like the Works Progress Administration and the Public Works Administration. The FDIC (choice B) supported regulation of banking, the FHA (choice C) supported housing regulation, and the Social Security Act (choice D) addressed help for the elderly.

18. **The correct answer is C.** Many of the policies during the first 100 days were focused on protecting and regulating the banking industry in hopes of addressing the causes of the Great Depression. Although there are examples that show housing (choice A), farming (choice B), and conservation (choice D) being addressed, there are more policies focused on banking than any other area.

19. **The correct answer is C.** As the passage notes, in terms of what a US dollar can buy, its value has declined steadily since 1950. Although 1967 does not appear in the actual illustration, it is the only year listed among the choices that could be the base year used for comparison with the others.

20. **The correct answer is A.** The growing buying power of the euro compared to the US dollar means that goods and services in the United States are relatively inexpensive to Europeans. It makes sense that they would take advantage of the weak US dollar by spending their money in the United States.

21. **The correct answer is A.** The United States was concerned with the spread of Communism and hoped to continue its protection of democracy at home and abroad. Choice B is incorrect because The United States hoped to contain the spread of Communism. Choice C is incorrect because the United States wanted to spread and protect the ideas of the Constitution, democracy—not the document itself. Choice D is incorrect because the speech had nothing to do with immigration.

22. **The correct answer is C.** The Three-Fifths Clause was a measure taken to ease tensions about population at the Constitutional Convention. Because the North was more heavily populated, southerners were concerned with lack of representation in Congress. By counting black slaves (not immigrants, Protestants, or Native Americans) as three-fifths of a person, southerners were appeased.

23. **The correct answer is A.** If Southern states included slaves in their population counts, they would have greater representation in Congress. If slaves were not counted, they would lack representation as the North was much more heavily populated. The Three-Fifths Clause was an attempt to remedy this situation, albeit at the expense of black slaves. Choice B is incorrect because there was no mention of slavery in the Constitution. Choices C and D are incorrect because the clause was a compromise meant to give equal representation to both the North and the South.

24. **The correct answer is A.** By establishing judicial review, *Marbury v. Madison* ensured that the judicial branch had as much power and influence as the legislative and executive branches. Choice B is incorrect because the political party of the judge was not relevant. Choices C and D are incorrect because the ruling did not limit nor did it grant uncontrolled power to the judicial branch.

25. **The correct answer is B.** A writ of mandamus is an order from the court to an inferior government official. Habeas corpus (choice A) is due process. Judicial review (choice C) is the process of the Supreme Court determining the constitutionality of laws. Finally, Marshall did not issue any warrants for arrest (choice D).

26. **The correct answer is A.** The Sons of Liberty organized in numerous places, but all had the same reason for organizing: resistance to the Stamp Act. Choice B is incorrect because a common goal was found. Choice C is incorrect because, while the *colonies* were divided, the "Sons of Liberty" were united. Choice D is incorrect because the organization was more focused on protests and boycotts, not a large military resistance.

27. **The correct answer is *House of Representatives*.** The US Congress ratified the Twelfth Amendment in 1804. The amendment states that "the House of Representatives shall choose immediately, by ballot, the President" and "the Senate shall choose the Vice-President." The process is also used in the event that no candidate wins 270 or more Electoral College votes.

28. **The correct answer is B.** While the swastika was grossly offensive to the Jewish people of Skokie, Collins and the other members of the neo-Nazi party were protected by the First Amendment's right to assemble peacefully.

29. **The correct answer is *Manifest Destiny* (B).** The reasons for moving Native Americans off their land was focused on obtaining the land for US residents and expanding America from ocean to ocean. Trail of Tears is incorrect because it was the name for the event, not the reason behind it. "Southern Manifesto" is incorrect because the term relates to racial discrimination during the Civil Rights Movement. The Emancipation Proclamation was given by Abraham Lincoln to make slaves free.

30. **The correct answer is A.** Jose bartered with a store owner. He offered help with the store's books in exchange for space. The other choices are not mentioned as viable options in the passage.

31. **The correct answer is A.** Rising property taxes forced the closure of many of the Paivo family's restaurants. The passage does not mention unionization (choice B), poor management (choice C), or the unavailability of inventory (choice D).

32. **The correct answer is D.** The Bill of Rights seeks to protect, not limit, personal freedoms. Choices A, B, and C are all reasons that the Bill of Rights was included.

33. **The correct answer is B.** The Third Amendment protects citizens from having to house and feed troops during peacetime. The Second Amendment (choice A) is the right to bear arms. The Ninth Amendment (choice C) provides power not otherwise described to the people. The Tenth Amendment (choice D) gives power not otherwise described to the states.

34. **The correct answer is B.** China is the closest mainland to Japan, and it is 115 miles away. Japan is not a neutral or isolationist nation, and while the history of Japan includes migration from other Asian countries, this would not diminish threats from foreign invaders.

35. **The correct answer is C.** Cultural influence from Korea, the Mongolians, and the Chinese have all played a part in molding Japanese culture. The passage does not indicate this cultural blend was tenuous (choice A), nor did it create a class system (choice B). Korean migrants introduced advanced weaponry and the use of horses in combat (choice D).

ARE YOU READY TO TAKE THE GED® TEST?

Now that you have completed the Diagnostic Test, it's time to see if your scores indicate if you are ready to take the GED test. Remember, this diagnostic practice test is not only designed to give you a testing experience, but to help you pinpoint your strengths and weaknesses. Check your scores against the table below to see where you stand.

GED Test	All Set—Well-Prepared	Possibly Ready	Need More Preparation
Reasoning Through Language Arts	37–49	25–36	0–24
Mathematical Reasoning	34–36	23–33	0–22
Science	26–33	18–25	0–17
Social Studies	26–35	18–25	0–17

If your scores are in the "All Set—Well-Prepared" column, you are probably ready to take the actual GED test, and you should apply to take it soon. If some of your scores are in the "Possibly Ready" column, you should focus your study on those areas where you need to improve most. "Possibly Ready" means that you are probably ready enough to earn a GED diploma, but it's not a bad idea to spend a little more time brushing up and improving your chances to pass the actual GED test.

If any of your scores fell in the "Need More Preparation" category, take more time to review the pertinent chapters in this book—and in any high school textbooks, if necessary. Good luck!

PART III

REASONING THROUGH LANGUAGE ARTS

Mastering Reading Comprehension

Chapter 3

OVERVIEW

- **Taking the Reasoning Through Language Arts Test—Reading Comprehension**
- **Understanding Nonfiction**
- **Understanding Fiction**
- **General Test-Taking Strategies**
- **Summing It Up**
- **Practice Questions**
- **Answer Key and Explanations**

THE REASONING THROUGH LANGUAGE ARTS TEST—READING COMPREHENSION IN A NUTSHELL

Time allowed: 150 minutes for the entire Reasoning Through Language Arts Test, which includes 45 minutes for the Extended Response as well as a 10-minute break.

Number of passages: Expect 6 to 8 (the number can vary)

Length of each passage: 400–900 words

Total number of questions: 45–50 questions total for Reading Comprehension, Language Conventions, and Writing (question types include multiple-choice, select-an-area, drag-and-drop, drop-down, and extended response)

Number of questions per passage: Expect 6 to 8 (the number can vary)

TAKING THE REASONING THROUGH LANGUAGE ARTS TEST—READING COMPREHENSION

The Reasoning Through Language Arts Test gauges your ability to understand, interpret, evaluate, synthesize, and apply information contained in nonfiction as well as fiction texts. The test consists of several reading passages, each one followed by six to eight questions (multiple-choice, technology-enhanced, or a combination of both). Passages are drawn from a wide variety of sources.

Regardless of what sort of passage you're dealing with, all the questions will cover the same basic reading skills. Here is the breakdown of the broad skill areas covered by the test questions. As indicated by the percentage numbers, some areas receive greater emphasis than others.

- **Comprehension (20 percent):** Understanding and recalling specific information from the passage
- **Analysis and Interpretation (30–35 percent):** Understanding what is suggested or implied in the passage and drawing reasonable inferences and conclusions from passage information
- **Evaluation and Synthesis (30–35 percent):** Understanding the passage's central idea and concern; inferring the author's intent or purpose; recognizing the purpose of and relationships among various parts of the passage; characterizing the passage as a whole
- **Application (15 percent):** Applying what is stated and implied in the passage to other contexts; applying the author's reasoning to other situations

During the test, expect several passages and 6 to 8 questions per passage—49 questions in total, which include the language conventions questions and the extended response question. Each passage will be 400 to 900 words in length (about one to two pages, on average). One feature common to all passages is that every fifth line of each passage will be numbered. Some questions might refer to portions of the passage by line number.

In the pages ahead, you'll learn how to read and understand the various types of fiction and nonfiction passages you'll encounter on the test. For each type, you'll read sample passages and attempt test-style questions based on them. At the end of the lesson, you'll review some general strategies—ones that apply to every kind of reading passage.

UNDERSTANDING NONFICTION

A written work of **nonfiction** is one that involves real people and events, either past or present. Nonfiction can take a variety of different forms, from a brief article or diary entry to a book, or even a multivolume work. On the GED Reasoning Through Language Arts Test, you can expect at least four nonfiction reading passages involving informational text. Each passage will range from about 400–900 words in length. The passage may provide an entire work if it is brief, or it may be excerpted from a longer work. Nonfiction passages reflect real-world experiences that are drawn from the following categories:

- **Informational science passages** are texts that revolve around human health and living systems and energy and related systems.
- **Informational social studies passages** are excerpts from or texts related to the theme "the Great American Conversation." These could include excerpts from historical documents, public speeches, Supreme Court decisions, and other primary or secondary documents that reflect concepts in American history, civics, and culture.
- **Informational workplace passages** are examples of documents from real-life situations. They could include work-related documents (e.g., emails, procedural documents, cover letters, and so forth) as well as community-related documents (e.g., letters to the editor or public postings).

All categories of informational nonfiction text will present a **main idea** or **central point.** You might find that the main idea is neatly expressed in either the opening or closing sentences. Or you might need to synthesize all of the information in the text to determine the main idea. The main idea will be broad enough to encompass the entire text without going beyond or off the topic.

Related to the text's main idea (central point) is its **central concern** or focus. To determine a text's central concern, ask yourself what issue, problem, events, or developments the text mainly addresses. The central concern will embrace the text's main idea and all supporting information, without departing from the topic at hand. In other words, a text's central concern is one that is neither too broad nor too narrow in focus.

Also related to the text's main idea is the author's **primary purpose** or **objective**, as revealed in the text. In the case of a purely informational text, the primary purpose might be to:

- Inform of facts
- Summarize and apply concepts
- Relate observations
- Provide explanations

Some texts express an opinion or point of view. In these cases, the author is clearly interested in accomplishing more than simply presenting facts. The author is also trying to convince or persuade the reader (or listener) in some way. In this case, the primary purpose might be to:

- Argue for or defend a certain position on an issue
- Advocate for a cause or a course of action
- Promote an ideology or a value system
- State problems and recommend solutions
- Forecast, predict, or warn of future events

After reading a passage for the first time, think about what the author wrote. Ask yourself what the overall topic is and why the author might have written the text. Formulate a sentence or two that expresses the main idea. You may even wish to jot it down in your test booklet.

Understanding the main idea, central concern, and primary purpose of a passage will help you handle many different types of test questions—not just ones that ask "What is the main idea of the passage?" or "What is the central concern of the text?" For example, understanding the "big picture" will help you apply the author's viewpoint to new situations as well as to determine what else the author would agree and disagree with.

In informational text, the main ideas are facts, which are supported by **reasons and examples**. As you read the text, try to follow the author's line of reasoning, from main idea to the evidence used to support it.

You might find it helpful to jot down supporting points, so you can answer questions about them without reading the passage again. But don't try to jot down or remember every small detail from the passage. Instead, note where different kinds of details are located in the passage, so you can find them quickly if you need them to answer certain questions.

In some passages, it may help to pay attention to the author's **attitude** toward the subject being discussed. For example, in a letter to the editor, speech, or essay, the author's attitude may be highly critical or judgmental, or it may be supportive, admiring, or even praising. In the following sections, you'll learn more about all of these types of nonfiction, and you'll learn how best to read nonfiction in order to understand it in ways that will help you most on the GED Reasoning Through Language Arts Test. For each category, you'll also read a variety of sample passages and answer test-style questions based on them.

Informational Science

The informational science passages you will see on the GED Reasoning Through Language Arts Test are related to either human health and living systems or energy and related systems. They may include diagrams or graphics, and some may tend to be academic in nature. Others will be geared toward a more general audience, but they will be relevant to living in the twenty-first century.

These passages, like other general nonfiction texts, have a purpose with a main idea and supporting details, along with other general features that you will be asked to analyze. Passages in this category are designed to inform the reader and are usually objective; that is, they relate facts in order to support a scientific concept or idea.

The following passage provides the reader with specific information. As you read, note the main ideas and how they are connected. If you come across an unfamiliar scientific term, don't focus on its specific meaning; instead, try to analyze its context and how it fits into the rest of the text. Then try to answer the accompanying questions.

Questions 1–3 refer to the following passage.

The following article is from Cancer.gov: National Cancer Institute website, January 3, 2012.

Obesity and Cancer Risk

Obesity is a condition in which a person has an abnormally high and unhealthy proportion of body fat.

To measure obesity, researchers commonly use a scale known as the body mass index (BMI). BMI is calculated by dividing a person's weight (in kilograms) by their height (in meters) squared. BMI provides a more accurate measure of obesity or being overweight than weight alone.

Guidelines established by the National Institutes of Health (NIH) place adults age 20 and older into the following categories based on their BMI:

BMI	BMI Categories
Below 18.5	Underweight
18.5 to 24.9	Normal
25.0 to 29.9	Overweight
30.0 and above	Obese

The National Heart Lung and Blood Institute provides a BMI calculator.

For children and adolescents (less than 20 years of age), overweight and obesity are based on the Centers for Disease Control and Prevention's (CDC) BMI-for-age growth charts:

BMI	BMI Categories
BMI-for-age at or above sex-specific 85th percentile, but less than 95th percentile	Overweight
BMI-for-age at or above sex-specific 95th percentile	Obese

Compared with people of normal weight, those who are overweight or obese are at greater risk for many diseases, including diabetes, high blood pressure, cardiovascular diseases, stroke, and certain cancers.

How common is overweight or obesity?

Results from the 2007–2008 National Health and Nutrition Examination Survey (NHANES) show that 68 percent of US adults age 20 years and older are overweight or obese. In 1988–1994, by contrast, only 56 percent of adults age 20 and older were overweight or obese.

In addition, the percentage of children who are overweight or obese has also increased. Among children and teens ages 2 to 19, 17 percent are estimated to be obese, based on the 2007–2008 survey. In 1988–1994, that figure was only 10 percent.

What is known about the relationship between obesity and cancer?

Obesity is associated with increased risks of the following cancer types, and possibly others as well: esophagus, pancreas, colon and rectum, breast (after menopause), endometrium (lining of the uterus), kidney, thyroid, and gallbladder.

One study, using NCI Surveillance, Epidemiology, and End Results (SEER) data, estimated that in 2007 in the United States, about 34,000 new cases of cancer in men (4 percent) and 50,500 in women (7 percent) were due to obesity. The percentage of cases attributed to obesity varied widely for different cancer types but was as high as 40 percent for some cancers, particularly endometrial cancer and esophageal adenocarcinoma.

A projection of the future health and economic burden of obesity in 2030 estimated that continuation of existing trends in obesity will lead to about 500,000 additional cases of cancer in the United States by 2030. This analysis also found that if every adult reduced their BMI by 1 percent, which would be equivalent to a weight loss of roughly 1 kg (or 2.2 lbs) for an adult of average weight, this would prevent the increase in the number of cancer cases and actually result in the *avoidance* of about 100,000 new cases of cancer.

Several possible mechanisms have been suggested to explain the association of obesity with increased risk of certain cancers:

- Fat tissue produces excess amounts of estrogen, high levels of which have been associated with the risk of breast, endometrial, and some other cancers.
- Obese people often have increased levels of insulin and insulin-like growth factor-1 (IGF-1) [a protein made by the body that stimulates the growth of many types of cells] in their blood (a condition known as hyperinsulinemia or insulin resistance), which may promote the development of certain tumors in their blood.
- Fat cells produce hormones, called adipokines, that may stimulate or inhibit cell growth. For example, leptin, which is more abundant in obese people, seems to promote cell proliferation, whereas adiponectin, which is less abundant in obese people, may have antiproliferative effects.
- Fat cells may also have direct and indirect effects on other tumor growth regulators, including mammalian target of rapamycin (mTOR) [a protein that helps control several cell functions, including cell division and survival] and AMP-activated protein kinase [a type of enzyme (a protein that speeds up chemical reactions in the body)].
- Obese people often have chronic low-level, or "subacute," inflammation, which has been associated with increased cancer risk.

Other possible mechanisms include altered immune responses, effects on the nuclear factor kappa beta system, and oxidative stress [a condition in which antioxidant levels are lower than normal].

TIP

A **correlation** is a mutual relationship or a connection between two or more things. **Causation** indicates a cause-and-effect outcome in which an event is the result of another event. In other words, a correlation is simply a relationship; causation involves an action causing an outcome. Understanding these two terms will aid in answering GED test questions.

1. Which of the following statements represents a reasonable conclusion you could draw from the passage?

A. Obesity is a medical condition that requires treatment.

B. Obese people are more likely to get some form of cancer and other diseases.

C. Fat cells have a negative effect on the body.

D. Obesity causes many types of cancer.

Although statement A may be true, the passage doesn't talk about treating obesity; it discusses the correlation between obesity and cancer and other illnesses. The passage describes the role of fat tissue and fat cells, which may be implicated in some cancers but are not always negative—it depends on the quantity of these cells. Obesity is not a cause of cancer, but obesity has medical consequences that increase the odds of contracting cancer. **The correct answer is B.**

2. According to the passage, which statement is true?

A. The incidence of obesity in the United States is increasing in both adults and children.

B. If you lose weight you will not get cancer.

C. Fat cells make people obese.

D. The risk of getting cancer is the same for people who are overweight and those who are obese.

The passage cites statistics that indicate how the incidence of obesity has grown over the last two decades. The cancer risk is higher for people with obesity, and while losing weight can reduce that risk, it cannot eliminate it. Obese people have more fat cells, and the passage talks about how fat cells behave to increase the likelihood of tumor formation, but fat cells in and of themselves don't make people obese. Cancer risk is lower for people who are of normal weight. The passage says both people who are overweight and people who are obese are at higher risk for many different diseases, but the link it discusses is that between obesity and cancer. **The correct answer is A.**

3. A person who is in the 90th percentile for their age and sex has a BMI of

A. below 18.5.

B. between 18.5 and 24.9.

C. between 25.0 and 29.9.

D. 30.0 or higher.

Reading both charts, we can put the data together. *Overweight* and *obesity* are the two categories shown with BMIs. A person in the 90th percentile is in the overweight category, which would mean he or she has a BMI of between 25.0 and 29.9. **The correct answer is C.**

The next passage is about space and what scientists are learning about our solar system from space probes. As you read the passage, think about what you already know about our solar system.

Questions 4–7 refer to the following passage.

This passage is the text of a slide show created by NASA scientist Dr. Tony Phillips. It is one of NASA's web-based science features. (Science@NASA)

Mystery of the Missing Waves on Titan

One of the most shocking discoveries of the past 10 years is how much the landscape of Saturn's moon Titan resembles Earth. Like our own blue planet, the surface of Titan is dotted with lakes and seas; it has river channels, islands, mud, rain clouds and maybe even rainbows. The giant moon is undeniably wet.

The "water" on Titan is not, however, H_2O. With a surface temperature dipping 290 degrees F below zero, Titan is far too cold for liquid water. Instead, researchers believe the fluid that sculpts Titan is an unknown mixture of methane, ethane, and other hard-to-freeze hydrocarbons.

The idea that Titan is a wet world with its own alien waters is widely accepted by planetary scientists. Nothing else can account for the observations: NASA's Cassini spacecraft has flown by Titan more than 90 times since 2004, pinging the Moon with radar and mapping its lakes and seas. ESA's Huygens probe parachuted to the surface of Titan in 2005, descending through humid clouds and actually landing in moist soil.

Yet something has been bothering Alex Hayes, a planetary scientist on the Cassini radar team at Cornell University.

If Titan is really so wet, he wonders, "Where are all the waves?"

Here on Earth, bodies of water are rarely still. Breezes blowing across the surface cause waves to ripple and break; raindrops striking sea surfaces also provide some roughness. Yet on Titan, the lakes are eerily smooth, with no discernible wave action down to the millimeter scale, according to radar data from Cassini.

"We know there is wind on Titan," says Hayes. "The moon's magnificent sand dunes [prove] it."

Add to that the low gravity of Titan—only one-seventh that of Earth—which offers so little resistance to wave motion, and you have a real puzzle.

Researchers have toyed with several explanations. Perhaps the lakes are frozen. Hayes thinks that is unlikely, however, "because we see evidence of rainfall and surface temperatures well above the melting point of methane." Or maybe the lakes are covered with a tar-like substance that damps wave motion. "We can't yet rule that out," he adds.

The answer might be found in the results of a study Hayes and colleagues published in the July 2013 online edition of the journal *Icarus.* Taking into account the gravity of Titan, the low viscosity of liquid hydrocarbons, the density of Titan's atmosphere, and other factors, they calculated how fast wind on Titan would have to blow to stir up waves: A walking-pace breeze of only 1 to 2 mph should do the trick.

This suggests a third possibility: the winds just haven't been blowing hard enough. Since Cassini reached Saturn in 2004, Titan's northern hemisphere (where most of the lakes are located) has been locked in the grip of winter. Cold heavy air barely stirs, and seldom reaches the threshold for wave-making.

But now the seasons are changing. In August 2009 the sun crossed Titan's equator heading north. Summer is coming, bringing light, heat and wind to Titan's lake country.

"According to [climate models], winds will pick up as we approach the solstice in 2017 and should be strong enough for waves," he says.

If waves appear, Cassini should be able to detect them. Radar reflections from wavy lake surfaces can tell researchers a great deal. Wave dimensions, for instance, may reveal the viscosity of the underlying fluid and, thus, its chemical composition. Also, wave speeds would track the speed of the overlying winds, providing an independent check of Titan climate models.

Hayes is excited about "bringing oceanography to another world. All we need now," he says, "are some rough seas."

4. How do scientists get their information about Titan?

A. By observing the changes in data and photos sent back from *Cassini*

B. By comparing it to Earth

C. By using climate models

D. By measuring and comparing the temperatures to those on Earth

The article explains the role of the space probe, *Cassini*, to ping the moon with radar and map its lakes. These data are then used by scientists to form hypotheses about the data. Scientists may compare the data to Earth, but they do this after they have received data about Titan. It is not a direct comparison, and it is not one that is used to get information about Titan. Scientists do use climate models, and they use them with the data received from *Cassini*, but they don't use the climate models to get the information. The scientists use what they know about Earth for comparison, but they don't get information about Titan from knowledge about Earth. **The correct answer is A.**

5. Why was the discovery of Titan's resemblance to Earth shocking to scientists?

A. They didn't think they would be able to see the surface closely enough to map it.

B. They didn't expect to find that the surface was wet.

C. They expected it to look like Earth's moon.

D. They expected it to be completely frozen because of the extremely low temperatures.

The passage doesn't tell us what the expectations were before the probe started, but scientists were surprised when they saw photos that resembled Earth's surface, which indicate the presence of liquid in order to give Titan its contours. The passage tells us that they were shocked by this discovery. **The correct answer is B.**

6. What is the question about Titan that Alex Hayes is trying to figure out?

A. What is the composition of the surface?

B. Why are the lakes on Titan frozen?

C. Why aren't there waves in the bodies of liquid on Titan?

D. What is the density of the atmosphere of Titan?

The data received from the space probe tell scientists the composition of the surface, Titan's temperatures, and its density, along with other data. Hayes already knows about these data. His question is about the appearance of the surface of Titan's lakes. They are very smooth, unlike bodies of water on Earth, which have waves formed by wind and gravity. He asks why this may be and forms some hypotheses to help figure it out. **The correct answer is C.**

7. Why do scientists think waves may appear on Titan after 2017?

A. Because the seasons will change by then, and there should be more wind activity

B. Because the cold air will stimulate wind activity

C. Because scientists predict that the lakes will be frozen solid by then

D. Because the methane will begin to melt as the moon completes its orbit

The article says that one of the reasons that there may be no waves is that everything may be frozen. They expect the temperatures to rise as the season changes, which will occur as Titan moves closer to the sun in its orbit. It is the warm air that scientists think will stimulate wind activity as the liquids on the surface begin to thaw. The methane is not frozen—the article says the temperatures are above the melting point of methane. **The correct answer is A.**

The next passage represents one of the shorter informational science passages. The article is about a plant species and its uses. The italicized text indicates the Latin names for species. When you see terms like this in your reading, don't focus on them. Note how they are used and, if they are used multiple times, you can refer back to the part of the passage in which they are located in order to clarify your understanding. Overall, however, you will not be expected to interpret such terms, and they are not important to the main ideas in the information provided.

Questions 8–10 refer to the following passage.

Adam's Needle

The Catawba, Cherokee, Nanticoke, and other Native American tribes used *Yucca filamentosa* [Adam's needle] for a variety of purposes including food, medicine, cordage, and even soap. The roots, which contain saponin [a soapy lather substance in some plants], were prepared by boiling and pounding for use as soap. Roots were beaten into a salve or poultice that would then be used to treat sprains or applied to sores on the skin. The roots were used to treat gonorrhea and rheumatism. Skin diseases were treated by rubbing the roots on the skin and by taking a decoction of the roots. The plant was used as a sedative to induce sleep. An infusion of the plant was used to treat diabetes. The flowers were eaten both raw and cooked. The pounded roots were thrown into fishing waters to "intoxicate fish" allowing for easier catch. The green leaves are easily split into long strips that can be plied into cord. The leaves have long, very strong fibers, a type of sisal, which were twisted into strong thread used as cordage for binding and to construct baskets, fishing nets, fishing lines and clothing. The leaves of *Yucca filamentosa* contain the strongest fibers native to North America. . . .

Yuccas are pollinated by small, white Yucca moths (*Tegeticula yucasella* and related species) with which they have a special plant-insect mutualism. At night, the fragrant flowers attract the female moth that feeds on the nectar. She then rolls pollen from the flowers into a ball that is three times the size of her head and carries the pollen ball to the next flower. There, she first lays eggs inside the immature ovary and then deposits the pollen on the flower's stigma insuring that seeds will form to feed her progeny. Because the larvae mature before they are able to consume all of the seeds (60 to 80% of the seeds remain viable), the plants are able to reproduce as well.

Adam's needle is a native, evergreen, perennial shrub. The plants have long, thick underground stems and rarely have an aboveground stem. The grayish-green leaves appear from a rosette at or near the ground. The leaves are stiff and sword-shaped (30 to 76 cm long and 2.5 cm wide) with sharp, pointed tips and long, curly, filamentous threads at the margins. The bell-shaped flowers (5 to 8 cm wide) are a creamy white to pale yellow or green with broadly ovate petals (4 to 5 cm). The flowers, which appear in late spring and summer, hang loosely in clusters from a large, central spike (1 to 4 m tall) that emerges from the rosette. The fruits are capsules that contain 120 to 150 small black seeds that are dispersed by wind.

—US Department of Agriculture

8. The **best** subheading for the second paragraph is

A. Historical Use of Plants.

B. Reproduction.

C. Unusual Facts.

D. How Plants Thrive.

The first paragraph talks about ways that the Native Americans used Adam's needle. The second paragraph describes the specific pollination process used by this plant. There are no unusual facts given here, and the paragraph does not provide an overview of how plants thrive. **The correct answer is B.**

9. The flowers in an Adam's needle

A. bloom in the fall.

B. have thick, long, above-ground stems.

C. have curly, filamentous threads.

D. bloom annually.

The third paragraph provides information about the characteristics of the plant. It does not bloom in the fall; rather, it blooms in the spring and summer, so it is an annual plant. Its stems are generally underground, not above-ground, and it is the leaves that are described as curly with filamentous threads. **The correct answer is D.**

10. What conclusion could you draw about Native Americans from the information in the first paragraph?

A. They were vegetarians.

B. They knew how to identify plants that were edible and plants that were poisonous.

C. They learned how to use natural resources for multiple purposes.

D. They had a wide variety of food in their diet.

Although the paragraph says the Native Americans used Adam's needle for food, it does not say they did not also eat meat, and it does indicate that they ate fish. They knew that Adam's needle was edible, but there's no information given about poisonous plants. The passage does not discuss other aspects of the Native Americans' diets, so we don't know how much variety there was. The overall text shows ingenuity in using the Adam's needle for a wide variety of purposes, from food, to tools, to clothing, to medicines. **The correct answer is C.**

The next passage documents some of the problems of lead in our environment. It contains a lot of details. One technique for reading such a passage includes reading the questions first to note which details are covered in the questions. Then pay extra attention to these parts of the passage.

Questions 11–14 refer to the following passage.

Lead in the Environment

Lead is a naturally occurring element that can be harmful to humans when ingested or inhaled, particularly to children under the age of six. Lead poisoning can cause a number of adverse human health effects, but is particularly detrimental to the neurological development of children. . . .

Line

For hundreds of years, lead has been mined, smelted, refined, and used in products (e.g., as an additive in paint, gasoline, leaded pipes, solder, crystal, and ceramics). Natural levels of lead in soil range between 50 parts per million (ppm) and 400 ppm. Mining, smelting, and refining activities have resulted in substantial increases in lead levels in the environment, especially near mining and smelting sites. For example, near some types of industrial and municipal facilities, and adjacent to highways[1], soil lead concentrations have been reported to be more than 11,000 ppm[2].

Lead particles in the environment can attach to dust and be carried long distances in the air. Such lead-containing dust can be removed from the air by rain and deposited on surface soil, where it may remain for many years. In addition, heavy rains may cause lead in surface soil to migrate into ground water and eventually into water systems. . . .

Lead poisoning can be a serious public health threat with no unique signs or symptoms. Early symptoms of lead exposure may include: persistent fatigue, irritability, loss of appetite, stomach discomfort and/or constipation, reduced attention span, insomnia. Failure to treat lead poisoning in the early stages can cause long-term or permanent health damage, but because of the general nature of symptoms at early stages, lead poisoning is often not suspected.

In adults, lead poisoning can cause: poor muscle coordination, nerve damage to the sense organs and nerves controlling the body, increased blood pressure, hearing and vision impairment, reproductive problems (e.g., decreased sperm count [in males], retarded fetal development [in pregnant females] even at relatively low exposure levels).

In children, lead poisoning can cause: damage to the brain and nervous system, behavioral problems, anemia, liver and kidney damage, hearing loss, hyperactivity, developmental delays, and, in extreme cases, death.

Although the effects of lead exposure are a potential concern for all humans, young children (less than seven years old) are most at risk.[3] This increased vulnerability results from a combination of the following factors:

- Children typically have higher intake rates (per unit body weight) for environmental media (such as soil, dust, food, water, air, and paint) than adults, since they are more likely to play in dirt and put their hands and other objects in their mouths;
- Children tend to absorb a higher fraction of ingested lead from the gastrointestinal tract than adults;
- Children tend to be more susceptible than adults to the adverse neurological and developmental effects of lead; and
- Nutritional deficiencies of iron or calcium, which are common in children, may facilitate lead absorption and exacerbate the toxic effects of lead.

The national average blood lead levels in children have dropped over time as our understanding of lead risk has evolved, and as efforts are undertaken to reduce exposure to lead. While banning of lead paint and lead in gasoline were national efforts to stop childhood lead poisoning, contaminated sites require site-specific cleanups to reduce exposure to populations nearby.

The Centers for Disease Control (CDC) has identified that the current blood lead level of concern in children is 10 micrograms (μg) of lead per deciliter (dL) of blood (10 μg/dL); however, adverse effects may occur at lower levels than previously thought. In January of 2012, an advisory panel to the CDC recommended lowering the level that triggers intervention.

If you have concerns about possible lead exposure, contact your personal physician or county/state health department. Your doctor can conduct blood tests to determine lead concentrations in your blood. Blood tests are inexpensive and sometimes free; however, please consult your insurance provider to determine coverage of such tests. Lead in bone and teeth can be measured using x-ray techniques, but this test is not used very often. In communities where houses are old and deteriorating, residents are encouraged to take advantage of available screening programs offered by local health departments and to have children living in the residence checked regularly for lead poisoning. Because the early symptoms of lead poisoning are similar to those of other illnesses, it is difficult to diagnose lead poisoning without medical testing.

---

[1] Chaney et al., 1984; Shacklette et al., 1984
[2] National Research Council, 1980
[3] Reagan and Silbergeld, 1989

—From the US EPA Office of Superfund Remediation and Technology Innovation. www.epa.gov/superfund

11. Why is lead considered a serious public health threat?

A. Lead can poison people quickly before they know they have been exposed.

B. Lead gets washed into the soil and then works its way into water systems, and people drink the contaminated water.

C. Lead exposure causes many illnesses that others can catch, causing a wide-scale epidemic.

D. Lead is dangerous because there's no way to diagnose it in your system.

A public health hazard is created when lead gets in waterways and the water supply, but it also can be inhaled (choice B). Lead exposure does make people sick, but not with the kind of diseases that can be transmitted to other people (choice C). There are tests to diagnose lead in the blood (choice D). One danger of lead poisoning is that because of general symptoms at early stages, lead poisoning is often not suspected immediately. **The correct answer is A.**

12. Why are children at greater risk of exposure to lead?

A. Children are more likely to have direct contact with soil that is lead contaminated.

B. Children can ingest lead, while adults can't.

C. Children are more likely to be anemic.

D. Children's immune systems are not as well developed as that of adults.

Anyone can ingest lead from many different sources (choice B). Children are not more likely to be anemic (choice C). Although children's immune systems are less developed than those of adults, that is not what puts them at higher risk (choice D). Children are more likely to play in dirt and other sites of contamination, leading to an increased risk of exposure. **The correct answer is A.**

13. Which of the following is true about the relationship between lead and the environment?

A. Because rain removes lead from the air, lead is only hazardous in dry climates.

B. Because lead is no longer an ingredient in gasoline or paint, it is no longer a big problem.

C. Because lead is a natural element, there is nothing people can do to prevent lead poisoning.

D. Because lead can get into the soil and the water supply, it remains a hazard for a long time.

Rain does remove lead from the air, but it then deposits it in the soil, where it can remain for years and can even contaminate the water supply (choice A). Government regulation forced the removal of lead from paints and gasoline, but there are other sources (choice B). It is true that lead is a natural element, but the toxic levels are present in man-made items, which is something that can be reduced or even eliminated (choice C). Lead remains in older homes and commercial and industrial structures, and it can stay in the soil and water; the damage can remain for a long time (choice D). **The correct answer is D.**

14. Lead poisoning in children can cause

A. hyperactivity.

B. cancer.

C. diabetes.

D. blindness.

According to the article, the health effects of lead exposure on children include brain and nervous system damage, behavioral problems, anemia, liver and kidney damage, hearing loss, hyperactivity, developmental delays, and, in extreme cases, death. **The correct answer is A.**

Informational Social Studies

This section of the test will contain reading passages broadly related to American history and civics. Some will be excerpts from primary sources—original historical documents, the text of public speeches, or other such original writings. Primary sources are documents that were created at the time of the event; for example, a letter or an interview conducted at the time of an event. Others will be secondary sources—analyses and interpretations about the primary source; for example, a newspaper or magazine articles about a historical event. These sources may quote the primary source or others related to the event. Examples of secondary sources include biographies or journal articles about a primary source.

Author's Point of View

Personal accounts can tell us much about the history of a particular period. They can fill in details about events and provide a human perspective to the narrative. Primary sources like journals and memoirs, because of their personal natures, give the author's point of view about the events and the time in which the person was living. Combined with other sources, this information can give us a more balanced record of actual events.

Questions 15–19 refer to the following passage.

The following excerpt is from the memoir, The Narrative of Sojourner Truth. *Sojourner Truth was born into slavery in New York State before laws there abolished slavery in 1827. She escaped from her master and eventually became an active member of the abolition movement. As a former slave, Sojourner Truth had never learned to read or write; thus, her memoir was dictated to a friend. Truth's given name was Isabella, and she is referred to by that name in the passage.*

After emancipation had been decreed by the State, some years before the time fixed for its consummation, Isabella's master told her if she would do well, and be faithful, he would give her "free papers," one year before she was legally free by statute. In the year 1826, she had a badly diseased hand, which greatly diminished her usefulness; but on the arrival of July 4, 1827, the time specified for her receiving her "free papers," she claimed the fulfillment of her master's promise; but he refused granting it, on account (as he alleged) of the loss he had sustained by her hand. She plead that she had worked all the time, and done many things she was not wholly able to do, although she knew she had been less useful than formerly; but her master remained inflexible. Her very faithfulness probably operated against her now, and he found it less easy than he thought to give up the profits of his faithful Bell, who had so long done him efficient service.

But Isabella inwardly determined that she would remain quietly with him only until she had spun his wool—about one hundred pounds—and then she would leave him, taking the rest of the time to herself. "Ah!" she says, with emphasis that cannot be written, "the slaveholders are TERRIBLE for promising to give you this or that, or such and such a privilege, if you will do thus and so; and when the time of fulfillment comes, and one claims the promise, they, forsooth, recollect nothing of the kind; and you are, like as not, taunted with being a LIAR; or, at best, the slave is accused of not having performed his part or condition of the contract." "Oh!" said she, "I have felt as if I could not live through the operation sometimes. Just think of us! so eager for our pleasures, and just foolish enough to keep feeding and feeding ourselves up with the idea that we should get what had been thus fairly promised; and when we think it is almost in our hands, find ourselves flatly denied! Just think! how could we bear it?"

... The question in her mind, and one not easily solved, now was, "How can I get away?" So, as was her usual custom, she "told God she was afraid to go in the night, and in the day every body would see her." At length, the thought came to her that she could leave just before the day dawned, and get out of the neighborhood where she was known before the people were much astir. "Yes," said she, fervently, "that's a good thought! Thank you, God, for *that* thought!" So, receiving it as coming direct from God, she acted upon it, and one fine morning, a little before day-break, she might have been seen stepping stealthily away from the rear of Master Dumont's house, her infant on one arm and her wardrobe on the other; the bulk and weight of which, probably, she never found so convenient as on the present occasion, a cotton handkerchief containing both her clothes and her provisions.

As she gained the summit of a high hill, a considerable distance from her master's, the sun offended her by coming forth in all his pristine splendor. She thought it never was so light before; indeed, she thought it much too light. She stopped to look about her, and ascertain if her pursuers were yet in sight. No one appeared, and, for the first time, the question came up for settlement, "Where, and to whom, shall I go?" In all her thoughts of getting away, she had not once asked herself whither she should direct her steps. She sat down, fed her infant, and again turning her thoughts to God, her only help, she prayed him to direct her to some safe asylum.

15. What does the narrative of Isabella imply about slaveholders?

The slaveholders' cruelty toward their slaves was based on

A. twisted emotions.

B. desire for profit.

C. fear of confrontation.

D. racism.

The idea that slaveholders' cruelty was based on their desire for profit is implied in lines 6–7 ("the loss he had sustained by her hand") and in line 10 ("to give up the profits of his faithful Bell…"). **The correct answer is B.**

16. What is it about Truth's slaveholder that she mainly objects to?

A. His harassment

B. His brutality

C. His unfairness

D. His bigotry

In the passage, the author clearly depicts Isabella's slaveholder as unfair: he breaks his promises despite Isabella's faithfulness. On the other hand, nowhere in the passage does the author suggest that her slaveholder harassed or brutalized her (choices A and B). And though he may have been a bigot or a hypocrite (choice D), the passage does not indicate that Isabella noted that trait or objected to it. **The correct answer is C.**

17. What did Truth believe about her master that made her plan her escape?

A. She believed he was not trustworthy.

B. She thought he would continue to punish her.

C. She thought he was going to sell her to someone else.

D. She believed he would grant her freedom but she didn't want to wait any longer.

Truth realized that her master had lied and broken his promises to let her go free, in spite of the law. The date of her freedom came and went, and her master found excuses to keep her. There is no indication that he planned to sell her to someone else or that he had caused her injury. He had broken his word, and she realized that she could not trust him. **The correct answer is A.**

18. What can you infer about Truth's beliefs based on her plan for escape?

A. The law would be enforced, and she would be free.

B. The only way to become free was to go where she would not be recognized.

C. She would be freed but would have to leave the state.

D. She would be able to find safety with neighbors.

Truth's master did not free her after the law went into effect; he continued to hold her as an enslaved person (choice A). The text doesn't say the law specified that freed slaves had to leave the state (choice C). Truth's behavior indicates that she was afraid that people who knew her and her master would see her, and they would capture her and bring her back to him. Consequently, she did not feel safe taking refuge with her neighbors (choice D). She hoped that once she was in a place where she was not known, she would be safe, because the law said she was free. **The correct answer is B.**

19. Though *The Narrative of Sojourner Truth* is told in the third person by a narrator, what indications are there to show it's Truth's personal story?

A. The narrator quotes Truth's words and thoughts about her experience.

B. The narrator injects her own perspective that confirms Truth's experience.

C. The narrator keeps the story in the third person to be objective.

D. The narrator shows both her own and Truth's views, but only Truth's views are in the first person.

The narrator of *The Narrative of Sojourner Truth* uses the third person except where she includes direct quotes from Truth. The narrator does not inject her own perspective; she describes what Truth tells her and occasionally quotes Truth's own words. The narrator uses third person to tell the story from Truth's perspective, not to be objective. The narrator shows only Truth's views. **The correct answer is A.**

Secondary Sources

A secondary source provides us with further information about historical events, eras, and cultures. A source of this type tells us about events after they have occurred and may or may not contain objective accounts. A secondary source can be an analysis, a summary, or an interpretation of a primary source. In some cases, it might describe or explain primary sources. For example, a textbook or an encyclopedia could be considered a secondary source.

The following passage is an example of a secondary source. Think about what primary sources the author might have used to obtain the information needed to write the text. When reading these kinds of texts, the same skills are needed.

Questions 20–23 refer to the following passage.

The following passage, written by James H. Bruns, appeared in the January-March 1992 [vol 1, issue 1] issue of EnRoute, *the National Postal Museum's newsletter.*

Titanic's Mail

America's history is in the mail. This is no idle boast. From its beginnings, the post office helped make American history, and its growth parallels the history of the United States itself. This is true of major events, as well as many of the fascinating footnotes of our history . . .

Line This April marks the 80th anniversary of the loss of the R.M.S. *Titanic*, the world's most famous mail ship. (The abbreviation stood for "Royal Mail Ship.") On April 14, 1912, the ship went down with more than 1,500 lives, including clerks of the Sea Post Service.

Aboard the *Titanic* was a Sea Post Office with a crew of five clerks. Two of the clerks, Jago Smith and J. B. Williamson, were English. The others, John S. March, William L. Gwinn, and Oscar S. Woody, were Americans employed by the United States Post Office Department. On any ocean crossing, the receiving and sending countries would each assign clerks to the shipboard office. On the *Titanic*, the majority of the clerks were American because the ship was sailing to America, and American clerks were used to sort mail coming into the States.

American sea post clerks basically earned about $1,000 a year in 1912. They also ate their meals free with the passengers and were allotted an allowance for their board while awaiting the return of their ship.

For several hours before sailing, the *Titanic* clerks carried out the routine task of checking all of the mail sacks and storing those that did not need to be opened during the voyage. As soon as the liner set sail on April 10, they would have begun making distributions, much like the crew of a railway mail train would do.

The postal crew aboard the *Titanic* worked well together, especially in those last hours of April 14. From available information, within minutes after the collision, the mail storage room, which was located well below the ship's water line, began flooding, sending some of the mail sacks adrift. Frantically, the clerks brought as many sacks as possible up to the sorting room in preparation for moving the mailbags onto the deck for possible recovery by a rescue ship. According to the Postmaster General's 1912 *Annual Report:* "The last reports concerning their actions show that they were engaged in this work . . . to the last moment."

The entire ship's cargo was lost, including 3,423 sacks of mail. The mailbags contained over 7 million pieces of mail, including an estimated 1.6 [million] registered letters and packages. Within weeks of the sinking, postal officials began feeling the effects of the loss. About $150,000 in postal money orders had gone to the bottom of the sea. These would have to somehow be processed. Four days after the sinking, Third Assistant Postmaster General James J. Britt advised local postmasters:

Among the millions of pieces of mail matter carried on the lost Titanic, there were doubtless thousands of dollars' worth of international money orders, together with descriptive lists of such orders. It is assumed that many of the remitters of those orders will communicate with the payees in this country concerning them, and that these payees, in turn, will take up the matter through their respective postmasters.

It is the earnest desire of the department that in all such cases postmasters give careful attention to the inquiries made and promptly report the facts to the Third Assistant Postmaster General (Division of Money Orders), to the end that every effort may be made to insure early payments to the intended beneficiaries.

One of the first to be reimbursed for a lost money order was Miss Ethel Clarke, a maid who worked for President William Howard Taft's family. Her lost money order was for seven pounds. Based upon an examination of available postal records, a replacement US money order was issued to her from postal service headquarters for $35.

20. What can you infer about the author's attitude toward postal workers from the passage?

A. He thought postal workers should handle international mail only on a special mail ship.

B. He thought the postal workers were doing important work competently.

C. He thought the work of the postal workers was routine and boring.

D. He thought only Americans postal workers should handle American mail.

The author describes the tragedy of the *Titanic* in terms of the loss of one of its cargoes—that of the US mail carried on the ship bound for the United States. The postal workers were free to eat their meals with the passengers, and the author gives no indication that he thinks they should be on a separate ship. The author explains that they were engaged in their normal work routines when the ship started to flood, not that their work was routine and boring. He describes how incoming international mail is handled by American postal clerks but does not state any objections to other nationalities. Overall, the author describes workers who were good at their jobs—jobs that he showed to have an impact on others. **The correct answer is B.**

21. Which of the following details from the passage shows that the author's belief that the development of the United States Postal Service had a significant impact on the course of American history?

A. The author claims that he is not boasting when he says "history is in the mail."

B. People, including President Taft's maid, were refunded their money for lost money orders.

C. The fact that the *Titanic* was carrying so much mail showed that Europeans wanted to communicate with Americans.

D. Millions of pieces of mail were lost, but the postal service was able to recoup some of the monetary claims.

The author says that his opening statement is not a "boast," showing that he believes that the growth and success of the postal service is tied to the growth and success of the nation (choice A). People were able to file their claims and get money orders refunded (choices B and D), but that detail is not related to the overall history of the event. New technology meant faster and larger ships that could deliver goods more quickly. The postal service was able to take advantage of the new service, but in this case, the technology was what contributed to the country's growth. **The correct answer is A.**

22. What can you conclude about American life at the beginning of the twentieth century, based on the passage?

A. Mail service was quick and efficient if you had money to pay for it.

B. Many people wrote letters to friends and family.

C. Travel was dangerous, so most people stayed home.

D. The *Titanic* was carrying only wealthy passengers and crew.

We can infer that mail service was faster because of the advent of new technology that included large ships like the *Titanic*, which could carry millions of pieces of mail, making it easier and faster to send mail across the ocean. But nowhere does the author suggest that its cost was prohibitive (choice A). The *Titanic* is only one of many ships that would have carried mail. The more than 7 million pieces of mail that the author documents as having been lost indicates that large numbers of people were sending letters and packages to and from Europe. Some kinds of travel may have been dangerous by today's standards, but many people continued to travel (choice C). The author doesn't talk about the passengers, except to say that the postal workers were allowed to have their meals with them. We may have an image of wealthy people aboard the ship (choice D) from reading about it or seeing a film, but the passage alone does not give us this information. **The correct answer is B.**

23. What primary sources would the author **most likely** have used to get the facts for this article?

A. A diary from a passenger

B. A survivor's story

C. A book about the building of the ship

D. The captain's log from the ship

A passenger's diary (choice A) would be a primary source, but it would not supply the information provided in the article. Passengers would not have known how much mail was on board. A survivor's story (choice B) could also be a primary source, but not one that could have provided the kinds of details that are included in the passage. A book about building the ship (choice C) is a primary source, but such a book would be focused on how the ship was built and would not have information about the ship's voyage, including the mail it was carrying and the people who died. A captain's log would list passengers and cargo, so the author might have consulted this as a primary source. **The correct answer is D.**

Interpreting Images and Words

Primary sources can also be photographs or other original material. Observing the details in an image can help you to interpret what was going on when the photograph was taken. Look for details that give clues to the setting and note the expression(s) of the photo's subject(s) to give you clues about who they are. A written description with an image can often yield a lot of detailed information.

Questions 24–26 refer to the following photograph and passage.

The following passage describes how this photograph, entitled "Migrant Madonna," came about. This information is a secondary source, and the photograph is a primary source.

Migrant Madonna

On a raw, soggy day in March 1936, Dorothea Lange was driving home to Berkeley after six weeks spent photographing migrant workers in California, New Mexico, and Arizona. Her staff position at the Resettlement Administration (RA), an agency set up to help tenant farmers during the Depression, was tenuous: since there was no budget for a photographer, Lange had been hired as a clerk-stenographer, and she invoiced her film and travel expenses under "clerical supplies."

As Lange drove along the empty California highway that day, she noticed a sign that said Pea-Pickers Camp. Knowing that the pea crop had frozen, she debated for 20 miles before finally turning back. After pulling into the camp's muddy lane, Lange approached a female migrant worker, requested and got permission to photograph her and shot just five exposures. Lange's field notes read in part: "I did not ask her name or her history. She told me her age, that she was 32. She said that they had been living on frozen vegetables from the surrounding fields and birds that the children killed. She had just sold the tires from her car to buy food."

Back home, Lange developed the images and, clutching the still-wet prints, told the editor of the San Francisco *News* that migrant workers were slowly starving to death in Nipomo, California. The story the *News* ran about them featured Lange's pictures; UPI picked it up, and within days the federal government supplied the workers with 20,000 pounds of food. By that time, however, the woman and her family, desperate to find work, had moved on . . .

—Excerpt from *Smithsonian* magazine, March 2002, by Rebecca Maksel

24. How is the text enhanced by the photograph?

A. The text describes the woman's situation, but the photo communicates the harsh reality of it.

B. The text describes her diet, but the photo shows that although the woman looks poor, she's not starving.

C. The text gives information about the mother and family, but the photo shows what her three children look like.

D. The text gives information about the photographer, but the photograph shows her talent with photography.

The photo reinforces the reality of the description in the text (choice A). The family looks ragged, poor, and miserable, and the mother has a look of hopelessness; we can't tell from the photo whether the woman is starving or not (choice B). The children can be seen, but they are hiding from the camera—whether out of fear or shyness, we don't know, but we can't see what they look like in the picture (choice C). We can only glean a sense of the extent of their exhaustion. While the text does give us information about the photographer, and the photo is haunting, her talent does not inform the text (choice D). **The correct answer is A.**

25. How does the image combined with the text give us a better understanding of the Great Depression?

A. The text fills in details about the period that the photo can't provide by itself.

B. The text explains how the photograph started Lange's career.

C. The words and the image together describe the family's situation.

D. The photograph shows the effects of the Depression on real people described in the text.

The image shows us the victims of the Depression, and the text provides more details about the period; together, they give a broader picture (choice A). How Lange's career started (choice B) is irrelevant to understanding the Great Depression. The words and image do describe the family's situation (choice C), but understanding the Great Depression goes beyond one family, which part of the text describes briefly. The photo poignantly illustrates the effects of the Depression on real people; it is the additional text about other aspects of the Depression that creates a more complete picture of the era. **The correct answer is A.**

26. What was the role of the Resettlement Administration (RA) during the Depression?

A. To find work for farm laborers

B. To document migrant workers

C. To help tenant farmers

D. To deport migrant workers

The text describes the Resettlement Administration as an "agency set up to help tenant farmers." Farm laborers could be included in the category of tenant farmers, but the agency's role was not to find work for them (choice A). The mother in the photo was a migrant worker; that is, a farm worker who moves from place to place to find work. Lange's job was, on paper, as a clerk for the agency. She was not paid to document migrant workers (choice B). The agency was not designed to deport anyone (choice D). **The correct answer is C.**

Finding Evidence

The next passage is a primary document that represents one of the most important Supreme Court cases in US history, *Brown v. Board of Education*. The case was decided in 1954, a period when public schools across the country were mostly segregated, by law in the South and by practice in the North. The *Brown* case changed that and started a new era of civil rights. When you read the passage, notice the way details are used to support the main idea and the conclusion.

Questions 27–31 refer to the following passage.

This is an excerpt from the Supreme Court opinion written by Chief Justice Earl Warren in the Brown v. Board of Education landmark case.

Segregation of white and Negro children in the public schools of a State solely on the basis of race, pursuant to state laws permitting or requiring such segregation, denies to Negro children the equal protection of the laws guaranteed by the Fourteenth Amendment—even though the physical facilities and other "tangible" factors of white and Negro schools may be equal . . .

(a) The history of the Fourteenth Amendment is inconclusive as to its intended effect on public education.

(b) The question presented in these cases must be determined, not on the basis of conditions existing when the Fourteenth Amendment was adopted, but in the light of the full development of public education and its present place in American life throughout the Nation.

(c) Where a State has undertaken to provide an opportunity for an education in its public schools, such an opportunity is a right which must be made available to all on equal terms.

(d) Segregation of children in public schools solely on the basis of race deprives children of the minority group of equal educational opportunities, even though the physical facilities and other "tangible" factors may be equal. . . .

In approaching this problem, we cannot turn the clock back to 1868 when the Amendment was adopted, or even to 1896 when *Plessy v. Ferguson* was written. We must consider public education in the light of its full development and its present place in American life throughout the Nation. Only in this way can it be determined if segregation in public schools deprives these plaintiffs of the equal protection of the laws.

Today, education is perhaps the most important function of state and local governments. Compulsory school attendance laws and the great expenditures for education both demonstrate our recognition of the importance of education to our democratic society. It is required in the performance of our most basic public responsibilities, even service in the armed forces. It is the very foundation of good citizenship. Today it is a principal instrument in awakening the child to cultural values, in preparing him for later professional training, and in helping him to adjust normally to his environment. In these days, it is doubtful that any child may reasonably be expected to succeed in life if he is denied the opportunity of an education. Such an opportunity, where the state has undertaken to provide it, is a right which must be made available to all on equal terms.

We come then to the question presented: Does segregation of children in public schools solely on the basis of race, even though the physical facilities and other "tangible" factors may be equal, deprive the children of the minority group of equal educational opportunities? We believe that it does. . . .

To separate them from others of similar age and qualifications solely because of their race generates a feeling of inferiority as to their status in the community that may affect their hearts and minds in a way unlikely ever to be undone. The effect of this separation on their educational opportunities was well stated by a finding in the Kansas case by a court which nevertheless felt compelled to rule against the Negro plaintiffs:

"Segregation of white and colored children in public schools has a detrimental effect upon the colored children. The impact is greater when it has the sanction of the law; for the policy of separating the races is usually interpreted as denoting the inferiority of the negro group. A sense of inferiority affects the motivation of a child to learn. Segregation with the sanction of law, therefore, has a tendency to [retard] the educational and mental development of negro children and to deprive them of some of the benefits they would receive in a racial[ly] integrated school system."

Whatever may have been the extent of psychological knowledge at the time of *Plessy v. Ferguson,* this finding is amply supported by modern authority. Any language in *Plessy v. Ferguson* contrary to this finding is rejected. . . .

We conclude that in the field of public education the doctrine of "separate but equal" has no place. Separate educational facilities are inherently unequal. Therefore, we hold that the plaintiffs and others similarly situated for whom the actions have been brought are, by reason of the segregation complained of, deprived of the equal protection of the laws guaranteed by the Fourteenth Amendment. This disposition makes unnecessary any discussion whether such segregation also violates the Due Process Clause of the Fourteenth Amendment. . . .

27. What reason does Chief Justice Warren give to show that segregation in public schools creates unequal opportunities for learning?

A. The Fourteenth Amendment bans segregation.

B. Prior Supreme Court decisions show that segregation creates unequal schools.

C. Separate is not equal.

D. Education is naturally unequal.

Warren cites both the Fourteenth Amendment (choice A) and prior Supreme Court decisions (choice B) as legal support for making the decision, but the reason he uses to illustrate why segregation can't be tolerated is that it deprives minority group children of equal educational opportunities. Although he states that education is important to a democratic society, he does not cite natural inequality (choice D) as evidence for his argument. **The correct answer is C.**

28. According to Warren's decision, why is segregation a violation of the Fourteenth Amendment?

A. Because segregation has a negative effect on modern society

B. Because segregation prevented minorities from becoming US citizens

C. Because segregation is a form of slavery, and the Fourteenth Amendment ended slavery

D. Because segregation denies equal opportunity for an education

Segregation may have had a negative effect on society (choice A), but Warren's decision explains that the policy violates the equal protection clause of the Fourteenth Amendment. The passage doesn't discuss the citizenship aspects (choice B) of the Fourteenth Amendment. Segregation is not the same as slavery (choice C), and it was the Thirteenth Amendment that abolished slavery. The first section of the Fourteenth Amendment guarantees all people in the United States equal opportunity for an education, and according to Warren, "separate educational facilities are inherently unequal." **The correct answer is D.**

29. According to Warren's decision, public education is a(n)

A. privilege.

B. opportunity.

C. right.

D. responsibility.

Warren never refers to education as a privilege (choice A). He says that minorities should not be denied equal opportunities in education, not that education is an opportunity (choice B). He does not describe it as a responsibility (choice D). Warren describes education as a right that must be made available to everyone equally. **The correct answer is C.**

30. At the time of the *Brown* decision, Warren believed that segregation in public schools had to change because

A. we can't apply rules and ideas of the past to the way we live today.

B. the Fourteenth Amendment was applicable regardless of the time period.

C. public education is more important in modern society.

D. state laws were outdated.

Warren explains that the prior *Plessy* decision and the time period when the Fourteenth Amendment was passed can't be used as the basis for current ideas and decisions, which contradicts choice B. He does not compare public education of the past to that of the time of the decision, so choice C is incorrect. Warren says that states can't violate the rights of minority children by educating them in segregated schools by law because such laws, by design, deny minority children of equal protection and are therefore against the Fourteenth Amendment; he doesn't say the laws are outdated (choice D). **The correct answer is A.**

31. What is Warren's view of segregation in public schools?

A. It is unjust and unfair, but since it is legal, the Court can't change it.

B. Once examined, it can be defended.

C. It's an unfortunate offshoot of our past that can't be changed.

D. It is inherently unequal and has no place in public education.

Warren argues that segregation can't be held constitutional because it violates the Fourteenth Amendment. Once it is declared unconstitutional, it is not legal, and laws will need to be taken off the books, so choice A is incorrect. He examines the historical evidence that was used to maintain segregated schools and finds that the arguments don't hold up, so choice B is incorrect. Warren talks about the negative effects of past segregation but does not conclude that they cannot change (choice C). The past policy of "separate but equal" was shown not to be equal on any level and therefore could not continue. **The correct answer is D.**

Informational Workplace

The third type of nonfiction text on the test is what the test makers call **workplace and community documents.** The text might be a statement of policy, guidelines or rules for workplace behavior, an excerpt from an employee handbook or training manual, a statement of employee benefits, a communication (email, written memorandum, or letter), or even a legal document, such as an employment contract. Also, depending on the document type, the text might contain headings or numbered lists.

This category also includes what is referred to as "community" documents. These are communications such as letters to the editor of a local newspaper, complaint letters, and public notices. For example, a notice sent to people in the community about an upcoming event to be held in a municipal park or building would fall into this category.

All of these documents are drawn from real or simulated workplace and community documents. Applying reading skills to these types of documents is no different from other types of reading material. Your task is the same: to apply your comprehension, analysis, synthesis, and application skills to the text. As you read a workplace or community document, try to answer the following questions for yourself:

- Who is the intended *audience*? (A specific individual? All or only certain employees? A general community?)
- What is the overall *scope* of the document? (Does it address only specific policies, procedures, or problems? Or is it broader in scope?)
- What *goal* or *objective* of the institution is the document intended to further? (For example, the document's purpose might be to enhance workplace efficiency, thwart employee misconduct, increase profits or revenues, obtain funding, or attract new clients or customers.)
- What is the writer's *point of view*? (Does the document express an opinion about any specific issue, or does it simply provide information?)
- What is the overall *tone* of the document? (The overall tone might be objective; but if a document serves as a warning—to employees, for example—the tone might be somewhat sharp or even accusatory.)

Also, if the document has a title, ask yourself what it suggests about the document's audience, scope, and purpose.

If you encounter a statement of policy on the test, expect at least one question asking what the broad policy is. (A **policy** is a general principle or broad course of action adopted by an institution as a guide for conducting its affairs.)

To understand the policy, you may need to synthesize information from various parts of the document. Also, policy statements typically provide details explaining how the institution implements its policy. So expect test questions about those supporting details as well. A policy is typically implemented through specific rules, regulations, and guidelines. When reading a policy statement, try to:

- Distinguish between a general policy and a specific policy, which is a rule or guideline that supports a general policy.
- Distinguish between *rules*, which require or prohibit certain behavior, and *guidelines*, which are merely suggestions as to how to further a policy.
- Pay attention to any consequences (discipline or punishment) for violating a rule or regulation. If consequences are discussed, pay attention to whether they vary, depending on the specific violation.

A policy statement that provides rules and regulations may contain so-called "legalese," which refers to words and phrases used in legal documents. If you run across legalese, don't be surprised if one of the test questions focuses on it. Don't worry: you should be able to figure out what the legalese means from its context. In fact, this skill is exactly what you're being tested on.

The following excerpt could be part of a policy statement, an employee handbook or training manual, or even an employment agreement. All of these types of documents can contain statements of policy as well as specific rules, regulations, or guidelines.

Questions 32–34 refer to the following document excerpt.

[*The document begins with Section 1, and then continues with Section 2, as follows.*]

Section 2

2.1. Metacorp has a no-tolerance policy with respect to employee pilfering. As used in this section, "pilfering" means the taking of any company property, regardless of its monetary value, for personal rather than company use, whether temporarily or permanently.

2.2. Any employee who is determined to have pilfered company property will be subject to disciplinary action in accordance with the guidelines set forth herein concerning warnings and subsequent termination of employment, and with applicable state and federal laws.

2.3. If an employee submits a false report of a violation under this section, that employee will be subject to immediate disciplinary action, which may include termination of employment without warning. For purposes of this provision, a "false report" is any report that the reporting employee knew or should have known was untrue or inaccurate, either in whole or in part.

32. Why did the company include Section 2 in the document?

A. To catch employees suspected of pilfering

B. To discourage employees from pilfering

C. To encourage employees to report pilfering incidents

D. To attract employees who are trustworthy

The first sentence of paragraph 2.1 expresses the company's general policy that it will not tolerate pilfering, while the rules that follow warn employees of harsh consequences should they violate the policy. Clearly, the main purpose of the section is to discourage employees from pilfering. Choices A and D both provide advantages of having this type of policy, but neither expresses the *purpose* of the policy. Choice C is incorrect because paragraph 2.3 actually *discourages* the reporting of pilfering. **The correct answer is B.**

33. A Metacorp employee borrows a coffee carafe from work but forgets to return it. Under Section 2, the employee would probably

A. be required to replace the company's carafe with a new one.

B. be fired by Metacorp because the company has a no-tolerance policy.

C. not be subject to discipline, because the employee intended to return the item.

D. receive a warning if this was the employee's first violation of Section 2.

To answer this question, you need to distinguish between consequences for pilfering (Section 2.2) and those for falsely reporting pilfering (Section 2.3). The applicable section is 2.2, which mentions "warnings" as a pre-termination procedure. Assuming this was a first offense, the pilfering employee's only discipline would probably be a warning. **The correct answer is D.**

34. For which behavior would a Metacorp employee **most likely** be disciplined?

A. Taking home a company desk that was just thrown away

B. Reporting a pilfering incident that was never actually observed

C. Using a company telephone to make long-distance, personal calls

D. Driving a company vehicle to a business-related conference

To answer this question correctly, you need to understand the definition of "false report." Its definition, provided in paragraph 2.3, contains some legalese. Choice B describes what might be considered submitting a false report, depending on the circumstances. If the reporting employee had absolutely no reason to suspect a coworker of pilfering, then it is possible that the employee knew or *should have known* that the report was false *in whole or in part*. **The correct answer is B.**

Another type of workplace or community document you might encounter is a communication such as an email, memo, or letter. The communication might be to a particular person, or it might be to a group, or a response to another communication. It could even be a letter to the editor of a newspaper. In its ideas and its tone, this type of a communication is more likely than other workplace and community documents to be *subjective*—that is, to communicate a distinct point of view and attitude toward the topic at hand, and possibly toward the recipient of the communication as well.

Here are some suggestions for reading and understanding these more subjective communication documents:

- Try to identify its main idea, and note the details provided in support of that idea.
- Ask yourself: Why did the author compose this email, memo, or letter? What was the author trying to accomplish by doing so?
- As with other workplace and community documents, look for policy statements, and distinguish between supporting rules and supporting guidelines.
- If the communication begins by identifying the sender, recipient, and/or the subject, pay attention to those lines. They can provide clues about the communication's topic and point of view.

Questions 35–37 refer to the following memo.

From: Jason Renaldi <jason.renaldi@theberwyngroup.com>

To: All Berwyn Corporation employees

Subject: Employee dress code and lunchtime policy

Beginning on Wednesday, January 17, our company dress code requiring all men and women to wear business suits will not apply on Wednesdays. All employees will be permitted to dress casually each Wednesday, at their option. Jeans will be considered appropriate attire, but T-shirts and/or shorts will be considered inappropriate. Women may wear open-toed shoes, but men may not. Management encourages you to enjoy the freedom of "casual Wednesdays" while still dressing in good taste.

Also beginning on January 17, you may take up to one-and-a-half hours for lunch, between 11:30 to 2:00. To make up the half-hour of work lost due to a longer lunch, you must either arrive up to 30 minutes earlier to start your Wednesday workday or leave 30 minutes later to end your workday. If you prefer a relatively late Wednesday lunch, management has arranged for the mobile food vendor Cuisine on Wheels to serve lunch in our parking lot from 12:45 to 1:45 every Wednesday—again, starting on January 17. For those of you leaving the premises for Wednesday lunch, as always we encourage you to carpool and to dine with your coworkers.

I'm confident that a more leisurely lunch and casual attire will leave us all that much more excited about whatever challenges lie ahead during the rest of the work week. As always, I welcome your continuing feedback on these and other working conditions.

Jason Renaldi
Human Resources Director
Berwyn Corporation

35. Which is the **most likely** purpose of the email?

A. To announce policies designed to improve employee morale

B. To inform workers of recent company developments

C. To introduce incentives for job performance

D. To defend the company's dress code and lunch-hour policy

The closing paragraph reveals the purpose of the new policies: to help workers face the second half of the work week with a positive outlook—in other words, to improve their morale. **The correct answer is A.**

36. How is this memo structured to enable Berwyn employees to get the information?

A. The memo describes the changes in company policies in two detailed paragraphs.

B. The memo explains the consequences of not conforming to the dress code as part of the detail of the new dress code.

C. The memo's author made the memo short so that employees would be able to read it quickly.

D. The memo describes two new related policies so that employees understand their connection.

The main idea of the memo is to communicate updated and revised company policy. This is accomplished in two detailed paragraphs (choice A), one for each change. The memo does not mention consequences for not following the dress code (choice B). The memo is short but clear in its details and intent. The intent is to have employees conform to the new policies, so it is not to be skimmed over and read quickly (choice C). The two changes are unrelated to each other, so choice D is incorrect. **The correct answer is A.**

37. What will be required of Berwyn Corporation employees in the future?

On Wednesdays, employees of Berwyn Corporation must

A. eat lunch off the Berwyn premises.

B. carpool to lunch.

C. wear jeans to work.

D. work as long as on other work days.

The author implies that workers must compensate for a longer lunch by either starting the workday earlier or ending it later. All other details mentioned in the email are guidelines, or suggestions, rather than rules or requirements. **The correct answer is D.**

The following is a typical letter of complaint. Companies receive these kinds of letters regularly, and generally they respond to them. They are by nature subjective, since they refer to the unique experience of the customer who is making the complaint.

Questions 38–40 refer to the following complaint letter.

October 20, 2016

Mr. Henry Jones, Manager
ABC Appliances
555 Main Street
Somewhereville, VA 55555

Dear Mr. Jones:

On September 15, I purchased from your store a GEM dishwasher (model GM249). I was told that it was as good—if not better than—the other name brands you sell. And it was considerably less expensive, so I was delighted with my purchase. I have attached a copy of my receipt for your information.

I am writing to you because

- The dishwasher is very noisy.
- The dishwasher sometimes stops before the timer has finished, making it impossible to get my dishes clean.

On October 1, I called your store and spoke to Cindy Smith, who said she didn't know the return policy. She stated that she would discuss the problem with you and would call me back. However, I received no return call from anyone in the company. I called again on October 8 and got your company voicemail, even though I called during business hours. I left a message but again have not received a call. On October 12, I called again and spoke to Ms. Smith, who apologized and said she would call back after discussing it with you. That was over a week ago, and I have still not heard from anyone.

It is now more than 30 days since my date of purchase, even though I informed your company of the problem well before that time period expired.

The dishwasher you sold me is poor quality, doesn't work properly, and is useless as is. Under consumer law, my contract is with the seller of the goods and, as such, I am writing to you to seek a full refund.* At this point, given my experience with your customer service, I do not wish to exchange it for another unit of the same brand or even another brand. Thus far, your company has been totally unresponsive to my inquiries and complaints. This is not the kind of customer service I expect.

I would appreciate your response within 10 working days. If you wish to discuss by phone, I am contactable by phone at 555-555-5555.

If you choose to continue to ignore my complaint, I will seek alternative options.

Yours sincerely,

Susan Smith

---

* "As a consumer, if you purchase faulty goods, the law entitles you to seek either a repair, replacement, or a refund. It is a matter for you to negotiate with the seller for your redress. However, if a repair is offered, then it should be permanent. If not, and if the same fault occurs again, then the buyer is entitled to seek another form of redress. If you cannot agree on the form of redress, your next step after a letter may be the Small Claims Procedure—see our website/booklets for full details."

38. What action will Ms. Smith **most likely** take if she gets no response from Mr. Jones?

- **A.** She'll give up and drop it.
- **B.** She'll call a lawyer.
- **C.** She'll file a claim in small claims court.
- **D.** She'll call again and insist that she talk to Mr. Jones directly.

The tone of the letter is one of frustration and anger, so it is unlikely that Susan Smith will drop it completely (choice A). She could call a lawyer (choice B), but in general, this would not be the outcome for a small item and a limited complaint. The footnote refers to small claims court (choice C) as an option. Smith included the footnote in the letter, letting Jones know that she is aware of this option as a consumer. This implies that it might be her next step. While it's possible that she may try calling again and insisting that she talk directly to Mr. Jones (choice D), she has already tried calling multiple times with no desirable result, so it is more likely she will choose to file a claim in small claims court. **The correct answer is C.**

39. What evidence does Smith provide to support her claim that she should get a refund?

- **A.** The timer doesn't work properly.
- **B.** She found a less expensive model elsewhere.
- **C.** No one has returned her calls.
- **D.** The dishwasher is still under warranty.

Smith documents the specific problems she has found with the dishwasher, one of which is the timer (choice A). Because it is not working properly, and consumer law gives her the right to seek redress, she wants her money back. She does not mention that she found a less expensive model elsewhere, so choice B does not support her claim. In spite of Smith's calls, no one ever called her back (choice C), but that's not the basis for her refund. The letter doesn't mention what kind of warranty is on the appliance (choice D). **The correct answer is A.**

40. Why would Smith include in her letter the statement: "I was delighted with my purchase"?

- **A.** She wanted to tell them what a good shopper she is.
- **B.** She wanted to let them know that she did not start off being negative and disgruntled.
- **C.** She needed to give the manager information about her purchase.
- **D.** She didn't want to show her anger.

Smith starts her letter by giving the store proof of her purchase (choice C) so they can look it up in their records. Her feelings about her consumer skills (choice A) are not part of that information, but they indicate good faith in her expectations for a positive experience with the store (choice B). She does show her anger (choice D) in the last part of the letter ("This is not the kind of customer service I expect."), but she does not start off that way. **The correct answer is B.**

A letter to the editor is another form of communication that people may use to voice their complaints or concerns. These letters usually address a broader concern about the community rather than a very specific complaint directed at one person or company. These communications could even be in the form of a response to a political situation or an editorial position taken by the paper.

As you read the following letter to the editor, notice how the author argues his point of view. Ask yourself what facts he uses to support his position and note how he organizes his argument.

Questions 41–44 refer to the following letter to the editor.

Dear Editor,

This letter is in response to the recent letter in your publication disparaging bicycle drivers' use of roadways.

Different vehicle types have different advantages and disadvantages, and different people have different needs and preferences. Fortunately, our roadways and traffic laws allow accommodation of a diversity of vehicle types for transportation. If this were not the case, many people would be limited to vehicles they don't need, don't want, can't afford, or can't use.

An unfortunate reality of our roadway system is that all forms of traffic affect all other forms of traffic. No road user is immune to traffic delays or innocent of creating them for others. Although the cause and nature of the delays generated by traffic may appear different from one vehicle type to the next, comparison of the total induced delays caused by different vehicle types fails to reveal any significant net difference long-term. Time and time again, our free society has found that the advantages of allowing transportation via a diversity of vehicle types outweighs convenience-oriented arguments for prohibition of certain vehicle types on the surface streets that provide essential access to our local destinations. This is especially true for those vehicles that are the most affordable, are the most environmentally friendly, occupy the least space, do the least damage to roadways, generate the least noise, and create the least danger for other innocent road users.

When issues of traffic-related inconvenience arise, the prudent response is to improve or supplement the transportation facility, not ban a segment of the population from travel. If some motorists feel that they are unreasonably delayed by slow traffic, they can lobby for construction of extra road space for passing or promote a redundant system of expressways that slower travelers won't need to use. Many communities have elected to incorporate improved passing facilities into their roadways via construction of wide (14' or wider) outside travel lanes. In other locations, delays caused by slower traffic may be too small to warrant the costs of roadway widening, and taxpayer money may be better spent in other ways.

Some motorists who wish to avoid the responsibilities and occasional inconveniences of motor vehicle travel have claimed that use of slow, open vehicles on roadways is unreasonably dangerous. However, analysis of safety data for bicycle transportation shows this to be untrue. Bicycle drivers who follow the vehicular rules of the road when traveling on roadways enjoy a safety record similar to automobile users, safer than sidewalk cyclists, and much safer than motorcycle users. Our society's respect for the travel rights of vulnerable but lawfully operating road users is what keeps these bicyclists safe. Those impatient road users who treat bicycle drivers with disrespect and make inflammatory statements intent on depriving other groups of their equal right to travel upon our public street system are the ones creating the real danger.

Often we hear claims from very vocal individuals that bicyclists are not taxed enough or regulated enough to deserve to use public streets. Advocates for bicyclists are willing to entertain these concerns when they are presented in a constructive manner, but once a realistic discussion of the costs and benefits of various revenue collection and regulation schemes begins, the vocal complainants usually lose interest. It appears that these individuals are not really interested in ensuring that the system is fair or effective; rather, they are only interested in changes that will discourage bicycling. If these bicycling critics are primarily interested in their own convenience as motorists, perhaps their efforts would be better spent lobbying for improved roadway facilities such as wide outside lanes. Bicycling critics may also point out that some bicycle operators create hazards for other road users by habitually violating the rules of the road. Lawfully operating bicycle drivers share this concern and advocate better education and enforcement of the traffic laws we already have as they apply to all drivers of vehicles.

Sometimes members of the motoring public will express empathy for utilitarian bicyclists who don't use cars, but exhibit anger toward recreational cyclists who use popular roads at popular times. Some of these motorists suggest that the government place prohibitions on recreational bicycle travel. This concept is fraught with problems. First, it is impossible to tell one's trip purpose simply from appearance, since many utilitarian cyclists use the same bicycles and clothing as recreational cyclists, and second, the government has never been granted an interest in the citizens' trip purpose for everyday travel on public streets. Do we wish to open a Pandora's box of civil liberty infringements where our government can stop citizens for their appearance, demand to know their trip purpose, and arrest them for traveling for unapproved reasons? If recreational travel is subject to prohibition, does that mean that trips to sporting events and vacations may be prohibited to reduce traffic? May the government ban "sports cars," "sport utility vehicles," and "RVs" in order to spare the public from their impact on roads? It seems far better to allow everyone to use our roadways, and to design and regulate them to make them as safe and efficient as possible for mixed traffic. That way we can continue to enjoy living in a free country, with equal opportunity for all.

Sincerely,

Your friendly neighborhood bicycle driver, Tom

41. What is the author's purpose in addressing the critics of bicycle riders on the roadways?

A. To suggest ways to reduce congestion on the roads

B. To show that his critics are all wrong

C. To answer all of the critics in one letter

D. To make a stronger argument

The author cites the critics and provides evidence to show why each claim is not supportable. This makes a stronger argument (choice D), since there are fewer ways to punch holes in it. The author does suggest some ways to reduce congestion (choice A), but these are given as part of his overall argument. The author's argument does show the specific ways in which his critics are wrong (choice B), but the purpose of refuting their arguments is to make his own argument stronger, not merely to prove critics wrong. Although critics may not all be included, the author counters their arguments but does not address the critics themselves (choice C). Putting it all in one letter or essay makes it easier to read and makes the argument more understandable, but it is not the author's purpose. **The correct answer is D.**

42. What prompted the author's letter to the editor?

A. A proposal to tax bicycles on the road

B. A letter that was insulting to bicycles on the roadways

C. The increasing traffic congestion

D. Road rage toward bicycle riders

The first sentence in the passage says that the letter is a response to an earlier letter that "disparages" bicycle riders on the road (choice B). All of the other options are ideas that are mentioned as details in one of the counterarguments, but none is what the author says prompted his letter. **The correct answer is B.**

43. Which phrase in the last paragraph is an example of figurative language that the author uses to help drive home his point?

A. "recreational cyclists who use popular roads at popular times"

B. "simply from appearance"

C. "a Pandora's box of civil liberty infringements"

D. "prohibitions on recreational bicycle travel"

Figurative language is language that is not literal; that is, it has meaning beyond the specific meaning of the words themselves. In the last paragraph, the author gets more emphatic and uses hyperbole (exaggeration) to show how ridiculous the argument would be if one were to carry it to its logical conclusion. An example of such a phrase is "a Pandora's box of civil liberty infringements," in which he refers to a Greek myth in which a box that seems harmless turns out to contain the evils of the world. Referring to Pandora's box symbolizes opening the door to something that has unexpected and perhaps severe consequences. None of the other phrases are used figuratively. **The correct answer is C.**

44. Which of the claims made by the author's critics does he think has some validity?

A. Bicycles on the roads should be taxed to discourage their use.

B. Bicycles on the road are a hazard to road safety.

C. Bicyclists do not follow the rules of the road.

D. Only bicyclists who use their bikes to get to work should be allowed on the roads.

The author addresses each critic with counterarguments. He shows that those who want to tax bicycle use (choice A) are really only interested in reducing or even eliminating bicycles on the roads—these critics usually disappear when anyone actually tries to talk to them about such a policy. To the claim that bicycles are dangerous to road safety (choice B), the author counters statistics that show that this is not true, so long as bicyclists are following road rules. To the claim that bicyclists don't follow the rules of the road (choice C), he says that bicyclists who obey the rules share this concern. This statement implies that some (but not all) bicyclists do not follow the rules. To the claim that bicycles for recreational use should not be allowed on the roads at certain times (choice D), the author provides several different statements that expose the lack of logic to this argument. **The correct answer is C.**

UNDERSTANDING FICTION

A work of **fiction** is one that is made up; in other words, it involves imaginary people and events. Works of fiction can take a variety of different forms, but the Reasoning Through Language Arts—Reading Comprehension test focuses on prose. You can expect one reading passage involving fiction, with approximately eight questions.

A passage may provide an entire work of fiction if the work is brief. Generally, however, passages are excerpted from longer works of fiction, whether novels or short stories.

In the following sections, you'll learn more about prose fiction, and you'll learn how best to read this type of fiction in order to understand it in ways that will help you most on the GED Reasoning Through Language Arts Test. You'll also read a variety of sample passages and answer test-style questions based on them.

The Elements of Fiction

As was just noted, a fictional work is a work based on someone's imagination. In other words, the story, characters, and other elements of a fictional work are made up by the author. Even stories based on real people or real situations can be fiction. A work of fiction can be in the form of a short story, a novel, a poem, or a drama. The term **prose fiction** is generally used in reference to short stories and novels, as opposed to plays or poems, and it is this type of fiction that will be used in the test. (The word *prose* refers to the ordinary form of writing or speaking.)

The **plot** in fiction is the story line—the story's events strung together in a particular sequence or order. A story's events can flow chronologically (in the order they occur in time) or they can be revealed out of order or sequence. Works of fiction usually begin with the first event and trace subsequent events chronologically. However, the author may choose a different sequence instead. For instance, the author may begin the story with the final event and then unravel the plot by going back to the first event in order to explain what led up to the event.

A story's **narrator** is the voice that tells the story—the storyteller. The narrator relates the story's events as he or she sees them unfold, from his/her *point of view*. Usually a story is told from either a first-person or a third-person point of view. A work written in **first person** is told from the narrator's own perspective. Throughout the story, the narrator speaks in terms of *I* or *me*, so the reader follows the story as seen through the narrator's eyes. When reading fiction that is written in first person, the reader is limited by the narrator's limited knowledge. The reader knows only what the narrator sees and thinks and must interpret the actions and thoughts of the other characters through the narrator's eyes, responding to events and other characters through the narrator's subjective perspective. In contrast, a work of fiction written in **third person** is told from the perspective of a narrator who knows and reveals *everything* to the reader. From this point of view, the narrator does not speak in terms of *I* but rather in terms of *he*, *she*, and *they*. The third-person point of view allows the reader glimpses of all the characters' actions and feelings through an all-knowing, or omniscient, narrator.

The figures involved in the plot are known as **characters**. The main characters are those around whom the plot revolves. Minor characters are incidental characters who become involved in the plot to a lesser extent. A story's characters are revealed to the reader in several different ways. Usually, the narrator describes what the characters look like and tells the reader about their personalities, either directly or indirectly. Characters are also revealed by how they act and what they say. For instance, a character might behave in a consistently shy manner, or continually talk about herself, or use poor grammar in his or her speech. Finally, characters are understood by what the others in the story say or think about them. A character's spoken words to another character are referred to as **dialogue.**

The **tone** of a story is the attitude of the narrator or the author toward the subject or event. The reader's impression of the subject or event may be colored by how the narrator or author feels about it. The **mood** is an overall atmosphere the author creates by carefully selecting certain words and details. The **setting** of a story is the author's description of the time and place in which the story occurs. Not only does the setting make the story more real for the reader, it also helps to create the mood of the story. An event that occurs at midnight on a rainy night creates more of a mood of mystery than the same event occurring on a sunny day.

Authors of fiction use a variety of **literary devices** to help convey ideas, emphasize certain points, incite the reader's imagination, and provide a more interesting and enjoyable reading experience. To help describe a story's setting or to describe how the story's characters experience certain events, fiction authors often employ **imagery**—the use of language to convey a sense experience (sight, sound, smell, taste, or touch). To help convey ideas and enhance interest, fiction authors often use **figurative language**—the use of language in ways that give words and phrases a meaning other than their common, or *literal*, meaning. A particular instance of figurative language is commonly referred to as a **figure of speech**.

Figurative language can be used to make an abstract idea concrete or to visualize an idea. Often a figure of speech will compare two seemingly different things to reveal their similarities. For instance, when someone says they are *on pins and needles* waiting for something to happen, that person is using a figure of speech. Obviously, the person is not literally on pins and needles. The expression, however, does convey the person's excitement about whatever might happen.

An author's use of figurative language might apply to larger elements of a story as well, perhaps even to the entire story. For example, an entire narrative might serve as a *metaphor* or as a *symbol*, by which the story's events are intended either to substitute for or represent some other story. Or a narrative might be intended as an *allegory,* which can either be understood literally or taken to mean something more, or deeper, as well.

Prose Fiction

The reading comprehension portion of the Reasoning Through Language Arts Test will include one prose fiction passage drawn from a short story or novel. The passage will be 400–900 words in length (one or two pages, more or less). Even a 900-word passage is a very manageable piece of text; you should have little difficulty reading 900 words and remembering the information within the passage.

The passage you will see on the test could reflect any number of characters, cultural settings, and historical references that could be from different time periods. A passage might contain only narrative, but could contain dialogue as well. A passage's style might be formal and heavy-handed, or it might be casual or even conversational. In short, expect anything. Keep in mind, though, that the goal is *not* to test you on your knowledge of literature, literary traditions, or specific authors. To answer the test questions, all you'll need to know will be expressed or implied in the passages and in the questions themselves.

Inferring context from the passage can help you interpret the passage's events and the characters' actions. Ask yourself: What events might have led to or might follow the ones described in the passage?

Regardless of when or by whom a work of prose fiction was written or what style of writing the author uses, the guidelines for reading and understanding prose fiction are essentially the same. As you read a passage of prose fiction, ask yourself the following questions that focus on the very same reading skills that the test covers:

- **Who is the narrator?** Is the story told in the first person—from the narrator's perspective? Or is it told in the third person—from the perspective of an all-knowing observer outside the story itself?
- **What is the setting and mood of the passage?** Through the narrator or the characters, the reader might infer when and where certain events are taking place. Are they occurring during a particular era, decade, year, or season? During wartime, a time of prosperity and optimism, or a time of strife and despair? In a big city, in a rural village, or on a remote island? In a modest apartment, a large mansion, or a restaurant? What are the weather and other environmental conditions? Is the overall mood somber, joyous, upbeat, or tense? Understanding the setting and mood can help you interpret the passage's events and the characters' actions.
- **What is the author's main concern in the passage?** Think about the passage as a whole. Ask yourself what the author's intent is, as revealed through the narrator. Here are just a few examples of what an author might be trying to accomplish:
    - Describe a predicament or difficult situation
    - Explain implicit causes and their consequences by recounting a series of events
    - Reveal the relationship between characters through their conversation
    - Reveal a character through his or her thoughts, actions, and reactions
- **How does the narrator set the mood and tone for the story?** Look for specific words or phrases that paint a picture of the setting or create the mood for the overall story. Think about how these words influence the reader's perspective of the characters or point of view. Are there specific words that suggest a particular tone? Ask yourself how changing one or several of these words would alter your perception of what's taking place and/or the motives of the characters.
- **What does the passage reveal about the story's characters?** A character's specific actions, spoken words, and thoughts can reveal a lot about his or her personality, motives, attitudes, and mood. They can also reveal how the character sees and relates to the story's other characters. They can reveal, too, how the character might behave in other situations. Pay careful attention to these details.

- **What events might have led to or might follow the ones described in the passage?** More specifically, ask yourself questions such as the following:
    - How might the situation described in the passage have come about?
    - Are the characters behaving in a way that certain prior events might help explain?
    - Do the characters' thoughts and their dialogue suggest what they might do later in the story?
    - Given the circumstances, what would naturally and logically occur next in time?
- **Beyond their literal meaning, what do the passage's words and ideas imply or suggest?** As noted earlier, fiction authors use a variety of literary devices to convey ideas. These could include using figurative language; that is, words that suggest a non-literal meaning. Figurative language points beyond the generally understood meaning of words so that the words mean something else. The device creates a contrast to reality and helps establish an author's ideas. Often, figurative language enhances the emotional intensity and imaginative appeal of the work, and it does so with fewer words, since the larger meaning is embedded in the language itself. For example, some passages may use devices like some of the following to create a mood, set a tone, or otherwise embellish the story:
    - *Irony:* a discrepancy between an actual situation and what one would normally expect under the circumstances. For example, dying of thirst while disabled within sight of a river could be considered ironic. Getting into a fender bender on the way to a driver's education class might also be thought of as ironic. Irony is a powerful tool because it allows the writer to convey an idea without asserting it directly. The irony of a situation is left to the reader to discover.
    - *Paradox:* a situation that seems contradictory, yet is not. In fact, once understood, something paradoxical actually makes sense on a deeper level. For example, the expression *youth is wasted on the young* is a paradox. While the expression seems to be contradictory upon first glance, the deeper meaning is that many who are young do not appreciate the benefits of youth until they are no longer young. A paradox is different from an oxymoron in that paradoxes are larger concepts, whereas an oxymoron is made up of a two-word phrase; for instance, *thunderous silence* or *noble theft*.
    - *Metaphor and simile:* techniques that both compare two unlike things. These literary devices are probably the most commonly used types of figures of speech. They are designed to heighten our senses and help the reader look at something in a new way. A simile makes a comparison by using the words *like* or *as*. A metaphor makes the comparison without these words. We all use similes every day without thinking about it—for example, when we refer to *being tired as a dog* or *sleeping like a baby*. Common metaphors can be found in lyrics to music as well as in poetry; for example, *a sea of grief*, *a bridge over troubled water*, *the light of my life*, and so on. In each of these examples, the metaphor enriches the image conveyed through the language chosen.

- *Personification:* attributing human qualities to an animal, an object, or even a concept. Here are a few examples:

  The setting sun sang its lullaby.

  The barn gate jeered and complained to the sudden gust.

  Using personification lends special powers to inanimate objects, injecting them with qualities that emphasize a point.
- *Symbolism:* one thing used to represent something else that is more abstract. In prose, symbols give an expanded meaning to a specific aspect of the text. For example, a boy's white shirt may symbolize his innocence.

When reading a prose fiction passage, look for use of the previously noted figures of speech. While you will not be tested on the definitions, you may be expected to understand and recognize their use.

Rest assured that prose fiction questions will not ask you to uncover obscure, hidden meanings behind the passage. Rather, the questions will focus on what we've just covered—the passage's main concern, setting, use of language to create mood and tone, sequence of events, and character development—all as stated or implied in the passage. It's important to read the passage carefully for what is implied as well as what is stated. As you read, try to develop an overview—a short who, what, where, when, why—so the passage has some context that will be assisted by the details given in the text.

In the following brief passage, imagery and figurative language are used effectively to establish setting, mood, and tone, all of which serve to make a point in a powerful way. Read the paragraph, and then answer the three questions that follow it.

Questions 1–3 refer to the following passage.

Dark spruce forest frowned on either side the frozen waterway. The trees had been stripped by a recent wind of their white covering of frost, and they seemed to lean towards each other, black and ominous, in the fading light. A vast silence reigned over the land. The land itself was a desolation, lifeless, without movement, so lone and cold that the spirit of it was not even that of sadness. There was a hint in it of laughter, but of a laughter more terrible than any sadness—a laughter that was mirthless as the smile of the Sphinx, a laughter cold as the frost and partaking of the grimness of infallibility. It was the masterful and incommunicable wisdom of eternity laughing at the futility of life and the effort of life. It was the Wild, the savage, frozen-hearted Northland Wild.

—from *White Fang*, by Jack London

1. What does the setting described in this paragraph lead you to expect about the story?

A. It will be bleak and dark.

B. It will be all about nature.

C. It will contain some humor, or at least some moments of laughter.

D. It will contain a moral lesson.

London provides vivid details of the setting, which, all told, give a dark and bleak picture. The use of specific language (for example, *desolation*—solitude, loneliness, and isolation) and imagery (for example, the *frowned* forest, the *black and ominous* trees, the *desolate* and *lifeless* land that is *lone and cold*) all suggest a stark and bleak picture. By identifying what is being described in the paragraph, the last sentence provides a clue that the story will not remain focused on nature (choice B) but will lead the reader into a story in which the Wild plays a major role. The tone of the passage is definitely not humorous (choice C) as the idea of laughter here is wicked and grim. Although the last line mentions wisdom, there is no hint of a moral to come (choice D). **The correct answer is A.**

2. How does the author's use of the simile *a laughter that was mirthless as the smile of the Sphinx* contribute to painting a picture of the setting?

A. He contrasts laughter with the cold landscape to show the human element in an otherwise stark environment.

B. He uses the Sphinx, made out of stone, to remind us of the cold and hardened atmosphere.

C. He uses the simile to show irony in the situation.

D. He describes the smile of the Sphinx to show that there is laughter in nature.

The author is using figurative language here to convey an idea. Notice that he is using a simile to draw a comparison between two very different things: a land's laughter and a Sphinx's smile. (In fact, each of these two things is a figure of speech in itself, not to be read literally.) The fact that the Sphinx is made of stone and that the narrator describes the scene as cold and lonely both indicate that the smile of the Sphinx is one without warmth, further emphasizing the bleak environment. There is nothing ironic in the description. The laughter is a figure of speech—a hardened and lifeless form in contrast to a human voice. **The correct answer is B.**

3. Which statement **best** captures the essential idea of the passage?

A. The North is wild beyond compare.

B. In the North, life is short and brutal.

C. In the North, time defeats all life.

D. Winter in the North can be deadly.

This deceptively difficult question essentially asks what the author's main point is in the passage. To answer it, you need to synthesize the passage's ideas and evaluate the passage as a whole. The narrator does refer to the "savage. . . Northland Wild", the futility of life, and the "lifeless" land. However, none of these observations captures the essence of the paragraph. The passage's main thrust is best expressed by the second-to-last sentence: "It was the masterful and incommunicable wisdom of eternity laughing at the futility of life and the effort of life" (lines 7–8). In other words, the passing of time ultimately defeats all life in the North. **The correct answer is C.**

The next paragraph follows the paragraph from London's *White Fang* in the previous passage. On the GED Reasoning Through Language Arts Test, the two paragraphs would be shown as one passage. Together, they are about half the length of an average passage on the test. Observe the contrast between the two paragraphs.

Questions 4–6 refer to the following passage.

In advance of the dogs, on wide snowshoes, toiled a man. At the rear of the sled toiled a second man. On the sled, in the box, lay a third man whose toil was over—a man whom the Wild had conquered and beaten down until he would never move nor struggle again. It is not the way of the Wild to like movement. Life is an offence to it, for life is movement; and the Wild aims always to destroy movement. It freezes the water to prevent it running to the sea; it drives the sap out of the trees till they are frozen to their mighty hearts; and most ferociously and terribly of all does the Wild harry and crush into submission man—man who is the most restless of life, ever in revolt against the dictum that all movement must in the end come to the cessation of movement.

—from *White Fang*, by Jack London

4. How does this paragraph extend the ideas of the first paragraph?

A. It adds humans to the setting.

B. It contrasts the dogs with the humans.

C. It contradicts the first paragraph in showing that life can exist in this environment.

D. It fills in details by describing what the men were carrying.

The main point of this paragraph is as a continuation of the story. The paragraph drops men and their dogs into the harsh environment described in the prior paragraph, which serves as a backdrop. The dogs and the men are part of the description; they are not compared. There is no contradiction described here, although the text says that life (the dogs and men) is defiant, trying to overcome the brutality of the land. The description of what the men were carrying is a detail about the men. **The correct answer is A.**

5. Which of the following statements correctly describes how the second paragraph advances the theme of the story thus far?

A. The brutal cold affects both the men and the dogs.

B. Men may try to conquer nature but don't always win.

C. Human ingenuity helps the men survive the cold and harsh environment.

D. In an environment of man against nature, the supplies will be very important to the men's survival.

This paragraph introduces the human element to the harsh environment and describes men who are trying to defy nature by surviving in the inhospitable Wild. The theme of man vs. nature starts to develop as the narrator describes not just how the cold affects the men and the dogs (choice A), but their attempt to live and overcome the obstacles (choices C and D). We see a hint of nature winning with the long and narrow oblong box—probably a coffin carrying someone who didn't survive. **The correct answer is B.**

6. Which figurative device is used throughout the paragraph?
   A. Irony
   B. Personification
   C. Simile
   D. Metaphor

Irony (choice A) is when a discrepancy occurs between what is expected and what actually happens; this is not shown in this passage. Similes and metaphors (choices C and D) are both ways of comparing unlike things in a descriptive way, with the former using *like* or *as* and the later making a direct comparison. Throughout the passage *Wild* is capitalized and personified (i.e., has human qualities attributed to it). A good example of the personification is saying that it "aims always to destroy movement." **The correct answer is B.**

Questions 7–11 refer to the following passage.

If ever a girl of the working class had led the sheltered life, it was Genevieve. In the midst of roughness and brutality, Genevieve had shunned all that was rough and brutal. She saw but what she chose to see, and she chose always to see the best, avoiding coarseness and uncouthness without effort, as a matter of instinct. To begin with, she had been peculiarly unexposed. An only child, with an invalid mother upon whom she attended, she had not joined in the street games and frolics of the children of the neighborhood. Her father, a mild-tempered, narrow-chested, anaemic little clerk, domestic because of his inherent disability to mix with men, had done his full share toward giving the home an atmosphere of sweetness and tenderness.

An orphan at twelve, Genevieve had gone straight from her father's funeral to live with the Silversteins in their rooms above the candy store; and here, sheltered by kindly aliens, she earned her keep and clothes by waiting on the shop. Being Gentile, she was especially necessary to the Silversteins, who would not run the business themselves when the day of their Sabbath came round.

And here, in the uneventful little shop, six maturing years had slipped by. Her acquaintances were few. She had elected to have no girl chum for the reason that no satisfactory girl had appeared. Nor did she choose to walk with the young fellows of the neighbourhood, as was the custom of girls from their fifteenth year. "That stuck-up doll-face," was the way the girls of the neighbourhood described her; and though she earned their enmity by her beauty and aloofness, she none the less commanded their respect. "Peaches and cream," she was called by the young men—though softly and amongst themselves, for they were afraid of arousing the ire of the other girls, while they stood in awe of Genevieve, in a dimly religious way, as a something mysteriously beautiful and unapproachable.

—from *The Game*, by Jack London

7. Which of the following does NOT account for Genevieve's character?

A. The fact she was an only child

B. The neighborhood children

C. Her mother's invalidity

D. Her father's domestic nature

All choices except for choice B list factors that influenced Genevieve's character. The children in the neighborhood did not influence her because she had little contact with them. **The correct answer is B.**

8. Which word **best** describes Genevieve?

A. Anemic

B. Predictable

C. Timid

D. Naive

Genevieve had clearly lived a sheltered life ("she had been peculiarly unexposed"). She intentionally avoided exposure to anything "rough and brutal" and to the "coarseness and uncouthness" of the real world. She preferred to keep to herself rather than joining in street games with other children. As a result, she was probably a bit innocent in the ways of the world, or *naive*. **The correct answer is D.**

9. Which job would Genevieve's father probably be **most** suited for?

A. School teacher

B. Business manager

C. Car salesman

D. Gentleman's butler

The father is described as "domestic because of his inherent disability to mix with men." What this probably means is that he lacked an ability to get along in the working world, where he would have to compete and deal with other men. Because he was accustomed to the domestic life, and in fact had provided a very nice home atmosphere, he would probably make an excellent gentleman's butler. **The correct answer is D.**

10. What words in the passage could you use as clues to determine the meaning of the word *enmity* (line 19)?

A. Because she had no friends, Genevieve made enemies of her peers.

B. Genevieve didn't find the other girls suitable as friends, and they thought she was stuck-up.

C. The girls were jealous because Genevieve was beautiful.

D. Genevieve chose always to see the best.

The passage states that Genevieve had no friends by her own choice. This made her peers brand her as "stuck-up." The narrator describes her beauty, which the other girls resented. These factors show that the feelings between Genevieve and the other girls were mutual, as they were all full of ill will, which is the meaning of *enmity.* Choice D indicates Genevieve's feelings; choice C describes the girls' feelings toward Genevieve. Choice A suggests an incorrect definition of *enmity* (making enemies). Only choice B shows the mutual dislike that defines the word. **The correct answer is B.**

11. What does Genevieve's rejection of brutality in the world imply about her nature?

A. That she is capable of ignoring what she doesn't like

B. That as a child she was brutalized by other children, causing her to be fearful

C. That she sees the world as a brutal place and became hardened to that reality

D. That her natural beauty can overcome brutality

Genevieve is shown to have had a hard life, especially compared to the other girls she sees during her regular days. But the narrator also describes her as someone who sees only what she chooses and is therefore unaware of the harsh realities that she doesn't want to see. She was not brutalized by other children (choice B), but instead by circumstances, although she opts not to see them and thus has not been hardened (choice C). Although she is described as beautiful, there is no indication that her beauty is a means of overcoming brutality (choice D). **The correct answer is A.**

Unlike either of the previous passages, the next passage consists mainly of dialogue. (Its word length would be on the shorter side of a GED Reasoning Through Language Arts Test reading passage, although it might appear longer due to its many paragraph breaks.) As you read the passage, ask yourself who the narrator is and how the three characters are related to one another. Also pay close attention to what their behavior suggests about each of them individually and about their relationship with one another. To follow the events as they unfold in the passage, try to visualize the scene. As is typical of the test's prose-fiction passages, the passage's concluding sentences leave you asking questions that are likely to be the focus of at least one or two test questions.

Questions 12–17 refer to the following passage.

On the 24th of May, 1863, my uncle, Professor Liedenbrock, rushed into his little house, No. 19 Konigstrasse, one of the oldest streets in the oldest portion of the city of Hamburg. Martha must have concluded that she was very much behindhand, for the dinner had only just been put into the oven.

"Well, now," said I to myself, "if that most impatient of men is hungry, what a disturbance he will make!"

"Mr. Liedenbrock so soon!" cried poor Martha in great alarm, half opening the dining-room door.

"Yes, Martha; but very likely the dinner is not half cooked, for it is not two yet. Saint Michael's clock has only just struck half-past one."

"Then why has the master come home so soon?"

"Perhaps he will tell us that himself."

"Here he is, Monsieur Axel; I will run and hide myself while you argue with him."

And Martha retreated in safety into her own dominions. I was left alone. But how was it possible for a man of my undecided turn of mind to argue successfully with so irascible a person as the Professor? With this persuasion I was hurrying away to my own little retreat upstairs, when the street door creaked upon its hinges; heavy feet made the whole flight of stairs to shake; and the master of the house, passing rapidly through the dining room, threw himself in haste into his own sanctum.

But on his rapid way he had found time to fling his hazel stick into a corner, his rough broadbrim upon the table, and these few emphatic words at his nephew: "Axel, follow me!"

I had scarcely had time to move when the Professor was again shouting after me: "What! not come yet?" And I rushed into my redoubtable master's study.

Otto Liedenbrock had no mischief in him, I willingly allow that; but unless he very considerably changes as he grows older, at the end he will be a most original character.

—from *Journey to the Center of the Earth*, by Jules Verne

12. The events are described from the point of view of

A. Martha.

B. Monsieur Axel.

C. an outside observer.

D. Otto Liedenbrock.

The narration is in first person—from the point of view of Monsieur Axel, who is Professor Liedenbrock's nephew. The narrator's identity is not clear until Martha says "Here he is, Monsieur Axel; I will run and hide myself while you argue with him," after which the narrator comments, "I was left alone." **The correct answer is B.**

13. Which description **best** characterizes the Professor, as he is revealed in the passage?

A. Absent-minded

B. Mischievous

C. Decisive

D. Demanding

In the passage, the narrator (Axel) uses the words *impatient* (line 5) and *irascible* (line 15) to describe Professor Liedenbrock. (The word *irascible* means "disagreeable.") However, none of the four answer choices matches these two descriptive words. To answer the question, you must infer some other trait from the Professor's behavior, as seen through Axel's eyes. Notice that Martha is worried that she might be in trouble with the Professor because dinner was late. Notice also that the Professor shouts to his nephew, "Axel, follow me!" These portions of the narrative both strongly suggest that the Professor is a *demanding* person. **The correct answer is D.**

14. What does the passage suggest about Martha?

A. She is often late cooking dinner.

B. She looks to Axel for support.

C. She is afraid of losing her job.

D. She is Otto Liedenbrock's niece.

When dinner is not ready for the Professor, Martha asks Axel to intercept the Professor while she hides in her quarters. Based on this narrative, we can infer that Martha looks to Axel to help her out in difficult situations. **The correct answer is B.**

15. The narrator remarks that unless Otto Liedenbrock changes as he grows older, "at the end he will be a most original character" (lines 24–25).

The narrator's point about Otto Liedenbrock is that as he grows older,

A. he will be known for his originality.

B. his students will no longer enjoy his teaching methods.

C. people will find him very difficult to be around.

D. he will begin imagining things due to old age.

Otto Liedenbrock's demeanor throughout the passage is hurried and impatient. The narrator acknowledges that while the professor "had no mischief in him" (i.e., his behavior was not meant to intentionally be annoying or cause harm or damage), it certainly instills alarm and upheaval in those around him. It can be inferred from the narrator's statement that, as Liedenbrock grows older, this behavior will only get worse unless he changes. Hence, he will become a "most original character" rather than a relatable person. **The correct answer is C.**

16. Based on his behavior, what can you conclude about why the Professor has come home early?

A. He is very hungry and wants to have his dinner right away.

B. He is angry at his nephew and wants to berate him immediately.

C. He isn't feeling well and needs to lie down and rest before dinner.

D. He has important news and wants to share it with Axel immediately.

We can see that the Professor is impatient and moves quickly, scattering his belongings about the house, illustrating that he is distracted. He doesn't demand food, so he has not come home early to eat (choice A). The Professor moves about with purpose. Though he appears to be in a rush, there is no indication that he is angry at anyone (choice B). He heads for his *own sanctum*—his study—so he has not come home to rest (choice C). He is in a hurry to speak to his nephew, since he impatiently calls him into his office. While we don't know the reason he is in such a hurry to speak to Axel, we can infer that it is so important that he has come home early, something he does not usually do. **The correct answer is D.**

17. Which of the following events is **most likely** to occur next?

A. The Professor will realize that dinner is not ready and will become angry.

B. The Professor will have a serious conversation with Axel.

C. Martha will apologize to the Professor for the half-cooked dinner.

D. Axel will sit down to eat with Martha but without the Professor.

Martha, who is probably the Professor's live-in cook, has hidden herself in her quarters. Meanwhile, the Professor has called his nephew Axel into his study. Since the Professor is nowhere near the dining area, he is not likely to suddenly realize that dinner is not ready (choice A). Nothing in the passage indicates that Martha will be rushing to the Professor's study with an apology (choice C). Martha is most likely the hired help and probably won't be eating with the Professor's family (choice D). Only choice B provides a plausible continuation of the story. **The correct answer is B.**

GENERAL TEST-TAKING STRATEGIES

Here are some general strategies for tackling the reading comprehension portion of the test. These points of advice generally apply to all types of passages and questions. Put these strategies to work on the practice tests in this book, and then review them again just before exam day.

Read the questions based on a passage before you read the passage itself.

Each reading comprehension passage will be followed by 6 to 8 questions that refer to it. Before you read the passage, read the question stems (the questions themselves, but not the answer choices). This task should only take you 20 seconds or so. Some of the questions will provide clues as to what you should look for and think about as you read.

Read each passage straight through before answering any questions based on it.

Read the passage from beginning to end. Focus mainly on the flow of ideas from one to another. Maintaining this mindset will help you understand the passage's main ideas, as well as the author's overall concern and purpose in mentioning various details—all of which in turn will help you answer the questions.

Don't get bogged down in details as you read a passage.

Some of the reading passages will be loaded with details: examples, descriptions, dates, and so forth. If you try to absorb all of the details as you read, you'll not only lose sight of the ideas behind the details, you'll also lose reading speed. Don't get bogged down in the details, especially those you don't fully understand. Instead, gloss over them. Note where examples, lists, and other details are located. Then, if you're asked a question involving those details, you can quickly and easily locate them and read them more carefully.

Sum up a passage after you read it.

After reading an entire passage, take a few seconds to recap it. If the passage is nonfiction, ask yourself what the author's main point and major supporting points are. If the passage is from a fictional story, recap events in your mind. Remind yourself about the flow of the discussion or events, without thinking about all the details. Seeing the "big picture" may be enough to answer as many as half the questions.

If possible, formulate your own answer to a question before reading the answer choices.

For each question, try to formulate your own response to it, and *then* scan the choices for something resembling your home-grown answer. This technique will keep you from becoming confused and distracted by incorrect answer choices.

To answer a question that quotes the passage, expect to "read around" the quoted text.

A particular question might quote a word, line, or entire sentence from the passage. If so, be sure you understand the *context* of the quote before answering the question. Re-read the sentences preceding and following the quote. Chances are, you'll need to understand what precedes and follows the quote to recognize the best answer choice.

To avoid skipping around the passage, answer the questions in sequence.

The sequence of questions generally corresponds to where the passage addresses each one. For example, a question about the first paragraph will probably appear earlier than a question about the second paragraph. Answering the questions in sequence helps you "go with the flow" of ideas as the passage presents them. So avoid "shopping around" for easy questions, unless you're running out of time. Keep in mind, however, that some questions *might* appear out of sequence and that questions involving the entire passage can appear anywhere in the sequence.

Pace yourself properly.

Your time limit for answering all 49 questions in the entire GED Reasoning Through Language Arts Test is 150 minutes. Try to answer 10 questions about every 30 minutes, on average. If you're falling behind, try to pick up your pace. In any event, try to answer all questions with a few minutes to spare, so you can go back and reconsider any responses you were unsure about.

SUMMING IT UP

- In the GED Reasoning Through Language Arts Test, the reading comprehension questions gauge your ability to understand, interpret, evaluate, synthesize, and apply information contained in fiction as well as nonfiction texts. This portion of the test consists of several reading passages, each one followed by several multiple-choice questions.
- Reading comprehension passages are drawn from a wide variety of sources, including fiction; informational nonfiction that includes topics of interest related to science; social studies; and workplace and community documents.
- The broad reading skill areas tested in the reading comprehension portion of the test include comprehension, analysis and interpretation, evaluation and synthesis, and application.
- The entire GED Reasoning Through Language Arts Test lasts 150 minutes. You should expect six to eight passages with a total of 45–50 questions. Each passage of prose will be 400 to 900 words in length (about one to two pages).

PRACTICE QUESTIONS

Directions: The following reading comprehension questions will help you practice the concepts presented in this chapter. After you read a passage, answer the questions that follow it, referring back to the passage as needed. Answer all questions based on what is stated and implied in the passage. Most questions are in multiple-choice format. Others are meant to prepare you for the electronically formatted questions that you will find on the test, such as drop-down, fill-in-the-blanks, and drag-and-drops.

Questions 1–6 refer to the following passage.

A Fable by Mark Twain

Once upon a time an artist who had painted a small and very beautiful picture placed it so that he could see it in the mirror. He said, "This doubles the distance and softens it, and it is twice as lovely as it was before."

The animals out in the woods heard of this through the housecat, who was greatly admired by them because he was so learned, and so refined and civilized, and so polite and high-bred, and could tell them so much which they didn't know before, and were not certain about afterward. They were much excited about this new piece of gossip, and they asked questions, so as to get at a full understanding of it. They asked what a picture was, and the cat explained.

"It is a flat thing," he said; "wonderfully flat, marvelously flat, enchantingly flat and elegant. And, oh, so beautiful!"

That excited them almost to a frenzy, and they said they would give the world to see it. Then the bear asked:

"What is it that makes it so beautiful?"

"It is the looks of it," said the cat.

This filled them with admiration and uncertainty, and they were more excited than ever. Then the cow asked:

"What is a mirror?"

"It is a hole in the wall," said the cat. "You look in it, and there you see the picture, and it is so dainty and charming and ethereal and inspiring in its unimaginable beauty that your head turns round and round, and you almost swoon with ecstasy."

The ass had not said anything as yet; he now began to throw doubts. He said there had never been anything as beautiful as this before, and probably wasn't now. He said that when it took a whole basketful of sesquipedalian adjectives to whoop up a thing of beauty, it was time for suspicion.

It was easy to see that these doubts were having an effect upon the animals, so the cat went off offended. The subject was dropped for a couple of days, but in the meantime curiosity was taking a fresh start, and there was a revival of interest perceptible. Then the animals assailed the ass for spoiling what could possibly have been a pleasure to them, on a mere suspicion that the picture was not beautiful, without any evidence that such was the case. The ass was not troubled; he was calm, and said there was one way to find out who was in the right, himself or the cat: he would go and look in that hole, and come back and tell what he found there. The animals felt relieved and grateful, and asked him to go at once—which he did.

But he did not know where he ought to stand; and so, through error, he stood between the picture and the mirror. The result was that the picture had no chance, and didn't show up. He returned home and said:

"The cat lied. There was nothing in that hole but an ass. There wasn't a sign of a flat thing visible. It was a handsome ass, and friendly, but just an ass, and nothing more."

The elephant asked:

"Did you see it good and clear? Were you close to it?"

"I saw it good and clear, O Hathi, King of Beasts. I was so close that I touched noses with it."

"This is very strange," said the elephant; "the cat was always truthful before—as far as we could make out. Let another witness try. Go, Baloo, look in the hole, and come and report."

So the bear went. When he came back, he said:

"Both the cat and the ass have lied; there was nothing in the hole but a bear."

Great was the surprise and puzzlement of the animals. Each was now anxious to make the test himself and get at the straight truth. The elephant sent them one at a time.

First, the cow. She found nothing in the hole but a cow.

The tiger found nothing in it but a tiger.

The lion found nothing in it but a lion.

The leopard found nothing in it but a leopard.

The camel found a camel, and nothing more.

Then Hathi was wroth, and said he would have the truth, if he had to go and fetch it himself. When he returned, he abused his whole subjectry for liars, and was in an unappeasable fury with the moral and mental blindness of the cat. He said that anybody but a near-sighted fool could see that there was nothing in the hole but an elephant.

MORAL, BY THE CAT

You can find in a text whatever you bring, if you will stand between it and the mirror of your imagination. You may not see your ears, but they will be there.

1. What is the main purpose of the passage?

A. To prove that every worthwhile story has a moral lesson

B. To amuse the reader with an absurd story of talking animals

C. To teach the reader a lesson about experiencing art

D. To imply that animals live complex lives when humans are not around

2. The cat's thoughts about the other animals reveal that

A. the cat was irritated by the animals' failure to understand him.

B. the cat had lied about the beautiful images in the mirror.

C. the cat was vain for thinking the image in the mirror was so beautiful.

D. the cat wished he had never said anything about the mirror to the animals.

3. For which activity would this fable be **most** useful?

A. Explaining why vanity leads to ruin

B. Illustrating how storytelling has evolved

C. Describing how different animals look to young children

D. Teaching the interpretation of literature to students

4. The cat's primary motivation for telling the other animals about the mirror is
- **A.** to make them look foolish by revealing their ignorance.
- **B.** to share something beautiful with them.
- **C.** to prove his superiority by telling them something they know nothing about.
- **D.** to instigate an argument among the animals.

5. Based on the passage, which word **best** describes Hathi's personality?
- **A.** Kindly
- **B.** Brilliant
- **C.** Hateful
- **D.** Fearsome

6. Which of the following lines from the passage reveals the animals' curiosity?
- **A.** "The subject was dropped for a couple of days, but in the meantime curiosity was taking a fresh start, and there was a revival of interest perceptible."
- **B.** "They were much excited about this new piece of gossip, and they asked questions, so as to get at a full understanding of it."
- **C.** "The ass had not said anything as yet; he now began to throw doubts."
- **D.** "Then Hathi was wroth, and said he would have the truth, if he had to go and fetch it himself."

Questions 7–12 refer to the following passage.

Excerpt from *Principles of Public Health* by Thos. D. Tuttle

These bodies of ours are built somewhat like automobiles. An automobile is made up of a framework, wheels, body, gasoline tank, engine, and steering-gear. The human body has much the same form of construction. We have a frame, which is made of the bones of the body. We have arms and legs, which correspond to the wheels of the automobile. We have many little pockets in our bodies in which fat is stored, and these little pockets answer to the gasoline tank of the automobile. We have an engine, which, like the automobile engine, is made up of many parts; and we have a head or brain, that plays the same part as the steering-gear of the automobile.

The automobile has a tank in which is carried the gasoline necessary to develop power for the machine. If the gasoline gives out, the engine will not run, and before the owner starts on a trip, he is always careful to see that the tank is well filled. In the same way, if we do not provide new fat for the pockets in our bodies in which the fat is stored, our supply will soon give out and our bodies will refuse to work, just as the engine of the automobile will refuse to work when the gasoline is used up.

What cells are like

The automobile is made of iron and wood and rubber, and each bit of iron and wood and rubber is made up of tiny particles. The body is made of bones and muscles, covered with skin, and all these are made up of very fine particles that we call cells. Every part of the body is made of these fine cells. The cells are so small that they can be seen only with a powerful microscope. If you look at your hand you cannot see a cell, because it takes a great many cells to make a spot large enough for you to see…

You can scratch some of the paint from your automobile and the machine will work just as well as ever. Apparently no harm has been done, but an opening has been made through which moisture and germs can enter and cause the wood to rot and the iron to rust. You can remove certain parts of the automobile and still the machine will do its work; but you cannot take away too much of any one part without weakening the automobile, and if certain parts are missing (such as the sparker, the battery, or the steering-gear), the usefulness of the machine is destroyed. So it is with the body. You can scratch off some of the skin and not do any apparent harm, but you have made an opening through which germs may get into the body. You can remove certain parts of the body, such as the arm or leg, and still the body will do efficient service. But there are certain parts of the body that are necessary to life, just as certain parts of the automobile are necessary to the usefulness of the machine. You cannot remove the heart and live; you cannot remove the brain and live.

How cells are killed

You are probably thinking that it must be easy to kill such a little thing as a cell; and so it is. Cells can be killed by too much heat or too much cold. When you skin your hand, you kill many cells, and at the same time make an opening for germs to get in and cause sickness. You can kill cells also by starving them, for they must have not only enough food, but the right kind of food. If you feed your bodies on nothing but candy, pie, and cake, most of the cells will refuse to perform their work and many of them will die. These cells must have also an abundance of air, and the air must be pure and fresh. If you breathe the air that others have breathed or that contains poison of any kind, you will soon find that you are not feeling well. This simply means that so many of the cells are being starved for fresh air, that not enough strong ones are left to do the necessary work. You can kill these cells by overwork, for they must have a proper amount of rest. If you go to school all day long and then sit up until midnight every night, you must not expect the cells of your body to keep strong and well.

7. In the context of the passage, the **best** synonym for *power* in the second paragraph is

A. energy.

B. authority.

C. control.

D. supremacy.

8. Which of the following is NOT discussed in the passage?

A. How cells can be damaged

B. How new cells form

C. Where cells are in the body

D. How to view cells

9. The author discusses automobiles in the passage mainly to

A. show how every part of an automobile is similar to a part of the human body.

B. illustrate how cells function in the human body.

C. prove that neither an automobile nor a human body can function without fuel.

D. make a comparison that may make the main topic easier to understand.

10. Which of the following quotes from the passage **best** illustrates the author's main point about cells ? Choose your answer from the drop-down menu.

Select ▼

A. "You are probably thinking that it must be easy to kill such a little thing as a cell; and so it is."

B. "Every part of the body is made of these fine cells."

C. "If you look at your hand you cannot see a cell, because it takes a great many cells to make a spot large enough for you to see."

D. "You cannot remove the heart and live; you cannot remove the brain and live."

11. When the author says, "If you go to school all day long and then sit up until midnight every night, you must not expect the cells of your body to keep strong and well," he means that

A. too much education can be a bad thing.

B. it is more important to exercise than to learn.

C. sitting is not the best way to rest.

D. the human body needs to take breaks.

12. Which person would **most likely** be required to read this passage?

A. A surgeon

B. A person with a terminal disease

C. An auto mechanic

D. A new biology student

Questions 13–19 refer to the following passages.

Presidential Addresses

The following passages are addresses presented by US presidents at different, yet crucial periods in American history.

Passage 1—Excerpt from *America and the World War* by Theodore Roosevelt

Peace is worthless unless it serves the cause of righteousness. Peace which consecrates militarism is of small service. Peace obtained by crushing the liberty and life of just and unoffending peoples is as cruel as the most cruel war. It should ever be our honorable effort to serve one of the world's most vital needs by doing all in our power to bring about conditions which will give some effective protection to weak or small nations which themselves keep order and act with justice toward the rest of mankind. There can be no higher international duty than to safeguard the existence and independence of industrious, orderly states, with a high personal and national standard of conduct, but without the military force of the great powers; states, for instance, such as Belgium, Holland, Switzerland, the Scandinavian countries, Uruguay, and others. A peace which left Belgium's wrongs unredressed and which did not provide against the recurrence of such wrongs as those from which she has suffered would not be a real peace.

As regards the actions of most of the combatants in the hideous world-wide war now raging it is possible sincerely to take and defend either of the opposite views concerning their actions. The causes of any such great and terrible contest almost always lie far back in the past, and the seeming immediate cause is usually itself in major part merely an effect of many preceding causes. The assassination of the heir to the Austro-Hungarian throne was partly or largely due to the existence of political and often murderous secret societies in Servia which the Servian government did not suppress; and it did not suppress them because the "bondage" of the men and women of the Servian race in Bosnia and Herzegovina to Austria was such a source of ever-present irritation to the Servians that their own government was powerless to restrain them. Strong arguments can be advanced on both the Austrian and the Servian sides as regards this initial cause of the present world-wide war.

Passage 2—Excerpt from *Address Before a Joint Session of the Congress* (February 24, 2009) by Barack Obama

I know that for many Americans watching right now, the state of our economy is a concern that rises above all others, and rightly so. If you haven't been personally affected by this recession, you probably know someone who has: a friend, a neighbor, a member of your family. You don't need to hear another list of statistics to know that our economy is in crisis, because you live it every day. It's the worry you wake up with and the source of sleepless nights. It's the job you thought you'd retire from but now have lost, the business you built your dreams upon that's now hanging by a thread, the college acceptance letter your child had to put back in the envelope. The impact of this recession is real, and it is everywhere.

But while our economy may be weakened and our confidence shaken, though we are living through difficult and uncertain times, tonight I want every American to know this: We will rebuild, we will recover, and the United States of America will emerge stronger than before.

The weight of this crisis will not determine the destiny of this Nation. The answers to our problems don't lie beyond our reach. They exist in our laboratories and our universities, in our fields and our factories, in the imaginations of our entrepreneurs and the pride of the hardest working people on Earth. Those qualities that have made America the greatest force of progress and prosperity in human history, we still possess in ample measure. What is required now is for this country to pull together, confront boldly the challenges we face, and take responsibility for our future once more.

Now, if we're honest with ourselves, we'll admit that for too long, we have not always met these responsibilities as a Government or as a people. I say this not to lay blame or to look backwards, but because it is only by understanding how we arrived at this moment that we'll be able to lift ourselves out of this predicament.

The fact is, our economy did not fall into decline overnight, nor did all of our problems begin when the housing market collapsed or the stock market sank. We have known for decades that our survival depends on finding new sources of energy, yet we import more oil today than ever before. The cost of health care eats up more and more of our savings each year, yet we keep delaying reform. Our children will compete for jobs in a global economy that too many of our schools do not prepare them for. And though all these challenges went unsolved, we still managed to spend more money and pile up more debt, both as individuals and through our Government, than ever before.

13. According to the first passage, under what circumstances was the assassination of the heir to the Austro-Hungarian throne made possible?

A. The safeguarding of industrious, orderly states
B. The attempt to maintain peace by crushing liberty
C. The thriving of dangerous secret societies in Servia
D. The releasing of men and women in Servia from bondage

14. In the context of the second paragraph of the first passage, what is the definition of the word *great*?

A. Wonderful
B. Countless
C. Major
D. Noble

15. Which of the following is NOT a country President Roosevelt describes as industrious but lacking military force?

A. Austria
B. Belgium
C. Uruguay
D. Switzerland

16. Which situation is **most** similar to the one President Obama describes in the second passage?

A. A married couple who have completely depleted their savings
B. A factory that has to lay off all of its employees
C. A business that is renovating its office with new equipment
D. An entrepreneur who plans to revive her faltering business

17. Which of the following is a likely reason Obama lists mistakes the country has made in the final paragraph?

A. To prove that the economic crisis could have been avoided
B. To explain which problems need to be corrected
C. To identify the institutions that should be blamed for the recession
D. To warn Americans that they should be anxious about the economy

18. What is Obama's point of view in the second passage?

A. Fear over the state of the economy
B. Concern that Americans do not care about the economy
C. Hopefulness about the future of America
D. Arrogance about America's ability to recover from a recession

19. Drag the characteristics that fit the description of President Roosevelt or President Obama to the correct space in the Venn Diagram. If there is a common characteristic, drag it into the center of the diagram. (Enter the answers in the diagram.)

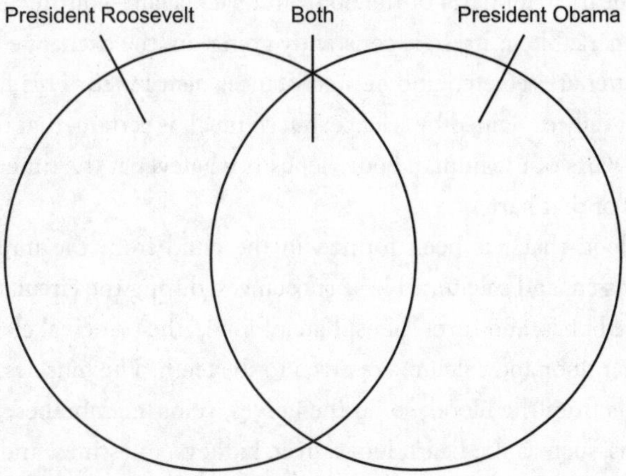

A. Concerned about protecting other countries

B. Focused on homeland issues only

C. Interested in pointing out the causes of political problems

D. Intent on maintaining peace amidst violent conflict

Questions 20–25 refer to the following passage.

Excerpted from *Popular Books on Natural Science*, by Aaron Bernstein

One would be well justified in calling the blood "man's body in a liquid state." For the blood is destined to become the living solid body of man.

People were astonished, when Liebig, the great naturalist, called blood the "liquid flesh"; we are correct even in going further and calling the blood "man's body in a liquid state." From blood are prepared not only muscles and flesh, but also bones, brain, fat, teeth, eyes, veins, cartilages, nerves, tendons, and even hair.

It is utterly wrong for anybody to suppose that the constituents of all these parts are dissolved in the blood, say as sugar is dissolved in water. By no means. Water is something quite different from the sugar dissolved in it, while the blood is itself the material from which all the solid parts of the body are formed.

The blood is received into the heart, and the heart, like a pump, forces it into the lungs. There it absorbs in a remarkable manner the oxygen of the air, which comes into the lungs by breathing. This blood, saturated now with oxygen, is then recalled to another part of the heart by an expansive movement of that organ.

This part of the heart contracts again and impels the oxygenated blood into the whole body by means of arteries, which branch out more and more, and become smaller and smaller, until at last they are no longer visible to the naked eye. In this manner the blood penetrates all parts of the body and returns to the heart by means of similar thread-like veins, which gradually join and form larger veins. Having reached the heart, it is again forced into the lungs, and absorbs there more oxygen, returns to the heart, and is again circulated through the whole system.

During this double circulation of the blood from the heart to the lungs and back, and then from the heart to all parts of the body and back again—during all this, the change of particles, so remarkable in itself, is constantly going on: the exchange by which the useless and wasted matter are secreted and new substances distributed. This fact is wonderful, and its cause not yet fully explained by science; but so much is certain, that the blood when being conveyed to all parts of the human body, deposits whatever at the time may be needed there for the renewal of that part.

Thus the blood that has been formed in the child from the mother's milk, contains phosphorus, oxygen, and calcium. These substances, during the circulation of the blood, are deposited in the bones, and form "phosphate of lime," the principal element in the bone. In the same manner fluor and calcium are given to the teeth. The muscles, or flesh, also receive their ingredients from the blood; so do the nerves, veins, membranes, brain, and nails; also the inner organs, such as the heart, lungs, liver, kidneys, intestines, and stomach.

They all, however, in return give to the blood their waste particles, which it carries to that part of the human body where they may be secreted.

If any member of the body is so bound, that the blood cannot circulate, it must decay; for the life of the body consists in its constant change and transformation, in the continual exchange of fresh substances for waste ones. But this vital exchange is only kept up by the constant circulation of the blood, which, while it decreases by being transformed into vital parts of the body, is always formed anew by our daily food.

Food is therefore very justly called "Means of Existence," and the blood may rightly be called the "Juice of Life."

20. What is the main purpose of this passage?

A. To explain how blood travels through and serves the body

B. To define the phrase "man's body in a liquid state"

C. To list which parts of the body are prepared from blood

D. To describe how blood interacts with the heart

21. Drag and drop the details about blood into the chart to show the order in which they occur in the passage. (Enter the letters that correspond to each idea in the box.)

1	2	3	4

A. Blood enters the arteries.

B. The heart expands to move blood.

C. Blood absorbs oxygen.

D. Blood travels to all the body parts.

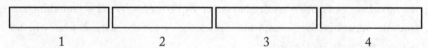

22. What are bones mainly composed of?

A. Phosphate of lime

B. Fluor

C. Calcium

D. Blood

23. The author's main argument in the third paragraph is that

A. water dissolves in sugar and body parts dissolve in blood.

B. most people believe that human body parts are basically dissolved in blood.

C. blood and body parts have a different relationship than water has with sugar.

D. blood and water are completely different liquids that do not share any properties.

24. When the author says that blood is "the juice of life," he means that blood

A. is rich in vitamins.

B. is a liquid that sustains the body.

C. travels through the heart.

D. is formed by food.

25. What is **least likely** to happen if blood permanently fails to circulate to someone's leg?

A. The leg will decay.

B. The leg will fail to receive oxygen.

C. The leg will receive oxygen by other means.

D. The leg will retain waste.

ANSWER KEY AND EXPLANATIONS

1. C	**6.** B	**11.** D	**16.** D	**21.** C,B,A,D
2. A	**7.** A	**12.** D	**17.** B	**22.** A
3. D	**8.** B	**13.** C	**18.** C	**23.** C
4. B	**9.** D	**14.** C	**19.** See explanation	**24.** B
5. D	**10.** A	**15.** A	**20.** A	**25.** C

1. **The correct answer is C.** The moral at the end of the story makes its purpose explicit: to teach the reader a lesson about experiencing art. While this passage does have a moral lesson, the purpose of the passage as a whole is more specific than proving anything about stories with morals in general, so choice A is not the best answer. This story is intended to be amusing, and the idea of talking animals may strike some readers as absurd, but the moral at the end of the passage suggests a different purpose from the one in choice B. Choice D implies that this fable is not meant to be taken literally, which is not the author's intention.

2. **The correct answer is A.** The statement that the cat was offended by how the other animals doubted him supports the conclusion in choice A. Choice B reveals something about the ass's opinion of the cat, not the cat's feelings about the other animals. Choice C is incorrect because the cat saw the painting in the mirror, not himself, and because this answer choice reveals nothing about the cat's ideas about the other animals. Choice D is an extreme conclusion to draw that information in the passage does not support sufficiently.

3. **The correct answer is D.** According to the moral at the end of the passage, the main idea of the passage is that how one interprets a text of any kind depends on perspective, so choice D is the best answer. Choice A is incorrect because the animals who see themselves in the mirror do not believe they have seen anything beautiful, so vanity is hardly a theme in this passage. While fables are hardly modern forms of storytelling, choice B describes a weak use of this passage. Choice C is incorrect because the passage never explains how the animals look.

4. **The correct answer is B.** The cat tells the other animals about the mirror because he sees something beautiful in it and wants to share that experience. Choice A is incorrect because the fact that the mirror ends up revealing the other animals' ignorance was not the cat's intention. Choices C and D similarly misinterpret the cat's benevolent motivations.

5. **The correct answer is D.** Hathi's anger and abuse of his subjects distinguish him as fearsome. His behavior contradicts choice A. While Hathi thinks he is the only one capable of figuring out the truth about the mirror, he fails to, so choice B is not the best answer. Hathi's anger is motivated more by frustration than hate, so choice C is not the best answer.

6. **The correct answer is B.** This line best illustrates the animals' curiosity. Choice A is not as a strong of an answer because it indicates only a "perceptible" level of interest from the animals, which indicates a low level of curiosity. Choice C suggests more about the animals' tendency to doubt than their curiosity. Choice D may suggest the animals' curiosity in a roundabout way, since it shows Hathi wanting to solve the mystery of the mirror, but it is not as clear of an illustration of the animals' curiosity as choice B is.

7. **The correct answer is A.** While each answer choice can be used as a synonym for *power*, only *energy* makes sense in this particular context. *Authority* (choice B), *control* (choice C), and *supremacy* (choice D) would not make as much sense as *energy* if used in place of *power* in the second paragraph.

8. **The correct answer is B.** How new cells form is never discussed in the passage. Choice A is the main topic of the final paragraph. Choice C is discussed in the third paragraph. Choice D is also explained in the third paragraph.

9. **The correct answer is D.** The author mainly discusses automobiles to compare them to human bodies to make that topic easier to understand for the reader. The author only states that "These bodies of ours are built *somewhat* like automobiles," so choice A is not the best answer. Choice B is incorrect because the author uses automobiles to illustrate something about more than just cells. Choice C may be an idea in the passage, but it does not explain the main reason the author compares human bodies to automobiles.

10. **The correct answer is A.** The author spends the most time discussing cells in terms of how easy they are to destroy, so choice A is the best answer. The author does not spend much time dwelling on the facts that cells are in every part of the body (choice B) or that they are small (choice C). Choice D is more about the removal of vital organs than the destruction of cells.

11. **The correct answer is D.** The author states this to illustrate how the human body needs to take breaks from activity. Choice A misinterprets this line. The author is not making a comparison between the value of exercise and the value of education, so choice B is not the best answer. Choice C is not the best answer because the author is not making any kind of assessment of sitting as a form of rest; he is making a broader statement about the body's need for rest.

12. **The correct answer is D.** This passage provides some very basic information about the human body, so it would be most appropriate for a new biology student. Choice A is incorrect because the passage is far too basic for a surgeon, who should have a very advanced understanding of the human body. A person with a terminal disease would not find much useful in this passage, so choice B is not the best answer. The author uses automobiles only to illustrate information about the human body, so auto mechanics are not the author's main audience.

13. **The correct answer is C.** In the first passage, President Roosevelt makes a direct connection between the assassination of the heir to the Austro-Hungarian throne and the thriving of dangerous secret societies in Servia. Choices A and B are not things Roosevelt mentions in connection with the assassination. Roosevelt does not state that the releasing of men and women in Servia from bondage led to the assassination, so choice D is incorrect.

14. **The correct answer is C.** While each answer choice can be used as a synonym for *great*, only *major* makes sense in this particular context. *Wonderful* (choice A), *countless* (choice B), and *noble* (choice D) would not make as much sense as *great* if used in place of *power* in the second paragraph.

15. **The correct answer is A.** Roosevelt does not use Austria as an example of an industrious country that lacks military force. However, he does use Belgium (choice B), Uruguay (choice C), and Switzerland (choice D) as examples of such countries.

16. The correct answer is D. In the passage, President Obama is discussing the United States' economic woes but also is insisting that the country will work to revive itself, which is most similar to an entrepreneur who plans to revive her faltering business. Since President Obama is saying only that the United States is having economic trouble and not that it is completely bankrupt, the situation he describes is not very similar to the one in choice A. Choice B describes a similarly dire situation that is far worse for the factory than the one President Obama describes for the United States. Choice C is not indicative of a business experiencing economic troubles.

17. The correct answer is B. Obama lists the problems after stating that "it is only by understanding how we arrived at this moment that we'll be able to lift ourselves out of this predicament." Since he also says that he is not interested in "looking back," choice A is not the best answer. He also says he does not want to "lay blame," which eliminates choice C. Based on the first paragraph of the speech, it is likely that most Americans are already anxious about the economy, so choice D is not the best answer.

18. The correct answer is C. President Obama states that "We will rebuild, we will recover, and the United States of America will emerge stronger than before" despite the recession, which supports choice C. While Obama says Americans have reason to be concerned, choice A overstates the president's own worries. He also acknowledges that most Americans are already concerned, so choice B is not the best answer. While Obama expresses confidence in America's ability to recover from the recession, he never makes any statements that suggest outright arrogance, so choice D should be eliminated.

19. Choices A and D should be placed in President Roosevelt's section (he is the only one concerned with global issues and maintaining peace amidst war), **choice B** should be placed in President Obama's circle (only he discussed homeland issues in his speech), and **choice C** should be placed in the center (both presidents discuss causes of the problems that are the focuses of their respective speeches).

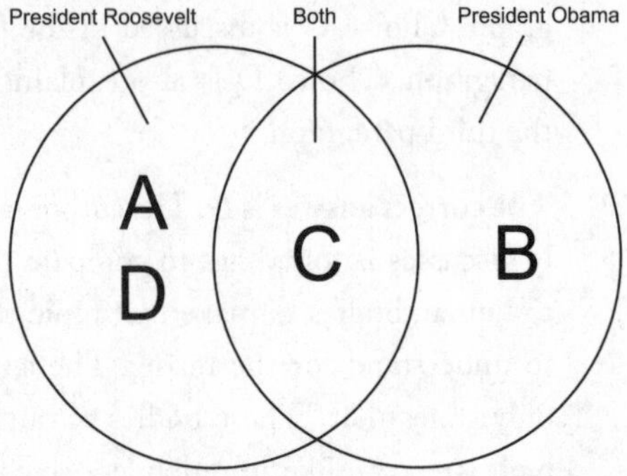

20. The correct answer is A. As a whole, the passage explains how blood travels through and serves the body. Choice B is not the best answer because this phrase is only used as an introduction to the discussion and is not quite a recurring focus of the entire passage. Choice C only describes a purpose of the second paragraph and not the passage as a whole. While a good deal of the passage describes how blood interacts with the heart, choice A does a more thorough job of covering the purpose of the entire passage than choice D does.

21. The correct order is C, B, A, D. The process this sequence describes is illustrated in the third and fourth paragraphs of the passage, which explain that blood first absorbs oxygen in the lungs (choice C) before the heart expands to move the blood into a part of the heart (choice B), and the blood then enters the arteries (choice A), where it is transported to all parts of the body to deliver oxygen (choice D).

22. **The correct answer is A.** This information is found in the seventh paragraph, which states "These substances, during the circulation of the blood, are deposited in the bones, and form 'phosphate of lime,' the principal element in the bone." Fluor (choice B) and calcium (choice C) are elements in teeth. While the passage specifies that all of the body consists of blood, it also specifies that phosphate of lime is "the principal element in the bone," so choice A is a better answer than choice D.

23. **The correct answer is C.** The author is arguing that despite an apparently popular belief, blood and body parts have a different relationship than water has with sugar. Choice A is the opposite of the author's argument. Choice B describes only what the author is arguing against; it does not state his argument. Choice D is too extreme; while the author does make a distinction between blood and water, he does not say that they are completely unlike liquids that share no properties.

24. **The correct answer is B.** The author uses this phrase to illustrate how blood sustains life in the body. While many juices are rich in vitamins, the author never discusses vitamins in the passage, so choice A cannot be correct. Blood does travel through the heart, but this is not directly responsible for the author's description of blood as "the juice of life," so choice C is incorrect. Choice D is similarly true, but it is not a clear explanation for why the author calls blood "the juice of life."

25. **The correct answer is C.** The passage never indicates that there is an alternate way for oxygen to travel through the body if blood fails to circulate. The ninth paragraph explains that stopping the circulation of blood by binding a limb will cause that limb to decay (choice A). Blood delivers oxygen throughout the body, so if blood cannot travel to a particular part of the body such as a leg, it is logical that the leg will not receive oxygen (choice B). Blood also carries away waste, so a leg without circulation will retain waste (choice D).

Mastering Language Conventions

OVERVIEW

- **All About the Reasoning Through Language Arts Test—Language Conventions**
- **Answering Questions**
- **General Test-Taking Strategies**
- **Summing It Up**
- **Practice Questions**
- **Answer Key and Explanations**

Chapter 4

THE REASONING THROUGH LANGUAGE ARTS TEST—LANGUAGE CONVENTIONS IN A NUTSHELL

Time allowed: 150 minutes for the entire Reasoning Through Language Arts Test, which includes 45 minutes for the Extended Response as well as a 10-minute break.

Number of passages: Expect 2 (the number can vary)

Length of each passage: 350–450 words

Total number of questions: 45–50 on the Reasoning Through Language Arts Test, which includes a reading component, language component, and extended response (question types include multiple-choice, select-an-area, drag-and-drop, drop-down, and extended response)

Number of questions per passage: Expect 6 to 8 (the number can vary)

ALL ABOUT THE REASONING THROUGH LANGUAGE ARTS TEST—LANGUAGE CONVENTIONS

The language conventions portion of the GED Reasoning Through Language Arts Test includes technology-enhanced questions such as drag-and-drop, select-an-area, and drop-down items. Drag-and-drop questions will require you to drag the "drag tokens" and place them on one or more correct "drop targets." Select-an-area items will be used so that you may select your answer by clicking or graphing a point on a designated sensor on graphs, maps, or diagrams. Drop-down questions will require you to chose the correct answer from a list of options in a drop-down menu.

Each passage for the language component of the test will be 400–900 words in length. Here is an example of a test-style workplace-related text. This one happens to come with a title, but some may not.

THANK YOU NOTE AFTER AN INTERVIEW

Dear [Select ▼],

I [Select ▼] meeting you to discuss the position as the administrative assistant at Colton & Smith Co. [Select ▼]—I appreciate your consideration for this position. After meeting with you, [Select ▼] My organizational and communication skills [Select ▼]

I look forward to [Select ▼] final decision regarding the position is made. Please feel free to contact me at any time if [Select ▼]. I can be reached at (123) 456-7890 or ksmith@email.com.

Thank you again for your time and consideration,

Sincerely,

Katherine

Regardless of what sort of text you're dealing with, the questions will all cover the same sorts of language convention issues. Below is the breakdown of the broad areas covered by the language component of the Reasoning Through Language Arts Test. Note that the test questions cover only certain topics within each area, as listed here. Don't worry if you are unfamiliar with some of the terms here; this book's grammar review explains many common issues.

- **Grammar and usage:** Subject-verb agreement and pronoun reference/antecedents
- **Sentence structure:** Sentence fragments, fused sentences, and run-ons; parallelism; coordination and subordination; placement of modifiers
- **Writing mechanics:** Spelling (homonyms, contractions, and possessives only); capitalization of proper nouns; use of commas for punctuation, use of apostrophes with possessive nouns, frequently confused words
- **Effective writing:** Informal usage, transitional words, words that support logic and clarity

ANSWERING QUESTIONS

The language conventions questions on the Reasoning Through Language Arts Test are used mainly to test grammar, usage, mechanics, and sentence structure. Within the structure of the passage, questions will focus on specific sentences that need correction using the drop-down menu feature. For example, look at a sentence correction question based on "Thank You Note After an Interview." In this online test, you would select the correct answer from the drop down menu. For this print version, you see all four answer choices as if you had clicked the select button.

In the pages ahead, you'll take a closer look at types of questions that would appear on the language component of the GED Reasoning Through Language Arts Test. The following are some useful strategies and tips for handling language questions:

- **Always consider all four choices before making your final selection.** The sentences might be flawed in more than one way. An answer choice might fix one flaw, but not another, or it may introduce an error. In addition, more than one proposed revision might be better than the original version. Without examining all choices, you can't know for sure which is best.
- **Resist the urge to "hyper-correct."** In some questions you will have the option to leave the wording alone. Always consider this option. If you see it, be especially wary of the proposed changes in the other choices. Each and every one of them might either be unnecessary or create an error where there was none.
- **Be sure to consider the entire sentence.** Keep in mind that all parts of a sentence are interrelated. By examining just one replaced part, or even that part along with what immediately precedes or follows it, you can easily overlook a problem. The same applies to each proposed revision as well.
- **Remember your task is to identify "the best way to revise the sentence."** This means that you should look not just for grammatical errors but also for other problems, such as awkwardness, misplaced modifiers, and problems in sentence sense or logic. Also, rule out any revision that distorts or alters the intended meaning of the sentence.

The following test-style paragraph and sample questions illustrate question types you may see on the language component of the GED Reasoning Through Language Arts Test. The analysis that follows each question explains how to apply one or more of the previously-listed strategies. (Note: sentences have been numbered for reference.) In the actual test, the unnumbered drop-down selections are integrated into the paragraph.

(1) When starting a job, [Select ▼] (2) Offices can be [Select ▼] (3) You should [Select ▼] (4) Most dress codes [Select ▼]

Choose the option that correctly completes sentence 1.

When starting a job, [Select ▼]

A. your bosses will tell you the dress code they prefers.

B. you're boss will tell you the dress code they prefers.

C. your boss will tell you the dress code he or she prefers.

D. your boss will tell you the dress code they prefer.

In sentence 1, the noun *boss* is singular, but the pronoun *they,* which refers to *boss,* is plural. Here's the applicable rule of grammar: a pronoun must agree in number (either singular or plural) with the noun to which it refers (called the *antecedent*).

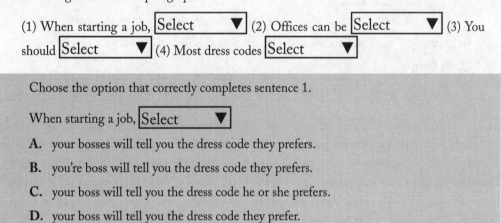

It might appear that choices A, C, or D correct the pronoun reference error in sentence 1. But does this mean that all three choices are correct? No. For example, trying out choice D, if you read the sentence again using *prefer*, you'll "hear" the incorrectly paired phrases "boss will tell you ... they prefer." Removing the *s* would correct the pronoun-verb agreement at the end of the sentence, but the pronoun and noun agreement is still incorrect. By changing *they* to *he or she,* the pronoun agrees with the antecedent and allows you to leave *prefers* as is. **The correct answer is C.**

Choose the option that correctly completes sentence 2.

Offices can be Select ▼

A. consider casual, considered formal, or a combination of the two.

B. considered casual, considered formal, or a combinations of the two.

C. considered casual, considered formal, or a combination of the two.

D. considered casual, formal, or a combination of the two.

Notice that sentence 2 lists a series of three features. Here's the applicable rule of grammar: all items in a series should be grammatically parallel. Read sentence 2 with this rule in mind, and you'll notice what is called "faulty parallelism." The second feature (*considered formal*) is not parallel to the third feature (*a combination*). One starts with the verb *considered,* while the other one does not. One way to fix the problem is to insert the word *considered* immediately after *or*. However, this option is not listed among the four choices. Another way to fix the problem is to remove the word *considered* after *casual,* which is what choice D suggests. The result is a series of three parallel items: (1) *casual,* (2) *formal,* and (3) *a combination.* **The correct answer is D.**

Choose the option that correctly completes sentence 3.

You should Select ▼

A. make sure you know the dress code rules, before going into work on you're first day.

B. make sure you know the dress code rules before going into work on your first day.

C. know the dress code rules before going into work on you're first day.

D. make sure you know of the dress code rules before going into work on you're first day.

In sentence 3, the phrase "make sure you know" might not be as concise as the same phrase without the words *make sure you.* But the phrase is not grammatically incorrect, and its meaning is clear enough. So the change proposed in choice C is not necessary, and you should look for a better answer. The word *you're* is a contraction of the two-word phrase "you are." Read the sentence with "you are," and you'll notice that the meaning of the sentence changes to "before going into work on you are first day." This is clearly incorrect, so eliminate choices A and D. As choice B suggests, *you're* should be replaced with *your.* **The correct answer is B.**

Choose the option that correctly completes sentence 4.

Most dress codes [Select ▼]

A. have been included in the employee handbook, can help you learn the rules.

B. are includes in the employee handbook, can help you learn the rules.

C. is included in the employee handbook, can help you learn the rules.

D. are included in the employee handbook, which can help you learn the rules.

In sentence 4, the time frame for the action in the first clause is the present ("most ... are included"). Choice A proposes to use the present-perfect tense ("have been included"). Here's the applicable rule of grammar: The present-perfect tense should be used to indicate action occurring in the past and ending at the present time. The present-perfect tense is not incorrect here, and it makes sense, especially since the second clause is framed in the same tense. However, the present tense works just as well, if not better. So the tense change that choice A proposes is unnecessary, and you should look for a better answer choice.

Read sentence 4 straight through. The clause after the comma sounds incomplete. Adding *which* after the comma completes the second clause and properly connects it to the main clause. **The correct answer is D.**

Here is the next part of the passage.

> (5) Whether your company [Select ▼] (6) [Select ▼] keep your shoulders covered, wear close-toed shoes, and always avoid jeans. (7) Also, try to choose neutral colors and solids, [Select ▼]

Choose the option that correctly completes sentence 5.

Whether your company [Select ▼]

A. requires formal, or casual, attire, choosing appropriate clothing is easy.

B. requires formal or casual attire, choosing appropriate clothing is easy.

C. requires formal or casual attire: choosing appropriate clothing is easy.

D. require formal, or casual attire choosing appropriate clothing is easy.

In sentence 5, the object of the verb *requires* is "formal or casual attire." Splitting this element with commas makes for an awkward and confusing clause. The pair of commas makes "or casual" an appositive phrase, implying that it can be removed without changing the meaning of the sentence. This is not true, because you need to know if your company requires formal or casual attire, so the commas should be removed. Choice D removes one of the incorrect commas but also deletes the necessary comma that connects the dependent and independent clauses in the sentence. Both choice B and choice C correctly remove the commas. However, choice C adds a colon after *attire*, making the sentence mechanically incorrect. By placing a colon after *attire*, it implies that the section of the sentence preceding the colon is an independent clause. This is untrue, and you can "hear" that it is incorrect by reading the section leading up to the colon, as if the second half is not there. **The correct choice is B.**

Choose the option that correctly completes sentence 6.

[Select ▼] keep your shoulders covered, wear close-toed shoes, and always avoid jeans.

A. To avoid confusion if any rules are unclear,

B. If any rules are unclear,

C. Avoided confusion if any rules are unclear,

D. To avoid being confused if any rules are unclear,

You can quickly rule out choice D because it provides a very awkward-sounding phrase. Choice C introduces the past-tense verb form *avoided.* But does the past tense make sense in the context of the sentence as a whole? No. The sentence clearly intends to establish a present-to-future time frame. By mixing tenses, choice C confuses the time frame of the sentence's action.

To improve the sentence, you can eliminate either "To avoid confusion" or "if any rules are unclear," but ask yourself, "Would making the clothing choices listed truly *avoid confusion*, and if so, for whom?" Clearly, "if any rules are unclear" is the more precise phrase. **The correct answer is B.**

As with the two previous examples (sentences 5 and 6), consider the four options in the context of the sentence below as a whole.

Choose the option that correctly completes sentence 7.

Also, try to choose neutral colors and solids, [Select ▼]

A. because employees should not be distracted by your wardrobe in the workplace.

B. because they are less distracting.

C. since employees should not be distracted by your wardrobe in the workplace.

D. because your wardrobe should not distract employees.

The problem in sentence 7 is use of the passive voice. If possible, it's preferable for the subject of sentence to be doing the action, not being acted upon. The first clause refers to colors and solids, so it's clear that the subject of this sentence is *wardrobe*, not *employees*. Choices A and C use the passive voice, saying that the employees should not be distracted *by* the wardrobe. Choice B creates an incomplete comparison and does not explain who might be distracted. Choice D removes the passive voice and states a fact as a result of the first clause. **The correct answer is D.**

GENERAL TEST-TAKING STRATEGIES

Here are some general strategies for tackling the language component of the GED Reasoning Through Language Arts Test. Most apply to all types of documents and questions. Put these strategies to work on the practice tests in this book, and then review them again just before exam day.

Read a document straight through before answering any questions based on it.

Read the document quickly from beginning to end. Don't bother to take notes, and don't pay too much attention to specific grammatical errors (you'll find plenty of them!). Instead, ask yourself the following questions:

- Is the sequence of ideas logical and easy to understand?
- Is the language and tone of the passage appropriate for the audience? For example, a business letter usually requires a formal tone and specific conventions.
- Are there any places in the text in which the meaning is lost or obscured?

This strategy will help you to focus and to anticipate at least some of the questions. The documents are short (from 350 to 450 words), so up to a minute should be ample time for this task.

"Listen" to sentences for anything that doesn't sound right.

In answering questions about particular sentences, listen to them—as if you were reading aloud—for anything that sounds awkward, confusing, or just plain weird. If you hear something wrong, trust your ear and your instinct.

Apply the four basic principles for error-spotting in GED test sentences.

If you're not sure what the problem with a particular sentence is, follow these four steps to uncover it:

1. Find the verb, then its subject. Check for subject-verb agreement, including collective nouns and compound subjects.
2. Examine all pronouns. Make sure each has a clear antecedent with which it agrees in person and number.
3. Examine sentence structure. Make sure modifiers are attached to what they modify, parallel ideas are grammatically parallel, and comparisons are clear and logical.
4. Listen for awkwardness or "gobbledygook" (anything that simply makes no sense).

Try to formulate an answer *before* reading the choices.

In tackling a replacement for part of a particular sentence, think about how you would write that part of the sentence. Do this before looking at any of the answer choices. Try rephrasing a faulty sentence part, figuring out what word or punctuation mark you'd eliminate, change, move, or add. You'll zero in on the correct choice more quickly this way, and you're less likely to become confused and tempted by wrong answer choices. Keep in mind that this strategy works for most, but not all, question types on the language component of the Reasoning Through Language Arts Test. Exceptions to the rule are noted in the grammar review, which follows this lesson.

Pace yourself properly.

The language portion of the test consists of several distinct question sets, each set based on a different document. The number of questions per set can vary from 6 to 8. You have about two minutes to answer each question on the GED Reasoning Through Language Arts Test (with the exception of the Extended Response). If you're falling behind, try to pick up your pace.

SUMMING IT UP

- The language component of the GED Reasoning Through Language Arts Test is basically an *editing* test that is designed to measure your ability to review a document and spot grammatical errors and other writing problems that need to be corrected or revised. Expect approximately two documents altogether and 6 to 8 questions based on each document. Each document will be 350–450 words in length.
- The language component of the test covers grammar and usage, sentence structure, and writing mechanics.
- Be on the lookout for answer choices that fix one error but create another, and avoid correcting a sentence that doesn't need to be corrected.
- In addition to grammatical errors, look for other problems, such as awkwardness, misplaced modifiers, and problems in sentence sense or logic. Also, rule out any revision that distorts or alters the intended meaning of the sentence.
- Most sentence construction questions focus on sentence structure. However, some might cover usage and/or mechanics as well. Sentence construction questions vary in format; make sure you become familiar with these different types of questions, including the different styles of technology-enhanced items as outlined at the beginning of the book.

PRACTICE QUESTIONS

Directions: The following is a document you might find in the workplace. The passage contains errors in grammar, spelling, and punctuation. For questions 1–10, choose the option from the drop-down menu that correctly completes or rewrites the sentence.

Gail Benning
34 Sherwood Drive
Bethpage, New York 11714
516-555-6789
gb@scopenet.com

March 13, 2018
(1) Luisa Benez

(2) Chief Instructor

(3) [Select ▼]

(4) 1313 E. Marie Street
(5) Hicksville, New York 11801

(6) [Select ▼]

(7) I am writing in response to your recent advertisement in the *Long Island Post* for a studio assistant at Artwood Arts Education. (8) The description of the position for an assistant [Select ▼] (9) I am available for an interview at your convenience and can start the position immediately if necessary.

(10) I have extensive experience in various avenues of the art [Select ▼] (11) [Select ▼] having recently earned a degree in Art Therapy, I am looking to break into this stimulating field, and assisting in your classroom would be an ideal entry into a field that promises to be both stimulating and gratifying.

(12) As assistant to the Chief Director, I gained extensive experience in facilitating her ability to execute projects and guide my fellow employees through every step of the artistic process. (13) My ten years of experience at Gentry Arts, a nonprofit organization based in Levittown, has provided me with a great deal of experience in dealing with various aspects of the art environment. (14) Among my duties were analyzing legal issues that might effect our company, arranging creative displays, writing proposals, coordinating volunteers, and developing fundraising strategies. (15) These duties involved a great deal of multitasking, critical thinking, collaborating, time managing, and both receiving and providing constructive criticism. (16) I not only handled an abundance of challenges on a daily basis, [Select ▼]

(17) I believe my education in art therapy has not only provided me with the knowledge necessary to overcome the new challenges that will doubtlessly arise at your art therapy institution, but has also deepened my understanding of my fellow humans in ways that will surely make me a more [Select ▼]

(18) I would be thrilled to meet with you to discuss this exciting opportunity further. (19) Ms. Benez, please contact me so that we can set up an interview at [Select ▼] (20) I look forward to meeting you [Select ▼]

(21) Thank you so much for your time and consideration.

Respectfully,
Gail Benning

1. **Sentence 3:** [Select ▼]
   A. Artwood arts Education
   B. Artwood arts education
   C. artwood arts education
   D. Artwood Arts Education

2. **Sentence 6:** [Select ▼]
   A. Dear Ms. Benez
   B. Dear Ms. Benez,
   C. Dear Ms. Benez:
   D. Dear Ms. Benez;

3. **Sentence 8:** The description of the position for an assistant [Select ▼]
   A. suit my particular qualifications perfectly.
   B. suits my particular qualifications perfectly.
   C. suited my particular qualifications perfectly.
   D. will suit my particular qualifications perfectly.

4. **Sentence 10:** I have extensive experience in various avenues of the art [Select ▼]
   A. world, I have worked as a commercial artist, had my work displayed as a fine artist, and most recently, spent ten years as an assistant at Gentry Arts.
   B. world I have worked as a commercial artist, had my work displayed as a fine artist, and most recently, spent ten years as an assistant at Gentry Arts.
   C. world: I have worked as a commercial artist, had my work displayed as a fine artist, and most recently, spent ten years as an assistant at Gentry Arts.
   D. world. I have worked as a commercial artist, had my work displayed as a fine artist, and most recently, spent ten years as an assistant at Gentry Arts.

5. **Sentence 11:** [Select ▼] having recently earned a degree in Art Therapy, I am looking to break into this stimulating field, and assisting in your classroom would be an ideal entry into a field that promises to be both stimulating and gratifying.

   A. Therefore,

   B. As a result,

   C. For starters,

   D. However,

6. The sentences in the third paragraph appear below as they are in the letter. Drag and drop them into the chart to put them in the order that makes the most sense. (Enter the sentence numbers in order on your answer sheet.)

   Sentence 12. As assistant to the Chief Director, I gained extensive experience in facilitating her ability to execute projects and guide my fellow employees through every step of the artistic process.

   Sentence 13. My ten years of experience at Gentry Arts, a nonprofit organization based in Levittown, has provided me with a great deal of experience in dealing with various aspects of the art environment.

   Sentence 14. Among my duties were analyzing legal issues that might effect our company, arranging creative displays, writing proposals, coordinating volunteers, and developing fundraising strategies.

   Sentence 15. These duties involved a great deal of multitasking, critical thinking, collaborating, time managing, and both receiving and providing constructive criticism.

7. **Sentence 16:** I not only handled an abundance of challenges on a daily basis, [Select ▼]

   A. but I look forward to such situations as opportunities to expand my experience.

   B. but I looked forward to such situations as opportunities to expand my experience.

   C. but I look forward to expanding my experience.

   D. but we looked forward to such situations as opportunities to expand my experience.

8. **Sentence 17:** I believe my education in art therapy has not only provided me with the knowledge necessary to overcome the new challenges that will doubtlessly arise at your art therapy institution, but has also deepened my understanding of my fellow humans in ways that will surely make me a more [Select ▼]

   A. effective assistant to you.

   B. affective assistant to you.

   C. effective assistance to you.

   D. affective assistance to you.

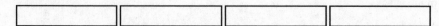

9. **Sentence 19:** Ms. Benez, please contact me so that we can set up an interview at Select ▼

   A. her soonest convenience.

   B. your soonest convenience.

   C. their soonest convenience.

   D. its soonest convenience.

10. **Sentence 20:** I look forward to meeting you Select ▼

    A. like crazy.

    B. a lot.

    C. so much.

    D. with the keenest anticipation.

ANSWER KEY AND EXPLANATIONS

1. D	**3.** B	**5.** D	**7.** B	**9.** C
2. C	**4.** D	**6.** 13,12,14,15	**8.** A	**10.** D

1. **The correct answer is D.** All words in the name of this business are proper nouns and should be capitalized, especially when used formally in an address.

2. **The correct answer is C.** This is a cover letter, which requires a colon after the salutation.

3. **The correct answer is B.** In this sentence, the verb *suits* must agree with the singular subject *description*. Choice A is incorrect because *suit* would only agree with a plural subject. Choice C is written in the past tense, and choice D is in the future tense; this letter takes place in the present.

4. **The correct answer is D.** The two clauses of the sentence must be divided into separate sentences with a period. Choice A is a run-on. Choice B eliminates the punctuation completely and fails to correct the error. Choice C incorrectly uses a colon to separate the clauses in the sentence.

5. **The correct answer is D.** The transition word *however* is used to indicate a shift, and such a shift occurs when the writer transitions from discussing her present job to discussing how she wants a new job in a somewhat different field. *Therefore* (choice A) and *As a result* (choice B) are used to indicate consequences, not shifts. *For starters* (choice C) is used to indicate a beginning and is too informal for a cover letter.

6. **The correct order is (13), (12), (14), (15).** This is the only order that clarifies who the Chief Director is.

7. **The correct answer is B.** A past tense verb is used in the first part of the sentence, so the second part should use a past tense verb also. The usage of past tense is also in line with the previous sentences in the cover letter. Choice A and C incorrectly use the present tense instead of the past tense. Choice D erroneously uses the plural *we*, instead of the singular *I* in the second part of the sentence.

8. **The correct answer is A.** The sentence is correct as written. The words *effective* and *affective* are frequently confused, but they have very different meanings: *effective* means "successful," while *affective* means "emotional," so choices B and D don't make much sense. Choice C is incorrect because assistance is not a kind of person like an assistant is.

9. **The correct answer is C.** The pronoun in this sentence must agree with the antecedent *Ms. Benez*, and *your* is the only pronoun that accomplishes this. Because the writer is addressing Ms. Benez directly, *her* (choice A) is incorrect. Since Ms. Benez is one person, *their* (choice C) is in the wrong number and point of view. *Its* (choice D) is used only to refer to a non-human antecedent.

10. **The correct answer is D.** This is a business letter, so it must use formal language; "like crazy" (choice A) is far too informal, while "a lot" (choice B) and "so much" (choice C) lack the professional finesse of "with the keenest anticipation" (choice D).

Mastering Extended Response

Chapter 5

OVERVIEW

- All About the Reasoning Through Language Arts Test—Extended Response
- How Extended Response Items Are Evaluated
- What's Not Tested
- How Extended Response Items Are Scored
- The Extended Response Topic
- Writing Your Extended Response: From Brainstorm to Final Product
- Developing and Connecting Your Paragraphs
- Writing Style
- Suggestions for Writing and Evaluating Your Extended Response
- General Test-Taking Strategies
- Summing It Up
- Practice Extended Response
- Sample Responses and Analysis

THE REASONING THROUGH LANGUAGE ARTS TEST—EXTENDED RESPONSE IN A NUTSHELL

Time allowed: 150 minutes for the entire Reasoning Through Language Arts Test, which includes 45 minutes for the Extended Response as well as a 10-minute break

Total number of questions: One written analysis based on two reading passages that offer opposing views

ALL ABOUT THE REASONING THROUGH LANGUAGE ARTS TEST—EXTENDED RESPONSE

The extended response component of the GED Reasoning Through Language Arts Test assesses your ability to communicate your ideas and thoughts in writing. You will be asked to present your opinion in response to a paired passage on a specific topic. You will not be given a choice of topics to write on, and you *must* write only about the topic provided.

Here are the basic rules and procedures for the extended response component of the GED Reasoning Through Language Arts Test:

- **The allotted time to plan, write, and revise your extended response is 45 minutes**. However, if you finish the first part of the test early, you can start work on the extended response right away. Note that when you complete your extended response, you cannot go back to any earlier part of the test.
- **An erasable note board will be provided for jotting down notes, making an outline, and writing out a rough draft**. The notes you make on the note board will not be read or scored. If a new note board is needed, a test taker can trade in the old board for a fresh one. The note boards take the place of scratch paper and are more environmentally friendly and secure, as the boards cannot be taken from the testing center.
- **You must write your extended response in the space provided on the computer screen**. Passages will be broken up into tabbed pages for longer texts. Also, the question or prompt and instructions will be visible as you read the passage, through use of a split screen.

HOW EXTENDED RESPONSE ITEMS ARE EVALUATED

The Extended Response item will be evaluated on the basis of three rubrics, each one emphasizing a different aspect (trait) of the essay, as follows:

- **Trait 1:** Creation of arguments and use of evidence
- **Trait 2:** Development of ideas and organizational structure
- **Trait 3:** Clarity and command of standard English conventions

Each trait is worth up to 2 points, so responses will be scored on a 6-point scale. The final raw score on the Extended Response item is then double-weighted so that it represents up to 12 raw score points on the overall GED Reasoning Through Language Arts Test.

Extended Response Scoring Rubric

Score	Description
	Trait 1: Creation of Arguments and Use of Evidence
2	• Generates **text-based argument(s)** and establishes **a purpose that is connected** to the prompt • Cites relevant and specific **evidence from source text(s)** to support argument (may include few irrelevant pieces of evidence or unsupported claims) • **Analyzes the issue** and/or **evaluates the validity of the argumentation** within the source text(s) (e.g., distinguishes between supported and unsupported claims, makes reasonable inferences about underlying premises or assumptions, identifies fallacious reasoning, evaluates the credibility of sources, etc.)
1	• Generates an **argument** and demonstrates some connection to the prompt • Cites some **evidence from source text(s)** to support argument (may include a mix of relevant and irrelevant citations or a mix of textual and non-textual references) • Partially **analyzes the issue** and/or **evaluates the validity of the argumentation** within the source text(s); may be simplistic, limited, or inaccurate
0	• May attempt to create an **argument** OR **lacks purpose or connection** to the prompt OR does neither • Cites minimal or no evidence from source text(s) (sections of text may be copied from source)
	Non-Scorable Responses (Score of 0/Condition Codes) Response exclusively contains text copied from source text(s) or prompt; shows no evidence that test taker has read the prompt; is incomprehensible; is not in English; has not been attempted (blank)

Extended Response Scoring Rubric *(continued)*

Score	Description
	Trait 2: Development of Ideas and Organizational Structure
2	• Contains **ideas that are well developed** and generally logical; most ideas are **elaborated** upon • Contains a sensible **progression of ideas** with clear connections between details and main points • Establishes an **organizational structure** that conveys the message and purpose of the response; applies **transitional devices** appropriately • Establishes and maintains a **formal style** and **appropriate tone** that demonstrates awareness of the audience and purpose of the task • **Chooses specific words** to express ideas clearly
1	• Contains **ideas that are inconsistently developed** and/or may reflect simplistic or vague reasoning; **some ideas are elaborated** upon • Demonstrates **some evidence of a progression of ideas,** but details may be disjointed or lacking connection to main ideas • Establishes an **organizational structure that may inconsistently** group ideas or is partially effective at conveying the message of the task; **uses transitional devices inconsistently** • May **inconsistently** maintain a formal style and appropriate tone to demonstrate an **awareness of the audience** and **purpose of the task** • May occasionally **misuse words** and/or choose words that express ideas in vague terms
0	• Contains **ideas that are insufficiently or illogically developed,** with **minimal or no elaboration** on main ideas • Contains **unclear or no progression of ideas**; details may be absent or irrelevant to the main ideas • Establishes **ineffective or no discernible organizational structure**; does not apply transitional devices, or does so inappropriately • Uses an **informal style** and/or **inappropriate tone** that demonstrates **limited or no awareness of audience and purpose** • May **frequently misuse words,** overuse slang, or express ideas in a vague or repetitious manner
	Non-Scorable Responses (Score of 0/Condition Codes) Response exclusively contains text copied from source text(s) or prompt; shows no evidence that test taker has read the prompt; is incomprehensible; is not in English; has not been attempted (blank)

Extended Response Scoring Rubric *(continued)*

Score	Description
	Trait 3: Clarity and Command of Standard English Conventions
2	• Demonstrates **mostly correct sentence structure** and a **general fluency** that enhances clarity with specific regard to the following skills: 1) Varied sentence structure within a paragraph or paragraphs 2) Correct subordination, coordination, and parallelism 3) Avoidance of wordiness and awkward sentence structures 4) Usage of transitional words, conjunctive adverbs, and other words that support logic and clarify 5) Avoidance of run-on sentences, fused sentences, or sentence fragments • Demonstrates **competent application of conventions** with specific regard to the following skills: 1) Frequently confused words and homonyms, including contractions 2) Subject-verb agreement 3) Pronoun usage, including pronoun antecedent agreement, unclear pronoun references, and pronoun case 4) Placement of modifiers and correct word order 5) Capitalization (e.g., proper nouns, titles, and beginnings of sentences) 6) Use of apostrophes with possessive nouns 7) Use of punctuation (e.g., commas in a series or in appositives and other non-essential elements, end marks, and appropriate punctuation for clause separation) • **May contain some errors in mechanics and conventions,** but they do not interfere with comprehension; overall, standard usage is at a level appropriate for on-demand draft writing
1	• Demonstrates **inconsistent sentence structure**; may contain some repetitive, choppy, rambling, or awkward sentences that may detract from clarity; demonstrates inconsistent control over skills 1–5 as listed in the first bullet under Trait 3, Score Point 2 above • Demonstrates **inconsistent control of basic conventions** with specific regard to skills 1–7 as listed in the second bullet under Trait 3, Score Point 2 above • **May contain frequent errors in mechanics and conventions** that occasionally interfere with comprehension; standard usage is at a minimally acceptable level of appropriateness for on-demand draft writing
0	• Demonstrates **consistently flawed sentence structure** such that meaning may be obscured; demonstrates minimal control over skills 1–5 as listed in the first bullet under Trait 3, Score Point 2 above • Demonstrates **minimal control of basic conventions** with specific regard to skills 1–7 as previously listed in the second bullet under Trait 3, Score Point 2 • Contains **severe and frequent errors in mechanics and conventions** that interfere with comprehension; overall, standard usage is at an unacceptable level for on-demand draft writing OR • **Response is insufficient** to demonstrate level of mastery over conventions and usage
	Non-Scorable Responses (Score of 0/Condition Codes) Response exclusively contains text copied from source text(s) or prompt; shows no evidence that test taker has read the prompt; is incomprehensible; is not in English; has not been attempted (blank)

NOTE

Because test takers will be given 45 minutes to complete Extended Response tasks, there is no expectation that a response should be completely free of conventions or usage errors to receive a score of 2.

Also, keep in mind that the automated scoring engine will evaluate your essay based on the *quality*, and not the quantity, of your writing, specifically taking into account how well you meet the criteria in the three rubrics. So a brief response that is fully developed, well-organized, and well-written will, in all likelihood, earn a higher score than a much longer response that is poorly developed, disorganized, and poorly written.

Finally, notice that Rubric 3 covers the same knowledge areas as those covered by the language component of the GED Reasoning Through Language Arts Test. So knowing the rules and guidelines for grammar, usage, sentence structure, paragraph and document structure, and writing mechanics will serve double duty: it will help you to edit the documents in the language component of the test *and* to write your extended response item.

WHAT'S NOT TESTED

In evaluating and scoring your response, the GED test automated scoring engine focuses only on the three rubrics previously described. Many test takers will make the mistake of trying to write in an impressive manner, which will not be noticed by the automated scoring engine. Other test takers will be too concerned about saying the "right thing" and not concerned enough about how they say it. To avoid these mistakes, here's what you need to keep in mind:

- **There is no "correct" answer.** First and foremost, remember that there is no "best" response or "correct" answer to the extended response question. What's important is how effectively you present and support your ideas. The response is ***expected*** to be in paragraph form, and the following pages clearly state that you need at least one introductory paragraph, one body paragraph, and one summary paragraph. (A minimum of two body paragraphs is strongly suggested.)
- **Special knowledge about the topic at hand won't matter.** The extended response component of the GED Reasoning Through Language Arts Test is a *skills* test. So you don't need any special knowledge of the topic presented in order to produce a high-scoring response. Besides, the extended response topics are not technical in nature. So though you'll need to know something about the subject, common everyday knowledge will be enough.
- **The extended response component is not a vocabulary exercise.** You won't score points from the automated scoring engine by using obscure or so-called "big" words. When it comes to vocabulary, all that matters is that the words you use make sense in context.
- **The extended response component is not a creative writing exercise.** Some test takers will make the mistake of using an imaginative writing style or essay structure in order to receive a better score for originality. Simply put, this is a bad idea. The GED test is not the place to experiment with imagery, to display wit or humor, or to show that you have "Hemingway potential." Focus on writing with strong organization and communication skills—not astounding creativity.
- **Occasional, minor mechanical errors will not hurt your score.** In evaluating your essay, the automated scoring engine will focus on how well you meet the criteria in the rubrics. The automated scoring engine will overlook the occasional punctuation error, awkward sentence, or even misspelled word.

HOW EXTENDED RESPONSE ITEMS ARE SCORED

An automated scoring engine will use the three rubrics to score the extended response question. These rubrics measure creation of arguments and use of evidence, development of ideas and organizational structure, and clarity and command of standard English conventions. This automated scoring engine uses algorithms to mimic the human scoring process. It has been programmed based on a computer evaluation of hundreds of responses that align to all possible scores on the rubrics. To ensure the accuracy of this engine, readers will manually score a sample of responses. Also, if the engine flags an essay as being unusual, it will be sent to a reader to be evaluated and scored.

THE EXTENDED RESPONSE TOPIC

The topic for your GED Reasoning Through Language Arts Test extended response question will be based on two passages offering opposing viewpoints on a subject. The text for these passages will not exceed 650 words. Your task will be to determine which essay's argument is best presented and supported with relevant and persuasive details. To complete the extended response, you will write a response comparing the two writings you are given.

Comparative Response

A comparative response compares and contrasts the ideas and opinions of two different reading selections about a similar or related issue. Your task will be to analyze both passages to determine which author best supports his or her position on the given issue. Below is a list of possible passage topics you might encounter in the prompt of the extended response.

1. A passage about the importance of teamwork paired with a passage about individual initiative
2. A passage about the benefits of high school students holding part-time jobs paired with a passage about why high school students should not hold part-time jobs
3. A passage about how colleges should focus on teaching real-world job skills paired with a passage on how colleges should focus on providing a general education
4. A passage about how innate talent is essential to individual success paired with a passage about how perseverance and effort is essential to individual success
5. A passage about how high school students should be required to wear uniforms combined with a passage about why uniforms do more harm than good
6. A passage about how digital books are better than printed books paired with a passage about how printed books are better than digital books
7. A passage about how smartphones, tablets, and other gadgets save us time paired with a passage about how these devices rob us of time

WRITING YOUR EXTENDED RESPONSE: FROM BRAINSTORM TO FINAL PRODUCT

Writing is probably something you do every day without giving it much thought. Whether you write letters, emails, or memos, you know that writing is simply putting your thoughts into written form. Some people get intimidated when they are required to write a formal essay that will be read and graded. You shouldn't be intimidated at all, though. For the extended response, you just need to follow certain steps to ensure you've hit the marks on the rubric and will receive a good score from the automated scoring engine.

In writing their GED Test extended response, many test takers make the mistake of diving in head first. They immediately start typing in the designated box without planning their writing ahead of time. While a few may be able to compose a good response this way, the vast majority won't. Writing essays "on the fly" usually produces poorly written and disorganized essays. Rather than expressing and developing a central idea in a clear, well-organized manner, they tend to lose focus and ramble, without a clear train of thought, and sometimes without a clear beginning or end.

Instead of simply jumping in and starting to type, you should spend some time up front thinking about what you should write and how you should organize your ideas. And you should save some time at the end to proofread your response. Below is a 7-step plan to help you budget your time and produce a solid response within your 45-minute time limit.

7-Step Plan for Writing a GED® Test Extended Response Item

Plan (5 minutes):

1. Brainstorm ideas and make notes.
2. Review your notes and decide on a central idea or viewpoint.
3. Decide the sequence in which you will present your main points. If you find outlines helpful, write your main points in outline format.

Write (35 minutes):

4. Write a brief introductory paragraph.
5. Write the body paragraphs of your essay.
6. Write a brief summary or concluding paragraph.

Review (5 minutes):

7. Proofread to find errors you can easily fix, and fix them.

The suggested time limits for each step are merely guidelines, not hard-and-fast rules. As you practice composing your own responses under timed conditions, start with these guidelines, and then adjust to a pace that works best for you personally.

In the following pages, you'll walk through each step in turn, using a GED test-style prompt.

Extended Response Topic

Debating Hybrid Cars

The following passages represent two views of the value of hybrid cars, cars that are powered by gasoline or by electricity depending on whether they are in traffic or on the open road. Analyze both positions presented to determine which one is best supported. Use relevant and specific evidence from both passages to support your response.

Enter your response in the answer sheets provided. You should expect to spend up to 45 minutes to plan, draft, and edit your response.

Passage 1

Advocates of hybrids believe that the cars offer the best short-term solution to some long-term problems. By combining a regular gasoline-powered engine with an electric engine, hybrids cut down on costly gas consumption and decrease the pollution caused by gasoline engines. These cars help automakers meet government regulations for fuel efficiency and emissions controls—in some states, hybrid owners do not need an emission test for registration at all, which will amount to further savings for the hybrid owner. Not only are the cars more gas efficient, but they are more efficient in the city: Hybrid cars can generate more electricity at lower speeds, also making them a good choice for heavy commuter traffic. This may put wear and tear on brakes for gas-powered cars, but hybrids use brakes that also regenerate electricity. This means that when a driver brakes, the mechanism that slows down the car creates energy that can be used or stored. Standard cars dispel this energy via friction in the brake linings, wasting the energy and wearing down the brakes. Most hybrids have warranties on their batteries that are good for up to 150,000 miles, and some hybrid models have been known to perform just as well at over 200,000 miles as they did when brand new. Automakers do not think that hybrids are the answer for the future, but these small cars provide a way for conservation-conscious consumers to do something for the environment. Automakers see another benefit to the development process for hybrids. The technology that has gone into creating and refining the dual-powered hybrid will help with the longer-term development of cars powered by hydrogen fuel cells.

Passage 2

I think automakers should be focusing on a longer-term solution to the ideal automobile than hybrids. Really, hydrogen fuel cells or diesel fuel or both are better alternatives than hybrids. The cost of hybrids is higher than comparably sized gasoline-powered cars, forcing consumers who want "green" cars to pay anywhere from $2,500 to $4,000 more. Another big problem with hybrids is that the higher sticker price means lower demand and less likelihood of automobile companies making their development dollars back. Just look at Europe to get an idea of how little demand there is for hybrids. Gas prices are much higher there than in the United States, but no mass movement from gasoline-powered cars to hybrids has occurred. Not all hybrids are equal, causing discrepancies about their accessibility for a large buyer's market. Some hybrids perform better than others in terms of gas mileage and electric efficiency, and some heating and air conditioning systems do not operate when the gasoline engine stops. Aside from temperature control issues, not many models come with a third row of seats, making them unsuitable for large families. These large hybrids do not get very good gas mileage compared to other hybrids as far as I'm concerned.

Step 1: Brainstorm Ideas and Make Notes

Your first step in developing an extended response essay is to brainstorm ideas that are relevant to the topic. Be aware of how much room on the erasable board these notes take up since you only have one to use. To decide on which viewpoint you think is best supported, and to come up with ideas for your comparative response, you should consider the following:

- Evidence each author presents
- Conclusions each author draws
- Attitude each author adopts
- Language each author uses

As you think of ideas, don't try to filter out what you think might be unconvincing reasons or weak examples. Just let all your ideas flow onto your erasable note board, in no particular order. (You can sort through them during steps 2 and 3.) Here's what your notes on the topic might look like after a few minutes of brainstorming:

PASSAGE 1

Cut down on gas consumption

Decrease pollution

Fuel-efficient

Emissions controls

Good in heavy traffic

Clear language

Gets technical about brakes

Gets technical about brakes

CONCLUSION: Pro hybrids

PASSAGE 2

Hydrogen fuel cells and diesel fuel better than hybrids

Hybrids are too expensive

Companies won't make money back

Hybrids don't sell in Europe

Not all hybrids are the same

Bad for big families

Clear language

First person point-of-view

CONCLUSION: Author is clearly anti hybrids

Notice that some notes are grouped together to reflect one train of thought. Other notes reflect assorted, random ideas. The notes aren't well organized, but that's okay. The point of brainstorming is just to generate a bunch of ideas—the raw material for your essay. Let your ideas flow freely, and you'll have plenty of material for your essay.

Step 2: Review Your Notes and Decide Which Passage You Will Choose as the Most Effective

Decide on which passage you intend to support in your essay. Your notes from step 1 should help you decide. Review the ideas you jotted down, and then ask yourself for which viewpoint you can make a strong case.

Pick the three or four ideas from your notes that best support your view. These should be ideas that you think make sense and that you know enough about to write at least a few sentences on. Put a checkmark next to those ideas, to signify that these are the ones you're certain you want to use in your essay. If you don't have enough ideas, try elaborating one or two of your existing ideas. Think of items that may be related, add details or examples, and use these to fill out your list.

Step 3: Organize Your Ideas into an Outline

Next, decide on a sequence for the ideas. They should flow naturally and logically from one to another. Once you've decided on a sequence for your ideas, number them accordingly in your notes. At this point, you might want to create a separate outline, or you might be able to transform your notes from step 1 into an outline. Use the outline structure that works best for you; you may find numbers and bullet points easier and faster than the traditional hierarchy of roman numerals and letters.

For example, if you decide that you agree that hybrid cars offer the best short-term solution to some long-term problems, your outline might look something like this:

PROS:

(1) Save on gas money

(2) Better for the environment

- Less fuel used
- Decrease in pollution

(3) Last a long time (fewer repairs)

- Brakes regenerate
- Batteries last a long time

(4) No smog tests

(5) Good practice for developing hydrogen-powered cars

CONS:

(1) Costs more to buy

(2) Hydrogen or diesel fuels are better than gas/electric combination

(3) Companies lost money

(4) Some don't have efficient air and heat while operating under electricity

(5) Not big enough for large families

As previously mentioned, you might prefer to create a separate outline based on your notes. Doing so shouldn't take much time, and it will give you another chance to think about your ideas and how you should organize them into paragraphs. Here's what an outline based on your initial notes might look like:

Hybrid cars are a helpful invention: the pros outweigh the cons.

(1) Money saved on gas will make up for the extra expense of buying the car.

(2) Also, companies may lose money up front, but will be pioneers for the technology, leading to profits in the long run.

(3) Even though they might not be the *most* efficient, they are the best on the market right now:

- Less fuel used, so no smog test needed
- Decrease in pollution
- By making hybrid cars we can learn about developing better models. Practice makes perfect.
- Ones with a third row big enough for a large family, don't get as good of gas mileage as other hybrids, but they still get better gas mileage than standard cars.

(4) Last a long time (fewer repairs)

- Brakes regenerate.
- Batteries last a long time.
- Some don't have efficient air and heat while operating under electricity, so do your research in choosing between hybrids . . . in temperate areas this wouldn't be a problem.

(5) Passage 1 uses a more neutral tone than Passage 2, which is from first-person point of view. This makes passage 1 seems more objective.

Notice that we've combined a few points, jotted down the ideas in sequence, and filled out the notes a bit.

Following this outline, our best plan of action is to compose four body paragraphs, one for each numbered point. (The *body* of an essay includes all paragraphs except for an introductory and a concluding paragraph.) There is no "correct" or "best" number of body paragraphs for an extended-response essay. Three or four body paragraphs is a manageable number for a 45-minute essay. The prompt itself may help you decide on how many body paragraphs to include. But no matter which prompt you get, be sure to include *at least two* body paragraphs.

Step 4: Write a Brief Introductory Paragraph

Once you've spent about five minutes planning your essay, it's time to write it. You'll begin with a brief introductory paragraph. In your initial paragraph, try to accomplish the following:

- Show that you understand both sides of the argument.
- Show that you have a clear view of why you chose one side as better presented than the other.
- Provide a glimpse of how you will support your ideas in your essay.

You can probably accomplish all three goals in two to three sentences. Don't go into details yet by listing specific reasons or examples that support your view. This is what your essay's body paragraphs are for. Also, don't begin your introductory paragraph by repeating the essay prompt word-for-word. Show from the very first sentence that you're thinking for yourself. Here's a good introductory paragraph for the provided essay topic:

> With the increasingly popular go-green movement and the controversy surrounding global warming, people are becoming more aware of their effect on the earth. The environmentally aware who seek out both short-term and long-term solutions may find hybrid cars a good stepping-stone to a healthier world. However, others argue that hybrid cars are a weak solution to a serious issue. Each of the two passages argue for opposing positions in this debate, though one clearly presents more effective evidence than the other.The opening paragraph is an important part of the essay, so take great care in writing it. To help ensure that it's as good as it can be, consider writing a rough draft of the paragraph on your erasable white board first.

Step 5: Write the Body Paragraphs of Your Essay

During step 5, your task is to get your supporting points out of your brain and off your erasable note board and into the space allotted for your extended response. Here's what you need to keep in mind as you write:

- Be sure the first sentence of each paragraph begins a distinct train of thought and clearly conveys the essence of the paragraph.
- Arrange your paragraphs so your essay flows logically and persuasively from one point to the next. Try to stick to your outline, but be flexible.
- Try to devote at least two, but no more than three or four sentences to each main point in your outline.
- Don't stray from the topic at hand, or even from the points you seek to make. Be sure to stay well focused on both.

The following are the body paragraphs of a response to the topic. These paragraphs are based on our notes from step 3, but there are a few differences.

One of the biggest arguments against standard cars is the depletion of fossil fuels—otherwise known as gasoline. This is such a strong argument that the author of Passage 2 does not even attempt to refute it. The author of Passage 1 argues that by buying a hybrid car, less of this precious fuel will be used and owners of hybrid cars can save money. The author of Passage 2 argues that buying such vehicles is more expensive, but the money saved on gas will make up for the initial expense. Even though companies may lose money initially in creating the cars, these companies are pioneers for the technology: long-term financial goals may prove profitable as theories are tested and models are perfected.

The author of Passage 2 tends to focus too much on the expense of hybrid cars, failing to address their environmental benefits sufficiently. According to Passage 1, because hybrids use less gas, there is a decrease in pollution. This is not only good for the environment, but it also means that some states do not require hybrid cars to go through an emissions test. The author of Passage 1 mentions that this can save hybrid owners even more money, dealing another blow to the author Passage 2's fixation on the expense of hybrid cars.

Passage 1 also makes a strong case for hybrids in its discussion of how they may not need brake or battery replacements as often as standard cars. According to the passage, hybrid brakes are designed to be regenerative, meaning they use the energy created from braking rather than wasting it, which damages the brakes. In terms of batteries, most hybrid models are protected under extensive warranties—hybrid cars that were analyzed once they reached 200,000 miles reportedly performed as well as new models of the same brand, something standard cars cannot live up to. This is yet another key issue in terms of the environmental and financial benefits of owning a hybrid car that Passage 2 fails to address. Instead it makes a weak argument regarding how hybrids may be too small for large families that might require three rows of seats instead of the much more common two rows.

The relatively weak evidence in Passage 2 is also less effectively presented because of the author's more personal language. While the ideas in the passage may be have been well researched, the author's use of phrases such as "I think" and "as far as I'm concerned" make some of the passage's details seem more like personal opinions than neutral evidence. Passage 1 uses a more neutral, authoritative tone, making its arguments seem less like the author's opinions and more like indisputable facts.

Step 6: Write a Brief Summary or Concluding Paragraph

Make sure that your essay has a clear ending. Reserve time to wrap up your essay. Convey your main supporting ideas in a clear, concise, and forceful way. Two or three sentences should be enough for this purpose. If an especially insightful concluding point occurs to you, the final sentence of your essay is a good place for it.

Here's a brief but effective concluding paragraph for the response to the topic. Notice that this brief summary does not introduce any new reasons or examples. Instead, it simply provides a quick recap, which is all you need to accomplish with your final paragraph.

Passage 1 makes a clear, well-supported argument for how hybrid cars are more gas efficient, reduce the effect humans have on the environment, and can save drivers money if they are committed to the project's long-term efforts. Passage 2's argument against hybrids by dwelling on the cost of buying one fails to undermine the conclusions in passage 1, and Passage 2's more personal tone does not assist its argument either. That author's argument that something better than a hybrid car may be released eventually may have some validity, but until that happens, these cars are strong contenders for a short-term solution that can teach creators about how to develop and perfect future models.

From beginning to end (including the introductory, body, and concluding paragraphs), the preceding sample essay is fewer than 650 words. So it's not especially lengthy. Nor is it a literary masterpiece. Nevertheless, it expresses a clear viewpoint, supports a viewpoint with relevant reasons and examples, is well organized, and is written in a clear and effective manner. In short, it contains all the elements of a high-scoring GED Reasoning Through Language Arts Test extended response essay.

Step 7: Proofread to Find Errors You Can Easily Fix

Save the last few minutes to proofread your essay from start to finish for mechanical problems that you can quickly and easily fix, such as errors in spelling, punctuation, and word choice.

DEVELOPING AND CONNECTING YOUR PARAGRAPHS

An effective extended response essay will contain much more than just a series of general statements. Ideally, you will have only a few general statements, and the majority of your writing will be dedicated to creating purposeful, specific details that will support your premise.

Topic Sentences

Each body paragraph in your essay should help explain and support your extended response essay's central idea, of course. But each body paragraph should have its own central idea as well, which you should express in a **topic sentence**. The topic sentence of each paragraph should be a major point in support of the central idea. The paragraph's other sentences should all relate directly to the topic sentence, providing information that explains or supports the topic sentence's idea.

The sentences that make up a paragraph should be presented in a logical order. An essay that flows logically from one paragraph to another so that its ideas are easily understood is said to be *coherent*. Your body paragraphs should flow from and support your central idea, as well as flow logically from one to the next. As you introduce new ideas, use a consistent structure from one paragraph to the next. Repeating key words or phrases, or using variations of the same phrases, can be especially helpful. Here is an example:

First body paragraph:

One way that spending too much time on the internet can be harmful . . . .

Second body paragraph:

A second problem with spending too much time on the internet is . . . .

Third body paragraph:

A final problem with internet overuse is . . . .

Try to develop your own arsenal of words and phrases that connect ideas together so they flow from one to another. Certain words and phrases move the extended response essay forward and imply the building of an idea or thought. Certain other words and phrases work to compare ideas or draw conclusions from the preceding thoughts. Following are several lists of words and phrases that writers often use as bridges between ideas.

Words and phrases that help connect ideas of *equal weight*:

first, second, . . .	finally	likewise
additionally	further	next
also	furthermore	similarly
equally important	in addition	what's more

Words and phrases that signal *comparison* and *contrast*:

although	conversely	on the other hand
but	however	rather
by comparison	in contrast	to the contrary
by the same token	in spite of	whereas
compared to	more importantly	while

Words and phrases used to *qualify* or point out an *exception* to an assertion of fact:

depending on	in rare instances	nevertheless
despite	in some circumstances	sometimes
infrequently	in spite of	yet

Words and phrases that signal *sequence* (chronological, logical, or rhetorical):

first, second, third, . . .	concurrently	previously
	consequently	simultaneously
after	finally	subsequently
beforehand	next	then

Words and phrases that signal the use of a supporting *example*:

as an illustration	in another case	one possible scenario
consider	in this case	take the case of
for example	in this situation	to demonstrate
for instance	on this occasion	to illustrate

Words and phrases that signal a *conclusion*:

accordingly	hence	therefore
as a result	it follows that	thus

Use these phrases for your concluding or *summary paragraph*:

all things considered	in essence	on balance
in a nutshell	in short	on the whole
in brief	in sum	summing up
in conclusion	in the final analysis	to recapitulate

It takes practice to develop a knack for writing paragraphs that use connecting words effectively. Be sure to complete all three extended response items on the practice tests provided.

WRITING STYLE

Your writing style refers to the words and phrases you choose to use and how you use them, how you structure your sentences, and the overall voice and tone you use in your writing. To ensure yourself a high score on your extended response question, strive for writing that is:

- appropriate in tone and "voice" for academic writing.
- clear and concise (easy to understand and direct rather than wordy or verbose).
- varied in sentence length and structure (to add interest and variety as well as to demonstrate maturity in writing style).
- correct and appropriate in word choice and usage.

All of this is easier said than done, of course. Don't worry if you're not a natural when it comes to writing the kind of prose that's appropriate for the GED test. You *can* improve your writing for your exam, even if your time is short. Start by reading the suggestions and guidelines that follow. But, keep in mind: improvement in writing comes mainly with practice. So you'll also need to apply what you learn here to the practice tests in this book and to the supplementary writing prompts provided at the end of this lesson.

Overall Tone and Voice

In general, you should try to maintain a somewhat *formal* tone throughout your response. A response that comes across as casual or conversational—like a personal email or blog entry—is probably a bit too informal for the GED test. Here are some specific guidelines:

- The overall tone should be analytical, which means it should be a detailed explanation of your viewpoint. Don't overstate your view or opinion by using extreme or harsh language that appeals to emotions instead.
- When it comes to your main points, a very direct, even forceful, voice is perfectly acceptable. Just don't overdo it.
- It is perfectly acceptable, though optional, to refer to yourself from time to time in your essay. Just be consistent. For example, be sure not to mix phrases such as *I disagree with* or *In my view* with phrases such as *We cannot assume that*.

- Avoid puns, double-meanings, plays on words, and other forms of humor. Sarcasm is also entirely inappropriate for your extended response essay. The automated scoring engine will not realize that you're trying to be humorous, in which case your remark might be confusing.

Clear and Concise Writing

With enough words, anyone can make a point; but it requires skill and effort to make a point with concise phrases. Before you commit to any sentence you have in mind, ask yourself whether you can express the same idea more concisely and clearly. You can use your erasable note board to write a rough draft of the sentence or sentences you're not sure how to write, or you can revise them as you type your essay.

Sentence Length and Variety

Sentences that vary in length make for a more interesting analysis. Your sentences should be varied in style and length. Abrupt, short sentences might be appropriate for making crucial points, but an entire paragraph written in short, choppy sentences is distracting and suggests a certain immaturity. Compare the following two passages:

Ineffective:

Some television shows have too much violence. This is not good for young children. They may learn to be violent themselves. They see too much fighting and shooting on television.

More effective:

The television shows that have too much violence may not be good for young children. The fighting and shooting on these shows may teach children to be violent themselves.

Effective Use of Language

To earn a high score on your essay, you'll need to show that you can use the English language correctly and clearly. By all means, use a strong vocabulary, but don't resort to obscure, high-level vocabulary just to be impressive. Also avoid **colloquialisms** (i.e., slang and vernacular). Instead of nailing your essay, it'll turn out lousy, and you'll be totally out of luck and end up on the skids, big time. (Did you catch the *four* colloquialisms in the preceding sentence?)

Your **diction**—your choice of words as well as the manner in which the words are used—also will be evaluated on your extended response essay. When you commit an error in diction, you might be confusing one word with another because the two words look or sound similar. Or you might be using a word that isn't the best choice to convey the idea you have in mind. Although it is impossible to provide an adequate diction review in these pages, here are some guidelines:

- If you're the least bit unsure about the meaning of a word you're thinking of using in your response, don't use it. Why risk committing a diction error just to use a high-level vocabulary word?
- If a phrase sounds wrong to your ear, change it until it sounds correct to you.
- The fewer words you use, the less likely you'll commit an error in diction. So when in doubt, go with a relatively brief phrase that still conveys your point.

Persuasive Writing

As noted at the beginning of this lesson, the GED Reasoning Through Language Arts Test extended response item will prompt you to read two opposing viewpoints and select the one that makes the most effective argument. In order for your essay to be effective, it must be persuasive. The best way to persuade the reader, of course, is to provide good ideas supported by sound reasons and relevant examples, all presented in a logical sequence. But you can also persuade the reader through your writing style. The art of persuasive writing (or speaking) is referred to as **rhetoric**. Effective rhetorical writing makes its points clearly and forcefully by placing appropriate emphasis on different ideas.

The main way to make a rhetorical point effectively is to use appropriate connecting words between ideas. In the first example that follows, notice that it is difficult to determine the writer's point because of a structure that gives both ideas equal weight. The second and third examples clarify the point by using appropriate connecting words (in italics), as well as by a few other revisions.

Equal weight on both ideas (ineffective):

We try to plan out every detail of our lives. We often change plans because of events we did not foresee.

Greater emphasis on one idea (effective):

It is futile to try planning out every detail of our lives, *since* we often end up changing our plans due to events we did not foresee.

Greater emphasis on the other idea (effective):

People often change their plans due to events they did not foresee. *Nevertheless*, most people continue trying, often in vain, to plan out every detail of their lives.

Another way to emphasize a point is by using an abrupt, short sentence. Good topic sentences for paragraphs are often written in this style. Just be sure that the sentences supporting that point are longer; otherwise, the emphasis will be lost. You should not have any trouble identifying the short, punchy topic sentence in either of the following two paragraphs.

Rhetorical emphasis on the last sentence:

While the richest people in our country find ways to add to their own wealth, thousands of people die on the streets in our nation each day, and thousands more go hungry or suffer from nearly intolerable living conditions. Millions have inadequate health insurance, and millions more have no health insurance at all. In short, we have an empathy crisis.

Rhetorical emphasis on the first sentence:

Corporations are not evil. The people who run them simply try to maximize profits for the corporation's owners. So when you hear complaints about a CEO cutting employee benefits or outsourcing jobs, remember that the CEO is only doing his job, which is what the company's owners want.

You can also use punctuation for rhetorical emphasis. To emphasize a particular idea, you can end a sentence with an exclamation mark instead of a period. Also, you can emphasize a particular word by italicizing it. But use these two rhetorical devices *very* sparingly; one of each in your essay is plenty! (Notice the use of both devices in the preceding sentence.)

Sentences that pose questions can also provide rhetorical emphasis. Like short, abrupt sentences, **rhetorical questions** can help persuade the reader—or at least help to make your point. They can be quite effective. They also add interest and variety. Yet how many GED test takers think to incorporate them into their essays? (By the way, the previous question is a rhetorical question.) Just don't overdo it: one rhetorical question is plenty for one essay. And be sure to provide an answer to your question.

Finally, you can emphasize a point using rhetorical words and phrases such as *undeniably*, *absolutely*, *clearly*, *without a doubt*, *the fact is*, and *anyone would agree that*. By themselves, these words and phrases mean very little; to be truly effective, they must be backed up by sound ideas and convincing reasons and examples. But they can help add rhetorical flair to your essay. Just don't overuse them.

SUGGESTIONS FOR WRITING AND EVALUATING YOUR PRACTICE EXTENDED RESPONSE

To improve your writing, there is no substitute for practice. Start by using the essay prompts in this book's practice tests.

Always practice under exam-like conditions. Limit your time to 45 minutes. Use an erasable note board for notes, outlines, and rough drafts of particular sentences as needed, but type your final draft on the computer. Experiment in allocating your time among your various tasks:

- Brainstorming (note-taking)
- Organizing your ideas (outlining)
- Writing rough drafts
- Writing the final draft
- Proofreading and fixing problems

Keep practicing until you've learned to allocate your time in a way that works best for you.

Be sure to evaluate each practice response you write. Be critical. Try to identify your weaknesses so that you can focus on eliminating them. A good way to improve on weaknesses is to *rewrite* an entire practice essay. Spend no more than 25 minutes to write your revised version; focus mainly on correcting the most glaring problems with your earlier draft.

You may find it difficult to judge your own writing objectively, so consider asking a friend, family member, coworker, or teacher to read and evaluate your responses as well. You might be surprised how useful their feedback can be. In any case, use the following 3-point checklist to evaluate your practice responses. This list provides all of the elements of an effective, high-scoring GED test extended response.

1. Does the response discuss each passage presented and go into why or why not each makes a good argument? (Does it clearly convey your selection, and does it cite evidence from the source texts to support your stance?)

2. Is the response well organized? (Are the ideas presented in a logical sequence, so they can be easily followed? Are transitions from one point to the next natural and logical? Does the response show awareness of purpose in making its points? Does it demonstrate appropriate vocabulary? Does it have a clear ending, or did you appear to run out of time?)
3. Does your response demonstrate fluency with the conventions of edited American English grammar, sentence structure, word choice, punctuation, and spelling?

Your extended response item will be scored based on how well it meets the traits outlined in each rubric. Responses are scored on a 6-point scale; each rubric is worth up to two points. The final raw score on the extended response item is then double-weighted so that it represents up to 12 raw score points on the overall GED Reading and Language Arts Test. When evaluating your practice response, look at the various points on the rubric. If your essay displays all of the characteristics in the 2-point cell on the rubric, you would get 2 points for that trait; if it meets all of the characteristics in the 1-point cell, you would get 1 point; and if it displays the characteristics of the 0-point cell, you would get 0 points for that trait. To earn a high score of 12, your response would have to match the description in the 2-point cell for each rubric.

GENERAL TEST-TAKING STRATEGIES

Here are some general strategies for writing GED Reasoning Through Language Arts Test extended response items. Most reiterate key points of advice made earlier in this lesson. Apply these strategies to the practice tests and then review this list again just before exam day.

Organize your thoughts before you write.

Use your erasable note board to make notes and to construct an outline of your major points and supporting examples. Before you start typing your final draft, consider writing a rough draft of at least the introductory and first body paragraphs. Just be sure to leave enough time to write your final draft.

Express a clear view based on evidence supported by the passages.

The prompt will ask you to analyze the texts and select the one that makes the best argument. Whatever position you take, you must support it logically based on the specific language used in the texts. Remember: in writing your response, there is no "correct" or "best" answer.

Develop each major point of your outline with reasons and/or examples.

Asserting your views and opinions without explaining or justifying them is not sufficient (or persuasive) and will not earn a high score. Develop your analysis and each major supporting point with sound reasons and relevant examples. In fact, the prompt will instruct you to do precisely that.

Stay well-focused on the topic at hand.

Don't digress from the specific topic that is presented. Your central idea must address the topic directly, and each body paragraph should relate directly to an aspect of the texts being analyzed.

Appeal to reason, not emotion.

The extended response item is an *intellectual* exercise. It's perfectly appropriate to criticize particular behaviors or viewpoints. But do not use the essay as a forum to "preach" on the subject or make an emotional appeal. Avoid extremes in tone and attitude. In particular, do not provide even a hint of racial prejudice or jingoism (excessive patriotism).

Keep it simple.

Don't make the extended response task more difficult than it needs to be for you to attain a solid score. Keep your sentences clear and simple. Use a simple, straightforward structure for your response. Avoid using fancy words just to be impressive.

Look organized and in control of the task.

Show that you know how to present your thoughts in an organized manner. Present your main points in a logical, easy-to-follow sequence, using logical paragraph breaks between major supporting points. Use a consistent voice and tone throughout your essay. Your introductory and concluding paragraphs are especially key to looking organized and in control. Be sure to include both, and make sure that both reveal your central idea.

It's quality, not quantity, that counts.

The only limitations on the length of your response are the time limit and the amount of space provided. You need to strive for quality, not length. Be sure to incorporate into your response all the elements recommended in this lesson, and the length of your response will take care of itself.

Don't lose sight of your primary objectives.

During the time you have to produce your response, remember your three main objectives:

1. Develop your analysis using sound evidence and relevant examples from the texts provided.
2. Present your ideas in a logical, well-organized manner.
3. Express your ideas through simple, clear writing that is correct in grammar, diction, spelling, and punctuation.

Never lose sight of these three objectives. Accomplish them all, and you can be assured that you've produced a solid, high-scoring GED test extended response.

SUMMING IT UP

- The extended response component of the GED Reasoning Through Language Arts Test assesses your ability to communicate your thoughts and ideas in writing. You will be asked to analyze two documents that contain opposing viewpoints and present your opinion or explain why one makes a better argument than the other. You will not be given a choice of essays to write on, and you must write *only* about the ideas that are presented in the documents provided.
- You will have 45 minutes to plan, write, and revise your response. Erasable note boards will be provided to jot down notes, but you must type your extended response in the space provided.
- There is no correct answer or best response, and there is no correct structure or number of paragraphs for a extended response. The response is ***expected*** to be in paragraph form, and the preceding pages clearly state that you need at least one introductory paragraph, one body paragraph, and one summary paragraph. (A minimum of two body paragraphs is strongly suggested.)
- An automated scoring engine will score your response on a scale of 0–6 based on how well it meets the traits on three rubrics, each one emphasizing a different aspect of the response, as follows:
    - Rubric 1: Creation of arguments and use of evidence
    - Rubric 2: Development of ideas and organizational structure
    - Rubric 3: Clarity and command of standard English conventions
- The final raw score (0–6) on the Extended Response item is double-weighted; it will represent up to 12 raw score points on the overall GED Reasoning Through Language Arts Test.
- When practicing your writing—and during the real test—be sure to remember the following important steps:
    - Brainstorming (note-taking)
    - Organizing your ideas (outlining)
    - Writing the rough draft
    - Writing the final draft
    - Proofreading and fixing problems

PRACTICE EXTENDED RESPONSE

Directions: Try the following prompt on your own. Enter your response in the answer sheets provided. You should expect to spend up to 45 minutes to plan, draft, and edit your response.

Debating Allowing Smartphones in the Classroom

The following passages represent two views of the value of allowing smartphones in the classroom. Analyze both positions presented to determine which one is best supported. Use relevant and specific evidence from both passages to support your response.

Passage 1

Statistics reveal that students tend to check their smartphones more than 11 times during the school day. So I'm sure you'll agree that to characterize smartphones as a distraction is something of an understatement. As a teacher, I would call the smartphones in the classroom downright antithetical to education. The idea that my school has not instated a policy preventing kids from using smartphones in the classroom is an absurdity.

There is no benefit to allowing smartphones in the classroom. Students waste class time giggling about nonsense they read on the internet, "zone out" of the lesson by focusing on their devices rather than the white board, and create an audible buzz worthy of a swarm of killer bees as their phones vibrate incessantly throughout the class period. The presence of smartphones is nothing but a hindrance to the students' learning and my ability to teach them.

To be clear, I have authority to ban smartphone use in my class. The school has no policy preventing teachers from using their personal discretions when it comes to phone use during class time. The problem is that too many teachers do not exercise that right, allowing the students we share to fall into patterns that are impossible to break. When a kid is allowed to check his phone as often as he likes in Ms. X's science class, what do you think that student will do after the bell rings and he takes a seat in my room?

Banning smartphones at Grant High School will take care of this problem completely. Students cannot slip into bad habits when those habits are disallowed outright. With support from my fellow teachers, I believe we can inspire a policy change at our school that will make it easier for teachers to do their jobs and students to do theirs.

Passage 2

Students apparently check their smartphones 11 times a day during school. Based on my own experience as a teacher, I can't say that this statistic is unconvincing. However, I believe that what may initially seem like a negative can be transformed into a positive with some creative thinking and adaptability on the part of my fellow teachers.

I won't argue that the texting, emailing student is not a nuisance. Young people are certainly addicted to their smartphones. However, expecting them all to go "cold turkey" during class time is a bit unrealistic. Banning smartphones will simply result in more students flouting the rules and clogging seats during after-school detention sessions.

Perhaps the solution is to think of ways to incorporate smartphones into our daily lessons. Smartphones are essentially mini personal computers. Think of it: a computer at every desk…and in every student's pocket at no extra expense for the school. A plethora of quality learning apps is at the fingertips of every student wielding a smart phone. Students can use their phones for research and to communicate with each other in creative ways while collaborating on projects.

Naturally, students cannot simply tap away on the phones all day, every day. There must be designated phone times during the class period. If students know they will be allowed—expected, even—to use their phones at some point during class, they will be less likely to whip them out during inappropriate times.

So I reject the old-fashioned notion that smartphones are an evil of the modern world that must be banished from the classroom. More importantly, most students will too. By allowing our lessons to keep up with the times, we will not have to enforce new rules that students are unlikely to follow in any event and we may even find that those students will begin learning more effectively than ever.

Extended Response

SAMPLE RESPONSES AND ANALYSIS

High-Scoring Analysis

For better or for worse, smartphones have seemingly infiltrated our lives for good. Everywhere you go you will see people of all ages and backgrounds hunched over the phones and furiously texting or skidding across the Internet. This is even true of that sanctuary of learning: the classroom. Along with their other multitudinous tasks, teachers must now also contend with students who are more interested in updating Instagram than learning. The question is: should teachers ban smartphones from the class completely or adapt to a new era and figure out creative ways to incorporate smartphones into lessons.

That question is at the heart of the two sides of the debate in Passages 1 and 2. Passage 1 unequivocally calls for a ban on smartphones in the class. Passage 2 takes a more measured approach, suggesting that portions of class time be set aside for smartphone use among students. While both authors make their cases with clarity, I find both to be flawed in significant ways.

Interestingly, both arguments draw on the same statistic to make their cases: the apparent fact that "students tend to check their smartphones more than 11 times during the school day." That there is no citation for this statistic could be a red flag that Passage 1 might be built on unreliable information. That the author of Passage 2 qualifies this statistic with the word "apparently" indicates that she or he questions it, but that author does not indicate why that might be the case. Both passages could use more specifics to strengthen their arguments.

They could also use more support that isn't based solely on personal experience. After dropping this uncited statistic, the author of Passage 1 dwells on his or her own classroom experiences to make generalizations such as "there is no benefit to allowing smartphones in the classroom." The author of Passage 2 makes some strong arguments to the contrary, though the reference to "a plethora of quality learning apps" begs for more specificity as well.

While I appreciated the more nuanced take on smartphones in the classroom in Passage 2, I also took issue with a glaring detail absent from it. What of students who do not have the wherewithal to purchase smartphones? The author seems to take for granted that all young people currently own smartphones, which would be the only way to incorporate them into daily lessons. However, this is simply unrealistic. What of students from low income families or students whose parents disallow smartphones? Would they be required to scrape together the funds to purchase smartphones if these devices become essential to lessons?

Considering our smartphone-addicted society, the debate regarding whether or not smartphones should be allowed in the classroom is a worthwhile one. However, arguments on both sides need to be crafted with greater attention to detail and sensitivity than these ones are. Passage 2 certainly displays less extreme thinking than Passage 1, but as it stands, the ultimate argument for or against allowing smartphones in the classroom is still waiting to be made.

Explanation

This analysis would receive a high score because it generates a text-based argument and uses relevant evidence from the passages to support it, contains ideas that are organized and well-developed, and demonstrates a command of standard English conventions. Specifically, this essay critiques both sides of the argument by citing information in the passages and details that they lack. The passage shows a logical and thoughtful progression of ideas. The essay demonstrates fluency in standard English and uses varied sentence structure.

Mid-Level-Scoring Analysis

I agreed with the conclusion of the first of the two passages. Smartphones should not be allowed in classrooms. This seems self-evident to me; something that does not even deserve to be debated. But since it was debated in these passages, it is worth noting that the first argument is the more convincing of the two.

As the author reveals, students check their phones on an average of 11 times during the school day. That is a tremendous distraction when they should be learning. The other author cites the same evidence and doesn't even spin it so that it supports his or her argument. So it is kind of self defeating. What's the point? I do not know.

I really cannot defend anything in the second passage. Not only is citing evidence that works against your own argument foolish, but the other arguments are weak too. The idea that students should use their smartphones in class is absurd. There is nothing they can do on their smartphones that can't be done by less distracting means. I think that if they take out their phones once to do an assignment in class, they'll just keep them out for the rest of the period and continue to play with them. Just look at everyone with a smartphone and tell me this isn't true. Even the author knows this, writing that "When a kid is allowed to check his phone as often as he likes in Ms. X's science class, what do you think that student will do after the bell rings and he takes a seat in my room?"

The first passage is written by an experienced teacher, and so that teacher should know what she or he is talking about. The other passage was written by a teacher as well, but I surmise that this teacher is not very experienced. If she or he was, he or she would not make the strange argument that students should be allowed to use their phones in class.

There's only one possible side to this debate and the author of the first passage is on the right side of it. Put away your smartphones in class! I cannot accept any other solution.

Explanation

This analysis would receive a medium-level score because it generates a mostly text-based argument that uses some relevant evidence from the passages to support it, contains ideas that are fairly organized and well developed, and demonstrates a reasonable command of standard English conventions. However, there are some significant flaws in the argument, as when the writer uses a quote from one passage to support an idea to which the quote isn't connected. There are also too many personal opinions, and the passage could be longer.

Low-Scoring Analysis

Passage 2 definitely makes the better argument. Smartphones should be allowed in the classroom, period. They can be used to help with learning as the author shows.

Passage 1 is not as good because it is basically black and white about the issue. It thinks smartphones are bad, period. It never even considers that there might be positive things about using smartphones to learn.

Still, I think that it is pretty extreme that kids check their phones 11 times every class period. That is a lot. Maybe they should be banned from the classroom.

Saying that, I still think Passage 2 is better. It shows that smartphones don't have to be banned. Think of all the excellent apps that can be used to teach kids that are on smartphones. Such apps can become a vital part of the learning experience. If only teachers would start thinking in a more modern way instead of the old fashioned belief that anything modern should be kept out of the classroom. That is basically what I thought when I read Passage 1.

Still, that writer is a teacher. If we learn one thing in class, its that teachers know what they're talking about. So there may be some validity to that argument. I still think that Passage 2 has a more positive attitude. Maybe that is what kids need more than anything else in the world.

Explanation

This analysis would receive a low score because it is far too short, with an argument that uses little to no evidence from the passage to support it and wavers on its conclusion more than once. It contains ideas that are confusing and not clearly organized, and demonstrates minimal command of Standard English conventions with several mistakes and only some varied sentence structure.

Chapter 6

Writing Review

OVERVIEW

- **Sentence Structure**
- **Usage**
- **Verb Tense**
- **Pronoun Case, Reference, and Agreement**
- **Writing Mechanics**
- **Summing It Up**

SENTENCE STRUCTURE

Sentence structure refers to how a sentence's parts fit together as a whole. In this section, you'll learn to spot these problems and how to correct or revise sentences on the GED Reasoning Through Language Arts Test. It is also important to understand sentence structure when answering the extended response item.

Structural Errors

A sentence on the test might be structured in a way that results in one of the following grammatical errors:

- Sentence fragments
- Run-ons and comma splices
- Faulty parallelism involving series
- Faulty parallelism involving correlatives

Don't worry if some of the terms listed above are unfamiliar to you. You'll learn what they mean in the pages ahead.

Sentence Fragments

A complete sentence must include both a subject and a predicate. The **subject** of a sentence is the word or phrase that describes what the sentence is about. A complete subject is a noun or pronoun and any of the words directly related to that noun or pronoun. The **predicate**, or complete verb, includes all the words that, together, say something about the subject.

Look at this sentence:

> *Aaron tried to start his car but couldn't.*

In this sentence, the word *Aaron* is the complete subject. The rest of the sentence, which says something about Aaron, is the predicate, or complete verb. The word *tried* is the verb that establishes the predicate.

An incomplete sentence is called a **sentence fragment**. On the test, you probably won't have any trouble recognizing and fixing a short sentence fragment like the next one, which lacks a predicate. In the complete sentence, notice that the verb *are* establishes a predicate.

> **fragment (incorrect):** Expensive private colleges, which for most families are out of financial reach.
>
> **complete sentence (correct):** Expensive private colleges are out of financial reach for most families.

A longer fragment is more likely to escape your detection, especially if you're not paying close attention:

> **fragment (incorrect):** As most of the engineers and other experts have agreed, their responsibility for building safe bridges, as well as for maintaining them.
>
> **complete sentence (correct):** As most of the engineers and other experts have agreed, they are responsible not only for building safe bridges but but also for maintaining them.

In the complete sentence, the subject is *they,* and the predicate is the verb *are* and the words that follow that verb.

If you're not sure whether a sentence is complete, ask yourself the following two questions: What is the subject? Where is the verb that establishes a predicate?

Run-ons and Comma Splices

An **independent clause** is a sentence part that can stand alone as a complete sentence. There's nothing wrong with combining two such clauses into one sentence, as long as you connect them properly.

Connecting two independent clauses without using a punctuation mark or any words to make the connection results in a grammatical error called a **run-on** sentence. One way to correct the error is to split the sentence in two using a period. Another solution is to add a comma, followed by an appropriate connecting word:

> **run-on (incorrect):** Dan ran out of luck Mike continued to win.
>
> **correct:** Dan ran out of luck. Mike continued to win.
>
> **correct:** Dan ran out of luck, but Mike continued to win.

Connecting two independent clauses with only a comma results in an error known as a **comma splice**. One way to correct the error is to insert an appropriate connecting word after the comma:

> **comma splice (incorrect):** Dan ran out of luck, Mike continued to win.
>
> **correct:** Dan ran out of luck, though Mike continued to win.

It can be easy to overlook a longer run-on or comma splice unless you're reading carefully. Here's an example of a longer comma splice:

> **comma splice:** The Aleutian Islands of Alaska include many islands near the populated mainland, the majority of them are uninhabited by humans.

In reading this sentence, it isn't until you reach the word *are* that the comma splice becomes apparent. One way to correct the error is to remove the word *are*. Another way to correct the error is to transform the second independent clause into a *dependent* clause by changing the word *them* to *which*.

Faulty Parallelism Involving Series

Sentence elements that are grammatically equal should be constructed similarly; otherwise, the result will be what is referred to as **faulty parallelism**. For example, whenever you see a list, or series, of items in a sentence, look for inconsistent or mixed use of:

- Prepositions (such as *in, with*, or *on*)
- Gerunds (verbs with an *-ing* added to the end)
- Infinitives (plural verb preceded by *to*)
- Articles (such as *a* and *the*)

In the following sentence, the preposition *to* is not applied consistently to every item in the series:

> **faulty:** Flight 82 travels first to Boise, then to Denver, then Salt Lake City.
>
> (The word *to* precedes only the first two of the three cities in this list.)
>
> **parallel:** Flight 82 travels first to Boise, then Denver, then Salt Lake City.
>
> **parallel:** Flight 82 travels first to Boise, then to Denver, and then to Salt Lake City.

In the next sentence, the gerund *being* is not applied consistently:

> **faulty:** Being understaffed, lack of funding, and being outpaced by competitors soon resulted in the fledgling company's going out of business.
>
> (Only two of the three listed items begin with the gerund *being*.)
>
> **parallel:** Understaffed, underfunded, and outpaced by competitors, the fledgling company soon went out of business.
>
> **parallel:** As a result of understaffing, insufficient funding, and outpacing on the part of its competitors, the fledgling company soon went out of business.

In the next sentence, the article *the* is not applied consistently:

> **faulty:** Among the mountains, the sea, and desert, we humans have yet to fully explore only the sea.
>
> **parallel:** Among the mountains, sea, and desert, we humans have yet to fully explore only the sea.
>
> **parallel:** Among the mountains, the sea, and the desert, we humans have yet to fully explore only the sea.

Faulty Parallelism Involving Correlatives

The preceding section described how a list of items in a series can suffer from faulty parallelism. A similar problem can occur in sentences that contain **correlatives**. Here are the most common ones:

either . . . or . . .

neither . . . nor . . .

both . . . and . . .

not only . . . but also . . .

When a correlative is used in a sentence, the element immediately following the first correlative term must be grammatically parallel to the element following the second term.

faulty: Students wishing to participate in the study group should *either* contact me by telephone *or* should email me.

parallel: Students wishing to participate in the study group should *either* contact me by telephone *or* email me.

faulty: Students wishing to participate in the study group *either* should contact me by telephone *or* email.

parallel: Students wishing to participate in the study group should contact me by *either* telephone *or* email.

Awkward and Confusing Sentence Structures

A sentence that is free of errors might nevertheless be structured in a way that makes the sentence's ideas confusing, vague, ambiguous, or even nonsensical. These sorts of structural problems include the following:

- Improper coordination or subordination
- Mixing of two structures together in one sentence
- Omission of a key word needed for sentence logic
- Improper placement of modifiers
- Dangling modifiers
- Improper splitting of a grammatical unit
- Stringing together too many subordinate clauses

Don't worry if some of the terms listed are unfamiliar to you. You'll learn what they mean in the following pages.

Improper Coordination or Subordination

A sentence that is free of grammatical errors may nevertheless be structured in a way that overemphasizes certain ideas, so that the reader misses the sentence's main point. If a sentence conveys two equally important ideas, they should be separated as two distinct clauses of similar length—to suggest equal importance.

mixed and unbalanced: Julie and Sandy, *who* are twins, are both volunteers.

separated but unbalanced: Julie and Sandy were the first two volunteers for the fund-raising drive, *and* they are twins.

separated and balanced: Julie and Sandy are twins, *and* they are both volunteers.

On the other hand, if a sentence involves only one main idea, that idea should receive greater emphasis as a main clause than the other ideas in the sentence.

balanced: Julie and Sandy, *who* are twins, were the first two volunteers for the fund-raising drive.

In the preceding sentence, notice that the less important idea (that Julie and Sandy are twins) is contained in a brief, modifying clause that describes Julie and Sandy. This is an effective way to deemphasize an idea that is not the main idea of the sentence.

To suggest similarity in ideas, a **coordinating conjunctive** such as *and* should be used. To suggest dissimilarity, or contrast, in ideas, a **subordinating conjunctive** such as *but, though, although,* or *whereas* should be used.

similar ideas: Julie and Sandy were identical twins, *and* they both liked to travel.

similar ideas: Julie and Sandy were identical twins, *and* so were Tracy and Judy.

dissimilar ideas: Julie and Sandy were identical twins, *but* they had completely different ambitions.

dissimilar ideas: Julie and Sandy were identical twins, *whereas* Tracy and Judy were merely fraternal twins.

Mixing Sentence Structures

If two or more clauses in the same sentence express parallel ideas, they should be grammatically parallel to each other. Otherwise, the sentence may be awkward and confusing.

This problem often occurs when a sentence mixes the **active voice** with the **passive voice**. In a sentence expressed in the active voice, the subject *acts upon* an object. Conversely, in a sentence expressed in the passive voice, the subject *is acted upon by* an object. Here are two sets of examples:

mixed: Although the *house was built by Gary, Kevin built the garage.*

parallel (passive): Although the *house was built by Gary*, the *garage was built by Kevin.*

parallel (active): Although *Gary built the house, Kevin built the garage.*

mixed: All hardback *books are to be sorted* today, but *wait* until tomorrow *to sort paperbacks.*

parallel (passive): All hardback *books are to be sorted* today, but *paperbacks are not to be sorted* until tomorrow.

parallel (active): *Sort all hardback books* today *and sort the paperbacks* tomorrow.

Sentence Logic

If a sentence excludes a necessary word, the omission can obscure or confuse the meaning of the sentence. The unintentional omission of "little" words—prepositions, pronouns, conjunctives, and especially the word *that*—can make a big difference.

omission: We decided after going to the movie, we would grab a snack.

(When was the decision made: before or after seeing the movie?)

clearer: We decided that, after going to the movie, we would grab a snack. (before)

clearer: After going to the movie, we decided that we would grab a snack. (after)

Look out especially for an omission that results in an illogical comparison, as in the following sentences. It can easily slip past you if you're not paying close attention.

illogical: The color of the blouse is different from the skirt.

logical: The color of the blouse is different from *that* of the skirt.

illogical: China's population is greater than any country in the world.

(This sentence draws an illogical comparison between a population and a country and illogically suggests that China is not a country.)

logical: China's population is greater than *that of* any *other* country in the world.

In many cases, the word *that* is optional. For example, here's a sentence that makes sense either with or without it:

Some evolutionary theorists believe [*that*] humans began to walk in an upright posture mainly because they needed to reach tree branches to obtain food.

Improper Placement of Modifiers

A **modifier** is a word or phrase that describes, restricts, or qualifies another word or phrase. Modifying phrases are typically set off with commas, and many such phrases begin with a relative pronoun (*which, who, that, whose, whom*).

In general, modifiers should be placed as close as possible to the word(s) they modify. Positioning a modifier in the wrong place can result in a confusing or even nonsensical sentence.

misplaced: His death shocked the entire family, *which occurred quite suddenly*.

better: His death, *which occurred quite suddenly*, shocked the entire family.

misplaced: *Nearly dead,* the police finally found the victim.

better: The police finally found *the victim, who was nearly dead.*

unclear: Bill punched Carl *while wearing a mouth protector*.

clear: *While wearing a mouth protector*, Bill punched Carl.

Modifiers such as *almost, nearly, hardly, just,* and *only* should immediately precede the word(s) they modify, even if the sentence sounds correct with the parts separated. For example:

misplaced: Their 1-year-old child *almost* weighs *40 pounds.*

better: Their 1-year-old child weighs *almost 40 pounds.*

Note the position of *only* in the following sentences:

unclear: The assistant was *only* able to detect obvious errors.

clear: *Only the assistant* was able to detect obvious errors.

unclear: The assistant was able to *only* detect *obvious errors.*

clear: The assistant was able to detect *only obvious errors.*

The general rule about placing modifiers near the words they modify applies most of the time. In some cases, however, trying to place a modifier near the words it modifies actually confuses the meaning of the sentence, as with the modifier *without his glasses* in the following sentences.

unclear: Nathan can read the newspaper and shave *without his glasses.*

(It is unclear whether *without his glasses* refers only to *shave* or to both *shave* and *read the newspaper.*)

unclear: *Without his glasses, Nathan* can read the newspaper and can shave.

(This sentence implies that these are the only two tasks Nathan can perform without his glasses.)

clear: *Even without his glasses,* Nathan can read the newspaper and shave.

So don't apply the rule without checking to see whether the sentence as a whole makes sense.

Dangling Modifiers

A *dangling modifier* is a modifier that doesn't refer to any particular word(s) in the sentence. The only way to correct a dangling modifier problem is to reconstruct the modifying phrase or the entire sentence.

dangling: *Set by an arsonist,* firefighters were unable to save the burning building.

(What was set by an arsonist?)

better: Firefighters were unable to save the burning building from *the fire set by an arsonist.*

dangling: *By imposing price restrictions on oil suppliers,* these suppliers will be forced to lower production costs.

(Who imposed the price restrictions?)

better: *If price restrictions are imposed on oil suppliers,* these suppliers will be forced to lower production costs.

Despite the rule against dangling modifiers, a dangling modifier may be acceptable if it is an **idiom**, which means it is considered correct because it has been in common use over a long period of time.

> **acceptable:** *Judging* from the number of violent crimes committed every year, our nation is doomed.
>
> (This sentence makes no reference to whomever is judging; but it is acceptable anyway.)
>
> **acceptable:** *Considering* its great distance from Earth, that star's brightness is amazing.
>
> (This sentence makes no reference to whomever is considering; but it is acceptable anyway.)

Splitting a Grammatical Unit

Splitting clauses or phrases apart by inserting other words between them often results in an awkward and confusing sentence.

> **split:** The value of the dollar *is not,* relative to other currencies, *rising* universally.
>
> **better:** The value of the dollar *is not rising* universally relative to other currencies.

> **split:** The government's goal this year *is to provide* for its poorest residents *an economic safety net.*
>
> **split:** *The government's goal* is to provide an economic safety net *this year* for its poorest residents.
>
> **better:** The *government's goal this year* is to provide an economic safety net for its poorest residents.

Sentences should not contain split infinitives. An **infinitive** is the plural form of an action verb, preceded by the word *to.* If *to* is separated from its corresponding verb, then you're dealing with a **split infinitive** and a sentence that is grammatically incorrect.

> **improper (split):** The executive was compelled *to,* by greed and ambition, *work* more and more hours each day.
>
> **correct:** The executive was compelled by greed and ambition *to work* more and more hours each day.

> **improper (split):** Meteorologists have been known *to* inaccurately *predict* snowstorms.
>
> **correct:** Meteorologists have been known *to predict* snowstorms inaccurately.

Strings of Subordinate Clauses

A *subordinate clause* is one that does not stand on its own as a complete sentence. Stringing together two or more subordinate clauses can result in an awkward and confusing sentence. If possible, these sentences should be restructured to simplify them.

awkward: Barbara's academic major is history, *which* is a very popular course of study among liberal arts students, *with whom* political science is the most popular major.

better: Barbara's academic major is history, *which is second only* to political science as the most popular major among liberal arts students.

USAGE

The language component of the GED Reasoning Through Language Arts Test involves verb and pronoun *usage*—that is, whether these types of words are used correctly in sentences. The test covers only the following areas of usage:

- Subject-verb agreement
- Pronoun case, reference, and agreement

In this section you'll review the rules for these aspects of usage. It is also important to understand usage when answering the extended response.

Subject-Verb Agreement

A verb should always agree in number—either singular or plural—with its subject. A singular subject takes a singular verb, while a plural subject takes a plural verb:

incorrect (singular): The *parade were* spectacular.

correct (singular): The *parade was* spectacular.

incorrect (plural): The parades *was* spectacular.

correct (plural): The parades *were* spectacular.

In the preceding examples, it's easy to tell whether the subject is singular or plural. But in other cases, it's not so easy, as you'll learn in the following sections.

Interrupting Phrases

Don't be fooled by any words or phrases that might separate the verb from its subject. In each sentence below, the singular verb *is* agrees with its subject, the singular noun *parade:*

incorrect: The *parade* of cars *are* spectacular.

correct: The *parade* of cars *is* spectacular.

incorrect: The *parade* of cars and horses *are* spectacular.

correct: The *parade* of cars and horses *is* spectacular.

An intervening phrase set off by commas can serve as an especially effective "smokescreen" for a subject-verb agreement error. Pay careful attention to what comes immediately before and after the intervening phrase. Reading the sentence without the phrase often reveals a subject-verb agreement error.

incorrect: *John*, as well as his sister, *were* absent from school yesterday.

correct: *John*, as well as his sister, *was* absent from school yesterday.

Pronoun Subjects

Determining whether a sentence's subject is singular or plural isn't always as simple as you might think. You can easily determine whether a personal pronoun such as *he, they,* and *its* is singular or plural. But other pronouns are not so easily identified as either singular or plural. Here are two lists, along with some sample sentences, to help you keep these pronouns straight in your mind:

Singular Pronouns
anyone, anything, anybody
each
either, neither
every, everyone, everything, everybody
nobody, no one, nothing
what, whatever
who, whom, whoever, whomever

correct: *Every* possible cause *has* been investigated.

correct: *Each* one of the children here *speaks* fluent French.

correct: *Neither* of the pens *has* any ink remaining in it.

correct: *Whatever* he's doing *is* very effective.

correct: *Everything* she touches *turns* to gold.

Even when they refer to a compound subject joined by *and,* the pronouns listed above remain *singular.*

correct: *Each adult and child* here *speaks* fluent French.

correct: *Every* possible *cause and suspect was* investigated.

Plural Pronouns
both
few
many
others
several
some

correct: *Few think* that line of reasoning makes sense.

correct: *Many claim* to have encountered alien beings.

correct: *Some thrive* on commotion, while *others need* quiet.

Compound and Other Types of Subjects

It's especially easy to overlook a subject-verb agreement problem in a sentence involving a compound subject (multiple subjects joined by connectors such as the word *and* or the word *or).* If joined by *and,* a compound subject is usually plural (and takes a plural verb). But if joined by *or*, *either*... *or,* or *neither*... *nor,* the verb tense depends on whether the subject closest to the verb is singular or plural.

plural: The teacher *and* the students are happy.

plural: The teacher *or* the students are happy.

singular (by position): *Neither* the students *nor* the teacher is happy.

In some cases, you can't tell whether a subject is singular or plural without looking at how it's used in the sentence. This is true of *collective* nouns and nouns of *quantity.* These special situations might call for either a singular verb or a plural verb, depending on whether the noun is used in a singular or plural sense.

correct: Four years *is* too long to wait. (*four years* used in singular sense)

correct: Four years *pass* by quickly. (*four years* used in plural sense)

Noun clauses are considered singular. A **noun clause** is one that starts with either a **gerund** (a noun ending in *-ing)* or an **infinitive** (a verb preceded by the word *to*). In each of the next two sentences, the italicized noun clause is accompanied by a singular verb (in bold):

correct: *Mastering several musical instruments* **requires** many years of practice.

correct: Among my least favorite chores **is** *to clean the bathroom.*

VERB TENSE

While verb tense is not specifically tested as part of the language component of the GED Reasoning Through Language Arts Test, it is expected that your extended response writing sample will illustrate your command of proper use of verb tenses. The following sections will help you to review this aspect of grammar and incorporate the rules into your writing.

Verb tense refers to how a verb's form indicates the *time frame* (past, present, or future) of a sentence's action. In this section, you'll focus specifically on the following topics:

- Choosing a verb tense
- Verb forms used for each tense
- Improper shifting and mixing of tenses (including conditional perfect tenses)

The first two topics listed above provide a foundation for the third topic, which is the main verb-tense issue that the GED Reasoning Through Language Arts Test examines.

Verb Tenses and Verb Forms

There are six regular verb tenses in total. A sentence should use one of three *simple* tenses—either *present, past,* or *future*—to "simply" indicate one of the three time frames.

simple present: They *have* enough money to buy a car.

simple past: They *had* enough money to buy a car.

simple future: They *will have* enough money to buy a car.

simple present: I *am losing* my mind.

simple past: I *was losing* my mind.

simple future: I *will lose* my mind.

The present-perfect tense is used for actions that began in the past and continued up until the present:

present perfect: He *has eaten* enough food (but *has continued* to eat anyway).

present perfect: She *has tried* to lose weight (for the past year).

The past-perfect tense is used for actions that began in the past and continued up until a more recent time in the past:

past perfect: He *had eaten* enough food (but *had kept eating* anyway).

past perfect: She *had tried* to lose weight (until recently).

The future-perfect tense is used for actions beginning in the future and continuing up until a more distant point in the future:

future perfect: He *will have eaten* enough food (once he *has finished eating* dessert).

future perfect: By year's end, she *will have tried* to lose weight (for nearly six months).

With many verbs, the same form is used for all tenses, except that *-ed* is added for the past tenses—as in *walk, walked.* However, other verbs take distinct forms for different tenses. Notice how forms of the following three verbs (in bold) vary, depending on the tense.

Tense	To Have	To Be	To See
present	has (have)	is (are)	see
past	had (had)	was (were)	saw
future	will have	will be	will see
present perfect	has had (have had)	has been (have been)	has seen (have seen)
past perfect	had had	had been	had seen
future perfect	will have had	will have been	will have seen

Determining the correct verb form for any tense is a matter of practice and experience with the English language. If a verb form sounds incorrect, your ear is probably telling you that it is. Test your ear by listening to the following incorrect sentences as you read them.

> **incorrect:** We *be* too far along to quit now; we *have went* past the point of no return.
>
> **correct:** We *are* too far along to quit now; we *have gone* past the point of no return.

> **incorrect:** The pilot *seen* the mountain but *flied* too low to avoid a collision.
>
> **correct (present tense):** The pilot *sees* the mountain but *is flying* too low to avoid a collision.
>
> **correct (past tense):** The pilot *saw* the mountain but *flew* too low to avoid a collision.
>
> **correct (past-perfect tense):** The pilot *had seen* the mountain but *had flown* too low to avoid a collision.

> **incorrect:** After we *gone* to the training session, we *begun* to work on the job assignment.
>
> **correct (present tense):** After we *go* to the training session, we *will begin* to work on the job assignment.
>
> **correct (past tense):** After we *went* to the training session, we *began* to work on the job assignment.
>
> **correct (future-perfect tense):** Even before we *go* to the training session, we *will have begun* to work on the job assignment.

If you have trouble hearing incorrect verb forms, consult an English usage book that contains lists of verbs and their conjugations (the word *conjugations* refers to verb forms for different tenses).

Shifting or Mixing Verb Tenses

A sentence should not needlessly *mix* tenses or *shift* tense from one time frame to another in a confusing manner.

> **incorrect:** If it rains tomorrow, we *cancel* our plans.
>
> **correct:** If it rains tomorrow, we *will cancel* our plans.

> **incorrect:** When Bill arrived, Sal still *did not begin* to unload the truck.
>
> **correct:** When Bill arrived, Sal still *had not begun* to unload the truck.

The problem with mixing and shifting tenses also applies to sentences like these:

> **incorrect:** *To go* to war is *to have traveled* to hell.
>
> **correct:** *To go* to war is *to go* to hell.
>
> **correct:** *To have gone* to war is *to have traveled* to hell.

incorrect: *Seeing* the obstacle *would have allowed* him to alter his course.

correct: *Having seen* the obstacle *would have allowed* him to alter his course.

correct: *Seeing* the obstacle *would allow* him to alter his course.

Conditional Perfect Tense

To indicate that something would be completed at some point in time (past, present, or future) *if* a certain condition were met, a sentence should use the *conditional perfect tense*.

To employ the conditional perfect tense properly, a sentence will use words such as *would, should,* or *could,* as well as words such as *if, had,* or *were.* Here are three pairs of examples (all sentences are correct):

Should the college lower its tuition, I *would* probably enroll.

If the college *were* to lower its tuition, I *would* probably enroll.

Had he driven slower, he *would* have noticed the new building.

If he *had* driven slower, he *would* have noticed the new building.

They *could have* reached home in time for dinner *were* it not for the sudden storm.

Had it not rained suddenly, they *could have* reached home in time for dinner.

If a sentence mixes a regular verb tense (either simple or perfect) with the conditional perfect tense, then it is grammatically incorrect. For example, look at these incorrect versions of the preceding examples:

incorrect: If the college *lowers* its tuition, I *would* probably enroll.

(The first clause uses the present tense, but the second clause implies the conditional perfect tense.)

incorrect: *Had* he driven slower, he *will* notice the new building.

(The first clause implies the conditional perfect tense, but the second clause uses the future tense.)

incorrect: They *will have* reached home in time for dinner *were* it not for the sudden storm.

(The first clause uses the future-perfect tense, but the second clause implies the conditional perfect tense.)

PRONOUN CASE, REFERENCE, AND AGREEMENT

Pronouns include **personal pronouns** and **relative pronouns**. Personal pronouns (words such as *they, me,* and *his*) refer to specific people, places, and things and indicate whether they are singular or plural. Relative pronouns (words such as *which* and *who*) are not specific in their reference.

Which personal or relative pronoun you should use in a sentence depends mainly on: (1) where the pronoun appears in the sentence, and (2) what noun, if any, the pronoun refers to.

Personal Pronoun Case

Personal pronouns take different forms, called *cases,* depending on how they're used in a sentence. You'll find all the various cases in the following table.

	Subjective case	Possessive case	Objective case	Objective case—reflexive
first-person singular	I	my, mine	me	myself
first-person plural	we	our, ours	us	ourselves
second-person singular	you	your, yours	you	yourself
second-person plural	you	your, yours	you	yourselves
third-person singular	he, she, it	his, hers, its	him, her, it	himself, herself, itself
third-person plural	they	their, theirs	them	themselves

You can generally trust your ear when it comes to detecting personal pronoun errors. In some cases, however, your ear can betray you, so make sure you are "tuned in" to the following uses of pronouns.

Any form of the verb *to be* is followed by a subject pronoun, such as *he.*

> **incorrect:** Either *him* or Trevor *would be* the best spokesman for our group.
>
> **correct:** Either Trevor or *he would be* the best spokesperson for our group.
>
> **incorrect:** The best spokesperson for our group *would be* either *him* or Trevor.
>
> **correct:** The best spokesperson for our group *would be* either *he* or Trevor.

The *possessive* form is used when the pronoun is part of a noun clause, such as "their cooperating."

> **incorrect:** One can't help admiring *them* cooperating with one another.
>
> **correct:** One can't help admiring *their cooperating* with one another.

A *reflexive* pronoun is used to refer to the sentence's subject.

> **incorrect:** In striving to understand others, *we* also learn more about *us.*
>
> **correct:** In striving to understand others, *we* also learn more about *ourselves.*

Choice of Relative Pronoun

The English language includes only the following handful of *relative* pronouns: *which, who, that, whose, whichever, whoever,* and *whomever.* Don't worry about what the term "relative pronoun" means. Instead, just remember the following rules about when to use each one.

Use *which* to refer to things. Use either *who* or *that* to refer to people.

> **incorrect:** Amanda, *which* was the third performer, was the best of the group.
>
> **correct:** Amanda, *who* was the third performer, was the best of the group.
>
> **correct:** The first employee *that* fails to meet his or her sales quota will be fired.
>
> **correct:** The first employee *who* fails to meet his or her sales quota will be fired.

Whether you should use *which* or *that* depends on what the sentence is supposed to mean.

> **one meaning:** The third page, *which* had been earmarked, contained several typographical errors.
>
> **different meaning:** The third page *that* had been earmarked contained several typographical errors.

Notice that the first sentence above merely describes the third page as earmarked, while the second sentence also suggests that the page containing the errors was the third earmarked page. So the two sentences carry two different meanings.

Whether you should use *who* (*whoever*) or *whom* (*whomever*) depends on the grammatical function of the person (or people) being referred to. This is a tricky area of English grammar, and the GED test makers are reluctant to test on it. But you should be ready for it anyway, so here are two good examples.

> When referring to the sentence's subject, the subjective pronoun *who* should be used.
>
> **incorrect:** It was the chairman *whom* initiated the bill.
>
> **correct:** It was the chairman *who* initiated the bill.
>
> When referring to the sentence's object, the objective pronoun *whom* should be used.
>
> **incorrect:** The team members from East High, *who* the judges were highly impressed with, won the debate.
>
> **correct:** The team members from East High, with *whom* the judges were highly impressed, won the debate.

Agreement with Antecedent

An **antecedent** is simply the noun to which a pronoun refers. In the sentences you encounter on the test, make sure that pronouns agree in number (singular or plural) with their antecedents.

> **singular:** Studying other artists actually helps a young *painter* develop *his* or *her* own style.
>
> **plural:** Studying other artists actually helps young *painters* develop *their* own style.

Singular pronouns are generally used in referring to antecedents such as *each, either, neither,* and *one.*

> **correct:** *Neither* of the two countries imposes an income tax on *its* citizens.
>
> **correct:** *One* cannot be too kind to *oneself.*

If a pronoun and its antecedent are far apart, it can be especially easy to overlook an agreement problem, as in this example:

> **incorrect:** *Neither* a brilliant movie *script nor* a generous *budget* can garner critical acclaim without a good director to make the most of *them.*

In the previous sentence, the antecedent of *them* (a plural pronoun) is *script* or *budget* (singular). One way to remedy the disagreement is to replace *them* with *it.* Since the antecedent and pronoun are so far apart, another solution is to replace the pronoun with its antecedent—for example, with *that script or budget.*

Ambiguous and Vague Pronoun References

Pronouns provide a handy, shorthand way of referring to identifiable nouns. But unless the identity of the pronoun's antecedent is clear, using a pronoun will leave the reader guessing what its intended antecedent is. In other words, *every pronoun in a sentence should have a clearly identifiable antecedent.*

Here's a sentence in which the pronoun could refer to either one of two nouns:

> **ambiguous:** Minutes before Kevin's meeting with Paul, *his* wife called with the bad news.

According to the sentence, whose wife called? Kevin's or Paul's? The answer is not clear. To correct this sort of ambiguous pronoun reference, either replace the pronoun with its antecedent or reconstruct the sentence to clarify the reference.

> **clear:** Minutes before Kevin's meeting with Paul, *Kevin's* wife called with the bad news.
>
> **clear:** *Kevin's* wife called with the bad news minutes before *his* meeting with Paul.

Another sort of ambiguous pronoun reference occurs when a sentence shifts from one pronoun to another in a way that leaves the reader confused. Here's an example:

> **ambiguous:** When *one* dives in without looking ahead, *you* never know what will happen.

In this sentence, *you* might refer either to the diver (*one*), to someone observing the diver, or to anyone in general. Here are two alternative ways of clearing up the ambiguity:

> **clear:** *One* never knows what will happen when *one* dives in without looking ahead.
>
> **clear:** When *you* dive in without looking ahead, *you* never know what will happen.

If a pronoun has no identifiable antecedent at all, the sentence should be reworked to eliminate the pronoun. Here's a sentence that makes this sort of vague pronoun reference, followed by a version that fixes the problem:

> **vague:** When the planets are out of alignment, *it* can be disastrous. (*It* does not refer to any noun.)
>
> **clear:** Disaster can occur when the planets are out of alignment.

WRITING MECHANICS

Part of the language component of the GED Reasoning Through Language Arts Test involves writing mechanics. The test covers only the following mechanics issues:

- Correct use of punctuation
- Use of the apostrophe for possessives and contractions
- Frequently confused words and homonyms (words that sound alike but are spelled differently)
- Capitalization (distinguishing between proper and common nouns, beginnings of sentences)

In this section, you'll review the rules for these aspects of writing mechanics, which are also important to keep in mind as you write your extended response.

You will not encounter test questions on any punctuation marks other than the comma and the apostrophe, or on the spelling of any words other than homonyms.

Proper and Improper Uses of Commas

A comma indicates a pause that should correspond to a pause in the logic of the sentence. The commas make it clear to the reader that the logic of the sentence is being (temporarily) interrupted. The GED Reasoning Through Language Arts Test tests four different uses (and misuses) of the comma.

- Overuse of the comma, resulting in the splitting of a grammatical unit
- Too few commas, resulting in a confusing sentence
- Commas in a series (a list of three or more items)
- Commas used in pairs to set appositives (parenthetical phrases) apart

Commas That Split a Grammatical Unit

Commas should not needlessly separate parts of the sentence that belong together, such as the subject and verb:

> **incorrect:** Former Secretary of State Henry Kissinger, is the author of several books on the history of diplomacy.

In the above sentence, the verb *is* should not be separated by a comma from its subject *Henry Kissinger* (unless a parenthetical phrase intervenes between them—not the case here).

Similarly, no comma should come between the verb and a subject complement that may follow it:

> **incorrect:** The nineteenth-century explorers Lewis and Clark may be, two of America's most-admired historical figures.

In the same way, a preposition should not be separated from its object by a comma:

> **incorrect:** As the storm continued, pieces of driftwood as well as, large quantities of sand were blown onto the front porch.

In the above sentence, the preposition *as well as* needs to remain connected to its object, the phrase "large quantities of sand."

When commas are overused on the test, it will usually be in sentences like these examples, where the commas jarringly separate parts of the sentence that belong together. These abuses are generally pretty easy to spot.

Commas for Sentence Sense

A tougher task is deciding whether a sentence uses too *few* commas, a problem that can easily confuse the reader. Here's the guideline: A sentence should use the minimum number of commas needed for a reader to understand the intended meaning of the sentence.

> **too few commas:** Chandra is learning Spanish although acquiring this new skill is not one of her job duties.
>
> **better:** Chandra is learning Spanish, although acquiring this new skill is not one of her job duties.

The first sentence is a run-on sentence, which connects two or more independent clauses with a conjunction (such as *but, and,* or *although*) but no comma. Some run-on sentences, such as the previous example, can be fixed by inserting a comma immediately before the conjunction. Others, like the next example, are better split into two sentences:

> **too few commas:** Chandra is learning Spanish but acquiring this new skill is not one of her job duties and she should not be paid for the time she devotes to this activity.
>
> **better:** Chandra is learning Spanish, but acquiring this new skill is not one of her job duties. Therefore, she should not be paid for the time she devotes to this activity.

Commas in a Series

When three or more words, phrases, or clauses are presented in sequence, or series, a comma should be used to separate them. Here are examples of each instance:

> **commas separating a list of words:** The Galapagos Islands boast some of the world's most unusual plants, birds, mammals, reptiles, and fish.
>
> **commas separating a list of phrases:** We looked for the missing gloves under the sofa, in the closet, and behind the dresser, but we never found them.
>
> **commas separating a list of clauses:** The plot of the movie was a familiar one: boy meets girl, boy loses girl, mutant from outer space devours both.

Commas for Setting Off Introductory Elements

Common introductory phrases such as *for example* and *first of all* should be followed by a comma; otherwise, the sentence won't make grammatical sense. For example, removing the comma from either of the next two sentences would confuse its meaning:

> To begin with, the new ordinance does nothing to protect tenants.
>
> However, we decided to drive west instead of east.

A longer introductory element, which is usually a dependent clause, can be more difficult to detect. Introductory dependent clauses typically begin with words and phrases such as the following:

Introductory Dependent Clauses		
Although	Whenever	Regarding
Though	If	As for
Unless	With respect to	Since

Regardless of the specific word or phrase used to begin the introductory clause, a "pause" (comma) will probably be helpful, and may be needed, at the end of the clause in order for the reader to follow the flow of ideas in the sentence. Here are two examples:

> Aside from the fact that his feet were blistered and swollen, there was no reason Jim should not have finished the race.
>
> Without first setting up an account, you won't be able to purchase that item from the website.

Commas for Setting Off Appositives

An **appositive** is a noun or noun phrase that renames or describes a noun. Appositives should be set off by commas; otherwise, the sentence won't make grammatical sense. In the following example, the phrase "the great left-handed Dodger pitcher" is an appositive that describes Sandy Koufax. Notice that without *both* commas, the sentence is rather confusing.

confusing: Sandy Koufax the great left-handed Dodger pitcher was the guest of honor at this year's sports club banquet.

still confusing: Sandy Koufax, the great left-handed Dodger pitcher was the guest of honor at this year's sports club banquet.

clear: Sandy Koufax, the great left-handed Dodger pitcher, was the guest of honor at this year's sports club banquet.

An appositive can be as brief as a few words. Or it can be quite lengthy, as in this example:

I was surprised to learn that Paula, my cousin Frank's former girlfriend and a well-known local artist, had decided to move to Santa Fe.

To determine the correct use of commas in sentences like the preceding ones, try this test: Read the sentence without the phrase. If it still makes grammatical sense and the meaning is basically the same, then the phrase is nonessential (or parenthetical) and should be set off by commas. Both of the preceding examples pass the test:

Sandy Koufax ... was the guest of honor at this year's sports club banquet.

I was surprised to learn that Paula ... had decided to move to Santa Fe.

The Apostrophe (for Possessives and Contractions)

The apostrophe is used for two purposes: possessives and contractions. Both are frequently tested on the language component of the GED Reasoning Through Language Arts Test and should be used correctly when writing your extended response. A **possessive** is used to indicate ownership or some other close connection between a noun or pronoun and what follows it. Form the possessive as follows:

- For a singular noun, add *'s* (apostrophe followed by the letter *s*):

  the company's employees

  the cat's meow

- For a plural noun ending in *s*, just add an apostrophe:

  the Jacksons' first home

  the wolves' pack leader

- For a plural noun that does not end in *s*, add *'s* (apostrophe followed by the letter *s*):

  the school alumni's favorite reunion spot

  the cattle's hooves

The possessive pronouns *his, hers, its, ours, yours,* and *theirs* contain no apostrophes.

- Be especially careful about positioning the apostrophe in plural nouns such as the following three:

  men's (not *mens'*)

  women's (not *womens'*)

  children's (not *childrens'*)

The other use of an apostrophe is in a **contraction**, which is a word made up of at least two words from which letters have been omitted for easier pronunciation.

The apostrophe is usually (but not always!) inserted in place of the letters omitted. If in doubt, mentally "expand" the contraction to determine which letters have been left out; this is often a useful guide to determine where the apostrophe belongs. For example:

We've got to go. = *We have* got to go.

She *won't* mind. = She *will not* mind.

The following is a list of common contractions, grouped according to the contraction's second word (in bold). Any of these contractions might be used on the GED test to test you on word usage. Notice that some of these contractions are homonyms (they sound just like one or more other words).

Common Contractions	
not can't = cannot (one word) couldn't = could not didn't = did not hadn't = had not hasn't = has not haven't = have not isn't = is not wasn't = was not weren't = were not won't = will not wouldn't = would not	**is** it's = it is (do not confuse with *its*) he's = he is she's = she is what's = what is whatever's = whatever is that's = that is there's = there is where's = where is who's = who is (do not confuse with *whose*)
have I've = I have they've = they have we've = we have who've = who have could've = could have would've = would have	**are** they're = they are (do not confuse with *their* and *there*) we're = we are you're = you are (do not confuse with *your*)
had (would) I'd = I had (I would) she'd = she had (she would) he'd = he had (he would) they'd = they had (they would) we'd = we had (we would) where'd = where had (where did) who'd = who had (who would)	**am** I'm = I am **will** I'll = I will he'll = he will she'll = she will they'll = they will it'll = it will

Homonyms and Easily Confused Words

A **homonym** is a word that sounds just like another word but is spelled differently. Here are two examples:

see and **sea**

Jonah went to *see* the ocean for the first time.

More than 1,000 of the cruise ship's passengers were lost at *sea*.

lead and **led**

Lead-based fishing sinkers are banned in all of US and Canadian National Parks.

The guide *led* us through the dense jungle terrain.

Closely related to homonyms are words that are easily confused. These words may sound similar depending on how you may pronounce them, but they are spelled differently. Here are two examples:

than and **then**

Gary was taller *than* Joshua but shorter *than* Michael.

First you should change your clothes, *then* you should eat dinner.

affect and **effect**

The blinking lights won't *affect* you if close your eyes.

The blinking lights had a slightly hypnotic *effect*.

On the language component of the GED Reasoning Through Language Arts Test, expect several corrections that will test you on recognizing the misuse of homonyms or easily confused words. To prepare for these questions, study the following lists. They contain many of the homonyms you should know for the language component of the test. You should also keep them in mind when writing your extended response.

Contractions and Their Homonyms

Be sure not to confuse certain contractions with their homonyms. These tricky words appear frequently on the test.

it's (it is)

There no secret to scoring high; *it's* all a matter of practice.

its

The groundhog saw *its* shadow, and so we can expect more cold weather ahead.

there's

In case *there's* any doubt on your part, I've brought a letter of reference with me.

theirs

Victory was once ours, but now it is *theirs.*

they're (they are)

Once *they're* gone, we can finally have peace and quiet.

their

The two employees set *their* differences aside and finished the project.

there

In order to go *there*, you'll need to take the ferry.

who's (who is)

Find out *who's* to blame for starting the fire.

whose

Find out *whose* car this is, and warn them that it might be towed.

Common Two-word Phrases and Their Homonyms

Be on the lookout for the following two-word phrases and their one-word homonym counterparts.

all ready

If the four of you are *all ready* to leave, then we can take the same bus.

already

Sherry has left *already*, so I need to find someone else to drive me home.

all together

Are we *all together*, then, in opposing the proposed law?

altogether

He counted six raccoons *altogether*, four gray and two red.

all ways

In *all ways*, the newly engaged couple seemed incompatible.

always

The problem with dessert is that it's *always* served last, when I'm already full.

any one

I'm sure *any one* of you can jump higher than I can.

anyone

Does *anyone* here know how to jumpstart a car?

every day

Tiffany runs three miles *every day* before work.

everyday

Gang violence is an *everyday* occurrence in this part of town.

every one

Each and *every one* of you must keep quiet, or else they'll hear us.

everyone

If *everyone* talks at once, we'll never accomplish anything.

there for

I will always be *there for* you.

therefore

I think, *therefore* I am.

Some Challenging Homonyms and Easily Confused Words You Might Find on the GED® Test

You're probably familiar with most, if not all, of the following words. Nevertheless, it's remarkably easy to confuse any of these words. Be sure you know the difference in spelling and meaning between the words in each pair.

accept and **except**

Please *accept* this gift as a token of my appreciation.

Every staff member *except* Bruce attended the office party.

capital and **capitol**

The nation's *capital* is Washington, D.C.

Through its stock offering, the company was able to raise more *capital.*

The dome of the *capitol* building shone brightly in the afternoon sun.

cast and **caste**

Jim was in a skiing accident, and his leg will be in a *cast* for two months.

The fisherman *cast* his line toward the river, hoping to catch his dinner.

The movie's *cast* included Daniel Day-Lewis and Penelope Cruz.

People born into a *caste* social system find it impossible to improve their standard of living.

complement and **compliment**

The brick driveway is a perfect *complement* to the house's metal trim.

She paid him a *compliment* by telling him that he had good fashion sense.

council and **counsel**

The head of the community *council* made the final decision.

A married couple wanting to divorce should seek separate legal *counsel.*

dual and **duel**

Immigrants with *dual* citizenship can easily land a job in this country.

The final tennis match turned out to be a long, drawn-out *duel.*

principal and **principle**

Gwen's incompetence was the *principal* reason she was fired from her job.

The elementary school *principal* knew every student's name.

My guiding *principle* is to treat others how I would like to be treated.

stationary and **stationery**

Riding a *stationary* bike is good exercise, but I prefer riding a real bike.

Since email has become popular, few people buy *stationery* for writing letters.

Other Common GED® Test Homonyms

Here's a list of many of the other homonyms you might encounter on the language component of GED Reasoning Through Language Arts Test. They're all common, everyday words, so you probably know what they mean. Nevertheless, you can easily confuse any of these words with its homonym if you're not paying careful attention. Also be aware of these when writing your extended response.

Common Homonyms		
aisle, isle	dear, deer	plain, plane
ate, eight	earn, urn	profit, prophet
bare, bear	for, fore, four	read, red
based, baste	know, no	right, write
based, baste	ladder, latter	seas, sees, seize
blew, blue	lead, led	steal, steel
boar, bore	meat, meet	to, too, two
brake, break	might, mite	waist, waste
cell, sell	miner, minor	ware, wear
clause, claws	pair, pare, pear	weather, whether
coarse, course	peace, piece	would, wood

Capitalization of Proper Nouns

Of course, the first word in each new sentence is capitalized. But there are many instances where a word that falls somewhere within the sentence should be capitalized as well, and these are the words that the GED test covers. Here's the general rule for capitalizing words:

> Capitalize all **proper nouns** and words derived from them, such as adjectives. Do not capitalize **common nouns**. A proper noun is the name of a specific person, place, or thing. All other nouns are common nouns.

This section covers the types of proper nouns you're most likely to encounter on the GED test.

People

Any particular person's name is capitalized. Any title accompanying a person's name is also capitalized. Study and compare the italicized words in these sentences:

> Send copies of the letter to *Mr. and Mrs. Stefanski* and to *Dr. Reed.*
>
> While in the US Army, *Corporal Yates* served directly under an ambitious *captain* who later became *General* Eisenhower and, eventually, *President* Eisenhower.
>
> *Peter Innis* was *president* of the company the year that *Chairman Stanton* resigned as board *chairman*.

Titles for named relatives are capitalized. Otherwise, a word that identifies a family relationship is considered a common word. Study and compare the italicized words in these sentences:

> We went to the art museum with *Father* and *Aunt Janice.*
>
> Yesterday my *father* took my sister and me to the art museum. I think any *father* should take his child to an art museum at least once.

Institutions, Organizations, and Groups

Names of schools, businesses, and other organizations are capitalized. Specifically named offices, branches, and agencies are also capitalized. Study and compare the italicized words in these sentences:

> Prior to Dr. Kingston's tenure as head of the *Office of Transportation,* he served as head of the *School of Architecture* at *Drysdale College.*
>
> The chief financial officer of *Unicost Corporation* attended this state's most prestigious *university,* where she majored in *sociology.*
>
> After graduating *Franklin High School,* he went to work for the US *government,* at the *Bureau of Printing and Engraving.*
>
> If you join the *US Army,* the government will pay for your college tuition. Even so, I refuse to join an *army* that invades other countries.

Names that identify groups of people by nationality, ethnicity, religion, tribe, or other such category are capitalized.

> Sioux City, which is Iowa's capital city, is named for the *Sioux* tribe of *American Indians.*
>
> You'll find *Danes* to be most hospitable, although the *Danish* pastries alone are worth the trip.

Artistic and Other Creative Works

Titles of literary works (books, poems, short stories, treaties, etc.), as well as magazines, movies, songs, visual art works, and other similar works are capitalized.

> The new issue of *Time* includes an interesting article entitled "Movie Rags to Movie Riches."
>
> Apparently, *The Wizard of Oz* did not make a profit until a decade after the movie was released.

Depending on the type, a named artistic work is also italicized (or underlined) or enclosed in quotation marks. The GED test does not cover these rules.

Specifically named artifacts (documents, treasures, etc.) are also capitalized.

> Every grade-school student in the United States learns to recite the *Pledge of Allegiance.* But very few students ever memorize the *Bill of Rights* or the *Gettysburg Address.*
>
> The *Dead Sea Scrolls* and the *Shroud of Turin* are subjects of great controversy among scholars.

Time Periods and Events

Days of the week, months of the year, and specific holidays are capitalized (even when preceded by the word *a*). But the words *week, month,* and *year* themselves are not.

> This year, *Thanksgiving* will fall on a *Thursday,* and *Christmas* will fall on a *Monday.* But next year they'll both fall on the last *Thursday* of the month.
>
> It rained every Sunday during the *month* of *April.*

Seasons of the year are not capitalized.

I look forward to *autumn* and the brisk weather it will bring.

The temperature has risen into the eighties nearly every day this *summer.*

Only specifically named historical events, periods, and eras are capitalized.

The South's surrender to the North marked the end of the *Civil War.*

The nation's bloody *civil war* claimed more than a half-million lives.

During the *Great Depression,* unemployment among working-age men reached 25 percent.

The current recession might turn out to be as bad as the *depression* of the 1930s.

Times of the day, such as *dawn, noon,* and *midnight,* and the word *o'clock* are common nouns (not capitalized).

Geographic Regions

Words involving compass direction (north, south, east, west, northeast, etc.) are capitalized when they refer to a specific geographical section or region (or, for example, when they are part of a street name).

The *Southeast* is more humid than the *Southwest.*

The *East* Coast of *North America* receives more annual rainfall than the continent's *West* Coast.

This restaurant is located on *South* Park Street.

But these words are not capitalized when used to merely indicate direction.

Hike up the *eastern* flank of the mountain, and you'll be treated to a spectacular view of the valley.

Turn *north* when you reach the stop sign, then look for City Hall on the *east* side of *West* 75th Street.

Specifically named municipalities (cities, townships, and counties), states, regions, and countries are capitalized. Otherwise, words such as *city, county,* and *state* are not capitalized. Study and compare the italicized words in these sentences:

When driving along *Thompson County's* main highway, expect to encounter numerous speed traps, especially within *Hilltown's city* limits.

Our entire *Scandinavian* excursion was a worthwhile experience. The fiords along the *Norway* coast were magnificent.

Streets, Landmarks, and Geographic Features

Only specifically named streets, roads, highways, freeways, and others are capitalized.

> If you're driving south on *Skyline Parkway*, merge onto the *freeway,* and then look for the *Lake Street* exit.
>
> We live near *Roosevelt Avenue,* which parallels *Park Lane.* You can take either *street* to get to our house.

Buildings and other landmarks, parks and monuments, mountains and valleys, and bodies of water (rivers, lakes, seas, and oceans) are capitalized. Study and compare the italicized words in these sentences:

> No trip to Washington, D.C., is complete without a visit to the *Capitol* and the *Lincoln Memorial.* After seeing the *memorial,* be sure to take a stroll along the *Potomac River.*
>
> The *Great Lakes* are the world's largest bodies of fresh water. Among the five *lakes, Lake Superior* is the largest.
>
> As they approached Earth, the shuttle crew could clearly observe the *Great Wall of China* and even the *Three Gorges Dam.*

Celestial Bodies

Specifically named celestial bodies (planets, moons, stars, etc.) are also capitalized. Study and compare the italicized words in these sentences:

> In a solar eclipse, *the moon* travels directly between *Earth* and *the sun.* During this type of eclipse, the moon blocks out almost all *sunlight.*
>
> Ganymede is the largest *moon* orbiting the planet *Jupiter.*
>
> We could not dig any deeper because just beneath the *earth* we hit an impervious layer of hardpan.

SUMMING IT UP

- **Sentence structure** refers to how a sentence's parts fit together as a whole. Sentence structure questions account for a portion of the language component of the GED Reasoning Through Language Arts Test.
- Sentence structure questions on the GED Reasoning Through Language Arts Test might present errors such as:
    - Sentence fragments
    - Run-ons and comma splices
    - Faulty parallelism involving series
    - Faulty parallelism involving correlatives
- Part of the language component of the GED Reasoning Through Language Arts Test involves verb and pronoun *usage*—that is, whether these types of words are used correctly in sentences.
- The test covers the following language components:
    - Subject-verb agreement and pronoun case
    - Reference
    - Agreement
- The language component of the GED Reasoning Through Language Arts Test also covers the following mechanics issues:
    - Use of punctuation
    - Use of the apostrophe for possessives and contractions
    - Homonyms (words that sound alike but are spelled differently)
    - Capitalization (distinguishing between proper and common nouns)
- You will not encounter test questions on any punctuation marks other than the comma or the apostrophe, or on the spelling of any words other than homonyms and easily confused words.
- In addition to being tested on the language component of the GED Reasoning Through Language Arts Test, these skills are also important to know when writing the extended response.

PART IV

THE SOCIAL STUDIES TEST

Mastering the Social Studies Test

Chapter 7

OVERVIEW

- **All About the Social Studies Test**
- **Formats Used for GED® Social Studies Test Questions**
- **Subject Areas for GED® Social Studies Test Questions**
- **Source Material for GED® Social Studies Test Questions**
- **Question Types on the Social Studies Test**
- **Questions Based on Visual Depictions**
- **General Test-Taking Strategies**
- **Summing It Up**

THE SOCIAL STUDIES TEST IN A NUTSHELL

Time allowed: 70 minutes

Total number of questions: 30–35 questions

Format: Each question is based on a text passage and/or visual depiction

Length of text passages: Up to 150 words

Number of questions per passage or visual: Expect 1 to 5 (1 or 2 is most common)

ALL ABOUT THE SOCIAL STUDIES TEST

The broad academic field of **social studies** includes a wide variety of subjects, all involving human activity and relations. These subjects include history, civics and government, economics, sociology, anthropology, psychology, and geography (as well as some others). The GED Social Studies Test is designed to measure a variety of abilities within the context of just four of these subject areas: history, political science (civics and government), economics, and geography.

The test consists of a range of 30–35 multiple-choice questions. Here's an approximate breakdown in terms of the subject areas that the test covers (percentages and numbers may vary slightly):

50%	Civics and Government
20%	US (or Canadian*) History
15%	Economics
15%	Geography

*Subject matter is based on the history and/or government of the country in which the test is administered.

The test questions are *not* grouped by content area. Instead, questions from all areas listed above are mixed together. Responding to the questions in each of these areas will enable you to demonstrate the following set of skills:

- Reading and writing in Social Studies (33%)
- Social Studies concepts (33%)
- Mathematical reasoning in Social Studies (33%)

These skill areas are designed to measure your abilities in comprehending information (recalling and understanding), analyzing information (drawing inferences and conclusions), evaluating information (synthesizing), and applying concepts and ideas to a variety of situations. Keep in mind that with prior knowledge of the content areas listed above, you can expect to handle the questions with greater ease and confidence. The review materials later in this part of the book are designed to help you in this respect.

FORMATS USED FOR GED® SOCIAL STUDIES TEST QUESTIONS

The GED Social Studies Test utilizes an electronic format that provides for a variety of question formats. While the majority of your questions will be presented in a traditional multiple-choice format, others (such as drop-downs, select-an-area, drag-and-drops, and fill-in-the-blanks) will allow you to provide a specific response in certain subject areas. Each multiple-choice question will list four choices. Most questions will be based on brief passages of text, which may vary in length from a few sentences to as many as 150 words (about one-fourth of a page). A question involving a passage of text might refer to it either as a "passage" or as "information" or as "text." The remaining questions will be based on maps, charts, cartoons, diagrams, and other visual depictions. Some (but not all) visual depictions will be accompanied by a brief passage of text. At times, you will be asked to analyze the text itself in terms of identifying fact and opinion, bias, and elements of propaganda. Finally, many of the questions will be presented in groups of two to five based on the same passage and/or visual depiction.

Drop-down questions consist of passages with blanks that can be filled by selecting the correct answer from a drop-down menu. This text will simulate those questions by providing answer choices similar to that of a multiple-choice question. Comparably, fill-in-the-blank questions will include a blank space for you to provide the correct response. Drag-and-drop and select-an-area questions are based on maps or charts. The former challenges you to supply the correct content, while the latter challenges you to locate a specific area on a map.

SUBJECT AREAS FOR GED® SOCIAL STUDIES TEST QUESTIONS

As outlined earlier, the subject areas you'll encounter on the Social Studies Test are limited to civics and government, history, economics, and geography. Though you can review each area in depth later in this part of the book, here's an initial survey of each one.

Civics and Government

Questions about **civics and government,** both of which are aspects of political science, account for about 50 percent of the test. On the US version of the GED test, you might encounter questions dealing with any of the following aspects of civics and government:

- Types of modern and historical governments
- Principles that have contributed to the development of American constitutional democracy
- Structure and design of the United States government
- Individual rights and responsibilities
- Political parties, campaigns, and elections in American politics
- Contemporary public policy

On the US version of the GED test, many civics and government questions will be based on the concepts embodied in the following important documents:

- The US Declaration of Independence
- The original (unamended) US Constitution
- Amendments to the US Constitution
- The Federalist Papers
- Landmark US Supreme Court decisions

A question involving one of these documents might quote the document, or it might paraphrase or summarize the document.

History

History can be defined as the record of past events or as the subject matter that makes up those records. On the GED test, you'll review historical facts and records and glean information from them by applying reading-comprehension and analytical skills. The questions will not require you to recall random historical facts such as names, dates, or other trivial information, so you need only be able to work within a historical context to succeed in answering history questions. However, if you have a good background in history, particularly in US history (or Canadian history if you are taking the test in Canada), you will have an advantage when dealing with these questions.

History questions account for about 20 percent of the test. Of these questions, expect three or four to involve US (or Canadian) history. If you're taking the US version of the test, expect at least one question involving the following broad eras of US history:

- European settlement and population of the Americas
- Key historical documents that have shaped American constitutional government
- Revolutionary and Early Republic Periods
- The Civil War and Reconstruction
- Civil Rights
- World Wars I and II
- The Cold War
- American foreign policy since 9/11

Economics

Economics questions, or those dealing with the study of how humans use resources to meet their material needs, will account for about 15 percent of the test. Some questions deal with how economics relates to government policy or key events in history. Here are the broad aspects of economics you can expect these questions to involve:

- Key economic events that have shaped American government and policies
- Relationship between political and economic freedoms
- Fundamental economic concepts
- Macroeconomics and microeconomics
- Consumer economics
- Economic causes and impacts of wars
- Economic drivers of colonization and exploration
- Scientific and industrial revolutions

An economics question might be framed in a historical context (such as the Great Depression of the 1930s), or it might present a hypothetical scenario instead. Expect some economics questions to refer to tables, charts, and graphs. Finally, note that some economics questions might incorporate certain psychology concepts—especially those relating to advertising or consumer behavior.

Geography

Expect about 15 percent of the social studies questions to focus on **geography**, which is the study of Earth's physical features and the way humans adapt to those features through the development of cultures and communities. Among possible topics for a GED test geography question are the following:

- Development of classical civilizations
- Relationships between the environment and societal development
- Borders between peoples and nations
- Human migration

On the GED Social Studies Test, you'll probably encounter some geography questions based solely on textual information, while other questions will involve a visual depiction—a map, globe, graph, chart, or table—in addition to, or instead of, text.

SOURCE MATERIAL FOR GED® SOCIAL STUDIES TEST QUESTIONS

The source material for the GED Social Studies Test includes primary as well as secondary sources. **Primary sources** are those that are original and contemporary to whatever event or development the source documents. Examples of primary sources include historical documents, laws, speeches, newspaper articles, political cartoons, and maps. **Secondary sources** are those that are based on primary sources or other secondary sources. A textbook is a good example of a secondary source.

A question may be from a textual source, a visual source, or a combination of textual and visual sources. Regardless of the source, remember that you will *not* need to recognize or identify any document or the source of any information. Rather, your task will be to understand, evaluate, analyze, or apply the source information you are given.

QUESTION TYPES ON THE SOCIAL STUDIES TEST

The Social Studies Test measures your skills in three main skill areas: reading and writing, social studies concepts, and mathematical reasoning in social studies. You'll find these skills all throughout the test. In the next few pages, you'll examine each question type more closely. Note that the GED test-style example questions here are all based on passages of text, rather than on visuals. In the next section, you'll learn how to handle questions involving visuals.

Comprehension Questions

Comprehension questions require that you read and recall information contained in a passage. In most cases, they also require that you *understand* and *interpret*—in other words, grasp or comprehend—the ideas and concepts that the passage's words convey. Some comprehension questions will require you to understand the main idea of a passage—much like a main idea question in the Reasoning Through Language Arts Test. To handle this sort of question, look for an answer choice that sums up the passage. Other comprehension questions focus instead on the passage's details.

Though the correct answer choice might repeat a phrase from the passage word-for-word, more likely it will either paraphrase or provide an interpretation of passage information. In other words, comprehension questions typically focus on a passage's *ideas* rather than on exactly how those ideas are expressed. Incorrect answer choices will often contradict passage information or provide assertions that are unsupported by the passage or that do not respond to the specific question that is asked.

To understand how a comprehension question might require that you interpret—rather than merely recall—what you've read in a passage, study the following two examples.

Question 1 refers to the following information.

During the 1700s, Europeans reaped many benefits of the agricultural revolution. New methods of farming increased food production and variety on many farms. New foods added much-needed variety to the diets of many Europeans. Larger and more balanced diets bolstered the immune systems of many Europeans and helped them become stronger and healthier.

1. Which development occurred in eighteenth-century Europe?

A. Over-farming left the soil unfertile for subsequent generations.
B. Advances in farming technology enhanced the health of the population.
C. Severe droughts resulted in famine throughout farming and other rural areas.
D. Industrialization left Europe with relatively few farmers.

Notice that choice B does not simply repeat a particular part of the passage, word-for-word. Instead, it combines and paraphrases two closely related ideas: first, that new farming methods increased food variety, and, second, that greater food variety led to better health among many Europeans. The passage does not include the word *technology*, nor does it refer to the "population." Nevertheless, choice B provides a good interpretation of these two closely related ideas from the passage. None of the other three statements is supported by the passage. **The correct answer is B.**

Question 2 refers to the following information.

International trade occurs when goods manufactured in a country are sent elsewhere, or *exported*, for sale, while goods manufactured elsewhere are brought into the country, or *imported*, for sale in the country. Often, governments can raise money by imposing taxes (tariffs) on goods they import from other countries. Although tariffs are paid for by the manufacturers of the goods, the cost of the tax is usually built into the cost of the product itself, which means that the tax is passed on to the consumer. A manufacturer is often able to realize a profit by producing an excess of goods and then exporting the surplus. When the manufacturer can do this, often the cost of production is lowered on each unit produced, so the final selling price is reduced for the products sold in the country of production.

2. The lowest prices on manufactured goods are realized when a manufacturer can

Select ▼

A. impose a tariff on imported goods.
B. import materials it needs to make its products.
C. pass along a tariff to consumers.
D. export a surplus of goods.

Choice D essentially provides the point of the final two sentences of the passage: by producing more units, a manufacturer often can reduce its per-unit cost and then pass the savings on to domestic consumers while charging more for surplus sales in foreign countries. Though the passage does not explicitly state that this is how the lowest price on manufactured goods is realized, you can interpret the information in this way.

Choice A contradicts the passage: it is a government, not a manufacturer, that imposes tariffs. Choice B is unsupported by the passage—whether a manufacturer can save money by importing materials depends on the cost of those materials. Choice C indicates an activity that manufacturers can do, according to the passage. But choice C is incorrect because passing along a tax is not how the lowest price is realized. So choice C does not answer the question. **The correct answer is D.**

As the second of the previous two examples illustrates, when handling comprehension questions involving lengthier passages, be sure to focus on the part of the passage that the question asks about. Some of the incorrect answer choices will probably involve other parts of the passage—parts that are not relevant to the question at hand.

Question 3 refers to the following information.

Critics and proponents of the Vietnam War were loud and vocal, and their opinions led to a wave of protests and theories regarding America's true intentions for getting involved in another major skirmish abroad. Proponents of the war claimed that American involvement was necessary to stop the spread of communism in Vietnam and neighboring countries abroad. Those who opposed the war claimed that it was a pointless overreach of American influence and power, and it led to the unnecessary loss of American and Vietnamese lives.

3. Which of the following is an informed hypothesis regarding the reason for American involvement in the Vietnam War?

A. America entered the war to secure access to the rice production business in North Vietnam.

B. America wanted to seize political power in South Vietnam when it decided to enter the war.

C. America was initially intimidated by Vietnamese military power when it was considering entering the war.

D. America wanted to help stop communism from spreading across South Vietnam.

Choices A, B, and C all are unsupported claims regarding American involvement in the Vietnam War, as there is no credible evidence to support these notions. Only choice D is a reasonable and informed hypothesis—one that was supported by the American government at the time the country entered the war, when it provided its rationale for entering. **The correct answer is D.**

Comprehension questions may task you with distinguishing between unsupported claims and informed hypotheses on a wide range of key historical events, some of which are steeped in controversy.

Analysis Questions

Analysis questions go beyond understanding the information in a passage or visual. Analysis involves organizing the information; explaining how ideas, facts, or data connect together; identifying patterns;

and recognizing inferences, conclusions, and meanings beyond what is stated. Some analysis questions may require you to *infer* historical or economic causes or effects. (To infer is to draw a reasonable conclusion based on certain information.) Other analysis questions might require you to point out similarities and differences between two events, eras, systems, or other phenomena. Still other analysis questions may require you to distinguish fact from opinion. These are just some of the many possibilities for analysis questions.

Question 4 refers to the following information.

Determining the intent of the Founding Fathers of the United States when they drafted the language contained in the Second Amendment (*"A well regulated militia being necessary to the security of a free state, the right of the people to keep and bear arms shall not be infringed."*) has been at the crux of the gun control debate, which still rages on. Those who support unfettered gun ownership claim that the Second Amendment directly and explicitly provides citizens with the freedom and right to own guns as they see fit, while some proponents of gun control claim that the language of the Second Amendment does not deny the government the right to regulate ownership or to legislate gun control laws that evolve to reflect both the times and innovations in gun technology (the Founding Fathers could have hardly envisioned the power and capability of weapons available today compared to those available at the time the amendment was written).

4. Which of the following reflects a fact regarding the language contained in the Second Amendment to the US Constitution?

A. The Founding Fathers believed that the security of a free state required a well-regulated militia.

B. The Founding Fathers believed that all citizens should be able to keep and bear arms.

C. The Founding Fathers believed that a nation without guns can never be truly secure.

D. The Founding Fathers believed that all types of weapons should be made available for purchase by citizens of the United States.

There are many opinions in the ongoing debate regarding gun control, with vocal proponents on both sides offering their views regarding the intent of the Founding Fathers when drafting the language contained in the Second Amendment of the US Constitution. However, among the answer choices provided exists an irrefutable fact—that the Founding Fathers believed that the security of a free state required a well-regulated militia (*"A well regulated militia being necessary to the security of a free state…"*). The other answer choices reflect opinions regarding the language contained in the amendment. **The correct answer is A.**

Expect to encounter questions that task your ability to distinguish among fact, opinion, and reasoned judgment in a primary source document, such as an Amendment to the Constitution, and be ready to analyze the accuracy of secondary source interpretations of both meaning and intent.

Question 5 refers to the following information.

Industrialized countries need uninterrupted supplies of oil in order for their economies to function. The Organization of Petroleum Exporting Countries (OPEC) has made major inroads in helping certain less-industrialized countries become more self-sustaining. Because these countries have a virtual monopoly on the export of oil, they have been able to raise oil prices substantially.

5. Why do some industrialized nations oppose OPEC?

A. They don't want competition in the production of oil.

B. Higher oil prices can raise the cost of running an economy.

C. Some non-industrialized nations have little or no oil reserves.

D. OPEC is not a member of the United Nations.

To answer the question, you must infer an effect, or consequence, of what OPEC has achieved. Because oil is a valuable commodity in almost every area of an industrialized nation's economy, the cost of running such an economy would rise proportionately to the cost of oil, hurting the nation's economy (which is obviously a result that no nation would want for itself). **The correct answer is B.**

Question 6 refers to the following information.

Communism is both a political and an economic system in which the major means of production and distribution of goods and products are shared in common by all the people. In its purest form, communism would mean even the sharing of all property. The term is generally used to describe the economic systems in Soviet Russia and China. *Socialism* is an economic system in which the majority of productive resources, both human-made and natural, are owned and controlled by the state or its agencies. Because production is divided among the population under socialism, production is assumed to be more equitable (fairer) and more efficient than under Western-style capitalism.

6. What do communism and socialism have in common?

A. A preference for private ownership of resources

B. A preference for competition over cooperation

C. The fact that both are political as well as economic systems

D. The division of production among all the people

To answer this question, you must note the similarities and differences between the two systems. Neither communism nor socialism promotes private ownership of resources (choice A) nor does either promote competition in business (choice B). Only communism is considered both a political as well as an economic system (choice C). Both systems, however, believe in the division of production among all the people (choice D). How the division is made may differ, but both support the theory that division of production is good. **The correct answer is D.**

Question 7 refers to the following information.

After the Great War, later referred to as World War I, the United States, Great Britain, and France joined forces and drew up terms for the defeated Germany. The terms, known as the Treaty of Versailles, reflected the allies' position that Germany was to blame for the war. Consequently, the treaty provided that Germany was forbidden to have a military air force and that the German army and navy were to be strictly limited in size. In addition, under the treaty, Germany was required to pay 132 billion gold marks in reparations to nations it had harmed during the war. Germany had no choice but to abide by all these terms.

7. Which of the following is an opinion, rather than a fact, about the conclusion and immediate aftermath of World War I?

A. Germany had little or no say when it came to the terms of the treaty.

B. Germany's punishment was unfair since other nations had harmed Germany as well.

C. After the Great War, Germany was left without an air force to defend itself.

D. France was one of the nations that participated in the Great War.

Based on the passage information, choices C and D are clearly accurate, and so you can eliminate them. Choice A is not a fact provided in the passage. So does this mean that the statement in choice A is merely an opinion? No. The passage makes it clear that the treaty was drawn up by the countries that had opposed Germany, and that Germany "had no choice but to abide by" the terms of the treaty. So you can infer that Germany had little or no say in the treaty negotiations. In contrast, choice B is merely on opinion. Whether the treaty terms were fair may very well depend on one's perspective on the war. **The correct answer is B.**

You may also be asked to analyze relationships between texts that offer different perspectives or opinions on a social studies topic.

Questions 8 and 9 are based on the following information.

Document 1

"... Thus the constituted compact has been deliberately broken and disregarded by the non-slaveholding States, and the consequence follows that South Carolina is released from her obligation...

... We, therefore, the People of South Carolina, by our delegates in Convention assembled, appealing to the Supreme Judge of the world for the rectitude of our intentions, have solemnly declared that the Union heretofore existing between this State and other States of North America, is dissolved, and that the State of South Carolina has resumed her position among the nations of the world, as a separate and independent State; with full power to levy war, conclude peace, contract alliances, establish commerce, and to do all other acts and things which independent States may of right do."

Source: Declaration of Immediate Causes Which Induce and Justify the Secession of South Carolina from the Federal Union. 1860. From Docsteach.org

Document 2

"...I hold that, in contemplation of universal law, and of the Constitution, the Union of these States is perpetual. Perpetuity is implied, if not expressed, in the fundamental law of all National Governments. It is safe to assert that no Government proper ever had a provision in its organic law for its own termination. Continue to execute all the express provisions of our National Constitution, and the Union will endure forever—it being impossible to destroy it except by some action not provided for in the instrument itself...

...It follows, from these views, that no State, upon its own mere motion, can lawfully get out of the Union; that resolves and ordinances to that effect are legally void; and that acts of violence, within any State or States, against the authority of the United States, are insurrectionary or revolutionary, according to circumstances."

Source: Inaugural Address. 1860. Pamphlet of [President Abraham] Lincoln Speeches. 1912. From Docsteach.org

8. These two documents led to which of the following events in United States history?

A. The French and Indian War

B. The American Revolution

C. The Mexican War

D. The Civil War

Secession of South Carolina and other southern states would start a four-year civil war in America that split the country in two. While the French and Indian War (choice A), the American Revolution (choice B), and the Mexican War (choice C) involved the people of the United States of America, only the Civil War pitted countrymen solely against themselves, resulting in casualties of more than 620,000 men, more than any other war in American history. **The correct answer is D.**

9. The author of the first document believes in which type of theory regarding secession?

A. Contract

B. Compact

C. Natural law

D. Constitutional

This question requires general knowledge of the political theories that relate to the development of federal constitutions. In his Inaugural Address, Abraham Lincoln asserted his belief in the contract theory, meaning all people signed an agreement with the Constitution, not the states, and thus the states had no right to secede. In contrast, South Carolina argued that compact theory justified its secession, as the states came together or "compacted" to form the union and thus had the right to determine if the government had overstepped its limits of authority as set forth in the compact. **The correct answer is B.**

Evaluation Questions

Evaluation involves drawing on your comprehension and analytical skills in order to make an assessment, judgment, or critique or to draw a conclusion. An evaluation question might ask you to characterize an event, era, or system described or outlined in a passage. Or it might ask you to recognize a potential benefit or drawback of an economic or political policy, or with a particular statute (law). An evaluation question might present a point of view, along with numbered statements that either reflect or oppose that point of view. An evaluation might ask you to determine whether statements made in a passage are facts or opinions, or whether the author of a passage seems to be a reliable expert or someone with biased opinions. Evaluation questions often involve quotations and historical documents.

In handling these questions, what's just as important as recognizing a fair assessment of the information is recognizing unfair assessments and judgments. Be on the lookout for incorrect answer choices that speculate too much or that jump to conclusions or judgments that are unreasonable based solely on the information provided.

Question 10 refers to the following information.

> "The ostensible cause of the war was the issue of slavery. However, slavery was just one of many issues that drove a wedge between the two sides. One of the main points of contention between the two sides was the issue of states' rights. Another issue was the favoritism shown in Congress toward the North. The final straw, though, was the election of Abraham Lincoln, a candidate who did not receive a true mandate of the people based on the number of votes he received."

10. The war to which the quoted words referred was the US Civil War. Which of the following is **most likely** true about the author of the quoted words?

The author

A. sympathized with the South.

B. was opposed to slavery.

C. saw many causes of the war.

D. participated in the war.

The question asks you to make an assessment or draw a conclusion about the author based on what he or she wrote. So you need to understand the quotation's specific points as well as the author's broader point. Because the author identifies several possible contributing factors leading to the Civil War, it is fair to conclude that the author, in fact, recognized that the war had many causes. Though some of the points that the author makes might be the same ones that a Southern sympathizer might have pointed out, it is unfair to conclude, based solely on the passage, that the author sympathized with the South. **The correct answer is C.**

Question 11 refers to the following information.

The Fourteenth Amendment to the US Constitution states in part: ". . . (C) No person shall be a Senator or Representative in Congress, or elector of President and Vice President, or hold any office, civil or military, under the United States, or under any State, who, having previously taken an oath, as a member of Congress, or as an officer of the United States, or as a member of any State legislature, or as an executive or judicial officer of any State, to support the Constitution of the United States, shall have engaged in insurrection or rebellion against the same, or given aid or comfort to the enemies thereof. But Congress may by a vote of two thirds of each House, remove such disability. . . ."

11. What is the intent of this portion of the Fourteenth Amendment?

A. To encourage criminal prosecution of elected officials

B. To ensure party loyalty at all levels of government

C. To enhance the security of the nation and its states

D. To encourage patriotic citizens to run for Congress

The question requires you to evaluate and characterize the quoted portion of the Fourteenth Amendment. The portion lists a number of government offices, and then forbids any person who poses a threat to the government from holding any of the listed public offices. Choice C provides a good characterization of what this provision was intended to accomplish. Notice that choices A and D go too far. The purpose of the quoted part of the Fourteenth Amendment is more limited than either choice A or choice D suggests. Choice B is incorrect because the provision is concerned with loyalty to the state and federal governments, not to any political party. **The correct answer is C.**

Application Questions

Application questions require you to use information from a passage (or visual) in a way that is different from the way it is presented to you. In other words, your task is to apply the ideas to new situations and contexts. Use your understanding of the concept described in the passage, along with common sense, to identify the correct answer.

Question 12 refers to the following information.

During a period of economic recession, the nation's gross national product (GNP) is in decline, which means that the economy as a whole is producing fewer goods and providing fewer services than previously.

12. How is a small business **least likely** to behave during an economic recession?

A. By putting its products on sale

B. By giving loyal employees a pay raise

C. By limiting the kinds of products it sells

D. By depleting its inventory of goods

This question requires you not only to understand the definition of a recession, but also to apply the concept to a situation not specifically described in the passage. When fewer goods and services are produced, everyone makes less money and, in turn, everyone has less money to spend. The behaviors described in choices A, C, and D make perfect sense in this situation. Eliminate those choices. **The correct answer is B.**

Question 13 refers to the following information.

A *lobbyist* is a person who represents a group of people and whose job it is to work for the special interests of that group. A lobbyist will contact members of Congress in order to make sure that money is allocated for the group's work. The lobbyist will try to persuade them that the interests he or she represents are more worthy than others to receive a share of available financial resources.

13. Which activity would be **most** closely associated with lobbying?

A. Explaining to a legislator why he or she should run for reelection

B. Petitioning the city council to pass a law outlawing smoking in public places

C. Convincing the boss to throw an office party that will improve worker morale

D. Staging a labor-union strike in protest of unfairly low wages

Choice C is the only one that describes an interest held in common by a group of people (employees), and where someone representing the group attempts to obtain a benefit (a party) for the group from someone in a position to give it to them (the boss) by persuading that person of the benefits of doing so (improvement in worker morale). **The correct answer is C.**

Question 14 refers to the following information.

On August 2, 1990, Iraqi president Saddam Hussein invaded Kuwait, an oil-rich neighboring state roughly the size of New Jersey, and ignited a conflict that would, ultimately, lead to his downfall. Until that time, the United States had turned a blind eye to the repressive policies of Saddam's regime. National Security Directives advised "economic incentives," such as food supplies, to urge Iraq towards more humane policies. Following Iraq's invasion of Kuwait, the Bush administration denounced the "naked aggression" of Iraq's actions even as it feared an invasion of oil-rich Saudi Arabia. Economic sanctions were issued, but Saddam would not withdraw his forces from Kuwait. In November, the United States appealed to the United Nations Security Council for authorization for military intervention. In Resolution 678, the Security Council gave Iraq until January 15, 1991, to withdraw. Saddam Hussein promised that military invasion would result in the "mother of all battles," and critics at home warned of a long and bloody war. President Bush had claimed that an order by him for an American invasion to liberate Kuwait did not require Congressional approval, but he changed policy and asked Congress for authorization, which he received on January 12. The United States began an air war against Baghdad and Iraqi footholds in Kuwait. When Iraq responded by attacking Israel, the Bush administration provided Patriot missiles operated by American personnel. When Iraq set fire to Kuwaiti oil fields, American forces invaded Kuwait on February 23, an invasion that lasted for 100 hours. Thousands of Iraqis were killed and tens of thousands surrendered or fled north. On February 27, President Bush declared that Kuwait had been liberated.

14. According to the author, President George H.W. Bush's decision to invade Kuwait

A. was done without Congressional approval.

B. reversed earlier American policy towards Iraq.

C. incurred widespread United Nations disapproval.

D. was ignored by Saddam Hussein.

In the earlier years of Bush's presidency, his administration had used economic incentives and diplomatic means to attempt to influence Iraqi policy. In a reversal of earlier policy, Bush ultimately decided to invade Kuwait, which was done with Congressional approval as well as UN support. Iraq responded to initial warnings by promising a bloody war and retaliated against American bombings with air strikes against Israel and incinerating Kuwaiti oil fields. **The correct answer is B.**

Question 15 refers to the following information.

The political discourse that followed the United States' invasion of Iraq in 2003 was especially vitriolic and included a diverse array of viewpoints—some of which were bolstered by factual evidence and others unsubstantiated theories. Among the most extreme theories, which many experts argue is bereft of credible evidence, is the notion that the Bush administration planned and initiated the 9/11 attack to galvanize the populace to support a "justified" military invasion of Iraq, which the government then used to profit from oil reserves in the region as well as in contract-based rebuilding efforts, and to advance its political agenda abroad.

15. Which of the following is a credible source of information on the Iraq War following the events on September 11, 2001?

A. A personal blog dedicated to uncovering conspiracies among the world's governments

B. A student essay that reflects her opinion regarding the war and its aftermath

C. Documentation detailing the war released directly by the CIA

D. An anarchist group's newsletter, which is focused on critiquing the world's existing power structures

This question asks you to evaluate the credibility of authors in historical and contemporary political discourse, a common theme on the exam. The only credible and verifiable source of information regarding the Iraq War following the events on September 11, 2001, among the answer choices is documentation directly from a government department, like the CIA. The secondary sources among the other answer choices are not credible sources of information. **The correct answer is C.**

QUESTIONS BASED ON VISUAL DEPICTIONS

Approximately 40 percent of the questions on the GED Social Studies Test are based on a visual depiction of some sort or on a brief passage of text accompanied by a visual depiction. The "visual" may be a chart, graph, or table; or it might be a political cartoon, photo, or other illustration; or it might be a map, diagram, or timeline.

Questions based on visuals are designed to gauge your ability to interpret the meaning of the visual (as well as the accompanying text, if any). Even if you do not recognize the visual or don't understand it initially, you can still figure out the best answer by looking for clues or for things you do recognize.

In the following pages, you will examine the types of visuals appearing most frequently on the test. You'll see some examples of each type, and you'll learn how to handle them.

Editorial Cartoons

The cartoons on the GED Social Studies Test are not the sort you'll find in the comics section of your newspaper. Instead, they're the type that appear in a newspaper's editorial section, which contains articles, essays, and cartoons expressing opinions about current events. These editorial cartoons are sometimes referred to as *political cartoons*, even though they often deal with a much wider range of issues—from political and economic to social and cultural.

Editorial cartoonists are not concerned with providing information. Instead, through their cartoons, they express their opinions and perspectives (their "slant") on current events and issues of the day. Their cartoons carry messages that are usually critical of prevailing ideas, well-established institutions, and influential individuals—especially political figures in the public eye at the moment. Editorial cartoonists often employ humor, sarcasm, and irony to convey their messages.

As for how these cartoonists convey their messages, their cartoons often show human-like characters, which the artist typically uses to depict a specific, well-known public figure—for example, a president or presidential candidate, a dictator or leader from another country, a high-ranking government official, or even an influential commentator from the media. The editorial cartoonist will usually portray the specific person as a **caricature**, which exaggerates the person's prominent physical features.

Of course, when a cartoon shows a caricature of a specific, well-known person, you know that the message of the cartoon has to do with that person. But editorial cartoonists often use human-like characters, animals, and even objects to represent, or *symbolize,* something else, such as the following:

- A group of specific individuals—for example, the Supreme Court or a legislative body (such as the US Senate)
- A geographically defined entity—for example, a particular state or nation, the North or the South (as during the US Civil War), or the European Union
- An organization or alliance—for example, a political party, the United Nations, an oil cartel such as OPEC, political lobbyists, or big business
- An abstract idea, an ideology, or a cause—for example, free-market capitalism, religious fundamentalism, social welfare, environmentalism, the so-called "war on terror," or gun control

Here are just a few of the symbols often used in editorial cartoons:

- An eagle, to represent democracy or freedom
- A hammer-and-sickle, to represent Communism
- A donkey, to represent the Democratic political party
- An elephant, to represent the Republican political party
- A soldier, to represent one of the countries involved in a war
- A judge, to represent the concept of justice
- A beggar, to represent social welfare
- A pile of money, to represent greed or capitalism

Sometimes, specific individuals become so closely associated with an ideology, cause, or concept that a cartoonist will use a caricature of that person as a symbol—especially if the readership is sophisticated enough to understand the symbolism. For example:

- Lenin has come to represent Soviet-style communism.
- Theodore Roosevelt has come to represent opposition to monopolies and big business.
- Adolf Hitler has come to represent persecution and is even seen as the embodiment of evil.
- Franklin D. Roosevelt has come to represent New Deal–style, or so-called "big" government.
- Richard Nixon has come to represent political scandal, secrecy, and dirty politics.

As you examine the characters and objects in an editorial cartoon, look for clues as to what they represent. The cartoonist may write a word or brief phrase directly on the characters (especially their clothing) as well as on other pictured objects to help the audience understand the symbolism. Look carefully for any such clues, as they typically appear in small print. Remember: if the cartoonist went to the trouble of writing words anywhere in the visual, those words will no doubt be useful in understanding the idea that the cartoonist was trying to convey.

Also pay close attention to how the characters appear and what they are doing or saying. A character might be drawn to appear noble and victorious or aggressive and evil; or a character might be drawn to appear defeated, injured, or victimized. Two characters may appear to be fighting or angry with each other, or they might appear friendly toward one another. Body postures, facial expressions, modes of dress, objects carried or held, and other visual clues can be useful in understanding a cartoon's message. In addition, spoken words—usually written in bubbles above the characters—are even more crucial to that message.

Finally, editorial cartoons sometimes come with **captions**—words appearing below the illustration. A caption might indicate what a character is saying, or it might provide a clue as to how to interpret or evaluate the cartoon. If the cartoon includes a caption, you can be certain that it is crucial in understanding the message of a cartoon.

Question 16 refers to the following cartoon.

WONDER HOW LONG THE HONEYMOON WILL LAST?

16. What idea is the artist who created the cartoon trying to convey?

Hitler and Stalin

A. should be partners because they have a lot in common.

B. were on unfriendly terms before forming a partnership.

C. have formed an alliance that they hope to keep secret from their mutual enemies.

D. have formed a partnership whose prospects are uncertain.

Your knowledge of twentieth-century history may be useful in interpreting the cartoon, yet it isn't needed to answer the question at hand. You may not have recognized Stalin in the cartoon. But notice the hammer-and-sickle symbol, together with the swastika, on the wedding cake. These symbols provide a clue as to the identity of both characters. In any event, the question provides this information.

In this question, the caption is crucial to understanding the message. Posing the question "Wonder how long the honeymoon will last?" suggests that a new marriage, though happy at first, might turn sour over time. The cartoon implies that the relationship is good at the onset, but the future of the relationship is uncertain (choice D). Choice A is incorrect because the cartoon shows Hitler and Stalin already partners. Choices B and C may or may not provide accurate historical information, but since the cartoon provides no clue as to the past relationship between Hitler and Stalin (choice B), or about whether their alliance was secret (choice C), you can rule out both choices. Again: if a cartoon provides a caption, you can be sure that it is crucial to understanding the cartoonist's intended meaning. **The correct answer is D.**

Maps

During the Social Studies Test, you'll encounter at least one or two geography and/or history questions based on maps. Don't expect to find the kinds of maps you use in your everyday life to help you find your way across town or from one city to another. Instead, what you're likely to see are any of the following kinds of maps, depending on the sort of information the map is intended to provide:

- **Political map:** This is the most familiar type of map to most people. It shows political boundaries of cities, states, and countries as well as capitals and other major cities. On the GED Social Studies Test, a map of this type might cover a multi-state region, an entire country, a multi-country region, or an entire continent (and possibly the seas and oceans around it).
- **Topographical map:** This type of map shows the locations of natural features such as rivers, lakes, seas, mountain ranges, and deserts. It may also focus on the locations of natural resources such as minerals, timber (forests), and other forms of vegetation or crops, and even animal life. A topographical map may also provide elevations (altitude) at various locations.
- **Historical map:** This type of map provides a timeline of key historical events according to where they took place. Historical maps often provide callouts, which list events and/or dates and point to the places on the map where the events occurred.

The three categories listed above are not mutually exclusive. For example, a map may provide political boundaries as well as geographical features. Historical maps typically show politically defined regions such as colonies, provinces, nations, territories, kingdoms, and even empires.

Regardless of which type of map a test question involves, you should start by reading the title of the map. The title will provide clues as to what information the map conveys. Next, locate the map key, or **legend** (if any). The legend is often located off to the side or at the bottom of the map. It will explain the symbols used on the map as well as any colors or shading used on the map. The legend may also contain a map **scale** that indicates distances on the map. Here's an example of a typical map legend:

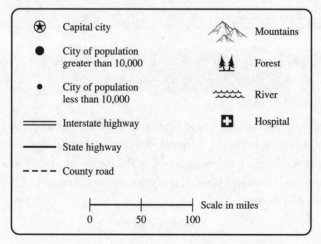

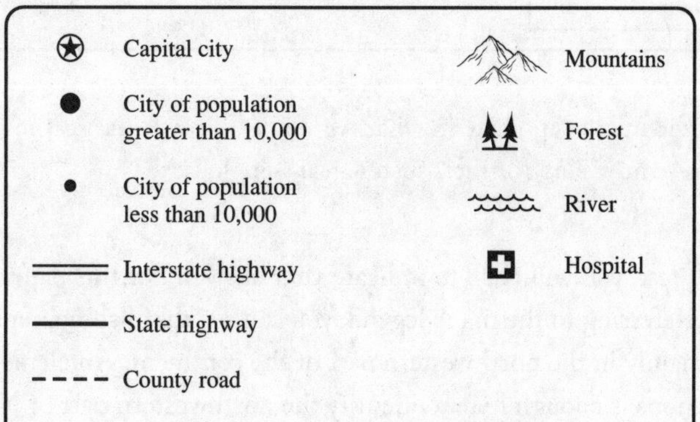

Since maps can be used to display any sort of geographically, anthropologically, or historically specific information, a myriad of specialized map types are possible. Remember, the select-an-area or drag-and-drop interactive features allow you to pinpoint exactly where on a map a specific event occurred or specific information can be verified. The following two maps, each of which is accompanied by two GED test-style questions, illustrate two such types.

Questions 17 and 18 refer to the following map.

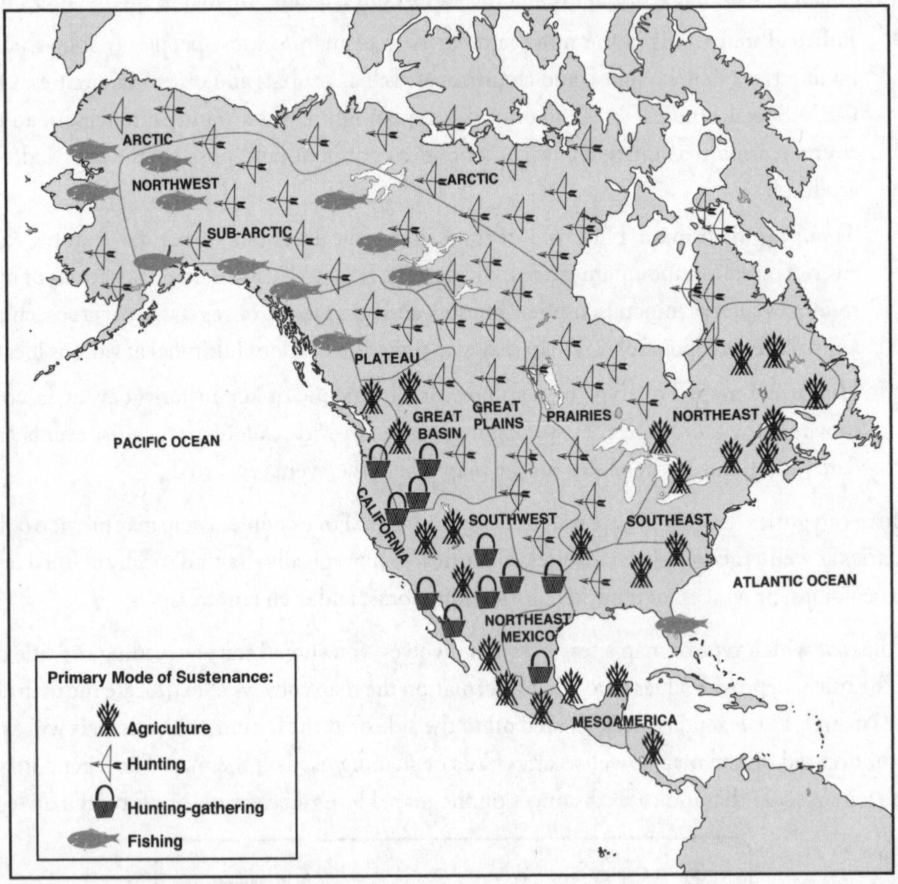

17. Click on the map to indicate in what region of North America the majority of Native Americans who fished for their sustenance were located.

On the online GED test, you will click to indicate your answer. For this paper version, write your answer on the map. Referring to the map's legend, you can see that fishing, represented by the fish symbol, took place mainly in the northwestern part of the continent. An elementary knowledge of geography and directions is enough here to identify the northwestern part of North America. **The correct answer is the Northwest.**

18. [ ] were available to the early Native Americans of the Great Basin as a means of sustenance.

When taking the GED test online, you will type your answer in the box. For this paper test, please write it in. To answer this question, you need to locate the Great Basin area on the map (in the map's left-central region). In that area, you'll find the symbols for agriculture, hunting, and hunting-gathering. **The correct answer is hunting, gathering, and agriculture.**

Questions 19 and 20 refer to the following map.

Percentage of Renter-Occupied Units Spending 30 Percent or More of Household Income on Rent (2008)

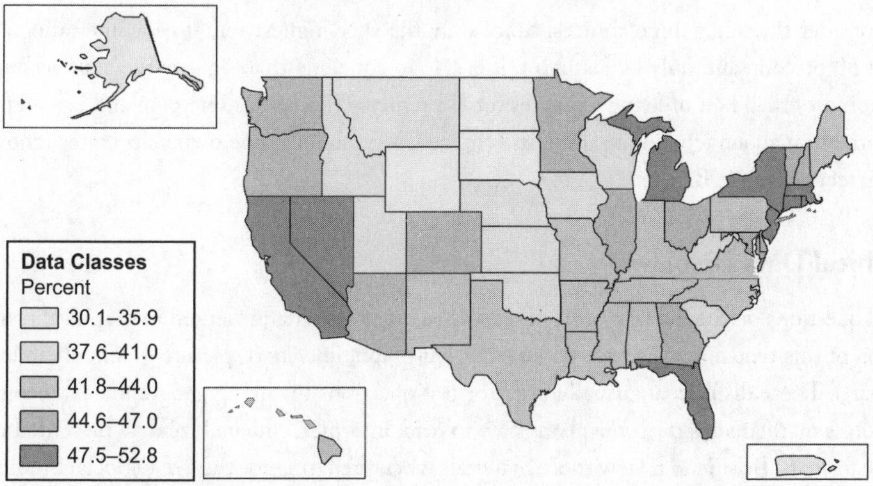

United States: Estimate 45.9 Percent, Margin of Error: +/– 0.1 Percent
Source: US Census Bureau, 2006–2008 American Community Survey

19. In how many states, including Alaska and Hawaii, is the percentage of households who rent their residence rather than own it 30.1 to 41.0 percent?

A. 11

B. 15

C. 46

D. Not enough information is provided.

This question illustrates the importance of reading the title of a map. According to this map's title, the map provides only the rent-to-income ratio in each state, which is entirely different from the renter-to-owner ratio. Not enough information is provided to answer this question. **The correct answer is D.**

20. The map **best** supports which of the following conclusions?

A. On average, US renters pay more for rent than for all other living expenses combined.

B. Arizona rental housing is less affordable than rental housing in most other states.

C. The average rent in Georgia is greater than in most other states.

D. States with the highest rent-to-income ratio have the highest home ownership rates.

This is a relatively difficult question. Focusing on choice B, the rent-to-income ratio for Arizona residents is in the second-highest category (44.6–47.0 percent) among the five provided in the legend. Estimating the total number of states in the top two categories, you'll find that the total is far less than half of 51 (the total number of states, as well as Puerto Rico). Interpreting rent-to-income ratio as an indication of "affordability," Arizona is clearly less affordable than most states when it comes to rental housing (choice B).

Now consider the other three choices. Since only the very highest rent-to-income ratio category exceeds 50 percent, and only by just a bit, it is safe to conclude that, on average, rent accounts for *less* (not more) than half of living expenses for US renters (choice A). The map and legend provide no information about actual rent amounts (choice C), or about home ownership rates (choice D). **The correct answer is B.**

Graphical Data Displays

Several questions on the Social Studies Test will be based on data presented in graphical format. A question of this type might be based on a table, bar graph, line chart, picture graph, or circle graph (pie chart). These displays are usually used for test questions involving geography and economics. This book's mathematics review explains how to read, interpret, and analyze data presented in each of these formats. Be sure to review those materials when preparing for the GED Social Studies Test. Keep in mind, however, that on the Social Studies Test, the emphasis is not on number-crunching but, rather, on the following skills:

- Understanding what the graphical display is intended to show
- Reading and interpreting the data
- Understanding the significance of the data
- Drawing general conclusions from the data

Though you may need to perform simple arithmetic tasks, such as counting or adding, you won't need to calculate precise percents, ratios, or averages. (These skills are measured on the Mathematical Reasoning Test.) In addition to multiple-choice questions, chart and graph items may ask you to use the interactive drag-and-drop feature.

The next two GED test-style questions are based on the same picture graph and illustrate that the focus of data-display questions on the Social Studies Test is far more on understanding and interpreting graphs in a social studies context than on applying math.

Questions 21 and 22 refer to the following graphs.

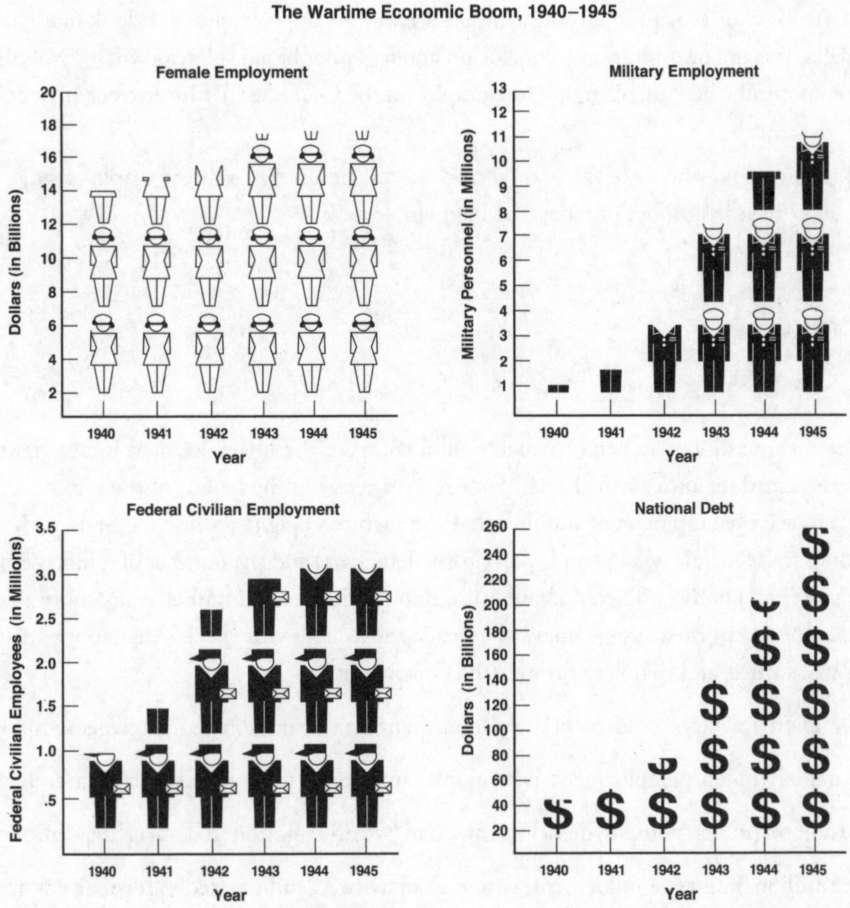

21. What conclusion can you draw from the information presented in the charts?

From 1940 through 1945,

A. the employment rate among males was greater than among females.

B. all of the US military personnel were males.

C. a rise in federal civilian employment contributed to increased government spending.

D. the greatest increase in employment was among females.

Focusing on choice C, the upper-right and lower-left charts show that military employment and federal civilian employment both rose over the course of the war. The lower-right chart shows that government *debt* rose over the course of the war. Together, the three charts strongly support the inference that the rise in federal civilian employment (as well as the rise in military employment) contributed to increased government spending. Though you cannot draw this conclusion with absolute certainty, the data strongly support it.

Now consider the other three choices. Notice that the upper-left chart expresses female employment in terms of *dollars* (in billions), not in terms of the number of females employed. So you cannot draw any conclusions about how many females were employed from 1940 through 1945. Eliminate choices A and D. As for choice B, although the symbols used in the upper-right chart look more like males than females, it is unfair to draw any conclusion about gender based solely on these symbols. (Keep this lesson in mind when analyzing picture graphs on the GED test.) **The correct answer is C.**

22. During how many of the years shown was the number of military employees more than double the number of federal civilian employees?

A. One

B. Two

C. Three

D. Four

To answer this question, you need to analyze and compare the lower-left and upper-right charts. (You can disregard the other two charts.) For each year, look at the height of the picture, then look to the left to see the employment number that the picture's height represents. Start with the year 1940. Notice that federal civilian employees (lower-left chart) and the number of military employees (upper-right chart) both numbered about 1.0 million. The second number is *not* more than twice the first number. Perform a similar analysis for each subsequent year (notice that approximating the numbers will suffice, and that very little math is involved):

1941: 2.0 million (military employment) is *not* more than twice 1.5 million (federal civilian employment).

1942: 3.5 million (military employment) is *not* more than twice 2.6 million (federal civilian employment).

1943: 8.0 million (military employment) is more than twice 3.0 million (federal civilian employment).

1944: 10.5 million (military employment) is more than twice 3.2 million (federal civilian employment).

1945: 12.0 million (military employment) is more than twice 3.3 million (federal civilian employment).

As you can see, during three of the six years, military employment was more than double the federal civilian employment. **The correct answer is C.**

GENERAL TEST-TAKING STRATEGIES

Here are some general strategies for tackling the GED Social Studies Test as a whole. These points of advice generally apply to all types of questions. Put these strategies to work on the practice tests in this book, and then review them again just before exam day.

First, read the question(s) based on a passage of text or visual depiction.

Before you look at a visual or read even a brief passage, read the question stem (the question itself, but not the answer choices). If the passage or visual comes with more than one question, read all the question stems first. This task should only take 10 to 15 seconds. The question(s) may provide clues as to what you should focus on and think about as you read the text or analyze the visual.

Read a passage of text straight through before answering any questions based on it.

If a question or group of questions refers to a passage of text, read the passage from beginning to end without interruption. Pay careful attention to how the ideas connect together. Think about what the overall message, or main idea, of the text is. Also think about whether the ideas lead naturally to any conclusion or inference. If they do, the chances are good that the question(s) will focus on this feature.

Use your note board as you read a longer passage.

Passages can run up to 150 words in length (about one-fourth of a page)—long enough to merit taking notes while reading. Jotting down key words and phrases helps you think actively while reading, which will help you answer the questions about the passage.

When reading charts, graphs, maps, and timelines, don't get bogged down in every detail.

Some visual depictions will contain more information than you'll need to answer the question(s) based on them. In fact, one of the skills you're being tested on is your ability to sort through that information to determine what is relevant (and what is not relevant) to the question at hand. So don't waste time analyzing every detail in a visual. Instead, focus your attention on what the question asks about.

Read any title or caption accompanying a map, chart, graph, or cartoon.

Many times, the title or caption will give you a clue about the true meaning of the visual. You can then use this clue to help clarify the question and eliminate incorrect answers.

Apply common sense.

Many questions, especially about economics and geography, may be unfamiliar to you at first glance. However, remember that you use and make decisions concerning economics and geography every day. Use your real-life, practical economics and geography skills to help you on the test.

If possible, formulate your own answer to a question before reading the answer choices.

For each question, try to formulate your own response to it, and *then* scan the choices for something resembling your home-grown answer. This technique will keep you from becoming confused and distracted by incorrect answer choices.

Pace yourself properly.

You have 70 minutes to answer all questions on the GED Social Studies Test. The questions are not presented in any set order of difficulty. So after 35 minutes, you should have answered about 18 questions. If you're falling behind, pick up the pace. In any event, try to answer all questions with at least five minutes to spare, so you can go back and reconsider any responses you were unsure about.

SUMMING IT UP

- GED Social Studies Test questions test your knowledge of important principles, concepts, events, and relationships. The questions cover history, civics and government, economics, and geography.
- The Social Studies Test contains up to 35 questions, including drop-down, fill-in-the-blank, drag-and-drop, and two select-an-area questions.
    - The Social Studies Test focuses on three main skill areas: reading and writing, social studies concepts, and mathematical reasoning in social studies.
- Most questions are based on brief passages of text, which vary in length from a few sentences to as many as 150 words (about a quarter of a page).
    - A question involving a passage of text might refer to it either as a "passage" or as "information" or "text."
- Other questions are based on maps, charts, cartoons, diagrams, and other visual depictions.
    - Some visual depictions are also accompanied by a brief passage of text.
- The GED Social Studies Test requires you to demonstrate that you can do the following:
    - Comprehend the material
    - Draw inferences and conclusions
    - Evaluate the information
    - Apply concepts and ideas to other situations
- The best way to do well on this test is to read the front-page section of a trustworthy newspaper or news source every day, watch the news on TV, listen to serious discussions of current events on public radio, and think about current issues. It may also be helpful to visit your local library and look at the atlases, maps, and news magazines.

Chapter 8

Social Studies Review

OVERVIEW

- US History
- Civics and Government
- The US Government
- Canadian Government
- Economics
- Geography
- Historical Documents on the GED® Social Studies Test
- Canadian History
- Summing It Up
- Practice Questions
- Answer Key and Explanations

The GED Social Studies Test is designed to measure critical-thinking skills rather than knowledge. Nevertheless, with some prior familiarity with the four content areas covered on the test (history, civics and government, economics, and geography) you can expect to handle the questions with greater ease and confidence. The review materials in this part of the book are designed to help you in this respect. Keep in mind that this review is intended only to highlight the four content areas listed above. It is by no means intended to be a comprehensive examination of these areas.

Questions are provided throughout this social studies review. As you answer them, keep in mind that the passages of text on which they are based are longer than those on the actual GED Social Studies Test. To assist readers preparing for the GED test in Canada, sections focusing on Canadian government and history are included in this review. Also later in the review are summaries of key US historical documents covered on the Social Studies Test.

US HISTORY

This history focuses mainly on US history, although some of that history is presented in the context of the world affairs and relations between the United States and other nations. It begins with the European colonization of the Americas and includes questions about the Native American population that inhabited North America. It concludes with American foreign policy after 9/11.

European Settlement and Population of the New World

Beginning in the late fourteenth century, European explorers embarked on a series of expeditions of discovery and conquest. Their goals were to amass great wealth by conquering indigenous peoples, to bring fame to their monarchs and themselves for their daring exploits, and to bring

Christianity to the regions that they explored and exploited. The first explorers were motivated by fabulous tales from the Orient brought back by Marco Polo and other Italian traders, and especially by the valuable products they brought with them, such as spices, silk, gold, and silver. Portugal's Prince Henry sought a sea route to India around Africa so that Portuguese traders could bypass the Italian middlemen who had monopolized the Oriental luxury trade. Under his direction, Portuguese explorers explored much of the African coast and established profitable trading posts in the Niger delta and farther south in Angola. Eventually, Portuguese explorers reached Southern India's trading cities. Within a mere 50 years, Portugal essentially controlled the Indian Ocean with strategically located trading posts and naval military might.

While Portugal set its sights on dominating the Indian Ocean, Spain also began to explore and seek colonies. **Christopher Columbus**, an enterprising Italian merchant with sailing experience on Portuguese trade vessels in the Indian Ocean, attempted to voyage across the Atlantic to India and break the Portuguese trade monopoly. Columbus landed in the Bahamas, not in India, though he thought he had reached India.

By the end of the fifteenth century, Spain and Portugal dominated trade and territories in Asia and the Americas. Portugal controlled most of the Indian Ocean trade, as well as the spice plantations in Indonesia, while Spain controlled extensive parts of Central and South America. Fearing a war between the two rivals, Pope Alexander VI (Rodrigo Borgia) helped negotiate the Treaty of Tordesillas, which essentially divided the world in half, with both countries receiving exclusive rights in their respective hemispheres. England, France, and the Netherlands refused to comply with the Treaty of Tordesillas and began to explore and establish their own colonies in the Americas.

France founded colonies in much of eastern North America, on a number of Caribbean islands, and in South America, primarily as trading posts for exporting products such as fish, sugar, and furs. Through the explorers Cartier and Champlain, France established a fur trading post in 1608 that would grow into the city of Quebec. Extending their reach, the French claimed a large territory in Canada and the Great Lakes region. Then "New France" grew west of the Great Lakes into Wisconsin and south to the Gulf of Mexico. In 1682, the entire Mississippi River watershed was claimed for France. Named Louisiane, it gave France control of the Mississippi Valley and the Great Plains in addition to its holdings in the Great Lakes and Canada.

NOTE

On the actual GED Social Studies test, you will need to click on the computer screen to select your answer from the drop-down menu provided. For your ease in using this book and checking your answers, we have provided answer choices as A, B, C, and D.

1. The European explorers of the fourteenth and fifteenth centuries were motivated by all of the following with the possible exception of

Select ▼

A. converting native peoples to their religion.

B. acquiring new land for their countries.

C. the possibility of personal fame.

D. papal proclamations to go forth and explore.

European explorers were enlisted and supported in their explorations by their monarchs. They were not following any directives from the Pope. **The correct answer is D.**

The New World

By 1700, the Portuguese, Spanish, French, and British had all established colonies in the New World. In 1607, Jamestown, Virginia, became the first permanent British settlement in the New World. Jamestown and other early settlements and colonies were created as joint-stock companies. Joint-stock companies were business ventures in which a large number of people invested small amounts of money. This allowed the investors to avoid the risk of losing huge sums of money. A total of 13 British colonies appeared on the eastern coast of North America over the next 125 years, each with its own identity. The British sponsored the colonies and the journeys of the colonists because the British hoped to create trade revenues through trade with the colonies. The colonists from England who sailed to the New World sought freedom of worship, a voice in their government, and a fresh start with land of their own. Some colonists, many of those in Georgia, for example, sought refuge from the law in the New World. By 1763, after an armed conflict with the French (known in the Americas as the French and Indian War and known in Europe as the Seven Years War), the British controlled a large portion of the North American continent. Unfortunately for those Native Americans who occupied the lands of North America before the arrival of the Europeans, colonization meant the end of many Native American cultures. Partly because of armed conflict and partly because of the introduction of European diseases into North America, the Europeans caused the death of many, many Native Americans.

Native Americans

Many thousands of years before the arrival of the Europeans, Native Americans formed settlements in distinct regions around the continent. Each tribe or nation had a different culture, language, governing system, religion, and clothing, as well as their own types of dwellings and customs, such as feasts.

Northeast Woodland tribes lived in enormous longhouses, and hunted and grew corn, beans, and squash. On the opposite coast, tribes in the Northwest Coastal region built cedar houses, and hunted, fished, and gathered plants and clams. Native Americans living on the Great Plains lived in portable tepees, and harvested plants, hunted buffalo, and tamed horses. Tribes in the Southwest lived in multistory adobe houses, farmed crops, raised turkeys, and hunted. In the Southeast, tribes built homes with thatched roofs. They farmed, hunted, fished, and gathered berries and nuts.

2. It was important for tepees to be easily moved to different locations so tribes could

A. fish in Northwest streams.

B. raise turkeys across the Southwest.

C. trade throughout the Northeast.

D. hunt buffalo across the Great Plains.

Tribes who lived on the Great Plains lived in tepees that could quickly be disassembled and relocated. These tribes had a nomadic lifestyle, following herds of buffalo that were their primary food source. **The correct answer is D.**

3. Regional variations affected all of the following aspects of Native American life, EXCEPT:

Select ▼

A. Style of housing

B. Type of crops raised

C. Trading with white settlers

D. Species of animals hunted

Different types of housing, crops, and animal species characterized Native Americans in different regions; however, trade with settlers was not dependent upon location. **The correct answer is C.**

TIP

The GED® Social Studies Test will assess your ability to put relevant key historical events in chronological order, so make sure you're familiar with the timeline of this struggle for independence and freedom.

The Struggle for American Independence

The sequence of events that led colonists in the "New World" of North America to galvanize and collectively rebel against the authoritarian governance of the British Empire ultimately led to the birth of the United States:

- 1754–1763: The French and Indian War—This war ended with the Treaty of Paris and France ceding its control over key eastern portions of North America to Great Britain.
- 1765: Stamp Act—The heavy losses incurred as a result of the French and Indian war directly led to the creation of new, draconian taxes on the colonists, such as the Stamp Act, which enraged colonists.
- 1767: Townshend Acts—These laws were passed in attempt by the British Empire to assert its authority and diminish colonists' representation in government.
- 1770: Boston Massacre—A small group of British troops in North America reacted to colonial protestors and detractors by killing five people, further igniting tensions.
- 1773: Boston Tea Party—A protest of the tea tax by Bostonians, their actions resulted in the passing of the Intolerable Acts by the British Parliament.
- 1774: The First Continental Congress is convened.
- 1775: The battles of the American Revolution are fought.
- 1776: The Declaration of Independence is signed and adopted.
- 1783: The Treaty of Paris is signed, effectively ending the war for American independence.

4. Which of the following events in American history preceded the formation of the First Continental Congress?

A. The signing of the Declaration of Independence

B. The Townshend Acts

C. The American Revolution

D. The signing of the Treaty of Paris

The question asks you to identify the proper sequence of events pertaining to America's struggle for independence; specifically, we're looking for the event that preceded, or occurred before, the formation of the First Continental Congress. A solid knowledge of American history will lead you to the conclusion that the Townshend Acts preceded the formation of the First Continental Congress. **The correct answer is B.**

Between the time of their arrival in the New World and the years prior to the War for American Independence, the colonists developed their own ideas about the way the colonies should be governed. Consequently, many of the colonists disagreed with the way the British governed the colonies. Among these points of contention was the problem of taxation without representation. In other words, the colonists did not like the fact that they were being forced to pay increasing British taxes, but they were never allowed much, if any, say in the way the British governed the colonies. Many of the colonists also resented the presence of British troops throughout the colonies. These disagreements, among others, caused tension between the colonies and the British government and led to one of the most monumental events in history, the War for American Independence (also known as the American Revolution or Revolutionary War).

5. Why did the British sponsor expeditions and colonists in the New World?

A. The British population explosion forced the British to seek relief from high population density by sending some of its population elsewhere.

B. The British encouraged the expeditions and colonists so that the colonists could escape the widespread famine facing the British Isles.

C. The British wanted to establish colonies and find new goods to bolster the British economy.

D. The British government wanted to give the colonists an opportunity to experiment with new religions.

The British saw the potential economic benefits of establishing colonies and supporting exploring expeditions based on the examples of the Spanish and Portuguese. **The correct answer is C.**

6. What was the colonists' main point of contention with the British government?

A. Taxation without being allowed a fair voice in the government of the colonies

B. The brutality of the British soldiers against the Native Americans

C. The high taxes on tea

D. The slow communications between the British government and the colonies

The colonists thought it was unfair that they paid taxes to the British government yet had no say in the way they were governed by the British. **The correct answer is A.**

Between 1765 and 1776, the British imposed a number of taxes on the colonies that the colonists viewed as unfair. Some of the items taxed by the British included sugar, playing cards, newspapers, and tea. In many cases, the colonists displayed their displeasure and anger by burning officials in effigy, tarring and feathering officials, and even throwing massive amounts of tea into British harbors. In response, the British government tried to limit and control the trade of the American colonies. In further attempts to keep the colonies from straying too far from British rule, the British attempted to reduce the power of the American lawmaking assemblies. To discourage protest even further, the British legislature passed special bills targeting specific troublesome colonists for imprisonment and stripping them of their wealth, which was then given to the Crown.

After much debate within the colonies, the colonial leaders, with the support of many of the colonists, decided to cut ties with Great Britain and declare the colonies' independence from British rule. Some of the colonists, known as loyalists, however, did not want to break away from the mother country; they still felt a sense of duty and loyalty toward England. In 1776, the colonial leaders signed the **Declaration of Independence**, which officially declared that the colonies were no longer under British rule. The carefully considered and effectively executed language of the Declaration of Independence perfectly captured the desire of its creators—to break free from the tyranny of British rule and establish independent, sovereign states with the freedom to choose their own destinies. The British refused to recognize the independence of the colonies. As a result, war broke out in the colonies between the American colonists and the British soldiers.

TIP

By analyzing the language used in a historical document, you should be able to identify the writer's purpose and point of view.

7. Which of the following excerpts from the Declaration of Independence makes clear that the colonies stood united in their desire for freedom from harsh British rule?

A. "We hold these truths to be self-evident, that all men are created equal"

B. "He has refused his Assent to Laws, the most wholesome and necessary for the public good"

C. "Prudence, indeed, will dictate that Governments long established should not be changed for light and transient causes"

D. "And for the support of this Declaration, with a firm reliance on the protection of divine Providence, we mutually pledge to each other our Lives, our Fortunes and our sacred Honor"

From the document's stirring opening lines ("When in the Course of human events, it becomes necessary for one people to dissolve the political bands which have connected them with another, and to assume among the powers of the earth, the separate and equal station to which the Laws of Nature and of Nature's God entitle them, a decent respect to the opinions of mankind requires that they should declare the causes which impel them to the separation.") to its assertion that the colonies stand firmly united in the closing sentence ("And for the support of this Declaration, with a firm reliance on the protection of divine Providence, we mutually pledge to each other our Lives, our Fortunes and our sacred Honor."), the Declaration of Independence is a vivid and powerful expression of the hunger for basic human rights and freedom shared by its creators. **The correct answer is D.**

The colonists mustered an army made up of many militiamen, or citizen soldiers, but very few professional soldiers. The British, on the other hand, fielded an army of professionally trained soldiers along with a formidable navy. Although the revolutionary army was outnumbered and perhaps outclassed, they had a few advantages. The revolutionists had great leadership, they were fighting from a defensive position, and they passionately believed in the cause for which they fought. With the aid of the French, Dutch, and Spanish—all of whom were enemies of the British—the Americans won an improbable victory over the British and gained their independence. Interestingly, by the end of the war, the colonies were only a minor concern for the British as they were also in the midst of a global conflict, fighting against the nations of France, Holland, and Spain. Tired of war, American and British diplomats met in Paris and signed the **Treaty of Paris of 1783**, in which Britain recognized the independence of the colonies. After the dust settled, the 13 colonies stood loosely united as the United States of America.

8. From the Declaration of Independence: "The history of the present King of Great Britain is a history of repeated injuries and usurpations, all having in direct object the establishment of an absolute Tyranny over these States."

All of the following are "injuries and usurpations" to which the Declaration of Independence refers, EXCEPT:

A. Controlling trade

B. Limiting lawmaking authority

C. Imprisoning protesters

D. Prohibiting public assembly

The British engaged in the activities described in choices A through C. However, they did not prohibit public assembly. **The correct answer is D.**

9. Which of the following conclusions can be drawn concerning the War for American Independence?

A. The Americans might not have won the war without the aid of foreign countries.

B. The British would have lost the colonies in America even if the French and Spanish had not declared war on the British.

C. Every colonist wanted independence from British rule.

D. Almost no colonists wanted independence from British rule.

If France, Spain, and Holland had not supplied money and supplies, and if these countries had not declared war on the British, the colonies might have lost the war and remained under British control. **The correct answer is A.**

The Early US Government

Over the next several years, the states worked hard to settle their differences and agree on a system of government that best suited all of the states. Since 1781, the colonies had operated under the **Articles of Confederation**, the first constitution of the United States. Under the Articles, the colonies were united as a loose union of states, the Congress held the majority of the political power, and there was no executive branch of the government. The entire national government was weak. In 1787, leaders from each of the states met at the Constitutional Convention and outlined a plan for a new government. Some argued for a weak central government that was unlike the British government, while others argued for a very strong central government. Eventually the states compromised. The resulting plan was the **US Constitution**.

In many ways, the newly constructed US Constitution was a vivid reflection of how leaders can effectively compromise and work together to achieve a larger purpose and collective goals. It demonstrated how a diverse set of states with different needs could agree upon the fundamental construction of

TIP

Analyzing how various historical events, processes, and ideas develop and interact within the language of an historical document is a skill you'll want to sharpen as you prepare to take the GED® Social Studies Test.

a prevailing national government, with three distinct but interconnected branches (the executive, legislative, and judicial branches) that checked and balanced each other, as well as protected the individual freedoms and liberties of the people. From the opening words of the document (*We the people...*), its writers made clear that the newly formed country stood united in its effort to create "a more perfect Union." The drafters of the Constitution were also aware that the document should be flexible enough to evolve over time, as new historical events and ideas unfold, and allow for amendments to be included (since its creation, the Constitution has been amended 27 times).

10. Which of the following does NOT reflect the will of the designers of the US Constitution to create a strong and "more perfect union," despite the diverse needs of the states?

A. The document's opening language: *"We the people..."*

B. The ability to add amendments to the Constitution

C. The formation of three branches of government that check and balance each other

D. Having an expiration date for the original 10 amendments to the constitution

The development of the Constitution reflected the desire of its drafters to create a strong nation with a unified central government. To help foster this "more perfect union," the document's creators included unifying language (choice A) and the ability to amend the constitution as needed (choice B), and they provided for the creation of three branches of government that check and balance each other (choice C). However, there is no expiration date for the original 10 amendments to the Constitution. **The correct answer is D.**

Eventually, all of the states ratified, or approved, the Constitution, or plan of government; it became the official plan of government in 1789. In 1791, the United States adopted 10 amendments, or changes, to the Constitution. These changes, known as the **Bill of Rights**, protected the rights of individuals.

About the same time, the nation's first political parties were forming as a result of disagreements over the proper political and financial policies for the new nation. The two parties that emerged were the **Federalists** and the **Republicans**. The Federalists, who were led by the wealthy and educated, sought a strong central government steered by the elite. The Republicans, on the other hand, believed in the ability of the common people to govern themselves. Republican leaders like James Madison and Thomas Jefferson wanted to limit the powers of the federal government and protect states' rights. The two parties also differed in the area of foreign policy. The Republicans supported the French Revolution, while the Federalists thought that the French Revolution was a terrifying act against an established government. Disputes between the Federalists and the Republicans reached new heights in the election of 1800. The Republican candidate Thomas Jefferson was elected president. This election showed that the American people believed in the power of the people to determine the course the country would take. The Federalists, though they had won the 1796 election, never won another presidential election.

11. Those opposed to a strong central government in the early days of the United States were concerned **most** about which of the following?

A. The possibility of the government becoming oppressive the way that King George had been to the colonists

B. The possibility that no good candidates could be found to run such a government

C. The possibility that the states could not agree on a leader for such a government

D. The idea that the states had to be a part of a single nation instead of each forming its own country

Anti-Federalists did not want a government with the potential to oppress its constituents the way the king had done to the colonists. **The correct answer is A.**

12. Disagreement over the correct path for the new government to take resulted in the

Select ▼

A. US Civil War.

B. creation of the first two American political parties.

C. Bill of Rights.

D. Articles of Confederation.

There were two predominant ideas about the direction in which the new government should go. The politicians chose sides, and those two sides became the Federalists and the Republicans. **The correct answer is B.**

US Expansion and Growing Pains

One of the most important decisions Jefferson made as president was to expand westward. Jefferson acquired a huge amount of land; the acquisition became known as the **Louisiana Purchase**. For a bargain price, Jefferson bought from France all the land between the Mississippi River in the east and the Rocky Mountains in the west, from the Gulf of Mexico in the south to the Canadian border in the north. For only $15 million, the United States doubled the size of its territory. Eventually, the United States would create 14 more states in the land of the Louisiana Purchase. The growing size of the United States helped earn international respect. The westward expansion of the United States was a difficult task. Settlers faced uncharted land, harsh climates, and Native Americans who did not welcome those who might drive them out of their homeland. Nevertheless, the Americans pressed onward and gradually adapted to life on the frontiers.

As the new nation continued to grow and become more self-sufficient, it struggled with policies concerning international trade. The United States passed legislation that hurt trade between the United States and Great Britain and France. The British took exception to this and responded with animosity. The British navy made it a common practice to stop American ships on the open seas, claiming that it was searching for deserters, those who had illegally left the British navy. Often the British captured Americans on these ships and forced them into the British navy. They also confiscated American ships and goods. These actions, along with reports of British aid to hostile Native Americans, moved Congress to declare war on the British. Known as the **War of 1812**, this conflict did not settle any of the issues that started it, but the United States emerged victorious. The war brought the nation together and earned the United States respect in the eyes of many European countries. The period of time that followed the war was marked by further expansion, with the addition of Florida, and an increased American role in international diplomacy and politics. President Monroe issued the **Monroe Doctrine** and declared that the United States would not allow any further European colonization or expansion in the Western Hemisphere. As the United States earned a reputation as an up-and-coming nation, it was able to increase its trade with other nations. This helped stimulate the country's economy and that of each of the states. The northern states concentrated on manufacturing and production, while the southern states focused on agriculture, or farming. The northern states, most of whose population was urban (in cities), became a society centered on industry and big business. The southern states, most of whose population was rural (in the countryside), became a society centered on plantations and the production of crops such as cotton and sugar. Large plantations grew throughout the South and became the backbone of the southern economy. Although all the states maintained loyalty to the nation, the two regions were often very competitive. The two sections of the country competed for political power within the Congress and for the presidency. As a result of this competition, along with other major issues such as slavery, tensions between the North and the South grew.

In the West, the United States continued to expand by annexing Texas and Oregon. The **annexation** of these two regions stirred great emotion. Adding Texas to the Union meant the addition of a slave territory. This possibility angered many in the North until the potential addition of Oregon to the Union presented an opportunity for compromise: if the United States added Oregon, a non-slave territory, it could add Texas, a slave territory, and maintain equilibrium between the slave states and non-slave states. By 1846, both territories were added to the United States. However, Mexico went to war with the United States over Texas. Eventually, the United States negotiated a treaty with Mexico that added California, New Mexico, and part of Arizona to US holdings in exchange for $15 million. The issue of **slavery** moved front and center again as both the North and the South argued over whether the new territories should allow slavery. In an attempt to divert or delay major problems between the North and the South, politicians passed legislation such as the **Compromise of 1850**, which made sure the number of free states and slave states remained equal as new states were added to the nation. After 1850, some of the new territory prohibited slavery, while other territories permitted the settlement of both those who owned slaves and those who did not. The United States then passed fugitive slave laws that required runaway slaves to be returned to their owners. Then the Supreme Court issued the ***Dred Scott* decision**, which opened all new territories to slavery. The decision also determined that African Americans whose ancestors were imported and sold as slaves, whether enslaved or free, could not be American citizens and thus had no right to sue. The South felt that the North was trying to abolish slavery, an act the southern states saw as a violation of their state rights.

TIP

On the GED® Social Studies Test, you will be expected to analyze key historical issues involving bias or propagandizing.

By arguing against the notion of popular sovereignty, denying the freedom of a slave and his family who resided in a freed territory, and declaring that African Americans would not be afforded rights as citizens of the United States, the *Dred Scott* decision—often harshly criticized by legal scholars—reflected the bias of the US Supreme Court at the time the decision was rendered.

13. The *Dred Scott* decision revealed that the US Supreme Court, at the time its decision was rendered,

A. had a conservative bias that tended to support the South's beliefs that slavery was acceptable.

B. had a progressive bias that tended to support the North's anti-slavery beliefs.

C. did not want to pass judgment on issues involving slavery.

D. was made up of judges who could not agree on key issues.

In the years leading up to the Civil War, the composition of the Supreme Court, under Chief Justice Roger B. Taney, reflected a conservative bias that tended to support the South's beliefs that slavery was acceptable, which helped escalate the tension between the North and the South. In addition to the *Dred Scott* decision, several key rulings by Taney and the court at the time—including the declaration of the Missouri Compromise as unconstitutional, arguing that its prohibition of slavery violated the Fifth Amendment by depriving individuals of private property without due process of law—reflected a bias that persisted until President Lincoln appointed Salmon P. Chase as Chief Justice in 1864. **The correct answer is A.**

14. The majority of new territory added to the United States was added to by means of [ ].

Although some US territory came as spoils of war, most land was purchased from other countries. The Louisiana Purchase is a good example of such an acquisition. **The correct answer is *purchases*.**

15. Perhaps the **most** controversial issue surrounding new territories that were added to the United States was whether the new territory would [Select ▼]

A. be Federalist or Republican.

B. be industrial or agricultural.

C. be hostile or friendly to Native Americans.

D. allow slavery or prohibit slavery.

Slave states wanted all the new territories to be open to slavery, while non-slave states wanted slavery prohibited in the new territories. **The correct answer is D.**

NOTE

On the actual GED Social Studies test, you will type in your answer in the space provided. For purposes of this book, write your answer in the box provided.

The Civil War and Reconstruction

The nation's diametrically opposed ideas regarding slavery revealed a sharp internal division within the country. There were key differences in the sociocultural, political, and economic makeups between the northern states and southern states that bolstered opposition regarding slavery. The industrialized northern states were less reliant on slave labor to fuel the engines of economic prosperity than the more agriculturally based economies of the South; in addition, slavery was an interwoven aspect of the South's cultural fabric, while in the North it was largely prohibited. Because of these sharply contrasting views, it would take many decades—and a civil war—for the nation to even begin to heal and come together as a union.

In the presidential **election of 1860**, the issue of slavery came to a head. The southern Democrats split into two factions, or groups, and put forth two different candidates, each with different beliefs, though both were pro-slavery. The Republicans nominated Abraham Lincoln, a candidate who did not support the idea of slavery in the new territories. A fourth party put forth yet another candidate. With American votes scattered among the four candidates, Lincoln won the controversial election with less than 40 percent of the popular vote. After Lincoln won, South Carolina seceded, or withdrew, from the Union. Shortly thereafter, 10 more southern states followed South Carolina and created the **Confederate States of America.**

Lincoln made it clear that he had no intention of allowing any state to secede from the Union. He called up troops from the remaining loyal states and went to war to preserve the Union. In 1861, the South was at a disadvantage in the **Civil War** because it lacked the manufacturing power and transportation that the North had. In addition, most of the fighting was done in the South. After four years of bloody fighting, in what was often known as the War Between the States, the South surrendered. Slavery ended, and the United States survived. Although America suffered heavy casualties in both the North and the South, the war resolved two important issues. First, the authority of the federal government took precedence over the states. Second, slavery was abolished throughout the United States.

Lincoln, thankful that the Union was still intact, intended to allow the southern states back into the Union with relatively easy terms. However, he was assassinated before he could put his plan into effect. After Lincoln's death, a vindictive Congress initiated a period known as Reconstruction, during which time the South lived under very oppressive conditions. The Union had been saved, but the South harbored great resentment against the North for the harsh treatment it endured after the war. Many Southerners were especially resentful of having to allow African Americans to vote and hold public office. These feelings endured in the southern states for several generations after the war.

TIP

You may be expected to compare different views related to political, historical, economic, geographic, or societal ideas, and their impact, through the lens of history on the GED® Social Studies Test.

16. Which of the following was a key economic difference between the northern and southern states that bolstered opposition regarding slavery?

A. The South's industrialized economy relied upon slave labor.

B. The South's agricultural economy relied upon slave labor.

C. The northern economy was too weak to pay workers any wages.

D. The North refused the south's plan to industrialize the entire country.

A key difference between northern and southern states involved their economic makeup—the industrialized North had less of a reliance on slave labor than the agricultural South, which helped to contribute to southern opposition to eradicate slavery. **The correct answer is B.**

17. Which of the following statements is true?

A. The South seceded from the Union because Southerners feared Reconstruction.

B. The South seceded from the Union because of the issue of slavery.

C. The South seceded from the Union because of the issue of slavery, its concern about states' rights, and other issues.

D. The South seceded from the Union because the North threatened to take all political power away from the South.

The issues of slavery, states' rights, the threat of new free territories upsetting the equilibrium, and other issues all played a part in the South's secession. **The correct answer is C.**

18. President Lincoln decided to go to war with the South in order to

Select ▼

A. end slavery.

B. punish the South for having slaves.

C. confiscate its wealth.

D. preserve the Union.

Lincoln refused to allow the nation to be dissolved over any issue, so he sent troops into the South to preserve the Union. **The correct answer is D.**

Reconstruction

After the Civil War ended, the United States entered a Reconstruction period from 1865 through 1877. Although the war had ended, the North and South were still divided; Reconstruction helped to repair the country's fragile union, as all the former Confederate states pledged their allegiance to the United States and its government; these states also acknowledged the legitimacy of the Thirteenth, Fourteenth, and Fifteenth Amendments to the US Constitution. During this period, the southern states that had composed the defeated Confederacy were incorporated into the Union in an attempt to rebuild the South. The southern states, attempting to rebuild after the devastation caused by the war, viewed Reconstruction as an unreasonable penalty.

How the nation approached the concept of Reconstruction further reflected the deep division amongst the states. These ideological differences had a profound effect on how Reconstruction would unfold. As a result, Reconstruction led to several key advances as well as challenges, which persisted in the aftermath of one of the most devastating wars in American history.

The driving force behind Reconstruction was the nearly four million slaves who had been freed following the Civil War. Issues involving slavery proved to be challenging and ultimately prevented the Reconstruction from achieving all its goals. The sociocultural associations of slavery in the South were deeply ingrained in its culture, and rights for newly freed slaves in the southern states took much longer to achieve, as anti-progressive sentiment and legislation served to suppress southern transformation in key ways.

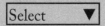

President Abraham Lincoln had recommended that the South's African American slaves be given the right to vote; however, he was assassinated before his plans were put into action. Lincoln's successor, President Andrew Johnson, vetoed the Civil Rights Act of 1866, which Congress had enacted, although his veto was overridden. The southern states enacted laws called "black codes" that restricted freed blacks' activities, enraging Northerners.

During the period of Reconstruction, Congress passed a Reconstruction Act in 1867 that temporarily divided 10 Confederate states into 5 military districts. The act required that these states ratify the Fourteenth Amendment to the Constitution, which stated that all people born in the United States are citizens granted equal protection under the law, including the right to vote, regardless of race. The southern states were readmitted to the Union by 1870, although Reconstruction didn't come to an end until 1877, when Rutherford B. Hayes became president.

19. Reconstruction can be summed up in which of the following statements?

A. Southern states that had seceded during the Civil War were reorganized under Congress and later restored to the Union.

B. Freed slaves in the South were given equal opportunities for employment throughout the region.

C. The Northern states did not recognize the rights of former slaves from the South.

D. President Lincoln rejected the Civil Rights Act of 1866.

TIP

Learn to recognize key historical cause-and-effect relationships, including those with multiple factors, as you prepare for the test.

The former Confederacy, composed of 11 southern states that seceded from the United States, was readmitted into the Union during the Reconstruction period. **The correct answer is A.**

20. Which of the following is a reason why Reconstruction following the Civil War was only partially successful?

A. The Union refused to help fund reconstruction initiatives in the South.

B. The roots of slavery were strong in the South.

C. The North refused to acknowledge the legitimacy of southern states.

D. The country lacked a central government following the war.

Reconstruction faced a number of key challenges in the years following the Civil War—among them was the issue of slavery. The strong tradition of slavery was woven into the economic and sociocultural fabric of the South, and made resolutions regarding this issue difficult to achieve, and exacerbated the deep divisions between the North and the South. **The correct answer is B.**

21. What does the Fourteenth Amendment define?

A. How many terms the president is allowed to serve

B. Which branch of the government can collect income tax

C. What it means to be a US citizen

D. At what age people are allowed to vote

The Fourteenth Amendment defines what it means to be a citizen of the United States and protects the rights of African Americans to citizenship. **The correct answer is C.**

World Wars I and II

The beginning of the twentieth century saw more reform in many areas of life in the United States. Trusts, or combinations of companies that reduced competition, came under government scrutiny. Conditions in factories drew much attention, and the government responded by passing laws that required businesses to clean up unsanitary conditions. These laws made working conditions better for the factory and food-packing plant workers and made the products safer for consumers. The government set aside many acres of land for national parks and wildlife preserves. The United States also began construction of the **Panama Canal** to join the Atlantic and Pacific Oceans; this would allow ships to pass through the canal instead of rounding the entire South American continent.

During the early twentieth century, the United States devoted much time and energy to international diplomacy. American foreign policy, based on President Theodore Roosevelt's maxim, "Speak softly and carry a big stick," meant that the United States let its policies and intentions be known through diplomacy, and it backed that up with military action when needed. This approach to foreign policy, which comprised an effort to negotiate with foreign powers peacefully whenever possible, while possessing the capability to vigorously defend and protect the country as needed, is a cornerstone of American foreign policy.

TIP

Understanding the meaning and intention of key words and phrases—within their proper historical context—is an often-tested component of the GED® Social Studies Test.

22. Which of the following policy examples **best** reflects Roosevelt's maxim for America to "speak softly and carry a big stick"?

A. Deploying naval ships to a key strategic area near a country that is threatening to pull out of critical negotiations to reduce tensions between nations.

B. Attacking a country with an aerial assault for refusing to sign an agreement to reduce its trade tariffs.

C. Ignoring human rights violation atrocities within a war-torn country.

D. Providing every American with a protective stick to carry when they leave their homes.

Engaging meaningfully and thoughtfully with other nations around the world while protecting the country's freedom and interests—at home and abroad—is what Roosevelt was referring to when he described his approach to foreign policy as "the exercise of intelligent forethought and of decisive action sufficiently far in advance of any crisis." Deploying US naval ships to a key strategic area near a country that is threatening to pull out of critical negotiations to reduce tensions between nations—a clear urging to continue negotiations in an effort to avoid an escalation—is an example of this approach to foreign policy. **The correct answer is A.**

When World War I, or the Great War as it was known then, erupted in Europe, the United States faced a dilemma. President Wilson wanted to maintain **neutrality** in the war. However, after German submarines sank the *Lusitania*, a British passenger ship that carried 128 American passengers, the United States entered the war on the side of the Triple Entente (Great Britain, France, and Russia). The United States tipped the scales in favor of the Triple Entente, and US troops returned home victorious. At the conclusion of World War I, the United States led a failed attempt to establish the

League of Nations as an international peacekeeping organization; the US Congress refused to allow the United States to join, so the League proved ineffective.

In the years following the war, the United States enjoyed a period of terrific prosperity. Business and industry grew and expanded. Individuals invested heavily and spent large sums of money on things like sporting events, parties, movies, nightclubs, and other forms of entertainment. Politically, the United States implemented many new tariffs on imports to protect its interests at home. The government began regulating public utilities and the rates they charged both businesses and consumers. The government used a Constitutional amendment to ban the production and sale of alcoholic beverages; this period was known as **Prohibition.** Another Constitutional amendment gave women the right to vote for the first time in the United States. Millions of immigrants flocked to the United States from war-torn Europe seeking new financial opportunities.

During this era of prosperity, many individuals purchased stocks by putting up a small percentage of the stock purchase price and borrowing the rest of the purchase price from a stockbroker. This was a very risky investment strategy. Stock prices continued to rise and investors continued to borrow money to buy stocks. Then in 1929, the stock market crashed, and banks failed in the United States and in Europe. In other words, panicked investors began selling off their high-priced stocks at a feverish pace. The feeling of panic struck not only the United States but also the rest of the world. By 1932, many banks had failed, factories closed, workers found themselves unemployed, and many lost their homes and other properties to foreclosure. Facing record unemployment and economic hardships, Americans elected **Franklin D. Roosevelt** as president in 1932. He instituted reforms and economic recovery programs in his **New Deal**. Roosevelt's New Deal programs included relief for businesses and individuals through new government agencies that put people to work on public works projects. These measures, along with the onset of World War II, eventually led the United States out of the Great Depression.

On December 7, 1941, the Japanese attacked the US military base at Pearl Harbor in Hawaii. Almost immediately, the United States entered **World War II** on the side of the Allies (Great Britain and the Union of Soviet Socialist Republics, or USSR) against the Axis Powers (Germany, Italy, and Japan). The massive war effort stimulated the economy and created millions of jobs for Americans. In 1945, after four years of fierce fighting against the Axis Powers in Europe and in the Pacific, the United States dropped two **atomic bombs** on Japan. Shortly thereafter the war ended, and the United States stood victorious alongside the other Allied Powers. The United States emerged from World War II not just as a legitimate world power but as a superpower. After the war, with the influence and leadership of the United States, world leaders divided Germany into different zones of influence, established the United Nations, and launched efforts to help rebuild war-torn nations. The United States joined the International Court of Justice, launched the National Security Council, and established the CIA, or Central Intelligence Agency.

In the years that followed World War II, the United States found itself in an ideological disagreement with the **Soviet Union** and the Eastern Bloc, or eastern European nations under the influence of communism in the Soviet Union. The United States committed itself to stopping the spread of communist ideas and eventually became the enemy of the Soviet Union and its allies. For years, the United States remained deadlocked in a Cold War, or a war of rhetoric and ill will, with the Soviet Union. The fear of nuclear holocaust and communism marked the next 45 years.

American troops did not stay home long after they returned from World War II. Only five years after World War II, American troops were deployed to South Korea to fight against the communist threat posed by the North Koreans in an undeclared war (the **Korean War**) that ended in 1953 with no real winner. Then, in the 1960s, the United States deployed more troops to **Vietnam** in another controversial, undeclared war. The American troops were eventually brought home in 1975, and Vietnam fell to the communists. Each time the troops returned home from fighting in Vietnam, they had a difficult time readjusting to civilian life. The troops were not received as heroes the way World War II and Korea troops were, and many of the soldiers faced emotional problems as a result of their experiences abroad.

23. Why was the League of Nations formed after World War I?

A. To promote trade among nations

B. To prevent another world war

C. To pressure Germany into surrendering to the Allied Forces

D. To prevent the spread of communism

At the close of World War I, US President Wilson insisted that all countries signing the Treaty of Versailles agree to form the League of Nations for the purpose of keeping world peace through deterrence, so that another world war would not happen again. (Congress, which under the Constitution must ratify all treaties that the president enters, refused to agree to US membership in the League.) **The correct answer is B.**

24. The Great Depression followed an era of which of the following?

A. Careful financial planning by individuals but not by businesses

B. Widespread corruption with the savings and loan corporations

C. Carefree lifestyles, risky investing, and poor financial management on the part of brokers

D. World war

It was an era of carefree lifestyles, risky investing, and poor financial management. Investors speculated wildly, and brokers unwisely issued credit to individuals who wanted to purchase a large number of stocks. **The correct answer is C.**

Civil Rights

The 1950s were a tumultuous decade in the United States, as many Americans reacted to the struggle for civil rights. A progressive cultural awakening began to occur, bringing with it a desire for equal rights and treatment for African Americans and all citizens. Executive and judicial action at the time helped lead the way, shaping America's desire for reform. President Truman established the President's Committee on Civil Rights and in 1948 signed an executive order to desegregate the military. This ideological shift helped shape subsequent policy decisions and paved the way for important social and cultural progression.

TIP

Be sure to familiarize yourself with how historical context shapes the points of view of leading thinkers, authors, activists, and policy makers.

25. Which of the following is an example of America's ideological shift towards expanding basic rights for all citizens?

A. The Eighteenth Amendment to the Constitution, which prohibited the sale of alcohol

B. *Smith v. Allwright*, in which the Supreme Court ruled against the notion of an all-white Democratic primary, helping to reduce the disenfranchisement of African American voters

C. The Vietnam War, which is often described as an effort to stop the flow of communism across the world

D. The creation of the electoral college system in America's voting process

By reducing voter disenfranchisement among African Americans, the Supreme Court's ruling in *Smith v. Allwright* reflected the court's—and the nation's—desire to advance the civil rights and liberties of American citizens, a powerful mid-twentieth century ideological shift. **The correct answer is B.**

In 1954, the Supreme Court desegregated schools in the landmark decision *Brown v. Board of Education of Topeka*. The civil rights movement built on that momentum. As people like Rosa Parks and Martin Luther King, Jr. led the **civil rights movement** in a dignified and peaceful manner, groups like the Ku Klux Klan promoted violence against African Americans and those who fought for the rights of African Americans, and individuals like Arkansas Governor Orval Faubus inhibited progress toward equal rights for American citizens. In 1957, Congress created the Civil Rights Commission, which investigated civil rights violations. As a result of the Commission's investigations, the government appointed officials to safeguard the voting rights of African Americans.

The Cold War

The 1960s saw heightened tensions between the United States and the Soviet Union reach a boiling point during the **Cuban Missile Crisis.** The two world powers moved dangerously close to nuclear war as President Kennedy forced the Soviets to remove missiles from Cuba. Then, in 1963, to the horror of the nation, President Kennedy was assassinated. The rest of the decade was marked by domestic problems concerning the deployment of troops to Vietnam to fight communism. Many Americans disagreed with American involvement there, and they took to the streets in protest. The civil rights situation improved during the 1960s with the passage of the Twenty-Fourth Amendment, which eliminated the poll tax, and the **Voting Rights Act of 1965**, which aided African Americans in the voting process. The 1960s ended with a cultural phenomenon known as Woodstock, a massive free concert in New York, where thousands of young Americans spent days reveling in art, drugs, sex, and rock and roll.

Many Americans grew wary of the government as corrupt officials and oil shortages marked the 1970s. **President Nixon** resigned following a scandal in which several people were arrested for breaking into the Democratic National Headquarters at the Watergate Hotel in Washington, DC. Nixon and his advisers knew about the break-in and about illegal wiretaps. In 1973, Vice President Spiro Agnew was indicted for tax evasion and bribery, further damaging citizens' trust in the government. The tension between the United States and the USSR declined in the 1970s in what became known as détente. Economically, the end of the 1970s brought further recession, an unfavorable balance of trade, high unemployment, and a very high rate of inflation.

In the 1980s, conservative Republican leadership under **President Ronald Reagan** pushed for less government and more military spending. The economy recovered, but the government's deficit spending caused national debt to spiral. Relations with the Soviets grew tense again as the United States unveiled its "Star Wars" program, a missile defense system. At the end of the decade, US and Soviet leaders agreed to reduce existing stockpiles of nuclear weapons and proposed to create no future stockpiles.

During the 1990s, the United States enjoyed the end of the Cold War and celebrated the collapse of the Soviet Union. However, the 1990s also saw the liberal use of US military power in many places around the world, including Panama, Iraq, Bosnia, and Somalia. Eventually, the government cut military spending, along with some social programs, in an attempt to reduce the national debt. **President Bill Clinton**'s administration (1993–2001), was marked by personal scandal as the millennium drew to a close.

American Foreign Policy Since 9/11

The new millennium brought with it a presidential election unlike any that the United States had ever seen. By a very controversial margin of just a very few votes, **George W. Bush** defeated **Al Gore**. Less than a year later came the terrorist attacks on the Pentagon, the World Trade Center, and in Pennsylvania. In the immediate aftermath of the "9/11" event, the United States sent forces to Afghanistan to flush out Osama Bin Laden and his terrorist group. Shortly thereafter, the Bush administration convinced the Congress that in order to prevent further terrorist attacks on US soil and to stem the development of nuclear weapons by dictator enemies, the United States should invade Iraq and topple Saddam Hussein's regime. In April 2003, the United States invaded Iraq, and in December of that year Hussein was finally captured.

The US occupation of Iraq grew controversial over the next few years. Widely publicized abuse of Iraqi prisoners captured by US forces and generous "no-bid" contracts given to US companies loyal to the Bush administration brought the occupation under increasing scrutiny and criticism. In the meantime, Osama bin Laden, the apparent mastermind of the 9/11 terrorist attacks, remained at large, and loose networks of terrorist organizations were proliferating throughout the Middle East, especially in Afghanistan. In November 2008, Barack Obama was elected president, and by the close of the decade, the United States had begun to take affirmative steps to extricate the country from Iraq and return to a policy of diplomacy rather than unilateral military action against would-be enemy states—while at the same time increasing US presence in Afghanistan for the purpose of defeating terrorist organizations that pose a threat to US security.

On the economic front, the first decade of the new millennium saw federal economic policies that were decidedly favorable to big business. The Federal Reserve Bank lowered interest rates to historically low levels in order to bring the nation out of the recession that followed the "dot-com" era collapse and the events of September 2001. Low interest rates encouraged spending and borrowing, which stimulated economic growth. Nevertheless, real economic growth remained stagnant throughout the decade. The only growth occurred in the health care, financial, and real estate sectors. At the same time, true production declined. Traditional manufacturing jobs continued to move overseas, leaving middle-class Americans worse off economically at the end of the decade than when it began.

At the same time, federally chartered banks were permitted to engage for the first time in high-risk, high-return leveraged investing. A combination of lax lending standards for home loans (mortgages), upon which many of the banks' investments hinged, and low interest rates created a debt "bubble" in which consumers and large businesses alike would ultimately be unable to repay their debts. By the end of 2008, the US economy was on the verge of collapse—a collapse that was prevented only by a massive infusion of credit from the federal government to save the large commercial banks. As the decade came to a close, a home-foreclosure crisis and an escalating unemployment rate had left **President Barack Obama**'s administration little choice but to engage in a massive spending, or stimulus, campaign to create new jobs, bolster the manufacturing sector, help struggling homeowners, and rein in the imprudent investments and lending practices of previous years.

26. The Twenty-Fourth Amendment, which was ratified in 1964, outlawed the use of a tax as a precondition to voting in any federal election. Given the historical context in which the Twenty-Fourth Amendment became law, whose rights were advocates of the amendment most concerned with protecting?

A. Tax evaders

B. Unwed mothers

C. Convicted felons

D. African Americans

It was during the 1960s that the struggle for civil rights on the part of African Americans came to a head, led by individuals such as Martin Luther King, Jr. Poll taxes levied by certain southern states had the effect of disenfranchising poor people, and in the South, that meant that a disproportionate number of African Americans were effectively denied the right to vote. **The correct answer is D.**

27. What was responsible for the collapse of the Soviet Union in the late 1980s and early 1990s?

A. Civil war among its states

B. Overthrow of the central government by an Eastern European alliance

C. The Soviet leaders' decision that a democratic government would work better

D. Economic and military burdens that weakened the Soviet Union internally

By the mid-1980s, the centralized, or command, economy of the Soviet Union was becoming too burdensome and expensive to manage. At the same time, the Soviets were draining their resources fighting a losing war in Afghanistan. Ultimately, the Soviet Union collapsed under the weight of these burdens it had put on itself. **The correct answer is D.**

CIVICS AND GOVERNMENT

Simply put, **political science** is the study of government, the methods of governing, and those who lead governments. As long as people have been organized into states, people have needed a government to maintain order. The form of government each society has used throughout history has depended on a number of factors, including the size of the state and the traditions of the state.

Many of the forms of government used throughout history, though, have been determined, directly affected, or influenced by the means the leader used to assume the leadership of a government. Although there are many different types of government, there are a few basic political systems in which all governments may be classified.

Types of Modern and Historical Governments

One very old political system is **democracy.** Democracy means "rule by the people." In a democracy, the people make decisions in matters of government. Democracy dates back to ancient Greece and has changed only slightly since its birth so many years ago. There are two types of democracies that exist: a true democracy and a representative democracy. In a **true democracy**, also called a direct democracy or pure democracy, the people make all the decisions. A true democracy is only possible within a small geographic area, such as a small country or a small town, because a large area makes the exchange of information slow and inefficient. In a **representative democracy**, the people elect representatives to make decisions for them. A republic is a representative democracy. The United States is a good example of a representative democracy.

Another very old political system, even older than democracy, is a **monarchy.** Monarchy means "rule by monarch," which can be either a king or queen. In a monarchy, the right to rule is hereditary, meaning that the right is passed down through a king's or queen's family from generation to generation. There are a few types of monarchies that exist. An **absolute monarchy** is one in which the monarch controls every aspect of life within his or her kingdom. The absolute monarch controls every facet of economics, politics, diplomacy, and, often, religion and culture. Louis XIV of France was the epitome of an absolute monarch. A **constitutional monarchy**, such as Great Britain, is a monarchical government in which the power of the monarch is limited by a constitution, written laws, and legislative bodies such as a parliament.

Dictatorship is a third form of government. The ruler of a dictatorship, a dictator, has complete rule over his state. Often the dictator assumes control of the state after a military takeover of a government and then maintains control through military force. A dictator usually rules strictly and controls most aspects of the government, often to the point of being oppressive. Cuba under Fidel Castro and Iraq under Saddam Hussein are good examples of dictatorships.

A fourth political system is an **oligarchy.** Oligarchy means "rule by a few." The "few" is often a group of people who lead in the style of a dictator. This group is not a group that is elected. Rather, the group usually takes control in much the same way as a dictator, after a military takeover. Also like a dictator, an oligarchy maintains control with the military. If the group takes control after a revolution, the group is referred to as a junta. Ancient Sparta, a very militaristic society, maintained an oligarchy.

A form of government rarely seen anymore is an **aristocracy.** An aristocracy, ruled by aristocrats, is a system in which those who are presumed best suited to rule have the power to rule. The best suited to rule, according to the aristocrats, are those who are of privileged birth and who are well educated. Usually aristocrats have great wealth and vast amounts of land.

28. The most efficient form of government in a time of crisis would **most likely** be which of the following?

A. Dictatorship

B. Oligarchy

C. Democracy

D. Aristocracy

Because one person with total control of a government can make decisions much more quickly than any other kind of government, a dictatorship is the most efficient, especially in a time of war or other emergency. **The correct answer is A.**

29. Which of the following political systems allows citizens the **most** opportunities to participate in the political process?

A. Dictatorship

B. Oligarchy

C. Democracy

D. Aristocracy

Democracy is the political system built on the idea that the people should control the government. **The correct answer is C.**

THE US GOVERNMENT

The US government can be classified as a **republic**, an indirect democracy. The men who created the foundations of the US government believed the government should be carefully laid out in a written plan, or constitution. According to the Constitution, the US government is a **federal government.** In other words, the power and authority of the government is divided between the national government, state governments, and local governments. Each level of government has certain authority and responsibilities. Also, according to the Constitution, each level of government is split into three branches, each with separate duties. The three branches include the legislative branch, the executive branch, and the judicial branch. This is known as **separation of powers.** The founders of the United States deliberately divided all the power between the different levels and the different branches of government so that no one person or part of the government could assume too much power. In addition, the founders made sure that each branch of government had the authority to limit the power of the other two branches. This, too, was a preventive measure against any one branch becoming too powerful.

The Three Branches of Government

As you have already learned, the Constitution divides the government into three branches, each with its own responsibilities and duties. The **legislative branch** makes the laws, the **executive branch** enforces the laws, and the **judicial branch** interprets the laws. Let's examine each of the three branches more closely.

The Legislative Branch

According to Article I of the Constitution, the power to make laws belongs to the legislative branch of government. The word *legislative* means "law making," so the legislative branch of government is the one that makes laws. The legislature, or the law-making body, is the US Congress. The US Congress is known as a bicameral legislature. In other words, the Congress has two parts, or houses. These are the House of Representatives and the Senate. Although their powers are practically the same, the House of Representatives, sometimes referred to as the House, is the lower house, while the Senate is the upper house of the legislature. The legislators, or lawmakers, in the **House of Representatives** total 435. The members represent each of the 50 states, and the number of representatives from each state is based on that state's population. Each state is guaranteed at least one representative, regardless of population. Each representative is elected from a district within his or her home state. Representatives serve two-year terms of office, and all of the representatives are elected in their states every two years. In order to run for the office of US Congressional Representative, a person must meet three criteria or qualifications. The candidate must

- be at least 25 years old.
- have been a citizen of the United States for at least seven years.
- live in the state he or she intends to represent.

There are no limits on the number of terms that a representative may serve.

The **Senate** is slightly different from the House of Representatives. There are 100 senators in the Senate, two from every state, regardless of how large or small a state's population. Senators serve six-year terms, and one-third of the senators are elected every two years. In order to be a US senator, a candidate must meet some stricter requirements than those for a candidate for the House. A candidate for the US Senate must

- be at least 30 years old.
- have been a citizen of the United States for at least nine years.
- be a resident of the state he or she intends to represent.

Currently, there is no limit on the number of terms a senator may serve.

As you just learned, the legislative branch of government makes laws. Let's look at exactly how the legislature creates a law. First, a legislator must present an idea for a potential law in the form of a **bill.** After the legislator—senator or representative—writes the bill, the bill goes to either the clerk of the House or the clerk of the Senate, where the bill receives a name and a number. From here, the bill travels to a committee. A committee is a small group of members of Congress who specialize in a particular area of legislation. For example, the Armed Services Committee deals specifically with legislation concerning the US armed forces. If the committee does not like the bill, it may "pigeonhole" it or "table" it by setting it aside and not dealing with it again. If this happens, the bill is said to have died in committee. If the committee likes the bill, it sends the bill to the House and Senate where the members of Congress debate the bill, make any changes they feel are necessary, and then vote on the bill. If either house votes against the bill, or defeats the bill, the bill dies. If majorities of both houses approve the bill, the bill goes before the entire Congress for a vote. If a majority of Congress approves the bill, it goes before the president for his approval. The president may sign the bill and make it law, or he can veto, or kill, the bill. However, another majority vote in

Congress can override the veto and make the bill law. This process may seem slow and inefficient, but this slow process prevents the government from making any hasty decisions.

The Constitution grants Congress a number of powers that are clearly defined in the text of the Constitution. These powers are known as enumerated powers, expressed powers, or delegated powers. Some of these powers include the authority to tax and collect taxes from the American people, coin or print money, declare war on another country, borrow money, and maintain a proper national defense with an army and a navy. Some powers of Congress are limited to only one house or the other. For example, only the House can impeach, or bring formal charges against, the president, but only the Senate can hold a trial for the president. In addition, only the Senate can approve treaties with other countries. The Constitution granted Congress other unnamed powers through the elastic clause. The elastic clause allows Congress some flexibility to deal with new issues that the founders could not foresee.

30. Which of the following may indicate that the Senate is the upper house of the US legislature?

- **A.** Senators must have graduate degrees.
- **B.** Candidates must be lawyers before they can be elected to the Senate.
- **C.** Requirements for senatorial candidates are a little stricter than requirements for those seeking a seat in the House.
- **D.** There are fewer senators than there are representatives.

The fact that senatorial candidates must meet more demanding qualifications indicates that the founders of the United States wanted senators to be more qualified than representatives. This indicates that the Senate must have been held in higher regard at one point in history. **The correct answer is C.**

31. Which of the following is a reason why California may have more influence than Alaska in the House of Representatives?

- **A.** California covers a larger geographical region than Alaska.
- **B.** California is located within the continental United States and Alaska is not.
- **C.** Alaska has not been a part of the United States as long as California.
- **D.** California has a larger population than Alaska.

Seats in the House are appropriated to states according to population. If a state has more representatives than another state, it likely also has more influence than that state. **The correct answer is D.**

The Executive Branch

Article II of the Constitution lays forth the powers of the executive branch of government. It is the responsibility of the executive branch to see that the laws of the land are carried out, or enforced. The head of the executive branch is the president. Below the president are the vice president and all the departments and agencies necessary to make sure that the country's laws are enforced and administered properly.

According to Article II, a candidate for president must meet only three qualifications or requirements. The presidential candidate must be

- a native-born (not naturalized) citizen.
- at least 35 years of age.
- a resident of the United States for at least 14 years.

Presidential elections are held every four years. Although the American people cast their votes for the president (and vice president), the Electoral College actually elects the president. The Electoral College consists of electors from each state who cast their votes for presidential candidates one month after the popular election. Originally, no law set a limit on the number of terms, although George Washington suggested that no president serve more than two terms so as not to build and maintain too much power. The Twenty-Second Amendment, ratified in 1951, set the term limit at two terms.

The president serves in three major roles during his term in office. First, the president serves as the **Chief Executive.** As the Chief Executive, the president is responsible for making sure that all the laws of the land are carried out properly. Obviously, one person cannot carry out all the laws. Therefore, the president must appoint officials to head executive agencies and departments to carry out and enforce the laws. The heads of the executive departments are members of the president's **cabinet**. Cabinet members are among the president's closest advisers, and they offer advice to the president about issues within their departments. As Chief Executive, the president can issue executive orders. An executive order is a directive or command that has the weight of law but does not require approval of either the Congress or the Supreme Court. Most often, executive orders are issued during times of war, crisis, or emergency. Second, the President serves as the **Chief Diplomat**. As the Chief Diplomat, the president has the responsibility of appointing ambassadors, meeting and greeting foreign dignitaries, and making treaties. The Senate must approve any appointments or treaties, though. The third major role of the president is that of **Commander in Chief** of the military. Although the president cannot declare war, the president can deploy troops to foreign lands or activate troops here in the United States to help in times of emergency. During war the president is the highest-ranking commander of all the US armed forces.

In addition to these major responsibilities, the president also plays many smaller roles. As the legislative leader, the president often introduces legislation into Congress, influences the direction of legislation, and vetoes, or rejects, proposed legislation. As the party leader, the president promotes his political party, appoints leadership positions within the party, and endorses party candidates who are seeking election. As the judicial leader, the president appoints justices to the Supreme Court and other federal courts. Furthermore, the president may grant a pardon to someone convicted of a crime. Finally, as Chief of State, the president serves as a symbol of the American people. For example, the president may visit another country on behalf of the United States or issue a public statement on behalf of the United States.

The immediate assistant to the president is the **vice president.** The vice president is the only other member of the executive branch mentioned in Article II of the Constitution. If for some reason the president dies, leaves office, or becomes unable to carry out the presidential duties, the vice president becomes the new president. In 1947, Congress decided to lay out a plan for exactly who is next in line for the presidency in the case of some emergency. After the vice president, the Speaker of the

House is next in line, followed by the President Pro Tempore of the Senate, the Secretary of State, Secretary of the Treasury, Secretary of Defense, the Attorney General, and the other cabinet members.

As you learned earlier, the president's closest advisers are the members of his cabinet. The cabinet members are the heads of the executive departments. Some of the departments include the following: Department of State, which carries out the nation's foreign policy; Department of the Treasury, which collects taxes and prints money; Department of Defense, which controls the US armed forces; Department of Justice, which heads national law enforcement; and Department of Education, which guides and provides funding for the nation's schools. In all, there are currently 15 cabinet positions. The cabinet members receive appointments from the president. Then, the cabinet members choose other worthy candidates to fill positions within the executive departments that they oversee.

The last part of the executive branch is the collection of agencies known as the executive agencies. Within each Executive Department, many smaller agencies exist. Some of these agencies include the Central Intelligence Agency (CIA), the National Aeronautics and Space Administration (NASA), and the Environmental Protection Agency (EPA). Some of these agencies, including the Federal Reserve System and the National Labor Relations Board, are called regulatory commissions. Some agencies, such as the US Postal Service, are government corporations.

32. Powers of the president include all EXCEPT:

A. The power to introduce legislation

B. The power to veto legislation

C. The power to send troops into a country

D. The power to declare war

Only Congress can declare war on another country. **The correct answer is D.**

33. Which of the following would be the responsibility of a cabinet member?

A. Overriding an executive order

B. Heading a department within the executive branch of government

C. Declaring war

D. Approving or rejecting a presidential appointment

Each member of the cabinet heads one of the executive departments within the executive branch. **The correct answer is B.**

The Judicial Branch

The third branch of the US government, outlined in Article III of the Constitution, is the judicial branch. The Constitution establishes the **Supreme Court** as the head of the judicial branch. The Supreme Court's main responsibility is to hear cases appealed from lower courts. However, the Supreme Court's other responsibility is to determine the constitutionality of the laws and actions of other branches of government and lower courts. This is the power of judicial review. The Supreme Court has eight justices, or judges, who are appointed by the president, and a Chief Justice, also appointed by the president. Although the president can appoint anyone to be a Supreme Court justice, the Senate has the power to reject a President's nomination. The justices maintain their seats on the Supreme Court for life.

The Supreme Court has the authority to hear, or has jurisdiction over, both criminal and civil cases that have been appealed to the high court. Criminal cases are those dealing with crimes, while civil cases are those that deal with disputes between two or more parties. The Supreme Court has original jurisdiction over cases in which a foreign diplomat is involved or in which a state is involved. In other words, these two kinds of cases may originate with the Supreme Court instead of being appealed to the Supreme Court. The Supreme Court is the highest court in the United States, while the lowest federal courts in the United States are known as Federal District courts. The District courts are the courts in which federal trials and lawsuits begin, or originate. Federal District courts hear both criminal and civil cases. If one of the parties involved in a case at the district-court level believes that an error occurred during the trial, the case can be appealed to a Federal Court of Appeals. If one of the parties involved in the appealed case still believes that the case needs to be heard by a higher court, the party can appeal the case to the Supreme Court. Federal Appeals Courts and the Supreme Court can decide to hear a case or dismiss a case and leave it as is.

34. Which of the following is true of the Supreme Court?

A. It hears only civil cases.

B. It hears only criminal cases.

C. It is the highest court in the United States.

D. It can be overruled by a presidential veto.

Once a case has been decided by the Supreme Court, there are no more courts to which the case may be appealed. **The correct answer is C.**

35. What is the main responsibility of the Supreme Court?

A. To hear and decide appealed cases

B. To hear and decide cases between foreign countries

C. To represent the United States in international court

D. To declare presidential acts unconstitutional

The Supreme Court's greatest responsibility is to hear and decide cases that have been appealed from the lower courts. **The correct answer is A.**

Checks and Balances

As you learned earlier, the writers of the Constitution divided the US government into three branches—the legislative, executive, and judicial—so that no one part of the government would develop too much power. The writers of the Constitution also included in the plan of government another system of safeguards against one branch dominating any other branch. This is known as the **system of checks and balances.** Each branch of government has the ability to check the power of the other two branches and that helps balance the powers of the branches.

Let's look at a few examples of some of the checks each branch has on the others. The executive branch can check the power of the legislative branch by vetoing legislation and can check the power of the judicial branch by appointing judges. The legislative branch can check the power of the executive branch by overriding vetoes, by rejecting presidential appointments or nominations, and by impeaching the president. The legislative branch can check the power of the judicial branch by impeaching judges and by rejecting judicial appointments. The judicial branch can check the power of the executive branch by declaring acts of the president unconstitutional. The judicial branch can check the power of the legislative branch by declaring laws unconstitutional. This system may seem like it could cause inefficiency in the government, but it helps maintain a healthy balance of power among the three branches.

The US Federal System

When the 13 colonies first came together under the Articles of Confederation, they still governed themselves. Once they permanently united as the United States of America, the states retained the ability to continue governing themselves in some instances and to some extent. The government of the country became the shared responsibility of the national government and the state governments. Issues such as marriage laws, educational standards, and election laws were left to the discretion of the states. In addition, some powers were also set aside for local governments. This division of government on multiple levels is known as **federalism.**

State and Local Governments

The powers set aside specifically for the states are known as reserved powers and are provided for in the **Tenth Amendment.** To avoid any conflict between state and federal law, the writers of the Constitution made sure to include in Article VI a provision that states that the Constitution and the laws created by Congress take priority over any state or local laws. This clause in Article VI is known as the Supremacy Clause.

The United States requires that each state have a republican form of government. In other words, each state must operate as a republic. There are no other requirements for state governments than that. Most states, however, used the US Constitution as the model for their state constitutions. Therefore, most state governments are very similar to that of the US government, even though they do not have to be. All states have a governor who serves as the head of the executive branch in his or her state. All states, with the exception of Nebraska, have two legislative houses in their legislative branch (Nebraska has a unicameral system, with only one legislative house.). Each state has its own court system, although there are many variations of court system structures.

The Constitution requires that the state governments and the federal government work together. For example, a state law enforcement agency may work with a federal law enforcement agency on a special case. The Constitution also facilitates cooperation among states. The "full faith and credit clause" of the Constitution requires that states accept each other's legal decisions and documents. It is the "full faith and credit clause" that ensures that each state will recognize the marriage licenses or drivers licenses from other states. States also cooperate through the process of extradition. Extradition is when a state sends a suspected criminal back to the state in which the suspect is accused of committing a crime.

Although state governments tend to be very similar to the federal government, local governments vary greatly. Some local governments are headed by a mayor, or a chief executive officer, elected by the people of the city or town. In these municipalities, a city council often aids the mayor in the administration of the local government. In other municipalities, a council is elected, and then a city manager is hired to handle the business operations. Still other municipalities are run by elected commissioners; each commissioner is responsible for a certain area of operation, such as water or public safety.

36. Which of the following did the writers of the Constitution provide in their plan of government to ensure that no branch of government grew too powerful?

A. Government monitors who watch for corruption

B. Supreme Court elections

C. Three separate divisions of government, each with different responsibilities

D. Two houses in the legislature

With the political power divided three ways, no part of the government has the ability to dominate politically. **The correct answer is C.**

37. According to the Constitution, state governments must do which of the following?

A. Establish a pure democracy

B. Establish a republican form of government

C. Establish a federal system at the state level

D. Require municipalities to have a republican form of government

The only requirement a state government must meet according to the Constitution is that it have a republican form of government. **The correct answer is B.**

Political Parties, Campaigns, and Elections in American Politics

Since the earliest days of the United States, Americans have had differing opinions on the way the country should be governed. These differences in opinions in the formative years of the nation led to the development of the first two political parties, the Federalists and the Republicans. A political party is a group of people who hold similar values and have similar ideas about the proper leadership of the government. Often people form or join political parties based on beliefs about how weak or strong the central government should be, how much or how little the government should tax or spend, or how federal money is spent. Both political parties and members of political parties can be classified based on their ideas about government. On the one hand, liberals, who are often referred to as being on the left, generally advocate political change and social progress. Conservatives, on the other hand, generally advocate very slow change, if any, to the existing political and social order. Conservatives are often referred to as being on the right. Those individuals who fall somewhere in between liberal and conservative are often referred to as moderates.

The basic goal of a political party is to influence public policy in a way that is in line with its ideology. To do so, the parties try to get their candidates elected to public office. The political parties also have another important function in the US political system. In addition to influencing the policies of the government, political parties further strengthen the system of checks and balances. The parties keep a close eye on the actions of the other parties in power and help ensure that there is no abuse within the system. Furthermore, political parties give citizens a sense of belonging in the political arena and give citizens a voice in all levels of politics.

As you just learned, political parties want their candidates elected to office. In order to elect a candidate, the political party and the candidate must go through a long process. In many elections, candidates must first win a preliminary election called a primary. Each party holds a primary election in which voters choose a candidate to represent their party in the main election. For example, in a Republican primary, Republican voters choose from a list of potential Republican candidates. The winner of the Republican primary will run against candidates from other parties in the main election. Some primary elections, known as open primaries, are open to all voters. Closed primaries are primary elections in which voters must declare a party and choose from that party's candidates. One of the ways candidates get elected is by promoting their platforms. A platform is a list of beliefs, values, or ideas that a particular candidate or political party holds as their own. Voters usually use candidates' platforms to evaluate and choose the candidate they want to be in office.

Individuals who are not content with simply participating in a political party often form or join pressure groups. Pressure groups are those with a particular agenda or list of needs and wants. These pressure groups work diligently to persuade legislators in the lawmaking process. This active persuasion of legislators is known as lobbying. Lobbyists often try to meet with legislators to sway the legislators one way or the other during the lawmaking process. For example, an environmental lobbyist would try to persuade legislators to pass legislation that seeks to improve the environment.

38. People may join a political party for any of the following reasons EXCEPT:

A. To voice an opinion collectively instead of individually
B. To discover ideas of governing different from their own
C. To promote a particular candidate in an election
D. To vote in a closed primary

People do not join political parties to find new and different ideas. **The correct answer is B.**

39. Which of the following would **most likely** hire a lobbyist to persuade legislators to pass a new law?

A. The Boy Scouts of America
B. A church in Georgia
C. A tobacco company in North Carolina
D. A single parent on welfare

A tobacco company would want certain laws passed or certain laws changed, and they could afford to hire lobbyists to try to accomplish that goal. **The correct answer is C.**

CANADIAN GOVERNMENT

The Canadian Constitution establishes the responsibilities of the federal government, or a government in which responsibilities are divided between **national**, **provincial**, and **municipal** governments. In addition to those duties enumerated, or named, in the Constitution, the federal government also controls all issues not specifically charged to the provincial or territorial governments. Like the government of the United States, powers are divided among three separate branches of government.

Governor General

As a **constitutional monarchy**, Canada is governed by a monarch whose powers are defined by the Constitution. The monarch, or **Head of State**, is Queen Elizabeth II. The Queen, on the advice of Canada's prime minister, appoints a **governor general**. The governor general is traditionally appointed to a five-year term. The governor general then fulfills all of the duties of the Head of State on behalf of the Queen.

The duties of the governor general include executing orders-in-council and other state documents, appointing all superior court judges, and giving "royal assent" to bills passed by the House of Commons and the Senate before they can become law. The governor general also summons, prorogues (ends a session), and dissolves Parliament.

Prime Minister

The **prime minister** is the leader of the party with the most seats in the House of Commons. In addition to controlling the House of Commons, the prime minister advises the Queen on her appointment of the governor general and thus enjoys quite a bit of power. The prime minister also oversees the Cabinet. Members of the Cabinet include the heads of the Ministries, the Prime Minister's Office, and the Privy Council Office. Canada has 18 Ministries that cover all areas of government. Some of the Ministries are Finance, Canadian Heritage, Health, Justice, and Veteran Affairs. The Prime Minister's Office handles issues related to the prime minister's role as Party Leader. For example, the Prime Minister's Office handles public relations and decides which matters need the prime minister's attention and which do not. The Privy Council Office has a number of responsibilities that range from advising the prime minister on national security matters to working as a liaison between the prime minister and the Cabinet.

Parliament

Canada has a **bicameral** legislature, or a legislature with two houses. The two houses include the **House of Commons** and the **Senate**. The House of Commons, also called the Green Chamber, is made up of 338 members who are elected in general elections at least every five years. The number of members is based on population. At any given time, several different political parties may be represented in the House of Commons. However, the party with a majority of seats in the House of Commons is asked to form the government of Canada. If no party holds a majority, then the parties are asked to form a partnership to form a minority government.

The Senate, or Red Chamber, was created to protect regional, provincial, and minority interests. Unlike the House of Commons, senators are appointed by the governor general on the basis of "equal representation" and are not elected based on population. There are 105 seats in the senate. To be appointed as a senator, one must be at least 30 years old, be a Canadian citizen by birth or naturalization, have a net estate worth of at least $4,000, own property worth $4,000 in the province for which he or she is appointed, and be a resident of the province he or she is appointed to represent.

The Judiciary

The **Supreme Court** consists of a **Chief Justice** and eight justices. Each is appointed and holds office until the age of 75. A justice may be removed from office for incapacity or misconduct by the governor general (on address of the Senate and House of Commons). The Supreme Court issues judgments and advises on questions concerning constitutional interpretation, the constitutionality of legislation, and the powers of Parliament and the Provinces. Another important branch of the Judiciary is the **Tax Court**. Created in 1983, the Tax Court is the first level of appeals for taxpayers. Below the Supreme Court and the Tax Court is the **Federal Court**. A superior court of record with both civil and criminal jurisdiction, the Federal Court of Canada is divided into the Federal Court of Appeal and the Federal Court, Trial Division. The trial division hears lawsuits and applications to review government actions. The Court of Appeal hears appeals from the Trial Division and supervises the decisions of government tribunals. Appeals from the Court of Appeal are made to the Supreme Court.

The Provincial and Territorial Government

Each of the 10 provinces and the three territories has its own capital in which its government is centered. Each province is headed by a lieutenant governor, and a commissioner heads each territory. Generally speaking, provinces and territories differ in a few ways. All land in a **province** is controlled by the province itself, while land in a **territory** is controlled by the federal government. Also, provinces are included in the Constitutional amendment process, while territories are not. The governments of both provinces and territories are responsible for the education and welfare of their inhabitants, the administration of justice, and the protection of natural resources within the boundaries.

The Municipal Government

Below the provincial and territorial governments are the **municipal** governments. Within each province and territory there exist many municipalities in the form of regions, counties, and districts called "Upper Tier" municipalities. "Lower Tier" municipalities are cities and townships. The provincial and territorial governments have the power to create and modify the municipal, or local, governments. Also, the provincial and territorial governments have the power to assign certain responsibilities to the townships. These may include things such as animal control, water and sewage management, and economic development.

40. Which of the following statements concerning the Canadian federal government is true?

A. The Canadian government has loose ties with Great Britain, most notably its association with the Sovereign.

B. The Judiciary clearly has more power than the other two branches of Canadian government.

C. Because of the structure of the Canadian government, it would be relatively easy for one person or one party to abuse powers and take control of the government.

D. The municipal governments have nearly the same amount of authority as the provincial and territorial governments.

The Sovereign is still the highest position in the order of precedence in Canada, so it would be correct to state that the Canadian government has loose ties with Great Britain, most notably its association with the Sovereign. **The correct answer is A.**

41. Which of the following government positions indicates the importance of political parties in the Canadian government?

A. Mayor

B. Governor general

C. Queen

D. Prime minister

The prime minister is the leader of the party that has the most seats in the House of Commons. **The correct answer is D.**

ECONOMICS

Macroeconomics and Microeconomics

The study of **economics** is the study of the way society uses limited resources to meet its material needs. To be more specific, economics deals with the production, distribution, and consumption of goods. The field of economics can generally be divided into two major areas: **microeconomics** and **macroeconomics**. Microeconomics, also known as price theory, examines how supply, demand, and competition cause differences in prices, profits, wages, and other aspects of economics. In the area of microeconomics, economists assume that proprietors or entrepreneurs seek to make the most profit possible and that consumers spend their money while seeking the most value possible. Macroeconomics looks at the larger picture of economics and examines such things as employment and national income. Macroeconomics developed after the publication of a book called *The General Theory of Employment, Interest, and Money* in 1935 by a British economist named John Maynard Keynes.

Although economics has been a vital part of the life of every state in history, the academic field of economics did not take on a life of its own until a Scottish moral philosopher, Adam Smith, wrote *Inquiry into the Nature and Causes of the Wealth of Nations* in 1776. Smith's landmark work is still used today by economists and students of economics. Paramount to Smith's economic theory was the idea of the "invisible hand." Smith believed that the government should be directly involved in the economy as little as possible. He argued that if consumers were left alone to act in their own interests and on their own behalf, a natural force—an invisible hand, so to speak—would point the national economy in a direction that would benefit the greatest number of people. As a result, Smith was a critic of the economic policy of mercantilism. **Mercantilism**, a popular government practice during the time, was a system in which all national economic policy was directed by the goal of national self-sufficiency. In other words, a mercantilist nation sought to make its economy better by becoming less and less reliant on other nations' goods. Mercantilist nations sought to stockpile gold and silver, to keep wages as low as possible, and to keep the population growing. Smith disagreed with this policy of government manipulation of the economy.

A group of French economists, known as physiocrats, reacted to the mercantilists by advocating **free trade** and a **laissez-faire** approach to the economy. *Laissez faire* is a term that means the government takes a "hands off" approach to economic policy. Free trade means that the government allows both imports and exports to come and go freely. The physiocrats believed in a single tax to raise money for the state instead of the manipulation of the economy; Smith agreed with their ideas.

Other notable economists include Thomas Malthus, David Ricardo, and John Stuart Mill. Although these economists had some philosophical differences, they all basically agreed on some major principles. They all believed in a free market economy, the right to own private property, and the ability of competition to drive an economy. Another economist was Karl Marx. Marx took a different approach to economic theory, though. Marx, a socialist, believed that those who owned the means of production historically had exploited the working class. Therefore, Marx advocated the elimination of private property and the collective ownership of both property and industry. Marx outlined his economic theories in the historic *Communist Manifesto*, co-authored by Frederick Engels.

Basic Economic Concepts

Factors of Production

When economists talk about production within an economic system, they must consider the three factors of production. These factors are natural resources, capital, and labor. Usually the factors of production cannot fully meet the demands of the consumers, or people who use the goods produced. **Natural resources** are the raw materials necessary for the production of goods. For example, trees are necessary for the production of houses, paper, and wooden furniture.

Capital can be any equipment, factories, or property necessary for the conversion of raw materials into finished goods. This type of capital is referred to as fixed capital. Capital can also refer to money that is invested to support the production of goods. This type of capital, called circulating capital, can be wages paid to laborers or raw materials used in production. Any capital that can be sold for cash is considered liquid capital, while capital that cannot be easily converted to cash is known as frozen capital.

In economics, the term **labor** is used to describe the work it takes to convert raw materials into goods and services. Labor may refer to the people who actually do the work processing the raw materials and producing the goods. Laborers may be factory assembly line workers, truck drivers, sales agents, or other people involved in the production and distribution of goods. Labor may even refer to people in a service industry, such as doctors or teachers that provide services for others.

When considering productivity, economists also consider the **law of diminishing returns.** The factors of production, when used together in the correct proportions, will produce an end result sufficient for a society. However, according to the law of diminishing returns, at a certain point, any additional resources (raw materials, labor, or capital) fail to produce additional product with a value that is commensurate with the cost of the additional resources. In fact, according to the law, at a certain point, additional resources may even result in less production than before the additional resources were added.

42. The natural resources required to build a log home include which of the following?

A. Trees, land, and construction workers

B. Land and construction workers

C. Trees

D. Trees and land

Trees are the only natural resource listed among the answer choices because land is considered capital and construction workers are considered laborers. **The correct answer is C.**

43. The law of diminishing returns could be applied to which of the following situations?

A. Salaries of factory workers are raised.

B. New raw materials are supplied to a factory to produce a brand-new product.

C. The number of assembly line workers in an efficient factory is cut in half to reduce company spending.

D. The number of assembly line workers in an efficient factory is doubled while the amount of raw materials remains the same.

With twice as many workers in an already efficient factory, the workers will probably get in each other's way and reduce efficiency and production. **The correct answer is D.**

Supply and Demand

The primary force and one of the basic principles of economics is that of **supply and demand.** Supply can be defined as all the goods available regardless of price. Demand can be defined as the desire of the consumers to purchase goods. Producers supply goods with the hope that consumers will demand goods. Producers must set prices on the goods high enough that they still make a profit after paying for all the costs of production. Consumers seek to pay the lowest price possible for goods. Producers must set the amount of production based on the demand for goods. The price and the availability of goods determine the demand. These factors working together make up the principle of supply and demand.

If a given item, a car for example, has a high profit yield, a great number of producers will be interested in production of the good. The producers of the cars will compete for a share of the market. If the market is flooded with cars and the supply of cars is greater than the demand, buyers either cannot or will not buy all of the supply of cars. If this happens, there will be a surplus that will then cause car prices to fall. This may increase the demand for the cars. If an item, such as a car, has a price that is low enough to make consumers want the item, it will be in demand. If the price of the car falls too much, there may be such a demand that producers cannot supply the item fast enough to meet the demand. If the demand exceeds the supply, the prices will rise.

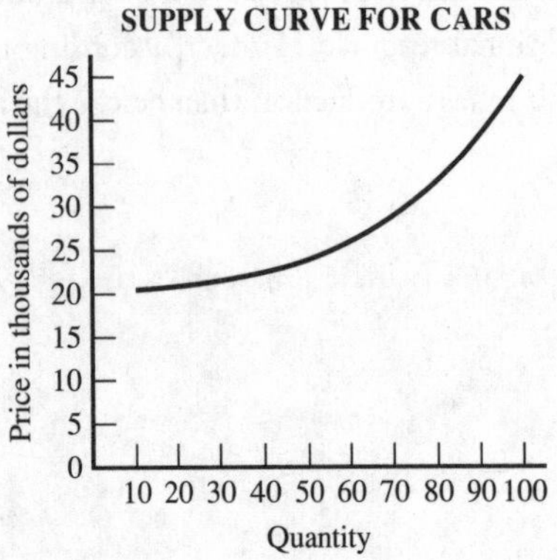

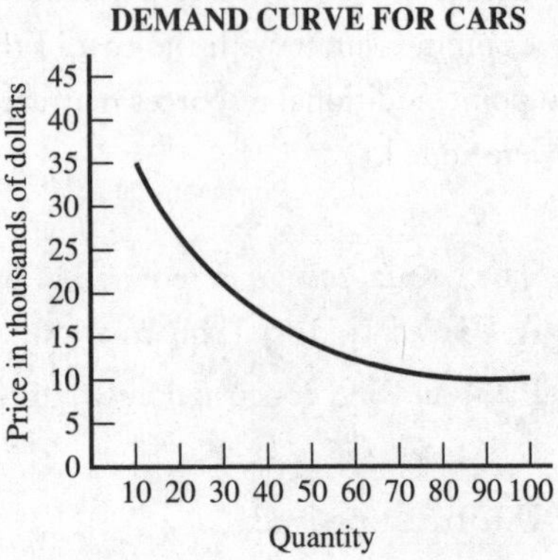

To make a market stable, producers must exactly determine the amount of goods that consumers will demand and the price that the consumers will pay for those goods. When this point is reached, it is called **equilibrium**. On the following chart, the point of equilibrium is the point at which the two curves intersect. When the price for goods rises above equilibrium, there is a decreased demand and, therefore, more goods than consumers want. This creates a surplus. If the opposite happens, that is, if the price falls below equilibrium, the demand increases, and there is a shortage. These are the laws of supply and demand.

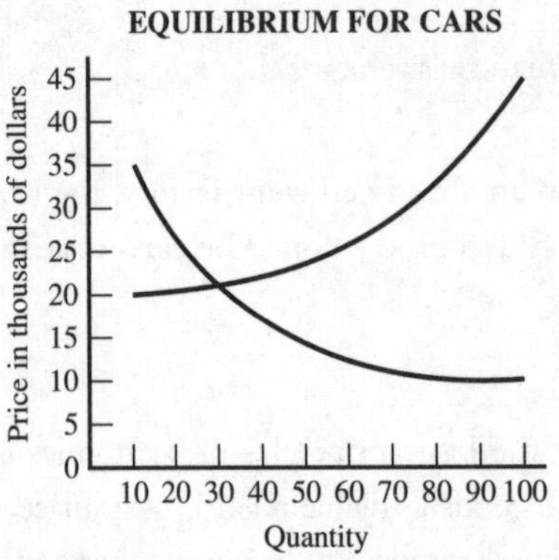

It should be noted that the laws of supply and demand are valid only in an economic system in which the markets are relatively undisturbed by the government. Because supply and demand depend on market conditions, an economy in which the government controls the market would not follow the laws of supply and demand. For example, during times of war in the United States or at any given time in the former USSR, the markets were somewhat manipulated by the government. That invalidated the mechanisms of supply and demand in those places.

44. What conclusion can be drawn from the principles of supply and demand?

A. The lower the profit an item generates, the more producers will be interested in producing that item.

B. The higher the price of an item, the higher the demand will be for that item.

C. The more consumers demand an item, the lower the prices will go.

D. The more consumers demand an item, the higher the prices will go.

If there is a high demand among consumers for an item, the producer can charge a higher price, and consumers will still buy the item. **The correct answer is D.**

45. Market stability will occur when which of the following occurs?

A. Prices rise above the point of equilibrium.

B. Producers produce the amount of goods that consumers want at the price that consumers want to pay.

C. A surplus is created.

D. A shortage is created.

Stability occurs when producers produce the amount of goods the consumers want at a price that consumers feel is fair. **The correct answer is B.**

Government and Economic Policy

The United States has a **free market** economy, yet the government still plays a vital role in steering that economy. Through the use of taxation, the government can create revenue for its own use or to control inflation. **Inflation** can be defined as a rise in prices or a devaluing of money, resulting in decreased buying power for consumers. By reducing government expenditures or by adjusting the tax rate, the government can help control or correct inflation. Taxation can also be used to increase or decrease consumer spending. By increasing the tax rate, the government can discourage consumer spending, thereby slowing the economy. By decreasing the tax rate, the government can stimulate or encourage consumer spending, investing, and business transactions because people have more money to spend and invest. It should be noted that not all inflation is bad, though. Slow and gradual inflation is normal and even good for an economy, but inflation of 10 percent annually coupled with high price increases would cause concern for economists. The government also controls social programs like welfare, unemployment benefits, Medicare, and Social Security. The government manages the funds used to operate these programs and distributes the funds to citizens who need assistance. All of these practices are part of the government monetary strategy known as the **fiscal policy**. The practice of increasing taxation or restricting public spending is called the **contractionary fiscal policy**. The practice of reducing taxation and stimulating public spending is known as the expansionary fiscal policy.

Money, Monetary Policy, and Financial Institutions

The use of money is the method of exchange employed in economic systems in lieu of bartering. Whatever currency an economic system uses is its money. The money supply of a nation is mostly coins and paper money, or bills, along with deposits made to banks. The use of money in an economic system is controlled through monetary policy. In the United States, the **Federal Reserve Board** controls the monetary policy. The Federal Reserve Board directs the monetary policy by regulating the money and credit available for use in the country. It does this by setting the reserve ratio and setting the discount rate. The **reserve ratio** is the amount of money that lending institutions can lend and the amount of money they must hold in reserve. By setting the reserve ratio, the Federal Reserve Board controls the supply of money that is available for banks and savings and loan associations to lend to consumers. The Federal Reserve Board tightens the supply of money by raising the reserve ratio. On the other hand, the Federal Reserve Board loosens the supply of money by dropping the reserve ratio. The **discount rate** is the interest rate that the Federal Reserve Board charges to member banks to borrow money. Banks then charge consumers a higher interest rate on loans than they pay to the Federal Reserve. The more money that banks want to borrow, the more it costs to borrow the money. The hike in the cost discourages banks from borrowing more and reduces bank demand for extra reserve money. The Federal Reserve Board also sets the margin requirement that determines the amount of cash a purchaser must pay up front when buying stocks; this helps deter speculation, as in the kind that led to the Great Depression.

Labor Relations

As you learned earlier, when speaking within the realm of economics, labor refers to the people who actually do the work and produce goods, or the people who provide services for others. All dealings between labor and management over labor issues are called **labor relations**. Many years ago, laborers constantly fought for better wages and working conditions, often with little or no success. One reason for the lack of success during pre-industrial America was because employers dealt directly with individual employees. As industrialization took over, though, employers faced many employees instead of just a few individuals. Government regulations eventually set limits on the number of hours workers had to work and the minimum wages workers could receive. These regulations helped curb dangerous working conditions. Labor, however, remained largely unorganized.

In the 1930s, the Wagner Act allowed laborers to organize and negotiate with management concerning disputes. The labor organizations became known as **unions**, and these negotiations became known as **collective bargaining.** Collective bargaining occurs when leaders of the labor unions meet with employers and management to negotiate wages, hours, conditions, benefits, or other issues. Collective bargaining is often successful. Many times independent arbitrators handle the negotiations between the two sides. However, when collective bargaining does not work, laborers may go on strike. When workers strike, or stop working, the government may intervene and end the strike, or the government may help facilitate successful negotiations. The threat of a strike is most successful during negotiations when the unemployment rate is relatively low. If there are plenty of unemployed workers who are willing to replace the strikers, the strike loses its effectiveness.

46. Government can control aspects of the economy by controlling which of the following?

A. Unemployment

B. Checking and savings accounts

C. Salary caps

D. Taxation

Taxation is the correct choice because a higher tax rate slows the economy, while a lower tax rate stimulates the economy. **The correct answer is D.**

47. The Federal Reserve Board is vital to the economy because of its policies concerning which of the following?

A. Labor disputes

B. Social Security

C. Interest rates

D. Minting and printing of new coins and bills

The Federal Reserve Board's policies on the reserve ratio and discount rate directly affect the nation's interest rates. **The correct answer is C.**

Consumer Economics

Historically, people around the world used the barter system to exchange goods and services in return for other goods and services that they needed. However, problems arose with bartering. Each trader needed to have goods or services that the other trader desired. Trading could be difficult and time-consuming. It could also be unfair, as when colonists adopted the Native American custom of trading with wampum. These small beads made from shells were easy for the colonists to produce, and they made so many that wampum declined in purchasing value.

Money facilitates a fair exchange for goods and services. It also has the advantage of being portable and accepted around the world by exchanging a unit of currency of one country for a unit of another country. Today, consumers use currency, coins, checks, and credit and debit cards to pay for goods and services. The use of "plastic," or debit or credit cards as a form of payment instead of cash or checks, has led to spiraling consumer debt and bankruptcy. The barter system is making a comeback in our nearly cashless society, but consumers still need to learn to make wise financial decisions.

Goods that are shipped out of a country to another country are known as **exports**; goods brought into a country from another country are called **imports**. To maintain a healthy economy, the goal of a country is to export more goods than it imports. Economists call this occurrence a favorable balance of trade. In order to protect domestic goods, countries often add a special tax, called a **tariff**, to imports so that domestic goods are more competitively priced. If the tariffs are too high, the country whose imports are being taxed will retaliate with tariffs of their own on imported goods. Another way that countries protect their interests is through the use of import quotas. Import quotas limit the number of particular foreign goods that may enter a country. Quotas are often very successful in reversing trade imbalances. On occasion, government health or safety standards prevent foreign goods from entering the domestic market. Government support of domestic industries provides additional advantages for those industries and puts foreign competitors at a disadvantage. It is very important that governments carefully manage their overseas trade; many workers in each country depend on producing goods for overseas trade.

48. Which of the following might occur as a result of relying too heavily on "plastic"?

A. The price of goods would be inflated.

B. The foreign exchange system would collapse.

C. The country would go bankrupt.

D. The consumer would be tempted to purchase without thinking.

The lure of debit and credit cards sometimes causes people to buy goods and services without consideration of paying back their debts. **The correct answer is D.**

49. Why did Native Americans have a disadvantage when colonists started trading with wampum?

A. The shells to make wampum became difficult to locate.

B. Colonists made countless beads, so they diminished in worth.

C. Native Americans preferred to trade with currency instead.

D. The beads couldn't be used to purchase food.

After colonists produced a plentiful supply of wampum, the purchasing value of these beads declined. **The correct answer is B.**

The Role of Economics in Social and Historical Events

Throughout history, economics has played a role in exploration and colonization of new territories. During the Age of Exploration, a period that began in the early fifteenth century and lasted until the seventeenth century, European explorers sailed from their homes in the Old World—Portugal, Spain, Great Britain, France, and Holland. Rulers of these nations financed the explorers' journeys, paying for ships, supplies, and crews. All of them anticipated wealth resulting from their investment. The European economy relied on gold and silver, yet these highly valued metals were a rare resource.

Along with precious metals, European explorers were searching for a new route to the Far East where the profitable spice trade flourished. Nutmeg, for example, was worth more than a comparable amount of gold. Prior to the Age of Discovery, Venice had been the trade port for spices harvested in the east and shipped to Europe. This city became wealthy by charging exorbitant tariffs on spices. Explorers, lead by the Portuguese, circumnavigated Africa and sailed to India, where they accessed spices without the additional high tariffs levied by the middlemen along the overland trade routes. Other explorers from different countries followed, and conflict broke out in a struggle for control of the spice trade.

At the same time, explorers such as Christopher Columbus explored new regions that Europeans would later colonize. Investors in sixteenth-century Europe set up chartered companies to encourage overseas trade and exploration in new territories such as Africa, Asia, the Caribbean, India, and

North America. The company would gain a trading monopoly in that region; the colonists would then establish settlements on the coast to facilitate trade.

Economics also is the motivation behind countless wars, as power over new territories leads to control of valuable commodities, such as minerals. Although victory can lead to increased wealth and trade, wars can be also costly and can disrupt trade. Supplies become scarce, with shortages causing food to be rationed and prices to skyrocket as living standards tumble. The consequences of war can be measured in economic terms. Military spending can spur economic growth or, at the other end of the spectrum, it can result in a devastated economy. After World War I, for example, Germany suffered a draining defeat, from which it attempted to recover by printing enormous amounts of money. This tactic backfired and led to extreme inflation and increasing unemployment. The poor economic state launched Hitler into a powerful position based on his promise of economic growth.

Wars can also lead to scientific and industrial innovations. New technologies developed by the military can lead to positive economic consequences when ordinary citizens use an invention commercially. To cite a modern example, the GPS navigation device was developed by the military and today has become a popular consumer product.

GEOGRAPHY

Geography is more than states and capitals or latitude and longitude. **Geography** is the study of Earth's physical features and the way people have adapted to these physical features. Geography is concerned not only with physical geographic features but also with cultural geographic features. Physical geographic features include things such as land, water, mountains, and plains. Cultural geographic features include things such as human architecture or man-made changes to Earth's physical features. The study of geography can also include how early civilizations developed within their environments, as well as the ways in which societies continue to develop in relation to their environments, including when environmental conditions require that peoples migrate elsewhere. The science of geography can be divided into two branches: systematic and regional. **Systematic geography** deals with individual elements of Earth's physical and cultural features. **Regional geography**, on the other hand, deals with the physical and cultural features within a particular region or area of Earth's surface.

Systematic geography includes a number of different fields within the realm of physical geography. Part of physical geography is cartography, or mapmaking. Another important part of physical geography is oceanography, or the study of Earth's oceans; climatology examines Earth's weather patterns; and geomorphology looks at the way Earth's surface has changed. Other areas of physical geography include biogeography, or the study of the distribution of plants and animals, and soil geography, or the study of the distribution of soil and soil conservation. Systematic geography also includes a number of fields within the realm of cultural geography, or the study of how human social and cultural life affects geography. Economic geography, for example, examines how business and industry have affected the geographic environment. Political geography looks at nations, states, cities, and other man-made areas and examines how geography influences these political units; political geography often involves some political science, too. Military geography is the study of how the geography of a particular area may affect military operations, and it is especially important today in light of the events in the Middle East. Historical geography studies how the Earth's geography has changed over time and the role that human civilizations have played in that change.

Development of Classical Civilizations

Beginnings and Early Civilizations

It is generally believed that at the start of the most recent Ice Age, which lasted from about 20,000 years ago until about 12,000 years ago, the world's entire human population numbered less than 1 million. Their existence revolved around hunting and gathering rather than growing plants or raising animals for food. Hunter-gatherer families belonged to larger groups of tribes. Though the cold temperatures of the Ice Age killed off some tribes, others moved toward the equator, seeking warmer temperatures. Yet, at the end of the Ice Age, humans were finding life even more difficult. As temperatures and sea levels rose, Earth's plant and animal life dwindled. To survive, humans learned to control the development of various plant and animal species. By cultivating small plots of land through what is called **horticulture**, human families could accumulate surplus food, and by breeding animals according to traits they found desirable, they could cultivate a predictable source of meat and other animal products.

Around 4500 BCE, **agriculture** began making rapid inroads in five areas worldwide. These five areas are sometimes called cultural hearths because of their role in establishing both culture and civilization in their regions of the world. Four of these areas came into existence in river valleys. One area was Egypt, in which the Nile River became a garden country quite early. The second region was Mesopotamia, located in the Tigris and Euphrates river valley. The third area was the Indus River valley in India, and the fourth area was in China. The fifth region was Mesoamerica, or what is now southern Mexico and Central America. This area followed a substantially different pattern from the other four. It had no vast river systems in which to build elaborate agricultural systems. Here, agriculture grew out of horticulture, as the gardens needed to sustain the local populations that became larger and larger.

Known as the ancient Near East, the areas of Egypt and Mesopotamia are considered to be the cradle of Western civilization. The people of the Near East were the first to practice intensive year-round agriculture. They produced the first writing system, invented the potter's wheel and then the vehicular and mill wheels, and created the first centralized governments, law codes, and empires. The people of the Near East also introduced social stratification, slavery, and organized warfare, and they laid the foundations for the fields of astronomy and mathematics.

Between 5000 BCE and 500 BCE, the Near East was home to successive waves of cultures, borrowing from and cooperating with one another for resources, ideas, and culture as well as competing with one another militarily for land and prestige. The Near East is where the first cities appeared. Near the confluence of the Tigris and Euphrates Rivers, several city-states competed for land, power, and prestige while fending off barbarians. These city-states became the ancient Greece of the region, providing written language, architecture, religion, and cultural norms to the societies that followed. Babylon, located not far from modern-day Baghdad, was the first city-state to assemble a true kingdom around itself in Mesopotamia. The Babylonians used the waterways for communication and to control their wide empire, which spread across the river valleys.

In the area of Greece, from around 3000 to 1100 BCE, the Minoan civilization inhabited the Aegean island of Crete, and, from around 1600 to 1100 BCE, the Mycenaean culture dominated the mainland. Mycenaean civilization began with the arrival of many tribes, which by around 1600

BCE had established themselves as political units. The Mycenaeans quite possibly lived under Minoan dominance until around 1400 BCE, when they conquered Crete. Sometime around 1100 BCE, the Dorian tribe from the north invaded and destroyed the Mycenaean civilization. Greece was subsequently thrown into a Dark Age, from which it took several centuries to recover. It was during the Dark Ages that the city-state began to develop.

Around the Nile River, even by 6000 BCE, advanced agricultural practices had developed, as did large-scale building construction. By about 3000 BCE, Egypt had become united as a kingdom under a single monarch, ushering in a thousand-year period of great order and stability. Protected from outside forces by impassible desert, and immune to change because of the orderly, predictable nature of life, Egypt thrived and advanced in all aspects of culture—from religion and art to language, customs, and overall quality of life. It was during this time that the Egyptian dynasties erected the pyramids as monuments to their god-kings. By around 1500 BCE, Egypt had risen to become an international power, solidifying its power on a regional scale.

Classical Traditions, Empires, and Religions

The classical civilizations (roughly the first millennium BCE) differed from earlier civilizations in that their basic need for water and food was met. Freed from a preoccupation with mere survival, civilizations of this period could devote more attention to the arts, architecture, religion, and philosophy and to developing systems of law and government that divided decision-making power. They could also turn their attention outward—toward overseas trade and toward expanding their territories by military force. Still, classical civilizations in many ways developed in terms of the physical environment that surrounded them.

The Rise of Rome

By the beginning of the ninth century BCE, the seven hills that rose from the marshy land along the Tiber River's eastern shore were occupied by people in village communities who kept farms in the low-lying areas and retreated to their hilltops for defense. Once the seven villages united, they constructed a wall around their territory and began charging a toll for the use of a ford (and later the bridge) across the marshy lowland. This toll was to prove an early source of Rome's wealth. The city of Rome itself was founded sometime between 850 and 700 BCE. It remained a minor town for a hundred years or so, until the Etruscans—a confederation of towns to the north—took over the city relatively peacefully around 640 BCE. A series of kings governed the town for more than a century thereafter. In 509 BCE, the Romans expelled their king and established a Republic that ruled Rome for the next four centuries. The Republic was in essence a broad oligarchy, with the city's aristocrats dominating politics, economics, and social life. The Romans developed effective military and foreign policies, which enabled them to conquer Italy, and then, between 394 and 290 BCE, to engage in three wars with another early superpower, Carthage, for control of the western Mediterranean Sea.

The Emergence of Classical Greece from Its Dark Ages

Little is known with certainty about ancient Greece during its Dark Age, since the Dorian tribes, which had destroyed and replaced the Mycenaean civilization, had no written language. They were a warring people, who devoted themselves instead to developing tools for battle. (They replaced bronze with a lighter material, iron, for weaponry and armor, thereby ushering in the Iron Age.) During the Dark Age, the region was a collection of warring city-states called *poleis* (singular: *polis*). Two of the more important poleis were Athens and Sparta, which spoke different dialects of Greek and had different cultural bases and histories. Ultimately, these differences expressed themselves in distinct forms of government. (Athens is credited with creating democracy: equal rule by all citizens.)

Despite their warring ways and the mountains that separated them, the various independent poleis of ancient Greece developed commonalities in culture, language, religion, and government. It was during this time period that Greeks began to identify themselves and each other as *Hellenes*. In spite of their rivalries, they became culturally united. Contributing to this sense of loose unity were the Olympic Games, which began in 776 BCE and featured athletes from the various poleis who competed against one another as a religious ritual. Eventually, around 600 BCE, Greece's Dark Age came to an end, and what followed was an explosive surge of Greek culture.

Classical Greek culture held a distinct set of ideals concerning beauty, life, and the world in general. During the classical era, Greek playwrights and poets came to express the harsh realities of the human condition through various gods and goddesses. The Greek ideals found physical expression in architecture and art that emphasized simplicity and realism. Greek scholars established a study of history emphasizing a communal identity among humankind. And philosophers laid the groundwork for modern ideas of government, law, and justice, which emphasized reason, intellectual inquiry, and the pursuit of wisdom over superstition and religion.

While flourishing culturally, the Greek poleis lost interest in maintaining a strong and unified military. The Greek independent city-states and loose confederations were no match against Philip of Macedon or his son Alexander the Great. They also were ineffective against the rising power of Rome, which, under its generals, would eventually come to conquer Greece. But the Romans would come to adapt the classical Greek culture, keeping it alive.

The Decline and Fall of Egypt

Drought, famine, and the rise of an aristocracy helped bring about the end of the Old Kingdom of dynastic rule in Egypt and usher in a period of new prosperity, in which nobles and ordinary citizens began to share in Egypt's wealth. The appearance of foreign invaders, the Hyksos, also changed and renewed Egyptian culture. The resurgence of Egyptian power after the pharaohs of the Sixteenth Dynasty drove out the Hyksos and led to Egyptian imperialism and major building programs that proclaimed the might of the pharaohs and the gods who watched over them.

However, new ideas in religion and political changes in the wider world tended to limit Egyptian power in unexpected ways. Successive waves of invasion made Egypt a land of outward-looking leadership and inward-looking commoners, and it widened the divide between governors and those governed. Egypt became the breadbasket of two successive empires, but the very nature of its wealth—in agriculture and critical products—made it a tempting target to Persian and Islamized Arab alike. At the same time, lacking in other material resources it needed (particularly iron and straight timber), Egypt had no choice but to import these items, thereby depleting its wealth and losing control of the Africa-Asia trade routes. Regular conflicts with other states sapped Egypt's military resources. Eventually, in the sixth century BCE, Egypt fell to the Second Babylonian Empire. The Persians added Egypt to their empire in the fifth century BCE, Alexander the Great conquered Egypt in the third century BCE, and then Julius Caesar and Octavian Augustus Caesar annexed Egypt to the Roman Empire in the first century BCE. Egypt would not achieve independence from outside forces until the seventh century CE.

50. The origins of the Roman Empire can be traced to Rome's distinctive [ ].

Rome's village communities could keep farms in the low-lying areas along the Tiber River's eastern shore while retreating to their hilltops for defense. Moreover, once they united and constructed a bridge across the marshy lowland, they began to amass wealth by charging a toll for accessing the mountains from the river. **The correct answer is *geography*.**

51. A student of classical Greek literature would **most likely** read a

Select ▼

A. poem about the fall of the Roman Empire.

B. battle tale written by a Dorian warrior.

C. philosophical essay about the meaning of life.

D. ballad once sung by traveling troubadours throughout Europe.

Classical Greek literature includes philosophical works by Plato, Socrates, Aristotle, and their contemporaries about life's larger questions. **The correct answer is C.**

Africa: The Cradle of Civilization

Africa is often referred to as the cradle of civilization, giving rise to ancient Egypt. Nomads settled along the banks of the Nile River, which flooded annually and left rich silt behind. The rise and fall of the river caused the land to cycle from fertile to barren. This was mirrored in the Egyptians' belief in death and rebirth. They preserved the dead through mummification, and buried the bodies along with "grave goods," such as food, tools, and weapons to assist the journey into the afterlife. Egyptian pharaohs were entombed in enormous triangular stone tombs, such as the pyramids of Giza, which are the oldest of the Seven Wonders of the Ancient World.

Ancient Egyptians formed an advanced society with culture and customs. They created decorative art, including pottery painted with hieroglyphics, an ancient form of writing using symbols and pictures. They also used metal tools and sculpted in stone. The ancient Egyptians also built ships, performed surgeries, and developed plows to harvest wheat and barley.

China: A Trio of Dynasties

In ancient China, three dynasties—the Zhou, Qin, and Han—ruled for centuries. Members of these dynasties were ranked in a hierarchy, from kings to nobles to commoners to slaves. The ancient Chinese settled along the Huang He, the second longest river in the country, which is known as the cradle of Chinese civilization.

Ancient Chinese created decorative art such as pottery, and invented silk and wheels. They also created calendars and religions such as Confucianism, which emphasizes self-control and social and political order. They also excelled in technology, inventing the compass, paper, gunpowder, and mechanical clocks.

India: Two Major Religions

Classical India encompassed two major religions. Hinduism, one of the oldest religions in the world, is characterized by a belief in reincarnation. Buddhism, a world religion based on the teachings of a prince called Buddha, encourages a state of enlightenment by rejecting worldly desires. Artists created Buddhist shrines called *stupas*. Ancient Indians also made important discoveries, such as the mathematical concept of zero, the world's first university, and furnaces to make steel products.

Latin and South America: Three Ancient Cultures

Three vital ancient cultures flourished in Latin and South America: the Mayan, Aztec, and Incan. Each of these civilizations created distinct societies and achievements.

The Maya built pyramids and temples, used a system of hieroglyphic writing, and developed accurate calendars. Similarly, the Aztecs excelled in math and science, especially astronomy. Their sophisticated calendar stone contains pictorial symbols for 12 months and 365 days of the year. They also used healing herbal remedies gathered from Central American plants. Along the same lines, the Inca gained fame for their agricultural engineering feats. They constructed tiers of terraces up mountainsides to grow corn, potatoes, and other crops.

52. Which of the following did NOT characterize ancient Latin and South American cultures?

A. Precise calendars

B. Silk fabrics

C. Herbal medicines

D. Terrace cultivation

The ancient Chinese culture was renowned for developing silk fabrics. Luxurious silks were reserved for royalty. **The correct answer is B.**

53. Ancient Egyptians reinforced their belief in death and rebirth by all of the following, with the possible EXCEPTION of

Select ▼

A. practicing cannibalism.

B. entombing in pyramids.

C. preserving through mummification.

D. burying objects with the dead.

The Egyptians believed in an afterlife following death; therefore, they treated the deceased with dignity to ensure eternal life. They did not practice cannibalism. **The correct answer is A.**

Environment and Societal Development

Societal Development

The Fertile Crescent is known as the cradle of civilization because the earliest known cultures originated there. Located in the modern-day Middle East, this crescent-shaped area of land was a lush, fertile slice in an arid region. Here, the Tigris and Euphrates rivers converged, and this source of water irrigated the land to help crops grow. This ancient region, known as Mesopotamia, was the site of an advanced society with cultural and social organization.

The first civilization in Mesopotamia was Sumer, where its residents, the Sumerians, rose to power and prosperity around 3000 BCE. A dozen city-states had separate walled cities and villages until one king united them following a great flood. Sumerians were prolific inventors. They invented new technologies, such as the sundial, potter's wheel, and wheeled carts and wagons. They built reservoirs to store water, and canals to carry it to farmland. They also created cuneiform, the earliest writing system, in which wedge-shaped characters were made on clay tablets. In addition, this advanced civilization created the first codes of law. Sumer faced frequent invasions from neighboring communities. It fell into decline around 1760 BCE, when it was absorbed into Babylonia.

Other civilizations, including Babylonia, took over the Fertile Crescent. Its most famous leader was Hammurabi, who established a code of laws dealing with various aspects of Babylonian culture. He wrote numerous laws about water rights, which were crucial in a region that depended upon irrigation agriculture.

As in ancient Mesopotamia, the world's topography continues to influence regional borders, with many borders delineated by natural features such as deserts, rivers, and mountains. For example, the Rio Grande forms part of the border between Mexico and the United States.

Human Migration

Humans often move from one country to another in response to environmental issues. People have been forced to migrate from their home territories due to changes in their environment. Desertification, droughts, earthquakes, floods, global warming, and rising sea levels can trigger migration. All of these issues can have a detrimental effect on food production and can lead to water shortages.

Scientists speculate that around 12,000 years ago, humans migrated from Asia to North America by passing over the Bering Strait on a temporary land bridge. According to archeologists, the most likely reason that these early Native Americans left the continent of Asia to walk far into a new land was due to climate change. Temperatures rising or plummeting would affect human survival. The migrating hunter-gatherers may have tracked herds of hoofed creatures from Siberia into Alaska, ensuring that their food supply would continue.

Food was also the motivating factor behind the Irish emigration of the 1840s. In 1845, a destructive fungus raged throughout Ireland, destroying the potato crop that formed the backbone of the Irish diet, and, therefore, economy. More than a million people starved during the Irish potato famine. Approximately two million Irish emigrated to new countries, with one-quarter of that number settling in the United States.

54. Ancient Sumerians were renowned for all of the following inventions EXCEPT:

Select ▼

A. Classical guitar

B. Written language

C. Reservoirs

D. Wheeled vehicles

Cuneiform, reservoirs, and wheeled carts and wagons all were Sumerian inventions; however, they did not invent the guitar. **The correct answer is A.**

55. Mass migration might be caused by all of the following factors EXCEPT:

Select ▼

A. Food shortages

B. Desertification

C. Rising sea levels

D. Safe drinking water

Shortages of food, desertification, and rising sea levels due to climate changes could cause millions of people to migrate. However, safe drinking water is not a cause, although an unsafe water supply would lead to mass migration. **The correct answer is D.**

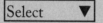

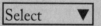

HISTORICAL DOCUMENTS ON THE GED® SOCIAL STUDIES TEST

The Social Studies Test will contain excerpts from at least one of the following key historical documents relating to the American constitutional form of government: the Declaration of Independence, the US Constitution, the Federalist Papers, or landmark Supreme Court cases. To help you become more familiar with each of these documents, we will examine them closely here. Before you take the Social Studies Test, take time to read some of each of these documents just to familiarize yourself with the language and the style of each one.

The Declaration of Independence

On July 4, 1776, the members of the Philadelphia Congress adopted a motion that "The united colonies are, and of right ought to be, free and independent states." Thomas Jefferson led a committee appointed to write a statement declaring the 13 colonies officially free of British reign. The resulting document was the Declaration of Independence. Jefferson's task was not an easy one, however. He needed to clarify the colonies' purpose in fighting Britain. He succeeded, and by doing so, he appealed to other colonies to declare their independence and encouraged other nations to support the colonies against Britain.

Jefferson begins the Declaration of Independence by asserting that all people have rights to which they are entitled by nature. He states that governments are established to protect those rights, and when a government fails to do so, people should abolish it and create a new government that will protect their rights.

The Declaration of Independence then takes on a more personal tone, stating that the King of Great Britain, George III, has misused his power in a number of specific ways. Basically, half of the Declaration is devoted to listing the ways in which King George abused his power. Pointing out that their previous attempts to compel the king to respect human rights had failed, Jefferson asserts that logically the Americans did the only thing they could do to preserve the rights of all people—they declared independence from Great Britain. The Declaration, a moving document, had the desired effect and enticed great support for the war against Britain.

The US Constitution

The Preamble

"We, the People of the United States, in Order to form a more perfect Union, establish Justice, insure domestic Tranquility, provide for the common defense, promote the general Welfare, and secure the Blessings of Liberty to ourselves and our Posterity, do ordain and establish this Constitution for the United States of America."

A preamble is a statement of purpose. The Preamble to the Constitution paraphrases the purpose of the Constitution. It answers the question of why the Constitution was created.

Articles of the Constitution

The Articles of the Constitution outline the plan for the government under which US citizens currently live. As discussed earlier, three branches of government, the executive, legislative, and judicial, divide the power and keep any one part of the government from dominating another. Each branch keeps a check on the others, thus the terms "separation of powers" and "checks and balances." To balance the power of the three branches of government, each has a "check" to limit the powers of the other two. For example, although Congress may pass a bill, the president has the power to veto it. Congress may, however, override a presidential veto by a two-thirds majority vote. Finally, the Supreme Court may declare a law unconstitutional. These powers are named, or enumerated, in Articles I, II, and III of the Constitution. Let's look more closely at each of these Articles.

ARTICLE I. LEGISLATIVE BRANCH

The legislative branch is outlined in Article I of the Constitution. The US legislature, called Congress, is made up of two houses—the House of Representatives and the Senate. Both houses are made up of representatives elected from the states. The House representation is based on state population, while the Senate consists of two senators from each state. The representatives are elected to two-year terms, while the senators are elected to six-year terms. The legislative branch "creates" the law under which we are governed.

ARTICLE II. EXECUTIVE BRANCH

Article II of the Constitution details the executive branch of government. The executive branch consists of the president, vice president, and various agencies and departments that administer and enforce the laws.

The president serves a four-year term and cannot serve more than two terms. The president and the vice president are elected by a vote of the people. However, there is a process known as the Electoral College, through which the results of the popular election must be certified. A president can, although it is rare, receive a majority of the popular vote and still lose the election because of the Electoral College vote. The executive branch "enforces" the laws under which we live.

ARTICLE III. JUDICIAL BRANCH

Article III of the Constitution provides that the "judicial power belongs to the federal courts." It is in this Article that the Supreme Court and inferior, or lower level, courts are created. As you've already learned, the Supreme Court "checks" the other two branches of government by declaring certain laws unconstitutional. The Supreme Court has the power to rule on cases involving a state and a citizen of another state, disputes between states, between citizens of different states, between a state and its citizens, or between a foreign state and US citizens. It also may consider conflicts arising at sea or regarding patents and copyrights. Most of the time, the Supreme Court hears "appeals" of decisions made by "inferior" courts. However, the Court does have "original" jurisdiction, or the right to hear an original case and not an appealed case, in some instances. These include cases involving ambassadors or other public ministers, consuls, and those cases in which a state is a party.

Although originally created with a Chief Justice and five associate judges, the Supreme Court is now composed of nine justices, each appointed for life by the president with approval from the

Senate. The Court acts by issuing decisions that explain why the Court makes particular rulings. The judiciary interprets the law.

ARTICLE IV. RELATIONS OF THE STATES TO ONE ANOTHER

The goal of this article is to promote respect between the states, also known as "full faith and credit." It requires that the citizens of different states be treated similarly. It also requires states to honor the legal decisions and legal documents of other states.

ARTICLE V. THE PROCESS OF AMENDMENT

This article explains the manner in which the Constitution may be amended or changed.

ARTICLE VI. GENERAL PROVISIONS

Article VI notes that the United States took on debts of the Confederacy, confirms that the Constitution, federal laws, and treaties "are the supreme law of the land," and requires federal and state officers to take an oath to support the Constitution.

ARTICLE VII. RATIFICATION OF THE CONSTITUTION

The authors of the Constitution wrote this article with an eye toward putting the Constitution into action. Article VII provides that the Constitution becomes effective when ratified by the conventions of nine (of the 13) states.

The Amendments

In the years following the ratification, or approval, of the Constitution, many leaders wanted to make sure that the rights of individuals were protected. The Constitution did not specifically list those protected rights, so the states' leaders decided to add amendments, or changes and additions, to the Constitution. The first 10 amendments are known collectively as the **Bill of Rights**. The other amendments were added periodically as the need arose throughout the course of American history. Let's look at each one of those amendments.

THE BILL OF RIGHTS

The first 10 amendments to the Constitution are known as the Bill of Rights. Many states ratified the Constitution only because they believed it would be amended to include the rights outlined in the Bill of Rights.

First Amendment—Religious and Political Freedom: The First Amendment prevents Congress from interfering with the freedom of religion, speech, and the press. It also incorporates the right to assemble and to petition the government.

Second Amendment—Right to Bear Arms: This amendment gives citizens a limited right to arm themselves, or keep weapons. There is some debate over whether this right is intended to refer to the right of the states or the right of individuals.

Third Amendment—Quartering of Troops: The purpose of the Third Amendment was to stop soldiers from taking over homes for their own use without the consent of the owner. The amendment provides that such "quartering," or "room and board," may occur "in a manner to be prescribed by law."

Fourth Amendment—Searches and Seizures: The Fourth Amendment forbids "unreasonable searches" and the issuance of warrants without "probable cause," or good reason.

Fifth Amendment—Right to Life, Liberty, and Property: The Fifth Amendment guarantees a citizen's rights while on trial as well as the rights to life, liberty, and property. When someone refuses to testify at trial and "takes the Fifth," they are said to be invoking their rights as established in the Fifth Amendment. It is also called a right against self-incrimination. The Fifth Amendment also provides that an individual must not be held for committing a crime without being "indicted." In addition, the Fifth Amendment protects against "double jeopardy," or the risk of being tried twice for the same offense. The Fifth Amendment also ensures individuals' "due process" rights, or the right to be moved through the criminal justice system in a proper fashion.

Sixth Amendment—Protection in Criminal Trials: Citizens are guaranteed a right to a speedy trial, an impartial jury, and the right to an attorney in the Sixth Amendment. The accused also has a right to "confront witnesses" against him or her at trial.

Seventh Amendment—Suits at Common Law: If there is a dispute over something valued at $20 or more, then the Seventh Amendment provides that citizens have a right to a jury trial in federal court. However, this type of case is not normally heard in federal court now.

Eighth Amendment—Bail and Punishment: The Eighth Amendment prohibits fines and punishments that, in essence, "don't fit the crime." It is said to be "cruel and unusual" to sentence someone unfairly, and the Eighth Amendment prohibits this.

Ninth Amendment—Considering Rights Not Enumerated: Fearing that the enumeration of certain rights would lead to the exclusion, or omission, of other rights, the authors of the Bill of Rights included the Ninth Amendment, which establishes that citizens are not limited to the rights specifically listed in the Constitution.

Tenth Amendment—Powers Reserved to States and to People: Similar to the rationale behind the Ninth Amendment, the Tenth Amendment was created to reassure the states that they would retain power in those areas not specifically granted to the Federal Government.

THE OTHER AMENDMENTS

Eleventh Amendment—Suits Against a State: The Eleventh Amendment clarifies the original jurisdiction of the Supreme Court concerning a suit brought against a state by a citizen of another state.

Twelfth Amendment—Election of the President and Vice President: The Twelfth Amendment explains how the Electoral College chooses the president and vice president. It also states that the two should work together, and that the vice president should become president if the president can no longer stay in office.

Thirteenth Amendment—Slavery Prohibited: Slavery was abolished in the United States by the addition of the Thirteenth Amendment.

Fourteenth Amendment—Civil Rights for Ex-Slaves and Others: The Fourteenth Amendment ensures that all citizens of all states enjoy rights on the state level as well as the federal level. It has also been interpreted as providing for "due process" at the state level.

Fifteenth Amendment—Suffrage for Blacks: This amendment prohibits the use of race as a requirement or disqualification for voting.

Sixteenth Amendment—Income Taxes: The Sixteenth Amendment authorizes the collection of income taxes.

Seventeenth Amendment—Direct Election of Senators: Prior to the Seventeenth Amendment, senators were selected by the legislatures of the various states. Since its passage, they are elected by the vote of the citizens.

Eighteenth Amendment—National Prohibition: This amendment prohibited the sale or manufacture of alcohol in the United States. It was later repealed by the Twenty-First Amendment.

Nineteenth Amendment—Woman Suffrage: Just as the Fifteenth Amendment prohibits the use of race as criteria for voting, the Nineteenth Amendment prohibits the use of gender as a requirement or disqualification for voting.

Twentieth Amendment—Presidential and Congressional Terms: The Twentieth Amendment sets new start dates for congressional terms and also addresses what to do if a president dies before he is sworn into office.

Twenty-First Amendment—Prohibition Repealed: The Twenty-First Amendment repealed the Eighteenth Amendment, which had prohibited the sale or manufacture of alcohol in the United States.

Twenty-Second Amendment—Anti-Third Term Amendment: This amendment limits a president to two four-year terms in office. There is an exception for a vice president who takes over because the president is unable to continue. In that case, the limit is a total of 10 years as president.

Twenty-Third Amendment—District of Columbia Vote: This amendment gave Washington, DC, representation in the Electoral College.

Twenty-Fourth Amendment—Poll Tax: The Twenty-Fourth Amendment prohibits charging a tax for placing a vote in a federal election.

Twenty-Fifth Amendment—Presidential Succession and Disability: This amendment states the order of succession should the president be unable to continue holding office.

Twenty-Sixth Amendment—Lowering Voting Age: Citizens who were 18 years old could vote after the passage of this amendment.

Twenty-Seventh Amendment—Congressional Pay Increases: The Twenty-Seventh Amendment requires that any law that increases the pay of legislators may not take effect until after the next election.

The Federalist Papers

The Federalist Papers are a collection of 85 essays written by John Jay, James Madison, and Alexander Hamilton. They are considered one of the most important contributions made to American political thought. The papers were intended to persuade states, particularly New York, to adopt the Constitution.

The delegates who signed the Constitution stipulated that it would take effect only after approval by ratifying conventions in nine of thirteen states. Because New York and Virginia were big and powerful, a vote against ratification from either of them would have been disastrous. The New York governor, George Clinton, clearly was opposed to the Constitution.

Hoping to persuade the New York convention to ratify the Constitution, Jay, Madison, and Hamilton wrote a series of letters defending the Constitution to New York papers under the pseudonym Publius. These letters are known collectively as The Federalist Papers. Historian Clinton Rossiter said, "The message of *The Federalist* reads: no happiness without liberty, no liberty without self-government, no self-government without constitutionalism, no constitutionalism without morality—and none of these great goods without stability and order."

Landmark Supreme Court Cases

The Supreme Court has issued many rulings of historical significance that have directly affected our rights as individuals. Let's look at a summary of some of those "landmark" cases that definitely changed rights in America.

Marbury v. Madison—1803

Prior to his death, President John Adams attempted to fill a number of judicial vacancies. Some of the commissions were not delivered to the appointees prior to Adams's death. One of the appointees who did not receive his commission, William Marbury, sued Secretary of State James Madison to get his commission as Justice of the Peace.

This issue came before the Court on its "original jurisdiction" (i.e., it was not on appeal from an inferior court), and it placed the Court in a difficult position. If the Court were to issue a writ of mandamus, or order, forcing Madison to turn over the commission, and he refused, the power of the Court would be weakened. On the other hand, to refuse to issue the writ of mandamus could be perceived as weakness or fear of the executive branch.

Ultimately, the Court's decision declared that Madison should have delivered the commission to Marbury but held that it did not have the power to issue a writ of mandamus. The Court declared that such power exceeded the Court's authority as granted in Article III of the Constitution. The writ of mandamus authority had been given to the Court by the Judiciary Act of 1789, a congressional act. Thus, the Court held an act of Congress unconstitutional. Ironically, by declaring that it did not have the power to order Madison to turn over the commission, the Court effectively strengthened its power over the other two branches of government.

This case exemplifies the Court's power as the "last word" on the meaning of the Constitution. It established the judicial branch as an equal power in the three branches of government. The power to declare acts of Congress unconstitutional is one that the Court has used sparingly over the years. The legislature is, however, always aware that the Court could declare a law unconstitutional.

Dred Scott v. Sandford—1857

Dred Scott was a black slave who lived on free (non-slavery) land with his owner for several years. He tried, unsuccessfully, to sue in state court for his freedom. He then filed suit in federal court. The basis of his claim to establish his freedom was that he had lived on free soil for more than five years in an area of the country where the Missouri Compromise of 1820 forbade slavery.

The Supreme Court ruled that Scott was a slave and not a citizen and therefore did not have the right to sue in federal court. The right to file suit is a right limited to citizens in Article III of the Constitution. A majority of the Court held that, because a slave was the private property of his master, the Missouri Compromise unconstitutionally took the slave owner's property without due process of law. Thus, a slave could be taken into any territory and held there. The reason? The Fifth Amendment clearly forbids Congress from depriving people of their property without due process. To allow Scott his freedom would be to deprive his owner of his "property." The Court found the Missouri Compromise unconstitutional, and Dred Scott remained a slave.

Plessy v. Ferguson—1896

Homer Adolph Plessy was a resident of Louisiana and a citizen of the United States. He was of partial African descent. He paid for a first-class ticket on the East Louisiana Railway, a passenger train that ran through Louisiana. When he boarded the train, Plessy found a seat in a car that was filled with white people and was designated for white passengers. The train conductor informed Plessy that he would have to find a seat in a car not designated for white people or he would be forced to leave the train. Plessy refused and was arrested.

Plessy was found guilty of violating a state statute that required passenger trains to provide "separate, but equal" accommodations for white and black people. The statute also imposed criminal punishment on those passengers who refused to comply. Plessy brought suit challenging the Louisiana statute as an unconstitutional violation of his due process rights under the Fourteenth Amendment. The Supreme Court held that the statute requiring "separate but equal" facilities was constitutional, rationalizing that separate facilities for blacks and whites satisfied the Fourteenth Amendment as long as they were equal. In other words, the Court found that segregation does not in itself constitute unlawful discrimination.

Brown v. Board of Education of Topeka, Kansas—1954

Linda Brown, a black third-grade student, walked a mile every day to get to her "black" school, even though a school designated for white children was much closer to her home. Linda's father tried to enroll her in the "white" school, but the school refused to accept Linda as a student. The Browns got help from the National Association for the Advancement of Colored People (NAACP) and sued the school board. The Supreme Court, hearing the case on appeal, ordered oral arguments in the case twice before reaching a decision. The question before the court: "Does segregation of children in public schools solely on the basis of race, even though the physical facilities and other 'tangible' factors may be equal, deprive the children of the minority group of equal educational opportunities?"

Thus, the question of "separate but equal" was once again before the court. The Court's decision in *Plessy v. Ferguson,* a finding that separate facilities are not unconstitutional as long as they are equal, seemed to hold the answer in this case as well. However, 58 years had passed, and this time, the Court's ruling was quite different. Significantly, the opinion of the Court was unanimous. The decision: "We conclude that in the field of public education, the doctrine of 'separate but equal' has no place. Separate educational facilities are inherently unequal."

The *Brown* decision did not abolish segregation in any areas other than public schools, but it was a start toward integrating the races in many areas of life. The Court did not overrule *Plessy v. Ferguson,* because it limited the decision in Brown to public schools. The ruling did, however, have a significant impact on the segregation of the races in many public facilities. Slowly, integration began. We can only imagine how different integration might have been if the Court's decision in *Plessy* over 100 years ago had held separate facilities to be "inherently unequal."

Miranda v. Arizona—1966

Ernesto Miranda was arrested for raping an 18-year-old girl. The police arrived at Miranda's home at night and asked him to go with them to the police station. Miranda, claiming he did not realize he had a choice, went with the police. After two hours of interrogation, Miranda confessed to the crime.

On appeal to the Supreme Court, Miranda argued that he would not have confessed to the crime if he had been advised of his right to remain silent and to have an attorney. In a 5-4 decision, the Court determined that a suspect must be warned prior to custodial interrogation of his right to remain silent, that any statement he does make may be used against him, and that he has a right to an attorney. Specifically, the Court stated: "He must be warned prior to any questioning that he has the right to remain silent, that anything he says can be used against him in a court of law, that he has the right to the presence of an attorney, and that if he cannot afford an attorney one will be appointed for him prior to any questioning if he so desires." Thus, the controversial "Miranda" warnings were created.

Roe v. Wade—1973

Roe was a single, pregnant woman who brought suit to challenge the constitutionality of the Texas laws that made getting an abortion or performing an abortion illegal. The laws did allow exceptions for those abortions performed on medical advice to save the mother's life.

The Court held that the law violated the due process clause of the Fourteenth Amendment, which protects the right to privacy against state action. This right, the Court found, includes a woman's qualified right to terminate her pregnancy. The Court acknowledged that the state has a legitimate interest in protecting both the pregnant woman's health and the potentiality of human life, and placed those rights on a scale that tips further to the state's interests as the pregnancy progresses.

During the first trimester, the Court stated, the decision should be left to the attending physician. After that, the state could regulate the abortion procedure in ways "reasonably related" to the mother's health. Subsequent to "viability," or the ability of the child to live outside of the womb, the Court held that the state could regulate abortion and even prohibit it except where necessary to save the life of the mother. Many abortion cases have followed *Roe,* but this was the first to hold that a woman's right to privacy outweighs the state's interest in protecting her health and the unborn child.

Nixon v. United States—1974

During the presidential election of 1972, burglars broke into the Democratic National Committee's headquarters in Washington, DC's Watergate Hotel. A federal grand jury indicted the Attorney General and others, alleging conspiracy and obstruction of justice. The grand jury named President Richard Nixon as a co-conspirator.

Investigations revealed that Nixon taped many conversations that took place in the oval office. The tapes were subpoenaed, and Nixon released edited transcripts but refused to release anything more, claiming "executive privilege." Executive privilege protects the president from being compelled by the judicial branch to turn over confidential executive branch material.

The question before the Court: Does the president have the right under executive privilege to refuse to surrender material to federal court? In a unanimous (8-0, Justice Rehnquist did not participate) decision, the Court held that Nixon had to turn over the tapes. The Court stated: "[N]either the doctrine of Separation of Powers, nor the need for confidentiality of high-level communications, without more, can sustain an absolute, unqualified presidential privilege of immunity from judicial process under all circumstances. The president's need of complete candor and objectivity from advisors calls for great deference from the courts. However, when the privilege depends solely on the broad, undifferentiated claim of public interest in the confidentiality of such conversations, a confrontation with other values arises. Absent a claim of need to protect military, diplomatic, or sensitive national security secrets, we find it difficult to accept the argument that even the very important interest in confidentiality of presidential communications is significantly diminished by production of such material for in camera inspection with all the protection that a district court will be obliged to provide." With this decision, the Court limited the president's use of "executive privilege" to the need to protect military secrets, diplomatic secrets, or national security. The rationale is based on the idea that the courts will protect the information and treat it as confidential.

Hustler Magazine, Inc. v. Falwell—1988

Reverend Jerry Falwell filed suit against *Hustler* magazine because the magazine published a cartoon that portrayed Falwell as engaging in an incestuous relationship with his mother in an outhouse.

The Supreme Court held that, in order to protect the free flow of ideas and opinions, the First and Fourteenth Amendments prohibit public figures and public officials from recovering for "intentional infliction of emotional distress" when the speech that causes the distress could not reasonably be taken as implying the truth. In essence, because the cartoon was obviously a joke, and because Falwell was a "public figure," *Hustler* had the right to print the cartoon under the First Amendment to the Constitution. If an individual places himself in a position to be known by the public, then he takes on the risk of being the topic of jokes.

Boy Scouts of America v. Dale—2000

The Boy Scouts revoked Dale's position as assistant scoutmaster in a New Jersey troop after learning that he was homosexual. Dale sued, claiming violation of a state statute prohibiting discrimination on the basis of sexual orientation. The Supreme Court held that the Boy Scouts could not be required to include Dale in its organization. The Court stated that to require mandatory inclusion of unwanted individuals into the organization would violate the Boy Scouts' First Amendment right of "expressive association." Forced membership, the Court found, is unconstitutional if it affects the group's ability to advocate its collective viewpoints. Because the Boy Scouts believed that a homosexual lifestyle conflicted with its philosophies, the inclusion of Dale would have hindered the Boy Scouts' ability to teach its views. Thus, to protect the Boy Scouts' First Amendment rights, it could not be forced to include Dale in its membership.

CANADIAN HISTORY

The Earliest Canadians

The earliest inhabitants of Canada most likely traveled from Asia to North America across a land bridge that once spanned the Bering Strait. The nomadic hunters probably followed large game into North America at least 10,000 years ago. Once in North America, they scattered across the continent and formed their own communities, each with its own distinct language. A new wave of nomads probably migrated to North America about 4,000 years ago. The earliest concentrations of Canadians were located along the Pacific Coast and in what is now Ontario. Over the centuries, the inhabitants of Canada developed a number of languages and cultures unique to Canada, including the Algonquian and the Athapaskan language groups. These groups, and others, interacted only with each other until 985 CE.

The Arrival of Europeans

In approximately 985, the first Europeans, the Vikings, landed on, explored, and settled Greenland. They also explored the northeastern coast of Canada. About 15 years later, the famous Viking Leif Ericson sailed from Greenland to a place he called Vinland, which was probably modern-day Newfoundland. Although exploration and trade continued along the northeast coast of Canada, the Viking colonies did not last long, and by the early fifteenth century, Europeans no longer maintained contact with North America.

Toward the end of the fifteenth century, European explorers began exploring North America's eastern coast again. John Cabot unsuccessfully searched the coast for the Northwest Passage, a sea route that Europeans believed would lead to the wealthy Asian trade empires. In the sixteenth century, France sponsored Jacques Cartier to continue the search for the Northwest Passage. Cartier was also unsuccessful in locating a sea route to Asia and was later unsuccessful at establishing a colony in North America.

Later attempts at colonization also met with little success. However, the Europeans discovered the vast wealth of fish and whales available to commercial fishermen off the coast of Labrador, in the Gulf of St. Lawrence, and in the Grand Banks. Fishermen from Spain, France, England, and Portugal took advantage of the bountiful catch found here. Eventually, the English explorer Sir Humphrey Gilbert claimed Newfoundland for England. After the Spanish and Portuguese left the area, the English settled the northern part of Newfoundland and the French settled the southern part. These settlers entered into a trade relationship with the natives. The bulk of the trading was for furs, especially beaver furs. The European demand for beaver products, particularly hats, launched an industry in Canada that remained a vital part of its economy for many years to follow.

The indigenous, or native, peoples of Canada traded with the European settlers and formed many alliances with the Europeans. Because of the large amount of Canadian territory and the relatively small number of Europeans in Canada, few conflicts emerged between Europeans and the indigenous nations they encountered in Canada. The Europeans made some attempts to Christianize the natives, but they found little success. The greatest negative effect of the trade relationship was the transmission of European diseases to the indigenous people of Canada. Diseases in epidemic proportions spread quickly and decimated vast numbers of natives wherever the Europeans went. The indigenous population of Canada continued to decline even into the twentieth century.

56. Which of the following is **most likely** true of the first inhabitants of Canada?

A. The first inhabitants of Canada were probably civilized.

B. The first inhabitants of Canada were probably of Asian descent.

C. The first inhabitants of Canada settled in permanent shelters as soon as they arrived in Canada.

D. The first Canadians were indigenous to North America.

The first people in Canada likely crossed the land bridge that then existed between Asia and modern-day Alaska. **The correct answer is B.**

57. Which of the following **best** describes the relationship between the Europeans who explored North America and the natives of Canada?

A. The two groups were involved in nearly incessant warfare.

B. The two groups formed a military alliance.

C. The two groups had a relationship based on trade.

D. The two groups freely exchanged information about cultures and farming techniques.

The Europeans and the natives exchanged many goods and generally maintained a good relationship. **The correct answer is C.**

Early Canadian Colonies

As France began to see the huge dividends paid by the fur trade in Canada (which was known at the time as New France), it officially claimed and began defending the area. England, a perennial enemy of France, disputed the claim. France realized that new, permanent settlements needed to be built if the claim to New France was going to be legitimate. Therefore, France used the fur trade to finance the construction of new forts and settlements. France settled at Quebec, an inland site well protected from foreign aggression. France then employed an economic policy known as mercantilism. Under mercantilism, a trade company was given control over New France. In exchange, the company agreed to ship all exports to France and to purchase all of its raw materials and supplies from France. The French also created strong alliances with the Huron and the Algonquin, two local nations of indigenous peoples. With the help of these two peoples, the French colony grew and prospered. The French also created many maps of the area, and in the 1630s and 1640s, they established colonies at Trois-Rivières and Montreal. The colonies remained dependent upon the fur trade and their relationship with the natives. This presented a problem in the mid-1600s, though, when the French aided the Huron in a losing effort against the Iroquois. The devastation of the Huron nearly cost France the colonies.

Conflict with the British

In the second half of the seventeenth century, the French increased their defenses and population in New France. Also during the late seventeenth century, the French sponsored significant exploration of North America, both westward across Canada and southward along the Mississippi River in the Louisiana territory. The English re-entered the picture during this same time period when the Hudson Bay Company, an English trade company, began competing with the French for the fur trade. The French responded by building more forts in French territory and along the frontier.

In the 1680s, the French found themselves in conflict with the British in several parts of the world, including North America. In King William's War during the 1690s, the French and British troops in North America exchanged guerrilla raids and attacks for nearly a decade before signing a treaty that returned the territorial borders of North America to the way they were before the war. In 1702, Queen Anne's War erupted between the two powers and later ended with France giving up some of its territory. The next half-century or so was a period of high tensions but no war. France continued to expand its fur trade and its relationship with the indigenous peoples in and around New France.

However, in 1754, the French and Indian War broke out between the French and the British. Many natives fought on both sides of the conflict. The French held their ground well against the British, who greatly outnumbered the French. However, at the war's end in 1763, France ceded its territory to Great Britain. Quebec, Nova Scotia, Newfoundland, and Rupert's Land were now under British control. Great Britain immediately sought to ease tensions between the British and the natives in Canada by signing treaties with them.

58. The French and the English competed **most** for which of the following in Canada?

A. The fur trade

B. Indian alliances

C. The western territories

D. Access to the Mississippi River

Both nations wanted control of the lucrative fur trade, which brought about fierce competition between the two rivals. **The correct answer is A.**

59. Which of the following is true about the situation after the end of the French and Indian War?

A. No indigenous peoples had become involved in the conflict between France and Great Britain.

B. The French territories remained unchanged from the beginning of the war.

C. The French added to their territories much land formerly under British rule.

D. France lost much land to Britain.

Rupert's Island, Quebec, Nova Scotia, and Newfoundland all went to Great Britain after the war. **The correct answer is D.**

Early British Rule

At first, Britain hoped to institute British customs and British-style government in its new territory. However, that plan did not work because of the resistance of the Canadian people, most of whom were originally French. With the Quebec Act of 1774, Great Britain allowed French law, French customs, and even Catholicism to continue in Canada. This went a long way toward reconciliation between the French Canadians and the British government. The Quebec Act also returned some land to Quebec and saved Montreal's fur trade, the backbone of its economy. The Canadian colonies grew, but they remained only loosely linked to each other.

With relative peace and security in Canada, the bulk of British forces left Canada. This opened the door for trouble with the 13 British colonies to the south. In 1775 and 1776, the British colonies along the Atlantic coast (now known as the United States) decided to break away from British control. During the time the colonies fought the British, they also invaded Quebec and Montreal. The British eventually drove the Americans out of Canada, but they failed to prevent the colonies from winning their independence. During and after the war, many loyalists—those Americans still loyal to Great Britain—fled the colonies and sought refuge in Canada. The British government rewarded these refugees for their loyalty by granting them land and other financial benefits.

The loyalists who settled in Canada expected they would be living in a British land, but what they found was an unfamiliar and uncomfortable French-style society. By 1791, these loyalists had voiced their displeasure with the situation on many occasions. The British government responded by dividing Quebec into two separate colonies called Upper Canada and Lower Canada. Each colony received a new constitution. The predominantly French Lower Canada retained its French culture and laws while the mostly British Upper Canada received new English laws that favored both the English nobility and the Protestant religion.

When the United States declared war on Great Britain in 1812, the United States thought it might be able to take advantage of the perceived vulnerability of Canada. US troops invaded Upper Canada but were soundly defeated by British forces and natives allied with the British. This act of aggression created an anti-American sentiment throughout much of Canada, particularly in Upper Canada.

60. For which of the following reasons might the Canadian people have been resistant to British rule?

A. Most of the people in Canada liked the government that they had already established there.

B. Most of the people in Canada did not like people who spoke English.

C. Most Canadians at the time were of French descent, and the French and British generally have never gotten along very well.

D. The British refused to allow French customs and traditions to be practiced in Canada.

The French and British had a long history of disputes. **The correct answer is C.**

61. What steps did the British take to give aid to refugees from the thirteen colonies during the War for American Independence?

A. The government gave them safe passage back to Great Britain.

B. The government granted them tracts of land in Canada.

C. The government refused to give them any aid and encouraged them to return to America.

D. The government took land and wealth away from the natives and gave it to the refugees.

The British government wanted to reward the loyalists for their loyalty to Great Britain. **The correct answer is B.**

Westward Expansion and Immigration

In the late eighteenth and early nineteenth centuries, two companies battled for control of the fur trade and sparked westward expansion in Canada. The Hudson Bay Company had been granted a monopoly on the fur trade, but a company founded by French-Canadian fur traders defied the monopoly. The North West Company explored, mapped, and tapped the natural resources of Canada all the way to the Pacific Coast. Both companies struggled for influence throughout the western territories. Friction between the two companies often resulted in outbreaks of violence in frontier towns. Finally, in 1821, the two companies merged and the Hudson Bay Company assumed control of the Canadian fur trade. However, by the end of the nineteenth century, the timber industry replaced the fur trade as the leading industry in Canada.

During the nineteenth century, millions of Europeans migrated to North America to seek new opportunities. Perhaps 1 to 2 million of these people, most from England, Ireland, and Scotland, migrated to Canadian territories. They were willing to take the risk of moving to the frontier because of the promise of free farmland. Upper Canada grew faster than any other part of the Canadian territory. Relatively few immigrants, on the other hand, moved to the far north or the far west. Not until the gold rush in the second half of the nineteenth century did a significant number of settlers move to the Pacific region. As the immigration continued, the native peoples of British North America gradually became the minority of the population.

62. Which of the following statements could be made concerning the competition between the two trade companies in Canada?

A. The competition between the two companies nearly caused a civil war.

B. The indigenous people were caught in the middle of the war between the two trade companies.

C. The two trade companies encouraged good, healthy competition in the marketplace.

D. The competition between the two companies ultimately led to the mapping and exploration of some of the western parts of Canada.

In order to find more resources and stay competitive with the Hudson Bay Company, the North West Company moved westward, exploring and mapping as it went. **The correct answer is D.**

63. Which of the following was the primary reason for the massive immigration to Canada during the early 1800s?

A. The government offered land grants to anyone who wanted to settle on the frontier.

B. World War in Europe drove millions from their homes.

C. The prospects of finding a job in the factories of Canada prompted many Europeans to immigrate.

D. The gold rush compelled many people to seek their fortunes.

Immigrants to Canada received large tracts of land on which they could settle and build homes. **The correct answer is A.**

Radicals, Reformers, the Act of Union, and Confederation

Because most of the non-indigenous inhabitants of Canada during the early 1800s were hardworking farmers and fishermen, the traditional British aristocratic system of government did not please many of the Canadians. In the early 1800s, two groups called for a change in the government. The members of the moderate group of people who sought change were known as reformers. The reformers liked the British system of government, but they wanted a parliamentary system with an elected legislature instead of one that was appointed. The radicals, the more liberal of the two groups, sought publicly elected officials within a republic modeled after the governments of France and the United States. Many in Canada, especially in Lower Canada, pointed to Britain as the root of many of the social, political, and economic problems that Canada faced. These feelings erupted in an armed rebellion in 1837 that eventually ended in victory for the British. The political climate in Lower and Upper Canada convinced Great Britain that something needed to be done in order to maintain peace.

In 1841, the British passed the Act of Union, which created the province of Canada. This province had two sections, Canada East and Canada West (formerly Lower Canada and Upper Canada, respectively). The act gave Canada West the same representation as the larger Canada East, and it made English the official language. Eventually, the government, which the Act of Union created, was dissolved. The Canadian provinces won the right to local self-government, and Britain retained the right to manage foreign affairs, defense, and the appointment of provincial governors.

During this time, a two-party system emerged in Canadian politics. Also during this time, industry began to grow in Canada. Trade restrictions and tariffs were eased, and North American trade flourished. Railroads were built across Canada to carry both passengers and cargo. Telegraph lines connected many parts of Canada and North America. Shipbuilding reached an all-time high in British North America. For some parts of Canada, this period was a golden age.

During the 1850s, the possibility of unifying the Canadian provinces was a topic of great debate. In the 1860s, when the Southern states of the United States tried to secede from the United States, talk of Canadian unification intensified. Canada, Nova Scotia, New Brunswick, Prince Edward Island, and Newfoundland met to discuss unification, or Confederation, as it came to be known. The legislative leaders approved the Seventy-two Resolutions, which was a draft of a constitution.

Under the Confederation, the governmental responsibilities would be split between a national government and provincial governments. The Confederation was not a move toward independence, though. Leaders wanted to maintain ties with Britain to prevent aggression from the United States. After ratification of the Seventy-two Resolutions, the Dominion of Canada was created in 1867. The new Canada had four provinces: Quebec, Ontario, New Brunswick, and Nova Scotia. Ottawa was chosen as the national capital. Great Britain did not repeal the Confederation, so in 1871, the last British troops left Canada.

The new nation moved immediately to expand westward. In 1869, Canada added the Northwest Territories, land that Canada purchased from the Hudson Bay Company. In 1871, British Columbia joined Canada, followed by Prince Edward Island two years later. Canada later added the Arctic Archipelago, Newfoundland, and Labrador. Two other important steps taken by the new Canada were the creation of what would eventually become the Royal Canadian Mounted Police and the beginning of the transcontinental railroad.

64. Which of the following was one of the major concerns about the Act of Union?

A. It did not preserve the heritage and culture of Quebec.

B. It gave two areas the same vote even though the populations of the two areas were not the same.

C. It allowed for no more than two parties in the Canadian political system.

D. It united all of Canada under a new government and not under the British monarch.

Upper and Lower Canada received equal representation, but the populations of the two were not equal, thus making the representation unfair. **The correct answer is B.**

65. Which of the following statements **best** defines *confederation*?

A. Confederation meant that Canada would no longer have ties with Britain.

B. Confederation meant that Britain and Canada would become united as one nation under God.

C. Confederation meant that the Canadian provinces would be loosely united but still under the monarch.

D. Confederation meant that some of the Canadian provinces would secede from the British Empire the way the Southern states did in the United States.

Confederation meant that the provinces would be united, but they would remain under the control of the British monarch. **The correct answer is C.**

Industrialization and Immigration

The late 1800s proved to be a time of industrial growth for many parts of Canada. Many cities located along the railroad benefited by having their goods shipped by rail. The main areas of industrial growth were in Montreal and Ontario. The populations in those two cities grew as people flocked to the cities in search of work. Many people made the transition from rural workers to urban wage laborers. This brought with it organized labor in the form of unions. The Atlantic cities, however, suffered during this time because their wooden ships were becoming obsolete, superseded by the new steel ships. The government also implemented tariffs during this time to help boost the Canadian economy. Another economic boost to the Canadian economy was the discovery of gold in the Yukon Territory just before the turn of the century. People rushed by the thousands to the Yukon Territory to seek their fortunes. Further economic boosts came with the development of Canada's natural mineral and hydroelectric resources in central Canada.

As the economy boomed in Canada at the turn of the twentieth century, immigrants flocked to Canada. Many of these immigrants moved to Canada from Britain and the United States. However, for the first time, many immigrants moved to Canada from other European nations, particularly from Eastern Europe. The Canadian government granted many tracts of land in the far west to the immigrants, and the immigrants began to develop the frontier. Many Canadians distrusted the immigrants who did not come from Britain, though. This fear and distrust caused backlash against the immigrants several times in the late 1800s and the early 1900s.

Canada, the British Empire, and Problems in Quebec

In the 1890s, a new prime minister adopted the popular Conservative political view that Canada should stand by the British Empire no matter what, even in matters of imperialism, or expansion into other lands. This policy was popular with most of the Canadians of British descent, but many of the French-speaking Canadians strongly opposed the policy. When Great Britain entered the Boer War in South Africa, many Canadians were ready to fight alongside the British. However, the French-speaking population opposed the popular policy because they were not willing to fight in Britain's wars on other continents. Furthermore, the French-speaking Canadians, most of whom were in Quebec, believed that the rest of Canada did not respect them, which caused a deep rift between Quebec and the other provinces.

The Canadian government felt pressure from both French and British Canadians over the extent to which Canada should help the British Empire. In 1910, Britain expected Canada to contribute to its navy. Instead of contributing, Canada built a small fleet of its own to sail alongside the British navy. Popular opinion turned to outrage again when Canada ratified a treaty with the United States that reduced tariffs and duties, a treaty that US officials saw as a step toward the annexation of Canada. The people of Canada expressed their displeasure, which led to the Conservative Party winning the election of 1911.

In 1914, the British declared war on Germany. This meant that all British holdings, including Canada, were at war, too. Canada responded quickly to Britain's call and sent tens of thousand of Canadians to help with the war effort. The war had a huge impact on Canada. The government imposed Canada's first income tax in 1917. Also, women replaced men in the factories and subsequently earned the right to vote. Another result of the war was the increased tension between Quebec and the rest of Canada. One of the biggest points of contention was the conscription, or draft, that began in 1918. This draft practically split the country because it proved to Quebec that English-speaking Canada would ignore French-speaking Canada in matters of national importance.

After the war, Canadians felt a deeper sense of nationalism than they ever had before, due mostly to the large number of Canadian casualties in the war. Canada began to act as an independent, sovereign nation during treaty negotiations. In 1926, the British government acknowledged Canada's equality with Great Britain. Then, in 1931, Canada was declared a sovereign state; however, it remained under the British monarch.

66. Which of the following was a result of industrialization in Canada?

A. People moved from urban areas to rural areas in search of jobs.

B. People moved from rural areas to urban areas in search of jobs.

C. Railroads were built after Canada completed all of its factories.

D. Millions of people lost their jobs because machines replaced humans at work.

People moved from the country into cities to find work in factories. **The correct answer is B.**

67. Which of the following was a major concern of Quebec during the late eighteenth and early nineteenth centuries?

A. Quebec feared that the United States would annex its territory.

B. Quebec feared that the rest of Canada did not respect its heritage and culture and, therefore, did not respect Quebec in important matters.

C. Quebec feared that French would be outlawed within its own borders.

D. Quebec feared that all its inhabitants would be drafted for World War I.

English-speaking Canada often ignored the needs and wants of French-speaking Quebec. **The correct answer is B.**

The Twentieth Century After World War I

Canada faced many problems after the First World War. Returning soldiers had a difficult time returning to a normal life in Canada. The economy did not boom during the 1920s in Canada as it did in the United States. Industry had difficulty making the transition from wartime production to peacetime production. Unemployment was high, and labor unrest loomed large, especially in the Atlantic regions. To make matters worse, Canada felt the effects of the Great Depression immediately. Many of Canada's trade partners closed their doors to Canadian goods, and foreign investors no longer had money to invest in Canada.

Even though the economic decline slowed in the 1930s, the economy did not fully recover until World War II. Canada was initially hesitant to become involved in the war, but the government felt it had no other choice. As the war progressed, the government put the issue of conscription to a vote by the people. All of Canada, with the exception of Quebec, favored the draft. Canada launched a major war effort, and the economy bounced back and did well during the war years.

After the war, the Canadian government moved more and more toward governmental control of the economic and financial aspects of the country. Government spending increased to compensate for the lack of business investments in Canada. A number of major social programs, including medical insurance and health care, were launched in the 20 years after the war. The economy boomed because Canada suddenly found itself with a seemingly endless number of markets for Canadian goods in Europe. Both industry and the population increased greatly after the soldiers returned from the war.

Also after the war, Canada joined the North Atlantic Treaty Organization (NATO) and played a greater role in international politics.

Problems in Quebec refused to go away, even after World War II. Many in Quebec wanted to break away from English-speaking Canada. Quebec wanted self-government and reduced Canadian control over affairs within Quebec. The situation in Quebec came to a head in the early 1970s when terrorism, kidnappings, and mass arrests occurred as a result of the Quebec dispute. Other provinces and indigenous peoples followed the lead of Quebec and demanded more provincial control and less national control over provincial affairs.

In 1982, Canada cut its final formal legislative ties with Britain by earning the right to amend its constitution. In 1987, the subject of Quebec came up again. Quebec asked for special legislation that would protect its special culture and heritage. The accord, however, did not survive. Again in 1992, Canada had an opportunity to recognize Quebec as a "distinct society," yet, that, too, failed to succeed. Throughout the 1990s, Quebec talked of secession, but the highest court in the land declared secession unconstitutional.

Indigenous peoples did reap one reward in the late 1990s as a new province, Nunavut, was added. Nunavut is largely populated by indigenous peoples, and Inuit is one of its official languages. In addition, Canada established a Healing Fund to help apologize to the indigenous peoples for the many years of injustice. Even today, the subjects of indigenous peoples' rights and an independent Quebec are at the forefront of Canadian issues.

68. Which of the following can be said of Canada after World War I?

A. Canada strengthened its ties to Great Britain.

B. Canada moved to cut all ties with Great Britain.

C. Canada cut some of the last ties with Great Britain.

D. Canada had the strongest military in the Western Hemisphere.

Although Canada did cut some ties, it remained under the British monarchy after World War I and remains so even today. **The correct answer is C.**

69. Which of the following is true of Canada immediately after World War II?

A. The Canadian economy declined tremendously because of the Canadian war efforts.

B. The Canadian economy boomed because of an increase in foreign markets for Canadian goods.

C. Canada's role in international politics dwindled until Canada no longer had any input in the international political arena.

D. Canada's population doubled because of Eastern European immigration.

Following World War II, Canada shipped many of its goods to the war-torn countries of Europe. **The correct answer is B.**

SUMMING IT UP

- The GED Social Studies Test is designed to measure critical-thinking skills rather than knowledge.
- Reviewing the following four content areas covered on the test will help you handle the questions with greater ease and confidence:
    1. History
    2. Civics and government
    3. Economics
    4. Geography
- The **history** review focuses mainly on US history, although some of that history is presented in the context of world affairs and relations between the United States and other nations.
- The **civics and government** review focuses on types of modern and historical governments, branches of the US government, the US Federal system, state and local governments, political parties, campaigns, and elections in American politics. For Canadian test takers, an overview of the structure of the Canadian government is provided.
- The **economics** review provides information regarding macroeconomics and microeconomics, as well as coverage of basic economic concepts such as supply and demand; production; government, economic, and monetary policy; labor relations; and consumer economics.
- The **geography** review focuses on the development of classical civilizations as well as environmental and societal development.
- An excerpt from at least one of the following historical documents will be included on the test. Read through parts (if not all) of each of these documents to familiarize yourself with their language and style.
    - Declaration of Independence
    - US Constitution
    - Federalist Papers
    - Landmark Supreme Court cases
- The Canadian history review focuses on the early Canadian colonies, British rule and conflicts with the British, westward expansion, industrialization, immigration, and tensions with French-speaking Canadians.

PRACTICE QUESTIONS

Directions: The following practice questions will cover general social studies concepts. The questions are based on brief passages of text and visual information (graphs, charts, maps, cartoons, and other figures). Some questions are based on both text and visual information. Study the information provided and answer the question(s) that follow it, referring back to the information as needed.

Most questions are in multiple-choice format. Others are meant to prepare you for the technology-enhanced questions that you will find on the test, such as drop-down questions, select-an-area maps, and fill-in-the-blanks.

Question 1 refers to the following information.

Following the Civil War, African Americans saw economic, political, and social changes. With the passage of the Thirteenth Amendment, slavery was outlawed in the United States, but African Americans were by no means treated equally. Jim Crow laws created legal segregation of the races, and Black Codes restricted the political and economic freedom of blacks by forcing African Americans into a low-wage, labor economy.

1. Which of the following is an example of "Jim Crow"?

A. Sharecropping

B. Separate white and black water fountains

C. The Freedmen's Bureau

D. Carpetbagging

Question 2 refers to the following information.

"So, first of all, let me assert my firm belief that the only thing we have to fear is fear itself—nameless, unreasoning, unjustified terror which paralyzes needed efforts to convert retreat into advance. In every dark hour of our national life a leadership of frankness and of vigor has met with that understanding and support of the people themselves which is essential to victory. And I am convinced that you will again give that support to leadership in these critical days.

In such a spirit on my part and on yours we face our common difficulties. They concern, thank God, only material things. Values have shrunken to fantastic levels; taxes have risen; our ability to pay has fallen; government of all kinds is faced by serious curtailment of income; the means of exchange are frozen in the currents of trade; the withered leaves of industrial enterprise lie on every side; farmers find no markets for their produce; and the savings of many years in thousands of families are gone."

—Excerpt from FDR's first inaugural address of March 4, 1933

2. Which of the following **best** summarizes the context for the president's speech?

A. The United States was in the midst of a Great Depression.

B. The United States was in the midst of a Great World War.

C. The United States was in the midst of a religious revival.

D. The United States was in the midst of a political revolution.

Question 3 and 4 refer to the following information.

The Cold War between the United States and the Soviet Union (USSR) was a difference in ideologies following World War II. The countries had fought as Allies against the Axis powers, but following the war engaged in multiple conflicts that expressed their economic and political differences. The United States, a democracy believing in capitalism, opposed the spread of Soviet communism across the Eastern hemisphere. While none of these conflicts were direct, they would offer result in these countries becoming involved in proxy wars that symbolized their competing philosophies.

3. Which of the following would NOT be an example of conflict in the Cold War?
   - **A.** The Korean War
   - **B.** The Space Race
   - **C.** The Cuban Missile Crisis
   - **D.** The Bolshevik Revolution

4. Which of the following **best** summarizes how the availability of markets factored into creating conflict during the Cold War?
   - **A.** Competition between countries intensified when oil was discovered in the Middle East.
   - **B.** Both countries wanted economic partners to protect from falling into another Great Depression.
   - **C.** When the Open Door of trade was closed, both countries fought to find another large trade partner for their products.
   - **D.** The United States held a worldwide monopoly on trade and was being challenged by the Soviet Union.

Question 5 refers to the following information.

"Small islands, not capable of protecting themselves, are the proper objects for kingdoms to take under their care; but there is something absurd, in supposing a continent to be perpetually governed by an island."

—Thomas Paine, *Common Sense*

5. Which of the following was **most likely** the catalyst for the excerpt above?
   - **A.** The intrusion of European powers into Native American lands during the early-16th century.
   - **B.** The attempts of Great Britain to rule the colonies during the mid-18th century.
   - **C.** The failure of the Articles of Confederation during the late 18th century.
   - **D.** The Mexican government refusing to grant Texas annexation during the mid-19th century.

6. Complete the missing information in the chart below.

Branch of Government	Member(s)
Executive	President, Vice President
Legislative	Senate, ______
Judicial	Supreme Court

7. Which of the following **best** defines the type of government under the United States Constitution?
   A. Constitutional monarchy
   B. Oligarchy
   C. Republic
   D. Confederation

8. Which of the following qualifications for a senator is incorrect?
   A. Must be at least 30 years old
   B. Must have been a citizen of the United States for at least nine years
   C. Must be a resident of the state he or she intends to represent
   D. Must serve for less than six terms in office

Question 9 refers to the following information.

AMENDMENT XXII SECTION 1

"No person shall be elected to the office of the President more than twice, and no person who has held the office of President, or acted as President, for more than two years of a term to which some other person was elected President shall be elected to the office of President more than once. But this Article shall not apply to any person holding the office of President when this Article was proposed by Congress, and shall not prevent any person who may be holding the office of President, or acting as President, during the term within which this Article becomes operative from holding the office of President or acting as President during the remainder of such term."

9. For what reason would the Constitution have this provision instituted?
   A. Fear of one person becoming too powerful and ruling like a monarch
   B. Belief that holding more than two terms would favor one state too muchh
   C. To prevent the formation of a one-party system, thus removing democracy from the government
   D. To ensure a vice president becomes president

Question 10 refers to the following information.

Dred Scott was a black slave who lived on free (non-slavery) land with his owner for several years. He tried, unsuccessfully, to sue in state court for his freedom. He then filed suit in federal court. The basis of his claim to establish his freedom was that he had lived on free soil for more than five years in an area of the country where the Missouri Compromise of 1820 forbade slavery.

10. Select the amendment that was used to support the ruling in the *Dred Scott v. Sandford* case.

A. First Amendment

B. Fifth Amendment

C. Tenth Amendment

D. Thirteenth Amendment

Questions 11 and 12 refer to the following information.

Article Two of the United States Constitution requires the President of the United States to nominate Supreme Court Justices and, with Senate confirmation, requires Justices to be appointed: "he shall nominate, and by and with the Advice and Consent of the Senate, shall appoint ... Judges of the supreme Court ... "

11. Based on the information provided in the previous passage, which of the following is true?

A. The president has total power to unanimously appoint anyone to the title of Justice.

B. The Senate may reject the nomination of the president.

C. The selection of Supreme Court Justices is merely a formality.

D. The process of Judicial Review was created by Article Two.

12. The passage serves as evidence for which key element of the United States government as established by the Constitution?

A. Federalism

B. Aristocracy

C. Bicameral legislature

D. Checks and balances

13. Drag each choice into the correct place within the table. (*Note: When taking the GED test online, you will drag and drop your answers into the table. For this paper version, please write them in.*)

	A preliminary election
	Election where voters must declare a party and choose from those candidates
	A list of beliefs, values, or ideas
	Works to persuade legislators in the law-making process

Choices:

- Platform
- Pressure Group
- Primary
- Closed Primary

Question 14 refers to the following information.

The question of "separate but equal" was once again before the court in the *Brown v. Board of Education of Topeka, Kansas,* case. The Court's decision in *Plessy v. Ferguson*, a finding that separate facilities are not unconstitutional as long as they are equal, seemed to hold the answer in this case as well. However, 58 years had passed, and this time, the Court's ruling was quiet different. Significantly, the opinion of the Court was unanimous.

14. Which of the following **best** explains the reason for the ruling in the *Brown v. Board of Education* case?

A. Racism remained in the country, and the ruling resulted in the continuation of legal segregation in schools.

B. The growing civil rights movement in the country brought to light the injustice of the "separate but equal" doctrine established by *Plessy v. Ferguson.*

C. The previous case was thrown out on account of a technicality.

D. Private and public schools had long been deemed unequal and the Court addressed this issue.

15. Which of the following is NOT a way in which the United States and Canadian governments are alike?

A. They both divide powers between three branches of government.

B. They both have a bicameral legislature.

C. They both have an executive branch governed as a constitutional monarchy.

D. They both have a Supreme Court.

Question 16 refers to the following information.

The United States president serves three major roles during his time in office: the president is responsible for making sure that all the laws of the land are carried out properly, for appointing ambassadors while also meeting foreign dignitaries, and responsible for making treaties.

16. Select the third major role of the president, which is absent from the description above.

A. Chief Executive

B. Chief Diplomat

C. Commander in Chief

D. Chief of Staff

17. The Department of State, Department of the Treasury, Department of Defense, Department of Justice, and Department of Education would be considered members of the President's ________.

Question 18 refers to the following graph.

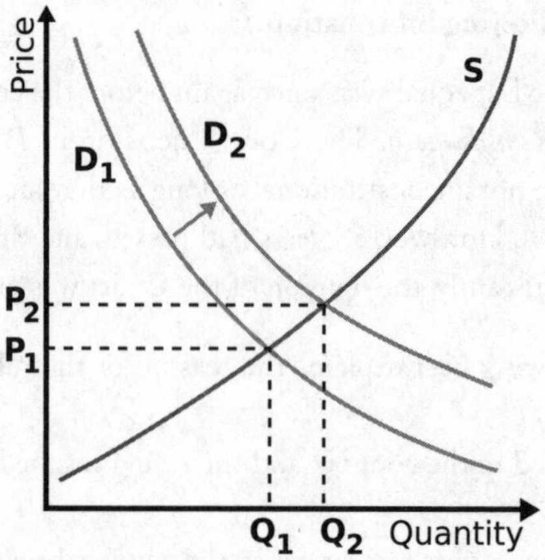

By SilverStar at English Wikipedia, CC BY 2.5, https://commons.wikimedia.org/w/index.php?curid=7159492

18. Select the point on the graph that would be considered equilibrium.

A. D_1

B. D_2

C. S

D. Q_1-P_1

19. Which of the following would NOT be considered a factor of production?

A. Supply and demand

B. Natural resources

C. Capital

D. Labor

20. As labor usage increases, total output increases. But if labor usage is increased by the same amount again, output goes up by less, implying [ ] to the use of labor as an input.

Question 21 refers to the following information.

"...by protecting the exercise by workers of full freedom of association, self-organization, and designation of representatives of their own choosing, for the purpose of negotiating the terms and conditions of their employment or other mutual aid or protection."

—Excerpt from the Wagner Act of 1935

21. Which of the following is correct about the excerpt above?

A. It was ruled unconstitutional as part of FDR's court packing agenda.

B. Unions were allowed to organize and negotiate with management in what is known as *collective bargaining*.

C. Strikes were made obsolete as workers now enjoyed greater freedoms and protections under federal law.

D. Unemployment declined greatly as a result of the new hiring practices created by the act.

Question 22 refers to the following information.

Human migration is the movement of people from one place to another, often as a result of environmental issues. Most often the issues result in detrimental effects on food production, even leading to shortages. Climate change can also be a factor in forcing the migration of humans from place to place.

22. Which of the following is considered an example of climate change that results in human migration?

A. Unemployment rate

B. Global warming

C. Food shortage

D. Hurricane

23. Which of the following would be considered a key Roman contribution to later civilizations?
   A. Their establishment of a Republic
   B. Their establishment of the Olympic games
   C. Their discovery of the mathematical concept of zero
   D. Their achievement of building the pyramids

Question 24 refers to the following information.

Field of Geography	Subfields or Explanation
Physical	Cartography, oceanography
Cultural	The effect of human social and cultural life on geography
Economic	Business and industry's effect on the geographical environment
Political	Geography's influence on the political units of nations, cities, and states
Military	Geography's effects on military operations
Climatology	Weather patterns

24. Which of the following fields is incorrectly placed in the chart above?
   A. Cultural
   B. Political
   C. Military
   D. Climatology

25. Select the **best** example of what would be considered political geography.
   A. An examination of the three branches of government and their separation of powers
   B. A map placing individual tribes and their rulers in different areas and their proximity to one another
   C. A timeline of different kings of the early civilizations and their length of rule
   D. An examination of the man-made changes to government throughout time

ANSWER KEY AND EXPLANATIONS

1. B	6. House of Representatives	11. B	16. C	21. B
2. A	7. C	12. D	17. cabinet	22. B
3. D	8. D	13. See explanation	18. D	23. A
4. B	9. A	14. B	19. A	24. D
5. B	10. B	15. C	20. diminishing returns	25. B

1. **The correct answer is B.** The laws that legitimized segregation, or separating the races between white and black facilities, were known as Jim Crow. An example of this practice was separate white and black water fountains. Sharecropping (choice A) is an example closer to Black Codes. The Freedmen's Bureau (choice C) was an organization that was created to help African Americans combat discrimination. Carpetbaggers (choice D) were politicians seeking election (usually traveling from the North to the South) in a district that was not their home.

2. **The correct answer is A.** FDR became President during the Great Depression and attempted to address the people regarding the economic turmoil they faced. America would not enter into war (choice B) until later in FDR's term. Religion (choice C) was not an overwhelming issue at the time. While political parties did change with the election of FDR, choice D is incorrect because the government saw a change in philosophy but not a total removal and overhaul.

3. **The correct answer is D.** The Bolshevik Revolution took place in 1917 and was not a source of conflict between the United States and the Soviet Union during the Cold War period. Choices A, B, and C are all examples of conflict during the Cold War between the United States and the USSR.

4. **The correct answer is B.** The desire to obtain foreign markets for trade following a worldwide depression was a major source of conflict between the capitalist United States and communist Soviet Union. Oil in the Middle East (choice A) was not a source of large conflict between the countries during the Cold War period. Choice C is incorrect because Russia had refused the Open Door much earlier than the Cold War and trade became a separate issue between the United States and China. While the United States was a large benefactor of trade, it did not hold a monopoly (choice D).

5. **The correct answer is B.** Paine wrote that it was "common sense" for the colonies to declare independence from the island of Great Britain following its repeated attempts to unfairly tax the colonists. Choices A, C, and D are incorrect because they are not the context in which Paine was writing about.

6. **The correct answer is House of Representatives.** The Legislative branch consists of 100 senators and 435 members of the House of Representatives, known collectively as "Congress."

7. **The correct answer is C.** The United States Constitution created a republic, or indirect democracy. Choice A is not the best answer because the United States does not have a monarch. Choice B is incorrect because the United States is ruled by the people electing its representatives, not by a small group of people that rule like a dictator. Choice D is not the best answer because a confederation was replaced by the Constitution.

8. **The correct answer is D.** Senators, like members of the House of Representatives, currently have no term limits in the United States. Choices A, B, and C are all proper qualifications for US Senators.

9. **The correct answer is A.** The fear of an executive tyranny consumed the country following World War II, and politicians mandated Washington's tradition of two terms. State favoritism (choice B) was not a concern, and there had been cases of consecutive presidents coming from the same state previously. Concern about the rise of a one-party government system (choice C) was not the reason this amendment was instituted; it was concern about giving the president too much power. Term limits would not ensure that the current vice president would become president (choice D); unless the vice president takes office by succession, election into the office is the only way to become president.

10. **The correct answer is B.** The Fifth Amendment was cited in forbidding Congress from depriving people of their property (slaves) without due process. Choice A is incorrect because Freedom of Speech and Religion (the First Amendment) was not cited in the case. Choice C is incorrect because Powers Reserved to the State and the People (the Tenth Amendment) was not cited. Choice D is incorrect because the prohibition of slavery (the Thirteenth Amendment) had not occurred yet and would not be applicable.

11. **The correct answer is B.** The Senate must confirm, or consent, to the selection of a Justice, meaning that they also have the power to reject the selection. Choice A is incorrect because the president must receive support and approval from the Senate. Choice C is incorrect because the Senate reserves the right to reject or question the selection. Choice D is incorrect because judicial review was established in the 1803 *Marbury v. Madison* case.

12. **The correct answer is D.** The separation of powers by the president's ability to "check" the judicial branch by appointing its judges is an important part of the government created by the Constitution. Federalism (choice A) is the division of power between multiple levels of government, such as between federal and state. An aristocracy (choice B) gives power to those presumed best suited to rule, such as the elite. A two-house legislature (choice C) is part of the Congress and was established as part of another article in the Constitution.

13. **Correct answer:**

Primary	A preliminary election
Closed Primary	Election where voters must declare a party and choose from those candidates
Platform	A list of beliefs, values, or ideas
Pressure Group	Works to persuade legislators in the lawmaking process

14. **The correct answer is B.** The Civil Rights Movement of the 1950s was bolstered by the ruling that initiated integration in public schools and, by extension, addressed segregation in public facilities. Choice A is incorrect because legal segregation in schools was deemed unconstitutional. Choice C is incorrect because the original case was not thrown out; *Brown v. Board of Education* overturned it. Choice D is inaccurate and was not the focus of the ruling.

15. **The correct answer is C.** The United States is not a constitutional monarchy; it is a republic. Its executive branch has a president, not a monarch as does Canada. Choices A, B, and D are examples in which the United States and Canadian governments are, in fact, alike.

16. **The correct answer is C.** The president is considered Commander in Chief of the military and is responsible for deploying troops to foreign lands or activating troops in the United States. As Chief Executive (choice A), the president makes sure all the laws of the land are carried out properly, while as Chief Diplomat (choice B), the president appoints ambassadors, meets with foreign dignitaries, and makes treaties. The Chief of Staff (choice D) works with the president to run day-to-day operations.

17. **The correct answer is cabinet.** The president chooses his own advisors that are the heads of executive departments.

18. **The correct answer is D.** Equilibrium is the point at which two curves intersect, making P_1-Q_1 and P_2-Q_2 points of equilibrium. D_1 (choice A) and D_2 (choice B) are demand curves, while S (choice C) is a supply curve.

19. **The correct answer is A.** Supply and demand is a primary principle of economics that is a result, not a factor, of production. Natural resources (choice B), capital (choice C), and labor (choice D) are factors of production.

20. **The correct answer is diminishing returns.** The law of diminishing returns states that at a certain point, any additional resources (raw materials, capital, or labor) fail to produce additional product with a value that is proportionate with the cost of the additional resources.

21. **The correct answer is B.** Collective bargaining was protected as part of the National Labor Relations (Wagner) Act and became a strong negotiating tool for workers and unions. Choice A is incorrect because the act was not deemed unconstitutional. Choice C is incorrect because strikes were (and are) still utilized by unions as a negotiating tool. Choice D is incorrect because unemployment rates and hiring practices were not part of the bill.

22. **The correct answer is B.** The change in weather patterns that result in rising temperatures would be considered a climate-related reason for migration. Unemployment (choice A) and food shortages (choice C) are reasons that humans migrate from one place to another but are not related to climate, and while the intensity and severity of a hurricane (choice D) may be affected by changes in climate, the hurricane itself is not an example of climate change.

23. **The correct answer is A.** The Roman Republic, while not completely modeled again, created important precedents for how future governments would be successfully run. Choice B is incorrect because the Greeks established the games. Choice C is incorrect because India discovered the concept of zero. Choice D is incorrect because the Maya of Latin and South America built the pyramids.

24. The correct answer is D. The study of weather patterns, climatology, is classified as a subfield of physical geography. Choices A, B, and C are all examples of separate fields of geography.

25. The correct answer is B. A location and its impact on creation of rulers within numerous tribes would be considered an example of political geography. Choices A, C, and D are incorrect because they simply examine government or ruling leaders without analyzing the impact of geography.

PART V

THE SCIENCE TEST

Mastering the Science Test

Chapter 9

OVERVIEW

- All About the Science Test
- What's Tested—and What's *Not* Tested
- Formats Used for GED® Science Test Questions
- Subject Areas for GED® Science Test Questions
- Question Types Based on the Three Skill Areas
- Understanding Science Concepts Questions
- Using Numbers and Graphics in Science Questions
- General Test-Taking Strategies
- Summing It Up

THE SCIENCE TEST—IN A NUTSHELL

Total time allowed: 90 minutes

Total number of questions: 30–35 questions

Format: Each question is based on a text passage and/or graphic. Question types include multiple-choice and technology-enhanced items.

Length of text passages: Up to 250 words (but most are 2 to 4 sentences)

Number of questions per passage or graphic: 1 to 4 (1 or 2 is most common)

ALL ABOUT THE SCIENCE TEST

The broad academic field of science includes a wide variety of subjects, all involving the **natural sciences** (as opposed to the social sciences, which are covered on the Social Studies Test). These subjects include life science (biology), Earth science (geology and oceanography), space science (astronomy), and physical science (chemistry and physics). The GED Science Test is designed to measure a variety of abilities within the context of all of these subject areas. The test consists of a range of 30–35 questions. Here's an approximate breakdown in terms of the subject areas that the test covers (percentages and numbers may vary slightly):

40%	Life science (biology)
20%	Earth and space science
40%	Physical science (chemistry and physics)

The test questions are *not* grouped by content area. Instead, questions from all areas listed previously are mixed together.

WHAT'S TESTED—AND WHAT'S *NOT* TESTED

The most important point to keep in mind about the GED Science Test is that it is *not* primarily a knowledge test. Regardless of content area—life science, Earth and space science, or physical science—all but the most basic information you'll need to answer a question will be provided. That said, the test assumes, or presupposes, a certain level of common knowledge about the physical world around us. For example:

- All animals require food, which they convert to energy, in order to grow and survive.
- Gravity works to keep us grounded, and the earth has an atmosphere of air, which becomes thinner with altitude.
- The moon revolves around the earth, which revolves around the sun in 365 days.
- Water freezes (or melts) and vaporizes (boils) at different temperatures.
- Pushing an object up a steep incline requires more total force than pushing it across flat ground.

But beyond these sorts of everyday facts, which most people know from observation and experience, no specific knowledge of science is required to perform well on the test. (In this respect, the GED Science Test is a lot like the GED Social Studies and Reasoning Through Language Arts tests.) Rather than demonstrating subject knowledge, your primary task during the Science Test will be to apply the following scientific reasoning skills:

- Reading for meaning in science
- Understanding science concepts
- Using numbers and graphics in science

Approximately 30% of the questions on the test involve reading for meaning in science, 40% involve understanding science concepts, and the remaining 30% involve using numbers and graphics in science. Though the Science Test is designed to measure skills rather than knowledge, keep in mind that with some prior knowledge of the subject areas covered on the test, you can expect to handle the questions with greater ease and confidence.

FORMATS USED FOR GED® SCIENCE TEST QUESTIONS

The GED Science Test consists of multiple-choice questions (presented with four answer choices) and the following technology-enhanced question formats:

- **Select-an-area:** Click on a value on a graph or number scale to indicate a numerical answer to a question, or click on an area of a diagram to indicate the correct answer to a question.
- **Drag-and-drop:** Use the mouse pointer to move objects, words, or numbers across the screen to positions that answer the question.
- **Fill-in-the-blank:** Type words or numbers in one or more blank spaces to correctly complete a statement.

- **Drop-down:** Use a drop-down menu embedded in the text to select the choice needed to correctly complete a statement.

Most of the questions you will encounter on this test are based on brief passages of text, which will vary in length from a few sentences to as many as 250 words (about one-third of a page). A question involving a passage of text might refer to it either as a "passage" or as "information" or "text." You will also encounter questions that will be based on graphs, charts, tables, diagrams, illustrations, and other graphics. Some graphics will be accompanied by a brief passage of text. Finally, some of the questions will be presented in groups of two to four (two is most common); all questions in a group are based on the same passage and/or graphic.

SUBJECT AREAS FOR GED® SCIENCE TEST QUESTIONS

As outlined earlier, the subject areas you'll encounter on the Science Test include life science (biology), Earth and space science, and physical science (chemistry and physics). Here we provide a brief overview.

Don't be intimidated by the scope of any one of these subject areas, or by the technical terminology and complex concepts they often involve. Rest assured: The GED covers only the most basic concepts taught in basic high school science classes. And, as noted earlier, all technical definitions and other information you'll need to answer the questions will be provided. Remember: the GED Science Test is not a trivia or science knowledge quiz; rather, its main purpose is to measure your reading, critical-thinking, and reasoning skills within the context of science subject matter.

Life Science (Biology)

Biology can be defined as the scientific study of living organisms, including plants and animals. Biology is a broad and deep field, which is why a greater portion of GED science questions involves biology than any of the other fields. One way to break down this vast field of study is into its three major branches:

1. **Zoology:** the scientific study of animals, including their structural characteristics, physiology (vital functions for growth, sustenance, and development), reproduction, and pathology (diseases)
2. **Botany:** the scientific study of plants, including their structural characteristics, physiology (vital functions for growth, sustenance, and development), reproduction, and pathology (diseases)
3. **Ecology:** the scientific study of how plants and animals interact with their environment

Another way to break down the field of biology is by scale:

- **Cellular biology** involves the cell as the basic structural unit of living matter.
- **Molecular biology** involves the structure and actions of proteins and nucleic enzymes as well as heredity and how organisms process the energy needed to sustain life.
- **Organism biology** explores the individual forms of life (for example, an oak tree or a human being).

- **Population biology** studies the organism as a member of a community and as part of an environment, or ecosystem.

Biology questions account for approximately 40 percent of the Science Test—about 12 to 14 questions. Among these questions, there is no set number from each branch listed above, although you can expect a fairly even distribution.

Earth and Space Science

Earth science is the study of origins, composition, and physical features of the earth. Like life science (biology), Earth science can be broken down into various branches:

- **Geology:** the scientific study of the earth's rocks, minerals, land forms, and the processes that have directed them since the earth's origins
- **Oceanography:** the scientific study of the oceans' physical characteristics and composition, the movement of their waters, and the topography of ocean floors; oceanography also includes the study of ocean life (in this respect, oceanography and biology overlap)
- **Meteorology:** the scientific study of the earth's atmosphere and of atmospheric conditions (weather and climate)
- **Mineralogy:** a branch of geology that involves the study of minerals—their composition and properties, as well as where they are found and their extraction

Space science refers to the following two related fields:

1. **Astronomy:** the scientific study of the universe and of the size, composition, motion, and evolution of celestial bodies (stars, planets, galaxies, and nebula)
2. **Astrophysics:** a branch of astronomy that deals with the physical and chemical processes that occur in the universe and in interstellar space, including the structure, evolution, and interactions of stars and systems of stars

On the GED, questions about Earth and space science account for about 20 percent of the test (6 or 7 questions). Expect to encounter more questions dealing with Earth science than with space science, although there is no fixed proportion.

Physical Science (Chemistry and Physics)

Physical Science includes the fields of chemistry and physics. **Chemistry** is the scientific study of the composition, properties, and interactions (or reactions) of elements and compounds (combinations of elements), and of the changes that elements and compounds undergo.

Physics is the scientific study of matter, energy, space, and time—and how they are interrelated. Physics is closely related to all other fields of science, since its laws are universal. The living systems of biology are made of matter particles that follow the laws of physics. Chemistry explores how atoms, small units of matter, interact to form molecules according to the laws of physics. And, to a great extent, the study of geology and astronomy deals with the physics of the earth and celestial bodies, respectively.

Chemistry and physics questions account for about 40 percent of the test (12 to 14 questions). Expect about the same number of questions from each of these two fields.

QUESTION TYPES BASED ON THE THREE SKILL AREAS

To succeed on the GED Science Test, you will need to demonstrate proficiency in three scientific reasoning skills: reading for meaning in science, understanding science concepts, and using numbers and graphs in science. You will use all three skills throughout the test. In the next few pages, you'll examine each skill more closely. Note that the GED-style example questions in the next two sections are all based on passages of text, rather than on graphics. Later in the chapter, you'll learn how to handle questions involving graphics.

Reading for Meaning in Science

Reading for meaning in science questions require that you read and recall information contained in a passage. The material to be comprehended may include science text, data, illustrations, or symbols. In most cases, they also require that you *understand* and *interpret* that information—in other words, grasp or comprehend—the ideas and concepts that the passage's words convey. Some reading for meaning questions will require you to understand the main idea of a passage, much like a main-idea question in the reading comprehension portion of the Reasoning Through Language Arts Test. To handle this sort of question, look for an answer choice that sums up the passage. However, most reading for meaning questions on the Science Test focus instead on the passage's details.

Reading for meaning in science questions usually involve passages of text that are longer than average—at least four or five sentences, and sometimes more than one paragraph. You may discover that you need to read the passage more than once to answer these questions. That's perfectly okay, since the total time allowed for taking the test, 90 minutes, should provide enough time for you to read the passages more than once.

Though the correct answer choice might restate a phrase from the passage word-for-word, more likely it will either paraphrase or provide an interpretation of passage information. In other words, reading for meaning questions typically focus on a passage's *ideas* rather than on exactly how those ideas are expressed. Incorrect answer choices will often contradict passage information or provide assertions that are unsupported by the passage or that do not respond to the specific question that is asked.

Don't make reading for meaning questions more difficult than the test makers intend them to be. These questions are not meant to trick you, to test your ability to find underlying, "hidden" meanings within the language of the text, or to find out which test takers already possess in-depth knowledge of the complexities of the science topic at hand. To understand how reading for meaning questions require merely that you understand and interpret what you've read in a passage, study the following two example questions. Both questions are based on a brief passage involving physics.

Questions 1 and 2 refer to the following information.

Light travels in waves consisting of vibrating electric and magnetic fields. Stronger vibrations cause an increase in brightness. The frequencies of the waves can also be different. Blue light, for example, has a higher frequency than red light, and the distance between its vibrations, or its wavelength, is shorter than the wavelength of red light. Black is the absence of light, and white light is the mixture of all colors. When white light passes through a prism, it is split into a band of colors called the spectrum.

1. Which statement is **best** supported by the information provided?

A. Short waves have a stronger magnetic field than longer waves do.

B. Light waves vibrate more strongly and at a higher frequency than sound waves do.

C. White light, which lacks any color, has no measurable wavelength or wave frequency.

D. Short waves have higher frequencies than longer waves do.

This question focuses on the idea that frequencies among different colors of light waves vary. To illustrate this idea, the passage points out that a blue light wave has a higher frequency and a shorter length than a red wave does. Choice D provides a more general way of making this point. In other words, it captures the idea conveyed in the third and fourth sentences.

Let's briefly examine the other three answer choices. The passage makes no connection between magnetism and wave frequency (choice A), and it never mentions sound waves (choice B). Choice C contradicts the passage, which tells us that white light is a mixture of all colors—not that it lacks color. Besides, the passage does not state, nor does it suggest, that the frequency or length of a white light wave cannot be measured. **The correct answer is D.**

2. Which of the following explains why a rainbow occurs when drops of water act as a prism?

A. A rainbow is made up of white light.

B. There are a number of frequencies involved.

C. White light from the sun is dispersed through the drops.

D. The electric and magnetic fields have strong vibrations.

Answering this question requires that you read and understand the last sentence of the passage. Don't let the fact that the question involves a rainbow, which is not mentioned in the passage, confuse you. The question simply requires that you interpret a rainbow as one way to see the color spectrum—the band of colors mentioned in the paragraph's last sentence. The drops of water act as a prism when the white light from the sun is dispersed through the water; the drops split the light into bands of color. Of course, to answer this question you need to know what a rainbow looks like. But this is just the sort of common, everyday knowledge that the GED Science Test presumes you have. Choice C appears to provide a good explanation.

Let's examine the three other answer choices. Choice A is incorrect because we all know that a rainbow shows many colors. Choice B provides an accurate statement in that different color bands of the spectrum have different frequencies, but it does not explain why this occurs—in other words, it does not respond to the question. Choice D is incorrect because the passage makes no connection between a magnetic field (mentioned only in the first sentence) and a prism. **The correct answer is C.**

The preceding two questions demonstrate the sort of incorrect answer choices to look for in reading for meaning questions. Be on the lookout for any answer choice that contradicts the passage information, goes off the passage's topic, or provides true information that nevertheless does not answer the specific question asked.

UNDERSTANDING SCIENCE CONCEPTS QUESTIONS

Almost half of the questions on the GED Science Test (40%) are understanding science concepts questions. These questions go beyond simple reading for meaning and can ask you to analyze, synthesize and evaluate, or apply the scientific information and concepts presented in a passage. There are many possible tasks that are encompassed by this type of question, such as drawing conclusions, identifying experimental errors, or using information in a different way than it's presented. Let's learn more about each of these types of questions.

Analysis Questions

Analysis questions go beyond understanding the information in a passage or visual. Analysis involves organizing the information; explaining how ideas, facts, or data connect together; identifying patterns; and drawing inferences and conclusions from the information given. Many analysis questions will require you to *infer* cause or effect in terms of a biological, chemical, or physical process. (To infer is to draw a reasonable conclusion based on certain information.) Other analysis questions will require you to point out similarities and differences between two or more types of organisms, processes, or other scientific phenomena. You might also be asked to identify sources of error in an investigation or cite evidence to support a scientific claim. These are just some of many possibilities for analysis questions. The next question is based on a passage involving botany (the scientific study of plants). To analyze the question, you need to first understand different facts and then connect those facts together in order to draw a logical conclusion from them.

Question 3 refers to the following information.

All of the earth's energy is produced through photosynthesis, which is the process by which green plants, algae, and some bacteria take light from the sun and convert it to chemical energy. Only organisms that contain chlorophyll can undergo photosynthesis. Chlorophyll is the pigment that makes plants green. The process of photosynthesis usually occurs in the leaves of plants.

3. What can you conclude from the information provided?

A. If a plant does not have leaves, it cannot produce energy.

B. If a plant is not green, it cannot produce energy.

C. On cloudy days, photosynthesis does not occur.

D. Photosynthesis does not occur in the winter.

NOTE

You may be aware that there are plants that are not green that are photosynthetic and thus produce energy, but you must answer GED test questions based only on the information given in their related passage.

The paragraph does not answer this question explicitly. To answer the question, you must draw an inference, or conclusion, from the information provided. According to the paragraph, only organisms with chlorophyll can undergo photosynthesis—the process by which plants produce energy—and it is chlorophyll that gives plants their green color. Thus, you can conclude that only green plants produce energy. Stated differently, this process cannot occur in anything other than a green plant (choice B).

Compared to choice B, the other answer choices provide unreasonable, poorly supported conclusions based on the information provided. Choice A goes too far, by assuming that chlorophyll exists only in the *leaves* of plants. But the paragraph does not say this is so, and our everyday observations suggest otherwise. For example, most of us have observed the green color in cacti, which do not have leaves. In order for choice C or choice D to be correct, you must assume that absolutely no light is available for photosynthesis on cloudy days (choice C) or during the winter (choice D). These are not reasonable assumptions, as they violate common sense as well as our everyday experience. **The correct answer is B.**

The next two questions ask you to analyze experiments that may or may not contain errors in design. When reading a given experiment on the exam, be mindful of its setup and whether the experimenter is making a mistake. Even if an experiment is technically correct, there are often times when it could be made stronger by tweaking certain elements.

Questions 4 and 5 are based on the following information.

Hannah's lab group believes that a particular gene in the worm *C. elegans* produces a protein in response to anoxia, the absence of oxygen. The protein produces chemical X, which produces a strong UV-Vis signal at an uncommon wavelength of 460 nm. Hannah's group decides to incubate *C. elegans* tissue in the presence (normal atmospheric level) and absence of oxygen, then lyse (burst) the cells and measure the UV-Vis signal at 460 nm of the resulting solution in order to determine how strongly the gene is expressed. Two trials were conducted in the presence of oxygen and in the absence of oxygen. The results are shown below:

	UV-Vis Signal (460 nm) in the Absence of Oxygen	UV-Vis Signal (460 nm) in the Presence of Oxygen
Trial 1	0.30	0.29
Trial 2	0.34	0.75
Average	0.32	0.52
Standard Deviation	0.0283	0.325

4. Which of the following represents a strength of the experiment?
   - **A.** The amount of protein was directly measured, increasing reliability.
   - **B.** Cells from a variety of different organisms were used, increasing sample diversity.
   - **C.** The measured wavelength was unique to the measured chemical, increasing specificity.
   - **D.** Excess materials were removed from the solution after bursting the cells, reducing background signal.

This example asks you to read an experiment and analyze its strengths. Let's look at the answer choices. Choice A could represent a strength of an experiment, but it is not true of this particular experiment. The protein is not directly measured; rather, the amount of chemical X, produced by the protein, is what is measured. Choice B is incorrect because the procedure indicates that all tissue samples were taken from the same organism, *C. elegans*. Choice D is a little more complex, but it refers to a step that was not taken according to the procedure, so it is not correct. The procedure indicates that the signal was measured at 460 nm because it is an uncommon signal specific to chemical X. **The correct answer is C.**

5. Hannah noticed that the standard deviation for the data in the presence of oxygen was much higher than that in the absence of oxygen. Which of the following changes would resolve this issue?
   - **A.** Repeat the experiment using the same gene in human tissues.
   - **B.** Change the UV-Vis wavelength that is measured.
   - **C.** Repeat the experiment in the presence of a higher concentration of oxygen.
   - **D.** Increase the number of trials for each condition.

This example asks you to select an improvement to the experiment based on information provided. Choice A describes an entirely different experiment rather than an improvement to the current one. Choice B is incorrect because this change would no longer measure chemical X, the foundation of the experiment. Choice C may improve the experiment by providing additional information, but it would not resolve the specific issue described in the question. In the two trials in the presence of oxygen, the two obtained numbers are completely different, so additional trials could confirm which value (higher or lower) is correct. This would, in turn, improve the standard deviation by supplying more numbers and potentially allowing for the elimination of an outlier. **The correct answer is D.**

The next question is based on a passage involving astronomy. To analyze the question, you first need to understand and organize various facts about two different things. Then you need to analyze the differences between those two things.

Question 6 is based on the following information.

Like Earth, Mercury—the smallest planet—revolves around the sun. It takes Mercury nearly 88 days to make one revolution around the sun. Earth takes 365 days to complete one revolution around the sun. Earth completes one revolution on its own axis in 24 hours, or one day. Mercury, on the other hand, takes 58.5 Earth days to slowly make one turn on its axis.

6. Based on the information, which is an accurate distinction between Mercury and Earth?

A. Any spot on Mercury's equator is sunlit longer than any spot on Earth's equator.

B. Earth passes Mercury as they both revolve around the sun.

C. Mercury's orbit around the sun is circular, whereas Earth's orbit is elliptical.

D. Mercury orbits the sun at a slower speed than Earth does.

Any spot on the surface of Mercury's equator is exposed to the sun for longer periods of time because it takes Mercury 58.5 Earth days to make one turn on its axis. (A spot on Mercury's equator faces the sun for approximately 29 hours at a time, whereas on Earth the maximum is approximately 12 hours.) So choice A is a good answer.

Let's examine the other three choices. Choice B contradicts the information in the passage. Choice C is completely unsupported by the passage, which tells us nothing about the shape of either orbit. Choice D is more difficult to assess than the others. We know from the paragraph that Mercury orbits the sun in fewer days than Earth does. But does this mean that Mercury is moving at a faster or slower speed than Earth? We don't know, at least not from the information provided. The answer depends not only on the time of one orbit around the sun but also on the distance traveled during one such orbit. The passage does not give enough information to compare the speed of the two planets. **The correct answer is A.**

The preceding questions demonstrate the sort of answer choices to be wary of when handling analysis questions:

- A choice that contradicts the passage information
- A choice that relies on crucial facts that the passage does not provide
- A choice that violates common sense or simple logic
- A choice that is inconsistent with your everyday observations and experiences

Synthesis and Evaluation Questions

Synthesis and evaluation questions involve drawing general assessments and conclusions from specific information. To "synthesize" science information is to understand what various pieces of information mean when you consider them all together, as a whole. In the context of the Science Test, a synthesis question might ask you to characterize a phenomenon, process, or system described in a passage. An evaluation question might ask you to recognize a potential benefit or drawback with a new science technology, or with the way that technology is applied. Or it might ask you to recognize a flaw in a scientific claim or hypothesis, possibly related to a certain experiment, or to assess the features of an experimental design. Other possible synthesis questions might require reasoning from data to evidence, making a prediction based on data, evaluating a theory, or reconciling multiple findings.

In handling these questions, what's just as important as recognizing a reasonable assessment or conclusion is recognizing unfair assessments and conclusions. Be on the lookout for incorrect answer choices that speculate too much—answer choices that jump to conclusions that are unwarranted based solely on the information provided.

Here is a synthesis question based on a passage involving mineralogy, one of the Earth sciences.

Question 7 refers to the following information.

There are three types of rocks on Earth's surface: igneous, metamorphic, and sedimentary. Igneous rocks have been formed by the cooling of molten magma where temperatures are extremely high. Metamorphic rocks have been formed by the compression of older rocks. They are formed below Earth's surface where both the temperature and pressure are high. Sedimentary rocks are formed by weathering or the remains of living organisms. These are formed on Earth's surface under low pressures.

7. Based on the information, which of the following is **most** probably true about the three types of rocks?

The three types of rocks

A. can be found only on Earth.

B. look very much the same.

C. are found in different places.

D. are all approximately the same age.

This question doesn't focus on just one part of the passage. To answer it, you instead need to read and understand all the details, and then synthesize them to form a broader perspective. The passage tells us that some rocks are formed below Earth's surface, that some come from volcanoes, and that some are the result of weathering or the remains of living organisms that have been found in different locations. Because the three types of rocks are all formed differently under different conditions, they cannot all be found in the same location. Choice C is a good answer.

Let's examine the other answer choices. The passage mentions nothing about whether these types of rocks are found on other celestial bodies (choice A), about what the three types look like (choice B), or their relative ages (choice D). **The correct answer is C.**

Next, look at an evaluation question based on a passage involving meteorology, another one of the Earth sciences.

Question 8 refers to the following information.

Water moves through a natural cycle of evaporation, cloud formation, rainfall, collection, and evaporation. In this cycle, water is self-purifying. Thus, smoke from industrial sites that is brought to the earth by rainfall is not a problem because the water purifies itself of the pollutants.

8. Which of the following, if true, would weaken the claim that water purifies itself through the cycle described above?

A. The polluters creating the industrial smoke are unwilling to reduce the amount of their pollution.

B. When the pollutants enter the clouds, much of them stay there.

C. Many of the pollutants evaporate with ground water into the air.

D. Water vapor containing industrial pollutants can travel great distances through the air.

This question asks you to assess, or critique, the assertion made in the brief passage. Your task is to recognize additional evidence that would weaken the conclusion that the smoke is not a problem because the water purifies itself. The passage describes a self-purifying cycle. But if smoke from industrial sites is brought back to the earth by rainfall and then evaporates with the water, it will return to the clouds where it becomes part of the cycle. In this event, the water would not purify itself properly. So choice C provides information that, if true, would weaken the conclusion in the passage.

Let's examine the other answer choices. Choice A is incorrect because the fact the industrial pollution carries on does nothing to disprove the claim that water rids itself of that pollution. The statement in choice B, if true, would actually make the purification cycle easier, since the pollutants would not cycle around with the water. Choice D is incorrect because the distance that the pollutants travel before falling to the earth in rain has nothing to do with the process of evaporation—water can evaporate anywhere. **The correct answer is C.**

Application Questions

Application questions require you to use information in a passage (or visual) in a way that is different from the way it is presented to you. For example, a question might ask about the effect of a particular biological or chemical process or a law of physics under specific conditions. Or, a question might ask you to identify an example or a practical use of a concept, principle, or process. You might also be asked to apply sampling techniques, models, theories, formulas, or statistical analysis to solve a problem or make a prediction. These are just some of the possibilities. Use your understanding of the information in the passage, along with your everyday experience and common sense, to identify the correct answer.

Here are two application questions involving physics.

Question 9 refers to the following information.

A fluid can exert a buoyant force, helping an object to float, but it can also exert a compressing force because of the weight of the fluid above it. The suit of a deep-sea diver resembles a rigid suit of armor that is watertight and can maintain an internal pressure of 1 atmosphere.

9. Why do deep-sea divers wear rigid, watertight suits?

A. They protect a diver from high levels of surrounding external pressure.

B. They make a diver more buoyant in the water.

C. They allow a diver to defy gravity.

D. They protect a diver from drowning by being leakproof.

The information to be taken from the passage and applied is that pressure increases with depth. It is logical that this is dangerous to a diver. The only protection against external pressure would be a rigid, watertight enclosure. Noting the similarity to the design of submarines is helpful. The explanation provided by choice A makes sense.

Let's examine the other three answer choices. The suit might make the diver more buoyant (choice B), which means that it would help the diver to float. But deep-sea divers want to go deep into the water rather than float, and so it makes no sense that a diving suit would be used mainly for buoyancy. You can eliminate choice C for essentially the same reason. Choice D asserts a true fact: the suit is designed to prevent leaks. But this function has nothing to do with external water pressure, which the passage indicates is the reason for the design of this type of suit. **The correct answer is A.**

Question 10 refers to the following information.

Newton's First Law: An object will remain in motion or in a state of rest unless something influences it and changes its course. (This property is referred to as inertia.)

Newton's Second Law: The change of motion is proportional to the force of change. (The greater the applied force, the greater the change in motion.)

Newton's Third Law: For every action (or applied force) there is an equal and opposite reaction.

10. Which is an example of Newton's Second Law?

A. Two shopping carts colliding in a grocery store

B. The whiplash you would experience in a car by suddenly applying the brake

C. A car coming to a stop at a stop sign

D. Allowing air to escape from a balloon

The force applied by the brakes causes a change in the motion of the car, so choice C seems an apt illustration of Newton's Second Law.

Let's examine the other answer choices. Choice A is an example of the first law, while choices B and D are examples of the third law. **The correct answer is C.**

USING NUMBERS AND GRAPHICS IN SCIENCE QUESTIONS

The GED Science Test is more visually oriented than any of the other tests in the GED battery. Nearly half of the questions on the Science Test will be based on a graphic or visual depiction of some sort. Some of these questions will also be accompanied by a brief passage of text. The "graphic" might be a chart, graph, or table displaying quantitative information (data); it might be a flowchart showing a biological or chemical system or process; it might be a diagram or table that organizes information into classes, categories, or characteristics; it might provide a sequence of illustrations showing multiple steps, phases, or stages in a biological, geological, or chemical process, or it may be a drawing, photo, or even a cartoon showing science as it applies to our everyday lives.

Questions based on graphics are designed to gauge your ability to understand what these graphics depict and what they mean, to analyze the information they contain, and to apply them to real-world situations. Even if you do not recognize a graphic or don't understand it initially, you can still figure out the best answer to the question at hand by looking for clues in the graphic, the accompanying text (if any), and the question itself.

On the following pages, you'll examine some of the types of graphics that appear frequently on the test. You'll see some examples of each type and learn how to handle them. At the end of this section you'll learn more about how you'll use numbers and math on the GED Science Test.

Illustrations That Include Arrow Symbols

The arrow symbol is used extensively in the Science Test. Arrows are used in physics questions to show the direction of physical flow or travel, as from a light or sound source, and to show the direction of pressure or other force on an object. Arrows are used in astronomy questions to show direction of travel, rotation, and orbit. Arrows are used in Earth science and biology questions to indicate flow and circulation in oceans, the atmosphere, organ systems, and ecosystems. Arrows are even used in chemistry questions to indicate chemical reactions.

Pay careful attention to any arrows in an illustration, as you can be sure that they will be crucial to answer the question at hand. Note whether an arrow is pointing:

- Upward (against gravity) or downward (pulled by gravity)
- Toward or away from an object (possibly suggesting the direction of a force)
- In a straight line versus a bent line (which might suggest *reflection, deflection,* or *refraction*)
- Through an opening versus a membrane or wall (which might suggest *permeability*)
- In a one-way circular pattern (possibly suggesting *rotation* or a continuous *cycle*)
- In each of two opposite directions (possibly suggesting an *exchange* of energy, gases, liquids, etc.)
- In a single, continuous line versus a line that splits in different directions (which might suggest a *dispersion* pattern for light or sound waves, or the dispersion of atoms or molecules)

Questions 11 and 12 refer to the following illustration and brief passage of text.

The following diagram illustrates three types of levers. All three are dependent on the effort (E), load (L), and fulcrum (F). Any lever in which the load and effort balance each other is said to be in equilibrium.

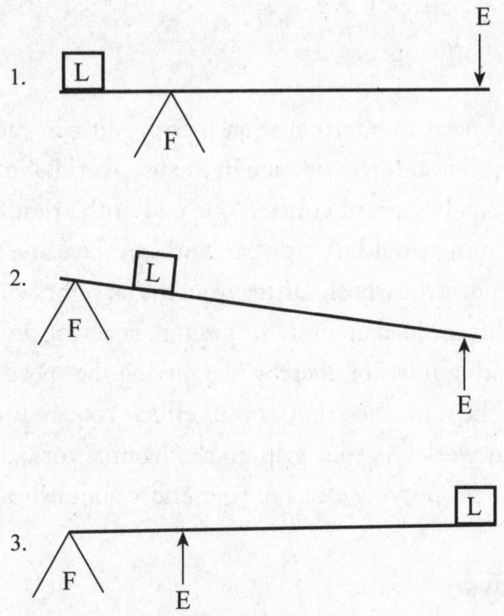

11. Which general principle do all three illustrations help demonstrate?

A. The function of a fulcrum is to balance effort and load.

B. Effort and load are equal physical forces.

C. A load is pulled down toward the earth by effort and gravity.

D. Effort and load are opposing physical forces.

To answer this question, you need to compare the pictures and note their similarities and differences. In all three pictures, the fulcrum provides a fixed point of rotation for the plank and the load. Apply your common sense and everyday experience to visualize what is happening in each picture. Pictures 2 and 3 show the effort pushing *up* to counteract the weight of the load. Picture 1 shows a *downward* effort that serves to push the load *up*, as in a seesaw. So in all three pictures, the effort and load are opposing physical forces. Choice D is a good answer, but let's examine the other three answer choices. Only in Picture 1 does the fulcrum balance the effort and the load, and so choice A is an incorrect general principle. None of the three pictures assumes that the effort and load are equal in force, and so choice B provides an unfair generalization. Choice C is only partially correct. It is true that the gravity works to push the load downward; however, all three pictures show the effort working to lift the load upward. **The correct answer is D.**

12. Which of the following provides one example of each of the three types of levers shown in the three pictures, in the order they are shown?
   A. Pliers, diving board, crane
   B. Hammer, wedge, seesaw
   C. Crowbar, wheelbarrow, baseball bat
   D. Saw, forklift, bottle opener

To answer this question, you need to interpret what is happening in each of the three pictures by applying your sense of how physical forces operate in the real world. Notice that Picture 1 shows a seesaw type of lever: you apply downward effort at one end of the rigid object, and move the load on the other side of the fulcrum upward. A crowbar works in the same way. Picture 2 resembles a wheelbarrow, where the fulcrum is the wheel. Lifting from the far right, where the handles are located, reduces the effort needed to lift the load up from the ground. Focusing on Picture 3, imagine yourself applying effort near the pivoting fulcrum, thereby magnifying the speed with which the other end of the rigid object moves in the same direction as your effort. You are imagining how tools such as a hammer and a baseball bat work. As your grip on the hammer or bat moves farther up toward the load (the nail or ball), the magnifying effect of your effort diminishes. **The correct answer is C.**

Graphical Data Displays

Several questions on the Science Test are based on data presented in graphical format. A question of this type might be based on a table, bar graph, line chart, or circle graph (pie chart). These displays may be used for any of the subject areas covered by the test.

This book's mathematics section explains how to read, interpret, and analyze data presented in each of these formats. Be sure to review those materials when preparing for the GED Science Test. Keep in mind, however, that on the Science Test the emphasis is not on number-crunching but on the following skills:

- Understanding what the graphical display is intended to show
- Reading and interpreting the data
- Understanding the significance of the data
- Drawing general conclusions from the data
- Applying the ideas conveyed by the display to specific scenarios

Though you may need to perform simple arithmetic tasks such as counting or adding, you won't need to calculate precise percentages, ratios, or averages. (These skills are measured on the Mathematical Reasoning Test instead.)

The next two GED-style questions both illustrate that the focus of data-display questions on the Science Test is far more on understanding and interpreting scientific data than on performing math on the data.

Question 13 refers to the following charts.

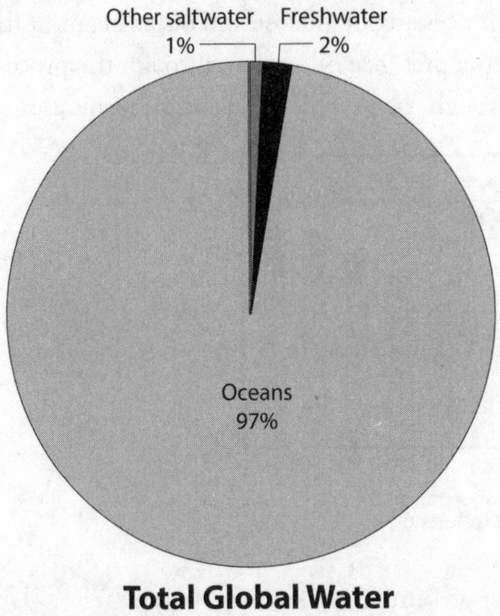

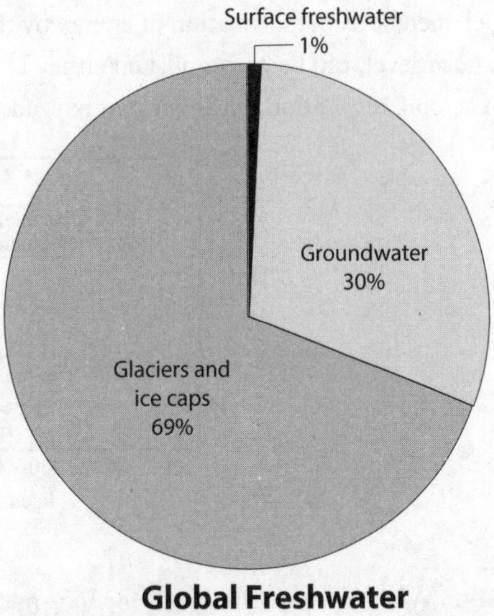

13. The freshwater sources that humans can use are surface freshwater and groundwater. The freshwater sources that humans can use make up what percentage of Earth's total water?

A. 2%

B. 31%

C. 31% of 69%, or 21%

D. 31% of 2%, or 0.62%

According to the chart on the right, surface freshwater makes up 1% of global freshwater, while groundwater makes up 30% of it. Together they make up 31% of global freshwater. However, according to the chart on the left, freshwater makes up only 2% of all of Earth's water. Therefore, the freshwater that humans can use makes up 31% of 2% of all of Earth's water, or (0.31)(2%) = 0.62%. **The correct answer is D.**

Note that the question is more about understanding what each chart shows and how their numbers are related to each other, and not about doing math; the answer choices do the math for you.

Question 14 refers to the following information and chart.

Cell metabolism, the creation of energy by the processing of glucose and other sugars at the cellular level, can be accomplished either 1) in the presence of oxygen, through the process of aerobic respiration, or 2) without oxygen, through the process of anaerobic respiration.

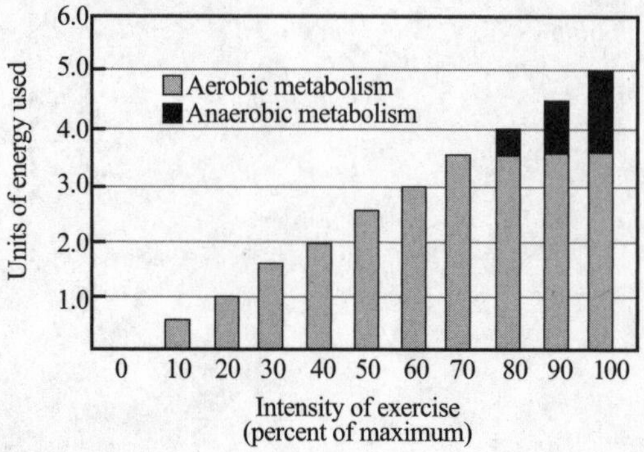

14. What can you infer from the information presented in the previous passage?

A. Intense exercise uses more anaerobically metabolized energy than light exercise.

B. Most of the energy you spend is through some form of exercise.

C. The longer you exercise, the more fuel you metabolize anaerobically.

D. Intense exercise requires less oxygen than moderate exercise.

This question requires application of the information displayed in the graph to everyday physical activity. Only choice A has the possibility of reaching high intensity. Some of the others use a large total amount of energy, but none of them have the possibility of reaching high intensity. **The correct answer is A.**

Illustrations That Show Spatial Relationships

Some questions on the Science Test focus on how the physical world around us (as well as inside us) arranges itself spatially. Showing where different distinct objects or other masses are located in relation to one another is usually best accomplished with a graphic, which might show, for example:

- Locations and distances involving celestial bodies
- Layers of Earth's atmosphere
- Stratification (layering) of rocks, minerals, and sediments that form the earth
- Configurations of chemical compounds, in which molecules link together in specific ways
- Separation of gases, liquids, or solids, either naturally or in a laboratory experiment
- Layers of cells and tissues in a plant or animal

The possibilities listed above are just some of many. The next GED-style question involves the Earth sciences as well as physics. As with most questions based on both textual and graphic information, you'll need both to help you answer the question.

Question 15 refers to the following diagram and information.

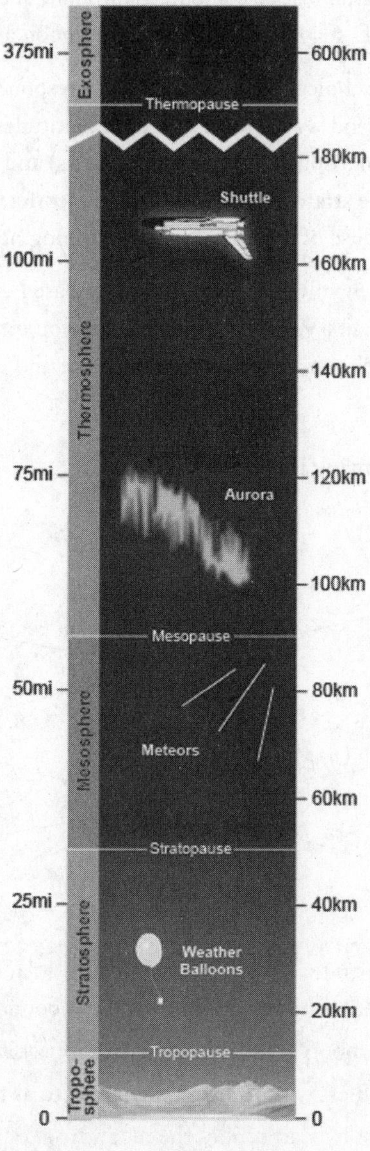

National Oceanic and Atmospheric Administration

Temperature levels fall from ground level to the top of the troposphere, but then they rise with altitude in the stratosphere.

15. Which of the following statements, assuming it is true, would **best** account for the rise in temperature?

A. The troposphere blocks the sun's rays.

B. Earth's surface is warming gradually.

C. Air is thinner at higher altitudes than at lower ones.

D. Gases in the upper stratosphere trap radiant heat from Earth.

One knows from experience that temperature falls with altitude. Pictures of snowcapped mountains in the tropics confirm this. There must be something different about the gases in the stratosphere to reverse this trend, as choice D suggests. So choice D is a good answer.

Let's examine the other answer choices. Choice C does not respond to the question because it does not explain why temperature trend would reverse at upper altitudes. Choice A is incorrect because the troposphere is below the stratosphere (as the figure shows) and hence cannot interfere with the amount of sunlight reaching the stratosphere. Choice B is incorrect because global warming makes sense as a *result* rather than a cause of the atmosphere's trapping heat. **The correct answer is D.**

The next GED-style question involves astronomy and is based solely on graphical information. Don't be concerned that it contains very few words to help you interpret it. Rest assured: all you'll need to answer the question, aside from your common sense and everyday experience, is provided in the picture.

Question 16 refers to the following illustration.

Solar Eclipse

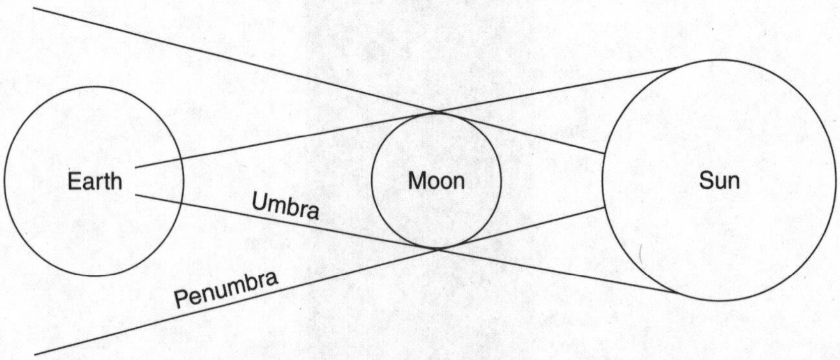

> **16.** Referring to the illustration, what is true during a solar eclipse?
> **A.** The moon appears brightest from within the boundaries of the penumbra.
> **B.** The side of the moon not seen from Earth is cast in darkness.
> **C.** Sunlight is dimmest within the field referred to as the umbra.
> **D.** The shadow cast by Earth hides the moon from our view.

If you are unfamiliar with solar eclipses, use your everyday experience to figure out what is happening in the illustration. You know that when any object is lit from one direction, it casts a shadow in the opposite direction. Use this common knowledge along with the illustration to figure out what happens during a solar eclipse. The moon is positioned between the earth and sun, thereby casting a shadow on the earth. It makes sense that the area at the center of the shadow (identified in the illustration as the umbra) will be darkest, while the shadow around its periphery (the penumbra) will be somewhat lighter. Choice C is a good answer.

Let's examine the other answer choices. Choice A contradicts what the illustration shows: the moon is casting a shadow within the boundaries of the field labeled as the penumbra. Choice B contradicts what the illustration shows: the side of the moon facing away from the earth is bathed in direct sunlight. Choice D is incorrect because the illustration shows the moon's shadow cast on the earth, not the other way around. **The correct answer is C.**

In the preceding example, did you notice that the illustration was accompanied by a title? Remember: some (but not all) illustrations on the Science Test will come with a title or descriptive caption that may help you understand and interpret the illustration.

Math and the GED® Science Test

As noted earlier, though some Science Test questions will involve numbers, you won't be asked to calculate precise ratios, percentages, or averages or to do any number-crunching to speak of. Those skills are measured by the Mathematical Reasoning Test. For example, consider the following table, which involves the eight planets within our solar system:

	Mercury	Venus	Earth	Mars	Jupiter	Saturn	Uranus	Neptune
Years to revolve around sun	0.24	0.62	1	1.88	11.86	29.46	84	164.79
Radius (Earth = 1)	0.38	0.45	1	0.53	11.2	9.42	4.01	3.88

A Mathematical Reasoning Test question based on the data in this table might ask you to calculate a ratio of one radius to another, or it might ask you to calculate a time difference (measured perhaps in Earth days) between one planet's year and another planet's year. But the Science Test would not pose these sorts of questions. Instead, a Science Test question might ask you how many of the planets other than Earth have a greater radius than that of Earth—or a longer year than Earth's year. Or the question might ask you what kinds of conclusions you can, or cannot, draw from the data. (For example, the table provides no information about rotation, distance between planets, or distance from the sun.)

But this does not mean that math plays absolutely no part on the Science Test. For at least a few questions, expect to perform some arithmetic such as counting or adding numbers. For example, a chemistry question might ask for the total mass of a chemical compound, in which case you would add up the atomic masses of the elements that make up the compound, accounting for the number of molecules per element. (Don't worry: the question will provide all the information you need.)

A physics question might ask you to apply the definition of a unit of measurement to a specific situation. Here's a GED-style example involving *hertz*, which is the unit of measurement used for soundwave frequency. As you can see, all the information about sound waves you need to answer the question is provided.

Question 17 refers to the following information.

The frequency of a sound wave is measured in units referred to as the *hertz*. One hertz is equal to one wave per second, and 1 kilohertz is equal to 1,000 hertz. If you tune your radio dial to 89.0, that number would signify the frequency of the radio station, in kilohertz.

17. What is the frequency of radio waves received at 98.6 on the radio dial?

A. 9,800 waves per second

B. 98,600 waves per second

C. 98.6 hertz

D. 98,600 hertz

If the radio dial is tuned to 98.6, this would mean that the waves are traveling at 98,600 waves per second because 1 kilohertz is equal to 1,000 waves per second: 1,000 × 98.6 = 98,600. **The correct answer is B.**

A Science Test question might ask you to apply one of the simple formulas that expresses the basic laws of physics. Here are just some of those formulas:

$v = \frac{d}{t}$	velocity = distance ÷ time
$a = \frac{9.80\text{ m}}{s^2}$	acceleration during freefall = 9.80 m / (number of seconds)^2
$F = m \cdot a$	force = mass × acceleration
$w = F \cdot d$	work = force × displacement
$v = l \cdot f$	velocity = wavelength × frequency
$P = \frac{W}{t}$	Power = work ÷ time

Don't worry: you won't need to memorize any formulas for the test. If a question requires you to apply a formula, it will provide that formula, along with the numbers you need to answer the question.

18. An object of mass m is at rest until a force, F, acts on it for a period of 10 seconds. Which expression shows the average velocity of the object during those 10 seconds?

A. $5F$

B. $10Fm$

C. $\frac{5F}{m}$

D. $\frac{10F}{m}$

$F = ma$, so $a = \frac{F}{m}$. $v = at$, and $t = 10$, so final $v = 10a = \frac{10F}{m}$. Because acceleration is constant, average v = final $\frac{v}{2} = \left(\frac{1}{2}\right)\frac{10F}{m} = \frac{5F}{m}$. **The correct answer is C.**

GENERAL TEST-TAKING STRATEGIES

Here are some general strategies for tackling the Science Test. Put these strategies to work on the practice tests in this book, and then review them again just before exam day.

First read the question(s) based on a passage of text or graphic.

Before you look at a graphic or read even a brief passage, read the question stem (the question itself, but not the answer choices). If the passage or graphic comes with more than one question, read all the question stems first. This task should only take 10 seconds or so. The question(s) may provide clues as to what you should focus on and think about as you read the text or analyze the graphic.

Read a passage of text straight through before answering any questions based on it.

If a question or group of questions refers to a passage of text, read the passage from beginning to end without interruption. Pay careful attention to definitions. If more than one term is defined, pay special attention to any differences between the two concepts, processes, or features defined. Think about whether the information in the passage leads logically to a particular conclusion or inference. If it does, the chances are good that you'll be asked about this feature.

Take notes when reading longer passages.

You will be given an erasable note board before you start the test. Use it to jot down key words and phrases and other notes. It will help you find information in the passage you need as you answer the question(s).

When examining graphics that provide quantitative information, don't get bogged down in the data.

A Science Test question may refer to a table, chart, or graph that presents quantitative information. The graphic may very well contain more data than you'll need to answer the question(s) based on it. In fact, one of the skills you're being tested on is your ability to sort through that data to determine what is relevant (and what is not relevant) to the question at hand. So don't waste time analyzing every piece of data in a graphic. Instead, focus your attention on what the question asks about.

Review diagrams and illustrations for helpful clues for answering the questions.

Many graphics will include arrows showing cause-and-effect, sequence of events in a process, or direction of motion, energy, or force. Pay special attention to these arrows, as they are often crucial to analyzing the question at hand. Also pay attention to labels used for various objects shown in an illustration. Finally, some graphics will come with a descriptive title or caption, which you should use to help you interpret the graphic, understand the question, and eliminate incorrect answers.

Make realistic assumptions when interpreting illustrations.

Some questions will involve illustrations depicting aspects of the physical world, but in a simplified manner. Make commonsense assumptions when interpreting these figures. For example, you can assume that lines that appear straight are intended to depict straight lines, that the natural forces of gravity, motion, and energy operate normally, and so forth. In other words, don't try to outsmart the test makers by splitting hairs; you'll only defeat yourself.

Apply your common sense and real-world experience—up to a limit.

Many questions on the Science Test—whether they involve physics, Earth sciences, ecology, biology, chemistry, and even astronomy—deal with phenomena that most of us have observed or experienced in our own lives. Use your life experiences, along with your common sense, to help you answer these questions. But don't use your outside knowledge as a *substitute* for reading and trying to understand the text and/or the graphic depiction provided. Rather, use that knowledge to safeguard against selecting answer choices that are contrary to common sense and real-life experience—in other words, that simply don't make sense.

Take care when handling questions stated in the negative.

Some questions may be stated in the negative rather than the affirmative. These questions are likely to use capitalized words in phrases such as "NOT accurate," or "EXCEPT which one," or in bold text as in "**least likely**." These questions are not intended to trick you, but they can be confusing. Take great care not to turn these questions around in your head when answering them.

Pace yourself properly.

You're allowed 90 minutes to answer all 30–35 questions. GED Science Test questions are not presented in any set order of difficulty. So after 30 minutes you should have answered at least 12 questions and after 60 minutes you should have answered at least 24 questions. If you're falling behind, pick up the pace. In any event, try to answer all 30–35 questions with at least 5 minutes to spare, so you can go back and reconsider any responses you were unsure about.

SUMMING IT UP

- The GED Science Test consists of multiple-choice questions and technology-enhanced questions. The subject areas covered include life science (biology), Earth and space sciences, and physical science (chemistry and physics).
- GED Science Test questions require that you read passages and comprehend or analyze the material presented in the passages, along with the charts, diagrams, graphs, illustrations, tables, and other graphics.
- The GED Science Test is more visually oriented than any of the other tests in the GED battery. Pay careful attention to any arrows in an illustration; you can be sure that they will be crucial as you answer the question at hand.
- Understanding science concepts questions involve drawing general assessments and conclusions from specific information. You will need to be able to recognize unfair assessments and conclusions—incorrect answer choices that jump to conclusions that are unwarranted given the information provided.
- You won't need to memorize any formulas for the GED Science Test. If a question requires you to apply a formula, it will provide that formula, along with the numbers you need to answer the question.
- Some GED Science Test questions will involve numbers, but you won't be asked to calculate precise ratios, percentages, or averages, or to do any serious number-crunching.
- Many questions on the GED Science Test deal with phenomena that you have observed or experienced in your everyday life. Use your experiences, along with your common sense, to help you answer these questions.

Science Review

Chapter 10

OVERVIEW

- **What You'll Find in This Review**
- **Science and the Scientific Method**
- **Life Science: Biology**
- **Earth and Space Science**
- **Chemistry**
- **Physics**
- **Summing It Up**
- **Practice Questions**
- **Answer Key and Explanations**

WHAT YOU'LL FIND IN THIS REVIEW

The GED Science Test is designed primarily to measure critical-thinking skills rather than knowledge. Nevertheless, with some prior familiarity with the three content areas covered on the test (life sciences, Earth and Space science, and physical science) you can expect to handle the questions with greater ease and confidence. The review materials in this part of the book are designed to help you in this respect. Keep in mind that this review is intended only to highlight the content areas listed above. It is by no means intended to be a comprehensive examination of these areas.

Review questions are provided throughout this review. As you answer them, keep in mind that the sections of text on which they are based are longer than selections of text on the actual GED Science Test.

SCIENCE AND THE SCIENTIFIC METHOD

Since the dawn of humankind, people have searched for explanations as to why the physical world around them is the way it is. Early explanations were most often based on religious and superstitious ideas. **Science** attempts to provide explanations for natural phenomena through investigation—more specifically, through observation and experimentation, as well as through theoretical explanation.

In order to sort out unreasonable explanations from plausible ones, scientists apply logic and common sense by means of a process called the **scientific method**. This method involves four fundamental steps:

1. **Observation:** During this first step, the scientist carefully observes a particular natural phenomenon, either directly (by using the five senses) or with the aid of any number of tools, such as telescopes, microscopes, temperature and pressure gauges, and other recording and measuring devices.
2. **Hypothesis:** During this second step, the scientist thinks about the set of facts obtained through observation, and he or she formulates a statement (the *hypothesis*) or series of statements that appear to logically explain the set of facts in a unified way. A good hypothesis is a simple statement intended to apply to a general set of circumstances.
3. **Experiment:** During the third step, the scientist designs and conducts experiments to determine whether the hypothesis is acceptable or whether it should be rejected or modified—in other words, to test the hypothesis.
4. **Conclusion:** During the fourth step, the scientist analyzes the results of the experiment(s) conducted during the third step. The results might support the hypothesis, or they might suggest that the hypothesis should be rejected or modified.

The proper conclusion (the final step described above) depends on whether the experimental results are consistent with the hypothesis. If the hypothesis is rejected or needs to be modified to fit the experimental results, new experiments are then designed and conducted to test a modified or new hypothesis in light of the experimental results. It is through a continuous cycle of new observations, new hypotheses, and further experimentation that scientists arrive at the best answers to their questions about the natural world.

Most people, including non-scientists, apply the scientific method in their everyday lives, often without realizing it. For example, assume that you are experiencing a stinging sensation in your stomach (an *observation*). You would probably want to know its cause so that you can remedy the problem. You might *hypothesize* that drinking coffee is the cause. In order to test your hypothesis, you might *experiment* by discontinuing coffee consumption for a period of days and monitoring the results. You would then reach a *conclusion* based on the results.

Reliable scientific conclusions depend on properly designed and conducted experiments. In the preceding experiment, for example, suppose you had discontinued coffee *and* alcohol consumption and observed that your stomach discomfort disappeared after a week. You could not reliably conclude that it was the coffee—rather than the alcohol or a combination of coffee and alcohol—that caused your stomach discomfort. A good test of your hypothesis would require that all possible factors other than coffee consumption remain unchanged, or constant, during the experiment. Researchers refer to such factors as **controls**, and they refer to factors that are changed to test the hypothesis as **variables**.

Question 1 refers to the following information.

A researcher combines equal amounts of three different clear liquids—X, Y, and Z—in a beaker, and she observes that the mixture turns blue in color. The researcher hypothesizes that liquid X turns blue when combined with any other liquid.

1. Which is the **best** way to test the hypothesis?
- **A.** Repeat the experiment, but change the proportions of the three liquids.
- **B.** Combine liquid X with a liquid other than Y or Z.
- **C.** Perform the same experiment again.
- **D.** Heat liquid X by itself, and observe its color response.

Liquid X is the control, and the other liquids are the variables. Change the variable to test the hypothesis. **The correct answer is B.**

LIFE SCIENCE: BIOLOGY

Biology is the scientific study of living organisms, including plants and animals. This field consists of three major branches: *zoology* (the study of animals), *botany* (the study of plants), and *ecology* (the study of how plants and animals interact with each other and their environment).

Cell Theory

The **cell** is the basic unit of structure and function for most living things. Cells arise from pre-existing cells by independent self-reproduction. All living organisms are composed of one or more cells. Cells vary in size, shape, and function. A bacterial cell, for instance, is invisible to the naked eye. Bacteria become visible only when they appear as colonies of millions of cells. At the other extreme, a single muscle cell can reach 9 inches in length (about a million times larger than a bacterial cell). It is estimated that the human body is composed of some 100 trillion cells.

Cell Structure

Cells are the basis of life, heredity, structure, and function of every organism. Each cell contains a variety of different structures called **organelles** ("little organs"). The **nucleus** of a cell is one of the most important organelles. The nucleus is the control center for all cellular activity. Within the *nucleoplasm* of a nucleus are long, thin fibers called *chromatin* on which are found *genes,* which contain all the genetic information for each cell. (This topic is examined in greater detail later in this review.)

Every cell has a **membrane** that encloses the cell and is selectively permeable to what enters and exits the cell. Inside the membrane, organelles are embedded in a gelatinous substance called **cytoplasm,** which fills the cell. The cytoplasm is the cell's manufacturing area and contains small *vacuoles,* which are storage areas; *mitochondria,* which release energy for cell operations; and *ribosomes,* which combine amino acids into proteins.

Cells are classified as **prokaryotic** (before a nucleus) and **eukaryotic** (possessing a true nucleus). Prokaryotic cells lack a nuclear membrane and membrane-bound organelles. They are unicellular, mainly microscopic organisms, such as bacteria and cyanobacteria. It is estimated that prokaryotes appeared some 3.5 billion years ago, and many scientists hypothesize that prokaryotic organisms evolved into eukaryotic cells. Eukaryotes include all cells in animals and plants, as well as in *protists*, unicellular organisms that can be plant-like or animal-like in unique ways. Eukaryote cells are characterized by a true nucleus that is bound by a membrane and membrane-bounded subcellular organelles. Eukaryotes can be unicellular, as in the case of the amoeba, or multicellular, as seen in humans. Eukaryotic cells possess many organelles to carry out cellular processes such as energy production, waste disposal, cellular transport, and product production.

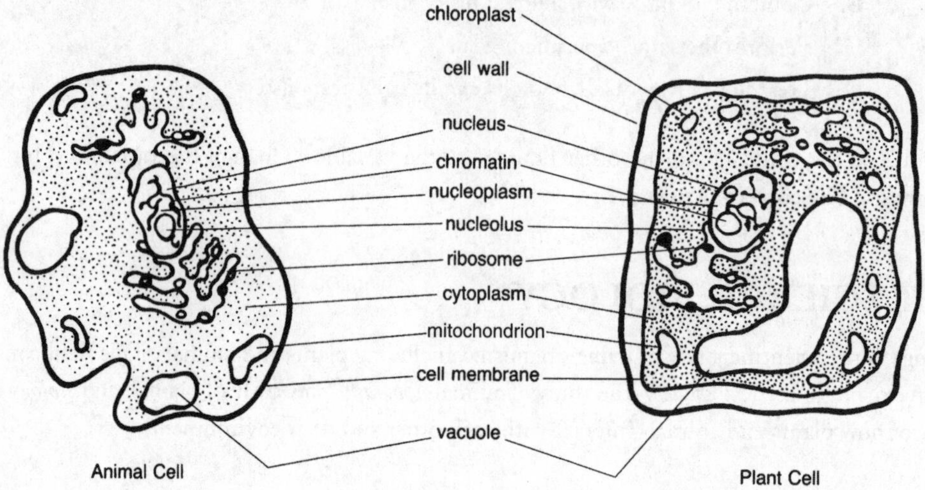

Although all eukaryotic cells are similar in structure, plant cells differ from animal cells in three important respects:

1. Plant cells have a firm outer boundary called the *cell wall.* This wall supports and protects the plant cell.
2. Vacuoles (storage areas) in the plant cell are much larger than those in the animal cell.
3. Within the cytoplasm, many plant cells contain small green structures called *chloroplasts.* These chloroplasts contain *chlorophyll,* which enables the plant cell to make food.

Cell Membrane and Transport

As noted earlier, cell membranes control the movement of materials into and out of the cell. The cell membrane is semi-permeable and allows only certain materials to enter and leave the cell. A cell membrane is a fluid-like sheet that is embedded with proteins and carbohydrate chains. This sheet creates an effective barrier against lipids (fats), while the sheet's proteins and carbohydrates act as receptors or identifiers for the movement of molecules from external sources.

While many factors are necessary for cell survival, **cellular transport**—the movement of particles into and out of the cell—is one of the most important. Cellular transport can be either passive or active. Movement by **passive transport** is accomplished through **diffusion**, by which particles move from an area of high concentration to an area of lower concentration until equilibrium is reached. The diffusion of water (the largest component of the cell cytoplasm) through a semi-permeable membrane is known more specifically as **osmosis**. Diffusion is a "passive" form of transport because it requires no energy. In contrast, **active transport** is used when a cell needs to move a substance from an area of lower concentration to an area of higher concentration; to do this, a cell must use energy.

Cellular Functions—Metabolism and Energy Pathways

All cells require a constant source of energy. Gathering, storing, and using this energy is referred to as a cell's **metabolism**. We consume nutrients to provide our bodies with the building blocks necessary to synthesize new materials needed by our cells. Unlike plants and some microscopic organisms, humans and other animals can't simply absorb energy through our skin. Instead, animal cells have to break food down in order to release the energy stored in the food.

Both plant and animal cells rely on metabolic pathways to convert substances into forms of energy that can be used by each cell. These conversions are controlled through **enzymes**, which are proteins that act as biological catalysts. What this means is that enzymes speed up the rate of a reaction by lowering the amount of activation energy needed. Without enzymes it would take weeks, even months, for foods to break down completely.

Enzymes are also necessary in order for the vital cellular reactions of **photosynthesis** and **cellular respiration** to occur.

Cells are the first level of the hierarchy of levels of organization in an organism. These levels are cells, which make up tissues, which make up organs, which make up organisms. Cells that make up tissues are specialized to perform a specific function. For example, muscle cells can release large amounts of energy needed to contract a muscle. Muscles made of such cells are part of the musculoskeletal system.

Energy for Life Functions

Photosynthesis is the food-manufacturing process by which green plants convert carbon dioxide (CO_2) from the air and water (H_2O) from the soil into glucose ($C_6H_{12}O_6$), which is a simple sugar, and oxygen (O_2). The sugars that the plant produces through photosynthesis can be used to make other compounds needed for the plant to sustain itself and grow. The green pigment in plants, called **chlorophyll**, captures the sun's light energy, which fuels this manufacturing process. Oxygen is a by-product of this reaction and is released into the atmosphere or used in cellular respiration (see below). Here's the chemical equation for photosynthesis:

$$6CO_2 + 6H_2O \rightarrow C_6H_{12}O_6 + 6O_2$$

Note that one molecule of glucose (sugar) combined with six molecules of oxygen to form six molecules of carbon dioxide and six molecules of water. The energy produced by this reaction is used by the cell.

Cellular respiration is used to free chemical energy from molecules of glucose for biological work. There are many types of respiration, but the most familiar is **aerobic respiration**, which converts carbohydrates (glucose) into carbon dioxide, water, and high-energy molecules of Adenosine triphosphate (**ATP**), which is the source of energy for many metabolic processes. Here's the chemical equation for aerobic respiration:

$$C_6H_{12}O_6 + 6O_2 \rightarrow 6CO_2 + 6H_2O + ATP$$

Respiration begins in the cytoplasm of the cell in a process known as **glycolysis** (sugar-breaking). The products of glycolysis then move to the mitochondria, where they are converted into energy-rich ATP molecules. Catabolic reactions such as respiration produce energy by the breakdown of larger molecules.

Cellular respiration occurs outside aerobic conditions as well. **Fermentation** and other forms of **anaerobic respiration** occur daily in fungi, bacteria, and even in the human body. While much of the inputs and outputs of cellular respiration are present in anaerobic respiration, the lack of oxygen is critical to the process.

The most well-known form of fermentation takes place through use of the common fungus, yeast (*Saccharomyces*). In this form of cellular respiration, glucose is broken down through catabolic reactions to provide energy for the fungus. However, the by-product of this form of respiration is not water, but *ethanol*—drinking alcohol. The formula for this reaction looks like this:

$$C_6H_{12}O_6 \rightarrow 2C_2H_5OH + 2CO_2 + 2ATP$$

Yeasts and other fermenters convert sugars like glucose to ethanol and carbon dioxide (note the lack of water as a by-product). This process is utilized in the food and alcohol industries.

Our bodies can also ferment sugar when oxygen is lacking, albeit only for short periods of time. When normal cellular respiration occurs in an oxygen-depleted environment, the breakdown of glucose stops at a three-carbon sugar—*pyruvate*. Pyruvate is converted to a carboxylic acid—*lactic acid*. The formula for this reaction looks like this:

$$C_6H_{12}O_6 \rightarrow 2C_3H_6O_3 + 2ATP$$

Lactic acid genesis can last for only a short time period in animals, as the need for oxygen is essential to life. However, the process can be sustained for brief intervals. This process actually occurs any time a person exercises beyond their conditioning level. As the body is stressed for oxygen, the lactic acid buildup increases. This buildup causes muscle soreness, and the effects of the lack of oxygen can be felt for days later. As conditioning increases, it takes longer for the body to start the fermentation process.

Another important form of anaerobic respiration is **methanogenesis**. As the name suggests, this is a process that creates methane. There are a number of bacteria species that can convert organic molecules into methane. Two examples of methanogenesis are carbon dioxide conversion and acetic acid conversion:

$$CO_2 + 4H_2 \rightarrow CH_4 + 2H_2O$$

$$CH_3COOH \rightarrow CH_4 + CO_2$$

Unlike other forms of cellular respiration, bacteria responsible for methanogenesis—*methanogens*—do not begin their respiration with sugars, but with products of other organismal cellular respiration. These bacteria often live in symbiotic relationships with other animals within the animals' digestive tracts. For example, methanogens can live within cows and aid in the digestion of cellulose—the sugar that makes up plant cell walls. This relationship can produce up to 250 liters (about 66 gallons) of methane a day.

Questions 2 and 3 refer to the following diagram and information.

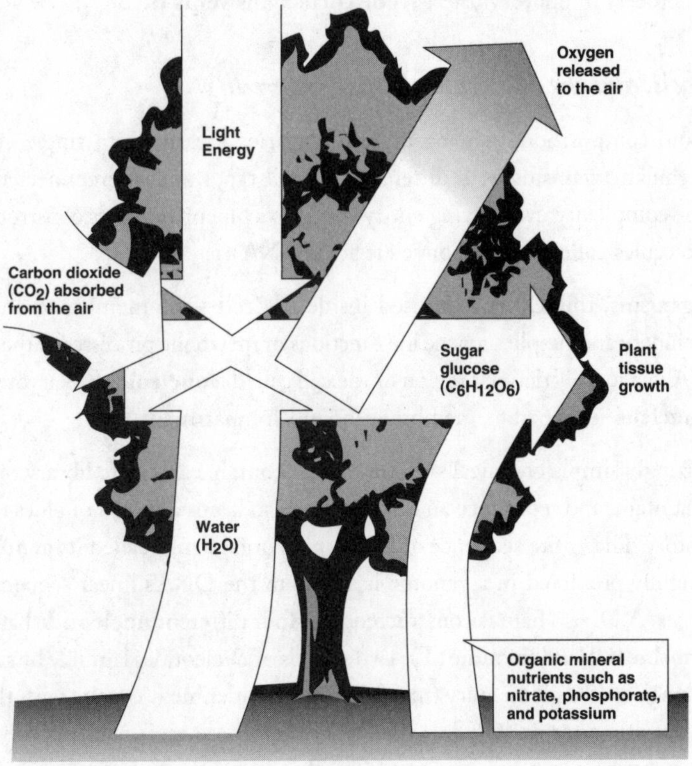

The oxygen produced by photosynthesis is necessary for cellular respiration, and the carbon dioxide produced by respiration is necessary for photosynthesis. In short, photosynthesis and cellular respiration are the yin and yang of energy: they are two complementary parts of a cycle of energy that is necessary for life to exist.

2. Which of the following exhibits passive cellular transport in a plant?
   - **A.** The plant's chloroplasts absorb light energy from the sun.
   - **B.** The plant's leaves emit oxygen into the air as a waste product.
   - **C.** The plant's roots absorb water from nearby soil.
   - **D.** The plant's stem delivers ATP molecules to the plant's leaves.

Passive transport involves a natural diffusion process, by which water moves from an area of higher concentration to one of lower concentration until equilibrium is reached. When you water a plant, the roots absorb it through osmosis, a form of diffusion, as needed to deliver that water to drier parts of the plant. **The correct answer is C.**

3. Which is NOT required in order for a plant to carry out photosynthesis?
   - **A.** Carbon dioxide
   - **B.** Glucose
   - **C.** Water
   - **D.** Chlorophyll

Glucose is a product of photosynthesis. Carbon dioxide, sunlight, water, and chlorophyll are all essential for the process of photosynthesis. **The correct answer is B.**

Mitosis, Meiosis, and the Molecular Basis of Heredity

The structure and composition of living organisms varies greatly, from single-celled bacteria to complex multicellular organisms with differentiated cell types and interconnected organ systems. Regardless of the complexity, every living entity contains a blueprint for its construction in the form of a chain of molecules called deoxyribonucleic acid (**DNA**).

In all living organisms, this DNA is housed inside the cell—the membrane-enclosed unit that contains the machinery and supplies for the life functions or metabolic processes of the cell. Prokaryotes house their DNA in a loosely defined region of the cell called a **nucleoid**. Eukaryotes sequester their DNA inside a **nucleus**—a separate, membrane-bound compartment.

DNA is an amazingly simple chemical structure, yet it contains an entire library of information on how to make, maintain, and reproduce an organism; it also keeps a record of clues to the organism's evolutionary history. The entire sequence of DNA in an organism is called its **genome**. The genetic blueprint so carefully preserved in a genome is stored in the DNA's linear sequence of molecules, referred to as **bases**. A DNA chain is constructed with four different **nucleotide** bases: **adenine (A), guanine (G), cytosine (C)**, and **thymine (T)**. Two strands of nucleotides lain side by side are connected by chemical pairings of complementary (matching) bases: adenine (A) pairs with thymine (T), and guanine (G) pairs with cytosine (C). The bonds between these molecules impose a twisting force (torsion) on the structure and cause it to wind slightly, much like a spiral staircase. This creates the familiar **double helix** shape of a DNA molecule.

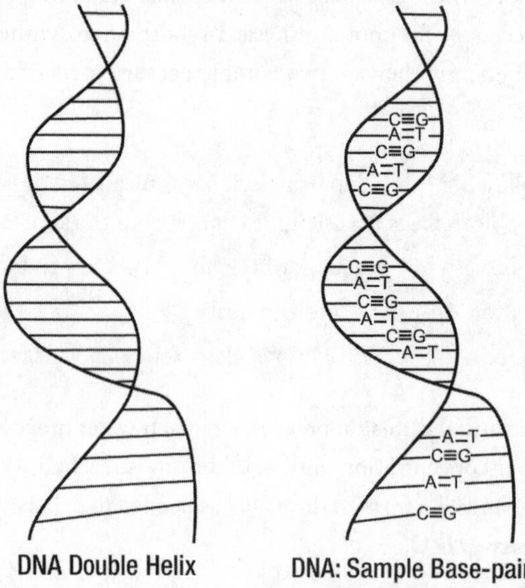

DNA Double Helix   DNA: Sample Base-pairing

Duplication of a cell's DNA is required both for cellular replication—to replenish dying cells—and for reproduction. In unicellular organisms, these two processes are the same. DNA is duplicated before the cell divides to produce two separate organisms, each with the original amount of DNA. This asexual method of reproduction is known as **binary fission**.

In multicellular organisms, a similar process called **mitosis** is used to replenish lost cells. However, reproduction is more complex and begins with specialized cells called **gametes** (eggs and sperm in animals), each of which provide only half of the DNA contained in other cells.

Mitosis

All cells must have a mechanism for perpetuation, growth, maintenance, and repair. If you've ever had a bad haircut or painful sunburn, in time your hair grew back and your skin peeled to reveal new skin. You can thank cellular division for this.

This process begins first with nuclear division—before the remainder of the cell divides. In cells of eukaryotic organisms, the nucleus normally carries two sets of genetic information. In this case the cell is said to be **diploid**. If a cell carries only one set of genetic information, it is said to be **haploid**. To begin cell division, unorganized DNA exits the nucleus in the strand-like form called **chromatin**. Once a cell is ready to divide, this chromatin coils and condenses into structures called **chromosomes**, which carry units of inheritance called **genes**. A chromosome in a non-dividing cell exists in a duplicated state where two copies—sister **chromatids**—are attached together at a central point. A nonreproductive human cell contains 46 chromosomes altogether—23 pairs of chromatids.

The process of mitosis consists of four sequential stages:

1. **Prophase:** The nuclear envelope dissolves; chromatin organizes into chromosomes; a fibrous spindle forms to connect opposite ends of the cell.
2. **Metaphase:** Duplicated chromosomes align at the equatorial plane of cell, along the spindles.
3. **Anaphase:** The two chromatids of a duplicated chromosome separate and move toward opposite ends of the cell.
4. **Telophase:** A nuclear envelope develops around a "daughter" cell, the chromosomes uncoil and revert back to chromatin, and the entire cell divides into two. (This division of the entire cell is called **cytokinesis**.)

Between cell divisions is a period referred to as **interphase**, during which the cell increases in volume, makes proteins and other crucial components, and replicates its DNA in preparation to divide again. The following illustration shows what the different phases of mitosis, including interphase, actually look like.

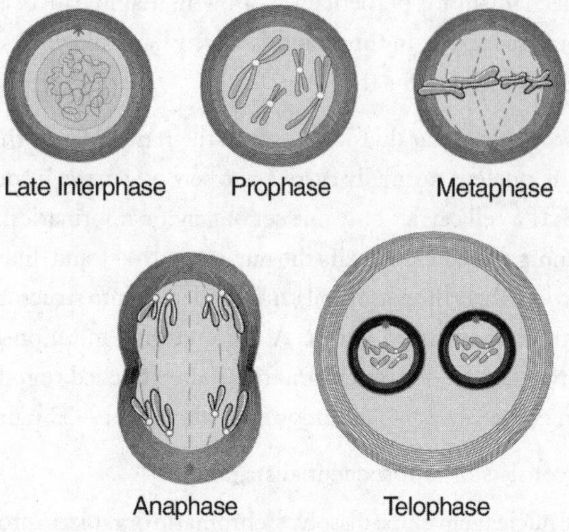

Mitosis

Animal cell division is similar to plant cell division, but there are a few differences. In animal cells, cytokinesis results in a **cleavage furrow** (shown below), which divides the cytoplasm. In plant cells, a **cell plate** forms in the center and progresses to the cell membrane. The result is a cell wall separating the two cells.

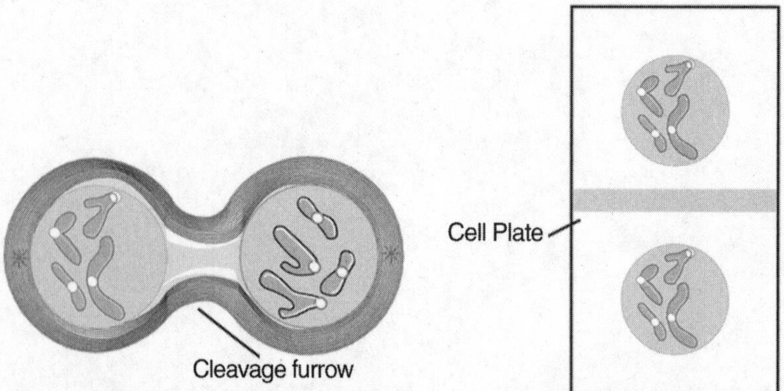

Telophase in animal cell **Telophase in plant cell**

After mitosis in an animal cell is complete, a cell has replicated the same genetic information initially donated by the egg and sperm cells. Except for random mutations, all of an organism's cells produced by mitosis have the same genes. The earliest cells created by mitosis are referred to as **stem cells**. Cells then differentiate into specialized cells by activating certain genes while repressing others. For example, muscle cells produce contractile proteins, while thyroid cells produce hormones that control metabolism. Each of these types of cells has a specific function, but it cannot perform the function of the other. The differentiating process is crucial—it explains why hair cells replace hair cells while skin cells replace skin cells.

Meiosis

The process of cell division known as **meiosis** occurs only in specialized reproductive cells of eukaryotic plants and animals. In animals, organs called **gonads** produce these reproductive cells, which are called **gametes**. In humans, the testes produce sperm, and the ovaries produce ova (eggs).

Human nonreproductive cells contain 23 pairs of chromosomes, as noted earlier. Of these 23 pairs, 22 are non-sex-related, or **autosomal**, while the 23rd pair is exclusively responsible for determining sex (male or female) and sex-related traits. A reproductive cell (sperm or ovum), however, does not carry a duplicate of any of the 23 chromosomes. Instead, it contains a total of only 22 *single* chromosomes and one *single* sex chromosome—23 chromosomes altogether. (The genetic complement is later restored once an egg is fertilized by a sperm cell.)

Meiosis, like mitosis, is a multiphase process. However, meiosis involves two divisions—**meiosis I** and **meiosis II**—rather than just one, and the *four* resulting daughter cells are each genetically different from the parent cell. This important distinction ultimately explains why you are uniquely different from each of your two parents.

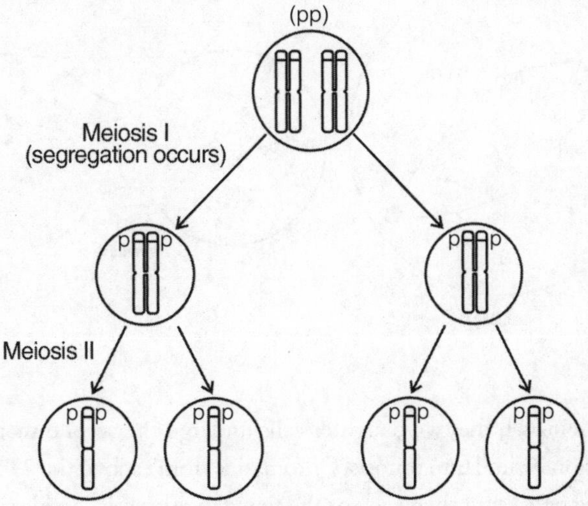

Meiosis Summary

The first step in meiosis I is **Interphase**, during which DNA is replicated in preparation for division. The chromatin organizes into chromosomes—each of 46 chromosomes consisting of two identical chromatids (diploids), just as in cells about to undergo mitosis. Then comes **Prophase I**, during which the nuclear envelope dissolves and **homologous** chromosomes (which have genes for the same trait) pair up and exchange genetic material in a process called "crossing over." This process does not occur during mitosis. Next comes **Metaphase I**, during which the chromosomes line up as a unit along an equatorial line.

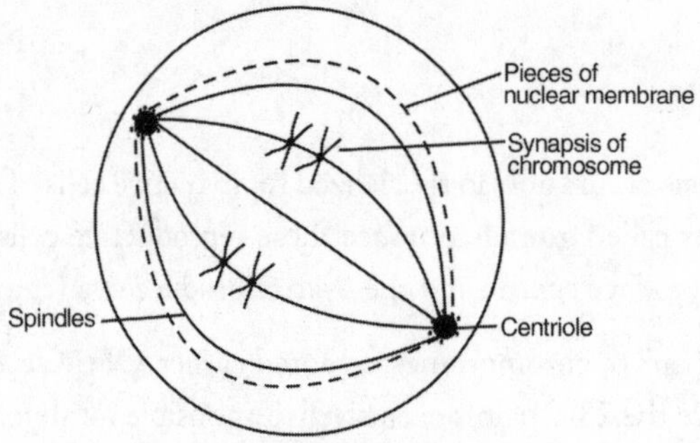

Prophase I

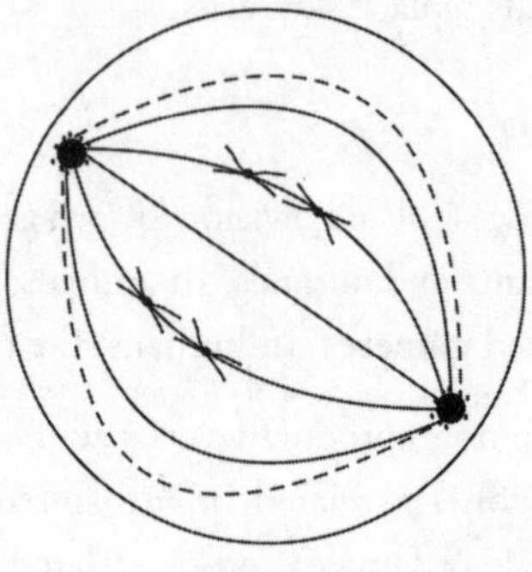
Metaphase I

In the next phase, **Anaphase I**, each chromosome pair separates, its two sister chromatids moving toward opposite poles of the cell. Thus, 23 chromosomes end up at one end of the cell, and 23 end up at the other end. During the final phase, **Telophase I**, a nuclear envelope re-forms around each new daughter nucleus, and the cell itself divides. Each of the two daughter cells has one set of 23 chromosomes. However, every chromosome still consists of two chromatids at this point. In other words, each of the two daughter cells is diploid.

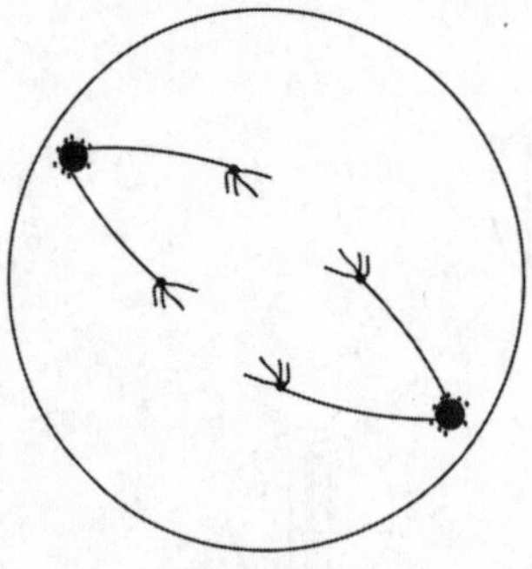
Anaphase I

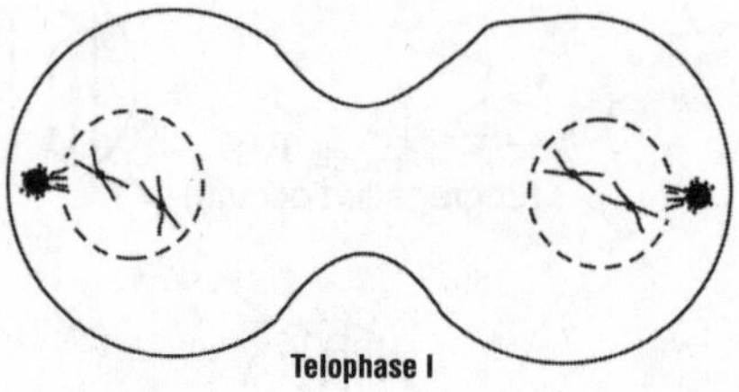
Telophase I

Immediately after Meiosis I, the two daughter cells undergo the second meiotic division (Meiosis II). This second division is similar to mitosis. Chromatids from each of the 23 chromosomes separate and move to opposite poles, and then each of the two daughter cells divides. The 23 chromatids in each of the four new cells form the chromosomes of those cells. At this point each daughter cell is haploid.

The four new cells become gametes (reproductive cells), each with 23 chromosomes that vary genetically from the original parent cell. In a human female, just one of these new reproductive cells can become a functional gamete (an egg). In the human male, however, all four new cells become viable sperm cells. The union of the egg and one of the sperm restores the full complement of 46 chromosomes in the fertilized human cell, or **zygote**.

4. In what respect is reproduction in unicellular organisms different from reproduction in multicellular organisms?
   A. Unicellular organisms reproduce simply by replacing dying cells.
   B. Unicellular organisms divide before their DNA is duplicated.
   C. Unicellular organisms depend on egg fertilization for reproduction.
   D. Unicellular organisms duplicate their DNA before they divide into separate organisms.

Before dividing into two separate organisms, a unicellular organism duplicates its DNA. In contrast, multicellular organisms do not simply duplicate their DNA but rather combine one half and another half of DNA from two different gametes, such as a sperm cell and an egg cell. **The correct answer is D.**

5. In terms of cell reproduction, which of the following helps explain the genetic differences between a child and its parents?
   A. Chromosome pairs exchange genes before the first meiotic cell division occurs.
   B. Reproductive cells create new chromosomes, which are unique to the child.
   C. After the initial meiotic cell division, all chromosomes break apart and reconfigure in a random manner.
   D. During the second meiotic division, each pair of chromosomes fuses together to become one.

In meiosis, the "crossing over" process that occurs just before the first meiotic cell division results in an exchange of genes between each of the 23 pairs of chromosomes. It is this exchange that all but ensures that daughter cells will differ genetically from their "mother" cell. **The correct answer is A.**

Genetic Inheritance

Genetics is the study of the principles of heredity and the variation of inherited traits among related organisms. These principles, upon which the field of modern genetics is based, were established in the nineteenth century by Austrian monk Gregor Mendel. In 1866, Mendel performed a number of simple but ingenious breeding experiments with garden pea plants and observed consistent, predictable patterns in terms of what traits are passed down from generation to generation. Mendel understood that some sort of hereditary factor was involved.

Mendelian Inheritance

We now know that the traits (or **phenotypes**) Mendel discovered are controlled by **genes**. Genes exist as heritable units on a chromosome. A chromosome may possess thousands of genes. Since each human is a product of the combination of both maternal and paternal chromosomes—23 from the egg and 23 from the sperm—we carry genes from both parents. Genes play a large role in our physical and mental development and dictate all of our individual characteristics or traits, everything from eye and hair color to blood type to the ability to roll your tongue. Genes come in alternative forms called **alleles**. We receive one allele from each parent. These alleles determine how each specific phenotype (such as eye color) is expressed. For example, the gene governing eye color can take the form of an allele for brown eyes or an allele for blue eyes.

Mendel proposed that a gene can be either a **dominant** allele for a certain trait or a **recessive** allele for that trait. The distinction between them is key to understanding heredity. Dominant alleles are expressed, which means they are actually shown as a trait. What's more, dominant alleles can "mask" the expression of recessive alleles. Recessive alleles can be expressed only when they are in the **homozygous** state, which means that alleles from both parents are the same. (A **heterozygous** state exists when the alleles are different.)

These principles, set forth by Mendel based on his observations of pea plants, are referred to today as Mendel's Laws of Inheritance:

The Law of Segregation: Each allele possessed by a parent will be passed into separate gametes (for example, egg and sperm cells in animals) during meiosis.

The Law of Independent Assortment: In each gamete, alleles of one gene separate independently of all other genes, allowing for new combinations of alleles through recombination.

The Law of Dominance: Each gene has two alleles, one inherited from each parent. Alleles are either **dominant** or **recessive** in their expression; dominant alleles "mask" the expression of recessive alleles.

Statistical Predictions of Individual Inheritance

Based on the patterns of inheritance that Mendel observed, it is possible to make predictions about the probability of a particular allele being passed on to an offspring and to make predictions about the phenotypic expression of an allele in the next generation.

All the genes that dictate the expression of a person's phenotypes are referred to collectively as the person's **genotype**. When certain genotypes of the parents are known for a specific trait, a simple diagram called a **Punnett square** can be used to predict the probability that the trait will be expressed in their offspring. Consider, for example, a genetic cross between the genes of two parents involving a single trait: the ability to roll the sides of one's tongue to form a "U" shape. We will designate **R** as the dominant allele, representing tongue-rolling ability, and **r** as the recessive allele representing a lack of tongue-rolling ability. Assume, for example, that the genotype of one parent is **RR** and the genotype of the other parent is **rr**. To construct a Punnett square for a cross such as this, the genes for one parent are placed along the side of the square and the genes for the other parent are placed along the top:

(Parents) **RR × rr**

The Punnett square for this cross:

	R	**R**
r	**Rr**	**Rr**
r	**Rr**	**Rr**

All the resulting offspring of this cross are heterozygous dominant (Rr)—this is their genotype. As a result, all offspring will be tongue rollers—this is the expression of their phenotype. Now, members of this second generation can be crossed to assess the probability that their offspring will be tongue-rollers if they produce offspring with an individual who is also heterozygous dominant:

(Parents) **Rr × Rr**

The Punnett square for this cross:

	R	**r**
R	**RR**	**Rr**
r	**Rr**	**rr**

Notice in this cross that three of the four squares are dominant—either RR or Rr. This means that there is a 75 percent probability that any member of this generation will be a tongue-roller. This is a phenotypic probability, of course, since it involves the actual expression of the trait.

You can also determine genotypic probabilities by examining the square:

- Homozygous dominant (RR)—25 percent probability
- Heterozygous dominant (Rr)—50 percent probability
- Homozygous recessive (rr)—25 percent probability

In genetics, phenotypic and genotypic probabilities are often expressed as ratios. Referring to the preceding Punnett square, the phenotypic ratio for tongue-rolling is 3:1, while the genotypic ratio for tongue-rolling is 1:2:1.

A Punnett square can also be used for crosses involving two traits that are independent of each other. The number of possible combinations is greater, yet the method is the same. Consider, for example, the texture and color of pea plants. Suppose that a yellow wrinkled pea will be crossed with a green smooth pea. The yellow color (Y) is dominant to green (y), and the smooth texture (S) is dominant to wrinkled (s). A cross between a purebred green, smooth pea plant and a yellow, wrinkled pea plant yields the following results:

(Parents) SSYY × ssyy

The Punnett square for this cross:

	SY	SY	SY	SY
sy	SsYy	SsYy	SsYy	SsYy
sy	SsYy	SsYy	SsYy	SsYy
sy	SsYy	SsYy	SsYy	SsYy
sy	SsYy	SsYy	SsYy	SsYy

All the offspring from this cross will be green and smooth (these are their phenotypes). Genotypically, they will all be heterozygous dominant for both traits (Ss and Yy). If we cross two heterozygous peas with one another, though, the offspring will not all look alike. In the following cross, notice all the different genotypes produced:

SsYy × SsYy

	SY	Sy	sY	sy
SY	SSYY	SSYy	SsYY	SsYy
Sy	SSYy	SSyy	SsYy	Ssyy
sY	SsYY	SsYy	ssYY	ssYy
sy	SsYy	Ssyy	ssYy	ssyy

Tallying up each different phenotype, you will find four different specific types, in a 9:3:3:1 ratio:

- 9 squares show dominance for both traits (SYYY, SSYy, SsYY, or SsYy)
- 3 squares show dominance for one trait and recessive for the other (SSyy or Ssyy)
- 3 squares show recessive for one trait and dominance for the other (ssYY or ssYy)
- 1 square shows recessive for both traits (ssyy)

As several generations pass, it is important to note which individuals carry or have a specific trait. This can help develop an understanding of the trait as well as enable scientists to estimate the chance that a trait will be passed on. When a map of several generations is created, we call this a **pedigree**. A pedigree is a chart that shows direct and extended family members and highlights who has a specific trait. In medicine, genetic counselors use pedigrees to help expecting parents understand the probability that a child may have a specific trait. By looking at family histories, the counselor can advise the parents on these inheritable traits.

The following diagram is an example of a pedigree. To understand the way a pedigree works, it is important to understand the symbols used: squares represent males, circles represent females, blank shapes indicate a lack of the trait, while shaded shapes indicates having a trait; some pedigrees will also have half-shaded shapes indicating people who are carriers for the trait. The lines in a pedigree are also significant. Horizontal lines directly connecting a male and a female indicate that these two individuals had children together, while shapes that are all connected via vertical lines to a common horizontal line indicate that these individuals are siblings. These siblings are listed from left (oldest) to right (youngest).

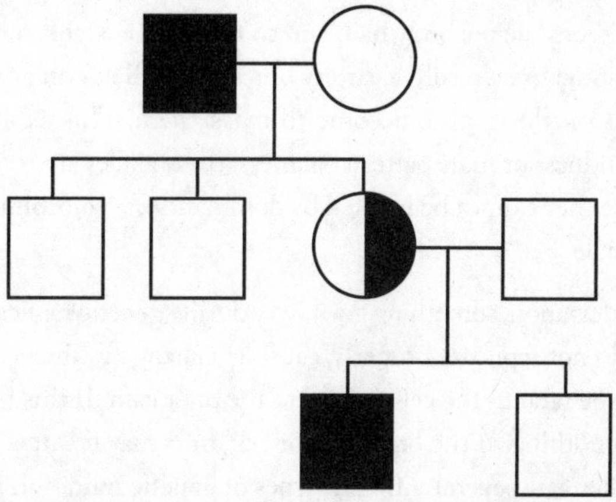

6. Assume that two parents are both heterozygous for a certain physical trait, which can either be present or absent in its expression. What is the expected genotypic ratio among their offspring?

A. 1:1

B. 2:1

C. 1:2:1

D. 3:1

Since both parents are heterozygous, the cross would be Tt × Tt (where T = dominant and t = recessive). Constructing a Punnett square would reveal the following: **TT** (one possibility), **Tt** (two possibilities), and **tt** (one possibility). The ratio is 1:2:1. **The correct answer is C.**

Deviations from Classic Mendelian Patterns

Since Mendel's discoveries, other patterns of gene expression have been identified that deviate from the "classic" Mendelian dominant/recessive patterns. Noteworthy among these are the following:

Co-dominance: In this deviation, neither of the two different alleles governing the same trait is dominant over the other, and *both* are expressed. For example, three alleles—A, B, and O—determine human blood type. The A and B alleles are co-dominant, and the O allele is recessive. Individuals with the AB genotype are phenotypically distinct (type AB blood) from individuals with the AA or AO (type A), BB or BO (type B), and OO (type O) genotype.

Incomplete dominance: In this deviation, neither of the two different alleles governing the same trait is dominant over the other, and the heterozygote is an intermediate between the two homozygous phenotypes—for example, a mix or hybrid of two colors. A snapdragon homozygous for a red allele (RR) has a red flower, and one that is homozygous for a white allele (WW) has a white flower. But a heterozygous (RW) cross results in a pink flower.

Sex linkage: One of our 23 pairs of chromosomes determines our sex—either male (**X**) or female (**Y**). The combination XX results in a female, while XY results in a male. These sex chromosomes carry the genes that govern the development of sex organs as well as secondary sex characteristics—body shape, body hair, and so forth. The X chromosome is much larger than the Y chromosome. As a result, a variety of recessive alleles on an X chromosome have no dominant alleles on the Y chromosome to mask them. This explains why only males experience color blindness or male pattern baldness: these alleles are recessive but will always be expressed because they cannot be masked by dominant *non*-colorblindness or *non*-balding alleles from the female.

Mutations: In this deviation, something goes awry during genetic replication. During mitosis, the genes of a cell do not replicate properly, causing a change in the genetic code of the new cell. This effect can be fatal to the cell or fatal to the organism. If this mutation continues to replicate, it may do nothing to the organism or cell, or it may create a new gene within the organism or cell. There are several different types of genetic mutation that can occur. Three common ones are deletion, insertion, and base substitution. As the name suggests, in **deletion mutations**, the mutated part of the DNA is deleted from the sequence. When **insertion mutations** occur, a portion of genetic material is added. Meanwhile, in **base substitution mutations**, the nucleotide bases—C, G, T, or A—are switched around.

Environmental Altering of Traits: There are two different forms of this deviation: one in which climatic events affect the gene, and one in which an agent in the environment—often a chemical—causes some form of mutation. An example of the first deviation can be seen in the arctic fox. During winter periods, when the temperatures can be well below freezing, the coat of the fox is all white, allowing the fox to blend into its environment. However, as summer—and warmer weather—approaches, the change in temperature alters the coat color genes, and the fox's hair takes on a reddish-brown color.

A **mutagen**—an agent that causes a mutation—can cause great, and even fatal, harm to the individual. Radiation (even as common as solar radiation) and the common solvent benzene are two such agents. While one is naturally occurring and the other is not (or at least not as readily available), both attack the genetic code and can lead to alterations to the code.

Chromosomal Crossover: In this deviation, portions of two non-sister chromosomes are swapped. This event happens almost exclusively during Prophase I of meiosis. A non-sister chromosome is a homologous chromosome that is not part of the other chromosome. For example, portions of the first 21st chromosome may switch with part of the second 21st chromosome. This can create new traits that are not present, even in a carrier form, in either parent.

Epigenetics: *Epigenetics* literally means "outside of genetics" and is a form of gene expression where traits are expressed differently from the parent cell, but the DNA sequence stays the same. In this deviation, a biochemical reaction within the DNA causes slight changes to the

DNA; this may be the addition of a methyl group or a change in a protein. Regardless of the alteration, the DNA base pairs are not altered. This leaves an identical set of DNA sequence with a completely different trait expressed. An epigenetic change is hereditable and reversible.

7. When neither of two different alleles governing the same trait is dominant over the other, what could be the result (each choice considered individually)?

I. Both alleles will be distinctly expressed.
II. The alleles will be expressed as a hybrid.
III. A genetic mutation will express itself in a unique way.
IV. Neither allele will be expressed.

A. I and II only
B. II and III only
C. III and IV only
D. I, II, III, and IV

The alleles might be co-dominant, in which case both will be distinctly expressed, as noted in statement A. Or they might be incomplete dominance, in which case a mix or hybrid will result, as noted in statement B. **The correct answer is A.**

Transmission of Disease and Pathogens

Beginning in this section, this review enlarges the scale on which it examines biological life from the molecular level to that of the individual organism. At this level, a good starting point is with two of the smallest such forms—bacteria and viruses.

Bacteria and Viruses

Bacteria, also known as *microbes* or *germs*, are microscopic organisms that reproduce primarily asexually. Most other organisms, including humans, are covered inside and out with what is referred to as a normal **flora** of bacterial populations. **Viruses** differ from bacteria in their simplified body structure and composition, their mode of replication, and in their dependence on a living host cell for replication.

Types of Bacteria

Bacteria are neither animals nor plants—they occupy their own pigeonhole in the modern classification system for biological life. (The system is outlined later in this review.) Bacteria can be either **autotrophic** (they synthesize food by converting light to chemical energy) or **heterotrophic** (they require other organisms to serve as a food source). Bacteria can be classified by their shape, the nature of their cell walls, motility, metabolism, and mode of reproduction.

Eubacteria (true bacteria) come in three shapes: coccus (spherical), bacillus (rod-shaped), and spirillum (spiral-shaped). One example of eubacteria is *Escherichia coli*, or *E. coli*, a bacterium that grows in small numbers as a part of the natural flora of human skin, intestinal tract, and genital tract. Under a compromised immune system, however, overgrowth of this bacterium can result in illness or even death.

Cyanobacteria perform photosynthesis to convert light energy into chemical energy for food. The green gooey stuff you sometimes see in standing pools of water (also known as pond scum) is an example of cyanobacteria.

Bacteria have simple structures. Since they are prokaryotes, they lack a membrane-bound nucleus and membrane-bound organelles. The following diagram shows the basic body plan for a typical bacterium. A bacterium cell contains strands of DNA, a plasma membrane, a cell wall, and a capsule. This simple structure allows for the rapid division of the bacterium, usually by way of binary fission—a form of asexual reproduction.

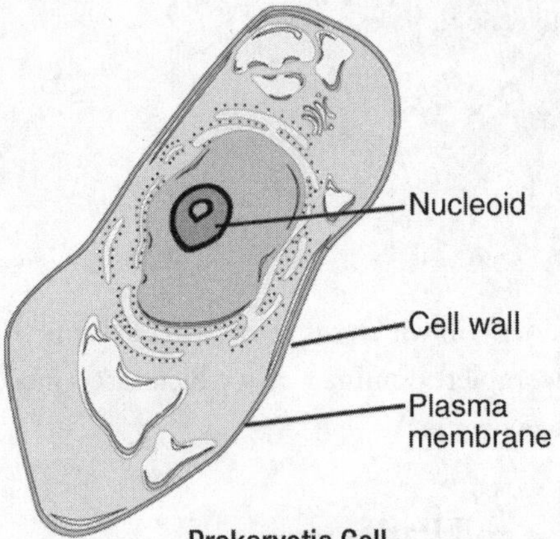

Prokaryotic Cell

Bacteria that are parasitic are called **pathogens**, meaning that they are disease-causing. Pathogenic bacteria invade healthy tissues. Their metabolic processes release enzymes that destroy the normal physiology of this tissue. Human diseases caused by pathogenic bacteria include leprosy, syphilis, gonorrhea, tuberculosis, strep throat, and Lyme disease—to list just a few. Through their bacterial metabolism, other pathogens produce toxins that are poisonous to humans. Botulism, for example, is caused by a toxin that infects food and liquids. When ingested, it can cause illness and even death.

To combat pathogens, scientists have developed a host of different kinds of **antibiotics** that disrupt bacterial metabolism. An antibiotic works by weakening and rupturing the cell wall of a bacterium, thereby killing the cell. But bacteria often develop immunity to a particular antibiotic, especially when the antibiotic is overused. As bacteria divide rapidly, they can develop into new and more virulent strains. For example, antibiotics such as penicillin are now ineffective against more resistant strains of some bacteria. Researchers are continually developing new and stronger antibiotics to combat the ability of bacteria to develop immunity to existing antibiotics.

Viruses

A **virus** cannot reproduce on its own accord or perform basic cellular tasks such as protein synthesis, and so most scientists do not consider them to be independent living organisms. A virus is simply a strand of genetic material, either DNA or RNA, encapsulated in an outer protein shell. Viruses act as intracellular parasites in all types of organisms. They can only reproduce inside a living cell. Once inside the host cell, viruses take over the replication machinery of the host cell. They transfer their genome into the cell of the host organism, integrate their DNA sequence into the host DNA, and let the host cell replicate, transcribe, and translate the virus's genes. Viral genomes contain genes for directing the replication and packaging of complete copies of the virus, so that eventually the host cell bursts open and releases new viruses to infect other cells.

The living host upon which viruses absolutely depend for replication can be of plant, bacterial, or animal origin. Viruses are host-specific in that they invade only one type of cell, which provides necessary **receptor sites** for the virus to attach itself. For example, the virus that causes polio attaches to neurons, the virus responsible for mumps attaches to salivary glands, and the virus that causes chicken pox attaches to skin cells. Though they are the smallest infectious agents known to humans, what they lack in size they more than make up for in destructive power. They are responsible for a wide variety of devastating human diseases, such as HIV/AIDS, hepatitis B, and herpes.

To treat viral infections, prevention is the key. Early investigations into the spread of disease, in particular smallpox, prompted the development of **vaccines**. In 1796, Dr. Edward Jenner discovered that milkmaids who contracted cowpox from cows showed a natural immunity against the more virulent smallpox. From this discovery, a new form of disease prevention was born. Vaccines are developed by using nonpathogenic strains of viruses or killed viral strains. The vaccine is introduced into an organism, and then the organism's immune system produces antibodies to fight the inactive virus. Later, if the organism encounters these particles again, it has already developed a defense, or immunity, to them.

Through genetic engineering in recent decades, scientists have devised ways for organisms other than the infected one to independently produce inactive components of a virus. For example, plants such as bananas can be engineered to become "edible vaccines" by splicing genes from a bacterium or virus with a bacterium that naturally occurs in the soil in which the banana plant grows. The bacterium in the soil then infects the growing plant, transferring the foreign gene along with it. Scientists hope that in this way, large quantities of vaccines can be produced inexpensively and distributed to areas of the world that lack conventional health care. Through this and other innovative approaches, researchers hope to eventually win the ongoing battle against these unseen and potentially deadly invaders.

8. Bacteria reproduce at a higher rate than any other organism. What allows bacteria to replicate so rapidly?

A. Their cell structure is very simple.

B. They feed on host organisms without providing any benefit in return.

C. Vaccines are generally ineffective in killing bacteria.

D. They can reproduce in nearly any environment, no matter how hostile.

The simple cell structure of bacteria is the key to their ability to replicate so rapidly. **The correct answer is A.**

9. A vaccine prevents a viral infection by

A. boosting the immune system with viral-fighting vitamins.

B. introducing a bacterium that encounters and kills the virus.

C. stimulating the production of antibodies to fight the virus.

D. strengthening cell walls so that the virus cannot enter the cells.

A vaccine introduces an inactive strain of the virus. The body's immune system then produces antibodies to fight the inactive virus. If the body is later exposed to a pathogenic strain of the virus, the appropriate antibodies are already there to fight it off. **The correct answer is C.**

Species Relationships

Symbiosis

Bacteria provide an ideal illustration of **symbiosis** in action. Two different types of organisms are said to have a **symbiotic** relationship when there is an ongoing, close association between them. A symbiotic relationship can be either **mutualistic** or **parasitic**. In a mutualistic relationship, each organism obtains a benefit from its association with the other. In a parasitic relationship, one organism obtains a benefit while the other organism is harmed by the relationship. (In a third type of symbiosis, called **commensalism**, one organism benefits while the other is neither benefited nor harmed.)

Bacteria maintain mutualistic relationships with many different species of plants. For example, the roots of bean plants form a mutualistic relationship with bacteria that are capable of converting atmospheric nitrogen into a usable form, which not only benefits the plant, but also the soil surrounding the plants. This process is known as **nitrogen fixation**.

Bacteria maintain mutualistic relationships with animals as well—including humans. For example, the digestive system in humans relies on intestinal bacteria to aid in digestion and to produce antibiotics that prevent the growth of pathogenic bacteria. Another example involves herbivores such as cows, which lack the enzyme needed to digest cellulose and thus depend on certain bacterial microbes to convert their food into simple sugars.

Bacteria are not the only species to form symbiotic relationships. For example, lichens are formed by a mutualistic symbiosis between fungus and algae. The two grow and live together in lichen form in some of the most hostile terrestrial environments on the planet. Their symbiotic relationship enables them to anchor on rocks and trees, provide nutrients, and survive the harsh climate. Ant species also form a number of mutualistic relationships. Some species of ants raise and care for aphids so that the ants may feed on the dew that aphids produce. Remoras and sharks share a mutualistic symbiotic relationship as well. Remoras attach themselves to the bottom of a shark and eat bits of food that the shark misses or that get caught on the shark. Meanwhile, the shark is cleaned by the remoras.

Parasitic relationships are classified into three types (although some classify up to five): endoparasites, ectoparasites, and brood parasites. Endoparasites live inside of their hosts. Examples of these include the tapeworm, pinworm, trypanosoma (the protozoan responsible for malaria), and even some flies, such as the botfly. Some parasites like the tapeworm and pinworm harm the host only slightly while they feed. Others, like trypanosoma, will eventually kill their hosts as they reproduce within the body. Some, like the botfly, only spend their larval stage within vertebrates where they grow and eat. Once mature, the botfly flies off and lives like other flies. Ectoparasites live outside of the body. For example, the tick bites and burrows its head into the skin of its host, drawing blood to feed. Other examples include fleas, mites, mosquitoes, and lice.

Brood parasites are animals that leave their eggs to be raised by other closely related organisms. Given the opportunity, the cowbird will push the eggs out of a host bird's nest and lay her own eggs before the host returns. If the host does not notice the switch, it will raise the parasite's young as its own. Cuckoo birds as well as cuckoo wasps have a similar method of raising their young.

The last type of symbiosis is known as commensalism. In a commensalistic relationship, one member of the relationship benefits, while the other is unaffected. For example, barnacles are sedentary crustaceans that, as adults, attach to objects for life. Barnacles attach to numerous animals, including whales and clams, without affecting the host. Another example is the relationship between clownfish and anemones. The clownfish, which is immune to the anemone's sting, finds safety and shelter from predators within the anemone's tentacles. Meanwhile, the anemone is not affected by the clownfish.

It should be noted that some scientists do not consider the latter two types of symbiosis, parasitism and commensalism, to be actual forms of symbiosis. These scientists cite mutualism as the only form of symbiosis because the prefix *sym-* means "together" or "united." Since parasitism and commensalism benefit only one member of the relationship, these species are not together or united.

Predator-Prey

Predator and prey interactions occur at all trophic levels throughout a food web. For example, a mouse in a grassland habitat may be the prey of a snake that is in turn preyed on by a hawk. That same mouse also preys upon insects, worms, and larvae. In a simple predator-prey relationship, such as that of the hare and the lynx, the interdependence of their populations can be seen. If the rabbit population is low, there is not enough food for the lynx and its population will stay relatively low. If the population of rabbits increases, the lynx population will also soon increase. Increased lynx population will then be followed by a decrease in hare population, and the cycle will repeat.

The changes in the population of a single species can result in the alteration of a number of other species' populations by a process known as **trophic cascade**. This effect was apparent when the gray wolf was reintroduced into Yellowstone National Park. When the wolf, an **apex predator**, went extinct in that region, the entire food web was altered. The gray wolves' primary prey population, the elk, increased rapidly in number. This affected the growth of many trees, such as the cottonwood, and the populations of other herbivores such as beavers. A lesser predator, the coyote, also increased its population. Shortly after the reintroduction of the wolf in 1995, the elk population returned to its former level. Populations of cottonwoods, beavers, and coyotes also returned to their old levels.

However, the balance of a healthy ecosystem can be disrupted a number of ways. Two general ways that an ecosystem's stability can be affected are climatic/structural and organismal events. In the latter, species are added or removed, thus disrupting the food chain. For example, invasive species are species that are not native to a particular ecosystem. They may be very similar to another species in the ecosystem, but since they are not native to this ecosystem, they often do not have the stresses that a native species has. For example, the vining plant kudzu was introduced in the South years ago as an erosion prevention plant. It grows rapidly and is adapted to warm, humid climates. However, since it is not native to the area, there are no, or few, organisms that feed on the kudzu. Because of this lack of stress on the plant, it has grown and smothered other plants and trees out of existence with little mechanism, outside of human interaction, to slow its growth. Kudzu now runs rampant in the South, and its range is growing. Other examples of invasive species include zebra mussels, flying carp, snakehead fish, and Chinese mantises.

Climatic and structural changes can also disrupt an ecosystem. These events can include flooding, desertification, and habitat destruction. In climatic events like flooding and desertification, the *biogeoclimate*—the climate involving the soil and biotic community—of the region is altered and can no longer support the ecology that was once present. Flooding kills plants and many animals via drowning, while desertification, marked by arid climate conditions and a loss of soil fertility, does the same via dehydration. Structural changes like deforestation and habitat destruction in general destroy an ecosystem that may have taken several hundred to several thousand years to establish. This requires the ecosystem to change or start over.

Common Ancestry and Cladograms

Besides interspecies and intraspecies competition like predation and finding mates, animal populations are also affected by disease. Some diseases kill only a few species every year. For example, chronic wasting disease, CWD, is an infectious protein disease (prion) that affects cervids like elk, whitetail deer, and mule deer. The disease is always fatal and turns a normally healthy animal into a slowly starving animal. There is no known cure and no known method of transmission. While this disease is always fatal, it does little to the overall population. Meanwhile, some diseases, such as Dutch elm disease, have had detrimental effects on the elm population since it was introduced in America in the late 1920s. Once the disease, a form of fungus spread by the elm beetle, infected the first native American elm tree, it spread rapidly. Since its introduction, nearly 40 million elm trees in North America have died from the disease, devastating the natural elm stock.

Attempts to categorize or classify all life forms date back to ancient times. Our current classification system is based on the one developed by Carolus Linnaeus, who in the 1700s took a major step in bringing order to the natural world. He laid the foundation for modern **taxonomy**, our system of classification and nomenclature (naming). Linnaeus used Latin to name organisms, so that everyone involved in the field of science could use a universal language for the names of organisms. He then created a system of **binomial nomenclature**, which uses a two-part name that illustrates the special characteristics of each organism. The binomial later evolved into the **genus** and **species** of modern taxonomic classification (see the following passage).

Our modern classification scheme starts with three major groups called **domains**. This is the largest grouping category. As classification continues, it becomes increasingly specific. The eight main hierarchical levels in this classification system are as follows (note that in plants the term *division* is used instead of *phylum*):

<u>Modern Taxonomy</u>

Domain
Kingdom
Phylum
Class
Order
Family
Genus
Species

The three domains are Bacteria, Archaea, and Eukarya. Organisms in the Bacteria and Archaea domains are **prokaryotes**—single-celled organisms that lack a cell nucleus and membrane-bound organelles. Organisms in the Eukaryota domain—**eukaryotes**—can be either single- or multicellular; cells of organisms in this domain have a nucleus and membrane-bound organelles.

The following is a brief overview of the six kingdoms: Archaebacteria, Eubacteria, Protista, Fungi, Plantae (plants), and Animalia (animals).

Kingdom Archaebacteria (Archaea)

Archaea are single-celled microscopic organisms. Formerly classified as bacteria, archaea were discovered to have molecular characteristics distinct from bacteria and now are classified as both a domain and kingdom to themselves. Archaea are characterized by their ability to survive in extreme habitats and toxic environments. The archaea can be classified by the environments in which they thrive:

- **Acidophiles** live in highly acidic environments
- **Alkaliphiles** live in highly basic environments
- **Barophiles** grow best under high pressure
- **Halophiles** are tolerant of high salt concentration environments
- **Methanogens** produce methane as a metabolic by-product
- **Psycrophiles** live in extremely low temperatures
- **Thermophiles** and **hyperthermophiles** are tolerant of extreme heat

Kingdom Eubacteria

Eubacteria are simple, single-celled, microscopic organisms and are the most primitive and ancient of all life forms. They lack a distinct cell nucleus, and their DNA is not organized into chromosomes. Eubacteria play a variety of roles in the biological world:

- Some are pathogenic (disease-causing).
- Some serve to break down gaseous nitrogen into inorganic compounds that are biologically usable (through a process called **nitrogen fixation**).
- Some serve to decompose organic matter, so that it can enrich the soil and nourish plant life.

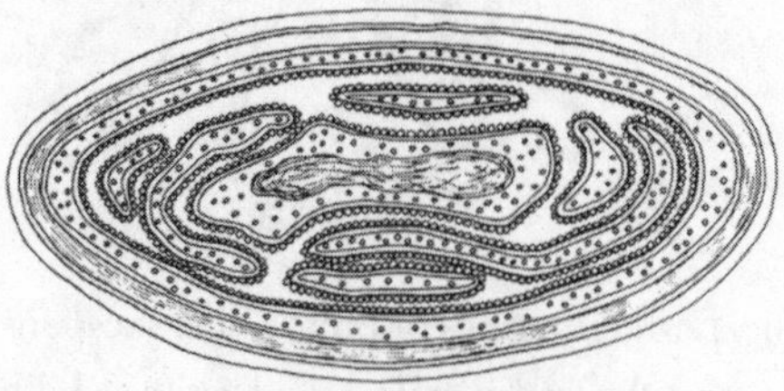

Typical Prokaryotic Cell

Members of Kingdom Eubacteria include **bacteria** and **cyanobacteria** (a special form of bacteria). There are more than 4,800 known kinds of bacteria. Most need oxygen to live, but other bacteria do not. Within the latter group, some can withstand small amounts of oxygen, while others find oxygen poisonous and will die if subjected to large amounts. (Bacteria are examined in more detail elsewhere in this review.)

Cyanobacteria are a special type of bacteria that are autotrophic and photosynthetic, which means that they manufacture their own food by harnessing the sun's light and absorbing inorganic substances such as carbon dioxide and ammonia. The most common cyanobacteria are blue-green algae (though they belong to a different kingdom than other types of algae). If a body of water contains appropriate and abundant nutrients, a growth explosion of blue-green algae can occur, creating a "floating carpet," or algal bloom. Much—perhaps even most—of the earth's oxygen is attributable to the photosynthetic activity of these great masses of cyanobacteria, which come in nearly 8,000 known species.

Kingdom Protista

Many members of this kingdom are single-celled and move about freely as individual organisms. Others, however, form colonies with other organisms of their type. The latter are eukaryotic cells—they have a distinct nucleus as well as other structures found in more advanced cells.

Protozoa

Protozoa are distinguished from other protists in their locomotive ability and by how they obtain food. Two common protozoa are the amoeba and the paramecium. An **amoeba** is a formless cell that uses **pseudopods** to move and to obtain food by simply engulfing it. A **paramecium** moves about by using hairlike **cilia**, which is also used by the paramecium to direct a current of water containing food into the organism's gullet (like a mouth and stomach all in one).

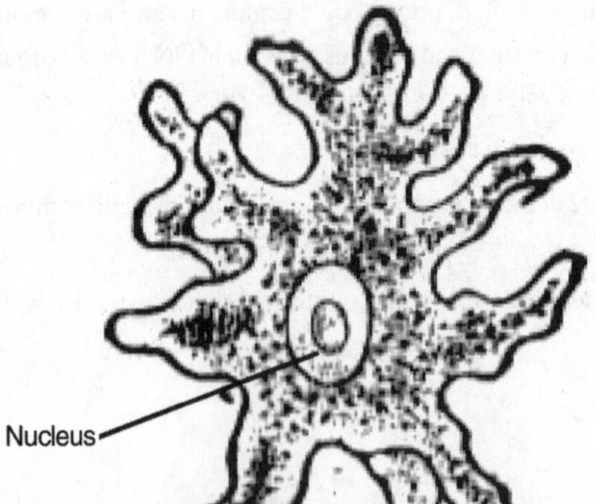

Amoeba

Some protozoa are pathogenic. Different types of protozoa are responsible for serious diseases such as amoebic dysentery, malaria, and African sleeping sickness (a debilitating, wasting disease).

Algae (Plant-like Autotrophs)

Algae are classified in the Kingdom Protista, but algae are quite different from amoebas and paramecia. Algae are autotrophic—they contain chloroplasts with pigment for photosynthesis—and include green, brown, red, and golden algae, as well as diatoms, euglena, and dinoflagellates. Most seaweed is a collection of algal cells. Due to seaweed's high nutritional value, it accounts for a major portion of the human diet in many parts of the world, especially near the coasts in Asia.

- **Diatoms** are widely used commercially for the reflective and abrasive nature of their shells. Paints used for marking highway lanes often contain **diatomaceous** earth, and many types of toothpaste contain diatom shells because of their abrasive quality.
- **Euglena** are perhaps the most curious of the various forms of algae. Euglena are normally autotrophic—they contain chloroplasts with pigment for photosynthesis. However, under low light or the absence of light, they can switch to a heterotrophic mode, meaning they can obtain their energy by consuming other organisms. They move by flagella, which is more characteristic of protozoa.
- **Dinoflagellates** are one of the main components of plankton. Some species can undergo explosive population growth, creating seas of red or brown referred to as "red tide" and producing great amounts of neurotoxins that kill both marine and human life.

Slime Molds (Fungus-like Heterotrophs)

You may have seen **slime molds** when camping or hiking. These amoeba-like cells dwell in dark, warm, moist areas—on damp soil or in decaying plant matter such as rotting leaves and logs—and move about, often in slug-like colonies, when food becomes scarce. During a portion of its lifecycle, one type of slime mold develops into a multicellular structure that produces and releases spores. In this form, a slime mold resembles a fungus, which is discussed next.

Kingdom Fungi

Members of the Kingdom Fungi are mainly non-motile, non-photosynthetic heterotrophic organisms. What this means is that they have no independent means of mobility, and they obtain the energy they need by consuming other organisms. Most fungi, including molds and mushrooms, are multicellular. However, this kingdom does include a few unicellular types as well, such as yeast. Fungi survive and spread by producing and releasing spores, which are made sexually or asexually. When released, the spores are carried by wind or water and can travel hundreds of miles from their point of origin.

Fungi can be either **saprophytic** or **symbiotic**. Saprophytes absorb nutrients from dead organisms. Symbiotic fungi are either parasitic (causing, for example, athlete's foot and ringworm) or mutualistic. Lichens are a form of mutualistic fungus; they afford protection to algae and cyanobacteria in exchange for the food energy that algae and cyanobacteria provide.

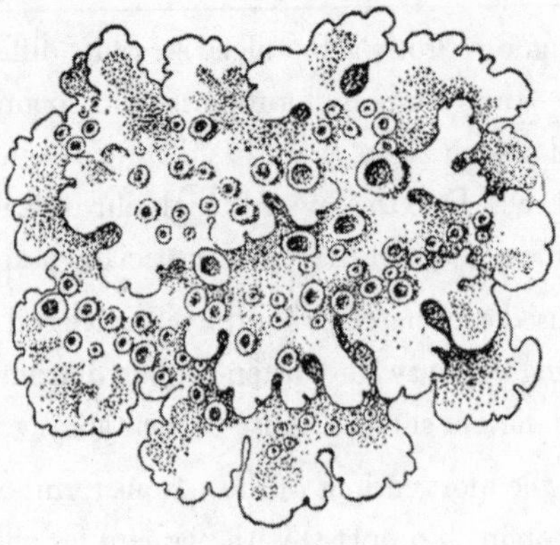

Lichen

A variety of commercial foods—mushrooms, blue cheese, beer, and soy sauce, to name a few—are fungi products.

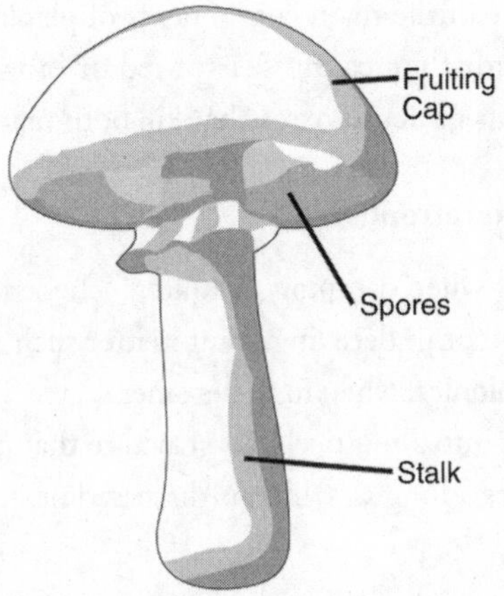

Mushroom

10. Of the following classifications, which is the **most** specific?

A. Class

B. Family

C. Phylum

D. Order

In hierarchical order, the classification choices listed are Phylum, Class, Order, and Family. Recall that as modern taxonomic classification continues, it becomes increasingly specific. Therefore, Family is the most specific. **The correct answer is B.**

11. What do all protists share in common?

A. They are a food source for humans living near the ocean.

B. They must consume organic matter to survive.

C. They can reproduce either asexually or sexually.

D. They dwell in water or in watery tissues of organisms.

Protozoa and algae are water dwellers, and slime molds dwell in the moist tissues of rotting leaves or logs. Choices A, B, and C each describe some, but not all, protists. **The correct answer is D.**

Kingdom Plantae (Plants)

Organisms in the three kingdoms previously discussed are very simple compared to the organisms in Kingdom Plantae (plants). All plants are multicellular, and they all are autotrophic, which means that they generate their own food. Nearly all plants do so by using their photosynthetic pigment **chlorophyll** found in organelles called **chloroplasts**.

Nonvascular Plants and Vascular Plants

Plants have adapted to live in practically every type of environment. They evolved in form, activity, and function over millions of years. The multitude of plants within this kingdom is staggering. But they all fall into two major groups of plants: nonvascular and vascular. By far, the simpler of the two forms is **nonvascular** (division *Bryophyta*). Nonvascular plants have no true roots, stems, or leaves. Lacking these structures, they are limited in two ways. First, they cannot grow very high—only a few inches in height, on average. Second, they can dwell only in a consistently moist environment. Nonvascular plants include mosses, liverworts, and hornworts. Among these forms, only mosses contain specialized tissues for transporting water or other nutrients from one part of the plant to another, and only to a limited extent.

A **vascular** plant is one that contains specialized tissues for carrying water, dissolved nutrients, and food from one part of the plant to another. Vascular plants represent the vast majority of plants. Their complex vascular tissues show that they have successfully adapted to living on land. They are mainly diploid throughout their lifecycle, which means that they reproduce sexually—one pair of chromosomes from each parent is inherited by offspring.

Vascular plants generally have roots, stems, and leaves. **Roots** anchor a plant into soil, from which the plant draws water and nutrients through osmosis. Humans eat a variety of roots, including carrots and radishes, to name just a few. **Stems** support leaves and transport raw materials from roots to leaves and synthesized food from leaves to roots and other parts of the plant. Humans eat the stems of a variety of plants, including celery, sugar cane, and several others.

Leaves are the major photosynthetic portion of a plant. Their chlorophyll—the pigment that gives plants their green appearance—receives sunlight, while the underside of the leaf takes in carbon dioxide through tiny openings called **stomata**. The plant then combines the carbon dioxide with water to produce energy in the form of glucose. As a waste product of the process, oxygen is then released through the leaf's pores. (The process by which a leaf exchanges gases in this way is called **transpiration**.)

The major parts of a typical leaf are as follows:

- **Epidermis**: Outer layer of stomata and hair cells, as well as a waxy cuticle that prevents water loss
- **Guard cells**: Epidermal cells that change shape according to the amount of water in a leaf; create tiny openings called stomata, which close or open to control the rate of water loss and gas exchange
- **Palisade layer**: Contains chloroplasts, arranged vertically for maximum photosynthesis
- **Spongy layer**: Loosely arranged chloroplasts that allow for water, oxygen, and carbon dioxide circulation
- **Vascular bundles**: Xylem and phloem tissues in bundles

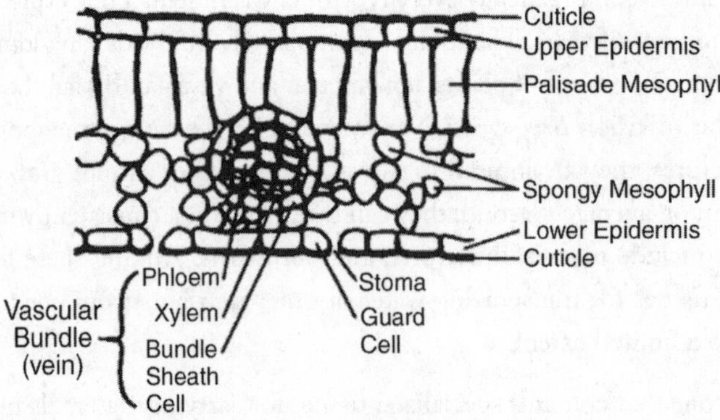

Cross section of a typical leaf

Vascular bundles of xylem and phloem are present in most other parts of a vascular plant as well. A plant's **xylem** consists of hollow cells that form tubes for carrying water from soil into roots and for transporting water to above-ground portions of the plant. A plant's **phloem** consists of thickened sieve-like cells that transport organic molecules produced in one part of the plant to storage regions in another part (for example, the sugars produced by photosynthesis in the leaf move to the root for storage).

Seedless and Seed-Bearing Vascular Plants

Some vascular plants are seedless. These plants propagate by producing and disseminating spores. Examples include club mosses, horsetails, and ferns. Other vascular plants are seed-producing. A **seed** is actually a reproductive organ—a specialized structure that contains an embryo enclosed in an outer, protective seed coat. Under the right conditions and with water, the seed can germinate and grow into an adult plant.

Seed-producing vascular plants include gymnosperms and angiosperms. Literally translated as "naked seed," **gymnosperms** produce seeds on the surfaces of woody, leaf-like structures called cones. The pine tree is one well-known example of a gymnosperm. Gymnosperm cones are reproductive structures: male cones produce pollen, and female cones produce ovules on the same tree. During the process of pollination, pollen is transferred by wind, insects, or rain from a male cone to the eggs of the female cone.

Angiosperms produce fruits, which attract animals that eat the fruit and then disperse its seeds. This group of plants is considered the highest order of evolution in the plant kingdom. Unlike gymnosperms, angiosperms produce coated seeds that are enclosed by tissues of an ovary, which is part of the plant's flower. The ovary and other tissues develop into the mature structure that is the fruit. When you eat a piece of fruit, you are actually consuming a plant's mature ovary.

There are approximately 300,000 varieties of plants that produce flowers, fruits, and seeds. All flowering plants are considered angiosperms. The two major categories of angiosperms are **monocots** and **dicots**. The distinction between the two involves a structure called a **cotyledon**. The cotyledon contains the embryo and stores nutrients for germination of the embryo. A monocot's seed contains only one cotyledon. Examples include orchids as well as grasses such as rye, corn, wheat, and rice. A dicot's seed contains two cotyledons. Dicots account for the majority of angiosperms—about 180,000 varieties—including most herbaceous (non-woody) plants, flowering shrubs, and trees. Examples of dicots include legumes (beans), apples, and oak trees.

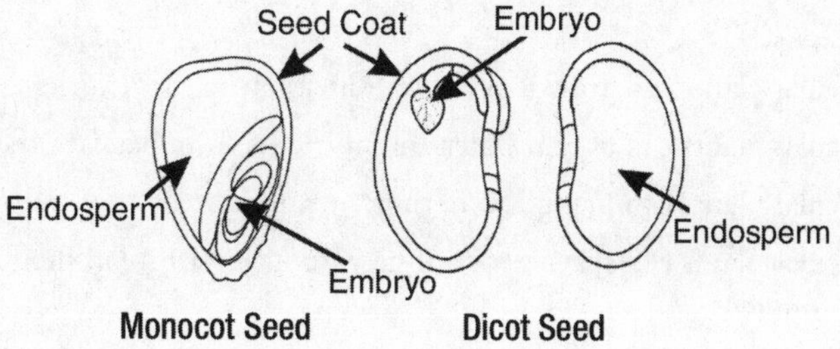

Flowers are the specialized reproductive organs for flowering plants. They contain both the male and female portions of the plant, as shown and described in the following diagram:

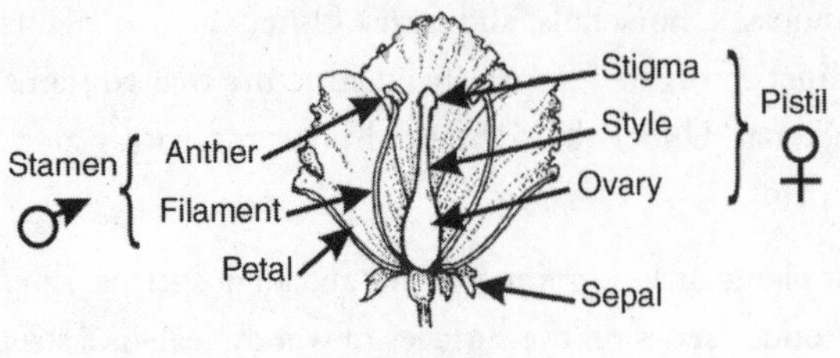

- **Petals:** The floral portions of the plant, usually ornate to attract pollinators
- **Pistil:** The female reproductive parts (stigma, style, ovary)
  - Stigma—the portion on which pollen lands
  - Style—the slender tube-like portion between the stigma and ovary
  - Ovary—contains the egg and site of fertilization; the ovary matures into the fruit with seeds
- **Stamen:** The male reproductive parts (anther, filament)
  - Anther—produces pollen
  - Filament—the stalk on which the anther sits
- **Sepals:** The protective portion of the unopened flower

In an angiosperm, pollination occurs when pollen is transferred from the anther to the stigma. Some angiosperms can self-pollinate, while others rely on insects, birds, or wind to carry pollen from the anther of one plant to the stigma of another.

12. All of the following characteristics clearly distinguish vascular plants from nonvascular plants EXCEPT:

A. Vascular plants can grow in a vertical direction.

B. Vascular plants can obtain water and nutrients from beneath the earth.

C. Vascular plants can manufacture their own food.

D. Vascular plants can survive for a time without moisture in their immediate environment.

All plants, vascular and nonvascular alike, can manufacture their own food. **The correct answer is C.**

13. Which statement about a typical vascular plant is **least** accurate?

A. The roots store water and other nutrients.

B. The leaves exchange carbon dioxide for oxygen.

C. The xylem regulates the plant's water intake.

D. The xylem transports glucose from leaves to roots.

The xylem is the hollow, tube-like portion of a plant's vascular bundle that carries water from the root system up to the leaves, where the water is combined with carbon dioxide to produce glucose. The phloem is responsible for transporting glucose from one part of the plant to another. **The correct answer is D.**

Kingdom Animalia (Animals)

Animals have adapted to live in practically every environment on Earth. From habitat to size and from form to color, animals show amazing variety. There are at least 4 million known species of animals. But all are multicellular; and all are heterotrophic, meaning they must obtain food by consuming other organisms. All members of the animal kingdom share the following characteristics:

- They are motile, which means they can move from place to place during at least some part of their life; they can also move one part of their body in respect to the other parts.
- They are not photosynthetic (they do not produce their own energy but rather obtain that energy by consuming other organisms).
- They reproduce sexually (although some may reproduce asexually as well).
- They consist of multiple cells (they are multicellular), many of which organize into tissues and then into complex organ systems.

Within the animal kingdom are different phyla (the next level down in the taxonomic classification system). Following are the main features and representative members of each phylum. Note that the phyla listed here begin with the more basic forms and advance to more complex forms. The phylum Chordata, the last one listed here, is examined in greater detail than the others.

Phylum Porifera (Sponges)

- **Features:** Stationary (sessile) organisms as adult; contain pores for circulation of water and food
- **Members:** Marine and freshwater sponges

Phylum Cnidaria (Cnidarians)

- **Features:** Secrete a hard, protective covering that surrounds the organism; have a two-form lifecycle (a stationary, or sessile, *polyp* produces a free-floating *medusae*); radial symmetry (body forms symmetrical around a center); stinging tentacles surround a mouth used for both ingesting food and eliminating waste
- **Representative members:** Hydra, jellyfish, corals, sea anemone

Phylum Platyhelminthes (Flatworms)

- **Features:** Free-living, nonsegmented carnivores with a sac-type digestive system
- **Representative members:** Planarian, tapeworm, fluke (Tapeworms are segmented parasites that live in the digestive tract of vertebrates and have no digestive system; flukes are both external and internal parasites with flattened bodies that live off of fluids from their host.)

Phylum Aschelminthes (Roundworms)

- **Features:** Cylindrical bodies and a complete digestive tract; not segmented; can be free-living or parasitic; especially useful for recycling in soil habitats
- **Representative members:** Nematode, pinworm

Phylum Annelida (Segmented Worms)

- **Features:** Occupy marine environments (exception: earthworms); segmented bodies; can be parasitic (example: blood-sucking leech); have developed organ systems, including circulatory, muscular, digestive, and nervous system
- **Representative members:** Earthworm, leech, polychaetes

Phylum Arthropoda (Arthropods)

- **Features:** Some possess a head, thorax, and abdomen (insects, spiders); have appendages such as jointed legs, antennae, mouthparts, and wings; have external exoskeleton armor; metamorphose from egg, larva, and pupa to adult; most are terrestrial, but some are marine dwellers (Class *Crustacea*)
- **Members:** Class *Insecta* (insects), Class *Arachnida* (spiders), Class *Diploda* (millipedes), Class *Chilopoda* (centipedes), Class *Crustacea* (crustaceans)

Phylum Mollusca (Mollusks)

- **Features:** Soft bodies (some are protected by shells); some have a ventral, muscular foot (example: bivalves, in which two shells are hinged together); have well-developed circulatory and nervous systems
- **Representative members:** Bivalves (clam, mussel), squid, snail, octopus

Phylum Echinodermata (Echinoderms)

- **Features:** Marine dwelling; possess tubular feet and a water-circulating system; lattice-like internal skeleton and usually a hard, spiny outer covering; adults exhibit radial body symmetry (a five-pointed body form)
- **Representative members:** Starfish, sand dollar, sea cucumber, sea urchin

Phylum Chordata Vertebrata (Vertebrates)

This is the most advanced phylum in terms of evolutionary development. Three evolutionary developments make the Chordata phylum so advanced:

- A *notochord*—a flexible rod that provides structural support
- A *dorsal nerve chord* on the back or upper surface, which in some animals differentiates into a brain and spinal cord
- One or more *pharyngeal gill slits* for carbon dioxide/oxygen exchange (in higher animals, these slits can appear as passages leading from the nose and mouth to the esophagus)

The phylum Chordata includes several different classes—the taxonomic system's next level down—as listed and briefly described below. Animals in the first four classes are **ectothermic** (*cold-blooded*), which means that their internal body temperature varies directly with external temperature. Animals in the remaining two classes are **endothermic** (*warm-blooded*), meaning they normally maintain a constant internal body temperature. (Note that only two of several classes of fish are listed here.)

- **Class Chondrichthyes (cartilaginous fish)**
  - **Features:** Cold-blooded; cartilage skeleton and fins
  - **Members:** Sharks and rays
- **Class Osteichthyes (bony fish)**
  - **Features:** Cold-blooded; bony skeleton, fins, and scales; use gills to process oxygen from water; mainly external fertilization
  - **Members:** trout, bass, carp
- **Class Amphibia (amphibians)**
  - **Features:** Cold-blooded; moist skin with no scales; external fertilization; undergo **metamorphosis** (dramatic change from fishlike form to four-legged, air-breathing terrestrial form) during development after birth or hatching; three-chambered heart
  - **Members:** Frog, salamander, toad
- **Class Reptilia (reptiles)**
  - **Features:** Cold-blooded; body covering of scales and horns; internal egg fertilization
  - **Members:** Snake, turtle, crocodile, lizard
- **Class Aves (birds)**
  - **Features:** Warm-blooded; wings and forelimbs; hard bill that covers the jaw; covering of feathers; internal fertilization; eggs enclosed in calcium-enriched shell; four-chambered heart
  - **Members:** Chicken, crow, eagle
- **Class Mammalia (mammals)**
  - **Features:** Warm-blooded; hair covers body, feed young with mammary glands; internal fertilization; four-chambered heart
  - **Members:**
    - ***Monotremes*** (primitive egg-laying)—duck-billed platypus
    - ***Marsupials*** (mother carries young in body pouch)—kangaroo
    - ***Rodents*** (incisor teeth that grow continually)—rat, squirrel, mouse
    - ***Cetaceans*** (marine; forelimbs modified to flippers)—dolphin, porpoise, whale
    - ***Carnivores*** (meat-eaters)—dog, wolf, cat
    - ***Primates*** (large brain; stand erect; ability to grasp and hold objects)—human, ape, monkey, lemur

14. Animals belonging to which of the following phyla have body forms that exhibit radial symmetry?

I. Cnidaria (cnidarians)
II. Aschelminthes (roundworms)
III. Arthropoda (arthropods)
IV. Echinodermata (echinoderms)

A. I and II only
B. I and IV only
C. II and III only
D. II, III, and IV only

All cniderians and echinoderms have body forms that exhibit radial symmetry. In this shape, the body extends symmetrically outward from a central mouth or other opening. **The correct answer is B.**

15. Which class in phylum Chordata could be characterized as a "hybrid," exhibiting a combination of characteristics from two other such classes?

A. Cartilaginous fish
B. Amphibians
C. Reptiles
D. Birds

Amphibians undergo a metamorphosis after birth or hatching, beginning as water-breathing, fishlike animals and then transforming into terrestrial, air-breathing animals with four legs. In this respect, they are a hybrid of fish and reptiles, both of which are also cold-blooded. **The correct answer is B.**

To better understand the relationship of one class of animals to another, scientists use a method of mapping known as a **cladogram**. A cladogram essentially creates an evolutionary family tree. The base of a cladogram depicts a common ancestor of the animals represented. As the cladogram moves up, branches shoot out, representing groups of animals that branched away from the common ancestor; these branches start from the earliest or least evolved organisms and move upward toward the most evolved organism. Cladograms can be very general, covering an entire animal kingdom, or very specific, covering only a single genus. Most cladograms are based on physiological differences, such as scales, feathers, and mammary glands. However, with the increase in genetic mapping, cladograms based on genetic relationships are also sometimes used. The cladogram below shows the ancestry of humans.

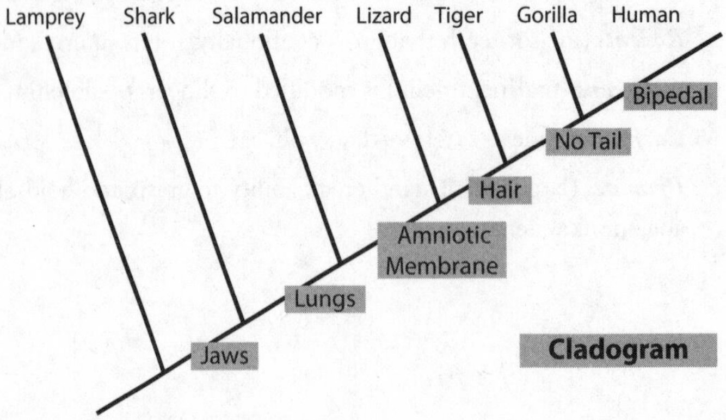

Cladogram

Natural Selection and Adaptation

Evolution is the process by which species of plants and animals arise from earlier life forms and undergo change over time. Our understanding of evolution is rooted largely in the theories of nineteenth-century scientist Charles Darwin. Based on his observations of different traits among certain animal species, Darwin theorized that species evolve as a result of **natural selection**—a process by which the strongest, or "fittest," among offspring survive to reproduce, passing on to the next generation the particular traits that helped them survive. When a species's environment changes, those members that have inherited traits that help them survive the change are more likely to survive. These survival traits are called **adaptations**. Darwin's theory has been verified by studies of the fossil record and by DNA studies. **Artificial selection** refers to human manipulation of traits in a species by selective breeding. This is done most often to produce desired traits in crop, livestock, and pet species. Over many, many generations, genetic traits that help a species adapt to its environment become increasingly common among individuals, while less useful traits wither.

Darwin's theories of evolution and natural selection have since been refined to accommodate the theories of punctuated equilibrium, sexual selection, and genetic drift.

- **Punctuated equilibrium:** Darwin proposed that species evolution is a gradual, nearly constant process. Recent investigations involving fossil evidence suggest, however, that evolution occurs in spurts (**punctuations**), between which are long time periods of stability (**equilibrium**) when no change in the species occurs. Environmental events such as sudden and dramatic climate changes, which we know have occurred many times both globally and regionally throughout our planet's history, lend support to this idea: it is when a species confronts a sudden environmental change that it is forced to adapt to that change by evolving.
- **Sexual selection:** This type of selection occurs when individuals in a population compete not for resources and survival, but rather for mates. For example, males with characteristics such as aggressiveness, great size, strength, or colorful feathers might be more successful in attracting mates, and thus their genetic traits will ultimately survive over many generations.
- **Genetic drift:** Studying isolated and relatively small populations, researchers have shown that certain genetic traits sometimes survive or wither over time by random chance. Like rolling genetic dice and getting the same trait many times in a row, against the statistical odds, a species can evolve in an aimless, or drifting, manner that has nothing to do with survival of the fittest.

Given that populations continually evolve, at what point does a population evolve into a new species? The generally accepted definition of the biological species concept is a population of organisms that is reproductively isolated from all other populations. This definition is generally accepted for vertebrate species, although other legitimate alternative definitions exist that take into account the diversity of reproductive biology (sexual, asexual, budding, etc.), and natural histories and life cycles.

Speciation occurs in three stages:

1. **A population becomes isolated**. Speciation begins when a group of individuals separates into an isolated population that no longer exchanges individuals with the parent population. Physical or geographical barriers to migration can occur from changes in the environment, such as a new stream resulting from a storm, creating allopatric (living separately) species.

Isolation can also be due to a change in a trait, such as behavior or coloration that prevents individuals from interbreeding with dissimilar individuals in the population, even if they are living together in the same geographical area.

2. **The isolated population evolves independently**. Once isolated, individuals will naturally accumulate random mutations, but they will also be subjected to a different set of selective pressures and/or evolutionary processes than that of the original population, and thus evolve differently than the parent population.
3. **Reproductive isolating mechanisms evolve**. Eventually the separated populations will evolve to a point where they can no longer interbreed because of reproductive isolating mechanisms. These are grouped into two categories: **Pre-zygotic mechanisms** prevent reproduction and include physical mechanisms that prevent successful copulation or fertilization; behavioral mechanisms that prevent successful solicitation of a mate; or temporal mechanisms in which mating seasons or fertility patterns are no longer synchronized. **Post-zygotic mechanisms** result in offspring with gene combinations that are fatal, cause sterility, or otherwise prevent reproduction.

16. Which of the following is **least likely** to contribute to the development of a new species?
    - **A.** Volcanic activity that reforms a region's landscape
    - **B.** A shift in a population's sexual selection criteria
    - **C.** An adaptive response to the appearance of a new predator
    - **D.** A local climate change that alters a population's breeding season

Choice C simply describes natural selection, whereby the traits of a species' fittest and most adaptable individuals are the ones that are passed on to subsequent generations. In itself, natural selection does not cause speciation. **The correct answer is C.**

Energy Flows in Ecosystems

Ecology is the scientific study of the interactions among organisms and between communities of organisms and the environment. All of these interactions determine where organisms are found, in what numbers they are found, and why they are found where they are. In this section, we will briefly explore the main concepts in this field of study.

The Biosphere

The term **biosphere** refers to the entire part of the earth that supports life. The biosphere consists of the surface of the earth, of course, but it also encompasses the lithosphere (the rocky crust of the earth), atmosphere (the air we breathe, which consists mainly of nitrogen and oxygen), and the hydrosphere (all of the water on the earth). This section examines the part of the biosphere appearing on the earth's surface. The lithosphere, atmosphere, and hydrosphere are examined in the Earth science review.

Environments, Ecosystems, and Biomes

Ecologists define an **environment** as any external factor that can influence an organism during its lifetime. These environmental influences can be divided into two categories:

- **Biotic factors:** living things that affect an organism
- **Abiotic factors:** nonliving things, such as water, air, geology, and the sun, that can affect an organism

Biotic and abiotic factors are interrelated. For example, plants rely on many abiotic factors, including rainfall and temperature, for proper growth. If either should change dramatically in a particular region, plant growth will decline, which in turn will reduce food sources and habitats for animals.

The term **ecosystem** refers to an entire community of organisms, their physical environment, and the interactions among that community and between the community and that environment.

Flow of Energy and Matter in Ecosystems

Ecosystems are structured according to each organism's main source of food. **Producers** are autotrophic—they manufacture their own food from inorganic substances. Autotrophs include green plants and photosynthetic bacteria, both of which use solar energy to convert nutrients into glucose. (Autotrophs include other types of bacteria as well.) **Consumers** are heterotrophic, which means that they rely on other organisms as their food source. There are three sub-types of consumers:

- **Primary consumers** (herbivores), which feed directly on producers
- **Secondary consumers** (carnivores), which feed only on primary consumers
- **Tertiary consumers** (carnivores), which feed on secondary consumers

Decomposers are heterotrophic but feed on waste or dead material: dead plants of all kinds, fecal waste, and dead animals; they recycle raw materials to the ecosystem. A simple feeding pathway among organisms in an ecosystem can be shown in a **food chain**. Here is an example of a simple food chain:

Humans (secondary consumer) → fish (primary consumer) → plankton (producer)

Food chains represent a transfer of energy from one organism to another. All organisms need a source of food to survive, so all organisms participate in food chains. Energy (food) moves through a series of levels—from producer to herbivore to carnivore. These levels are called **trophic levels** (the word *trophic* means "feeding"). The following diagram shows the hierarchy of the feeding levels:

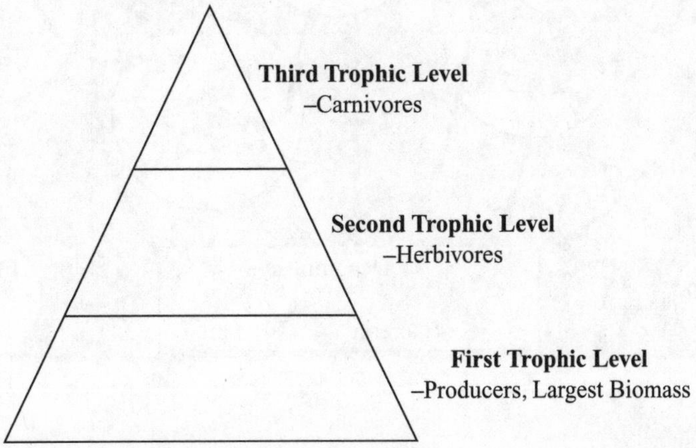

Producers account for the main portion of the **biomass**—the total amount of food available for consumption in the ecosystem. On average, producers pass only about 1 percent of their biomass to primary consumers, which in turn pass about 10 percent of their biomass to secondary consumers. At each higher level, again, about 10 percent of biomass is passed up to the next trophic level. The great majority of biomass is not consumed but rather is converted to energy used for growth and survival.

Of course, humans don't eat only fish, herbivore populations don't eat only one kind of plant, and carnivore populations don't consume only one type of herbivore. Thus the simple food chain is an oversimplification for most ecosystems. A more complete model is a **food web**, which links many food chains together into a matrix that represents complex feeding relationships.

Energy is not recycled, but matter is. This cycling is usually studied in terms of the paths of several chemical elements found in organic compounds. For example, producers take in carbon as carbon dioxide and convert it into glucose. Consumers extract energy from glucose and release carbon back into the atmosphere as carbon dioxide, where it is once again available to producers. Carbon also takes long, complicated side trips, as when it is converted to fossil fuel over millions of years, but it never disappears. Other elements, such as nitrogen and oxygen, also have complex cycles. These are explained in greater detail in the pages on Earth science.

As mentioned previously, energy relationships among trophic levels can almost never be described completely by simple, one-to-one linear food chains. To see the complete picture, we must construct a food web that combines the energy exchanges among all producers, consumers, and decomposers. In the food web shown here, the arrows show the direction of energy transfer.

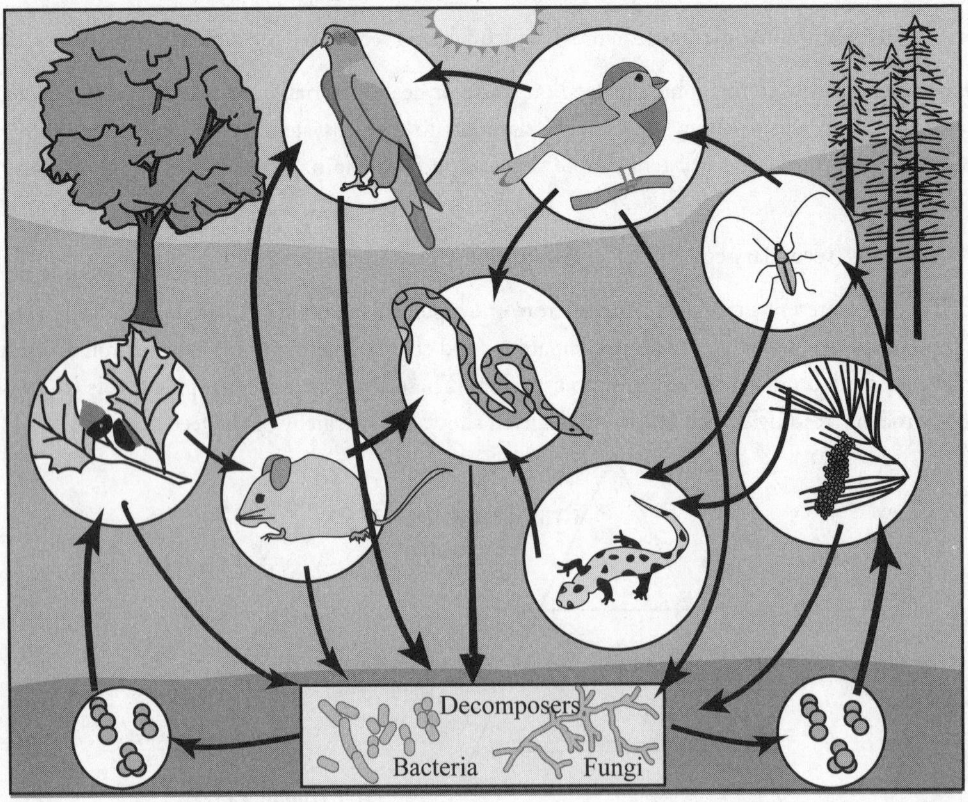

Pick any member of the food web and think about what would happen if that species were removed or if their population changed. Take the mouse, for example. A decrease in mouse population will mean a decrease in snake population but also a decrease in lizard population because snakes will have to prey more heavily on them. This will lead to an increase in insect population, and so forth. If you continue with this line of reasoning, you will see that changing the population of any one species in an ecosystem affects the populations of all other species.

17. Which of the following **best** helps to explain why feeding structures in most ecosystems are better described as food "webs" rather than food "chains"?

A. Many different types of plants can exist in the same community.

B. Without a sufficient food source, animals will move to another community.

C. If animal life disappears, then so does plant life.

D. Many animals consume plants as well as other types of animals.

The simple model of linear food "chain" does not account for the fact that the same animal might be a primary consumer (plant-eater) in one chain *and* a secondary consumer (meat-eater) in other chain. A "web" in which various chains are interconnected better represents a community's complete feeding structure. **The correct answer is D.**

Habitats and Niches

Feeding relationships dominate the structure of an ecosystem. However, an ecosystem isn't just one giant free-for-all characterized by severe interspecies competition for food. Each population of animals occupies a particular **habitat**—a particular locale such as a forest community or an arid, grassy plain in which a species is best suited to live according to its biological adaptations. Different species can even become "specialists" within their habitats by occupying a **niche**. A niche refers to all specific biotic and abiotic elements an organism incorporates for its survival, such as feeding location, food source, feeding schedule, source of shelter, and nesting location. For example, many birds may occupy a forest habitat, but some eat seeds and others eat worms and insects; some birds eat high up in a tree and others closer to the ground. In other words, various types of birds in the same habitat occupy different niches.

Carrying Capacity

A **population** is a group of individuals of the same species occupying the same geographical region.

A population's growth depends largely on its male-female ratio and on the portion of the population that is at or below reproductive age. With too few individuals capable of reproduction, population growth will slow or even decline.

Just as the growth rate of any population is limited, so is its size. A given environment has only so many resources to support a population. The maximum population of a particular organism that a given environment can support is referred to as **carrying capacity**. The most significant limiting factors in carrying capacity are food resources and physical space. A population may exceed its carrying capacity temporarily if the birth rate is extremely great, though eventually the population will decline to reflect the scarcity of food resources and/or space.

18. A colony of termites feeds off the wood frame of an old house for several years, but then the colony disappears. Assuming that the termites were not exterminated by humans, what **most likely** happened?

Eventually, the termite population

A. exceeded its life span.

B. was consumed by secondary consumers.

C. exhausted all of its available biomass.

D. exceeded its carrying capacity.

The termites' environment (the house's wood frame) contained a limited amount of food resources to support the growing termite population. Once this carrying capacity was exceeded, in all likelihood the termites died off. **The correct answer is D.**

Body Systems

The body's organ systems work together in many other ways. The best way to understand these connections is to examine each of the organ systems, in turn. This section briefly describes the structure, components, and functions of the body's various organ systems, as well as how they function together with one or more of the other systems.

The Integumentary System

The integumentary system includes skin, sweat glands, oil glands, hair, and nails. Skin is the largest organ in the body. Our skin is a barrier between our bodies and the external environment. It prevents water loss, mechanical and chemical damage, and microbial invasion. Skin is composed of two distinct regions: the **epidermis** and the **dermis**. These two regions are further divided into several functional layers. The third region just beneath the skin is the **hypodermis**. It is not considered a part of the skin, but it serves a protective function similar to skin.

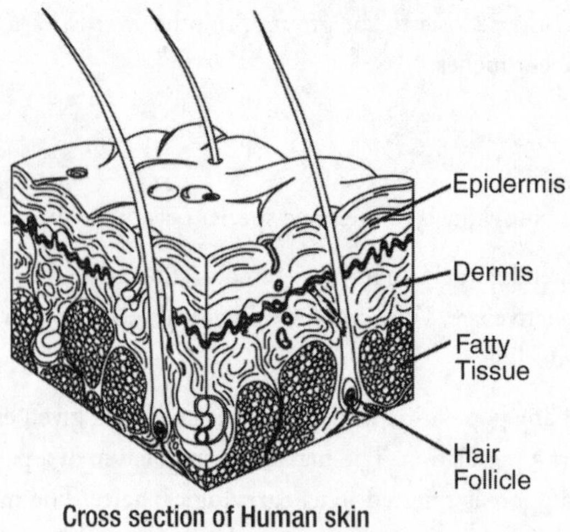

Cross section of Human skin

The Skeletal System

The skeletal system supports the body and acts as a lever system for the muscles, creating movement at joints. This system contains **bones**, of course, which provide for movement and support. But bones also serve as a mineral depository. What's more, the marrow, located in the center of the bones, is where new blood cells are formed. The 206 bones in the normal human body can be divided into two major groups: the *axial* skeleton (80 bones that run along the axis of the skeleton) and the *appendicular* skeleton (126 bones that include the limbs and the pectoral and pelvic girdles).

Bones articulate, or meet, with one another at joints. **Cartilage** lines the joints to prevent bones from rubbing against each other. Depending on the type of movement at a joint, the cartilage can provide either a smooth articulating surface or a strong adhesion between bones. **Ligaments**, band-like connective tissues, help stabilize movable joints. Finally, **tendons** attach muscles to bone at joints.

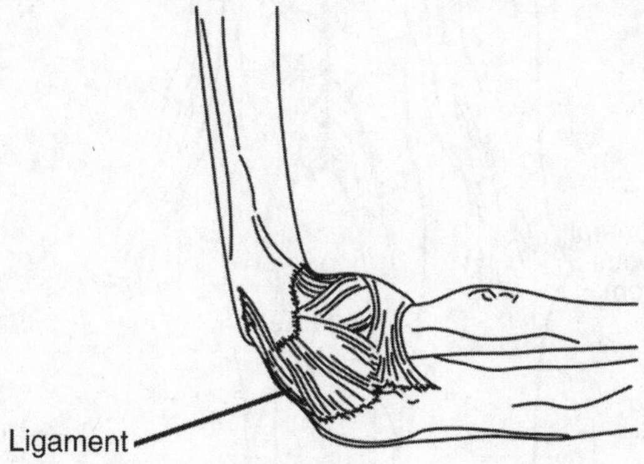

The Muscular System

The more than 600 muscles in the human body come in three types: skeletal, cardiac, and smooth. **Skeletal muscles** are responsible for the body's movement and are attached to bone at either end by tendons. On a microscopic level, the fibers that make up skeletal muscles are elongated, cylindrical, multinucleate cells that are encased by a **sarcolemma:** a membrane similar to the cell membrane of other cells containing a single nucleus. A muscle is composed of many bundles of these fibers working together. Each time a muscle contracts and shortens itself, it moves the body part it is attached to. **Cardiac muscle** is found in the walls of the heart. This muscle allows for the strong pumping action of the heart's ventricles. **Smooth muscle** is found in the walls of hollow organs, such as the stomach and intestines. Cardiac and smooth muscles coordinate with the nervous system in an entirely different way than skeletal muscles do. The movement of skeletal muscle is voluntary—you have conscious control over it. Cardiac and smooth muscles, however, move involuntarily—you can't control them consciously. They work without your even thinking about it.

The Nervous System

The nervous system, along with the endocrine system (you will read about this next), is responsible for coordinating all of the physiological processes in the body. The nervous system responds rapidly to external stimuli and to messages from the brain. It regulates a myriad of actions from breathing and digestion to the blink of an eye and the beating of the heart.

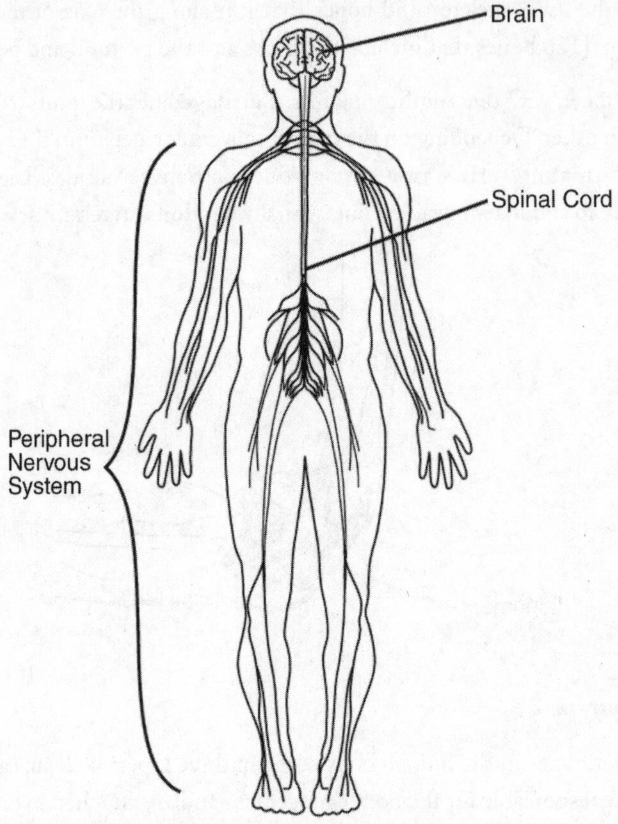

Peripheral Nervous System

The **peripheral nervous system** extends away from the spine and into the limbs. It carries impulses from sensory neurons to the **central nervous system**, which consists of the brain and spinal cord. The brain processes incoming sensory information and translates it into instructions. It then sends those instructions to the appropriate organs of the body, so the body can respond to the initial sensory information. The **neuron** is the functional unit of nervous tissue that is used by the central and peripheral nervous systems.

Taste, vision, hearing, balance, and smell are integral parts of the nervous system. They allow us to interact with and interpret external stimuli as well as monitor internal changes of a chemical or physical nature. Different animals utilize these senses to different degrees. Also, some nonhuman animals possess senses that humans lack altogether. For instance, some species of birds detect the magnetic field of the earth; honeybees see ultraviolet light; and rattlesnakes sense infrared radiation from objects at a distance.

The Eye

Visual perception in humans is like a camera lens. Light enters through an adjustable lens that focuses the image on a receptor called the **retina,** much as in a camera, the image is focused on film or—in a digital camera—on an image sensor array. Within the retina are specialized photoreceptors called **rods** and **cones** that detect different properties of light. Cones allow for color vision and visual acuity, and rods are responsive in low light conditions. Some of the simpler organisms, such as euglena, use eyespots that merely detect light intensity. Arthropods such as grasshoppers possess a compound eye that lets light enter at different angles; this enhances their sight in dim light. Other animals, such as deer and mice, are colorblind (as are many people) and cannot reliably distinguish certain colors.

The Ear

In higher animals, the ear is subdivided into three regions: the outer, the middle, and the inner ear. The outer ear consists of the **pinna** (a cartilaginous, funnel-like structure), the external auditory **meatus** (the ear canal), and the **tympanic membrane** (the eardrum). The middle ear contains the three ear ossicles: the **malleus** (hammer), the **incus** (anvil), and the **stapes** (stirrup). The **Eustachian tube** in the middle ear opens into the throat and allows for pressure stabilization. The inner ear contains the receptors for hearing, balance, and equilibrium.

Hearing is both a mechanical and neural event. Sound waves are funneled into the ear via the external auditory meatus and arrive at the tympanic membrane. The tympanic membrane sends the vibratory motion at the same frequency it was received to the ear ossicles. The motion is transferred to the middle ear, from the malleus to the incus to the stapes. The stapes sends this energy through the oval window and into the inner ear. The fluids in the inner ear are displaced by this motion, which in turn stimulates hair cells that synapse with sensory neurons. These neurons then send messages to the auditory centers of the brain.

The Endocrine System

The **endocrine system** is composed of specialized organs called **glands**, which secrete chemical messengers called **hormones.** These hormones are carried throughout the body by the circulatory system, but they have only site-specific responses and can attach only to recognized receptor molecules of certain cells. The response time of hormones varies according to the outcome that is needed. For instance, epinephrine and norepinephrine (released from the adrenal medulla gland) can cause a rapid behavioral response known as the "fight or flight" response. This causes the heart rate, blood pressure, and breathing rate to increase as well as directing blood to skeletal muscle. The following table lists each major gland, the major hormones it releases, and its function.

Major Endocrine Glands and Functions

Endocrine Gland	Hormones Released	Functions
Pituitary (both anterior and posterior)*	1. Growth hormone 2. Anti-diuretic hormone	1. Regulator of muscle, bone, and connective tissue growth 2. Increases re-uptake of water into blood from renal tubules; increases blood pressure
Thyroid	1. Thyroxin 2. Calcitonin	1. Regulates cellular metabolism 2. Decreases calcium ions in blood
Parathyroid	Parathyroid hormone	Increases calcium ions in blood
Pancreas	1. Insulin 2. Glucagon	1. Lowers blood sugar levels; increases rate of metabolism of stored sugar 2. Increases blood sugar levels by converting glycogen to glucose; synthesizes glucose; and releases glucose to blood from liver cells
Adrenal glands	1. Corticosteroid 2. Epinephrine	1. Decreases sodium ion excretion; influences cellular metabolism and provides resistance stressors; contributes to secondary sexual characteristics during puberty 2. Increases blood sugar levels, heart rate, blood pressure, and respiratory rate; shunts blood to skeletal muscle; mobilizes the sympathetic nervous system for short-term stressors or emergencies
Testes	Testosterone	Starts the maturation of male reproductive organs, secondary sexual characteristics at puberty, and sex drive
Ovaries	1. Estrogen 2. Progesterone	1. Initiates maturation of female reproductive organs and secondary sexual characteristics at puberty 2. Promotes breast development and menstrual cycle

* The pituitary gland has an effect on all of the major glands. The few listed in this table do not represent the total number of hormones released from the pituitary.

19. Which of the following is the **best** analogy to the nervous system?

A. A motor

B. A radio broadcast

C. A computer

D. A bee hive

A computer receives input, which is transmitted to a central processor, which then provides instructions as to the proper response to that input. The nervous system functions in a similar way. **The correct answer is C.**

The Cardiovascular System

Many multicellular organisms, such as humans, consist of trillions of cells that need a rapid and efficient way to meet their physiological needs. During cellular metabolism, cells take in nutrients, create waste, and store, make, and use molecules—all of which need to be transported to other parts of the body. The cardiovascular system provides transportation by using several integrated parts. The heart pumps blood into **arteries,** which distribute the blood to the organs. Blood is pumped into successively smaller arteries until it enters thin-walled vessels called **capillaries.** Blood is diffused through capillary beds so material can be exchanged between the blood and organ tissues. Blood then percolates through the capillary beds and into **veins,** which gradually merge with larger veins until the blood returns to the heart.

Cardiac Physiology

The lower right side of the heart, the **right ventricle**, pumps blood to the lungs, which are near the heart. The larger **left ventricle** sends blood to the **aorta,** the main artery that delivers blood to the rest of the body. The left ventricle must contract with greater force, and this force creates a higher pressure in the arteries. Each contraction of the heart is reflected in the heartbeat. (When you take your pulse, you are actually measuring your heartbeat rate.)

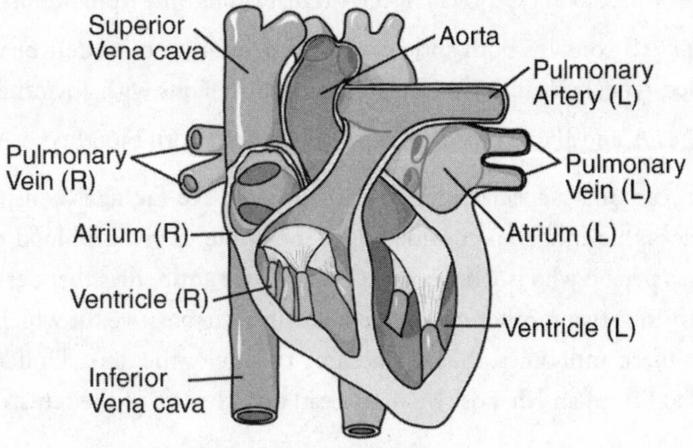

Heart and Associated Vessels

Blood pressure is measured through the heartbeat. There are two phases to a heartbeat. The first is referred to as **systolic pressure** and is the result of the strong contraction of the ventricles as blood is pumped into the aorta. The second phase is **diastolic pressure**, which is the result of ventricular relaxation.

Blood

The largest component of blood is a fluid matrix called **plasma**. Blood plasma, which is mostly water, transports a host of materials, including wastes, nutrients, hormones, electrolytes, and proteins, cells, and heat from one body region to another. Most notably, within the plasma are erythrocytes (red blood cells), leukocytes (white blood cells), and thrombocytes (platelets), each of which performs a unique function:

- **Red blood cells** consist mainly of **hemoglobin**, which are the molecules that transport oxygen throughout the bloodstream.
- **White blood cells** serve as a defense mechanism against disease, tumors, parasites, toxins, and bacteria; they move from blood to tissues, and they produce antibodies for long-term protection.
- **Platelets** are tiny disk-shaped cells that seal small ruptures in blood vessels and assist in blood clotting.

Human blood is categorized by four types—A, B, AB, and O—according to which type of antigens are present on the surface of a person's red blood cells. (Letters A and B represent different types of antigens.) An **antigen** is a substance that stimulates the production of an **antibody** when introduced into the body. Antibodies circulating throughout a person's bloodstream normally recognize the antigens in that same person's blood and do not react with them. However, if one type of blood is transfused with another type of blood, antibodies in the new blood can react with the foreign antigens by binding to them, resulting in clumping of the blood. Thus, a safe **blood transfusion** requires that the antigens of the donor's blood match those of the recipient's blood:

- Blood type O contains no antigens and thus can safely be used for any blood transfusions, regardless of the blood type of the person receiving the transfusion. On the other hand, individuals with blood type O can receive transfusions only from donors with type O blood.
- Blood type AB contains both antigens A and B and thus can safely be transfused with any other blood type, but cannot be donated for transfusions with any other blood type.
- Blood types A and B can be donated for transfusion with blood type AB.

Human blood that contains a special antigen known as the **Rh factor** is considered **Rh-positive**, while blood that lacks this antigen is considered **Rh-negative**. If given a blood transfusion from an Rh-positive donor, a person who is Rh-negative can produce antibodies that destroy red blood cells. The fetus of an Rh-negative mother can nevertheless be Rh-positive, in which case the mother's blood will produce these antibodies, thus threatening the life of the fetus. Under this circumstance, a transfusion of blood from an Rh-positive donor can save the life of the fetus.

The Respiratory System

The cyclic exchange of respiratory gases within an organism is known as **respiration**. Most vertebrates use lungs for gas exchange, although animals such as frogs use both a lung and moist skin to exchange gases.

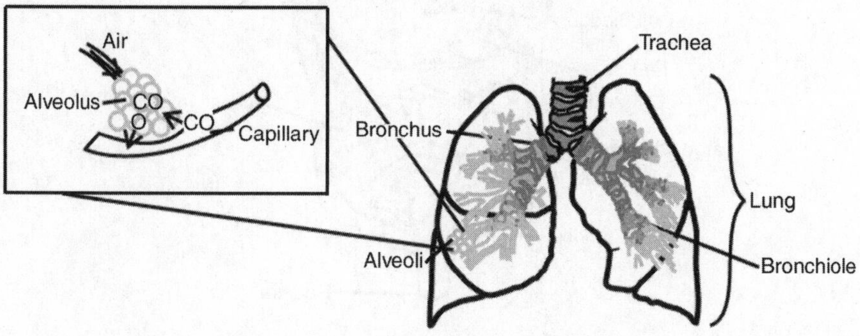

Lungs

Mammals have the most complex respiratory systems of all animals, with successively smaller branching tubes that open into vascularized sacs. Oxygen enters the lungs through the **bronchi**—two large tubes that branch off the trachea—which phase into smaller **bronchioles**, which then terminate in **alveolar sacs**. These sacs are covered with capillaries to facilitate gas exchange across the thin walls of the **alveoli**.

The Digestive System

Cells need a constant supply of nutrients for energy and as building blocks to assemble macromolecules. The **digestive system** allocates and processes these nutrients. The human digestive system, in all its complex functions, is nothing more than a long muscular tube extending from the mouth to the anus. Along this pathway are several modified pouches and segments to perform specific tasks, including nutrient intake, mechanical and chemical processes of digestion, nutrient uptake, and the elimination of undigested material.

When food reaches the stomach, both mechanical and chemical functions go to work on it. The muscles in the walls of the stomach churn, mixing the food with gastric juice and pepsin, which digests proteins. The majority of chemical digestion and nutrient absorption occurs in the **small intestine**. To assist with this process, the **pancreas** delivers several enzymes: **trypsin**, which breaks large polypeptides into amino acids; **amylase**, which changes polysaccharides to simpler forms; and **lipase**, which breaks fat down into glycerol and fatty acids. The **liver** assists by producing **bile**, which physically emulsifies fats to improve digestion. Virtually all nutrient absorption occurs in the small intestine, where the nutrients pass through the walls into the blood vessels. The nutrient-laden blood is taken to the liver and then to the body tissue.

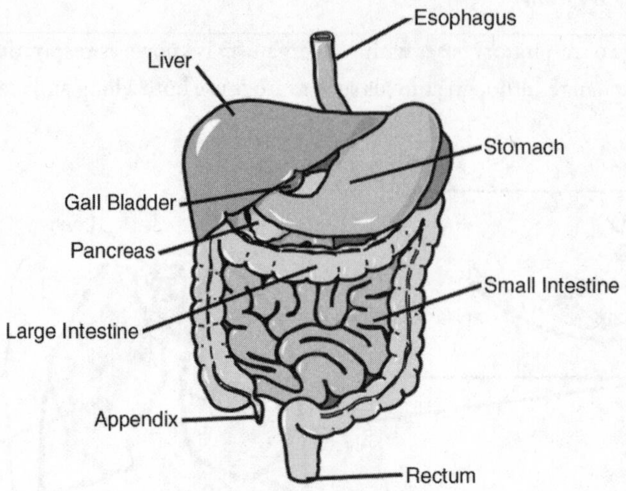

Digestive System

Not all food is digested, of course. Some moves into the **large intestine** to be processed. Any water and available minerals from the food are absorbed into the blood vessels of the walls of the large intestine and are returned to circulation. Bacterial action produces vitamin K, which is also absorbed into blood vessels and returned to circulation. The remainder of bacteria and undigested food forms the main component of feces, which is passed as waste from the body.

The Renal System

Cellular metabolism of every organism produces fluid waste products, such as urea and nitrogenous wastes, which need to be separated from useful products, such as water, and then disposed of. Simple organisms perform this task by diffusing waste directly into their surrounding environment. More complex organisms, on the other hand, use a tube system, or **renal system**, to excrete fluid wastes.

Vertebrates have one of the most complex renal systems of all organisms. It centers on the **kidney**, which is responsible for several functions:

- Blood filtration (the kidneys separate the filtrate from cellular components within blood)
- Monitoring of waste concentrations in blood
- Reabsorption from filtrate
- Return of reusable components back to blood
- Secretion for eventual removal of filtrate

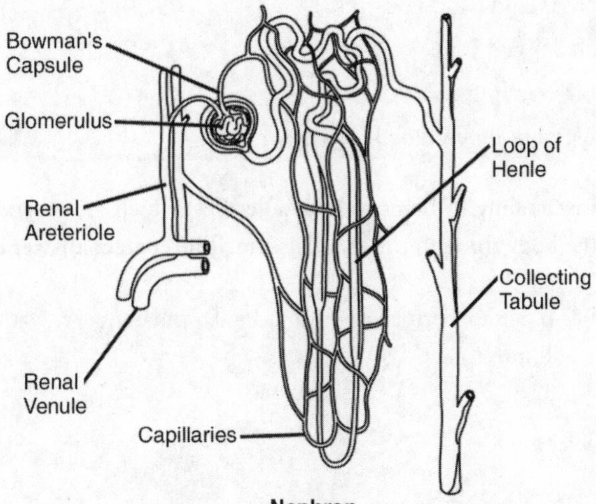

Nephron

Each kidney is composed of more than 2 million specialized units called **nephrons**, which play a large role in maintaining homeostasis by retaining useful substances and getting rid of waste products. Any usable molecules, including water, are reabsorbed and returned to circulation. Whatever is still left after this reabsorption process is waste, which is moved through the ureter to the bladder, where it waits to be passed from the body.

The Reproductive System

The primary goal of the reproductive system is the continuation of a species. There are many forms of reproduction, yet the degree of an organism's complexity is a good indicator of how it reproduces. **Asexual reproduction** does not require any of the complex structures used by eukaryotic cells. **Binary fission** is a type of asexual reproduction that is used by prokaryotic cells like bacteria. These cells merely replicate a simple loop of DNA and then undergo cytokinesis. **Fragmentation**, as seen in phylum Porifera (sponges), is another asexual form of reproduction. In this form, a piece of the body breaks away and matures into a larger form.

Vertebrates reproduce sexually by producing **gametes** (eggs and sperm) through their reproductive organs, called **gonads**. Females produce **ova**, or eggs, within their main reproductive structures, the **ovaries**. A hormone released by the pituitary gland stimulates egg production. An **embryo** develops from the initial **zygote**, a fertilized egg. If fertilization does not occur, the egg and its newly created uterine lining are sloughed off the walls of the uterus and moved out of the body. Males manufacture sperm within their major reproductive organ, the **testes**. The hormone **testosterone** signals and maintains sperm production. As with the female reproductive system, a pituitary hormone stimulates the production of sperm cells.

20. Which of the following is responsible for oxygen transport throughout the body?

A. Nephrons in the kidneys

B. Capillaries and veins

C. Alveolar sacs in the lungs

D. Hemoglobin in red blood cells

Red blood cells consist mainly of hemoglobin molecules, which are responsible for transporting oxygen throughout the body through the bloodstream. **The correct answer is D.**

21. Where does **most** nutrient absorption occur in the body?

A. The small intestine

B. The stomach

C. The liver

D. The large intestine

It is through the lining in the long, serpentine small intestine that the nutrients from the food we eat are absorbed into the bloodstream and transported to cells throughout the body. **The correct answer is A.**

Homeostasis

The body is a remarkable complex of various organ systems that function together in unison—like the components of a properly calibrated and well-oiled machine. For example, the organ systems naturally work together to ensure that the body's internal conditions remain stable and, if conditions deviate from their normal ranges, to return them to normal. Appropriate organ responses to internal changes help ensure steady body temperature, blood pressure, and the chemical composition of body fluids. The body's tendency to maintain the stability of these and other internal conditions is referred to as **homeostasis**.

There are many homeostatic mechanisms within the body, including temperature and water regulation. When the body gets overheated, sweat glands are activated and the body releases water. As air moves over the water that is being released through pores, the water evaporates, cooling the body. Conversely, when the body is too cold, the muscles will begin to contract involuntarily, causing the body to shiver. These small muscle contractions create heat via movement. By either sweating or shivering, the body will attempt to stay within the homeostatic range until it can no longer do so or until environmental conditions change.

Another homeostatic mechanism is water regulation, which is done primarily in the kidneys. Nephrons filter the blood for excess water and nutrients and then flush this excess out in the form of urine. Depending on the ratio of nutrients to water in the blood, the nephrons will regulate the amount of each it removes from the blood. When the body is slightly dehydrated, the urine is more concentrated, and when the body has plenty of water, the urine is less concentrated. This is an attempt at maintaining proper water levels throughout the body.

22. Which of the following helps ensure homeostasis in the human body?

A. Cardiac muscles, which pump more blood to skeletal muscles when you sense danger

B. Retinal cones, which allow you to see the difference between red and green traffic lights

C. Sweat glands, which help cool your body on a hot summer day

D. Inner ear receptors, which help you keep your balance during a tennis match

Through the process of homeostasis, your body seeks to maintain optimal states, including an optimal internal body temperature. When your body heats up too much, the integumentary system goes to work to secrete sweat, which helps reduce body temperature. **The correct answer is C.**

In order to carry out basic functions and maintain homeostasis, the body must have fuel. This fuel comes in the form of food. But not all foods are the same nutritionally. Foods are divided into three basic categories: **carbohydrates**, **proteins**, and **fats**. Comparatively, fats have more than twice the calories per gram (9 calories per gram) than either carbohydrates or proteins (4 calories per gram each). To put this into perspective, the United States Department of Agriculture (USDA) recommends a daily intake of approximately 2,600 calories for the moderately active man and approximately 2,000 calories for the moderately active woman. Rarely does a person eat a food that is fully a carbohydrate, protein, or fat. Because foods can have a mixture of these basic groups, the USDA breaks all food into six categories: grains; vegetables; fruits; milk/dairy; oils; and meat and beans (proteins). Each group is labeled with recommended serving amounts for a balanced daily diet. These servings amounts are: 6 oz. of grains; 5.5 ounces of proteins; 2 cups of fruit; 2.5 cups of vegetables; 3 cups of dairy; and a sparing amount of oils. A diet based on these portions would provide a person with approximately 2,000 calories. The USDA's MyPlate illustrates the relative amounts of the various food groups.

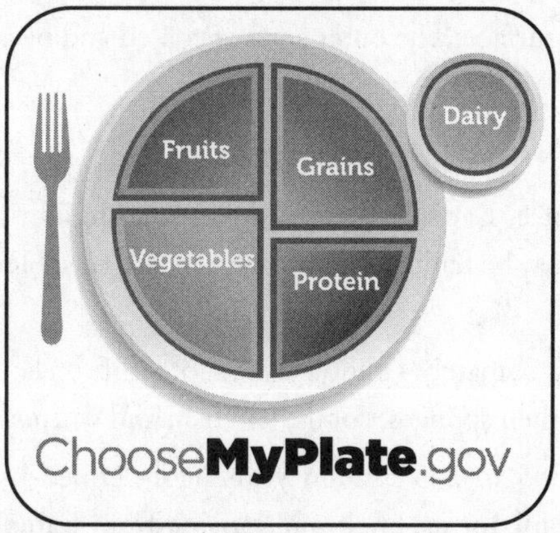

By eating a variety of foods within these guidelines, a person is also more apt to ingest essential vitamins and minerals. Vitamins are divided into two groups: water soluble and water insoluble. **Water-soluble vitamins** include Vitamin C and the B vitamins. Vitamin C is found in citrus fruits such as oranges, among other foods. While no food has all eight B-complex vitamins, they are found in a variety of foods, ranging from leafy greens to meats and beans to potatoes. **Water-insoluble vitamins** include A, D, E, and K, and are found in a variety of foods as well, ranging from leafy greens to meats and grains.

Minerals are also divided into two groups: **macronutrients** and **micronutrients**. This division is not based on the size of the mineral itself but on the amount needed in order for the body to function properly. Macronutrients, of which the body may require up to 1 to 2 grams daily, include sodium, potassium, calcium, and chloride. In contrast, the body may only require a few micrograms per day of micronutrients, also known as **trace minerals**. These include chromium, copper, iron, and zinc. By eating a variety of food, the body is able to ingest all the vitamins and nutrients it needs to operate at optimal levels.

EARTH AND SPACE SCIENCE

The study of our planet and outer space encompasses several fields of science. **Geology** deals with the composition of the earth and past and present events (both interior and exterior) that have shaped it. **Oceanography** involves physics, biology, chemistry, and geology as they pertain to ocean-related processes. **Meteorology** is the study of the earth's atmosphere, weather, and climate. **Astronomy** is the study of the universe and the objects in it, including stars, planets, nebula (dust particles), and so forth.

The Earth's History

Among physicists, the prevailing theory today about the formation of the earth is that our solar system was born out of a rotating cloud of dust and gas, a **nebula**, that flattened into a disk, rotated, and then contracted under the influence of gravity. This theory would explain how the planets' orbits came to lie in nearly the same plane as they move around the sun. Scientists think it took more than 1 billion years for gravity to cause the earth to settle and contract. Once this occurred, a sorting process called **differentiation** took place in which materials making up the forming proto-planets were sorted by densities. Materials with heavier densities sank to become the core material, and the lighter materials rose to the surface. The outer surface cooled and became the crust.

Earth's History

Based on radiometric evidence, Earth is estimated to be 4.5 billion years old. Earth's history has been divided into eras. You may be familiar with some of these eras. Here are the four major geologic eras of Earth's history:

1. **Precambrian:** Approximately 4 billion years ago; no life on land; life flourished in the ocean, first with bacteria, then sponges, corals, jellyfish, and worms
2. **Paleozoic:** From 545 to 245 million years ago; defined by the advent, evolution, and extinction of many life forms; life began moving from water to land as land emerged and formed; the first plants and amphibians emerged
3. **Mesozoic:** From 245 to 66 million years ago; spans the Triassic, Jurassic, and Cretaceous periods; each period has unique characteristics, but one unifying element is the presence of dinosaurs, which first appeared in the Triassic period but experienced mass extinction by the end of the Cretaceous period
4. **Cenozoic:** From 66 million years ago to the present; characterized by extensive evolution and natural selection; many distinct species began to form; hominids (a branch of animals that includes modern humans) first began to develop

Radiocarbon Dating

Much of what we know about past life forms and eras has been gathered from fossil evidence. **Fossils** represent the remains of living things preserved in layers of ancient rock, or **strata**. Fossils can be petrified when deposited minerals replace the original organism; petrified wood is one example. Other fossils are created when impressions form through compression, leaving a carbonaceous film of an organism. Sometimes an entire plant or organism is preserved, such as when a piece of amber (petrified tree sap) traps an insect. When strata are exposed, as they are on the walls of the Grand Canyon, fossils can be put in chronological order. This is based on the law of **superposition**, which is simply that the deeper the layer, the older it is.

Fossils provide proof that different life forms have existed at different times throughout Earth's history. Geologists can use the mineral and biological samples in various strata to determine the age of rock layers through a method referred to as **absolute dating** or **radiocarbon dating**. In general terms, this dating method involves the element carbon, which is found in all biological life. Carbon-12, the normal form of the element, contains 6 protons and 6 neutrons. However, the isotope carbon-14 contains 8 neutrons and hence is unstable. It decays radioactively into other elements at a certain rate. The time required for 50 percent of a pure sample of a radioactive isotope, such as carbon-14, to decay is referred to as the isotope's **half-life**. Through radiocarbon dating, the amount of a particular radioactive isotope in a sample can be measured and used to determine the age of the sample.

Composition of the Earth

The earth consists of several layers. The earth's **lithosphere**, or outer shell, is made of the crust and upper mantle. The **crust** is the outermost, thinnest layer, and shows the greatest degree of variation; the average thickness of the crust is 3 to 25 miles. It is composed of rocks enriched with silicon, potassium, and sodium. The oceanic crust is denser than the continental crust.

The **mantle** is a middle layer that extends halfway to the earth's center at a depth of 1,800 miles. It is composed of silicate enriched with magnesium and iron and is slightly denser than the crust. Due to high temperatures and pressure, the rocks in the mantle tend to be fluid.

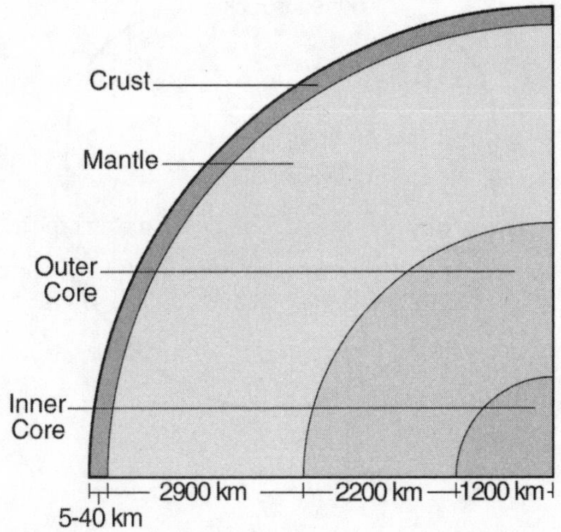

The **core**, which is the innermost layer, consists of an outer and an inner core. The **outer core** is mainly molten and consists of nickel, iron, and sulfur. It is 1,400 miles thick. The **inner core** is solid and is composed of iron and nickel. The core is much denser than either the mantle or the crust.

23. Which of the following is a possible objective of radiocarbon dating?

A. To determine the composition of layers deep beneath the earth's surface

B. To compare the length of one geologic era to another

C. To determine the age of extinct species of animals

D. To determine the age of the earth

Fossils are remains of living organisms and contain carbon that decays over time. By determining the extent of the decay through radiocarbon dating, it is possible to calculate how long ago the organism lived. **The correct answer is C.**

24. Which of the following statements about the earth's composition is **true**?

A. The outer crust is uniform in its thickness.

B. The earth's core is a fiery, gaseous ball.

C. Deeper layers are colder because they receive less warmth from the Sun.

D. Deeper layers are denser than layers nearer the surface.

The earth's core is denser than the mantle (the middle layer), which is denser than the crust. **The correct answer is D.**

Rocks, Soil, and Changes to the Land

Rocks are composed of combinations of different minerals. As described next, there are three basic categories of rock: **igneous**, **sedimentary**, and **metamorphic**. As the earth undergoes gradual changes, each type of rock is constantly, but slowly, transformed into one of the other types in a continuous process called the **rock cycle**.

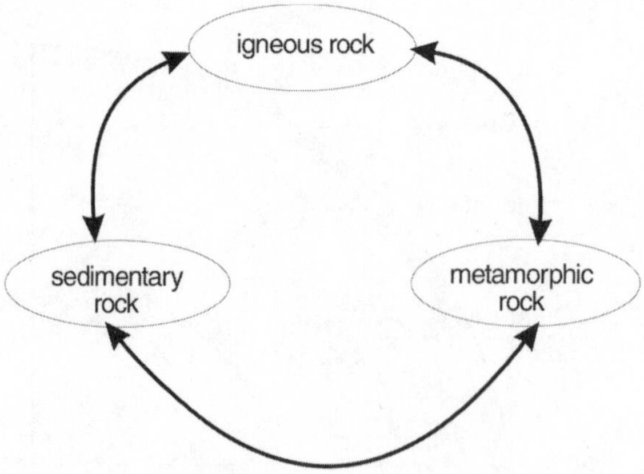

Igneous rock forms from the cooling and solidifying of molten rock, or magma, which becomes lava once it reaches the earth's surface. *Intrusive* igneous rock, such as granite, forms from magma cooling slowly below the earth's surface. This allows for a larger crystal size. *Extrusive* igneous rock forms when magma cools quickly on the earth's surface, resulting in a finer texture. Volcanic rock in the form of basalt is an example of extrusive igneous rock.

Sedimentary rock appears as small rock fragments formed from the deposition of sediment due to erosion or weathering, or by chemical processes. These small fragments can be carried into bodies of water (by wind or rain), where they sink to the bottom and deposit in layers. Sedimentary rock can be classified further into the following three types:

- **Clastic** rocks are formed by bits of previously existing rock. The pieces can be small and sand-like or larger pebbles. Sandstone is one example of clastic rock.
- **Organic** rocks are formed from previously living life forms.
- **Chemical** rocks are formed from dissolved minerals left from evaporated water. Limestone and chalk are examples of chemical rocks.

Metamorphic rock, like the other types, forms from preexisting rock. The unique feature of metamorphic rock is that it is formed when rocks are subjected to high temperatures and pressure, which chemically change the original rock into a new material. Marble is one example of a metamorphic rock.

Weathering

Weathering encompasses a variety of mechanical and chemical events that slowly disintegrate and decompose rocks. **Mechanical events** such as the freezing and thawing of water within the cracks of rocks can cause the rocks to expand and crack. Rocks can be mechanically worn away by the movement of wind as well. Fine sand particles act as an abrasive and wear rock away over time. Water that flows continuously over rocks can also result in mechanical weathering. Rock particles scrape against each other in the flow of water in a lake or river, smoothing one another.

Rocks can also weather as a result of **chemical events** that act to dissolve rocks. One example of such an event involves **acid rain**, which occurs when human-made pollutants in the atmosphere combine with rainwater and become acidic. The acid compounds that are formed, including sulfuric acid, can be strong enough to weather rocks.

Soil

Soil is created from weathered rocks. There are two main types of soil. **Residual soil** is found on top of the rock from which it formed. **Transported soil** has moved from its rock of origin, so it may not resemble the underlying rock. Another type of soil, **humus**, is created from dead organisms such as animals—especially worms, insects, bacteria, and fungi—and decayed plant matter. This form of soil is very important for plant growth. So soil is actually a mixture of weathered rock and organic material, and hence varies depending on the type of rock from which it formed and the organisms in the soil.

Forces of Erosion and Deposition

Erosion is a major force that is responsible for the gradually changing landscape of the earth. Erosion occurs when rocks and soil are moved from one place and are ultimately deposited in another place. Erosion can be caused by a variety of forces, including water, wind, gravity, and glaciers.

Water

Running water produced as run-off by rain flows downhill, carrying particles with it as it moves. When the water moves onto land, it can erode the land and create gullies. Arid regions that do not have much vegetation to hold down the soil (by roots) or to absorb the water experience even more erosion. The gullies can become deep enough to form streams that cause further erosion by the abrasion of moving sediments against rocks. Rapidly moving water can carry a huge amount of sediment, and over time it can completely change a landscape. Hillsides that lack any vegetation show the most pronounced effects of water erosion. The Grand Canyon was formed over the course of many millennia in this way.

The term **alluvium** refers to the silt, clay, sand, gravel, and other sedimentary material deposited by flowing water. Alluvium can be deposited in riverbeds or at the mouths of rivers to form **deltas**. It can also be spread out across a plain in a fan-shaped way that is referred to as an **alluvial fan**.

Wind

Wind carries sediments many miles, and the abrasive effects of the sediments can create new sediments.

Gravity

The force of gravity is a constant on Earth—and it plays a role in erosion. Just as we are pulled by gravity, so, too, are land masses. Gravity pulls on rocks and soil, sending them down slopes in an action called **mass wasting**. Rapid mass wasting occurs in the forms of landslides and mudslides. Landslides result when earthquakes loosen soil or when rain water pushes rocks down a slope.

Glaciers

The size of glaciers makes it easy to understand how they can cause erosion. Glaciers are like huge rivers of ice moving slowly across a landscape and pushing large rocks on a layer of ice and mud. This results in heavy glacial abrasion. Glaciers also leave large boulders or foreign particles from different regions behind as they melt and move. An example of glacial abrasion is Yosemite Valley in California.

25. Which would NOT be considered a cause of rock weathering?

A. Compression at high temperatures

B. The freezing of water in cracks between rocks

C. Fine windblown sand particles

D. Rapidly flowing water, as in a river

The force of compression does not aid in the disintegration of rocks. To the contrary, at high temperatures compression forms metamorphic rocks such as marble. Choices B, C, and D are causes of rock weathering. **The correct answer is A.**

26. How was the Grand Canyon formed?
   A. By soil erosion
   B. By the natural rock cycle
   C. By glacial abrasion
   D. By water erosion

The Grand Canyon was formed by the continuous downhill water flow that carried away rock sediments, resulting in gullies that grew deeper and deeper over time. **The correct answer is D.**

Global Change—Plate Tectonics and Land Forms

Approximately 225–250 million years ago, the continents were joined together as one major continent called Pangea. This land mass eventually broke up into several smaller land masses that drifted apart until they became today's seven continents. On a map or globe, the continents look as though they could fit together, like pieces of a jigsaw puzzle. This and other evidence gave birth to the **continental drift** theory, where scientists are convinced that the continents are continuing to shift, driven by the interactions between tectonic plates.

Plate tectonics is the scientific theory explaining the movement of the earth's crust. As noted earlier, the earth's lithosphere, or outer shell, is made of the crust and upper mantle. The crust is separated into seven major plates and dozens of minor plates. The location where two plates meet is called a **plate boundary**. A plate boundary is also known as a **fault**, which is defined as a fracture in rock where there has been movement and displacement. It's important to note here that while plate boundaries are faults, faults can and do occur elsewhere on the earth's crust.

The movement of the tectonic plates is likely caused by **convection** currents in the molten rock in the earth's mantle below the crust. Within the upper mantle, differences in temperature cause currents to form. **Magma** heated by the core rises toward the crust, while magma close to the crust cools off and sinks. The result of this cycle is convection currents that pull apart or compress the plates, transferring heat from one place to another by mass motion of a fluid such as water, air, or molten rock.

There are four basic types of movement that can occur between adjacent plates:

1. **Collision** occurs when two continental plates are pushed together. These **convergent** boundaries may produce earthquakes, but its more gradual effect is the formation of mountains. The compression forces cause the two plates to lift up and form mountains. The Himalaya Mountains in Central Asia provide the earth's most conspicuous demonstration of plate collision.
2. **Subduction** occurs when a denser plate (such as oceanic crust) slides under another plate that is less dense (such as a continental plate). As the denser plate is forced down, it melts, and periodically, the molten material erupts to the earth's surface. The 1980 eruption of Mount Saint Helens in Washington State is a good example of an eruption caused by subduction.
3. **Spreading** occurs when two plates are pulling away from each other. These **divergent** boundaries create a rift zone, an area that is defined by high volcanic activity. Convection currents can move magma to the surface, splitting apart the surface and creating a gap that is filled with molten material. The Horn of Africa is a rift zone on land, and the mid-Atlantic Ridge is a deep underwater rift zone.

4. **Shearing** occurs when two plates gradually slide past one another. Known as a **transform** boundary, this sliding movement can cause shallow earthquakes and volcanic ridges. The San Andres Fault in California is a prime example of this type of lateral movement.

Let's look more closely at how the forces of plate tectonics transform the earth's surface.

Mountains

Folded mountains develop by the slow compression of sedimentary and/or volcanic rock layers. This process results in mountains that are wavelike—they look like a carpet that has been pushed together. Examples of this type of mountain range include the Appalachians, Alps, and Northern Rockies. **Fault mountains** develop when tensile force is exerted along a crack in the crust. Over time, a mountain is formed, with one side bounded by a normal fault of a medium- to high angle. The spreading of the crust segments by tensile force causes cracking, and the crust is lifted up. An example of this sort of mountain formation is the Sierra-Nevada range in California.

Volcanoes

Volcanoes are formed by igneous activity—the cooling and hardening of magma—below the lithosphere. When the hot magma beneath the lithosphere is under great pressure and high temperatures, it erupts to the surface and forms a volcano. When the magma reaches the surface of the lithosphere, it is called **lava**. Not all volcanic activity is the same. Some eruptions are violent, while others are calm. Most major volcanic eruptions, as well as major earthquakes, occur in three major zones of the world where most of the earth's plates meet.

Earthquakes

Pressures built up within the earth can also result in **earthquakes**. When the crust shifts and moves, vibrations of varying degree—earthquakes—are created. As noted earlier, tectonic plates move along boundaries. Plates can push together, pull apart, or slide along each other. These movements reduce the tension and compression forces created by convection currents within the upper mantle. The released tension is the earthquake.

The strength of earthquakes is measured and compared based on the amplitude of the waves they create, called **seismic waves**. These waves are divided into three types:

1. **Primary waves** (P, or longitudinal, waves) are compressed waves that travel very fast, especially through denser materials of a solid, liquid, or gaseous nature. The damage they cause is moderate.
2. **Secondary waves** (S, or transverse, waves) are side-to-side waves that travel at speeds slower than P waves. S waves only travel through solids and cause more damage than P waves. We know that the earth's outer core is molten because these waves are lost in seismograph analysis.
3. **Surface waves** (L, or Love and Rayleigh, waves) cause a shifting and shaking in the earth's crust, both up and down and side to side. L waves are the slowest waves, but they cause the most extensive damage.

An earthquake or volcanic eruption occurring on the ocean floor can cause massive waves called **tsunamis**.

27. Plate tectonics theory explains all of the following phenomena EXCEPT:

A. The direction of ocean currents

B. Earthquake activity

C. Volcanic eruptions

D. The formation of mountain ranges

Ocean currents have nothing to do with plate tectonics. On the other hand, the shifting of the plates that make up the earth's crust are what causes the earth to quake, volcanoes to erupt, mountain ranges to form, and continents to move. **The correct answer is A.**

28. Which force is at work both in earthquakes and volcanic eruptions?

A. Subduction

B. Gravity

C. Pressure

D. Shearing

Convection currents are created when magma nearer the core heats up and rises while magma closer to the crust cools and sinks. These currents create compression (pressure), as well as tension (pulling) on the plates, resulting in earthquakes. When magma beneath the lithosphere becomes hot enough, sufficient pressure to cause a volcanic eruption can build up. **The correct answer is C.**

Natural Resources

A **natural resource** is anything we obtain from the natural environment to meet our basic needs of food, energy, clothing, and shelter. Renewable resources, such as air and water, are replenished in the environment through natural cycles. Many natural resources are finite or nonrenewable—when the supply is depleted, they are gone forever. Nonrenewable resources include copper, iron, oil, coal, and natural gas.

Renewable Energy

Renewable energy sources can be replenished in a short period of time. The five types of renewable sources used most often are the following:

1. **Biomass:** Biomass is organic material that has stored sunlight in the form of chemical energy. It includes wood, straw, and manure.
2. **Solar:** Solar energy is the sun's solar radiation that reaches the earth. It can be converted directly or indirectly into other forms of energy, such as heat and electricity.
3. **Hydropower:** Hydropower is created when moving water, such as a river or a waterfall, is directed, harnessed, or channeled. Water flows through a pipe and then turns the blades in a turbine to spin a generator that produces electricity.
4. **Wind:** Humans have used the wind as an energy source for thousands of years. For example, sails capture wind to propel boats, and wind turbines use wind to generate electricity.

5. **Geothermal:** When steam and hot water have been naturally trapped in the earth's crust, engineers drill into the crust and allow the heat to escape, either as steam or very hot water. The steam then turns a turbine that generates electricity. This is known as geothermal energy.

Nonrenewable Energy

Nonrenewable energy sources are extracted from the earth as liquids, gases, and solids. Oil, coal, and natural gas are called **fossil fuels** because they are created from the carbon in the buried remains of plants and animals that lived millions of years ago.

- **Oil:** Oil is formed from the remains of marine animals and plants that have been covered by layers of mud. Heat and pressure from these layers turn the remains into crude oil. After the oil is removed from the ground, it is sent to a refinery, where the different parts of the crude oil are separated into usable products ranging from motor gasoline and propane to ink, bubble gum, and dishwashing liquid.
- **Coal:** Coal beds are found near the ground's surface. Power plants burn coal to make steam; the steam then turns turbines to generate electricity. Separated ingredients of coal (such as methanol and ethylene) are used to make plastics, tar, and fertilizers. Coal also plays an integral role in the steel-making process.
- **Natural gas:** Like oil and coal, natural gas is formed when plant and animal remains decay and are covered by mud and soil. Pressure and heat change this organic material to natural gas. The main ingredient in natural gas is methane. It is used to heat homes and is an essential material for products such as paints, fertilizer, and antifreeze.

Uranium ore is the source of fuel for nuclear reactors that is mined and converted to a fuel. Uranium is not a fossil fuel. **Nuclear power** plants produce energy through the fission or splitting of uranium atoms, which creates heat. That heat boils water to make the steam that turns a turbine-generator. The part of the plant where the heat is produced is called the reactor core.

The distinction between renewable and nonrenewable resources is explained in the energy section of physical science. For renewable resources, it is also important to note the difference between sustainable and unsustainable use. If a renewable resource is being used more quickly than it is being renewed, it is being used unsustainably. In some places on Earth, water, wood, and soil are being used unsustainably.

29. Which of the following is involved in the process of converting renewable as well as nonrenewable natural resources to energy?

A. Steam
B. Carbon
C. Wind
D. Fossils

Geothermal energy is produced when steam (a renewable resource) is released from the earth's crust; energy is produced from coal (a nonrenewable resource) by burning the coal to make steam; and energy is produced by nuclear fission when the heat from fission boils water to make steam. In all three processes, steam is used to drive turbines that generate electric power. **The correct answer is A.**

Oceanography

Oceans cover just over 70 percent of the earth's surface and account for about 97 percent of the planet's total water. Globally, the composition of ocean water includes a variety of ions, including chloride, sodium, sulfate, magnesium, calcium, potassium, and bicarbonate. The average salinity (salt concentration) of ocean water worldwide is 3.5 percent.

Oceans produce **currents** that have predictable patterns worldwide (see map below). These currents, which develop from global wind patterns and water-temperature differences, help determine temperatures within the oceans as well as in the atmosphere.

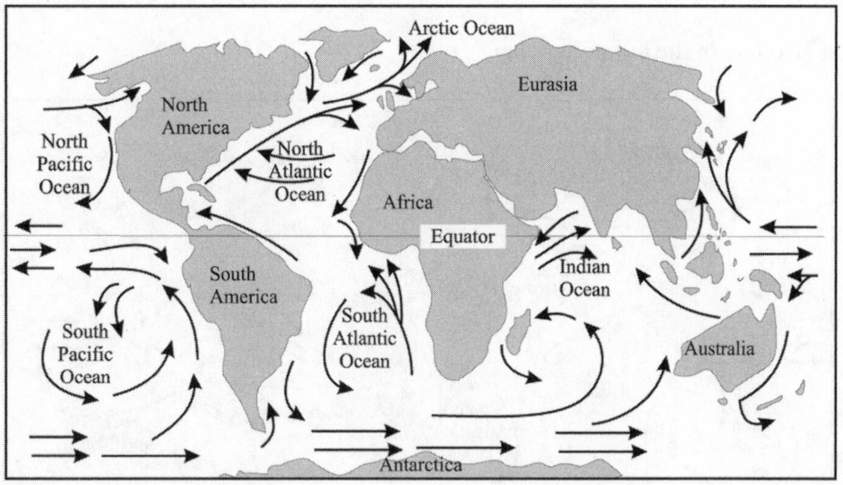

Continental margins are areas where the continents meet the oceans. Continental margins are made of continental shelves, which are submerged extensions of the continental crust beneath the oceans. The **continental shelf** projects outward from the coast at a depth of about 100 meters (325 feet). It is thought that the continental shelf may have been dry land at one time when oceans were smaller than their present sizes. The continental shelf gives way to the **continental slope**, which drops steeply to the ocean's bottom. The continental shelf then becomes the **abyssal plain** of the deep ocean floor. The abyssal plain is about 4,000–5,000 meters below sea level. This depth does not make it habitable for most forms of sea life. In fact, the abyssal plain is like a barren desert. Most sea life and vegetation are clustered closer to shallow shore waters where sunlight is more abundant.

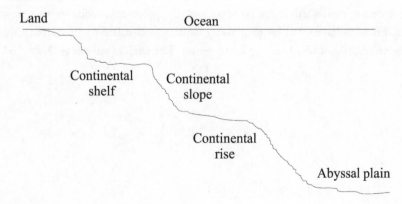

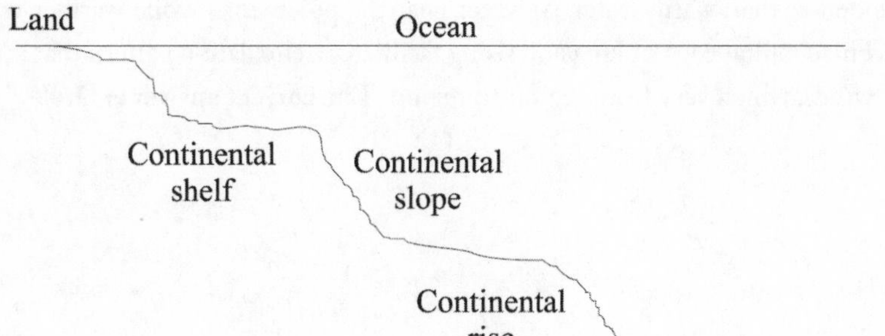

Notable topographical features of sea floor include the following:

- **Seamounts:** Submarine volcanic peaks that, above sea level, form islands (Hawaii is an example of a seamount.)
- **Mid-ocean ridges:** Long linear walls that can rise about 1.5 miles above the surrounding ocean floor and are formed by pronounced seismic and volcanic activity (when the ocean floor spreads apart and new ocean crust is created)
- **Trenches:** Narrow, steep-sided depressions in the ocean floor that can reach depths of more than 7 miles

Question 30 refers to the following map.

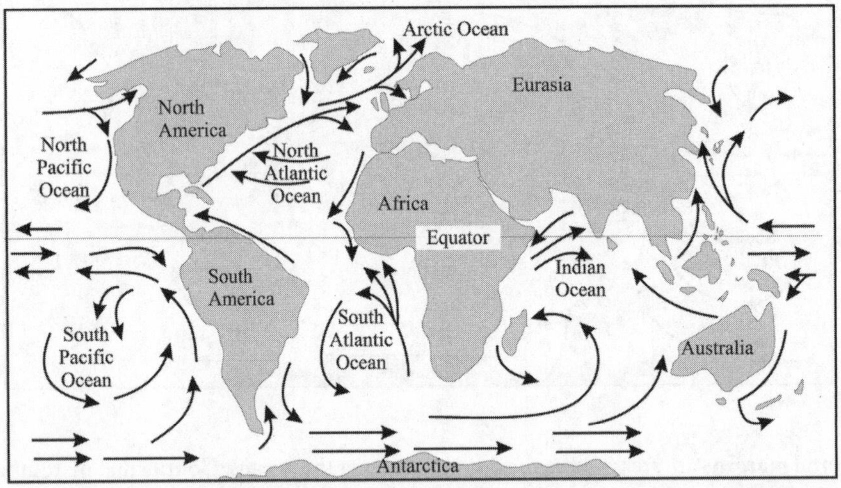

30. Which of the following helps explain the ocean-current patterns shown on the map above?

A. Rainfall is heaviest near the equator and lightest near the poles.

B. Global winds generally blow from north to south.

C. The narrow ocean straits between some continents increase current speed.

D. Cold water tends to sink, while warm water tends to rise.

Cold water is denser than warm water, so water near the poles sinks while warmer water near the equator rises. This simultaneous sinking and rising facilitates a circulation pattern that is then directed by prevailing winds, which vary from region to region. **The correct answer is D.**

31. What is the main reason that sea life CANNOT thrive near the deep ocean floor?

A. The water is too cold.

B. There is not enough sunlight.

C. The ocean current is too strong.

D. The pressure of overhead water is too great.

The ocean depths receive practically no sunlight. Green plants need sunlight to produce their own food through photosynthesis, and animal life in the sea relies on those plants for food. Thus, life cannot thrive near deep ocean floors. **The correct answer is B.**

Meteorology

Meteorology is the scientific study of Earth's atmosphere and atmospheric conditions, especially as they relate to weather and climate. Earth's atmosphere not only sustains life, but it also acts as a shield that filters out harmful radiation and small meteors. The atmosphere is dominated by two major gases, nitrogen at 78 percent and oxygen at 21 percent.

Earth's Atmosphere

There are four layers to the earth's atmosphere: the **troposphere**, **stratosphere**, **mesosphere**, and **thermosphere** (see the following figure). Generally speaking, both air pressure and temperature drop as altitude (distance from the earth's surface) increases. However, at certain altitudes, temperatures increase instead, as discussed next.

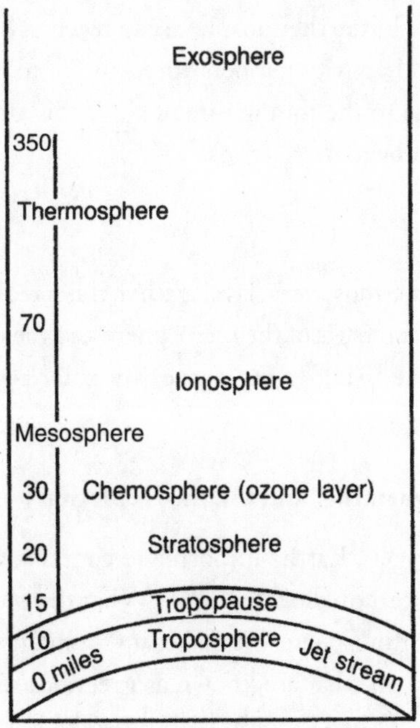

The Troposphere

The **troposphere** is the lowest layer and accounts for about 80 percent of Earth's atmosphere by weight. From ground level, it extends to an altitude that varies from 4 to 10 kilometers (6.2 miles). The troposphere is the main layer of atmospheric circulation. The lowest portion of the troposphere (the "jet stream" in the figure) is where most of Earth's weather occurs.

The Stratosphere

The **stratosphere** is above the troposphere. Though air temperature generally drops with altitude, in the stratosphere it remains constant and actually increases up to the mesosphere. The reason for the increase is that greenhouse gases at this level trap heat radiating from Earth's surface (discussed in more detail under "Greenhouse Gases, Global Warming, and Ozone Depletion").

The Mesosphere

The **mesosphere** lies above the stratosphere and is the layer where meteors first start to burn upon entering the atmosphere. The boundary between the mesosphere and stratosphere marks the outer limit of the high ozone concentration, so it is at this boundary where temperature once again begins to drop as altitude increases.

The Thermosphere

Above the mesosphere and ranging from 311 to 621 miles above the earth's surface, is the **thermosphere**. The air at this level is thin and highly reactive to incoming solar radiation. Within this layer, temperatures rise again as the air molecules absorb short-wave radiation produced by **solar wind**. Solar wind is a stream of ionized gases blown from the sun at supersonic velocities. During periods of peak velocity, the temperature in the thermosphere can reach as high as 1,225°C (2,237°F), while during periods of low solar wind activity temperatures can fall to as low as 225°C (437°F). These temperature fluctuations are due to the thin nature of air at this altitude—there are few molecules present to absorb and distribute heat.

The Ionosphere

The **ionosphere** is not a distinct atmospheric layer; rather, it is a region of Earth's upper atmosphere that includes the thermosphere and parts of the mesosphere and the exosphere, the earth's uppermost layer. The ionosphere is ionized (hence its name) by solar radiation that is formed in the thermosphere.

Greenhouse Gases, Global Warming, and Ozone Depletion

In addition to nitrogen and oxygen, Earth's atmosphere contains trace amounts of other gases as well. One of these trace gases is carbon dioxide (CO_2). What this gas lacks in abundance—it is only about 0.035 percent of the total atmosphere—it makes up for in impact. Carbon dioxide, along with water vapor and methane, make up what are known as **greenhouse gases**, which are also naturally occurring in Earth's atmosphere. When sunlight is absorbed by Earth's surface, the surface heats up and emits infrared rays (heat waves). Much of this thermal energy cannot pass through the greenhouse gases and warms the atmosphere. In other words, the effect occurs because the atmosphere is transparent to visible light rays but not to infrared rays. The resulting global warmth, called the

greenhouse effect, plays a vital role in maintaining Earth's hospitable climate and its fragile ecosystems. In fact, without these gases, Earth would be quite a bit colder, rendering it an ice-cold planet unsuitable for many forms of life.

Since the early twentieth century, and especially in recent decades, polluting emissions from cars, factories, and homes have increased the amount of carbon dioxide in the atmosphere. Because carbon dioxide traps heat, scientists believe that there is a direct cause-and-effect relationship between increased carbon dioxide and increased temperatures around the world. This phenomenon is known as **global warming** or, more generally, as **climate change**. Current trends indicate that the atmospheric temperatures are on the rise. At the same time that humans have been producing more and more greenhouse gases through industrialization, they have been stripping the world's forests. Trees and other plants absorb CO_2 during photosynthesis, and then emit the oxygen we breathe as a waste product. But fewer forests means more carbon dioxide accumulation in the atmosphere, which contributes further to global warming.

Along with global warming is another human-induced atmospheric problem referred to as **ozone depletion**. The earth's ozone layer acts as a natural filter in the stratosphere, protecting life on Earth from overexposure to the sun's harmful ultraviolet radiation. However, the stratosphere's ozone layer has become compromised by human use of harmful chemicals, especially a group of chemicals called **chlorofluorocarbons (CFCs)**, which are used in refrigerants, foam, solvents, and propellants. The overuse of CFCs has actually caused "holes" to appear in the ozone layer. The problem has recently reached an alarming level, and most of the world's developed nations have agreed by treaty to drastically limit their use and production of CFCs.

32. What accounts for increasing temperatures in the thermosphere?

A. Friction from incoming meteors

B. Variations in air pressure

C. Exposure to short-wave solar radiation

D. A high concentration of ozone

As the atmosphere's outermost layer, the thermosphere absorbs the sun's short-wave radiation (solar wind), which can increase temperatures dramatically there. **The correct answer is C.**

33. Which is an accurate statement about greenhouse gases?

A. They protect us from the sun's harmful radiation.

B. They are toxic to most humans and therefore pose a threat to our species.

C. They keep the earth warm enough to sustain life.

D. They are harmful to many plants that humans depend on for food.

Greenhouse gases trap some of the sun's radiation after it reflects off the earth's surface, thereby helping to keep the earth warm enough to sustain life as we know it. **The correct answer is C.**

Weather and Climate

Although the sun hits the earth everywhere, solar energy is strongest at the equator, where light rays are received most directly, and weakest at the poles, where the Sun's light waves hit the surface at a slant. The air in the earth's atmosphere circulates, which has the effect of making temperatures less extreme. It is this circulation that initiates what we call **weather**—the many atmospheric conditions at any one place in a given time frame.

Atmospheric (Air) Pressure

The earth's atmosphere has a mass of 5 thousand million tons. Most of this is in the troposphere, within 18 kilometers (11 miles) of the planet's surface. Gravity maintains this mass in an envelope surrounding the earth. The mass of the atmosphere applies pressure, called **atmospheric pressure**. The greater the air density, the greater the atmospheric pressure. Pressure decreases with altitude because density decreases. Temperature and humidity affect air pressure as well. Colder temperatures produce denser air and greater air pressure; moist air has a lower density and pressure than dry air.

Air Masses

Air masses are large bodies of air distinguished by their temperature, pressure, and humidity. Air masses develop due to local conditions in their place of origin. For instance, if an air mass develops over the tropics, it is going to be warm. If an air mass develops over the poles, it will be cold.

When two air masses of different characteristics collide and mix, fluctuating weather conditions result. This meeting of two air masses is called a **front**. A **cold front** develops when cold, dry air pushes under warmer, moister air, forcing the warmer air up. A **warm front** develops when warm, moist air pushes over colder, dryer air. In either case, the warm air, being lighter than cold air, rises and cools, then condenses along the boundary, resulting in precipitation such as rain or snow. Thunderstorms are often associated with cold fronts. Other front types include a **stationary front** (when air masses move parallel to one another without mixing) and the **occluded front** (when a fast-moving cold front overtakes a warm front).

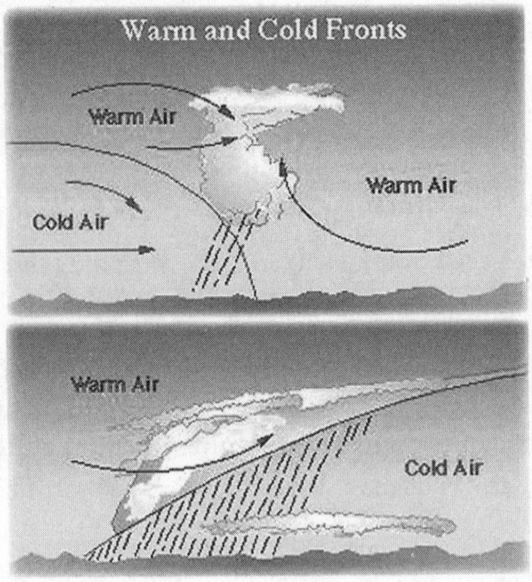

Humidity

Humidity increases when the sun's energy warms up a body of water, and then the water evaporates into the air as vapor. At any given temperature, the air can hold only a limited amount of moisture. If the saturation point is surpassed, water vapor condenses and returns back to the earth as precipitation (rain or snow).

Relative humidity refers to the ratio between the amount of water vapor in the air and the maximum amount of water vapor the air can hold without condensing, at a given temperature. The ratio is expressed as a percentage. As relative humidity reaches 100 percent, precipitation is likely because the air cannot hold any additional water vapor. Warm air can hold more water vapor than cold air, which explains why humidity is usually associated with warm temperatures, especially near large bodies of water.

The temperature at which water vapor condenses and turns to liquid is called its **dew point**. At dew point, large droplets of water may appear on surfaces as **dew**, while smaller droplets may remain suspended in the air as **fog**. As just suggested, humid air, which is usually warm, has a higher dew point than dry air. This explains why dew and fog tend to form when the air temperature is relatively cold.

Cloud Formation

Clouds form when warm air rises and then cools below the dew point, forming fine water droplets or ice particles suspended in the atmosphere. Clouds almost always form along weather fronts, where cold and warm air masses collide. **Cumulus clouds**, which appear puffy, are the type most often associated with the unstable weather conditions of weather fronts. By observing the movement of cumulus clouds, it is possible to assess the movement of fronts. (The suffix *–nimbus* signifies a certain type of storm cloud. For instance, cumulonimbus clouds are cumulus clouds that are likely to produce violent thunderstorms.)

There are other types of clouds as well. The two most common types are **cirrus** and **stratus**. Cirrus clouds are wispy and are composed mainly of ice crystals. Stratus clouds are relatively flat and occur in moist, stable air; these clouds are composed of water droplets.

Wind

Wind is created when air moves from an area of high atmospheric pressure to one of lower atmospheric pressure. Large-scale wind patterns on Earth are mainly the result of uneven heating of the Earth's surface by the sun. More solar radiation is received near the equator than at the poles. As the warm air at the equator rises, it creates a zone of low pressure that draws air up toward it. After the warm air rises, it moves toward the poles, cooling along the way until it is dense enough to descend, about midway between the equator and the two poles. From there, some of the air continues toward the poles, where it meets colder, dry air flowing away from the poles toward the equator. In this way, a continuous cycle of air currents is created between the poles and the equator.

Of course, global wind patterns are actually a bit more complex than just described. The earth's rotation is the most significant additional factor in these patterns. When the winds descending near the Tropic of Cancer and Tropic of Capricorn reach the earth's surface, they are deflected east by the earth's rotation, creating **prevailing westerly** winds, which move from west to east. (In meteorology, wind direction is indicated by the directional source of the wind, not the direction that the wind is moving.) Conversely, winds that are returning from the poles to the equator are deflected west. These **prevailing easterlies** generally blow from about 30° north of the equator to 30° south of the equator. Broad-scale wind patterns are determined to a lesser extent by other factors as well—including ocean currents, the arrangement of continents and oceans, and topography.

Climate

Climate refers to a region's general weather conditions, such as temperature, winds, and rainfall. A region's climate is affected mainly by **latitude** (distance from the equator). In general, regions located at or near the equator experience continuous warming and high rainfall and are virtually seasonless. Regions farther above and below the equator become more seasonal, with warm-to-hot summers and cool-to-cold winters. Near the poles, winters become increasingly longer.

Latitude is not the only determining factor in a region's climate. Broad-scale wind patterns play a significant role as well, as do temperature differences between land and sea. Warm ocean currents affect the climate of regions near the ocean. In general, coastal regions experience more moderate temperatures than inland regions. The relatively warm water near these regions warms the air above the water, which in turn raises temperatures of the air above the nearby land.

A region's topography also plays a role in determining its climate. Elevation is especially significant. It is not uncommon to see snow-capped mountains in regions near the equator. The higher the elevation, the more likely a region is subjected to thin air, which does not hold heat well.

Cycles of Matter

The Water Cycle

The process that begins when the sun's energy warms a body of water to the point of evaporation and ends when the vapor condenses and returns to Earth is referred to as the **water cycle**. Water moves to the atmosphere by **evaporation** in the form of water vapor. If the air is warmer, it rises through the atmosphere, where it is cooled. **Condensation** occurs when this cooled air becomes saturated and the water vapor condenses into water droplets or ice particles, which then return to the earth's surface as **precipitation**.

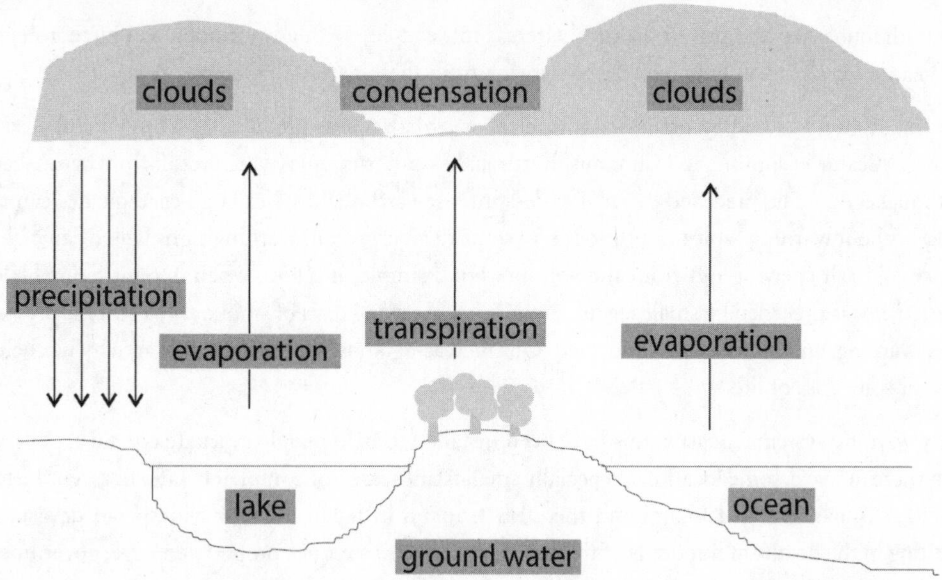

Alongside this component of the water cycle is a second component involving plants. Ground water is absorbed by plant roots, which make use of the nutrients contained in the water. Then, through the process of **transpiration**, the plant gives off vapor containing water as well as waste products. The water vapor rises, cools, and condenses, resulting in precipitation that returns the water to Earth, and the cycle repeats.

Other Cycles

In addition to water, several important elements are cycled. Carbon and oxygen are cycled continuously by the processes of photosynthesis and respiration. These cycles also include several long side trips that can take millions of years. Dead plants and animals can sink to the ocean floor where these elements spend long periods as oil, coal, or sedimentary rocks.

Natural Hazards

Many natural disasters originate in Earth's atmosphere, including hurricanes, tornadoes, floods, and blizzards. Natural disasters such as these can cause widespread injury and fatalities among humans and can cause enough property damage to affect the national economy. Tornadoes, floods, and hurricanes generally occur in the late spring and summer months when temperatures are increasing and snow packs are melting. There is a designated hurricane season, from late June to until October, during which hurricanes typically occur.

To mitigate the damage and loss of lives, governments have implemented safety regulations and evacuation plans. For example, Florida, which is prone to hurricanes, has special building codes for roofs and framing. These include hurricane straps for roof trusses, special plate anchors and straps for corner beams, and additional nails in shingles. The state has also established well-defined evacuation routes to help move large numbers of people from coastal areas such as Miami to inland areas. In the Midwest, where tornadoes are prevalent, tornado sirens are located around towns to warn people of approaching tornadoes. Other natural-disaster preparations can include levees, flood gates, and both municipal and private storm shelters. This, coupled with advancements in meteorological predication models, can help reduce the damage from these natural disasters.

Natural disasters caused by processes within the earth are not as predictable. These include earthquakes, volcanic eruptions, and tsunamis. Earthquakes and tsunamis (which result from ocean-based earthquakes) may be preceded by smaller, less intense earthquakes, but large earthquakes can also strike without warning. Volcanic eruptions, to some degree, give off warning signs which can include smoke and ash spewing out from the volcano. For example, in 1980, when Mount Saint Helens erupted, it was preceded by small seismic activities and several days of smoke and ash. This provided some warning, and most people evacuated. Our increasing knowledge of volcanic activity has helped prevent some loss of life.

Early warning systems for tsunamis have been installed to help people evacuate coastal areas. Even with these in place, some locations, especially small islands, are not completely safe. In recent history, the 2004 Indian Ocean tsunami and the 2011 tsunami in Japan brought widespread devastation resulting in the deaths of hundreds of thousands of people. To reduce property damage, governments have altered building codes to help structures withstand earthquakes. These design changes generally make a building less rigid, allowing it to sway and move with seismic shocks. Preventive measures, such as building codes and warning systems combined with individual preparedness (storing emergency supplies and learning evacuation routes) have made people better able to cope with natural disasters.

34. Warm, moist air is generally associated with which of the following?

A. Low air pressure

B. Easterly winds

C. Cirrus clouds

D. A stationary front

Warm air is less dense than colder air, and moist air is less dense than dry air. Air density is related directly to air pressure: the higher the density, the heavier the air and the more downward pressure it exerts. **The correct answer is A.**

35. Which of the following does NOT contribute to the earth's broad-scale wind patterns?

A. Air temperatures

B. The presence or absence of clouds

C. Atmospheric pressure

D. The earth's rotation on its axis

The presence or absence of clouds is partly the result rather than the cause of wind patterns. Each of the other answer choices provides a contributing factor in the earth's broad-scale wind patterns. **The correct answer is B.**

Astronomy

Astronomy is the scientific study of the universe and of the size, composition, motion, and evolution of celestial bodies: stars, planets, galaxies, and nebula (fine gas and dust particles). **Astrophysics**, a branch of astronomy, deals with the physical and chemical processes that occur in the universe and in interstellar space, including the structure, evolution, and interactions of stars and systems of stars.

The Universe

Current theories propose that the universe began about 14.4 billion years ago in an event called the **Big Bang**. Scientists have arrived at this age by extrapolating backward from background radiation thought to be left over from that event. The universe began as an infinitely small point and has been expanding rapidly outward ever since. Astrophysicists believe that this continued expansion is propelled by what they call **dark energy**. This is energy that is undetectable but must be there because, if it were not, the gravitational pull of all the mass in the universe would cause it to shrink instead of expand.

Earth's Orbit, Rotation, and Tilt

Earth exhibits two kinds of movement: **rotation** and **revolution**. Rotation is the spinning action of Earth on its **axis**, an imaginary line extending from pole to pole through the earth's center. The Earth rotates once every 24-hour period. This produces daily cycles of daylight and night. Day and night exist because only half the planet can face the Sun at any one time. **Revolution** is the movement of Earth around the sun. It takes Earth about 365 days to complete one revolution around the sun at a distance of 93 million miles. This orbit is in an oval, or **elliptical**, pattern. Planets closer to the sun take less time to orbit the sun than planets farther away. For example, Mercury's complete orbit takes only eighty-eight "Earth days," whereas Jupiter's complete orbit takes about twelve "Earth years." The sun's gravitational pull keeps the planets within their orbital paths.

Term	Definition	Diagram
Rotation	the spinning of a body on its axis, like a top	
Revolution	the movement of a body around another body	

The seasonal variations experienced between the equator and each of the two poles are mainly due to rotational **tilt** of the earth. The earth's axis is not perpendicular to the elliptical plane that defines its orbit around the sun. The earth's axis is inclined at a tilt of about 23° from perpendicular. This tilt causes some parts of the earth to receive more sunlight and other parts to receive less, accounting for the different seasons.

The Moon

Except for Mercury and Venus, all of the planets in our solar system have satellites, or **moons**. Earth's moon (referred to simply as "the moon") is about 238,000 miles from Earth and orbits Earth once every twenty-eight days in a slightly elliptical orbit. The moon's rate of rotation as it orbits Earth is such that from Earth we see only the same half of the moon. The so-called "dark side" of the moon always faces away from Earth.

The moon does not emit its own light; rather, it reflects light from the sun. As the moon orbits Earth, it appears to cycle through a series of **phases** as the sun lights it at different angles in relation to Earth's position. On nights when we do not see any of the sunlit portion of the moon, the side of the moon facing the planet is completely dark. This is called a **new moon**. As the moon continues its 28-day orbit of Earth, more and more of it becomes visible to us. When half of the moon's circular face is visible, it is known as a **quarter moon**. When the entire circular face of the moon is visible, it is known as a **full moon**. During the second half of each month, we see less and less of the moon's face until, at the end of a 28-day cycle, the sunlit portion of the moon is entirely out of our view, and the cycle renews with the new moon.

The gravity on the moon is about one-sixth that of Earth. It is the gravitational attraction of the moon and, to a lesser extent, the sun, that causes **tides** here on Earth. The highest high tides occur when the moon and sun are in the same direction from Earth, so that their gravitational pulls reinforce each other. The lowest high tides occur when the moon and sun are at right angles in relation to Earth, so that their gravitational forces counteract each other.

Solar and Lunar Eclipses

The sun and moon appear to be approximately the same size in our sky. This is because the sun is about 400 times wider than the moon *and* about 400 times farther than the moon from Earth. When the moon is positioned directly between the sun and Earth, the moon blocks our view of the sun. This infrequent alignment of the sun, moon, and Earth is referred to as a **solar eclipse**. During this type of eclipse, the moon casts a shadow on the earth. At the center of the shadow, where the sun is entirely hidden from view, the shadow is darkest. (This area is referred to as the **umbra**.) Farther away from the shadow's center, where only part of the sun is hidden from view, the shadow is lighter. (This area is referred to as the **penumbra**.) A solar eclipse is the only event during which stars are clearly visible in the daytime sky. Since the moon and Earth both travel in elliptical orbits, the moon is closer to Earth during some solar eclipses than during others. The duration of a solar eclipse is longer when the moon is closer to Earth. The maximum duration of a total solar eclipse is between 7 and 8 minutes. A **lunar eclipse** occurs when Earth is positioned directly between the sun and the moon so that Earth's shadow is cast upon the moon.

The Solar System

Our **solar system** includes all celestial bodies that orbit around the sun. The planets in our solar system can be divided into two categories based on physical characteristics. The **terrestrial planets** include Mercury, Venus, Earth, and Mars. They are composed of the same basic rock materials—hence the name "terrestrial." The **Jovian** (Jupiter-like) planets are Jupiter, Saturn, Uranus, and Neptune. They are made mostly of gases such as hydrogen, helium, and methane.

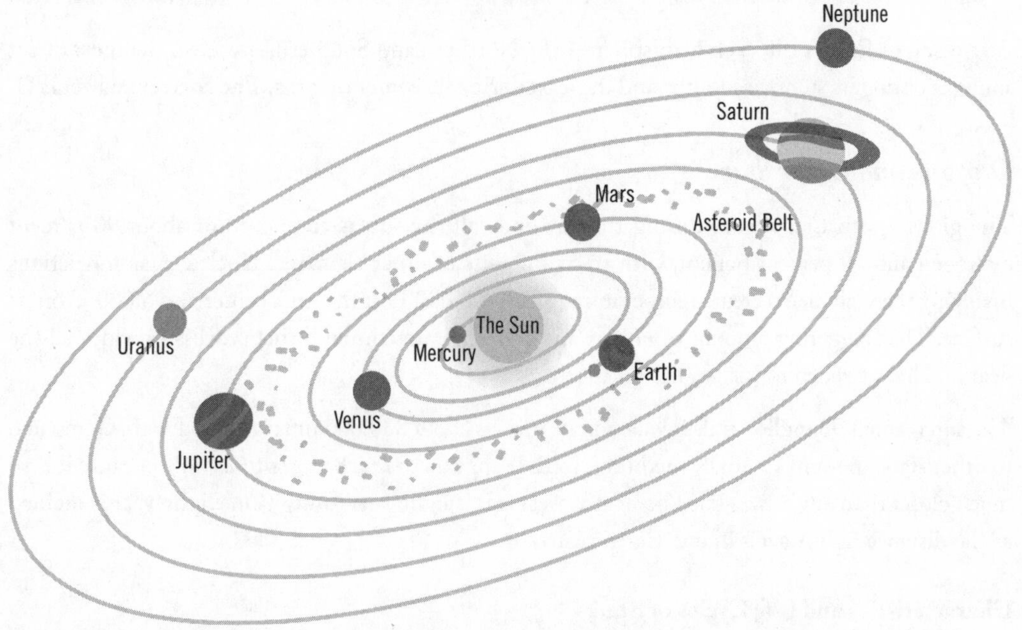

Mainly due to differences in size and distance from the sun, the two type of planets—terrestrial and Jovian—differ in their basic characteristics. Because the terrestrial planets are much smaller than the Jovian planets, they have weaker gravitational fields, which account for their lighter atmospheres. Terrestrial planets have high densities and consist mainly of a solid mineral crust with metals, along with some gases and ice. The Jovian planets are characterized by lower densities because they consist mainly of gaseous emission and varying concentrations of ice.

Between Mars and Jupiter is a great **asteroid belt**, as shown in the preceding illustration. The largest of these rocky, irregularly shaped bodies is about 620 miles in diameter. The total number of asteroids in this belt may be as high as a million, but their total mass is believed to be less than 3 percent of the moon's mass. It is generally thought that during the formation of our solar system, a plethora of smaller planets were drawn outward by Jupiter's gravitational pull. Through frequent collisions with one another, they fragmented into smaller bodies and then established their own belt of orbit about the sun, just inside Jupiter's orbit.

Comets are yet another type of object that orbits the sun. They are small compared to planets and moons and are composed of ice and other materials. Comets travel in very elongated, elliptical orbits, with one end close to the sun and the other far beyond the orbits of the planets. As they near the sun, they begin to glow and exhibit a long, cone-shaped tail. Comets return after a predictable span of time. One of the most well-known comets is Halley's Comet, which returns every 76 years.

36. Which of the following is a result of the tilt of Earth's axis in relation to Earth's elliptical orbit around the sun?
   A. The ebb and flow of tides along ocean and sea shores
   B. The difference in temperatures between equatorial regions and polar regions
   C. Differences in total glacial accumulations between the two polar ice caps
   D. Clearly seasonal weather patterns midway between the equator and each pole

As a result of Earth's tilt, each hemisphere—the Northern and Southern—receives the most direct sunlight during its summer months and the least during its winter months. **The correct answer is D.**

Our Sun and Other Stars

The glowing orb that we see during the day and call **the sun** is composed of about 90 percent hydrogen and 10 percent helium, with trace amounts of other elements. Nuclear fusion reactions involving these elements create temperatures of 15,000,000°C at the sun's center and 6,000°C on its surface. The staggering amount of energy the sun generates through this process provides all the heat and light needed to sustain life on Earth.

The sun is about 93 million miles away, and its mass is about 330,000 times that of Earth. Compared to other stars, the sun is actually medium-sized. It appears so much larger to us only because it is so much closer than any other star. The next closest star is light-years away. (One light-year is defined as the distance light travels in one Earth year.)

Characteristics and Life Cycles of Stars

Scientists are now able to measure and analyze stars to distinguish among star types according to various characteristics. Following is one version of the **Hertzsprung-Russell (H-R) diagram** (named for its creators). The H-R diagram organizes and presents key characteristics of stars in graphical form. The diagram plots stars according to luminosity (brightness), surface temperature, and spectral class (color). Absolute magnitude and luminosity measure the same phenomenon, except that absolute magnitude is measured on an inverted scale. (Notice that the numbers at the right side decrease as you move up the scale.) The temperature scale is given across the top of the diagram. Notice that temperatures *decrease* from left to right, so that stars with the highest surface temperatures are plotted at the *left* end of the diagram.

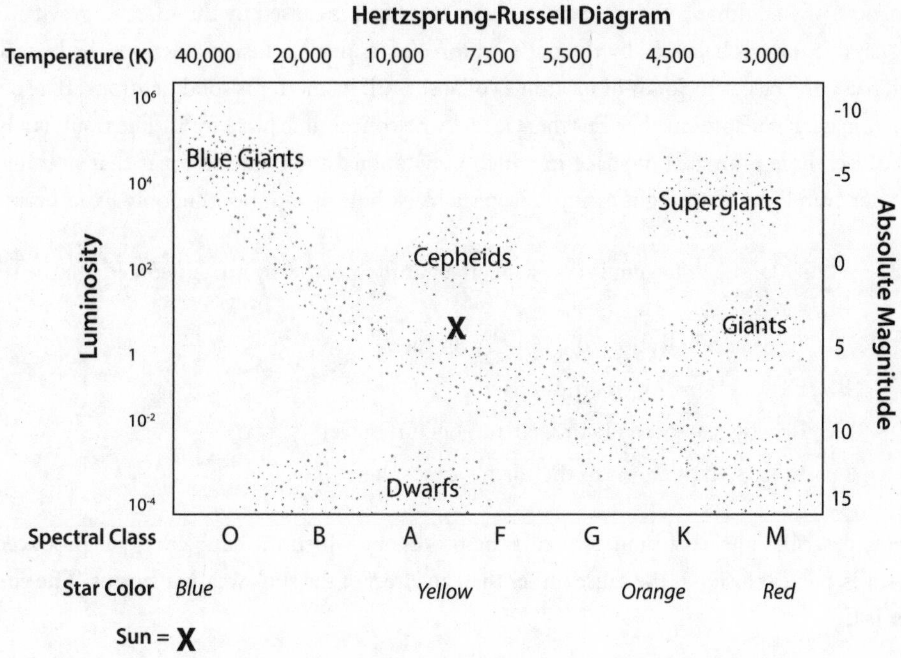

The Hertzsprung-Russell diagram shows most stars plotted in a large cluster that sweeps from the diagram's upper left to its lower right. This swath of stars is referred to as the **main sequence**. This swath suggests that brighter stars are generally hotter and, conversely, that darker stars are cooler. The sun—marked by an X on the diagram—is classified as a yellow main-sequence star. Notice that the sun is a fairly average star in terms of its temperature and brightness. Relative to the main sequence, stars classified as **giants** and **supergiants** are relatively bright in comparison to their temperature. Conversely, stars classified as **dwarfs** are relatively dark in comparison to their temperature.

The life of a star is sustained by the thermonuclear reactions in its core. The energy produced by these reactions prevents gravitational collapse of the core onto its own center. Referring to the H-R diagram, main-sequence stars are believed to be in the middle phase of their development, when a star's nuclear reactions are stable and its fluctuations in temperature and luminosity are minor.

As a star increases in age, the nuclear fuel of its core runs low and eventually exhausts itself. At this point, it is thought, the star moves off the main sequence and may become either a white dwarf, a giant, or a supergiant—depending on the star's mass:

- **Low-mass stars** (lower right in the main sequence) continue to burn until all fuel is used and then collapse into **white dwarfs**.
- **Medium-mass stars** (middle of the main sequence) temporarily expand into **red giants** as their gravitational energy is converted to heat. Once the red giant has exhausted its remaining energy, it will also shrink into a white dwarf. In some cases, the gas released as a red giant collapses and creates a glowing sphere of gas called a **planetary nebula**.
- **High-mass stars** (upper left in the main sequence) collapse, releasing a tremendous amount of energy. This creates a rapid expansion as the star becomes a **supergiant**, and it dies in a spectacular explosion known as a **supernova**.

The collapse of a star that follows the exhaustion of its fuel is caused by the force of gravity. In an active star, this force is balanced by the outward force of its nuclear fusion reactions. If the star has enough mass, the electron clouds of its atoms collapse until its matter is solid neutrons. If a star has even *more* mass, it collapses further, but there is really no conceivable place for it. The result is a **black hole**. A black hole is an area of space in which gravitational forces are so great that nothing can escape, not even light. Since light cannot escape, a black hole cannot be seen, only hypothesized.

37. Which of the following is NOT an effect of the weather storms that occur on the sun's surface?

A. Telecommunications disruptions on Earth

B. Explosive hydrogen eruptions

C. Reactions between hydrogen and helium nuclei

D. Ionization of atoms in the earth's atmosphere

Choice C describes nuclear fusion, which is the process by which the sun's energy is produced. In other words, nuclear fusion is the cause rather than an effect of the sun's weather storms. **The correct answer is C.**

Question 38 refers to the following diagram.

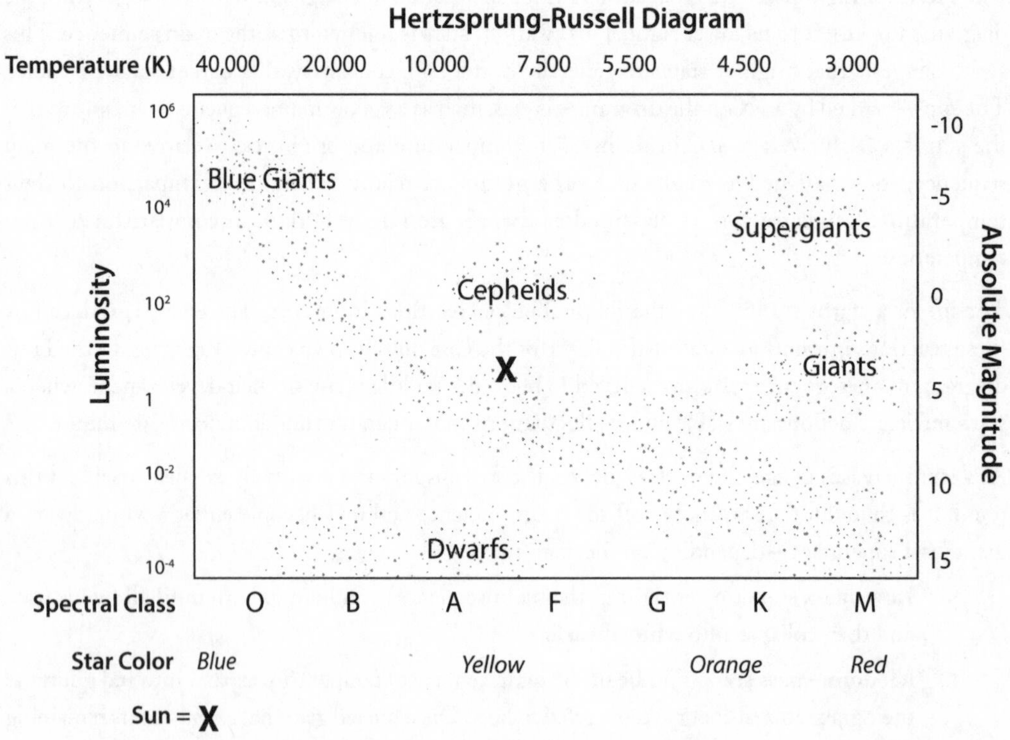

38. According to the Hertzsprung-Russell diagram shown, how can main-sequence stars be characterized?

Main-sequence stars are

A. similar to one another in temperature.

B. relatively bright compared to their age.

C. medium-sized for their age.

D. stable in temperature and luminosity.

Main-sequence stars are believed to be in the middle phase of their development, when a star's nuclear reactions are stable and its fluctuations in temperature and luminosity are minor. **The correct answer is D.**

Physical Science

Properties and Physical States of Matter

Matter describes anything that occupies space and has mass (defined below). It is found in everything, but not all matter is the same. For instance, compare the matter found in concrete to the matter in a cheesesteak. Both are considered matter, yet each has properties that make it uniquely different. There are three basic properties that are shared by all matter (although these are physics concepts, they are essential in chemistry as well):

1. **Mass** is a measure of the amount of matter in an object. In everyday language, mass is "stuff." Mass gives objects weight because weight is caused by gravitational attraction. The force of gravity is the force of attraction between the masses of two objects. Your own weight, for example, is the force of attraction between your mass and the entire mass of the planet Earth. Your mass is constant, but your weight is not. If you were on a planet with a different mass, you would have the same mass but a different weight. On Earth, mass can be converted to weight by multiplying by the constant *g*, the acceleration due to gravity, which equals 9.80 m/s^2. The relationship is $w = gm$.
2. **Volume** is the measure of space something occupies. An empty glass can potentially hold a specific amount of fluid, and, when empty, it can hold air. When the space of the glass is occupied by either the fluid or air, it represents the volume.
3. **Density** is a measure of how much mass is contained in a given volume and is measured in units of mass divided by units of volume. Density is most often expressed in grams per cubic centimeter, g/cm^3. Density is calculated by the simple formula: $D = \frac{\text{mass}}{\text{volume}}$

Some other common properties of matter are shape, color, hardness, thermal and electrical conductivity, melting point, boiling point, viscosity, malleability, and ductility.

There are four possible physical states of matter:

1. **Gas:** Matter in the gaseous state (e.g., steam) relies on its container for both shape and volume.
2. **Liquid:** Matter in the liquid state (e.g., water) takes on the shape of whatever container it is put in. However, a liquid has a definite volume that does not depend on the container it is put in.

3. **Solid:** Matter in the solid state (e.g., ice) has a definite shape and volume regardless of the container.
4. **Plasma:** A unique state of matter that only appears to be solid. In reality, it is an ionized gas. (To *ionize* an atom or collection of atoms is to give it an electrical charge either by adding or removing one or more electrons.)

The states of gas, liquid, and solid can be better understood by considering the states of motion of the particles (atoms and molecules) that make up materials. In the solid state, particles are close together and vibrate back and forth but cannot change position. This explains why a solid cannot take the shape of its container.

In a liquid, particles are still close together but can change position, which explains why liquids take the shape of their container.

In a gas, particles are much farther apart, can change position, and move much faster. Gas particles are not close enough to be attracted to one another, which explains why gases take up as much space as they are given.

Matter can change both physically and chemically. A **physical change** is a change in a substance's shape, size, or state. No chemical reaction is involved with a physical change. The particles that make up the substance remain essentially the same. So a diamond that is pulverized into diamond powder, or a potato that gets mashed are both examples of a physical change. In each instance, the diamond and potato take on a different appearance, but they are still made of the same particles.

A **chemical change** is a bit different. When matter experiences a chemical change, it actually changes into a new substance with different properties from its former self. For example, when you crack an egg shell, the egg comes out translucent and fluid. However, when you scramble the egg in a pan and start cooking it, the egg turns yellow and becomes solid. It has changed chemically and cannot return to its former composition.

39. Which of the following illustrate chemical rather than physical changes to matter?

I. A car chassis rusting from overexposure to water
II. Butter melting in a pan
III. Gasoline burning and becoming vapor
IV. Water vapor condensing and turning to rain

A. I and II only
B. I and III only
C. II and IV only
D. II, III, and IV

Melted butter can be cooled to return it to its former solid state. Rain water can be boiled to return it to its former gaseous state (water vapor.) On the other hand, water reacts chemically with the iron in a car chassis to disintegrate it, and, as gasoline burns, it becomes oxygen and carbon dioxide, which cannot be recombined to form gasoline. **The correct answer is B.**

40. Assume that you poured two liquids—one green and one yellow—in a glass. Then, no matter how much you stir the mixture, the green liquid settles to the bottom, and the yellow liquid rises to the top. What can you reliably conclude from this observation?

A. The two liquids are incapable of reacting chemically with each other.

B. The green liquid is denser than the yellow liquid.

C. The green liquid has more mass than the yellow liquid.

D. The green liquid contains solid matter, whereas the yellow liquid does not.

The density of a liquid determines whether it will float or sink when mixed with another liquid. This means that you can reliably conclude that the green liquid is denser than the yellow liquid. There is not enough information given to reliably conclude the observations given in choices A, C, and D. **The correct answer is B.**

CHEMISTRY

Chemistry is the study of the composition, interactions, properties, and structure of matter and the changes that matter undergoes. It involves looking at ways to take substances apart and put the parts together again in new ways. For example, scientists are able to create substances as varied as metal alloys, paint, plastics, medicine, and perfumes by manipulating elements and compounds.

The Universe of the Atom

All matter is made up of atoms. The **atom** is the smallest particle of matter that cannot be broken into smaller parts by chemical processes. (The word atom is derived from the Greek *atomos,* meaning "not cuttable.") Though theories about atoms date back to ideas proposed by ancient Greek philosophers, it would be another 2,000 years before researchers would develop a provable atomic theory. In the eighteenth century, building upon the work of his contemporaries, John Dalton proposed that the essential difference between atoms is their mass. Dalton proposed the Law of Conservation of Mass and constructed the first table of relative atomic weights and postulated the Law of Multiple Proportions. During the nineteenth century, Russian scientist Dmitri Mendeleev correctly ordered atoms by mass. In the early twentieth century, Ernest Rutherford discovered the "empty" nature of atoms, meaning that the mass of an atom concentrated at a positively charged central core, which he named the *nucleus.* And in 1913, Danish scientist Niels Bohr proposed that energy levels of an atom were like the orbits of planets—a proposal that led to the "solar system" model of the atom. While some of these scientists' proposals and theories have since been disproved, by providing the fundamentals upon which their successors could build, they were invaluable in advancing modern atomic theory.

Atomic Structure

All matter is made up of atoms, and all atoms are made up of subatomic particles: **electrons, protons,** and **neutrons.** All three particles have mass:

- Protons and neutrons have about the same mass.
- The mass of an electron is only about $\frac{1}{2,000}$ that of a proton or neutron.

Subatomic particles can be differentiated by their charges:

- Electrons have a negative charge (–).
- Protons have a positive charge (+).
- Neutrons have no charge.

Electrons and protons can repel and attract each other without physically touching. Opposite charges attract (electron to proton), and like charges repel (proton to proton or electron to electron).

Each atom has a specific arrangement for its subatomic particles. The nucleus of an atom, or central core, contains protons and neutrons. The electrons occupy several energy levels around the nucleus. In the past, scientists thought these energy levels orbited the nucleus like the planets orbit the sun. Today, the location of an electron in an atom is described as a "cloud," based on calculated probabilities of an electron being at various locations. The denser parts of the cloud are the places the electron is most likely to be found. It is experimentally and mathematically impossible to determine the exact speed and the exact position of an electron at a given point in time. This problem is called *Heisenberg's uncertainty principle*. The uncertainty arises from the fact that we can't tell how something really behaves because the act of observing it changes its behavior.

Electron Configuration

The term **electron configuration** refers to the distribution of electrons among available levels of an atom. Electrons reside in energy levels called **atomic orbitals**. The number and location of electrons in any atom determine how atoms of that element react chemically with other atoms. Different types of atoms vary in their number of energy levels. The outermost energy level is also called the **valence shell**. An atom will seek to complete its outer valence shell by reacting to or bonding with other atoms:

- The first energy level (level 1) is completed when it holds 2 electrons.
- The second energy level (level 2) is completed when it holds 8 electrons.
- The third energy level (level 3) is completed when it holds 18 electrons.

The next figure shows examples of Bohr models for four types of atoms that have relatively simple structures (the inner circle represents the nucleus, where protons and neutrons reside):

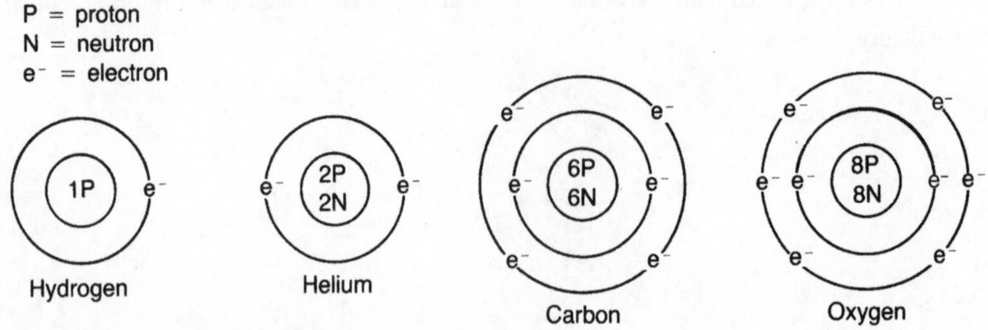

Notice that hydrogen and helium atoms have only one energy level, whereas carbon and oxygen have two energy levels. Also notice that of the four types of atoms, only helium has a completed valence shell. The other three types—hydrogen, carbon, and oxygen—will seek to complete their outer valances by reacting to or bonding with other atoms.

Protons, Neutrons, Atomic Mass, and Isotopes

An **element** is a substance that cannot be broken down into simpler substances by chemical processes. The number of protons in an atom defines the atom as a specific element. For example, the nucleus of a carbon atom *always* contains six protons, and this number of protons is exclusive and unique to carbon. The number of protons can be used as an identifying marker for an element. This marker is referred to as an element's **atomic number**. The following table ranks the first 22 elements by their atomic number—that is, by the number of protons. For each element, the table also shows the element's symbol and electron distribution among orbitals.

ATOMIC NUMBER	ELEMENT	SYMBOL	ELECTRON DISTRIBUTION
1	Hydrogen	H	1
2	Helium	He	2
3	Lithium	Li	2 – 1
4	Beryllium	Be	2 – 2
5	Boron	B	2 – 3
6	Carbon	C	2 – 4
7	Nitrogen	N	2 – 5
8	Oxygen	O	2 – 6
9	Fluorine	F	2 – 7
10	Neon	Ne	2 – 8
11	Sodium	Na	2 – 8 – 1
12	Magnesium	Mg	2 – 8 – 2
13	Aluminum	Al	2 – 8 – 3
14	Silicon	Si	2 – 8 – 4
15	Phosphorus	P	2 – 8 – 5
16	Sulfur	S	2 – 8 – 6
17	Chlorine	Cl	2 – 8 – 7
18	Argon	Ar	2 – 8 – 8
19	Potassium	K	2 – 8 – 8 – 1
20	Calcium	Ca	2 – 8 – 8 – 2
21	Scandium	Sc	2 – 8 – 9 – 2
22	Titanium	Ti	2 – 8 – 10 – 2

All neutral atoms of an element have the same number of protons (which are positively charged) and electrons (which are negatively charged). However, they do not necessarily have the same number of neutrons. When atoms of a specific element differ in the number of neutrons in their nuclei, they are said to be **isotopes** of that element. For example, here are three isotopes of the element hydrogen:

Hydrogen's neutral form (*Hydrogen*): 1 proton, no neutrons

One hydrogen isotope (*Deuterium*): 1 proton, 1 neutron

Another hydrogen isotope (*Tritium*): 1 proton, 2 neutrons

Neutrons have no charge, but they have the same mass as protons. The **atomic mass**, or **mass number**, of an atom is the number of protons plus the number of neutrons (the unit of measurement is called the *Dalton*). For example, hydrogen has an atomic mass of 1, whereas deuterium and tritium have atomic masses of 2 and 3, respectively.

41. If atom X has an atomic mass of 19, which of the following is a possible combination of particles within that atom?

A. 19 electrons, 19 protons, and 8 neutrons

B. 9 electrons, 9 protons, and 18 neutrons

C. 10 electrons, 9 protons, and 9 neutrons

D. 9 electrons, 9 protons, and 10 neutrons

The atomic mass is the sum of the number of protons and neutrons. Only in choice D do those two numbers total 19. **The correct answer is D.**

42. What is the distinguishing feature of each different element?

A. The number of protons it contains

B. The number of neutrons it contains

C. The number of atoms it contains

D. The total number of protons and neutrons it contains

The number of protons is what distinguishes each element from all the others. **The correct answer is A.**

Elements and Compounds

As mentioned previously, an element is a substance that cannot be broken down into simpler substances by chemical processes. Elements joined by chemical bonds in certain proportions form a **compound**.

Elements

As of 2019, there are 118 known elements; 92 of these elements are known to occur in nature. Elements include such substances as hydrogen, carbon, potassium, and lead. Each element has been assigned a one-letter or two-letter symbol. Most of these symbols include the first letter of the element's name, though some do not. For example, the symbol for carbon is **C**, and the symbol for iron is **Fe**. Each element is composed of atoms having the same **atomic number**, which means that each atom contains the same number of protons as all other atoms of that element. Atoms of each element also share the same electron configurations.

The modern **periodic table of elements** ranks all of the elements according to the atomic number and organizes them into **families** based on similar chemical and physical properties. Each horizontal row in the periodic table is called a **period**. Moving from left to right in a row, the elements in a period transition from metals to nonmetals, and atomic numbers and mass increase. The elements in each column are together called a **group**. Groups contain elements that have the same number of electrons in their outermost energy level (valence shell).

The following figure shows a left-hand and a right-hand portion of the Periodic Table. Notice that hydrogen (H), lithium (Li), sodium (Na), and potassium (K) are in the far left column (group) because they each have just one valence electron. Also notice that the gases in the right-hand group have completed outer valance shells. These gases are called **noble gases** and are completely inert, meaning that they seldom react or bond with other types of atoms. This is because atoms of these elements have a complete valence shell, which is a very stable configuration. Finally, notice that each element has its own "calling card" on the periodic table, showing its symbol, electron distribution, atomic weight, and atomic number.

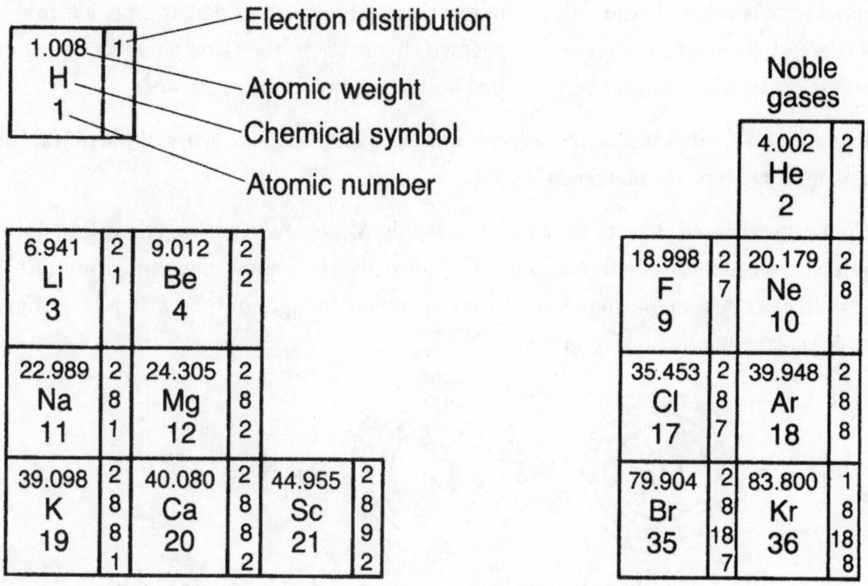

Elements fall into three major categories: **metals, nonmetals**, and **metalloids**.

1. **Metals** conduct electricity, are malleable, and can be drawn into wires or flattened into sheets. Metals can also be polished for shine and have high melting points (although mercury turns liquid at room temperature). Elements such as copper, silver, and iron are just a few examples of metals.
2. **Nonmetals** (such as carbon, phosphorus, and sulphur) are unsuitable for conducting electricity, and they are non-shiny. Also, some solid nonmetals are not very malleable and can shatter on impact. Finally, nonmetals have lower melting points than metals. (Nonmetals occupy the upper right-hand corner of the periodic table.)

3. **Metalloids** are elements such as silicon and boron that have properties similar to both metals and nonmetals.

A common, more detailed breakdown of the elements incorporates these three major categories into the following groupings of elements: alkalai metals, alkaine-earth metals, lanthanides, actinides, transition metals, post-transition metals, metalloids, nonmetals, halogens, and noble gases.

Compounds and Bonds

There are two major types of bonds that atoms form: **ionic bonds** and **covalent bonds**. In this section, you'll learn what each term means, and you'll learn the laws related to these relationships.

Ions: Formation and Compounds

Electrical forces of attraction hold matter together. As noted earlier, however, an element's atoms are electrically neutral, but an atom will seek to change its neutral state (i.e., fill its outer valence shell) by transferring or bonding its electrons with other atoms to form **compounds**. When atoms reorganize their electrons in this way, they are "reacting" to other atoms and are no longer called "atoms." At this point, they become **ions**. An ion is an atom with a charge, either positive or negative. The neutral state is altered because the atom has either gained or lost one or more electrons. In the nomenclature of chemistry, an ion with a positive charge keeps the same name as the atoms from which it was made, while a negatively charged ion is renamed to end with *-ide.*

Now is the time to clarify some terms: Atoms, ions, and molecules are types of **particles**. Elements and compounds are types of **materials**.

Ions of opposite charges attract one another strongly. When they get together, they form **ionic compounds**. Consider table salt, for example. Normally, the parent elements, sodium (Na) and chlorine (Cl), can't be brought together. However, certain changes in their electron configurations can take place, creating the ionic compound NaCl.

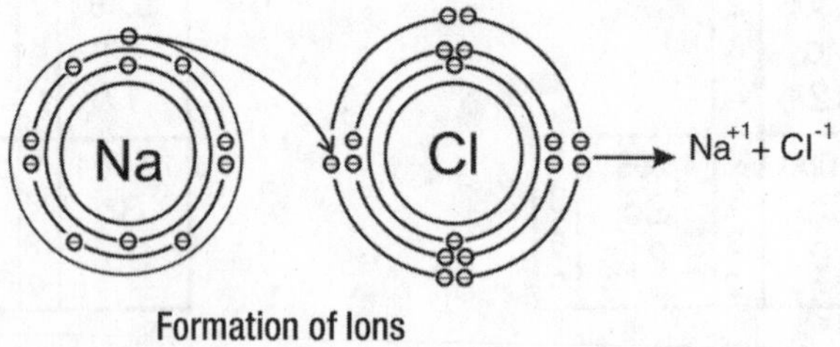

Formation of Ions

As the previous illustration shows, the single electron in the outermost energy level in the sodium ion (Na) is transferred to the outer valance shell of the chlorine ion (Cl). The outer valance shell of the chloride ion gains an electron from the sodium ion. This forms a stable ionic bond with an *octet* formation (four pairs of two electrons in the outer valance shell). Atoms and ions whose outer valance shell contains eight electrons enjoy more stability than those that lack eight electrons at this level.

Because like charges repel, all the new sodium ions move away from one another. The same is true for all the chloride ions. But the chloride and sodium ions attract each other, thereby becoming a stable compound we know as sodium chloride, or table salt. The net force of attraction between the oppositely charged ions is called the **ionic bond**.

Redox Reactions and Ionic Compounds

The simple reaction that drives the formation of ionic compounds is a **redox reaction**. This reaction draws its name from two important chemical events that occur during electron transfer:

- ***Red*uction:** The gaining of electrons
- ***Ox*idation:** The losing of electrons

In a redox reaction, one substance is the **oxidizer**—it causes the oxidation of the other substance by accepting electrons from it. The other substance is the **reducer**—it reduces a substance by giving it electrons. In table salt, sodium is the reducer because it gives electrons to the chlorine atom, which makes the chloride ion. Chlorine is the oxidizer; by accepting electrons from sodium, it oxidizes sodium atoms to ions. The oxidizing agent is the one that is always reduced. Look at another example:

2Mg	+	O_2	→	2MgO
electron configuration		electron configuration		Magnesium Oxide
2 8 ②		2 ⑥		

In this example, magnesium (Mg) is the reducing agent. It reduces oxygen and loses two electrons, becoming Mg^{2+}, a magnesium ion. Oxygen is the oxidizing agent. It oxidizes magnesium and gains two electrons, becoming O^{2-}, an oxide ion. Here are some additional examples of ionic compounds:

Sodium fluoride (NaF)—prevents cavities

Silver chloride (AgCl)—photographic film

Magnesium sulfate ($MgSO_4$)—laxative

Calcium carbonate ($CaCO_3$)—antacid

Molecules: Formation, Compounds, and Covalence

There are some nonmetals whose atoms cannot become ions by the transfer of electrons (as described in the previous section). So some other form of bonding must occur. Compounds that are composed only of nonmetals consist of **molecules** instead of ions. Molecules are small particles of neutral charge, consist of at least two atoms, and have enough electrons to make the system neutral (no net charge). A compound consisting of molecules is called a **molecular compound**.

Note, however, that some elements exist with two atoms to each molecule—in other words, they react with themselves. These are called **diatomic molecules** and contain atoms of only one element. Notable examples include the following (the right-hand column shows how the molecule is illustrated):

Cl_2	Cl—Cl
O_2	O═O
N_2	N≡N
I_2	I—I
Br_2	Br—Br
F_2	F—F
H_2	H—H

NOTE

In the symbol for a compound, a subscript number indicates the number of atoms if that number is greater than one. For example, calcium carbonate ($CaCO_3$) contains one calcium atom, one carbon atom, and three oxygen atoms.

Covalent bonds are formed by the sharing pairs of electrons between atoms. One outer-valance electron from each atom can be shared between their atomic nuclei. The following diagrams show two ways covalent bonds can be depicted in the phosphorous trichloride (PCl_3) molecule:

$$\ddot{:Cl} : \ddot{P} : \ddot{Cl:} \qquad \ddot{:Cl} - \ddot{P} - \ddot{Cl:}$$
$$\ddot{:Cl:} \qquad\qquad\qquad | $$
$$\qquad\qquad\qquad\qquad \ddot{:Cl:}$$

The left-hand diagram shows an electron-dot configuration where only outer electrons are shown. The right-hand diagram shows the bond-line structure. If you count the shared pair for each atom in the PCl_3 molecule, you notice that each has eight electrons in the outermost energy level (the outer valance shell). Atoms whose outer valance shell contains eight electrons are most stable.

In the list of diatomic molecule formulas, the double lines between the oxygen atoms indicate that they are sharing two pairs of electrons, which is called a **double bond**. Likewise, the three lines in the nitrogen formula indicate three pairs of electrons being shared to form a **triple bond**. Atoms of nonmetal elements differ in their ability to share electrons. Oxygen can form two bonds, nitrogen can form three bonds, and carbon can form four bonds. The term *valence* refers to the number of valence shell electrons an atom of an element can share to form bonds in a way that will complete the valence shell. In most cases, the outer shell holds eight electrons, and so this is called the **octet rule**. The exception is hydrogen, which has two electrons in its valence shell; it has a valence of 1 because it completes its shell by sharing its one electron. Here are four different element families and the valence number of each:

Carbon family: 8 − 4 = valence of 4

Nitrogen family: 8 − 5 = valence of 3

Oxygen family: 8 − 6 = valence of 2

Halogen family: 8 − 7 = valence of 1

Balancing Chemical Equations

Chemical reactions obey the law of conservation of mass. This means that not only does the mass of reactants equal the mass of the products, but that the number of atoms of each element involved is the same on both sides of the equation for a reaction. Consider the reaction of sodium metal (Na) with chlorine gas (Cl_2), $Na + Cl_2 \rightarrow NaCl$.

This equation is not balanced because there are two Cl atoms on the left and only one on the right. This is fixed by adding coefficients, that is, the numbers before the symbols that indicate the number of atoms of that element.

$$2Na + Cl_2 \rightarrow 2NaCl$$

To check whether an equation is balanced, count the numbers of atoms of each element on both sides of the equation. Consider a more complicated example:

$$2Al(OH)_3 + 3H_2SO_4 \rightarrow Al_2(SO_4)_3 + 6H_2O$$

The subscript after a parenthesis means that everything inside the parentheses is multiplied by that number. Now count the atoms of each element:

Al: 2 left = 2 right

O: 6 + 12 left = 12 + 6 right

H: 6 + 6 left = 12 right

S: 3 left = 3 right

Limiting Reactant

What if the reactants are not present in the ratio indicated by the equation? Charcoal, which is mostly carbon (C), reacts with oxygen (O_2) in the air according to the simple equation: $C + O_2 \rightarrow CO_2$. The amount of carbon dioxide (CO_2) produced depends only on the carbon available because the amount of oxygen is practically unlimited. Carbon is the limiting reactant.

If we know the mass of each reactant, we can calculate which is the limiting one and how much product will be produced. In such calculations, masses are converted to moles (mol). A mole is the atomic or molecular mass expressed in grams. What is true for atom ratios is true for mole ratios. Look back to the equation for the sodium-chlorine reaction. Suppose 23 g of Na reacted with 71 g of Cl_2. The atomic mass of Na is 23 g/mol and the molecular mass of Cl_2 is 71 g/mol. This means that we have 1 mol of Na and 1 mol of Cl_2. The balanced equation shows that each mole of Cl_2 requires 2 moles of Na, but we have only one. Therefore, Na is the limiting reactant, and there will be Cl_2 left over. Furthermore, there will be only 1 mole of NaCl produced, which is equal to 58.5 g.

43. What is the difference between an atom and an ion?

A. An atom is positively charged, but an ion is negatively charged.

B. An atom is neutral, but an ion has an electrical charge.

C. An atom has an electrical charge, but an ion does not.

D. An atom is negatively charged, but an ion is positively charged.

An atom has the same number of protons as electrons, and so it has no net charge (it is neutral). When an atom gains or loses an electron to a different atom, it becomes an ion—with either a positive or negative charge. **The correct answer is B.**

44. Which of the following **best** explains why carbon atoms form covalent bonds with atoms of many other elements?

A. Carbon is the only element that has enough electrons to bond with more than four other atoms.

B. Carbon's valence of 4 leads to several possible ways to complete its outer shell.

C. Carbon is present in every kind of living organism on Earth.

D. A carbon atom contains the same number of protons as outer-shell electrons.

Carbon has a valence of 4, which means it will seek to add four additional electrons for its outer shell. Several combinations are possible—for example: 4, 3 + 1, 2 + 2, or 1 + 1 + 1 + 1. Thus atoms with a valence of 1, 2, 3, or 4 are all candidates for covalent bonding with carbon. **The correct answer is B.**

Mixtures, Solutions, and Solubility

A **solution** is a uniform mixture of two or more substances that are mixed at the molecular level. Salt water is a good example of a solution. This solution consists of NaCl (table salt) and water. The salt seems to disappear into the water, but it is still there. You could physically separate them by evaporating the water, leaving the salt behind.

Solutions are **homogeneous mixtures**. Materials, such as soil, that are not uniformly mixed are called **heterogeneous mixtures**.

Solubility

The **solute** of a solution is the substance that dissolves. A solute can be a liquid, a gas, or a solid. The **solvent** is the medium in which the solute dissolves. In chemistry, water is referred to as the "universal solvent," which means that the properties of water give it the ability to dissolve many substances. In the case of salt water, salt is the solute that dissolves in water, the solvent.

Soluble refers to the ability of a solute to dissolve in a solvent under certain conditions, such as a given temperature or pressure. If additional solute can be dissolved in a volume of solvent, then the solution has not yet reached **saturation**. The maximum amount of solute that dissolves in a given volume of solvent is called its **solubility**. Solubility is usually measured in moles (of solute) per liter (of solvent) and also in grams of solute per hundred grams of solvent. In saturated solutions, a point has been reached in which no more solute can be dissolved in the solvent.

In some cases, creating a solution can result in a net temperature change. For example, calcium chloride releases heat upon dissolving. On the other hand, ammonium nitrate decreases in temperature, becoming cooler upon dissolving. Chemical processes that release heat (increase temperature) are referred to as **exothermic reactions**, and those that absorb heat (decrease temperature) are referred to as **endothermic reactions**. This is the chemistry behind many of the hot and cold packs that are used to ease swelling tissue and soothe pulled muscles.

In both cases, a certain amount of energy, called the **activation energy**, must be added to get the reaction started. In the case of an exothermic reaction, after it has gotten over the "hump," the reaction produces its own activation energy. This explains why a match is needed to light a candle but can be taken away after the wick begins to burn. If you subtract the energy of the products from the energy of the reactants, the difference is the energy released by an exothermic reaction. For an endothermic reaction, the result will be a negative number equal to the energy absorbed.

Temperature and pressure can affect solubility. For most solid solutes, an increase in temperature will lead to an increase in solubility. For gases, the effect of temperature is opposite: gases become less soluble at higher temperatures. This is why carbonated drinks are served with ice to keep them cool longer; the cooler temperature decreases the formation of carbon dioxide bubbles. Changes in pressure have a very small effect on the solubility of a liquid or a solid, but for gases, an increase in pressure increases solubility.

Increasing temperature not only increases solubility, it also increases the rate at which a solute dissolves. Stirring and increased surface area also increase the rate of dissolving but do not change the solubility.

45. A powdery substance is added to pure hot water and seems to disappear. The mixture remains clear but now has a distinct odor. What conclusion can be drawn from this observation?

A. The water has not yet reached boiling point.

B. The water is not beyond full saturation with the powder.

C. Any additional powder will settle to the bottom of the water.

D. The mixture has absorbed heat and is now cooler.

The fact that the powder disappears, leaving clear water, strongly suggests that it has dissolved in the water. Thus, the mixture is a solution that has not surpassed its saturation point at the current water temperature. **The correct answer is B.**

PHYSICS

Physics is the scientific study of matter, energy, space, and time—and how they are interrelated. Physics is closely related to all other fields of science, since its laws are universal. The living systems of biology are made of matter particles that follow the laws of physics. Chemistry explores how atoms, small units of matter, interact to form molecules according to the laws of physics. And the study of geology and astronomy deal to a great extent with the physics of Earth and other celestial bodies.

Motion: Velocity, Mass, and Momentum

Our universe is filled with objects in motion. **Motion** is described in terms of speed, velocity, and acceleration. **Speed** refers to rate of motion and can be either instantaneous—as recorded by the speedometer of a car, for instance—or an average rate over a period of time. Speed can be expressed in many ways—for example, as kilometers per hour (km/h) or centimeters per second (cm/sec). **Velocity** refers to speed *in a given direction:* for example, 50 miles per hour *east*. Velocity can change if either speed or direction changes. So a body in motion along a curved path is undergoing a continuous change in velocity, whether or not the speed is changing. **Acceleration** is the rate at which velocity changes. Acceleration is determined by dividing the change in velocity by the change in time:

$$a = \frac{V_2 - V_1}{T}$$

An increase in velocity over a period of time is referred to as **positive acceleration**, while a decrease in velocity over time is referred to as **negative acceleration**. Referring to the preceding formula, if the initial velocity (V_1) is greater than the subsequent velocity (V_2), then the acceleration over time T is negative. Since acceleration is expressed in terms of velocity, any change in direction is also a change in acceleration. A body in motion along a curved path is undergoing a continuous change in acceleration, whether or not the speed is changing.

Mass and Momentum

The term *mass* does not mean the same thing as the term *weight*. **Mass** refers to the amount of matter contained in a particular object or body. **Weight** is the force of attraction between the mass of the planet Earth and an object near its surface. The mass of an object is constant; its weight changes if the force of gravity changes.

Momentum is defined as mass multiplied by velocity (*mass* × *velocity*) and remains constant unless an outside force—such as friction—acts upon it. In other words, to change the momentum of an object, a force is required. For example, in a vacuum (a "closed system"), a 10-pound object moving in a straight path at 50 meters per second has the same momentum as a 25-pound object moving in the same straight direction path at a speed of 20 meters per second.

Momentum is conserved during collisions, according to the equation

$$m_{A1}v_{A1} + m_{B1}v_{B1} = m_{A2}v_{A2} + m_{B2}v_{B2}\ ,$$

where m and v are the masses and velocities of objects A and B before (1) and after (2) a collision. Suppose a 60-kg roller skater rolling along at $6\frac{m}{s}$ overtakes a 50-kg skater traveling $4\frac{m}{s}$. They clasp hands and continue to roll along together. What is their final velocity? Since $v_{A2} = v_{B2}$, the equation can be rearranged and solved for v_2, the final velocity.

$$v_2 = \frac{(m_{A1}v_{A1} + m_{B1}v_{B1})}{(m_{A2} + m_{B2})}$$

$$v_2 = \frac{(60 \cdot 6 + 50 \cdot 4)}{(60 + 50)} = 5.1 \text{ m/s}$$

Objects in motion under the influence of gravity are in freefall. Objects released from rest, thrown upward, or thrown downward, are in freefall once released. All objects in a near-vacuum, regardless of their mass, accelerate at the same rate of 9.8 m/sec^2. This is a constant on or near Earth's surface. It is called acceleration due to gravity and given the symbol g. It is the proportionality constant used to convert mass, m, to weight, w: $w = mg$.

Energy and Work

There are two major types of energy. **Potential energy** is energy that results from the position or condition of an object rather than from its motion. In general, potential energy is stored energy and includes chemical and nuclear energy. A coiled spring, a charged battery, or a weight held above the ground are all examples of this potential energy. In contrast, **kinetic energy** refers to the energy an object (or wave) possesses due to its motion. The amount of the kinetic energy depends on the object's velocity and mass—or, in the case of waves, the wave's velocity, frequency, and amplitude. **Thermal energy** is basically kinetic energy because it is the energy of motion of atoms and molecules.

Sources of Energy

Most sources of energy can be traced back to the sun. Plants convert solar energy to chemical energy and store it in the form of carbohydrates. In the short term, this energy can be used as food energy, biomass energy, and firewood. In the very long term, plants are converted to fossil fuels: coal, oil, and natural gas. The sun also drives the winds that power wind turbines, and it powers the water cycle that fills hydroelectric dams with water. Photovoltaic cells capture solar energy directly. Only geothermal and nuclear energy do not come in some way from the sun.

Fossil fuels are nonrenewable and are the source of pollution problems. Fuel for nuclear power is also nonrenewable, but the reserves are much greater than those of fossil fuels. There are concerns about the safety of nuclear power and about what to do with the radioactive waste products. Wind, geothermal, solar, hydroelectric, and biomass are all renewable. Availability and cost are sometimes problems with renewable sources. The amount of energy that can be derived from a given mass of fuel (energy density) varies widely.

Work

In physics, the word ***work*** refers to the transfer of energy from one object to another. Potential energy can be transferred to kinetic energy. In most instances, work is performed in order to move the other object over a distance. To accomplish work, the application of **force** is required. Pushing a lawn mower across the lawn, lifting a bucket of water, and pulling open a refrigerator door are all examples of work. In each case, you transfer your potential energy to another object by applying force upon it. Of course, applying a force upon an object does not always result in work done on that object. For example, pushing on a stationary wall results in no work because the wall doesn't move.

Work is equal to the amount of force multiplied by the distance over which it is applied:

$$\text{Work} = \text{Force} \times \text{Distance}$$

Work and energy are generally measured in a unit called the *joule* (j), although other units are used as well, depending on the forms of energy involved—for example, light, heat, chemical, mechanical, or electrical.

Power (P) is the rate at which work is done and is measured in joules per second (J/s). 1 J/s = 1 watt (W). Since Work = Force × Distance, P = fd/t. If a 600-N man climbs a 3-m flight of stairs in 6 s, he generates 300 W of power. P = (600)(3)/6. If the same man runs up the stairs in 3 s, he generates twice as much power, but does the same amount of work.

46. Which is **most likely** to occur if a loose bundle of feathers and a golf ball, each having a mass of 1 kilogram, are thrown straight up with equal but slight force from the moon's surface?

A. The golf ball will fall to the moon's surface before the feathers.

B. The feathers will fall to the moon's surface before the golf ball.

C. Neither object will return to the moon's surface.

D. They will fall to the moon's surface at the same time.

The two objects have the same mass and velocity, and so they have the same constant momentum. Without atmospheric air friction to alter the momentum of either one, both will maintain the same velocity regardless of their form or shape. Eventually, however, both will fall to the moon's surface—and at the same time—but only because of the moon's gravitational pull. **The correct answer is D.**

Question 47 refers to the following graph.

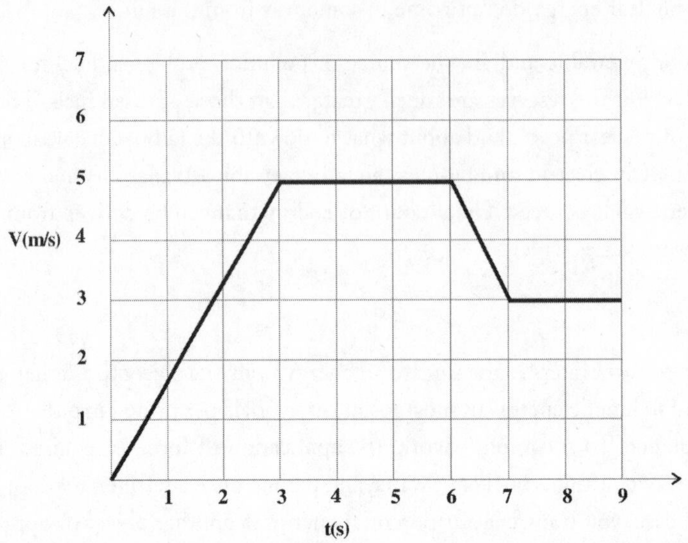

47. The graph shows a track athlete running a race along a straight track. Velocity as a function of time is shown for the first 9 seconds of the race. What is occurring from 3 to 6 seconds into the race?

A. Negative acceleration

B. Positive acceleration

C. Constant velocity

D. A change in direction

Up to second 3, the runner is accelerating (velocity is increasing). From second 3 through second 5, velocity is constant at 5 meters per second. During second 6, negative acceleration is occurring, and during seconds 7 through 9, velocity is once again constant. **The correct answer is C.**

Inertia, Force, and the Laws of Motion

Force refers to any of a variety of factors that cause an object to change speed or direction. It can be a push or pull that starts, stops, or changes the direction in which an object may be traveling. You apply force when you lift a can of soda to your mouth or when you slam a door shut. Motion or a change in direction only occurs when there is a non-zero *net* force. For example, if 2 people are pulling on opposite sides of a rope, both applying equal force, no motion occurs because the net force is zero (0). The most ubiquitous force in nature is gravity; in order to stand, a person must continually apply an opposing force to counteract gravity.

Sir Isaac Newton, a seventeenth-century English physicist, proposed three fundamental laws concerning the relationship between force, motion, mass, and inertia. These laws provided the foundation for classical mechanics and are referred to as **Newton's Three Laws of Motion**:

1. Newton's First Law of Motion, also known as the **Law of Inertia**, states that objects at rest and objects in uniform motion will remain at rest or in motion at a constant velocity unless acted on by an external force such as gravity, friction, or other resistance. The greater the inertia, the greater the force required to start, stop, or change the object's direction of motion. An object of great mass has more inertia than an object of lower mass.
2. Newton's Second Law of Motion states that the net force acting on an object is equal to its mass times its acceleration, or $F = m \times a$. This law is also called the **Law of Force**. The unit of force is known as a *Newton*. In this formula, m is the mass of the object, measured in kilograms, and a is the acceleration in meters per second per second m/s^2. Thus, a force of 1 newton (N) = 1 kg m/s^2.
3. Newton's Third Law of Motion states that for every action there is an equal and opposite reaction. In other words, when one object exerts a force on a second object, the second object exerts an equal force on the first in an opposing direction. This law is also called the **Law of Action and Reaction**. For example, when you hit a tennis ball with a racket, the racket exerts a forward force on the ball while the ball exerts an equal backward force on the racket. Another way to look at the third law is to understand that a force never appears out of nowhere, acting alone. Rather, forces always occur in pairs.

As explained in the discussion of properties, mass is not the same as weight. The mass of an object is constant, but weight changes if the force of gravity changes. The pull of gravity on mass (m) gives an object its weight (w), according to the equation $w = mg$, where g is acceleration due to gravity, equal to 9.80 m/s^2 at Earth's surface.

The force of gravity is the force of attraction between the masses of two objects. If the masses of objects A and B are m_A and m_B, that are separated by a distance, d, then the force of gravitational attraction between the objects is given by:

$$F = \frac{G(m_A m_B)}{d^2}$$

where G is a universal constant equal to 6.67×10^{-11} Nm^2/kg^2. This is Newton's law of universal gravitation. The squared distance in the denominator shows that gravitational force decreases very rapidly with distance. For example, if the moon was twice as far away from Earth, the gravitational attraction between these two bodies would only be one-fourth as great.

48. What force must a baseball bat exert on a baseball with a mass of 0.2 kg to give it an acceleration of 8,500 m/sec^2 ?

A. 42.5 newtons

B. 170 newtons

C. 425 newtons

D. 1,700 newtons

Apply the equation $F = m \times a$:

F = 0.2 × 8,500 = 1,700 Newtons. **The correct answer is D.**

49. Which of the following demonstrate(s) Newton's First Law of Motion?

I. The thrust of a rocket engine during liftoff

II. The exertion of a weightlifter pressing a barbell overhead

III. The lean of a motorcyclist in the direction of a turn

IV. The effort needed to stop yourself after stepping off a moving bus

A. II only

B. IV only

C. I and IV only

D. III and IV only

A moving motorcycle and a moving bus passenger both have inertia—they tend to remain in motion in the same direction and at the same velocity. Force is required to change a motorcycle's direction, or to stop forward movement after jumping off a moving bus. Scenario I demonstrates Newton's Third Law, and scenario II demonstrates Newton's Second Law. **The correct answer is D.**

Heat and Thermodynamics

Heat refers to the energy that flows from a body of higher temperature to one of lower temperature. The physical tendency is for energy to continue to flow in this direction until **thermal equilibrium** is reached—in other words, until the temperatures of the two systems are equal. For example, if you mixed two glasses of water of unequal temperatures together, the warmer portion becomes cooler until the entire mixture is equal in temperature. Heat is energy that is transferred. The energy itself is correctly called **thermal energy**.

An object has thermal energy because of the motion of its atoms and molecules. The faster they move the more thermal energy the object has. Thermal energy, then, is really a form of kinetic energy. The thermal energy of an object is equal to the total kinetic energy of its particles. The temperature of an object is a measure of the average kinetic energy of its molecules. The standard unit of heat is the **calorie**, defined as the amount of heat required to increase the temperature of 1 gram of water by 1° Celsius. (Another type of calorie, the food Calorie, is defined as 1,000 calories.) The preferred unit of measurement for thermal energy in most science applications is the joule (J): one calorie equals 4.186 J.

Transfer of Heat

The scientific study of heat transfer is called **thermodynamics**. Among the four laws of thermodynamics, the first two are the most fundamental. The first law states that the amount of energy added to a system is equal to the sum of its increase in heat energy and the work done to the system. The second law states that heat energy cannot be transferred from a body at a lower temperature to a body at a higher temperature without additional energy.

Heat can be transferred in three ways:

1. **Conduction** is the transfer of heat through a solid material. In conduction, kinetic energy is transferred from faster molecules to slower molecules by direct contact. But the positions of the molecules change very little, if any, so the solid material (the conductor) maintains

its structure. Conduction explains how the handle of a cooking pan or the portion of a teaspoon sticking out of a hot cup of tea heats up, even though the handle or spoon is not in direct contact with the heat source. Different solid materials vary greatly in their ability to conduct heat. Poor conductors absorb more heat than they transfer and hence make good heat insulators.

2. **Convection** refers to the transfer of heat through a fluid (either a liquid or gas). The liquid or gas near the heat source heats up, and then expands outward from the source, resulting in currents. The heated (less dense) liquid or gas rises, and cooler (denser) liquid or gas moves inward toward the heat source, where it is then heated. It is this circulatory process that is at work in convection ovens and many ocean currents.
3. **Radiation** is the transfer of heat by electromagnetic waves. The molecules of a substance receiving these waves of energy absorb that energy, thereby increasing their own kinetic energy and thus the temperature of the substance. Radiant energy is widely used in everyday life. For example, microwaves provide the energy for heating food in a microwave oven, and ultraviolet waves provide the energy that can tan and burn your skin.

Substances often undergo changes of state—solid to liquid (or vice versa) or liquid to gas (or vice versa). During the time that a change of state occurs, a substance either absorbs or releases heat while the temperature actually remains constant. This type of heat is called **latent heat**. The latent heat absorbed by the air when water condenses is what is behind the power of thunderstorms and hurricanes. A cold drink with ice cubes stays at 0°C until all the ice is melted. This is because of the latent heat of melting. The ice absorbs heat from the surroundings to free the water molecules from their rigid arrangement in the solid state.

50. Which of the following statements is NOT accurate?

A. Heat can flow only from a body of higher temperature to one of lower temperature.

B. Heat energy is produced by the vibrations of molecules.

C. Kinetic energy in a solid substance is transferred from faster molecules to slower molecules by direct contact.

D. Thermal equilibrium occurs when the temperature under a shade tree drops as the surrounding air becomes warmer.

The statements in choices A, B, and C are accurate. The statement in choice D, however, contradicts the first law of thermodynamics. **The correct answer is D.**

51. A steel spoon and a silver spoon are put into a cup of hot coffee at the same time. The silver spoon rapidly approaches the temperature of the coffee, while the steel spoon increases in temperature only slightly. What explains the difference?

A. The steel spoon has a lower specific heat.

B. The silver spoon has a lower specific heat.

C. The steel spoon retains more latent heat than the silver spoon.

D. The silver spoon retains more latent heat than the steel spoon.

The steel spoon has a lower thermal capacity, as measured by specific heat. **The correct answer is B.**

Waves

The concept of a **wave** is one of the most important in physics. A wave can be an oscillation or vibration that creates a disturbance in a medium, such as water or air, as in the case of sound waves. Or a wave can be a series of quantitative values moving through space, as in the case of electromagnetic waves.

Scientists measure waves in various ways, and these measurements are used to identify such phenomena as the visibility and color of light, the pitch and loudness of a sound, and the strength of an electromagnetic wave. These measurements are based on the various features of any wave, as shown in the following diagram.

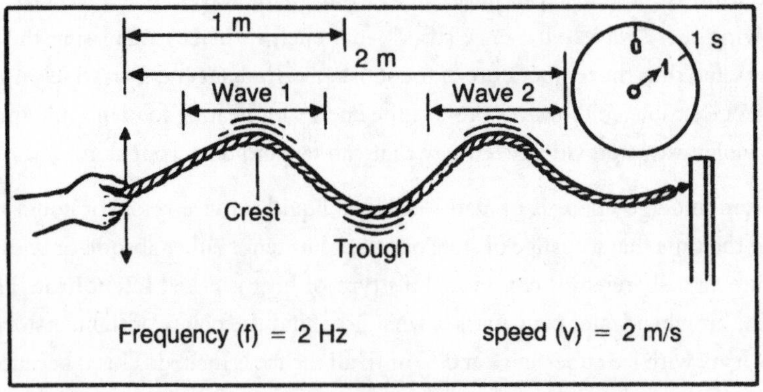

As you can see in this diagram, the **crest** of a wave is its top, and the **trough** of the wave is its bottom. A wave's **amplitude** is *half* the vertical distance from peak to trough and is used to measure the strength, or magnitude, of a wave. The **wavelength** is the distance between consecutive troughs or consecutive crests. Referring to the diagram, assume that the wavelength is 1 meter. Visualize the waves moving from left to right at 2 meters per second, which is the wave's velocity. The number of crests passing a certain point per unit time (a "cycle") is the **frequency** of a wave. At a given wave velocity, the shorter the wavelength the higher the frequency. Each of the following two equations expresses a wave's frequency:

$$\text{frequency} = \frac{\text{velocity}}{\text{wavelength}}$$

$$\text{frequency} = \frac{\text{wave cycles}}{\text{unit of time}}$$

Wavelength is generally measured in meters, while frequency is measured in *hertz.* (1 hertz = 1 cycle per second.) Electromagnetic waves vary in wavelength and frequency, but in a vacuum they all travel at the speed of light, which is 3×10^8 m/sec. Note that the rope only moves up and down, not right or left. This illustrates the fact that all waves transfer energy, but waves never transfer matter. This is even true of waves, such as ocean waves, that appear to be moving toward the shore.

Light Waves

Light travels in waves. The variations of colors we see are a result of different frequency ranges of light. The light spectrum ranges from long radio waves to short gamma rays. Humans can see color only within a particular range called the **visible spectrum**. The visible spectrum for humans ranges from low-frequency red waves to high-frequency violet waves.

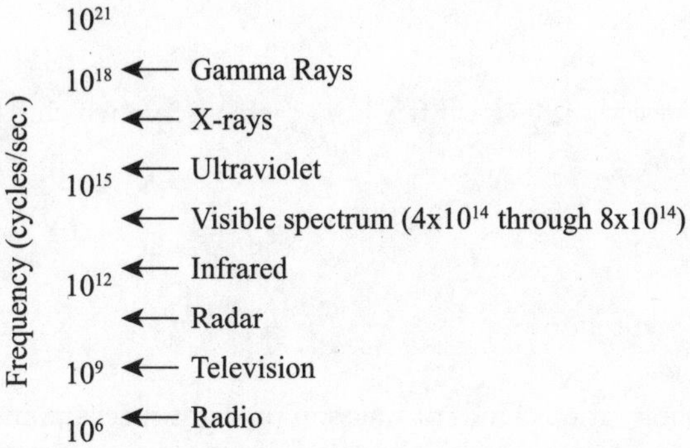

As shown above, the invisible spectrum is composed of many different rays, each one marked by a distinct frequency range. Infrared rays are detectable though as heat; X-rays travel through matter and are used to view structures beneath the skin; ultraviolet rays from the sun can damage skin; and gamma rays—the shortest rays—originate from radioactive substances. Gamma rays and x-rays are the most dangerous because their high frequency gives them high energy, which makes them more penetrating.

Light normally moves along a straight line called a **ray**. When a ray of light hits a surface such as a mirror, the light is reflected back. The light ray moving toward the mirror is the **incident ray**. The ray of light bouncing back is the **reflected ray**. As the next figure shows, the angle of the incident ray and the angle of the reflected ray are equal.

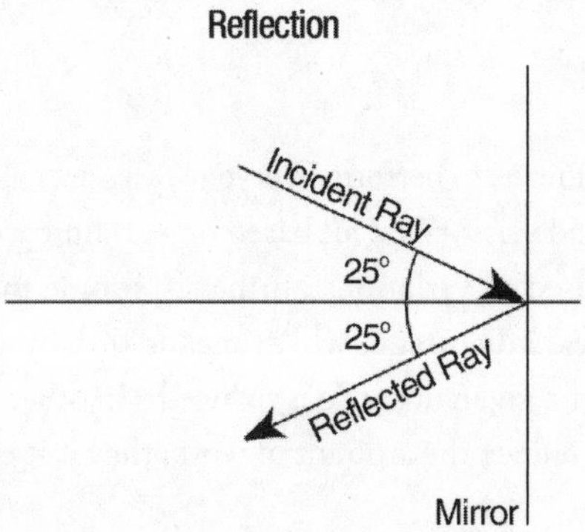

Sound Waves

Sound waves are created by vibrations from a source such as vocal chords or speaker cones. Unlike light waves, sound waves require a medium such as air, water, or an elastic solid through which to travel. The vibrations at the sound's source push the air or other medium away from the source, resulting in variations in pressure, density, and even temperature. It is these variations that our ears perceive as distinct sounds.

Like other types of waves, sound waves vary in frequency. High-frequency sound waves are higher in pitch than lower-frequency waves. The frequency of a sound wave is measured in hertz, where 1 hertz (Hz) = one cycle per second. The normal range for human hearing is between 20 and 20,000 hertz. Dogs can typically hear frequencies of 50,000 Hz. Ultrasound technology uses a very high frequency of 106 Hz. Sound waves also vary in amplitude. The greater the amplitude of the wave, the "louder" the sound, as measured in **decibels**. Look back to the diagram of the rope for a graphic illustration of amplitude.

52. Ultraviolet waves and X-rays differ from each other in which respect?

A. Wavelength

B. Amplitude

C. Velocity

D. Angle of reflection

The key distinction among various kinds of waves in the light spectrum involves their frequencies, which depend on wavelength. They all travel at the same speed, and so the longer the wavelength the lower the frequency. **The correct answer is A.**

53. A certain AM radio station broadcasts at a frequency of 550 kHz. What does this mean in terms of the radio wave that carries the station's broadcast?

A. The wavelength is 0.55 meters.

B. The wavelength is 0.55 millimeters.

C. The wave is received by radios at a rate of 550 cycles per second.

D. The wave is received by radios at a rate of 550,000 cycles per second.

One kilohertz = 1,000 hertz. ($550 \times 1{,}000 = 550{,}000$) So the wave frequency is 550,000 cycles per second. **The correct answer is D.**

Simple Machines

The mechanical devices that allow us to perform everyday tasks are called machines. Everyday devices such as door knobs, zippers, and scissors are all based on certain basic mechanical principles. Most mechanical devices are composed of variations on the six **simple machines** described next. These machines provide a **mechanical advantage**, which means that by using them properly, the force required to move an object over a given distance is reduced. (In other words, they make work easier.) Be clear that machines do not reduce the amount of work; they just change the amount of force and the time needed to do work.

The Lever

A **lever** consists of a rod or pole that rests on an object at a fixed point called a **fulcrum**. The object to be lifted is referred to as the **load** and may be placed at various positions with respect to the fulcrum. There are three types of levers based on fulcrum placement, as illustrated and described here:

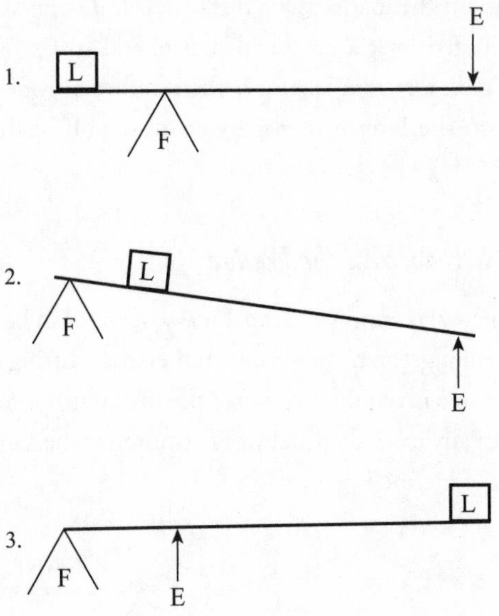

1. **First-class levers** have a fulcrum that is positioned centrally, between the load (what is being lifted) and the **force** (the exertion applied to do the lifting). Examples of this class of lever include a seesaw, scissors, pliers, and a crowbar.
2. **Second-class levers** have a fulcrum at one end, the force at other end, and the load in the middle. A wheelbarrow is a good example of this type of lever.
3. **Third-class levers** have a fulcrum and force at one end and the load at the other. Examples of this type of lever include a baseball bat, an axe, and a hammer.

The mechanical advantage (MA) of a lever can be calculated in two ways:

1. The load force divided by the effort force: $MA = L \div E$
2. The effort-fulcrum distance divided by the load-fulcrum distance: $EF \div LF$

The Pulley

A **pulley** alters the direction in which a force moves a load so the load moves upward as the force is applied downward. The basic pulley consists of a single wheel over which a belt, chain, or rope is run to change the direction of the pull on the load.

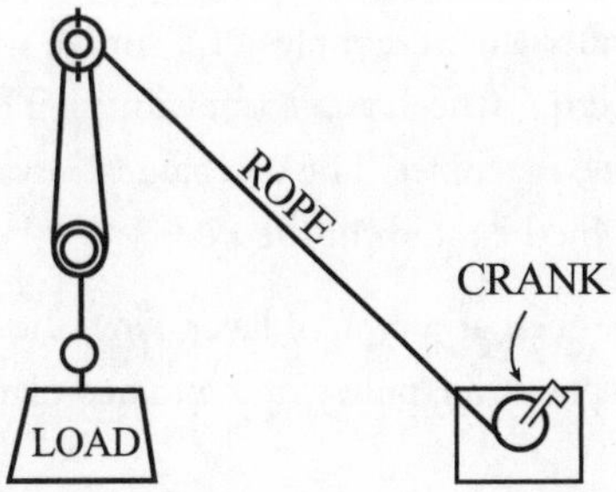

As shown above, a pulley system that consists of two or more wheels further reduces the force needed to lift a load by distributing the work over a longer length of belt, rope, or chain. The total amount of work that must be done to lift the load a given distance is the same as with a single-wheel pulley. However, the work is distributed over a greater distance, and so less force (exertion) is required. Mechanical advantage of a pulley system is simply the number of ropes attached to the load. The mechanical advantage is also the length of rope you must pull in divided by the distance the load rises.

The Inclined Plane, the Screw, and the Wedge

An **inclined plane** (shown below) is simply a ramp. Heavy objects can be moved to a higher position more easily by pushing or pulling them up a ramp rather than lifting them vertically. The more gradual the incline, the less force is required to move the load but the more distance the load must be moved to reach the top. In any case, the total work required is the same. A sloping driveway and a staircase are two examples of inclined planes.

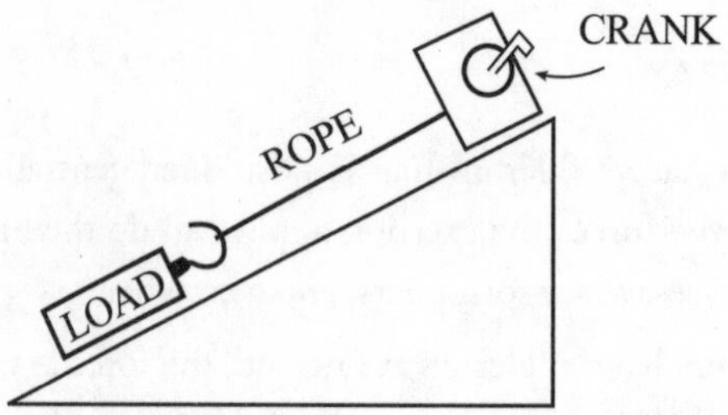

A **screw** is an inclined plane in a spiral rather than a straight-path configuration. Drilling into a piece of wood at the gradual angle of the screw's threads requires less force (exertion) than hammering a nail straight down into the wood. A **wedge** is another specialized inclined plane, actually two inclined planes back-to-back. When you use a wedge, you apply force to the plane to move it under the load, thereby lifting the load up onto the plane (the wedge). Examples of a wedge include a letter opener and an axe. Mechanical advantage of an inclined plane equals the length of the ramp surface divided by the height the load is raised.

The Wheel and Axle

The mechanical advantage of a **wheel-and-axle** machine is provided by the large diameter of the wheel compared to that of the axle. The wheel's circular path is greater, but less force is required to rotate it than to rotate the smaller axle. Examples of a simple wheel-and-axle machine include a door knob, bicycle pedals, a steering wheel, and a screwdriver. The cranks shown in the preceding diagrams are also wheel-and-axle machines. The mechanical advantage of a wheel-and-axle equals the radius of the wheel divided by the radius of the axle.

The wheel-and-axle can also be seen as a type of lever. Now the six types of simple machines can be reduced to just three basic types: lever, pulley, and inclined plane.

54. How might you enhance the mechanical advantage of a first-class lever?

A. Move the fulcrum closer to the load to be lifted.

B. Increase the load and decrease the force.

C. Move the fulcrum closer to where the force is to be applied.

D. Shorten the bar that rests on the fulcrum.

Moving the fulcrum closer to the load (and farther from where the force is applied) increases the leverage—less force is required to lift the load. **The correct answer is A.**

55. What do a double-wheel pulley, an inclined plane, a screw, a wedge, and a wheel-and-axle device share in common?

Each type of machine provides a mechanical advantage by

A. applying force more directly on an object to be moved.

B. distributing the same work over a greater distance.

C. reducing resistance of an object by circular motion instead of straight-line motion.

D. decreasing the distance over which an object must be moved.

Each type of machine reduces the force required to move an object by distributing the total work over a greater distance. **The correct answer is B.**

SUMMING IT UP

- The GED Science Test measures critical-thinking skills rather than knowledge. However, a review of the three content areas—**life sciences**, **Earth and space science**, and **physical science**—will help you to handle the test questions with greater ease and confidence.
- **Science** attempts to provide explanations for natural phenomena through investigation. In order to sort out unreasonable explanations from plausible ones, scientists apply logic and common sense by means of the **scientific method**, which involves four fundamental steps: observation, hypothesis, experiment, and conclusion.
- **Biology** is the scientific study of living organisms, including plants and animals, and consists of three major branches: **zoology**, **botany**, and **ecology**. This review began by examining biological life at the cellular and molecular level; then, biological organisms were examined in terms of organ systems and as individuals. The review concluded by examining individual organisms as members of a community and as part of an ecosystem.
- **Geology** deals with the composition of the earth and past and present events (both interior and exterior) that have shaped it. **Oceanography** involves physics, biology, chemistry, and geology as they pertain to ocean-related processes. **Meteorology** is the study of Earth's atmosphere, weather, and climate. **Astronomy** is the study of the universe and the objects in it.
- **Chemistry** is the study of the composition, interactions, properties, and structure of matter and the changes that matter undergoes. It involves looking at ways to take substances apart and put the parts together again in new ways.
- **Physics** is the scientific study of matter, energy, space, and time—and how they are interrelated. Physics is closely related to all other fields of science, since its laws are universal. The living systems of biology are made of matter particles that follow the laws of physics. Chemistry explores how atoms, small units of matter, interact to form molecules according to the laws of physics. The study of geology and astronomy deal to a great extent with the physics of the earth and other celestial bodies.

PRACTICE QUESTIONS

Directions: The following practice questions will cover general science concepts. The questions are based on brief passages of text and visual information (charts, graphs, diagrams, and other figures). Some questions are based on both text and visual information. Study the information provided, and answer the question(s) that follow, referring back to the information as needed.

Questions 1 and 2 refer to the following illustration and brief passage of text.

The following pedigree shows the occurrence of color blindness in a family. Circles represent females, and squares represent males. Open symbols represent individuals who do not have the condition, while filled-in symbols represent those who are colorblind.

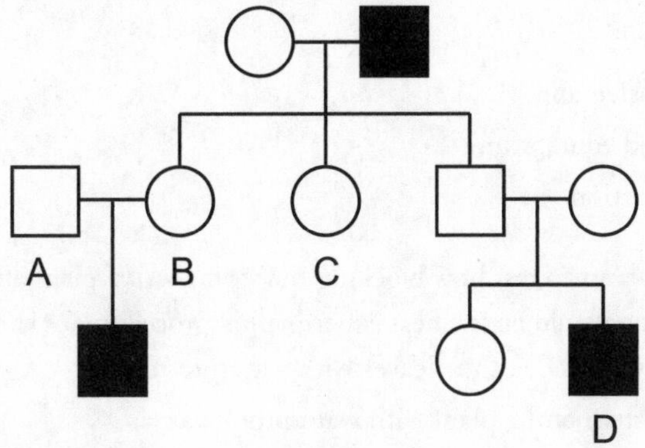

1. What is the sex and status of individual D?
   A. Male, not colorblind
   B. Male, colorblind
   C. Female, not colorblind
   D. Female, colorblind

2. Which individuals are siblings?
   A. A and B
   B. A and C
   C. B and C
   D. B and D

3. A new species of bacterium is discovered in the deep ocean, in an environment without sunlight, oxygen, or sugars. What type of metabolism is this bacterium **most likely** to use?
   A. Aerobic respiration
   B. Fermentation
   C. Methanogenesis
   D. Photosynthesis

4. Which of the following is an example of a mutualistic relationship?
   A. Bacteria living in termite guts that consume cellulose from the termite's food and break them down into simpler sugars that the termite can use
   B. Tapeworms living in pig guts that consume nutrients from the pig's food, depriving the pig of those nutrients
   C. Ticks burrowing into a deer's skin and sucking its blood, weakening the deer
   D. Lions hunting and eating zebras, controlling their population

5. Over time, male elephant seals have gradually evolved huge body size and larger bulbous, fleshy noses to better compete for and attract mates. Female elephant seals are much smaller and do not have large noses. The body form of male elephant seals **most likely** evolved through
   A. genetic drift.
   B. artificial selection.
   C. punctuated equilibrium.
   D. sexual selection.

6. A researcher wants to test how blocking the stomata of a plant affects its growth. Which of the following would be the **best** experimental procedure for the researcher to perform?
   A. Coat the underside of the leaves with waterproof wax
   B. Coat the stem of the plant with waterproof wax
   C. Pull the leaves off of the plant
   D. Cut the tips off of the plant's roots

7. A newly discovered animal is warm-blooded, covered with hair, and carries its young in a body pouch. It is **most likely** a
   A. rodent.
   B. monotreme.
   C. bird.
   D. marsupial.

Question 8 refers to the following illustration.

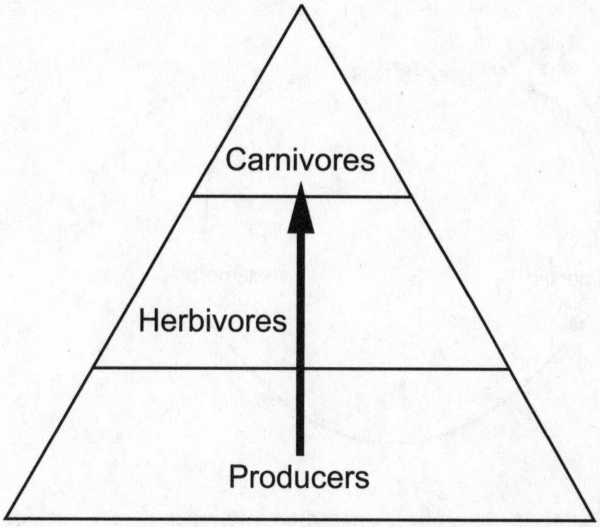

8. In the diagram of trophic levels in an ecosystem, the arrow represents the flow of

A. waste.

B. energy.

C. oxygen.

D. consumers.

9. Most scientists do not consider viruses to be living organisms because they

A. do not contain genetic material.

B. cannot insert their genetic material into a host cell.

C. cannot reproduce on their own.

D. contain an outer protein shell.

10. Prolactin is secreted by a gland in the brain and attaches to receptors on the mammary glands. This process is **most likely** part of which body system?

A. Cardiovascular

B. Endocrine

C. Nervous

D. Reproductive

11. The planets of our solar system lie in almost the same plane because they condensed from a cloud of dust and gas that was shaped like a

A. disk.

B. sphere.

C. line.

D. sun.

12. In the following diagram of the rock cycle, what do the arrows mean?

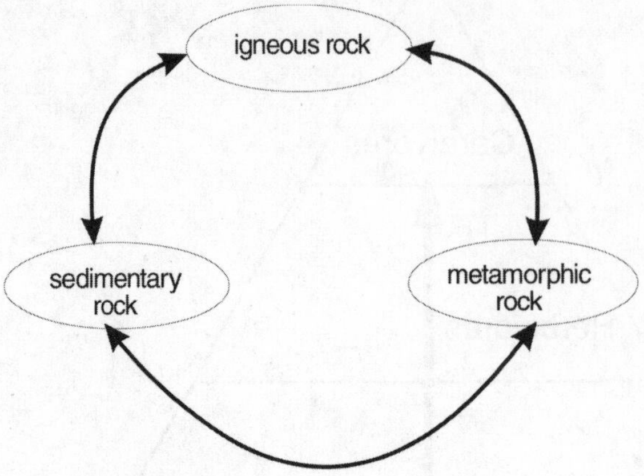

A. Sedimentary rock can be transformed into igneous rock but not metamorphic rock.

B. Igneous rock can be transformed into sedimentary rock but not metamorphic rock.

C. Metamorphic rock can be transformed into igneous rock but not sedimentary rock.

D. Sedimentary rock can be transformed into metamorphic rock and metamorphic rock can be transformed into sedimentary rock.

13. One line of evidence for continental drift is how the continents fit together like pieces of a jigsaw puzzle. When the continents are fitted together, which of the following pieces of evidence would also support continental drift theory?

A. The presence of the same kinds of living plants on all continents

B. The presence of sedimentary rock on all continents

C. Fossils that are only found on one continent

D. Mountain ranges that start on one continent and continue on another

14. If the abyssal plain is like a barren desert, then which part of the ocean is like a tropical rain forest and full of life?

A. Shallow coastal waters

B. Continental shelf

C. Continental slope

D. Continental rise

15. The difference between weather and climate is that

A. air circulation affects weather but not climate.

B. weather is affected by latitude but climate is not.

C. climate describes long-term atmospheric conditions while weather is short-term.

D. the amount of solar energy received by a region affects its climate but not its weather.

16. Which of the following compounds is **most likely** to be ionic?

A. NH_3

B. KCl

C. CO

D. PCl_3

17. To balance the following equation, which coefficient should be placed before Br_2?

$2Al + \_\_Br_2 \rightarrow 2AlBr_3$

A. 1

B. 2

C. 3

D. 6

18. When sugar is dissolved in water, a new [ ] is created.

A. element

B. compound

C. homogeneous mixture

D. heterogeneous mixture

19. The atomic orbitals within a single atom can differ in

A. the kind of subatomic particle they hold.

B. the number of protons they hold.

C. the number of neutrons they hold.

D. the number of electrons they hold.

20. Which of the following procedures would be the **best** way to measure the volume of fluid that a glass can hold?

A. Weigh the empty glass.

B. Fill the glass with water and weigh the filled glass.

C. Place the glass in a large graduated beaker that is half-filled with water and calculate how much water the glass displaced.

D. Fill the glass with water and measure how many milliliters of water were needed to fill the glass.

21. Which of the following is an accurate description of an object's velocity?
A. 70 meters per minute south
B. 120 kilometers per hour
C. 6 meters per second squared
D. 55 centimeters per minute

22. Which of the following is an example of something that possesses potential energy?
A. A ball rolling down a hill
B. A person standing on the edge of a diving board
C. A bird flying through the air
D. A hammer swinging into a nail on the wall

23. When a person steps out of the bathtub onto a tiled bathroom floor, the person's foot feels cold because heat is transferred from the foot to the floor. This is an example of heat transfer by
A. acceleration.
B. conduction.
C. convection.
D. radiation.

24. In the diagram below, which letter indicates the wavelength of this wave?

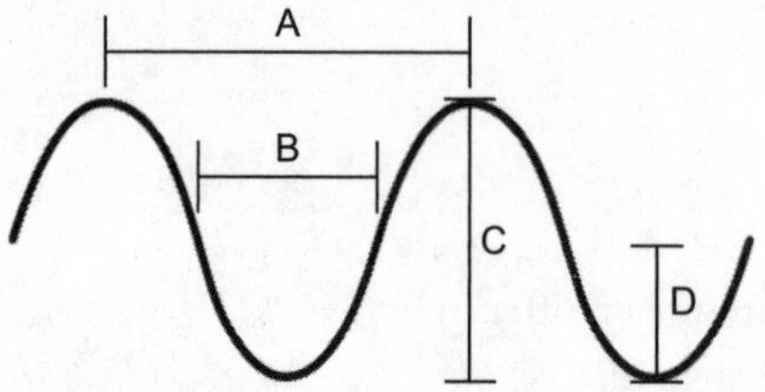

A. A
B. B
C. C
D. D

25. The screw and wedge are specialized versions of what basic type of simple machine?
A. Lever
B. Pulley
C. Inclined plane
D. Wheel-and-axle

ANSWER KEY AND EXPLANATIONS

1. B	**6.** A	**11.** A	**16.** B	**21.** A
2. C	**7.** D	**12.** D	**17.** C	**22.** B
3. C	**8.** B	**13.** D	**18.** C	**23.** B
4. A	**9.** C	**14.** A	**19.** D	**24.** A
5. D	**10.** B	**15.** C	**20.** D	**25.** C

1. **The correct answer is B.** Squares represent males, and filled-in symbols represent those individuals who are colorblind. Therefore individual D is a male who is colorblind.

2. **The correct answer is C.** In a pedigree, individuals connected by vertical lines to a common horizontal line are siblings. This common horizontal line will be connected by another vertical line to a horizontal line directly connecting their parents. Individuals B and C are connected by vertical lines to a common horizontal line, so they are siblings (sisters, to be exact). Individuals A and B (choice A) are directly connected by a horizontal line, but only individual B has an upward vertical line connecting to the parents. Individuals A and C (choice B) are not connected by any lines at all. Individual A is individual C's brother-in-law. Individuals B and D (choice D) are not in the same generation. Individual B is individual D's aunt.

3. **The correct answer is C.** The bacterium lives in an environment with no sunlight, so it cannot use photosynthesis (choice D). It also lives in an environment with no oxygen, so it cannot use aerobic respiration (choice A). Finally, it also lives in an environment with no sugars, so it cannot use fermentation (choice B), even though fermentation does not require oxygen. Therefore, the bacterium must use methanogenesis, which does not require sunlight, oxygen, or sugars.

4. **The correct answer is A.** Termites eat plant material that contain a lot of cellulose, a complex sugar. They cannot use the cellulose directly as an energy source. However, bacteria living in their guts can eat the cellulose and break it down into simpler sugars that the termite can use. Both the termite and the bacteria benefit, making this a mutualistic relationship. Choices B and C are both parasitic relationships: one organism benefits (the tapeworm and tick) while the other one is harmed (the pig and deer). Choice D describes a predator-prey relationship.

5. **The correct answer is D.** When individuals in a population compete for mates, sexual selection is the strongest influence on their evolution. Characteristics that help individuals attract mates, like large body and nose size in elephant seals, are selected for in populations undergoing sexual selection. Sexual selection often leads to differences in male and female individuals of the same species, a phenomenon called sexual dimorphism. Genetic drift (choice A) occurs randomly, and it is clear that the male elephant seals' characteristics are beneficial to mating and do not occur due to chance. Artificial selection (choice B) is performed by humans, which are not mentioned in the question. There is no evidence given that the evolution of elephant seals occurred in quick jumps, or punctuated equilibrium (choice C). In fact, the stem states that male elephant seals gradually evolved their distinctive body forms.

6. **The correct answer is A.** The stomata are located on the undersides of the leaves of a plant and are openings that control water and gas exchange with the environment. By coating the underside of the leaves with wax, the stomata will be blocked and the effects of this blockage can be studied. Coating the stem of the plant with wax (choice B) will not affect the stomata because there are no stomata on the stem of a plant. Pulling the leaves off entirely (choice C) will not isolate the stomata; the researcher will be studying what happens when a plant has no leaves at all, not just no stomata. Cutting the tips off of the plant's roots (choice D) is not the best procedure because there are no stomata in the roots.

7. **The correct answer is D.** The newly described animal is a mammal, since it is warm-blooded and covered with hair. This eliminates choice C; while birds are warm-blooded, they are covered with feathers, not hair. Marsupials are the only mammals that carry their young in body pouches. Rodents (choice A) do not carry their young in body pouches and are characterized by ever-growing incisor teeth. Monotremes (choice B) are primitive mammals that lay eggs and do not carry their young in pouches.

8. **The correct answer is B.** The arrow in the trophic diagram represents the flow of energy from lower trophic levels to higher trophic levels. When herbivores eat producers, energy from the producers flows into the herbivores, and when carnivores eat the herbivores, energy flows into the carnivores. Waste and oxygen (choices A and C) do not flow between tropic levels. Consumers (choice D) is a term that describes herbivores and carnivores.

9. **The correct answer is C.** Viruses are intracellular parasites that depend on a host cell to perform basic cellular tasks like protein synthesis and to reproduce. They cannot reproduce on their own and are not made out of cells, so most scientists do not consider them to be alive. Viruses do contain genetic material, either DNA or RNA, so choice A is not true. Viruses can insert their genetic material into a host cell; this is how they reproduce. Thus, choice B is also not true. While viruses do contain an outer protein shell, this is not a characteristic that determines whether or not they are alive, so choice D is incorrect.

10. **The correct answer is B.** In the endocrine system, chemical messengers called hormones are secreted by glands and carried in the bloodstream to distant targets, where they attach to specific receptors and generate an effect. In this case, the endocrine gland is in the brain (the pituitary gland, to be exact), prolactin is the hormone, and the target is a mammary gland. While the cardiovascular system (choice A) takes part in this process by delivering the hormone to its target, the overall process is part of the endocrine system. Even though the source gland is in the brain, this process is part of the endocrine system, not the nervous system (choice C). The reproductive system (choice D) is involved in generating offspring, and while hormones are involved in many of its processes, this specific process is part of the endocrine system.

11. **The correct answer is A.** The modern theory of solar system formation states that the sun and planets formed from a rotating disk of dust and gas. Because they formed out of the same disk, they lie in almost the same plane in space. If the planets formed from a sphere (which is also the shape of a sun), they would lie in different planes at the same distance from the sun, so choices B and D are incorrect. The dust and gas cloud was not shaped like a line, and this would be impossible to maintain under the

laws of physics if planets were to form, so choice C is incorrect.

12. **The correct answer is D.** The double-ended arrows in the rock cycle diagram indicate that each type of rock can be transformed into the other two types, and the reverse reactions can happen as well. Thus, sedimentary rock can be transformed into metamorphic rock, and the reverse is also true: metamorphic rock can be transformed into sedimentary rock. Sedimentary rock can also be transformed into igneous rock and vice versa. Therefore, the other answer choices are incorrect.

13. **The correct answer is D.** The fact that the continents fit together like pieces of a jigsaw puzzle suggests that they were once grouped together into a single continent that then broke up and drifted apart. So when the continents are put together again, large geological features like mountain ranges can start on one continent and continue onto another. The mountain range was broken up too when the continents drifted apart. Living plants would not provide any clues about the past, so choice A does not support the theory. Sedimentary rocks are such a broad category of rock that its presence on all the continents would not give any clues about their past positions, so choice B does not support the theory either. If specific sequences of distinctive sedimentary rocks were found on two different continents where they touch, then that would be evidence for continental drift. Fossils that are found on only one continent (choice C) would not provide evidence for the relative positions of other continents.

14. **The correct answer is A.** The abyssal plain is the deepest part of the ocean floor, so it is completely dark and supports very little life. In contrast, the shallow coastal waters are well-lit by sunlight and can support many species of organisms. Shallow waters are also rich in nutrients that have washed in from the land, which further supports life. The continental shelf, slope, and rise (choices B, C, and D) are increasingly deeper parts of the continental margin (the edge of the continent where the ocean meets the land) and do not support as much life as shallow coastal waters.

15. **The correct answer is C.** Climate describes the long-term, general weather conditions of an area on Earth. Weather is the day-to-day, localized atmospheric conditions in a given place. Climate is determined from the average weather conditions of a place over many years, but the weather on any given day is unpredictable. Just because it rains on one day does not mean a region has a rainy climate. Air circulation, latitude, and the amount of solar energy received all affect both weather and climate, so the other choices are incorrect.

16. **The correct answer is B.** Ionic compounds are made up of elements with opposite charges. Potassium (K) is in the first column of the periodic table, so it has one valence electron. It is likely to lose that valence electron and become an ion with a charge of +1 to have a stable octet as its valence shell. Chlorine (Cl) is in the next-to-last column of the periodic table, so it has seven valence electrons. It is likely to gain a valence electron to form a stable octet and become an ion with a charge of −1. Therefore, $K+$ and Cl^- could easily share electrons and form the ionic compound KCl. As a general rule, compounds formed entirely of nonmetals are not ionic because their elements either do not form ions or form ions with the same charge. In these nonmetallic compounds, covalent bonds form between the elements. The other answer choices are all formed from nonmetals, so none of them are ionic compounds.

17. The correct answer is C. On the right side of the equation, there are $2 \times 3 = 6$ Br atoms (there are 3 atoms of Br in each molecule of $AlBr_3$). To get 6 Br atoms on the left side, we need to multiply Br_2 by 3, since there are 2 atoms of Br in each molecule of Br_2. Therefore, the coefficient that should be placed before Br_2 is 3.

18. The correct answer is C. When sugar is dissolved in water, their molecules mix with each other on a molecular level and form a solution, but they still retain their individual properties and do not change chemically. The sugar and water can still be separated by allowing the water to evaporate. They form a homogeneous mixture because they mix completely and evenly. A heterogeneous mixture (choice D), like soil or trail mix, is not evenly mixed like a solution. Since the sugar and water do not change chemically, neither a new element (choice A) nor a new compound (choice B) is formed.

19. The correct answer is D. The atomic orbitals, or energy levels, within a single atom can differ in the number of electrons they hold. The innermost energy level can hold a maximum of 2 electrons, the second energy level can hold up to 8, and the third energy level can hold up to 18. Atomic orbitals hold only electrons, not protons or neutrons, so the other answer choices are incorrect.

20. The correct answer is D. The volume of fluid a that a glass can hold is also considered to be the volume of the glass; when you fill it with water, the amount of water it holds is its volume. Volume is measured in cubic units like cm^3 or in liters and its subdivisions, like milliliters. The choices that involve weighing things will give you that thing's mass, not its volume. Weighing the empty glass (choice A) would just give you the mass of the glass, and weighing the filled glass (choice B) would give you the mass of the glass plus the water inside. Placing the glass in a large beaker that is half-filled water and seeing how much water is displaced (choice C) will give you the volume of the empty glass itself—that is, how much material makes up the glass. This is not the same as the volume of fluid that the glass can hold.

21. The correct answer is A. Velocity is the rate of motion in a given direction. The rate of motion is also known as speed, so velocity is speed in a given direction. Speed is distance traveled per unit time. The only answer choice that specifies a direction is choice A, so this is the only choice that is a velocity. Choices B and D only give distance traveled per unit time, so they are both speeds, not velocities. Choice C is a description of acceleration, which is velocity multiplied by time.

22. The correct answer is B. A person standing on the edge of a diving board contains stored energy—potential energy—that can be used to generate motion. This potential energy exists because of the person's position high above the water. Once they jump off of the diving board, their potential energy turns into the kinetic energy of motion as they fall toward the water. The other choices are all objects that are in motion, so they all possess kinetic energy, not potential energy.

23. The correct answer is B. Conduction is the transfer of heat through direct contact between solid materials. The foot is in direct contact with the floor and transfers heat to the floor, so this is an example of conduction. Acceleration (choice A) is not a method of heat transfer; it is a measure of how quickly something increases its velocity. Convection (choice C) is the transfer of heat through fluids, so it does not apply in this case. Radiation (choice D) is the transfer of heat by electromagnetic waves, so it does not apply in this case either.

24. The correct answer is A. The wavelength of a wave is the distance between two co secutive crests or consecutive troughs. Choice B indicates only half a wavelength. Choice C is twice the amplitude of the wave. Choice D is the amplitude of the wave.

25. The correct answer is C. A screw is an inclined plane arranged in a spiral instead of a straight line. A wedge is two inclined planes placed back-to-back. A wheel-and-axle (choice D) is a type of lever (choice A). Pulleys (choice B) are the third basic type of simple machine and are unrelated to screws and wedges.

PART VI

THE MATHEMATICAL REASONING TEST

Mastering the Mathematical Reasoning Test

Chapter 11

OVERVIEW

THE MATHEMATICAL REASONING TEST—IN A NUTSHELL

Time allowed: 115 minutes

Total number of questions: 46

ALL ABOUT THE MATHEMATICAL REASONING TEST

The GED Mathematical Reasoning test is based on Common Core State Standards for Mathematics and Principles and Standards for School Mathematics. The test is designed to measure a variety of skills, including:

- Understanding and applying mathematical concepts and formulas
- Quantitative reasoning and problem solving
- Translating verbal language into mathematical terms
- Manipulating and evaluating arithmetic and algebraic expressions
- Analyzing and interpreting graphical data (charts, graphs, tables)

To measure these skills, content will focus on:

- Quantitative problem solving (approximately 45%)
    - Demonstrating fluency with operations using rational numbers
    - Using rational numbers to formulate solutions to problems set within real-world contexts
    - Solving problems with rational numbers that involve proportionality
    - Engaging with geometric figures in a variety of graphic presentations
    - Engaging with descriptive statistics in a variety of graphic presentations
    - Using formulas or decomposition to calculate perimeter, area, surface area, and volume of figures
- Algebraic problem solving (approximately 55%)
    - Writing linear mathematical expressions and equations that correspond to given situations
    - Evaluating the expressions for specific values of the variable
    - Solving linear equations, inequalities, and systems of linear equations and finding the equation of a line with varying criteria
    - Interpreting the slope of a line as rate of change or unit rate
    - Understanding and applying the concept of a function
    - Using function notation
    - Translating a variety of representations of a function, including tables and equations
    - Solving quadratic equations
    - Interpreting key features of both linear and nonlinear functions

These two subject areas cover a variety of topics that you will be questioned on, including:

- Basic operations with numbers
- Integers, divisibility, factoring, and multiples
- Number signs, absolute value, the real number line, and ordering
- Decimals, place value, and scientific notation
- Percents and fractions
- Exponents (powers) and roots
- Ratio and proportion
- Undefined numerical expressions
- Measures of central tendency (mean, median, mode, and range)
- Frequency distribution
- Probability
- Setting up and evaluating algebraic expressions
- Linear equations and equation systems
- Algebra word problems
- Algebraic inequalities

- Factorable quadratic expressions
- Functional relationships, including series and patterns
- Parallel lines, transversals, and perpendicular lines
- Properties of triangles, quadrilaterals, and other polygons
- Properties of circles (area, circumference, interior degree measures)
- The Pythagorean theorem
- Right triangle trigonometry
- Three-dimensional figures (rectangular solids, right cylinders, square pyramids, cones)
- Coordinate geometry
- Systems of measurement for length, area, volume, weight, and mass

Keep in mind that many of these questions will involve more than one of the areas listed above. For example, solving a geometry problem might also require algebra.

FORMAT AND FEATURES OF THE MATHEMATICAL REASONING TEST

The GED Mathematical Reasoning test consists of 46 questions, and you will have 115 minutes to answer them. The test content is broken up into two categories: 45 percent of the exam focuses on quantitative problem solving, while the other 55 percent is made up of algebraic problem solving.

Five of the questions you have to answer without the help of a calculator. For the rest of the questions, you are permitted to use an on-screen calculator. The calculator you will use is the TI-30XS Multiview Scientific calculator. (You'll examine that calculator's functions starting on the next page.) You will also be provided with an on-screen formula sheet for the entirety of the test, as well as a symbol tool, which will allow you to enter mathematical symbols for fill-in-the-blank problems.

A large portion of the questions on the Mathematical Reasoning test are multiple-choice questions with four choices. The remaining questions will require you to provide your own answer using alternative formats: select-an-area, fill-in-the-blank, drop-down, and drag-and-drop. These question types are used for a variety of subject skills and will be addressed later in the math chapters.

Here are some additional features of the Mathematical Reasoning test:

- Many of the questions are presented in "real-world" settings involving practical, everyday situations.
- Expect at least a third of the questions to refer to charts, graphs, tables, and geometry figures. These figures are drawn to scale unless otherwise noted.

As with every other part of the GED test, you will be provided with an erasable note board to jot down notes and make calculations. You will also be able to access the same list of formulas on-screen as the one that appears before each of the Mathematical Reasoning practice tests in this book. You may or may not need all of these formulas during the test.

Finally, during each part of the Mathematical Reasoning test, easier questions generally appear before more challenging questions. This is only a general rule; you may find some earlier questions to be more difficult for you than some of the subsequent questions.

MEASUREMENTS AND THE MATHEMATICAL REASONING TEST

During the Mathematical Reasoning test, you will be solving problems involving measurement of currency (money), time, length, weight, volume, and possibly mass. Some of these questions will require you to convert one unit of measurement to another. You will be expected to know the most commonly used conversion rates—the ones that people in the United States use in their everyday lives and that are listed next.

NOTE: An asterisk (*) signifies that the test question might provide the conversion rate.

Currency (money) conversions:

100 cents = 1 dollar

10 dimes = 1 dollar

20 nickels = 1 dollar

4 quarters = 1 dollar

Time conversions:

60 seconds (sec.) = 1 minute (min.)

60 minutes = 1 hour (hr.)

24 hours = 1 day

7 days = 1 week (wk.)

12 months (mo.) = 1 year (yr.)

365 days = 1 year

Length conversions:

12 inches (in.) = 1 foot (ft.)

3 feet = 1 yard (yd.)

Weight conversions:

16 ounces (oz.) = 1 pound (lb.)

* 2,000 pounds = 1 ton (T)

Liquid measure conversions:

* 8 ounces (oz.) = 1 cup

* 2 cups = 1 pint (pt.)

* 2 pints = 1 quart (qt.)

* 4 quarts = 1 gallon (gal.)

Answering a test question may require you to convert numbers from one *system* of measurement to another—especially to and from the metric system. You will not be expected to know these sorts of conversion rates. The question at hand will provide the rate you should use.

USING THE TEXAS INSTRUMENTS TI-30XS CALCULATOR

During the GED Mathematical Reasoning test, a calculator will be allowed for all but five questions. The use of a calculator is not *required*, but in order to avoid careless computational mistakes, it is suggested you use a calculator for all but simple calculations.

You will be provided with an on-screen, multiview, scientific calculator. The easy-to-use qualities of the Texas Instruments TI-30XS calculator have made it a standard mathematics tool used in middle and high school math courses. You will not be permitted to bring and use your own calculator during the test. It is highly recommended that you become familiar with the TI-30XS before your testing date.

You are permitted to use the calculator for 41 of the 46 questions. When you come across a question in which you need your calculator, click the "Calculator" button in the top left-hand corner of the screen. The on-screen TI-30XS will appear as a pop-up for use in your calculations for that question. You can move the pop-up by clicking and dragging the window with your mouse. To close the calculator window, click the X in the top right-hand corner of the pop-up window. The "Calculator" button will not be activated during the five questions you must answer without the help of a calculator.

NOTE

GED provides printed materials and online tutorials to help familiarize you with the calculator's functions so you will be comfortable with this tool on test day. Go to **https://ged.com/practice-test/en/calculator/** to view the interactive calculator tutorial.

When the calculator appears, it will be on and ready for use in the standard settings. To enter numbers or operations symbols, use your mouse to click on the keys. Click the **enter** key to view the answer to your calculation, which is located in the bottom right-hand corner of the calculator window.

Basic Operations

To add or subtract numbers, enter the numbers and the + or – keys.

+ –

To multiply or divide, use the × or ÷ keys.

× ÷

To use parentheses in your calculation, click the keys indicating parentheses in the order you see the problem written.

( )

To enter a negative number, click the – key located to the left of the enter key.

–

To find the square of a number, click the x^2 key located to the left of the 7 key.

x^2

Using the 2nd Key

Looking at the TI-30XS, you will see yellow symbols, letters, and functions around the larger, white or black keys. If you wish to use these functions, you must first click the yellow 2nd key in the upper left-hand corner of the calculator, and then the key that the function is located above. The two functions that involve this sequence that you are most likely to use are *percent* and *square root.*

The percent symbol (%) is located above the left parenthesis button. To show a number as a percent, click the number, then click the 2nd key, and then the left parenthesis key.

The square root function is located above the x^2 key. To find the square root of a number, enter the number, then click the 2nd key, and then the x^2 key.

Clearing the Memory

In order to perform a new calculation, you'll need to clear the calculator of the previous one. To do this, press the clear key, located above the division key and below the arrow pad. Clicking this key will clear the calculator's memory of all previous calculations.

ALTERNATE-FORMAT QUESTIONS

The newest edition of the GED Mathematical Reasoning test includes technology-enhanced questions such as drag-and-drop, select-an-area, drop-down, and fill-in-the-blank items. Drag-and-drop questions will require you to drag the "drag tokens" and place them on one or more correct "drop targets." Select-an-area items will be used so that you may select your answer by clicking or graphing a point on a designated sensor on graphs, maps, or diagrams. Drop-down questions will require you to choose the correct answer from a list of options in a drop-down menu. Fill-in-the-blank questions will require you to write a word or phrase in a box in order to complete a sentence.

STRATEGIES FOR SOLVING MATH PROBLEMS

About 50 percent of the questions on the Mathematical Reasoning test will involve problem solving—in other words, working to a solution expressed as either a number or an expression containing variables (such as x and y). In this section, you'll learn specific strategies for solving problems. Most of these strategies apply only to multiple-choice questions, which account for 80 percent of all questions on the test.

The examples you'll see here run the gamut in terms of the concepts covered. If you don't fully understand a certain concept illustrated here, you can come back and review it later.

Scan the Answer Choices for Clues

Scan the answer choices to see what all or most of them have in common—such as radical signs, exponents, factorable expressions, or fractions. Then try to formulate a solution that looks like the answer choices.

EXAMPLE 1 (EASIER):

If $a \neq 0$ or 2, then the expression $\dfrac{\frac{1}{a}}{2-a}$ is equivalent to which of the following?

A. $\dfrac{1}{2a-a^2}$

B. $\dfrac{2}{a-2}$

C. $\dfrac{1}{a^2}$

D. $\dfrac{2}{2a-1}$

Notice what all the answer choices have in common: Each one is a fraction in which the denominator contains the variable *a*, but the numerator doesn't. And there are no fractions in either the numerator or the denominator. That's a clue that your job is to manipulate the expression given in the question so that the result includes these features. Multiplying the numerator fraction by the reciprocal of the denominator will give you a result that has these features:

$$\frac{\frac{1}{a}}{2-a}=\frac{1}{a}\times\frac{1}{2-a}=\frac{1}{2a-a^2}$$

The correct answer is A.

EXAMPLE 2 (MORE CHALLENGING):

A team of archeologists and engineers plans to build a pyramid using ancient construction materials and methods. As shown below, the base of the pyramid is to be square, and each of the four angles at the apex of the pyramid is to measure 90°.

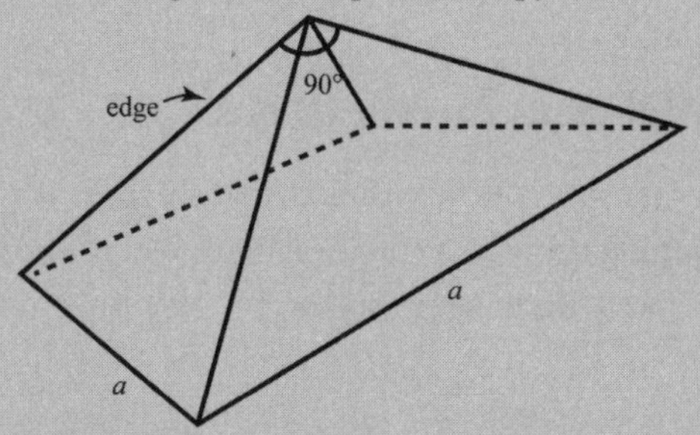

If the pyramid's base measures *a* meters on each side, which of the following represents the length of any of the four edges that extend from the pyramid's base to its apex?

A. $\frac{a}{3}\sqrt{2}$

B. $\frac{a}{2}\sqrt{2}$

C. $\frac{3}{4}a$

D. $\frac{12}{13}a$

Notice that $\sqrt{2}$ appears in two of the four expressions listed among the answer choices. With sufficient knowledge of the Pythagorean theorem, you will recognize this value as the hypotenuse of a certain right-triangle shape. With this clue in mind, bisect any triangular face of the pyramid into two smaller right triangles, as shown below.

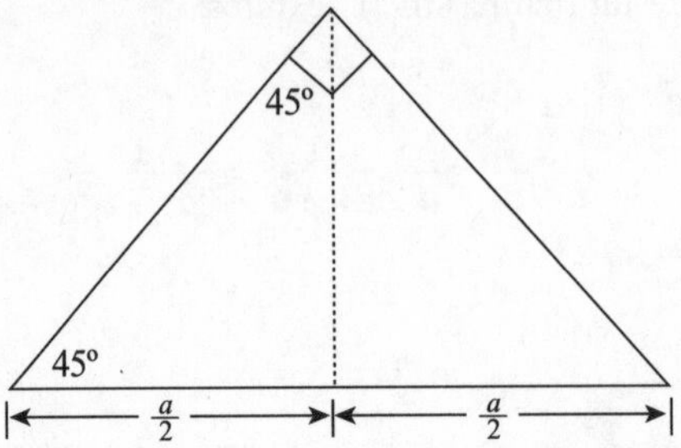

The length of each leg of a smaller triangle is $\frac{a}{2}$. From the Pythagorean theorem, you know that the length of the hypotenuse of any 90°-45°-45° triangle is the product of $\sqrt{2}$ and the length of either leg. So in this case, the hypotenuse, or "edge" of the pyramid, measures $\frac{a}{2}\sqrt{2}$ meters. **The correct answer is B.**

Don't Be Lured by Obvious Answer Choices

Expect to be tempted by incorrect answer choices that are the result of common errors in reasoning, in calculating, and in setting up and solving equations. Never assume that your solution is correct just because you see it among the answer choices.

EXAMPLE 3 (EASIER):

What is the value of $(8 + 8)^2 - (7 + 7)^2$?

A. 30

B. 60

C. 256

D. 452

Each incorrect answer choice is the result of a common error:

If you make the mistake of distributing the power to each term in parentheses, you might select choice A: $8^2 + 8^2 - 7^2 - 7^2 = 64 + 64 - 49 - 49 = 30$.

If you make the mistake of distributing the subtraction sign to both 7's before squaring, you might select choice C: $(8 + 8)^2 - (7 - 7)^2 = 16^2 - 0 = 256$.

If you make the mistake of adding instead of subtracting, you might select choice D: $(8 + 8)^2 + (7 + 7)^2 = 16^2 + 14^2 = 256 + 196 = 452$.

Here is the correct calculation: $16^2 - 14^2 = 256 - 196 = 60$.

The correct answer is B.

EXAMPLE 4 (MORE CHALLENGING):

The average of six numbers is 19. When one of those numbers is taken away, the average of the remaining five numbers is 21. What number was taken away?

A. 2

B. 6.5

C. 9

D. 20

In this example, two of the incorrect answer choices are especially enticing. Choice A would be the correct answer to the question: "What is the difference between 19 and 21?" But this question asks something entirely different. Choice D is the other too-obvious choice. 20 is simply 19 + 21 divided by 2. If this solution strikes you as too simple, you've got good instincts. You can solve this problem quickly by simply comparing the two *sums*. Before the sixth number is taken away, the sum of the numbers is 114 (6×19). After taking away the sixth number, the sum of the remaining numbers is 105 (5×21). The difference between the two sums is 9, which must be the value of the number taken away. **The correct answer is C.**

Size Up the Question to Narrow Your Choices

If a multiple-choice question asks for a number value, you can probably narrow down the answer choices by estimating the size and type of number you're looking for. When handling word problems, use your common sense and real-world experience to formulate "ballpark" estimates.

Also keep in mind that if the answer choices are all numbers, they'll be listed in order—from least in value to greatest in value. This feature can help you zero in on viable choices.

EXAMPLE 5 (EASIER):

Stephanie deposited $1,000 in an account that earns 5% **compound** interest. If she made no additional deposits, what was Stephanie's account balance after two years?

A. $1,050

B. $1,100

C. $1,102.50

D. $1,152.25

If you understand that compound interest is an *annual* rate that applies interest not only to the principal balance, but also to any previous interest earned, and if you know that 5% of $1,000 is $50, then you can narrow your choices. The account earned $50 in interest the first year, but *slightly more* than $50 the second year because it earned interest on the first year's interest. So the correct answer must be a bit greater than $1,100. You can eliminate choices A and B. All that's left is to perform the calculation:

$$5\% \text{ of } \$1{,}050 = 0.05 \times \$1{,}050 = \$52.50.$$

Add this amount of interest to the $50 earned during the first year:

$1,000 (initial deposit) + $50 (year 1 interest) + $52.50 (year 2 interest) = $1,102.50.

The correct answer is C.

EXAMPLE 6 (MORE CHALLENGING):

A container holds 10 liters of a solution that is 20% acid. If 6 liters of pure acid are added to the container, what percent of the resulting mixture is acid?

A. 20

B. $33\frac{1}{3}$

C. 40

D. 50

Common sense should tell you that when you add more acid to the solution, the percentage of the solution that is acid will increase. So you're looking for an answer that is a percentage greater than 20. Only choices B, C, or D fit the bill. If you need to guess at this point, your odds are one in three of answering the question correctly. Here's how to solve the problem:

The original amount of acid is (10)(20%) = 2 liters. After adding 6 liters of pure acid, the amount of acid increases to 8 liters, while the amount of total solution increases from 10 to 16 liters. The new solution is $\frac{8}{16}$, or 50%, acid. **The correct answer is D.**

Know When to Plug In Numbers for Variables

If the answer choices contain variables such as x and y, the question might be a good candidate for the "plug-in" strategy. Pick simple numbers (so the math is easy), and substitute them for the variables. You'll need your pencil and scratch paper (and your erasable note board on test day) for this strategy.

EXAMPLE 7 (EASIER):

If one dollar can buy m pieces of paper, how many dollars are needed to buy p reams of paper? [1 ream = 500 pieces of paper]

A. $\frac{500}{p+m}$

B. $\frac{m}{500p}$

C. $\frac{500p}{m}$

D. $\frac{p}{500m}$

You can solve this problem conventionally or by using the plug-in strategy.

The conventional way: The question is essentially asking: "1 is to *m* as what is to *p*?" Set up a proportion (equate two ratios, or fractions). Then convert either pieces of paper to reams (divide *m* by 500) or reams to pieces (multiply *p* by 500). The second conversion method is used below. Cross-multiply to solve for *x*:

$$\frac{1}{m} = \frac{x}{500p}$$
$$mx = 500p$$
$$x = \frac{500p}{m}$$

The plug-in strategy: Pick easy-to-use values for *m* and *p*. Let's try $m = 500$ and $p = 1$. At \$1 for 500 sheets, it obviously takes exactly \$1 to buy one ream of paper. Start plugging these values into each of the five expressions in turn. The correct choice will provide a value of 1. Choice A doesn't work, and neither does choice B. But choice C works:

$$\frac{500p}{m} = \frac{500(1)}{500} = 1$$

There's no need to test choice D. **The correct answer is C.**

EXAMPLE 8 (MORE CHALLENGING):

If a train travels $r + 2$ miles in *h* hours, which of the following represents the number of miles the train travels in 1 hour and 30 minutes?

A. $\frac{3r+6}{2h}$

B. $\frac{3r}{h+2}$

C. $\frac{r+2}{h+3}$

D. $\frac{r}{h+6}$

This is an algebraic word problem involving rate of motion (speed). As in the previous problem, you can solve this problem either conventionally or by using the plug-in strategy.

The conventional way: Notice that all of the answer choices contain fractions. This is a clue that you should try to create a fraction as you solve the problem. Given that the train travels $r + 2$ miles in *h* hours, you can express its rate in miles per hour as $\frac{r+2}{h}$. In $\frac{3}{2}$ hours, the train would travel $\left(\frac{3}{2}\right)\left(\frac{r+2}{h}\right) = \frac{3r+6}{2h}$ miles.

The plug-in strategy: Pick easy-to-use values for *r* and *h*. Let's try $r = 8$ and $h = 1$. Given these values, the train travels 10 miles $(8 + 2)$ in 1 hour. So in $1\frac{1}{2}$ hours, the train will travel 15 miles. Start plugging these *r* and *h* values into the answer choices. For this question, you won't need to go any further than choice A: $\frac{3r+6}{2h} = \frac{3(8)+6}{2(1)} = \frac{30}{2}$, or 15.

The correct answer is A.

The plug-in strategy can be very useful when you don't know how to set up the algebraic expression or equation that the problem requires. But keep in mind that this strategy can be time-consuming if the correct answer is far down in the list of choices. So use it only if you don't know how to set up the correct algebraic expression or equation.

Know When—and When Not—to Work Backward

If a multiple-choice question asks for a number value, and if you draw a blank as far as how to set up and solve the problem, don't panic. You might be able to work backward by testing the answer choices, each one in turn.

On the GED Mathematical Reasoning test, numerical answer choices are always listed in order of value, from least to greatest. So when working backward from the answer choices, the best place to start is with choice C, which provides a value close to the middle. If choice C provides a number that is too great, then the correct answer must be either choice A or choice B. Conversely, if choice C provides a number that is too small, then the correct answer must be choice D.

EXAMPLE 9 (EASIER):

A ball is dropped from 192 inches above level ground. After the second bounce, it rises to a height of 48 inches. If the height to which the ball rises after each bounce is always the same fraction of the height reached on its previous bounce, what is this fraction?

A. $\frac{1}{8}$

B. $\frac{1}{4}$

C. $\frac{1}{3}$

D. $\frac{1}{2}$

The fastest route to a solution is to plug in an answer. Try choice C, and see what happens. If the ball bounces up $\frac{1}{3}$ as high as it started, as choice C provides, then after the first bounce it will rise up $\frac{1}{3}$ as high as 192 inches, or 64 inches. After a second bounce, it will rise $\frac{1}{3}$ as high, or about 21 inches. But the problem states that the ball rises to 48 inches after the second bounce, so choice C cannot be the correct answer. We can see that the ball must be bouncing higher than one third of the way; that eliminates choices A and B and leaves you with only one possible answer. Try plugging in choice D, and you'll see that it works: $\frac{1}{2}$ of 192 is 96, and $\frac{1}{2}$ of 96 is 48. **The correct answer is D.**

Although it would be possible to develop a formula to answer the question in the example, doing so would be senseless, considering how quickly and easily you can work backward from the answer choices.

Working backward from numerical answer choices works well when the numbers are easy and few calculations are required, as in the preceding question. In other cases, applying algebra might be a better approach.

EXAMPLE 10 (MORE CHALLENGING):

How many pounds of nuts selling for 70 cents per pound must be mixed with 30 pounds of nuts selling at 90 cents per pound to make a mixture that sells for 85 cents per pound?

A. 8.5

B. 10

C. 15

D. 16.5

Is the easier route to the solution to test the answer choices? Let's see. First of all, calculate the total cost of 30 pounds of nuts at 90 cents per pound: $30 \times 0.90 = \$27$. Now, start with choice C. At 70 cents per pound, 15 pounds of nuts costs $10.50. The total cost of this mixture is $37.50, and the total weight is 45 pounds. Now you'll need to perform some long division. The average cost of the mixture turns out to be between 83 and 84 cents—too low for the 85-cent average given in the question. So you can at least eliminate choice C.

You should realize by now that testing the answer choices might not be the most efficient way to tackle this question. In addition, there are ample opportunities for calculation errors. Instead, try solving this problem algebraically by writing and solving a system of equations. Here's how to do it:

The cost (in cents) of the nuts selling for 70 cents per pound can be expressed as $70x$, letting x equal the number that you're asked to determine. You then add this cost to the cost of the more expensive nuts ($30 \times 90 = 2{,}700$) to obtain the total cost of the mixture, which you can express as $85(x + 30)$. You can state this algebraically and solve for x as follows:

$$\begin{aligned} 70x + 2{,}700 &= 85(x + 30) \\ 70x + 2{,}700 &= 85x + 2{,}550 \\ 150 &= 15x \\ 10 &= x \end{aligned}$$

At 70 cents per pound, 10 pounds of nuts must be added in order to make a mixture that sells for 85 cents per pound. **The correct answer is B.**

Look for the Simplest Route to the Answer

For many GED Mathematical Reasoning test questions, there's a long way and a short way to get to the correct answer. When it looks like you're facing a long series of calculations or a complex system of equations, always ask yourself if there's an easier, more intuitive way of answering the question.

EXAMPLE 11 (EASIER):

Type your answer in the box. You may use numbers and/or a decimal point (.) in your answer.

What is the value of $\frac{150}{450} \times \frac{750}{300} \times \frac{450}{1500}$? [ ]

Whether or not you use a calculator for this question, multiplying and dividing these large numbers is needlessly time-consuming. What's more, the more calculations you make, the more likely it is that you'll commit a computation error. Look carefully at the numbers involved. Notice that you can factor all of these numbers across fractions. After factoring, the three fractions that remain can be easily combined. Here's one possibility:

$$\frac{150}{450} \times \frac{750}{300} \times \frac{450}{1500} = \frac{1}{1} \times \frac{1}{2} \times \frac{1}{2} = \frac{1}{4}$$

The correct answer is 1/4 or 0.25. To receive credit for a correct answer, you would enter either **1/4** or **0.25** in the blank box.

EXAMPLE 12 (MORE CHALLENGING):

What is the difference between the sum of all positive **even** integers less than 32 and the sum of all positive **odd** integers less than 32?

A. 0

B. 1

C. 15

D. 16

To answer this question, should you add up two long series of numbers on your scratch paper or with the calculator? No. In this case, it is a waste of time, and you risk committing calculation errors along the way. A smart test taker will notice a pattern and use it as a shortcut. Compare the initial terms of each sequence:

even integers: 2, 4, 6, . . . , 30

odd integers: 1, 3, 5, . . . , 29, 31

Notice that for each successive term the odd integer is one less than the corresponding even integer. There are a total of 15 corresponding integers, so the difference between the sums of all these corresponding integers is 15. But the odd-integer sequence includes one additional integer: 31. So the difference is 31 – 15 = 16. **The correct answer is D.**

Keep in mind: GED Math test questions are not designed to gauge your ability to make lengthy, repetitive calculations on your erasable note board or with the calculator. Combining three or four numbers using basic operations will probably be the limit of what is expected of you. So again, if you're facing a long series of computations, especially with large numbers, look for a faster, easier way to answer the question.

Solve Problems by Starting with What You Know

It's easy to get lost in a complex math problem requiring several steps to solve. If you're at a loss as to how to begin, start with the information you know. Then ask yourself what you can deduce from that information. This approach will very likely lead you, step-by-step, to the solution.

EXAMPLE 13 (EASIER):

Type your answer in the box. You may use numbers and/or a decimal point (.) in your answer.

Cassie can assemble 4 computers in one hour, and Hillary can assemble 12 computers in one hour. Working at the same time, Cassie, Hillary, and a third worker, Jodie, can assemble 192 computers during an 8-hour shift. How many computers can Jodie assemble in one hour? [ ]

Two of the numbers are given as an hourly rate of work, and the other number is given as a rate of work per 8-hour shift. A good place to start is to convert one rate to the other. Let's try converting the total per-shift work rate to an hourly rate: $192 \div 8 = 24$. So you know that Hillary, Jodie, and Cassie can assemble 24 computers in an hour. Now ask yourself what else you know. You know that Cassie's hourly rate of work is 4 and that Hillary's hourly rate of work is 12. Now ask yourself what you deduce from this information. If you subtract those two numbers from 24, you'll find Jodie's hourly rate of work, which is the answer to the question:

$$24 - 4 - 12 = 8$$

The correct answer is 8. To receive credit for a correct answer, you would enter **8** in the blank box.

EXAMPLE 14 (MORE CHALLENGING):

In a group of 20 singers and 40 dancers, 20 percent of the singers are under 25 years of age, and 40 percent of the entire group is under 25 years of age. What portion of the dancers is under 25 years of age?

A. 20 percent

B. 24 percent

C. 40 percent

D. 50 percent

To answer this question, you need to know the total number of dancers as well as the *number* of dancers under 25 years in age. The question provides the first number: 40. To find the second number, start with what the question provides, and figure out what else you know. Keep going, and eventually you'll arrive at your destination. Of the whole group of 60, 24 are under 25 years in age (40% of 60 is 24). Of the 20 singers, 20 percent, or 4 singers, are under 25 years in age. Hence, the remaining 20 people under 25 must be dancers. That's the second number you need to answer the question: 20 is 50% of 40. **The correct answer is D.**

Search Geometry Figures for Clues

Some GED Math test geometry questions will be accompanied by figures. They are there for a reason: the pieces of information a figure provides can lead you, step-by-step, to the answer.

EXAMPLE 15 (EASIER):

This is how you will see the question worded on the online GED test. For this print version, mark the grid to show the correct coordinates.

$\overline{PQ}$ has a midpoint M. $\overline{PM}$ is congruent to $\overline{MQ}$. Click on the grid to show the correct (x, y) coordinates of point M.

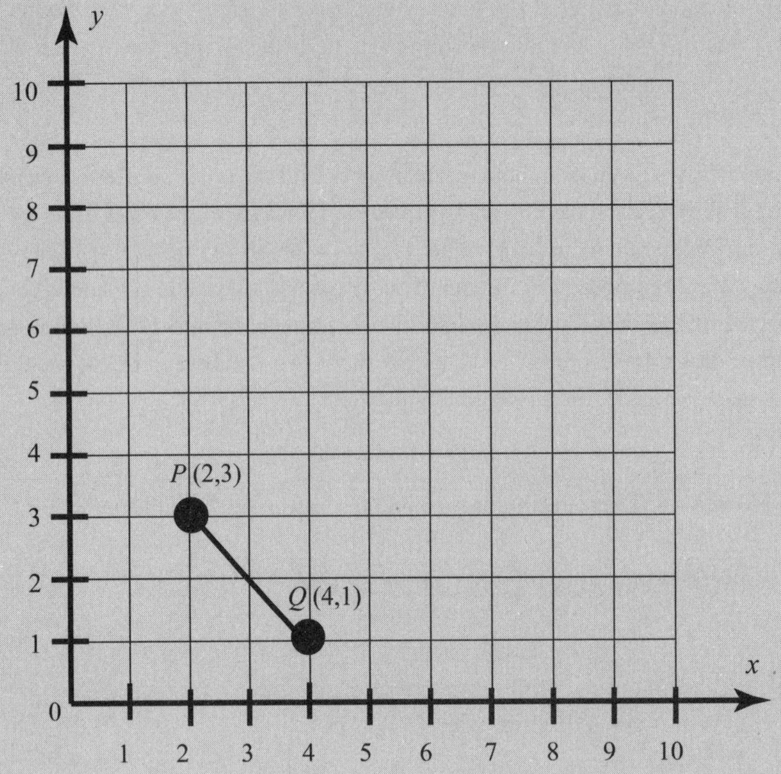

To answer the question, you need to examine the specific coordinates provided in the figure. Given that $\overline{PM}$ is congruent, or equal in length, to $\overline{MQ}$, the x-coordinate of point M is half the horizontal distance from 2 to 4 (P to Q), at 3. Similarly, the y-coordinate of point M is half the vertical distance from 3 to 1 (P to Q), at 2. The (x, y) coordinates of point M are (3, 2). **The correct answer is (3, 2).**

EXAMPLE 16 (MORE CHALLENGING):

Type your answer in the box.

Point *O* lies at the center of the circle shown in the figure.

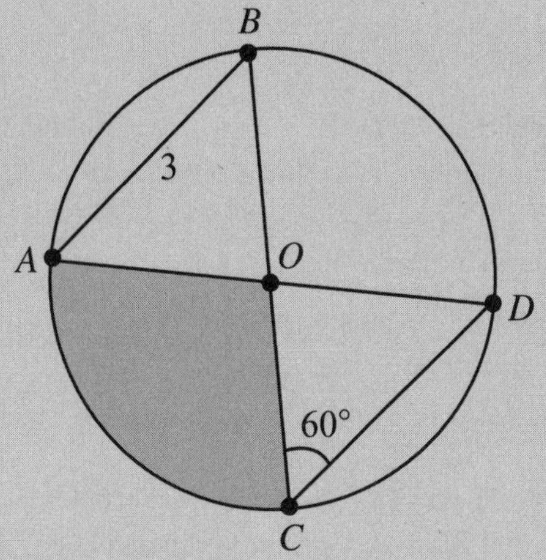

What is the area of the circle's shaded region, expressed in square units?

[ ] π

This question asks for the area of a portion of the circle defined by a central angle. To answer the question, you'll need to determine the area of the entire circle as well as what portion (fraction or percent) of that area is shaded. Search the figure for a piece of information that might provide a starting point. If you look at the 60° angle in the figure, you should recognize that both triangles *COD* and *AOB* areequilateral (all angles are 60°) and, extended out to their arcs, form two segments, each $\frac{1}{6}$ the size of the entire circle. What's left are the two largest segments, each of which is twice the size of a small segment. So the shaded area must account for $\frac{1}{3}$ the circle's area.

Now you've reduced the problem to the simple mechanics of calculating the circle's area, then dividing it by 3. In an equilateral triangle, all sides are congruent. Examining the figure once again, notice length 3, which is also the circle's radius (the distance from its center to its circumference). The area of any circle is πr^2, where *r* is the circle's radius. Thus, the area of the circle is 9π. The shaded portion accounts for $\frac{1}{3}$ the circle's area, or 3π. **The correct answer is 3.**

As the preceding examples show, GED Math test geometry figures are intended to provide information helpful in solving the problem. But they're not intended to *provide* the answer through visual measurement. Make sure you solve the problem by working with the numbers and variables provided, not simply by looking at the figure's proportions.

Sketch Your Own Geometry Figure

A geometry problem that doesn't provide a figure might be more easily solved if it had one. Try drawing a figure based on the information provided. It will be easier than trying to visualize it in your mind.

EXAMPLE 17 (EASIER):

Line A is perpendicular to line B, and the intersection of line B and line C forms a 35° angle. Which statement about the relationship between line A and line C is correct?

A. Line A is perpendicular to line C.

B. The intersection of line A and line C forms a 35° angle.

C. The intersection of line A and line C forms a 125° angle.

D. The intersection of line A and line C forms a 145° angle.

It's difficult to visualize all the lines and angles in your head in order to answer this question. So first draw perpendicular lines A and B. Then draw line C through line A at an acute angle of approximately 35° (a rough approximation will suffice), and mark that angle measure. You can now see a *right* triangle with interior angles 90°, 35°, and 55°. (The interior angles of any triangle total 180° in measure.)

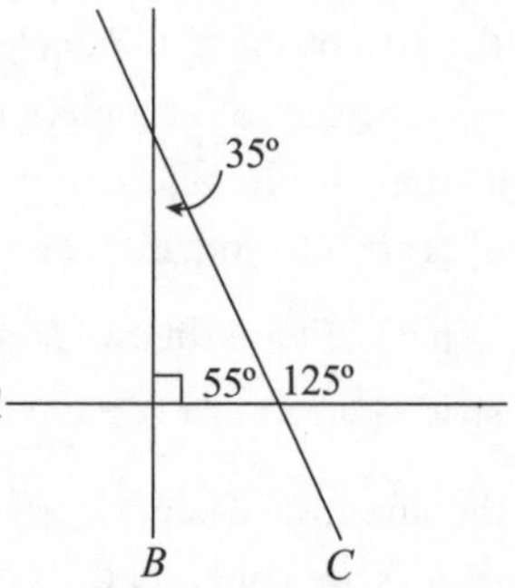

Since 55° is not among the answer choices, you need to determine the measure of either adjacent angle, which is *supplementary* to the 55° angle. (This means that the two angles combine to form a straight, 180° line.) Either of the two exterior angles adjacent to the 55° angle must measure 125° (180° – 55°). **The correct answer is C.**

EXAMPLE 18 (MORE CHALLENGING):

On the *xy*-coordinate plane, points R (7, –3) and S (7, 7) are the endpoints of the longest possible chord of a certain circle. What is the area of the circle?

A. 7π

B. 16π

C. 20π

D. 25π

There are lots of 7's in this question, which might throw you off track without at least a rough picture. To keep your thinking straight, sketch out your own rough *xy*-grid and plot the two points. You'll see that *R* is located directly below *S*, so chord $\overline{RS}$ is vertical.

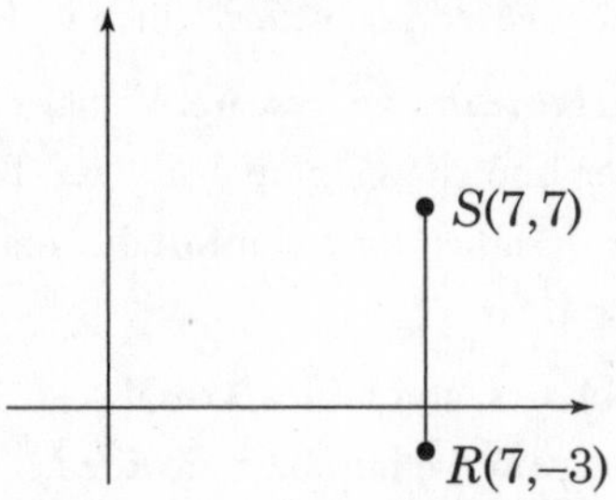

Accordingly, the length of $\overline{RS}$ is simply the vertical distance from –3 to 7, which is 10. By definition, the longest possible chord of a circle is equal in length to the circle's diameter. In this case, the circle's diameter is 10, and thus its radius is 5. The circle's area is $\pi(r)^2 = 25\pi$. **The correct answer is D.**

ANALYZING GRAPHICAL DATA (GRAPHS, CHARTS, AND TABLES)

GED Math test data analysis questions are most often based on the following types of data displays:

- Bar graphs
- Line charts
- Picture graphs
- Circle graphs (pie charts)
- Tables

Data analysis questions are designed to gauge your ability to read, compare, and interpret charts, graphs, and tables, as well as to calculate numbers such as percentages, ratios, fractions, and averages based on data presented in a graphical format. Here are some features of the GED Math test data analysis questions you should know about:

- **The number of displays per question and questions per display can vary.** The questions usually come in sets of 2–3, each question in a set referring to the same graphical data. Some questions or sets may involve just *one* chart, graph, or table; other questions or sets may involve *two or more* charts, graphs, or tables.
- **Important additional information may be provided.** Any additional information that you might need to know to interpret the graphical display will be indicated above, below, or to the side of it. Be sure to read this information!
- **Some questions might ask for an approximation.** The test makers are trying to gauge your ability to interpret graphical data, not your ability to crunch numbers to the "*n*th" decimal place.

- **Answering a question often involves multiple steps.** Though an easier question might simply involve locating a certain number value on a chart or graph, most questions ask you to perform one or more calculations as well. You also may need to refer to more than one graph or chart in order to answer a question, which will involve additional steps.
- **Bar graphs and line charts are drawn to scale.** Visual *estimation* is part of what's required to analyze a bar graph or line chart's graphical data. But they aren't drawn to test your eyesight. Instead, they're designed for a comfortable margin for error in visual acuity. Just don't round up or down too far.
- **For picture graphs, pie charts, and tables, visual scale is not important.** You'll interpret these displays based strictly on the numbers provided.

Bar Graphs

A **bar graph** looks like what the name implies: it consists of a series of vertical or horizontal bars representing number values. The higher (or longer) the bar, the greater the number value.

A bar graph includes a **vertical axis** and a **horizontal axis.** Each scale shows a different measure or other variable. Examine the following graph. The vertical scale indicates a number expressed in *thousands*. The numbers on this vertical scale range from 0 to 22,000. The horizontal scale indicates ages ranging from 25 to 65+ (which means 65 and older). Notice that the ages are given in five-year intervals; ages falling between these intervals are not represented.

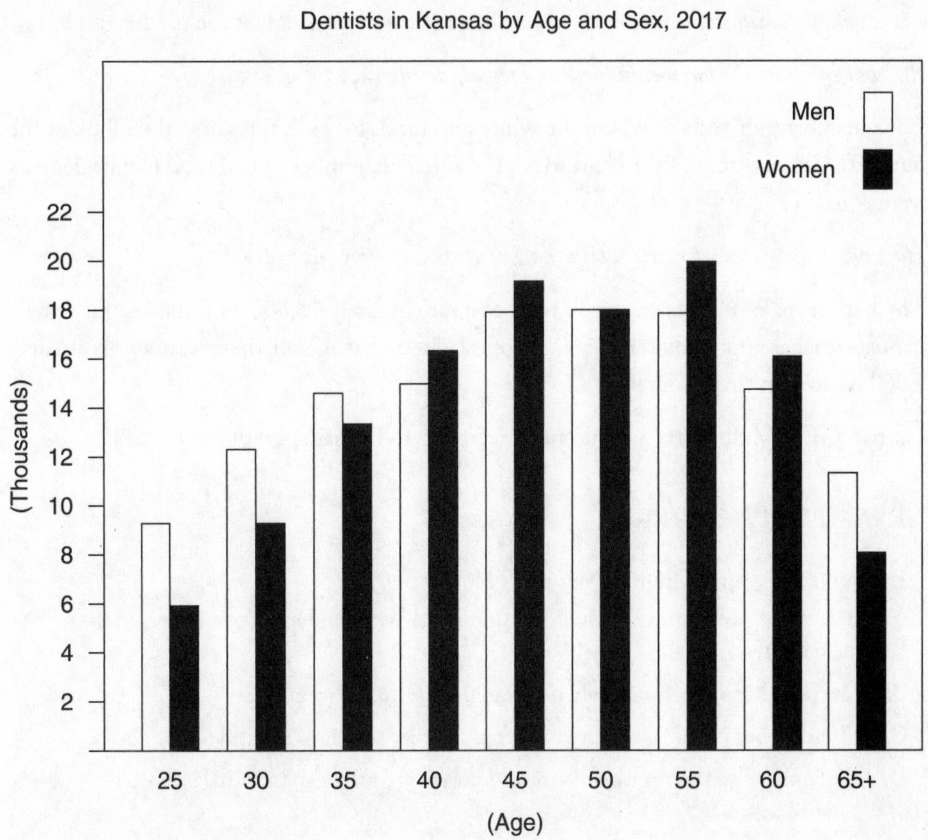

But what do the "thousands" (vertical scale) and the ages (horizontal scale) involve? Examine the information above the illustration. This is the label, or title, for the graph. It tells you that the vertical scale indicates the number of *dentists* (in thousands), while the horizontal scale indicates *age* categories for dentists. It also tells you that these numbers involve one state during one year only: Kansas in 2017.

Finally, what is the distinction between a white bar and a black bar? Examine the **legend** in the upper-right corner. It tells you that for each age interval, the white bar represents the number of dentists who are men, and the black bar represents the number of dentists who are women.

So by examining the height of a white (or black) bar in each age category, you can "see" the approximate number of male (or female) dentists at each age interval. For example, in Kansas during 2017:

- Approximately 15,000 dentists were 40-year-old men
- Approximately 20,000 dentists were 55-year-old women
- Just over 8,000 dentists were women 65 years of age or older

Notice that these numbers are approximations, or estimates. Remember: when analyzing GED Math test bar graphs, you won't need to provide precise values for numbers appearing on scales such as the vertical scale in this example.

Now answer a few questions involving a bit more than identifying a single value on the graph:

At what age were the number of male and female dentists equal?

Look at the graph and see where the white and black bars are the same, then look at the numbers at the bottom of the chart to see the age. The number of male and female dentists were equal at age 50.

How many more male dentists than female dentists were there at age 30?

The bar for male dentists at age 30 reaches approximately 12,500, and the bar for female dentists reaches approximately 9,500. So of the dentists at age 30, there were approximately 3,000 more men than women.

Now look at two GED Math test-style questions referring to the same graph.

EXAMPLE 19 (EASIER):

Based on the graph, which statement is NOT accurate?

A. Between ages 40 and 60, the total number of female dentists was greater than male dentists.

B. Overall, there are more male dentists than female dentists.

C. The number of female dentists decreased between ages 60 and 65+.

D. The only time the number of male dentists is greater than female dentists is prior to age 40.

All of the statements are true according to the graph except choice D. When examining the graph carefully, the number of male dentists is also greater than female dentists in the 65+ age group. **The correct answer is D.**

EXAMPLE 20 (MORE CHALLENGING):

At which age did the number of male dentists increase the **least** over the number of female dentists?

A. Age 30

B. Age 35

C. Age 45

D. Age 65+

First, notice that in the age 45 group, there were more female dentists than male dentists. Therefore, you can eliminate choice C on this basis alone. No calculations are necessary when comparing choices A, B, and D. For each of these age groups (30, 35, and 65+), examine the height difference between the two bars. The question asks for the *least* increase. At ages 30 and 65+, the differences in the heights of the bars is clearly greater than at age 35. Therefore, choices A and D can be eliminated. The only remaining group is age 35, where the difference between the number of male and female dentists is small. **The correct answer is B.**

Line Charts

A **line chart** consists of one or more lines running from left to right. Line charts are constructed by first plotting points at regular intervals, then connecting those points with **trend lines** (lines that suggest increases and decreases from one interval to the next). But the only data you know for sure are those indicated by the points themselves, and not by the lines. The higher the point on a line, the greater the number value the point represents.

Like bar graphs, line charts include a vertical axis and a horizontal axis, each showing a different measure or other variable. Examine the following line chart. The vertical scale indicates a number expressed in *thousands*. The numbers on this vertical scale range from 0 to 45,000. The horizontal scale indicates months of the years; all 12 months are represented.

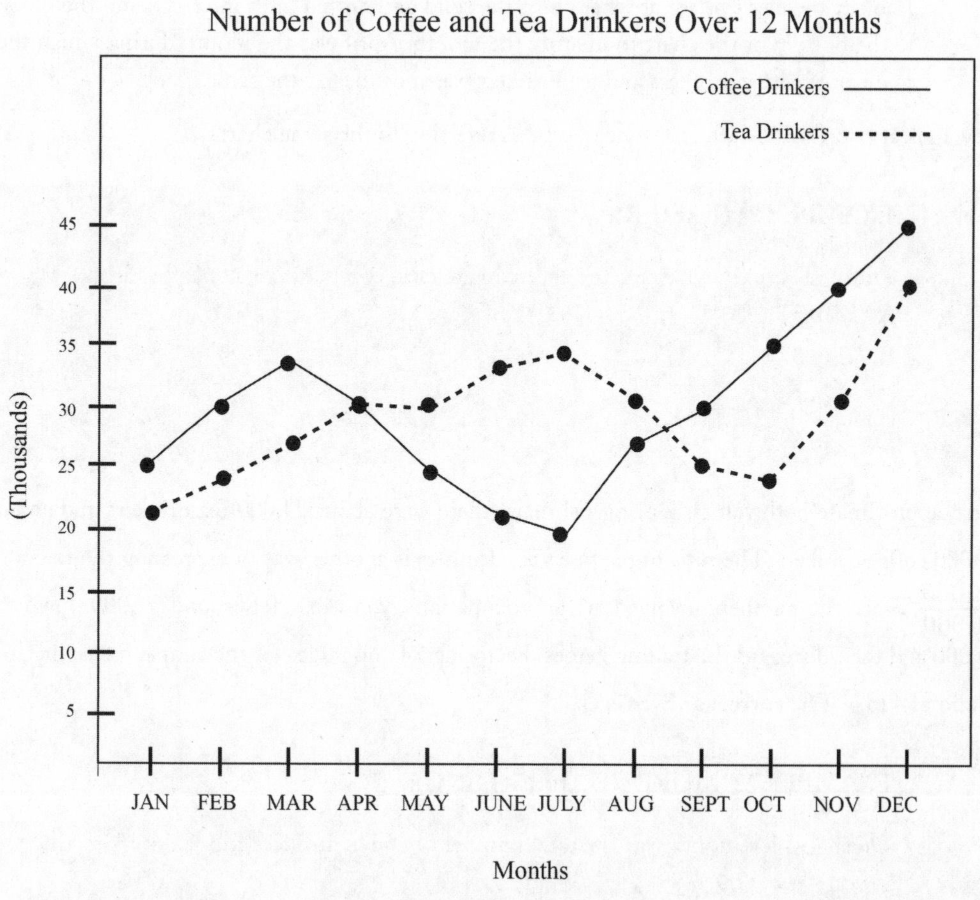

The chart's label, or title, above the illustration tells you that the vertical scale indicates the number of *coffee and tea drinkers* in thousands. The legend in the upper-right corner tells you that the solid line represents coffee drinkers, while the dotted line represents tea drinkers. By examining the height of the solid (or dotted) line at each point, you can "see" the approximate number of coffee (or tea) drinkers for that month. For example:

- The number of coffee drinkers in May was approximately 25,000.
- The number of tea drinkers in November was approximately 32,000.

These numbers are approximations, or estimates. As with bar graphs, analyzing GED Math test line charts won't require identifying precise values for numbers appearing on scales such as the vertical scale in this example.

Now answer a few questions involving a bit more than identifying a single number value on the chart:

During what month was the number of coffee drinkers greatest?

Look at the solid line and follow it to the highest point (dot) on the chart. Then look to the bottom of the chart to see the month. December saw the greatest number of coffee drinkers.

During what month were the number of coffee drinkers and tea drinkers most nearly the same?

Look at the chart to see at what point the solid and dotted lines intersect, and then look to the bottom of the chart to identify the month. April was the month during which the number of coffee drinkers and tea drinkers was most nearly the same.

Now look at two GED Math test-style questions referring to the same chart.

EXAMPLE 21 (EASIER):

During February, what was the approximate ratio of tea drinkers to coffee drinkers?

A. 2 to 5

B. 2 to 3

C. 4 to 5

D. 5 to 3

First, approximate both values: During February, there were about 24,000 tea drinkers and about 31,000 coffee drinkers. The *ratio* of tea to coffee drinkers is another way of expressing the fraction $\frac{24,000}{31,000}$. Since the numbers involved are approximations, you can safely round 31,000 down to 30,000 and then disregard the trailing zeroes. Factoring 24 and 30 leaves the simple fraction $\frac{4}{5}$, or a ratio of 4 to 5. **The correct answer is C.**

EXAMPLE 22 (MORE CHALLENGING):

During which month was the total number of coffee drinkers and tea drinkers the lowest?

A. January

B. May

C. August

D. September

Your task here is to add together the number of coffee drinkers and tea drinkers. But there's no need to perform calculations for each of the months listed. Instead, focus on the months when the number of both coffee and tea drinkers were both low—in other words, where both points are low on the chart. January is a viable choice, and so is September. Combine *approximate* numbers for each of these two months:

January: 21,000 (tea) + 25,000 (coffee) = 46,000

September: 20,000 (tea) + 30,000 (coffee) = 50,000

Thus, January saw the lowest combined consumption. **The correct answer is A.**

Circle Graphs

Circle graphs are sometimes referred to as **pie charts.** They show the parts, or segments, of a whole. Most often, the parts are expressed as percents of the whole. The parts of the whole add up to 100 percent. Reading circle graphs should not involve visual estimation. Rely only on the numbers provided, not on the visual size of any segment in relation to the whole. Here's an example of a circle graph:

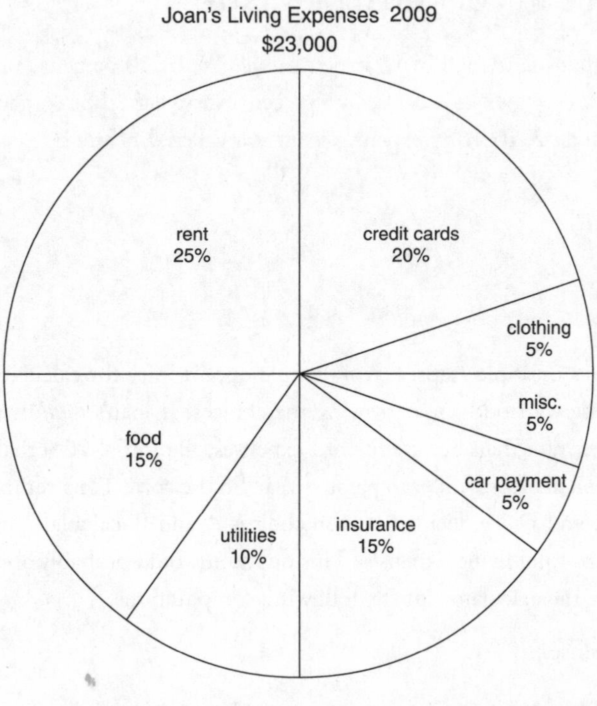

The label, or title, above the graph tells you that each segment on the graph represents a percent of Joan's total living expenses ($23,000) for 2009. To determine her expenditures for each category, you would multiply the percent by her total living expenses.

Now answer a few simple questions involving the data in this graph:

How much did Joan spend for insurance?

Insurance accounted for 15% of Joan's living expenses. Convert 15% to a decimal number, then multiply: Joan spent $23,000 × 0.15 = $3,450 on insurance.

How much did Joan spend on rent and utilities combined?

You can add the two percentages first: 25% (rent) + 10% (utilities) = 35%. Calculate the combined dollar amount: Joan spent $23,000 × 0.35 = $8,050 on rent and utilities.

Now look at two GED Math test-style questions referring to the same chart.

EXAMPLE 23 (EASIER):

How much more did Joan spend on food than on clothing?

A. \$560

B. \$1,150

C. \$2,300

D. \$3,450

First, subtract 5% from 15%. Joan spent 10% more of her total expenses on food than on clothing. Then express 10% as a dollar amount: \$23,000 × 0.10 = \$2,300. **The correct answer is C.**

EXAMPLE 24 (MORE CHALLENGING):

Assume that Joan's total living expenses increase by 10 percent every year and that her credit card expenses increase by 5 percent every year. Approximately what portion of Joan's total 2010 living expenses went toward credit cards?

A. 18%

B. 19%

C. 20%

D. 21%

This question requires multiple steps, leaving ample opportunity for calculation errors. However, you can easily increase your odds by narrowing the choices. If Joan's *total* living expenses increase every year at a greater rate than her credit card expenses, the initial 20% that constitutes just the credit card portion will *decrease* with each passing year. So the correct answer must be less than 20%. Eliminate choices C and D. To decide between choices A and B, calculate Joan's 2010 credit card expenses and her 2010 total living expenses. This question would probably appear on Part II of the test, so you could use the calculator for the following computations.

2010 credit card expenses:

$$\$4{,}600 + (0.05)(\$4{,}600) = \$4{,}830$$

2010 total living expenses:

$$\$23{,}000 + (0.10)(\$23{,}000) = \$25{,}300$$

To determine Joan's 2010 credit card expenses as a percentage of her total living expenses, divide. The question asks for an approximate percentage, so you can round your answer a bit:

$$\frac{4{,}830}{25{,}300} \approx 0.19, \text{ or } 19\%.$$

The correct answer is B.

Tables

A **table** consists of rows and columns of data. Beside each row and above each column is a heading that tells you what the numbers in the row or column signify. Most of us read tables every day: television, bus, and work schedules; menus; and even calendars are all everyday examples of tables. So you should have little trouble reading GED Math test tables. Nevertheless, the tables on the test will be unfamiliar to you, and some of the questions can be a bit more challenging than you might expect.

Look at the following table.

Resort	Snowfall (2017)	Snowfall (2018)	No. of Visitors (2017)	No. of Visitors (2018)
Blue Mountain	14.8 ft.	18.6 ft.	28,300	31,350
High Top	12.8 ft.	19.0 ft.	12,720	11,830
Crystal Hill	20.6 ft.	15.3 ft.	22,440	25,100
Snow Ridge	21.2 ft.	16.4 ft.	9,580	12,360

Notice that for each of the four resorts, two pieces of data are provided for each of the two years: 2017 and 2018. This table does not come with a title or other explanatory information, but you don't need any to understand the table. Now answer a few simple questions involving the tabular data:

Which resort saw the least snowfall in 2017?

High Top saw only 12.8 feet of snowfall in 2017. All three other resorts saw more than that.

How much more snow fell in High Top than in Crystal Hill in 2018?

Subtract the amount at Crystal Hill (15.3) from the amount at High Top (19.0). The difference is 3.7 feet.

How many more visitors came to Crystal Hill in 2018 than in 2017?

Subtract the number in 2017 (22,440) from the number in 2018 (25,100). The difference is 2,660.

Now look at two GED Math test-style questions referring to the same table.

EXAMPLE 25 (EASIER):

Which resort experienced the greatest *percentage* change in number of visitors from 2017 to 2018?

A. Blue Mountain
B. High Top
C. Crystal Hill
D. Snow Ridge

To answer the question, you don't need to calculate precise percentage changes. Instead, compare changes among the resorts by rough estimation. Notice that for each of three resorts—Blue Mountain, Crystal Hill, and Snow Ridge—the change was roughly 3,000. (For High Top, the change was far less, so you can rule out choice B.) Also notice that the actual numbers are lowest for Snow Ridge, which means that the *percentage* change at Snow Ridge was the highest. **The correct answer is D.**

EXAMPLE 26 (MORE CHALLENGING):

Based on the 2017 and 2018 data, what can be inferred about the four resorts?

A. The higher a resort's elevation, the greater the snowfall at that resort.

B. The four resorts received more visitors altogether in 2017 than in 2018.

C. The numbers of visitors were not consistently related to snowfall amounts.

D. The four resorts received more snowfall altogether in 2018 than in 2017.

The data in the table contradicts statements B and D, and the table contains no data about elevation (choice A). In contrast, the data strongly supports choice C. Only at Blue Mountain did the number of visitors vary directly with the amount of snowfall. (Both increased from 2017 to 2018.) At each of the other three resorts, the two variables varied *inversely*. At High Top, snowfall increased from 2017 to 2018, but the number of visitors decreased from one year to the next. At Crystal Hill and Snow Ridge, snowfall decreased from 2017 to 2018, but the number of visitors increased from one year to the next. **The correct answer is C.**

ROUNDING, SIMPLIFYING, AND CHECKING YOUR CALCULATIONS

No GED test taker is immune to committing number-crunching errors—with or without a calculator. In this section, you'll learn how to approximate and round numbers to help you solve problems quickly. You'll also learn how to simplify certain kinds of operations to make calculating numbers easier. Finally, you'll learn when it's best to use the calculator during Part II, as well as how best to check your calculations.

Approximations and Rounding

Some multiple-choice questions will clearly indicate that an approximate value will suffice. For example, a question might ask which choice is "most nearly equal to" a given expression. Or it might ask for "the approximate area" of a certain geometric figure. Read the question carefully for phrases such as these. If you see this sort of phrase, it tells you that you can *round* some of your calculations yet work to a solution that is closest to the value provided as the correct answer.

How to Round a Number

When you round a number, you eliminate one or more of the digits from the right end of the number. But this doesn't mean that you ignore those digits. Consider the number **4,834.826**. If you simply ignore all digits to the right of the decimal point, you're left with 4,834. But you have not rounded the number to the nearest unit, because **".826"** is closer to 1 than to 0. In this case, rounding this number to the nearest unit requires increasing the "ones" digit from 4 to 5, so that the entire rounded number would be **4,835**. For the record, here's the same number rounded to all possible places:

4,834.826 rounded to:	**equals:**	**what we've done:**
the nearest hundredth	4,834.83	round .826 up to .830
the nearest tenth	4,834.8	round .82 down to .80
the nearest unit	4,835	round 4.8 up to 5.0
the nearest ten	4,830	round 34 down to 30
the nearest hundred	4,800	round 834 down to 800
the nearest thousand	5,000	round 4,834 up to 5,000
the nearest ten thousand	0	round 4,834 down to 0

But what about rounding the number 5, which lies midway between 0 and 10. Do you round it up or down? It doesn't matter. Don't worry: the correct response to a GED test math question will *not* depend solely on whether you round the number 5 up or round it down. For example, if the solution to a problem is 4.5, you won't be asked to choose between 4 and 5 as the closest approximation.

Numbers with Non-repeating Decimal Places

Many numbers, especially square roots, include an infinite number of non-repeating decimal places. $\sqrt{2}$, $\sqrt{3}$, and π are three examples that appear frequently on the GED Math test because they are essential to certain geometry formulas. So how should you handle them? You will find that answer choices often express such numbers "as is" rather than as their decimal or fractional equivalents, so that you won't have to deal with their values at all. But if a question should require you to estimate the values of such numbers, rounding them to the nearest tenth will usually suffice, unless the question tells you the approximate value you should use in your calculation. Here's a simple example involving the value of π.

EXAMPLE 27:

Which of the following **most** closely approximates the area of a circle with a radius of 3 centimeters?

A. 18 cm^2

B. 28 cm^2

C. 30 cm^2

D. 36 cm^2

The phrase "most closely approximates" tells you that you can round some numbers and still narrow the choices to the correct answer. Notice that the answer choices are integers—a further clue that you can probably round your calculation and work to the correct solution. The area of a circle is equal to πr^2, where r represents the circle's radius. To the nearest tenth, $\pi = 3.1$. Substituting 3.1 for π:

$$\text{Area} = 3.1 \times 3^2 = (3.1)(9) = 27.9$$

If you're uncomfortable with rounding π to just one decimal place, use a slightly more precise value for π. To the nearest hundredth, $\pi = 3.14$. Substitute 3.14 for π in the same equation:

$$\text{Area} = 3.14 \times 3^2 = (3.14)(9) = 28.26$$

As you can see, either rounded value (3.1 or 3.14) leads you to the closest approximation among the five choices. **The correct answer is B.**

In the preceding example, what if the two closest values among the answer choices were 28 and 28.5? Using 3.1 as an approximate value of π would have resulted in the wrong answer. 27.9 is closer to 28 than to 28.5, while 28.26 is closer to 28.5 than to 28. Don't worry; you won't be required to slice the numbers this finely on the test.

Rounding Numerators and Denominators

Nowhere is rounding more valuable than in dealing with fractions. Assume, for example, that a certain question for which you are not allowed to use the calculator requires you to divide 47 by 62. The quotient can be expressed as the fraction $\frac{47}{62}$. Since 47 is a prime number, you can't simplify the fraction or the division. And if you apply long division, you'll find it time consuming to find the precise quotient:

$$62\overline{)47} = 0.7580645$$

But this is not the sort of number that you'll be required to compute on the GED Math test—with or without a calculator. If you face an operation such as this one, an approximation will almost always suffice to answer the question. If you're on a question for which the calculator may not be used, decide whether to round the numbers up or down, and by how far. But be sure to round both numbers *in the same direction* (either up or down), in order to minimize the change to the value of the overall fraction.

For example, in performing the operation 47 ÷ 62, you can round 47 *down* to 45 and 62 *down* to 60, or you can round 47 *up* to 50 and 62 *up* to 65. Either method will result in a close enough approximation of the quotient 0.7580645:

$$\frac{47}{62} \approx \frac{45}{60} = \frac{3}{4}\text{, or } 0.75$$

$$\frac{47}{62} \approx \frac{50}{65} = \frac{10}{13}\text{, or approximately } 0.77$$

Whether you should round up or down depends on how easy it is to divide the revised numerator by the denominator. In the operation 47 ÷ 62, rounding *up* is easier because you can simplify the resulting fraction. To underscore this idea, consider the fraction $\frac{42}{83.8}$. You can round both numbers *up*, and then simplify:

$$\frac{42}{83.8} \approx \frac{45}{85} = \frac{9}{17}$$

Better still, though, you can round both numbers *down*:

$$\frac{42}{83.8} \approx \frac{40}{80} = \frac{1}{2}$$

The second result is an easier fraction to work with and might suffice if the answer choices are expressed only to the nearest half unit.

Techniques for Combining Numbers

Here you'll learn some grouping techniques that can help you add, subtract, and multiply numbers efficiently. You'll also learn how to simplify multiplication and division of numbers that contain "trailing zeros." These techniques can be especially helpful for questions for which the use of the calculator is not allowed. But you can also apply them to calculator-allowed questions in order to check your calculator work.

Cancel Numbers if Possible (Addition and Subtraction)

When combining a series of numbers by addition and/or subtraction, look for number pairs or larger groups that "cancel out"—in other words, that add up to 0 (zero). Consider this series of numbers:

$$17 + 10 - 14 - 3$$

The conventional method is to add each term to the next one, from left to right. But since –14 – 3 = –17, those two terms cancel out the number 17. In other words, the three numbers add up to 0 (zero). So you know that all four numbers must add up to 10.

Combine Similarly Signed Numbers First (Addition and Subtraction)

Another technique for combining by addition and subtraction is to add positive and negative numbers separately, and then subtract the second sum from the first. Consider this series of numbers:

$$23 - 12 - 14 + 7 - 8$$

The conventional method is to subtract 12 from 23, then subtract 14, then add 7, then subtract 8—in other words, to move from left to right. If pressed for time, it's remarkably easy to overlook minus signs and to add when you should be subtracting. So instead (or to check the work you performed the conventional way), combine the positive numbers and the negative numbers separately, then subtract the sums as follows:

$$23 + 7 = 30 \text{ (sum of positive terms)}$$
$$12 + 14 + 8 = 34 \text{ (sum of negative terms)}$$
$$30 - 34 = -4 \text{ (total sum)}$$

Round One Number Up and Another Down (Addition and Subtraction)

Yet another method of combining by addition or subtraction is to round one number up and another one down by the same amount. For example, 89 is 11 *less* than 100, while 111 is 11 *greater* than 100. So 89 + 111 is the same as 100 + 100 = 200. Here's an example with four terms instead of just two:

$$251 + 423 + 749 + 77$$

Notice that 251 + 749 is the same as 250 + 750 = 1,000. Also notice that 423 + 77 is the same as 425 + 75 = 500. So the calculation boils down to 1,000 + 500 = 1,500, which can be performed quickly yet accurately.

Multiply Numbers in the Easiest Sequence

You can multiply three or more numbers together most efficiently by looking for number pairs that combine easily. Consider the following expression:

$$25 \times 3\frac{1}{2} \times 16$$

To combine all three numbers, you can start with any pair. But the operation 25 × 16 is the easiest one to start with: 100 × 16 = 1,600, and so 25 × 16 must equal one-fourth of 1,600, or 400. Now perform the second operation:

$$400 \times 3\frac{1}{2} = (400 \times 3) + \left(400 \times \frac{1}{2}\right) = 1{,}400$$

Strip Away Trailing Zeros When Multiplying or Dividing

When facing multiplication involving large numbers ending in zeros, called "trailing zeros," many test takers will include the zeros in their calculation (whether using the calculator or pencil and paper). But this method can easily result in a calculation error. Instead, strip away the trailing zeros before doing the math.

Consider the operation 4,200 × 6,000. Follow these three steps to make sure you handle the zeros correctly:

1. Ignore all the trailing (consecutive) zeros at the end of the numbers.
2. Multiply whatever numbers are left: 42 × 6 = 252.
3. Add back the zeros to the end of your product. In this example, we ignored five zeros, so the answer is 252 with five zeros to the right: 25,200,000.

Now consider the same two numbers, except that the operation is division: 4,200 ÷ 6,000. Follow these three steps to make sure you handle the zeros correctly:

1. Ignore the zeros, and divide what's left: 42 ÷ 6 = 7.
2. Cancel (cross out) every trailing zero in the numerator for which there is also a trailing zero in the denominator. In this example, all zeros cancel out except for one zero in the denominator.
3. For every extra zero in the denominator, move the decimal point in your quotient to the *left* one place. In this case, take the quotient, 7, and move the decimal point one place to the left. The answer is 0.7.

   or

   For each extra zero in the numerator, move the decimal point to the right one place. (This step doesn't apply to this particular example, but see below.)

Let's try this method again, this time reversing the numerator and the denominator (6,000 ÷ 4,200):

1. Ignore the zeros, and divide what's left: $\frac{6}{42} = \frac{1}{7}$, or about 0.14.
2. Cancel trailing zeros in the numerator and denominator.
3. You're left with one extra zero in the numerator, so move the decimal point to the right *one* place. The answer is about 1.4. (To express the answer as a fraction, you would add the extra zero to the numerator: $\frac{10}{7}$.)

Remember: you can ignore trailing zeros, but only temporarily. You'll have to tag them back onto your final number. And you can't ignore zeros between non-zero numbers (like 308).

Using the Calculator to Your Advantage

As noted earlier, you will have online access to the TI-30XS calculator and you should make sure you are thoroughly familiar with this calculator before taking the test.

For many questions, the calculator may be helpful. For some of these questions, however, using the calculator may be unnecessary or may actually slow you down. In any event, remember that a calculator is only a tool to avoid computing mistakes; it cannot take the place of understanding how to set up and solve a mathematical problem.

Here's a question for which a calculator might be helpful:

The price of one dozen roses is $10.80. At this rate, what is the price of 53 roses?

The simplest way to approach this question is to divide $10.80 by 12, which gives you the price of one rose, then multiply that price by 53:

$$\$10.80 \div 12 = \$0.90$$
$$\$.90 \times 53 = \$47.70$$

Although the arithmetic is fairly simple, using a calculator might improve your speed and accuracy. But in some questions involving numbers, using the calculator might actually slow you down because the question is set up to be solved in a quicker, more intuitive manner. Here's an example:

If $x = \frac{1}{2} \times \frac{1}{3} \times \frac{3}{2} \times \frac{4}{81}$, what is the value of $\sqrt{x}$?

To answer this question, you could use a calculator to perform all the steps:

1. Multiply the numerators.
2. Multiply the denominators.
3. Divide the product of the numerators by the product of the denominators.
4. Compute the square root.

But using a calculator is far more trouble than it's worth here. The problem is set up so that all numbers but 81 cancel out, so it's more quickly and easily solved this way (without a calculator):

$$x = \frac{1}{\cancel{2}} \times \frac{1}{\cancel{3}} \times \frac{\cancel{3}}{\cancel{2}} \times \frac{\cancel{4}}{81} = \frac{1}{81}; \sqrt{\frac{1}{81}} = \frac{1}{9}$$

Checking Your Calculations

Computation errors are the leading cause of incorrect answers on the GED Mathematical Reasoning test. Take this fact as your cue to check your work on every question before proceeding to the next one. If answering a question involved only one simple calculation, then by all means perform that calculation again; it should only take a few seconds of your time.

For questions involving multiple calculations, checking your work does not necessarily mean going through all the steps in the same sequence a second time. You're less likely to repeat the same mistake if you use some other approach. Try reversing the computational process. If you've added two numbers together, check your work by subtracting one of the numbers from the sum:

$$56 + 233 = 289$$
$$289 - 233 = 56 \text{ (check)}$$

If you've subtracted one number from another, check your work by adding the result to the number you subtracted:

$$28.34 - 3.8 = 24.54$$
$$24.54 + 3.8 = 28.34 \text{ (check)}$$

If you've multiplied two numbers, check your work by dividing the product by one of the numbers:

$$11.3 \times 6.65 = 75.145$$
$$75.145 \div 11.3 = 6.65 \text{ (check)}$$

If you've divided one number by another, check your work by multiplying the quotient by the second number:

$$789 \div 3 = 263$$

$$263 \times 3 = 789 \text{ (check)}$$

And if you simply don't have time to recalculate, whether forward or in reverse, you may still have time to recalculate the *smallest digit* (the one farthest to the right) to make sure it's correct. This check is quick and easy since you don't have to think about carried numbers. For example:

$$289 - 233 + 4722 \text{ (the last digit should be 8)}$$

$$11.3 \times 6.65 \text{ (the last digit should be 5)}$$

GENERAL TEST-TAKING STRATEGIES

Here are some general strategies for tackling the GED Mathematical Reasoning Test. Some of the points of advice encapsulate specific strategies you learned in the preceding pages. Apply all the strategies from this lesson to the practice tests in this book, and then review them again just before exam day.

Size up each question to devise a plan for handling it.

After reading a question, scan the answer choices (if any) and devise a plan of action for answering the question. Decide what operations or other steps are required to solve the problem. After some brief thought, if you still don't know where to start, try making a reasonable guess, and then move on to the next question. (Remember: you won't be penalized for incorrect answers.)

Be certain you know what the question is asking.

On the Mathematical Reasoning Test, careless reading is a leading cause of wrong answers. So be doubly sure you answer the precise question being asked. For example, does the question ask for the mean or the median? Circumference or area? A sum or a difference? A perimeter or a length of one side only? A total or an average? Feet or inches? Gallons or liters? Multiple-choice questions often bait you with incorrect answer choices that provide the *right* answer but to the *wrong* question. Don't fall for this ploy: know what the question is asking.

Look around for clues as to how to answer each question.

Be sure to read *all* information pertaining to the question. This includes not just the question itself, but also the answer choices and all information above, below, and beside a chart, graph, table, or geometry figure. Though you may not need every bit of information provided in order to answer the question at hand, reviewing it all helps ensure that you don't overlook what you need.

Don't hesitate to use your erasable note board.

You will be provided with an erasable note board, and by all means use it! Draw diagrams for geometry problems that don't supply them. Drawing a diagram often helps you visualize not only the problem but also the solution. Jot down any formulas or other equations needed to answer the question at hand. Remember also that you will not be allowed to use the calculator for five of the questions. For these, use the note board for all but the simplest calculations. (Immediately after the test, the test administrator will collect the note boards and erase your writing, so nothing you jot down on the note board will affect your score or be read by anyone.)

Save time by estimating and rounding.

If a question asks for an approximate value, you can safely round your calculations. Just be sure not to round too far or in the wrong direction. Either the question itself or the answer choices should tell you how far you can round. Even if the question doesn't ask for an approximate value, you might be able to use estimation and rounding to zero in on the correct answer—or at least eliminate choices that are too far off the mark.

Take the easiest route to the correct answer.

For some multiple-choice questions, it may be easier to work backward from the answer choices. For some algebra word problems, it might be easier to plug in numbers for variables instead of setting up and solving equations. When facing a long series of calculations, try to think of a shortcut. Avoid precise calculations when rough estimates will suffice. In short, be flexible in your approach: use whatever method reveals the answer.

Check your work before leaving any question.

The most common mistakes on math tests result not from lack of knowledge but from carelessness, and the GED Mathematical Reasoning Test is no exception. So before recording any response on your answer sheet:

- Do a reality check. Ask yourself whether your solution makes sense for what the question asks. (This check is especially appropriate for word problems.)
- Make sure you used the same numbers as were provided in the question and that you didn't inadvertently switch numbers or other expressions.
- For questions that require you to solve algebraic equations, plug your solution into the equation(s) to make sure it works.
- Confirm *all* your calculations. It's amazingly easy to commit errors in even the simplest calculations, especially under pressure. Using an erasable note board the first time around makes this task easier.

Pace yourself properly.

You won't be penalized for incorrect answers, so don't spend too much time on any one question. Use your time to answer all the questions that are not difficult for you, and then go back and work on the tougher ones if there's time.

SUMMING IT UP

- You will have 115 minutes to answer the 46 questions on the Mathematical Reasoning test.
- The Mathematical Reasoning test measures the following skills:
    - Understanding and applying mathematical concepts and formulas
    - Quantitative reasoning and problem solving
    - Translating verbal language into mathematical terms
    - Manipulating and devaluating arithmetic and algebraic expressions
    - Analyzing and interpreting graphical data (charts, graphs, tables)
- The calculator you will use during this test is the TI-30XS on-screen calculator. GED has provided printed materials and online tutorials to help you familiarize yourself with the calculator's functions so you will be comfortable with this tool on test day.
- There are 5 questions on the test where you will NOT be able to use a calculator. For the rest of the questions, you may use a calculator when it's indicated by the clickable icon. The icon will not appear with questions for which you may not use a calculator.
- You will be given an erasable note board at the test site to jot down notes and calculations; however, it will be collected at the end of the test, and your handwritten calculations will not have any effect on your score.
- You will also receive a list of formulas that you may or may not need to refer to during the test.
- The following are helpful strategies for solving math problems:
    - Scan the answer choices for clues
    - Don't be lured by obvious answer choices
    - Size up the question to narrow your choices
    - Know when to plug in numbers for variables
    - Know when, and when not, to work backward
    - Look for the simplest route to the answer
    - Solve problems by starting with what you know
    - Search geometry figures for clues
    - Sketch your own geometry figure
- Some multiple-choice questions on the Mathematics test will clearly indicate that an approximate value will suffice. Rounding and simplifying numbers will help you to solve math problems quickly and make calculations easier.

Math Review: Numbers

Chapter 12

OVERVIEW

WHAT YOU'LL FIND IN THIS REVIEW

In this review, you'll focus on:

- **Properties** of numbers (signs, integers, absolute value, and divisibility)
- **Forms** of numbers (fractions, mixed numbers, decimal numbers, percentages, ratios, exponential numbers, and radical expressions)
- **Operations** on numbers (the four basic operations and operations on exponential numbers and radical expressions)

Although this review is more basic than the next two in this part of the book, don't skip over it. The knowledge areas covered here are basic building blocks for all types of GED Mathematical Reasoning Test questions.

The GED test-style questions throughout this review are multiple-choice questions. The actual exam also includes questions in an alternative format in which you supply the numerical answer to the question.

ORDER AND LAWS OF OPERATIONS

The following rules apply to all operations on numbers as well as on variables (such as x and y).

Order of Operations

1. Operations inside parentheses
2. Operations with square roots and exponents

3. Multiplication and division
4. Addition and subtraction

Examples:

$(2 + 4) \times (7 - 2) = 6 \times 5$ (operate inside parentheses before multiplying)

$3 \times 4^2 = 3 \times 16$ (apply exponent before multiplying)

$5 + 7 \times 3 - 2 = 5 + 21 - 2$ (multiply before adding or subtracting)

$6 - 8 \div 2 + 3 = 6 - 4 + 3$ (divide before adding or subtracting)

The Commutative Law (addition and multiplication *only*)

$a + b = b + a$

$a \times b = b \times a$

Examples:

$3 + 4 = 4 + 3$

$3 \times 4 = 4 \times 3$

The Associative Law (addition and multiplication *only*)

$(a + b) + c = a + (b + c)$

$(ab)c = a(bc)$

Examples:

$(6 + 2) + 5 = 8 + 5 = 13$

$6 + (2 + 5) = 6 + 7 = 13$

$(3 \times 2) \times 4 = 6 \times 4 = 24$

$3 \times (2 \times 4) = 3 \times 8 = 24$

The Distributive Law

$a(b + c) = ab + ac$

$a(b - c) = ab - ac$

Examples:

$2(3 + 4) = 2 \times 7 = 14$

$(2)(3) + (2)(4) = 6 + 8 = 14$

$9(4 - 2) = 9 \times 2 = 18$

$(9)(4) - (9)(2) = 36 - 18 = 18$

NUMBER SIGNS AND THE FOUR BASIC OPERATIONS

A **positive number** is any number *greater than zero*, and a **negative number** is any number *less than zero*. The **sign** of a number indicates whether it is positive (+) or negative (–).

Be sure you know the sign—either positive or negative—of a non-zero number that results from combining numbers using the four basic operations (addition, subtraction, multiplication, and division). Here's a table that includes all the possibilities. A number's sign is indicated in parentheses. A question mark (?) indicates that the sign depends on which number is greater.

Addition:	**Examples:**
(+) + (+) = +	5 + 3 = 8
(–) + (–) = –	–5 + (–3) = –8
(+) + (–) = ?	5 + (–3) = 2 but 3 + (–5) = –2
(–) + (+) = ?	–5 + 3 = –2 but –3 + 5 = 2

Subtraction:	**Examples:**
(+) – (–) = (+)	6 – (–1) = 7
(–) – (+) = (–)	–6 – 1 = –7
(+) – (+) = ?	6 – 1 = 5 but 1 – 6 = –5
(–) – (–) = ?	–6 – (–1) = –5 but –1 – (–6) = 5

Multiplication:	**Examples:**
(+) × (+) = +	7 × 2 = 14
(+) × (–) = –	7 × (–2) = –14
(–) × (–) = +	(–7) × (–2) = 14

Division:	**Examples:**
(+) ÷ (+) = +	8 ÷ 4 = 2
(+) ÷ (–) = –	8 ÷ (–4) = –2
(–) ÷ (+) = –	–8 ÷ 4 = –2
(–) ÷ (–) = +	–8 ÷ (–4) = 2

Multiplying and Dividing Negative Terms

Multiplication or division involving any *even* number of negative terms gives you a positive number. On the other hand, multiplication or division involving any *odd* number of negative terms gives you a negative number.

Examples (*even* number of negative terms):

$(5) \times (-4) \times (2) \times (-2) = +80$ (two negative terms)

$(-4) \times (-3) \times (-2) \times (-1) = +24$ (four negative terms)

Examples (*odd* number of negative terms):

$(3) \times (-3) \times (2) = -18$ (one negative terms)

$(-4) \times (-4) \times (2) \times (-2) = -64$ (three negative terms)

Absolute Value

A number's **absolute value** refers to its distance from zero (the origin) on the real-number line. The absolute value of x is indicated as $|x|$. The absolute value of any number other than zero is always a positive number. The concept of absolute value boils down to these two statements:

1. If $x \geq 0$, then $|x| = x$

   Example: $|3| = 3$

   Example: $|0| = 0$

2. If $x < 0$, then $|x| = -x$

   Example: $|-2| = -(-2) = 2$

GED Mathematical Reasoning Test questions that involve combining signed numbers often focus on the concept of absolute value.

EXAMPLE 1 (EASIER):

What is the value of $|-2-3| - |2-3|$?

A. -2

B. -1

C. 1

D. 4

Remember, the absolute value of any number other than zero is always a positive number, so $|-2-3| = |-5| = 5$, and $|2-3| = |-1| = 1$. Performing subtraction: $5 - 1 = 4$. **The correct answer is D.**

EXAMPLE 2 (MORE CHALLENGING):

The number M is the product of seven negative numbers. The number N is the product of six negative numbers and one positive number.

Which of the following holds true for all possible values of M and N?

A. $M-N>0$

B. $M\times N<0$

C. $N+M<0$

D. $N\times M=0$

The product of seven negative numbers is always negative (M is a negative number). The product of six negative numbers is always a positive number, and the product of two positive numbers is always a positive number (N is a positive number). Thus, the product of M and N must be a negative number. Choices A and C may or may not hold true, depending on the specific values of M and N. Choice D cannot hold true. **The correct answer is B.**

INTEGERS AND THE FOUR BASIC OPERATIONS

An **integer** is any non-fraction number on the number line: {. . . –3, –2, –1, 0, 1, 2, 3, . . .}. Except for the number zero (0), every integer is either positive or negative and either even or odd. When you combine integers using a basic operation, whether the result is an odd integer, an even integer, or a non-integer depends on the numbers you combine. Here are the possibilities:

Addition and Subtraction:

- integer ± integer = integer
- even integer ± even integer = even integer (or possibly zero)
- even integer ± odd integer = odd integer
- odd integer ± odd integer = even integer (or possibly zero)

Multiplication and Division:

- integer × integer = integer
- integer ÷ non-zero integer = integer, but only if the numerator is divisible by the denominator (if the result is a quotient with no remainder)
- odd integer × odd integer = odd integer
- even integer × non-zero integer = even integer
- even integer ÷ 2 = integer
- odd integer ÷ 2 = non-integer

GED Mathematical Reasoning Test questions that test you on the preceding rules sometimes look like algebra problems, but they're really not. Just apply the appropriate rule. If you're not sure of the rule, plug in simple numbers to zero in on the correct answer.

EXAMPLE 3 (EASIER):

The numbers M and N are both integers. Without knowing the values of M and N, what formula would always determine the correct distance between M and N on a number line?

A. $M - N$

B. $N - M$

C. $|M - N|$

D. $|M| - |N|$

The distance between two points on a number line is expressed as a positive number. The distance is found by subtracting the lesser number from the greater number. Since the values of M and N are unknown, choices A and B provide no way to be certain that they will be subtracted in the correct order. Knowing that a positive value is required is an indication that you should apply absolute value. Choice D is not a good choice because it uses absolute value to make both numbers positive before subtracting them, which can result in a negative number if $|N| > |M|$. We know that distance must be positive. Choice C correctly subtracts one value from the other, and then makes that value positive by taking the absolute value. **The correct answer is C.**

EXAMPLE 4 (MORE CHALLENGING):

If P is an odd integer, and if Q is an even integer, which of the following expressions CANNOT represent an even integer?

A. $3P - Q$

B. $3P \times Q$

C. $2Q \times P$

D. $3Q - 2P$

Since 3 and P are both odd integers, their product ($3P$) must also be an odd integer. Subtracting an even integer (Q) from an odd integer results in an odd integer in all cases except where $3Q = P$, in which case the result is 0 (zero). **The correct answer is A.**

FACTORS, MULTIPLES, AND DIVISIBILITY

A **factor** (of an integer n) is any integer that you can multiply by another integer for a product of n. The factors of any integer n include 1 as well as n itself. Figuring out whether one number (f) is a factor of another (n) is simple: Just divide n by f. If the quotient is an integer, then f is a factor of n (and n is **divisible** by f). If the quotient is not an integer, then f is not a factor of n, and you'll end up with a **remainder** after dividing.

For example, 2 is a factor of 8 because $8 \div 2 = 4$, which is an integer. On the other hand, 3 is not a factor of 8 because $8 \div 3 = \frac{8}{3}$, or $2\frac{2}{3}$, which is a non-integer. (The remainder is 2, which you put over the divisor, 3, to form $\frac{2}{3}$.) Keep in mind these basic rules about factors, which are based on their definition:

RULE 1: Any integer is a factor of itself.

RULE 2: 1 and –1 are factors of all integers (except 0).

RULE 3: The integer zero (0) has no factors and is not a factor of any integer.

RULE 4: A positive integer's largest factor (other than itself) will never be greater than one half the value of the integer.

On the "flip side" of factors are **multiples**. If *f* is a factor of *n*, then *n* is a multiple of *f*. For example, 8 is a multiple of 2 for the same reason that 2 is a factor of 8: because $8 \div 2 = 4$, which is an integer.

A **prime number** is a positive integer that is divisible by only two positive integers: itself and 1. Zero (0) and 1 are not considered prime numbers; 2 is the first prime number. Here are all the prime numbers less than 50:

2 3 5 7

11 13 17 19

23 29

31 37

41 43 47

As you can see, factors, multiples, and divisibility are simply different aspects of the same concept. So a GED test question about factoring or prime numbers is also about multiples and divisibility.

EXAMPLE 5 (EASIER):

The number 24 is divisible by how many different positive integers other than 1 and 24?

A. three

B. four

C. five

D. six

The question asks for the number of different factors of 24 (other than 1 and 24). A good way to answer the question is to begin with 2 and work your way up to the largest possible factor, 12, which is half the value of 24:

$2 \times 12 = 24$

$3 \times 8 = 24$

$4 \times 6 = 24$

If you continue in this manner, you'll see that you've already accounted for all factors of 24, which include 2, 3, 4, 6, 8, and 12. **The correct answer is D.**

EXAMPLE 6 (MORE CHALLENGING):

If $n > 6$, and if n is a multiple of 6, which of the following is always a factor of n?

A. $n + 6$

B. $\frac{n}{3}$

C. $\frac{n}{2} + 3$

D. $\frac{n}{2} + 6$

Try the first multiple of 6 greater than 6, which is 12. This eliminates choice A because it is greater than 12 and therefore cannot be a factor. You can eliminate choices C and D because the largest factor of any positive number (other than the number itself) is half the number, which in this case is $\frac{n}{2}$. **The correct answer is B.**

Every time you're dealing with fractions, you have to pay attention to the denominators. Because you cannot divide by zero, any expression that has zero in the denominator is considered undefined. For example, you may see a question that asks "For what values of x is the rational expression undefined?" What you are being asked to find is the values of x that will result in a denominator of 0. A fraction such as $\frac{x}{5}$ will always be defined, whereas $\frac{x}{0}$ will be undefined.

The **greatest common factor** of a list of whole numbers is the largest whole number that can be divided evenly into every number in the list, and the **least common multiple** is the smallest whole number into which each number in the list divides evenly. For example, the greatest common factor of {18, 36, 63} is 9, and the least common multiple is 504.

The distributive property and greatest common factor can be used together to rewrite numeric expressions in different ways. For instance, $(24 + 54) = (6 \times 4 + 6 \times 9) = (6)(4 + 9)$.

Take a look at a more complicated example involving the use of the commutative property of multiplication (that is, the fact that the order of a product can be changed without affecting the outcome):

$$\begin{aligned}(18+24)\cdot(35+15) &= \underbrace{(6\cdot 3+6\cdot 4)}_{6\cdot(3+4)}\cdot\underbrace{(5\cdot 7+5\cdot 3)}_{5\cdot(7+3)}\\ &= \left[6\cdot(3+4)\right]\cdot\left[5\cdot(7+3)\right]\\ &= 6\cdot 5\cdot(3+4)(7+3)\end{aligned}$$

DECIMAL NUMBERS, FRACTIONS, AND PERCENTAGES

Any number can be expressed in the form of a decimal number, a fraction, or a percent. You use **decimal numbers** in your daily life every time you make a purchase at a store. Most of us are familiar with decimals in terms of money. When you have $5.87, you have 5 whole dollars, 8 dimes (or 8 tenths of a dollar), and 7 cents (or 7 hundredths of a dollar). When a number is written in decimal form, everything to the left of the decimal point is a whole number, and everything to the right of the decimal point represents a part of the whole (a tenth, hundredth, thousandth, and so on). Adding zeros to the *end* of a decimal number does not change its value. For example, the decimal number 0.5 is the same as 0.50 or 0.5000. But adding a zero to the *front* (the left) of the number *will* change the number's value. For example, 0.5 means "five tenths," but 0.05 means "five hundredths."

A **fraction** is a part of a whole. There are 10 dimes in each dollar, so one dime is one-tenth of a dollar—one of ten equal parts. The fraction to represent one-tenth is written $\frac{1}{10}$. The top number of a fraction is called the **numerator**, and the bottom number is called the **denominator**. A **proper fraction** is one in which the numerator is less than the denominator. An **improper fraction** is one in which the numerator is the same as or greater than the denominator. $\frac{1}{10}$ is a proper fraction, but $\frac{12}{10}$ is an improper fraction. Sometimes you will see a whole number and a fraction together. This is called a **mixed number**. $4\frac{3}{5}$ is an example of a mixed number.

A **percent (%)** is a fraction or decimal number written in a different form. 25% written as a decimal number is 0.25. A percent expressed as a fraction is the number divided by 100. For example, 25% written as a fraction is $\frac{25}{100}$. The number before the percent sign is the numerator of the fraction.

Converting One Number Form to Another

GED Mathematical Reasoning Test questions involving fractions, decimal numbers, or percentages often require you to convert one form to another as part of solving the problem at hand. You should know how to convert quickly and confidently. For percent-to-decimal conversions, move the decimal point two places to the *left* (and drop the percent sign). For decimal-to-percent conversions, move the decimal point two places to the *right* (and add the percent sign). Percentages greater than 100 convert to numbers greater than 1.

Examples (converting percents to decimal numbers)

9.5% = 0.095

95% = 0.95

950% = 9.5

Examples (converting decimal numbers to percents)

0.004 = 0.4%

0.04 = 4%

0.4 = 40%

4.0 = 400%

For percent-to-fraction conversions, *divide* by 100 (and drop the percent sign). For fraction-to-percent conversions, *multiply* by 100 (and add the percent sign). Percentages greater than 100 convert to numbers greater than 1.

Examples (converting percents to fractions)

$8.1\% = \frac{8.1}{100}$, or $\frac{81}{1000}$

$81\% = \frac{81}{100}$

$810\% = \frac{810}{100} = \frac{81}{10}$, or $8\frac{1}{10}$

Example (converting fractions to percents)

$\frac{3}{8} = \frac{300}{8}\% = \frac{75}{2}\%$, or $37\frac{1}{2}\%$

To convert a fraction to a decimal number, divide the numerator by the denominator, using long division or your calculator. Keep in mind that the result might be a precise value, or it might be an approximation with a never-ending string of decimal places. Compare these three examples:

$\frac{5}{8} = 0.625$ The equivalent decimal number is precise after three decimal places.

$\frac{5}{9} \approx 0.555$ The equivalent decimal number can only be approximated (the digit 5 repeats indefinitely).

$\frac{5}{7} \approx 0.714$ The equivalent decimal number can only be approximated; there is no repeating pattern by carrying the calculation to additional decimal places.

EXAMPLE 7 (EASIER):

What is the sum of $\frac{3}{4}$, 0.7, and 80%?

A. 1.59

B. 1.62

C. 2.04

D. 2.25

Since the answer choices are expressed in decimal terms, express all terms as decimals:

$$\frac{3}{4} = 0.75 \text{ and } 80\% = 0.8.$$

Then add:

$$0.75 + 0.7 + 0.8 = 2.25.$$

The correct answer is D.

EXAMPLE 8 (MORE CHALLENGING):

What is 150% of the product of $\frac{1}{8}$ and 0.4?

A. 0.075

B. 0.25

C. 0.75

D. 2.5

One way to solve the problem is to first express $\frac{1}{8}$ as its decimal equivalent 0.125. Next multiply: $0.125 \times 0.4 = 0.05$. Then, express 150% as the decimal number 1.5, and calculate the product: $1.5 \times 0.05 = 0.075$. **The correct answer is A.**

Fraction-Decimal-Percent Equivalents

Certain fraction-decimal-percent equivalents appear on the GED Mathematical Reasoning Test more often than others. The numbers in the following tables are especially common. You should memorize this table, so that you can convert these numbers quickly during the test.

Percent	Decimal	Fraction
50%	0.5	$\frac{1}{2}$
25%	0.25	$\frac{1}{4}$
75%	0.75	$\frac{3}{4}$
10%	0.1	$\frac{1}{10}$
30%	0.3	$\frac{3}{10}$
70%	0.7	$\frac{7}{10}$
90%	0.9	$\frac{9}{10}$
$33\frac{1}{3}\%$	$0.33\frac{1}{3}$	$\frac{1}{3}$
$66\frac{2}{3}\%$	$0.66\frac{2}{3}$	$\frac{2}{3}$

Percent	Decimal	Fraction
$16\frac{2}{3}\%$	$0.16\frac{2}{3}$	$\frac{1}{6}$
$83\frac{1}{3}\%$	$0.83\frac{1}{3}$	$\frac{5}{6}$
20%	0.2	$\frac{1}{5}$
40%	0.4	$\frac{2}{5}$
60%	0.6	$\frac{3}{5}$
80%	0.8	$\frac{4}{5}$
$12\frac{1}{2}\%$	0.125	$\frac{1}{8}$
$37\frac{1}{2}\%$	0.375	$\frac{3}{8}$
$62\frac{1}{2}\%$	0.625	$\frac{5}{8}$
$87\frac{1}{2}\%$	0.875	$\frac{7}{8}$

Decimal Numbers and Place Value

Place value refers to the specific value of a digit in a decimal number. For example, in the decimal number 682.793:

The digit 6 is in the "hundreds" place.
The digit 8 is in the "tens" place.
The digit 2 is in the "ones" place.
The digit 7 is in the "tenths" place.
The digit 9 is in the "hundredths" place.
The digit 3 is in the "thousandths" place.

So you can express 682.793 as follows: $600 + 80 + 2 + \frac{7}{10} + \frac{9}{100} + \frac{3}{1000}$.

EXAMPLE 9 (EASIER):

The number 40.5 is 1,000 times larger than which of the following numbers?

A. 0.405

B. 0.0405

C. 0.0450

D. 0.00405

To find the solution, divide 40.5 by 1,000 by moving the decimal point 3 places to the left. **The correct answer is B.**

EXAMPLE 10 (MORE CHALLENGING):

The letter *M* represents a digit in the decimal number 0.0*M*, and the letter *N* represents a digit in the decimal number 0.0*N*. Which expression is equivalent to $0.0M \times 0.0N$?

A. $\frac{1}{10{,}000} \times M \times N$

B. 0.000*MN*

C. 0.00*MN*

D. $\frac{1}{100} \times M \times N$

Suppose digits *M* and *N* are both 1. To find the product of 0.01 and 0.01, you multiply 1 by 1 ($N \times M$), then add together the decimal places in the two numbers. There are four places altogether, so the product would be 0.0001, which is equivalent to $\frac{1}{10{,}000}$. Thus, whatever the values of *N* and *M*, $0.0M \times 0.0N = \frac{1}{10{,}000} \times (M \times N)$. **The correct answer is A.**

Simplifying Fractions

A fraction can be simplified to its *lowest terms* if its numerator number and denominator number share a common factor. Here are a few simple examples:

$\frac{6}{9} = \frac{(3)(2)}{(3)(3)} = \frac{2}{3}$ (you can "cancel" or "factor out" the common factor 3)

$\frac{21}{35} = \frac{(7)(3)}{(7)(5)} = \frac{3}{5}$ (you can "cancel" or "factor out" the common factor 7)

Before you perform any operation with a fraction, always check to see if you can simplify it first. By reducing a fraction to its lowest terms, you'll simplify whatever operation you perform on it.

Adding and Subtracting Fractions

To combine fractions by addition or subtraction, you combine numerators over a **common denominator.** If the fractions already have the same denominator, simply add (or subtract) numerators:

$\frac{3}{4} + \frac{2}{4} = \frac{3+2}{4} = \frac{5}{4}$ (the two fractions share the common denominator 4)

$\frac{1}{7} - \frac{3}{7} = \frac{1-3}{7} = \frac{-2}{7}$, or $-\frac{2}{7}$ (the two fractions share the common denominator 7)

If the fractions don't already have a common denominator, you'll need to find one. You can always multiply all of the denominators together to find a common denominator, but it might be a large number that's clumsy to work with. So instead, try to find the **least (or lowest) common denominator (LCD)** by working your way up in multiples of the largest of the denominators given. For denominators of 6, 3, and 5, for instance, try out successive multiples of 6 (12, 18, 24 . . .), and you'll hit the LCD when you get to 30.

When combining fractions by either addition or subtraction, pay close attention to the + and – signs. Also, don't let common numerators fool you into thinking you can add or subtract without a common denominator.

EXAMPLE 11 (EASIER):

The equation $\frac{5}{3} - \frac{5}{6} + \frac{5}{2}$ is equal to

Select ▼

A. $\frac{5}{2}$

B. $\frac{15}{6}$

C. $\frac{10}{3}$

D. $\frac{15}{3}$

To find the LCD, try out successive multiples of 6 until you come across one that is also a multiple of both 3 and 2. The LCD is 6 itself. Multiply each numerator by the same number by which you would multiply the fraction's denominator to give you the LCD of 6.

$$\frac{5}{3}-\frac{5}{6}+\frac{5}{2}=\frac{5(2)-5+5(3)}{6}=\frac{10-5+15}{6}=\frac{20}{6}, \text{ or } \frac{10}{3}$$

The correct answer is C.

EXAMPLE 12 (MORE CHALLENGING):

If $\frac{x}{3}, \frac{x}{7}$, and $\frac{x}{9}$ are all positive integers, what is the **least** possible value of x ?

A. 42

B. 54

C. 63

D. 72

The answer to the question is the least value of x that is a multiple of all three denominators. In other words, the question asks for the least common denominator. Working your way up in multiples of the largest denominator, 9, you'll find that 63 is the lowest multiple that is also a multiple of both 7 and 3. Thus, $x = 63$. **The correct answer is C.**

Multiplying and Dividing Fractions

To combine fractions by multiplication, multiply the numerators, and multiply the denominators. The denominators need not be the same.

$$\frac{1}{2}\times\frac{5}{3}\times\frac{1}{7}=\frac{(1)(5)(1)}{(2)(3)(7)}=\frac{5}{42}$$

To divide one fraction by another, first invert the divisor (the number after the division sign) by switching its numerator and denominator. (This new fraction is called the **reciprocal** of the original one.) Then combine by multiplying.

$$\frac{\frac{2}{5}}{\frac{3}{4}}=\frac{2}{5}\times\frac{4}{3}=\frac{(2)(4)}{(5)(3)}=\frac{8}{15}$$

To simplify the multiplication or division, cancel factors common to a numerator and a denominator before combining fractions. You can cancel across fractions. Take, for instance, the operation

$\frac{3}{4}\times\frac{4}{9}\times\frac{3}{2}$. Looking just at the first two fractions, you can factor out 4 and 3, so the operation simplifies to $\frac{{}^{1}\not{3}}{{}_{1}\not{4}}\times\frac{{}^{1}\not{4}}{{}_{3}\not{9}}\times\frac{3}{2}$. Now, looking just at the second and third fractions, you can factor out 3, and the operation becomes even simpler: $\frac{1}{1}\times\frac{1}{{}_{1}\not{3}}\times\frac{{}^{1}\not{3}}{2}=\frac{1}{2}$.

Apply the same rules in the same way to variables (letters) as to numbers.

EXAMPLE 13 (EASIER):

Which expression is equal to $\frac{2}{a} \times \frac{b}{4} \times \frac{a}{5} \times \frac{8}{c}$?

A. $\frac{10b}{9c}$

B. $\frac{8}{5}$

C. $\frac{16b}{5ac}$

D. $\frac{4b}{5c}$

Since you're dealing only with multiplication, look for factors and variables (letters) in any numerator that match those in any denominator. Canceling common factors leaves $\frac{2}{1} \times \frac{b}{1} \times \frac{1}{5} \times \frac{2}{c}$. Combining numerators and combining denominators gives you the answer $\frac{4b}{5c}$.

The correct answer is D.

EXAMPLE 14 (MORE CHALLENGING):

Which is a simplified form of the complex fraction $\dfrac{\frac{3}{5}+\frac{3}{4}}{\frac{3}{4}-\frac{3}{5}}$?

A. $\frac{27}{10}$

B. 5

C. $\frac{27}{4}$

D. 9

Convert all four fractions to fractions with the least common denominator, 20. Then, add together the two numerator fractions and the two denominator fractions.

$$\dfrac{\frac{3}{5}+\frac{3}{4}}{\frac{3}{4}-\frac{3}{5}} = \dfrac{\frac{12}{20}+\frac{15}{20}}{\frac{15}{20}-\frac{12}{20}} = \dfrac{\frac{27}{20}}{\frac{3}{20}}$$

Then, multiply the resulting numerator fraction by the reciprocal of the resulting denominator fraction:

$$\dfrac{\frac{27}{20}}{\frac{3}{20}} = \left(\frac{27}{20}\right)\left(\frac{20}{3}\right) = \frac{27}{3} = 9$$

The correct answer is D.

Mixed Numbers

As noted earlier, a **mixed number** consists of a whole number along with a simple fraction. The number $4\frac{2}{3}$ is an example of a mixed number. Before combining fractions, you might need to convert mixed numbers to improper fractions. To do so, follow these three steps:

1. Multiply the denominator of the fraction by the whole number.
2. Add the product to the numerator of the fraction.
3. Place the sum over the denominator of the fraction.

For example, here's how to convert the mixed number $4\frac{2}{3}$ to a fraction:

$$4\frac{2}{3} = \frac{(3)(4)+2}{3} = \frac{14}{3}$$

To add or subtract mixed numbers, you can convert each one to a fraction, then find their LCD and combine them. Or, you can add together the whole numbers, and add together the fractions separately. To perform multiple operations, always perform multiplication and division before you perform addition and subtraction.

EXAMPLE 15 (EASIER):

What is the sum of $2\frac{1}{6}$, $3\frac{1}{5}$, and $2\frac{1}{15}$?

A. $7\frac{13}{30}$

B. $7\frac{4}{5}$

C. $11\frac{3}{10}$

D. $12\frac{17}{20}$

One way to combine these mixed numbers is to first convert the mixed numbers to fractions:

$$2\frac{1}{6} + 3\frac{1}{5} + 2\frac{1}{15} = \frac{13}{6} + \frac{16}{5} + \frac{31}{15}$$

But as you can see, to combine numerators over an LCD, you'll be dealing with large numbers. An easier method is to add together the whole numbers, and add together the fractions separately:

$$(2+3+2) + \frac{1}{6} + \frac{1}{5} + \frac{1}{15} = 7 + \frac{5+6+2}{30} = 7\frac{13}{30}$$

The correct answer is A.

EXAMPLE 16 (MORE CHALLENGING):

If you subtract $3\frac{2}{3}$ from $\dfrac{4\frac{1}{2}}{1\frac{1}{8}}$, what is the resulting fraction?

A. $\frac{1}{4}$

B. $\frac{1}{3}$

C. $\frac{11}{6}$

D. $\frac{17}{6}$

First, convert all mixed numbers to fractions. Then, eliminate the complex fraction by multiplying the numerator fraction by the reciprocal of the denominator fraction (cancel across fractions before multiplying):

$$\frac{\frac{9}{2}}{\frac{9}{8}} - \frac{11}{3} = \left(\frac{9}{2}\right)\left(\frac{8}{9}\right) - \frac{11}{3} = \left(\frac{1}{1}\right)\left(\frac{4}{1}\right) - \frac{11}{3} = \frac{4}{1} - \frac{11}{3}$$

Then, express each fraction using the common denominator 3. Finally, subtract:

$$\frac{4}{1} - \frac{11}{3} = \frac{12-11}{3} = \frac{1}{3}$$

The correct answer is B.

Fractions and decimal numbers can be arranged in increasing order along a number line in the same manner as whole numbers and integers. If a, b, c, and d are positive integers, we say $\frac{a}{b} < \frac{c}{d}$ if $ad < bc$. For instance, $\frac{2}{3} < \frac{4}{5}$ because $2(5) = 10$ is less than $3(4) = 12$. So $\frac{2}{3}$ lies to the left of $\frac{4}{5}$ on the number line. When comparing two mixed numbers, the one with the larger whole part is the larger number; if two mixed numbers have the same whole part, the one with the larger fractional part (determined as above) is the larger of the two numbers.

Decimal numbers can be compared by methodically comparing the digits in respective places until you come to a place in which the digits are different; in such cases, the one with the larger digit has the larger value and lies further to the right along the number line. For instance, 2.5561 is less than 2.55634 because, while the whole part and digits in the tenths, hundredths, and thousandths places are the same, the digits in the ten thousandths places are different, with 2.5561 having the smaller digit in that place.

Fractions and decimal numbers can be compared as well. In such cases, convert all numbers to the same format and then make the comparison as previously described.

Problems Involving Percentages

A question involving percentages might involve one of these three tasks:

1. Finding the percentage of a number
2. Finding a number when a percentage is given
3. Finding what percentage one number is of another

Regardless of the task, four distinct numbers are involved: the part, the whole, the percentage, and 100. The problem will give you three of the numbers, and your job is to find the fourth. An easy way to deal with percentage problems is to set up a grid to decide which number is missing, and then solve for that missing number. Arrange the grid as follows:

part	percent
whole	100

The left column is actually a fraction that is equal to the right-column fraction. (Think of the middle horizontal line as a fraction bar.) The two fractions have the same value. Once you set up the problem in this way, you can solve it by these steps:

1. Simplify the known fraction, if possible.
2. Multiply the diagonally situated numbers that you know.
3. Divide the product by the third number you know.

To see how this is done, study the following three examples.

Finding the Percentage

30 is what percent of 50?

In this question, 50 is the whole, and 30 is the part. Your task is to find the missing percent:

30	?
50	100

First, simplify the left-hand fraction $\frac{30}{50}$ to $\frac{3}{5}$. Then, multiply the two diagonally situated numbers you know: $3 \times 100 = 300$. Finally, divide by the third number you know: $300 \div 5 = 60$. This is the answer to the question. **The correct answer is 30 is 60% of 50.**

Finding the Part

What number is 25% of 80?

In this question, 80 is the whole, and 25 is the percentage. Your task is to find the part:

?	25
80	100

First, simplify the right-hand fraction $\frac{25}{100}$ to $\frac{1}{4}$.

?	1
80	4

Then multiply the two diagonally situated numbers you know: $1 \times 80 = 80$. Finally, divide by the third number you know: $80 \div 4 = 20$. **The correct answer is 25% of 80 is 20.**

Finding the Whole

75% of what number is 150?

In this question, 150 is the part, and 75 is the percentage. Your task is to find the whole:

150	75
?	100

First, simplify the right-hand fraction $\frac{75}{100}$ to $\frac{3}{4}$.

150	3
?	4

Then multiply the two diagonally situated numbers you know: $150 \times 4 = 600$. Finally, divide by the third number you know: $600 \div 3 = 200$. **The correct answer is 75% of 200 is 150.**

Percent Increase and Decrease

The concept of percent change is familiar to everyone. For example, investment interest, sales tax, and discount pricing all involve percent change. Here's the key to answering GED Mathematical Reasoning Test questions involving this concept: percent change always relates to the value before the change. Here are two simple examples:

10 increased by what percent is 12?

1. The amount of the increase is 2.
2. Compare the change (2) to the original number (10).
3. The change in percent is $\frac{2}{10}$, or 20%.

12 decreased by what percent is 10?

1. The amount of the decrease is 2.
2. Compare the change (2) to the original number (12).
3. The change is $\frac{2}{12}$, or $\frac{1}{6}$ (or $16\frac{2}{3}$%).

Notice that the percent increase from 10 to 12 (20%) is *not* the same as the percent decrease from 12 to 10 ($16\frac{2}{3}$%). That's because the original number (before the change) is different in the two questions.

Percent-change problems typically involve tax, interest, profit, discount, or weight. In handling these problems, you might need to calculate more than one percent change.

EXAMPLE 17 (EASIER):

A computer originally priced at $500 is discounted by 10%, then by another 10%. What is the price of the computer after the second discount, to the nearest dollar?

A. $400

B. $405

C. $425

D. $450

After the first 10% discount, the price was $450 ($500 minus 10% of $500). After the second discount, which is calculated based on the $450 price, the price of the computer is $405 ($450 minus 10% of $450). **The correct answer is B.**

EXAMPLE 18 (MORE CHALLENGING):

A merchant discounts an item priced at \$80 by 25%. Later, the merchant discounts the item again, this time to \$48. What *percent* was the second discount?

A. 20

B. 25

C. 27.5

D. 30

After the first discount, the price was \$60 (the difference between \$80 and 25% of \$80 [\$80 – \$20]). The second discount was \$12 (the difference between \$60 and \$48). Calculate the discount rate using the price *before* the *second* discount: $\frac{12}{60}=\frac{1}{5}$, or 20%. **The correct answer is A.**

RATIO AND PROPORTION

A **ratio** expresses proportion or comparative size—the size of one quantity *relative to* the size of another. Write a ratio by placing a colon (:) between the two numbers. Read the colon as the word "to." For example, read the ratio 3:5 as "3 to 5." As with fractions, you can reduce ratios to lowest terms by canceling common factors. For example, given a menagerie of 28 pets that includes 12 cats and 16 dogs:

- The ratio of cats to dogs is 12:16, or 3:4 ("3 to 4").
- The ratio of dogs to cats is 16:12, or 4:3 ("4 to 3").
- The ratio of cats to the total number of pets is 12:28, or 3:7 ("3 to 7").
- The ratio of dogs to the total number of pets is 16:28, or 4:7 ("4 to 7").

Another way of saying that two ratios (or fractions) are equivalent is to say that they are **proportionate**. For example, the ratio 12:16 is proportionate to the ratio 3:4. Similarly, the fraction $\frac{12}{16}$ is proportionate to the fraction $\frac{3}{4}$.

Determining Quantities from a Ratio

You can think of a ratio as parts adding up to a whole. In the ratio 5:6, for example, 5 parts + 6 parts = 11 parts (the whole). If the actual total quantity were 22, you'd multiply each element by 2: 10 parts + 12 parts = 22 parts (the whole). Notice that the ratios are the same. In other words, 5:6 is the same ratio as 10:12.

Another way to think about a ratio is as a fraction. Since you can express any ratio as a fraction, you can set two equivalent, or proportionate, ratios equal to each other, as fractions. So the ratio 16:28 is proportionate to the ratio 4:7 because $\frac{16}{28}=\frac{4}{7}$. If one of the four terms is missing from the equation (the proportion), you can solve for the missing term using the same method that you learned for solving percent problems:

1. Simplify the known fraction, if possible.
2. Multiply the diagonally situated numbers you know.
3. Divide the product by the third number you know.

For example, if the ratio 10:15 is proportionate to 14:?, you can find the missing number (?) by first setting up the following grid (which expresses an equation with two fractions):

10	14
15	?

Reading the ratio 10:15 as a fraction, simplify it to $\frac{2}{3}$.

2	14
3	?

Then, multiply the two diagonally situated numbers you know: $3 \times 14 = 42$. Finally, divide by the third number you know: $42 \div 2 = 21$. The ratio 10:15 is equivalent to the ratio 14:21.

In a ratio question, even if the quantities initially appear difficult to work with, it's a good bet that doing the math will be easier than it might seem.

EXAMPLE 19 (EASIER):

A class of students contains only freshmen and sophomores. 18 of the students are sophomores. If the ratio between the number of freshmen and the number of sophomores in the class is 5:3, how many students altogether are in the class?

A. 30
B. 40
C. 48
D. 56

Let's apply a part-to-whole analysis to answer this question. Look first at the ratio and the sum of its parts: 5 (freshmen) + 3 (sophomores) = 8 (total students). These aren't the actual quantities, but they're *proportionate* to those quantities. Given 18 sophomores altogether, sophomores account for 3 parts—each part containing 6 students. Accordingly, the total number of students must be $6 \times 8 = 48$. **The correct answer is C.**

EXAMPLE 20 (MORE CHALLENGING):

If 3 miles are equivalent to 4.83 kilometers, then 11.27 kilometers are equivalent to how many miles?

A. 8.4
B. 7.0
C. 5.9
D. 1.76

The decimal numbers may appear daunting, but they simplify nicely. This feature is typical for the GED Mathematical Reasoning Test. The question essentially asks: "a ratio of 3 to 4.83 is equivalent to a ratio of *what* to 11.27?" Set up a proportion grid (which expresses an equation with two fractions):

3	?
4.83	11.27

You might notice that the ratio (or fraction) $\frac{3}{4.83}$ simplifies to $\frac{1}{1.61}$. Using this simplified ratio might help you multiply and divide the numbers accurately. Otherwise, first multiply the diagonally situated numbers you know: $3 \times 11.27 = 33.81$. Then, divide by the third number you know: $33.81 \div 4.83 = 7$. A ratio of 3 to 4.83 is equivalent to a ratio of 7 to 11.27. **The correct answer is B.**

RATIOS INVOLVING MORE THAN TWO QUANTITIES

A more complex ratio problem might involve a ratio among three (or possibly more) quantities. The best way to handle these problems is with a part-to-whole approach, where the "whole" consists of more than two "parts."

EXAMPLE 21 (EASIER):

Machine X, Machine Y, and Machine Z each produce widgets. Machine Y's rate of production is one-third that of Machine X, and Machine Z's production rate is twice that of Machine Y. If Machine Y can produce 35 widgets per day, how many widgets can the three machines produce per day working simultaneously?

A. 105
B. 180
C. 210
D. 224

The key to handling this question is to convert ratios to fractional parts that add up to 1. The ratio of X's rate to Y's rate is 3 to 1, and the ratio of Y's rate to Z's rate is 1 to 2. You can express the ratio among all three as 3:1:2 (X:Y:Z). Accordingly, Y's production accounts for $\frac{1}{6}$ of the total widgets that all three machines can produce per day. Given that Y can produce 35 widgets per day, all three machines can produce (35)(6) = 210 widgets per day. **The correct answer is C.**

EXAMPLE 22 (MORE CHALLENGING):

Three lottery winners—Alan, Brenda, and Carl—are sharing a lottery jackpot. Alan's share is one-fifth of Brenda's share and one-seventh of Carl's share. If the total jackpot is $195,000, what is the dollar amount of Carl's share?

A. $15,000

B. $35,000

C. $75,000

D. $105,000

At first glance, this problem doesn't appear to involve ratios. (Where's the colon?) But it does. The ratio of Alan's share to Brenda's share is 1:5, and the ratio of Alan's share to Carl's share is 1:7. So you can set up the triple ratio: A:B:C = 1:5:7.

Alan's winnings account for 1 of 13 equal parts (1 + 5 + 7) of the total jackpot. $\frac{1}{13}$ of $195,000 is $15,000. Accordingly, Brenda's share is 5 times that amount, or $75,000, and Carl's share is 7 times that amount, or $105,000. **The correct answer is D.**

Proportion Problems Requiring Unit Conversions

Ratio or proportion problems often involve units of measurement, such as inches, ounces, or gallons. These problems sometimes require that you convert one unit to another—for example, feet to inches, pounds to ounces, or quarts to gallons. The problem will provide the conversion rate if it is not commonly known.

The problem might ask for nothing more than a conversion. To solve, set up a proportion and then cross-multiply and divide. Here are two examples for review:

4.8 ounces is equivalent to how many pounds? [1 pound = 16 ounces]

Set up the proportion $\frac{4.8}{x} = \frac{16}{1}$. Cross-multiply (diagonally) what you know: $4.8 \times 1 = 4.8$. Then divide by the third number: $4.8 \div 16 = 0.3$. (4.8 ounces is equivalent to 0.3 pounds.)

If Trevor hiked 13.6 kilometers, how many miles did he hike? [1 mile = 1.6 kilometers]

Set up the proportion $\frac{1}{1.6} = \frac{?}{13.6}$. Cross-multiply (diagonally) what you know:

$13.6 \times 1 = 13.6$. Then divide by the third number: $13.6 \div 1.6 = 8.5$.

(Trevor hiked 8.5 miles.)

Not all conversion-rate questions on the test are as simple as the two preceding examples. A question might require *two* conversions, or it might use *letters* instead of numbers—in order to focus on the process rather than the result. Though these problems may seem intimidating, they are actually not very difficult. You can easily solve them by applying the same method you would use to solve simpler conversion-rate problems.

EXAMPLE 23 (EASIER):

The distance from City 1 to City 2 is 840 kilometers. On an accurate map showing both cities, 1 centimeter represents 75 kilometers. On the map, how many millimeters separate City 1 and City 2? [1 centimeter = 10 millimeters]

A. 11

B. 45

C. 89

D. 112

First, set up the proportion $\frac{1 \text{ cm}}{75 \text{ km}} = \frac{?}{840}$. Then cross-multiply (diagonally) what you know: $840 \times 1 = 840$. Then divide by the third number: $840 \div 75 = 11.2$. On the map, the distance from City 1 to City B = $840 \div 75 = 11.2$ centimeters. But 11.2 is *not* the answer to the question. Your final step is to convert centimeters to millimeters. The problem provides the conversion rate: $11.2 \times 10 = 112$. **The correct answer is D.**

EXAMPLE 24 (MORE CHALLENGING):

A candy store sells candy only in half-pound boxes. At *c* cents per box, which of the following is the cost of *a* ounces of candy? [1 pound = 16 ounces]

A. $\frac{ac}{8}$

B. $\frac{a}{16c}$

C. $\frac{c}{a}$

D. $\frac{8c}{a}$

This question is asking: "*c* cents are to one box as *how many cents* are to *a* ounces?" Set up a proportion, letting "?" represent the cost of *a* ounces. Because the question asks for the cost of *ounces*, convert 1 box to 8 ounces (a half pound). $\frac{c}{8} = \frac{?}{a}$. Next, cross-multiply (diagonally) two terms that are provided (in this case, they are variables rather than numbers): $c \times a = ca$. Then divide by the third term that is provided: $\frac{ca}{8}$. (The expression *ca* , which signifies $c \times a$, is equal to *ac*, which signifies $a \times c$.) **The correct answer is A.**

Unit Rates

A **unit rate** is a ratio in which a value is compared to 1. In words, it represents "how much per one unit."

Say you are given that a bag of chips has 1,305 calories and contains about 9 servings. Let's write an equation that expresses the number of calories *y* for *x* servings.

The number of calories, *y*, is directly proportional to the number of servings, *x*. So the equation has the form $y = kx$. The slope, *k*, is the quotient $\frac{1,305}{9} = 145$. The equation is $y = 145x$.

EXPONENTS (POWERS) AND SCIENTIFIC NOTATION

An **exponent** refers to the number of times that a number (referred to as the **base number**) is multiplied by itself. In the exponential number 2^4, the base number is 2 and the exponent is 4. To calculate the value of 2^4 means: $2^4 = 2 \times 2 \times 2 \times 2 = 16$. An exponent is also referred to as a **power.** So you can express the exponential number 2^4 as "2 to the 4th power."

On the GED test, questions involving exponents usually require you to combine two or more exponential numbers using one of the four basic operations. To do so, you need to know certain rules. Can you combine base numbers *before* applying exponents to the numbers? The answer depends on which operation you're performing.

Combining Exponents by Addition or Subtraction

The rules for combining exponential numbers by addition or subtraction are very restrictive. You *can* combine exponential numbers *if* the base numbers and powers (exponents) are all the same. Here is the general rule, along with a simple example showing two ways to combine the numbers:

$$a^x + a^x + a^x = 3(a^x)$$

$$3^2 + 3^2 + 3^2 = (3)(3^2) = 3 \times 9 = 27$$

$$3^2 + 3^2 + 3^2 = 9 + 9 + 9 = 27$$

Otherwise, you cannot combine either base numbers or exponents. It's as simple as that. Here's the rule in symbolic form as it applies to different base numbers:

$$a^x + b^x \neq (a + b)^x$$

$$a^x - b^x \neq (a - b)^x$$

Substituting some simple numbers for *a*, *b*, and *x* illustrates the rule. In the following two examples, notice that you get a different result depending on which you do first: combine base numbers or apply each exponent to its base number.

Combining by addition:

$(4 + 2)^2 = 6^2 = 36$

$4^2 + 2^2 = 16 + 4 = 20$

Combining by subtraction:

$(4 - 2)^2 = 2^2 = 4$

$4^2 - 2^2 = 16 - 4 = 12$

EXAMPLE 25 (EASIER):

$a^7 + a^7 + a^7$ is equivalent to which of the following?

A. a^{21}

B. $3^7 \times a^7$

C. $3 \times a^7$

D. $21a$

You can combine terms here because base numbers and exponents are all the same. Adding together 3 of any quantity is the same as 3 *times* that quantity. **The correct answer is C.**

EXAMPLE 26 (MORE CHALLENGING):

If $x = -2$, what is the value of $x^5 - x^2 - x$?

A. –70

B. –58

C. –34

D. 26

You cannot combine exponents here, even though the base number is the same in all three terms. Instead, you need to apply each exponent, in turn, to the base number, then subtract:

$$x^5 - x^2 - x = (-2)^5 - (-2)^2 - (-2) = -32 - 4 + 2 = -34$$

The correct answer is C.

Combining Exponents by Multiplication or Division

Follow two basic rules for combining exponential numbers by multiplication and division.

RULE 1: You can combine base numbers first, but only if the exponents are the same. Here's the rule in symbolic form:

$$a^x \times b^x = (ab)^x$$

$$a^x \div b^x = (a \div b)^x \text{ or } \frac{a^x}{b^x} = \left(\frac{a}{b}\right)^x$$

Substituting some simple numbers for a, b, and x illustrates Rule 1. In the following two examples, notice that you get the same result whether or not you combine base numbers first.

Combining by multiplication:

$(4 \times 2)^2 = 8^2 = 64$

$4^2 \times 2^2 = 16 \times 4 = 64$

Combining by division:

$(10 \div 2)^2 = 5^2 = 25$

$10^2 \div 2^2 = 100 \div 4 = 25$

RULE 2: You can combine exponents first, but only if the base numbers are the same. When multiplying these terms, add the exponents. When dividing them, subtract the denominator exponent from the numerator exponent:

$$a^x \times a^y = a^{(x+y)}$$

$$a^x \div a^y = a^{(x-y)} \text{ or } \frac{a^x}{a^y} = a^{(x-y)}$$

Substituting some simple numbers for *a*, *b*, and *x* illustrates Rule 2. In the following two examples, notice that you get the same result whether or not you combine exponents first.

Combining by multiplication:

$2^3 \times 2^2 = 8 \times 4 = 32$

$2^{(3+2)} = 2^5 = 2 \times 2 \times 2 \times 2 \times 2 = 32$

Combining by division:

$2^5 \div 2^2 = 32 \div 4 = 8$

$2^{(5-2)} = 2^3 = 2 \times 2 \times 2 = 8$

When the same base number appears in a division problem, or in both numerator and denominator of a fraction, you can factor out (cancel) the number of powers common to both. To illustrate, consider the operation $9^6 \div 9^4$, or its equivalent fraction $\frac{9^6}{9^4}$. To find the quotient, you can either combine exponents, applying Rule 2, or you can factor out (cancel) 9^4 from each term:

Combining exponents first:

$\frac{9^6}{9^4} = 9^{(6-4)} = 9^2 = 81$

Canceling common factors first:

$\frac{9^6}{9^4} = \frac{9^4 \times 9^2}{9^4} = \frac{9^2}{1} = 81$

EXAMPLE 27 (EASIER):

When you divide $\frac{a^2b}{b^2c}$ by $\frac{a^2c}{bc^2}$, what is the result?

A. $\frac{1}{b}$

B. 1

C. $\frac{b}{a}$

D. $\frac{c}{b}$

First, cancel common factors in each term. Then you'll see that the numerator and denominator are the same, which means that the quotient must equal 1:

$$\frac{a^2b}{b^2c} \div \frac{a^2c}{bc^2} = \frac{a^2}{bc} \div \frac{a^2}{bc} = 1$$

The correct answer is B.

EXAMPLE 28 (MORE CHALLENGING):

What is the value of $\frac{x^3 - y^4}{x^3y^4}$, where x = 2 and y = −2 ?

A. $-\frac{1}{16}$

B. $\frac{1}{32}$

C. $\frac{1}{16}$

D. 1

One way to answer this question is to simplify the fraction by distributing the denominator to each term in the numerator, then cancel common factors. But an easier way to solve the problem is to plug in the *x* and *y* values that are provided, and do the math:

$$\frac{x^3 - y^4}{x^3y^4} = \frac{2^3 - (-2)^4}{2^3 \times (-2^4)} = \frac{8 - 16}{8 \times 16} = \frac{-8}{128} = -\frac{1}{16}$$

The correct answer is A.

Additional Rules for Exponents

For the GED test, you should also keep in mind these three additional rules for exponents.

1. When raising an exponential number to a power, multiply exponents:

   Rule: $\left(a^x\right)^y = a^{xy}$

   Example: $\left(2^2\right)^3 = 2^{(2)(3)} = 2^6 = 64$

2. Any number other than zero (0) raised to the power of 0 (zero) equals 1:

   Rule: $a^0 = 1\ [a \neq 0]$

   Example: $13^0 = 1$

3. Raising a base number to a negative exponent is equivalent to 1 divided by the base number raised to the exponent's absolute value:

   Rule: $a^{-x} = \frac{1}{a^x}$

   Example: $4^{-2} = \frac{1}{4^2} = \frac{1}{16}$

These three rules are all fair game for the GED test. In fact, a GED test question might require you to apply more than one of these rules.

EXAMPLE 29 (EASIER):

What is the value of $5^{-2} \times 5^{-1} \times 5^{0}$?

A. −125

B. $-\frac{1}{25}$

C. 0

D. $\frac{1}{125}$

Rewrite each of the first two terms under the numerator 1, but with a positive exponent. Then multiply:

$$\frac{1}{5^2} \times \frac{1}{5} \times 1 = \frac{1}{25} \times \frac{1}{5} \times 1 = \frac{1}{125}$$

The correct answer is D.

EXAMPLE 30 (MORE CHALLENGING):

What is the value of $\left(2^3\right)^2 \times 4^{-3}$?

A. $-\frac{1}{8}$

B. 1

C. $\frac{3}{2}$

D. 16

Multiply exponents in the first term. Rewrite the second term under the numerator 1, but with a positive exponent:

$$\left(2^3\right)^2 \times 4^{-3} = 2^{(2)(3)} \times \frac{1}{4^3} = \frac{2^6}{4^3} = \frac{2^6}{\left(2^2\right)^3} = \frac{2^6}{2^6} = 1.$$

The correct answer is B.

Exponents and the Real Number Line

Raising numbers to powers can have surprising effects on the size and/or sign (negative versus positive) of the number. You need to consider four separate regions of the real-number line.

For numbers greater than 1 (right of 1 on the number line):

Raising the number to a power greater than 1 gives a higher value. The greater the power, the greater the value. For example:

$$9^2 < 9^3 < 9^4 \text{ (and so on)}$$

For numbers less than –1 (left of –1 on the number line):

If the number is raised to an **even** power (such as 2, 4, or 6), the result is a number greater than 1. The greater the power, the greater the value. For example:

$$-3 < -3^2 < -3^4 < -3^6 \text{ (and so on)}$$

If the number is raised to an **odd** power (such as 3, 5, or 7), the result is a number less than –1. The greater the power, the smaller the value (the farther *left* on the number line). For example:

$$-2 > -2^3 > -2^5 > -2^7 \text{ (and so on)}$$

For fractional numbers between 0 and 1:

Raising the number to a power greater than 1 gives a *smaller positive* value. The greater the power, the smaller the value. For example:

$$\frac{2}{3} > \left(\frac{2}{3}\right)^2 > \left(\frac{2}{3}\right)^3 > \left(\frac{2}{3}\right)^4 \ldots > 0$$

For fractional numbers between –1 and 0:

Raising the fractional number to an **odd** power greater than 1 gives a *greater negative* value. The greater the power, the greater the value (approaching zero). For example:

$$-\frac{2}{3} < \left(-\frac{2}{3}\right)^3 < \left(-\frac{2}{3}\right)^5 \ldots < 0$$

Raising the fractional number to an **even** power greater than 1 gives a *positive fractional value* between 0 and 1. The greater the power, the lower the positive value (approaching zero). For example:

$$-\frac{2}{3} < 0, \text{ but } > \left(-\frac{2}{3}\right)^4 \ldots > 0$$

GED test questions involving exponents and the number line can be confusing. Nevertheless, they can be quite manageable if you keep in mind the four different regions of the number line.

EXAMPLE 31 (EASIER):

If $-1 < x < 0$, which of the following must be true?

A. $x^4 < -1$

B. $x^4 > 1$

C. $0 < x^4 < 1$

D. $x^4 = 1$

This question tests you on the rule that a negative fractional value raised to an even power (in this case 4), results in a fractional positive number, between 0 and 1. **The correct answer is C.**

EXAMPLE 32 (MORE CHALLENGING):

If $x^2 > 1 > y^2$, which of the following must be true?

A. $x > y$

B. $x^3 < y^3$

C. $x < y$

D. $-1 < y^2 < 1$

Given $x^2 > 1$, we know that x is either greater than 1 or less than –1. We also know that y must be a fraction less than 1 if y^2 is less than 1, but y also has to be a negative fraction greater than –1 for y^2 to be > –1. There are several situations in which choice A would be false, such as if $x = -5$ and $y = -\frac{1}{2}$. Choice B and C would be false if $x = 2$ and $y = -\frac{1}{2}$. Choice D is the only answer that must be true. **The correct answer is D.**

Exponents You Should Know

For the GED test, memorize the exponential values in the following table. These are the ones you're most likely to see on the exam.

Power and Corresponding Value

Base	2	3	4	5	6	7	8
2	4	8	16	32	64	128	256
3	9	27	81	243			
4	16	64	256				
5	25	125	625				
6	36	216					

Scientific Notation

Scientific notation is a system for writing extremely large or extremely small numbers. In scientific notation, an integer or decimal number between 1 and 10 is written to the power of 10. For example, the number 380,000,000 can be written as 3.8×10^8. The number between 1 and 10 that you are working with is 3.8. When you count the number of zeros plus the number to the right of the decimal point, you can see that there are 8 digits. That means that the exponent is 8. A negative exponent signifies a fractional number.

To illustrate further, here's a list of related decimal numbers and their equivalents in scientific notation:

837,000	$= 8.37 \times 10^5$ (decimal point shifts 5 places to the left)
8,370	$= 8.37 \times 10^3$ (decimal point shifts 3 places to the left)
837	$= 8.37 \times 10^2$ (decimal point shifts 1 place to the left)
8.37	$= 8.37 \times 10^0$ (decimal point unchanged in position)
0.837	$= 8.37 \times 10^{-1}$ (decimal point shifts 1 place to the right)
0.0837	$= 8.37 \times 10^{-2}$ (decimal point shifts 2 places to the right)
0.000837	$= 8.37 \times 10^{-4}$ (decimal point shifts 4 places to the right)

A GED test question might ask you to simply convert a number to scientific notation form, or the other way around.

EXAMPLE 33 (EASIER):

A computer can process data at the rate of 3.9×10^8 bits per second. How many bits can the computer process in 0.02 seconds?

A. 7.8×10^4

B. 7.8×10^6

C. 1.95×10^7

D. 7.8×10^8

To answer the question, first multiply the rate by the number of seconds: $(0.02)(3.9 \times 10^8) = 0.078 \times 10^8$. Since the answer choices are in proper scientific notation, shift the decimal point to the right two places and lower the power accordingly: 7.8×10^6. **The correct answer is B.**

EXAMPLE 34 (MORE CHALLENGING):

A particle travels at the rate of 52,500 meters per second. Expressed in millimeters, how far will the particle travel in 7×10^{-7} seconds?

[1 meter = 1,000 millimeters]

A. 0.3675

B. 3.675

C. 7.5

D. 36.75

Express 52,500 in scientific notation: 5.25×10^4. To convert this number from meters to millimeters, multiply by 1,000 (or 10^3):

$$(5.25 \times 10^4)(10^3) = 5.25 \times 10^7.$$

To answer the question, apply the following formula: distance = rate × time.

$$\begin{aligned} D &= (5.25\times10^{7})(7.0\times10^{-7}) \\ &= (5.25)(7)\times10^{(7-7)} \\ &= 36.75\times10^{0} \\ &= 36.75\times1 \\ &= 36.75 \end{aligned}$$

The correct answer is D.

SQUARE ROOTS (AND OTHER ROOTS)

The **square root** of a number n is a number that you "square" (multiply it by itself, or raise to the power of 2), to obtain n. The **radical sign** signifies square root and looks like this: $\sqrt{\ }$. Here's a simple example of a square root:

$2 = \sqrt{4}$ (the square root of 4) because 2×2 (or 2^2) = 4

The **cube root** of a number n is a number that you raise to the power of 3 (multiply by itself twice) to obtain n. You determine higher roots (for example, the "fourth root") in the same way. Except for square roots, the radical sign will indicate the root to be taken. For example:

$2 = \sqrt[3]{8}$ (the cube root of 8) because $2 \times 2 \times 2$ (or 2^3) = 8

$2 = \sqrt[4]{16}$ (the fourth root of 16) because $2 \times 2 \times 2 \times 2$ (or 2^4) = 16

Simplifying and Combining Radical Expressions

For the GED test, you should know the rules for simplifying and for combining radical expressions. Look for the possibility of simplifying radicals by moving what's under the radical sign to the outside of the sign. Check inside square-root radicals for **perfect squares**, which are factors that are squares of nice tidy numbers or other terms. The same advice applies to perfect cubes, and so on. Study the following three examples:

$\sqrt{4a^2} = 2a$

4 and a^2 are both perfect squares. Therefore, you can remove them from under the radical sign, and change each one to its square root.

$\sqrt[3]{27a^6} = 3a^2$

27 and a^6 are both perfect cubes. Therefore, you can remove them from under the radical sign, and change each one to its cube root.

$\sqrt{8a^3} = \sqrt{(4)(2)a^3} = 2a\sqrt{2a}$

8 and a^3 both contain perfect-square factors; remove the perfect squares from under the radical sign, and change each one to its square root.

The rules for combining terms that include radicals are quite similar to those for exponents. Keep the following two rules in mind; one applies to addition and subtraction, while the other applies to multiplication and division.

RULE 1 (addition and subtraction): If a term under a radical is being added to or subtracted from a term under a different radical, you cannot combine the two terms under the same radical.

$$\sqrt{x} + \sqrt{y} \neq \sqrt{x + y}$$
$$\sqrt{x} - \sqrt{y} \neq \sqrt{x - y}$$
$$\sqrt{x} + \sqrt{x} = 2\sqrt{x}\text{, not } \sqrt{2x}$$

RULE 2 (multiplication and division): Terms under different radicals can be combined under a common radical if one term is multiplied or divided by the other, but only if the radical is the same.

$$\sqrt{x}\sqrt{x} = \left(\sqrt{x}\right)^2\text{, or } x$$
$$\sqrt{x}\sqrt{y} = \sqrt{xy}$$
$$\frac{\sqrt{x}}{\sqrt{y}} = \sqrt{\frac{x}{y}}$$
$$\sqrt[3]{x}\sqrt{x} = \text{?} \quad \text{(you cannot combine)}$$

EXAMPLE 35 (EASIER):

$\left(2\sqrt{2a}\right)^2$ is equivalent to which of the following expressions?

A. $4a$

B. $4a^2$

C. $8a$

D. $8a^2$

Square each of the two terms, 2 and $\sqrt{2a}$, separately. Then combine their squares by multiplication: $\left(2\sqrt{2a}\right)^2 = 2^2 \times \left(\sqrt{2a}\right)^2 = 4 \times 2a = 8a$. **The correct answer is C.**

EXAMPLE 36 (MORE CHALLENGING):

$\sqrt{24} - \sqrt{16} - \sqrt{6}$ simplifies to which of the following expressions?

A. $\sqrt{6} - 4$

B. $4 - 2\sqrt{2}$

C. $\sqrt{6}$

D. $2\sqrt{2}$

Although the numbers under the three radicals combine to equal 2, you cannot combine terms this way. Instead, simplify the first two terms, then combine the first and third terms:

$$\sqrt{24} - \sqrt{16} - \sqrt{6} = 2\sqrt{6} - 4 - \sqrt{6} = \sqrt{6} - 4$$

The correct answer is A.

Roots You Should Know

Square roots, cube roots, etc. can be expressed using fractional exponents. The following notation is used:

$$\sqrt{a} = a^{\frac{1}{2}}$$
$$\sqrt[3]{a} = a^{\frac{1}{3}}$$
$$\vdots$$
$$\sqrt[n]{a} = a^{\frac{1}{n}}$$

Using the exponent rules, we have the more general definition:

$$\sqrt[n]{a^m} = \left(a^m\right)^{\frac{1}{n}} = a^{\left(m \cdot \frac{1}{n}\right)} = \left(a^{\frac{1}{n}}\right)^m = a^{\frac{m}{n}}$$

For instance:

$$8^{\frac{2}{3}} = \left(8^{\frac{1}{3}}\right)^2 = (2)^2 = 4$$

$$16^{\frac{3}{2}} = \left(16^{\frac{1}{2}}\right)^3 = 4^3 = 64$$

The following list of common roots is for your reference. You don't need to memorize these roots for the GED test. However, for those questions for which you may not use a calculator, it may be useful to commit to memory the first three roots in each column. Notice that the cube root of a positive number is positive, and the cube root of a negative number is negative.

Square roots of "perfect square" integers:	**Cube roots of "perfect cube" positive integers:**	**Cube roots of "perfect cube" negative integers:**	**Other roots you should know:**
$\sqrt{121} = 11$	$\sqrt[3]{8} = 2$	$\sqrt[3]{-8} = -2$	$\sqrt[4]{16} = 2$
$\sqrt{144} = 12$	$\sqrt[3]{27} = 3$	$\sqrt[3]{-27} = -3$	$\sqrt[4]{81} = 3$
$\sqrt{169} = 13$	$\sqrt[3]{64} = 4$	$\sqrt[3]{-64} = -4$	$\sqrt[5]{32} = 2$
$\sqrt{196} = 14$	$\sqrt[3]{125} = 5$	$\sqrt[3]{-125} = -5$	
$\sqrt{225} = 15$	$\sqrt[3]{216} = 6$	$\sqrt[3]{-216} = -6$	
$\sqrt{256} = 16$	$\sqrt[3]{343} = 7$	$\sqrt[3]{-343} = -7$	
$\sqrt{625} = 25$	$\sqrt[3]{512} = 8$	$\sqrt[3]{-512} = -8$	
	$\sqrt[3]{729} = 9$	$\sqrt[3]{-729} = -9$	
	$\sqrt[3]{1000} = 10$	$\sqrt[3]{-1000} = -10$	

SUMMING IT UP

- For the Mathematical Reasoning Test, it is important to review **properties** (signs, integers, absolute value, and divisibility), **forms** (fractions, mixed numbers, decimal numbers, percentages, ratios, exponential numbers, and radical expressions), and **operations** (the four basic operations and operations on exponential numbers and radical expressions). The knowledge areas that are covered here are basic building blocks for all types of GED test math questions.
- Questions involving fractions, decimal numbers, or percents often require you to convert one form to another as part of solving the problem at hand. Do your best to learn how to convert quickly and confidently.
- Certain **fraction-decimal-percent equivalents** appear on the GED test more often than others. The numbers in the tables in this chapter are especially common. Try to memorize them so that you can convert these numbers quickly during the test.
- Questions involving percentages might involve one of the following tasks:
    - Finding the percent of a number
    - Finding a number when a percent is given
    - Finding what percent one number is of another
- **Ratio** or **proportion** problems often involve units of measurement, such as inches, ounces, or gallons. These problems sometimes require that you convert one unit to another.
- An **exponent** refers to the number of times that a number (referred to as the **base number**) is multiplied by itself, *plus 1*. On the GED test, questions involving exponents usually require you to combine two or more exponential numbers using one of the four basic operations.
- Remember these three rules for exponents:
    - When raising an exponential number to a power multiply exponents.
    - Any number other than zero (0) raised to the power of 0 (zero) equals 1.
    - Raising a base number to a negative exponent is equivalent to 1 divided by the base number raised to the exponent's absolute value.
- Memorize the exponential values in the table that appears in this chapter. These are the ones you're most likely to see on the exam.
- Look for the possibility of simplifying radicals by moving what's under the radical sign to the outside of the sign. Check inside square-root radicals for **perfect squares**—factors that are squares of nice tidy numbers or other terms. The same advice applies to perfect cubes, and so on.

PRACTICE QUESTIONS

Directions: The following practice questions will cover the general math and numbers concepts that will appear on the GED Mathematical Reasoning Test. Choose the best answer to each problem presented.

SHOW YOUR WORK HERE

1. Simplify: $-(-5)^3 - 2^2(1 - 4)$.

A. −363

B. −113

C. 27

D. 137

2. Compute 300% of 0.03.

A. 0.009

B. 0.09

C. 3.03

D. 9.0

3. Which of these digits can be substituted for p in the number $45{,}2p8$ so that the resulting number is divisible by both 3 and 4?

A. 2

B. 3

C. 4

D. 5

4. Assuming b is not equal to zero, which of the following is equivalent to $\frac{a}{4} + \frac{3}{2b}$?

A. $\frac{a+3}{4+2b}$

B. $\frac{a+6}{4b}$

C. $\frac{ab+6}{4b}$

D. $\frac{ab+6b}{4b}$

5. Assuming that w and y are not equal to zero, which of these is equivalent to

$\dfrac{\left(w^{-3}\right)^2 y^{-4}}{\left(w^2 y^{-3}\right)^{-3}}$?

A. $\dfrac{1}{y^{13}}$

B. y^2

C. $\dfrac{w^{12}}{y^{13}}$

D. $w^{10}y^2$

6. What condition on a ensures that the expression $\dfrac{-2a^3}{1-a^2}$ is negative?

A. $-1 < a < 1$

B. $-1 < a < 0$

C. $a > 1$

D. $0 < a < 1$

7. Simplify: $\dfrac{|0.02 - 1.2| - |-0.08|}{-|1.01 - 1.11|}$

A. −12.6

B. −11

C. 9.2

D. 11

8. Assuming x, y, and z are positive, which of the following expressions is equivalent to

$\sqrt{48x^5\left(y^6z^3\right)^3}$?

A. $4x^2y^3z\sqrt{xz}$

B. $4x^2y^{3\sqrt{2}}z^{2\sqrt{2}}\sqrt{3xz}$

C. $4\sqrt{3}\,x^{\sqrt{5}}y^{3\sqrt{2}}z^3$

D. $4x^2y^9z^4\sqrt{3xz}$

SHOW YOUR WORK HERE

9. Assuming x and y are not equal to zero, which of these is equivalent to $\dfrac{\frac{2}{x}-\frac{1}{y}}{\frac{2}{y}+\frac{1}{x}}$?

SHOW YOUR WORK HERE

A. $\frac{1}{3}$

B. $\dfrac{3}{(x-y)(x+y)}$

C. $\dfrac{(2y-x)(2x+y)}{x^2y^2}$

D. $\dfrac{2y-x}{2x+y}$

10. $2\frac{1}{4}$ inches per minute =

A. $\frac{5}{6}$ yards per hour

B. $1\frac{21}{60}$ yards per hour

C. $3\frac{3}{4}$ yards per hour

D. $11\frac{1}{4}$ yards per hour

11. Compute: $\left(\frac{2}{3}\right)^{-2}-\left(\frac{1}{2}\right)^{-3}$

A. $-5\frac{3}{4}$

B. $-3\frac{1}{2}$

C. $\frac{1}{6}$

D. $\frac{1}{4}$

12. Which of the following expressions is equivalent to $20\frac{1}{2}\%$ of the sum of $2\frac{3}{8}$ and $4\frac{3}{4}$?

A. 20.5×7.125

B. 0.205×7.125

C. 20.5×6.5

D. 0.205×6.5

13. Suppose n is a positive, even integer. Which of the following is NOT definitely an integer?

A. $\frac{n}{2}$

B. $3n - 1$

C. n^{-1}

D. $\sqrt{n^2}$

14. Compute: $\frac{12 - 3(1-4)}{2(5-2^2)+1}$

A. –9

B. 1

C. $\frac{21}{19}$

D. 7

15. What is the value of $-a^2 + b^c$ if $a = -3$, $b = -2$, and $c = -3$?

A. $-9\frac{1}{8}$

B. –3

C. $-\frac{9}{8}$

D. $8\frac{5}{6}$

16. A map uses the scale $\frac{1}{4}$ inch = $1\frac{1}{2}$ miles. If two historical landmarks are $3\frac{1}{8}$ inches apart on the map, how many miles apart are they?

A. $2\frac{1}{4}$

B. $4\frac{11}{16}$

C. $12\frac{1}{2}$

D. $18\frac{3}{4}$

SHOW YOUR WORK HERE

SHOW YOUR WORK HERE

17. Which of the following is the smallest?

A. 10^3

B. 1,000%

C. $\frac{1}{0.01}$

D. $\frac{1}{10^{-2}}$

18. A botanical exhibit contains four different types of orchids; call them types A, B, C, and D. The ratio of the number of type A to the number of type B to the number of type C to the number of type D is 1:2:4:5. If there are 200 orchids of type C, how many orchids of type B are there?

A. 50

B. 100

C. 250

D. 600

19. If the whole number m is divisible by 6 and the whole number n is divisible by 4, what is the largest whole number that must divide $\frac{mn}{3}$?

A. 4

B. 6

C. 8

D. 24

20. Solve for m: $\frac{9 \times 10^m}{0.03} = 0.3$

A. –4

B. –3

C. 1

D. 3

SHOW YOUR WORK HERE

21. Sandy purchased a new sound system for \$900 last year. At the same time this year, the sound system has decreased in value by 18%. Which of these expressions represents its current value?

A. \$900(1.18)

B. 0.18(\$900)

C. \$900(1 – 0.18)

D. $\frac{\$900}{1-0.18}$

22. What is the value of $\frac{\frac{a}{b+c}+\frac{a}{b-c}}{abc}$ when $a=-3$, $b=4$, and $c=-2$?

A. $-\frac{3}{2}$

B. $-\frac{1}{32}$

C. $-\frac{1}{12}$

D. $\frac{1}{24}$

23. Compute: 25% of 20% of 2×10^{-2}

A. 1×10^{-3}

B. 9×10^{-3}

C. 1×10^{-2}

D. 9×10^{-2}

24. A store charges \$50 for 4 square yards of carpeting. What would be the cost for 369 square feet of carpeting?

A. \$170.83

B. \$512.50

C. \$1,476.00

D. \$4,612.50

SHOW YOUR WORK HERE

25. Which of these expressions is equivalent to $\left(\frac{a}{6b} - \frac{2b}{3a}\right)^{-2}$?

A. $\frac{(a-2b)^2}{(6b-3a)^2}$

B. $\frac{(6b-3a)^2}{(a-2b)^2}$

C. $\frac{12ab}{a^2-4b^2}$

D. $\frac{36a^2b^2}{\left(a^2-4b^2\right)^2}$

ANSWER KEY AND EXPLANATIONS

1. D	6. D	11. A	16. D	21. C
2. B	7. B	12. B	17. B	22. C
3. A	8. D	13. C	18. B	23. A
4. C	9. D	14. D	19. C	24. B
5. A	10. C	15. A	20. B	25. D

1. **The correct answer is D.** Use the order of operations to simplify:

$$\begin{aligned}-(-5)^3 - 2^2(1-4) &= -(-125) - 4(1-4)\\ &= -(-125) - 4(-3)\\ &= 125 + 12\\ &= 137\end{aligned}$$

Choice A is incorrect because you did not use the order of operations; you just computed from left to right. Choice B is incorrect because $-(-5)^3 = 125$, not -125. Choice C is incorrect because $(-5)^3 \neq -15$.

2. **The correct answer is B.** 300% is equal to the decimal 3.0. So 300% of 0.03 equals 3.0(0.03) = 0.09. In choice A, the decimal point is one too many places to the left. Choice C is incorrect because you multiply 3.0 and 0.03 to compute 300% of 0.03; you do not add them. Choice D is incorrect because 300% does not equal 300; you must move the decimal point two places to the left.

3. **The correct answer is A.** A whole number is divisible by 3 if the digit sum (that is, the sum of the digits of which the number is comprised) is divisible by 3. Here, the digit sum is $4 + 5 + 2 + p + 8 = 19 + p$. Here, 2 or 5 both work for p, which means you can eliminate choices B and C as correct. Next, a whole number is divisible by 4 if the number formed using its last two digits is divisible by 4. Here, that number is $p8$. This is divisible by 4 if $p = 2$ but not if $p = 5$. Choice D can be eliminated and you are left with choice A as the correct answer.

4. **The correct answer is C.** The least common denominator is $4b$. Express both fractions as equivalent with this denominator and add:

$$\begin{aligned}\frac{a}{4}+\frac{3}{2b} &= \frac{a}{4}\cdot\frac{b}{b}+\frac{3}{2b}\cdot\frac{2}{2}\\ &= \frac{ab}{4b}+\frac{6}{4b}\\ &= \frac{ab+6}{4b}\end{aligned}$$

Choice A is incorrect because you cannot add numerators and denominators to add fractions; you must first get a least common denominator. Choice B is incorrect because you did not multiply the first fraction by b when converting the fractions to equivalent ones with the least common denominator $4b$. Choice D is incorrect because you should not multiply the second fraction by b when converting the fractions to equivalent ones with the least common denominator $4b$.

5. **The correct answer is A.** Apply the exponent rules to simplify as follows:

$$\frac{\left(w^{-3}\right)^2 y^{-4}}{\left(w^2 y^{-3}\right)^{-3}} = \frac{\cancel{w^{-6}}\, y^{-4}}{\cancel{w^{-6}}\, y^{9}} = \frac{1}{y^4 y^9} = \frac{1}{y^{13}}$$

Choice B is incorrect because $\left(x^a\right)^b \neq x^{a+b}$. Choice C is incorrect because the w-terms cancel, since the same power of w appears in the numerator and denominator. Choice D is incorrect because the w-terms cancel because the same power of w appears in the numerator and denominator and $\left(x^a\right)^b \neq x^{a+b}$.

6. **The correct answer is D.** The denominator is positive when $-1 < a < 1$ and negative if $a < -1$ or $a > 1$. The numerator is positive when $a < 0$ and negative when $a > 0$. For the given fraction to be negative, the numerator and denominator must have opposite signs. This occurs when $0 < a < 1$.

7. **The correct answer is B.** Use the order of operations with the definition of absolute value as follows:

$$\begin{aligned}\frac{|0.02-1.2|-|-0.08|}{-|1.01-1.11|} &= \frac{|-1.18|-|-0.08|}{-|-0.1|}\\ &= \frac{1.18-0.08}{-0.1}\\ &= \frac{1.1}{-0.1}\\ &= -11\end{aligned}$$

Choice A is incorrect because $-|-0.08| \neq 0.08$; the absolute value does not apply to the negative sign that appears before it. Choice C is the result of an error with decimal point placement when computing $0.2 - 1.2$. Choice D is incorrect because the sign is wrong.

8. **The correct answer is D.** When computing the square root of an algebraic expression, any factor of the radicand that is squared comes outside the radical as the expression without the square; other quantities remain part of the radicand. Simplifying the expression using the exponent rules and then applying this principle yields:

$$\begin{aligned}\sqrt{48x^5\left(y^6z^3\right)^3} &= \sqrt{48x^5y^{18}z^9}\\ &= \sqrt{16 \cdot 3 \cdot x^4 \cdot x \cdot y^{18} \cdot z^8 \cdot z}\\ &= 4x^2y^9z^4\sqrt{3xz}\end{aligned}$$

Choice A does not account for the exponent 3 to which the quantity y^6z^3 is being raised. Choices B and C are incorrect because $\sqrt{x^a} \neq x^{\sqrt{a}}$.

9. **The correct answer is D.** Simplify the expressions in the numerator and denominator using the least common denominator *xy*. Then, compute the quotient:

$$\begin{aligned}\frac{\frac{2}{x}-\frac{1}{y}}{\frac{2}{y}+\frac{1}{x}} &= \frac{\frac{2}{x}\cdot\frac{y}{y}-\frac{1}{y}\cdot\frac{x}{x}}{\frac{2}{y}\cdot\frac{x}{x}+\frac{1}{x}\cdot\frac{y}{y}}\\ &= \frac{\frac{2y-x}{xy}}{\frac{2x+y}{xy}}\\ &= \frac{2y-x}{xy} \div \frac{2x+y}{xy}\\ &= \frac{2y-x}{\cancel{xy}} \cdot \frac{\cancel{xy}}{2x+y}\\ &= \frac{2y-x}{2x+y}\end{aligned}$$

Choices A and B are incorrect because you do not add or subtract fractions by adding or subtracting the numerators and denominators; you must get a least common denominator. In addition, choice B is incorrect because the quotient was not converted to an equivalent product by flipping the fraction after the division sign. Choice C is the result of making this same error.

10. The correct answer is C. Use the conversion factors 1 hour = 60 minutes and 1 yard = 36 inches, and convert the mixed number $2\frac{1}{4}$ to the improper fraction $\frac{9}{4}$, to obtain the following:

$$\frac{\frac{9}{4}\ \cancel{\text{inches}}}{1\ \cancel{\text{minute}}} \times \frac{60\ \cancel{\text{minutes}}}{1\ \text{hour}} \times \frac{1\ \text{yard}}{36\ \cancel{\text{inches}}}$$

$$= \frac{\frac{9}{4} \cdot 60}{36} \text{ yards per hour}$$

$$= \frac{15}{4} \text{ yards per hour}$$

$$= 3\frac{3}{4} \text{ yards per hour}$$

Choice A is the result of not interpreting the mixed number correctly. Choice B is the result of using the correct conversions, but incorrectly using their reciprocals in the unit conversion computation. Choice D is incorrect because 1 yard equals 36 inches, not 12 inches.

11. The correct answer is A. Apply the exponent rules and simplify, as follows:

$$\left(\frac{2}{3}\right)^{-2} - \left(\frac{1}{2}\right)^{-3} = \left(\frac{3}{2}\right)^{2} - 2^{3}$$

$$= \frac{9}{4} - 8$$

$$= -\frac{23}{4}$$

$$= -5\frac{3}{4}$$

Choice B is incorrect because if a fraction is raised to a power, you must apply that power to both the numerator and denominator. Choice C is incorrect because you do not multiply the base and exponent when computing the power of a quantity. Choice D is incorrect because you must first get a least common denominator before subtracting fractions.

12. The correct answer is B. Note that $20\frac{1}{2}\% = 20.5\% = 0.205$. Also,

$$2\frac{3}{8} + 4\frac{3}{4} = 2\frac{3}{8} + 4\frac{6}{8}$$

$$= 6\frac{9}{8}$$

$$= 7\frac{1}{8}$$

$$= 7.125$$

So $20\frac{1}{2}\%$ of 7.125 equals 0.205(7.125). Choice A is incorrect because you must convert $20\frac{1}{2}\%$ to a decimal. Choice C is incorrect because you must convert $20\frac{1}{2}\%$ to a decimal and you added the fractions incorrectly. Choice D is incorrect because you added the fractions incorrectly.

13. The correct answer is C. Observe that $n^{-1} = \frac{1}{n}$. Since n is a positive, even integer, this is always a fraction strictly between 0 and 1 and so is, in fact, never an integer. Choice A is incorrect because every even integer is divisible by 2. Choice B is incorrect because a multiple of an integer is an integer and subtracting 1 from an integer also produces an integer. Choice D is incorrect because this equals n, because n is positive.

14. **The correct answer is D.** Use the order of operations to solve, as follows:

$$\begin{aligned}\frac{12-3(1-4)}{2(5-2^2)+1} &= \frac{12-3(-3)}{2(5-4)+1}\\ &= \frac{12-(-9)}{(2)(1)+1}\\ &= \frac{21}{2+1}\\ &= \frac{21}{3}\\ &= 7\end{aligned}$$

Choice A is the result of not applying the order of operations correctly in the numerator; you subtracted 12 – 3 first but should have first computed 3(–3). Choice B is incorrect because of an error involving negative signs in the numerator. Choice C is incorrect because $5 - 2^2 \neq 5 + 4$; the exponent does not apply to the negative.

15. **The correct answer is A.** Substitute the given values for *a*, *b*, and *c* into the expression and simplify using the order of operations:

$$\begin{aligned}-a^2 + b^c &= -(-3)^2 + (-2)^{-3}\\ &= -9 + \frac{1}{(-2)^3}\\ &= -9 + \frac{1}{-8}\\ &= -9 - \frac{1}{8}\\ &= -9\frac{1}{8}\end{aligned}$$

Choice B is incorrect because you do not multiply base and exponent when computing (–2)–3. Choice C is incorrect because in the last step, you did not interpret the mixed number correctly; $-9\frac{1}{8} \neq -\frac{9}{8}$. Choice D is incorrect because –(–3)2 = –9, not 9, and (–2)3 = –8, not –6.

16. **The correct answer is D.** Let *x* be the number of miles between the two landmarks. Set up and solve the proportion:

$$\frac{\frac{1}{4}\text{ inch}}{1\frac{1}{2}\text{ miles}} = \frac{3\frac{1}{8}\text{ inches}}{x\text{ miles}}$$

$$\left(\frac{1}{4}\right)x = \left(1\frac{1}{2}\right)\left(3\frac{1}{8}\right)$$

$$\frac{1}{4}x = \frac{3}{2} \cdot \frac{25}{8}$$

$$x = \frac{\frac{3}{2} \cdot \frac{25}{8}}{\frac{1}{4}}$$

$$x = \frac{75}{16} \cdot 4 = \frac{75}{4} = 18\frac{3}{4}$$

Choice A is the result of not interpreting the mixed number $3\frac{1}{8}$ correctly; it does not equal $\frac{3}{8}$. Choice B is incorrect because you must divide by $\frac{1}{4}$. Choice C is the result of not using $1\frac{1}{2}$ in the calculation; you must set up a proportion.

17. The correct answer is B. Observe that $\frac{1}{10^{-2}} = 100$, 1,000% = 10, $\frac{1}{0.01} = 100$, and $10^3 = 1{,}000$. So 1,000% is the smallest.

18. **The correct answer is B.** Let x be the number of type A orchids. Then, there are 2*x* type B, 4*x* type C, and 5*x* type D. We are given that 4*x* = 200 and so, *x* = 50. Thus, the number of type B orchids is 2(50) = 100. Choice A is the number of type A. Choice C is the number of type D. Choice D is the total number of orchids in the exhibit.

19. **The correct answer is C.** Because *m* is divisible by 6, there must be some whole number *k* so that *m* = 6*k*. Similarly, because *n* is divisible by 4, there must be some whole number *l* so that *n* = 4*l*. So $\frac{mn}{3} = \frac{(6k)(4l)}{3}$ $= 8kl = 8 \times$ (some whole number). So 8 must divide this quantity.

20. The correct answer is B. Simplify the given equation as follows:

$$\frac{9 \times 10^m}{0.03} = 0.3$$
$$\frac{9}{0.03} \times 10^m = 0.3$$
$$300 \times 10^m = 0.3$$
$$m = -3$$

Choice A is incorrect because this would put the decimal point one too many places to the left. Choice C is incorrect because $\frac{9}{0.03} = 300$, so m cannot be 1. Choice D is incorrect because the sign is wrong; this would move the decimal point 3 units to the right.

21. The correct answer is C. A decrease by 18% is represented by 1 – 0.18. To get the current value, multiply this by the amount paid initially, which is \$900. This yields the expression \$900(1 – 0.18). Choice A represents an increase in value by 18%. Choice B is the amount of the decrease. Choice D is incorrect because you should multiply by (1 – 0.18), not divide by it.

22. The correct answer is C. Substitute the given values into the expression and simplify using the order of operations:

$$\frac{\frac{a}{b+c}+\frac{a}{b-c}}{abc} = \frac{\frac{-3}{4-2}+\frac{-3}{4-(-2)}}{(-3)(4)(-2)}$$
$$= \frac{\frac{-3}{2}+\frac{-3}{6}}{24}$$
$$= \frac{\frac{-3}{2}-\frac{1}{2}}{24}$$
$$= -\frac{2}{24}$$
$$= -\frac{1}{12}$$

Choice A is incorrect because this is just the numerator of the expression, albeit as the result of adding those fractions incorrectly. Choice B is incorrect because you do not add fractions by adding their numerators and denominators. Choice D is incorrect because $\frac{a}{b+c} \neq \frac{3}{2}$.

23. The correct answer is A. Observe that $2 \times 10^{-2} = 2 \times 0.01 = 0.02$. So 20% of 0.02 equals 0.2(0.02) = 0.004. Then 25% of this quantity is 0.25(0.004) = 0.001, which can be written as 10^{-3}. Choice B is incorrect because 25% of 20% of a quantity is different from 45% of that quantity. Choice C is incorrect because you moved the decimal point one too few places to the left. Choice D is incorrect because 25% of 20% of a quantity is different from 45% of that quantity, and you moved the decimal point one too few places to the left.

24. The correct answer is B. Before setting up the proportion, convert square yards to square feet using the conversion factor 1 square yard = $(3 \text{ feet})^2$ = 9 square feet. So the store charges \$50 for 4(9) = 36 square feet. Let x be the cost for \$369 square feet of carpeting. Set up this proportion:

$$\frac{\$50}{36 \text{ square feet}} = \frac{\$x}{369 \text{ square feet}}$$
$$x = \frac{(\$50)(369)}{36}$$
$$x = \$512.50$$

Choice A is incorrect because 1 square yard equals 9 square feet, not 27 square feet. Choice C is incorrect because the product 4(369) does not consider the cost (\$50) for 36 square feet of carpeting; set up a proportion. Choice D is incorrect because you did not convert square yards to square feet.

25. **The correct answer is D.** Combine the fractions inside the parentheses using the least common denominator $6ab$. Then, apply the power:

$$\left(\frac{a}{6b}-\frac{2b}{3a}\right)^{-2}=\left(\frac{a}{6b}\cdot\frac{a}{a}-\frac{2b}{3a}\cdot\frac{2b}{2b}\right)^{-2}$$

$$=\left(\frac{a^2}{6ab}-\frac{4b^2}{6ab}\right)^{-2}$$

$$=\left(\frac{a^2-4b^2}{6ab}\right)^{-2}$$

$$=\left(\frac{6ab}{a^2-4b^2}\right)^{2}$$

$$=\frac{(6ab)^2}{\left(a^2-4b^2\right)^2}$$

$$=\frac{36a^2b^2}{\left(a^2-4b^2\right)^2}$$

Choice A is incorrect because you did not add the fractions correctly and you did not apply the negative portion of the exponent correctly. Choice B is incorrect because you did not add the fractions correctly. Choice C is incorrect because you do not multiply the base times the exponent when computing a power.

Math Review: Algebra and Descriptive Statistics

Chapter 13

OVERVIEW

- What You'll Find in This Review
- Evaluating Expressions
- Linear Equations in One Variable
- Linear Equations in Two Variables
- Linear Equations That Can't Be Solved
- Solving Algebraic Inequalities
- Factorable Quadratic Expressions (One Variable)
- Factorable Quadratic Expressions (Two Variables)
- Functions
- Measures of Central Tendency (Mean, Median, and Range)
- Arithmetic Series
- Probability
- Counting Principles
- Graphing Data Sets
- Word Problems Involving Formulas
- Summing It Up
- Practice Questions
- Answer Key and Explanations

WHAT YOU'LL FIND IN THIS REVIEW

This review focuses on algebra and descriptive statistics. First, you'll review the following algebra skills:

- Evaluating linear, polynomial, and rational expressions
- Solving a linear equation in one variable
- Solving a system of two equations in two variables by substitution and addition-subtraction
- Recognizing unsolvable equations
- Handling algebraic inequalities
- Factoring quadratic expressions
- Finding the roots of quadratic equations by factoring
- Handling functions
- Solving formula word problems (weighted average, simple interest, and rate)

Later, you'll examine the concepts of mean, median, range, arithmetic series, and probability.

The GED Mathematical Reasoning Test-style questions throughout this review are multiple-choice questions. The actual exam also includes questions in an alternative format, in which you supply the numerical answer to the question.

EVALUATING EXPRESSIONS

Linear Expressions

A **linear expression** has the form $Ax + B$, where A and B are real numbers. They can be added and subtracted by combining like terms. For example:

$$\begin{aligned}\left(\frac{2}{3}x-\frac{3}{4}\right)+\left(\frac{1}{6}x+\frac{5}{12}\right)&=\left(\frac{2}{3}x+\frac{1}{6}x\right)+\left(-\frac{3}{4}+\frac{5}{12}\right)\\&=\left(\frac{4}{6}x+\frac{1}{6}x\right)+\left(-\frac{9}{12}+\frac{5}{12}\right)\\&=\frac{5}{6}x-\frac{4}{12}\\&=\frac{5}{6}x-\frac{1}{3}\end{aligned}$$

Using the distributive property, we can also multiply a linear expression by a single term:

$$1.4(0.3x-1.4)=1.4(0.3x)-1.4(1.4)=0.42x-1.96$$

Using the distributive property twice in succession enables us to multiply two linear expressions. A usual mnemonic device is the so-called FOIL method; the acronym stands for multiplying First terms, Outer term, Inner terms, and Last terms, and summing them. For example:

$$\begin{aligned}\left(2x-\frac{1}{4}\right)\left(3x-\frac{5}{3}\right)&=(2x)(3x)+(2x)\left(-\frac{5}{3}\right)+\left(-\frac{1}{4}\right)(3x)+\left(-\frac{1}{4}\right)\left(-\frac{5}{3}\right)\\&=6x^2-\frac{10}{3}x-\frac{3}{4}x+\frac{5}{12}\\&=6x^2+\left(-\frac{10}{3}-\frac{3}{4}\right)x+\frac{5}{12}\\&=6x^2+\left(-\frac{40}{12}-\frac{9}{12}\right)x+\frac{5}{12}\\&=6x^2-\frac{49}{12}x+\frac{5}{12}\end{aligned}$$

Such expressions arise when modeling real-world contexts, and often the desired solution is obtained by evaluating the expression at a specific value of the variable.

Example:

Evaluate $\frac{3}{4}x-\frac{5}{6}$ at $x=-2$.

To solve, replace every occurrence of the variable with the number and simplify the arithmetic expression using the order of operations:

$$\frac{3}{4}(-2)-\frac{5}{6}=-\frac{3}{2}-\frac{5}{6}=-\frac{9}{6}-\frac{5}{6}=-\frac{14}{6}=-\frac{7}{3}$$

Real-World Application

Sometimes, you will need to formulate a linear expression as part of solving a word problem. You simply need to look for key words and interpret accordingly. Here are some examples:

Scenario	Linear Expression
One cable is two-thirds the length of one-half of another piece.	Let x represent the length of the second piece. The word *of* means multiply, so the length of the cable is $\frac{2}{3}\left(\frac{1}{2}x\right)$.
Caty is three years older than twice her sister's age.	Let x be Caty's sister's age (in years). Then, Caty's age is $(2x + 3)$ years.
The length of a rectangle is one meter more than one-fourth the width.	Let w be the width of the rectangle (in meters). Then, the length is $\left(1+\frac{1}{4}w\right)$ meters.

Polynomial Expressions

Working with **polynomial expressions** is like working with linear expressions; the only difference is that there are more terms. To add or subtract polynomial expressions, you simply combine like terms (that is, terms with the same variable term). To multiply polynomial expressions, you use the distributive property to ensure each term of one expression is multiplied by each term of the other. Then, you add the results.

Example:

$$\left(3x^4 - 2x^2 + \frac{2}{3}x - 5\right) - \left(3x - 4x^2 + \frac{4}{3}x^3 - x^4\right)$$
$$= 3x^4 - 2x^2 + \frac{2}{3}x - 5 - 3x + 4x^2 - \frac{4}{3}x^3 + x^4$$
$$= \left(3x^4 + x^4\right) + \left(-\frac{4}{3}x^3\right)\left(-2x^2 + 4x^2\right) + \left(\frac{2}{3}x - 3x\right) + (-5)$$
$$= 4x^4 - \frac{4}{3}x^3 + 2x^2 - \frac{7}{3}x - 5$$

Example:

$$\left(3x - 2x^2\right)\left(x^3 - \frac{1}{4}\right) = (3x)\left(x^3\right) + (3x)\left(-\frac{1}{4}\right) + \left(-2x^2\right)\left(x^3\right) + \left(-2x^2\right)\left(-\frac{1}{4}\right)$$
$$= 3x^4 - \frac{3}{4}x - 2x^5 + \frac{1}{2}x^2$$
$$= -2x^5 + 3x^4 + \frac{1}{2}x^2 - \frac{3}{4}x$$

Just as with linear expressions, polynomials arise when modeling real-world contexts, and often, the desired solution is obtained by evaluating the expression at a specific value of the variable. To do so, replace every occurrence of the variable by the number and simplify the arithmetic expression using the order of operations.

For example, to evaluate the polynomial $3x^4 - 2x^2 + \frac{2}{3}x - 5$ at $x = -1$, simply replace every instance of x with -1, then solve:

$$3(-1)^4 - 2(-1)^2 + \frac{2}{3}(-1) - 5 = 3 - 2 - \frac{2}{3} - 5 = -4 - \frac{2}{3} = -\frac{14}{3}$$

Factoring Polynomials

Factoring polynomials involves writing a polynomial expression as a product of simpler polynomials. There are several techniques used to do this; the most common are factoring out a greatest common factor (GCF), using difference of squares formula, and factoring trinomials.

First let's look at the polynomial $12x^3 + 24x$.

The term $12x$ is common to both terms. Using the distributive property, it can be factored out of both terms:

$$12x^3 + 24x = 12x(x^2 + 2).$$

When you come across a polynomial, always check to see if it is a difference of squares. Take the polynomial $4x^2 - 121$:

$$4x^2 - 121 = (2x)^2 - 121$$

Then, using the formula $a^2 - b^2 = (a - b)(a + b)$, this further factors as $(2x - 11)(2x + 11)$.

What about trinomials? **Factoring trinomials** is a bit trickier. In general, you will need to apply the FOIL method *in reverse.*

Let's walk through the process with trinomial $10x^2 + 21x - 10$.

The relationships between the general quadratic form $ax^2 + bx + c$ and FOIL are as follows:

(F) is the first term (ax^2)

(O + I) is the second term (bx)

(L) is the third term (c)

To factor trinomial $10x^2 + 21x - 10$, first identify its components:

(F) $= 10x^2$

(O + I) $= 21x$

(L) $- 10$

Now you create a binomial shell to fill in numbers. In this example, since **(F)** is $10x^2$, the first term in each binomial must be x and a factor of 10:

$$(5x + \ ?)(2x + \ ?)$$

Since (**L**) is –10, the product of the two last terms (signified by "?") must be –10. The possibilities are 2 and –5, and–2 and 5. Let's try the first combination to see if it works:

$$\begin{aligned}(5x+2)(2x-5) &= (5x)(2x)-(5x)(5)+(2)(2x)-(2)(5)\\ &= 10x^2-25x+4x-10\\ &= 10x^2-21x-10\end{aligned}$$

As you can see, this isn't the right combination. Now let's try –2 and 5 to see if it works:

$$\begin{aligned}(5x-2)(2x+5) &= (5x)(2x)+(5x)(5)-(2)(2x)+(-2)(5)\\ &= 10x^2+25x-4x+10\\ &= 10x^2+21x-10\end{aligned}$$

This second combination works.

$$10x^2+21x-10=(5x-2)(2x+5)$$

In some cases, a GCF should be factored out before attempting to factor the trinomial.

In the trinomial $12x^3 - 22x^2 + 6x$, $2x$ is common to all three terms. Factor it out first, then factor the trinomial:

$$\begin{aligned}12x^3-22x^2+6x &= 2x\left(6x^2-11x+3\right)\\ &= 2x(3x-1)(2x-3)\end{aligned}$$

Real-World Application

Let's now look at an example where solving a word problem requires you to formulate a more complicated polynomial.

Example:

The edges of a rectangular box are such that the longest side is twice the length of the shortest side, and the third side is two meters longer than the shortest side. What is an expression for the volume of such a box?

Define all parts of the given situation. Let x be the length of the shortest side (in meters). Then, the longest side has length $2x$ meters and the third side has length $(x + 2)$ meters. The volume of a rectangular box is the product of these three edges, namely $V = x(2x)(x + 2)$ cubic meters.

Rational Expressions

A **rational expression** is a fraction in which the numerator and denominator are both polynomials. The arithmetic of rational expressions mimics that of numerical fractions. Here are some basic rules:

- To **simplify** a rational expression, factor the numerator and denominator and cancel any like factors.
- When **adding or subtracting** rational expressions, first get a least common denominator (LCD) of all rational expressions involved. Once all rational expressions are converted to equivalent ones in which the denominator is this LCD, simply add/subtract the numerators as you would any polynomials.

- To **multiply** rational expressions, it is easiest to factor all numerators and denominators and cancel any factor that appears in the numerator on one of the rational expressions and the denominator of a (possibly) different one. Once all such common factors have been eliminated, multiply numerators, and multiply denominators to obtain the final product.
- To **divide** two rational expressions, start by converting the quotient to a product by replacing the rational expression following the division sign by its reciprocal. Then, multiply the rational expressions as previously described.

Let's walk through how to compute some rational expressions.

Example: Subtracting a rational expression

Let's look at the rational expression $\frac{2}{x+2}-\frac{3}{x}$.

This expression involves subtraction, so you need to first find an LCD. For this example, the LCD is $x(x+2)$. Convert both fractions to equivalent ones with this LCD and proceed:

$$\frac{2}{x+2}-\frac{3}{x}=\frac{2x}{x(x+2)}-\frac{3(x+2)}{x(x+2)}=\frac{2x-3(x+2)}{x(x+2)}=\frac{2x-3x-6}{x(x+2)}=\frac{-x-6}{x(x+2)}$$

Example: Multiplying a rational expression

Let's look at the expression $\frac{125x}{4x^2-1}\bullet\frac{6x^2+5x-4}{25x^3}$.

When multiplying, you do not have to find an LCD; simply factor if possible, cancel out terms to simplify, and multiply across.

$$\frac{125x}{4x^2-1}\bullet\frac{6x^2+5x-4}{25x^3}=\frac{\cancel{25x}\bullet 5}{\cancel{(2x-1)}(2x+1)}\bullet\frac{\cancel{(2x-1)}(3x+4)}{\cancel{25x}\bullet x^2}=\frac{5(3x+4)}{x^2(2x+1)}=\frac{15x+20}{2x^3+x^2}$$

Rational expressions can be evaluated at any value of the variable that does not make the denominator equal to zero, since division by zero is not allowed.

Example:

Evaluate the expression

$$\frac{x-4}{x(x-3)(2x+1)}.$$

Can you evaluate it at $x = 4$?

When you plug in 4 for all instances of x, the value does not make the denominator equal to zero, so you can evaluate the rational expression at $x = 4$. Substituting it in results in a zero in the numerator, which means the fraction equals zero.

Can you evaluate it at $x = 3$?

Plugging in 3 for all instances of x makes the denominator equal to zero. Therefore, the rational expression cannot be evaluated at $x = 3$ and is undefined.

Can you evaluate it at $x = -1$?

This value does not make the denominator equal to zero, so you can evaluate the rational expression at $x = -1$. Substituting it in yields the following:

$$\frac{-1-4}{-1(-1-3)(2(-1)+1)} = \frac{-5}{(-1)(-4)(-1)} = \frac{-5}{-4} = \frac{5}{4}$$

Real-World Application

Sometimes, solving a word problem requires you to formulate a rational expression.

Example:

A group of x friends shares a taxi. If the entire trip costs 50 dollars, how much does each person owe?

To figure out the cost per person, you would divide the total cost (given as 50) by the number of people sharing the bill (given only as x). Here, this is expressed as $\frac{50}{x}$.

LINEAR EQUATIONS IN ONE VARIABLE

Algebraic expressions are usually used to form **equations,** which set two expressions equal to each other. Equations contain at least one **variable:** a letter such as x or y that represents a number that can *vary*. Most equations you'll see on the test are **linear equations**, in which the variables don't come with exponents.

To find the value of a linear equation's variable (such as x) is to **solve the equation**. To solve any linear equation containing only one variable, your goal is always the same: isolate the variable on one side of the equation. To accomplish this, you may need to perform one or more of the following operations on both sides, depending on the equation:

1. Add or subtract the same term on both sides.
2. Multiply or divide both sides by the same term.
3. Clear fractions by cross-multiplication.
4. Clear radicals by raising both sides to the same power (exponent).

Whatever operation you perform on one side of an equation you must also perform on the other side; otherwise, the two sides won't be equal. Performing any of these operations on *both* sides does not change the equality; it merely restates the equation in a different form.

Solving an Equation Using the Four Basic Operations

To find the value of the variable (to solve for x), you may need to either add a term to both sides of the equation or subtract a term from both sides. Here are two examples:

Adding the same number to both sides:

$$x - 2 = 5$$
$$x - 2 + 2 = 5 + 2$$
$$x = 7$$

Subtracting the same number from both sides:

$$\frac{3}{2} - x = 12$$

The objective is to isolate the variable x. To do this, like terms must be combined.

$$\begin{array}{rcl} \frac{3}{2} - x &=& 12 \\ -\frac{3}{2} & & -\frac{3}{2} \\ \hline -x &=& 10\frac{1}{2} \end{array}$$ (divide by -1 to make the variable positive)

$$x = -10\frac{1}{2}$$

The first system isolates x by adding 2 to both sides. The second system isolates x by subtracting $\frac{3}{2}$ from both sides. In some cases, solving for x requires that you either multiply or divide both sides of the equation by the same term. Here are two examples:

Multiplying both sides by the same number:

$$\frac{x}{2} = 14$$
$$2 \times \frac{x}{2} = 14 \times 2$$
$$x = 28$$

Dividing both sides by the same number:

$$3x = 18$$
$$\frac{3x}{3} = \frac{18}{3}$$
$$x = 6$$

The first system isolates x by multiplying both sides by 2. The second system isolates x by dividing both sides by 3. If the variable appears on both sides of the equation, first perform whatever operation is required to position the variable on just one side—either the left or the right. The next system positions both x-terms on the left side by subtracting $2x$ from both sides:

$$16 - x = 9 + 2x$$
$$16 - x - 2x = 9 + 2x - 2x$$
$$16 - 3x = 9$$

Now that x appears on just one side, the next step is to isolate it by subtracting 16 from both sides, and then dividing both sides by −3:

$$16 - 3x = 9$$
$$16 - 3x - 16 = 9 - 16$$
$$-3x = -7$$
$$\frac{-3x}{-3} = \frac{-7}{-3}$$
$$x = \frac{7}{3}$$

EXAMPLE 1 (EASIER):

For what value of x does $2x - 6$ equal $x - 9$?

A. −6

B. −3

C. 2

D. 6

First, write the verbal description as the equation $2x - 6 = x - 9$. Then position both x-terms on the same side. To place them both on the left side, subtract x from both sides. Then combine x-terms:

$$2x - 6 - x = x - 9 - x$$
$$x - 6 = -9$$

Finally, isolate x by adding 6 to both sides:

$$x - 6 + 6 = -9 + 6$$
$$x = -3$$

The correct answer is B.

Linear equations with rational coefficients are solved in the same way as those with integer coefficients—don't be intimidated because they look more complex! Just treat them as you would any rational expression. Let's walk through a couple of examples.

Example:

Say you are given the following equation:

$$\frac{2}{3}x - \frac{3}{2} = 3 - \frac{5}{6}x$$

Gather the x-terms on the left-side and constant terms on the right. Then, proceed as follows:

$$\frac{2}{3}x - \frac{3}{2} = 3 - \frac{5}{6}x$$
$$\frac{2}{3}x + \frac{5}{6}x = 3 + \frac{3}{2}$$
$$\frac{9}{6}x = \frac{9}{2}$$
$$x = 3$$

Example:

Solve for x:

$$\frac{3}{4}\left(\frac{9}{2}-2x\right)-3\left(\frac{4}{3}x+2\right)=-1$$

This example may look complicated, but it really is just testing your knowledge of working with rational expressions. First, apply the distributive property to simplify the left side. Then, take the constant terms to the right side and solve as follows:

$$\frac{3}{4}\left(\frac{9}{2}-2x\right)-3\left(\frac{4}{3}x+2\right)=-1$$

$$\frac{27}{8}-\frac{3}{2}x-4x-6=-1$$

$$\left(-\frac{3}{2}-4\right)x=-1+6-\frac{27}{8}$$

$$-\frac{11}{2}x=\frac{13}{8}$$

$$x=-\frac{2}{11}\cdot\frac{13}{8}$$

$$x=-\frac{13}{44}$$

EXAMPLE 2 (MORE CHALLENGING):

If $12=\frac{11}{x}-\frac{3}{x}$, then what is the value of x ?

A. $\frac{3}{11}$

B. $\frac{1}{2}$

C. $\frac{2}{3}$

D. $\frac{11}{3}$

First, combine the x-terms: $12=\frac{11-3}{x}$. Next, clear the fraction by multiplying both sides by x:

$$12x = 11-3$$

$$12x = 8$$

Finally, isolate x by dividing both sides by 12:

$$x=\frac{8}{12}\text{, or }\frac{2}{3}$$

The correct answer is C.

Cross-Multiplying and Clearing Radicals to Solve an Equation

If an equation equates two fractions, use **cross-multiplication** to eliminate the fractions. Combine each numerator with the denominator on the other side by multiplying diagonally across the equation. Then set one product equal to the other. (In effect, cross-multiplication is a shortcut method of multiplying both sides of the equation by both denominators.) Here's a simple example:

$$\frac{x}{3} = \frac{12}{2}$$
$$(2)(x) = (3)(12)$$
$$2x = 36$$
$$x = \frac{36}{2}, \text{ or } 18$$

If the variable appears under the square-root radical sign $\sqrt{\ }$, eliminate ("clear") the radical sign by squaring both sides of the equation. Use the same method to clear cube roots and other roots:

$$\sqrt[3]{2x} = 4$$
$$\left(\sqrt[3]{2x}\right)^3 = 4^3$$
$$2x = 64$$
$$x = 32$$

Be careful when you square both sides of an equation. In some instances, doing so will produce a variable such as x^2, in which case the equation is *quadratic* rather than linear. This means that it might have more than one solution. You'll examine quadratic equations later in this review.

EXAMPLE 3 (EASIER):

If $3\sqrt{2x} = 2$, then what is the value of x ?

A. $\frac{1}{18}$

B. $\frac{2}{9}$

C. $\frac{1}{3}$

D. $\frac{5}{4}$

First, clear the radical sign by squaring all items. In order to clear radicals, it is necessary to raise the radical to the index of the radical. Then the radical and its index cancel each other out.

$$3\sqrt{2x} = 2$$
$$9(2x) = 2^2$$
$$18x = 4$$
$$x = \frac{4}{18} = \frac{2}{9}$$

The correct answer is B.

EXAMPLE 4 (MORE CHALLENGING):

For what value of a does $\frac{7a}{8}$ equal $\frac{a+1}{3}$?

A. $\frac{8}{13}$

B. $\frac{7}{8}$

C. 2

D. $\frac{7}{3}$

First, cross-multiply (multiply diagonally across the equation) and equate the two products:

$$(3)(7a) = (8)(a + 1)$$

Next, combine terms (distribute 8 to both a and 1):

$$21a = 8a + 8$$

Next, isolate a-terms on one side by subtracting $8a$ from both sides; then combine the a-terms:

$$21a - 8a = 8a + 8 - 8a$$

$$13a = 8$$

Finally, isolate a by dividing both sides by 13:

$$\frac{13a}{13} = \frac{8}{13}$$

$$a = \frac{8}{13}$$

The correct answer is A.

LINEAR EQUATIONS IN TWO VARIABLES

In the preceding section, you examined linear equations in one variable only. Now we will consider linear equations in two variables x and y of the form $Ax + By = C$, where A, B, and C are real numbers. The left side of the equation is called a **linear combination of x and y.** Before, you were able to find the value of the variable by isolating it on one side of the equation. This is not so, however, for a linear equation in two (or more) different variables. Consider the following equation, which contains two variables:

$$x + 3 = y + 1$$

What is the value of x? It depends on the value of y, doesn't it? Similarly, the value of y depends on the value of x. Without more information about either x or y, you simply cannot find the other value. However, you *can* express x in terms of y, and you can express y in terms of x:

$$x = y - 2$$

$$y = x + 2$$

The two equations previously shown are really the same. You can't solve it because it contains two variables. Look at a more complex example: $4x - 9 = \frac{3}{2}y$.

Solve for *x* in terms of *y*:

$$4x = \frac{3}{2}y + 9$$

$$x = \frac{3}{8}y + \frac{9}{4}$$

Solve for *y* in terms of *x*:

$$\frac{4x - 9}{\frac{3}{2}} = y$$

$$\frac{2}{3}(4x - 9) = y$$

$$\frac{8}{3}x - 6 = y$$

To determine numerical values of *x* and *y*, you need a system of two linear equations with the same two variables. Given this system, there are two different methods for finding the values of the two variables: the substitution method and the addition-subtraction method.

The Substitution Method

To solve a system of two equations using the **substitution method**, follow these steps (we'll use *x* and *y* here):

1. In *either* equation isolate one variable (x) on one side.
2. Substitute the expression that equals x in place of x in the other equation.
3. Solve that equation for y.
4. Now that you know the value of y, plug it into *either* equation to find the value of x.

Consider these two equations:

Equation A: $x = 4y$
Equation B: $x - y = 1$

In equation B, substitute $4y$ for x, and then solve for y:

$$4y - y = 1$$

$$3y = 1$$

$$y = \frac{1}{3}$$

To find x, substitute $\frac{1}{3}$ for y into either equation. The value of x will be the same in either equation.

Equation A: $x = 4\left(\frac{1}{3}\right) = \frac{4}{3}$

Equation B: $x - \frac{1}{3} = 1;\ x = \frac{4}{3}$

The Addition-Subtraction Method

Another way to solve for two variables in a system of two equations is with the **addition-subtraction** method. Here are the steps:

1. "Line up" the two equations by listing the same variables and other terms in the same order. Place one equation above the other.
2. Make the coefficient of *either* variable the same in both equations (you can disregard the sign) by multiplying every term in one of the equations. (A **coefficient** is a variable's number. For example, in the term $7x$, the coefficient of x is 7.)
3. Add the two equations (work down to a sum for each term), or subtract one equation from the other, to eliminate one variable.

Consider these two equations:

Equation A: $x = 3 + 3y$
Equation B: $2x + y = 4$

In equation A, subtract $3y$ from both sides, so that all terms in the two equations "line up":

Equation A: $x - 3y = 3$
Equation B: $2x + y = 4$

To solve for y, multiply each term in Equation A by 2, so that the x-coefficient is the same in both equations:

Equation A: $2x - 6y = 6$
Equation B: $2x + y = 4$

Subtract Equation B from Equation A, thereby eliminating x, and then isolate y on one side of the equation:

$$\begin{array}{r} 2x - 6y = 6 \\ \underline{2x + y = 4} \\ 0x - 7y = 2 \\ -7y = 2 \\ y = -\frac{2}{7} \end{array}$$

Which Method Should You Use?

Which method you should use, substitution or addition-subtraction, depends on what the equations look like to begin with. To understand this point, look at this system of two equations:

$$\frac{2}{5}p + q = 3q10$$
$$q = 10 - p$$

Notice that the second equation is already set up nicely for the substitution method. But you could use addition-subtraction instead; you'd just have to rearrange the terms in both the equations first:

$$\frac{2}{5}p - 2q = -10$$
$$p + q = 10$$

Now, look at the following system:

$$3x + 4y = -8$$
$$x - 2y = \frac{1}{2}$$

Notice that the *x*-term and *y*-term already line up nicely here. Also notice that it's easy to match the coefficients of either *x* or *y*: multiply both sides of the second equation by either 3 or 2. This system is an ideal candidate for addition-subtraction. To appreciate this point, try using substitution instead. You'll discover that it takes far more number crunching.

In short, to solve a system of two linear equations in two variables, use addition-subtraction if you can quickly and easily eliminate one of the variables. Otherwise, use substitution.

EXAMPLE 5 (EASIER):

If $q = \frac{p}{10}$ and $q = 4.4 - p$, what is the value of $\frac{p}{q}$?

A. –4.4

B. 1.1

C. 2.2

D. 10

Since the question asks for $\frac{p}{q}$ (rather than either *p* or *q*), you can answer it by applying just the first of the two equations:

$$q = \frac{p}{10}$$
$$10q = p$$
$$10 = \frac{p}{q}$$

The correct answer is D.

EXAMPLE 6 (MORE CHALLENGING):

If $3x + 4y = -8$, and if $x - 2y = \frac{1}{2}$, what is the value of *x*?

A. –12

B. 9

C. $\frac{14}{5}$

D. $-\frac{7}{5}$

To solve for x, you want to eliminate y. You can multiply each term in the second equation by 2, and then add the equations:

$$\begin{array}{r} 3x + 4y = -8 \\ \underline{2x - 4y = 1} \\ 5x + 0y = -7 \\ x = -\frac{7}{5} \end{array}$$

The correct answer is D.

Let's walk through a graphing problem together.

$$\begin{cases} 3x - y = 1 \\ 4x - 2y = -1 \end{cases}$$

Solve the following system of equations using the graphing method:

First, solve both equations for y. Doing so puts the equations in **slope-intercept form**, which is the form from which it is easiest to graph a line.

$$\begin{cases} y = 3x - 1 \\ y = 2x + \frac{1}{2} \end{cases}$$

The first line has y-intercept of $(0, -1)$ and slope of 3, while the second line has y-intercept of $\left(0, \frac{1}{2}\right)$ and a slope of 2. The graphs are as follows:

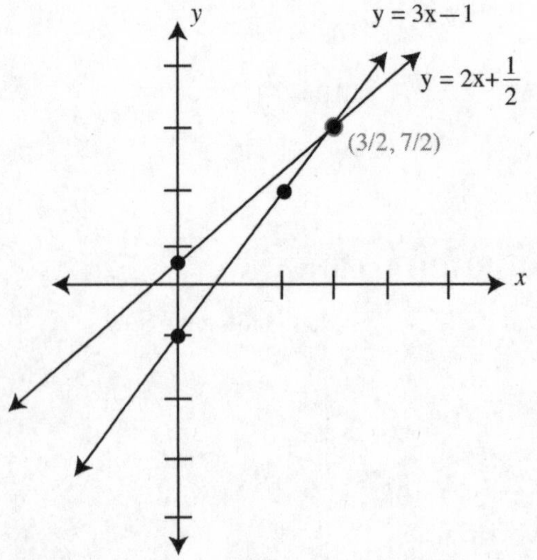

The intersection point of the graphs is the solution of the system. This point has coordinates $x = \frac{3}{2}$, $y = \frac{7}{2}$.

LINEAR EQUATIONS THAT CAN'T BE SOLVED

Never assume that one linear equation with one variable is solvable. If you can reduce the equation to $0 = 0$, then you can't solve it. In other words, the value of the variable could be any real number. Here's a simple example:

$$3x - 4 = 5x - 4 - 2x$$
$$3x - 4 = 3x - 4$$
$$0 = 0$$

In some cases, what appears to be a system of two equations in two variables might actually be the same equation expressed in two different ways. In other words, what you're really dealing with are two equivalent equations, which you cannot solve. Consider these two equations:

Equation A: $x + 4y = 16$
Equation B: $y = 4 - \frac{x}{4}$

If you multiply each term in Equation B by 4, you'll see that Equations A and B are the same:

Equation A: $x + 4y = 16$
Equation B: $4y = 16 - x$

Whenever you encounter a question that calls for solving one or more linear equations, and one answer choice provides something other than a numerical answer, size up the equation to see whether it's one of these two types of unsolvable problems. If so, then you have found your correct answer.

EXAMPLE 7 (EASIER):

If $-1 < x < 1$, and if $3x - 3 - 4x = x - 7 - 2x + 4$, then how many real numbers does the solution set for x contain?

A. 0
B. 1
C. 2
D. infinitely many

All terms on both sides cancel out:

$$3x - 3 - 4x = x - 7 - 2x + 4$$
$$-x - 3 = -x - 3$$
$$0 = 0$$

Thus, x could equal any real number between -1 and 1 (not just the integer 0).
The correct answer is D.

EXAMPLE 8 (MORE CHALLENGING):

$2b = 60 - 2a$, and $a + b = 30$. What is the value of a?

A. –10

B. 10

C. 12

D. No solution is possible.

An unwary test taker might assume that the values of both a and b can be determined with both equations together, because they appear at first glance to provide a system of two linear equations with two unknowns. But they don't. You can rewrite the first equation so that it is identical to the second:

$$2b = 60 - 2a$$
$$2b = 2(30 - a)$$
$$b = 30 - a$$
$$a + b = 30$$

As you can see, the equation $2b = 60 - 2a$ is identical to the equation $a + b = 30$. Thus, a and b could each be any real number. You can't solve one equation in two variables. **The correct answer is D.**

SOLVING ALGEBRAIC INEQUALITIES

You solve algebraic inequalities in the same manner as equations. Isolate the variable on one side of the equation, factoring and canceling wherever possible. However, one important rule distinguishes inequalities from equations:

RULE: Whenever you multiply or divide by a negative number, you must *reverse* the inequality symbol. Expressed in symbolic form: if $a > b$, then $-a < -b$.

The following simple example demonstrates this important rule:

$12 - 4x < 8$ (original inequality)

$-4x < -4$ (subtract 12 from both sides; inequality unchanged)

$x > 1$ (both sides divided by – 4; inequality reversed)

Here are some additional rules for dealing with algebraic inequalities.

1. Adding or subtracting unequal quantities to (or from) equal quantities:

   If $a > b$, then $c + a > c + b$

2. Adding unequal quantities to unequal quantities:

   If $a > b$, and if $c > d$, then $a + c > b + d$

3. Comparing three unequal quantities:

   If $a > b$, and if $b > c$, then $a > c$

4. Combining the same **positive** quantity with unequal quantities by multiplication or division:

   If $a > b$, and if $x > 0$, then $xa > xb$

   If $a > b$, and if $x > 0$, then $\frac{a}{x} > \frac{b}{x}$

   If $a > b$, and if $x > 0$, then $\frac{x}{a} < \frac{x}{b}$

5. Combining the same **negative** quantity with unequal quantities by multiplication or division:

   If $a > b$, and if $x < 0$, then $xa < xb$

   If $a > b$, and if $x < 0$, then $\frac{a}{x} < \frac{b}{x}$

   If $a > b$, and if $x < 0$, then $\frac{x}{a} > \frac{x}{b}$

EXAMPLE 9 (EASIER):

If $-2x > -5$, then which of the inequalities holds true?

A. $x > \frac{5}{2}$

B. $x < \frac{5}{2}$

C. $x > -\frac{2}{5}$

D. $x < \frac{2}{5}$

Divide both sides of the equation by –2, and reverse the inequality:

$$-2x > -5$$
$$\frac{-2x}{-2} < \frac{-5}{-2}$$
$$x < \frac{5}{2}$$

The correct answer is B.

Now that you know how to solve inequalities, let's go one more step and work on graphing them on a number line.

Take the following inequality: $\frac{1}{2}\left(\frac{5}{2} - 4x\right) < -10$.

First, solve:

$$\frac{1}{2}\left(\frac{5}{2} - 4x\right) < -10$$
$$\frac{5}{4} - 2x < -10$$
$$5 - 8x < -40$$
$$-8x < -45$$
$$x > \frac{45}{8}$$

Note that the inequality is reversed because you divided both sides by –8.

Next, graph the inequality on a number line. The dot over the $\frac{45}{8}$ is empty because the inequality sign is a >, not a ≥:

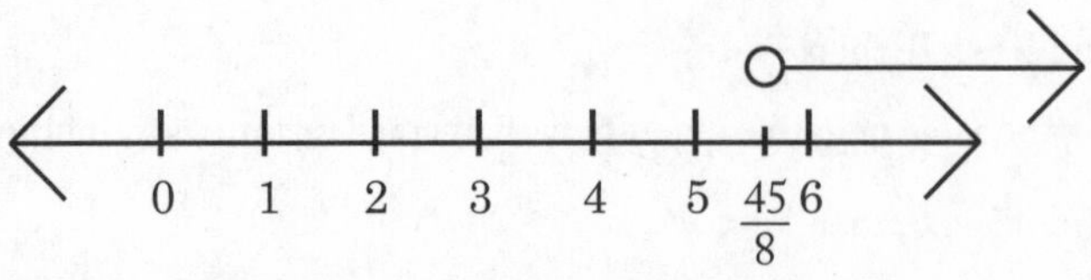

EXAMPLE 10 (MORE CHALLENGING):

Dave has \$150 to spend to buy tickets to go to a baseball game. The stadium charges a \$12 fee for buying tickets. The inequality $12 + 30n \leq 150$ represents the number of tickets, n, Dave can afford. Graph all possible numbers of tickets that Dave can buy.

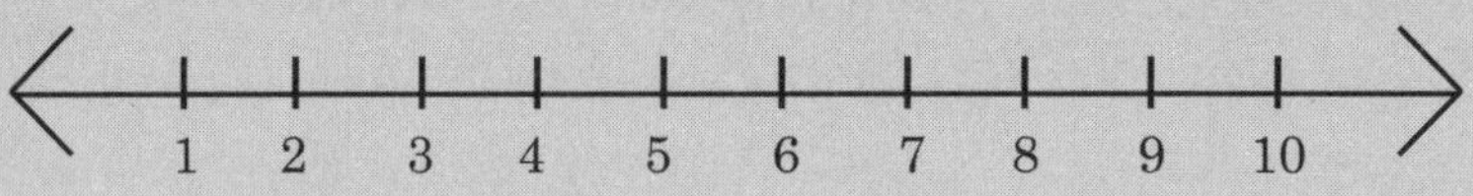

To solve the inequality $12 + 30n \leq 150$, subtract the one-time cost of \$12 from both sides of the inequality. This results in a new inequality: $30n \leq 138$. Dividing both sides by 30 will result in $n \leq 4.6$. Since tickets can only be purchased in whole number quantities, the range of valid answers would be 1, 2, 3, 4 and plotted on a number line like this:

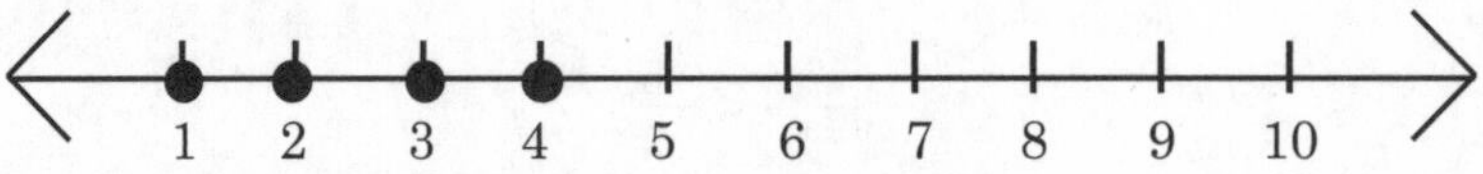

The correct answers are 1, 2, 3, and 4.

EXAMPLE 11 (MORE CHALLENGING):

Jennifer is moving from Boston to New York City, a distance of 220 miles. She needs to rent a truck one way to move her belongings. The rental of a truck is \$100 and the cost for fuel for this trip is \$75. Depending on where she rents the truck, there will be a varying fee per mile driven. If her moving budget is \$400, which inequality below shows how big a fee per mile she will be able to afford when renting a truck?

A. $175x + 220 \geq 400$

B. $175x + 220 \leq 400$

C. $220x + 175 \geq 400$

D. $220x + 175 \leq 400$

Add the fixed costs of \$175 (fuel + truck rental) to the variable cost per mile (x) multiplied by 220 and put it in a ≤ relationship with the total budget of \$400. **The correct answer is D.**

FACTORABLE QUADRATIC EXPRESSIONS (ONE VARIABLE)

A **quadratic expression** includes a squared variable, such as x^2. An equation is quadratic if you can express it in the general form $ax^2 + bx + c = 0$, and a linear inequality is quadratic if you can express it in the general form $ax + bx < c$ (or with any of the other three inequality signs), where:

x is the variable

a, b, and c are integers

$a \neq 0$

b can equal 0

c can equal 0

Examples: (Notice that the b-term and c-term are not essential; in other words, either b or c, or both, can equal 0.)

Equation: $2w^2 = 16$

General quadratic form: $2w^2 - 16 = 0$ (no b-term)

Equation: $x^2 = 3x$

General quadratic form: $x^2 - 3x = 0$ (no c-term)

Equation: $3y = 4 - y^2$

General quadratic form: $y^2 + 3y - 4 = 0$

Equation: $7z = 2z^2 - 15$

General quadratic form: $2z^2 - 7z - 15 = 0$

Every quadratic equation has exactly two solutions, called **roots**. (But the two roots might be the same.) On the test, you will probably be able to find the two roots by **factoring**.

To solve any factorable quadratic equation, follow these three steps:

1. Put the equation into the standard form: $ax^2 + bx + c = 0$.
2. Factor the terms on the left side of the equation into two linear expressions (with no exponents).
3. Set each linear expression (root) equal to zero and solve for the variable in each one.

Some quadratic expressions are easier to factor than others. If either of the two constants b or c is zero, factoring is very simple. In fact, in some cases, no factoring is needed at all.

A factorable quadratic equation with no *c*-term:

$$2x^2 = x$$
$$2x^2 - x = 0$$
$$x(2x - 1) = 0$$
$$x = 0, \quad 2x - 1 = 0$$
$$x = 0, \frac{1}{2}$$

A factorable quadratic equation with no *b*-term:

$$2x^2 - 4 = 0$$
$$2(x^2 - 2) = 0$$
$$x^2 - 2 = 0$$
$$x^2 = 2$$
$$x = \sqrt{2}, -\sqrt{2}$$

When dealing with a quadratic equation, your first step is usually to put it into the general form $ax^2 + bx + c = 0$. But keep in mind: The only essential term is ax^2.

A **binomial** is an algebraic expression that contains *two* terms. You can rewrite the product of two binomials by multiplying each term in one binomial by each term in the other, adding together all four terms. To organize this task, apply the **FOIL** method:

(F) the product of the **first** terms of the two binomials

(O) the product of the **outer** terms of the two binomials

(I) the product of the **inner** terms of the two binomials

(L) the product of the **last** (second) terms of the two binomials

Here are two simple demonstrations of the FOIL method:

$(x + 2)(x + 3) = x^2$ **(F)** $+ 3x$ **(O)** $+ 2x$ **(I)** $+ 6$ **(L)** $= x^2 + 5x + 6$

$(2x - 1)(x + 1) = 2x^2$ **(F)** $+ 2x$ **(O)** $- x$ **(I)** $- 1$ **(L)** $= 2x^2 + x - 1$

In both examples, notice that the two middle terms, **(O)** and **(I)**, can be combined. The simplified result is a **trinomial**, which is an algebraic expression that contains *three* terms. On the test, quadratic trinomials are generally *factorable* into two binomials.

Factoring trinomials often involves a bit of trial and error. You need to apply the FOIL method *in reverse*. To accomplish this task, keep in mind the following relationships between the general quadratic form $ax^2 + bx + c$ and the FOIL method:

(F) is the first term (ax^2) of the quadratic expression

(O + I) is the second term (bx) of the quadratic expression

(L) is the third term (c) of the quadratic expression

To factor the quadratic expression $x^2 + 3x + 2$, for example, first identify its components:

(F) $= x^2$

(O + I) $= 3x$

(L) $= 2$

Then create a binomial "shell" to fill in numbers as you determine them. Remember: in the general quadratic form, a, b, and c are all *integers*, so all coefficients and other numbers in both binomials must be integers. In this example, since **(F)** is x^2, the first term in each binomial must be x:

$$(x + ?)(x + ?)$$

Since **(L)** is 2, the product of the two last terms (signified by "?") must be 2. The only possibilities are 2 and 1 or –2 and –1. Try them both:

$$(x + 2)(x + 1) = x^2 + 2x + x + 2$$

$$(x - 2)(x - 1) = x^2 - 2x - x + 2$$

As you can see, the first option is the one that simplifies to $x^2 + 3x + 2$.

Remember that on the GED Mathematical Reasoning Test, quadratic trinomials will probably be factorable into two binomials, so you can apply the FOIL method to determine them.

EXAMPLE 12 (EASIER):

Which of the following is a factor of $x^2 - x - 6$?

A. $(x + 1)$

B. $(x - 3)$

C. $(x - 2)$

D. $(x + 3)$

Notice that x^2 has no coefficient. This makes the process of factoring into two binomials easier. Set up two binomial shells: $(x + ?)(x + ?)$. The product of the two missing second terms (the 'L' term under the FOIL method) is –6. The possible integral pairs that result in this product are (1, –6),

(–1, 6), (2, –3,), and (–2, 3). Notice that the second term in the trinomial is $-x$. This means that the sum of the two integers whose product is –6 must be –1. The pair (2, –3) fits the bill. Thus, the trinomial is equivalent to the product of the two binomials $(x + 2)$ and $(x - 3)$. To check your work, multiply the two binomials, using the FOIL method:

$$\begin{aligned}(x+2)(x-3) &= x^2 - 3x + 2x - 6 \\ &= x^2 - x - 6\end{aligned}$$

The correct answer is B.

EXAMPLE 13 (MORE CHALLENGING):

How many different values of x does the solution set for the equation $4x^2 = 4x - 1$ contain?

A. none

B. one

C. two

D. four

First, express the equation in standard form: $4x^2 - 4x + 1 = 0$. Notice that the *c*-term is 1. The only two integral pairs that result in this product are (1,1) and (–1,–1). Since the *b*-term $(-4x)$ is negative, the integral pair whose product is 1 must be (–1,–1). Set up a binomial shell:

$$(? - 1)(? - 1)$$

Notice that the *a*-term contains the coefficient 4. The possible integral pairs that result in this product are (1, 4), (2, 2), (–1, –4), and (–2, –2). A bit of trial-and-error reveals that only the pair (2, 2) works. Thus, in factored form, the equation becomes $(2x - 1)(2x - 1) = 0$.

To check your work, multiply the two binomials, using the FOIL method:

$$\begin{aligned}(2x-1)(2x-1) &= 4x^2 - 2x - 2x + 1 \\ &= 4x^2 - 4x + 1\end{aligned}$$

Since the two binomial factors are the same, the two roots of the equation are the same. In other words, x has only one possible value. **The correct answer is B.**

(Although you don't need to find the value of x in order to answer the question, solve for x in the equation $2x - 1 = 0$; $x = \frac{1}{2}$.)

When solving quadratic equations with rational coefficients, it is most effective to first eliminate the fractions by multiplying both sides by the LCD of all fractions involved. Then, proceed to solve the resulting quadratic equation as you would one with integer coefficients.

For example, take the quadratic equation $\frac{3}{4}x^2 - \frac{5}{2}x - 2 = 0$.

To solve, first multiply both sides by 4 to clear the fractions. Doing so yields the equivalent equation $3x^2 - 10x - 8 = 0$. Now, factor the left side and solve:

$$3x^2 - 10x - 8 = 0$$
$$(3x + 2)(x - 4) = 0$$
$$x = -\frac{2}{3}, 4$$

FACTORABLE QUADRATIC EXPRESSIONS (TWO VARIABLES)

In the world of math, solving nonlinear equations in two or more variables can be *very* complicated. But for the test, all you need to remember are these three general forms:

Sum of two variables, squared:
$(x + y)^2 = x^2 + 2xy + y^2$

Difference of two variables, squared:
$(x - y)^2 = x^2 - 2xy + y^2$

Difference of two squares:
$x^2 - y^2 = (x + y)(x - y)$

You can verify these equations using the FOIL method:

$$\begin{aligned}&(x + y)^2\\&= (x + y)(x + y)\\&= x^2 + xy + xy + y^2\\&= x^2 + 2xy + y^2\end{aligned}$$

$$\begin{aligned}&(x - y)^2\\&= (x - y)(x - y)\\&= x^2 - xy - xy + y^2\\&= x^2 - 2xy + y^2\end{aligned}$$

$$\begin{aligned}&(x + y)(x - y)\\&= x^2 + xy - xy - y^2\\&= x^2 - y^2\end{aligned}$$

Memorize the three equation forms listed here. When you see one of these forms on the exam, you will probably need to convert it to another form.

EXAMPLE 14 (EASIER):

If $x^2 - y^2 = 100$, and if $x + y = 2$, then what is the value of $x - y$?

A. –2
B. 10
C. 20
D. 50

If you recognize the difference of two squares when you see the form, you can handle this question with ease. Use the third equation you just learned, substituting 2 for $(x + y)$, then solving for $(x - y)$:

$$x^2 - y^2 = (x + y)(x - y)$$
$$100 = (x + y)(x - y)$$
$$100 = (2)(x - y)$$
$$50 = (x - y)$$

The correct answer is D.

EXAMPLE 15 (MORE CHALLENGING):

If $\frac{x+y}{x-y} = \frac{x+y}{x}$, which of the following expresses the value of x in terms of y?

A. $-y$

B. y^2

C. $\frac{y}{2}$

D. $y-1$

Apply the cross-product method to eliminate fractions. Rewrite the equation in its unfactored form. (If you recognize the difference of two squares, you'll rewrite more quickly.) Simplify, and then solve for x:

$$x(x + y) = (x - y)(x + y)$$
$$x^2 + xy = x^2 - y^2$$
$$xy = -y^2$$
$$x = -y$$

The correct answer is A.

FUNCTIONS

In a **function** or **functional relationship**, the value of one variable depends upon the value of, or is "a function of," another variable. In mathematics, the relationship is expressed in the form $y = f(x)$—where y is a function of x.

To find the value of the function for any value of x, simply substitute the x-value for x wherever it appears in the function. In the following function, for example, the function of 2 is 14, and the function of –3 is 4.

$$f(x) = x^2 + 3x + 4$$
$$f(2) = 2^2 + 3(2) + 4 = 4 + 6 + 4 = 14$$
$$f(-3) = (-3)^2 + 3(-3) + 4 = 9 - 9 + 4 = 4$$

Determine the function of a variable expression the same way—just substitute the expression for x throughout the function. In the function above, here is how you would find $f(2 + a)$:

$$\begin{aligned} f(2+a) &= (2+a)^2 + 3(2+a) - 4 \\ &= 4 + 4a + a^2 + 6 + 3a - 4 \\ &= a^2 + 7a + 6 \end{aligned}$$

A challenging function question might ask you to apply the same function twice.

EXAMPLE 16 (EASIER):

If $f(a) = 9$, then for which function does $a = 6$?

A. $f(a) = 9a$

B. $f(a) = 3$

C. $f(a) = a + 3$

D. $f(a) = \frac{2}{3}a$

In each answer choice, substitute 9 for $f(a)$, and substitute 6 for a. Of the four functions listed, only the one in choice C holds true: $9 = 6 + 3$. **The correct answer is C.**

EXAMPLE 17 (MORE CHALLENGING):

If $f(x) = 2x$, then $\frac{1}{f(x)} \times f\left(\frac{2}{x}\right)$ is equal to which of the following expressions?

A. $\frac{1}{x}$

B. 1

C. $\frac{x^2}{2}$

D. $\frac{2}{x^2}$

To rewrite the first term, simply substitute $2x$ for $f(x)$. To rewrite the second term, substitute $\frac{2}{x}$ for x in the function $f(x) = 2x$. Then combine the terms by multiplication:

$$\frac{1}{f(x)} \times f\left(\frac{2}{x}\right) = \left(\frac{1}{2x}\right)\left(2 \times \frac{2}{x}\right) = \frac{4}{2x^2} = \frac{2}{x^2}$$

The correct answer is D.

A function is a relationship between two quantities. It can be expressed using a table of values, a formula, or a graph. Its domain is the set of inputs that can be substituted in for the variable and produce a meaningful output. A function can have only *one output* for each input. The following are examples of relationships between two variables that are NOT functions.

x	-1	2	-1	1	1	3	0
y	4	1	3	2	3	4	1

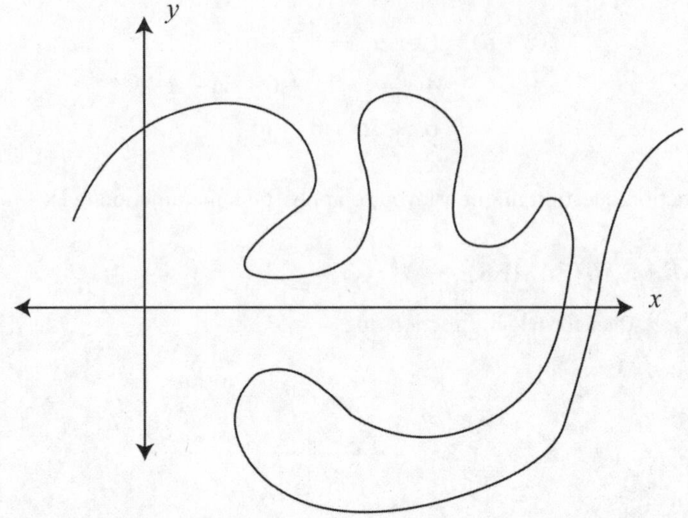

If you are given a formula for a function, you can evaluate it at any value in its domain. Once you substitute a value for the variable, you simply simplify the resulting numerical expression using the order of operations.

For example, to evaluate $f(x) = -2x + 5$ at $x = -3$, substitute in -3 wherever there is an x term and then simplify:

$$f(-3) = -2(-3) + 5 = 6 + 5 = 11$$

To evaluate $g(x) = 3x^2 - 4x - 1$ at $x = -4$, substitute in -4 wherever there is an x term and then simplify:

$$g(-4) = 3(-4)^2 - 4(-4) - 1 = 3(16) + 16 - 1 = 48 + 16 - 1 = 63$$

Functions arise when modeling various situations. Certain features of their graphs have important meaning in applied contexts. Here are a few you should know:

- **Linear versus nonlinear**: If the points all lie on a straight line, the graph is *linear*. Otherwise, the graph is *nonlinear*.
- **Increasing versus decreasing**: If the graph rises from left to right, it is *increasing*. If the graph falls from left to right, it is *decreasing*.
- **Maximum versus minimum:** The point higher than all others is the *maximum*, while the point lower than all others is the *minimum*.

Let's look at how this might appear on your exam. Say the entranceway to a theater is shaped like a parabolic arc described by the quadratic function $f(x) = 8x - x^2$. Sketch the entranceway and indicate the height of the tallest part of the entranceway and the length of the base.

The function can be written as $f(x) = x(8 - x)$; the x-intercepts are 0 and 8, so the length of the base is 8 feet. The vertex occurs halfway between at $x = 4$; the height at this value is $f(4) = 8(4) - 4^2 = 16$ feet.

The graph is as follows:

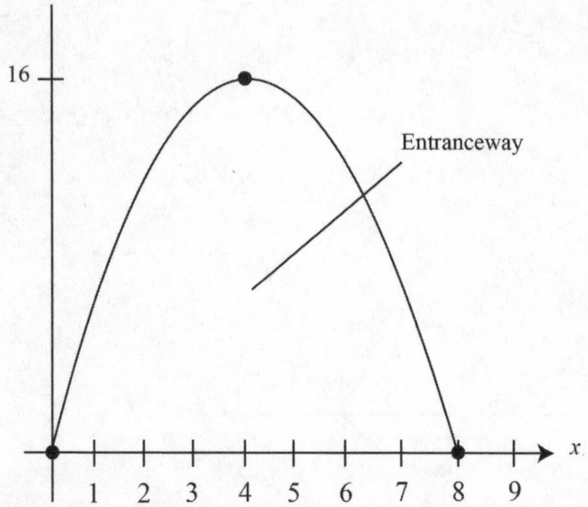

Often, you need to compare two linear functions or two quadratic functions expressed in different ways. That is, one might be graphed, and the other may be expressed using a table of values or an explicit formula. To make the comparison, you need to extract the important characteristics of each function. The first example below shows how to make a comparison for two proportional relationships. The second one shows how to do so for quadratic functions.

Compare the following two scenarios. Which car will have traveled farther after 8 hours?

Scenario I	Scenario II
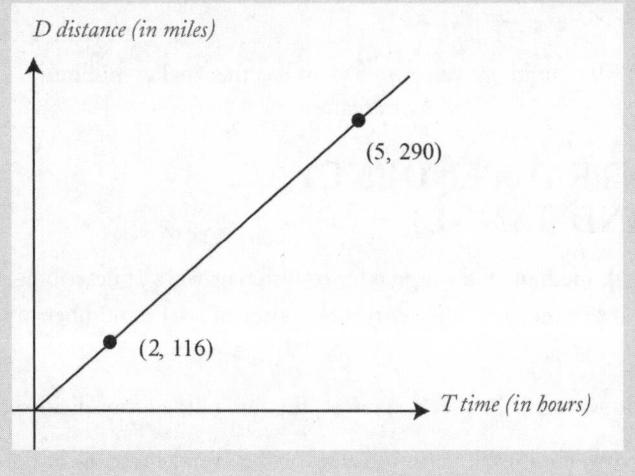	$D(t) = 62t$ t is the number of hours traveled $D(t)$ is the number of miles traveled after t hours

Since both linear functions have y-intercept (0, 0), the slope (which gives the speed) will determine which car traveled farther. The slope of the linear function in Scenario I is $\frac{290-116}{5-2} = \frac{174}{3} = 58$. The slope of the linear function in Scenario II is 62. So the car in Scenario II will have traveled farther after 8 hours.

Which of the following quadratic functions has the smaller minimum?

Scenario I	Scenario II
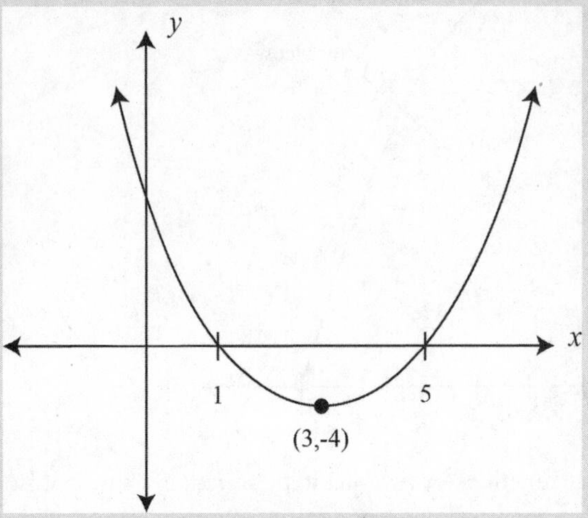	$f(x) = 2x^2 - 4x - 3$

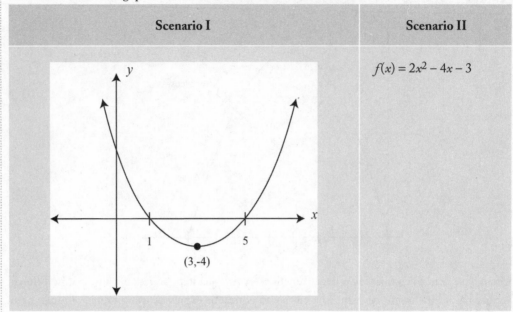

The minimum of a quadratic function that opens upward is the y-coordinate of the vertex. For Scenario I, this minimum value is –4. For Scenario II, you must complete the square to find the vertex:

$$\begin{aligned} f(x) &= 2x^2 - 4x - 3 \\ &= 2\left(x^2 - 2x\right) - 3 \\ &= 2\left(x^2 - 2x + 1\right) - 3 - 2 \\ &= 2(x-1)^2 - 5 \end{aligned}$$

The vertex in Scenario II is $(1, -5)$. Its minimum value is –5, so it has the smaller minimum.

MEASURES OF CENTRAL TENDENCY (MEAN, MEDIAN, AND RANGE)

Arithmetic mean (simple average), **median**, and **range** refer to different ways of describing a set of numbers with just one number. Each measures the **central tendency** of a set of numbers. Here's the definition of each term:

Arithmetic mean (simple average): In a set of n terms, the sum of the terms divided by n.

Median: In a set of n terms, the middle term in value, or the average (mean) of the two middle terms if the number of terms is even.

Range: The difference in value between the greatest and the least term in a set.

For example, given a set of six numbers {8, –4, 8, 3, 2, and 7}:

$$\textbf{mean} = \mathbf{4}\left(\frac{8-4+8+3+2+7}{6} = \frac{24}{6} = 4\right)$$

median = **5** (the average of 3 and 7, which are the two middle terms in value: {–4, 2, 3, 7, 8, 8}

range = **12** (the difference on the number line between 8 and –4)

The mean and median might be the same, or they might differ from each other (as in the previous example).

Questions involving arithmetic mean usually involve calculating the arithmetic mean by adding terms together ($a + b + c + \ldots$) and dividing the sum by the number of terms (n):

$$\text{mean} = \frac{(a + b + c + \ldots)}{n}$$

But a question might instead require you to find a missing term when the arithmetic mean of all the terms is known. To solve this type of problem, plug what you know into the arithmetic mean formula. Then, use algebra to find the missing number. For example, if the average of 2 and another number (N) is 5, here's how you would find the value of N:

$$5 = \frac{2+N}{2}$$
$$10 = 2 + N$$
$$8 = N$$

Approach arithmetic mean problems that involve variables (such as a and b) the same way as those involving only numbers.

EXAMPLE 18 (EASIER):

What is the mean (simple average) of $\frac{1}{5}$, 25%, and 0.09 ?

A. 0.18

B. $\frac{1}{4}$

C. 0.32

D. $\frac{1}{3}$

Since the answer choices are not all expressed in the same form, first convert numbers into whichever form you think would be easiest to work with when you add the numbers together. In this case, the easiest form to work with is probably the decimal number form. So convert the first two numbers into decimal form, and then find the sum of the three numbers:

$$0.20 + 0.25 + 0.09 = 0.54$$

Finally, divide by 3 to find the average:

$$0.54 \div 3 = 0.18$$

The correct answer is A.

EXAMPLE 19 (MORE CHALLENGING):

If A is the average of P, Q, and another number, which of the following represents the missing number?

A. $\frac{1}{3}(A+P+Q)$

B. $3A-P+Q$

C. $A-P+Q$

D. $3A-P-Q$

Let x = the missing number. Solve for x by the arithmetic mean formula:

$$A = \frac{P+Q+x}{3}$$
$$3A = P+Q+x$$
$$3A-P-Q = x$$

The correct answer is D.

ARITHMETIC SERIES

In an **arithmetic series** of numbers, there is a constant (unchanging) difference between successive numbers in the series. In other words, all numbers in an arithmetic series are evenly spaced on the number line. All of the following are examples of arithmetic series:

- Successive integers
- Successive even integers
- Successive odd integers
- Successive multiples of the same number
- Successive integers ending in the same digit

An arithmetic-series question might ask for the *mean* (average) of a series, or it might ask for the *sum*. Since the numbers are evenly spaced, the mean and median of the series are the same. To find the mean, instead of adding all the terms and then dividing, you can find the median or, even easier, compute the average of the least number and the greatest numbers (the endpoints of the series). Faced with calculating the average of a series of evenly spaced integers, you can shortcut the addition. Study the following examples:

The mean (and median) of all *even* integers 20 through 40 is $\frac{20+40}{2} = \frac{60}{2} = 30$.

The mean (and median) of all integers –11 through 20 is $\frac{-11+20}{2} = \frac{9}{2} = 4\frac{1}{2}$.

The mean (and median) of all positive two-digit numbers ending in the digit 5 is $\frac{15+95}{2}=\frac{110}{2}=55$.

The mean (and median) of all integers greater than −100 but less than 100 is $\frac{-99+99}{2}=0$. (The set's negative and positive numbers all cancel out.)

Finding the sum of an arithmetic (evenly spaced) series of numbers requires only one additional step: multiplying the average (which is also the median) by the number of terms in the series. When calculating the sum, be careful to count the number of terms in the series correctly. For instance, the number of positive *odd* integers less than 50 is 25, but the number of positive *even* integers less than 50 is only 24.

EXAMPLE 20 (EASIER):

What is the average of the first 20 positive integers?

A. $7\frac{1}{2}$

B. $10\frac{1}{2}$

C. 15

D. 20

Since the terms are evenly spaced (an arithmetic series), take the average of the first term (1) and the last term (20):

$$\frac{1+20}{2}=\frac{21}{2}\text{, or }10\frac{1}{2}$$

The correct answer is B.

EXAMPLE 21 (MORE CHALLENGING):

What is the sum of all odd integers *between* 10 and 40?

A. 250

B. 325

C. 375

D. 400

The average of the described numbers is $\frac{11+39}{2}=\frac{50}{2}$, or 25. The number of terms in the series is 15. (The first term is 11, and the last term is 39.) The sum of the described series of integers $= 25 \times 15 = 375$. **The correct answer is C.**

PROBABILITY

Probability refers to the statistical chances, or "odds," of an event occurring (or not occurring). By definition, probability ranges from 0 to 1. Probability is never negative, and it's never greater than 1. Here's the basic formula for determining probability:

$$\text{Probability} = \frac{\text{number of ways the event can occur}}{\text{total number of possible occurrences}}$$

Probability can be expressed as a fraction, a percent, or a decimal number. The greater the probability, the greater the fraction, percent, or decimal number.

Determining Probability (Single Event)

Probability plays an integral role in games of chance, including many casino games. In the throw of a single die, for example, the probability of rolling a 5 is "one in six," or $\frac{1}{6}$, or $16\frac{2}{3}\%$. Of course, the probability of rolling a certain other number is the same. A standard deck of 52 playing cards contains 12 face cards. The probability of selecting a face card from a full deck is $\frac{12}{52}$, or $\frac{3}{13}$. The probability of selecting a queen from a full deck is $\frac{4}{52}$, or $\frac{1}{13}$.

To calculate the probability of an event NOT occurring, just subtract the probability of the event occurring from 1.

EXAMPLE 22 (EASIER):

If you randomly select one candy from a jar containing two cherry candies, two licorice candies, and one peppermint candy, what is the probability of selecting a cherry candy?

A. $\frac{1}{6}$
B. $\frac{1}{3}$
C. $\frac{2}{5}$
D. $\frac{3}{5}$

There are two ways among five possible occurrences that a cherry candy will be selected. Thus, the probability of selecting a cherry candy is $\frac{2}{5}$. **The correct answer is C.**

EXAMPLE 23 (MORE CHALLENGING):

A bag of marbles contains twice as many red marbles as blue marbles, and twice as many blue marbles as green marbles. If these are the only colors of marbles in the bag, what is the probability of randomly picking from the bag a marble that is NOT blue?

A. $\frac{2}{9}$

B. $\frac{2}{5}$

C. $\frac{2}{7}$

D. $\frac{5}{7}$

Regardless of the number of marbles in the bag, the red-blue-green marble ratio is 4:2:1. As you can see, blue marbles account for $\frac{2}{7}$ of the total number of marbles. Thus, the probability of picking a marble that is NOT blue is $1 - \frac{2}{7} = \frac{5}{7}$.

The correct answer is D.

Determining Probability (Two Events)

To determine probability involving two or more events, it is important to distinguish probabilities involving **independent** events from an event that is **dependent** on another one.

Two events are independent if neither event affects the probability that the other will occur. The events may involve the random selection of one object from *each of two or more groups*. Or they may involve the random selection of one object from a group, then *replacing* it and selecting again (as in a "second round" or "another turn" of a game).

In either scenario, to find the probability of two events BOTH occurring, multiply together their individual probabilities:

probability of event 1 occurring

×

probability of event 2 occurring

=

probability of both events occurring

For example, assume that you randomly select one letter from each of two sets: {A, B} and {C, D, E}. The probability of selecting A and C $= \frac{1}{2} \times \frac{1}{3} = \frac{1}{6}$.

To calculate the probability that two events will NOT BOTH occur, subtract the probability of both events occurring from 1.

Now let's look at dependent probability. Two distinct events might be related in that one event affects the probability of the other one occurring—for example, randomly selecting one object from a group, then selecting a second object from the same group without replacing the first selection. Removing one object from the group increases the odds of selecting any particular object from those that remain.

For example, assume that you randomly select one letter from the set {A, B, C, D}. Then, from the remaining three letters, you select another letter. What is the probability of selecting both A and B? To answer this question, you need to consider each of the two selections separately.

In the first selection, the probability of selecting either A or B is $\frac{2}{4}$. But the probability of selecting the second of the two is $\frac{1}{3}$. Why? Because after the first selection, only *three* letters remain from which to select. Since the question asks for the odds of selecting both A and B (as opposed to either one), multiply the two individual probabilities: $\frac{2}{4} \times \frac{1}{3} = \frac{2}{12}$, or $\frac{1}{6}$.

EXAMPLE 24 (EASIER):

A gaming die is a cube with numbers 1–6 on its faces, each number on a different face. In a roll of two gaming dice, what is the probability that the two numbers facing up will total 12?

A. $\frac{1}{64}$

B. $\frac{1}{36}$

C. $\frac{1}{12}$

D. $\frac{1}{9}$

The only two-number combination on the dice that can total 12 is 6 + 6. The probability of rolling 6 on each die is $\frac{1}{6}$. Accordingly, the probability of rolling 6 on both dice is $\frac{1}{6} \times \frac{1}{6} = \frac{1}{36}$. **The correct answer is B.**

EXAMPLE 25 (MORE CHALLENGING):

Two pairs of socks are randomly removed from a drawer containing five pairs: two black, two white, and one blue. What is the probability of first removing a black pair and then, without replacement, removing a white pair from the drawer?

A. $\frac{1}{10}$

B. $\frac{1}{5}$

C. $\frac{1}{3}$

D. $\frac{2}{5}$

When removing the first pair, the probability that the pair removed will be black is $\frac{2}{5}$. Four pairs of socks remain, two of which are white. The probability of removing a white pair of socks from among those four is $\frac{2}{4}$. Combine the two probabilities by multiplying:

$$\frac{2}{5} \times \frac{2}{4} = \frac{4}{20}, \text{ or } \frac{1}{5}$$

The correct answer is B.

COUNTING PRINCIPLES

Determining the *total* number of possible outcomes in an experiment, whether tossing a coin 5 times, rolling a die twice, or randomly selecting colored balls from a bin, is an important step to assessing likelihood, or chance, of getting each possible outcome. Answering this question type requires a systematic way of counting that includes two main concepts: combinations and permutations.

A **permutation** of a set of objects is an arrangement of those objects in which each object is used once and only once. For example, if you have objects labeled A, B, C, D, and E, some permutations of these objects are ABCDE and DECBA. Any unique ordering of the letters produces a different permutation. The number of ways to arrange n objects in such a manner is $n!$.

Sometimes, we want to arrange only *some* of the objects in a given set. That is, what if we had n letters but we only wanted to arrange k of them? This is a "permutation of n objects taken k at a time." The number of such arrangements is written as:

$$P(n,k) = \frac{n!}{(n-k)!}$$

Before we look at an example, let's define $n!$.

$$n! = n \times (n-1) \times (n-2) \times \ \ldots \ \times 3 \times 2 \times 1.$$

For instance, $4! = 4 \times 3 \times 2 \times 1$. Let's look at an example.

EXAMPLE 26:

In how many ways can 4 books from a collection of 7 be arranged on a shelf?

A. 120

B. 210

C. 720

D. 840

We wish to arrange 4 of the 7 books, so we must calculate $P(7, 4)$:

$$P(7,4) = \frac{7!}{(7-4)!} = \frac{7!}{3!} = \frac{7 \times 6 \times 5 \times 4 \times \cancel{3} \times \cancel{2} \times \cancel{1}}{\cancel{3} \times \cancel{2} \times \cancel{1}} = 7 \times 6 \times 5 \times 4 = 840$$

The correct answer is D.

Sometimes, the order in which objects are arranged is not relevant, like when forming a committee of 4 people from a group of 10 people in which all committee members have the same influence, or when simply selecting 5 cards randomly from a standard deck of 52 cards. To determine the number of such selections, a **combination** is required.

The number of ways of selecting k objects from a group of n objects in which order does NOT matter is called the "number of combinations of n objects taken k at a time." The formula is as follows:

$$C(n,k) = \frac{n!}{k!(n-k)!}$$

EXAMPLE 27:

Max found 10 used books in a clearance bin that he likes equally well, but he only has enough money to purchase 3 of them. In how many different ways can he select 3 books to purchase?

A. 120

B. 500

C. 720

D. 910

Order does not matter here because Max is simply purchasing a collection of unrelated books. (He is not, as in the previous example, ordering them in a certain way on a shelf.) So we use the combinations formula with $n = 10$ and $k = 3$:

$$C(10,3) = \frac{10!}{3!(10-3)!} = \frac{10!}{3!7!} = \frac{10 \times 9 \times 8 \times \cancel{7!}}{(3 \times 2 \times 1) \times \cancel{7!}} = 120$$

The correct answer is A.

GRAPHING DATA SETS

Numerical data sets can be visualized in various ways. Three common types of graphs are **dot plots, histograms** and **box plots**. Let's take a look at each by illustrating the data set {1, 1, 1, 2, 3, 3, 6, 6, 6, 6, 6, 10} using a dot plot, histogram, and box plot.

A dot plot is plot obtained by illustrating each member of a data set as a point above the appropriate position on a number line, as follows:

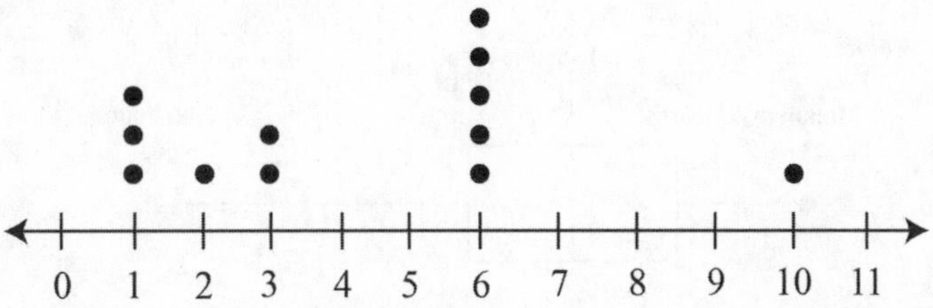

In a histogram, bars appear above each value of the data set. The height of each bar represents the number of times that data value appears in the set. The appearance resembles a dot plot, but the bars replace the stacks of dots. The bars on a histogram always touch, may or may not appear on a number line, and will most often have labels that identify the horizontal (x) and vertical (y) axes.

Here is an example of a histogram:

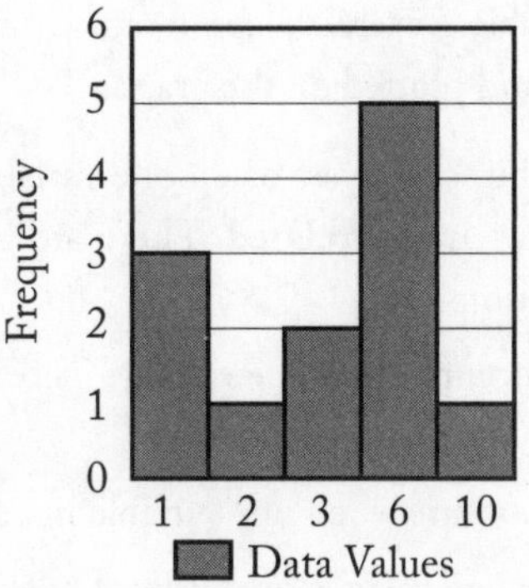

A box plot requires a bit more information to construct, but it tells you much more about the spread and center of a data set. Five numbers are needed to form a box plot:

1. **Minimum**: This is the smallest number in the data set. Here, this number is 1.
2. **First Quartile**: This is the 25th percentile, or number for which 25% of the data set is less than or equal to it. Assuming the data are arranged in increasing order, the position of the first quartile is obtained by dividing the number of values in the data set (here, 12) by 4. Doing so gives 3. So, the number in the third position from the left in the list of data is the first quartile. Here, this number is 1.
3. **Median**: This is the 50th percentile. Assuming the data are arranged in increasing order, the position of the median is obtained by averaging the middle two data values since there is an even number of data in this set. (If there is an odd number of data values, it is the single value in the middle of the data set.) The middle two values are those in the 6th and 7th positions, namely 3 and 6. The average is 4.5.

NOTE

Although similar in appearance, **bar graphs** and **histograms** serve different purposes. While histograms are used to represent the frequency of numerical data ranges, bar graphs are used to represent the frequency of categories of data. The data on the x-axis of a histogram will *always* be continuous and *always* be numerical values. The data on the x-axis of a bar graph will be distinct categories, each represented by a separate bar.

4. **Third Quartile**: This is the 75th percentile. Assuming the data are arranged in increasing order, the position of the first quartile is obtained by dividing the number of values in the data set (here, 12) by 4 and then, multiplying it by 3. Doing so gives 9. So the number in the ninth position from the left in the list of data is the third quartile. Here, this number is 6.
5. **Maximum**: This is the largest number in the data set. Here, this number is 10.

The box plot obtained is as follows:

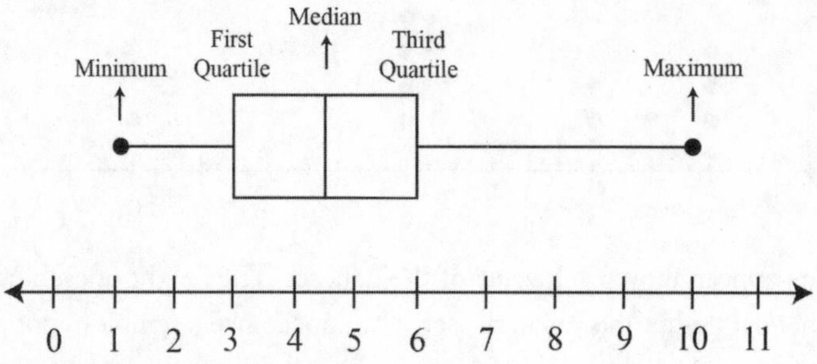

A **scatter plot** is another type of visual presentation used to show relationships or trends in data. A scatter plot is a graph in which the *x*-axis represents the values of one variable and the *y*-axis represents the values of the other variable. Several values of one variable and the corresponding values of the other variable are measured and plotted on the graph.

If two variables have a relationship such that when one variable changes, the other changes in a predictable way, the two variables are **correlated**. There are typically three types of correlation: positive, negative, and no correlation.

- A **positive correlation** occurs when one variable increases and the other variable increases as well.
- A **negative correlation** occurs when one variable increases and the other decreases.
- **No correlation** occurs when there is no apparent relationship between the variables.

Generally, the more tightly packed the points are in a scatter plot, the stronger the relationship. If the data points rise from left to right, we say the relationship is positive, while if they fall from left to right, we say the trend is negative.

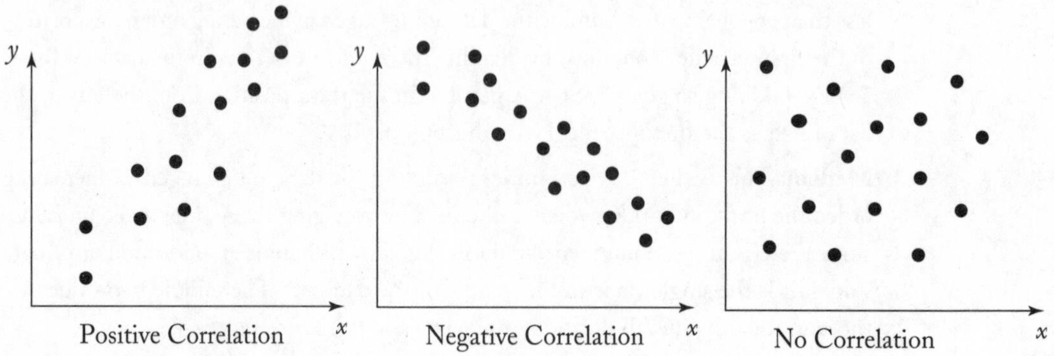

If there is a strong correlation in the data, it is likely that there will be a line that could be drawn on the scatter plot that comes close to all the points. This line is known as the **line of best fit**. Without performing any computations, it is possible to visualize the location of the line of best fit, as the following diagrams show:

Let's look at a few examples.

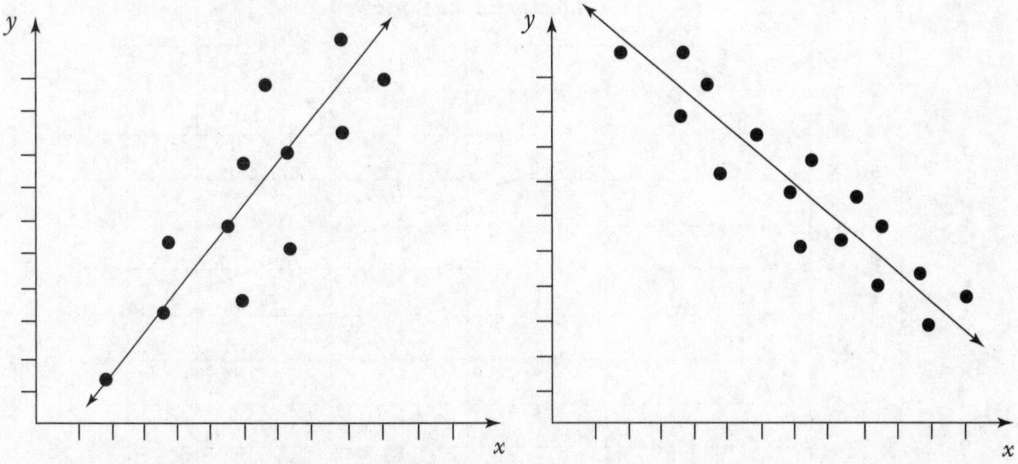

EXAMPLE 28 (EASIER):

Below is a scatter plot depicting the relationship between the variable *a* and the variable *b*.

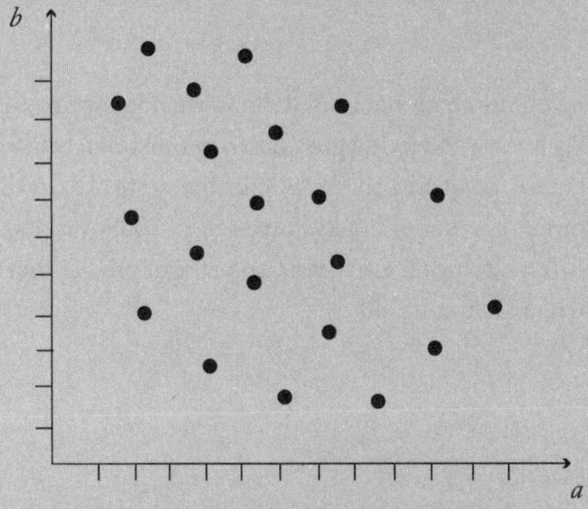

Which of the following **best** describes the relationship depicted in the graph?

A. There is a strong positive correlation between the two variables.

B. There is a strong negative correlation between the variables.

C. The two variables are not correlated.

D. As the value of *a* increase, the value of *b* decreases.

The points on the scatter plot appear to be randomly arranged on the graph. This is an indication that the values of *a* and *b* are not correlated. **The correct answer is C.**

EXAMPLE 29 (MORE CHALLENGING):

The following scatter plot shows the average number of books borrowed on a weekly basis for years 2000–2009 at a local library.

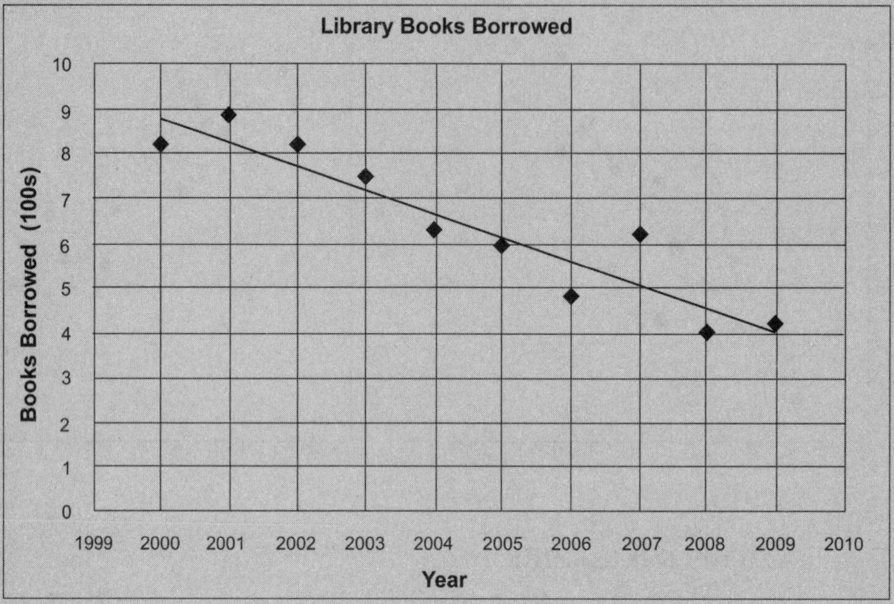

If the trend continued, about how many books were borrowed in 2010?

Use the slope of the line to make predictions about data points that are not shown. According to the slope, the average number of books borrowed weekly goes down approximately $0.6 \times 100 = 60$ books every year. Multiply by 100 because, according to the title of the vertical axis, the numbers are in the 100s. The expected value for the number of books borrowed in 2009 was 400. The slope says we should expect that number to decrease by 60 every year, so you can predict that there were 340 books borrowed in 2010. **The correct answer is 340.**

WORD PROBLEMS INVOLVING FORMULAS

Certain types of word problems call for you to apply a formula. Here are the three types of formulas you can expect to apply during the test:

1. Weighted average (based on the formula for arithmetic mean)
2. Simple interest (on a monetary investment)
3. Rate

The formulas for simple interest and rate will be on the formulas sheet provided during the test.

In the next few pages, you'll learn how to handle these three types of word problems. Remember: for any type of word problem, including these three, you might be able to work backward from the answer choices as well. Even if not, you can often narrow down your choices by estimating the size of the answer.

Weighted Average Problems

You solve **weighted average** problems using the arithmetic mean formula, except you give the set's terms different weights. For example, if a final exam score of 90 receives *twice* the weight of each of two mid-term exam scores 75 and 85, think of the final-exam score as *two* scores of 90—and the total number of scores as 4 rather than 3:

$$WA = \frac{75 + 85 + (2)(90)}{4} = \frac{340}{4} = 85$$

Similarly, when some numbers among terms might appear more often than others, you must give them the appropriate "weight" before computing an average. A weighted average problem might ask you to find the average, or it might provide the weighted average and ask for one of the terms. These questions sometimes require conversion from one unit of measurement to another.

EXAMPLE 30 (EASIER):

During an 8-hour trip, Brigitte drove 3 hours at 55 miles per hour and 5 hours at 65 miles per hour. What was her average rate, in miles per hour, for the entire trip?

A. 58.5

B. 60

C. 61.25

D. 62.5

Determine the total miles driven: (3)(55) + (5)(65) = 490. To determine the average over the entire trip, divide this total by 8, which is the number of total hours: 490 ÷ 8 = 61.25. **The correct answer is C.**

EXAMPLE 31 (MORE CHALLENGING):

A certain olive orchard produces 315 gallons of oil annually, on average, during four consecutive years. How many gallons of oil must the orchard produce annually, on average, during the next six years, if oil production for the entire 10-year period is to meet a goal of 378 gallons per year?

A. 240

B. 285

C. 396

D. 420

In the weighted average formula, 315 annual gallons receives a weight of 4, while the average annual number of gallons for the next six years (x) receives a weight of 6:

$$378 = \frac{1260 + 6x}{10}$$
$$3780 = 1260 + 6x$$
$$3780 - 1260 = 6x$$
$$420 = x$$

This solution (420) is the average number of gallons needed per year, on average, during the next six years. **The correct answer is D.**

Investment Problems

Investment problems on the GED Mathematical Reasoning Test involve interest earned (at a certain percentage rate) on money over a certain time period (usually a year). To calculate interest earned, multiply the original amount of money by the interest rate:

amount of money × interest rate = amount of interest on money

For example, if you deposit \$1,000 in a savings account that earns 5% interest annually, the total amount in the account after one year will be \$1,000 + 0.05(\$1,000) = \$1,000 + \$50 = \$1,050.

A investment question might involve more than simply calculating interest earned on a given principal amount at a given rate. It might call for you to set up and solve an algebraic equation. When handling this sort of problem, it's best to eliminate percent signs.

EXAMPLE 32 (EASIER):

Gary wishes to have \$2,970 in a savings account at the end of the year. How much must Gary deposit in his account at the start of the year if the account pays him 8% interest per year?

A. \$2,575

B. \$2,732

C. \$2,750

D. \$3,208

Letting x equal the original amount deposited, set up the following equation: $x + 0.08x = 2{,}970$. Combining terms on the left side of the equation: $1.08x = 2{,}970$. Solve for x:

$$x = \frac{2{,}970}{1.08} = 2{,}750$$

Thus, Gary must invest \$2,750 at the start of the year to end with \$2,970. **The correct answer is C.**

EXAMPLE 33 (MORE CHALLENGING):

Fiona deposits D dollars in a savings account that earns 10% interest per year. At the end of one year, she then deposits the total amount in another savings account, which earns 5% per year.

Which of the following represents the total amount in the account after the two-year period, in dollars?

A. $1.05D$

B. $1.155D$

C. $1.10D$

D. $1.5D$

The total dollar amount after the first year is $D + 0.10D$, or $1.1D$. Fiona deposits $1.1D$ in an account earning 5%. After one year, her total is $1.1D + 0.05(1.10)D$, which equals $1.10D + 0.055D$, or $1.155D$. **The correct answer is B.**

Problems Involving Rate

A **rate** is a fraction that expresses a quantity per unit of time. For example, the rate of travel is expressed this way:

$$\text{rate of travel} = \frac{\text{distance}}{\text{time}}$$

Similarly, the rate at which a machine produces a certain product is expressed this way:

$$\text{rate of production} = \frac{\text{number of units produced}}{\text{time}}$$

A rate question on the GED Mathematical Reasoning Test will usually provide two of the three terms, and then it will ask you for the value of the third term. A rate question might also require you to convert a number from one unit of measurement to another.

EXAMPLE 34 (EASIER):

If a printer can print pages at a rate of 15 pages per minute, how many pages can it print in $2\frac{1}{2}$ hours?

A. 1,500

B. 1,750

C. 2,250

D. 2,500

Apply the following formula: rate $= \frac{\text{\# of pages}}{\text{time}}$. The rate is given in terms of minutes, so convert $2\frac{1}{2}$ hours to 150 minutes. Determine the number of pages by applying the formula to these numbers:

$$\begin{aligned} 15 &= \frac{\text{\# of pages}}{150} \\ (15)(150) &= \text{\# of pages} \\ 2{,}250 &= \text{\# of pages} \end{aligned}$$

The correct answer is C.

EXAMPLE 35 (MORE CHALLENGING):

A passenger train and a freight train leave from the same station at the same time. Over 3 hours, the passenger train travels 45 miles per hour faster, on average, than the freight train.

Which of the following expresses the combined distance the two trains have traveled after 3 hours, where *x* represents the number of miles the freight train traveled per hour, on average?

A. $3x + 45$

B. $6x + 45$

C. $3x + 120$

D. $6x + 135$

Since x equals the rate (speed) of the freight train, you can express the rate of the passenger train as $x + 45$. Substitute these values for time and rate into the formula for each train:

Formula: rate × time = distance

Passenger: $(x + 45)(3) = 3x + 135$

Freight: $(x)(3) = 3x$

The combined distance that the two trains covered is $3x + (3x + 135) = 6x + 135$.

The correct answer is D.

More Word Problems

Linear and quadratic equations must be formulated to solve many types of word problems.

Let's walk through three practice questions.

1. Students in a science class are recording the growth of a lima bean plant once the seed sprouted. They recorded that the initial height of the plant was 2 inches and noted that the plant grew approximately 0.2 inch per day. Write a linear equation that expresses the height of the plant in terms of the number of days after the initial measurement is taken.

   Let y be the height of the plant and x the number of days after the initial measurement is taken. The y-intercept is the height on Day 0, which is the initial height; here, this is 2 inches. The rate of growth is inches per day, which is 0.2; this is the slope. So, using slope-intercept form $y = mx + b$, the desired equation is $y = 0.2x + 2$.

2. Dayle buys a quilting book for $18.50, which is a 25% discount off the regular price. Write an equation that can be used to find the regular price of the book.

   Let x be the regular price of the book. The price paid for the book after the 25% discount is given by $x - 0.25x = 0.75x$. Since this price is given to be $18.50, we have the equation $0.75x = 18.50$.

3. The base of a triangle is four inches less than three times its height. Formulate a quadratic equation that can be solved to give the height and base that will yield an area of 30 square inches.

   Let x be the height of the triangle (in inches). The base has length $(3x - 4)$ inches. Using the area formula for a triangle yields the equation $\frac{1}{2}x(3x - 4) = 30$. Simplifying yields the following quadratic equation in standard form:

$$\begin{aligned} \frac{1}{2}x(3x - 4) &= 30 \\ x(3x - 4) &= 60 \\ 3x^2 - 4x &= 60 \\ 3x^2 - 4x - 60 &= 0 \end{aligned}$$

SUMMING IT UP

- The GED Mathematical Reasoning Test assesses the following algebra skills:
    - Solving a linear equation in one variable
    - Solving a system of two equations in two variables by the substitution method and the addition-subtraction method
    - Recognizing unsolvable equations
    - Handling algebraic inequalities
    - Factoring quadratic expressions
    - Finding the roots of quadratic equations by factoring
    - Handling functions
    - Identifying measures of central tendency
    - Recognizing arithmetic series patterns
    - Solving formula word problems (weighted average, simple interest, and rate)
- Most algebraic equations you'll see on the test are linear. Remember the operations for isolating the unknown on one side of the equation. Solving algebraic inequalities is similar to solving equations: Isolate the variable on one side of the inequality symbol first.
- Weighted average problems and currency problems can be solved by using the arithmetic mean (simple average) formula.
- Investment problems involve interest earned (at a certain percentage rate) on money over a certain time period (usually a year). Investment and mixture problems can be solved using what you've learned about proportions and percentage questions.
- A rate question (a rate is a fraction that expresses a quantity per unit of time) will usually provide two of the three terms, and then it will ask you for the value of the third term. A rate question might also require you to convert a number from one unit of measurement to another.
- Rates of production and travel questions can be solved using the strategies you've learned about fraction problems.

PRACTICE QUESTIONS

Directions: The following practice questions will cover the algebra and descriptive statistics concepts that will appear on the GED Mathematical Reasoning Test. Choose the best answer to each problem presented.

SHOW YOUR WORK HERE

1. Solve for y: $4y + 3 = -9$

A. -12

B. -8

C. -3

D. -1.5

2. If $f(x) = 2 - x(1 - x)$, compute $f(-3)$.

A. -10

B. -4

C. 2

D. 14

3. Let a be a positive real number. If (x,y) is the solution of the following system, what is the value of $\frac{x}{y}$?

$$\begin{cases} y = ax - 1 \\ 2ax - y = 2 + a \end{cases}$$

A. $a + 1$

B. $\frac{1}{a}$

C. $\frac{a+1}{a^2}$

D. $\frac{1}{a-1}$

4. Consider the data set {0, 4, 2, 8, 4, 4, 13}. Which of the following is the correct relationship among the mode, median, and mean?

A. mode = median < mean

B. mode < mean < median

C. mode = median = mean

D. median = mean > mode

SHOW YOUR WORK HERE

5. Solve the inequality

$$3(2 - 4x) + 2(8x - 3) > -8.$$

A. $x < -4$

B. $x < -2$

C. $x > -\frac{11}{12}$

D. $x > -2$

6. Suppose you roll a fair 6-sided die three times in succession and record the result each time. What is the probability that you do NOT roll three 5s?

A. $\frac{215}{216}$

B. $\frac{35}{36}$

C. $\frac{125}{216}$

D. $\frac{1}{216}$

7. Which of these expressions is equivalent to the sum of the first 30 positive integers?

A. 30(31)

B. 29(30)

C. 15(31)

D. 15(29)

8. Solve for x: $\sqrt[3]{2x+5} = -5$

A. –65

B. –60

C. 10

D. 15

9. Factor completely: $4x^2 - 169$

A. $(4x - 13)(x + 13)$

B. $(2x - 13)^2$

C. $(2x - 169)(2x + 1)$

D. $(2x - 13)(2x + 13)$

10. The property tax for a house costing \$252,000 is \$4,200. At this rate, what would be the property tax for a house costing D dollars?

A. $D + 60$ dollars

B. $\frac{60}{D}$ dollars

C. $\frac{D}{60}$ dollars

D. $60D$ dollars

11. Jake attended a baseball card show four times over the course of the year and earned the following amounts in sales: \$450, \$600, \$240, and \$1,060. How much would he need to earn at the next show so that his average profit is \$800?

A. \$587.50

B. \$800.00

C. \$850.00

D. \$1,650.00

12. Aaron earns \$9.45 per hour plus an additional \$140 in tips working as a waiter on Friday evening. If he earns at least \$185 that night, which of these inequalities could be used to determine the least number of hours, h, he would need to work that night to earn this amount?

A. $9.45(h + 140) \geq 185$

B. $9.45h \geq 185$

C. $9.45h + 140 \geq 185$

D. $9.45 + 140h \geq 185$

SHOW YOUR WORK HERE

SHOW YOUR WORK HERE

13. In a certain high school, the following is the breakdown of the junior classes participation in electives this academic year: 40% take theater, 22% take electronic art, 10% take plant biology, 10% take creative writing, and 18% take German. What is the probability that a junior chosen at random did NOT select either plant biology or German as their elective?

A. 0.28

B. 0.72

C. 0.82

D. 0.90

14. Solve for z: $\frac{2-3z}{2} = \frac{1}{4}z - \frac{z-2}{4}$

A. –8

B. $\frac{1}{3}$

C. 2

D. 4

15. A bank offers 1.5% simple interest on a money market account. If $8,000 is deposited, which of the following expressions is the amount the account is worth after one year?

A. $8,000 + $8,000(0.015)

B. $8,000 + $8,000(1.5)

C. $8,000(0.015)

D. $8,000(1.5)

16. Two times the sum of three and a number is equal to ten less than six times that number. What is the number?

A. –1

B. $\frac{13}{4}$

C. 4

D. 12

SHOW YOUR WORK HERE

17. Factor: $18x^2 - 27xy + 4y^2$

A. $(3x - 4y)(6x - y)$

B. $(6x - 2y)(3x - 2y)$

C. $(9x - 4y)(2x - y)$

D. $(3x + 2y)(6x - 2y)$

18. Solve for x: $2x^2 + x - 4 = 0$

A. $\frac{1 \pm i\sqrt{31}}{4}$

B. $\frac{-1 \pm \sqrt{33}}{4}$

C. $\frac{1 \pm \sqrt{33}}{4}$

D. $\frac{-1 \pm \sqrt{31}}{4}$

19. Katie received \$20 for her birthday from her uncle. She saved the money and added \$4 to it every week for 15 consecutive weeks. She recorded the amount at the end of each week. What is the median of the amounts she recorded for these 15 weeks?

A. \$32

B. \$48

C. \$52

D. \$60

20. Which of these conditions relating a and b guarantees that the following system has no solution?

$$\begin{cases} 3y - ax = 1 \\ bx + 4y = 2 \end{cases}$$

A. $4a - 3b = 0$

B. $ab = 12$

C. $4a + 3b = 0$

D. $ab = -12$

SHOW YOUR WORK HERE

21. A vase contains 14 carnations and 11 daisies. If two flowers are selected at random without replacement, what is the probability of selecting two daisies?

A. $\frac{11}{25} \times \frac{10}{25}$

B. $\frac{11}{25} \times \frac{11}{25}$

C. $\frac{11}{14} \times \frac{10}{14}$

D. $\frac{11}{25} \times \frac{10}{24}$

22. Solve for z: $\frac{\frac{1}{w} + z}{2 + z} = \frac{3}{w}$

A. $z = \frac{5}{w - 3}$

B. $z = \frac{7}{w + 3}$

C. $z = \frac{5}{w + 3}$

D. $z = \frac{7}{w - 3}$

23. Which of the following expressions is equivalent to $\frac{x^3\left(x^2y^3\right)^3}{x^5y}$?

A. $x^{13}y^8$

B. x^6y^{26}

C. $x^{\frac{9}{5}}y^9$

D. x^4y^8

24. Scott and Micah play racquetball twice a week. So far, Micah has won 13 of 22 matches. Which equation can be used to determine the number of matches, z, Micah must win consecutively to improve his winning percentage to 90%?

A. $\frac{13+z}{22+z}=0.90$

B. $\frac{13+z}{22}=0.90$

C. $\frac{z}{22+z}=0.90$

D. $\frac{13}{22+z}=0.90$

25. If $f(x) = 2x - 3x^2$, then what is $f(x+1)$?

A. $-3x^2+4x+2$

B. $-3x^2-4x-1$

C. $-3x^2+2x-1$

D. $-3x^2+2x+1$

SHOW YOUR WORK HERE

ANSWER KEY AND EXPLANATIONS

1. C	**6.** A	**11.** D	**16.** C	**21.** D
2. D	**7.** C	**12.** C	**17.** A	**22.** A
3. C	**8.** A	**13.** B	**18.** B	**23.** D
4. A	**9.** D	**14.** B	**19.** C	**24.** A
5. D	**10.** C	**15.** A	**20.** C	**25.** B

1. The correct answer is C. Subtract 3 from both sides and then divide by 4:

$$4y + 3 = -9$$
$$4y = -12$$
$$y = -3$$

Choice A is incorrect because −12 is equal to 4*y*. In the first step, you should subtract 3, not add it, so −8 (choice B) is incorrect. In the second step, you should divide by 4, not add it to both sides, so −1.5 (choice D) is not correct either.

2. The correct answer is D. Substitute in −3 for *x* and simplify using the order of operations:

$$\begin{aligned} f(-3) &= 2 - (-3)(1 - (-3)) \\ &= 2 + 3(1 + 3) \\ &= 2 + 3(4) \\ &= 2 + 12 \\ &= 14 \end{aligned}$$

Choice A is incorrect because −(−3) = 3, not −3. Choice B is incorrect because 1 − (−3) = 1 + 3, not 1 − 3. Choice C is incorrect because to compute 2 − 3(−2), you must compute the product; you computed 2 − 3 first and then multiplied by −2.

3. The correct answer is C. Solve the system using the substitution method—substitute the expression for *y* given by the first equation into the second equation, and then solve for *x*:

$$2ax - (ax - 1) = 2 + a$$
$$2ax - ax + 1 = 2 + a$$
$$ax = a + 1$$
$$x = \frac{a+1}{a}$$

Now, substitute this in for *x* in the first equation to find the value of *y*:

$$y = a\left(\frac{a+1}{a}\right) - 1$$
$$y = a + 1 - 1$$
$$y = a$$

So $\frac{x}{y} = \frac{\frac{a+1}{a}}{a} = \frac{a+1}{a^2}$.

Choice A is *xy*. Choice B is incorrect because you cannot cancel like terms in the numerator and denominator of a fraction; you can only cancel factors. Choice D is incorrect because when solving the equation $ax = a + 1$, you should divide both sides by *a*, not subtract it from both sides.

4. **The correct answer is A.** The mode is the most frequently occurring value in the data set. Here, that value is 4. For the median, first arrange the data in increasing order:

$$0, 2, 4, 4, 4, 8, 13$$

Since there are seven data values, the median is the value in the fourth position in this list, which is 4. The mean is the average of the seven values:

$$\frac{0+2+4+4+4+8+13}{7}=\frac{35}{7}=5$$

So mode = median < mean.

5. **The correct answer is D.** Use the distributive property, gather like terms, and then divide by the coefficient of x:

$$\begin{aligned} 3(2-4x)+2(8x-3) &> -8 \\ 6-12x+16x-6 &> -8 \\ 4x &> -8 \\ x &> -2 \end{aligned}$$

Choice A is incorrect because you only reverse the inequality sign when you divide by a negative number, and when solving the inequality $4x > -8$, you should divide both sides by 4, not add it to both sides. Choice B is incorrect because you only reverse the inequality sign when you divide by a negative number. Choice C is incorrect because you did not use the distributive property when simplifying the expression on the left side.

6. **The correct answer is A.** The three rolls are independent of each other, and each has 6 possible outcomes. So there are (6)(6)(6) = 216 possible three-roll outcomes. There is only one way to get all 5s. So the probability of NOT getting three 5s is $\frac{215}{216}$. Choice B is the probability of not getting two 5s when rolling the die twice. Choice C is the probability that you do not roll any 5s in the three attempts. Choice D is the probability of rolling three 5s.

7. **The correct answer is C.** The formula for the sum of the first n positive integers is $\frac{n(n+1)}{2}$. Substituting $n = 30$ into the formula yields $\frac{30(31)}{2}=15(31)$. Choice A is incorrect because you must divide this by 2. Choice B is an attempt to compute the sum of the first 29 positive integers, but you forgot to divide by 2. Choice D is the sum of the first 29 positive integers.

8. **The correct answer is A.** Cube sides to get rid of the radical, and then solve for x as you would any linear equation:

$$\begin{aligned} \sqrt[3]{2x+5} &= -5 \\ 2x+5 &= (-5)^3 \\ 2x+5 &= -125 \\ 2x &= -130 \\ x &= -65 \end{aligned}$$

Choice B is incorrect because when solving an equation of the form $az + b = c$, subtract b from both sides, do not add it. Choice C is incorrect because you squared both sides, but that does not undo a cube root; you must raise both sides to the third power. Choice D is incorrect because you squared both sides, but that does not undo a cube root; you must raise both sides to the third power. Also, when solving an equation of the form $az + b = c$, subtract b from both sides, do not add it.

9. **The correct answer is D.** This is a difference of squares, since it can be written in the form $(2x)^2 - 13^2$. This factors as $(2x - 13)(2x + 13)$. The other choices are incorrect because while the squared term and constant terms are correct, each of them when multiplied out has a middle term not present in the original expression.

10. **The correct answer is C.** Let x be the amount of property tax for a house costing D dollars. Set up the proportion $\frac{252,000}{4,200} = \frac{D}{x}$. Solving for x yields $x = \frac{4,200D}{252,000} = \frac{D}{60}$ dollars. Choice A is incorrect because you should divide by 60, not add it. Choice B is the reciprocal of the correct expression. Choice D is incorrect because you should divide by 60, not multiply by it.

11. **The correct answer is D.** Let x be the earnings needed at the fifth show. Compute the average of the five amounts and set this equal to $800:

$$\frac{450 + 600 + 240 + 1,060 + x}{5} = 800$$
$$\frac{2,350 + x}{5} = 800$$
$$2,350 + x = 4,000$$
$$x = 1,650$$

So he must earn $1,650 at the fifth show. Choice A is incorrect because this is just the average of the earnings from the first four shows. Choice B is incorrect because this only works if the average of the first four shows is equal to $800, which is not the case. Choice C is incorrect because you divided the total earnings by 4, not 5.

12. **The correct answer is C.** The total amount earned from the hourly wage for h hours of work is $9.45h$ dollars. So the total earned on Friday evening is $9.45h + 140$ dollars. This must be greater than or equal to $185. This yields the inequality $9.45h + 140 \geq 185$. Choice A is incorrect because you should not multiply the amount earned in tips by the hourly wage. Choice B is incorrect because you did not include the amount earned in tips in the total amount earned on the left side of the inequality. Choice D is incorrect because you should interchange the 9.45 and 140.

13. **The correct answer is B.** The probability is $1 - (0.10 + 0.18) = 1 - 0.28 = 0.72$. Choice A is the probability of selecting a junior that *did* choose plant biology or German as their elective. Choice C is incorrect because you must also exclude the percentage who chose plant biology as their elective. Choice D is incorrect because you must also exclude the percentage who chose German as their elective.

14. **The correct answer is B.** First, clear the fractions by multiplying both sides by 4. Then, simplify both sides using the distributive property and combining like terms. Then, isolate the z-terms on one side and the constant terms on the right. Finally, divide both sides by the coefficient of z:

$$4 \bullet \frac{2 - 3z}{2} = 4 \bullet \left(\frac{1}{4}z - \frac{z - 2}{4} \right)$$
$$2(2 - 3z) = z - (z - 2)$$
$$4 - 6z = z - z + 2$$
$$4 - 6z = 2$$
$$-6z = -2$$
$$z = \frac{1}{3}$$

Choice A is incorrect because to solve an equation of the form $ax = b$, divide both sides by a, you should not add it. Choice C is incorrect because you did not use the distributive property correctly. Choice D is incorrect because to solve an equation of the form $ax = b$, divide both sides by a, do not subtract it.

15. **The correct answer is A.** The interest earned in one year at 1.5% on $8,000 is $8,000(0.015). Adding this to the original deposit of $8,000 shows the account is worth $8,000 + $8,000(0.015) after one year. Choice B is incorrect because 1.5% = 0.015. Choice C is just the amount of interest earned. Choice D is incorrect because 1.5% = 0.015, and this would just be the amount of interest earned.

16. **The correct answer is C.** Translating the sentence into symbols yields the following equation, where x is the unknown number:

$$2(x + 3) = 6x - 10.$$

Solve for x, as follows:

$$2(x + 3) = 6x - 10$$
$$2x + 6 = 6x - 10$$
$$16 = 4x$$
$$4 = x$$

Choice A is incorrect because to solve an equation of the form $az + b = c$, subtract b from both sides, do not add it. Choice B is incorrect because when translating the sentence into symbols, you incorrectly interpreted the phrase "two times the sum of three and a number" as $2x + 3$; it should be $2(x + 3)$. Choice D is incorrect because to solve an equation of the form $az = b$, divide both sides by a, do not subtract it from both sides.

17. **The correct answer is A.** This is the only pair of binomials that, when expanded, yields the given trinomial. Applying FOIL to $(3x - 4y)(6x - y)$ yields the following:

$$(3x)(6x) + (3x)(-y) + (-4y)(6x) + (-4y)(-y) =$$
$$18x^2 - 3xy - 24xy + 4y^2 = 18x^2 - 27xy + 4y^2$$

18. **The correct answer is B.** Use the quadratic formula $x = \dfrac{-b \pm \sqrt{b^2 - 4ac}}{2a}$ with $a = 2$, $b = 1$, and $c = -4$ to find the solutions:

$$x = \frac{-1 \pm \sqrt{1 - 4(2)(-4)}}{2(2)} = \frac{-1 \pm \sqrt{33}}{4}$$

Choice A is incorrect because the number before the "$\pm$" sign in the quadratic formula is $-b$, not b, and you made a sign error when simplifying the radicand. Choice C is incorrect because the number before the "$\pm$" sign in the quadratic formula is $-b$, not b. Choice D is incorrect because you made a sign error when simplifying the radicand.

19. **The correct answer is C.** The median of a data set containing 15 values that are arranged in increasing order is the one in the eighth position. Since Katie is adding 4 to the previous value each week, if we just list the new total amount saved each week, the data set will automatically be in increasing order. It is as follows: 24, 28, 32, 36, 40, 44, 48, 52 … 80. So the median is 52. Choice A is the amount she had saved by the eighth week, not including the amount she received as a gift from her uncle. Choice B is the seventh week's total, which is not the median. Choice D is the total amount she saved for these 15 weeks, not including the amount she received as a gift from her uncle.

20. **The correct answer is C.** Solve both equations for y:

$$3y - ax = 1 \Rightarrow y = \frac{1}{3}ax + \frac{1}{3}$$
$$bx + 4y = 2 \Rightarrow y = -\frac{1}{4}bx + \frac{1}{2}$$

Since these lines have different y-intercepts, they will not intersect if they have the same slope. In such case, the system will have no solution. Equating the slopes and simplifying yields the following:

$$\frac{1}{3}a = -\frac{1}{4}b$$
$$4a = -3b$$
$$4a + 3b = 0$$

Choice A is incorrect because the minus should be a plus. Choice B is incorrect because this condition would guarantee the lines are perpendicular, not parallel, and perpendicular lines intersect in one point, which corresponds to a solution of the system. Choice D is incorrect because this is close to the condition ensuring the lines are perpendicular—a minus sign is missing. But perpendicular lines intersect in one point, which corresponds to a solution of the system.

21. **The correct answer is D.** There are 11 daisies of 25 that could be chosen in the first selection; the probability of doing so is $\frac{11}{25}$. Once this flower is removed, there are 24 remaining in the vase, 10 of which are daisies. So the probability of choosing a second daisy is $\frac{10}{24}$. Since the selections are performed in succession, we multiply the probabilities. So the probability of randomly selecting two daisies is $\frac{11}{25} \times \frac{10}{24}$. Choice A is incorrect because the denominator of the second fraction in the product should be reduced by 1 since the flower selected first was not returned to the vase. Choice B is incorrect because this is the result if the first flower were returned to the vase before the second flower was chosen. Choice C is incorrect because the number of flowers in the vase is not 14; this is the number of carnations. Rather, there are 11 + 14 = 25 flowers in the vase from which to make the first selection.

22. **The correct answer is A.** First, cross-multiply. Then simplify each side using the distributive property and isolate z, as follows:

$$\frac{\frac{1}{w} + z}{2 + z} = \frac{3}{w}$$

$$\left(\frac{1}{w} + z\right)w = 3(2 + z)$$

$$1 + wz = 6 + 3z$$

$$wz - 3z = 5$$

$$z(w - 3) = 5$$

$$z = \frac{5}{w - 3}$$

The other choices are incorrect due to errors when solving equations of the form $x + a = b$ and $ax = b$.

23. **The correct answer is D.** Apply the exponent rules, as follows:

$$\begin{aligned}\frac{x^3\left(x^2y^3\right)^3}{x^5y} &= \frac{x^3x^{2\cdot3}y^{3\cdot3}}{x^5y}\\ &= \frac{x^3x^6y^9}{x^5y}\\ &= \frac{x^{3+6}y^9}{x^5y}\\ &= \frac{x^9y^9}{x^5y}\\ &= x^{9-5}y^{9-1}\\ &= x^4y^8\end{aligned}$$

Choice A is incorrect because $z^a \cdot z^b = z^{a+b}$, not $z^{a \cdot b}$. Choice B is incorrect because $\left(z^a\right)^b$ does not equal z^{a^b}. Choice C is incorrect because $\frac{z^a}{z^b}$ does not equal $z^{a/b}$.

24. **The correct answer is A.** Let z be the number of matches Micah needs to win consecutively to raise his winning percentage to 90%. Then, after playing these z matches, he will have won $13 + z$ out of $22 + z$ matches played. This yields the ratio $\frac{13 + z}{22 + z}$, which must equal 0.90. This yields the equation $\frac{13 + z}{22 + z} = 0.90$. Choice B is incorrect because z must be added to the denominator as well, since he will have played $22 + z$ matches. Choice C is incorrect because 13 must be added to the numerator. Choice D is incorrect because this ratio assumes Micah lost the next z matches.

25. The correct answer is B. Substitute $x + 1$ for x in the function $f(x) = 2x - 3x^2$ and simplify:

$$\begin{aligned} f(x+1) &= 2(x+1) - 3(x+1)^2 \\ &= 2x + 2 - 3\left(x^2 + 2x + 1\right) \\ &= 2x + 2 - 3x^2 - 6x - 3 \\ &= -3x^2 - 4x - 1 \end{aligned}$$

Choice A is incorrect because you did not use the distributive property correctly. Choice C is incorrect because $f(x + 1) \neq f(x) + f(1)$. Choice D is incorrect because $f(x + 1) \neq f(x) + 1$.

Math Review: Geometry

Chapter 14

OVERVIEW

WHAT YOU'LL FIND IN THIS REVIEW

In this review, you'll examine the areas of geometry covered on the GED Mathematical Reasoning Test. They include the following:

- Congruency and similarity
- Angles, parallel and perpendicular lines, and transversals
- Two-dimensional figures (triangles, quadrilaterals, polygons, and circles)
- Three-dimensional figures (cubes and other rectangular prisms, cylinders, cones, and square pyramids)
- Basic right-triangle trigonometry
- Coordinate geometry (points, lines, and other figures on the *xy*-coordinate plane)

The GED test-style questions throughout this review are multiple-choice questions, as well as technology-enhanced items. The actual exam includes both types of questions.

CONGRUENCY AND SIMILARITY

Two geometric figures that have the same size and shape are said to be **congruent.** The symbol for congruency is $\cong$. Two angles are congruent if their degree measure (size) is the same. Two line segments are congruent if they are equal in length. Two triangles are congruent if the angle measures and sides are all identical in size. (The same applies to figures with more than three sides.)

If a two-dimensional geometric figure, such as a triangle or rectangle, has exactly the same shape as another one, then the two figures are **similar.** Similar figures share the same angle measures, and their sides are proportionate (though not the same length). Look at the following figure.

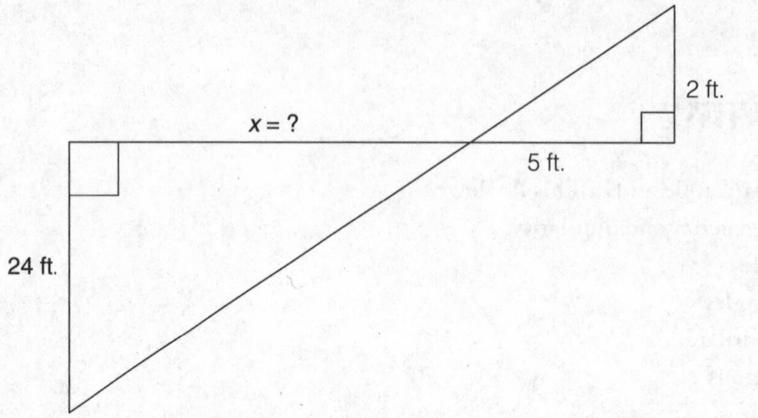

In order to find the length of the corresponding side of the larger triangle, you must set up a proportion. The triangles are similar, so their sides are in proportion: $\frac{2}{5} = \frac{24}{x}$. To solve the proportion, cross multiply: $2x = 120$. Then, to find x, divide 120 by 2: $120 \div 2 = 60$. The unknown side is 60 feet in length. (You'll examine triangles in greater detail later in this review.)

ANGLES

Angles are indicated by the angle symbol ($\angle$). They are measured in **degrees** (°). The letter 'm' is used to indicate the measure of an angle. The line that extends in only one direction from a point is called a **ray.** Lines, rays, or line segments meet at a point called the **vertex.** Angles are usually named by letters, as in the following figure.

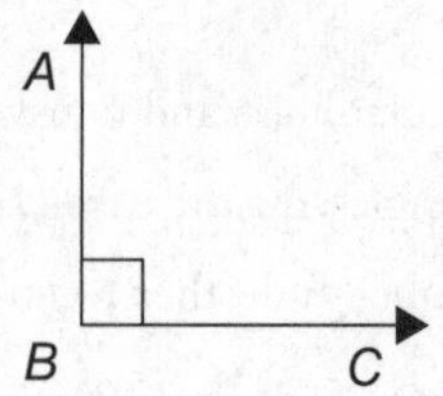

The name of the above angle is $\angle ABC$. This angle is called a **right angle** because $m\angle ABC = 90°$. The small square drawn in the angle indicates that it is a right angle. When two lines meet to form a right angle, they are said to be **perpendicular** to each other, as indicated by the symbol $\perp$. In the above figure, $\overline{BA} \perp \overline{BC}$.

An angle that measures less than 90° is called an **acute** angle. $\angle VWX$ in the following figure is an acute angle. An angle that measures more than 90° but less than 180° is called an **obtuse** angle. $\angle EFG$ in the following figure is an obtuse angle.

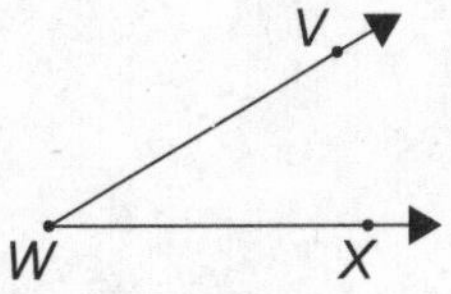

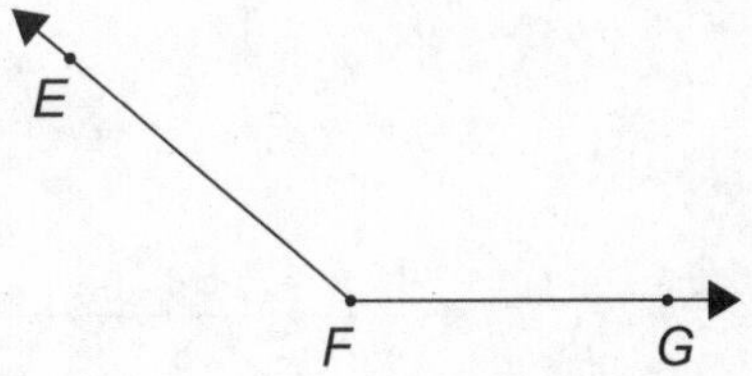

A **straight angle** measures 180°. $\angle XYZ$ below is a straight angle. Two or more angles whose measures add up to 180° are called **supplementary**. In the next figure, $\angle DEG$ forms a straight line and therefore measures 180°. $\angle DEF$ and $\angle FEG$ are supplementary angles; their measures add up to 180°.

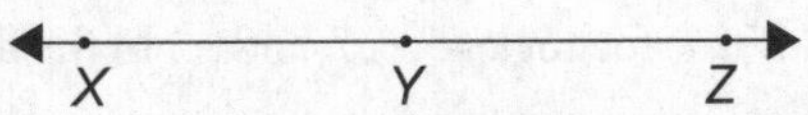

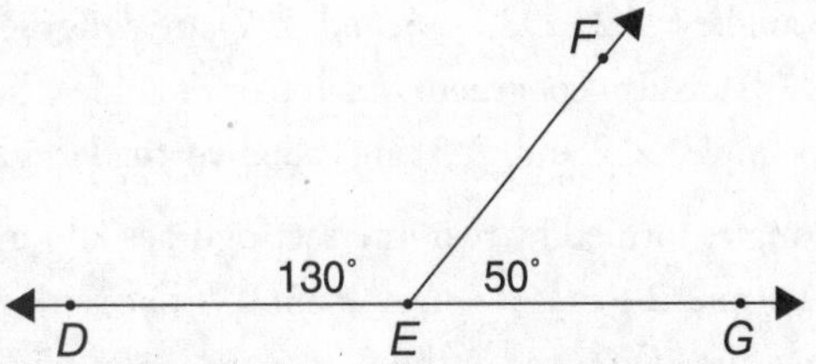

Two angles are called **complementary** angles when their measurements add up to 90° (a right angle). In the next figure, m$\angle ABC = 90°$. $\angle ABE$ and $\angle CBE$ are complementary because their measurements add up to 90°. You also know that m$\angle ABD = 90°$ because $\angle ABD$ and $\angle ABC$ combine to form a straight line, which measures 180°.

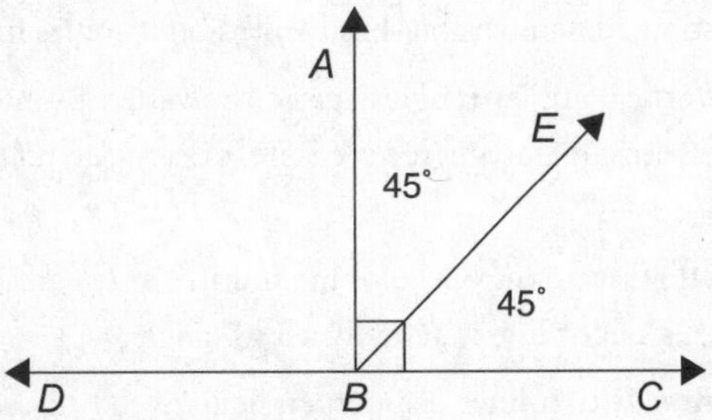

In geometry, the set of points that makes up a flat surface is referred to as a **plane.** When two lines in the same plane never meet, no matter how far they are extended, they are called **parallel lines** and are indicated by the symbol ||. If two parallel lines are intersected by a third line, eight angles are formed. A line that intersects two parallel lines is called a **transversal.** If a transversal intersects two parallel lines perpendicularly (at a 90° angle), all eight angles that are formed are right angles (90°). Otherwise, some angles are acute, while others are obtuse. Look at the next figure.

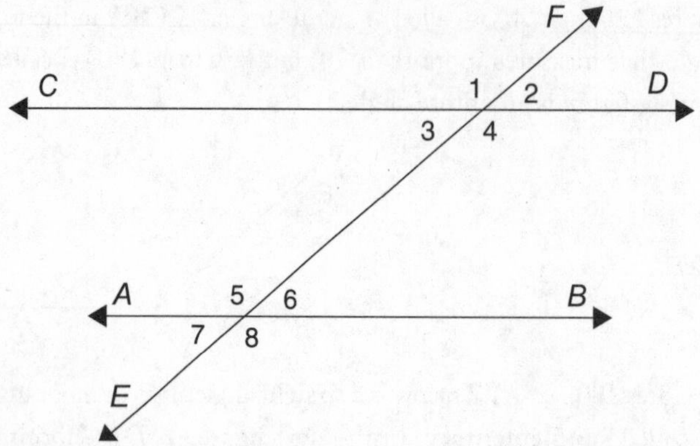

As noted earlier, angles that are equal in degree measure are called congruent angles (the symbol $\cong$ indicates congruency). In the figure above, you can see that eight angles have been formed. The four acute angles ($\angle 2$, $\angle 3$, $\angle 6$, and $\angle 7$) are congruent, and the four obtuse angles ($\angle 1$, $\angle 4$, $\angle 5$, and $\angle 8$) are also congruent. Each pair of angles that are opposite each other in relation to a vertex (for example, $\angle 2$ and $\angle 3$) are called **vertical angles**. Vertical angles are always congruent.

Four angles formed by two intersecting lines add up to 360° in measure. In the same figure above, $m\angle 1 + m\angle 2 + m\angle 3 + m\angle 4 = 360°$. (The same holds true for angles 5, 6, 7, and 8.) In the figure, the measure of any one of the four acute angles plus the measure of any obtuse angle equals 180°. If you know the measure of *any* one angle, you can determine the measure of all seven other angles. For example, if $m\angle 2 = 30°$, then $\angle 3$, $\angle 6$, and $\angle 7$ each measures 30° as well, while $\angle 1$, $\angle 4$, $\angle 5$, and $\angle 8$ each measures 150°.

A geometry question might involve nothing more than intersecting lines and the angles they form. To handle this type of question, remember four basic rules about angles formed by intersecting lines:

1. **Vertical angles:** Vertical angles (angles across the vertex from each other and formed by the same two lines) are equal in degree measure, or congruent ($\cong$). In other words, they're the same size.
2. **Adjacent angles:** If adjacent angles combine to form a straight line, their degree measures total 180. In fact, a straight line is actually a 180° angle.
3. **Perpendicular lines:** If two lines are perpendicular ($\perp$) to each other, they intersect at right (90°) angles.
4. **The sum of angles:** The sum of all angles formed by the intersection of two (or more) lines at the same point is 360°, regardless of how many angles are involved.

EXAMPLE 1 (EASIER):

The figure below shows three intersecting lines.

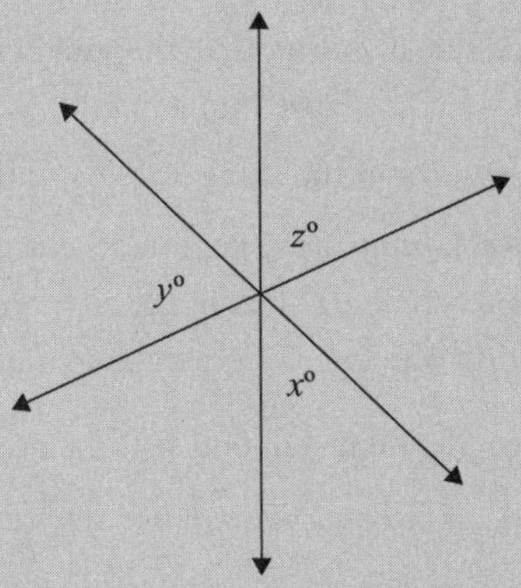

Which of the following expresses the value of $x + y$ in every case?

A. $2z$

B. $180 - z$

C. $360 - z$

D. $z + 90$

The angle vertical to the one whose measure is given as $z°$ must also measure $z°$. That angle and the angles whose measures are $x°$ and $y°$ combine to form a straight (180°) line. In other words, $x + y + z = 180$. Accordingly, $x + y = 180 - z$. **The correct answer is B.**

EXAMPLE 2 (MORE CHALLENGING):

Line R intersects line P and line Q at a 45° angle. Which statement must be true?

A. Line P is parallel to line Q.

B. Line P intersects line Q at a 45° angle.

C. Line P is perpendicular to line Q.

D. Line Q intersects line R at a 135° angle.

Lines P and Q may or may not be parallel. But any two lines intersecting at a 45° angle also form a 135° at the vertex because adjacent angles combine to form a straight, 180° line. **The correct answer is D.**

TRIANGLES

The **triangle** is a 3-sided shape. All triangles, regardless of shape or size, share the following four properties:

1. **Length of the sides.** Each side is shorter than the sum of the lengths of the other two sides. (Otherwise, the triangle would collapse into a line.)
2. **Angle measures.** The measures of the three interior angles total 180°.
3. **Angles and opposite sides.** Comparative angle sizes correspond to the comparative lengths of the sides opposite those angles. For example, a triangle's largest angle is opposite its longest side. (The sides opposite two congruent angles are also congruent.)
4. **Area.** The area of any triangle is equal to one-half the product of its base and its height (or "altitude"): Area $= \frac{1}{2} \times$ base $\times$ height. You can use any side as the base to calculate area.

The next figure shows three particular types of triangles. GED test questions often involve these three types.

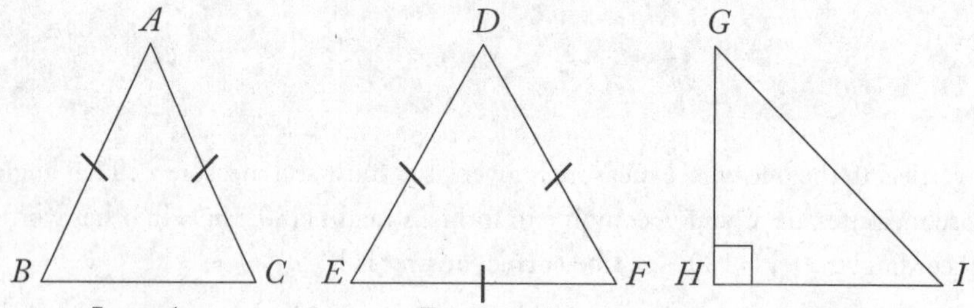

Isosceles Triangle | Equilateral Triangle | Right Triangle

An **isosceles triangle** is one in which two sides (and two angles) are congruent. In the figure above, ∠ B and ∠ C are congruent, and the sides opposite those two angles, $\overline{AB}$ and $\overline{AC}$, are congruent. In an **equilateral triangle**, all three angles are congruent, and all three sides are congruent. In a **right triangle**, one angle is a right angle, and the other two angles are acute angles. The longest side of a right triangle (in this case, $\overline{GI}$) is called the **hypotenuse**. In the pages ahead, you'll examine these three types of triangles in greater detail.

EXAMPLE 3 (EASIER):

The length of one side of a certain triangular floor space is 12 feet. Which of the following CANNOT be the lengths of the other two sides?

A. 1 foot and 12 feet

B. 8 feet and 4 feet

C. 12 feet and 13 feet

D. 16 feet and 14 feet

The length of any two sides combined must be greater than the length of the third side. **The correct answer is B.**

EXAMPLE 4 (MORE CHALLENGING):

In triangle *T*, the degree measure of one interior angle is three times that of each of the other two interior angles. What is the measure of triangle *T*'s largest interior angle?

A. 72°

B. 90°

C. 108°

D. 120°

The ratio among the three angles is 3:1:1. Letting x = the length of either short side:

$$x + x + 3x = 180$$
$$5x = 180$$
$$x = 36$$

The largest angle measures 3 × 36 = 108°. **The correct answer is C.**

Right Triangles and the Pythagorean Theorem

In a right triangle, one angle measures 90° and, of course, each of the other two angles measures less than 90°. The **Pythagorean theorem** involves the relationship among the sides of any right triangle and can be expressed by the equation $a^2 + b^2 = c^2$. As shown in the next figure, the letters a and b represent the lengths of the two **legs** (the two shortest sides) that form the right angle, and c is the length of the hypotenuse (the longest side, opposite the right angle).

Pythagorean theorem: $a^2 + b^2 = c^2$

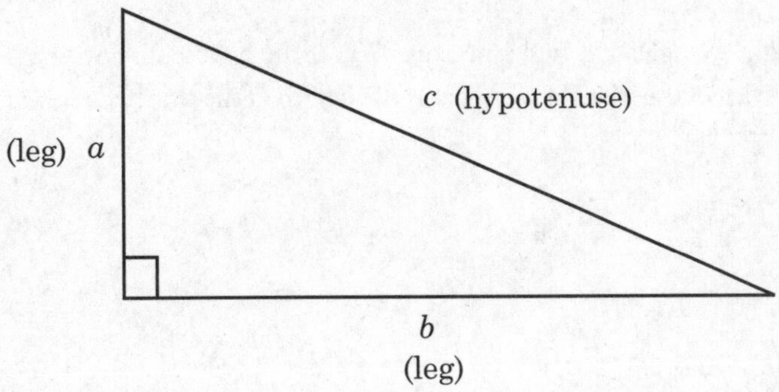

The Pythagorean theorem is included on the Formula Sheet provided during the test.

For any right triangle, if you know the length of two sides, you can determine the length of the third side by applying the Pythagorean theorem. Study the following two examples:

Example:

If the two shortest sides (the legs) of a right triangle are 2 and 3 inches in length, then the length of the triangle's third side (the hypotenuse) is $\sqrt{13}$ inches:

$$a^2 + b^2 = c^2$$
$$2^2 + 3^2 = c^2$$
$$4 + 9 = c^2$$
$$13 = c^2$$
$$\sqrt{13} = c$$

Example:

If a right triangle's longest side (hypotenuse) is 4 inches in length, and if another side (one of the legs) is 2 inches in length, then the length of the third side (the other leg) is $\sqrt{12}$ inches:

$$a^2 + b^2 = c^2$$
$$a^2 + 2^2 = 4^2$$
$$a^2 + 4 = 16$$
$$a^2 = 12$$
$$a = \sqrt{12}$$

EXAMPLE 5 (EASIER):

In a right triangle, one angle measures 90°. If the hypotenuse of a right triangle is *c* and one leg of the triangle is *a*, what is the length of the third side in terms of *a* and *c*?

A. $\sqrt{a^2 + c^2}$

B. $\frac{a + c}{2}$

C. $\sqrt{a \times c}$

D. $\sqrt{c^2 - a^2}$

Use the Pythagorean theorem to determine the length of the third side, which is the other leg of the triangle. Call the length of the third side *b*. The Pythagorean theorem says that $a^2 + b^2 = c^2$. Solve for *b*:

$$b^2 = c^2 - a^2$$
$$b = \sqrt{c^2 - a^2}$$

The correct answer is D.

EXAMPLE 6 (MORE CHALLENGING):

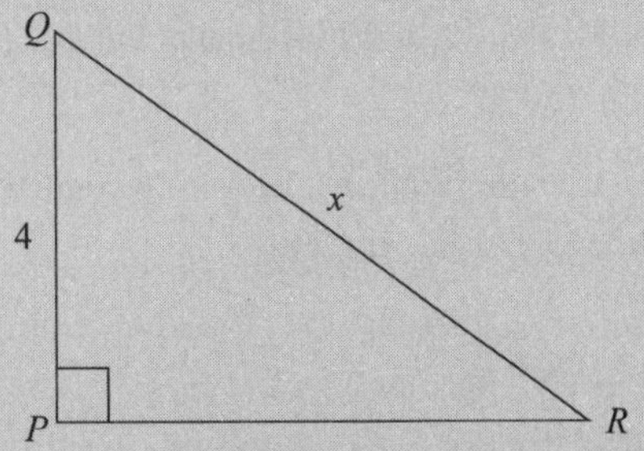

Which of the following expresses the unit length of $\overline{PR}$ in the figure above?

A. $\sqrt{x^2 - 4}$

B. $\sqrt{x + 16}$

C. $x - 4$

D. $\sqrt{x^2 - 16}$

The question asks for the length of leg $\overline{PR}$ in terms of the other two sides. Apply the Pythagorean theorem (let y = the length of $\overline{PR}$):

$$
\begin{aligned}
4^2 + y^2 &= x^2 \\
16 + y^2 &= x^2 \\
y^2 &= x^2 - 16 \\
y &= \sqrt{x^2 - 16}
\end{aligned}
$$

The correct answer is D.

Pythagorean Side Triplets

A **Pythagorean side triplet** is a specific side ratio that satisfies the Pythagorean theorem. In each of the following triplets, the first two numbers represent the ratio between the lengths of the two legs (*a* and *b*), and the third, and largest, number represents the length of the hypotenuse (*c*) in relation to the two legs:

Side ratio	**Pythagorean theorem**
$(a:b:c)$	$(a^2 + b^2 = c^2)$
$1:1:\sqrt{2}$	$1^2 + 1^2 = \left(\sqrt{2}\right)^2$
$1:\sqrt{3}:2$	$1^2 + \left(\sqrt{3}\right)^2 = 2^2$
3:4:5	$3^2 + 4^2 = 5^2$
5:12:13	$5^2 + 12^2 = 13^2$
8:15:17	$8^2 + 15^2 = 17^2$
7:24:25	$7^2 + 24^2 = 25^2$

Each triplet shown is expressed as a *ratio* because it represents a proportion among the triangle's sides. All right triangles with sides having the same proportion, or ratio, have the same shape. For example, a right triangle with sides of 5, 12, and 13 is smaller but exactly the same shape (proportion) as a triangle with sides of 15, 36, and 39.

To save valuable time on right-triangle problems, learn to recognize numbers (lengths of triangle sides) that are multiples of Pythagorean side triplets.

EXAMPLE 7 (EASIER):

Which of the following does NOT describe a right triangle?

A triangle with sides

A. 3 inches, 4 inches, and 5 inches

B. 5 inches, 12 inches, and 13 inches

C. 10 inches, 24 inches, and 26 inches

D. 6 inches, 10 inches, and 20 inches

Choice A describes a 3:4:5 triangle. Choices B and C describe 5:12:13 triangles. Choice D does not describe a right triangle ($6^2 + 10^2 \neq 20^2$). In fact, since the sum of the two sides (6 inches + 10 inches) is not greater in length than the third side (20 inches), this isn't even a triangle at all. **The correct answer is D.**

EXAMPLE 8 (MORE CHALLENGING):

Two boats leave the same dock at the same time, one traveling due west at 30 miles per hour and the other due north at 40 miles per hour. If they maintain those speeds, how far apart are the boats after three hours?

A. 90 miles

B. 120 miles

C. 150 miles

D. 210 miles

The distance between the two boats after three hours forms the hypotenuse of a triangle in which the legs are the two boats' respective paths. The ratio of one leg to the other is 30:40, or 3:4. So you know you're dealing with a 3:4:5 triangle. The slower boat traveled 90 miles (30 mph × 3 hours). The number 90 corresponds to the number 3 in the 3:4:5 ratio, so the multiple is 30 (3 × 30 = 90). 3:4:5 = 90:120:150. **The correct answer is C.**

Pythagorean Angle Triplets

In two (and only two) of the unique triangles identified in the preceding section as Pythagorean side triplets, all degree measures are *integers:*

The angles of a $1:1:\sqrt{2}$ triangle are 45°, 45°, and 90°.

The angles of a $1:\sqrt{3}:2$ triangle are 30°, 60°, and 90°.

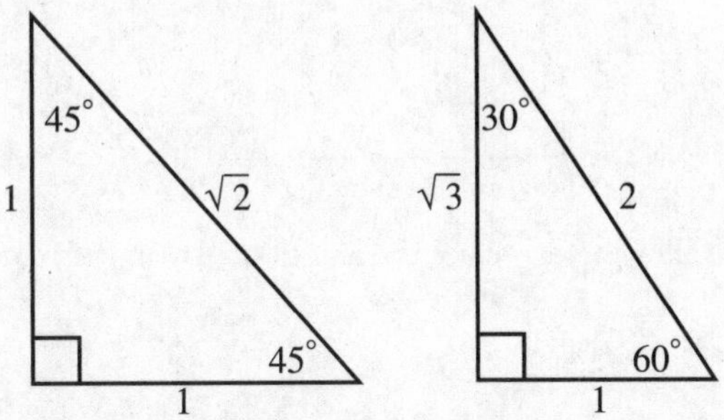

If one acute angle of a right triangle is given as 45°, and you know the length of one side, then you can find the lengths of the other sides. For example:

If one leg is 5, then the other leg must also be 5, while the hypotenuse must be $5\sqrt{2}$.

If the hypotenuse is 10, then each leg must be $\frac{10}{\sqrt{2}} = \frac{10}{\sqrt{2}} \times \frac{\sqrt{2}}{\sqrt{2}} = 5\sqrt{2}$

(divide the hypotenuse by $\sqrt{2}$ and clear the radical from the denominator).

Similarly, if you know that one acute angle of a right triangle is either 30° or 60°, then given the length of any side, you can find the lengths of the other sides. For example:

If the shortest leg (opposite the 30° angle) is 3, then the other leg (opposite the 60° angle) must be $3\sqrt{3}$, and the hypotenuse must be 6 units long (3×2).

If the hypotenuse is 10, then the shorter leg (opposite the 30° angle) must be 5, and the longer leg (opposite the 60° angle) must be $5\sqrt{3}$ (the length of the shorter leg multiplied by $\sqrt{3}$).

To save time on right-triangle problems, be on the lookout for either of the two Pythagorean angle triplets.

EXAMPLE 9 (EASIER):

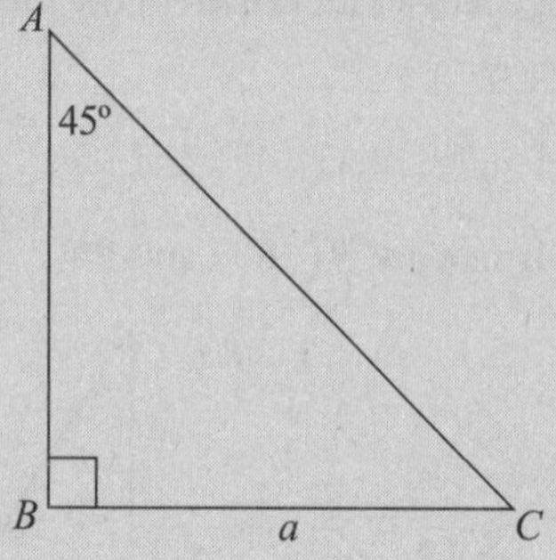

Which of the following expresses the length of $\overline{AC}$ in the figure above?

A. $2a$

B. $a\sqrt{2}$

C. $a\sqrt{3}$

D. $2\sqrt{a}$

The 45° angle tells you that $\overline{AB}$ and $\overline{BC}$ are congruent (equal in length). So the ratio of the three sides is $1:1:\sqrt{2}$. Given that each leg has a length of a, the ratio is $a : a : a\sqrt{2}$. **The correct answer is B.**

EXAMPLE 10 (MORE CHALLENGING):

As shown in the following figure, $\overline{AC}$ is 5 units in length, $m\angle ABD = 45°$, and $m\angle DAC = 60°$.

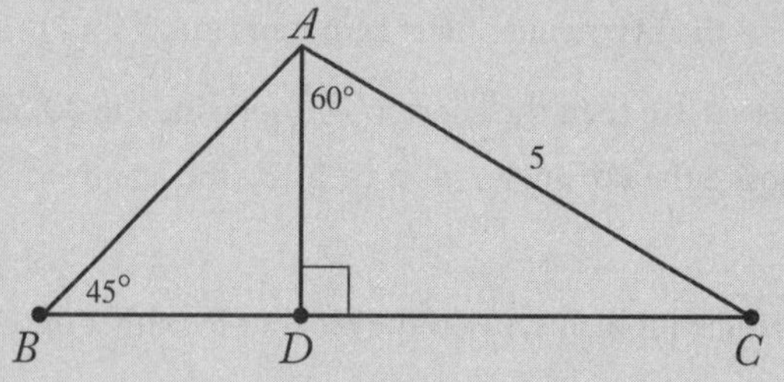

What is the unit length of $\overline{BD}$?

A. $2\sqrt{2}$

B. $\frac{5}{2}$

C. $\frac{7}{2}$

D. $\frac{7}{3}$

To find the length of $\overline{BD}$, you first need to find the length of $\overline{AD}$. Notice that ΔADC is a 30°-60°-90° triangle. The ratio among its sides is $1:\sqrt{3}:2$. Given that $\overline{AC}$ is 5, $\overline{AD}$ must be $\frac{5}{2}$. (The ratio 1:2

is equivalent to a ratio of $\frac{5}{2}$ to 5.) Next, notice that ΔABD is a 45°-45°-90° triangle. The ratio among its sides is $1:1:\sqrt{2}$. You know that $\overline{AD}$ is $\frac{5}{2}$ units in length. Thus, $\overline{BD}$ must also be $\frac{5}{2}$ units in length. **The correct answer is B.**

Isosceles and Equilateral Triangles

An *isosceles* triangle has the following special properties:

1. Two of the sides are congruent (equal in length).
2. The two angles opposite the two congruent sides are congruent (equal in size or degree measure).

If you know any *two* angle measures of a triangle, you can determine whether the triangle is isosceles. Subtract the two angle measures you know from 180. If the result equals one of the other two measures, then the triangle is isosceles. For example:

> If two of the angles are 55° and 70°, then the third angle must be 55° (180 – 55 – 70 = 55). The triangle is isosceles, and the two sides opposite the two 55° angles are congruent.
>
> If two of the angles are 80° and 20°, then the third angle must be 80° (180 – 80 – 20 = 80). The triangle is isosceles, and the two sides opposite the two 80° angles are congruent.

In any isosceles triangle, lines bisecting the triangle's three angles each bisect its opposite side. The line bisecting the angle connecting the two congruent angles divides the triangle into two congruent right triangles.

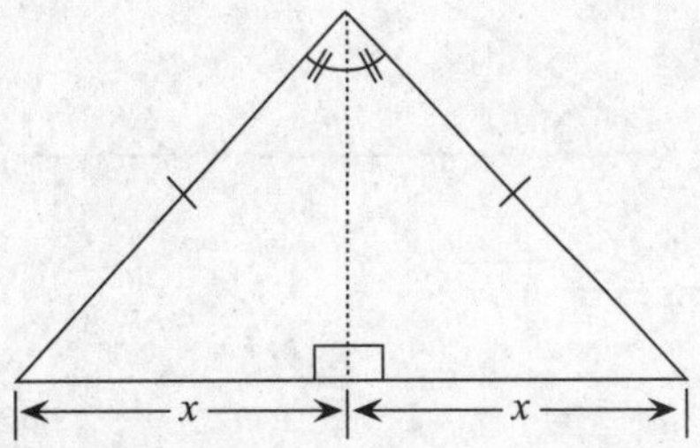

So if you know the lengths of all three sides of an isosceles triangle, you can determine the area of the triangle by applying the Pythagorean theorem.

All **equilateral triangles** share the following three properties:

1. All three sides are congruent (equal in length).
2. The measure of each angle is 60°.
3. Area $= \frac{s^2\sqrt{3}}{4}$ (s = any side)

The area formula for an equilateral triangle may or may not appear on the Formula Sheet provided during the exam. If you need to find an equilateral triangle's area but don't recall the formula, you can bisect the triangle and combine the two smaller areas.

As shown in the following diagram, any line bisecting one of the 60° angles divides an equilateral triangle into two right triangles with angle measures of 30°, 60°, and 90° (one of the two Pythagorean angle triplets). Accordingly, the side ratio for each smaller triangle is $1:\sqrt{3}:2$. The area of this equilateral triangle is $\frac{1}{2}(2)\sqrt{3}$, or $\sqrt{3}$.

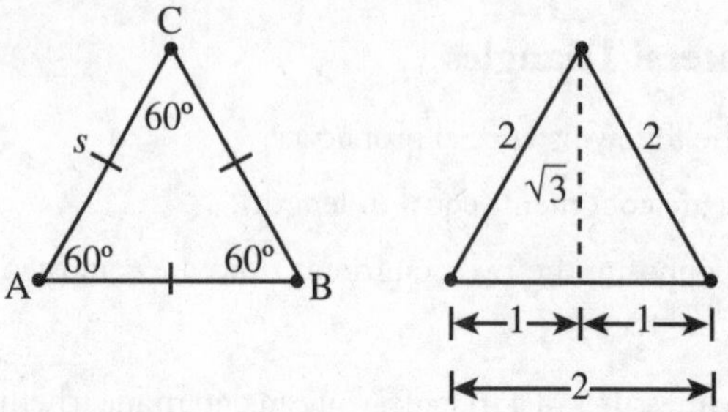

On the GED Mathematical Reasoning Test, equilateral triangles often appear in problems involving *circles*, which you'll examine later in this review.

EXAMPLE 11 (EASIER):

As shown in the figure, $\overline{BC}$ is 6 units in length, m $\angle A = 70°$, and m $\angle B = 40°$.

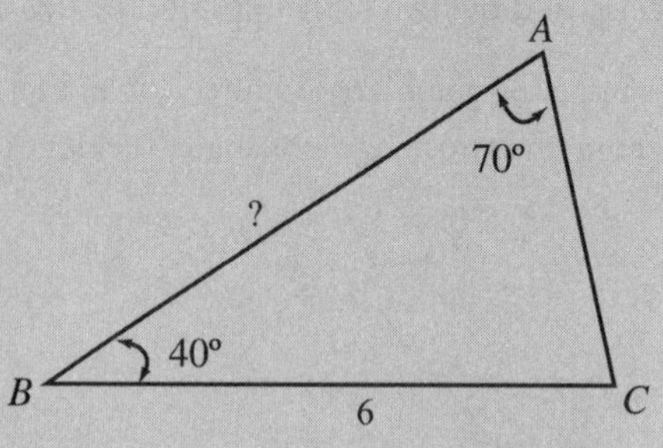

What is the unit length of $\overline{AB}$?

A. 5

B. 6

C. 7

D. $5\sqrt{2}$

Since m $\angle A$ and m $\angle B$ add up to 110°, m $\angle C = 70°$ (70 + 110 = 180), and you know the triangle is isosceles. Since m $\angle A =$ m $\angle C$, $\overline{AB} \cong \overline{BC}$. Given that $\overline{BC}$ is 6 units in length, $\overline{AB}$ must also be 6 units in length. **The correct answer is B.**

EXAMPLE 12 (MORE CHALLENGING):

Two sides of a triangle are each 8 units in length, and the third side is 6 units in length. What is the area of the triangle, expressed in square units?

A. 14

B. $12\sqrt{3}$

C. 18

D. $3\sqrt{55}$

Bisect the angle connecting the two congruent sides ($\overline{BC}$ and $\overline{AC}$ in ΔABC below). The bisecting line is the triangle's height (h), and $\overline{AB}$ is its base, which is 6 units long.

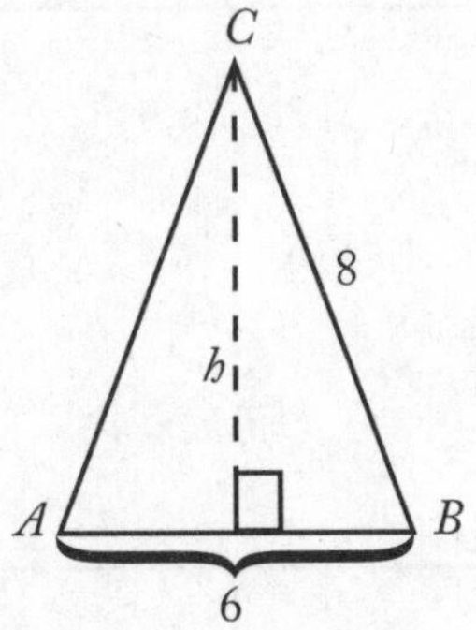

You can determine the triangle's height (h) by applying the Pythagorean theorem:

$$3^2 + h^2 = 8^2$$
$$h^2 = 64 - 9$$
$$h^2 = 55$$
$$h = \sqrt{55}$$

A triangle's area is half the product of its base and height. Thus, the area of ΔABC = $\frac{1}{2}(6)\sqrt{55} = 3\sqrt{55}$. **The correct answer is D.**

QUADRILATERALS

A **quadrilateral** is any four-sided figure. The GED Mathematical Reasoning Test emphasizes four specific types of quadrilaterals: the square, the rectangle, the parallelogram, and the trapezoid.

Rectangles, Squares, and Parallelograms

A **parallelogram** is a quadrilateral in which opposite sides are parallel. A **rectangle** is a special type of parallelogram in which all four angles are right angles (90°). A **square** is a special type of rectangle in which all four sides are congruent (equal in length). Certain characteristics apply to all rectangles, squares, and parallelograms:

- The sum of the measures of all four interior angles is 360°.
- Opposite sides are parallel.
- Opposite sides are congruent (equal in length).
- Opposite angles are congruent (the same size, or equal in degree measure).
- Adjacent angles are supplementary (their measures total 180°).

You should know how to determine the perimeter and area of these three types of quadrilaterals. Formulas for both area and perimeter are included on the Formula Sheet provided during the test.

The Square

To find the perimeter of a square, multiply any side by 4. To find the area, simply square any side.

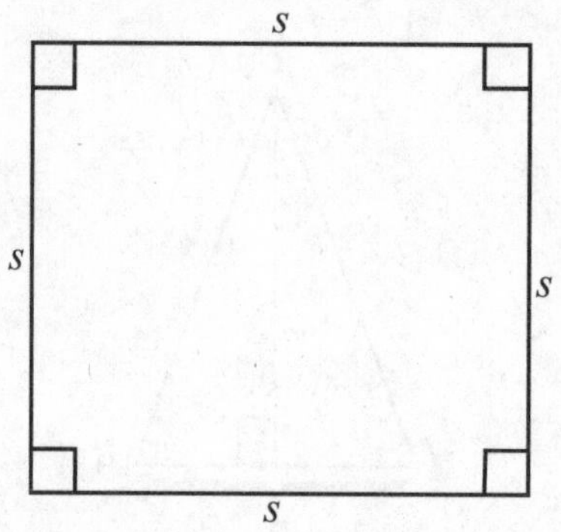

Perimeter = $4s$ [s = side]

Area = s^2

Questions involving squares come in many varieties. For example, you might need to determine an area based on a perimeter, or you might need to do just the opposite—find a perimeter based on a given area. For example:

The area of a square with a perimeter of 8 is 4.

$s = 8 \div 4 = 2$; $s^2 = 4$

The perimeter of a square with area 8 is $8\sqrt{2}$.

$s = \sqrt{8} = 2\sqrt{2}$; $4s = 4 \times 2\sqrt{2}$

Or, you might need to determine a change in area resulting from a change in perimeter (or vice versa). These are just some of the possibilities.

EXAMPLE 13 (EASIER):

Nine square tiles, each with an area of 25 square centimeters, have been arranged to form a larger square. What is the perimeter of the large square?

A. 60 centimeters

B. 100 centimeters

C. 150 centimeters

D. 225 centimeters

The side of each square = $\sqrt{25}$ or 5 cm. Aligned to form a large square, the tiles form three rows and three columns, each column and row with side 5 × 3 = 15. The perimeter = 15 × 4 = 60. **The correct answer is A.**

EXAMPLE 14 (MORE CHALLENGING):

If a square's sides are each increased by 50%, by what percent does the square's area increase?

A. 100%

B. 125%

C. 150%

D. 200%

The easiest way to answer this question is to plug in simple numbers. Assume that the square's original side length is 1. Its area is also 1. Increase the side length to 1.5, and then square it to find the new area: 1.5 × 1.5 = 2.25. Comparing 1 to 2.25, the percent increase is 125%. You can also solve the problem conventionally. Letting s = the length of each side before the increase, area = s^2. Let $\frac{3}{2}s$ = the length of each side after the increase, the new area = $\left(\frac{3}{2}s\right)^2 = \frac{9}{4}s^2$. The increase from s^2 to $\frac{9}{4}s^2$ is $\frac{5}{4}$, or 125%. **The correct answer is B.**

The Rectangle

To find the perimeter of a rectangle, multiply width by 2, and multiply length by 2, and then add the two products. To find area, multiply length by width.

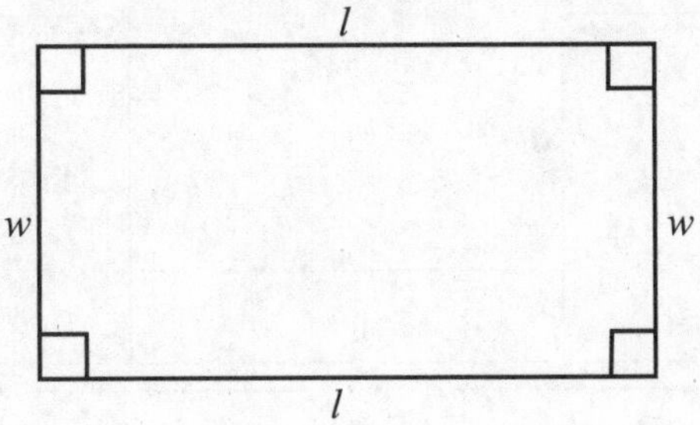

Perimeter = $2l + 2w$

Area = $l \times w$

Questions involving non-square rectangles also come in many possible varieties. For example, a question might ask you to determine area based on perimeter, or vice versa. Or, a question might require you to determine a combined perimeter or area of adjoining rectangles.

EXAMPLE 15 (EASIER):

In the following figure, all intersecting line segments are perpendicular.

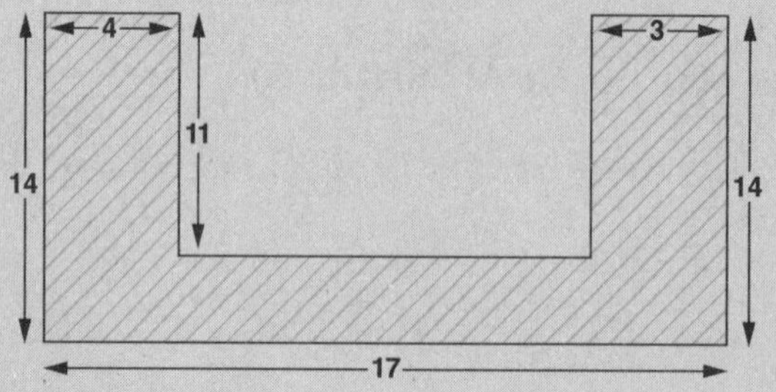

What is the area of the shaded region, in square units?

A. 84

B. 118

C. 128

D. 238

The figure provides the perimeters you need to calculate the area. One way to find the area of the shaded region is to consider it as what remains when a rectangular shape is cut out of a larger rectangle. The area of the entire figure without the "cut-out" is 14 × 17 = 238. The "cut-out" rectangle has a length of 11, and its width is equal to 17 – 4 – 3 = 10. Thus, the area of the cut-out is 11 × 10 = 110. Accordingly, the area of the shaded region is 238 – 110 = 128. **The correct answer is C.**

Another way to solve the problem is to partition the shaded region into three smaller rectangles, as shown in the next figure, and sum up the area of each.

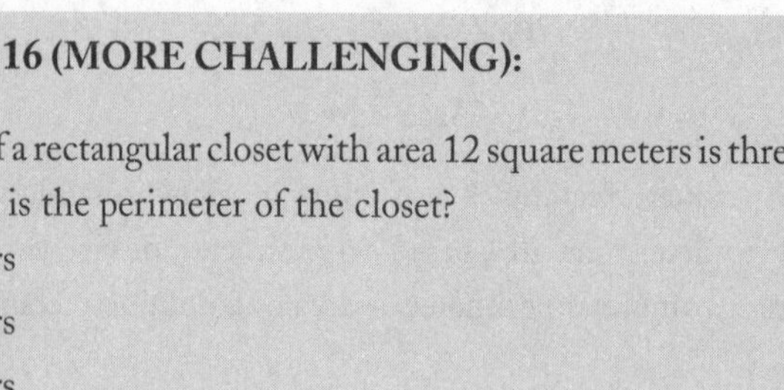

EXAMPLE 16 (MORE CHALLENGING):

The length of a rectangular closet with area 12 square meters is three times the closet's width. What is the perimeter of the closet?

A. 10 meters

B. 12 meters

C. 14 meters

D. 16 meters

The ratio of length to width is 3:1. The ratio 6:2 is equivalent, and 6 × 2 = 12 (the area). Thus, the perimeter = (2)(6) + (2)(2) = 16. **The correct answer is D.**

The Parallelogram

To find the perimeter of a parallelogram, multiply the width by 2, multiply the length by 2, and then add the two products. To find the area, multiply the base by the **altitude,** which is the parallelogram's *height*, not the length of any side. (*Note*: The base can be any of the four sides of the figure; just be sure to to use the altitude that goes with the base you've chosen.)

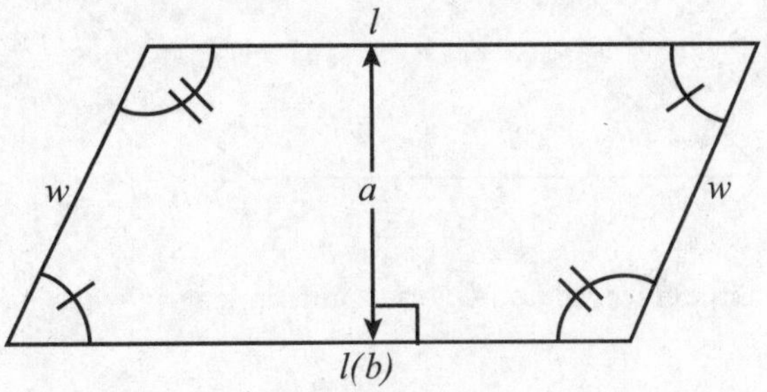

Perimeter = $2l + 2w$

Area = base (b) × altitude (a)

Of these two formulas, *only* the area formula is included on the Formula Sheet provided during the test.

A question about a non-rectangular parallelogram might focus on angle measures. These questions are easy to answer. In any parallelogram, opposite angles are congruent, and adjacent angles are supplementary. (Their measures total 180°.) So if one of a parallelogram's angles measure 65°, then the opposite angle must also measure 65°, while the two other angles each measure 115°.

A more difficult question about a non-rectangular parallelogram might focus on area. To determine the parallelogram's altitude, you might need to apply the Pythagorean theorem (or one of the side or angle triplets).

EXAMPLE 17 (EASIER):

If one of a parallelogram's interior angles measures a°, which of the following expresses the combined measures of its two adjacent angles?

A. $2a + 90$

B. $180 - a$

C. $180 + a$

D. $360 - 2a$

$\angle a$ is supplementary to both its adjacent angles. Thus, the degree measure of each adjacent angle = $180 - a$. Express their sum by adding: $(180 - a) + (180 - a) = 360 - 2a$. **The correct answer is D.**

EXAMPLE 18 (MORE CHALLENGING):

In the following figure, $\overline{AB} \parallel \overline{CD}$, $\overline{AD} \parallel \overline{BC}$, and $m\angle B = 45°$.

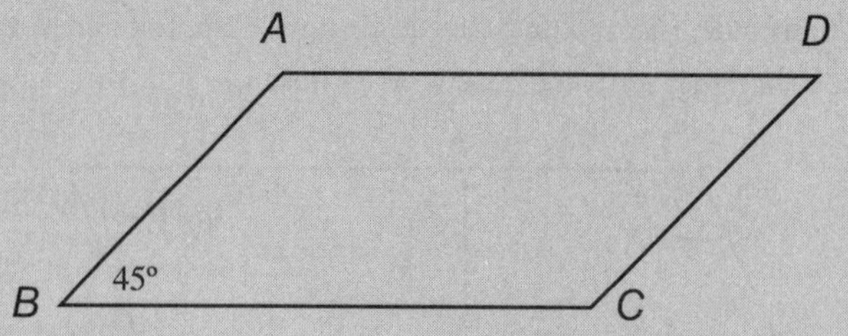

If $\overline{BC}$ is 4 units in length and $\overline{CD}$ is 2 units in length, what is the area of quadrilateral *ABCD*?

A. $4\sqrt{2}$

B. 6

C. 8

D. $6\sqrt{2}$

Since *ABCD* is a parallelogram, its area = base (4) × altitude. To determine altitude (*a*), draw a vertical line segment connecting point *A* to $\overline{BC}$, which creates a 45°-45°-90° triangle.

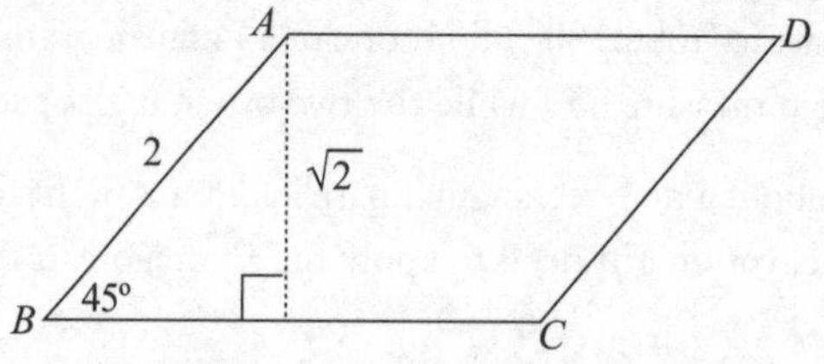

The ratio of the triangle's hypotenuse to each leg is $\sqrt{2}$:1. The hypotenuse $\overline{AB} = 2$. Thus, the altitude (*a*) of *ABCD* is $\frac{2}{\sqrt{2}}$, or $\sqrt{2}$. Accordingly, the area of $ABCD = 4 \times \sqrt{2}$, or $4\sqrt{2}$.

The correct answer is A.

Trapezoids

A **trapezoid** is a quadrilateral with only one pair of parallel sides. All trapezoids share these four properties:

1. Only one pair of opposite sides is parallel.
2. The sum of all four angles is 360°.
3. Perimeter = the sum of the four sides.
4. Area = half the sum of the two parallel sides, multiplied by the altitude (*a*).

The next figure shows a trapezoid in which $\overline{BC} \parallel \overline{AD}$.

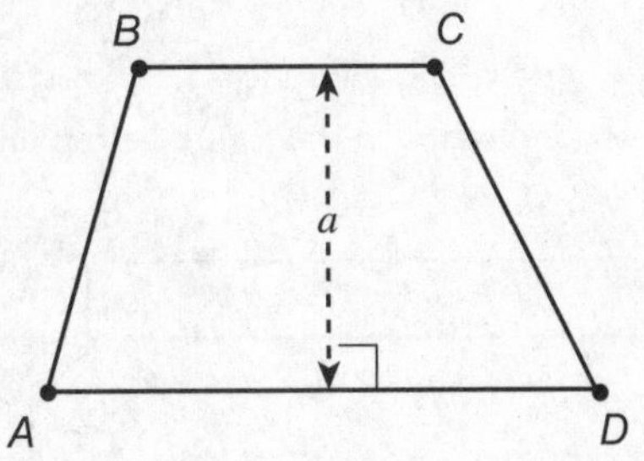

$$\textbf{Perimeter} = \overline{AB} + \overline{BC} + \overline{CD} + \overline{AD}$$

$$\textbf{Area} = \frac{\overline{BC} + \overline{AD}}{2} \times a$$

The area formula for a trapezoid is included on the Formula Sheet provided during the test.

Trapezoid problems on the GED Mathematical Reasoning Test generally provide all but one of the values in the area formula, and then ask for the missing value.

EXAMPLE 19 (EASIER):

A metal sheet in the shape of a trapezoid is to be assembled from a square piece and a triangular piece, as shown below.

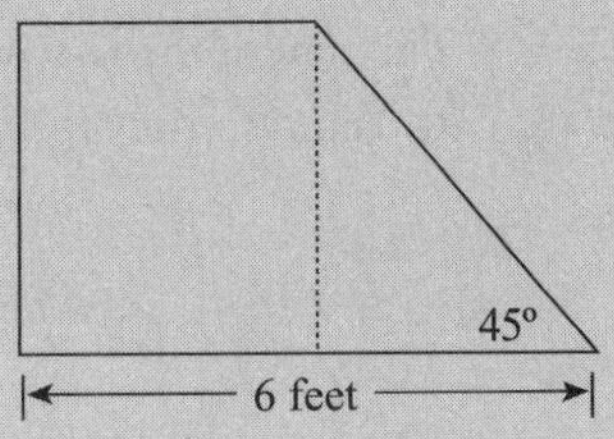

What is the area of the assembled product?

A. 12 square feet

B. $13\frac{1}{2}$ square feet

C. 15 square feet

D. $17\frac{1}{2}$ square feet

To answer this question, you don't need to apply the area formula. The 45° angle tells you that the triangle's two legs are the same length, which is also the height of the square. Since the two pieces together run 6 feet in length, each piece is half that length. Thus, the altitude (dotted line) is 3. The area of the square = $3^2 = 9$. The area of the triangle = $\frac{1}{2} \times 3^2 = \frac{9}{2}$. The combined area is $13\frac{1}{2}$ square feet. **The correct answer is B.**

EXAMPLE 20 (MORE CHALLENGING):

To cover the floor of an entry hall, a 1-foot × 12-foot strip of carpet is cut into two pieces, shown as the shaded strips in the figure below, and each piece is connected to a third carpet piece, as shown.

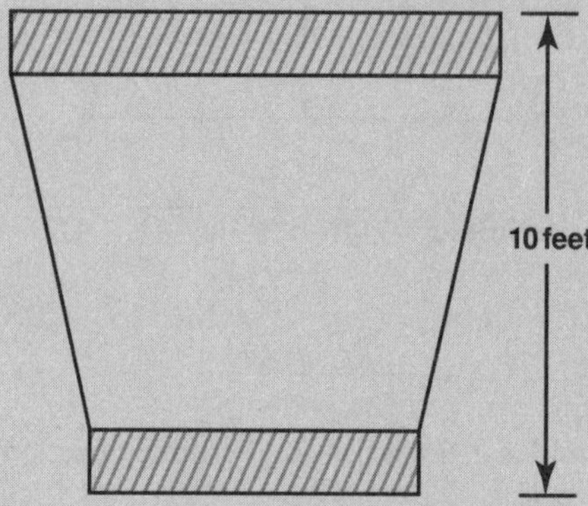

If the 1-foot strips run parallel to each other, what is the total area of the carpeted floor?

A. 48 square feet

B. 52.5 square feet

C. 56 square feet

D. 60 square feet

The altitude of the trapezoidal piece is 8. The sum of the two parallel sides of this piece is 12' (the length of the 1' × 12' strip before it was cut). You can apply the trapezoid formula to determine the area of this piece:

$$A = 8 \times \frac{12}{2} = 48$$

The total area of the two shaded strips is 12 square feet, so the total area of the floor is 60 square feet. **The correct answer is D.**

POLYGONS

Polygons include all two-dimensional figures formed only by line segments. The two most important points about polygons to remember are these two reciprocal rules:

1. If all angles of a polygon are congruent (equal in degree measure), then all sides are congruent (equal in length).
2. If all sides of a polygon are congruent (equal in length), then all angles are congruent (equal in degree measure).

A polygon in which all sides are congruent and all angles are congruent is called a **regular polygon**.

You can use the following formula to determine the sum of all interior angles of *any* polygon with angles that each measure less than 180° (n = number of sides):

$$(n-2)(180°) = \text{sum of interior angles}$$

This formula is NOT included on the Formula Sheet provided during the test. The test question will provide the formula if needed.

For regular polygons, the average angle size is also the size of every angle. But for *any* polygon (except for those with an angle exceeding 180°), you can find the average angle size by dividing the sum of the angles by the number of sides. One way to shortcut the math is to memorize the angle sums and averages for polygons with three to eight sides:

3 sides: $(3-2)(180°) = 180° \div 3 = 60°$

4 sides: $(4-2)(180°) = 360° \div 4 = 90°$

5 sides: $(5-2)(180°) = 540° \div 5 = 108°$

6 sides: $(6-2)(180°) = 720° \div 6 = 120°$

7 sides: $(7-2)(180°) = 900° \div 7 = 129°$

8 sides: $(8-2)(180°) = 1{,}080° \div 8 = 135°$

You can add up known angle measures to find unknown angle measures.

EXAMPLE 21 (EASIER):

The measures of a polygon's interior angles total $(n-2)(180°)$, where n = number of sides. If four of the interior angles of a five-sided polygon measure 100° each, what is the measure of the fifth interior angle?

A. 40°

B. 60°

C. 90°

D. 140°

The total number of degrees in the polygon = $(5-2)(180°) = 540°$. The four known angles total 400°, so the fifth angle must be 140°. **The correct answer is D.**

EXAMPLE 22 (MORE CHALLENGING):

The regular octagon pictured below is 12 inches on each side and has been divided into 9 smaller pieces.

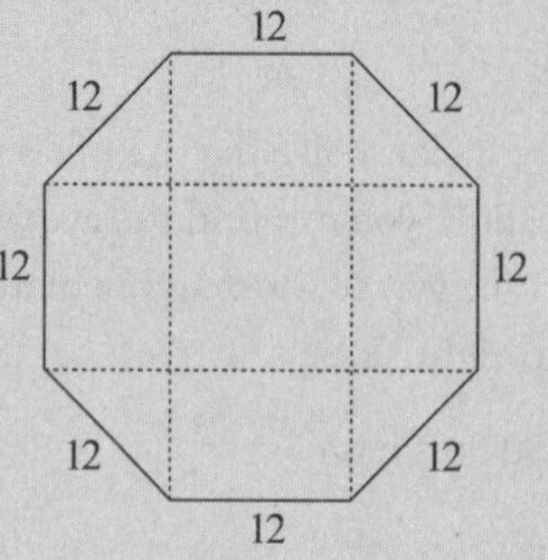

Which of the following **most nearly** approximates the area of the octagon?

A. 660 square inches

B. 790 square inches

C. 860 square inches

D. 1,000 square inches

The center segment, a square, is 12 inches on each side and thus has an area of 144 square inches. Each of the four triangles is an isosceles right triangle, with the hypotenuse given as 12 inches. The ratio of the hypotenuse's length to the length of each leg is $\sqrt{2}$:1. To determine the length of each base, divide 12 by $\sqrt{2}$. Using 1.4 as an approximate value for $\sqrt{2}$, the length of each base is approximately 8 inches. The approximate area of each triangle $= \frac{1}{2}(8)(8) = 32$ square inches. The approximate area of each of the four non-square rectangles is $8 \times 12 = 96$. Combine the approximate areas of the octagon's nine pieces:

$$\begin{aligned} 144 + 4(32) + 4(96) &= 144 + 128 + 384 \\ &= 656 \text{ square inches} \end{aligned}$$

Since the question asks for the closest approximation, the correct answer would then be 660 square inches. **The correct answer is A.**

CIRCLES

For the GED Mathematical Reasoning Test, you should be familiar with the following basic terminology involving circles:

- **circumference:** the distance around the circle (the same as "perimeter," but the word "circumference" applies only to circles, ovals, and other curved figures)
- **radius:** the distance from a circle's center to any point along the circle's circumference
- **diameter:** the greatest distance from one point to another on the circle's circumference (twice the length of the radius)
- **chord:** a line segment connecting two points on the circle's circumference (a circle's longest possible chord is its diameter, passing through the circle's center)

As noted previously, a circle's diameter is twice the length of its radius. The next figure shows a circle with radius 6 and diameter 12.

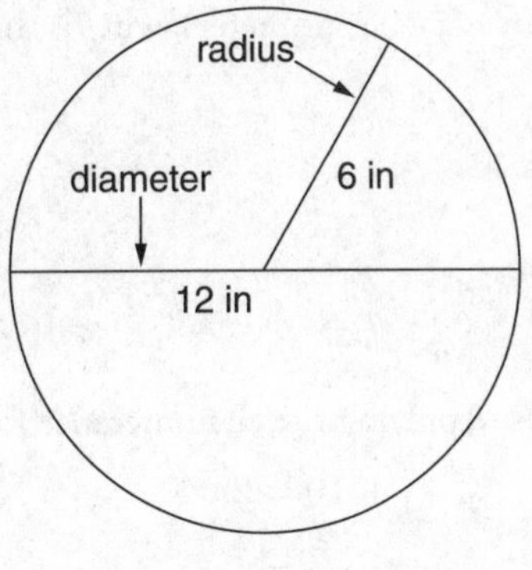

During the test, you'll apply one, or possibly both, of two basic formulas involving circles (r = radius, d = diameter):

Circumference = $2\pi r$, or πd

Area = πr^2

The value of π is approximately 3.14. A close fractional approximation of π is $\frac{22}{7}$.

With the circumference and area formulas, all you need is one value—area, circumference, diameter, or radius—and you can determine all the others. Referring to the circle shown above:

Given a circle with a diameter of 12:

radius = 6

circumference = 12π

area = $\pi(6)^2 = 36\pi$

For the test, you won't need to work with a value of π any more precise than 3.14 or $\frac{22}{7}$. In fact, you might be able to answer a circle question using the symbol π itself, without approximating its value.

EXAMPLE 23 (EASIER):

If a circle with radius r has an area of 4 square feet, what is the area of a circle whose radius is $3r$?

A. 6π square feet

B. 36 square feet

C. 12π square feet

D. 48 square feet

The area of a circle with radius $r = \pi r^2$, which is given as 4. The area of a circle with radius $3r = \pi(3r)^2 = 9\pi r^2$. Since $\pi r^2 = 4$, the area of a circle with radius $3r = (9)(4) = 36$. **The correct answer is B.**

EXAMPLE 24 (MORE CHALLENGING):

If a circle's circumference is 10 centimeters, what is the area of the circle?

A. $\frac{25}{\pi}$ cm^2

B. 5π cm^2

C. 22.5 cm^2

D. 25 cm^2

First, determine the circle's radius. Applying the circumference formula $C = 2\pi r$, solve for r:

$$10 = 2\pi r$$
$$\frac{5}{\pi} = r$$

Then, apply the area formula, with $\frac{5}{\pi}$ as the value of r:

$$A = \pi\left(\frac{5}{\pi}\right)^2$$
$$= \pi\left(\frac{25}{\pi^2}\right)$$
$$= \frac{25}{\pi^2} \cdot \frac{\pi}{1}$$
$$= \frac{25}{\pi}$$

The correct answer is A.

Arcs and Degree Measures of a Circle

An **arc** is a segment of a circle's circumference. A **minor arc** is the shortest arc connecting two points on a circle's circumference. For example, in the figure shown, minor arc $\widehat{AB}$ is the one formed by the 60° angle from the circle's center (O).

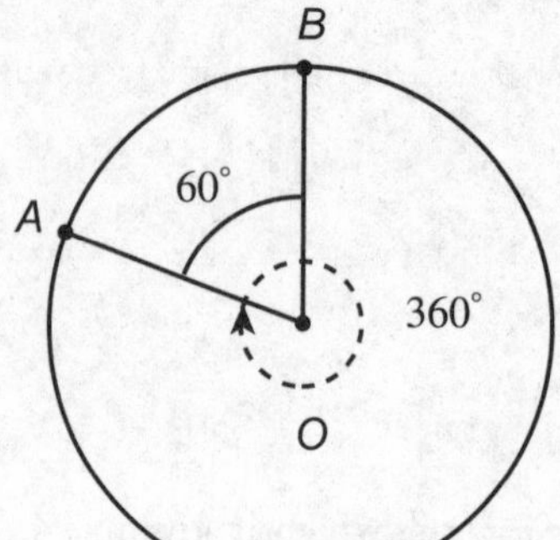

A circle, by definition, contains a total of 360°. The length of an arc relative to the circle's circumference is directly proportionate to the arc's degree measure as a fraction of the circle's total degree measure of 360°. For example, in the preceding figure, minor arc $\overset{\frown}{AB}$ accounts for $\frac{60}{360}$, or $\frac{1}{6}$, of the circle's circumference.

An arc of a circle can be defined either as a length (a portion of the circle's circumference) or as a degree measure. In the preceding figure, $\overset{\frown}{AB} = 60°$. If the circumference is 12π, then the length of minor arc $\overset{\frown}{AB}$ is $\frac{1}{6}$ of 12π, or 2π.

EXAMPLE 25 (EASIER):

Circle *O* has diameters $\overline{DB}$ and $\overline{AC}$, as shown in the figure below.

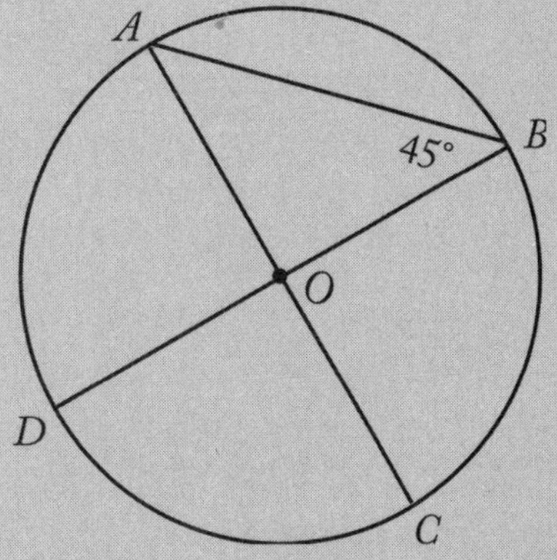

If the circumference of circle *O* is 12 inches, what is the length of minor arc $\overset{\frown}{BC}$?

A. 3 inches

B. $\frac{13}{4}$ inches

C. $\frac{11}{3}$ inches

D. 4 inches

Since $\overline{AO}$ and $\overline{BO}$ are both radii, ΔAOB is isosceles, and therefore $m\angle BAO = 45°$. It follows that $m\angle AOB = 90°$. That 90° angle accounts for $\frac{1}{4}$ of the circle's 360°. Accordingly, minor arc $\overset{\frown}{BC}$ must account for $\frac{1}{4}$ of the circle's 12-inch circumference, or 3 inches. **The correct answer is A.**

EXAMPLE 26 (MORE CHALLENGING):

A hexagon is inscribed in a circle whose center is *O*, as shown below.

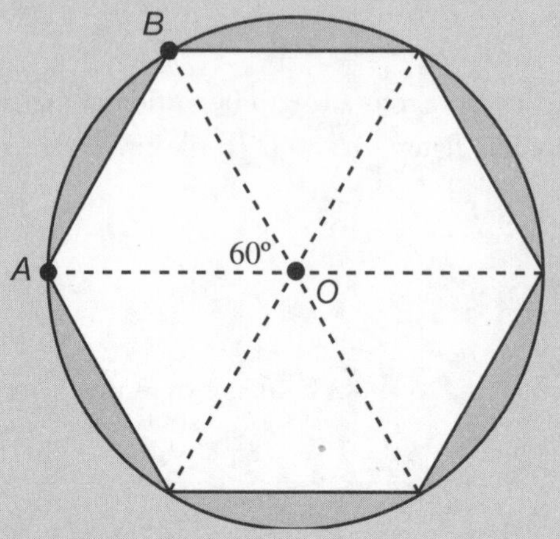

What is the unit length of $\overline{AB}$, expressed in terms of the diameter (d) of circle *O*?

A. $\frac{d}{3}$

B. $\frac{d}{\pi}$

C. $\frac{d}{2}$

D. $\frac{n}{d}$

Since $\overline{AO}$ and $\overline{BO}$ are both radii, the 60° central angle tells you that ΔABO is equilateral. Accordingly, the length of $\overline{AB}$ must equal the circle's radius, which is half its diameter, or $\frac{d}{2}$. **The correct answer is C.**

Circles and Tangent Lines

A circle is **tangent** to a line (or line segment) if the two intersect at one and only one point (called the **point of tangency**). Here's the key rule to remember about tangents: A line that is tangent to a circle is *always* perpendicular to the line passing through the circle's center and the point of tangency.

The figure shown shows a circle with center O inscribed in a square. Point P is one of four points of tangency. By definition, $\overline{OP} \perp \overline{AB}$.

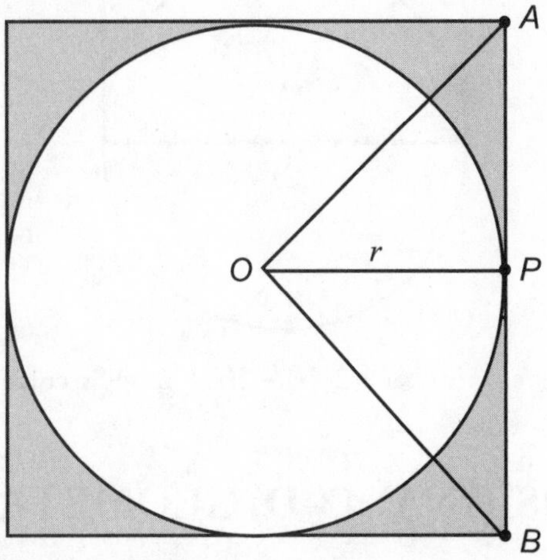

Also, notice the following relationships between the circle in the preceding figure and the inscribing square (r = radius):

Each side of the square is $2r$ in length.

The square's area is $(2r)^2$, or $4r^2$.

EXAMPLE 27 (EASIER):

Two parallel lines are tangent to the same circle. What is the shortest distance between the two lines?

A. The circle's radius

B. The circle's diameter

C. The circle's circumference

D. The product of the circle's radius and π

The two lines are both perpendicular to a chord that is the circle's diameter. Thus, the shortest distance between them is that diameter. **The correct answer is B.**

EXAMPLE 28 (MORE CHALLENGING):

One side of a rectangle forms the diameter of a circle. The opposite side of the rectangle is tangent to the circle. In terms of the circle's radius (r), what is the perimeter of the rectangle?

A. $2r$

B. $4r$

C. $6r$

D. $8r$

The information in the problem describes the following figure:

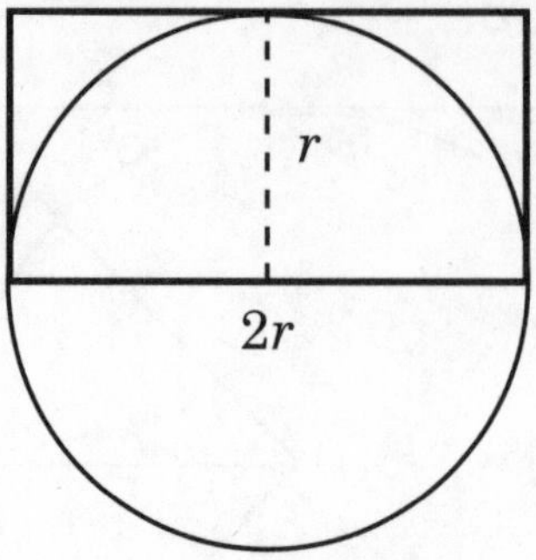

Given radius r, the rectangle's perimeter = $2(2r) + 2(r) = 6r$. **The correct answer is C.**

THREE-DIMENSIONAL (3-D) GEOMETRIC FIGURES

Three-dimensional (3-D) figures you might deal with on the GED Mathematical Reasoning Test include cubes and other rectangular prisms (box-shaped objects), cylinders, cones, and so-called "square" pyramids (pyramids that have a square base).

Rectangular Prisms

Rectangular prisms are box-shaped figures in which all corners are right angles. Any box-shaped figure has a total of six sides, or *faces*. The length of a side is generally referred to as an *edge*. A test question about a rectangular prism will involve one or both of two basic formulas (p = perimeter of base, B = area of base ($l \times w$), h = height):

Volume = Bh, or lwh

Surface Area = $ph + 2B$

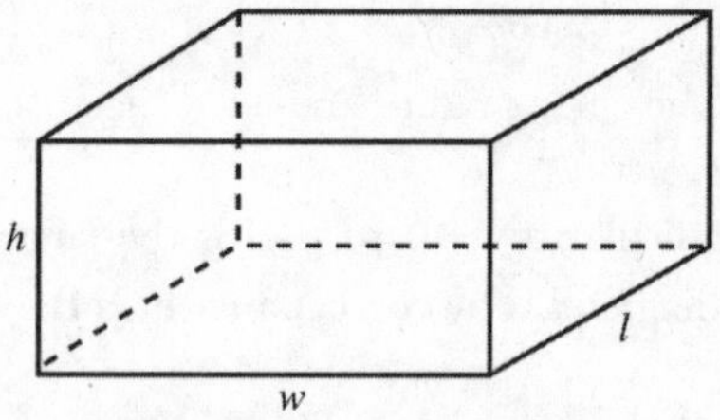

The volume formula is included on the Formula Sheet provided during the test.

To answer a question involving a rectangular prism, plug what you know into the appropriate formula—surface area or volume—and then solve for the missing term. Depending on the question, you might need to apply both formulas.

For example, when given the surface area of a cube, you can then find the length of one of its edges. Say you are given that a cube has surface area of 294 square inches. Since this is a cube, you know that all the edges are the same length. Let's call that length e:

$$SA = ph + 2B$$
$$SA = 4e(e) + 2(e^2)$$
$$SA = 4e^2 + 2e^2$$

So the formula for the surface area of a cube is $6e^2$. To find the length of an edge, solve the equation $6e^2 = 294$ for e, as follows:

$$6e^2 = 294$$
$$e^2 = 49$$
$$e = 7$$

The edges of this cube each measure 7 inches in length.

EXAMPLE 29 (EASIER):

Which of the following does NOT describe the dimensions of a rectangular box whose capacity is 120 cubic inches?

A. 6 inches, 6 inches, and $3\frac{1}{3}$ inches

B. 8 inches, 2 inches, and $7\frac{1}{2}$ inches

C. 5 inches, 10 inches, and $2\frac{2}{5}$ inches

D. 9 inches, 5 inches, and $2\frac{1}{2}$ inches

For each answer choice, multiply the three numbers. The only dimensions that do not equal 120 inches are $9 \times 5 \times 2\frac{1}{2}$, which equal $112\frac{1}{2}$. **The correct answer is D.**

EXAMPLE 30 (MORE CHALLENGING):

A closed rectangular box with a square base is 5 inches in height. If the volume of the box is 45 square inches, what is the box's surface area?

A. 66 square inches

B. 78 square inches

C. 81 square inches

D. 90 square inches

First, determine the dimensions of the square base. The box's height is given as 5. Accordingly, the box's volume (45) = $5lw$, and $lw = 9$. Since the base is square, the base is 3 inches long on each side. Now you can calculate the total surface area:

$$2lw + 2wh + 2lh = (2)(9) + (2)(15) + (2)(15) = 78$$

The correct answer is B.

Cubes

A **cube** is a rectangular prism whose length, width, and height are all the same—in other words, all six faces are squares. The volume and surface area formulas are even simpler than for other rectangular prisms (let s = any edge):

volume = s^3 , or $s = \sqrt[3]{\text{Volume}}$

surface area = $6s^2$

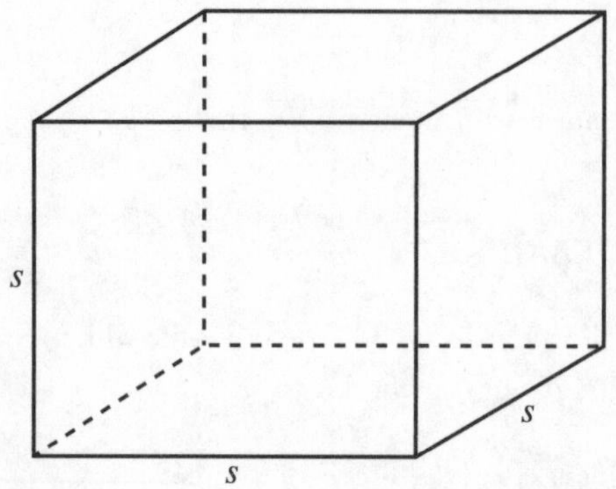

The volume formula is NOT included on the Formula Sheet provided during the test.

Questions involving cubes (or other box shapes) are sometimes presented as "packing" problems. In this type of problem, your task is to determine how many small boxes fit into a larger box. Another type of cube question focuses on the *ratios* among the cube's linear, square, and cubic measurements.

EXAMPLE 31 (EASIER):

How many cube-shaped boxes, each box 18 inches on a side, can be packed into a storage unit measuring 6 feet long, 6 feet wide, and 5 feet high?

A. 36

B. 42

C. 48

D. 64

First convert inches to feet: 18 inches $= 1\frac{1}{2}$ feet. You can pack 3 levels of 16 cube-shaped boxes, with a half-foot space left at the top of the storage unit. 3 × 16 = 48. **The correct answer is C.**

EXAMPLE 32 (MORE CHALLENGING):

If the volume of one cube is 8 times greater than that of another, what is the ratio of any edge of the larger cube to any edge of the smaller cube?

A. 2 to 1

B. 4 to 1

C. 8 to 1

D. 16 to 1

The ratio of the two volumes is 8:1. The edge ratio is the cube root of this ratio: $\sqrt[3]{8}$ to $\sqrt[3]{1}$, or 2:1. **The correct answer is A.**

Cylinders

A **cylinder** is a three-dimensional figure with a circular base. The only type of cylinder question you may encounter on the test might involve a **right cylinder**, in which the height and base are at 90° angles. The surface area of a right cylinder is the sum of three areas:

1. The circular base
2. The circular top
3. The rectangular surface around the cylinder's vertical face (visualize a rectangular label wrapped around a soup can)

The area of the vertical face is the product of the circular base's circumference (i.e., the rectangle's width) and the cylinder's height. The volume of a right cylinder is the product of the circular base's area and the cylinder's height. Given a radius r and height h of a cylinder:

Surface Area (SA) = $2\pi rh^2 + 2\pi r^2$

Volume = $\pi r^2 h$

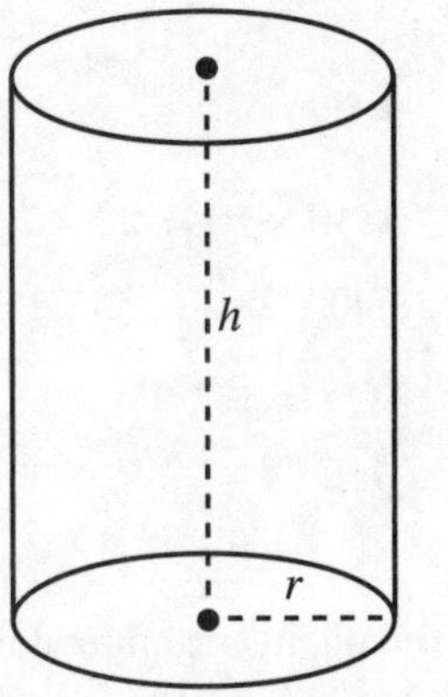

The volume and surface area formulas are included on the Formula Sheet provided during the test.

A cylinder problem might require little more than a straightforward application of either the surface-area or the volume formula. As with rectangular-solid questions, just plug what you know into the formula, then solve for what the question asks. A more complex cylinder problem might require you to apply other math concepts, or require you to convert one unit of measurement to another.

EXAMPLE 33 (EASIER):

What is the volume of a cylinder whose circular base has a radius of 3 centimeters and whose height is 7 centimeters?

A. 21π cm^3

B. 42π cm^3

C. 63π cm^3

D. 81 cm^3

The cylinder's volume = $\pi(3)^2(7) = 63\pi$ cm^3. **The correct answer is C.**

EXAMPLE 34 (MORE CHALLENGING):

A cylindrical pail with a diameter of 14 inches and height of 10 inches is filled to one-fourth its capacity with water. Which of the following **most** closely approximates the volume of water in the pail? [231 cubic inches = 1 gallon]

A. 0.8 gallons

B. 1.7 gallons

C. 2.9 gallons

D. 4.2 gallons

The volume of the pail = $\pi r^2 h \approx \frac{22}{7} \times 49 \times 10 = 22 \times 7 \times 10 = 1{,}540$ cubic inches. The gallon capacity of the pail is approximately 1,540 ÷ 231, or about 6.7 gallons. One-fourth of that amount is about 1.7 gallons. **The correct answer is B.**

Cones and Pyramids

Two other three-dimensional figures you might encounter during the GED Mathematical Reasoning Test are the **cone** and the **square pyramid** (a four-sided pyramid with a square base). Both are shown below, along with their volume formulas:

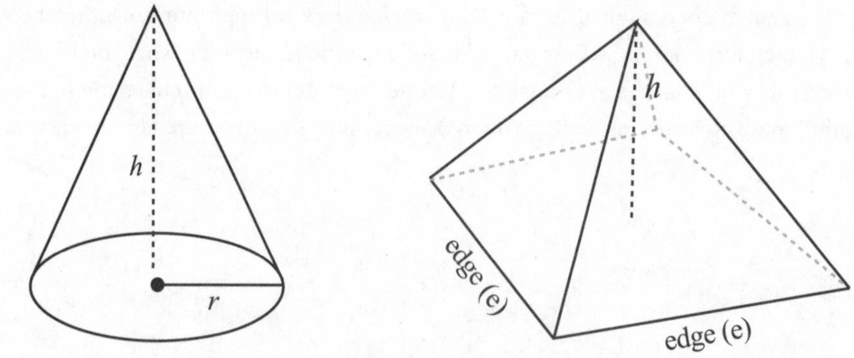

Volume of a cone: $\frac{1}{3}\ \pi \times \text{radius}^2 \times \text{height}\ (\pi \approx 3.14)$

Volume of a square pyramid: $\frac{1}{3} \times (\text{base edge})^2 \times \text{height}$

The Formula Sheet provided during the exam includes both of these equations, so you do not need to memorize them. Notice that the volume of a cone is simply one-third that of a right cylinder, and that the volume of a square pyramid is simply one-third that of a rectangular prism.

EXAMPLE 35 (EASIER):

What is the volume of a pyramid with a height of 24 feet and a square base that measures 10 feet on each side?

A. 240 cubic feet

B. 480 cubic feet

C. 760 cubic feet

D. 800 cubic feet

The volume of the pyramid $= \frac{1}{3} \times \text{edge}^2 \times \text{height} = \frac{1}{3} \times 100 \times 24 = 800$ cubic feet. **The correct answer is D.**

EXAMPLE 36 (MORE CHALLENGING):

Which of the following is nearest to the height of a cone with a diameter of 16 inches and a volume of 4,480 cubic inches?

A. 36 inches

B. 44 inches

C. 56 inches

D. 70 inches

Given a diameter of 16, the radius is 8. Letting h = height, the cone's volume $(4{,}480) = \frac{1}{3} \times \pi(8)^2(h) \approx \left(\frac{1}{3}\right)(3.14)(64)(h)$. Since the question asks for an approximation, try canceling out 3.14 and the denominator number 3. Solve for h:

$$4{,}480 \approx 64h$$

$$\frac{4{,}480}{64} \approx h$$

$$70 \approx h$$

The correct answer is D.

Spheres

The **sphere** is the final three-dimensional figure you may encounter on the GED Mathematical Reasoning Test.

The volume and surface area of a sphere with radius r are given by the following formulas:

Volume $= \frac{4}{3}\pi r^3$

Surface Area $= 4\pi r^2$

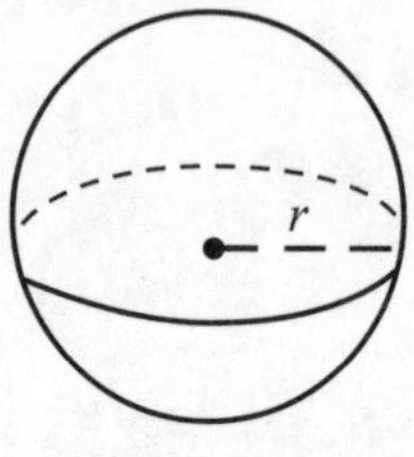

EXAMPLE 37:

What is the volume of a sphere with a surface area of 100π square meters?

A. $\frac{100}{3}\pi$ cubic meters

B. 166π cubic meters

C. $\frac{500}{3}\pi$ cubic meters

D. 500π cubic meters

We must determine the radius to compute the volume. Using the formula for the surface area enables us to do this:

$$4\pi r^2 = 100\pi$$
$$r^2 = 25$$
$$r = 5$$

So the volume of the sphere is $\frac{4}{3}\pi \cdot 5^3 = \frac{4}{3}\pi \cdot 125 = \frac{500}{3}\pi$ cubic meters.

The correct answer is C.

RIGHT-TRIANGLE TRIGONOMETRY

Right-triangle trigonometry involves the ratios between sides of right triangles and the angle measures that correspond to these ratios. Refer to the following right triangle, in which the sides opposite angles *A*, *B*, and *C* are labeled *a*, *b*, and *c*, respectively (*A* and *B* are the two acute angles):

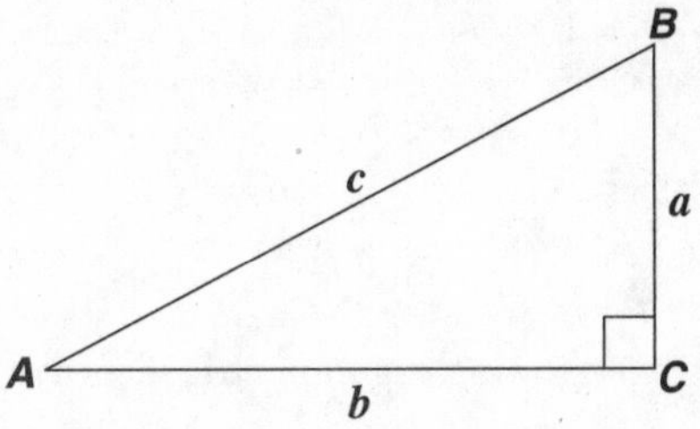

Referring to ΔABC, you express and define the six trigonometric functions **sine, cosine, tangent, cotangent, secant,** and **cosecant** for angle *A* as follows. Notice that each function in the right column is the **reciprocal**, or **multiplicative inverse**, of the function to the left of it.

$$\sin A = \frac{a}{c} \qquad \csc A = \frac{c}{a}$$

$$\cos A = \frac{b}{c} \qquad \sec A = \frac{c}{b}$$

$$\tan A = \frac{a}{b} \qquad \cot A = \frac{b}{a}$$

You would express and define the six functions for angle *B* similarly. The sine, cosine, and tangent functions are the most important ones. For the GED Mathematical Reasoning Test, you should memorize the following three general definitions:

$$\text{sine} = \frac{\text{opposite}}{\text{hypotenuse}}$$

$$\text{cosine} = \frac{\text{adjacent}}{\text{hypotenuse}}$$

$$\text{tangent} = \frac{\text{opposite}}{\text{adjacent}}$$

These definitions will NOT be included on the Formula Sheet provided during the exam.

You also won't find any trigonometric tables, which list angle measures and their corresponding trigonometric function values. Though a question might provide specific angle measures, it's more likely that you'll express solutions to problems in terms of trigonometric functions. If the lengths of only two sides are given, you might need to use the Pythagorean theorem to find the length of the third side. For example, look at the next figure:

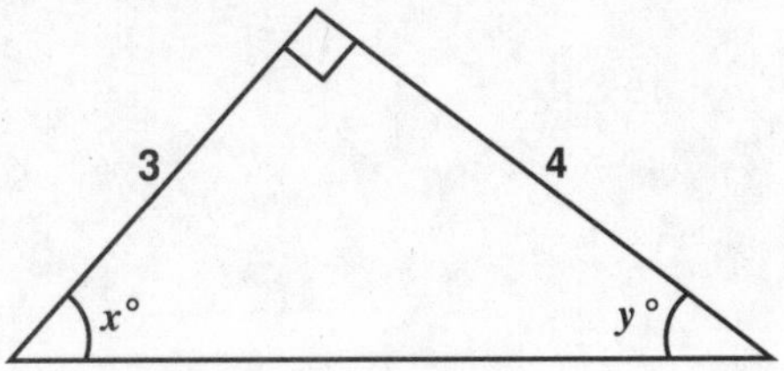

You should recognize the Pythagorean side triplet 3:4:5 in this figure ($3^2 + 4^2 = 5^2$). The length of the hypotenuse is 5. Applying the definitions of sine, cosine, and tangent to angles x and y, here are the results:

$$\sin x = \frac{4}{5} \qquad \sin y = \frac{3}{5}$$

$$\cos x = \frac{3}{5} \qquad \cos y = \frac{4}{5}$$

$$\tan x = \frac{4}{3} \qquad \tan y = \frac{3}{4}$$

You should also keep in mind the following trigonometric identity:

$$\text{tangent} = \frac{\text{sine}}{\text{cosine}}$$

The relationships among the sine, cosine, and tangent functions result in the following three additional observations for a triangle with acute angles A and B:

1. By definition, $\tan A \times \tan B = 1$.
2. For all right triangles, $\sin A = \cos B$ (and $\sin B = \cos A$). For all other triangles, $\sin A \neq \cos B$ (and $\sin B \neq \cos A$).
3. In a right isosceles triangle (in which A and B each measures 45°), $\sin A = \sin B = \cos A = \cos B = \frac{\sqrt{2}}{2}$ (you can apply the Pythagorean theorem to show this fraction).

EXAMPLE 38 (EASIER):

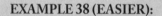

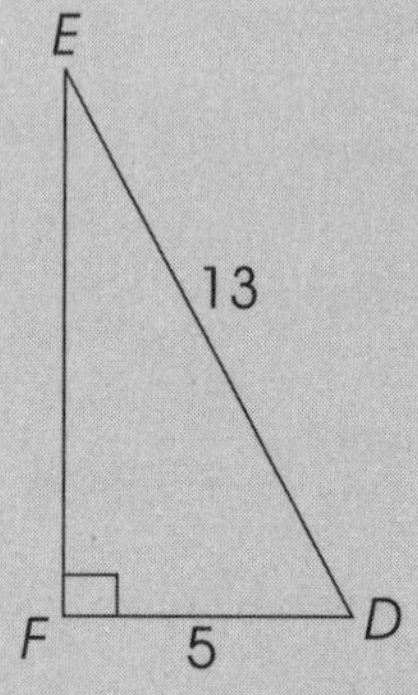

In ΔDEF, what is the value of $\tan D$?

A. $\frac{3}{5}$

B. $\frac{12}{13}$

C. $\frac{12}{5}$

D. $\frac{13}{5}$

You can find the length of $\overline{EF}$ by applying the Pythagorean theorem. Notice that the sides conform to the Pythagorean side ratio 5:12:13 ($5^2 + 12^2 = 13^2$). The length of $\overline{EF} = 12$. In ΔDEF, $\tan D = \frac{\text{opposite}}{\text{adjacent}} = \frac{12}{5}$. **The correct answer is C.**

EXAMPLE 39 (MORE CHALLENGING):

A 50-foot wire is attached to the top of a vertical electric pole and is anchored on the ground. If the wire rises in a straight line at a 70° angle from the ground, what is the height of the pole, in linear feet?

A. $50\sin 70°$

B. $50\cos 70°$

C. $\frac{\cos 70°}{50}$

D. $\frac{50}{\cos 70°}$

As shown in the figure, the height of the pole (x) is opposite the 70° angle, and the triangle's hypotenuse (length of the wire) is 50.

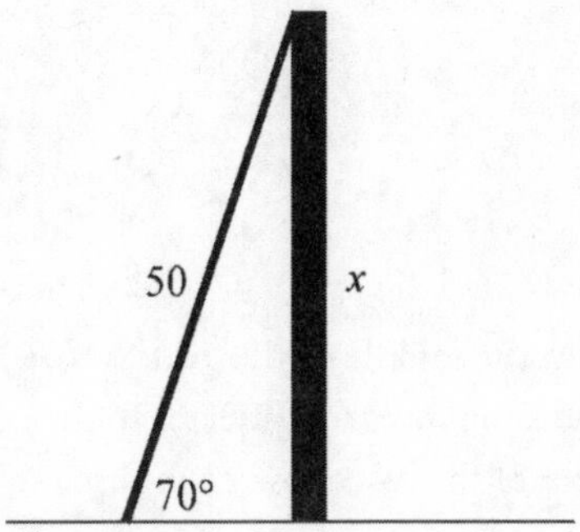

Apply the sine function: sine = opposite ÷ hypotenuse.

$$\frac{x}{50} = \sin 70°$$
$$x = 50\sin 70°$$

The correct answer is A.

COORDINATE GEOMETRY

Finding points on a plane is the study of **coordinate geometry**. A grid is commonly used to do this. The grid is divided into four sections. Each section is called a **quadrant**. The two number lines that divide the grid into quadrants are called the ***x*-axis** (the horizontal axis) and the ***y*-axis** (the vertical axis). The center of the grid, where the two axes meet, is called the **origin**. The points that are drawn on the grid are identified by **ordered pairs**. The *x*-coordinate is always written first. Look at the grid below.

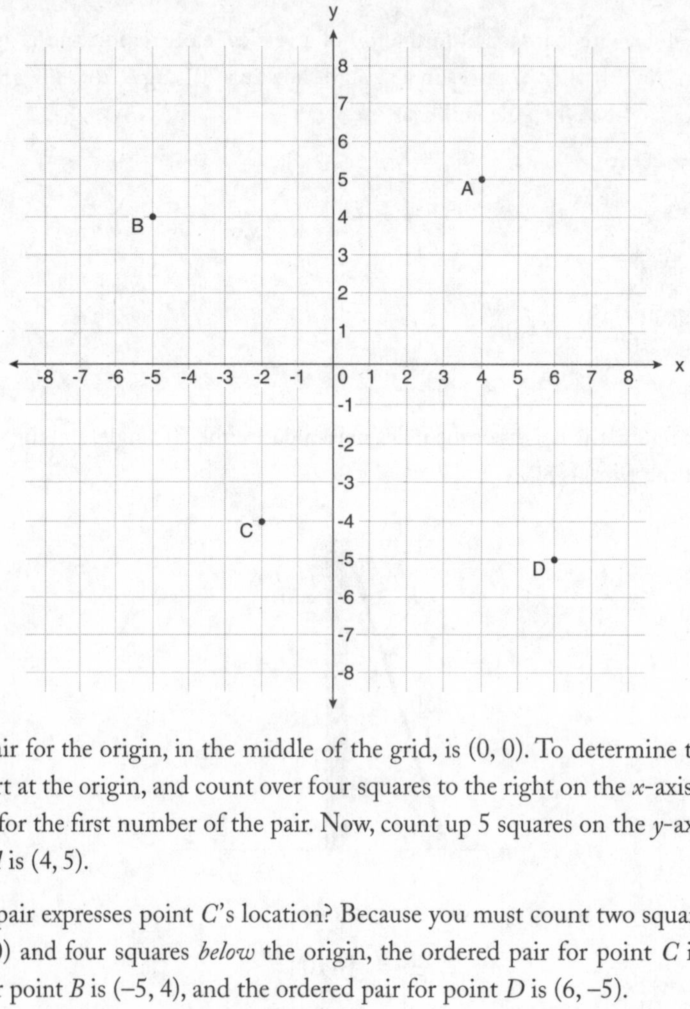

The ordered pair for the origin, in the middle of the grid, is (0, 0). To determine the ordered pair for point *A*, start at the origin, and count over four squares to the right on the *x*-axis. This gives you the coordinate for the first number of the pair. Now, count up 5 squares on the *y*-axis. The ordered pair for point *A* is (4, 5).

What ordered pair expresses point *C*'s location? Because you must count two squares to the *left* of the origin (0, 0) and four squares *below* the origin, the ordered pair for point *C* is (–2, –4). The ordered pair for point *B* is (–5, 4), and the ordered pair for point *D* is (6, –5).

Finding the Distance Between Two Points

Finding the distance between two points that are directly horizontal or vertical from each other is simply a matter of counting the number of squares that separate the points. In the next grid, for example, the distance between points *A*(2, 3) and *B*(7, 3) is 5. The distance between points *C*(2, 1) and *D*(2, –4) is also 5.

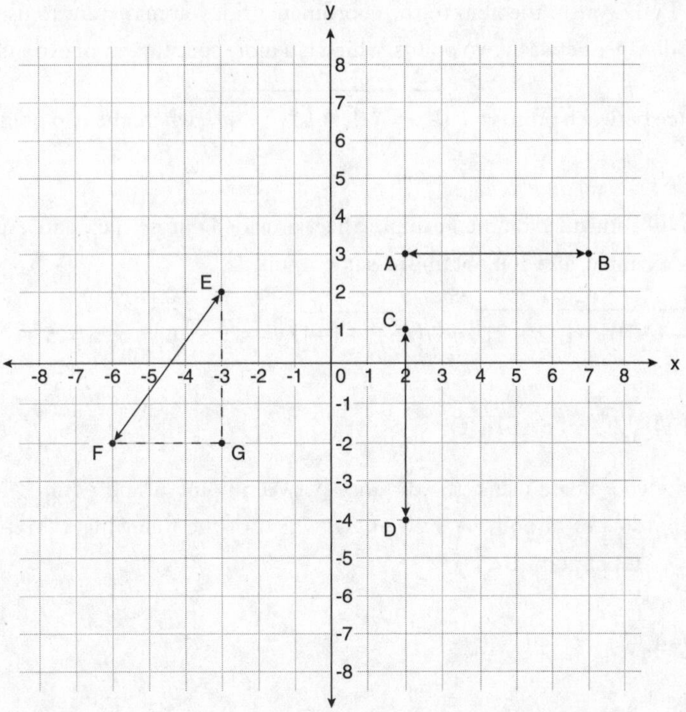

If you are asked to find the distance between two points that are not directly horizontal or vertical from each other, you can use the Pythagorean theorem. (The formula for the Pythagorean theorem is included in the Formula Sheet.) For example, to find the distance between points *E* and *F* on the preceding grid, follow these steps:

1. Draw a right triangle in which $\overline{EF}$ is the hypotenuse (as shown by the broken lines on the preceding grid).
2. Determine the distance between *E* and *G*. That distance is 4. This is the length of one leg of right triangle *EFG*.
3. Determine the distance between *F* and *G*. That distance is 3. This is the length of the other leg of a right triangle *EFG*.
4. Apply the Pythagorean theorem to find the hypotenuse of ΔEFG, which is the distance between *E* and *F*:

$$4^2 + 3^2 = c^2$$
$$16 + 9 = c^2$$
$$25 = c^2$$
$$5 = c$$

In applying the Pythagorean theorem to the coordinate grid, you may want to use the formula for determining the distance between two points, which is a more specific way of expressing the theorem.

Distance between points $=\sqrt{(x_2-x_1)^2+(y_2-y_1)^2}$, where the two points are (x_1, y_1) and (x_2, y_2)

The formula is NOT included on the Formula Sheet provided during the exam. Apply this formula to the preceding example, and you obtain the same result:

$$\sqrt{(-6-(-3))^2+(-2-2)^2}=\sqrt{(-3)^2+(-4)^2}=\sqrt{9+16}=\sqrt{25}=5$$

EXAMPLE 40 (EASIER):

On the coordinate plane, the distance between point A and point B is 8 units. If the coordinates of point A are (–4, 5), which of the following CANNOT be the coordinates of point B?

A. (4, 5)

B. (–4, –3)

C. (–4, 13)

D. (4, –3)

Point 1 is 8 units from point A, directly horizontal from point A. Points 2 and 3 are 8 units from point A, directly vertical from point A. Point 4 is diagonal to point 8 by more than 8 units. (Plotting the two points on the coordinate grid will show that the distance is greater than 8 units; there's no need to apply the formula.) **The correct answer is D.**

EXAMPLE 41 (MORE CHALLENGING):

What is the distance between (–3, 1) and (2, 4) on the coordinate plane?

A. 5

B. $\sqrt{29}$

C. $\sqrt{34}$

D. 6

Apply the formula for determining the distance between two points:

$\sqrt{(-3-2)^2+(1-4)^2}=\sqrt{25+9}=\sqrt{34}$. **The correct answer is C.**

Finding the Midpoint of a Line Segment

To find the coordinates of the midpoint (M) of a line segment, simply average the two endpoints' x-values and y-values:

$$x_M = \frac{x_1+x_2}{2} \text{ and } y_M = \frac{y_1+y_2}{2}$$

The **midpoint formula** is often used to find these coordinates:

$$M = \left(\frac{x_1+x_2}{2}, \frac{y_1+y_2}{2}\right)$$

These formulas are NOT included on the Formula Sheet provided during the test.

A question might simply ask you to find the midpoint between two given points. Or, it might provide the midpoint and one endpoint, and then ask you to determine the other endpoint.

EXAMPLE 42 (EASIER):

Click on the graph to plot the point that represents the midpoint between (–3, 1) and (–7, 5) on the coordinate plane. For this print version, mark the graph to plot the point that represents the midpoint.

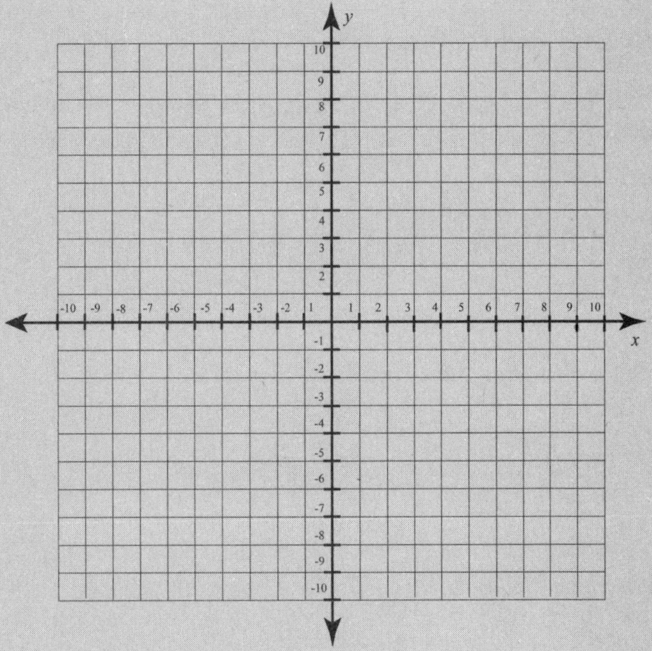

First apply the formula to the two x-values: $\frac{-3+(-7)}{2} = -\frac{10}{2} = -5$. Then apply the formula to the two y-values: $\frac{1+5}{2} = \frac{6}{2} = 3$. The midpoint is (–5, 3).

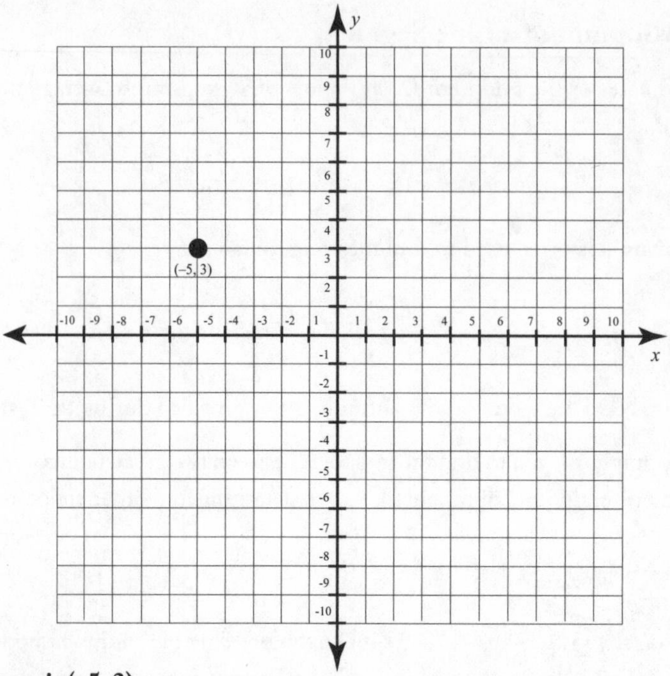

The correct answer is (–5, 3).

EXAMPLE 43 (MORE CHALLENGING):

On the coordinate plane, the point $M(-1, 3)$ is the midpoint of a line segment with endpoints $A(2, -4)$ and B. What are the xy-coordinates of point B?

A. (–3, 8)

B. (8, –4)

C. (5, 12)

D. (–4, 10)

Apply the midpoint formula to find the x-coordinate of point B:

$$-1 = \frac{x + 2}{2}$$
$$-2 = x + 2$$
$$-4 = x$$

Apply the midpoint formula to find the y-coordinate of point B:

$$3 = \frac{y + (-4)}{2}$$
$$6 = y - 4$$
$$10 = y$$

Thus, the xy-coordinates of point B are (–4, 10). **The correct answer is D.**

Defining a Line on the Plane

You can define any line on the coordinate plane by the following general equation:

$$y = mx + b$$

In this equation:

- The variable m is the **slope** of the line.
- The variable b is the line's ***y*-intercept** (where the line crosses the y-axis).
- The variables x and y are the coordinates of any point on the line. Any (x, y) pair defining a point on the line can substitute for the variables x and y.

Think of the slope of a line as a fraction in which the numerator indicates the vertical change from one point to another on the line (moving left to right) corresponding to a given horizontal change, which the fraction's denominator indicates. The common term used for this fraction is **rise over run**.

You can determine the slope of a line from any two pairs of (x, y) coordinates. In general, if (x_1, y_1) and (x_2, y_2) lie on the same line, calculate the line's slope according to the following formula:

$$\textbf{slope } (m) = \frac{y_2 - y_1}{x_2 - x_1}$$

This formula is included on the Formula Sheet provided during the test.

In applying the formula, be sure to subtract corresponding values. For example, a careless test taker calculating the slope might subtract y_1 from y_2 but subtract x_2 from x_1. Also be sure to calculate rise over run, and not run over rise.

A question might ask you to identify the slope of a line defined by a given equation, in which case you simply put the equation in the form $y = mx + b$, then identify the m-term. Or, it might ask you to determine the equation of a line, or just the line's slope (m) or y-intercept (b), given the coordinates of two points on the line.

For example, suppose that the following points lie on the same line.

x	2	5	–1	–3
y	1	$-\frac{7}{2}$	$\frac{11}{2}$	$\frac{17}{2}$

Since the points lie on the same line, you can use any pair of points to determine the slope. For convenience, use the first two:

$$m = \frac{y_2 - y_1}{x_2 - x_1} = \frac{-\frac{7}{2} - 1}{5 - 2} = \frac{-\frac{9}{2}}{3} = \frac{9}{2} \cdot \frac{1}{3} = -\frac{3}{2}$$

EXAMPLE 44 (EASIER):

On the coordinate plane, what is the slope of the line defined by the two points $P(2, 1)$ and $Q(-3, 4)$?

A. $-\frac{5}{3}$

B. -1

C. $-\frac{3}{5}$

D. $\frac{1}{3}$

Apply the slope formula:

$$\text{slope } (m) = \frac{4-1}{-3-2} = \frac{3}{-5}, \text{ or } -\frac{3}{5}$$

The correct answer is C.

EXAMPLE 45 (MORE CHALLENGING):

On the coordinate plane, at what point along the vertical axis (the y-axis) does the line passing through points (2, 4) and (–1, –5) cross the y-axis? Once you have calculated the answer, mark the intercept point on the coordinate grid.

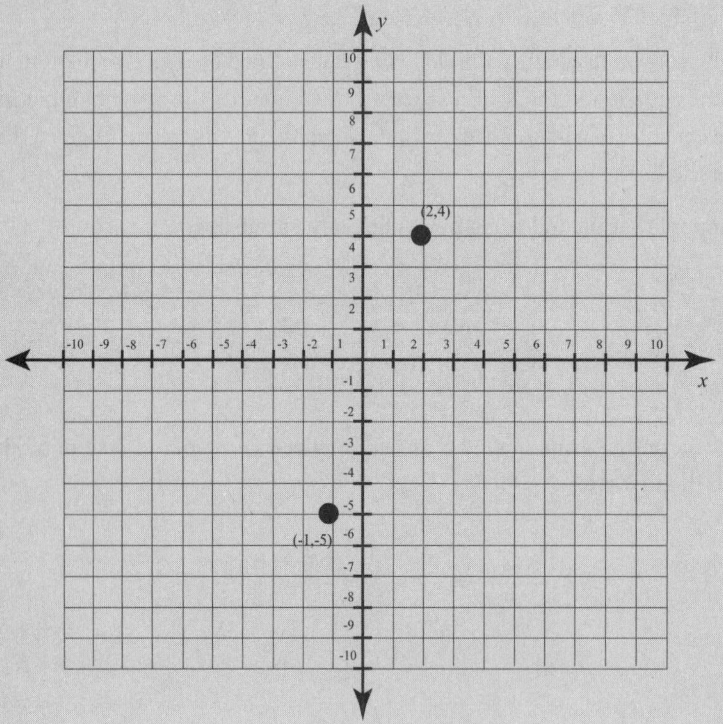

The question asks for the line's y-intercept (the value of b in the general equation $y = mx + b$). First, determine the line's slope:

$$\text{slope }(m) = \frac{y_2 - y_1}{x_2 - x_1} = \frac{-5-4}{-2-1} = \frac{-9}{-3} = 3$$

In the general equation ($y = mx + b$), $m = 3$. To find the value of b, substitute either (x, y) value pair for x and y, then solve for b. Substituting the (x, y) pair (2, 4):

$$y = 3x + b$$
$$4 = 3(2) + b$$
$$4 = 6 + b$$
$$b = -2$$

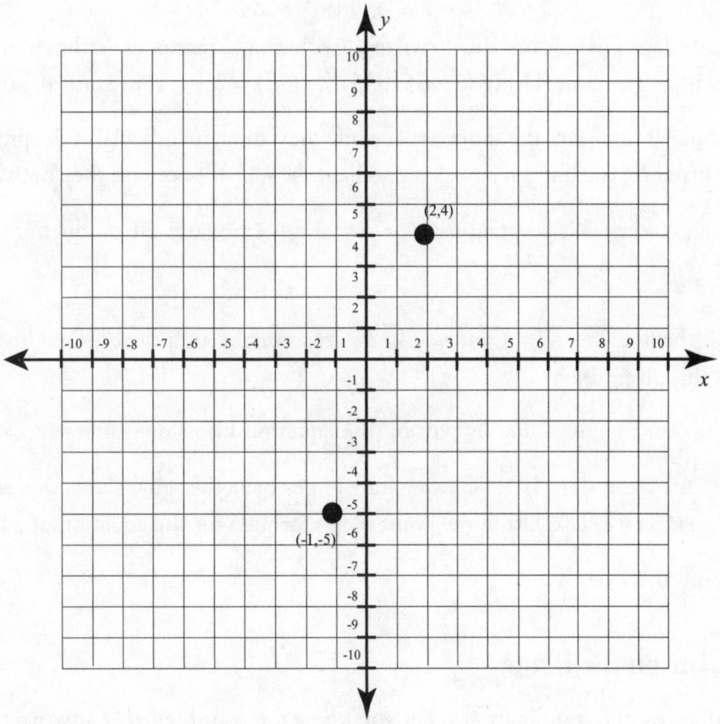

The correct answer is –2.

The slope and a point are needed to write the equation of a line.

Let's say you are asked to find the equation of the line with slope $-\frac{2}{3}$ that passes through the point (–1, –3).

The most efficient approach is to use the point-slope equation of the line. Precisely, a line with slope m passing through the point (x_1, y_1) has the equation $y - y_1 = m(x - x_1)$. Using the given information yields the equation $y - (-3) = -\frac{2}{3}(x - (-1))$. This can be simplified in different ways.

Slope-intercept form:

$$y+3=-\frac{2}{3}(x+1)$$
$$y=-\frac{2}{3}x-\frac{11}{3}$$

Standard form:

$$2x+3y=-11$$

You can also write the equation of a line when given 2 points on that line. For example, if you know the line passes through the points (2, –5) and (4, –1), first, determine the slope of the line:

$$m=\frac{-1-(-5)}{4-2}=\frac{-1+5}{2}=\frac{4}{2}=2$$

Now, use the point-slope formula of a line to write the equation. You can use either of the two points —the equation will be the same. Using (2, –5) yields $y-(-5)=2(x-2)$ or equivalently, $y=2x-9$.

Two lines are parallel if they have the same slope, while they are perpendicular if the product of their slopes is –1. For instance, the line $y=3x-1$ is parallel to $y=3x+4$ because they both have slope 3. Similarly, the line $y=-2x+3$ is perpendicular to $y=\frac{1}{2}x-1$ because the product of their slopes is $(-2)\left(\frac{1}{2}\right)=-1$.

Say you are given the line $2x-4y=1$ and you know it passes through the origin. How do you find a line parallel to this given line?

First, find the slope of the given line by putting the equation into slope-intercept form; doing so yields $y=\frac{1}{2}x-\frac{1}{4}$. So the slope is $\frac{1}{2}$. Since parallel lines have the same slope, this is the slope of the line whose equation we seek. Using the point-slope formula for the equation of a line with this slope and the point (0, 0) yields $y=\frac{1}{2}x$.

Graphing a Line on the Plane

You can graph a line on the coordinate plane if you know the coordinates of any two points on the line. Just plot the two points, and then draw a line connecting them. You can also graph a line from one point on the line, if you also know either the line's slope or its y-intercept.

A question might ask you to recognize the value of a line's slope (m) based on a graph of the line. If the graph identifies the precise coordinates of two points, you can determine the line's precise slope (and the entire equation of the line). Even without any precise coordinates, you can still estimate the line's slope based on its appearance.

Lines that slope upward from left to right:

- A line sloping *upward* from left to right has a positive slope (m).
- A line with a slope of 1 slopes upward from left to right at a 45° angle in relation to the x-axis.
- A line with a fractional slope between 0 and 1 slopes upward from left to right but at less than a 45° angle in relation to the x-axis.
- A line with a slope greater than 1 slopes upward from left to right at more than a 45° angle in relation to the x-axis.

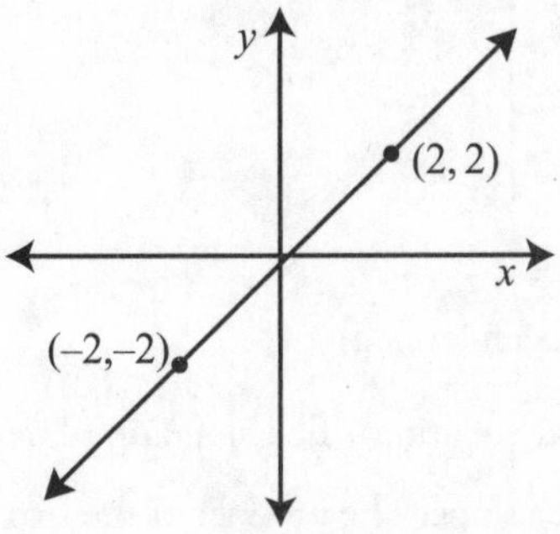

$y = x$
(Slope $= \frac{1}{1}$)

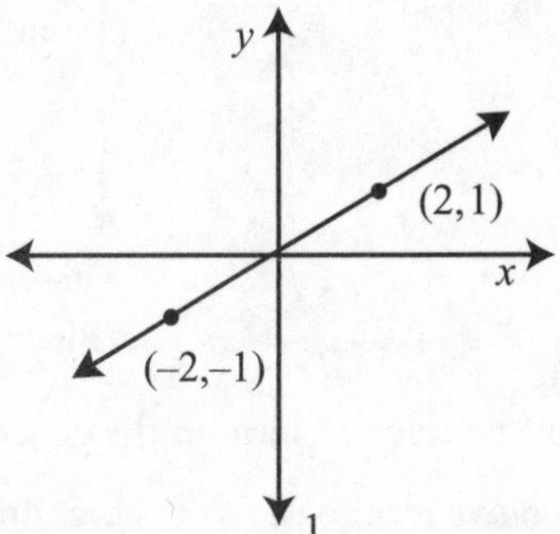

$y = \frac{1}{2}x$
(Slope $= \frac{1}{2}$)

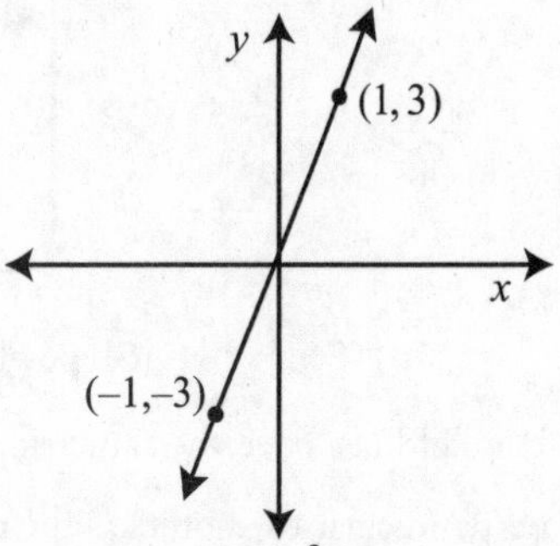

$y = 3x$
(Slope $= \frac{3}{1}$)

Lines that slope downward from left to right:

- A line sloping *downward* from left to right has a negative slope (m).
- A line with a slope of –1 slopes downward from left to right at a 45° angle in relation to the x-axis.
- A line with a fractional slope between 0 and –1 slopes downward from left to right but at less than a 45° angle in relation to the x-axis.
- A line with a slope less than –1 (for example, –2) slopes downward from left to right at more than a 45° angle in relation to the x-axis.

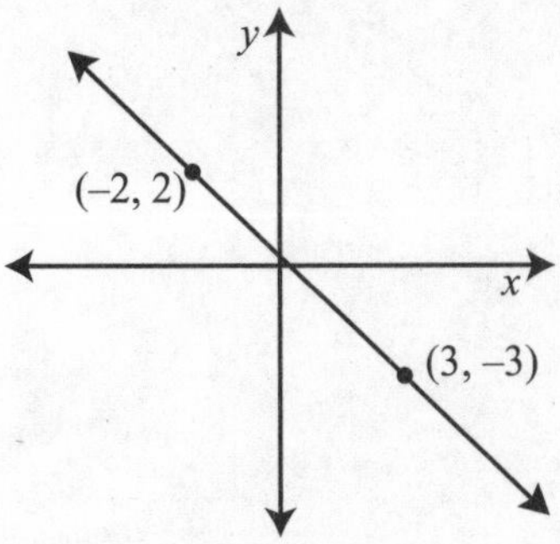

$y = -x$
(Slope $= -\frac{1}{1}$)

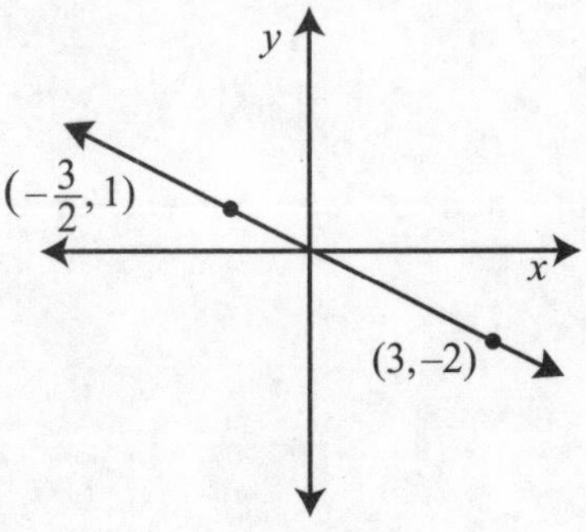

$y = -\frac{2}{3}x$
(Slope $= -\frac{2}{3}$)

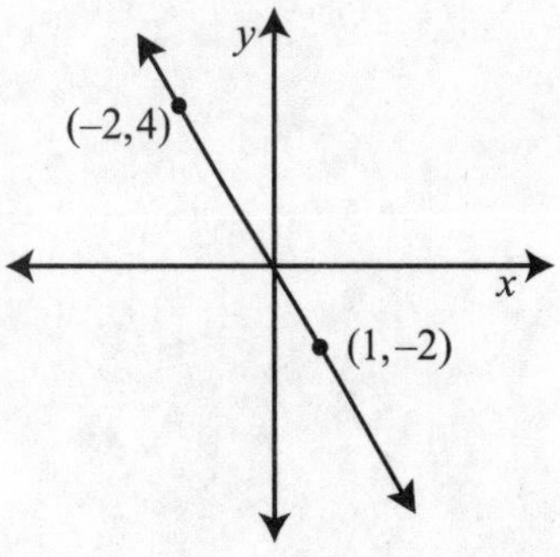

$y = -2x$
(Slope $= -\frac{2}{1}$)

Horizontal and vertical lines:

- A horizontal line has a slope of **zero** ($m = 0$, and $mx = 0$).
- A vertical line has either an **undefined** or an **indeterminate** slope (the fraction's denominator is 0), so the m-term in the equation is ignored.

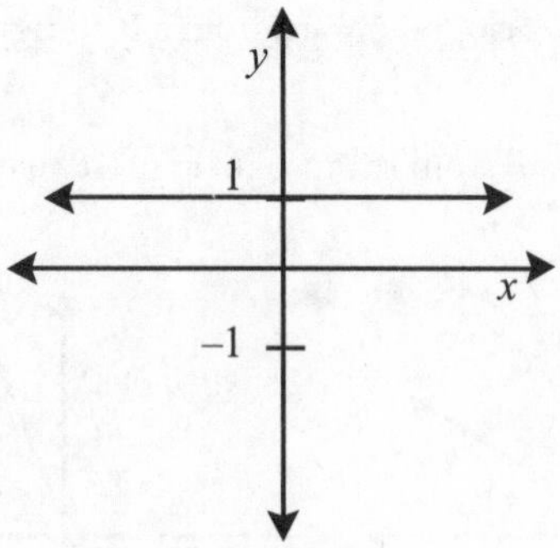

$y = 1$
(Slope=0)

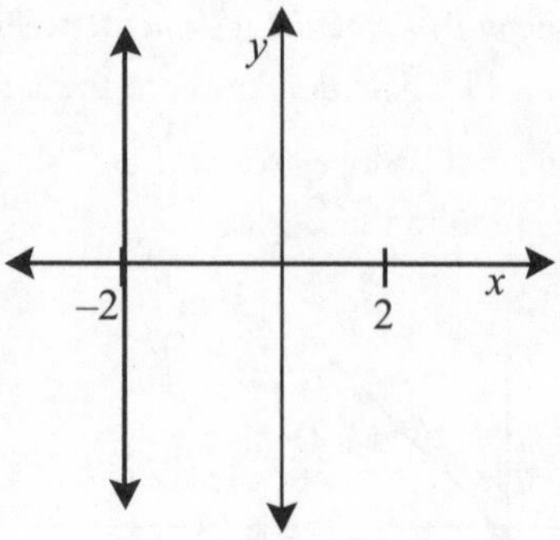

$x = -2$
(Slope is undefined)

Parallel lines have the same slope (the same m-term in the general equation). The slope of a line perpendicular to another is the negative reciprocal of the other line's slope. The product of the two slopes is 1. For example, a line with slope $\frac{3}{2}$ is perpendicular to a line with slope $-\frac{2}{3}$.

EXAMPLE 46 (EASIER):

Line P is shown on the coordinate plane below.

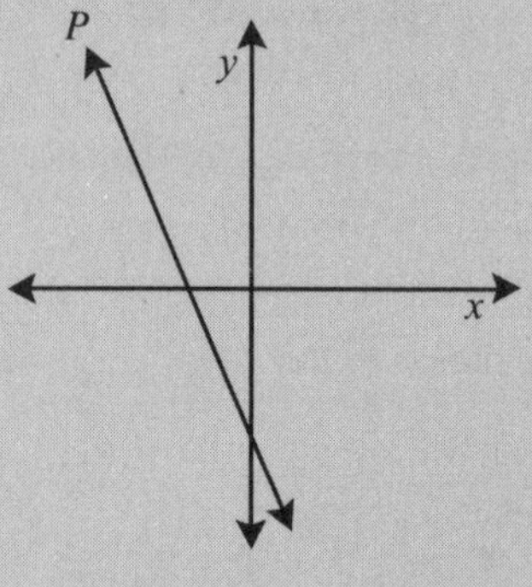

Which of the following could be the equation of line P?

A. $y = -\frac{5}{2}x + \frac{5}{2}$

B. $y = \frac{5}{2}x - \frac{5}{2}$

C. $y = \frac{2}{5}x + \frac{2}{5}$

D. $y = -\frac{5}{2}x - \frac{5}{2}$

Notice that line P slopes downward from left to right at an angle greater than 45° in relation to the x-axis. Thus, the line's slope (m in the equation $y = mx + b$) < -1. Also notice that line P crosses the y-axis at a negative y-value (below the x-axis). The line's y-intercept (b in the equation $y = mx + b$) is negative. Only choice D provides an equation that meets both conditions. **The correct answer is D.**

You can also jump right to the graph to solve.

For example, say you are asked to graph the line passing through the point (4, 0) that is perpendicular to the line $2x - 4y = 1$.

First, you need to find the slope of the line you are to graph. To do so, note that the line $2x - 4y = 1$ can be written as $y = \frac{1}{2}x - \frac{1}{4}$. Since the line you must graph is perpendicular to this one, its slope must be -2.

Next, use the point-slope equation of a line to see that the equation of the line is $y - 0 = -2(x - 4)$, which is equivalent to $y = -2x + 8$. From here, we see the slope is -2 and y-intercept is 8. Its graph will appear like so:

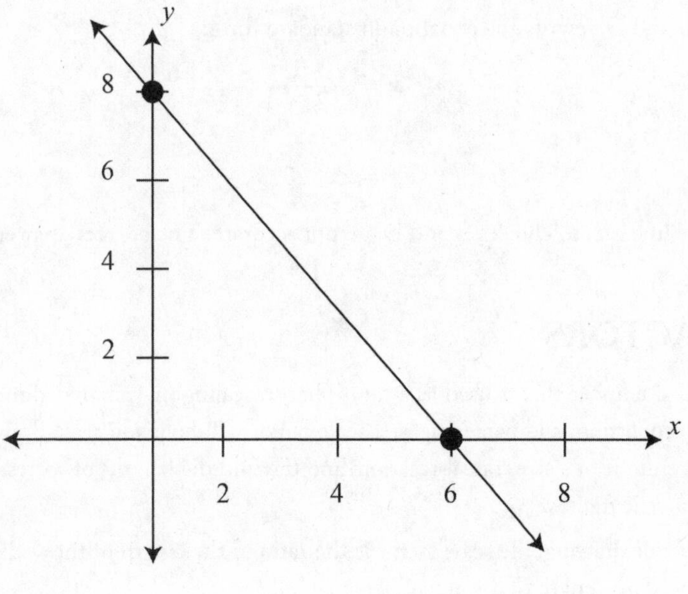

EXAMPLE 47 (MORE CHALLENGING):

If the equation $x = \frac{y+5}{2}$ is graphed as a line on the coordinate plane, which statement about the line is accurate?

A. The line crosses the y-axis at (3, 0).

B. The line is vertical.

C. The line crosses the x-axis at (0, –5).

D. The line is horizontal.

Before rewriting the equation to find the slope, quickly test the statements of choices A and C by plugging the x-value and y-value of each ordered pair into the equation. You'll see that the equation holds true for the ordered pair (0, –5):

$$0 = \frac{-5+5}{2}$$

(0, –5) is a point on the line, so choice C holds true. The point (3, 0) is not on the line because the equation does not hold true when these values are substituted, so choice A is incorrect. If you want to test choices B and D, rewrite the equation in standard form:

$$x = \frac{y+5}{2}$$
$$2x = y + 5$$
$$y = 2x - 5$$

The slope of the line is 2, so choices B and D are not accurate. **The correct answer is C.**

SCALE FACTORS

A **scale factor** is a number that is used as a multiplier in scaling in 1, 2, or 3 dimensions. Closely linked to ratio, proportion, and percentages, a scale factor will help you scale drawings or objects, compute the magnitude of a size transformation, and the find the lengths of corresponding sides in two similar geometric figures.

- When scale drawing, the scale factor is the ratio of the length of the scale drawing to the corresponding length of the actual object.
- In a size transformation, the scale factor is the ratio that expresses the amount of magnification from one figure to another.
- When comparing two similar geometric figures, the scale factor is the ratio of the lengths of the corresponding sides.

Real-life examples of using scale factors include increasing a recipe to feed a larger group of people, creating miniature replicas of life-sized objects, calculating the distance between two points on a map, or using a floor plan to build a building.

Let's look at how you would determine the magnitude of a size change, using the following triangles.

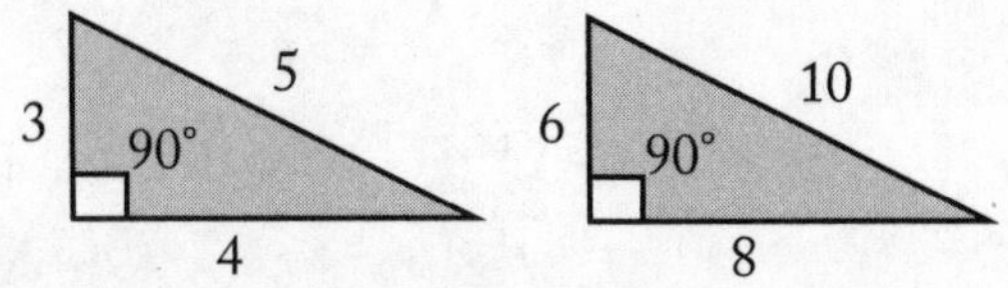

Note that the triangles shown are similar but they are not drawn to scale. While it is visually helpful to see the magnitude of a size change, geometric figures do not need to be shown scaled for you to find the scale factor.

The first triangle is a standard 3-4-5 right triangle. For this example, you do not need to know the mathematical formula for a scale factor to find the answer. Use simple multiplication to compare the corresponding sides to see how they relate.

$$3 \times ? = 6$$
$$4 \times ? = 8$$
$$5 \times ? = 10$$

Each side can be multiplied by 2, so the scale factor is 2 when scaling up to the larger right triangle. Conversely, to scale down, the scale factor would be $\frac{1}{2}$.

The actual mathematical formulas to find a scale factor are as follows:

To scale up:

$$\text{scale factor}\,(k) = \frac{\text{larger length}}{\text{smaller length}}$$

To scale down:

$$\text{scale factor}\,(k) = \frac{\text{smaller length}}{\text{larger length}}$$

Now let's look at how you can use the scale factor formula to find a missing side length. Take a look at the following triangles:

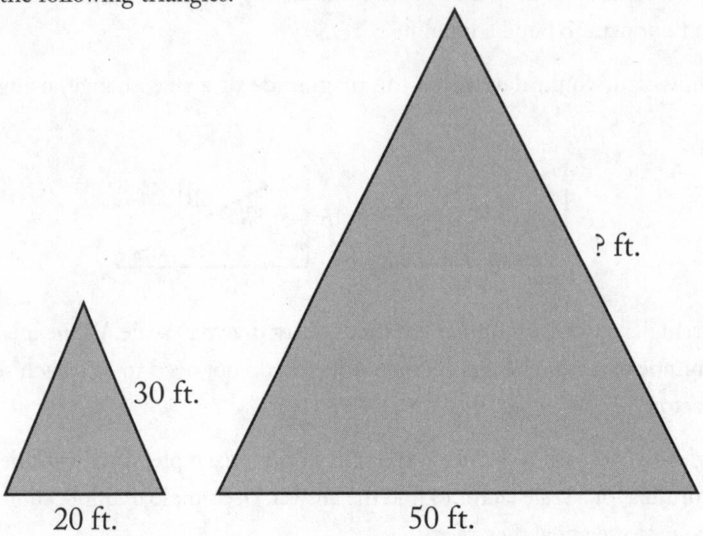

The two triangles are similar and we have one corresponding side to compare to find the scale factor.

$$\text{scale factor}\,(k) = \frac{\text{larger length}}{\text{smaller length}} = \frac{50}{20} = \frac{5}{2} \text{ or } 2.5$$

Now multiply 30 ft. by the scale factor of 2.5 to find the missing side in the larger triangle. The length of the missing side is 75 ft.

Let's examine a few more examples.

EXAMPLE 48 (EASIER):

Figure 1 is a scaled copy of Figure 2.

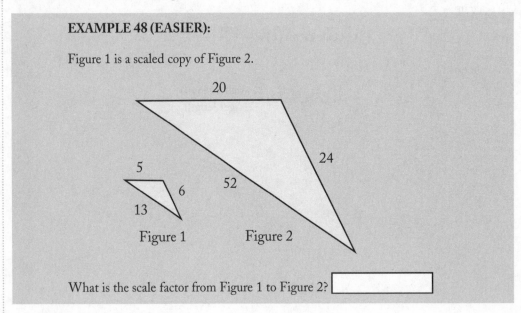

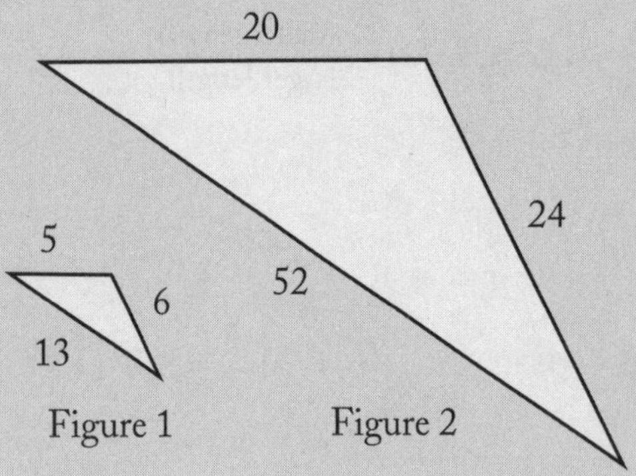

What is the scale factor from Figure 1 to Figure 2?

The two figures are similar so you can compare the corresponding sides and see how they relate. This will tell you what number you multiply each side length in Figure 1 to get to the corresponding length in Figure 2.

$$5 \times 4 = 20$$
$$6 \times 4 = 24$$
$$13 \times 4 = 52$$

The corresponding sides in Figure 2 are all 4 times the length of Figure 1. **The correct answer is 4.**

EXAMPLE 49 (MORE CHALLENGING):

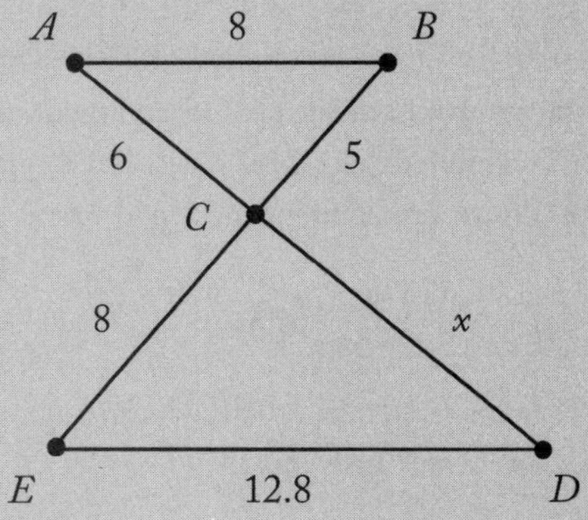

What is the value of x? [ ]

First find the scale factor by comparing the corresponding sides. If the scale factors match, the triangles are similar.

Line AB corresponds to line ED, so $\frac{12.8}{8} = 1.6$.

Line BC corresponds with line CE, so $\frac{8}{5} = 1.6$.

The scale factor matches for comparable sides, which means that these triangles are similar. Now multiply the value of line AC by the scale factor of 1.6 to find the missing value of x.

$$6 \times 1.6 = 9.6$$
$$x = 9.6$$

The correct answer is 9.6.

EXAMPLE 50 (MORE CHALLENGING):

On the weekends in the summer, Kyle rollerblades 5 miles from home to the skate park. Then, he rollerblades 1.75 miles to get to his friend's house. At the end of the day, he rollerblades 4.25 miles to get home. Kyle charts his progress on a map poster in his bedroom in which 1.25 inches corresponds to 0.5 miles. How far did Kyle rollerblade in terms of this smaller scale?

A. 11.0 inches

B. 13.75 inches

C. 20.25 inches

D. 27.5 inches

You must determine Kyle's total number of miles traveled, and then convert that to inches using the given scale factor. Altogether, Kyle rollerblades 11.0 miles. Let x represent the number of inches corresponding to this distance. We set up the following proportion:

$$\frac{11 \text{ miles}}{x \text{ inches}} = \frac{0.5 \text{ miles}}{1.25 \text{ inches}}$$

Cross-multiplying yields the equation $(11)(1.25) = 0.5x$, which is equivalent to $13.75 = 0.5x$. Solving for x then yields 27.5 inches. **The correct answer is D.**

SUMMING IT UP

- Geometry questions on the GED Mathematical Reasoning Test cover the following areas: congruency and similarity; angles, parallel and perpendicular lines, and transversals; two-dimensional figures (triangles, quadrilaterals, polygons, and circles); three-dimensional figures (cubes and other rectangular prisms, cylinders, cones, spheres, and square pyramids); basic right-triangle trigonometry; and coordinate geometry (points, lines, and other figures on the xy-coordinate plane).
- Lines and line segments are the fundamental elements of most geometry problems on the test, so it's important to be familiar with the basic rules of angles formed by intersecting lines.
- Most geometry formulas, such as the Pythagorean theorem, are included on the Formula Sheet that will be provided to you during the test. Other formulas, such as the definitions for the sine, cosine, and tangent functions, will NOT appear on the Formula Sheet, and you may want to memorize them before taking the test.
- Be sure you know the properties of all basic types of triangles. Not only will you encounter triangle problems on the test, you'll also need these skills for solving problems with four-sided figures, three-dimensional figures, and circles.
- Know how to determine the perimeter and area of squares, rectangles, and parallelograms. GED Mathematical Reasoning Test questions involving non-square rectangles may ask you to determine the area based on the perimeter, or vice versa.
- You won't need to work with a value of π any more precise than 3.14 or $\frac{22}{7}$. In fact, you might be able to answer a circle question using the symbol π itself, without approximating its value.
- Become familiar with the following basic terminology involving circles: circumference, radius, diameter, and chord. Circle problems typically involve other types of geometric figures as well, including triangles, squares, rectangles, and tangent lines. Learn the basics of circle problems, and you'll be a step ahead in solving the most advanced geometry problems.
- Test questions involving cubes (or other box shapes) are sometimes presented as "packing" problems, where you need to determine how many small boxes fit into a larger box. Another type of question involving cubes focuses on the **ratios** among the cube's linear, square, and cubic measurements.
- A cylinder problem might require little more than a straightforward application of either the surface area or the volume formula. As with rectangular solid questions, just plug what you know into the formula, then solve for what the question asks.
- Coordinate questions involve the xy-plane defined by the horizontal x-axis and the vertical y-axis. You will need to know how to determine the slope of a line, so remember to calculate it as "rise over run" and not "run over rise."

PRACTICE QUESTIONS

Directions: The following practice questions will cover the geometry concepts that will appear on the GED Mathematical Reasoning Test. Choose the best answer to each problem presented.

SHOW YOUR WORK HERE

1. Assume that *l* is parallel to *m*. Find the value of *y*.

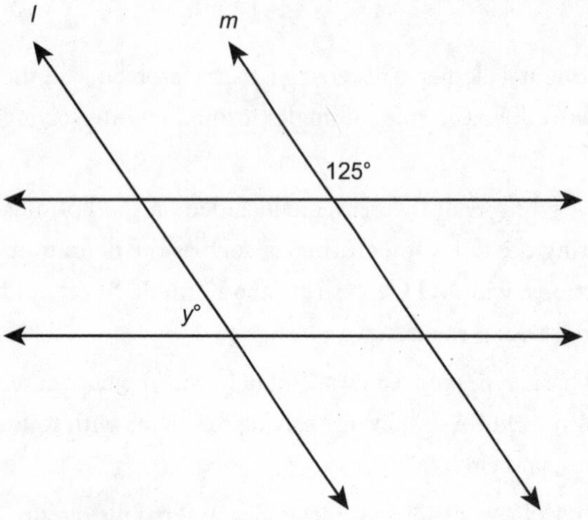

A. 45°

B. 55°

C. 90°

D. 125°

2. Suppose *a* and *b* are real numbers. What is the distance between the points in the *xy*-plane with coordinates $(2a, -b)$ and $(-a, 2b)$?

A. $3(a + b)$

B. $9a^2 + 9b^2$

C. $\sqrt{3a + 3b}$

D. $3\sqrt{a^2 + b^2}$

3. Find z:

SHOW YOUR WORK HERE

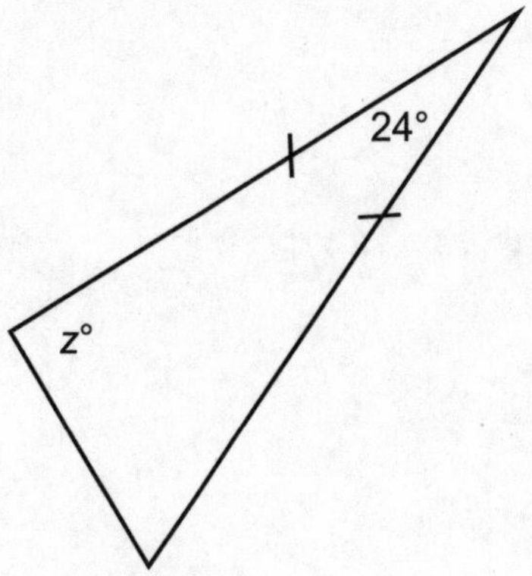

A. 24

B. 78

C. 90

D. 156

4. What is the equation of the graphed line?

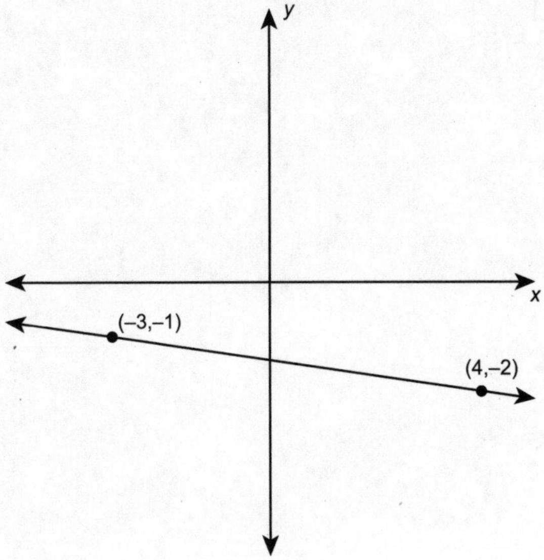

A. $x + 7y = -10$

B. $2x + 4y = -21$

C. $y + 7x = -22$

D. $y + 3x = -10$

SHOW YOUR WORK HERE

5. What is the sum of the interior angles of a regular decagon?

   A. 360

   B. 720

   C. 1,440

   D. 1,800

6. Assume a and b are positive real numbers. If triangle ABC is similar to triangle DEF, which of the following is the relationship between a and b?

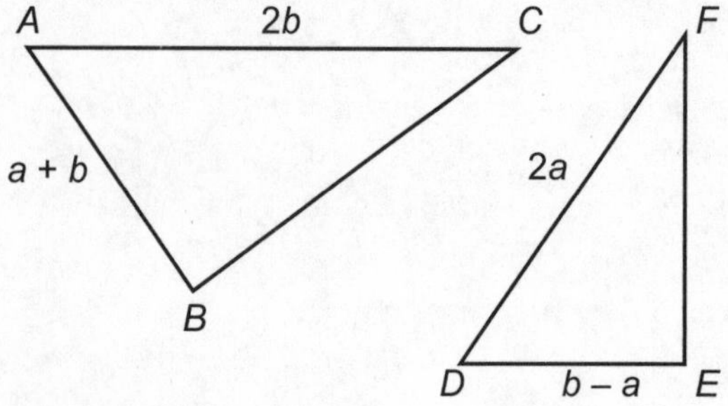

   A. $b^2 - a^2 - 2ab = 0$

   B. $2a^2 - 2b^2 + b + a = 0$

   C. $b^2 - a^2 - 4ab = 0$

   D. $a = b$

7. What is the area of the following parallelogram?

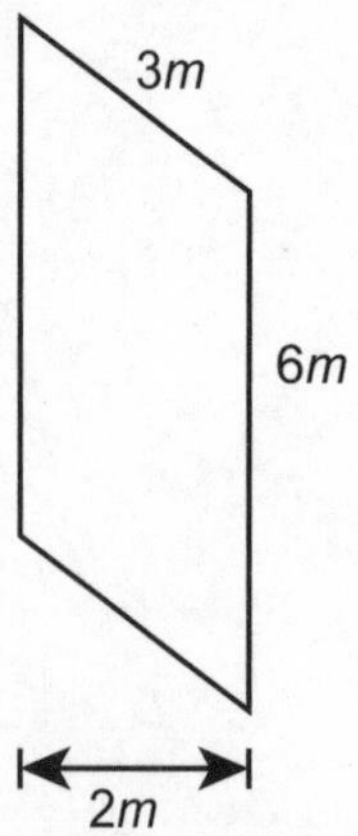

   A. 6 square meters

   B. 11 square meters

   C. 12 square meters

   D. 18 square meters

8. Which of the following expressions is equivalent to y?

SHOW YOUR WORK HERE

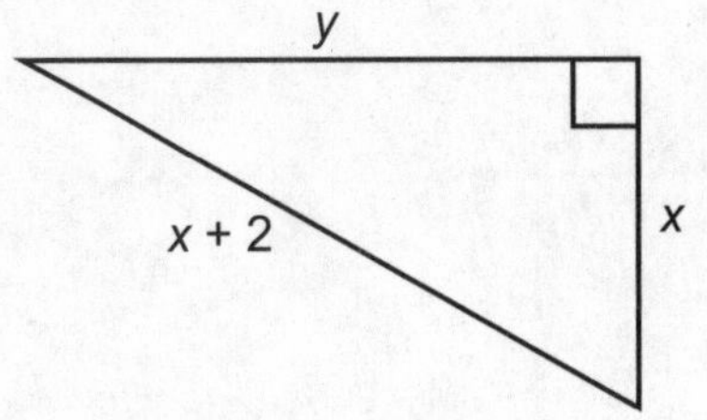

A. $2\sqrt{x+1}$

B. $4x + 4$

C. 2

D. $\sqrt{2x^2 + 4x + 4}$

9. The surface area of a cube is 13.5 square inches. What is its volume?

A. 4.5 cubic inches

B. 1.5 cubic inches

C. 3.375 cubic inches

D. 2.25 cubic inches

10. What is the measure of the largest angle in the following triangle?

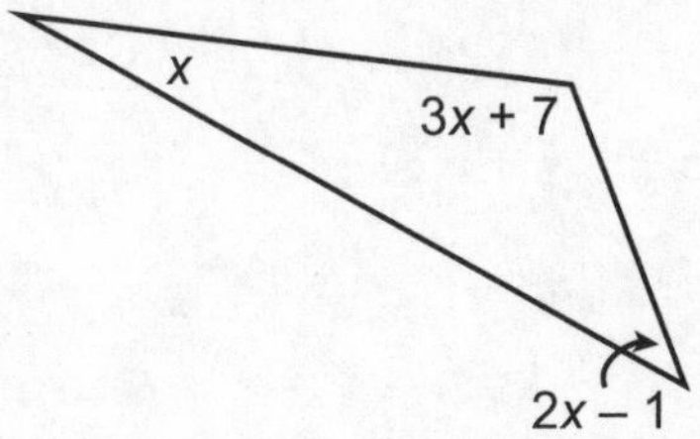

A. 29°

B. 57°

C. 94°

D. 117°

SHOW YOUR WORK HERE

11. Compute the area of the following composite figure:

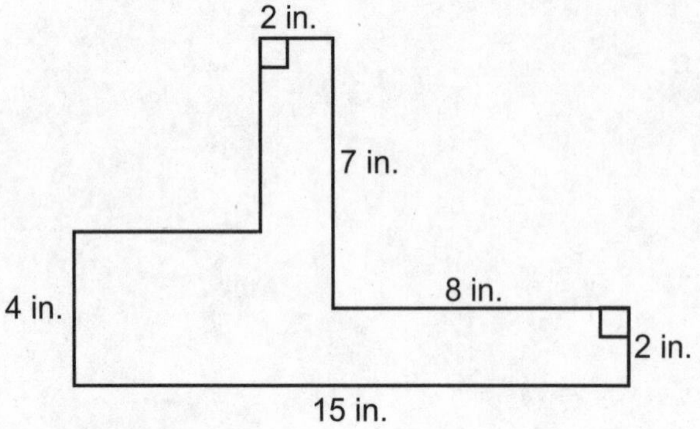

A. 38 square inches

B. 43 square inches

C. 54 square inches

D. 70 square inches

12. Find the area of this triangle:

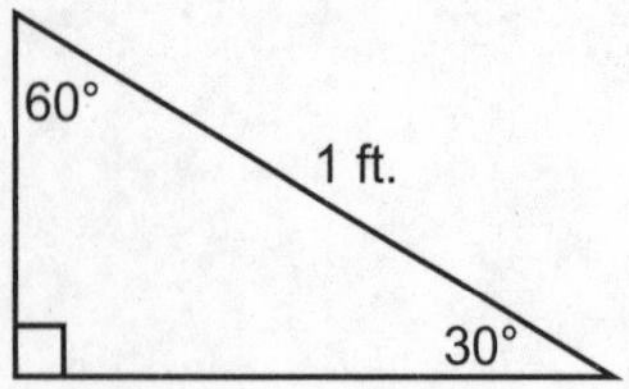

A. $\frac{3+\sqrt{3}}{2}$ square feet

B. $\frac{\sqrt{3}}{4}$ square feet

C. $\frac{1}{4}$ square feet

D. $\frac{\sqrt{3}}{8}$ square feet

13. What is the equation of the line passing through the points (0, –3) and (–6, 0)?

A. $y=-\frac{1}{2}x-3$

B. $y=-\frac{1}{2}x-6$

C. $y=-2x-6$

D. $y=-2x-3$

14. Suppose x is a positive real number less than 3. Compute $\cos\theta$.

SHOW YOUR WORK HERE

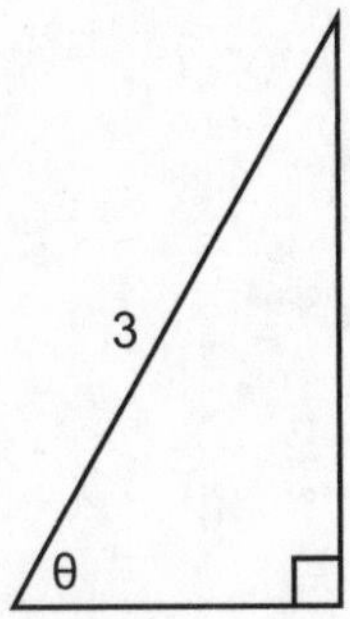

A. $\frac{3-x}{3}$

B. $\frac{x}{3}$

C. $\frac{\sqrt{9-x^2}}{3}$

D. $\frac{3}{\sqrt{9-x^2}}$

15. The sides of a square have a length of x inches. If they are decreased by 30%, what is the perimeter of the resulting square?

A. $0.49x$ inches

B. $0.70x$ inches

C. $1.20x$ inches

D. $2.80x$ inches

16. A statue honoring a town mayor is erected in the town square. The following diagram shows a person standing 28 feet from the statue with various measurements. What is the height of the statue?

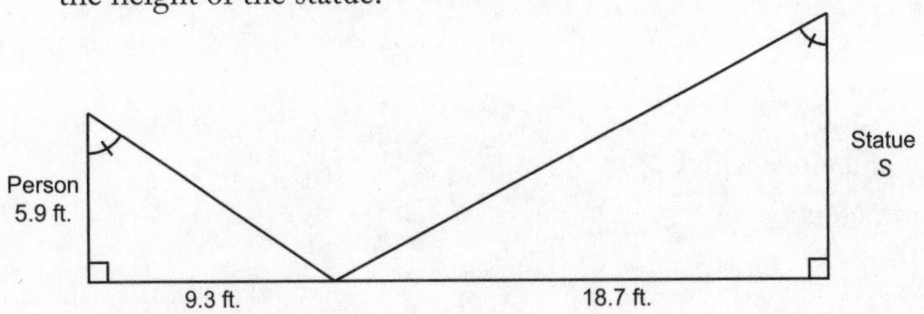

A. $\frac{(5.9)(18.7)}{9.3}$ feet

B. $\frac{(5.9)(9.3)}{18.7}$ feet

C. $\frac{(9.3)(18.7)}{5.9}$ feet

D. $(5.9)(18.7)(9.3)$ feet

17. Find the area of the following trapezoid:

SHOW YOUR WORK HERE

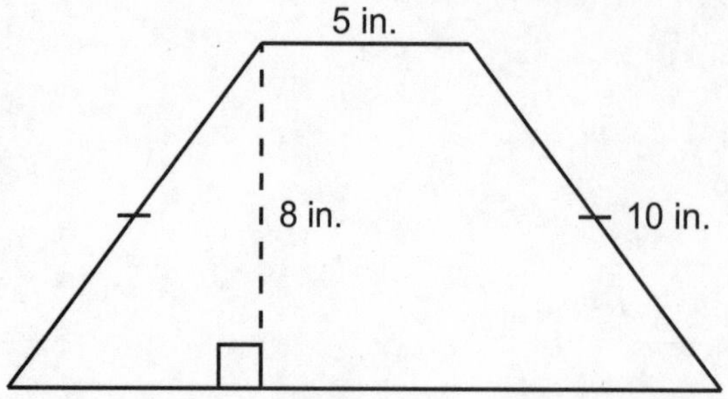

A. 23 square inches

B. 42 square inches

C. 88 square inches

D. 176 square inches

18. Suppose a is a positive real number. The diagonal of a square is a meters. If the length of the diagonal is increased by 40%, what would be the area of the resulting square?

A. a^2 square meters

B. $0.98a^2$ square meters

C. $0.36a^2$ square meters

D. $1.96a^2$ square meters

19. A slide at a playground measures 9 feet high. The base of the slide on the ground is 14 feet. Which of the following is the length of the slide?

A. $(14 - 9)$ feet

B. $(14 + 9)$ feet

C. $\sqrt{14^2 + 9^2}$ feet

D. $\sqrt{14^2 - 9^2}$ feet

20. What is the circumference of a circle with an area of $\sqrt{\pi}$ square centimeters?

A. $\frac{1}{\pi^{1/4}}$ centimeters

B. $2\pi^{1/2}$ centimeters

C. $2\pi^{5/4}$ centimeters

D. $2\pi^{3/4}$ centimeters

21. Which of the following triplets CANNOT be the lengths of the sides of a triangle?

A. 3, 4, 6

B. 2, 4, 4

C. 1, 1, 2

D. 5, 11, 13

22. The diameter and height of a right circular cylinder are in a 3:2 ratio. If the height is H feet, what is the volume of the cylinder?

A. $\frac{9}{16}\pi H^3$ cubic feet

B. $\frac{3}{4}\pi H^2$ cubic feet

C. $\frac{9}{4}\pi H^3$ cubic feet

D. $\frac{3}{2}\pi H^2$ cubic feet

23. What is the area of the following triangle?

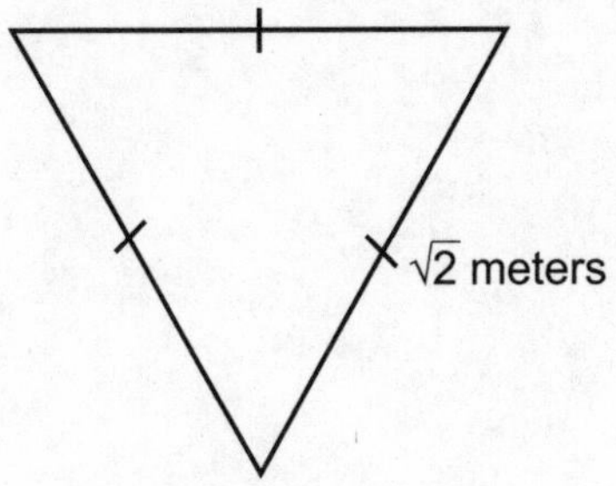

A. $\frac{\sqrt{3}}{4}$ square meters

B. $\frac{\sqrt{3}}{2}$ square meters

C. 1 square meter

D. $3\sqrt{2}$ square meters

24. A submarine traveling at a depth of 0.6 miles dives at an angle of 20° with respect to the surface of the ocean. If it travels a horizontal distance of 1.4 miles during the dive, what is the approximate depth of the submarine after the dive?

A. 0.5 miles

B. 1.1 miles

C. 3.8 miles

D. 4.4 miles

SHOW YOUR WORK HERE

25. Compute the area of the shaded region:

SHOW YOUR WORK HERE

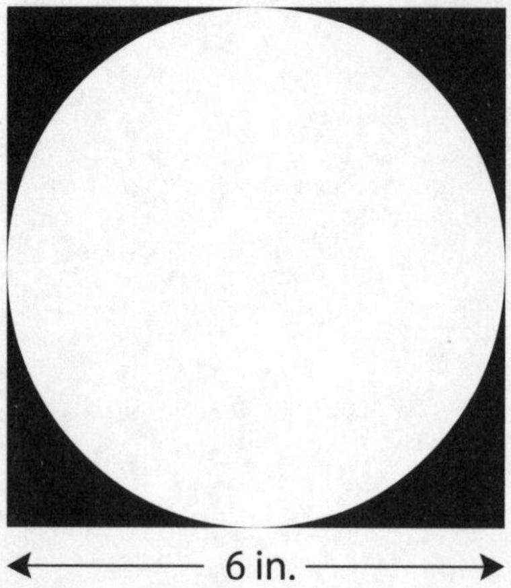

A. 9π square inches

B. $(36\pi - 36)$ square inches

C. $(36 - 9\pi)$ square inches

D. 36π square inches

ANSWER KEY AND EXPLANATIONS

1. B	6. A	11. C	16. A	21. C
2. D	7. C	12. D	17. C	22. A
3. B	8. A	13. A	18. B	23. B
4. A	9. C	14. C	19. C	24. B
5. C	10. C	15. D	20. D	25. C

1. **The correct answer is B.** The angles adjacent to the one labeled as 125° each measure 55° because they are supplementary angles. Because *l* is parallel to *y*, the angle labeled as *m* is the corresponding angle to one whose measure is 55°, so it also measures 55°. Choice A is incorrect because of an arithmetic error. Choice C is incorrect because there are no right angles marked in the diagram. Choice D is incorrect because the angle marked as *y* is not a corresponding angle to the one that measures 125°.

2. **The correct answer is D.** Use the distance formula:

$$\begin{aligned}&\sqrt{\left(2a-(-a)\right)^2+\left(-b-2b\right)^2}\\&=\sqrt{(3a)^2+(-3b)^2}\\&=\sqrt{9a^2+9b^2}\\&=\sqrt{9\left(a^2+b^2\right)}\\&=3\sqrt{a^2+b^2}\end{aligned}$$

Choice A is incorrect because the square root of a sum does not equal the sum of the square roots of the individual parts. Choice B is incorrect because the square root is missing around the entire quantity. Choice C is incorrect because the individual differences in the distance formula should be squared.

3. **The correct answer is B.** Angles opposite the congruent sides of an isosceles triangle are congruent. Using this fact, together with the fact that the sum of the three angles in a triangle is 180°, yields the equation $z + z + 24 = 180$. Solve for z, as follows:

$$\begin{aligned}z+z+24&=180\\2z+24&=180\\2z&=156\\z&=78\end{aligned}$$

Choice A is incorrect because the side opposite the angle with measure 24° is not marked as being congruent to the one opposite the angle with measure z. So z cannot be 24. Choice C is incorrect because you cannot have two right angles in the same triangle. Choice D is incorrect because 156 is $2z$.

4. **The correct answer is A.** The slope of the line is:

$$\begin{aligned}m&=\frac{-1-(-2)}{-3-4}\\&=\frac{-1+2}{-7}\\&=-\frac{1}{7}\end{aligned}$$

Using the point-slope form of the equation of a line, namely $y - y_1 = m(x - x_1)$ with the point $(x_1, y_1) = (-3,-1)$ yields

$$\begin{aligned}y-(-1)&=-\frac{1}{7}(x-(-3))\\y+1&=-\frac{1}{7}(x+3)\\-7(y+1)&=x+3\\-7y-7&=x+3\\x+7y&=-10\end{aligned}$$

Choice B is incorrect because the slope is incorrect. Choice C is incorrect because you used the reciprocal of the slope; remember, it is the difference in the y-coordinates of the two points divided by the difference in the x-coordinates. Choice D is incorrect because you added the y-coordinates and x-coordinates when computing the slope but should have subtracted them.

5. **The correct answer is C.** The sum of the interior angles in a regular polygon with n sides is $(n - 2)180$. A decagon has 10 sides. So the sum of its interior angles is $(10 - 2)180 = 8(180) = 1{,}440$. Choice A is incorrect because 360 is the sum of the exterior angles. Choice B is incorrect because 720 is half the correct sum. Choice D is incorrect because the formula is $180(n - 2)$, not $180n$.

6. **The correct answer is A.** Since triangle ABC is similar to triangle DEF, the ratios of the corresponding sides are equal. In particular, $\frac{AB}{AC} = \frac{DE}{DF}$. Using this fact and simplifying yields the following relationship:

$$\frac{a+b}{2b} = \frac{b-a}{2a}$$
$$2a(a+b) = 2b(b-a)$$
$$2a^2 + 2ab = 2b^2 - 2ba$$
$$a^2 + ab = b^2 - ab$$
$$b^2 - a^2 - 2ab = 0$$

Choice B is incorrect because you did not use the distributive property correctly when simplifying the relationship obtained from similarity of the triangles. Choice C is incorrect because when setting up the proportion obtained from similarity of the triangles, you flipped one of the fractions. Choice D is incorrect because a relationship of $a = b$ would require the base of triangle DEF to have length zero.

7. **The correct answer is C.** The height and base used in the area formula for a parallelogram must be perpendicular. Using $2m$ for the height and $6m$ for the base, we conclude the area is $(2m)(6m) = 12$ square meters. Choice A is incorrect because the sides with lengths $3m$ and $2m$ are not perpendicular. Choice B is incorrect because 11 is just the sum of the three labeled measurements, not the area. Choice D is incorrect because the sides with lengths $3m$ and $6m$ are not perpendicular.

8. **The correct answer is A.** Use the Pythagorean theorem:

$$y^2 + x^2 = (x+2)^2$$
$$y^2 + x^2 = x^2 + 4x + 4$$
$$y^2 = 4x + 4$$
$$y = \sqrt{4x+4}$$

Choice B is incorrect because the square root around the quantity is missing. Choice C is incorrect because $(x + 2)^2 \neq x^2 + 2^2$. Choice D is incorrect because you identified the side with length y as the hypotenuse in the Pythagorean theorem, but it is not the side opposite the right angle.

9. **The correct answer is C.** Let e be the edge of the cube. The surface area is $6e^2 = 13.5$. Solve for e:

$$6e^2 = 13.5$$
$$e^2 = 2.25$$
$$e = \sqrt{2.25} = 1.5$$

So the volume is $e^3 = (1.5)^3 = 3.375$ cubic inches. Choice A is incorrect because you do not multiply base and exponent when computing a power. Choice B is incorrect because 1.5 in. is the length of an edge of the cube. Choice D is incorrect because 2.25 square inches is the area of a single face of the cube; the volume is the cube of an edge, not the square.

10. The correct answer is C. The sum of the three angles in a triangle is 180°. Using this fact yields the following:

$$\begin{aligned} x + (2x - 1) + (3x + 7) &= 180 \\ 6x + 6 &= 180 \\ 6x &= 174 \\ x &= 29 \end{aligned}$$

So the three angles are 29°, 57°, and 94°. Choice A is incorrect because 29° is the smallest of the three angles. Choice B is incorrect because 57° is the middle of the three angles. Choice D is incorrect because the sum of the angles of a triangle is 180°, not 360°.

11. The correct answer is C. Decompose the figure into three smaller rectangles, as shown:

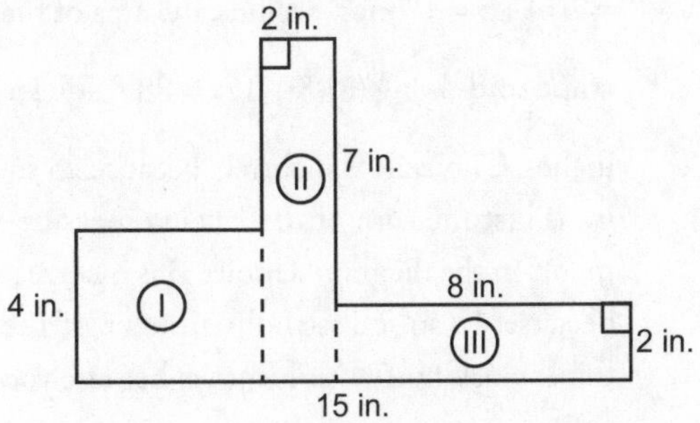

For rectangle I, the side adjacent to the one with length 4 inches has length 15 – (2 + 8) = 5 inches. So the area is (4)(5) = 20 square inches. For rectangle II, the side adjacent to the side with length 2 inches has length (7 + 2) = 9 inches. So the area is (2)(9) = 18 square inches. For rectangle III, the area is (2)(8) = 16 square inches. The sum of these three areas, 54 square inches, is the area of the composite figure. Choice A is incorrect because 38 is just the sum of the labeled measurements in the diagram. Choice B is incorrect because 43 inches is the perimeter of the composite figure, not the area. Choice D is incorrect because you seem to have partitioned the figure horizontally but then inadvertently used the bottom rectangle as one with sides 4 inches and 15 inches; this solution includes a portion that is not included in the figure.

12. The correct answer is D. Label the two legs of the triangle, as shown:

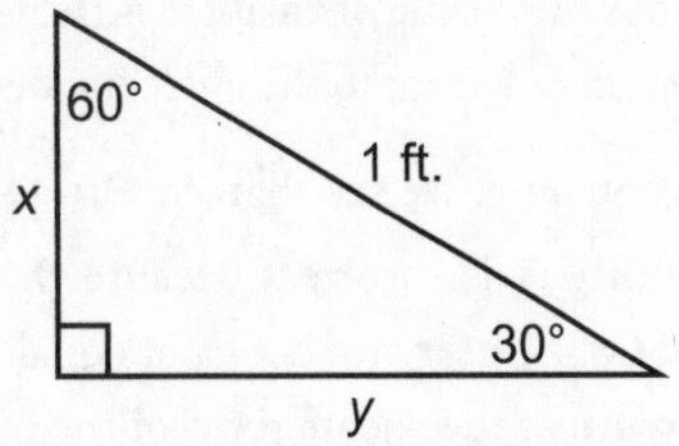

Use right triangle trigonometry to determine x and y:

$$x = \frac{x}{1} = \sin 30^\circ = \frac{1}{2}$$

$$y = \frac{y}{1} = \sin 60^\circ = \frac{\sqrt{3}}{2}$$

So the area of the triangle is $\frac{1}{2}\left(\frac{1}{2}\right)\left(\frac{\sqrt{3}}{2}\right) = \frac{\sqrt{3}}{8}$ square feet. Choice A is incorrect because $\frac{3+\sqrt{3}}{2}$ is the perimeter of the triangle. Choice B is incorrect because you forgot to multiply by $\frac{1}{2}$ in the area formula. Choice C is incorrect because you used the hypotenuse as one of the legs when computing the area.

13. The correct answer is A. The slope of the line is $m = \frac{-3-0}{0-(-6)} = -\frac{1}{2}$. Since the y-intercept is (0, –3), we know that b in the slope-intercept form for the equation of a line, which is $y = mx + b$, is –3. So the equation is $y = -\frac{1}{2}x - 3$. Choice B is incorrect because you used the x-intercept instead of the y-intercept for b in the slope-intercept form for the equation of a line, $y = mx + b$. Choice C is incorrect because you used the x-intercept instead of the y-intercept for b in the slope-intercept form for the equation of a line, $y = mx + b$, and you used the reciprocal of the slope. Choice D is incorrect because you used the reciprocal of the slope.

14. **The correct answer is C.** First, determine the length of the missing leg using the Pythagorean theorem: $\sqrt{3^2 - x^2} = \sqrt{9 - x^2}$. Since the cosine of an angle is the length of the side adjacent to the angle divided by the hypotenuse, we see that $\cos\theta = \frac{\sqrt{9-x^2}}{3}$. Choice A is incorrect because the square root of a difference does not equal the difference of the square roots of the individual terms. Choice B is incorrect because $\frac{x}{3}$ is $\sin\theta$. Choice D is incorrect because $\frac{3}{\sqrt{9-x^2}}$ is the reciprocal of the correct answer.

15. **The correct answer is D.** The new side (after the reduction) has length $x - 0.30x = 0.70x$. So the perimeter of the new square is $4(0.70x) = 2.8x$ inches. Choice A is incorrect because $0.49x$ is the area of the new square. Choice B is incorrect because 0.70 in. is the length of one side. Choice C is incorrect because you used $0.3x$ as the length of the side, but $0.3x$ is the amount to be subtracted from the original side length x to get the new side length.

16. **The correct answer is A.** The two right triangles are similar since their corresponding angles are congruent. So their sides are proportional. This yields the relationship $\frac{5.9}{9.3} = \frac{s}{18.7}$, so that $s = \frac{(5.9)(18.7)}{9.3}$. Choice B is incorrect because the 18.7 and 9.3 should be interchanged. Choice C is incorrect because the 9.3 and 5.9 should be interchanged. Choice D is incorrect because you should divide by 9.3, not multiply by it.

17. **The correct answer is C.** You must determine the length of the bottom base to find the area of the trapezoid. To this end, decompose the trapezoid in the following way:

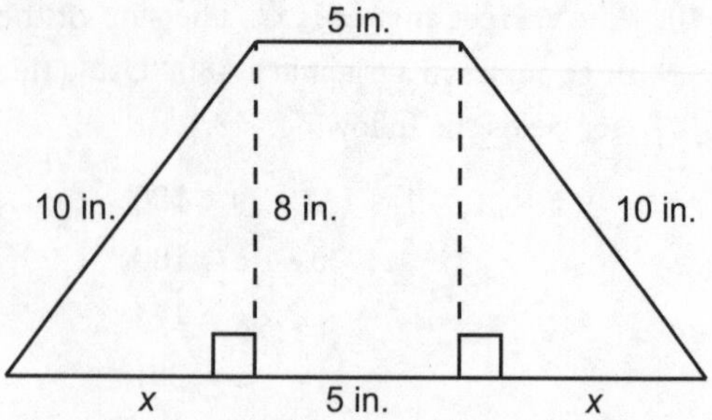

The right triangles are congruent because the diagonal sides of the trapezoid are congruent. Use the Pythagorean theorem to find x:

$$10^2 = 8^2 + x^2$$
$$100 = 64 + x^2$$
$$x^2 = 36$$
$$x = 6$$

So the length of the bottom base is $2x + 5 = 2(6) + 5 = 17$ inches. Thus, the area of the trapezoid is $\frac{1}{2}(8)(5+17) = 88$ square inches. Choice A is incorrect because 23 sq. in. is just the sum of the labeled measurements in the diagram. Choice B is incorrect because 42 sq. in. is the perimeter of the trapezoid. Choice D is incorrect because you need to multiply this amount (176) by $\frac{1}{2}$.

18. **The correct answer is B.** The length of the new diagonal is $a + 0.40a = 1.40a$. To find the area of the new square, you must find the length of a side, x, as shown:

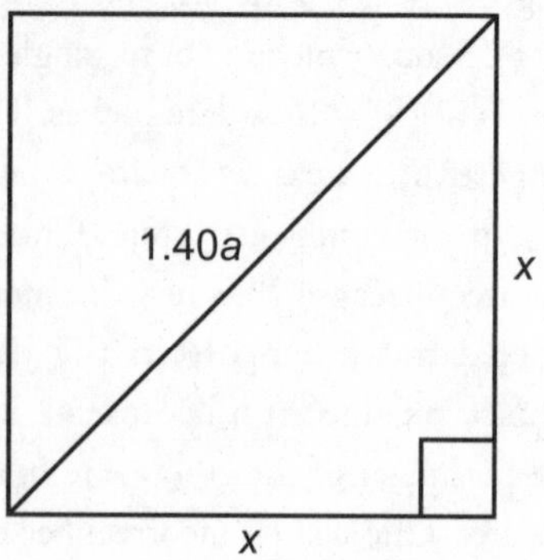

Use the Pythagorean theorem:

$$x^2 + x^2 = (1.4a)^2$$
$$2x^2 = 1.96a^2$$
$$x^2 = 0.98a^2$$

So the area is $0.98a^2$ square meters. Choice A is just the square of the length of the original diagonal. Choice C is incorrect because you decreased the length of the diagonal to $0.60a$ instead of increasing it. Choice D is incorrect because when using the Pythagorean theorem, you did not divide by 2.

19. **The correct answer is C.** This scenario is depicted in the following diagram:

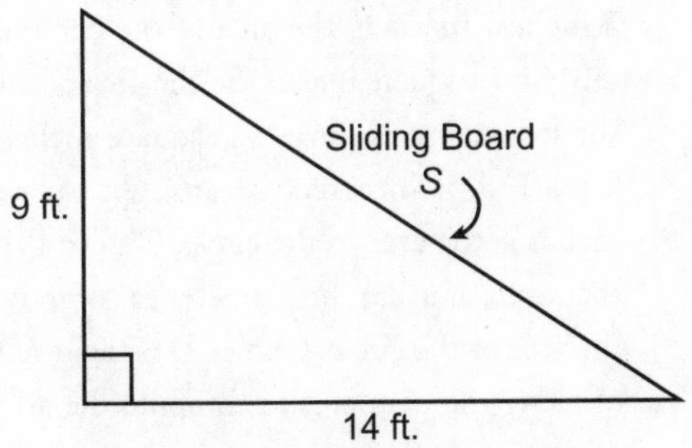

Applying the Pythagorean theorem yields $s^2 = 14^2 + 9^2$, so that $s = \sqrt{14^2 + 9^2}$ feet. Choices A and B are incorrect because the square root of a difference/sum does not equal the difference/sum of the square roots of the individual terms. Choice D is incorrect because you treated the sliding board as one of the legs of a right triangle instead of as the hypotenuse.

20. **The correct answer is D.** Using the area formula for a circle yields the equation $\pi R^2 = \sqrt{\pi}$, where R is the radius. Solve for R:

$$\pi R^2 = \sqrt{\pi}$$
$$R^2 = \frac{\sqrt{\pi}}{\pi} = \frac{1}{\sqrt{\pi}}$$
$$R = \sqrt{\frac{1}{\sqrt{\pi}}} = \left(\frac{1}{\pi^{1/2}}\right)^{1/2}$$
$$R = \frac{1}{\pi^{1/4}}$$

So the circumference is $2\pi\left(\frac{1}{\pi^{1/4}}\right) = 2\pi^{3/4}$ centimeters. Choice A is incorrect because $\frac{1}{\pi^{1/4}}$ is the radius. Choice B is incorrect because of an error involving exponent rules. Choice C is incorrect because you used the reciprocal of the radius.

21. **The correct answer is C.** The triangle law says that the sum of the lengths of any two sides must be greater than the length of the third side. The only choice for which this is not true is choice C, since 1 + 1 is not greater than 2.

22. **The correct answer is A.** The ratio between the diameter and height yields the proportion $\frac{3}{2} = \frac{\text{diameter}}{H}$. Solve for the diameter to see that diameter $= \frac{3H}{2}$ feet. So the radius of the bases of the cylinder is $\frac{1}{2}\left(\frac{3H}{2}\right) = \frac{3H}{4}$ feet. So the volume of the cylinder is $\pi\left(\frac{3H}{4}\right)^2 H = \frac{9}{16}\pi H^3$ cubic feet. Choice B is incorrect because you did not square the rad us. Choice C is incorrect because you used the diameter instead of the radius. Choice D is incorrect because you used the diameter instead of the radius and did not square it.

23. **The correct answer is B.** Extend a segment from the bottom vertex to the opposite side perpendicularly. Since the triangle is equilateral, this bisects the side. Label the length of this segment h, as shown:

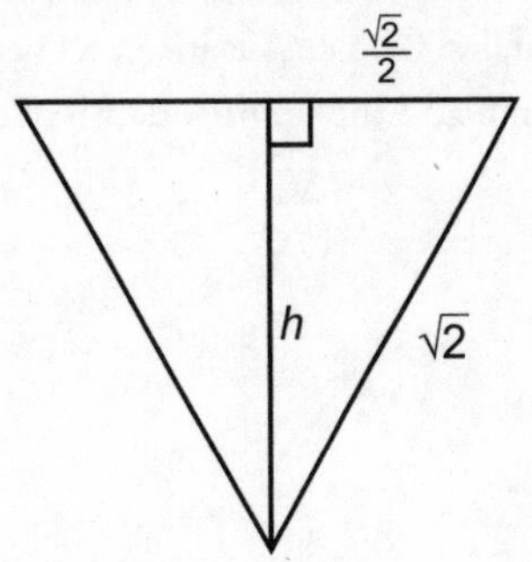

Use the Pythagorean theorem to find h:

$$h^2 + \left(\frac{\sqrt{2}}{2}\right)^2 = \left(\sqrt{2}\right)^2$$

$$h^2 + \frac{1}{2} = 2$$

$$h^2 = \frac{3}{2}$$

$$h = \sqrt{\frac{3}{2}}$$

The area is $\frac{1}{2}\left(\frac{\sqrt{3}}{\sqrt{2}}\right)\left(\sqrt{2}\right) = \frac{\sqrt{3}}{2}$ square meters. Choice A is incorrect because you used $\frac{\sqrt{2}}{2}$ meters as the length of the base instead of $\sqrt{2}$ meters. Choice C is incorrect because $\sqrt{2}$ meters cannot be used as the height, since it is not perpendicular to the base. Choice D is incorrect because this is the perimeter.

24. The correct answer is B. Start by drawing a diagram:

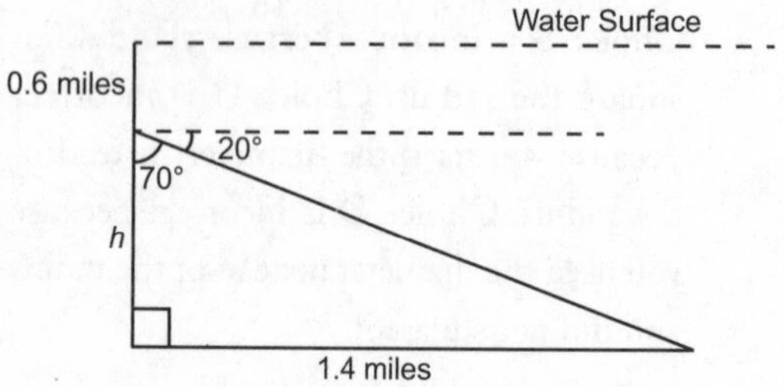

Observe that $\tan 70^\circ = \frac{1.4 \text{ miles}}{h}$, so that $h = \frac{1.4 \text{ miles}}{\tan 70^\circ} \approx$ miles. So the depth of the dive, all told, is approximately $(0.5 + 0.6) =$ 1.1 miles. Choice A is incorrect because you did not add the original depth of 0.6 miles.

Choice C is incorrect because this is $1.4 \tan 70^\circ$; you should have divided by $\tan 70^\circ$. Also, you did not add the original depth 0.6 miles. Choice D is incorrect because this is $1.4 \tan 70^\circ$; you should have divided by $\tan 70^\circ$. Choice A is incorrect because you did not add the original depth of 0.6 miles.

25. The correct answer is C. The area of the shaded region equals the difference between the area of the square and the area of the circle. The area of the square is $(6)(6) = 36$ square inches. Since the circle is inscribed in the square, the diameter of the circle is equal to the length of the side of the square; the diameter is 6 inches. Thus, the radius is 3 inches. As such, the area of the circle is $\pi(3)^2 = 9\pi$ square inches. So the area of the shaded region is $(36 - 9\pi)$ square inches. Choice A is incorrect because 9π square inches is the area of the circle. Choice B is the result of using the diameter to compute the area of the circle. Choice D is the result of using the diameter to compute the area of the circle and not subtracting it from the area of the square.

PART VII

TWO PRACTICE TESTS

Practice Test 2

DIRECTIONS FOR TAKING THE PRACTICE TEST

Directions: The Practice Test for the GED test has four separate subtests: Reasoning Through Language Arts, Mathematical Reasoning, Science, and Social Studies.

- Read and follow the directions at the start of each test.
- Stick to the time limits.
- Enter your answers to the multiple-choice questions in the appropriate circle on the answer sheets provided. Answer the technology-enhanced questions on the answer sheet as follows:
    - **Fill-in-the-blank questions** are designated by an empty box. When you see this box, write your answer in the blank that corresponds to the question number.
    - **Drop-down questions** appear with a drop-down menu icon. To answer these questions, write your answer (or the corresponding letter) in the blank that corresponds to the question number.
    - **Drag-and-drop questions** will appear with a diagram; for instance, a Venn diagram, flow chart, or series of boxes. To answer these questions, enter the answers (or the corresponding letter) into the correct space on the answer sheet.
    - **Select-an-area questions** will appear with an image that you are instructed to "Click" on or "Select," such as a number line. To answer these questions, you will write the answer in the blank that corresponds to the question number.
    - An **extended response question** will appear on the Reasoning Through Language Arts Test. To answer this question, you will write your response on the lined pages provided in the answer sheet.
- When you have completed the entire test, compare your answers with the correct answers given in the Answer Key and Explanations at the end of this Practice Test.
- Remember to check the "Are You Ready to Take the GED® Test?" section to gauge how close you are to mastering the GED test.

ANSWER SHEET: PRACTICE TEST 2

Reasoning Through Language Arts

Part I

1. Ⓐ Ⓑ Ⓒ Ⓓ
2. Ⓐ Ⓑ Ⓒ Ⓓ
3. Ⓐ Ⓑ Ⓒ Ⓓ
4. Ⓐ Ⓑ Ⓒ Ⓓ
5. Ⓐ Ⓑ Ⓒ Ⓓ
6. Ⓐ Ⓑ Ⓒ Ⓓ
7. Ⓐ Ⓑ Ⓒ Ⓓ
8. Ⓐ Ⓑ Ⓒ Ⓓ

9. 1st: ____________
2nd: ____________
3rd: ____________
4th: ____________

10. ____________

11. ____________

12. Ⓐ Ⓑ Ⓒ Ⓓ
13. Ⓐ Ⓑ Ⓒ Ⓓ
14. Ⓐ Ⓑ Ⓒ Ⓓ
15. Ⓐ Ⓑ Ⓒ Ⓓ
16. Ⓐ Ⓑ Ⓒ Ⓓ
17. Ⓐ Ⓑ Ⓒ Ⓓ

Part II

Write your response using the pages provided after this answer sheet.

Part III

18. Ⓐ Ⓑ Ⓒ Ⓓ

19. Jefferson: ____________
Adams: ____________

20. Ⓐ Ⓑ Ⓒ Ⓓ

21. ____________

22. Ⓐ Ⓑ Ⓒ Ⓓ
23. Ⓐ Ⓑ Ⓒ Ⓓ
24. Ⓐ Ⓑ Ⓒ Ⓓ

25. ____________

26. Ⓐ Ⓑ Ⓒ Ⓓ
27. Ⓐ Ⓑ Ⓒ Ⓓ

28. ____________

29. Ⓐ Ⓑ Ⓒ Ⓓ

30. ____________

31. Ⓐ Ⓑ Ⓒ Ⓓ
32. Ⓐ Ⓑ Ⓒ Ⓓ
33. Ⓐ Ⓑ Ⓒ Ⓓ
34. Ⓐ Ⓑ Ⓒ Ⓓ
35. Ⓐ Ⓑ Ⓒ Ⓓ
36. Ⓐ Ⓑ Ⓒ Ⓓ
37. Ⓐ Ⓑ Ⓒ Ⓓ
38. Ⓐ Ⓑ Ⓒ Ⓓ
39. Ⓐ Ⓑ Ⓒ Ⓓ
40. Ⓐ Ⓑ Ⓒ Ⓓ

41. ____________

42. ____________

43. ____________

44. ____________

45. ____________

46. ____________
____
____
____

47. ____________

48. ____________

Extended Response

answer sheet

Mathematical Reasoning

1. Ⓐ Ⓑ Ⓒ Ⓓ
2. Ⓐ Ⓑ Ⓒ Ⓓ
3. ____________
4. Ⓐ Ⓑ Ⓒ Ⓓ
5. Ⓐ Ⓑ Ⓒ Ⓓ
6. ____________
7. ____________

   ____
8. Ⓐ Ⓑ Ⓒ Ⓓ
9. Ⓐ Ⓑ Ⓒ Ⓓ
10. Ⓐ Ⓑ Ⓒ Ⓓ
11. Ⓐ Ⓑ Ⓒ Ⓓ
12. Ⓐ Ⓑ Ⓒ Ⓓ
13. Ⓐ Ⓑ Ⓒ Ⓓ
14. Ⓐ Ⓑ Ⓒ Ⓓ
15. Ⓐ Ⓑ Ⓒ Ⓓ
16. Ⓐ Ⓑ Ⓒ Ⓓ
17. Ⓐ Ⓑ Ⓒ Ⓓ
18. ____________
19. ____________
20. Ⓐ Ⓑ Ⓒ Ⓓ
21. Ⓐ Ⓑ Ⓒ Ⓓ
22. Ⓐ Ⓑ Ⓒ Ⓓ
23. Ⓐ Ⓑ Ⓒ Ⓓ
24. Ⓐ Ⓑ Ⓒ Ⓓ
25. Ⓐ Ⓑ Ⓒ Ⓓ
26. Ⓐ Ⓑ Ⓒ Ⓓ
27. Ⓐ Ⓑ Ⓒ Ⓓ
28. Ⓐ Ⓑ Ⓒ Ⓓ
29. Ⓐ Ⓑ Ⓒ Ⓓ
30. Ⓐ Ⓑ Ⓒ Ⓓ
31. Ⓐ Ⓑ Ⓒ Ⓓ
32. Ⓐ Ⓑ Ⓒ Ⓓ
33. Ⓐ Ⓑ Ⓒ Ⓓ
34. Ⓐ Ⓑ Ⓒ Ⓓ
35. ____________
36. ____________
37. Ⓐ Ⓑ Ⓒ Ⓓ
38. Ⓐ Ⓑ Ⓒ Ⓓ
39. ____________
40. Ⓐ Ⓑ Ⓒ Ⓓ
41. Ⓐ Ⓑ Ⓒ Ⓓ
42. ____________
43. ____________
44. Ⓐ Ⓑ Ⓒ Ⓓ
45. Ⓐ Ⓑ Ⓒ Ⓓ
46. Ⓐ Ⓑ Ⓒ Ⓓ

answer sheet

Science

1. Ⓐ Ⓑ Ⓒ Ⓓ	13. Ⓐ Ⓑ Ⓒ Ⓓ	25. Ⓐ Ⓑ Ⓒ Ⓓ
2. Ⓐ Ⓑ Ⓒ Ⓓ	14. Ⓐ Ⓑ Ⓒ Ⓓ	26. ________
3. Ⓐ Ⓑ Ⓒ Ⓓ	15. Ⓐ Ⓑ Ⓒ Ⓓ	27. Ⓐ Ⓑ Ⓒ Ⓓ
4. Ⓐ Ⓑ Ⓒ Ⓓ	16. Ⓐ Ⓑ Ⓒ Ⓓ	28. Ⓐ Ⓑ Ⓒ Ⓓ
5. Ⓐ Ⓑ Ⓒ Ⓓ	17. Ⓐ Ⓑ Ⓒ Ⓓ	29. Ⓐ Ⓑ Ⓒ Ⓓ
6. Ⓐ Ⓑ Ⓒ Ⓓ	18. Ⓐ Ⓑ Ⓒ Ⓓ	30. Ⓐ Ⓑ Ⓒ Ⓓ
7. Ⓐ Ⓑ Ⓒ Ⓓ	19. Ⓐ Ⓑ Ⓒ Ⓓ	31. Ⓐ Ⓑ Ⓒ Ⓓ
8. Ⓐ Ⓑ Ⓒ Ⓓ	20. Ⓐ Ⓑ Ⓒ Ⓓ	32. Ⓐ Ⓑ Ⓒ Ⓓ
9. ________	21. Ⓐ Ⓑ Ⓒ Ⓓ	33. Ⓐ Ⓑ Ⓒ Ⓓ
10. Ⓐ Ⓑ Ⓒ Ⓓ	22. Ⓐ Ⓑ Ⓒ Ⓓ	34. Ⓐ Ⓑ Ⓒ Ⓓ
11. ________	23. Ⓐ Ⓑ Ⓒ Ⓓ	35. Ⓐ Ⓑ Ⓒ Ⓓ
12. Ⓐ Ⓑ Ⓒ Ⓓ	24. Ⓐ Ⓑ Ⓒ Ⓓ	

Social Studies

1. Ⓐ Ⓑ Ⓒ Ⓓ	13. ________	25. ________
2. Ⓐ Ⓑ Ⓒ Ⓓ	14. Ⓐ Ⓑ Ⓒ Ⓓ	26. Ⓐ Ⓑ Ⓒ Ⓓ
3. Ⓐ Ⓑ Ⓒ Ⓓ	15. Ⓐ Ⓑ Ⓒ Ⓓ	27. Ⓐ Ⓑ Ⓒ Ⓓ
4. Ⓐ Ⓑ Ⓒ Ⓓ	16. Ⓐ Ⓑ Ⓒ Ⓓ	28. Ⓐ Ⓑ Ⓒ Ⓓ
5. Ⓐ Ⓑ Ⓒ Ⓓ	17. ________	29. Ⓐ Ⓑ Ⓒ Ⓓ
6. Ⓐ Ⓑ Ⓒ Ⓓ	18. Ⓐ Ⓑ Ⓒ Ⓓ	30. Ⓐ Ⓑ Ⓒ Ⓓ
7. Ⓐ Ⓑ Ⓒ Ⓓ	19. Ⓐ Ⓑ Ⓒ Ⓓ	31. ________
8. ________	20. Ⓐ Ⓑ Ⓒ Ⓓ	32. Ⓐ Ⓑ Ⓒ Ⓓ
9. ________	21. Ⓐ Ⓑ Ⓒ Ⓓ	33. ________
10. Ⓐ Ⓑ Ⓒ Ⓓ	22. Ⓐ Ⓑ Ⓒ Ⓓ	34. Ⓐ Ⓑ Ⓒ Ⓓ
11. ________	23. Ⓐ Ⓑ Ⓒ Ⓓ	35. Ⓐ Ⓑ Ⓒ Ⓓ
12. Ⓐ Ⓑ Ⓒ Ⓓ	24. Ⓐ Ⓑ Ⓒ Ⓓ	

REASONING THROUGH LANGUAGE ARTS

150 Minutes • 49 Questions

Directions: The Reasoning Through Language Arts Test consists of passages of fiction and nonfiction reading material. After you read a passage, answer the questions that follow it, referring back to the passage as needed. Answer all questions based on what is stated and implied in the passage.

Most questions are in multiple-choice format. Others are meant to prepare you for the technology-enhanced questions that you will find on the test, such as drop-down, fill-in-the-blanks, and drag-and-drops. There is also an extended response question that requires you to read a paired passage that represents two views on a topic and write a well-organized essay supporting one of the viewpoints. Record your answers on the Reasoning Through Language Arts section of the answer sheet provided. To review how to answer these questions on your answer sheet, please refer to "Directions for Taking the Practice Test" on page 653.

Part I

Questions 1–6 refer to the following passage.

Franklin Delano Roosevelt's First Inaugural Speech

The following speech has been adapted from President Franklin Delano Roosevelt's first inaugural speech on March 4, 1933. In the presidential election of 1932, Roosevelt had defeated President Herbert Hoover in a landslide. When Roosevelt took office, the United States was already in the midst of an economic crisis called The Great Depression.

President Hoover, Mr. Chief Justice, my friends:

This is a day of national consecration, and I am certain that on this day my fellow Americans expect that on my induction into the Presidency I will address them with a candor and a decision which the present situation of our people impels. This is preeminently the time to speak the truth, the whole truth, frankly and boldly. Nor need we shrink from honestly facing conditions in our country today. This great Nation will endure as it has endured, will revive and will prosper.

So, first of all, let me assert my firm belief that the only thing we have to fear is fear itself—nameless, unreasoning, unjustified terror which paralyzes needed efforts to convert retreat into advance. In every dark hour of our national life a leadership of frankness and of vigor has met with that understanding and support of the people themselves which is essential to victory. And I am convinced that you will again give that support to leadership in these critical days.

In such a spirit on my part and on yours we face our common difficulties. They concern, thank God, only material things. Values have shrunk to fantastic levels; taxes have risen; our ability to pay has fallen; government of all kinds is faced by serious curtailment of income; the means of exchange are frozen in the currents of trade; the withered leaves of industrial enterprise lie on every side; farmers find no markets for their produce; and the savings of many years in thousands of families are gone.

More important, a host of unemployed citizens face the grim problem of existence, and an equally great number toil with little return. Only a foolish optimist can deny the dark realities of the moment.

And yet our distress comes from no failure of substance. We are stricken by no plague of locusts. Compared with the perils which our forefathers conquered because they believed and were not afraid, we have still much to be thankful for. Nature still offers her bounty and human efforts have multiplied it. Plenty is at our doorstep, but a generous use of it languishes in the very sight of the supply. Primarily this is because the rulers of the exchange of mankind's goods have failed, through their own stubbornness and their own incompetence, have admitted their failure and have abdicated. Practices of the unscrupulous money changers stand indicted in the court of public opinion, rejected by the hearts and minds of men.

True they have tried, but their efforts have been cast in the pattern of an outworn tradition. Faced by failure of credit they have proposed only the lending of more money. Stripped of the lure of profit by which to induce our people to follow their false leadership, they have resorted to exhortations, pleading tearfully for restored confidence. They only know the rules of a generation of self-seekers. They have no vision, and when there is no vision the people perish.

1. What is the main idea of this passage?

A. Herbert Hoover's administration was a failure.

B. The United States' economic problems will be easily fixed.

C. High unemployment is due to natural disasters.

D. Economic challenges can be overcome with honest work.

2. In the context of paragraph 1, what does the word *candor* mean?

A. Honesty

B. Humor

C. Vagueness

D. Fear

3. What was **most likely** Roosevelt's motivation for talking about the economy?

A. He wanted to convince people to re-elect him in the next election.

B. He wanted to emphasize that he understood the challenges.

C. He wanted to distract from other problems going on in the country.

D. He wanted to blame farmers for causing the Great Depression.

4. Based on the passage, what **most likely** caused the Great Depression?

A. Natural disasters ruining crops.

B. High taxes paid by citizens.

C. High unemployment among citizens.

D. Poor leadership and outdated solutions.

5. What purpose does the discussion of "plenty" in line 52 serve in Roosevelt's speech?

   A. It contrasts the successes of the forefathers with the failures of modern government.

   B. It suggests that there is hope, even in the middle of a dark situation.

   C. It criticizes the economic policies of the previous presidential administration.

   D. It shows how some citizens are living the good life at the expense of others.

6. What does the following quote from the passage mean?

   "[L]et me assert my firm belief that the only thing we have to fear is fear itself—nameless, unreasoning, unjustified terror which paralyzes needed efforts to convert retreat into advance."

   A. Fear is the only way to fix the current situation.

   B. Americans should be afraid of what's about to happen.

   C. Fear is holding back necessary progress.

   D. Roosevelt has no fear about the future.

Questions 7–12 refer to the following passage.

Is There a Safe Level of Lead in Drinking Water?

The Safe Drinking Water Act requires the Environmental Protection Agency (EPA) to determine the level of contaminants in drinking water at which no adverse health effects are likely to occur with an adequate margin of safety. These non-enforceable health goals, based solely on possible health risks, are called maximum contaminant level goals (MCLGs). The EPA has set the maximum contaminant level goal for lead in drinking water at zero because lead is a toxic metal that can be harmful to human health even at low exposure levels. Lead is persistent, and it can bioaccumulate in the body over time.

Young children, infants, and fetuses are particularly vulnerable to lead because the physical and behavioral effects of lead occur at lower exposure levels in children than in adults. A dose of lead that would have little effect on an adult can have a significant effect on a child. In children, low levels of exposure have been linked to damage to the central and peripheral nervous system, learning disabilities, shorter stature, impaired hearing, and impaired formation and function of blood cells.

The Centers for Disease Control and Prevention (CDC) recommends that public health actions be initiated when the level of lead in a child's blood is 5 micrograms per deciliter (μg/dL) or more.

It is important to recognize all the ways a child can be exposed to lead. Children are exposed to lead in paint, dust, soil, air, and food, as well as drinking water. If the level of lead in a child's blood is at or above the CDC action level of 5 micrograms per deciliter, it may be due to lead exposures from a combination of sources. The EPA estimates that drinking water can make up 20 percent or more of a person's total exposure to lead. Infants who consume mostly mixed formula can receive 40 percent to 60 percent of their exposure to lead from drinking water.

7. What might be another title for this passage that summarizes its main ideas?

A. "Lead is Less Hazardous Than Previously Thought"

B. "The Dangers of Lead in Drinking Water"

C. "Sources of Clean Drinking Water"

D. "A History of Lead in Drinking Water"

8. What does the phrase "lead is persistent" in line 15 mean?

A. There is no way to get rid of lead.

B. Lead affects everybody the same way.

C. Once ingested, lead does not go away.

D. Lead takes a long time to accumulate.

9. Drag and drop the ideas about lead in drinking water in the chart to show the order in which they are presented in the passage. (Enter the letters that correspond to each idea on your answer sheet.)

A. Children are exposed to lead from various sources, including drinking water.

B. The highest amount of acceptable lead in drinking water is zero.

C. The EPA has the power to investigate the safety of levels of lead in drinking water.

D. Children are likely to experience more side effects of lead poisoning than adults.

10. In paragraph 1, how does the description of the acceptable amount of lead in drinking water affect the understanding of the passage? Choose the correct answer from the drop-down menu.

Select ▼

A. It illustrates that the consequences of lead are severe.

B. It suggests that the problem of lead in drinking water will never be solved.

C. It distracts from the main idea of the passage.

D. It shows the bias of the passage's writer.

11. What is the level of lead in a child's blood that should trigger action?

12. What additional information would fit in with this passage?

A. Which members of Congress sponsored the Safe Drinking Water Act

B. The effects of water pollution on drinking water

C. The number of children affected by lead in the past ten years

D. A description of the history of the Environmental Protection Agency

Questions 13–17 refer to the following document.

Ethics in the Workplace

Ethics Policy for Cutting Edge Industries, Inc.
June 2019

A. Overview

Cutting Edge Industries is committed to protecting employees, partners, vendors and the company from illegal or damaging actions by individuals, either knowingly or unknowingly. When Cutting Edge Industries addresses issues proactively and uses correct judgment, it will help set us apart from competitors.

Cutting Edge Industries will not tolerate any wrongdoing or impropriety at any time. Cutting Edge Industries will take the appropriate measures and act quickly in correcting the issue if the ethical code is broken.

B. Purpose

The purpose of this policy is to establish a culture of openness and trust and to emphasize the employee's and consumer's expectation to be treated to fair business practices. This policy will serve to guide business behavior to ensure ethical conduct. Effective ethics is a team effort involving the participation and support of every Cutting Edge Industries employee. All employees should familiarize themselves with the ethics guidelines that follow this introduction.

C. Scope

This policy applies to employees, contractors, consultants, temporaries, and other workers at Cutting Edge Industries, including all personnel affiliated with third parties.

D. Policy

D.1 Executive Commitment to Ethics

The company's senior leaders and executives must set a prime example. In any business practice, honesty and integrity must be top priority.

Executives must have an open-door policy and welcome suggestions and concerns from employees. This will allow employees to feel comfortable discussing any issues and will alert executives to concerns within the work force. Executives must also disclose any conflict of interests regarding their position within Cutting Edge Industries.

D.2 Employee Commitment to Ethics

Cutting Edge Industries employees will treat everyone fairly, have mutual respect, promote a team environment, and avoid the intent and appearance of unethical or compromising practices.

Every employee needs to apply effort and intelligence in maintaining the company's ethics value. Employees must disclose any conflict of interests regarding their position within Cutting Edge Industries.

Employees should consider the following questions to themselves when any behavior is questionable:

- Is the behavior legal?
- Does the behavior comply with all appropriate Cutting Edge Industries policies?
- Does the behavior reflect Cutting Edge Industries values and culture?
- Could the behavior adversely affect company stakeholders?
- Would you feel personally concerned if the behavior appeared in a news headline?
- Could the behavior adversely affect Cutting Edge Industries if all employees did it?

E. Company Awareness

Promotion of ethical conduct within interpersonal communications of employees will be rewarded. Cutting Edge Industries will promote a trustworthy and honest atmosphere to reinforce the vision of ethics within the company.

F. Maintaining Ethical Practices

Cutting Edge Industries will reinforce the importance of the integrity message and the tone will start at the top. Every employee, manager, director needs consistently maintain an ethical stance and support ethical behavior. Employees at Cutting Edge Industries should encourage open dialogue, get honest feedback, and treat everyone fairly, with honesty and objectivity.

The company has established a best practice disclosure committee to make sure the ethical code is delivered to all employees and that concerns regarding the code can be addressed.

G. Unethical Behavior

Cutting Edge Industries will avoid the intent and appearance of unethical or compromising practice in relationships, actions and communications. The company will not tolerate harassment or discrimination.

The company will not permit impropriety at any time and we will act ethically and responsibly in accordance with laws. Employees will not use corporate assets or business relationships for personal use or gain.

H. Policy Compliance

The Employee Resource Team will verify compliance to this policy through various methods, including but not limited to, business tool reports, internal and external audits, and feedback.

I. Exceptions

None. Any employee found to have violated this policy may be subject to disciplinary action, up to and including termination of employment.

13. Based on the document, what is the **most likely** outcome for someone who breaks the ethics rules?

   A. Reduction in pay
   B. Getting fired
   C. No consequences
   D. Promotion

14. What is meant by "The company has established a best practice disclosure committee" in Section F?

   A. The company is spying on its employees.
   B. The ethics rules apply only to committee members.
   C. The company wants to ensure fairness.
   D. Executives are exempt from the ethics rules.

15. Which of the following rules would be **most relevant** to add to the ethics policy?

   A. Employees are not allowed to accept gifts from vendors.
   B. Employees are required to wear appropriate attire at all times.
   C. Employees are eligible for 10 vacation days per year.
   D. Employees are not allowed to use personal social media accounts at work.

16. Based on the passage, which of the following is an example of what employees should NOT do?

   A. Keep quiet about other employees' ethical violations.
   B. Treat customers differently from other employees.
   C. Expect executives to maintain the same ethical standards.
   D. Expect to receive a reward for ethical behavior.

17. Which of the following questions could be added to the employee checklist in Section D?

   A. Can this behavior be used for personal gain?
   B. Do other employees get away with doing the same thing?
   C. Is there a chance that you could get away with this behavior without getting caught?
   D. Does the behavior reflect Cutting Edge Industries values and culture?

Part II

The following passages present two views on privatizing space travel. Analyze both viewpoints and determine which one is best supported. Use specific and relevant evidence from the passages to support your response. Use reasons and examples to support your position. Take 45 minutes to plan, draft, and edit your response.

Does the Government Belong in Space?

Passage 1—NASA Should be the Space Standard

Since the mid-twentieth century, the US government's NASA program has done things in space that few other nations have been able to match: moon landings, shuttle launches, interplanetary probes. Although priorities (and budgets) have shifted away from space travel in the early twenty-first century, it's time to start restoring NASA to its full space potential.

A number of private companies, like SpaceX, have started trying to move into the space sector, making it less about pushing the limits of scientific discovery and more about opening up new markets and money opportunities. Imagine a point fifty years from now when we're able to go to space on a regular basis, only to find ads and billboards there to greet us, like a zero-gravity Times Square.

Take the International Space Station, for example. As it exists now, it's a cooperative effort among nations. If it were run by private companies, this "space diplomacy" and shared effort would become secondary to whether the research and the facility are profitable or not, and which companies would be allowed to take part.

The reality is that the government has not only the decades of cutting-edge research and experience, but also the responsibility to push space science as far as it can go. The Cold War-era Space Race may seem quaint now, but it was backed by a genuine commitment to "go where no man has gone before."

In addition, there are serious economic benefits to funding NASA research. A recent study by the Space Foundation estimated that every dollar spent on NASA adds $10 to the US economy. The goods and services generated by the space agency contribute to the overall economy.

If the US starts ceding its space exploration and innovative research to private companies, it's an immeasurable loss. NASA has helped ensure that space belongs to all, not just those who can afford to be in the know.

Passage 2—Private Industry is the Wave of the Future

Space may be the "final frontier," but the time has come to let others explore. Since its creation, NASA and its government funding were an amazing tool to catapult us into space (literally as well as figuratively!). Now, as other government agencies and initiatives take priority in the federal budget, NASA's leading role in world space travel has begun to lapse—and maybe that's for the best.

Private companies, including Richard Branson's Virgin Galactic and Elon Musk's SpaceX, have gotten to the point where consumer space travel is no longer theoretical. Although these companies are still struggling with the mechanics of space travel, their research and development has gotten to the point where they're launching test rockets and conducting missions. This shows that the industry is ready to start taking over the space travel mantle, or at least will be ready in the coming decades.

Although many of these space programs are often treated like the pet projects of rich madmen, the fact is that they're willing to put in the money and time on projects that the US government is no longer willing to fund, like going back to the moon. The "been there, done that" attitude saves federal money, but shortchanges potential future research.

It all comes down to money, really. Federal space programs require budgets, sign-off, and limitations set by earthbound members of Congress. Private companies have more freedom to invest as they see fit, perhaps channeling more money into more attempts to get space travel right.

As we consider whether space funding should be privatized at this point in our history, it's important to consider that what the government *should* be doing (and has, in NASA's case) is creating a platform for the free market to take over eventually. The invaluable decades of NASA experience and research give companies the basics they need to take space travel to the next level.

It's time to let those private rockets fly.

Part III

Questions 18–24 refer to the following passage.

Passage 1—from Thomas Jefferson's "Declaration of Independence," published on July 4, 1776.

When in the Course of human events, it becomes necessary for one people to dissolve the political bands which have connected them with another, and to assume, among the Powers of the earth, the separate and equal station to which the Laws of Nature and of Nature's God entitle them, a decent respect to the opinions of mankind requires that they should declare the causes which impel them to the separation.

We hold these truths to be self-evident, that all men are created equal, that they are endowed by their Creator with certain unalienable Rights, that among these are Life, Liberty, and the pursuit of Happiness. That to secure these rights, Governments are instituted among Men, deriving their just powers from the consent of the governed, That whenever any Form of Government becomes destructive of these ends, it is the Right of the People to alter or to abolish it, and to institute new Government, laying its foundation on such principles and organizing its powers in such form, as to them shall seem most likely to effect their Safety and Happiness. Prudence, indeed, will dictate that Governments long established should not be changed for light and transient causes; and accordingly all experience hath shown, that mankind are more disposed to suffer, while evils are sufferable, than to right themselves by abolishing the forms to which they are accustomed. But when a long train of abuses and usurpations, pursuing invariably the same Object evinces a design to reduce them under absolute Despotism, it is their right, it is their duty, to throw off such Government, and to provide new Guards for their future security.

Such has been the patient sufferance of these Colonies; and such is now the necessity which constrains them to alter their former Systems of Government. The history of the present King of Great Britain is a history of repeated injuries and usurpations, all having in direct object the establishment of an absolute Tyranny over these States. To prove this, let Facts be submitted to a candid world.

Passage 2—from a letter written by John Adams to his wife, Abigail, on July 3, 1776.

Had a Declaration of Independency been made seven months ago, it would have been attended with many great and glorious effects. We might, before this hour, have formed alliances with foreign states. We should have mastered Quebec, and been in possession of Canada. You will perhaps wonder how such a declaration would have influenced our affairs in Canada, but if I could write with freedom, I could easily convince you that it would, and explain to you the manner how.

Many gentlemen in high stations, and of great influence, have been duped by the ministerial bubble of Commissioners to treat. And in real, sincere expectation of this event, which they so fondly wished, they have been slow and languid in promoting measures for the reduction of that province. Others there are in the Colonies who really wished that our enterprise in Canada would be defeated, that the Colonies might be brought into danger and distress between two fires, and be thus induced to submit. Others really wished to defeat the expedition to Canada, lest the conquest of it should elevate the minds of the people too much to hearken to those terms of reconciliation which, they believed, would be offered us. These jarring views, wishes, and designs occasioned an opposition to many salutary measures which were proposed for the support of that expedition, and caused obstructions, embarrassments, and studied delays, which have finally lost us the province.

All these causes, however, in conjunction would not have disappointed us, if it had not been for a misfortune which could not be foreseen, and perhaps could not have been prevented; I mean the prevalence of the small-pox among our troops. This fatal pestilence completed our destruction. It is a frown of Providence upon us, which we ought to lay to heart.

But, on the other hand, the delay of this Declaration to this time has many great advantages attending it. The hopes of reconciliation which were fondly entertained by multitudes of honest and well-meaning, though weak and mistaken people, have been gradually, and at last totally extinguished. Time has been given for the whole people maturely to consider the great question of independence, and to ripen their judgment, dissipate their fears, and allure their hopes, by discussing it in newspapers and pamphlets, by debating it in assemblies, conventions, committees of safety and inspection, in town and county meetings, as well as in private conversations, so that the whole people, in every colony of the thirteen, have now adopted it as their own act. This will cement the union, and avoid those heats, and perhaps convulsions, which might have been occasioned by such a Declaration six months ago.

18. How does Jefferson support his idea that it is time for the colonies to declare independence from England?

A. By describing the rights people hold

B. By making fun of the king

C. By describing the history of the colonies

D. By listing the people who support independence

19. Based on the different perspectives between the two writers in these passages, select which ideas would **most likely** be supported by which writer. Drag and drop the sentences into the correct location in the chart. (Enter the corresponding letters of the choices on the answer sheet.)

Jefferson	Adams

A. Declaring independence is the most noble thing to do.

B. Declaring independence now may not be the most effective action.

C. We need to consider our relationships with foreign governments.

D. Our own political needs are more important than any relationships.

20. What can the reader infer as the main similarity between Jefferson and Adams?

A. They are both loyal to the British king.

B. They are both supportive of independence.

C. They both want to be president.

D. They have the same goals for their new country.

21. Based on the passage, which writer **most likely** decided when to publish the Declaration of Independence on July 4: Jefferson, Adams, or both? ______

22. What does the phrase "it is a frown of Providence upon us, which we ought to lay to heart" in paragraph 3 of Passage 2 suggest?

A. Rhode Island supports the declaration.

B. The Declaration of Independence is a bad idea.

C. Those declaring independence should be cautious.

D. The colonists are weak and need rest.

23. Based on the context clues in Passage 1, what does *unalienable* mean?

A. Foreign

B. Sacred

C. Unnecessary

D. Changeable

24. What can we infer was Adams's intent in writing about the Declaration of Independence?

A. To vent his frustrations to a loved one

B. To criticize Thomas Jefferson's writing

C. To distance himself from the independence movement

D. To ensure that he gets credit for declaring independence

Questions 25–29 refer to the following passages.

Passage 1

Dr. Anna Howard Shaw was an early women's suffrage activist in the late nineteenth and early twentieth centuries. This excerpt is from The Story of a Pioneer, *her autobiography.*

The Washington convention of 1910 was graced by the presence of President Taft, who, at the invitation of Mrs. Rachel Foster Avery, made an address. It was understood, of course, that he was to come out strongly for woman suffrage; but, to our great disappointment, the President, a most charming and likable gentleman, seemed unable to grasp the significance of the occasion. He began his address with fulsome praise of women, which was accepted in respectful silence. Then he got round to woman suffrage, floundered helplessly, became confused, and ended with the most unfortunately chosen words he could have uttered: "I am opposed," he said, "to the extension of suffrage to women not fitted to vote. You would hardly expect to put the ballot into the hands of barbarians!"

The dropping of these remarkable words into a suffrage convention was naturally followed by an oppressive silence, which Mr. Taft, now wholly bereft of his self-possession, broke by saying that the best women would not vote and the worst women would.

In his audience were many women from suffrage states—high-minded women, wives and mothers, who had voted for Mr. Taft. The remarks to which they had just listened must have seemed to them a poor return. Someone hissed—some man, some woman—no one knows which except the culprit—and a demonstration started which I immediately silenced. Then the President finished his address. He was very gracious to us when he left, shaking hands with many of us, and being especially cordial to Senator Owens's aged mother, who had come to the convention to hear him make his maiden speech on woman suffrage. I have often wondered what he thought of that speech as he drove back to the White House. Probably he regretted as earnestly as we did that he had made it.

Passage 2

Theodore Roosevelt was the 26th president of the United States, and an early supporter of women's voting rights. This excerpt is from his autobiography.

The performance of duty, and not an indulgence in vapid ease and vapid pleasure, is all that makes life worthwhile.

Suffrage for women should be looked on from this standpoint. Personally I feel that it is exactly as much a "right" of women as of men to vote. But the important point with both men and women is to treat the exercise of the suffrage as a duty, which, in the long run, must be well performed to be of the slightest value. I always favored woman's suffrage, but only tepidly, until my association with women like Jane Addams and Frances Kellor, who desired it as one means of enabling them to render better and more efficient service, changed me into a zealous instead of a lukewarm adherent of the cause—in spite of the fact that a few of the best women of the same type, women like Mary Antin, did not favor the movement. A vote is like a rifle: its usefulness depends upon the character of the user.

25. Which sentence in Passage 2 describes why Roosevelt supports women's suffrage? Choose your answer from the drop-down menu.

Select ▼

A. The performance of duty, and not an indulgence in vapid ease and vapid pleasure, is all that makes life worthwhile.

B. Suffrage for women should be looked on from this standpoint.

C. Personally I feel that it is exactly as much a "right" of women as of men to vote.

D. But the important point with both men and women is to treat the exercise of the suffrage as a duty, which, in the long run, must be well performed to be of the slightest value.

26. Based on Passage 1, which of the following **best** describes President Taft?

A. He misjudged his audience.

B. He was a women's suffrage activist.

C. He was mean and unpleasant.

D. He was proud of his statements.

27. What is the purpose of the phrase, "The dropping of these remarkable words into a suffrage convention was naturally followed by an oppressive silence" in Passage 1?

A. To show how much the audience agreed with Taft's statement

B. To illustrate how few people were in the audience

C. To suggest that the audience did not like Taft's statement

D. To clarify the writer's personal opinion of Taft

28. Both passages present different presidents' perspectives on women's suffrage. Which of the following statements **best** describes what they have in common? Choose your answer from the drop-down menu.

Select ▼

A. Both support women's suffrage.

B. Neither supports women's suffrage.

C. Neither started out as a strong supporter.

D. Both feel that voting is a duty.

29. What evidence does Passage 1 provide that suggests that the author feels sympathetic for Taft?

A. The author assumes that Taft felt shame about the speech.

B. Taft was kind to Senator Owens's mother on his way out after the speech.

C. Someone in the crowd hissed at Taft's remarks on suffrage

D. Many women came to hear Taft speak about suffrage.

Questions 30–35 refer to the following passage.

How 3D Printers Work

Source: **https://www.energy.gov/articles/how-3d-printers-work**

What is 3D printing?

First invented in the 1980s by Chuck Hull, an engineer and physicist, 3D printing technology has come a long way. Also called "additive manufacturing," 3D printing is the process of making an object by depositing material, one tiny layer at a time.

The basic idea behind additive manufacturing can be found in rock formations deep underground (dripping water deposits thin layers of minerals to form stalactites and stalagmites), but a more modern example is a common desktop printer. Just like an inkjet printer adds individual dots of ink to form an image, a 3D printer only adds material where it is needed based on a digital file.

In comparison, many conventional manufacturing processes—which have recently been termed "subtractive manufacturing"—require cutting away excess materials to make the desired part. The result: Subtractive manufacturing can waste up to 30 pounds of material for every 1 pound of useful material in some parts, according to a finding from the Energy Department's Oak Ridge National Lab.

With some 3D printing processes, about 98 percent of the raw material is used in the finished part. Not to mention, 3D printing enables manufacturers to create new shapes and lighter parts that use less raw material and require fewer manufacturing steps. In turn, that can translate into lower energy use for 3D printing—up to 50 percent less energy for certain processes compared to conventional manufacturing processes.

Though the possibilities for additive manufacturing are endless, today 3D printing is mostly used to build small, relatively costly components using plastics and metal powders. Yet, as the price of desktop 3D printers continues to drop, some innovators are experimenting with different materials like chocolate and other food items, wax, ceramics, and biomaterial similar to human cells.

How does a 3D printer work?

Additive manufacturing technology comes in many shapes and sizes, but no matter the type of 3D printer or material you are using, the 3D printing process follows the same basic steps.

It starts with creating a 3D blueprint using computer-aided design (commonly called CAD) software. Creators are only limited by their imaginations. For example, 3D printers have been used to manufacture everything from robots and prosthetic limbs to custom shoes and musical instruments.

Once the 3D blueprint is created, the printer needs to be prepared. This includes refilling the raw materials (such as plastics, metal powders or binding solutions) and preparing the build platform (in some instances, you might have to clean it or apply an adhesive to prevent movement and warping from the heat during the printing process).

Once you hit print, the machine takes over, automatically building the desired object. While printing processes vary depending on the type of 3D printing technology, material extrusion (which includes a number of different types of processes, such as fused deposition modeling) is the most common process used in desktop 3D printers.

Material extrusion works like a glue gun. The printing material—typically a plastic filament—is heated until it liquefies and extruded through the print nozzle. Using information from the digital file—the design is split into thin two-dimensional cross sections so the printer knows exactly where to put material—the nozzle deposits the polymer in thin layers, often 0.1 millimeter thick. The polymer solidifies quickly, bonding to the layer below before the build platform lowers and the print head adds another layer. Depending on the size and complexity of the object, the entire process can take anywhere from minutes to days.

30. According to the passage, material extrusion works like a(n) ______.

31. Which phrase defines "subtractive manufacturing"?

A. Depositing material

B. Cutting away material

C. 3D printing

D. Dripping water

32. What is one reason 3D printing uses less energy than traditional manufacturing?

A. It takes much less time.

B. It requires fewer people.

C. It is innovative.

D. It requires less material.

33. Which example of 3D printing materials suggests that these processes could potentially be used in medicine?

A. Chocolate

B. Plastics

C. Wax

D. Biomaterial

34. Based on information given in the passage, how much material is NOT used in the finished part after the 3D printing process is completed?

A. 98%

B. 2%

C. 50%

D. 0.01%

35. According to the passage, which factor is leading to innovation in 3D printing?

A. Reduced prices for desktop printers

B. Widespread availability of 3D blueprints

C. Expensive raw material

D. More efficient use of materials

Questions 36–40 refer to the following passage.

The passage below is an excerpt from Charlotte Perkins Gilman's "The Yellow Wallpaper.

It is very seldom that mere ordinary people like John and myself secure ancestral halls for the summer.

A colonial mansion, a hereditary estate, I would say a haunted house, and reach the height of romantic felicity—but that would be asking too much of fate!

Still I will proudly declare that there is something queer about it.

Else, why should it be let so cheaply? And why have stood so long untenanted?

John laughs at me, of course, but one expects that in marriage.

John is practical in the extreme. He has no patience with faith, an intense horror of superstition, and he scoffs openly at any talk of things not to be felt and seen and put down in figures.

John is a physician, and perhaps—(I would not say it to a living soul, of course, but this is dead paper and a great relief to my mind)—perhaps that is one reason I do not get well faster.

You see, he does not believe I am sick! And what can one do?

If a physician of high standing, and one's own husband, assures friends and relatives that there is really nothing the matter with one but temporary nervous depression—a slight hysterical tendency—what is one to do?

My brother is also a physician, and also of high standing, and he says the same thing.

So I take phosphates or phosphites—whichever it is, and tonics, and journeys, and air, and exercise, and am absolutely forbidden to "work" until I am well again.

Personally, I disagree with their ideas.

Personally, I believe that congenial work, with excitement and change, would do me good.

But what is one to do?

I did write for a while in spite of them; but it does exhaust me a good deal—having to be so sly about it, or else meet with heavy opposition.

I sometimes fancy that in my condition if I had less opposition and more society and stimulus—but John says the very worst thing I can do is to think about my condition, and I confess it always makes me feel bad.

So I will let it alone and talk about the house.

The most beautiful place! It is quite alone, standing well back from the road, quite three miles from the village. It makes me think of English places that you read about, for there are hedges and walls and gates that lock, and lots of separate little houses for the gardeners and people.

There is a delicious garden! I never saw such a garden—large and shady, full of box-bordered paths, and lined with long grape-covered arbors with seats under them.

There were greenhouses, too, but they are all broken now.

There was some legal trouble, I believe, something about the heirs and co-heirs; anyhow, the place has been empty for years.

That spoils my ghostliness, I am afraid; but I don't care—there is something strange about the house—I can feel it.

I even said so to John one moonlight evening, but he said what I felt was a draught, and shut the window.

I get unreasonably angry with John sometimes. I'm sure I never used to be so sensitive. I think it is due to this nervous condition.

But John says if I feel so I shall neglect proper self-control; so I take pains to control myself,—before him, at least,—and that makes me very tired.

I don't like our room a bit. I wanted one downstairs that opened on the piazza and had roses all over the window, and such pretty old-fashioned chintz hangings! but John would not hear of it.

He said there was only one window and not room for two beds, and no near room for him if he took another.

He is very careful and loving, and hardly lets me stir without special direction.

I have a schedule prescription for each hour in the day; he takes all care from me, and so I feel basely ungrateful not to value it more.

He said we came here solely on my account, that I was to have perfect rest and all the air I could get. "Your exercise depends on your strength, my dear," said he, "and your food somewhat on your appetite; but air you can absorb all the time." So we took the nursery, at the top of the house.

It is a big, airy room, the whole floor nearly, with windows that look all ways, and air and sunshine galore. It was nursery first and then playground and gymnasium, I should judge; for the windows are barred for little children, and there are rings and things in the walls.

The paint and paper look as if a boys' school had used it. It is stripped off—the paper—in great patches all around the head of my bed, about as far as I can reach, and in a great place on the other side of the room low down. I never saw a worse paper in my life.

One of those sprawling flamboyant patterns committing every artistic sin.

It is dull enough to confuse the eye in following, pronounced enough to constantly irritate, and provoke study, and when you follow the lame, uncertain curves for a little distance they suddenly commit suicide—plunge off at outrageous angles, destroy themselves in unheard-of contradictions.

The color is repellant, almost revolting; a smouldering, unclean yellow, strangely faded by the slow-turning sunlight.

It is a dull yet lurid orange in some places, a sickly sulphur tint in others.

No wonder the children hated it! I should hate it myself if I had to live in this room long.

There comes John, and I must put this away,—he hates to have me write a word.

36. Based on the passage, which word would the narrator **most likely** use to describe the room?

A. Comfortable

B. Perfect

C. Ugly

D. Warm

37. How does the narrator feel about John and her brother's assessment of her medical condition?

A. She believes they're right.

B. She is angry about it.

C. She ignores them.

D. She disagrees with them.

38. "The Yellow Wallpaper" was published in 1892. What does the following sentence suggest about social expectations for husbands and wives at the time?

"If a physician of high standing, and one's own husband, assures friends and relatives that there is really nothing the matter with one but temporary nervous depression—a slight hysterical tendency—what is one to do?"

A. Husbands were expected to defer to their wives' thoughts.

B. Wives were expected to defer to their husbands' expertise.

C. Wives were not allowed to buy houses without their husbands' approval.

D. Husbands were not allowed to make medical decisions for their wives.

39. Based on the passage, what can be inferred about the relationship between the narrator and John?

A. The narrator feels controlled by John.

B. Their marriage is unhappy.

C. They share a dislike of the wallpaper.

D. They are in legal trouble.

40. Which of the following conclusions is supported by the passage?

A. The narrator is sicker than she thinks.

B. The narrator's house is haunted.

C. The narrator is frustrated with her current life.

D. The narrator is likely to leave her husband.

Questions 41–48 refer to the following passage.

Subject: Northchester Community Garden – Summer is Coming!
From: Jennifer.M.Milo@myemailserver.com
Date: May 1, 2019

(1) Greetings, [Select ▼] !

(2) I'm Jennifer Milo, a proud longtime resident of the Northchester neighborhood. (3) As the president of the local [Select ▼] I wanted to reach out to let you know of some great new programs and opportunities we have going on this summer.

(4) Our community garden on Franklin Street, now in its fifth year of existence, has grown from one half of an empty lot to almost an acre of greenspace. (5) We have a crew of more than 25 volunteers who help maintain the flower beds, organic vegetable garden, and composting center. (6) And thanks to generous donations from the Barker Garden Center, we [Select ▼] able to plant five new trees, six new types of vegetables, and 150 perennial plants this past summer.

(7) This spring, we still need more volunteers to take shifts working in the garden. We have shifts available on Mondays, Wednesdays, and Fridays. (8) If [Select ▼] interested, please contact me at Jennifer.m.milo@myemailserver.com to learn more and find a time that works for you. (9) We still need volunteers for the following task

- (10) raking
- (11) [Select ▼] and weeding
- (12) watering
- (13) collecting compostable materials

(14) Every Saturday from April to November, we have special Junior Gardener sessions where children and teens can literally get their hands dirty and learn the ins and outs of gardening. (15) Additionally, if you have some budding green thumbs in your family, you'll love our weekly programs for kids! (16) And every Friday night in July, we have

Community Garden Movie night, where volunteers and their families can watch movies in our beautiful outdoor space. (17) Seating is first come, first served. (18) There are [Select ▼] things happening in the Northchester Community Garden. (19) We hope [Select ▼] you this summer!

41. Sentence 1: Greetings, [Select ▼]!

A. Fellow neighbors

B. fellow neighbors

C. fellow Neighbors

D. Fellow Negihbors

42. Sentence 3: As the president of the local [Select ▼] I wanted to reach out to let you know of some great new programs and opportunities we have going on this summer.

A. Northchester Gardening Club,

B. Northchester Gardening, Club

C. Northchester Gardening Club;

D. Northchester Gardening Club…

43. Sentence 6: And thanks to generous donations from the Barker Garden Center, we [Select ▼] able to plant five new trees, six new types of vegetables, and 150 perennial plants this past summer.

A. was

B. would

C. were

D. is

44. Sentence 8: If [Select ▼] interested, please contact me at Jennifer.m.milo@myemailserver.com to learn more and find a time that works for you.

A. your

B. you're

C. you were

D. you

45. Sentence 11:

[Select ▼] and weeding

A. to plant

B. planters

C. plant

D. planting

46. The sentences in the fourth paragraph appear below as they are in the letter. Drag and drop them into the chart to put them in the order that makes the **most** sense. (Enter the sentence numbers in order on your answer sheet.)

Sentence 14: Every Saturday from April to November, we have special Junior Gardener sessions where children and teens can literally get their hands dirty and learn the ins and outs of gardening.

Sentence 15: Additionally, if you have some budding green thumbs in your family, you'll love our weekly programs for kids!

Sentence 16: And every Friday night in July, we have Community Garden Movie night, where volunteers and their families can watch movies in our beautiful outdoor space.

Sentence 17: Seating is first come, first served.

47. **Sentence 18:** There are [Select ▼] things happening in the Northchester Community Garden.

A. excepting

B. indication

C. addendum

D. exciting

48. **Sentence 19:** We hope [Select ▼] you this summer!

A. to seeing

B. to have seen

C. to see

D. too see

STOP! DO NOT GO ON UNTIL TIME IS UP.

MATHEMATICAL REASONING

115 Minutes • 46 Questions

Directions: The Mathematical Reasoning Test will have calculator-allowed questions mixed with calculator-prohibited questions, with the calculator tool available to use when it is an option. However, for this test, the calculator-prohibited questions are grouped together as the first five questions.

Most questions are multiple-choice, but to answer some questions, you will be required to fill an answer in a blank, drag and drop correct answers, and select answers on a given graphic. Record your answers on the Mathematical Reasoning section of the answer sheet provided. To review how to answer these questions on your answer sheet, please refer to "Directions for Taking the Practice Test" on page 653.

To answer some questions, you will need to apply one or more mathematics formulas. The formulas provided on the following page will help you to answer those questions. Some questions refer to charts, graphs, and figures. Unless otherwise noted, charts, graphs, and figures are drawn to scale.

Mathematics Formula Sheet

The GED Mathematical Reasoning Test contains a formula sheet, which displays formulas relating to geometric measurement and certain algebra concepts. Formulas are provided to test takers so that they may focus on *application*, rather than the *memorization*, of formulas.

Area of a:		
parallelogram	$A = bh$	
trapezoid	$A = \frac{1}{2}h(b_1 + b_2)$	
Surface Area and Volume of a:		
rectangular/right prism	$SA = ph + 2B$	$V = Bh$
cylinder	$SA = 2\pi rh + 2\pi r^2$	$V = \pi r^2 h$
pyramid	$SA = \frac{1}{2}ps + B$	$V = \frac{1}{3}Bh$
cone	$SA = \pi rs + \pi r^2$	$V = \frac{1}{3}\pi r^2 h$
sphere	$SA = 4\pi r^2$	$V = \frac{4}{3}\pi r^3$
	(p = perimeter of base B; $\pi \approx 3.14$)	
Algebra		
slope of a line	$m = \frac{y_2 - y_1}{x_2 - x_1}$	
slope-intercept form of the equation of a line	$y = mx + \mathrm{b}$	
point-slope form of the equation of a line	$y - y_1 = m(x - x_1)$	
standard form of a quadratic equation	$y = ax^2 + bx + c$	
quadratic formula	$x = \frac{-b \pm \sqrt{b^2 - 4ac}}{2a}$	
Pythagorean theorem	$a^2 + b^2 = c^2$	
simple interest	$I = prt$	
	(I = interest, p = principal, r = rate, t = time)	

The use of a calculator is prohibited for questions 1–5.

SHOW YOUR WORK HERE

1. The diameter D of the right circular cylinder pictured below is 12 feet. If the height H is one-third of three more feet than the radius, what is its volume?

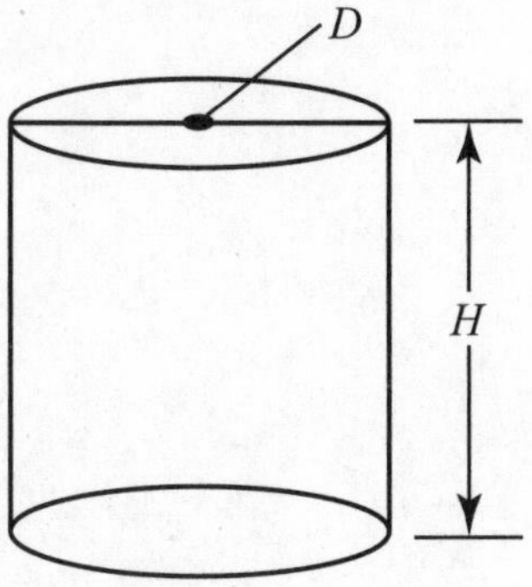

A. 36π cubic feet

B. 72π cubic feet

C. 108π cubic feet

D. 720π cubic feet

2. Compute: $\dfrac{\frac{3}{4}-\frac{2}{3}}{\frac{3}{4}+\frac{2}{3}}$

A. $\frac{1}{5}$

B. $\frac{7}{5}$

C. 0

D. $\frac{1}{17}$

3. Compute: $3\left(\frac{1}{8}+\frac{1}{4}\right)^2$

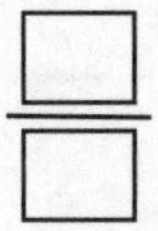

4. If $f(x) = 1 - \frac{x}{x+2}$, what is $f(x-1)$?

SHOW YOUR WORK HERE

A. $\frac{2-x}{x+1}$

B. $\frac{2}{x+1}$

C. $-\frac{x}{x+2}$

D. $\left(1 - \frac{x}{x+2}\right)(x-1)$

5. A map of the subway routes in a major metropolitan city uses a scale of $\frac{1}{16}$ – inch = 9 blocks. The length of the route from stop A to stop B is $\frac{3}{8}$ – inch and the length of the route from stop B to stop C is $\frac{1}{4}$ – inch. How many blocks, total, is a round trip from stop A to stop C, and back?

A. 54

B. 72

C. 90

D. 180

Use the following scenario for Questions 6 and 7:

Melanie and Rose collected seashells during their beach vacations each year. The number of shells, in hundreds, they each collected each year is pictured below:

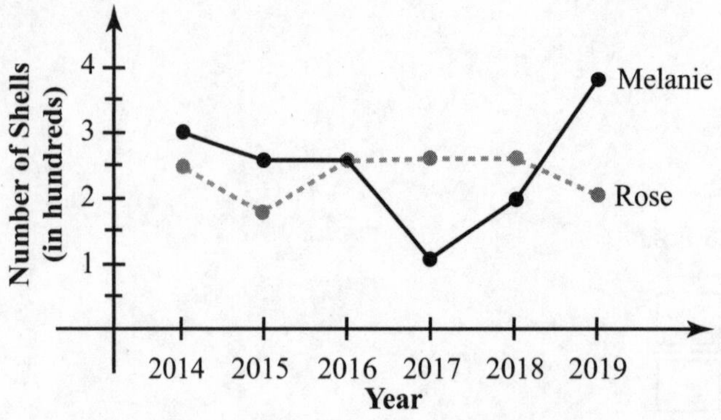

6. What is the absolute value of the difference between the total shells collected by Melanie and the total collected by Rose?

SHOW YOUR WORK HERE

[ ]

7. What is the simplified ratio of the number of years in which the number of shells collected by Melanie and Rose, combined, exceeds 500 to the number of years for which this is not the case?

Fill in the blanks to complete the ratio:
[ ] to [ ]

8. Determine the value of $x + y$:

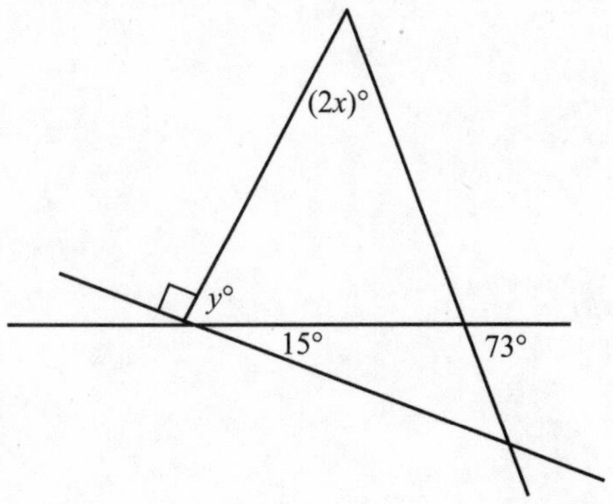

A. 32

B. 91

C. 105

D. 148

9. A photograph is enlarged to 125% of its original size. If its original dimensions are 10 inches by 14 inches, what are the new dimensions?

A. 7.5 inches by 10.5 inches

B. 10.25 inches by 14.25 inches

C. 12.5 inches by 17.5 inches

D. 14 inches by 17 inches

10. Seventy-five percent of the boys in the sophomore class play one sport during the school year. Forty percent play football, 25% play basketball, and the rest play tennis. If 20 boys play tennis, how many boys, total, in the sophomore class play one sport?

A. 100

B. 150

C. 200

D. 250

11. A solid sphere with diameter 1 foot is placed inside a square box with sides of length 1 foot. Sand is poured into the box to fill the space to the top of the box. What is the volume of sand in the box?

A. $\left(\frac{6-\pi}{6}\right)$ cubic feet

B. $\frac{\pi}{6}$ cubic feet

C. $\left(\frac{4\pi}{3}-1\right)$ cubic feet

D. $\frac{5\pi}{6}$ cubic feet

12. Suppose x is a positive irrational number. Which of these can be a rational number?

A. $x+\sqrt{5}$

B. x^2

C. $2x$

D. $x \div \frac{1}{5}$

13. Assume a and b are positive real numbers. To which of these expressions is $\left(a^{-2}-b^{-2}\right)^{-1}$ equivalent?

A. $\frac{1}{a^2-b^2}$

B. $\frac{a^2b^2}{b^2-a^2}$

C. $\frac{b^2-a^2}{a^2b^2}$

D. a^2-b^2

SHOW YOUR WORK HERE

14. Which of these is the graph of $x = 4 - 2y$?

SHOW YOUR WORK HERE

A.

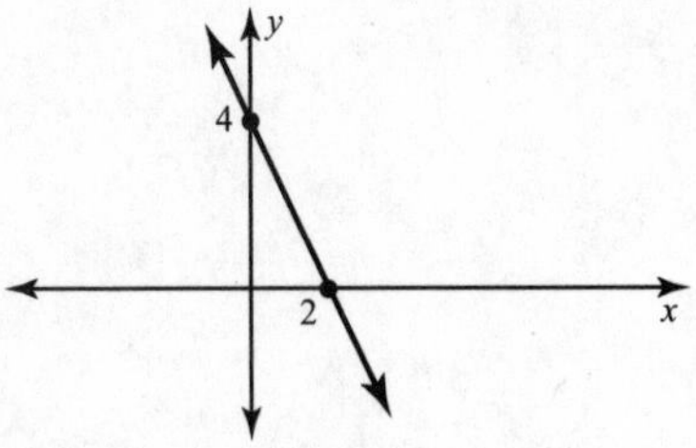

B.

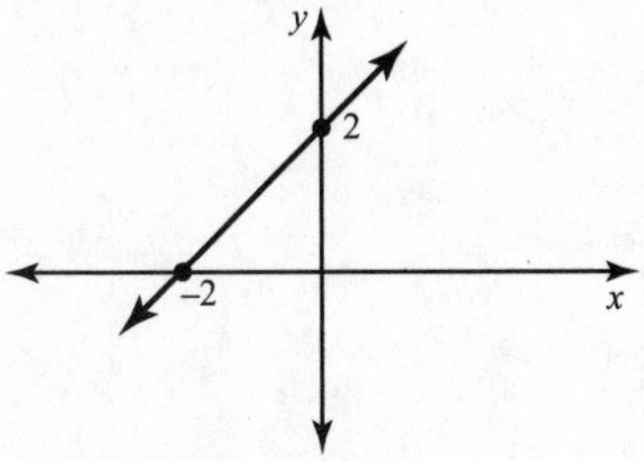

C.

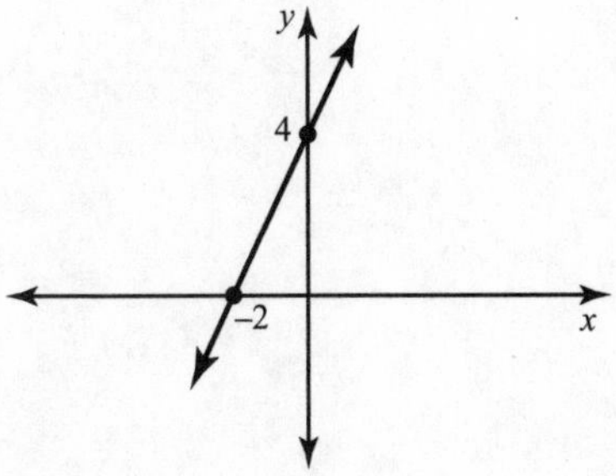

D.

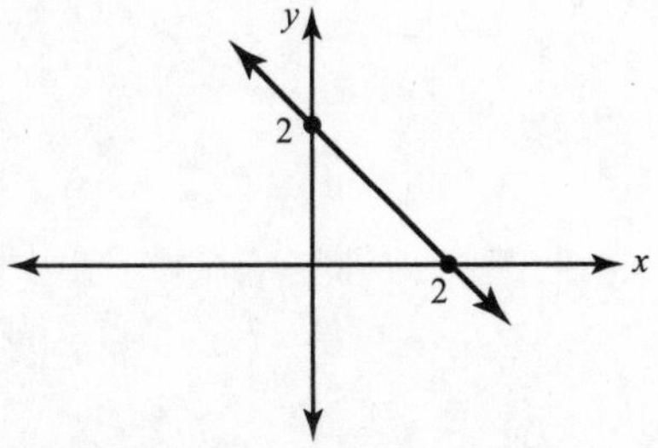

15. At what point does the graph of the function $f(x) = -3x^2 + 12x$ attain its maximum value?

A. (2, 12)

B. (2, 0)

C. (2, 4)

D. (−2, 4)

SHOW YOUR WORK HERE

16. A square is formed by decreasing the length of the diagonal of a given square by 20%. What is the ratio of the area of the newly formed square to the area of the given one?

A. 0.80 : 1.00

B. 0.60 : 1.00

C. 0.16 : 0.25

D. 0.50 : 0.32

17. The value of a rare computing magazine was \$80 on May 1 and increased in value by 36% by June 1. Which expression gives the value of the magazine on June 1?

A. 1.36(\$80)

B. $\frac{\$80}{0.36}$

C. \$80 + 1.36

D. (1 – 0.36)(\$80)

18. A weightlifter uses w 45-pound plates, x 25-pound plates, y 10-pound plates, and z 5-pound plates on a barbell. Create an algebraic expression representing the total amount of weight she has on the barbell.

[ ]

19. What is the x-intercept of the line passing through the points $\left(-3, \frac{1}{4}\right)$ and $\left(\frac{3}{2}, -2\right)$?

([ ] , [ ])

20. Determine the value of $m \cdot n$ based on this equation: $\frac{\left(x^{-3}\right)^m \cdot y}{\left(y^2\right)^{-2}} = x^{12} \cdot y^n$

A. –20

B. –12

C. 20

D. 60

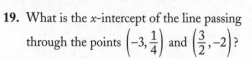

21. Suppose C_1 is a circle centered at O with radius R, point P is on C_2, and OP is a diameter of circle C_2. Determine the perimeter of the shaded region shown below:

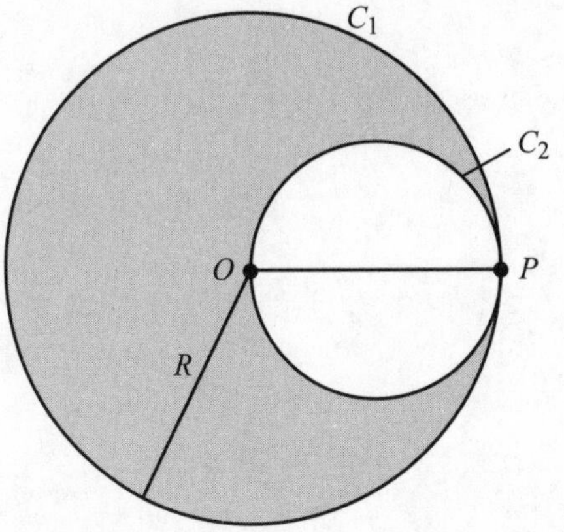

A. πR

B. $2\pi R$

C. $3\pi R$

D. $4\pi R$

22. Factor completely: $8x^3 - 40x^2 + 50x$

A. $(8x + 25)(x^2 - 2x)$

B. $2x(2x - 5)^2$

C. $(4x - 10)(2x^2 + 5x)$

D. $2x(2x - 5)(2x + 5)$

SHOW YOUR WORK HERE

23. A rectangular area rug has dimensions as shown:

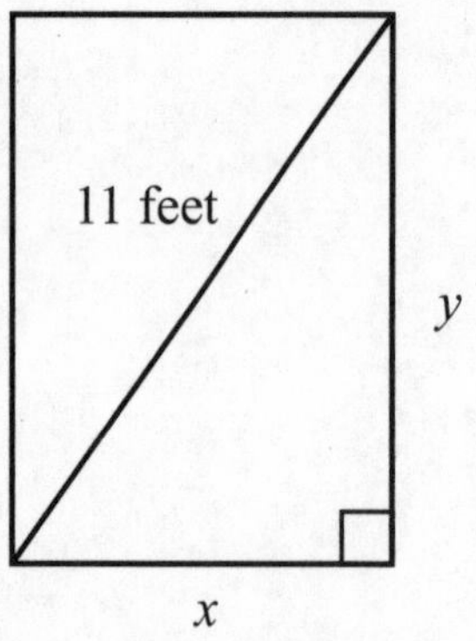

Which expression gives the length of y in terms of x?

A. $y = \sqrt{x^2 + 121}$

B. $y = \sqrt{121 - x^2}$

C. $y = \sqrt{x^2 - 121}$

D. $y = 11 - x$

24. What is the area of the shaded region?

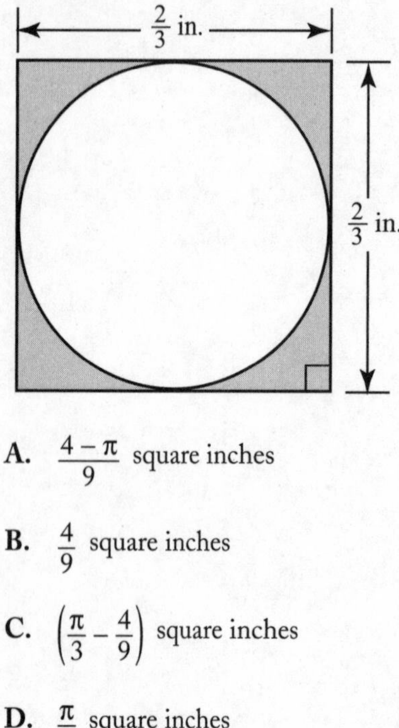

A. $\frac{4-\pi}{9}$ square inches

B. $\frac{4}{9}$ square inches

C. $\left(\frac{\pi}{3} - \frac{4}{9}\right)$ square inches

D. $\frac{\pi}{9}$ square inches

SHOW YOUR WORK HERE

SHOW YOUR WORK HERE

25. If $f(x) = x\left(2 + \frac{1}{x}\right)$, compute $f\left(-\frac{3}{2}\right)$.

A. -2

B. $-\frac{9}{8}$

C. $-\frac{3}{2}$

D. 0

26. The annual percentage yield, *APV*, on an investment is given by the formula,

$$APV = \left(1 + \frac{r}{m}\right)^m - 1$$

where r is the annual interest rate (as a decimal) and m is the number of times per year at which the interest is calculated. If the annual interest rate is 5% and the interest is computed monthly, which expression gives the *APV*?

A. $\left(\frac{1}{120}\right)^{12} - 1$

B. $\left(\frac{1}{240}\right)^{12}$

C. $\left(\frac{241}{240}\right)^{12} - 1$

D. $241 - 1$

27. Which expression is equivalent to $(2x - 3)(4 - x)$?

A. $-2x^2 + 11x - 12$

B. $2x^2 - 11x - 12$

C. $-2x^2 + 5x - 12$

D. $11x$

practice test 2 — Mathematical Reasoning

28. A computer server can process a task every s nanoseconds. If m computer labs each have n computers, all of which are connected to the server, and each computer sends t tasks to the server to be completed, how many nanoseconds does it take the server to process them all?

A. $s + m + n + t$

B. $(m + n)st$

C. $smnt$

D. $(m + n)(s + t)$

29. Solve for a: $\dfrac{1}{\dfrac{2a+b}{a} - b} = 1$

A. $a = \dfrac{b-1}{b}$

B. $a = \dfrac{b}{b-1}$

C. $a = b(b-1)$

D. $a = \dfrac{b-1}{b+1}$

30. Solve for w: $-2(2 - 3w) + 1 \leq -3(w + 2)$

A. $w \leq -\dfrac{1}{3}$

B. $w \leq 6$

C. $w \geq 6$

D. $w \geq -\dfrac{1}{3}$

SHOW YOUR WORK HERE

31. A salesperson earns a base salary of \$50,000 and a commission of 8% on his total sales, x dollars, for the year. Which equation can be used to determine the total sales he would need to make to earn \$120,000 for the year?

A. $50{,}000 + 8x = 120{,}000$

B. $0.08(x + 50{,}000) = 120{,}000$

C. $8(x + 50{,}000) = 120{,}000$

D. $50{,}000 + 0.08x = 120{,}000$

32. A skier starts on top of a mountain 3,200 feet high and descends at a rate of 15 feet per second. Which function gives the height of the skier above the ground in terms of the number of seconds, x, she has been skiing downhill?

A. $f(x) = 15 - 3{,}200x$

B. $f(x) = 3{,}200 - 15x$

C. $f(x) = 15x - 3{,}200$

D. $f(x) = -15(x + 3{,}200)$

33. What are the solutions of the equation $9x(x - 1) = -2$?

A. $x = -\frac{2}{9}, x = -1$

B. $x = \frac{2}{9}, x = 1$

C. $x = \frac{1}{3}, x = \frac{2}{3}$

D. $x = -\frac{1}{3}, x = -\frac{2}{3}$

SHOW YOUR WORK HERE

practice test 2—Mathematical Reasoning

34. An electrician charges a flat service fee of \$75 plus \$100 per hour for the installation of a home generator. Which of these graphs describes the total cost C as a function of the number of hours h it takes to complete the job?

A.

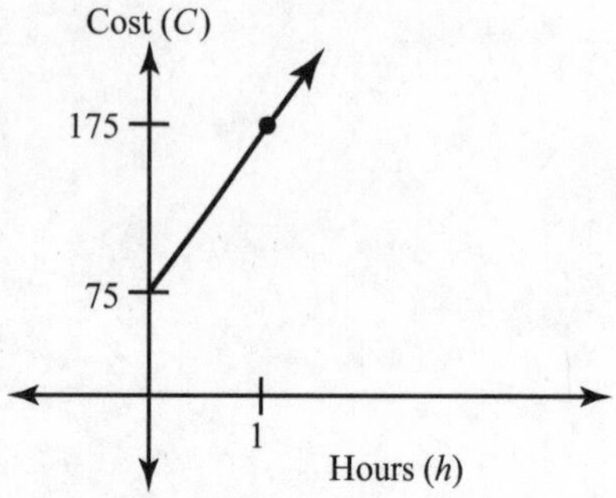

B.

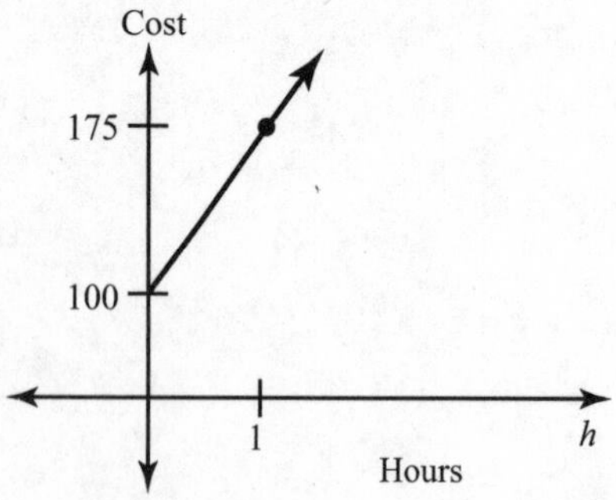

C.

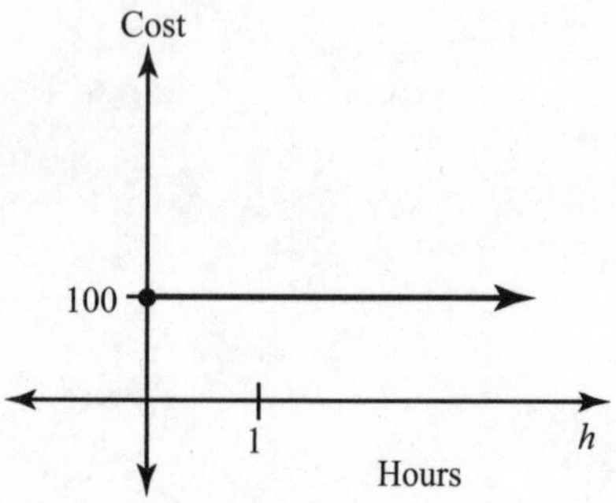

D.

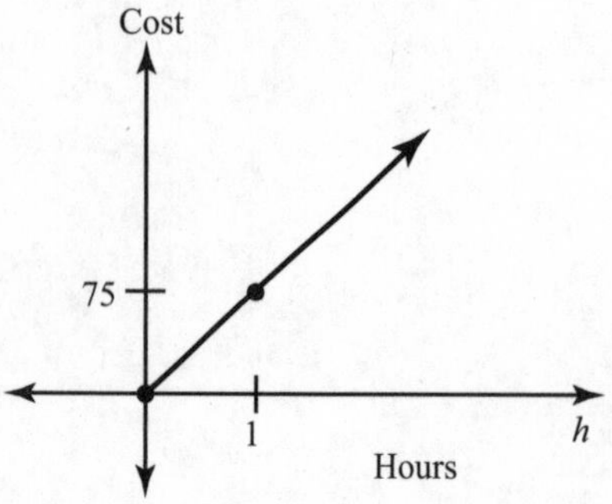

SHOW YOUR WORK HERE

35. The following table describes *y* as a function of *x*:

x	−1	1	3	4	?
y	0	1	4	−1	2

Which of the following values can be inserted into the blank cell in the last column so that the resulting table is NOT a function? Select all values that apply.

0 1 2 3 −2

36. What is the slope of a line passing through the point (3, −2) that is perpendicular to the line $5x = 2 - 10y$?

37. If $F(x) = \sqrt{x-1}$, where $x \geq 1$, which of the following expressions equals $F\left(\frac{1}{x}\right) \cdot F(x+1)$?

A. $\sqrt{x}$

B. $\sqrt{1-x}$

C. $\frac{1}{\sqrt{x}} - 1$

D. $\sqrt{x-1}$

38. Suppose $0 < x < 1$ and $y > 1$ are rational numbers. Which of the following must be greater than 1?

A. $y - x$

B. $\frac{x}{y}$

C. $x \cdot y$

D. y^2

SHOW YOUR WORK HERE

practice test 2 — Mathematical Reasoning

39. A petri dish contains 9.5×10^4 microbes of a new virus. Each of 10 labs at a research facility is given 1.2×10^3 petri dishes for study. How many microbes, total, are at the research facility?

Enter a decimal strictly between 0 and 10, accurate to the hundredths place, in the first box and an integer as the exponent of 10 to express the total in scientific notation:

$\square \times 10^{\square}$

40. A coffee shop requires customers to spend at least $5 before tax if they want to pay with a credit card. Jill wants a small coffee that costs $1.95. She will also buy biscotti that each cost $0.75. Which inequality describes the number of biscotti, *B*, Jill can buy so that she can pay with a credit card?

A. $0.75B + 1.95 > 5$

B. $1.95 + 0.75B \geq 5$

C. $0.75(1.95 + B) > 5$

D. $0.75(B + 1.95) \geq 5$

41. Jamil has 2,000 megabytes of data for use on his cell phone each month. Each video he downloads uses about 130 megabytes, each song he downloads uses 6 megabytes, and each photo uses 3 megabytes. Which inequality can be used to determine the different combinations of numbers of videos *V*, songs *S*, and photos *P* Jamil can download each month?

A. $VSP \leq 2,000$

B. $(130V)(6S)(3P) \leq 2,000$

C. $130V + 6S + 3P \leq 2,000$

D. $P + S + V \leq 2,000$

SHOW YOUR WORK HERE

42. Sixty percent of the freshmen class participates in an extracurricular activity. Of these, 15% take two or more honors classes. What fraction of the freshmen class participates in an extracurricular activity and takes at least two honors classes?

Give your answer in whole numbers to form a simplified fraction:

$\frac{\square}{\square}$

43. A lacrosse team played 24 games and lost 1 of every 4. If there are no tied games and the trend continues, how many wins would you expect the team to have in 36 games played?

$\square$

44. A homeowner needs to replace a triangular window on a side of her house, as shown:

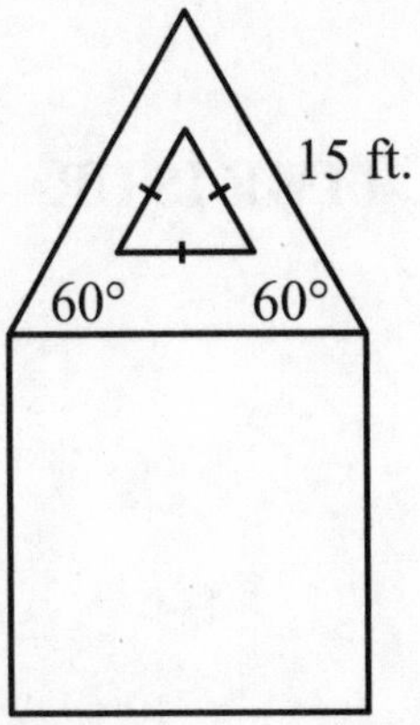

If the sides of the window are in a 1:5 correspondence with the sides of the triangular parts of the house, what is the area of the window?

A. $\frac{9\sqrt{3}}{4}$ square feet

B. $\frac{9}{2}$ square feet

C. $\frac{3\sqrt{3}}{4}$ square feet

D. $\frac{9}{4}$ square feet

SHOW YOUR WORK HERE

45. What is the sum of the even negative integers greater than −100?

SHOW YOUR WORK HERE

A. −2,500

B. −2,450

C. −2,400

D. −2,350

46. A spherical hot air balloon is inflated at such a rate that its radius, *r*, after *t* seconds is given by the function $r(t) = \frac{1}{4}t^{\frac{3}{2}}$ feet. Which of the following is the surface area *S* of the hot air balloon after *t* seconds?

A. $S = \frac{\pi}{48}t^{\frac{9}{2}}$

B. $S = \frac{\pi}{4}t^{3}$

C. $S = 2\pi t^{\frac{7}{2}}$

D. $S = \frac{\pi}{4}t^{\frac{7}{2}}$

STOP! DO NOT GO ON UNTIL TIME IS UP.

SCIENCE

90 Minutes • 35 Questions

Directions: The Science Test consists of questions in several formats designed to measure your knowledge of general science concepts. The questions are based on brief passages of text and visual information (charts, graphs, diagrams, and other figures). Some questions are based on both text and visual information. Study the information provided, and answer the question(s) that follow, referring back to the information as needed.

Most questions are multiple choice, but to answer some questions, you will be required to select from a drop-down menu, fill an answer in a blank, drag and drop correct answers, and select answers on a given graphic. Record your answers on the Science section of the answer sheet provided. To review how to answer these questions on your answer sheet, please refer to "Directions for Taking the Practice Test" on page 653..

Question 1 refers to the following information.

The lancet liver fluke is a flatworm parasite with a very complex life cycle. It lives its adult life in the liver of its definitive host, typically a cow. After it reproduces in the cow's liver, it lays eggs that pass into the cow's feces. It then moves on to its first intermediate host, land snails, when the snails eat its eggs. The eggs hatch into immature liver fluke larvae, which the snail packages into cysts (hard-walled spheres) in an attempt to protect itself from the parasite. The snail sheds the cyst-enclosed larvae in its slime trail. A second intermediate host, ants, unknowingly eat the fluke larvae cysts when they use the snail's slime trail as a source of moisture. The fluke larvae then infect the ant's nervous system and cause the ant to climb to the top of a blade of grass. In that position, the ant is more easily eaten by a cow, and the cycle starts over again.

1. Based on the information in the passage, what is the **best** definition of the liver fluke's definitive host?

   A. The animal in which the fluke spends its adult life

   B. The animal whose nervous system the fluke infects

   C. The animal in which the fluke spends its larval stage

   D. The animal that the fluke lives in after it first hatches from an egg

Questions 2 and 3 are based on the following information.

A student is observing the effects of temperature on the solubility of different substances in liquid water. When 1 tablespoon of sugar is added to 1 cup of water at 5°C and stirred 10 times, it does not completely dissolve. When 1 tablespoon of sugar is added to 1 cup of water at 100°C and stirred 10 times, it does completely dissolve. A can of soda at 5°C tastes very fizzy and is full of gas bubbles. A can of soda at 25°C tastes flat and contains few gas bubbles.

The student understands that when a solid solute (like sugar) is added to a liquid solvent (like water), the solute dissolves when the kinetic energy of the solvent molecules is greater than the forces that hold the solute molecules together. The student also understands that when a gas is combined with a liquid solvent, the gas dissolves when the kinetic energy of the gas is too low to keep it from escaping the liquid solution.

2. What conclusion is supported by these observations?

A. The solubility of both gases and solids increases as temperature increases.

B. The solubility of both gases and solids decreases as temperature increases.

C. The solubility of gases decreases as temperature increases.

D. The solubility of solids decreases as temperature increases.

3. Which statement correctly explains the energy relationships in the solutions described in the passage?

A. As temperature increases, the kinetic energy of the sugar molecules becomes greater than the forces that hold water molecules together.

B. As temperature increases, the kinetic energy of the water molecules becomes greater than the forces that hold sugar molecules together.

C. As temperature increases, the kinetic energy of the gas molecules becomes too low to keep it from escaping the soda.

D. As temperature increases, the kinetic energy of the water molecules becomes too low keep it from escaping the soda.

Questions 4 and 5 refer to the following information and diagrams.

Until the 1970s, all single-celled organisms without a nucleus or other membrane-enclosed organelles were classified as prokaryotes and thought to be different types of bacteria. Prokaryotes included common bacteria and methanogens, microorganisms that produce methane gas as waste. All other living organisms were classified as eukaryotes. Eukaryotes include more complex single-celled organisms like yeast and amoebas (which do contain a nucleus and other membrane-bound organelles), as well as plants and animals. In 1977, DNA analysis revealed that methanogens were not bacteria and were more closely related to eukaryotes than they were to bacteria. Methanogens and their closest relatives were renamed archaea to set them apart from bacteria.

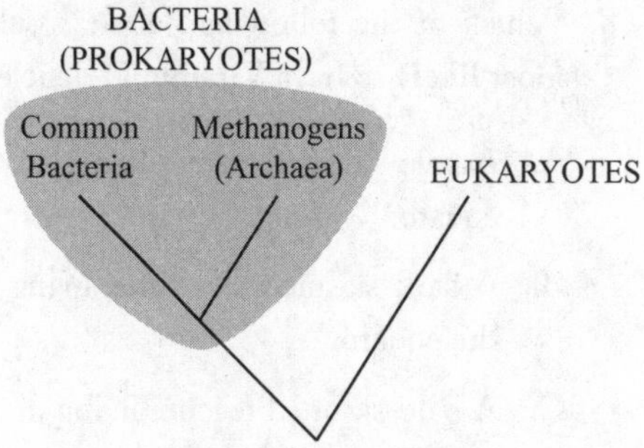

Traditional Classification

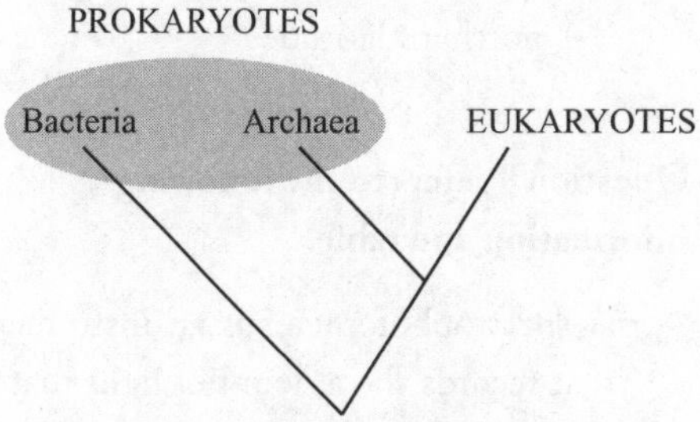

Current Classification

Since then, many other types of archaea have been discovered all over the world, including in extreme environments with conditions that would kill most other organisms, like boiling hot deep-sea vents, deep lakes under the ice in Antarctica, and extremely salty ponds.

4. Why were archaea originally classified as prokaryotes?

   A. They have only one cell.

   B. They produce methane as waste.

   C. They have no nucleus.

   D. They live in extreme environments.

5. What is the **best** general description of an extreme environment?

   A. A location deep under the ocean's surface

   B. A location found all over the world

   C. A location with very high or low temperatures

   D. A location that is deadly to most organisms

Question 6 refers to the following information.

In 2006, Pluto was downgraded from a planet to a dwarf planet, which surprised much of the world. Pluto is located in the outer part of the solar system in a region called the Kuiper belt. New discoveries of objects in the Kuiper belt that were the same size and bigger than Pluto led scientists to conclude that Pluto was not a planet after all. Scientists now have three requirements for planets: they must (1) orbit the sun, (2) have enough mass to become spherical as a result of their own gravity, and (3) have cleared their orbit of other objects of similar size. Dwarf planets meet requirements 1 and 2 for planets but not requirement 3, which is why Pluto is classified as a dwarf planet; there are many objects of similar size in its orbit. Smaller objects in the Kuiper belt that do not meet requirements 2 or 3 are simply called Kuiper belt objects.

On New Year's Day in 2019, the *New Horizons* spacecraft flew by an unusually shaped object in the Kuiper belt nicknamed Ultima Thule, pictured below.

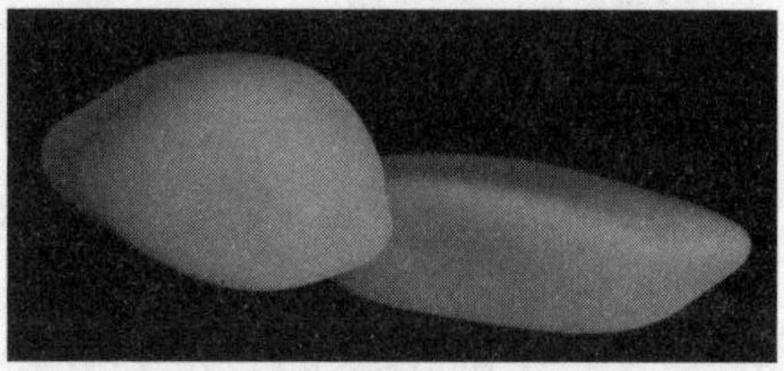

Source: https://solarsystem.nasa.gov/

6. Based on the information in the passage and the image, how should Ultima Thule be classified?

   A. As a planet

   B. As a dwarf planet

   C. As a Kuiper belt object

   D. As a spacecraft

Questions 7 and 8 refer to the following information.

All human skin cells can make Vitamin D when the ultraviolet (UV) radiation in sunlight strikes them. However, too much UV radiation can cause skin cancer. Pale skin cannot block UV radiation as well as dark skin can. Scientists hypothesize that pale skin evolved in people living in northern latitudes, where there is less sunlight, so that their skin could absorb more UV radiation and make enough Vitamin D to keep them healthy. Conversely, scientists hypothesize that dark skin evolved in people living near the equator, where there is the most sunlight year-round, so that they could be protected from skin cancer. Despite these adaptations, data shows that pale-skinned people living in northern latitudes are far more likely to have Vitamin D deficiency (not enough Vitamin D in their bodies) than dark-skinned people living near the equator. In fact, all people living in northern latitudes are much more likely to have too little Vitamin D in their bodies than all people living near the equator.

7. What conclusion is supported by the information in the passage?

A. People living near the equator are more likely to get enough sunlight to make the Vitamin D they need.

B. Dark-skinned people living in northern latitudes are more likely to get skin cancer than pale-skinned people living at the same latitude.

C. Pale skin does not block UV radiation as well as scientists thought.

D. People living in northern latitudes all have skin cells that cannot make Vitamin D.

8. Which of the following people would be **most likely** to have Vitamin D deficiency?

A. A pale-skinned farmer living near the equator

B. A dark-skinned fisherman living near the equator

C. A pale-skinned teacher living in northern latitudes

D. A dark-skinned lawyer living in northern latitudes

Question 9 refers to the following information and table.

A spectrophotometer is an instrument that records the amount of light that is absorbed by a solution, a measurement also known as absorbance. A purple dye is mixed with water in different concentrations. The absorbance of the different solutions is measured by a spectrophotometer and recorded in the table below.

Concentration (mol/L)	Absorbance
0.1	0.071
0.2	0.142
0.3	0.213
0.4	0.284

9. Based on the relationship shown in the table, drag the correct symbol into the statement below.

For a dye solution with a concentration of 0.5 mol/L, absorbance is ________ 0.284

= < >

10. Some plants have what are called induced defenses, which are defenses that occur only when the plants are directly attacked by herbivores. Which of the following scenarios suggests that a plant has induced defenses?

A. A bush flowers earlier in a valley than it does on the top of a mountain.

B. A tree produces toxic leaves in a forest with deer and in a forest without deer.

C. A grass forms spiky seed pods that are spread more widely in areas with sheep.

D. A cactus has spines on an island with cattle and no spines on an island without cattle.

Questions 11 and 12 refer to the following diagram and information.

A rock is placed into a large graduated cylinder that is filled with water. The water level before and after the rock is placed into the cylinder is shown in the diagram. The numbers on the cylinder indicate the volume in milliliters (mL).

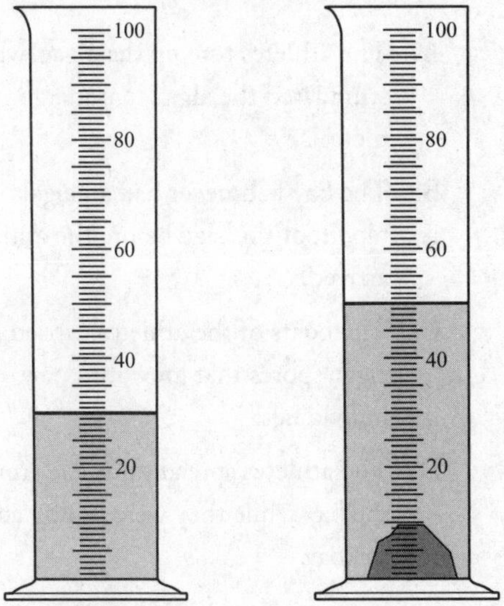

11. What is the volume of the rock in milliliters?

[ ] ml

12. Which statement about this method of determining volume is correct?

A. The volume of objects that are less dense than water can be measured with this method because the objects will sink.

B. The volume of objects that are less dense than water cannot be measured with this method because part of the object will float above the water.

C. The volume of objects that are denser than water cannot be measured with this method because the objects will sink.

D. The volume of objects that are denser than water can be measured with this method because part of the object will float above the water.

Question 13 refers to the following graph.

13. Which of the following statements is supported by the graph?

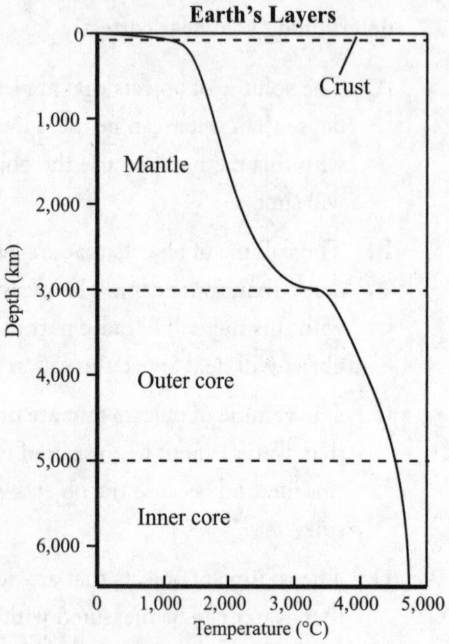

A. Temperature increases at a constant rate with depth in the earth.

B. Temperature increases at a higher rate in the crust than the outer core.

C. The maximum temperature in the mantle is around 5,000°C.

D. The minimum temperature in the inner core is around 3,500°C.

Question 14 refers to the following information.

During the 2008 Summer Olympics, the algae population in Qingdao Bay, where the sailing events were to be held, suddenly exploded. A few patches of algae grew to 1.5 million tons of living material covering 1,500 square miles in just a few weeks. Algal blooms of this size had never happened in Qingdao Bay before the Olympic athletes arrived. Research later determined that the athletes practicing sailing in the bay chopped up the first patches of algae into small pieces as they crossed the bay in their boats. Being cut into smaller pieces stimulated the cells at the edges of the torn pieces of algae to undergo meiosis. In algae, meiosis is the process of cell division that creates spores, which are the algae's reproductive cells. Each spore grows into a new individual. All these cells undergoing growth and reproduction led to the world's largest algal bloom.

14. How did the Olympic athletes cause the algal bloom?

A. The athletes tore up the algae, which stimulated the algae to undergo meiosis.

B. The bay had never had an algal bloom of this size before the athletes arrived.

C. The boats of the athletes carried algae spores that grew into new individuals.

D. The athletes spread the algae around the bay while they were sailing across the bay.

Questions 15 and 16 are based on the following information.

An object that oscillates is one that is attached to a stationary (unmoving) support at one end and that moves back and forth in a regular, predictable cycle. This type of motion is also known as periodic motion or oscillation. An initial force is required to start an object's oscillation. An oscillating object will continue to move forever in an air-free vacuum, but under ordinary conditions (like a classroom), the object will eventually stop moving if no additional force is applied to it.

15. Which of the following objects is undergoing periodic motion?

A. An ant walking to and from its nest

B. A ball thrown back and forth from one person to another

C. A child swinging back and forth on a playground swing

D. A shuttle bus driving from one stop to the other and back again

16. What is the **best** explanation for why an oscillating object eventually stops moving outside a vacuum if no additional force is applied to it?

A. Air particles in a vacuum cause periodic motion.

B. Atoms within the object slow its motion.

C. Air applies a force that keeps an object moving.

D. Air drags on the object, slowing it down.

Question 17 is based on the following map and information.

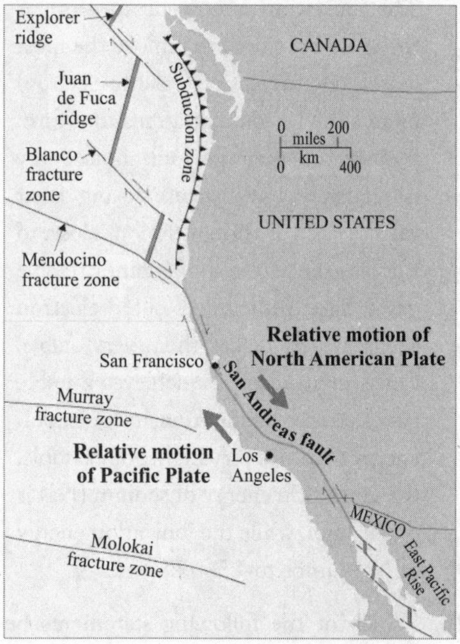

The cities of San Francisco and Los Angeles are on opposite sides of the San Andreas fault. This fault is located in one of the places where the Pacific Plate and North American Plate meet. The large arrows on the map show the relative direction of motion of each tectonic plate. The plates move at an average rate of about 25 millimeters per year.

17. San Francisco and Los Angeles are approximately 560 kilometers apart. One million years from today, what will be the relative positions of San Francisco and Los Angeles?

A. Los Angeles will be closer to Mexico.

B. San Francisco will be closer to Los Angeles.

C. Los Angeles will be farther from San Francisco.

D. San Francisco will be closer to Canada.

Practice Test 2—Science

Question 18 is based on the following information.

The ionization energy of an atom is the energy required to remove the most loosely bound electron (valence electron) of an atom or ion. For atoms that form positive ions, their first ionization energy is relatively low because losing their valence electrons brings the ions closer to a noble gas electron configuration. Noble gases have fully filled outer electron shells, which makes them very stable. Once an atom or ion achieves a noble gas electron configuration, its ionization energy becomes very high. For example, the ionization energy of sodium (Na) is 496 kJ/mol, while the ionization energy of Na^+ jumps to 4,560 kJ/mol.

18. Which of the following statements **best** explains why the ionization energy of Na^+ is so much higher than that of Na?

A. Na^+ is less stable than Na.

B. Na^+ has more total electrons than Na.

C. Na^+ has a noble gas electron configuration.

D. Na^+ has a partially filled outer electron shell.

Question 19 is based on the following information.

Chlorofluorocarbons (CFCs) can destroy ozone in the upper atmosphere through a chain reaction triggered by sunlight. UV light breaks down a CFC like $CFCl_3$ (Freon-11), releasing a single chlorine atom (Cl) that is highly reactive because it has a single unpaired electron:

$$CFCl_3 + \text{sunlight} \rightarrow CFCl_2 + Cl$$

This chlorine atom reacts with ozone (O_3) in a series of reactions that regenerates Cl:

$$Cl + O_3 \rightarrow ClO + O_2$$

$$ClO + O \rightarrow Cl + O_2$$

This Cl can react with another molecule of ozone and repeat this cycle many more times, quickly breaking down ozone in the atmosphere.

19. Similar compounds containing bromine (Br) undergo an analogous chain reaction and can also destroy ozone. For example, methyl bromide (CH_3Br) can be broken down by sunlight to release a single bromine atom:

$$CH_3Br + \text{sunlight} \rightarrow CH_3 + Br$$

This Br atom follows the same steps as Cl to react with ozone and regenerate itself. The first step in this chain reaction is:

$$Br + O_3 \rightarrow BrO + O_2$$

What is the final step of this process that regenerates Br?

A. $CH_3Br \rightarrow CH_3 + Br$

B. $Br + O_2 \rightarrow BrO + O$

C. $BrO + O_3 \rightarrow Br + 2O_2$

D. $BrO + O \rightarrow Br + O_2$

Question 20 is based on the following information.

Archosaurs are a group of reptiles that first appeared about 250 million years ago, with some archosaurs still alive today. Archosaurs include some of the most well-known reptiles, such as crocodiles, dinosaurs, and pterosaurs (winged reptiles). These reptile groups are defined by different characteristics; this means that a defining characteristic is present only in members of the group it defines. Archosaurs are defined by a hole in the skull in front of the eye and one in the lower jaw. Crocodiles are defined by two rows of bony plates on their backs. Dinosaurs are defined by a hole in the hip socket. Pterosaurs are defined by a wing that is supported by the fourth finger of the hand.

20. Birds are one group of archosaurs that is alive today. Birds are also classified as dinosaurs. According to the passage, what characteristic does a bird have that classifies it as a dinosaur?

A. Hole in lower jaw

B. Hole in hip socket

C. Wing supported by fourth finger

D. Two rows of bony plates on the back

Question 21 is based on the following information and table.

The power of a rocket fuel is indicated by its specific impulse, which is a measure of how much thrust is provided by burning one kilogram of the fuel. In simple terms, thrust is the amount of push provided by the rocket fuel. Specific impulse is measured in units of seconds (s). The table shows the specific impulse of several rocket fuels.

Specific Impulse of Different Rocket Fuels

Fuel	Specific Impulse (s)
Liquid oxygen (O_2) + Liquid hydrogen (H_2)	381
Liquid fluorine (F) + Liquid H_2	400
Nitrogen tetroxide + Kerosene	267
Nitric acid + Hydrazine	276

21. A team of engineers needs its rocket to weigh as little as possible. Which of the following fuels should the team use to keep the weight of the rocket to a minimum but to achieve the maximum possible thrust?

A. Liquid F + Liquid H_2

B. Liquid O_2 + Liquid H_2

C. Nitric acid + Hydrazine

D. Nitrogen tetroxide + Kerosene

Question 22 is based on the following information.

Igneous rocks are those that are formed from the cooling of molten rock. One of the ways that igneous rocks are classified is by their silica (SiO_2) and mineral content. The four major composition classes for igneous rock are ultramafic, mafic, intermediate, and felsic. The table below shows the composition classes of igneous rocks and their typical characteristics.

Characteristics of Igneous Rock Classes

	Ultramafic	Mafic	Intermediate	Felsic
Color	Very dark	Dark	Medium	Light
Silica content	< 45%	45–52%	52–66%	< 66%
Major minerals	• Olivine • Pyroxene	• Pyroxene • Plagioclase feldspar • Amphibole	• Plagioclase feldspar • Biotite •Quartz	• Quartz • Potassium and sodium feldspar • Muscovite

22. An igneous rock that is 60% silica and composed primarily of plagioclase feldspar and quartz is **most likely** to be what class of rock?

A. Ultramafic

B. Mafic

C. Intermediate

D. Felsic

Question 23 refers to the following information and graph.

The air pressure inside a car tire (also called tire pressure) depends on the temperature of the tire. The temperature of a tire can change if the temperature outside the car changes. The tire temperature can also increase if the car has been driven for a long time. The graph below shows how tire pressure, measured in pounds per square inch (psi), changes with temperature for a tire that is at 30 psi at room temperature (68°F).

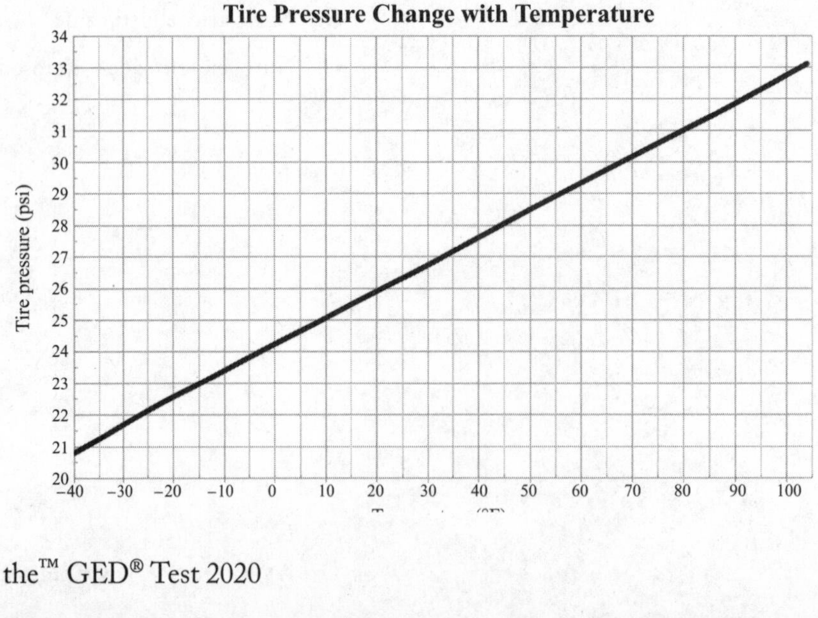

23. A tire's temperature is currently 90°F, and its pressure is 30 psi. About how much air must be added to the tire for it to be at 30 psi at 68°F?

   A. 0 psi
   B. 2 psi
   C. 4 psi
   D. 6 psi

Question 24 refers to the following information and table.

The complete set of DNA in an organism is called its genome. In prokaryotic organisms like bacteria, the genome size is calculated by counting all the base pairs in their single circular chromosome. In eukaryotic organisms like fungi, plants, and animals, the genome size is calculated by counting all the base pairs (bp) in the DNA in the nucleus of a haploid cell. The following table provides the genome size and number of genes for a variety of organisms.

Genome Size for Various Organisms

Species name	Organism Type	Genome Size (bp)	Number of Genes
Escherichia coli	Common lab bacterium	4,639,221	4,377
Saccharomyces cerevisiae	Baker's yeast (fungus)	12,110,000	5,770
Drosophila melanogaster	Fruit fly	130,000,000	17,000
Mus musculus	Common house mouse	2,717,000,000	23,000
Homo sapiens	Humans	3,200,000,000	21,000
Oryza sativa	Rice plant	4,311,000,000	56,000

24. Which statement is supported by the data in the table?

   A. The most structurally and behaviorally complex organisms have the largest genome sizes and the most genes.
   B. Animals have larger genomes and more genes than any other organisms.
   C. Fungi have smaller genomes and fewer genes than any other organisms.
   D. The number of genes usually increases as genome size increases.

Question 25 refers to the following information.

All animals except sponges have symmetrical bodies. This means that one side of the body is the mirror image of the other side. Animals display either radial symmetry or bilateral symmetry. With radial symmetry, the body can be sliced down several imaginary lines that create identical mirror-image sides. With bilateral symmetry, the body can only be sliced down a single line that creates identical mirror-image sides. For example, sea stars display radial symmetry, while humans display bilateral symmetry.

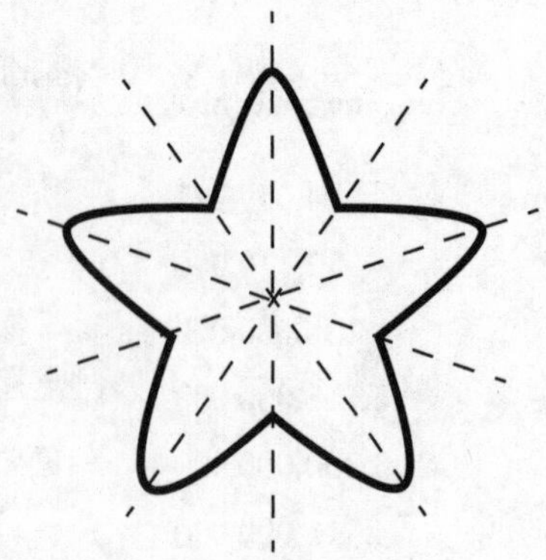

radial symmetry

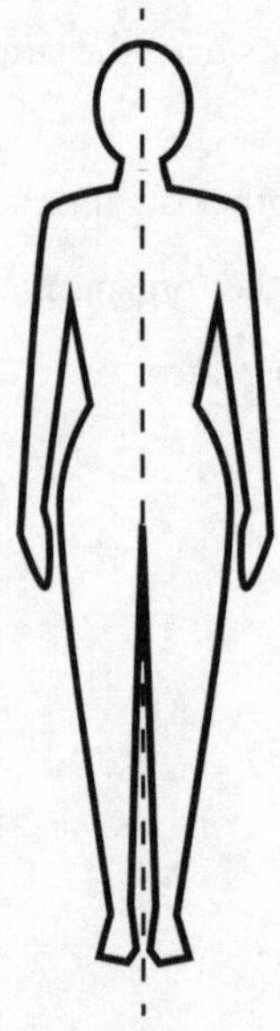

bilateral symmetry

25. Which of the following animals displays bilateral symmetry?

A. Sea anemone

B. Jellyfish

C. Sea urchin

D. Goldfish

Questions 26 and 27 refer to the following information.

In each of the world's major oceans, there is a system of rotating ocean currents called a gyre. These currents are shaped by the earth's rotation, global wind patterns, and the coasts of continents. Ocean currents start when the wind blows along the surface of the water and moves the water in the direction it is blowing. The earth's rotation causes the currents to curve as they travel north or south. The coastlines of continents act like the sides of a bowl; currents must flow along them because they cannot flow over or through them.

When lightweight debris from land falls into an ocean, some of it becomes trapped in the center of that ocean by its gyre's circular motion. Plastic waste has become a problem in the past few decades, forming enormous "garbage patches" in the ocean gyres.

26. A plastic bottle washes into the ocean from a beach on the west coast of North America. Click on the map to identify which gyre it is **most likely** to become trapped inside. (Enter the answer in the space provided on the answer sheet.)

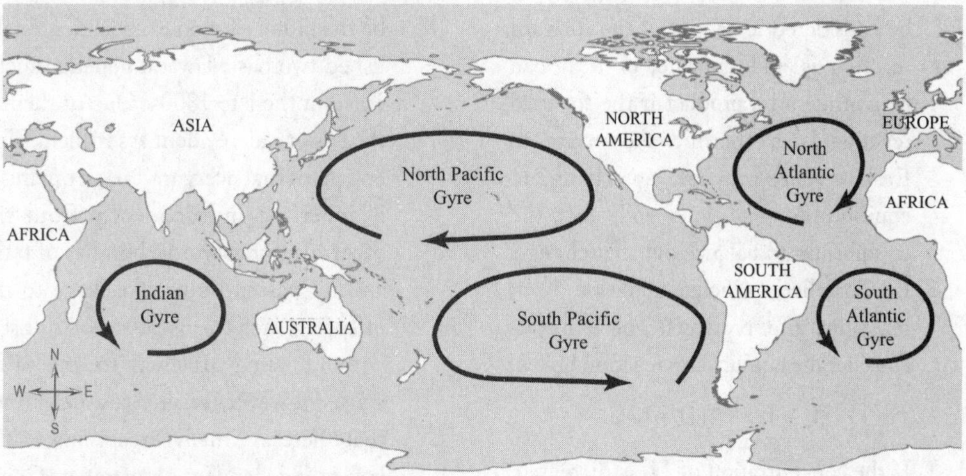

27. The Indian Gyre is controlled by which of the following factors?

A. East coast of Africa

B. East coast of Australia

C. Earth's orbit

D. Debris from land

Question 28 refers to the following information.

At a microscopic level, muscle contraction involves three proteins: actin, myosin, and troponin. Actin and troponin are on a part of the muscle fiber called the thin filament, while myosin is on a part called the thick filament. When calcium ions (Ca^{2+}) bind to troponin, troponin unblocks the myosin-binding site on actin. Myosin is then able to bind to actin and pull that part of the thin filament toward it. Then, ATP binds to myosin, causing it to release actin. Ca^{2+} binds troponin again and the process repeats as long as Ca^{2+} is present. Millions of these molecules working together generate the muscle contractions that allow us to perform everyday actions like walking, speaking, and lifting.

28. If Ca^{2+} were not present in the body, which process would be directly affected?

A. Myosin binding to actin

B. Myosin releasing actin

C. Troponin unblocking actin's binding site

D. Myosin pulling the thin filament toward it

practice test 2—Science

Question 29 refers to the following information.

For any reaction in equilibrium, heat can be considered a reactant if the forward reaction is endothermic, or heat can be considered a product if the forward reaction is exothermic. According to Le Châtelier's principle, any change to equilibrium conditions will shift the equilibrium to balance out that change. Le Châtelier's principle applies to heat, reactants, and products. For example, consider the equilibrium reaction below:

$$H_2 + I_2 \rightleftharpoons 2HI + \text{heat}$$

If the concentration of H_2 is increased, then the equilibrium will shift to the right, in the forward direction, producing more HI to balance out the increased H_2.

29. According to Le Châtelier's principle, what will happen if more heat is added to the equilibrium system shown in the passage?

A. The equilibrium will shift to the right; the concentration of HI will increase.

B. The equilibrium will shift to the right; the concentration of H_2 will decrease.

C. The equilibrium will shift to the left; the concentration of I_2 will increase.

D. The equilibrium will shift to the left; the amount of heat will increase.

Question 30 refers to the following information.

Gregor Mendel, widely considered to be the father of modern genetics, established two basic laws of genetic inheritance in the late 1800s. One of them is the law of independent assortment. This law states that every trait in an organism is inherited independently from the others. In other words, bundles of traits are not passed on as a package to the offspring; each trait is passed on by itself, without being attached to any other trait. However, recent research finds that there are many exceptions to the law of independent assortment. Genes (and their associated traits) that are close together on the same chromosome are often passed on together. This is called genetic linkage.

30. Which of the following procedures is **most likely** to introduce a source of error into a flame test?

A. They are inherited independently from each other.

B. They are close together on the same chromosome.

C. They follow the law of independent assortment.

D. They do not display genetic linkage.

Question 31 refers to the following information.

When metals or their ions are heated at high temperatures, their electrons are excited as they absorb energy from the heat source. When the electrons return to their normal state, they release that energy in the form of a photon, or light particle. If the photon has a wavelength in the visible spectrum, flashes of color will be seen when the metal is heated. Different metals display characteristic colors when they are heated. For example, sodium is yellow-orange, copper is bluish-green, and lithium is bright pink. The traditional method of testing the content of a metal salt solution is called a flame test, in which a metal loop is dipped into an unknown salt solution and then placed in a hot flame. The color that results when the loop is heated helps to identify the metal in the solution.

31. Which of the following procedures is **most likely** to introduce a source of error into a flame test?

- **A.** Using pure distilled water to make the salt solutions
- **B.** Thoroughly cleaning the loop when changing solutions
- **C.** Using different flames for different solutions
- **D.** Using a metal loop that is made of copper

Questions 32 refers to the following information.

Death-feigning, sometimes called "playing dead," or "playing possum," is a behavior observed in many animals where, when threatened by a predator, an animal pretends to be dead. The exact details of their behavior vary by species, but generally death-feigning animals become still and limp, sometimes rolling over and closing their eyes. This behavior carries enormous risks. If the predator continues its attack, an animal that is pretending to be dead may have given up its best opportunity to flee or fight back. Given the danger, scientists have long wondered why death feigning evolved as a defense strategy.

To try to answer this question, scientists examined a small species of beetle that often feigns death. The scientists collected 100 beetles and gave each of them a test of their flying abilities. They then presented those same 100 beetles with a threat and recorded the duration of their death-feigning behavior. After observing all 100 beetles in both tests, they noticed that the beetles that scored highest on the flying test feigned death for the shortest amount of time. The beetles that scored lowest feigned death for longer. Beetles with intermediate flying skills feigned death for moderate periods.

32. What is the **most likely** conclusion you can draw from this experiment?

- **A.** Death-feigning is the most successful way for beetles to escape a predator.
- **B.** Beetles are incapable of both flying and playing dead.
- **C.** Beetles decide whether to feign death based on their flying ability.
- **D.** Given the chance, beetles would always prefer to fly away from danger.

Question 33 refers to the following information and graph.

The paper nautilus is a rare type of octopus known for the beautiful shells built by its female individuals. They are the only type of octopus that swims long distances in open water.

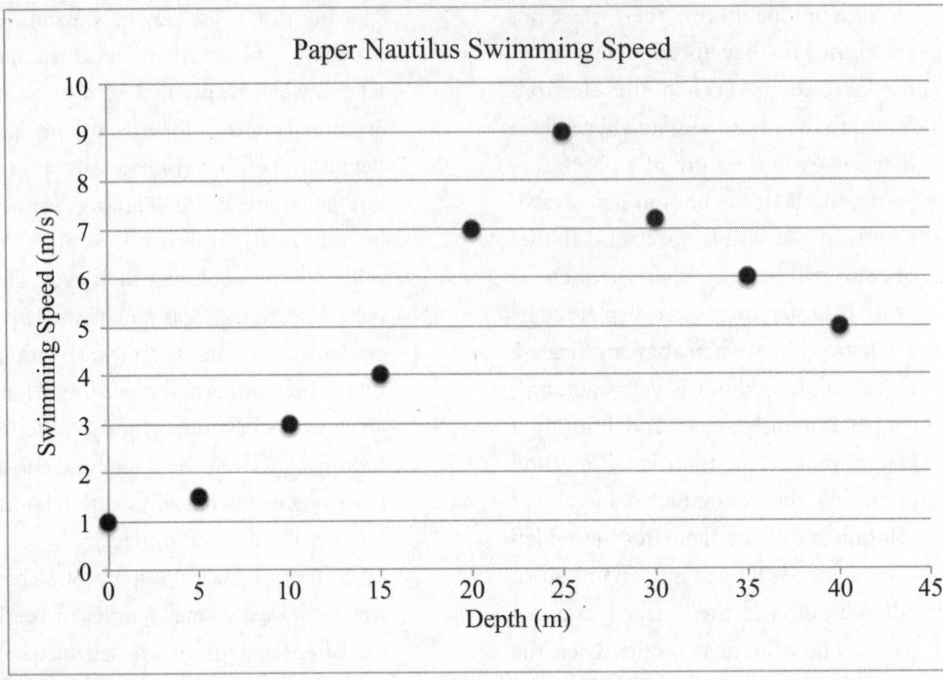

33. Based on the graph, which statement would **best** describe the relationship between ocean depth and paper nautilus swimming speed?

A. It is a negative correlation.

B. It is a positive correlation.

C. Paper nautilus do not swim below 40 m.

D. Swimming speed peaks at middle depths.

Question 34 refers to the following information.

The water cycle recycles water throughout the earth's atmosphere, oceans, and land. Locations where water builds up and is stored are called reservoirs. Water can move back and forth between reservoirs. Water passes through different phases in the water cycle as well, turning from gas to liquid to solid and back again. The amount of time that water spends in a reservoir is called its residence time. Residence time can vary from a few hours to millions of years. In general, residence times are shorter in reservoirs that can easily flow, evaporate, or condense. Residence times are longer in reservoirs that cannot easily move or change. Water often changes phase when moving from one reservoir to another.

34. Which fact from the passage supports the assumption that water's residence time in an ice cap is longer than that in a river?

A. Residence times are shorter in reservoirs that can easily flow or evaporate.

B. Water can move back and forth between reservoirs.

C. Water often changes phase when moving from one reservoir to another.

D. The amount of time that water spends in a reservoir is called its residence time.

Question 35 refers to the following information.

There are two main types of motion: linear and rotational. Linear motion is motion in a straight line. Rotational motion is circular motion around an unmoving center (an axis). The displacement, or distance traveled, in linear motion is represented by d. The displacement in rotational motion is represented by θ. Velocity for both types of motion is defined as displacement per unit time (t). Linear velocity is represented by v and rotational velocity is represented by ω.

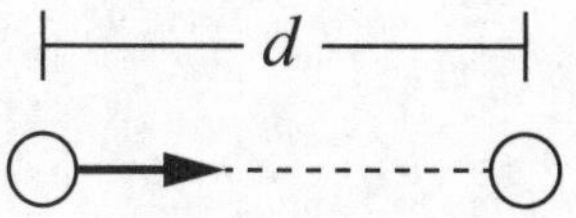

Linear motion

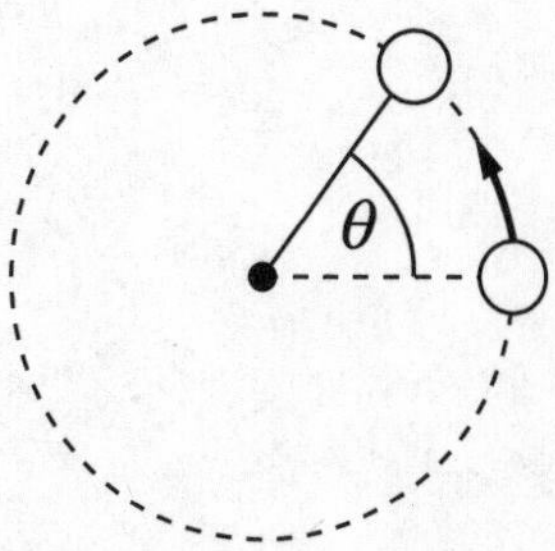

Rotational motion

35. What is the equation for rotational velocity?

A. $v = \frac{d}{t}$

B. $v = \frac{\theta}{t}$

C. $\omega = \frac{d}{t}$

D. $\omega = \frac{\theta}{t}$

STOP! DO NOT GO ON UNTIL TIME IS UP.

SOCIAL STUDIES

70 Minutes • 35 Questions

Directions: The Social Studies Test consists of a series of questions involving general social studies concepts. The questions are based on brief passages of text and visual information (graphs, charts, maps, cartoons, and other figures). Some questions are based on both text and visual information. Study the information provided and answer the question(s) that follow it, referring back to the information as needed.

Most questions are in multiple-choice format. Others are meant to prepare you for the technology-enhanced questions that you will find on the test, such as drop-down, select-an-area, and fill-in-the-blank questions. Record your answers on the Social Studies section of the answer sheet provided. To review how to answer these questions on your answer sheet, please refer to "Directions for Taking the Practice Test" on page 653.

Question 1 is based on the following chart.

British Action	British Rationale
Proclamation of 1763	Attempt to protect colonists from conflict with the Natives
Writs of Assistance 1763	Attempt to enforce Navigation Acts by allowing unrestricted search warrants
Stamp Act of 1765	Attempt to pay war debt by placing tax on legal documents; first direct tax on colonies
Townshend Duties of 1766	Attempt to gain revenue by taxing tea, paper, and other goods
Tea Act of 1773	Attempt to save British East India Company; lowered price of tea but also placed a tax upon it

1. Which of the following is the **best** title for the chart?

A. The American Reaction to British Taxation

B. The End of British Salutary Neglect

C. The Failure of Compromise

D. Colonial Revenue Collection

Question 2 is based on the following information.

1. The CIA exceeded its capabilities in developing the project from guerrilla support to overt armed action without any plausible deniability.
2. Failure to realistically assess risks and to adequately communicate information and decisions internally and with other government principals.
3. Insufficient involvement of leaders of the exiles.
4. Failure to sufficiently organize internal resistance in Cuba.
5. Failure to competently collect and analyze intelligence about Cuban forces.
6. Poor internal management of communications and staff.
7. Insufficient employment of high-quality staff.
8. Insufficient Spanish-speakers, training facilities, and material resources.
9. Lack of stable policies and/or contingency plans.

—"Survey of the Cuban Operation,"
CIA Inspector-General
Lyman B. Kirkpatrick

2. The event being described in the report above would be classified as which of the following?

A. The Bay of Pigs

B. The U-2 Incident

C. The Cuban Missile Crisis

D. The Haitian Revolution

Question 3 is based on the following passage and quote.

In response to the newly formed US government's difficulty raising funds, Congress passed an excise tax that placed a heavy tax on liquor within the country. The tax hit many in the frontiers of Pennsylvania hard, and soon pockets of resistance formed, including violence towards tax collectors. In response to the "Whiskey Rebellion," President Washington issued the following Proclamation.

"... I, George Washington, President of the United States, in obedience to that high and irresistible duty consigned to me by the Constitution 'to take care that the laws be faithfully executed,' ... do hereby declare and make known that... a militia...force which...is adequate to the exigency is already is motion..."

3. According to the quote, Washington believed in which of the following?

A. The urgency of the federal government's economic position justified its position in using the military to enforce the tax.

B. The militia that started the rebellion was justified in defending their Constitutional right to no taxation without representation.

C. Violent actions from citizens were to be dealt with swiftly by legislation.

D. The government's responsibility to enforce laws, such as taxes, justified his use of military force to put down the rebellion.

Question 4 is based on the following quotation.

"The oath that I have taken is the same oath that was taken by George Washington and by every President under the Constitution. But I assume the Presidency under extraordinary circumstances never before experienced by Americans. This is an hour of history that troubles our minds and hurts our hearts...

I am acutely aware that you have not elected me as your President by your ballots, and so I ask you to confirm me as your President with your prayers. And I hope that such prayers will also be the first of many.

If you have not chosen me by secret ballot, neither have I gained office by any secret promises. I have not campaigned either for the Presidency or the Vice Presidency. I have not subscribed to any partisan platform. I am indebted to no man, and only to one woman—my dear wife—as I begin this very difficult job...

Thomas Jefferson said the people are the only sure reliance for the preservation of our liberty. And down the years, Abraham Lincoln renewed this American article of faith asking, "Is there any better way or equal hope in the world?"...

In all my public and private acts as your President, I expect to follow my instincts of openness and candor with full confidence that honesty is always the best policy in the end.

My fellow Americans, our long national nightmare is over..."

—Gerald R. Ford's Remarks Upon Taking the Oath of Office as President (1974)

4. Which of the following events had the **greatest** influence on Gerald Ford's speech?

A. George Washington's Farewell Address

B. Thomas Jefferson's Inaugural Address

C. Abraham Lincoln's Gettysburg Address

D. Richard Nixon's Resignation Address

Questions 5 and 6 refer to the following passages.

Passage A

We consider the underlying fallacy of the plaintiff's argument to consist in the assumption that the enforced separation of the two races stamps the colored race with a badge of inferiority. If this be so, it is not by reason of anything found in the act, but solely because the colored race chooses to put that construction upon it.... The argument also assumes that social prejudice may be overcome by legislation, and that equal rights cannot be secured except by an enforced commingling of the two races.... If the civil and political rights of both races be equal, one cannot be inferior to the other civilly or politically. If one race be inferior to the other socially, the Constitution of the United States cannot put them upon the same plane.

—*Plessy v. Ferguson* (1896)

Passage B

Here . . . there are findings below that the Negro and white schools involved have been equalized, or are being equalized, with respect to buildings, curricula, qualifications, and salaries of teachers, and other "tangible" factors. Our decision, therefore, cannot turn on merely a comparison of these tangible factors in the Negro and white schools involved in each of these cases. We must look instead to the effect of segregation itself on public education. . . .

Today, education is perhaps the most important function of state and local governments. Compulsory school attendance laws and the great expenditures for education both demonstrate our recognition of the importance of education to our democratic society. . . . Today it is a principal instrument in awakening the child to cultural values, in preparing him for later professional training, and in helping him to adjust normally to his environment. In these days, it is doubtful that any child may reasonably be expected to succeed in life if he is denied the opportunity of an education. Such an opportunity, where the state has undertaken to provide it, is a right which must be made available to all on equal terms. . . .

—*Brown v. Board of Education* (1954)

5. The passages above are similar in their focus on which of the following issues?

A. Legal battles over segregation

B. The role of the Constitution in schools

C. Continued efforts to create equality

D. Differences in cultural values

6. Which of the following is at the heart of the difference between the passages?

A. Whether African Americans should be afforded schooling

B. Whether African Americans should be given equal treatment as whites

C. Whether racism exists in society

D. Whether the court has the right to determine the case

Question 7 refers to the following information.

Consider the typical consumer's budget problem. Consumers have a limited amount of income to spend on the things they need and want. Suppose Alphonso has $40 in spending money each week that he can allocate between bus tickets for getting to work and the burgers that he eats for lunch. Burgers cost $8 each, and bus tickets are $2 each.

Economists use the term **opportunity cost** to indicate what one must give up to obtain what he or she desires. The idea behind opportunity cost is that the cost of one item is the lost opportunity to do or consume something else. In short, opportunity cost is the value of the next best alternative.

7. Based on the information in the passage, what is the opportunity cost for Alphonso?

A. The opportunity cost of a burger is the four bus tickets he would have to give up.

B. The opportunity cost of a bus ticket is the two burgers he would have to give up.

C. The opportunity cost is going hungry or not having transportation.

D. The opportunity cost is only having enough money for four burgers and four bus tickets.

Question 8 is based on the following information.

In the landmark Supreme Court case of *McCulloch v. Maryland* (1819), the Court held that Congress had implied powers, powers that would allow for the creation of a National Bank.

8. The implied powers were derived from Article I, Section 8, and became known as the [ ] clause.

Questions 9–11 are based upon the following passage.

Preamble

We, the people of the Confederate States, each State acting in its sovereign and independent character, in order to form a permanent federal government, establish justice, insure domestic tranquility, and secure the blessings of liberty to ourselves and our posterity invoking the favor and guidance of Almighty God do ordain and establish this Constitution for the Confederate States of America.

Article I

Section I. All legislative powers herein delegated shall be vested in a Congress of the Confederate States, which shall consist of a Senate and House of Representatives.

Sec. 2. (I) The House of Representatives shall be composed of members chosen every second year by the people of the several States; and the electors in each State shall be citizens of the Confederate States, and have the qualifications requisite for electors of the most numerous branch of the State Legislature; but no person of foreign birth, not a citizen of the Confederate States, shall be allowed to vote for any officer, civil or political, State or Federal.

(2) No person shall be a Representative who shall not have attained the age of twenty-five years, and be a citizen of the Confederate States, and who shall not when elected, be an inhabitant of that State in which he shall be chosen.

(3) Representatives and direct taxes shall be apportioned among the several States, which may be included within this Confederacy, according to their respective numbers, which shall be determined by adding to the whole number of free persons, including those bound to service for a term of years, and excluding Indians not taxed, three-fifths of all slaves…

—Constitution of the Confederate States (March 11, 1861)

9. The type of government described in the passage places the majority of power with the [ ] government(s).

10. Which of the following represents continuity with the United States Constitution?

A. Both Constitutions place heavy emphasis on granting powers to state governments.

B. Both Constitutions place heavy emphasis on granting powers to the federal government.

C. The Confederate States Constitution continues to place restrictions on the institution of slavery.

D. Both Constitutions provide for a two-house legislature.

11. In the Confederate States Constitution, legislative representation continued to account for the states' slave populations using the [ ] compromise agreed upon during the Constitutional Convention.

Question 12 refers to the following passage.

The nation demanded a response to the bombings, and the Attorney General—who had his eye on the White House in 1920—was ready to oblige. He created a small division to gather intelligence on the radical threat and placed a young Justice Department lawyer named J. Edgar Hoover in charge. Hoover collected and organized every scrap of intelligence gathered by the Bureau of Investigation (the FBI's predecessor) and by other agencies to identify anarchists most likely involved in violent activity. The young Bureau, meanwhile, continued to investigate those responsible for the bombings.

Later that fall, the Department of Justice began arresting, under recently passed laws like the Sedition Act, suspected radicals and foreigners identified by Hoover's group, including well-known leaders Emma Goldman and Alexander Berkman. In December, with much public fanfare, a number of radicals were put on a ship dubbed the "Red Ark" or "Soviet Ark" by the press and deported to Russia.

—Excerpt from "Palmer Raids," (www.fbi.gov/history/famous-cases/palmer-raids)

12. Which of the following **best** summarizes the passage?

- **A.** "A period of high anxiety in the United States"
- **B.** "Creation of the FBI"
- **C.** "Public pressure leads to communist arrests"
- **D.** "Political aspirations create false witch hunt"

Questions 13 and 14 refer to the following map and information.

The map of the world's population density is shown below. Densities are indicated by the shading on the geographic areas, from light (representing less density) to dark (representing greater density).

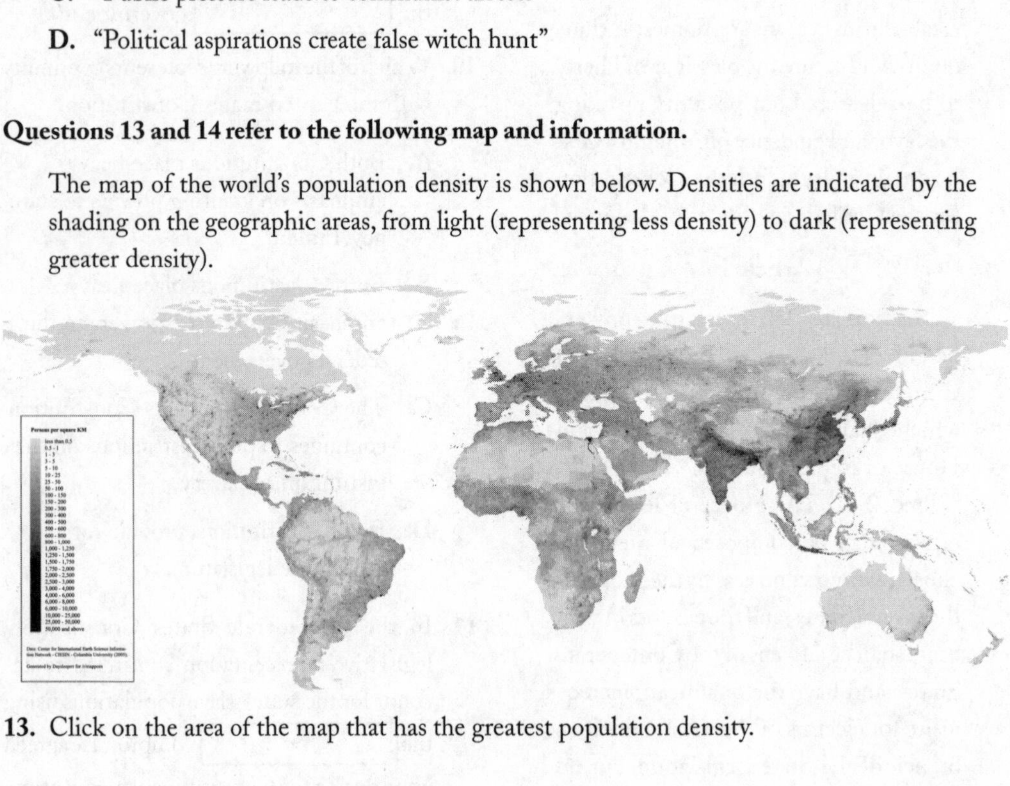

13. Click on the area of the map that has the greatest population density.

14. According to the map, which part of the United States has the greatest population density?

A. Northeast

B. Southwest

C. Southeast

D. Northwest

Question 15 refers to the following chart.

United States Constitution

Legislative Branch	Executive Branch	Judicial Branch
Writes laws	Enforces laws	Interprets laws

15. Which of the following concepts **best** represents the information in the chart shown?

A. System of checks and balances

B. Separation of powers

C. Federalism

D. Judicial review

Question 16 refers to the following chart.

US Presidential Election, 2016

Party	Candidate	Vote %	Popular Votes	Electoral votes
Democratic	Hillary Clinton/ Tim Kaine	48.2%	65,853,514	227
Republican	Donald Trump/ Mike Pence	46.1%	62,984,828	304

16. Which of the following candidates would be the winner of the 2016 presidential election, according to the information in the chart?

A. Hillary Clinton, because of her popular votes

B. Donald Trump, because of his electoral votes

C. Hillary Clinton, because she had a higher vote percentage

D. Donald Trump, because he had more combined votes

Questions 17 and 18 are based on the following graph.

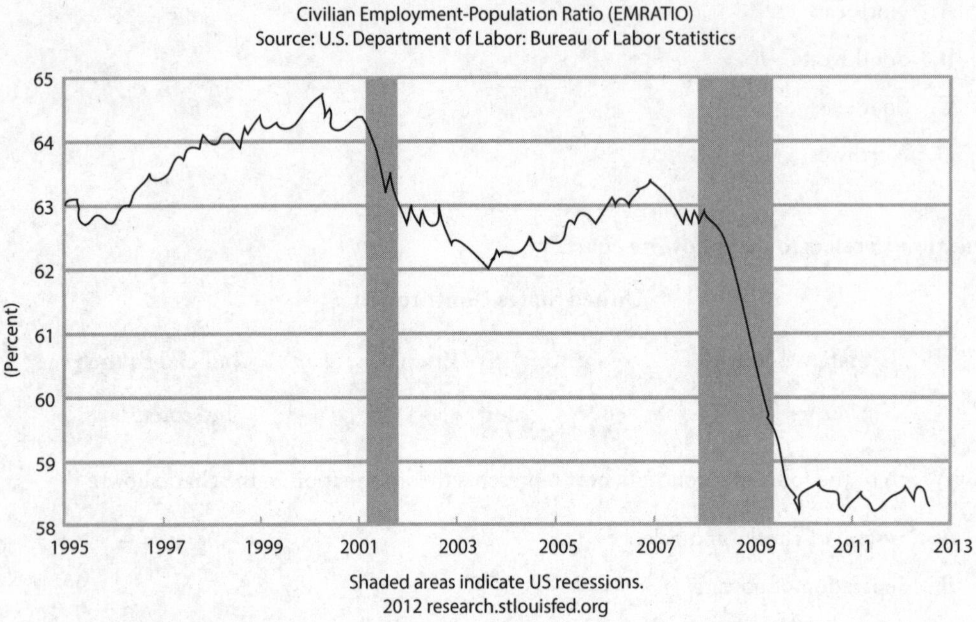

Source: https://commons.wikimedia.org/wiki/File:US_employment_1995-2012.png

17. According to the graph, the year ______ saw the sharpest decline in the unemployment rate.

18. Which relationship is **best** shown by the graph?

A. Unemployment decreases directly before a recession.

B. Recessions create unemployment.

C. Employment increases to prerecession rates after a recession ends.

D. Unemployment only increases after a recession.

Questions 19–21 are based on the following information.

Source for Political News by Age Group

	18–30	31–50	51 and over
CNN	10%	35%	19%
Local TV	3%	7%	31%
Fox News	17%	22%	25%
MSNBC	9%	29%	23%
Facebook	61%	7%	2%

19. According to the chart, what news source is **most** used for political information?

A. CNN

B. Local TV

C. Fox News

D. Facebook

20. Based on the information in the chart, baby boomers **most** utilize which news source for their political information?

A. CNN

B. Local TV

C. Fox News

D. MSNBC

21. Which of the following reasons **best** accounts for the differentiation in use of Facebook for political information?

A. Recent generations (those aged 18–30) have become more reliant on internet sources with instant access over local or cable programs.

B. Older generations are unwilling to utilize resources such as the internet.

C. Younger generations are unaware of the bias and unreliability of the internet, whereas older generations have more experience in news bias.

D. Facebook is a relatively new source of media and only younger generations are aware of the site.

Question 22 refers to the following graph.

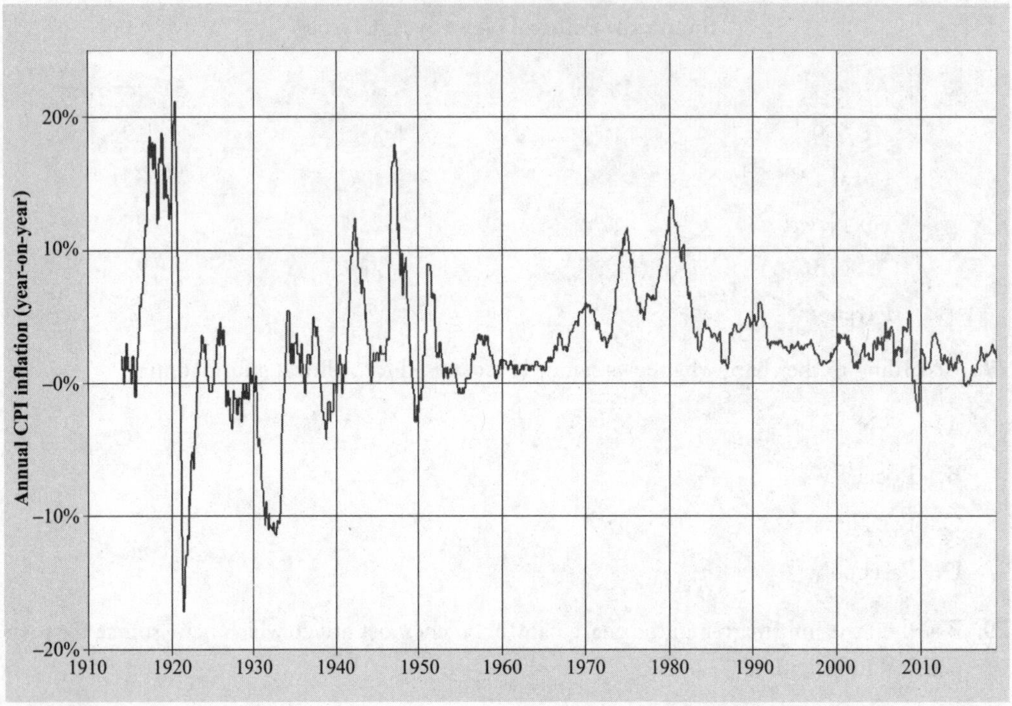

22. According to the graph, which of the following years saw the lowest general price level of goods?

A. Late 1910s

B. Early 1920s

C. Early 1930s

D. Late 1940s

Questions 23 and 24 refer to the following passage.

If two laws conflict with each other, the courts must decide on the operation of each. ... If then, the courts are to regard the Constitution, and the Constitution is superior to any ordinary act of the legislature, [then] the Constitution, and not such ordinary act, must govern the case to which they both apply.

—*Marbury v. Madison* (1803)

23. The ruling above would have the **most** influence on establishing which of the following?

A. Legislative powers

B. Separation of powers

C. Federalism

D. Judicial review

24. This ruling would give support to which of the following statements?

   A. The Supreme Court had the ability to check the other branches of government with regards to the US Constitution.

   B. The Supreme Court had the ability to rewrite the laws of the federal government.

   C. The Supreme Court had the ability to determine what acts could be brought before Congress.

   D. The Supreme Court is above the laws of the Constitution.

Question 25 refers to the following passage.

25. A map shows latitudes and longitudes of locations on a flat surface, or plane. The look, size, and shapes of the areas placed upon the map are projected and often become [Select ▼] due to the restrictions placed upon projecting such objects onto such a surface. Often the distance, shape, area, and direction are changed, or even lost.

   A. distorted

   B. diffused

   C. distributed

   D. decayed

Question 26 refers to the following quotation.

"Four score and seven years ago our fathers brought forth on this continent, a new nation, conceived in Liberty, and dedicated to the proposition that all men are created equal. Now we are engaged in a great civil war, testing whether that nation, or any nation so conceived and so dedicated, can long endure. We are met on a great battle-field of that war. We have come to dedicate a portion of that field, as a final resting place for those who here gave their lives that that nation might live. It is altogether fitting and proper that we should do this."

—Abraham Lincoln,
The Gettysburg Address
(Gettysburg, Pennsylvania.
November 19, 1863)

26. What event was President Lincoln referencing at the start of his address?

   A. The Puritans' arrival at Plymouth

   B. The Declaration of Independence

   C. The United States Constitution

   D. The creation of the Confederate States of America

Question 27 refers to the following chart.

Outlays for Mandatory and Related Programs: 1962–2024 (in millions of dollars)

Category and Program	1998	1999	2000	2001	2002
Mandatory Programs:					
Human Resource programs					
Education, training, employment, and social services	7,943	5,442	4,788	2,798	7,785
Health					
Medicaid	101,234	108,042	117,921	129,374	147,512
Refundable Premium Tax Credit and Cost Sharing Reductions	....	....	....	....	....
Children's Health Insurance	5	565	1,220	3,699	3,682
Other	5,292	5,464	5,441	6,003	5,889
Total Health	106,531	114,071	124,582	139,076	157,083
Medicare	190,233	187,694	194,115	214,061	227,699

Information from https://www.whitehouse.gov/omb/historical-tables/

27. According to the chart, which mandatory program had the greatest on average increase during the years 1998–2002?

A. Medicaid

B. Children's Health Insurance

C. Total Health

D. Medicare

Questions 28 and 29 refer to the Twenty-Second Amendment.

Section I

No person shall be elected to the office of the President more than twice, and no person who has held the office of President, or acted as President, for more than two years of a term to which some other person was elected President shall be elected to the office of the President more than once. But this Article shall not apply to any person holding the office of President, when this Article was proposed by the Congress, and shall not prevent any person who may be holding the office of President, or acting as President, during the term within which this Article becomes operative from holding the office of President or acting as President during the remainder of such term.

Section II

This article shall be inoperative unless it shall have been ratified as an amendment to the Constitution by the legislatures of three-fourths of the several States within seven years from the date of its submission to the States by the Congress.

28. According to the Twenty-Second Amendment, which of the following would constitute a President serving more than eight years in office?

A. If an official becomes president with one year remaining in another president's term

B. If an official becomes president in nonconsecutive terms

C. If an official has already been president

D. If an official has been a member of Congress

29. According to the amendment, for how many years total could a person be president?

A. Seven years

B. Eight years

C. Ten years

D. Twelve years

30. Which of the following economic concepts would utilize a graph that has a curve and concave to represent slope and equilibrium?

A. Supply and demand

B. Total revenue

C. Consumer surplus

D. Opportunity cost

Question 31 refers to the following image.

Source: https://commons.wikimedia.org/wiki/File:Jdr-king.JPG

31. The image infers that Rockefeller held a ________ on industries in the Gilded Age.

Question 32 is based on the following information.

There are many agents of socialization in politics, such as the family, television and mass media, friends or peers, and school. These agents are what help us develop our opinions, political positions, and to develop our beliefs that create our ideology on the political spectrum. It is a learning process that helps to develop our orientation and behaviors towards politics.

32. Based on the passage, which agent of change is the first to shape our political opinions?

A. Family

B. TV and mass media

C. Peers and friends

D. School

Questions 33 and 34 are based on the following map.

The following is a map of the world's religions.

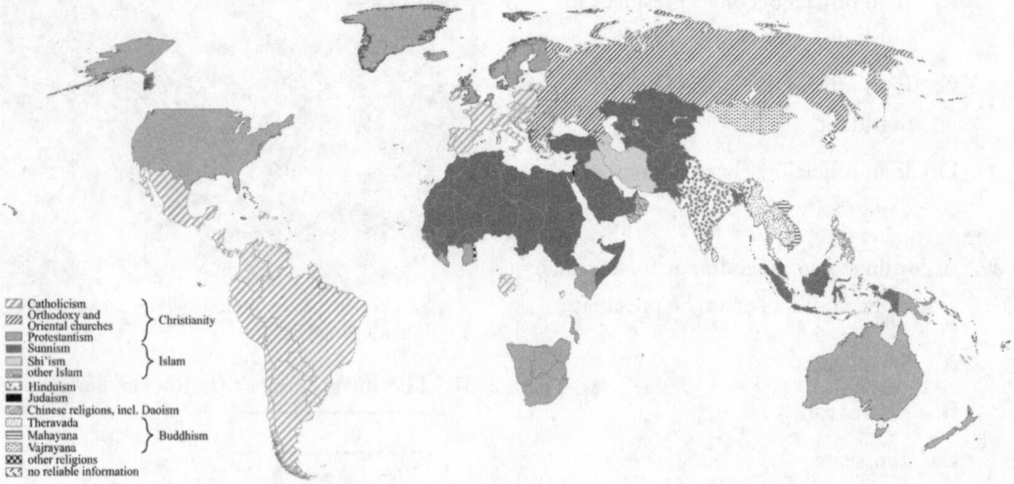

Source: https://commons.wikimedia.org/wiki/File:World_religions_map_en.svg

33. On the map, click on the region that is best understood as the Middle East.

34. There are many religions found across the continents, but according to the map, which of the following religions is **most** common to the Western Hemisphere?

A. Christianity

B. Islam

C. Buddhism

D. There is no common religion

Question 35 is based on the following image.

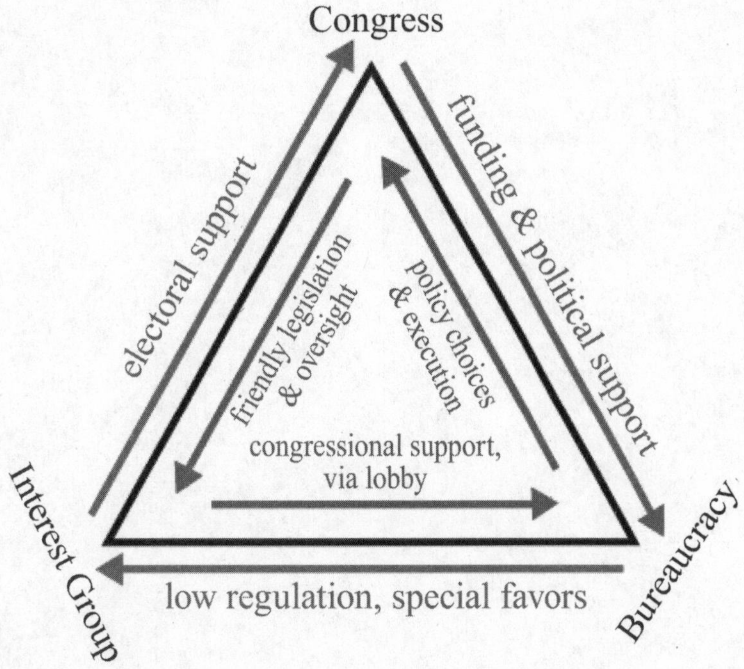

35. The image shown **best** represents which of the following political relationships?

A. Iron triangles

B. Super PACs

C. Advocacy groups

D. Party politics

STOP! DO NOT GO ON UNTIL TIME IS UP.

ANSWER KEYS AND EXPLANATIONS

Reasoning Through Language Arts

Part I	**14.** C	**24.** A	**39.** A
1. D	**15.** A	**25.** D	**40.** C
2. A	**16.** A	**26.** A	**41.** fellow neighbors (B)
3. B	**17.** D	**27.** C	**42.** Northchester Gardening Club, (A)
4. D	**Part II**	**28.** C	**43.** were (C)
5. B	See explanation	**29.** A	**44.** you're (B)
6. C	**Part III**	**30.** Glue gun	**45.** planting (D)
7. B	**18.** A	**31.** B	**46.** 15, 14, 16, 17
8. C	**19.** Jefferson is A and D, Adams is B and C	**32.** D	**47.** exciting (D)
9. C, B, D, A	**20.** B	**33.** D	**48.** to see (C)
10. A	**21.** Jefferson	**34.** B	
11. 5 micrograms per deciliter	**22.** C	**35.** A	
12. C	**23.** B	**36.** C	
13. B		**37.** D	
		38. B	

Part I

1. **The correct answer is D.** The main idea of the passage is that economic challenges can be overcome with honest work. Although the passage represents Roosevelt taking over the presidency from Hoover, there is no direct criticism of Hoover's administration (choice A). In the first paragraph, Roosevelt suggests that the path to "victory" will require honesty and hard work, which directly contradicts choice B. Paragraph 4 uses the example of locusts to suggest that the economic problems in the United States are *not* due to natural disasters, which contradicts the statement in choice C.

2. **The correct answer is A.** *Candor* means "honesty" or "straightforwardness." The tone of the speech is very serious, so *humor* (choice B) doesn't fit the context. In the rest of the paragraph, Roosevelt describes speaking the truth "frankly and boldly," so *vagueness* (choice C) and *fear* (choice D) do not fit the context either.

3. **The correct answer is B.** The Great Depression affected millions of Americans and was likely one of the main factors in Roosevelt's election victory. This speech is a promise to address those issues as a leader. Re-election (choice A) is not a likely motivation because this is Roosevelt's inaugural address (or first speech) at the start of his presidency, and there would not be another election for several years. Paragraph 1 talks about addressing problems openly and honestly, so it is unlikely he is trying to hide other issues as choice C suggests. Paragraph 3 discusses some of the problems facing farmers but does not blame them for the nation's economic issues (choice D).

4. **The correct answer is D.** In paragraph 6, Roosevelt mentions the "false leadership" of those in charge of money and finance, suggesting that their failed policies are dooming the country. Paragraph 5 discusses how there is no "plague of locusts," and that there are plenty of goods produced, so Roosevelt does not blame natural disasters (choice A) for the country's condition. High taxes (choice B) and high unemployment (choice C) are presented as aspects of the current state of things, but Roosevelt does not suggest these as causes of the Great Depression.

5. **The correct answer is B.** Paragraph 5 is meant to contrast the nation's resources with the poor way they've been managed, suggesting that the nation has the necessary elements to succeed again. The paragraph does compare the "perils" of the forefathers with modern people's but does not directly compare the success or failure of the forefathers and the 1933 government (choice A). The paragraph does allude to poor leadership, but the references to the plentiful resources available is not used to criticize the Hoover administration (choice C). The paragraph discusses "plenty" as the number of resources available but ruined by the "money changers," but does not suggest that some citizens are successful at the expense of others (choice D).

6. **The correct answer is C.** Roosevelt believes that moving past fear is the way to move forward. The way Roosevelt describes fear ("unreasoning, unjustified terror which paralyzes") suggests that fear is not a solution (choice A) or a productive emotion (choice B). There is no indication that Roosevelt is either afraid or not afraid, so choice D is not supported by the passage.

7. **The correct answer is B.** Much of the passage describes what happens to people when there is too much lead in drinking water. There is no information in the passage that suggests lead is less dangerous than researchers previously thought, so choice A does not fit. The passage also does not tell the reader where to find clean, lead-free drinking water, so choice C is not supported. The passage describes the current risks of lead in drinking water and does not describe history, so choice D is incorrect.

8. **The correct answer is C.** *Persistent* means "stubborn" or "tenacious," suggesting that once it's in the body, it stays. Although choice A is close, there is not enough information in the passage to support the statement that there is no way to get rid of lead. While the passage discusses the effects of lead on different groups of people, it does not say that each person has the same symptoms—and in paragraph 2, the passage says that children and adults can experience different effects, so choice B is incorrect. Paragraph 1 does say that lead bioaccumulates over time, but *persistent* refers to the presence of lead, not the time it takes to get there, so choice D is incorrect.

9. **The correct order is C, B, D, A.** Paragraph 1 describes how the EPA uses the Safe Drinking Water Act to investigate lead safety (choice C), then states how the maximum contaminant level goals are zero (choice B). Paragraph 2 describes how children are more vulnerable to the effects of lead (choice D). Paragraph 4 describes how drinking water is just one of the ways children can be exposed to lead (choice A).

10. **The correct answer is A.** By establishing that there is no safe level of lead in the water ("EPA has set the maximum contaminant level goal for lead in drinking water at zero because lead is a toxic metal that can be harmful to human health even at low exposure levels"), it shows the reader that having any lead can have major consequences. Although the passage describes the health risks of lead, the writer does not take a stance

on whether the issue can be fixed (choice B). The main idea of the passage is that lead is dangerous in drinking water, so explaining that there is no safe level of lead in water supports the understanding, not distracts (choice C) from it. The tone of the passage is informational, and there is no evidence that the writer is biased (choice D) one way or the other.

11. **The correct answer is 5 micrograms per deciliter.** Paragraphs 3 and 4 list this amount as the lead level at which action should be taken.

12. **The correct answer is C.** Because the main topic of the passage is the effect of lead on children, statistics about the number of children affected would fit well in the article. Although the Safe Drinking Water Act is mentioned, information about the members of Congress who passed it (choice A) would not be necessary or relevant. Because lead is the main subject of the passage, general information about water pollution (choice B) would not fit well. Information about the history of the EPA (choice D) would not be relevant either, given that the passage focuses on the specific topic of lead in drinking water, not the agency itself.

13. **The correct answer is B.** Section I describes what happens to employees who violate the policy, and the consequences include "termination of employment," or getting fired. Pay reduction (choice A) is not listed as an disciplinary option, in the document. Facing no consequences (choice C) is unlikely, because Section I also says that there are no exceptions to the policy. Earning a promotion (choice D) is a positive outcome, which is not likely at all, given the context of the passage.

14. **The correct answer is C.** The committee is meant to ensure that everyone is equally aware of the ethics policy, not to spy on employees (choice A). There is no indication in the passage that the committee members are more or less bound by the ethics rules than everyone else (choice B), or that the policy does not apply to executives (choice D). In fact, Section D specifically calls for executives to follow the policy.

15. **The correct answer is A.** The policy outlines policies for fairness and ethical behavior. Choice A is the only one that aligns with that topic. Choices B and C are about dress code and benefit policies, respectively, while choice D is about employee time management.

16. **The correct answer is A.** At multiple times in the passage, the policy calls for "openness," so you can infer that employees should not hide others' ethical violations. Section D calls for employees to treat everyone fairly (choice B), and calls for executives to behave ethically (choice C). Section E states that employees who work to improve ethical behavior at the company will be rewarded (choice D).

17. **The correct answer is D.** One of the recurring themes of the passage is using ethical behavior to support the company, so it makes sense to include a question about supporting the company's values. The policy discourages using company resources for personal gain, so choice A should not be added to the checklist. Paragraph B states that "effective ethics is a team effort," so choice B shouldn't be added either. Trying to get away with unethical behavior would violate the policy, so it doesn't make sense to add choice C to the checklist.

Part II

Extended response. Answers will vary. You will find two sample analyses on pages 839–840.

answers practice test 2

Part III

18. **The correct answer is A.** Throughout the passage, Jefferson describes "rights," "duties," and "truths" to emphasize that the colonies should declare independence. The tone is not mocking or humorous, so choice B is incorrect. There is no description of what is happening in the colonies, so choice C is incorrect. The passage as presented does not list any specific names of supporters, so choice D is incorrect.

19. **The correct answer is Jefferson is A and D, Adams is B and C.** Thomas Jefferson's writing is highly supportive of declaring independence right now as a statement of rights, while Adams's point of view is that the timing could be better, and that it could be used to get foreign support as well.

20. **The correct answer is B.** Although Adams is more skeptical of the timing and method of declaring independence, by the last paragraph, he is speaking admiringly of the "great question of independence." Neither passage suggests that the writers are loyal to the English king (choice A). There is nothing in either passage that discusses the writers' future ambitions or goals (choices C and D).

21. **The correct answer is Jefferson.** Because Adams uses sarcasm to complain about the timing, it is likely that Jefferson (and not Adams) made the decision to publish the document when he did.

22. **The correct answer is C.** In this phrase, Adams is recommending that everyone involved pay attention to the potential consequences of their actions. The use of "Providence" is figurative, not literal, so choice A is incorrect. Although Adams refers to a "frown," he is not condemning the whole idea of the declaration (choice B). He is also not referring to literal "lay[ing]," or rest, so choice D does not fit either.

23. **The correct answer is B.** Based on context phrases like "that they are endowed by their Creator," *sacred* is the best option.

24. **The correct answer is A.** Adams is writing to his wife, and by the mocking tone of some of the passage, it is clear this is not meant to be a public statement. He never mentions Jefferson by name or even indirectly (choice B), and from the context of the passage, you can infer that, although he doesn't agree with the the timing of the declaration, Adams supports independence and is not trying to distance himself from the movement (choice C). There is also nothing in the passage that suggests he wants credit for the declaration (choice D).

25. **The correct answer is D.** The sentence, "But the important point with both men and women is to treat the exercise of the suffrage as a duty, which, in the long run, must be well performed to be of the slightest value" describes why Roosevelt supports women's suffrage. Although Roosevelt eventually says that he believes voting is a duty for both men and women, his stating that the performance of duty makes life worthwhile (choice A) does not explain his support. Choices B and C restate that he supports the right to vote but does not explain why.

26. **The correct answer is A.** The second paragraph in Passage 1 describes how poorly Taft's remarks were received by the audience, upsetting Taft. The first paragraph talks about how Taft did *not* support women voting, so choice B is incorrect. The first paragraph describes Taft as "a most charming and likeable gentleman," so choice C is inaccurate. The second paragraph describes how the reaction to his statements changed his tone and demeanor, so choice D is not supported by the passage.

27. **The correct answer is C.** The phrase "oppressive silence" shows that the tone in the

room was not positive, suggesting that Taft's remarks were not received well. Choice A means the opposite, and there is no indication in the passage that the audience liked what he was saying. Choice B is too literal, implying that the silence was due to a lack of attendees, and it contradicts paragraph 3, which states that there were "many women" in attendance. Choice D does not offer a personal perspective, but rather describes what happened.

28. **The correct answer is C.** In Passage 1, you learn that although Taft is expected to support women's suffrage, he actually does not. Passage 2 describes how Roosevelt *does* support women's suffrage, so neither choice A nor choice B is correct. Only Roosevelt describes voting as a duty, so choice D is incorrect. Taft does not support women's suffrage, and Roosevelt describes himself as a "tepid" (or lukewarm) supporter early on, so choice C is the best choice of the options given.

29. **The correct answer is A.** By giving Taft the benefit of the doubt and assuming he understands why his speech was regrettable, the author creates a sympathetic tone. The remaining choices are facts that describe the audience (choice D), their reaction to Taft's speech (choice C), and what Taft did after the speech (choice B).

30. **The correct answer is *glue gun*.** This comparison is made in paragraph 10.

31. **The correct answer is B.** The second paragraph describes subtractive manufacturing as "cutting away excess materials." Depositing materials (choice A) describes additive manufacturing, 3D printing (choice C) describes the printing process, and dripping water (choice D) describes stalactites.

32. **The correct answer is D.** The fourth paragraph describes how 3D printing saves energy by using fewer materials, and lighter ones, than traditional manufacturing. Although the passage does say that there are fewer steps, there is not enough information given to tell you if it takes less time overall (choice A). There's also no mention of how many people are involved, so choice B is not supported. Choice C is an opinion, and the question is asking for a reason.

33. **The correct answer is D.** Biomaterials are described as being similar to human cells, suggesting that the technology could be used for medical procedures on humans. Chocolate (choice A) is a food, and plastics (choice B) and wax (choice C) are non-medical materials.

34. **The correct answer is B.** Paragraph 3 states that 98% of the material is used, which means 2% of the material is *not* used. Choice C (50%) describes the amount of energy saved in the 3D printing process. Choice D (0.01%) is a description of polymer width and is not a percentage given in the passage.

35. **The correct answer is A.** Paragraph 5 describes what is causing 3D manufacturers to experiment, and it lists the price of printers as a reason. There is not enough information in the passage to support choices B and D, and choice C is essentially the opposite of what the author is suggesting.

36. **The correct answer is C.** As the passage progresses, the narrator focuses on the ugliness of the wallpaper, using words like *unclean* and *sickly* to describe it. The words *comfortable* (choice A), *perfect* (choice B), and *warm* (choice D) would be used in a more positive context.

37. **The correct answer is D.** In line 39, the narrator states that she disagrees with her brother and John, so choice A can be eliminated as a correct answer. The tone is not angry (choice B) but calm. She talks about their beliefs versus her own, so she is not ignoring their advice (choice C).

answers practice test 2

38. **The correct answer is B.** The narrator disagrees with her husband's diagnosis of her problems, but she feels like she cannot contradict him. There is not enough evidence in the passage to support the idea that husbands should defer to wives (choice A). The narrator talks about finding a room, but there is not enough information given to support the idea that the narrator would not be allowed to buy a house on her own (choice C). The passage describes the ways that John makes medical decisions for the narrator, so choice D is not supported.

39. **The correct answer is A.** While the narrator seems to be frustrated with John's attempts to control every part of her day, she does not seem unhappy overall (choice B). While the narrator dislikes the wallpaper, there is no information given that illustrates how John feels about it (choice C). Although the passage mentions "legal trouble" (choice D), this reference is about the house itself, and not the two main characters.

40. **The correct answer is C.** The passage supports the conclusion that the narrator is frustrated with her current life. Because the narrator presents only her own perspective, there is not enough information to determine how sick she really is (choice A). Although haunting is mentioned briefly, there is no evidence to suggest that the house really is haunted (choice B). Although the narrator does seem upset by the way she's being treated, there is no evidence that she plans to leave (choice D).

41. **The correct answer is *fellow neighbors* (B).** "Fellow neighbors" is a general greeting, not a specific person, so it should be a common noun phrase, with both words lowercase.

42. **The correct answer is *Northchester Gardening Club,* (A).** A comma is the correct punctuation to show a pause in the sentence. Choice B puts the comma in the wrong place. Choices C and D create sentence fragments.

43. **The correct answer is *were* (C).** The sentence is talking about events that happened in the past, and the pronoun *we* is plural, so *were* is correct. *Was* (choice A) is past tense, but singular. *Would* (choice B) is the future tense. *Is* (choice D) is both current tense and singular.

44. **The correct answer is *you're* (B).** The sentence calls for a present-tense version of the noun-verb phrase *you are*, but *your* (choice A) is a possessive pronoun, *you were* (choice C) is past tense, and *you* (choice D) is lacking the verb. *You're* is the only answer that fits the sentence.

45. **The correct answer is *planting* (D).** The verb form should match the other verbs in the bulleted list, which are all verbs ending in *–ing*. Choice D is the only option that agrees with the rest of the verbs in the list.

46. **The correct order is 15, 14, 16, 17.** The paragraph makes more sense if the sentence with the transition word *additionally* opens the paragraph, introducing the concept of the garden's family programs before offering more details.

47. **The correct answer is *exciting* (D).** The answer should be an adjective describing how the author feels about the garden's upcoming activities, and *exciting* is the only option that fits the sentence.

48. **The correct answer is *to see* (C).** The verb should be future tense, because the writer is talking about something that will happen this summer. *To seeing* (choice A) is missing a helper verb (*be*). *To have seen* (choice B) is the future perfect tense and doesn't really fit. *Too see* (choice D) incorrectly uses the word *too* (meaning "also") instead of *to*.

Extended Response: Sample Essay

High-Scoring Analysis

Between the two perspectives on public funding for space travel, I found the first essay to be more compelling and better supported. The writer in Passage 1 used strong historical and cultural evidence to show why the United States should continue to fund the space program, while the writer of Passage 2 had a more limited argument.

While Passage 2 does make a valid argument that private industry may have more money and time to research and develop space programs, the financial piece was the only real argument presented. This ignores the government's past history of leadership when it comes to space, and basically ignores the contributions that have come from NASA as a publicly funded agency. This is important context when deciding whether or not to continue with government-funded space programs. The reality is that it's NOT all about the money, as the writer of Passage 2 insists it is. I found this argument to be worth considering, but not comprehensive enough.

Comparatively, Passage 1 provides much more information (and fewer opinions) for the reader to work with. By presenting information about specific things the space program has achieved, and tying it to current space initiatives, the writer presents a coherent perspective on how the space program fits into our current government landscape.

The writer of Passage 1 also uses concrete financial information to support his own point about funding NASA, while undercutting Passage 2's main point that space funding should boil down to a question of money. When the writer of Passage 1 shows that every federal dollar contributes $10 to the overall economy that is a very compelling point. A point that is not made in Passage 2. Passage 2 never tells you how what kind of economic advantages would come from privatizing the space program.

As a taxpayer myself, I'm interested in how government programs spend my money, and the writer of Passage 1 helps illustrate how space participation affects not only our economy, but also international diplomacy. By showing the usefulness of the space program, the writer helps to answer the question that all of us have: "how does this affect our lives?" It's not just space that's at issue here, but some core American ideals of international cooperation and programs that benefit other countries as well as our own.

For these reasons, the argument in Passage 1 triggered more agreement with me. I feel better informed by the statistics and information provided in the first passage. The second passage does make some good points about private industry, but it fails to convince me that having private companies manage space travel would be better…not just different

Explanation

This is a high-scoring analysis because it shows a thoughtful reading of both passages. The extended response takes a side (the writer clearly agrees more fully with the first passage) but explains this support by using evidence from both passages and expressing a coherent opinion. The flow of the response is clear and makes sense. Although there are some minor grammatical issues, the response demonstrates a command of standard English conventions as well.

Low-Scoring Analysis

I've read the passages, and I agree with #2. Government has too much power as it is. Let's the billionaires have a crack at space. Its not like we're going back to the moon anytime soon if we wait for Uncle Sam to pay for it.

The first passage states that space would be times Square, so what? I've visited Time Square and it was great. The ads don't bother me, why should they bother anyone else? Don't pay attention Most of us wont get to go anyway, so it's not a valid argument. NASA's history is in the passed. What have they done for us lately?

So passage 1 is not a valid reason to keep the government paying for the space program. Businessmen know how the business world. They have the money. They have the time to invest. All of these are listed as reasons in passage 2.

In conclusion, I like the argument that we should privitize space travel. Imagine where we could be in just a few short years!

Explanation

This is a low-scoring analysis because it is too short and shows little actual analysis on the writer's part. While the writer has read both passages and does compare/contrast some of the information in each passage, there is little original analysis. There are several personal diversions that are not tied back to the original passages. The argument that Passage 2 provides the better argument is not supported well, and is not presented in a clear, coherent way. The response writer also shows minimal command of standard English conventions, with many spelling, grammatical, and organizational issues throughout the response.

Mathematical Reasoning

1. C	10. C	19. $\left(-\frac{5}{2}, 0\right)$	28. C	38. D
2. D	11. A	20. A	29. B	39. 1.14×10^9
3. $\frac{27}{64}$	12. B	21. C	30. A	40. B
4. B	13. B	22. B	31. D	41. C
5. D	14. D	23. B	32. B	42. $\frac{9}{100}$
6. 50	15. A	24. A	33. C	43. 27
7. 1 to 2	16. C	25. A	34. A	44. A
8. B	17. A	26. C	35. 1 and 3	45. B
9. C	18. $45w + 25x + 10y + 5z$	27. A	36. 2	46. B
			37. B	

1. The correct answer is C. Since the diameter is 12 feet, the radius R is 6 feet. So the height H is $\frac{1}{3}(3+6) = 3$ feet, and so the volume is $\pi R^2 H = \pi(6)^2(3) = 108\pi$ cubic feet. Choice A is the result of not multiplying by the height. Choices C and D result from incorrect computations of the height.

2. The correct answer is D. Simplify the numerator and denominator separately by getting a least common denominator in each, and then divide the resulting fractions:

$$\frac{\frac{3}{4}-\frac{2}{3}}{\frac{3}{4}+\frac{2}{3}} = \frac{\frac{9}{12}-\frac{8}{12}}{\frac{9}{12}+\frac{8}{12}} = \frac{\frac{1}{12}}{\frac{17}{12}} = \frac{1}{17}$$

Choice A is incorrect because you do not add or subtract fractions by adding or subtracting the numerators and denominators. Choice B is the result of incorrectly multiplying one fraction in the top and bottom by the number needed to convert to a common denominator, not both. Choice C is the result of incorrect canceling—you cannot cancel like fractions in the top and bottom if they are being added.

3. The correct answer is $\frac{27}{64}$. Use the order of operations:

$$\begin{aligned} 3\left(\frac{1}{8}+\frac{1}{4}\right)^2 &= 3\left(\frac{1}{8}+\frac{2}{8}\right)^2 \\ &= 3\left(\frac{3}{8}\right)^2 \\ &= 3\left(\frac{9}{64}\right) \\ &= \frac{27}{64} \end{aligned}$$

4. The correct answer is B. Substitute $x - 1$ in for x in the formula for $f(x)$ and simplify:

$$\begin{aligned} f(x-1) &= 1 - \frac{(x-1)}{(x-1)+2} \\ &= 1 - \frac{x-1}{x+1} \\ &= \frac{x+1-(x-1)}{x+1} \\ &= \frac{x+1-x+1}{x+1} \\ &= \frac{2}{x+1} \end{aligned}$$

Choice A is the result of handling negative signs incorrectly. Choice C is incorrect because $f(x-1)$ does not equal $f(x) - 1$. Choice D is incorrect because the expression $x - 1$ in the notation $f(x-1)$ is an input for x in $f(x)$, not a multiple of $f(x)$.

5. **The correct answer is D.** The length from A to B on the map is $\frac{3}{8} = \frac{6}{16}$ – inch; this corresponds to 6(9) = 54 blocks. The length from B to C on the map is $\frac{1}{4} = \frac{4}{16}$ – inch; this corresponds to 4(9) = 36 blocks. So a one-way trip from A to C is 90 blocks. Therefore, a round trip is 2(90) = 180 blocks. Choice A represents the length from A to B. Choice B represents the length from A to B (54 blocks) added to half the length from B to C (18 blocks). Choice C represents one full trip there, not back.

6. **The correct answer is 50.** Add the *y*-values of the six points for Melanie and for Rose separately. Subtract these values and multiply the result by 100.

   Melanie: 3 + 2.5 + 2.5 + 1 + 2 + 3.5 = 14.5

   Rose: 2.5 + 2 + 2.5 + 2.5 + 2.5 + 2 = 14

   The difference in their totals is 0.5, which corresponds to 0.5(100) = 50 shells.

7. **The correct answer is 1 to 2.** Add the *y*-values of the two points on each of the six years. Those years for which the sum is greater than 5 are those for which the number of shells collected exceeds 500. These years are 2014 and 2019. The number of shells collected during the other four years is less than 500. So the ratio is 2 to 4, which simplifies to 1 to 2.

8. **The correct answer is B.** First, the missing angle in the triangle, as shown, is 73° because vertical angles are congruent.

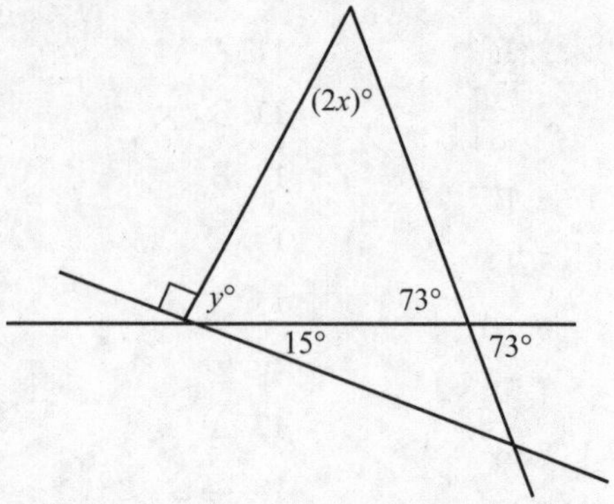

   Next, the three consecutive angles—90, *y*, and 15—form a straight angle, so their sum is 180. So 15 + 90 + *y* = 180, so that *y* = 75. Now, since the sum of the three angles of a triangle is 180°. This yields the equation *y* + 2*x* + 73 = 180. Using *y* = 75 in this equation and solving for *x* yields:

$$2x + 75 + 73 = 180$$
$$2x = 32$$
$$x = 16$$

   Thus *x* + *y* = 16 + 75 = 91. Choice A represents the value of 2*x*. Choice C represents the value of 180 – *y*. Choice D represents 180 – 2*x*.

9. **The correct answer is C.** 125% of 10 inches is 1.25(10) = 12.5 inches and 125% of 14 inches is 1.25(14) = 17.5 inches. The new dimensions are 12.5 inches by 17.5 inches. Choice A represents a 25% decrease in dimensions. Choice B is the result of using 25% = 0.25, rather than computing 25% of the actual dimensions. Choice D represents a larger increase than 25%.

10. **The correct answer is C.** Let *x* be the number of males who play one sport. Since 10% of this number is 20, we know that 0.10*x* = 20. Therefore *x* = 200. Choice A is half the correct number. Choices B is the result of incorrectly multiplying 75 (in 75%) by 2. Choice D is the result of an arithmetic error.

11. **The correct answer is A.** The volume of sand equals the volume of the box minus the volume of the sphere. The volume of the box is 1 cubic foot, and since the sphere has a radius of $\frac{1}{2}$, its volume is $\frac{4}{3}\pi\left(\frac{1}{2}\right)^3 = \frac{\pi}{6}$ cubic feet. The difference between these two volumes is therefore $1-\frac{\pi}{6}=\frac{6}{6}-\frac{\pi}{6}=\frac{6-\pi}{6}$ cubic feet. Choice B represents the volume of the sphere. Choice C is the result of computing the volume of the sphere incorrectly. Choice D is the result of incorrectly treating 1 as through it were π when computing the difference $1-\frac{\pi}{6}$.

12. **The correct answer is B.** For instance, if $x=\sqrt{2}$, then $x^2 = 2$, which is rational. Choice A cannot be correct because the sum of a rational number and an irrational number is always irrational. Similarly, choice C cannot be correct because the product of a nonzero rational number and an irrational number is always irrational. Choice D is incorrect because an irrational number divided by a nonzero rational number is always irrational.

13. **The correct answer is B.** Simplify the expression using the definition of negative exponents with the order of operations:

$$\begin{aligned}\left(a^{-2}-b^{-2}\right)^{-1} &= \left(\frac{1}{a^2}-\frac{1}{b^2}\right)^{-1} \\ &= \left(\frac{b^2-a^2}{a^2b^2}\right)^{-1} \\ &= \frac{a^2b^2}{b^2-a^2}\end{aligned}$$

Choice A is the result of dealing incorrectly with negative exponents. Choice C represents the reciprocal of the correct answer. Choice D is the result of incorrectly distributing the power −1 to both terms of the binomial.

14. **The correct answer is D.** Write the equation in the slope-intercept form:

$$y=-\frac{1}{2}x+2$$

The y-intercept is (0, 2) and x-intercept is (2, 0); the slope is negative, so the line falls from left to right. The only graph possessing these characteristics is the graph in choice D.

15. **The correct answer is A.** This is a quadratic function for which the coefficient of the squared term is negative; so, it opens downward. Its maximum value must occur at its vertex. To find the vertex, complete the square:

$$\begin{aligned}f(x) &= -3x^2+12x \\ &= -3\left(x^2-4x\right) \\ &= -3\left(x^2-4x+4\right)+12 \\ &= -3(x-2)^2+12\end{aligned}$$

The vertex is (2, 12). Choices B and C are incorrect because while the x-coordinate is correct, the y-coordinate is not, due to incorrect arithmetic. Choice D is incorrect because the x-coordinate of the vertex is 2, not −2.

answers practice test 2

16. The correct answer is C. Let x be the length of a side of the original square and d its diagonal, as shown:

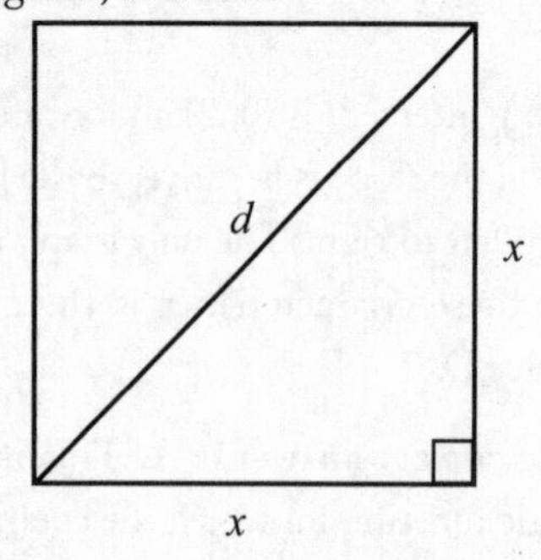

The area of the square is x^2. Using the Pythagorean theorem, we see that $x^2 + x^2 = d^2$, so that $x^2 = \frac{1}{2}d^2 = 0.5\,d^2$. Next, consider a square with side length y and whose diagonal has length $0.8d$, as shown:

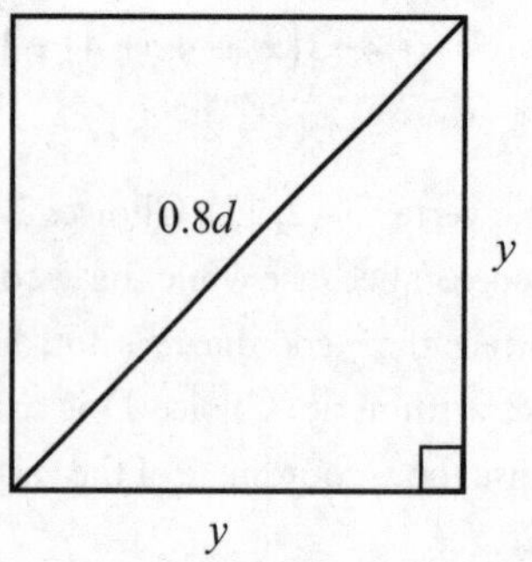

The area of the square is y^2. Using the Pythagorean theorem, we see that $y^2 + y^2 = (0.8d)^2$, so that $y^2 = \frac{0.64}{2}d^2 = 0.32d^2$. Thus, the desired ratio is $0.32\,d^2 : 0.50\,d^2$. Dividing both parts by $2d^2$ yields the equivalent ratio 0.16 : 0.25. Choice A represents the ratio of the percentages used of the original diagonal length for the two triangles. Choice C is the result of an arithmetic error. Choice D represents the ratio of the two diagonal lengths.

17. The correct answer is A. The new value is the original value on May 1 plus the increase. That is, $\$80 + 0.36(\$80) = 1.36(\$80)$. Choice B does not apply the percent correctly to the given dollar value. Choice C incorrectly shows addition, not multiplication. Choice D represents a decrease in value, not an increase.

18. The correct answer is $45w + 25x + 10y + 5z$. Multiply the weight of each plate by the number of that sized plate affixed to the barbell. Doing so yields $45w + 25x + 10y + 5z$.

19. The correct answer is $\left(-\frac{5}{2}, 0\right)$. First, the slope of the line is

$$m = \frac{\frac{1}{4} - (-2)}{-3 - \frac{3}{2}} = \frac{\frac{9}{4}}{-\frac{9}{2}} = -\frac{1}{2}$$

Using the point-slope formula with the point $\left(-3, \frac{1}{4}\right)$ yields

$$y - \frac{1}{4} = -\frac{1}{2}(x - (-3))$$

$$y = -\frac{1}{2}x - \frac{5}{4}$$

The x-intercept (when $y = 0$) is

$$0 = -\frac{1}{2}x - \frac{5}{4}$$

$$\frac{1}{2}x = -\frac{5}{4}$$

$$x = 2\left(-\frac{5}{4}\right) = -\frac{5}{2}$$

The x-intercept is $\left(-\frac{5}{2}, 0\right)$.

20. The correct answer is A. Simplify the left-side using the exponent rules:

$$\frac{\left(x^{-3}\right)^m \bullet y}{\left(y^2\right)^{-2}} = x^{12} \bullet y^n$$

$$\frac{x^{-3m} \bullet y}{y^{-4}} = x^{12} \bullet y^n$$

$$x^{-3m} \bullet y^5 = x^{12} \bullet y^n$$

Now equate the exponents of x and the exponents of y. This gives $-3m = 12$, so that $m = -4$ and $n = 5$. So $m \bullet n = -20$. Choice B is the result of incorrectly using the value of $n = 3$ instead of 5. Choice C is the result of incorrectly using the value of $m = 4$ instead of -4. Choice D is incorrect because it represents the product of the exponents on x and y, not of the values of m and n.

21. The correct answer is C. The perimeter of the shaded region is comprised of circumference of the two circles C_1 and C_2. The circumference of C_1 is $2\pi R$ and the circumference of C_2 is $2\pi\left(\frac{R}{2}\right) = \pi R$. So, the perimeter of the shaded region is $3\pi R$. Choice A represents the circumference of C_2 only. Choice B represents the circumference of C_1 only. Choice D is twice the circumference of C_1.

22. The correct answer is B. First, factor out the greatest common factor $2x$ to get

$$8x^3 - 40x^2 + 50x = 2x\left(4x^2 - 20x + 25\right)$$

Then, factor the trinomial as $(2x - 5)^2$. So the factored form is $2x(2x - 5)^2$. The other choices do not factor back to $8x^3 - 40x^2 + 50x$ when expanded.

23. The correct answer is B. Using the Pythagorean theorem yields

$$y^2 + x^2 = 11^2$$

$$y^2 + x^2 = 121$$

$$y^2 = 121 - x^2$$

$$y = \sqrt{121 - x^2}$$

Choice A is incorrect because the terms in the radicand should be added. Choice C is incorrect because the order of the terms in the difference inside the radicand should be reversed. Choice D is incorrect because the square root of a difference does not equal the difference of the square roots.

24. The correct answer is A. The area of the square is $\left(\frac{2}{3}\right)\left(\frac{2}{3}\right) = \frac{4}{9}$ square inches. Since the diameter of the inscribed circle is equal to the length of a side of the square, its radius is $\frac{1}{2}\left(\frac{2}{3}\right) = \frac{1}{3}$ inch. So the area of the circle is $\pi\left(\frac{1}{3}\right)^2 = \frac{\pi}{9}$ square inches, and the area of the shaded region is $\frac{4}{9} - \frac{\pi}{9} = \frac{4 - \pi}{9}$ square inches. Choice B represents the area of the square. Choice C is the result of subtracting the areas in the wrong order and not squaring the radius when computing the area of the circle. Choice D represents the area of the circle.

25. The correct answer is A. Substitute $-\frac{3}{2}$ for x in the expression for $f(x)$ and simplify:

$$f\left(-\frac{3}{2}\right) = \left(-\frac{3}{2}\right)\left(2 + \frac{1}{-\frac{3}{2}}\right)$$

$$= \left(-\frac{3}{2}\right)\left(2 - \frac{2}{3}\right)$$

$$= \left(-\frac{3}{2}\right)\left(\frac{4}{3}\right)$$

$$= -2$$

answers practice test 2

Choice B is the result of mistakenly computing $\left(2+\frac{1}{-\frac{3}{2}}\right)$ as $-\frac{9}{8}$. Choice C represents the input. Choice D is the result of computing $\left(2-\frac{2}{3}\right)$ by subtracting the twos rather than first getting a common denominator.

26. **The correct answer is C.** Here, $r = 5\% = \frac{5}{100} = \frac{1}{20}$ and $m = 12$. Substitute these into the given formula to obtain

$$\begin{aligned} APV &= \left(1+\frac{\frac{1}{20}}{12}\right)^{12} - 1 \\ &= \left(1+\frac{1}{20(12)}\right)^{12} - 1 \\ &= \left(\frac{20(12)+1}{20(12)}\right)^{12} - 1 \\ &= \left(\frac{241}{240}\right)^{12} - 1 \end{aligned}$$

Choice A is the result of incorrectly adding the whole number 1 to the numerator in the expression $1+\frac{1}{20(12)}$ without first getting a common denominator. Choice B is the result of subtracting the 1 inside the parentheses, not outside, in the expression $\left(1+\frac{\frac{1}{20}}{12}\right)^{12}-1$. Choice D is the result of incorrectly computing the exponentiated fraction by multiplying the fraction by the power.

27. **The correct answer is A.** Multiply the two binomials using the FOIL method to get

$$\begin{aligned} (2x-3)(4-x) &= 8x - 2x^2 - 12 + 3x \\ &= -2x^2 + 11x - 12 \end{aligned}$$

Choice B has the wrong signs on the first two terms of the expression. Choice C has the wrong coefficient on the x-term. Choice D is missing both the squared term and the constant term.

28. **The correct answer is C.** Using the multiplication rule, multiplying the four quantities to get the total time gives *smnt* nanoseconds. Choice A is incorrect because the quantities should be multiplied, not added. Choice B is incorrect because m and n should be multiplied. Choice D is incorrect because all four variables should be multiplied.

29. **The correct answer is B.** Solve for a, as follows:

$$\begin{aligned} \frac{1}{\frac{2a+b}{a} - b} &= 1 \\ \frac{2a+b}{a} - b &= 1 \\ \frac{2a+b-ba}{a} &= 1 \\ 2a+b-ba &= a \\ a - ba &= -b \\ a(1-b) &= -b \\ a &= \frac{-b}{1-b} \\ a &= \frac{b}{b-1} \end{aligned}$$

Choice A represents the reciprocal of the correct answer. Choice C represents the product of b and $(b-1)$ but should be their quotient. Choice D is the result of a factoring error when solving for b.

30. **The correct answer is A.** Start by using the distributive law and then isolate the variable, w, on one side of the inequality:

$$\begin{aligned} -2(2-3w)+1 &\le -3(w+2) \\ -4+6w+1 &\le -3w-6 \\ -3+6w &\le -3w-6 \\ 9w &\le -3 \\ w &\le -\frac{1}{3} \end{aligned}$$

Choices B and C are the result of adding 9 to both sides instead of dividing by it, and either keeping the same sign (choice B) or reversing it (choice C). Choice D has the inequality reversed.

31. The correct answer is D. First, 8% = 0.08. The total commission earned on x dollars of sales is $0.08x$. So the annual salary is $50{,}000 + 0.08x$ dollars. To earn \$120,000 in one year, this expression must equal \$120,000. This gives the equation $50{,}000 + 0.08x = 120{,}000$. Choice A is incorrect because 8% is not converted to the decimal 0.08. Choice B is incorrect because the 8% commission should be computed based on total sales (x dollars), and not include the \$50,000 base salary amount. Choice C has a similar issue and also does not convert 8% to the decimal 0.08.

32. The correct answer is B. The height at 0 seconds into the downhill run is 3,200 feet; this is the y-intercept of the line. The distance traveled down the hill after x seconds is $15x$ feet, so that the height above ground level is $3{,}200 - 15x$ feet. Choice A has the roles of the parameters 3,200 and 15 reversed. Choice C represents going uphill, not downhill, since the slope in this expression is positive. Choice D is incorrect because only x should be multiplied by -15.

33. The correct answer is C. Gather all terms to the left side, factor the resulting expression, and set each factor equal to zero:

$$9x(x-1) = -2$$
$$9x^2 - 9x + 2 = 0$$
$$(3x-2)(3x-1) = 0$$
$$x = \frac{2}{3}, \frac{1}{3}$$

Choices A and B are the result of incorrectly setting the factors on the left side equal to -2; one side of the equation must be zero to apply this property. Also, in choice B, the resulting linear equations are solved incorrectly. Choice D features the wrong signs on the solutions.

34. The correct answer is A. The linear function describing the cost of the job in terms of the number of hours, h, it takes to complete it is $C(h) = 75 + 100h$. This has y-intercept $(0, 75)$ and slope 100. In particular, the graph passes through the point $(1, 175)$. This is the case only with the graph in A.

35. The correct answer is 1 and 3. The only values you could insert into the missing cell to create a table that is NOT a function are the x-values that have already been used in other columns of the table. The reason is that a function can assign only one y-value to each value of x. Of the choices listed, the values that do this are 1 and 3.

36. The correct answer is 2. The slope of the desired line must be the negative reciprocal of the slope of the given line to be perpendicular to it. Write the given line in slope-intercept form:

$$5x = 2 - 10y$$
$$10y = 2 - 5x$$
$$y = \frac{1}{5} - \frac{1}{2}x$$

Since the slope of this line is $-\frac{1}{2}$, the slope of the desired line is 2.

37. The correct answer is B. Observe that

$$F\left(\frac{1}{x}\right) = \sqrt{\frac{1}{x} - 1} = \sqrt{\frac{1-x}{x}}$$
$$F(x+1) = \sqrt{(x+1) - 1} = \sqrt{x}$$

So

$$F\left(\frac{1}{x}\right) \cdot F(x+1) = \sqrt{\frac{1-x}{x}} \cdot \sqrt{x}$$
$$= \frac{\sqrt{1-x}}{\cancel{\sqrt{x}}} \cdot \cancel{\sqrt{x}}$$
$$= \sqrt{1-x}$$

Choice A represents the value of $F(x+1)$. Choice C is an attempt at computing just $F\left(\frac{1}{x}\right)$, but incorrectly splits up the radicand of the difference as the difference of the radicals. Choice D features the order of the terms in the difference in the radicand reversed.

38. **The correct answer is D.** If $y > 1$, then $y^2 = y \cdot y$ must be greater than 1 because the product of two rational numbers greater than one must be greater than one. Choice A can be less than 1 if you take $x = \frac{3}{4}$ and $y = \frac{5}{4}$. Choice B is always less than 1 because the choices for the numerator are all less than all choices for the denominator. Choice C can be less than 1 if you take $x = \frac{3}{4}$ and $y = \frac{5}{4}$.

39. **The correct answer is 1.14×10^9.** Multiply and then convert to proper scientific notation:

$$\left(9.5\times10^4\right)\left(1.2\times10^3\right)(10) = 11.4\times10^8$$
$$= 1.14\times10^9$$

40. **The correct answer is B.** The cost for B biscotti is $0.75B$ dollars. Adding this to the cost of the coffee gives a total bill of $1.95 + 0.75B$ dollars. This must be greater than or equal to 5 for Jill to be able to pay using a credit card. So the desired inequality is $1.95 + 0.75B \geq 5$. Choice A is almost correct, but does not allow for the possibility that the bill equal \$5 exactly. Choice C is incorrect because you should not multiply 1.95 times 0.75, and it does not allow for the possibility that the bill equal \$5 exactly. Choice D is incorrect because you should not multiply 1.95 times 0.75.

41. **The correct answer is C.** The number of megabytes of space used for V videos is obtained by multiplying the size of each video by the number of videos; doing so yields $130V$. Similarly, the number of megabytes of space used for S songs is $6S$, and the number of megabytes of space used for P photos is $3P$. The sum of these quantities, namely $130V + 6S + 3P$, must be less than or equal to 2,000. This yields the inequality $130V + 6S + 3P \leq 2{,}000$. Choice A is incorrect because each number of megabytes represented by the variables V, S, and P should be multiplied by the number of that particular medium, and the results should be added, not multiplied. Choice B is incorrect because the three terms in parentheses on the left-side should be added, not multiplied. Choice D is incorrect because each number of megabytes represented by the variables V, S, and P should be multiplied by the number of that particular medium.

42. **The correct answer is $\frac{9}{100}$.** Multiply the two percentages to solve. $(0.60)(0.15) = 0.09$. This is equivalent to $\frac{9}{100}$.

43. **The correct answer is 27.** Since the fraction of losses is $\frac{1}{4}$, it follows that the fraction of wins is $\frac{3}{4}$. So the number of wins in 36 games is $\frac{3}{4}(36) = 27$.

44. **The correct answer is A.** The window is an equilateral triangle because all three sides are congruent. Since the sides of the window are in a 1:5 correspondence, the length of the sides of the window must be 3 feet. Using the fact that the area of an equilateral triangle with side length s is $\frac{s^2\sqrt{3}}{4}$ with $s = 3$ feet, we see that the area of the window is $\frac{9\sqrt{3}}{4}$ square feet. Choice B is the result of using the wrong formula for the area of an equilateral triangle. Choice C is incorrect because the side length should be squared in the formula. Choice D is the result of forgetting to multiply by $\sqrt{3}$.

45. **The correct answer is B.** The mean of the set $\{-98, -96, \ldots, -2\}$ is $\frac{(-98)+(-2)}{2} = -50$. The number of terms in the list is 49. So the sum of the terms is $-50(49) = -2{,}450$. Choices A, C, and D are incorrect because the number of terms in the list is 49, not 50, 48, or 47, respectively.

46. The correct answer is B. Substitute $\frac{1}{4}t^{\frac{3}{2}}$ in for the radius r in the surface area formula $S = 4\pi r^2$ yields the formula:

$$S = 4\pi\left(\frac{1}{4}t^{\frac{3}{2}}\right)^2$$
$$= 4\pi \cdot \frac{1}{16}t^3$$
$$= \frac{\pi}{4}t^3$$

Choice A represents the volume, not the surface area. Choice C is the result of incorrectly multiplying $\frac{1}{4}$ by the power 2 and adding the powers (instead of multiplying) when simplifying the expression $\left(t^{\frac{3}{2}}\right)^2$. Choice D is the result of adding the powers (instead of multiplying) when simplifying the expression $\left(t^{\frac{3}{2}}\right)^2$.

Science

1. A	**8.** D	**15.** C	**22.** C	**29.** C
2. C	**9.** >	**16.** D	**23.** B	**30.** B
3. B	**10.** D	**17.** B	**24.** D	**31.** D
4. C	**11.** 20 mL	**18.** C	**25.** A	**32.** C
5. D	**12.** B	**19.** D	**26.** North Pacific Gyre	**33.** D
6. C	**13.** B	**20.** B	**27.** A	**34.** A
7. A	**14.** A	**21.** A	**28.** C	**35.** D

1. **The correct answer is A.** The passage states that the fluke lives its adult life in the liver of its definitive host. The passage also states that in its intermediate hosts, the fluke is a larva. The fluke infects the nervous system (choice B) of the ant, which the passage states is its second intermediate host. The fluke spends its larval stage (choice C) in *two* intermediate hosts—the snail and the ant. The fluke first hatches from an egg (choice D) in the snail, which the passage states is its first intermediate host.

2. **The correct answer is C.** The correct answer may seem counterintuitive because solids (such as sugar) dissolve more quickly in hot liquids than in cold liquids, but when it comes to solubility, most gases behave in the opposite way to solids. At lower temperatures, the soda is fizzy and full of gas bubbles, which suggests that there is a lot of gas dissolved in it. At higher temperatures, the soda is flat and not very bubbly, suggesting that there is less gas dissolved in it. Therefore, the solubility of gases decreases as temperature increases. The solubility of gases and solids trends in opposite ways as temperature increases, so choices A and B are incorrect. Choice D is incorrect because the solubility of solids increases as temperature increases.

3. **The correct answer is B.** As temperature increases, the sugar dissolves completely in the water, which must mean that the kinetic energy of the solvent (water) is greater than the forces that hold the solute (sugar) molecules together. Choice A confuses the solute and solvent, as water does not dissolve in sugar, so it is incorrect. As temperature increases, the soda seems flat and gas bubbles are few, which suggests that much of the gas has escaped and is no longer dissolved in the solution (the soda). Thus, the kinetic energy of the gas must be high enough for it to escape from the soda at higher temperatures; thus choice C is incorrect. Choice D mistakenly identifies the water as the solute.

4. **The correct answer is C.** Archaea were originally classified as prokaryotes because, like bacteria, they do not have a nucleus or other membrane-bound organelles. The passage states that some eukaryotes have only one cell. Therefore, being single-celled (choice A) is not a characteristic that is unique to the prokaryotes. Lacking a nucleus (choice B) and surviving in extreme environments (choice D) are characteristics of archaea, but they are not characteristics that they have in common with all prokaryotes.

5. **The correct answer is D.** The passage defines an extreme environment as an environment with conditions that would kill most organisms. In other words, it is a location that is deadly to most organisms. Locations deep under the ocean's surface (choice A)

and with very high or low temperatures (choice C) are *examples* of extreme environments, but they are not *general descriptions* of an extreme environment. Although extreme environments are found all over the world, choice B does not explain what an extreme environment is.

6. **The correct answer is C.** Ultima Thule is not spherical but is shaped like a flattened disk attached to a lumpy walnut. It is also located in the Kuiper belt with many objects of similar size. Therefore it does not meet requirements 2 or 3 for a planet and is a Kuiper belt object. Because Ultima Thule does not meet requirements 2 or 3, it cannot be classified as a planet (choice A) or a dwarf planet (choice B). Although the *New Horizons* spacecraft flew by it, Ultima Thule is not a spacecraft (choice D)—it is a natural object in the solar system.

7. **The correct answer is A.** Dark-skinned people living near the equator are less likely to have Vitamin D deficiency, which means that they get enough sunlight to make the Vitamin D they need. Despite having skin that evolved to block UV radiation, the year-round sunlight at the equator allows them to make enough Vitamin D. Choice B is incorrect because dark-skinned people are less likely to get skin cancer than pale-skinned people living at the same latitude because dark skin is better at blocking UV radiation. If pale skin did not block UV radiation as well as scientists thought (choice C), it would be even easier for them to make Vitamin D, and they would not have higher rates of Vitamin D deficiency. Choice D is incorrect because the passage states that all human skin cells can make Vitamin D. Just because a person is deficient in Vitamin D doesn't mean that they have *no* Vitamin D in their bodies; they just don't have enough. In addition, not all people living in northern latitudes have a Vitamin D deficiency, so at least some people have skin cells that can make Vitamin D.

8. **The correct answer is D.** The person most likely to be deficient in Vitamin D is the one whose skin will be exposed to the least amount of sunlight and UV radiation. People who work outside such as a farmer (choice A) or a fisherman (choice B) and live near the equator will get the most sunlight exposure. People who work inside such as a teacher or lawyer and live in northern latitudes will get the least sunlight exposure, so choices C and D are both possible. Dark skin will block more UV radiation than pale skin, so choice D will receive the least UV radiation out of all the choices and be the most likely to have Vitamin D deficiency.

9. **The correct answer is >.** From the table, you can see that absorbance increases as concentration increases. So for a dye solution with a concentration of 0.5 mol/L, which is greater than any of the concentrations in the table, the absorbance should be greater than the largest absorbance value in the table, which is 0.284.

10. **The correct answer is D.** The cactus grows spines only in the presence of cattle, which are herbivores (plant-eaters) that can attack it. This suggests that the cactus has the induced defense of spines to protect it from predators. The flowering bush scenario (choice A) does not suggest induced defenses because there is no mention of herbivores in this scenario. The bush likely flowers earlier in the valley because the valley gets warmer earlier in the year than the mountaintop. The tree scenario (choice B) does not suggest induced defenses because the tree produces its defense (toxic leaves) all the time, whether or not herbivores are present. The grass scenario (choice C) describes only how widely the seed pods are

spread, not where the seed pods are produced. It is implied that seed pods are produced by the grass all the time, and that the spikes may be an adaptation to help it spread its seeds rather than a defense.

11. **The correct answer is 20 mL.** Before the rock is placed in the cylinder, the water volume is 30 mL. The 20, 40, and 60 mL marks are labeled and there are 20 marks between each pair of labeled marks, which means that each labeled mark is 20mL apart. After the rock is placed in the cylinder, the water volume goes up to 50 mL (10 marks below the labeled 60 mL mark). An object that is completely submerged in water will increase the volume reading by the same amount as its own volume. Therefore the difference in volume readings before and after the rock is added to the water is the volume of the rock: 50 mL – 30 mL = 20 mL.

12. **The correct answer is B.** For this method of volume determination to work, the object must sink completely underwater so that it can displace a volume of water equal to its volume. For the object to sink completely, it must be denser than water. Objects that are less dense than water will float, so some part of the object will be above the water. Choice A is incorrect because less dense objects will not sink. Choice C is incorrect because the fact that denser objects will sink is the reason this method works. Choice D is incorrect because denser objects will sink, not float.

13. **The correct answer is B.** Temperature does not increase at a constant rate with depth within the earth. If this were true, the graph would be a straight line. Instead, the line changes steepness several times in the graph, so choice A is incorrect. The temperature increases much more quickly with depth in the crust than in the outer core. If you turn the graph sideways you can see that the line shoots up steeply in the crust, while being more level in the outer core. The maximum temperature in the mantle is around 3,500°C, not 5,000°C (choice C). The minimum temperature in the inner core is around 4,500°C, not 3,500°C (choice D).

14. **The correct answer is A.** The athletes chopped up the algae with their boats while they were practicing for their events. This caused the cells at the edges of the torn pieces of algae to undergo meiosis and produce spores. The spores grew into more algae, leading to the algal bloom. Choice B is incorrect because the fact that there had never been an algal bloom this big in Qingdao Bay supports the conclusion that the athletes caused the algal bloom, but it does not explain how they did it. Nowhere in the passage does it mention that the athlete's boats carried algae spores, so choice C cannot be correct. Choice D is incorrect because the athletes didn't merely spread the algae around the bay, they cut it up into small pieces that grew into more algae.

15. **The correct answer is C.** The key characteristic of an oscillating object (other than regular back-and-forth motion) is being attached at one end to an unmoving support. So while the ant (choice A), ball (choice B), and shuttle bus (choice D) might display back-and-forth motion, they are not attached at one end to a stationary support. They are free to move in all directions, so they are not oscillating objects. In addition, because all three are free to move in all directions, their motion is not perfectly regular. In contrast, a playground swing is attached at the top to an unmoving support, and the child moves back and forth in a predictable, regular pattern set by the length of the swing chain.

16. **The correct answer is D.** The difference between a vacuum and an ordinary environment like a classroom is the presence of air.

Outside of a vacuum, air molecules apply drag on an object, slowing it down and eventually stopping its motion completely. Choice A is incorrect because there are no air particles in a vacuum. Choice B cannot be correct because an object keeps moving in a vacuum, which means that it's not the atoms within an object that slow it down. The passage states that in air, an object slows down and does not keep moving, so choice C cannot be correct either.

17. **The correct answer is B.** The map shows that Los Angeles is located on the Pacific Plate and San Francisco is located on the North American Plate. The arrows on the map show that the Pacific Plate is moving to the north, toward San Francisco and Canada, while the North American Plate is moving to the south, toward Los Angeles and Mexico. Since the two cities are moving toward each other, in a million years they will be closer together. You can do some quick math to confirm this. The plates move 25 millimeters (mm) per year, so in 1,000,000 years they will be 25,000,000 mm closer. Since the question provides the distance between San Francisco and Los Angeles in kilometers, convert mm to km to find their relative positions in 1,000,000 years. Remember, 1 kilometer (km) = 1,000 meters (m), and 1 m = 1,000 mm. So if 25,000,000 mm + 1 m/1,000 mm = 25,000 m, then 25,000 m + 1 km/1,000 m = 25 km. This is far less than the distance that currently separates the two cities (560 km), so they will be closer together but will not have met up yet. Choice A is incorrect because Los Angeles is moving toward Canada. Choice C is incorrect because the two cities are moving toward each other. Choice D is incorrect because San Francisco is moving toward Mexico.

18. **The correct answer is C.** The sodium ion (Na^+) is a sodium atom (Na) that has lost its outermost electron. Losing this outermost electron gives Na^+ a completely filled outer electron shell and thus a noble gas electron configuration. This is why it is so difficult to remove a valence electron from Na^+ and why its ionization energy is so high. The opposite of choice A is true because with its noble gas electron configuration, Na^+ is much more stable than Na. Choice B is also not true because Na^+ is formed when Na loses an electron, which means that it has fewer total electrons than Na. Choice D is incorrect because Na^+ has a noble gas electron configuration, which means that it has a fully filled outer electron shell.

19. **The correct answer is D.** Recall that the series of reactions of Cl and O_3 are as follows:

$$Cl + O_3 \rightarrow ClO + O_2$$

$$ClO + O \rightarrow Cl + O_2$$

The first step of the analogous process for Br is provided:

$$Br + O_3 \rightarrow BrO + O_2$$

Since the processes for Br and Cl are analogous, simply substitute Br for Cl in the final reaction to get the correct answer:

$$BrO + O \rightarrow Br + O_2$$

$CH_3Br \rightarrow CH_3 + Br$ (choice A) is the initial reaction that breaks down methyl bromide to generate Br. $Br + O_2 \rightarrow BrO + O$ (choice B) is the reverse of the correct equation and does not have Br as one of the products. $BrO + O_3 \rightarrow Br + 2O_2$ (choice C) is incorrect because ozone does not react with BrO.

20. **The correct answer is B.** The passage says that dinosaurs are defined by a hole in the hip socket, which means that only dinosaurs have his characteristic. Therefore, if birds are dinosaurs, they must have a hole in the hip socket that classifies them as dinosaurs. A hole in the lower jaw (choice A) defines

answers practice test 2

archosaurs. This is the larger group that includes dinosaurs, so all archosaurs, not just dinosaurs, have this feature. A wing supported by the fourth finger (choice C) defines pterosaurs. Only pterosaurs have this characteristic, not dinosaurs. Two rows of bony plates on the back (choice D) defines crocodiles, not dinosaurs.

21. **The correct answer is A.** The rocket fuel with the highest specific impulse has the most thrust per kilogram burned. This means that a smaller amount of this fuel will provide more thrust than any other fuel. To keep the weight of the rocket to a minimum but thrust at a maximum, the engineers should use the smallest amount of fuel possible that provides the greatest amount of thrust. Therefore, the engineers should use the fuel with the greatest specific impulse, which is liquid fluorine (F) plus liquid hydrogen (H_2). The other choices are incorrect because they all have specific impulses that are less than that of liquid F + liquid H_2.

22. **The correct answer is C.** Igneous rocks with silica content between 52% and 66% are intermediate rocks. The presence of plagioclase feldspar and quartz confirms that the rock is intermediate. The color of the rock isn't given, but you don't need that information to determine the correct answer since you already have two pieces of data that confirm its classification. Ultramafic (choice A) and mafic (choice B) rocks contain less than 60% silica. Felsic (choice D) rocks contain more than 66% silica.

23. **The correct answer is B.** The graph shows that a tire that starts at 30 psi at 68°F goes up to around 32 psi at 90°F. This tire is only at 30 psi at 90°F, so you have to add 2 psi to the tire to get it up to 32 psi. This way, when it cools to 68°F, tire pressure will decrease to 30 psi. If you add no air (choice A) while the tire is currently at 30 psi, when it cools to 68°F, tire pressure will decrease to less than 30 psi (to 28 psi, to be exact). Adding 4 psi (choice C) and 6 psi (choice D) will cause tire pressures of 32 psi and 34 psi at 68°F, respectively.

24. **The correct answer is D.** In the table, as genome size increases, the number of genes usually increases. There is one exception: the mouse has a slightly smaller genome than humans, but slightly more genes. Choices A and B are incorrect because the largest genome belongs to the simple rice plant. Plants are much simpler structurally than animals, and they don't move or think, so their behaviors are much simpler as well. Choice C is incorrect because the smallest genome given in the table is for *Escherichia coli*, which is a bacterium, not a fungus.

25. **The correct answer is D.** If you draw a line down the back of a goldfish, the parts to either side of that line are identical. Each side has an eye, three sets of fins, and half of the tail fin. You can't draw a line anywhere else that will create two identical mirror-image halves. Therefore, goldfish have bilateral symmetry. All of the other animals display radial symmetry. Even if you are unfamiliar with some of the animals listed, a goldfish is most likely familiar to you. Since it has bilateral symmetry, none of the other answers can be correct.

26. **The correct answer is the North Pacific Gyre.** The west coast of North America is on the North Pacific Ocean. Therefore, any lightweight waste like a plastic bottle is most likely to be trapped in the North Pacific Gyre. The compass at the bottom of the map can help you orient yourself.

27. **The correct answer is A.** The passage states that three things control ocean currents: wind, Earth's rotation, and continental coastlines. The Indian Gyre is bounded by

the east coast of Africa, the west coast of Australia, and the south coast of Asia. These coastlines help control the shape of the Indian Gyre. It is the west, not east, coast of Australia (choice B) that helps control the Indian Gyre. It is Earth's rotation, not its orbit (choice C), that controls ocean currents. Debris from land (choice D) is moved by ocean currents, not the other way around.

28. **The correct answer is C.** Calcium ions (Ca^{2+}) bind to troponin and cause troponin to unblock actin's myosin-binding site. Ca^{2+} does not directly affect any of the other processes. Choice A is incorrect because myosin automatically binds to actin once actin's binding site is unblocked. Choice B is incorrect because ATP binding to myosin causes it to release actin. Choice D is incorrect because myosin pulls the thin filament toward it after it binds to actin.

29. **The correct answer is C.** In this equilibrium system, heat is a product. If more heat is added to the equilibrium system, the equilibrium will shift to the left, in the reverse direction, producing more H_2 and I_2, and decreasing both the concentration of HI and the amount of heat. Choices A and B are incorrect because the equilibrium will shift to the left. Choice D is incorrect because although the equilibrium will shift to the left, the amount of heat will decrease, not increase.

30. **The correct answer is B.** If two traits are always found together in a person, it means that their genes are always passed on together, and *not* passed on independently, thereby eliminating choice A as a correct answer. This suggests that these genes are close together on the same chromosome and show genetic linkage, so choice D is incorrect. Therefore they do not follow the law of independent assortment, and choice C can be eliminated as a correct answer.

31. **The correct answer is D.** The easiest way to introduce error into a flame test is to contaminate the solution that is being heated. Using pure water (choice A), cleaning the loop between solutions (choice B), and using different flames for different solutions (choice C) are all precautions that will avoid the chances of contamination. However, using a copper loop means that the copper in the loop will be heated along with the solution. The passage states that copper gives off a green color when it is heated, which could cover up the color of the solution's flame.

32. **The correct answer is C.** The experiment shows that death-feigning intensity varies depending on an individual beetle's flight skills. So given the option of escape or death-feigning, they will choose escape if they are better fliers, presumably since better fliers have a greater chance of escaping. Those beetles that are less likely to escape through flight will feign death. Since successful escapes are not recorded in the experiment, choice A is not a valid conclusion. The results state that beetles with moderate flight skills still play dead for moderate amounts of time, making choice B an invalid conclusion. The passage also states that some beetles clearly choose death-feigning instead of flight, making choice D an incorrect conclusion as well.

33. **The correct answer is D.** The graph shows that the paper nautilus's swimming speed slowly increases until a top speed of 9 m/s is recorded at a depth of 25 m. As depth increases further, its swimming speed starts to decrease again. A negative correlation (choice A) between depth and swim speed would mean that swimming speed steadily decreases as depth increases. A positive correlation (choice B) between depth and swim speed would mean that swimming speed steadily increases as depth increases. Choice

C is possible, but there is no way to tell from the graph if paper nautilus do not swim below 40 m.

34. The correct answer is A. The passage states that residence times are shorter in reservoirs that can easily flow or evaporate and longer in ones that cannot easily move or change. Rivers can flow, and they are open to the atmosphere, so they can evaporate easily as well. Ice caps, in contrast, are solid and thick, so they cannot easily move or change. This supports the assumption that water's residence time in an ice cap is longer than that in a river. The other choices do not explain why residence time varies between reservoirs.

35. The correct answer is D. Rotational velocity is represented by ω, so choices A and B can be eliminated as correct answers right from the start. Displacement in rotational motion is represented by θ, so choice C cannot be correct either. This leaves choice D as the only possible correct answer. When a value is said to equal some variable per unit time, it means that you divide that variable by time.

Social Studies

1. B	**8.** Necessary and Proper	**15.** B	**22.** B	**29.** C
2. A	**9.** state	**16.** B	**23.** D	**30.** A
3. D	**10.** D	**17.** 2008	**24.** A	**31.** monopoly
4. D	**11.** three-fifths	**18.** B	**25.** distorted (A)	**32.** A
5. A	**12.** A	**19.** D	**26.** B	**33.** See explanation.
6. B	**13.** See explanation.	**20.** B	**27.** C	**34.** A
7. A	**14.** A	**21.** A	**28.** A	**35.** A

1. **The correct answer is B.** The chart describes British actions following the French and Indian War, in which the crown incurred massive debt. Prior to the war Britain had practiced indifference, or salutary neglect, towards the colonists, especially regarding enforcement of taxation. The chart does not present information regarding American reactions or rationale, nor does it contain information regarding colonial response or compromise between the two parties, so choices A and C are incorrect. Not all the actions listed in the chart collected revenue, including the Proclamation Act and the Writs of Assistance, so choice D is incorrect.

2. **The correct answer is A.** The Bay of Pigs was a failed CIA invasion of Cuba in 1961 during which Cuban exiles were trained in an attempt to overthrow the government of Fidel Castro. The U-2 Incident (choice B), the Cuban Missile Crisis (choice C), and the Haitian Revolution (choice D) were not CIA missions, nor did any of the events require the organization of exile resistance or collection of intelligence about Cuban forces.

3. **The correct answer is D.** Washington's quote reflects his belief that the tax was constitutional and that the government has the authority to enforce said tax by any means necessary, including military force in the face of an insurrection. Washington cites the Constitution, not the nation's debt (choice A) as justification for use of the militia. Washington is on the side of the government, not the rebellion, and is focused on justification for use of the military, not legislation, so choices B and C are incorrect.

4. **The correct answer is D.** The Watergate Scandal forced President Nixon to resign the office of the Presidency, not only making Gerald Ford president but also creating a cloud of turmoil around the oval office. Ford's remarks are an attempt to create trust during a period of cynicism towards government. The events listed in choices A, B, and C do not make sense because Ford's message is in the wake of the Watergate Scandal and directly tied to Nixon's resignation.

5. **The correct answer is A.** Both court cases have different majority opinions on the role of equality within society, more specifically the belief about segregation and its legal place in society. Choice B is incorrect because school is not the focus of both passages, and in the second passage it is an example to showcase the greater issue of segregation in society. Choice C is incorrect because the passages reflect a growing challenge to inequity as the first passage justifies it, while the second contests it. Choice D is incorrect because cultural values are not

debated; they are cited only as an example within the greater context of segregation.

6. **The correct answer is B.** Both passages reflect the struggles within society stemming from segregation and racism, specifically what rights African Americans have. The first passage presupposes that African Americans are inferior and therefore should not expect access to the same facilities as whites, whereas the second passage asserts that African Americans should have equal access to the same facilities as whites, with a focus on access to schools. Schooling (choice A) is not the focus of the first passage, only the second. The existence of racism in society (choice C) is not being debated; rather, both passages acknowledge its existence. Neither passage questions the court's right to determine the case (choice D); that a majority opinion was given proves the court's belief that it has exercised its duty in determining the Constitution's position on the issue.

7. **The correct answer is A.** Based on the definition of opportunity cost, Alphonso would be giving up four bus tickets if he bought one burger. Choice B is incorrect because one bus ticket is less than a burger, so two burgers would cost $16, while one bus ticket is only $2. Choice C is incorrect because the definition of opportunity cost is not properly defined. Choice D is incorrect because the definition of opportunity cost is incorrect even though the math is correct.

8. **The correct answer is *Necessary and Proper*.** The "Necessary and Proper" clause referenced in *McCulloch v. Maryland* (1819) was established in the Constitution, giving Congress the ability to make laws required for the exercise of its other powers that are implied by the Constitution, such as the creation of a national bank in the case.

9. **The correct answer is *state*.** The Confederate States of America placed a heavy emphasis on states' rights, including a declaration that each state is sovereign and independent.

10. **The correct answer is D.** The Confederate States Constitution continued the model of the United States Constitution with regard to the legislative branch, consisting of two houses (Senate and House of Representatives) according to Article I, Section I. Choices A and B are incorrect because each Constitution places a different emphasis on power; the United States Constitution places emphasis on the federal government, whereas the Confederate States of America are focused on states' rights. Choice C is incorrect because the Confederate States continued to utilize the institution of slavery instead of placing restrictions on it, as the United States Constitution did in 1865 with the ratification of the Thirteenth Amendment.

11. **The correct answer is *three-fifths*.** The three-fifths compromise was agreed upon during the Constitutional Convention to appease southern states over their large slave population not being represented in congressional seats. Article I, Section I (3) references the compromise and includes it as part of counting for representation and taxes.

12. **The correct answer is A.** The passage is referencing a period of xenophobia and anxiety known as the Red Scare in post-WWI America. The passage relates the bombings and threats that set in motion many actions by the United States government to address public concern. The passage merely mentions the FBI being created (choice B) and does not focus on the bureau, only its actions. Choice C is incorrect because the passage addresses public reaction to the arrests, not a call for them. Choice D is incorrect because the passage does not imply the arrests were unwarranted or unjust.

13. **The correct answer is near India.** This is where the map shows the most density.

14. **The correct answer is A.** The Northeast has the greatest population density, or the most people concentrated in the smallest area as denoted by the darker color on the map. Choices B, C, and D are lighter in color, denoting a lower population density.

15. **The correct answer is B.** The chart reflects separation of powers, as each branch is given a different responsibility or power within the federal government. The system of checks and balances (choice A) involves how each branch checks the other, such as using a veto, which is not represented in the chart. Federalism (choice C) involves the shared responsibilities and powers of both the federal and state government, which is beyond the scope of the chart. The chart is not focused on the role of the Judicial Branch, which includes judicial review (choice D), but the entire federal government under the United States Constitution.

16. **The correct answer is B.** The higher vote total in the Electoral College column is what determines the Presidency in the United States. Even though Hillary Clinton had a higher number of popular votes and a higher vote percentage, Donald Trump was elected President. Choices A, C, and D cannot be correct because only the electoral votes determine the President.

17. **The correct answer is *2008*.** The graph shows the number of employed civilians, and it takes the largest drop between the years 2007 and 2009, meaning more people became unemployed during this period than at any other time on the graph.

18. **The correct answer is B.** The graph shows a relationship between the start of a recession and an increase in unemployment during and even after the recession ends. That unemployment decreases directly before a recession (choice A) is not supported by the graph, as years directly before a recession, such as in 2000, show decreases in employment from the previous year. The graph does not support the conclusion that employment increases to prerecession rates after a recession ends (choice C), as it shows that employment never again reaches prerecession levels. The graph also indicates that unemployment increases are not limited to times after a recession (choice D), for example in 1996.

19. **The correct answer is D.** Facebook, used by 70% of all ages, is the most utilized news source according to the chart. Although CNN (choice A), local TV (choice B), and

Fox News (choice C) have a more balanced age differentiation, they have a less total percentage of users.

20. **The correct answer is B.** Local TV news is most watched by the baby boomer generation, which is made up of people over the age of 55. CNN (choice A), Fox News (choice C), and MSNBC (choice D) do not have the highest viewing percentage for adults over 55 years old.

21. **The correct answer is A.** The discrepancy in use of Facebook largely falls on recent generations' focus on use of the internet over cable or local television programs. The claim that older generations are unwilling to utilize resources such as the internet (choice B) cannot be supported by the graph, as 2% of users over the age 51 reported using the site. News bias is present in many sites or television shows, making it difficult to support the claim that only one generation is aware of bias while another is not (choice C). The claim that Facebook is a relatively new source of media and only younger generations are aware of it (choice D) cannot be supported by the graph, as 2% of users over the age 51 reported using the site.

22. **The correct answer is B.** The inflation rate is the rate at which the price of goods is at its highest, meaning the lowest price of a good would correlate with the lowest spike in the graph, in this case, the early 1920s. According to the spikes on the graph, inflation was at its highest in the late 1910s (choice A) and the late 1940s (choice D), making the cost of goods very high. Although the prices of goods were low in the early 1930s (choice C), they were not as low as in the early 1920s.

23. **The correct answer is D.** Judicial review was established by John Marshall's ruling in *Marbury v. Madison*. Legislative powers (choice A) were not established by the ruling; they were only made to adhere to the system of checks and balances protected by judicial review. *Marbury v. Madison* did not establish separation of powers (choice B); rather, it provided the judicial branch a strong check within the system of checks and balances established by the Constitution. Federalism (choice C) is a system of checks and balances between federal and state powers, whereas *Marbury v. Madison* was focused on the powers of the Court over other federal branches.

24. **The correct answer is A.** *Marbury v. Madison* established the principle of judicial review and declared the Supreme Court the authority on the Constitution, including the constitutionality of laws created by other bodies of government. Although it has the power to declare the constitutionality of laws, the Court does not have the power to write laws (choice B) or to decide which acts can be brought before Congress (choice C). The Court has the ability to rule on the constitutionality of laws, but its rulings cannot extend above and beyond the laws of the Constitution (choice D).

25. **The correct answer is distorted (A).** The result of twisting or altering something out of its true, natural, or original state is known as geographic distortion, which is what happens when a map attempts to show physical or spatial features. In geography, diffusion (choice B) is the process of spread of a feature or trend from one place to another over time; distribution (choice C) is the arrangement of something across Earth's surface; and distance decay (choice D) occurs when contact between two groups diminishes because of the distance between them.

26. **The correct answer is B.** Lincoln's mention of "four score and seven years" is a direct time reference to the signing of the Declaration of Independence, which is further

underscored by his mention of liberty and equality. The time and the focus of the passage were not connected to Puritan values or their arrival (choice A). The Constitution (choice C) was not, at that point, considered a document of equality because of its position on slavery. Lincoln was focused on the liberty and equality of the nation as a whole, not on the creation of the Confederate States of America (choice D) or recognizing the legitimacy of southern secession; instead, he focused on the tolls that secession took on the nation.

27. **The correct answer is C.** Total Health had the greatest increase, growing by over $12,000 on average over the four years. Although Medicaid (choice A) grew at a large rate, that total would be added into the total amount of Health, making Total Health the overall greatest increase. Children's Health Insurance (choice B) grew at a small rate. Although Medicare (choice D) grew at very high rate of around $9,000 per year, it was not as high as Total Health; there was a year (1999) that Medicare decreased as well.

28. **The correct answer is A.** According to the Amendment, if an official has not been President for more than two years prior to being elected (in the case of an assassination or resignation), that person can continue to run for two more elected terms. Nonconsecutive terms (choice B) would still total two, four-year terms and, under the Amendment, would disqualify a person from running. Per the Amendment, a previous term as President (choice C) would remain part of the total number of terms and would prevent a person from running. Being a member of Congress (choice D) has no bearing on the Amendment or terms of office.

29. **The correct answer is C.** The amendment states a person can hold two terms if they have not already served more than two years. Each term is four years, making the allowed total (two) four-year terms plus two years, equaling ten total years. Seven (choice A), eight (choice B), and twelve (choice D) years do not satisfy the requirements allocated by the amendment.

30. **The correct answer is A.** A typical example of a supply and demand curve would show the elements that curve and concave to represent slope and equilibrium. Elements that curve and concave to represent slope and equilibrium would not reflect the concepts of total revenue (choice B) or consumer surplus (choice C). A graph using elements that curve and concave to represent slope and equilibrium does not show what is given up for something else (choice D), but how supply and demand affect one another.

31. **The correct answer is *monopoly*.** The image shows the vast number of railroads that Rockefeller controlled during the Gilded Age. It refers to his position as a monopolist and his company Standard Oil's stranglehold on the oil industry.

32. **The correct answer is A.** Family is the first agent of socialization that we encounter, and familial beliefs are placed upon us at a very young age, often to the extent of telling us what to believe until we can develop beliefs for ourselves.

33. **The correct answer is shown below.** The area known as the Middle East is in the region that lies between Africa, Europe, and parts of Northern and Southeast Asia, which includes the countries Afghanistan, Jordan, Iran, Israel, Lebanon, Kuwait, Pakistan, Qatar, Saudi Arabia, and Turkey.

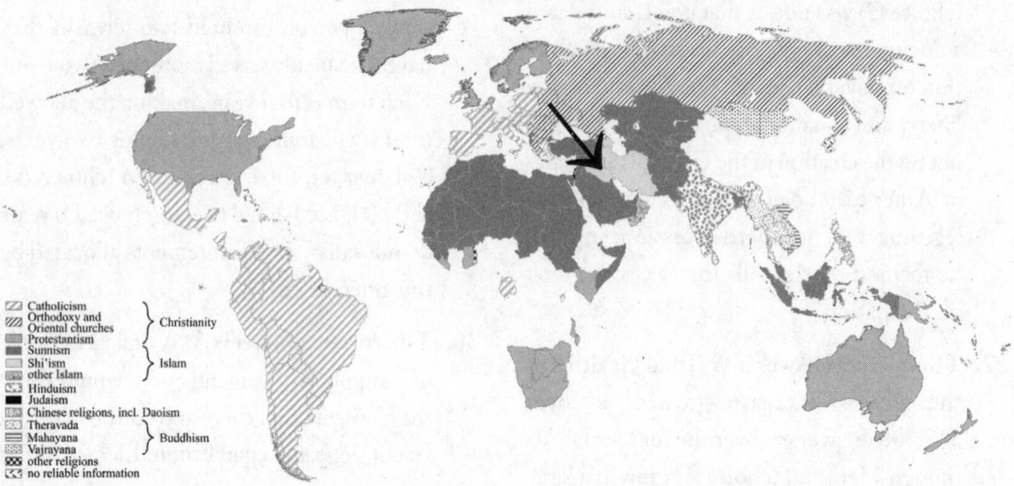

34. **The correct answer is A.** North and South America are found in the Western Hemisphere where, according to the map, Christian religions are practiced the most frequently, although many other religions are practiced on both continents. Islam (choice B) and Buddhism (choice C) are practiced in the Western Hemisphere but, according to the map, neither is practiced in as large numbers as Christianity.

35. **The correct answer is A.** The image represents an iron triangle, or a relationship between interest groups, congressional committees, and the bureaucracy to make policy while expanding their power base. While super PACs (choice B), advocacy groups (choice C), and party politics (choice D) can all be a part of the triangle, the entire relationship is known as the iron triangle.

ARE YOU READY TO TAKE THE GED® TEST?

Now that you have spent a great deal of time and effort studying for the GED® test and taking this Practice Test, hopefully you are well-prepared to take the GED® test. But, it's best to make sure that you are completely ready. Check your scores from this Practice Test on the table below to see where you stand.

	All Set—Well-Prepared	Possibly Ready	Need More Preparation
Reasoning Through Language Arts	37–49	25–36	0–24
Mathematical Reasoning	34–36	23–33	0–22
Science	26–33	18–25	0–17
Social Studies	26–35	18–25	0–17

If your scores are in the "All Set—Well-Prepared" column, you are probably ready to take the actual GED® test, and you should apply to take the test soon. If some of your scores are in the "Possibly Ready" column, you should focus your study on those areas where you need to improve most. "Possibly Ready" means that you are probably ready enough to earn a GED® diploma, but it's not a bad idea to spend a little more time brushing up and improving your chances to pass the actual GED® test.

If any of your scores fell in the lowest category, take more time to review the pertinent chapters in this book—and in any high school text books, if necessary. Good luck!

Practice Test 3

DIRECTIONS FOR TAKING THE PRACTICE TEST

Directions: The Practice Test for the GED test has four separate subtests: Reasoning Through Language Arts, Mathematical Reasoning, Science, and Social Studies.

- Read and follow the directions at the start of each test.
- Stick to the time limits.
- Enter your answers to the multiple-choice questions in the appropriate circle on the answer sheets provided. Answer the technology-enhanced questions on the answer sheet as follows:
    - **Fill-in-the-blank questions** are designated by an empty box. When you see this box, write your answer in the blank that corresponds to the question number.
    - **Drop-down questions** appear with a drop-down menu icon. To answer these questions, write your answer (or the corresponding letter) in the blank that corresponds to the question number.
    - **Drag-and-drop questions** will appear with a diagram; for instance, a Venn diagram, flow chart, or series of boxes. To answer these questions, enter the answers (or the corresponding letter) into the correct space on the answer sheet.
    - **Select-an-area questions** will appear with an image that you are instructed to "Click" on or "Select," such as a number line. To answer these questions, you will write the answer in the blank that corresponds to the question number.
    - An **extended response question** will appear on the Reasoning Through Language Arts Test. To answer this question, you will write your response on the lined pages provided in the answer sheet.
- When you have completed the entire test, compare your answers with the correct answers given in the Answer Key and Explanations at the end of this Practice Test.
- Remember to check the "Are You Ready to Take the GED® Test?" section to gauge how close you are to mastering the GED test.

ANSWER SHEET: PRACTICE TEST 3

Reasoning Through Language Arts

Part I

1. Ⓐ Ⓑ Ⓒ Ⓓ
2. Ⓐ Ⓑ Ⓒ Ⓓ
3. ____________
4. Ⓐ Ⓑ Ⓒ Ⓓ
5. Ⓐ Ⓑ Ⓒ Ⓓ
6. Ⓐ Ⓑ Ⓒ Ⓓ
7. Ⓐ Ⓑ Ⓒ Ⓓ
8. Ⓐ Ⓑ Ⓒ Ⓓ
9. Ⓐ Ⓑ Ⓒ Ⓓ
10. ____________
11. ____________
12. ____________
13. ____________
14. ____________
15. ____________
16. ____________
17. ____________
18. Use diagram below.

Part II

Write your response using the pages provided with this answer sheet.

Part III

19. Ⓐ Ⓑ Ⓒ Ⓓ
20. Ⓐ Ⓑ Ⓒ Ⓓ
21. Ⓐ Ⓑ Ⓒ Ⓓ
22. Ⓐ Ⓑ Ⓒ Ⓓ
23. Use diagram below.
24. Ⓐ Ⓑ Ⓒ Ⓓ
25. Ⓐ Ⓑ Ⓒ Ⓓ
26. Ⓐ Ⓑ Ⓒ Ⓓ
27. Ⓐ Ⓑ Ⓒ Ⓓ
28. Ⓐ Ⓑ Ⓒ Ⓓ
29. Ⓐ Ⓑ Ⓒ Ⓓ
30. ____________
31. Ⓐ Ⓑ Ⓒ Ⓓ
32. Ⓐ Ⓑ Ⓒ Ⓓ
33. Ⓐ Ⓑ Ⓒ Ⓓ
34. Ⓐ Ⓑ Ⓒ Ⓓ
35. Ⓐ Ⓑ Ⓒ Ⓓ
36. Ⓐ Ⓑ Ⓒ Ⓓ
37. Ⓐ Ⓑ Ⓒ Ⓓ
38. Ⓐ Ⓑ Ⓒ Ⓓ
39. Ⓐ Ⓑ Ⓒ Ⓓ
40. Use diagram below.
41. ____________
42. ____________
43. ____________
44. ____________
45. ____________
46. ____________
47. ____________
48. ____________

18.

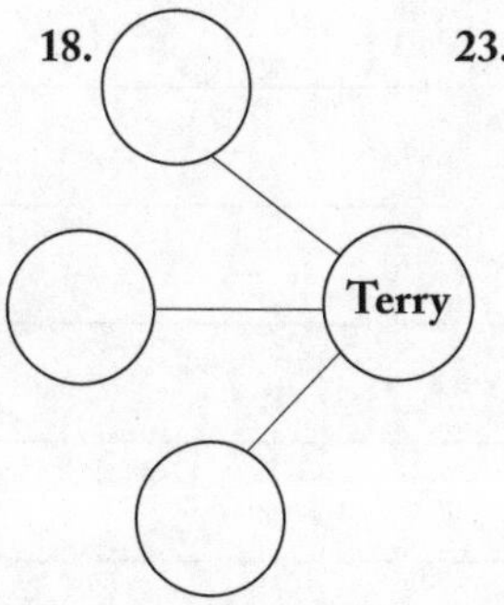

23.

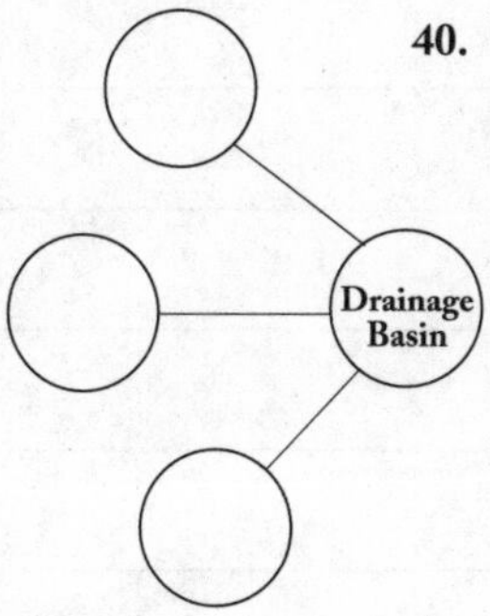

40.

Appropriate Clothing	Inappropriate Clothing

Extended Response

answer sheet

Mathematical Reasoning

1. ________	17. Ⓐ Ⓑ Ⓒ Ⓓ	33. ________
2. Ⓐ Ⓑ Ⓒ Ⓓ	18. Ⓐ Ⓑ Ⓒ Ⓓ	34. ________
3. Ⓐ Ⓑ Ⓒ Ⓓ	19. Ⓐ Ⓑ Ⓒ Ⓓ	35. Ⓐ Ⓑ Ⓒ Ⓓ
4. Ⓐ Ⓑ Ⓒ Ⓓ	20. Ⓐ Ⓑ Ⓒ Ⓓ	36. Ⓐ Ⓑ Ⓒ Ⓓ
5. Ⓐ Ⓑ Ⓒ Ⓓ	21. ________	37. Ⓐ Ⓑ Ⓒ Ⓓ
6. Use diagram below.	22. Ⓐ Ⓑ Ⓒ Ⓓ	38. Ⓐ Ⓑ Ⓒ Ⓓ
7. Ⓐ Ⓑ Ⓒ Ⓓ	23. ________	39. Ⓐ Ⓑ Ⓒ Ⓓ
8. ________	24. Ⓐ Ⓑ Ⓒ Ⓓ	40. Ⓐ Ⓑ Ⓒ Ⓓ
9. ________	25. Ⓐ Ⓑ Ⓒ Ⓓ	41. ________
10. Ⓐ Ⓑ Ⓒ Ⓓ	26. Ⓐ Ⓑ Ⓒ Ⓓ	42. ________
11. Ⓐ Ⓑ Ⓒ Ⓓ	27. Ⓐ Ⓑ Ⓒ Ⓓ	43. ________
12. Ⓐ Ⓑ Ⓒ Ⓓ	28. Ⓐ Ⓑ Ⓒ Ⓓ	44. Ⓐ Ⓑ Ⓒ Ⓓ
13. ________	29. ________	45. Ⓐ Ⓑ Ⓒ Ⓓ
14. Ⓐ Ⓑ Ⓒ Ⓓ	30. Ⓐ Ⓑ Ⓒ Ⓓ	46. ________
15. Ⓐ Ⓑ Ⓒ Ⓓ	31. Ⓐ Ⓑ Ⓒ Ⓓ	
16. ________	32. Ⓐ Ⓑ Ⓒ Ⓓ	

6.

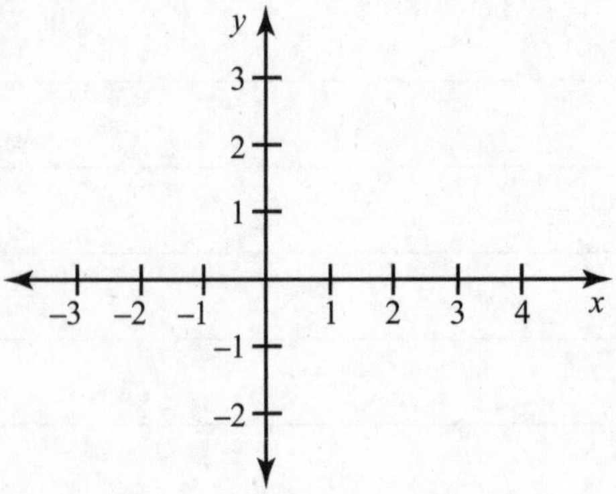

answer sheet

Science

1. Ⓐ Ⓑ Ⓒ Ⓓ	14. Ⓐ Ⓑ Ⓒ Ⓓ	27. Ⓐ Ⓑ Ⓒ Ⓓ
2. Ⓐ Ⓑ Ⓒ Ⓓ	15. ____________	28. Ⓐ Ⓑ Ⓒ Ⓓ
3. Ⓐ Ⓑ Ⓒ Ⓓ	16. Ⓐ Ⓑ Ⓒ Ⓓ	29. Ⓐ Ⓑ Ⓒ Ⓓ
4. Ⓐ Ⓑ Ⓒ Ⓓ	17. Ⓐ Ⓑ Ⓒ Ⓓ	30. Ⓐ Ⓑ Ⓒ Ⓓ
5. Ⓐ Ⓑ Ⓒ Ⓓ	18. Ⓐ Ⓑ Ⓒ Ⓓ	31. Ⓐ Ⓑ Ⓒ Ⓓ
6. ____________	19. Ⓐ Ⓑ Ⓒ Ⓓ	32. Ⓐ Ⓑ Ⓒ Ⓓ
7. Ⓐ Ⓑ Ⓒ Ⓓ	20. Ⓐ Ⓑ Ⓒ Ⓓ	33. Ⓐ Ⓑ Ⓒ Ⓓ
8. Ⓐ Ⓑ Ⓒ Ⓓ	21. Ⓐ Ⓑ Ⓒ Ⓓ	34. Ⓐ Ⓑ Ⓒ Ⓓ
9. Ⓐ Ⓑ Ⓒ Ⓓ	22. Ⓐ Ⓑ Ⓒ Ⓓ	35. ____________
10. Ⓐ Ⓑ Ⓒ Ⓓ	23. Ⓐ Ⓑ Ⓒ Ⓓ	____________
11. Ⓐ Ⓑ Ⓒ Ⓓ	24. Ⓐ Ⓑ Ⓒ Ⓓ	____________
12. Ⓐ Ⓑ Ⓒ Ⓓ	25. Ⓐ Ⓑ Ⓒ Ⓓ	
13. Ⓐ Ⓑ Ⓒ Ⓓ	26. Ⓐ Ⓑ Ⓒ Ⓓ	

Social Studies

1. Ⓐ Ⓑ Ⓒ Ⓓ
2. Ⓐ Ⓑ Ⓒ Ⓓ
3. Ⓐ Ⓑ Ⓒ Ⓓ
4. ____________
5. Ⓐ Ⓑ Ⓒ Ⓓ
6. Ⓐ Ⓑ Ⓒ Ⓓ
7. Ⓐ Ⓑ Ⓒ Ⓓ
8. Ⓐ Ⓑ Ⓒ Ⓓ
9. Ⓐ Ⓑ Ⓒ Ⓓ
10. ____________
11. Ⓐ Ⓑ Ⓒ Ⓓ
12. Ⓐ Ⓑ Ⓒ Ⓓ
13. ____________
14. ____________
15. ____________
16. ____________
17. Ⓐ Ⓑ Ⓒ Ⓓ
18. Ⓐ Ⓑ Ⓒ Ⓓ
19. Ⓐ Ⓑ Ⓒ Ⓓ
20. ____________
21. Ⓐ Ⓑ Ⓒ Ⓓ
22. Ⓐ Ⓑ Ⓒ Ⓓ
23. Ⓐ Ⓑ Ⓒ Ⓓ
24. Ⓐ Ⓑ Ⓒ Ⓓ
25. Ⓐ Ⓑ Ⓒ Ⓓ
26. Ⓐ Ⓑ Ⓒ Ⓓ
27. ____________
28. Ⓐ Ⓑ Ⓒ Ⓓ
29. ____________
30. Ⓐ Ⓑ Ⓒ Ⓓ
31. Ⓐ Ⓑ Ⓒ Ⓓ
32. Ⓐ Ⓑ Ⓒ Ⓓ
33. Ⓐ Ⓑ Ⓒ Ⓓ
34. Ⓐ Ⓑ Ⓒ Ⓓ
35. ____________

REASONING THROUGH LANGUAGE ARTS

150 Minutes • 49 Questions

Directions: The Reasoning Through Language Arts Test consists of passages of fiction and nonfiction reading material. After you read a passage, answer the questions that follow it, referring back to the passage as needed. Answer all questions based on what is stated and implied in the passage.

Most questions are in multiple-choice format. Others are meant to prepare you for the technology-enhanced questions that you will find on the test, such as drop-down, fill-in-the-blanks, and drag-and-drops. There is also an extended response question that requires you to read a paired passage that represents two views on a topic and write a well-organized essay supporting one of the viewpoints. Record your answers on the Reasoning Through Language Arts section of the answer sheet provided. To review how to answer these questions on your answer sheet, please refer to "Directions for Taking the Practice Test" on page 865.

Part I

Questions 1–9 refer to the following passage.

This passage is adapted from the novel Rilla of Ingleside *by L.M. Montgomery.*

Mrs. Blythe and her visitor, Miss Cornelia—alias Mrs. Marshall Elliott—were chatting together near the open door that led to the veranda, through which a cool, delicious breeze was blowing, bringing whiffs of phantom perfume from the garden, and charming gay echoes from the vine-hung corner where Rilla and Miss Oliver and Walter were laughing and talking. Wherever Rilla Blythe was, there was laughter.

There was another occupant of the living-room, curled up on a couch, who must not be overlooked, since he was a creature of marked individuality, and, moreover, had the distinction of being the only living thing whom Susan really hated.

All cats are mysterious but Dr. Jekyll-and-Mr. Hyde—"Doc" for short—was trebly so. He was a cat of double personality—or else, as Susan vowed, he was possessed by the devil. To begin with, there had been something uncanny about the very dawn of his existence. Four years previously Rilla Blythe had had a treasured darling of a kitten, white as snow, with a saucy black tip to its tail, which she called Jack Frost. Susan disliked Jack Frost, though she could not or would not give any valid reason therefor.

"Take my word for it, Mrs. Dr. dear," she was wont to say ominously, "that cat will come to no good.

"But why do you think so?" Mrs. Blythe would ask.

"I do not think—I know," was all the answer Susan would vouchsafe.

With the rest of the Ingleside folk Jack Frost was a favourite; he was so very clean and well groomed, and never allowed a spot or stain to be seen on his beautiful white suit; he had endearing ways of purring and snuggling; he was scrupulously honest.

And then a domestic tragedy took place at Ingleside. Jack Frost had kittens!

It would be vain to try to picture Susan's triumph. Had she not always insisted that that cat would turn out to be a delusion and a snare? Now they could see for themselves!

Rilla kept one of the kittens, a very pretty one, with peculiarly sleek glossy fur of a dark yellow crossed by orange stripes, and large, satiny, golden ears. She called it Goldie and the name seemed appropriate enough to the little frolicsome creature which, during its kittenhood, gave no indication of the sinister nature it really possessed. Susan, of course, warned the family that no good could be expected from any offspring of that diabolical Jack Frost; but Susan's Cassandra-like croakings were unheeded.

The Blythes had been so accustomed to regard Jack Frost as a member of the male sex that they could not get out of the habit. So they continually used the masculine pronoun, although the result was ludicrous. Visitors used to be quite electrified when Rilla referred casually to "Jack and his kitten," or told Goldie sternly, "Go to your mother and get him to wash your fur."

"It is not decent, Mrs. Dr. dear," poor Susan would say bitterly. She herself compromised by always referring to Jack as "it" or "the white beast," and one heart at least did not ache when "it" was accidentally poisoned the following winter.

In a year's time "Goldie" became so manifestly an inadequate name for the orange kitten that Walter, who was just then reading Stevenson's story, changed it to Dr. Jekyll-and-Mr. Hyde. In his Dr. Jekyll mood the cat was a drowsy, affectionate, domestic, cushion-loving puss, who liked petting and gloried in being nursed and patted. Especially did he love to lie on his back and have his sleek, cream-coloured throat stroked gently while he purred in somnolent satisfaction. He was a notable purrer; never had there been an Ingleside cat who purred so constantly and so ecstatically.

"The only thing I envy a cat is its purr," remarked Dr. Blythe once, listening to Doc's resonant melody. "It is the most contented sound in the world."

Doc was very handsome; his every movement was grace; his poses magnificent. When he folded his long, dusky-ringed tail about his feet and sat him down on the veranda to gaze steadily into space for long intervals the Blythes felt that an Egyptian sphinx could not have made a more fitting Deity of the Portal.

When the Mr. Hyde mood came upon him—which it invariably did before rain, or wind—he was a wild thing with changed eyes. The transformation always came suddenly. He would spring fiercely from a reverie with a savage snarl and bite at any restraining or caressing hand. His fur seemed to grow darker and his eyes gleamed with a diabolical light. There was really an unearthly beauty about him. If the change happened in the twilight all the Ingleside folk felt a certain terror of him. At such times he was a fearsome beast and only Rilla defended him, asserting that he was "such a nice prowly cat." Certainly he prowled.

Dr. Jekyll loved new milk; Mr. Hyde would not touch milk and growled over his meat. Dr. Jekyll came down the stairs so silently that no one could hear him. Mr. Hyde made his tread as heavy as a man's. Several evenings, when Susan was alone in the house, he "scared her stiff," as she declared, by doing this. He would sit in the middle of the kitchen floor, with his terrible eyes fixed unwinkingly upon hers for an hour at a time. This played havoc with her nerves, but poor Susan really held him in too much awe to try to drive him out. Once she had dared to throw a stick at him and he had promptly made a savage leap towards her. Susan rushed out of doors and never attempted to meddle with Mr. Hyde again—though she visited his misdeeds upon the innocent Dr. Jekyll, chasing him ignominiously out of her domain whenever he dared to poke his nose in and denying him certain savory tidbits for which he yearned.

1. What conclusion can you draw from the passage about Susan?

A. She is generally a mistrustful person.

B. She dislikes all cats, not just Doc.

C. She is unhappy working for the Blythes.

D. She has good instincts about the cat.

2. How does Mrs. Blythe react to Susan's gloomy prediction about Doc?

A. She agrees with Susan completely.

B. She is skeptical of Susan's dislike.

C. She disagrees with Susan's assessment.

D. She wants to get rid of the cat.

3. Susan's reaction to Mr. Hyde shows that she feels [Select ▼].

A. frightened

B. disgusted

C. relieved

D. excited

4. Which name represents the cat in his gentle, loveable mood?

A. Dr. Blythe

B. Dr. Jekyll

C. Mr. Hyde

D. Jack Frost

5. Which figure of speech in the passage **best** describes the cat's odd personality changes?

A. "an Egyptian sphinx"

B. "possessed by the devil"

C. "Cassandra-like croakings"

D. "an unearthly beauty about him"

6. Who was Jack Frost's owner?

A. Rilla

B. Susan

C. Miss Cornelia

D. Walter

7. Based on the context, what does *vouchsafe* (line 38) **most likely** mean?

A. Scream

B. Refuse

C. Offer

D. Silence

8. What reaction do guests have when learning that "Jack Frost" has given birth to a kitten?

A. Surprise

B. Happiness

C. Anger

D. Amusement

9. Based on the passage, Dr. Blythe's statement that Doc's purr is "the most contented sound in the world"

A. supports Susan's opinion of Doc.

B. contrasts with Doc's behavior.

C. illustrates Doc's true personality.

D. compares Doc with Jack Frost.

Questions 10–18 refer to the following passage.

The passage below contains errors in grammar, spelling, and punctuation. For questions 10–17, choose the option from the drop-down menu that correctly completes or rewrites the sentence.

Dear Ms. Gonzalez,

(1) [Select ▼] (2) [Select ▼] recommended that I reach out to you, given my work experience and skills.

(3) I am currently a receptionist at Best Roofing, Inc. (4) I've been there for three years, and [Select ▼] (5) In addition to answering phones and maintaining visitor records, I work closely with the office manager and the administrative assistants to coordinate visitor schedules, deliveries, and other scheduling tasks.

(6) My attached resume goes into more detail about my [Select ▼] (7) It also includes my past work experience as an intern and customer service representative. (8) With my history in customer service, I know how important it is to bring that service perspective to everything I do— [Select ▼] (9) I have also developed very strong technical skills, and am able to use advanced email, calendar, and task-tracking apps to ensure efficiency.

(10) [Select ▼] I am also very used to performing under pressure and on deadline. (11) I know how to create strong working relationships with a variety of people. (12) In my current [Select ▼], I work with people throughout sixteen different departments—which takes true teamwork!

(13) I would love to have to opportunity to join the team at Anderson Consulting, and bring my expertise in managing day-to-day office processes to your company. (14) I believe [Select ▼] the expectations you have for this role. (15) I look forward to speaking more with you about my application. (16) If there's any other information I can provide, please feel free to contact me at any time. (17) I can be reached at (999) 777-2222, or by email at TQFranklin@emaildomain.com. (18) Thank you for your time and consideration!

(19) Sincerely,

(20) Terry Franklin

10. Sentence 1: Select ▼

A. I am applying.

B. Please consider my application for your open administrative assistant position at Anderson Consulting.

C. You work for Anderson Consulting, and I would like to work there.

D. Please consider my amazing, winning application for the administrative assistant job at your fantastic company, Anderson Consulting, about which I've heard so many wonderful things.

11. Sentence 2: Select ▼ recommended that I reach out to you, given my work experience and skills.

A. My former colleague Vanessa Smith who works in your Marketing department

B. My former colleague; Vanessa Smith; who works in your Marketing department;

C. My former colleague Vanessa Smith, who works in your Marketing department,

D. My former colleague Vanessa Smith (she works in your Marketing department)

12. Sentence 4: I've been there for three years, and Select ▼

A. over that time, I have developed strong organizational and administrative skills.

B. my organizational skills have grown and over that time developed.

C. I have grown over that time.

D. the development and growing of my administrative and organizational skills are well known.

13. Sentence 6: My attached resume goes into more detail about my Select ▼

A. daily job duties and achieved.

B. daily job duties and achievements.

C. daily job, my duties, and my achievements.

D. daily job duties and achievement.

14. Sentence 8: With my history in customer service, I know how important it is to bring that service perspective to everything I do—Select ▼

A. whether that's working with, interacting, or handling internal teams, customers, or vendors.

B. whether that's working with internal teams, working with customers, or working with vendors.

C. whether that's when I worked with internal teams, or when I interact with customers or handled vendors.

D. whether that's working with internal teams, interacting with clients, or handling vendors.

15. Sentence 10: Select ▼ I am also very used to performing under pressure and on deadline.

A. As a busy medium-sized company,

B. With my experience at a busy medium-sized company,

C. A busy medium-sized company,

D. Life in a busy medium-sized company isn't easy,

16. **Sentence 12:** In my current [Select ▼], I work with people throughout sixteen different departments—which takes true teamwork!

A. roll

B. route

C. role

D. row

17. **Sentence 14:** I believe [Select ▼] the expectations you have for this role.

A. I can: meet and exceed

B. I can, meet and exceed

C. I can…meet and exceed

D. I can meet and exceed

18. Which of the following skills does Terry have experience doing? Drag and drop your choices in the blank circles. (Enter your choices in the blanks provided on the answer sheet.)

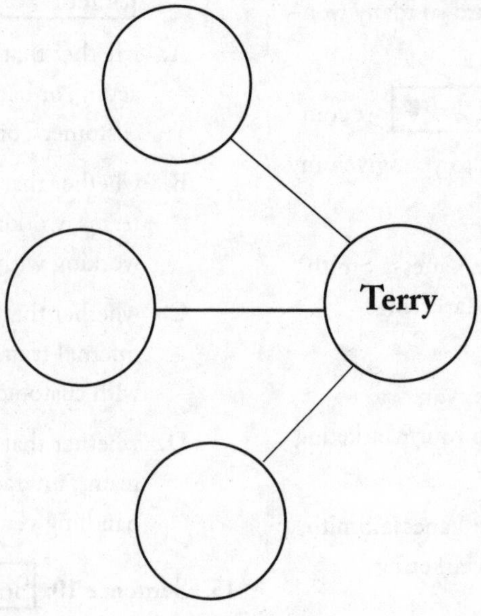

A. answering phones

B. managing interns

C. customer service

D. designing presentations

E. coordinating schedules

F. planning events

Part II

The following passages present two views on raising the federal minimum wage to $15 an hour. Analyze both positions presented to determine which one is best supported. Use relevant and specific evidence from both passages to support your response.

Enter your response in the answer sheets provided. You should expect to spend up to 45 minutes to plan, draft, and edit your response.

Should the Universal Minimum Wage Be $15?

Passage 1

A Minimum Wage Should Be a Living Wage

Having a federal minimum wage is supposed to guarantee that hard-working Americans have some financial security, and can't be taken advantage of by unscrupulous their employers. It was originally designed to help keep working people above the poverty line, but now it has stalled out at a number that is no longer viable for working families. Raising the federal minimum wage to $15 would help make up for that gap, and put workers on a stronger footing.

Since the federal minimum wage was introduced in the 1930s, it has been raised 22 times, from $0.25 per hour in 1938 to $7.25 per hour in 2019, where it remains to this day. More than ten years have passed since that last pay raise, and the US cost of living has continued to increase. For example, in a recent study, economists found that there isn't a single county in the US where a family of four can be supported on a single minimum-wage income.

Adjusted for inflation, the federal minimum wage peaked in 1968, when it was the equivalent of $11.68 in today's dollars. That we haven't even kept pace with 1968 standards is alarming. In addition, most Americans are in favor of raising the minimum wage; according to a 2016 poll, 71% of Americans favored increasing the minimum wage.

Although the federal minimum wage stays low, 29 states have created their own higher minimum wages, creating a discrepancy at the state and federal levels. It's time the federal government stepped up and raised its own minimum wage, to ensure a fair wage for its entire working population.

Passage 2

A $15 Minimum Wage Sounds Great, But Hurts in the Long Run

On the news and in political debates, we often hear about how raising the minimum wage to $15 will be the economic solution that our workers need. While that sounds good in theory, there are drawbacks that we should consider before making such a drastic economic change on the federal level.

In states and cities that have already increased their own minimum wages independent of the federal minimum wage, we're starting to see mixed results. For example, according to one study, Seattle (which was one of the first major cities in the country to adopt the $15 minimum wage) is seeing younger workers effectively pushed out of low-skilled jobs as older workers take jobs in food service or similar industries. So while the increased minimum wage could be adding a few more dollars to some workers' paychecks, the futures of other workers could be looking more bleak, as the younger workers struggle to build skills and experience.

Additionally, the calls to raise the minimum wage overlook one very important factor: the employers. A higher minimum wage affects any company's bottom line budget and profits. Many smaller, "mom and pop" businesses get by on the smallest of profit margins, and a huge shift in employment costs could put them out of business. Larger companies may be able to absorb a higher minimum wage more easily but will find ways to get around the costs. That could mean higher prices for consumers (taking that money right back from employees who have to buy these goods and services).

Increased minimum wage costs may also mean there are fewer jobs to be had. Many businesses, like fast food restaurants, are finding ways to automate and computerize their labor. That leads to fewer jobs open to human workers, and higher unemployment. Alternatively, companies may start outsourcing more of their labor to other countries, where the cost of doing business is lower.

While raising the minimum wage sounds like a simple solution for keeping Americans out of poverty, it is a far more complex issue. Before we dive in and make a $15 minimum wage the law of the land, it's important to step back and consider what could happen as a result.

Part III

Questions 19–24 refer to the following passage.

This passage is adapted from author Mark Twain's memoir Life on the Mississippi, *in which he recounts his time as a steamboat pilot on the Mississippi River.*

The Mississippi is well worth reading about. It is not a commonplace river, but on the contrary is in all ways remarkable. Considering the Missouri its main branch, it is the longest river in the world—four thousand three hundred miles. It seems safe to say that it is also the crookedest river in the world, since in one part of its journey it uses up one thousand three hundred miles to cover the same ground that the crow would fly over in six hundred and seventy-five. It discharges three times as much water as the St. Lawrence, twenty-five times as much as the Rhine, and three hundred and thirty-eight times as much as the Thames. No other river has so vast a drainage-basin: it draws its water supply from twenty-eight States and Territories; from Delaware, on the Atlantic seaboard, and from all the country between that and Idaho on the Pacific slope—a spread of forty-five degrees of longitude. The Mississippi receives and carries to the Gulf water from fifty-four subordinate rivers that are navigable by steamboats, and from some hundreds that are navigable by flats and keels. The area of its drainage-basin is as great as the combined areas of England, Wales, Scotland, Ireland, France, Spain, Portugal, Germany, Austria, Italy, and Turkey; and almost all this wide region is fertile; the Mississippi valley, proper, is exceptionally so.

It is a remarkable river in this: that instead of widening toward its mouth, it grows narrower; grows narrower and deeper. From the junction of the Ohio to a point half way down to the sea, the width averages a mile in high water: thence to the sea the width steadily diminishes, until, at the 'Passes,' above the mouth, it is but little over half a mile. At the junction of the Ohio the Mississippi's depth is eighty-seven feet; the depth increases gradually, reaching one hundred and twenty-nine just above the mouth.

The difference in rise and fall is also remarkable—not in the upper, but in the lower river. The rise is tolerably uniform down to Natchez (three hundred and sixty miles above the mouth)—about fifty feet. But at Bayou La Fourche the river rises only twenty-four feet; at New Orleans only fifteen, and just above the mouth only two and one half.

An article in the New Orleans 'Times-Democrat,' based upon reports of able engineers, states that the river annually empties four hundred and six million tons of mud into the Gulf of Mexico—which brings to mind Captain Marryat's rude name for the Mississippi—'the Great Sewer.' This mud, solidified, would make a mass a mile square and two hundred and forty-one feet high.

The mud deposit gradually extends the land—but only gradually; it has extended it not quite a third of a mile in the two hundred years which have elapsed since the river took its place in history. The belief of the scientific people is, that the mouth used to be at Baton Rouge, where the hills cease, and that the two hundred miles of land between there and the Gulf was built by the river. This gives us the age of that piece of country, without any trouble at all—one hundred and twenty thousand years. Yet it is much the youthfullest batch of country that lies around there anywhere.

19. How many feet tall would a structure made of Mississippi River mud be?

A. 87

B. 241

C. 4,300

D. 675

20. The author feels that the Mississippi River is

A. ordinary.

B. boring.

C. awe-inspiring.

D. frightening.

21. What is the author **most likely** describing with the phrase "flats and keels" (line 28)?

A. Different kinds of boats

B. The geography of the riverbed

C. The flow of the water

D. The narrowness of the river's

22. What is the effect of comparing the Mississippi River to world rivers in paragraph 1, lines 13–23?

A. It shows how inferior American rivers are.

B. It proves that no two rivers are alike.

C. It describes how far the Mississippi River runs.

D. It illustrates the Mississippi's superior qualities.

23. Which of the following nations are included in the list of those whose combined areas equal the area of the Mississippi drainage basin? Drag and drop your choices in the blank circles. (Enter your choices in the blanks provided on the answer sheet.)

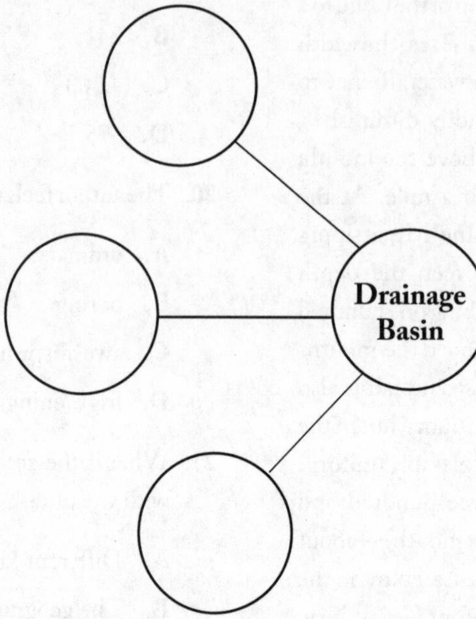

A. Ireland

B. Germany

C. Turkey

D. Mexico

E. Canada

24. What does this passage reveal about the author's relationship to the Mississippi River?

A. He respects it.

B. He wants to conquer it.

C. He is afraid of it.

D. He does not want to travel it.

Questions 25–32 refer to the following passage.

The following passage is adapted from a NASA article about global methods for dealing with climate change.

Responding to Climate Change

Climate change is one of the most complex issues facing us today. It involves many dimensions—science, economics, society, politics, and moral and ethical questions—and is a global problem, felt on local scales, that will be around for decades and centuries to come. Carbon dioxide, the heat-trapping greenhouse gas that has driven recent global warming, lingers in the atmosphere for hundreds of years, and the planet (especially the oceans) takes a while to respond to warming. So even if we stopped emitting all greenhouse gases today, global warming and climate change will continue to affect future generations. In this way, humanity is "committed" to some level of climate change.

How much climate change? That will be determined by how our emissions continue and also exactly how our climate system responds to those emissions. Despite increasing awareness of climate change, our emissions of greenhouse gases continue on a relentless rise. In 2013, the daily level of carbon dioxide in the atmosphere surpassed 400 parts per million for the first time in human history. The last time levels were that high was about three to five million years ago, during the Pliocene era.

Because we are already committed to some level of climate change, responding to climate change involves a two-pronged approach:

- Reducing emissions of and stabilizing the levels of heat-trapping greenhouse gases in the atmosphere ("mitigation");
- Adapting to the climate change already in the pipeline ("adaptation").

Mitigation—reducing climate change—involves reducing the flow of heat-trapping greenhouse gases into the atmosphere, either by reducing sources of these gases (for example, the burning of fossil fuels for electricity, heat or transport) or enhancing the "sinks" that accumulate and store these gases (such as the oceans, forests and soil). The goal of mitigation is to avoid significant human interference with the climate system, and "stabilize greenhouse gas levels in a timeframe sufficient to allow ecosystems to adapt naturally to climate change, ensure that food production is not threatened and to enable economic development to proceed in a sustainable manner."

Adaptation—adapting to life in a changing climate—involves adjusting to actual or expected future climate. The goal is to reduce our vulnerability to the harmful effects of climate change (like sea-level encroachment, more intense extreme weather events or food insecurity). It also encompasses making the most of any potential beneficial opportunities associated with climate change (for example, longer growing seasons or increased yields in some regions).

Throughout history, people and societies have adjusted to and coped with changes in climate and extremes with varying degrees of success. Climate change (drought in particular) has been at least partly responsible for the rise and fall of civilizations. Earth's climate has been relatively stable for the past 12,000 years and this stability has been crucial for the development of our modern civilization and life as we know it. Modern life is tailored to the stable climate we have become accustomed to. As our climate changes, we will have to learn to adapt. The faster the climate changes, the harder it could be.

While climate change is a global issue, it is felt on a local scale. Cities and municipalities are therefore at the frontline of adaptation. In the absence of national or international climate policy direction, cities and local communities around the world have been focusing on solving their own climate problems. They are working to build flood defenses, plan for heatwaves and higher temperatures, install water-permeable pavements to better deal with floods and stormwater and improve water storage and use.

25. Which of the following **best** expresses the main idea of the passage?

A. Climate change has two simple solutions: mitigation and adaptation.

B. Climate change is a complex problem that requires complex solutions.

C. Climate change is likely to be resolved in the near future.

D. Climate change is something to be handled on a global level, not local.

26. According to the passage, the level of carbon dioxide in the atmosphere is

A. increasing.

B. decreasing.

C. staying the same.

D. not important.

27. The phrase "adjusting to actual or expected future climate" refers to which approach to climate change?

A. Mitigation

B. Adaptation

C. Reducing drought

D. Stopping greenhouse gases

28. The author **most likely** believes that

A. we can solve climate change by cutting off all greenhouse gas emissions.

B. there is nothing humans can to do reduce the effects of climate change.

C. climate change solutions are best left to economists, not scientists.

D. humans can alter the future climate somewhat by taking action today.

29. The author argues that up until recently, Earth's climate has been

A. chaotic.

B. stable.

C. fast-changing.

D. extreme.

30. In paragraph 6, how does the description of climate change throughout history affect the reader's understanding of the passage? Choose your answer from the drop-down menu.

Select ▼

A. It creates a sense of urgency and a call to action.

B. It shows there is no reason to act now on climate change.

C. It adds a humorous tone to the passage.

D. It prompts the reader to question whether climate change is real.

31. Based on the passage, which of the following is NOT a local solution for adapting to climate change?

A. Creating large-scale policies

B. Planning for heatwaves

C. Dealing with stormwater

D. Improving water storage

32. Which of the following could be an alternative title for the passage?

A. Adapting to the Climates of the Future

B. How to Mitigate Climate Change

C. A History of Climate Change

D. Sensible Solutions for Climate Change

Questions 33–40 are based on the following passage.

The following passage is adapted from a corporate dress code document.

Universal Inc. Dress Policy

[1]

Universal Inc. strives to maintain a workplace environment that is productive, professional, respectful, and free from unnecessary distractions and annoyances. As part of that effort, the company expects and requires employees to maintain a clean, neat, professional appearance that is appropriate for the workplace setting and for the work being performed. Accordingly, Universal Inc. management and team leaders may determine and enforce guidelines for workplace-appropriate attire and grooming for their departments as they deem appropriate.

Overview

[2]

All Universal Inc. employees and contractors are expected to present a professional, businesslike image to clients, visitors, customers, and the public. Acceptable personal appearance, like proper maintenance of work areas, is an ongoing requirement of employment with Universal Inc.

[3]

Supervisors should communicate any department-specific workplace attire and grooming guidelines to staff members during new-hire orientation and evaluation periods. Any questions about the department's guidelines for attire should be discussed with the employee's immediate supervisor.

[4]

Any employee who does not meet the attire or grooming standards set by his or her department will be subject to corrective action and may be asked to leave the premises to change clothing. Hourly paid staff members will not be compensated for any work time missed because of failure to comply with designated workplace attire and grooming standards. Employees who violate these standards repeatedly may be subject to more severe corrective action, up to and including termination.

[5]

All staff members must carry or wear their Universal Inc. identification badge at all times while at work.

Standards

[6]

Business or business-casual is the standard expected attire for Universal Inc. employees. In special circumstances, staff members may be permitted to dress in a more casual fashion than is normally required. On these occasions, staff members are still expected to present a neat appearance and are not permitted to wear ripped, frayed or disheveled clothing or athletic wear. Likewise, tight, revealing or otherwise workplace-inappropriate dress is not permitted.

Casual Attire

[7]

Departments may adopt casual or dress-down days, at the department head's discretion.

[8]

The following guidelines apply to casual attire:

- Pants, jeans, or skirts must be must be clean and free of rips, tears and fraying; they may not be excessively tight or revealing. Shorts are not allowed, but skorts and capris are acceptable.
- Shirts should have sleeves (short sleeves are acceptable) and a collar. Shirts with the company logo are always appropriate.
- Low-rise pants, low-cut shirts, and midriff-baring tops are not appropriate.
- Casual shoes are acceptable, but athletic sneakers and open-toed sandals are not appropriate.
- Athletic clothing (including leggings and sweatshirts) and beachwear are not acceptable attire.

Business Attire

[9]

The following guidelines apply to business attire:

- For men, business attire includes a long-sleeved dress shirt, tie, and tailored sport coat worn with dress trousers (not khakis) and dress shoes.
- For women, business attire includes tailored pantsuits, businesslike dresses, coordinated dressy separates worn with or without a blazer, and conservative, closed-toe shoes.

How to Address Workplace Attire and Hygiene Problems

[10]

Violations of the policy can range from inappropriate clothing items to offensive perfumes and body odor. If a staff member comes to work in inappropriate dress, he or she will be required to go home, change into conforming attire or properly groom, and return to work.

[11]

If a staff member's poor hygiene or use of too much perfume/cologne is an issue, the supervisor should discuss the problem with the staff member in private and should point out the specific areas to be corrected. If the problem persists, supervisors should follow the normal corrective action process.

33. Based on the passage, when can employees wear casual clothing?

A. Every Friday

B. Whenever they want

C. When supervisors decide it's appropriate

D. At office social events or offsite activities

34. The purpose of the dress code is to

A. limit employees' individuality.

B. punish people for dressing offensively.

C. build team spirit among employees.

D. support how the company looks in public.

35. What is meant by the sentence, "Employees who violate these standards repeatedly may be subject to more severe corrective action, up to and including termination" (Paragraph 4)?

A. Consequences for breaking the dress code may include getting fired.

B. People can violate the rules many times before getting in trouble.

C. The dress code guidelines are only recommendations, and are not binding.

D. People who break the dress code will be immediately fired.

36. Which of the following would NOT be a violation of the dress code?

A. Wearing flip-flops on a casual Friday

B. Wearing strong cologne

C. Wearing a t-shirt with the Universal Inc. logo

D. Wearing a sleeveless shirt on a hot summer day

37. The passage suggests that Universal Inc. values its

A. laid-back attitude.

B. professional image.

C. maintenance of work areas.

D. employees' attractiveness.

38. Based on the passage, what does *conforming* (line 47) mean?

A. Inappropriate

B. Business

C. Original

D. Suitable

39. Which of the following additional guidelines would **best** support the ones in the dress code?

A. A guideline that discourages employees from wearing hats at work.

B. A guideline that describes what to do if employees experience workplace harassment.

C. A guideline that outlines the annual work performance review process.

D. A guideline that sets rules about personal email use while at work.

40. Based on the dress code outlined in the passage, decide which items of clothing would be appropriate, and which items would be inappropriate. Drag and drop the clothing items into the correct location in the chart. (Enter the corresponding letters of the choices on the answer sheet.)

Appropriate Clothing	Inappropriate Clothing

A. Yoga pants

B. Sneakers

C. Cargo shorts

D. Blazer

Questions 41–48 refer to the following passage.

The passage below contains errors in grammar, spelling, and punctuation. For questions 41–44, choose the option from the drop-down menu that correctly completes or rewrites the sentence.

Subject: Donaghy Design follow-up

From: Jeffrey Donaghy

To: Miriam Jefferson

(1) Hi Miriam,

(2) [Select ▼] (3) I enjoyed our conversation about the playoffs (go Cardinals!), and was glad to hear that you want to find a new design partner for your company. (4) As requested, I'd like to tell you a little more about what my company, Donaghy Design, can offer you.

(5) As a small-business owner myself, I know how much it means to have that personal touch with all clients. (6) My design firm started with just me and my laptop about six years ago; now we're twenty people [Select ▼] with firms of all sizes. (7) With this team in place, we provide [Select ▼] design services, including:

- Company logos and branded materials
- Website layout and design
- Social media page design
- Print brochures, posters, and templates

(8) I like too think of us as an "end-to-end" design firm, helping you put your company's mark on everything you need, from the smallest business cards to the logo wraps on your company's vans.

(9) Whether you're looking for cool simplicity or bright flash, we'll work with you to set the write tone in your design. (10) [Select ▼]

(11) To see some samples of our work, please visit our site at DonaghyDesign.org. (12) I'd love to set up some time to talk with you about your company and it's specific design needs, and show you some sample price plans and contracts. (13) Please let me know what time works best for you in the next few weeks, and we'll get the ball rolling.

(13) Regards,

Jeffrey

Practice test 3—Language Arts

41. Sentence 2: [Select ▼]

A. Meeting you at Andrew's party the other day, it was so nice!

B. It was so nice to meet you at Andrew's party the other day!

C. It was so nice when you and me met at Andrew's party the other day!

D. At Andrew's party the other day, it was so nice!

42. Sentence 6: My design firm started with just me and my laptop about six years ago; now we're twenty people [Select ▼] with firms of all sizes.

A. strong, and work

B. strong; work

C. strong and work

D. strong. And work

43. Sentence 7: With this team in place, we provide [Select ▼] design services, including:

A. both digital or print

B. either digital or print

C. either digital and print

D. both digital and print

44. Sentence 10: [Select ▼]

A. Innovative and creative, your highest standards will be met by my designers.

B. My innovative and creative designers know how to meet the highest standards, and your highest standards as well.

C. My designers are creative and innovative, and they know how to meet your highest standards.

D. Innovative and creative is how my designers meet the highest standards.

The following sentences appear in Jeffrey's email. The words displayed in brackets are homonyms—they sound the same as other words that have different meanings and may be spelled differently.

For questions 45–48, if the word in brackets is spelled correctly based on the context in which it appears, type "ok" in the box. If it is not, type the correct spelling in the box. (Enter your choices in the blanks on your answer sheet.)

45. Sentence 3: I enjoyed our conversation about the playoffs (go Cardinals!), and was glad to hear that you want to find a new design partner for [your] company.

[ ]

46. Sentence 8: I like [too] think of us as an "end-to-end" design firm, helping you put your company's mark on everything you need, from the smallest business cards to the logo wraps on your company's vans.

[ ]

47. Sentence 9: Whether you're looking for cool simplicity or bright flash, we'll work with you to set the [write] tone in your design.

[ ]

48. Sentence 12: I'd love to set up some time to talk with you about your company and [it's] specific design needs, and show you some sample price plans and contracts.

[ ]

MATHEMATICAL REASONING

115 Minutes • 46 Questions

Directions: The Mathematical Reasoning Test will have calculator-allowed questions mixed with calculator-prohibited questions, with the calculator tool available to use when it is an option. However, for this test, the calculator-prohibited questions are grouped together as the first five questions.

Most questions are multiple-choice, but to answer some questions, you will be required to fill an answer in a blank, drag and drop correct answers, and select answers on a given graphic. Record your answers on the Mathematical Reasoning section of the answer sheet provided. To review how to answer these questions on your answer sheet, please refer to "Directions for Taking the Practice Test" on page 865.

To answer some questions, you will need to apply one or more mathematics formulas. The formulas provided on the following page will help you to answer those questions. Some questions refer to charts, graphs, and figures. Unless otherwise noted, charts, graphs, and figures are drawn to scale.

Mathematics Formula Sheet

The GED Mathematical Reasoning Test contains a formula sheet, which displays formulas relating to geometric measurement and certain algebra concepts. Formulas are provided to test takers so that they may focus on *application*, rather than the *memorization*, of formulas.

Area of a:		
parallelogram	$A = bh$	
trapezoid	$A = \frac{1}{2}h\,(b_1 + b_2)$	
Surface Area and Volume of a:		
rectangular/right prism	$SA = ph + 2B$	$V = Bh$
cylinder	$SA = 2\pi rh + 2\pi r^2$	$V = \pi r^2 h$
pyramid	$SA = \frac{1}{2}ps + B$	$V = \frac{1}{3}Bh$
cone	$SA = \pi rs + \pi r^2$	$V = \frac{1}{3}\pi r^2 h$
sphere	$SA = 4\pi r^2$	$V = \frac{4}{3}\pi r^3$
	(p = perimeter of base B; $\pi \approx 3.14$)	
Algebra		
slope of a line	$m = \frac{y_2 - y_1}{x_2 - x_1}$	
slope-intercept form of the equation of a line	$y = mx + \mathrm{b}$	
point-slope form of the equation of a line	$y - y_1 = m(x - x_1)$	
standard form of a quadratic equation	$y = ax^2 + bx + c$	
quadratic formula	$x = \frac{-b \pm \sqrt{b^2 - 4ac}}{2a}$	
Pythagorean theorem	$a^2 + b^2 = c^2$	
simple interest	$I = prt$	
	(I = interest, p = principal, r = rate, t = time)	

The use of a calculator is prohibited for questions 1–5.

SHOW YOUR WORK HERE

1. The starting price for a copy of a classic novel with a misprint on the cover at an auction was $400. The price increased by 160% until the novel was finally sold. For what amount did the novel sell?

$ [ ]

2. Compute: $-1-[3(4-7)-(-3)(-2)]$

A. –15

B. –16

C. 14

D. 4

3. Evaluate $\left(\frac{x}{y}-\frac{y}{x}\right)^{-1}$ when $x=\frac{1}{2}$ and $y=-2$.

A. $-\frac{4}{15}$

B. $\frac{15}{4}$

C. $\frac{4}{15}$

D. $-\frac{15}{4}$

4. To which of these expressions is $\frac{2x-1}{x+2}-\frac{2x}{2x+1}$ equivalent?

A. $-\frac{4x+1}{5x+2}$

B. $-\frac{1}{x}$

C. $-\frac{1}{1-x}$

D. $\frac{2x^2-4x-1}{2x^2+5x+2}$

Practice test 3—Mathematical Reasoning

5. Carl invested \$750 in an account that pays 3% interest per year and \$500 in an account that pays 2.5% interest per year. What is the total interest earned at the end of one year?

A. \$12.50

B. \$22.50

C. \$35.00

D. \$68.75

6. What are the x-intercepts of the graph of the function $f(x) = 6x^2 - 9x$? Plot them on the xy-plane below:

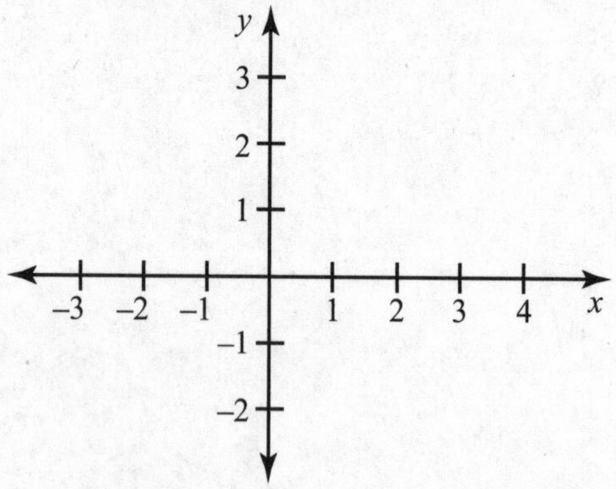

7. The volume of a closed right circular cylinder with base radius $\sqrt{2}$ meters is 8π cubic meters. What is the surface area of the cylinder?

A. $\pi\left(1 + 4\sqrt{2}\right)$ square meters

B. $4\pi\left(1 + 2\sqrt{2}\right)$ square meters

C. $8\sqrt{2}\,\pi$ square meters

D. $2\pi\left(1 + 4\sqrt{2}\right)$ square meters

8. Two-thirds of a group of puppies at an adoption center are male. Of them, three-fifths are mixed-breed dogs. And of these, four-ninths are part Shepherd. What proportion of the puppies satisfy all three conditions? Enter whole numbers in each box to form a simplified fraction:

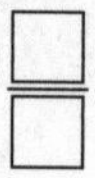

SHOW YOUR WORK HERE

9. What is the slope of any line parallel to the line with the equation $0.4(1.1-0.2y)=0.8x$?

[ ]

SHOW YOUR WORK HERE

10. For what value of A, if any, does this system have no solution?

$$\begin{cases} x = -\frac{1}{2}y + 1 \\ Ay - \frac{1}{2}x = -1 \end{cases}$$

A. $-\frac{1}{4}$

B. -4

C. -2

D. No such value of A

11. Rick has the following scores on a miniature golf course: 16, 11, 18, 16, 15.

Which of the following CANNOT be his score on a sixth game if the median of the six scores is 15.5?

A. 8

B. 12

C. 15

D. 16

12. Suppose $x > 2$. Which of the following can be a negative integer?

A. $-\frac{2}{x}$

B. $\frac{1}{x-2}$

C. $2-x$

D. $2x$

13. Suppose z is a negative integer less than −1. Drag and drop the following expressions into the appropriate boxes to create a correct comparison:

$-z \quad 3z \quad z^2 \quad \frac{1}{z}$

$\square < \square < \square < \square$

Practice test 3 — Mathematical Reasoning

SHOW YOUR WORK HERE

14. What is the area of the region shown?

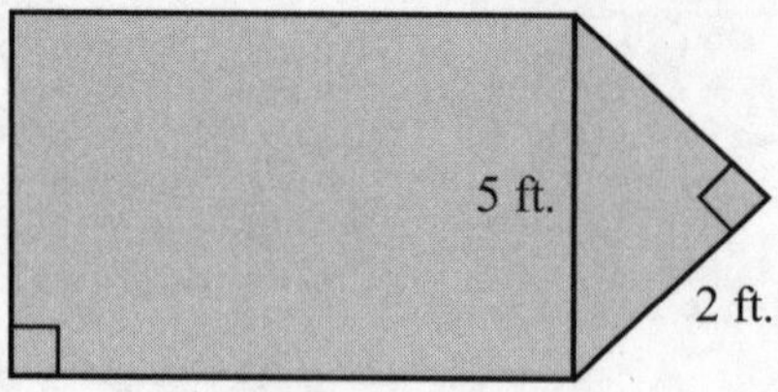

A. $\left(40+\sqrt{21}\right)$ square feet

B. 40 square feet

C. 26 square feet

D. $\left(26+\sqrt{21}\right)$ square feet

15. It takes Kyle 3 hours to sand a wooden floor. Tom can do the same job in 2.5 hours. Which equation can be used to determine the number of hours, x, it takes Kyle and Tom to complete the job if they work together?

A. $3+2.5=x$

B. $\frac{1}{3}+\frac{2}{5}=\frac{1}{x}$

C. $\frac{x}{3+2.5}=1$

D. $\frac{1}{3}+\frac{2}{5}=x$

16. If $f(x)=1-[x(1-2x)]^3$, compute $f(-1)$.

17. The diameter of the inside of a hemispherical dome of a planetarium is 400 feet. It costs \$25 per square foot to install projection screen on this dome. How much does it cost to cover the entire inside of the dome with projection screen?

A. $160{,}000\pi$ dollars

B. $640{,}000\pi$ dollars

C. $4{,}000{,}000\pi$ dollars

D. $16{,}000{,}000\pi$ dollars

18. Four discs are arranged in a straight line, each tangent to its neighbors. A rectangle is then circumscribed around the arrangement of discs, as shown.

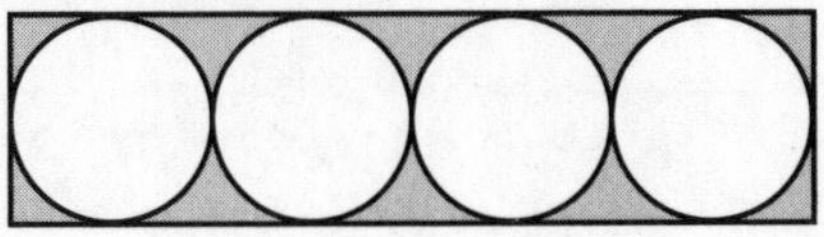

If the diameter of a disc is $\frac{3}{4}$ inch, find the area of the region within the rectangle between the discs.

A. $\left(\frac{9}{4}-\frac{\pi}{16}\right)$ square inches

B. $\frac{9}{4}\left(1-\frac{\pi}{4}\right)$ square inches

C. $\left(\frac{9}{4}-\frac{9}{4}\pi\right)$ square inches

D. $\left(\frac{9}{4}-\frac{9}{64}\pi\right)$ square inches

19. If the circumference of a circle is $\pi\sqrt{2}$ meters, what is the area of the circle?

A. 2π square meters

B. $\frac{\pi}{2}$ square meters

C. $\sqrt{2}\,\pi$ square meters

D. $\frac{\sqrt{2}}{2}\pi$ square meters

20. Marty has at most $450 to spend on groceries and household items. She spent $\frac{2}{5}$ of the money on household items and 60% of the remaining amount of groceries. How much money does she have left after these expenses?

A. $108

B. $162

C. $270

D. $390

SHOW YOUR WORK HERE

practice test 3 — Mathematical Reasoning

21. A new reality-television show had 7.1×10^7 viewers for the pilot episode and then 8.2×10^6 viewers for the second episode. How many fewer viewers were there for the second episode? Enter a decimal accurate to the hundredths place in the first box and an integer as the power of 10 to express your answer using proper scientific notation:

$\square \times 10^{\square}$

22. The length of a rectangular deck storage box is 2.5 feet. The height and width both measure *m* feet, as shown:

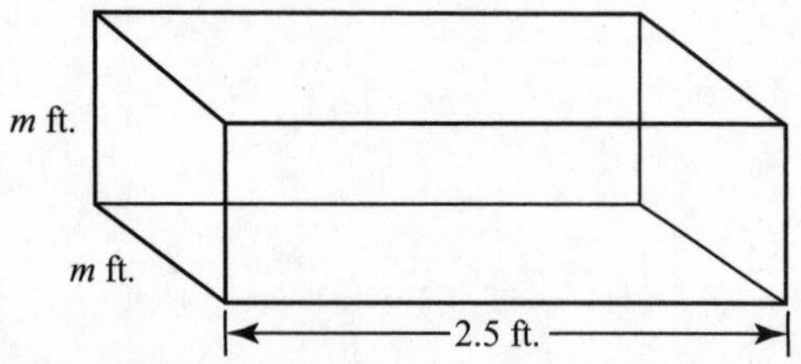

If the volume of the box is 5.625 cubic feet, what is the area of the top of the deck box?

A. 1.5 square feet

B. 2.25 square feet

C. 3.75 square feet

D. 4.00 square feet

SHOW YOUR WORK HERE

23. A cell phone accessories merchant has five different types of accessories for sale. The fraction that each type of accessory accounts for his entire inventory is described by this pie chart:

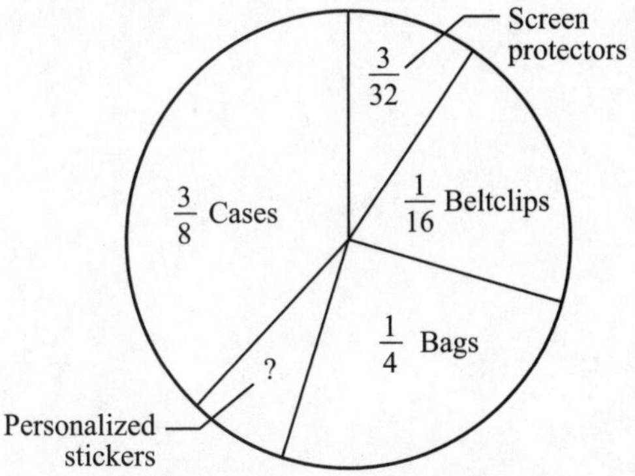

If the merchant has 6,400 individual items for sale, how many of them are personalized stickers?

24. Three fair 6-sided dice have faces labeled 1 through 6. They are rolled simultaneously. What is the probability that all three dice come to rest on the same number?

A. $\frac{1}{216}$

B. $\frac{1}{36}$

C. $\frac{1}{6}$

D. $\frac{1}{3}$

25. To which of these expressions is this product equivalent?

$$\sqrt[4]{27z^2w^5} \cdot \sqrt[4]{3z^6w^2}$$

A. $w^3 \cdot \sqrt[4]{3z^2w}$

B. $3z^2w \cdot \sqrt[4]{w^3}$

C. $3z^4w^3 \cdot \sqrt[4]{w}$

D. $3zw \cdot \sqrt[4]{3z^2w^2}$

SHOW YOUR WORK HERE

practice test 3 — Mathematical Reasoning

26. Solve for x: $\frac{1}{3}\left(\frac{5}{2}x-2\right) \geq \frac{1}{6}+x$

SHOW YOUR WORK HERE

A. $x \leq -\frac{3}{11}$

B. $x \leq -5$

C. $x \geq -5$

D. $x \geq -\frac{3}{11}$

27. A bungee jumper starts her descent from the top of a cliff 2,000 feet above a lake. She descends at a rate of 40 feet per second. Which expression gives her height above the lake s seconds after she jumps?

A. $2{,}000 + 40s$

B. $40(2{,}000 - s)$

C. $40s$

D. $2{,}000 - 40s$

28. Which of the following is NOT equivalent to $6(1-x^2)+3x(x^2-1)$?

A. $3(2-x)(1-x^2)$

B. $3(x-2)(x-1)(x+1)$

C. $(6+3x)(x^2-1)$

D. $(3x-6)(x^2-1)$

29. Evaluate the expression $\left(\frac{x}{3x-\frac{1}{3}}\right)^2$ at $x=-\frac{2}{3}$. Enter your answer as a simplified fraction:

$\frac{\square}{\square}$

30. Which of the following is the solution set of the inequality $x \le \frac{1}{2}y + 1$?

SHOW YOUR WORK HERE

A.

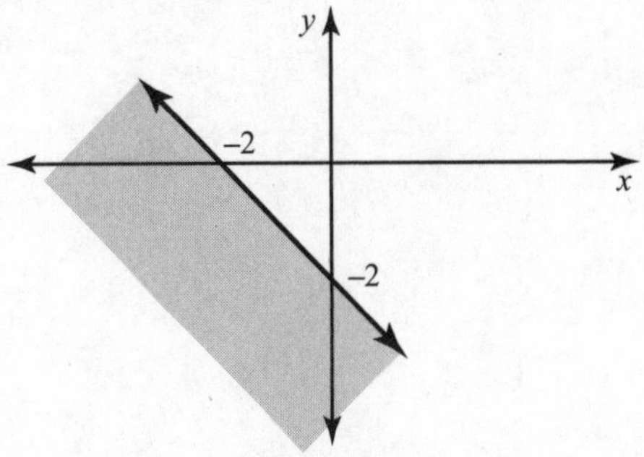

B.

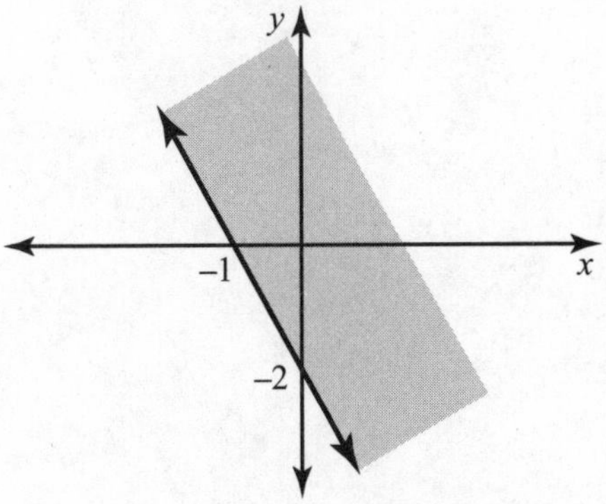

C.

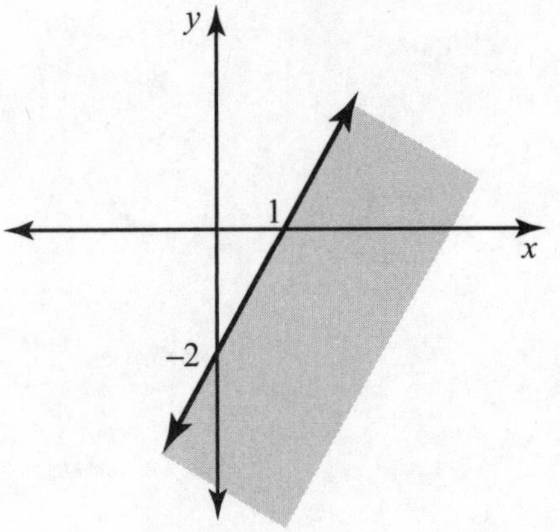

D.

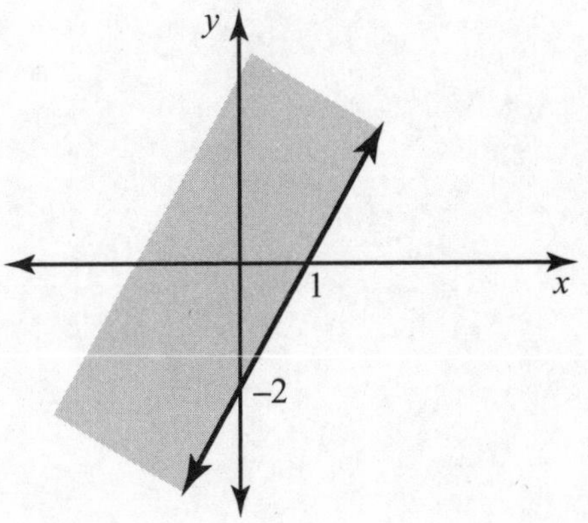

SHOW YOUR WORK HERE

31. One space heater can increase the room temperature from 55°F to 72°F in 3 hours working by itself. A second, more powerful, space heater can do so in 2 hours by itself. Which equation can be used to determine the number of hours, h, it takes them to raise the temperature together?

A. $\frac{1}{3}h+\frac{1}{2}h=1$

B. $2h+3h=1$

C. $\frac{1}{3h}+\frac{1}{2h}=1$

D. $\frac{3}{h}+\frac{2}{h}=1$

32. The length, l, of a picture window is $\frac{1}{2}$ foot longer than twice the width, w. If the area of the window must be between 6 square feet and 8 square feet, which inequality can be used to determine the possible values of the width of the window?

A. $6 \le w^2 \le 8$

B. $12 \le 1 + 6w \le 16$

C. $12 \le w + 4w^2 \le 16$

D. $6 \le 1 + 4w \le 8$

33. What is the x-intercept of the linear function $f(x) = 0.5(1.3 - 2.8x) - 1$?

[ ] , [ ] .

34. Select the value from the list $\{-17, -3, 1, 17\}$ to complete the following sentence:

The function $f(x) = -2x^2 - 12x - 17$ has a maximum value of [ ] .

35. What is the domain of the function $g(x) = \dfrac{x(x+2)}{(x^2+9)(x-5)}$?

A. All real numbers except 5

B. All real numbers except –3, 3, and 5

C. All real numbers except –3, –2, 3, and 5

D. All real numbers except –3, –2, 0, 3, and 5

36. What is the average rate of change of the function $f(x) = \dfrac{x}{x+1}$ on the interval $[1, 4]$?

A. 1

B. $\dfrac{1}{10}$

C. $\dfrac{3}{10}$

D. 3

SHOW YOUR WORK HERE

37. Which of these graphs does NOT represent a function with independent variable *x*?

SHOW YOUR WORK HERE

A.

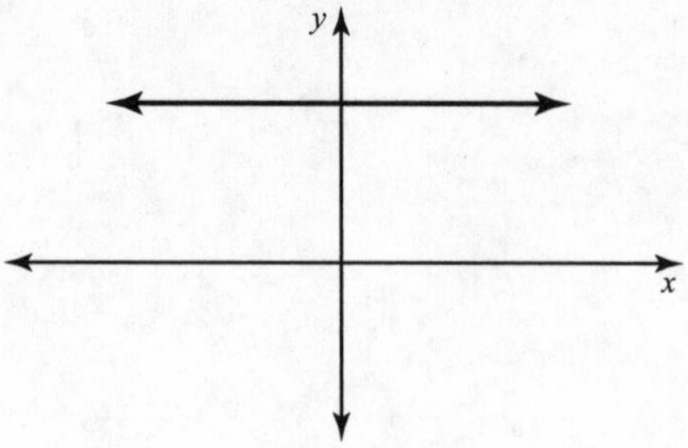

B.

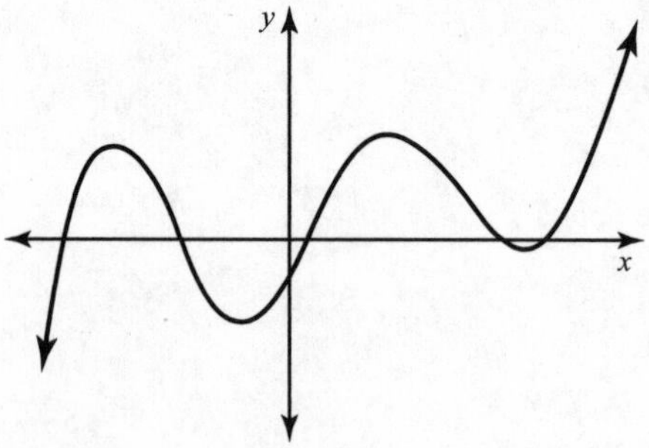

C.

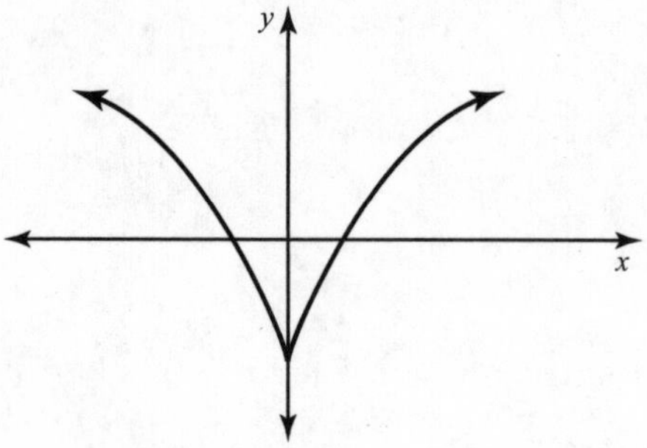

D.

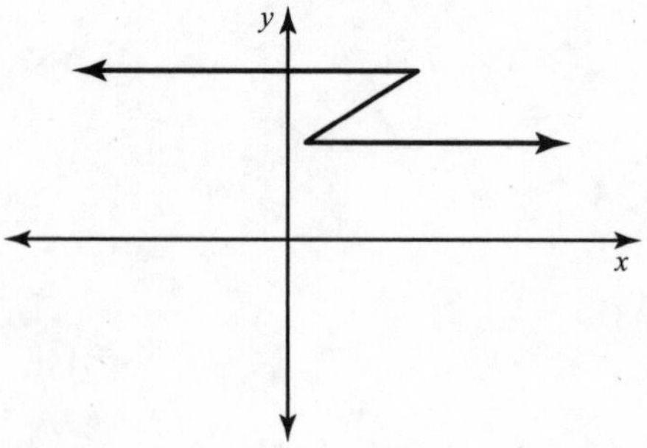

38. If $\frac{1}{2}$ cup of soup contains 15 mg of sodium, how much sodium is contained in $2\frac{3}{8}$ cups of soup?

A. $\frac{2 \times 15}{2\frac{3}{8}}$ mg

B. $2 \times \left(2\frac{3}{8}\right) \times 15$ mg

C. $\frac{2 \times \left(2\frac{3}{8}\right)}{15}$ mg

D. $\frac{\left(2\frac{3}{8}\right) \times 15}{2}$ mg

39. Suppose $10 < y < 100$. Which of these numbers must be larger than 100?

A. $y + 10$

B. $\frac{100}{y}$

C. $\frac{y}{0.1}$

D. $0.1y$

40. Which of these is the smallest?

A. 0.5% of 10,000

B. 1,000% of 0.5

C. 1% of 5,000

D. 500% of 0.10

SHOW YOUR WORK HERE

Practice test 3—Mathematical Reasoning

SHOW YOUR WORK HERE

41. A roll of paper labels 6 inches high, when unrolled, measures 6,525 inches in length. The cans for which these labels are used have the following dimensions:

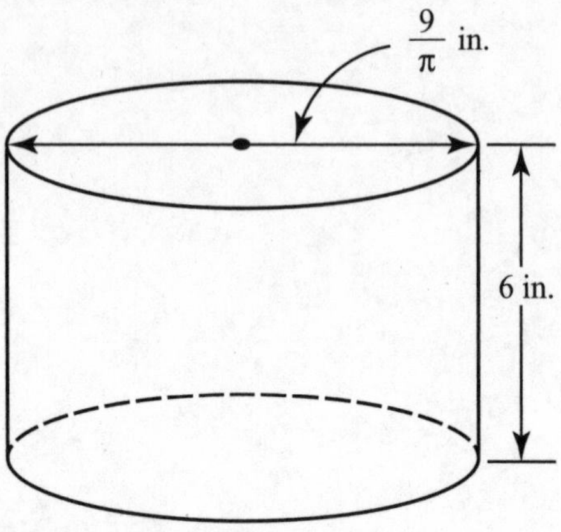

How many cans can be labeled with a single roll?

42. The owner of a small gym valued at \$750,000 pays \$4,500 in property taxes each year. At this tax rate, the owner of a larger gym valued at \$1,100,000 should expect to pay how much property tax? Let p be the property taxes paid for the \$1,100,000 gym. Fill in the boxes below to set up a proportion that can be used to determine p:

$$\frac{\square}{\square} = \frac{\square}{p}$$

43. On average, a single human hair grows approximately 0.50 inch per month. At this rate, how long would a hair grow in 3 years?

44. Two seasons ago, two running backs on a college football team rushed a combined 1,728 yards. One running back rushed three times as many yards as the other. Which system can be used to determine the number of yards rushed by each of the running backs?

SHOW YOUR WORK HERE

A. $\begin{cases} xy = 1{,}728 \\ y + 3x = 0 \end{cases}$

B. $\begin{cases} x + y = 1{,}728 \\ y + 3x = 0 \end{cases}$

C. $\begin{cases} x + y = 1{,}728 \\ y = 3x \end{cases}$

D. $\begin{cases} x + 3y = 1{,}728 \\ y = 3x \end{cases}$

45. A yo-yo bobs up and down along a vertical path at a steady pace. The position y of the yo-yo (in inches) below the person's hand (which is assumed to be at $y = 0$) for the first 6 seconds of its movement is described by the following graph:

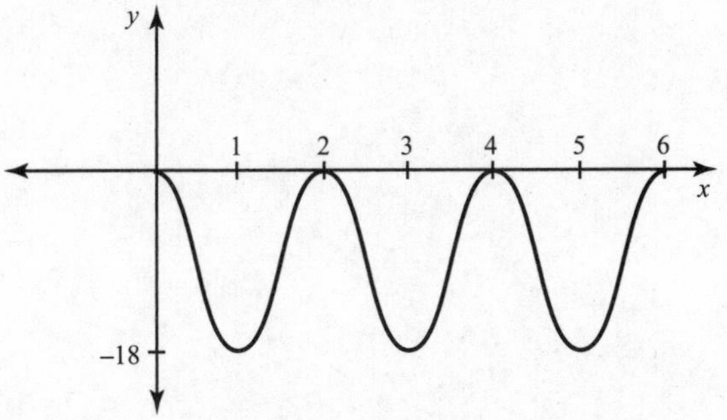

How far did the yo-yo move in the first four seconds?

A. 18 inches

B. 36 inches

C. 72 inches

D. 90 inches

Practice test 3 — Mathematical Reasoning

46. Glenn wants to build a 2-foot wide walkway along the perimeter of his pond, as shown.

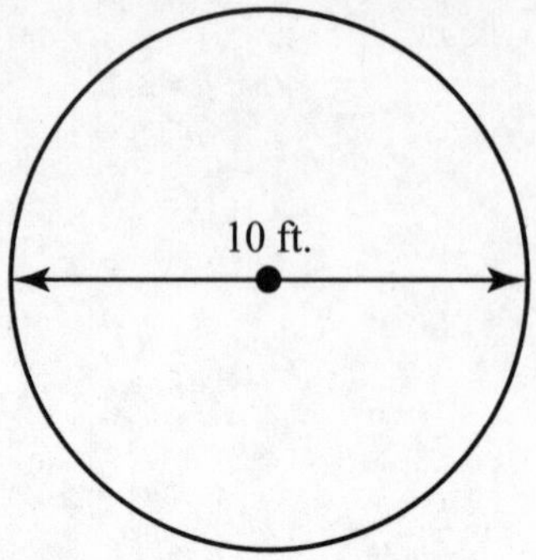

Paving stones cost $8 per square foot. Approximate what is the cost to install such a walkway to the nearest dollar?

$ ______

SHOW YOUR WORK HERE

SCIENCE

90 Minutes • 35 Questions

Directions: The Science Test consists of questions in several formats designed to measure your knowledge of general science concepts. The questions are based on brief passages of text and visual information (charts, graphs, diagrams, and other figures). Some questions are based on both text and visual information. Study the information provided, and answer the question(s) that follow, referring back to the information as needed.

Most questions are multiple-choice, but to answer some questions, you will be required to select from a drop-down menu, fill an answer in a blank, drag and drop correct answers, and select answers on a given graphic. Record your answers on the Science section of the answer sheet provided. To review how to answer these questions on your answer sheet, please refer to "Directions for Taking the Practice Test" on page 865.

Question 1 refers to the following information.

There are three main types of rocks—igneous, sedimentary, and metamorphic—that are classified based on how they are formed. Rocks that are made of tiny pieces of rock, such as sand, are called sedimentary. The tiny pieces become packed together over time. Sometimes additional layers of sediment pile on top of existing rocks, giving a striped appearance. Sedimentary rocks take many years to form. Igneous rocks are formed when molten rock, called magma when it is located inside the earth, cools down and forms solid rocks. Magma can cool slowly inside the earth to form igneous rocks. But sometimes magma is forced to the earth's surface, typically through volcanic eruptions or in places where the seafloor spreads apart. Once magma reaches the surface, it is called lava and can cool quickly to form igneous rock. The third type of rock, metamorphic, is formed when the structure of an existing rock is changed through forces, such as high heat and pressure. Any type of rock (sedimentary, igneous, or even an existing metamorphic rock) can become a metamorphic rock if subjected to enough heat and pressure. The conditions that form metamorphic rock typically occur deep within the earth.

1. Based on the information in the passage, which type of rock is **most likely** to be found on the side of a volcano a month after an eruption occurs?

   A. Sedimentary

   B. Igneous

   C. Metamorphic

   D. Magma

Question 2 refers to the following information.

Food that is consumed makes its way through the esophagus into the stomach, where it is churned up and partially digested by various enzymes. Chyme, a soupy mix of churned up food, water, and enzymes, exits the stomach into the small intestine. The small intestine is about four times longer than the large intestine, but the large intestine has a greater circumference. The inner lining of the small intestine is covered with tiny, soft, stationary projections called villi, and there are even tinier projections branching off from the villi called micro-villi. About 80–90% of the water and nutrients from the chyme are absorbed into the body as the chyme moves through the small intestine; most of the remainder is absorbed as the remaining chyme transits the large intestine.

2. What is the **most** probable reason that the small intestine is so long and has such a complicated interior surface?

   A. The structure continues to physically grind the chime.

   B. The structure moves chyme efficiently through the small intestine.

   C. The structure prevents chyme from moving backward into the stomach.

   D. The structure provides additional surface area for water absorption.

Question 3 refers to the following information and diagram.

A food web diagram illustrates the feeding relationships between the organisms in an ecosystem. Food webs can be complicated; even just a few organisms can have multiple, overlapping relationships. There are three main categories of organisms: 1. producers, which create their own food from solar energy; 2. consumers, which get energy by eating other organisms; and 3. decomposers, which break down the bodies of other organisms, both plants and animals. Within the consumer category, there are different trophic levels; the primary level eats only plants, while the apex level can eat any virtually anything else in the ecosystem. Each row in a food web diagram indicates a different trophic level.

The illustration below is a diagram of a simple food web. An arrow pointing from one organism to another indicates that the first organism is consumed by the second organism. For example, the arrow pointing from beetles to dragonflies indicates that dragonflies eat beetles.

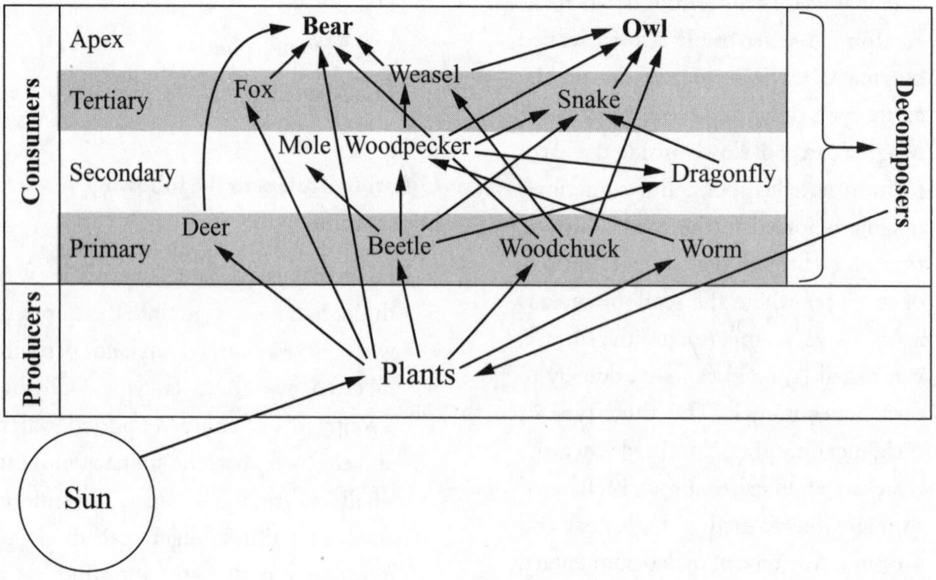

3. Which feeding relationship crosses the greatest number of trophic levels?

   A. Plants getting energy from the sun

   B. Decomposers breaking down consumers

   C. Bears eating berries

   D. Owls eating woodchucks

Questions 4 and 5 refer to the following information.

The brain is so important to the functioning of the body that it is isolated from most of the circulatory system by the blood–brain barrier (BBB). (Some parts of the brain, such as the pineal gland that produces the hormone melatonin, are not behind the BBB, so they can release hormones directly into the bloodstream.) This barrier is composed mostly of endothelial cells that line the capillaries along most of the central nervous system. Endothelial cells line most blood vessels, serving as the border between circulating fluids and the blood vessel wall, but these cells take on extra importance protecting the brain. The endothelial cells of the BBB are connected by tight junctions that prevent transport of soluble material from the blood into the brain. Necessary materials in the blood such as water, oxygen, and hormones can pass into the brain by diffusion, and waste products like carbon dioxide can diffuse out of brain tissue into the blood. Transport proteins, proteins that span the entire endothelial cell membrane, can move nutrients like glucose across the BBB by active transport. Other molecules and particles in the blood, particularly bacteria and other pathogens, cannot cross the barrier, so systemic illnesses of the body generally spare the brain. Infections of the brain can be very serious and difficult to eradicate, as antibodies and immune cells cannot cross the barrier to fight the infection. It is difficult to deliver medications or antibiotics to the brain, as most of these are also stopped at the BBB. Ultimately, it is a necessary tradeoff that some helpful chemicals must be prevented from entering the brain in order to ensure that harmful substances cannot cross the BBB.

4. According to the passage, what is the primary purpose of the blood–brain barrier?

   A. To keep blood and the nervous system completely separate

   B. To prevent autoimmune disease in the brain

   C. To control the flow of hormones to the brain

   D. To prevent pathogens from entering the brain

5. Where are endothelial cells located?

   A. In all tissues throughout the body

   B. In the lining of blood vessels

   C. Only in the blood-brain barrier

   D. Only in the central nervous system

6. Newton's second law of motion describes the relationship between the mass of an object and the force required to accelerate that object. The law is usually represented by the equation $F = ma$, where F is the force acting on the object (in newtons, N), m is the object's mass (in kilograms, kg) and a is the object's rate of acceleration (in m/s^2). Acceleration is the rate at which the object, once in motion, picks up speed. Assuming no friction, when a force of 24 N is applied to an object accelerating at a rate of 4 m/s^2, what is the mass of the object in kilograms (kg)?

   ______ kg

practice test 3 —Science

Question 7 refers to the following information.

In recent years, scientists have found increasing evidence that the bacteria living in the human gut play an important role in our health. This community of microorganisms is known as the microbiome. Research has shown possible links between the microbiome and important aspects of health such as proper digestion, healthy immune responses, maintaining body weight, and maybe even emotional well-being. Each person's microbiome is influenced by a variety of factors, including diet and the conditions present when the individual was born. However, not all gut bacteria are helpful. The key is the composition of the microbiome; a healthy population of "good" bacteria in the gut is needed to control the spread of "bad" bacteria that can cause illness.

The appendix, a small pocket located off the large intestine close to where the small and large intestines join, was long thought to be useless. More recent research suggests that its function may be connected to the gut microbiome. Medical researchers studied people who had been treated with a powerful antibiotic that wiped out virtually all the bacteria in the gut. After comparing patients who still had their appendix (group A) with patients whose appendix had been removed (group B), researchers concluded that the appendix might store good bacteria to repopulate the gut after an illness.

7. Which piece of evidence **best** supports the researchers' conclusion?

   A. There is a special immune response that specifically defends the appendix.

   B. A week after treatment, group A had a small but healthy microbiome.

   C. A week after treatment, all the patients in group B became sick.

   D. The patients in each group developed different microbiomes.

Question 8 refers to the following information and diagram.

Sometimes when humans need to move an object, they use a machine to provide some extra force to help. Any additional force provided by the mechanism is called mechanical advantage. A first-degree lever is a simple machine that can aid in lifting. It consists of a rigid bar that rests on a pivot called a fulcrum. The load is the object to be lifted; the pivot is between the load and the force being applied to lift it. When the load and the force are equal, they are in equilibrium, such as two equal weights on either side of a scale. The length of the bar across the pivot determines the ideal mechanical advantage (IMA) available for a specific lever, according to the formula

$$\text{IMA} = \frac{L_e}{L_r}$$

where L_e is the length of the bar between the fulcrum and the force, and L_r is the length of the bar between the fulcrum and the load. The farther the force has to move in relation to the distance traveled by the load, the less force is required to move the load.

The diagram below shows a first-degree lever.

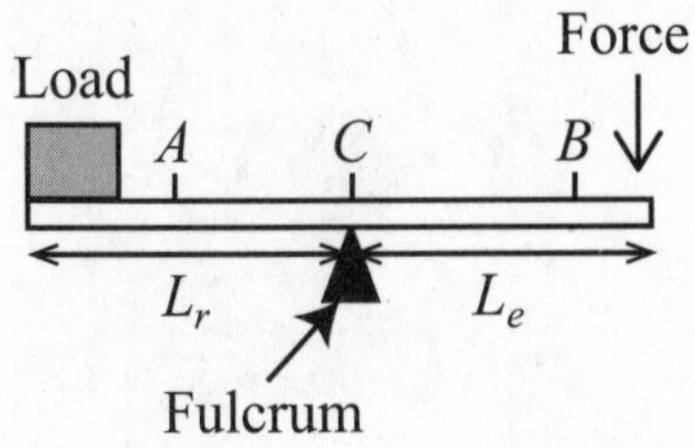

8. In order to achieve the highest mechanical advantage, how should the lever be positioned?

A. Move the fulcrum to position A.

B. Move the fulcrum to position B.

C. Move the load to position B.

D. Move the force to position C.

Questions 9 and 10 refer to the following information.

Light is a form of electromagnetic radiation that takes the form of a wave. Its speed seems instantaneous to the naked eye, but the speed at which light travels can be precisely measured. The speed of light can be influenced by outside factors such as molecules of matter in its path, so for precision, the speed of light is always measured in a vacuum, or an area where there is no other matter at all, not even air. Traveling through a vacuum, the speed of light is always constant and is approximately 186,000 miles/second. Light speed is used in many physics equations, denoted by *c*.

According to Einstein's theory of relativity, nothing can go faster than the speed of light, but that does not mean that only light can travel at *c*. There are different types of radiation and certain particles that may also travel just as fast as light. Some scientists theorize that a special particle called a tachyon can travel faster than light, but its existence has yet to be proven. Matter, such as a spaceship, a person, or any solid object, can never travel at the speed of light, as infinite energy would be required to make it happen, and infinite energy is impossible.

Tremendous speeds such as *c* can even affect time. As velocity increases toward *c*, time at the high speed slows down relative to a stationary object. For example, if it were possible to send a clock at light speed away from Earth for one year, according to the speeding clock only a few moments would pass while an identical clock on Earth would have advanced a whole year. This time difference has been tested using pairs of extremely precise clocks, keeping one on Earth and sending the other into orbit. An orbiting rocket does not travel at *c*, but it does travel fast enough that an orbiting clock is measurably slower than a stationary one. No matter how much distance is traveled at light speed, very little time will pass while traveling.

9. According to the passage, which of the following statements is true?

A. Only light can travel at light speed.

B. Light speed is constant in a vacuum.

C. Matter can travel at light speed.

D. Tachyons are faster than light.

10. The nearest star to Earth is Alpha Centauri, about 4.3 light years (the distance light can travel in a year) away. If a clock could be sent at light speed to Alpha Centauri while an identical clock stayed on Earth, how much time would pass on the moving clock?

A. A few minutes

B. 2.3 years

C. 4.3 years

D. 186,000 seconds

Question 11 refers to the following information.

In Mendelian genetics, particular traits in an organism such as eye color or leaf shape are controlled by a single gene. Each gene has two variants, called alleles, and every organism has two alleles, one inherited from each parent. The term *genotype* describes the organism's alleles for a trait; *phenotype* refers to what the trait actually looks like. In many cases, one allele is dominant over another, where the dominant allele determines the final phenotype. Just one copy of a dominant allele is enough to give an organism the dominant phenotype. Alleles are usually denoted by letters, with dominant alleles written as capital letters and nondominant, or "recessive," alleles denoted by lowercase letters.

Since every organism gets one allele from each parent, if the genotype of each parent is known, it is possible to predict the possible phenotypes of a given offspring. A Punnett square is a tool to help predict the possible phenotypes for a given trait. The mother's genotype is written across the top of the square, and the father's down the left. The trait is red eyes in flies, where allele combination *R* (*RR* or *Rr*) will be the red-eyed phenotype, and *rr* will be the white-eyed phenotype. Each square represents a possible genotype in the offspring.

Use the Punnett square to answer the question below. The first square has been filled in.

	R	*r*
R	*RR*	
r		

11. What proportion of offspring from two parents with the *Rr* genotype would be expected to have red eyes?

A. $\frac{1}{4}$

B. $\frac{1}{2}$

C. $\frac{3}{4}$

D. All will have red eyes

Question 12 refers to the following information.

Energy can be broadly divided into two main categories: potential energy and kinetic energy. Kinetic energy is the energy of motion, or the energy found in moving objects. The greater the force applied to an object, the greater the kinetic energy it will have. However, before an object has kinetic energy, it has potential energy. Potential energy is stored but unused energy that is ready to become kinetic energy. Anything that can move or power movement holds kinetic energy.

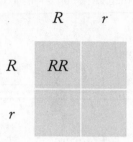

12. The image below shows a batter about to hit a ball during a game of baseball. Which number **best** indicates a source of potential energy?

A. 1

B. 2

C. 3

D. 4

Question 13 refers to the following information.

Mines are often dug in areas in which the ground is saturated with water, so water must constantly be pumped out of mines, or the mines will flood. In especially wet or abandoned mines, water can react with minerals in the mines and form a toxic liquid called acid mine drainage (AMD). The most common AMD is formed when pyrite (FeS_2, also known as fool's gold) reacts with oxygen and water and breaks down into iron(II) ions (Fe^{2+}) and sulfuric acid (H_2SO_4):

$$2FeS_2 + 7O_2 + 2H_2O \rightarrow 2Fe^{2+} + H_2SO_4$$

Iron(II) ions can be oxidized into iron(III) ions in this acidic solution:

$$4Fe^{2+} + O_2 + 4H^+ \rightarrow 2Fe^{3+} + 2H_2O$$

Iron(III) ions are soluble in AMD, but when the pH of the AMD increases above 3, as when it runs into a natural water source that dilutes its acidity, it forms insoluble iron(III) hydroxide, which is a bright yellow-orange color.

13. The Rio Tinto river in Spain flows through an area where mines have been operating for almost 5,000 years. In this area, the water is bright orange. Based on the information in the passage, what is the **most likely** explanation for the color of the river?

A. The river forms AMD that contains dissolved iron(II) ions.

B. AMD is diluted by the river and forms iron(III) hydroxide.

C. The river forms AMD that contains dissolved iron(III) ions.

D. The sulfuric acid in AMD is present in the river.

14. The earth's crust is broken into a number of huge plates floating on the earth's mantle. Areas where these plates are splitting apart are called divergent plate boundaries. In parts of East Africa, these divergent boundaries have formed deep valleys called rift valleys that are located between mountainous highlands. A scientist wants to determine how quickly these plates are splitting apart. Which experimental procedure would have the **best** chance of figuring out the rate of movement at the rift?

A. Identify the center of the boundary and measure the width of the valley at that location.

B. Look at historical rates of movement at other divergent boundaries.

C. Place a set of markers on each side of the boundary and regularly measure the distance between them.

D. Place several sets of markers on each side of the boundary and regularly measure the distance between each set.

Question 15 is based on the following information.

On a roller coaster, the first hill is the highest, and each rise and drop, or loop, is lower than the previous ones. This is because roller coasters rely on gravity to start them moving and a force called inertia to keep them moving. The only motor on a roller coaster controls the winch that hauls the train to the top of the first, highest hill; once the train is released, gravity provides all the force and acceleration necessary to move the train. Once it has started, inertia keeps the train moving forward. Inertia is the tendency of a moving object to stay moving in the same way and at the same velocity in the absence of a force that alters its motion or velocity. Once moving, the train also has momentum, which is the train's mass times its velocity. Momentum allows the train to pick up speed as it goes down the hill and overcome gravity to climb the subsequent hills on the track.

15. According to the passage, the roller coaster train enters the loops and turns of the track because of [Select ▼].

A. gravity

B. inertia

C. momentum

D. velocity

Question 16 refers to the following information.

Permanent hair dye (dye that does not wash out of hair) is a complex mixture of chemicals that play different roles. Hair color is due to the protein melanin. Hair with no melanin is white or gray. When permanent hair dye is applied to the hair, hydrogen peroxide, ammonia, and ammonium persulfate first open the outer cells of the hair strand and break down the natural melanin. This both allows the dye to get into the hair strand and bleaches the hair so that the dye can be more easily seen. The dye starts off as colorless small molecules (monomers) that can fit inside the opened hair strand. These monomers react with chemicals called couplers that link the monomers together to form larger intermediate dye molecules (polymers) that cannot easily be washed out of the hair. Oxidizers then react with the polymers to create the final dye color.

16. People who wish to avoid the strong odor of ammonia often opt for ammonia-free hair dye. However, most ammonia-free hair dyes are not permanent. Why is ammonia necessary for hair color to be permanent?

A. It links the dye monomers together into larger polymers.

B. It reacts with the intermediate dye polymers to create the final dye color.

C. It opens the outer cells of the hair strand to allow dye molecules to enter the hair.

D. It creates large intermediate dye molecules that cannot easily be washed out of hair.

Question 17 refers to the following information and graphic.

The graphic below is called the geologic time scale. This is a chart of all geologic time divided into sections based mostly on the types of fossils found in rocks of a given age.

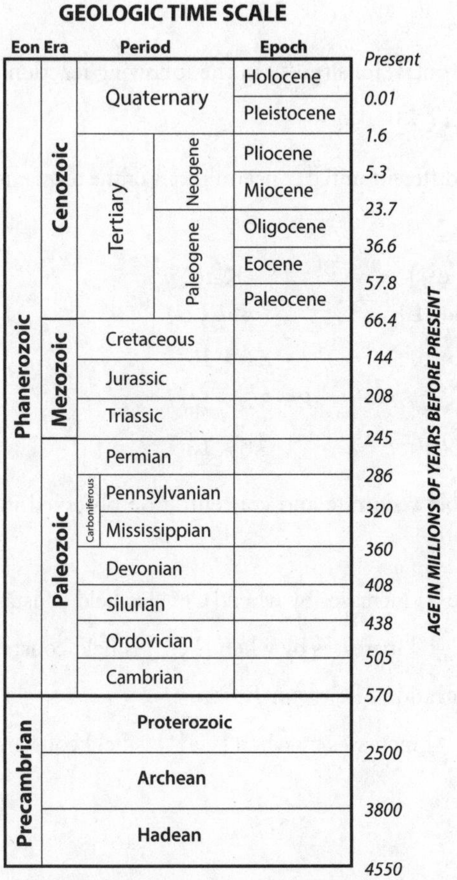

GEOLOGIC TIME SCALE
Eon Era
Period
Epoch
Present
Phanerozoic
Cenozoic
Quaternary
Holocene
0.01
Pleistocene
1.6
Tertiary
Neogene
Pliocene
5.3
Miocene
23.7
Paleogene
Oligocene
36.6
Eocene
57.8
Paleocene
66.4
Mezozoic
Cretaceous
144
Jurassic
208
Triassic
245
Paleozoic
Permian
286
Carboniferous
Pennsylvanian
320
Mississippian
360
Devonian
408
Silurian
438
Ordovician
505
Cambrian
570
Precambrian
Proterozoic
2500
Archean
3800
Hadean
4550
AGE IN MILLIONS OF YEARS BEFORE PRESENT

(From Decade of North American Geology, 1983)

Source: https://archive.usgs.gov/archive/sites/geomaps.wr.usgs.gov/parks/gtime/timescale.html

17. According to the graphic, which time division took place 316 million years ago?

A. Permian Period

B. Mesozoic Era

C. Pennsylvanian Period

D. Mississippian Period

Questions 18 and 19 refer to the following information.

Planets outside our solar system are called exoplanets. These planets are so far away that they cannot be directly observed by a telescope. Instead, astronomers must rely on indirect means of detection, or detecting the ways in which a planet can impact other nearby objects. For example, Neptune, the outermost planet of our solar system, was first discovered after astronomers realized that the orbit of the planet Uranus was being affected by a large, then unknown planet. Shortly afterward, astronomers observed Neptune through a telescope. Relative to Uranus, Neptune is fairly massive, but the distant objects that are easiest to observe are stars. The movement of massive objects, such as stars, is not easily impacted, but when a star's movement changes, the light emitted by that star can look different as well. This phenomenon, called "wobble," allows astronomers to record changes in the star's light and infer that an unseen planet is impacting the star's movement. The brightness of stars obscures smaller, nearby objects such as planets, so often the existence of a new planet is known but not directly confirmed.

18. It can be inferred from the passage that which kinds of planets are typically detected through wobble?

A. Small (in diameter), dim planets

B. Small (in diameter), bright planets

C. Large (in diameter), bright planets

D. Massive (mass-heavy) planets

19. Which of the following is a possible direct method of observing an exoplanet?

A. Measuring light from star wobble

B. Measuring starlight dimmed by a planet's shadow in front of a star

C. Using software to obscure a star's brightness

D. Using a telescope to view an exoplanet

Question 20 refers to the following information.

Cerium(IV) ions (Ce^{4+}) pull electrons from iron(II) ions (Fe^{2+}) in the following reaction:

$$Ce^{4+} + Fe^{2+} \rightarrow Ce^{3+} + Fe^{3+}$$

The initial rate for this reaction is measured at different initial concentrations of the reactants. The data is provided in the table below.

$[Ce^{4+}]$ (mol/L)	$[Fe^{2+}]$ (mol/L)	Rate (mol/L·s)
1.0×10^{-5}	2.0×10^{-5}	2.0×10^{-7}
1.0×10^{-5}	3.0×10^{-5}	3.0×10^{-7}
3.0×10^{-5}	3.0×10^{-5}	9.0×10^{-7}

20. Which statement describes the relationship between rate and concentration observed in the data?

A. Rate increases by the same factor that $[Fe^{2+}]$ increases by when $[Ce^{4+}]$ is held constant.

B. Rate increases by twice the factor that $[Ce^{4+}]$ increases by when $[Fe^{2+}]$ is held constant.

C. Rate is not affected by changes in concentration of Ce^{4+} or Fe^{2+}.

D. Rate decreases by half the factor that $[Fe^{2+}]$ increases by when $[Ce^{4+}]$ is held constant.

Questions 21 and 22 refer to the following information and graphs.

A species' population growth in the environment follows a few predictable patterns. Graphs A and B show two of the most common population growth models. Graph A shows exponential growth, where a population grows at an increasing rate regardless of population size. Exponentially growing populations tend to crash just as rapidly, entering periods of both rapid growth and decline. Graph B shows the logistic growth model, where growth is initially rapid but begins to slow down before eventually leveling off. In all cases, population size (*N*) is limited by the available resources; the maximum population an area can support is called the carrying capacity, *K*.

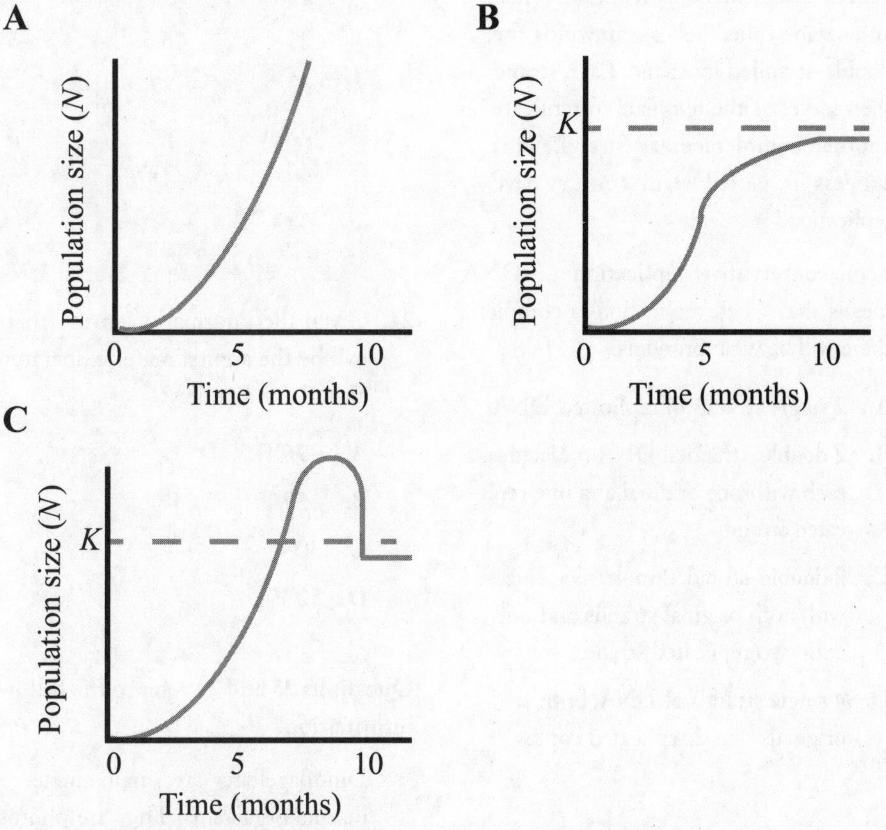

21. If $K = 5{,}000$, what would the approximate population be after 9 months if the population is following the logistic growth model?

A. 2,500

B. 4,900

C. 5,000

D. 10,000

22. What is the **best** interpretation of the growth curve shown in graph C?

A. Purely exponential growth

B. Purely logistic growth

C. Both exponential and logistic growth

D. Excessive growth followed by population collapse

Question 23 refers to the following information.

DNA, or the genetic blueprint for each organism, is a molecule composed of two strands that wind around each other in a specialized shape called a double helix. When a cell divides (splits into two), it needs to replicate its DNA so the two daughter cells will each have a complete genetic blueprint. DNA replicates when an enzyme called helicase unwinds the double-stranded molecule. Each strand then serves as the template to replicate another complementary strand. This process is called semi-conservative replication.

23. Semi-conservative replication of DNA means that when replication is complete, there will be what products?

A. 2 single strands of replicated DNA

B. 2 double-stranded DNA molecules, each with one original and one replicated strand

C. 2 double-stranded molecules, one with both original strands and one with two replicated strands

D. 4 single strands of DNA, both originals plus 2 replicated copies

Question 24 refers to the following information.

The table below lists temperature changes in the stratosphere, the second lowest level of Earth's atmosphere.

Altitude (km)	Altitude (miles)	Temperature (°F)
15	9	–75
20	12	–75
25	15.5	–57
30	19	–40
35	22	–22
40	25	–4
45	28	13
50	31	?

24. Given the information in the chart, what will be the approximate temperature at an altitude of 31 miles?

A. –75°F

B. –39°F

C. 30°F

D. 50°F

Questions 25 and 26 refer to the following information.

Dinoflagellates are small, single-celled marine organisms. They are photosynthetic, meaning they can create carbohydrates using sunlight, water, and carbon dioxide. They have many similarities to algae but are considered their own class of organism.

Dinoflagellates can live as free swimmers, but they can also live in cooperation with a host. A certain type of dinoflagellate, called zooxanthellae, engage with another organism in a mutualism, which is a mutually beneficial relationship between organisms. The relationship between two organisms associating in close physical proximity is called symbiosis. Zooxanthellae live inside the tissues of certain marine invertebrates such as corals, jellyfish, nudibranchs, sea anemones, and even giant clams. They may enter a host cell when the host cell is young, or sometimes zooxanthellae have a free-swimming stage of their life cycle before entering a host. Some corals even release chemicals that attract free-swimming zooxanthellae to them in order to start their mutualism.

Zooxanthellae provide the host and themselves with nutrients through photosynthesis, sometimes providing up to 90% of nutrition for the host. The remainder is obtained when the host acquires food directly through feeding. In return, zooxanthellae receive protection as well as the raw materials for photosynthesis from the host's respiration and a more favorable position in the water closer to sunlight then they might have on their own. Photosynthetic pigments in the zooxanthellae give them the red and yellow colors that their hosts share. Zooxanthellae are sensitive to rising water temperature, and a sharp increase can kill them. If favorable conditions do not return or the host cannot attract replacement zooxanthellae, the host will have insufficient nutrients and will eventually die.

25. According to the passage, what is the **most likely** difference between mutualism and symbiosis?

A. Only mutualism requires mutual benefit between organisms.

B. Only symbiosis requires close proximity between organisms.

C. Symbiosis is only between marine organisms.

D. There is no difference between mutualism and symbiosis.

26. Coral are colonial organisms that build elaborate skeletons out of limestone as they grow. How would a coral colony appear immediately following a sharp increase in water temperature?

A. White

B. Red or yellow

C. Thin or shrunken

D. Dead

Question 27 refers to the following information.

Water behaves differently from most liquids. When water freezes, it takes up a greater volume than when it is in its liquid form. Also, a volume of water freezes from the top down. In other words, in a cooling volume of water, a layer of solid ice forms at the surface first, while the water underneath remains liquid.

27. Density is the mass of a substance divided by its volume. How do the density differences between liquid and solid water explain why the top of a volume of water freezes first?

A. Liquid water is denser than ice, so liquid water floats to the surface.

B. Ice is denser than liquid water, so ice sinks to the bottom.

C. Liquid water is less dense than ice, so liquid water sinks to the bottom.

D. Ice is less dense than liquid water, so ice floats to the surface.

Question 28 refers to the following information.

A solution refers to a solute dissolved in a solvent. Colligative properties are properties of a solution that are dependent on the number of solute particles that are present, but not on the identity of the solute. Colligative properties do depend on the identity of the solvent. One well-known colligative property is freezing point depression. Solutions with a particular solvent have a lower freezing point than the pure solvent. For example, a NaCl solution in water freezes at a lower temperature than pure water. This is a colligative property because if the concentration of solute molecules or ions in solution is the same, the amount the freezing point is decreased is the same—it does not matter what the solute is. Therefore, a 1 M NaCl aqueous solution will freeze at the same temperature as a 1 M KCl aqueous solution. Both these salts break down into two ions in water, causing both solutions to have the same concentration of ions (2 moles of ions per liter of solution). However, a 1 M ethanol in water solution will have a different freezing point than a 1 M ethanol in benzene solution because the solvents are different.

28. Which of the following solutions will have the same freezing point as a 1 M Na_2SO_4 solution in water?

A. 1 M $CaCl_2$ solution in water

B. 0.1 M Na_2SO_4 solution in water

C. 1 M $MgSO_4$ solution in water

D. 1 M Na_2SO_4 solution in H_2O_2

Question 29 refers to the following chart.

The following chart depicts the average lifespan of mammals of different sizes. The numbers above each bar represent the average weight for that species in pounds.

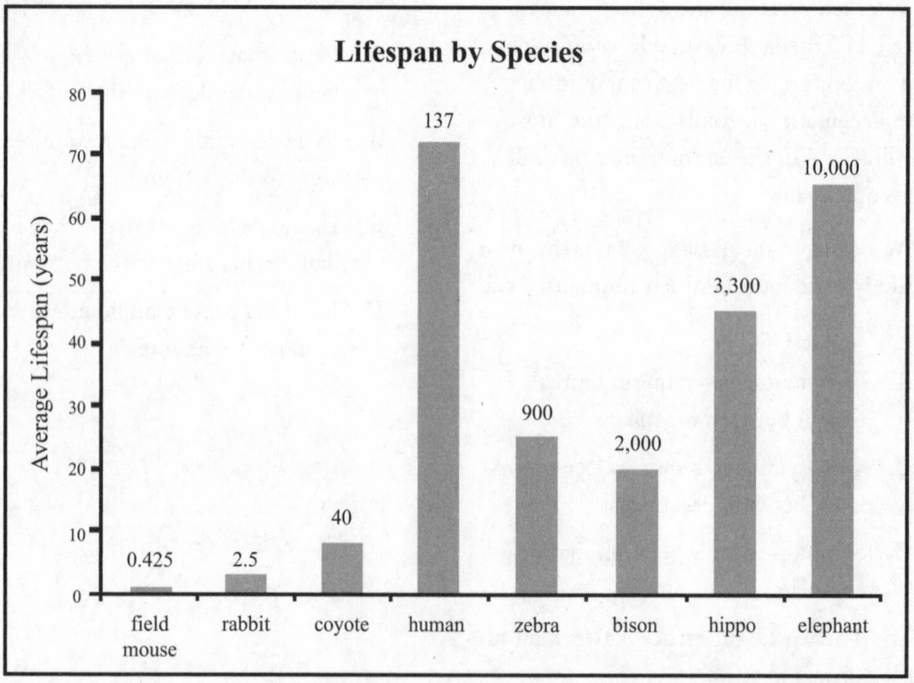

29. According to the chart, which species has the shortest lifespan relative to body size?

A. Human

B. Zebra

C. Bison

D. Elephant

Question 30 refers to the following information.

Lining the back of the vertebrate eye is the retina, a nerve layer responsible for sensing light and creating the nerve impulses that are sent to the brain via the optic nerve. Within the retina is a region containing the photoreceptor cells that actually receive the photons of light and provide visual acuity. There are two main types of photoreceptors in the retina—rods and cones—named for their general shape. There are generally far more rods than cones. Rods can be activated by just a few photons, giving humans the ability to see in low light. Rods perceive less detail and do not sense color. Cones come in three varieties, S-cones, M-cones, and L-cones, which correspond to the different wavelengths of light that activate them; each type of cone corresponds to a different range of color perception. Multiple photoreceptors must be active to provide color vision. The cones are also responsible for perceiving fine details and spatial relationships in our vision; higher numbers of cones correspond with greater visual acuity.

30. According to the passage, what is the **best** explanation for why humans see only in black and white at low light levels?

A. Only a few photons are activating the photoreceptors in low light.

B. Only one type of photoreceptor is activated in low light.

C. Humans do not possess photoreceptors to see color.

D. The ratio of activated rods to cones is higher in low light.

Questions 31 and 32 refer to the following information.

Modern plastics are usually made of polymers of hydrocarbon molecules. Hydrocarbons, as their name suggests, are molecules made up of mostly carbon and hydrogen atoms. Polymers are long chains of the same type of hydrocarbon. For example, polyethylene, which is used to make bottles, food containers, and toys, consists of tens of thousands of ethylene molecules linked together. (The dotted lines at the ends of the polyethylene molecule indicate that the molecule repeats itself many, many more times on each end.)

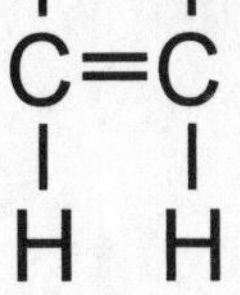

Ethylene

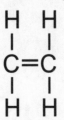

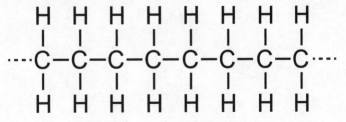

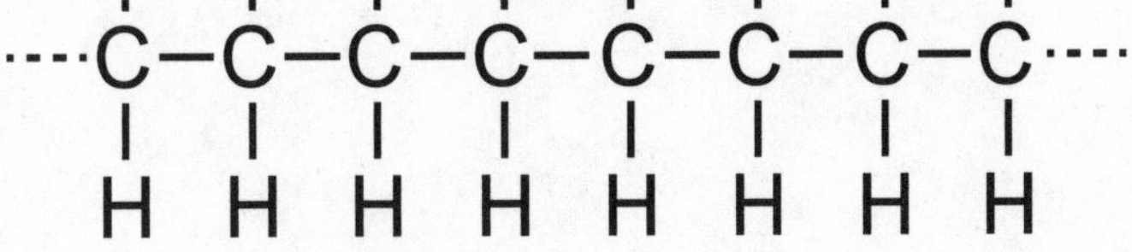

Polyethylene

Because plastic polymer molecules are so long, they are often arranged in a random, non-uniform way, also known as an amorphous structure. In some areas, the molecules may be in a more orderly, or crystalline, arrangement. Plastics with greater amounts of crystalline structure tend to be more rigid and opaque, while plastics that are more amorphous tend to be more flexible and transparent.

31. Which of the following statements is supported by the passage?

A. Contact lenses are made of a plastic with a high degree of crystallinity.

B. Plastic sandwich bags are made of a plastic that is highly amorphous.

C. The polymer molecules in a polyethylene toy car are arranged in a random way.

D. The polymer molecules in a clear seat cover are arranged in an orderly way.

32. How does ethylene change when it becomes part of a polyethylene polymer molecule?

A. Each carbon atom loses a hydrogen atom.

B. Each carbon atom gains another hydrogen atom.

C. The double bond between its two carbon atoms becomes a single bond.

D. One carbon atom is connected to a new carbon, while the other is connected to another hydrogen atom.

Question 33 refers to the following information.

The innermost layer of the earth is known as the core. The core is divided into an inner core, which is made of extremely hot but mostly solid iron, and an outer core made of hot liquid iron mixed with a few other metals.

The liquid outer core is not static. As parts of the liquid core cool, they solidify and sink toward the inner core. At the same time, warmer parts rise higher in the outer core. The up-and-down motion in the outer core creates circular convection currents. These currents in the liquid metal core create electrical currents, which lead to magnetic fields. The force created by the earth spinning on its axis, called the Coriolis force, causes all of the smaller magnetic fields to align in the same direction, creating one huge magnetic field for the earth.

33. Based on the information in the passage, what is the underlying cause of the earth's magnetic field?

A. The rotation of the solid inner core

B. Temperature and density differences in the outer core

C. The rotation of the earth around its axis

D. The precise temperature of the outer core

Question 34 refers to the following information and table.

Scurvy is a disease resulting from insufficient vitamin C. Symptoms include damaged gums, bruises, weakness, and fatigue; eventually death results if the deficiency persists. Vitamin C is acquired through fresh fruits and vegetables in the diet. During the days of sailing ships when sea voyages might take months and refrigeration was nonexistent, sailors at sea had very little access to fresh fruits and vegetables. Under those circumstances, sailors suffered high rates of injuries and death from scurvy. At the time, nobody knew about vitamins or understood the causes of scurvy.

In 1740, Scottish doctor James Lind performed an experiment to test if eating citrus fruits, such as oranges or limes could treat the illness, even though he did not understand the true cause of scurvy. He selected 12 sailors, all showing symptoms of scurvy. He divided them into 6 groups of 2 and put them on identical diets, except for the actions shown in the chart below. Only the sailors in Group 5 recovered.

Group	Action
1	Drink 1 quart of apple cider/day
2	Drink 25 drops of sulfuric acid/day
3	Take 6 spoonsful of vinegar/day
4	Drink half a pint of seawater/day
5	Eat 2 oranges and a lemon/day
6	Take 3 spoonsful of spice paste and barley water/day

34. By modern standards, what would be a valid control group(s) for this experiment?

A. Group 1 only

B. Groups 1, 2, and 3

C. A group that receives only 1 orange a day

D. A group that receives no intervention

Question 35 refers to the following information.

Acids and bases can be defined in several different ways. The most commonly used is the Brønsted-Lowry definition, which states that a Brønsted-Lowry acid is a chemical that can donate a hydrogen ion (H^+) and a Brønsted-Lowry base is a chemical that can accept a hydrogen ion. For example, the Brønsted-Lowry acid HCl donates H^+ to the Brønsted-Lowry base water (H_2O) in solution, forming a new acid (H_3O^+) and a new base (Cl^-).

$$\underset{\text{acid 1}}{HCl} + \underset{\text{base 1}}{H_2O} \rightarrow \underset{\text{acid 2}}{H_3O^+} + \underset{\text{base 2}}{Cl^-}$$

An acid without its H^+ is called the conjugate base of the acid, and a base after accepting H^+ is called the conjugate acid of the base. Thus, Cl^- is the conjugate base of HCl, while H_3O^+ is the conjugate acid of H_2O.

35. Consider the following reaction between a Brønsted-Lowry acid and base.

$$H_2SO_4 + OH^- \rightarrow HSO_{4^-} + H_2O$$

Drag and drop the correct molecule, ion, or word into the appropriate boxes in the statement below. (Enter the correct answers on the answer sheet.)

H_2SO_4 is a Brønsted-Lowry [ ] and [ ] is its conjugate [ ]. (Enter your choices in the blanks provided on the answer sheet.)

H_2O	acid
HSO_{4^-}	base
OH^-	

SOCIAL STUDIES

70 Minutes • 35 Questions

Directions: The Social Studies Test consists of a series of questions involving general social studies concepts. The questions are based on brief passages of text and visual information (graphs, charts, maps, cartoons, and other figures). Some questions are based on both text and visual information. Study the information provided and answer the question(s) that follow, referring back to the information as needed.

Most questions are in multiple-choice format. Others are meant to prepare you for the technology-enhanced questions that you will find on the test, such as drop-down, select-an-area, and fill-in-the-blank questions. Record your answers on the Social Studies section of the answer sheet provided. To review how to answer these questions on your answer sheet, please refer to "Directions for Taking the Practice Test" on page 865.

Question 1 refers to the following chart.

Senator (Article I, Section 3)	House Representative (Article I, Section 2)	President (Article II, Section 1)
• at least 30 years of age • a US citizen for at least nine years at time of election to Senate • a resident of the state one is elected to represent in the Senate	• at least 25 years of age • a US citizen for at least seven years prior to election to the House • a resident of the state one is elected to represent in the House	• at least 35 years of age • a native-born US citizen • must live in the US for at least 14 years

1. According to the chart, shared requirements between all political offices include all the following EXCEPT:

A. Age

B. Citizenship

C. US residency

D. State residency

Question 2 is based on the following map.

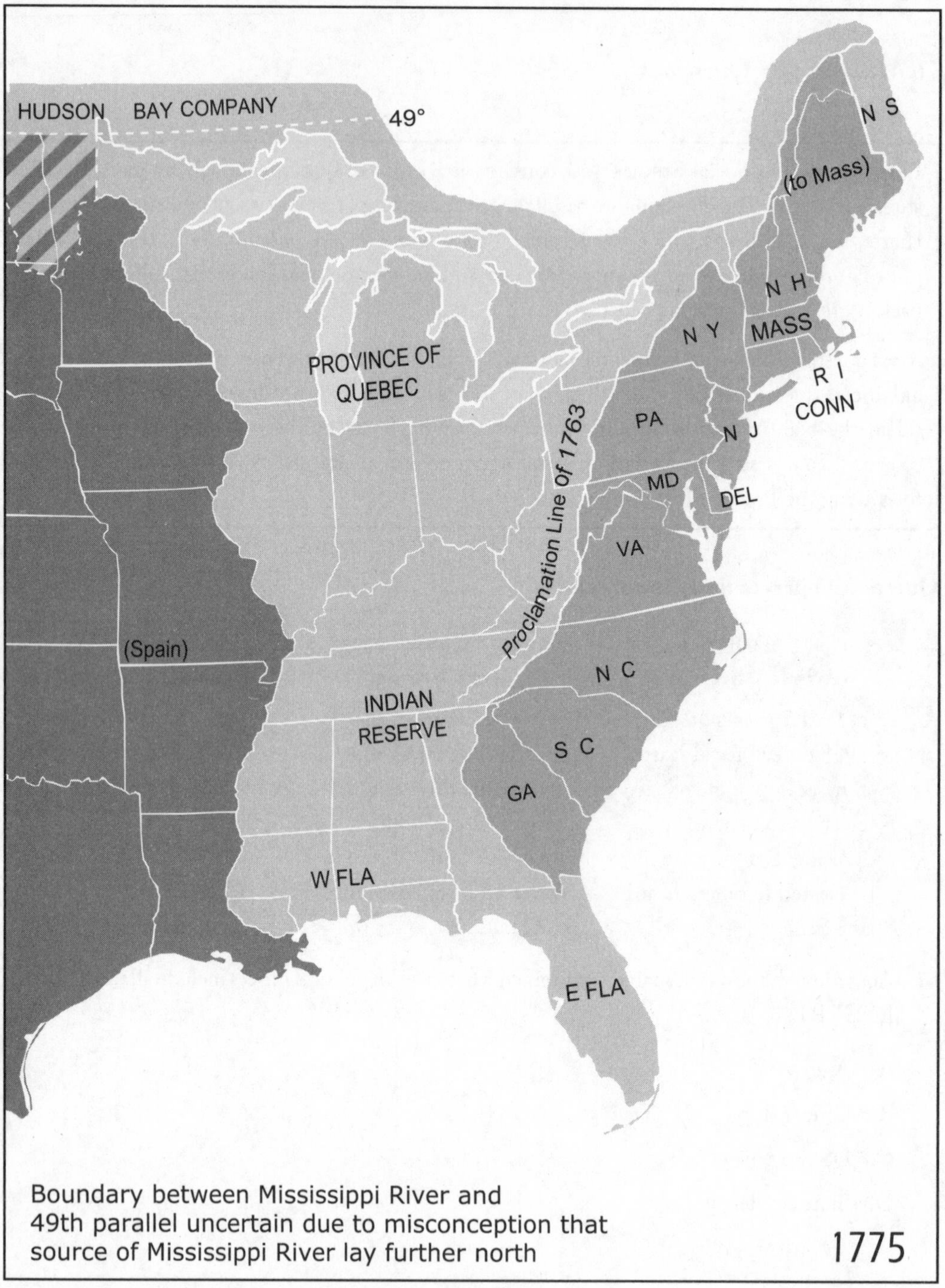

2. According to the map, which of the following was NOT an original British colony?

   A. Massachusetts

   B. Virginia

   C. Maine

   D. Pennsylvania

Questions 3 and 4 refer to the following passage.

This excerpt is taken from the People's Party Platform, July 4, 1892.

We declare, therefore—

First.—That the union of the labor forces of the United States this day consummated shall be permanent and perpetual; may its spirit enter into all hearts for the salvation of the Republic and the uplifting of mankind.

Second.—Wealth belongs to him who creates it, and every dollar taken from industry without an equivalent is robbery. "If any will not work, neither shall he eat." The interests of rural and civic labor are the same; their enemies are identical.

Third.—We believe that the time has come when the railroad corporations will either own the people or the people must own the railroads, and should the government enter upon the work of owning and managing all railroads, we should favor an amendment to the Constitution by which all persons engaged in the government service shall be placed under a civil-service regulation of the most rigid character, so as to prevent the increase of the power of the national administration by the use of such additional government employes.

FINANCE.—We demand a national currency, safe, sound, and flexible, issued by the general government only, a full legal tender for all debts, public and private, and that without the use of banking corporations, a just, equitable, and efficient means of distribution direct to the people, at a tax not to exceed 2 per cent, per annum, to be provided as set forth in the sub-treasury plan of the Farmers' Alliance, or a better system; also by payments in discharge of its obligations for public improvements.

1. We demand free and unlimited coinage of silver and gold at the present legal ratio of 16 to 1.
2. We demand that the amount of circulating medium be speedily increased to not less than $50 per capita.
3. We demand a graduated income tax.
4. We believe that the money of the country should be kept as much as possible in the hands of the people, and hence we demand that all State and national revenues shall be limited to the necessary expenses of the government, economically and honestly administered.
5. We demand that postal savings banks be established by the government for the safe deposit of the earnings of the people and to facilitate exchange.

3. Which of the following is NOT an area of concern for the People's Party?

A. Railroads

B. Banking

C. Distribution of wealth

D. Creation of a post office

4. The People's Party Platform is considered an important illustration in the creation of the type of political party known as a ______________ party.

Questions 5–7 refer to the following information.

"All too will bear in mind this sacred principle, that though the will of the majority is in all cases to prevail, that will, to be rightful, must be reasonable; that the minority possess their equal rights, which equal laws must protect, and to violate would be oppression. Let us then, fellow citizens, unite with one heart and one mind, let us restore to social intercourse that harmony and affection without which liberty, and even life itself, are but dreary things. And let us reflect that having banished from our land that religious intolerance under which mankind so long bled and suffered, we have yet gained little if we countenance a political intolerance, as despotic, as wicked, and capable of as bitter and bloody persecutions. . . [E]very difference of opinion is not a difference of principle. We have called by different names brethren of the same principle. We are all republicans: we are all federalists. If there be any among us who would wish to dissolve this Union, or to change its republican form, let them stand undisturbed as monuments of the safety with which error of opinion may be tolerated, where reason is left free to combat it."

—*Thomas Jefferson, Inaugural Address, 1801*

5. According to Jefferson, what must the nation "bear in mind"?
   A. Everyone must be a republican.
   B. The will of the majority must always be followed.
   C. The rights of all people must be recognized.
   D. The minority must be mindful of oppression.

6. Jefferson was speaking to a larger issue plaguing the young nation. What was the issue?
   A. The division created by political parties
   B. The large federal debt the nation faced
   C. The threat of foreign invasion
   D. The problems with the Articles of Confederation

7. What was the **most likely** cause of Jefferson's message?
   A. Fear of a dissolving Union
   B. Anger with the lack of protections afforded to those in the minority
   C. Threats of rebellion by the minority population
   D. His election as President by a narrow margin

Questions 8 and 9 refer to the following image.

Source: National Archives and Records Administration, no. 594360.

8. Which of the following would be the **most likely** time period for the image above?

A. Early 1950s

B. Late 1960s

C. Late 1980s

D. Early 1990s

9. Which of the following **best** describes the context of the image?

A. The contrast of antiwar protesters and soldiers during a controversial war

B. The oppression of the people at the hands of the military

C. The peaceful transition of power from one group to another

D. The willingness of one generation to forgive another for their actions of war

Question 10 refers to the following passage.

The current order of presidential succession was established by the Presidential Succession Act of 1947 and provides a plan for the executive office in the case of the following: incapacitation, death, resignation, or impeachment. The current line of succession follows the order of: Vice President, Speaker of the House, President pro tempore of the Senate, Secretary of State, Secretary of the Treasury, Secretary of Defense…

10. According to the passage, in the event of the death of the President, the resignation of the Vice President, the incapacitation of the Speaker and President pro tempore, the [ ] would become President.

Question 11 refers to the following passage.

> Now, [...] the right of property in a slave is distinctly and expressly affirmed in the Constitution. [...] Upon these considerations, it is the opinion of the court that the act of Congress which prohibited a citizen from holding and owning property of this kind in the territory of the United States north of the [36°N 36' latitude] line therein mentioned, is not warranted by the Constitution, and is therefore void.
>
> —*Dred Scott v. Sandford, 60 U.S. at 451–52.*

11. What resulted from the Supreme Court ruling cited above?

A. Slavery became legal.

B. The Missouri Compromise was invalidated.

C. The Constitution did not protect the right to own slaves.

D. Slavery was valid only in certain territories.

Question 12 refers to the political cartoon.

SOUTHERN CHIVALRY— ARGUMENT VERSUS CLUB'S.

Source: https://commons.wikimedia.org/wiki/File:Southern_Chivalry.jpg

12. The cartoon reflects which of the following circumstances during the mid-nineteenth century?

A. Debates over slavery were intensifying.

B. Outrage over southern secession from the Union.

C. The lengths to which political campaigns would go to win an election.

D. The continued violence that had overcome members of the minority party.

Questions 13–16 refer to the following chart.

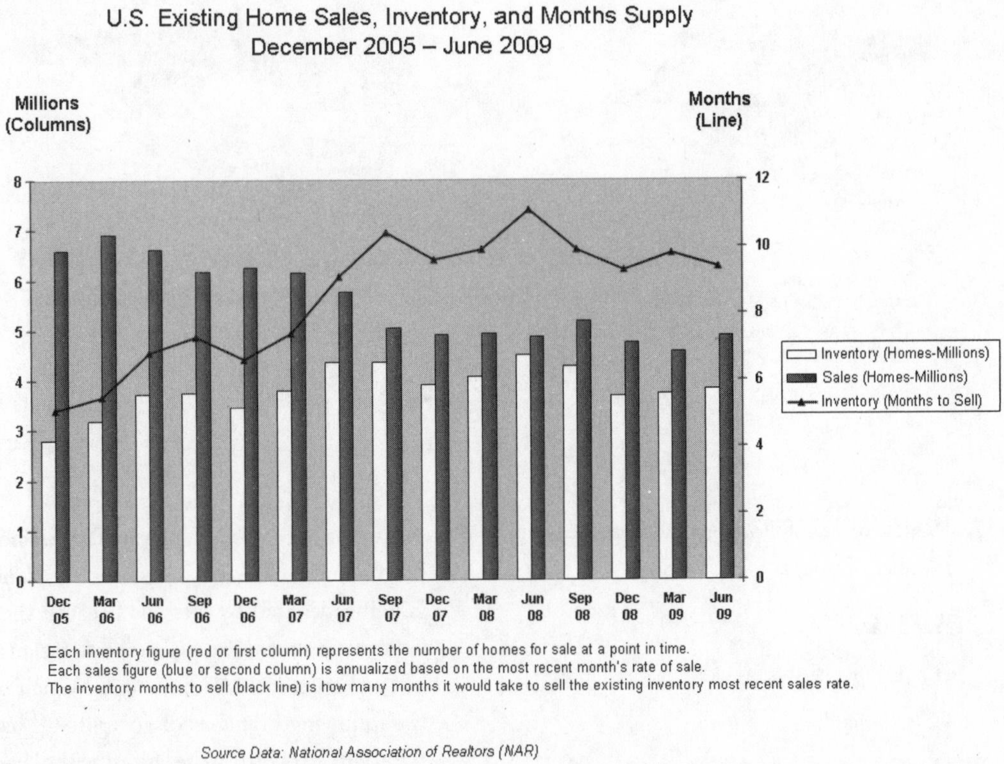

13. Select the month and year that was the **best** to sell a home. (Enter your answer on the answer sheet.)

14. Select the month and year that would be the **most** difficult time to sell a home. (Enter your answer on the answer sheet.)

15. Select the month and year that would be give a buyer the **most** negotiating power when buying a home. (Enter your answer on the answer sheet.)

16. Select the month and year that would cost the **most** for a buyer to purchase a home. (Enter your answer on the answer sheet.)

Questions 17 and 18 refer to the following map.

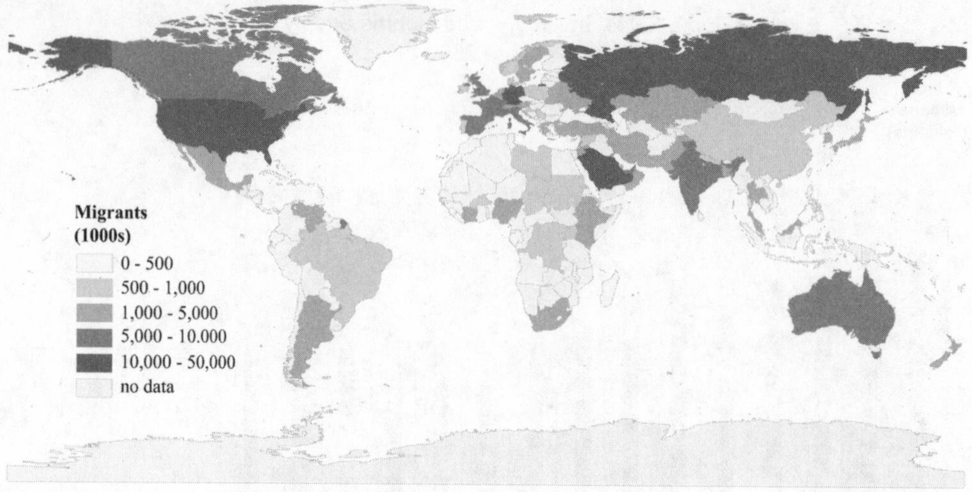

17. Which of the following had the greatest number of migrants?

A. Brazil

B. Egypt

C. Russia

D. Canada

18. According to the map, if someone were to migrate to the southern part of Asia, which country would they **most likely** migrate to?

A. India

B. China

C. Vietnam

D. Japan

19. A law has been passed and said law has not been vetoed. The law is controversial and is being debated by citizens because they believe it violates the equal protection clause of the Fourteenth Amendment. Which of the following branches of government has the ability to overturn the law using the basis of the Constitution as grounds?

A. Legislative

B. Executive

C. Judicial

D. State

20. A person has decided to vote for their favorite candidate based on their shared political views. The politician is pro death penalty, believes in a free-market economy, supports individuals' right to bear arms, and supports lower taxes from a smaller government. The politician would be considered a(n) ________.

Question 21 refers to the following electoral map of a Presidential election.

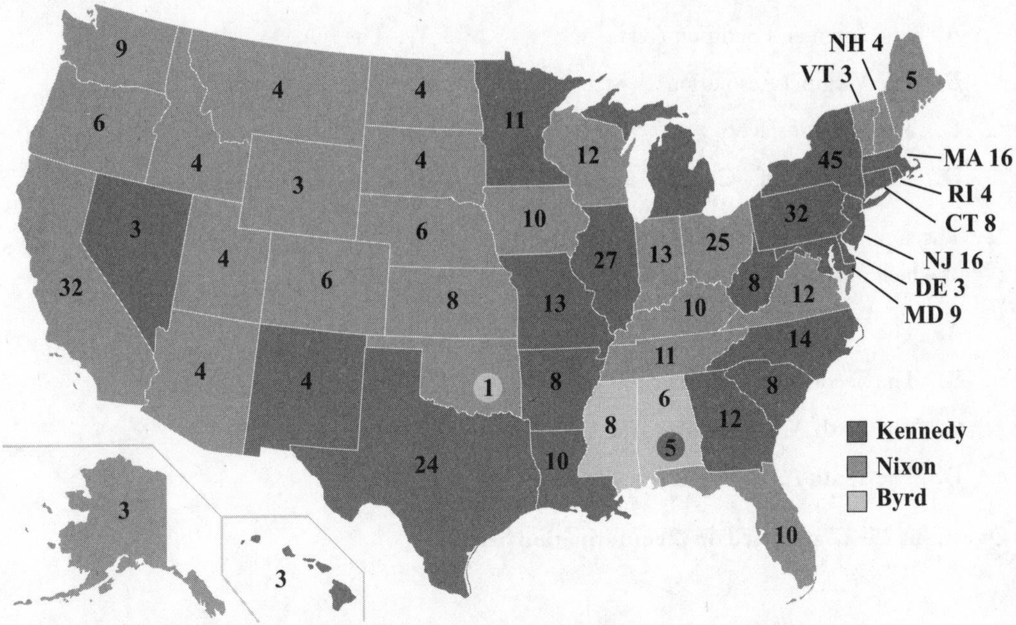

Source: https://en.wikipedia.org/wiki/File:ElectoralCollege1960.svg

21. The election results reflect an electoral victory for which candidate?

A. Richard Nixon

B. John F. Kennedy

C. Harry F. Byrd

D. No electoral victory; election went to the House of Representatives

Questions 22–24 refer to the following passage.

That the several states composing the United States of America are not united on the principle of unlimited submission to their general government; but that, by compact, under the style and title of a Constitution for the United States, and of amendments thereto, they constituted a general government for special purposes, delegated to that government certain definite powers, reserving, each state to itself, the residuary mass of right to their own self-government; and that whensoever the general government assumes undelegated powers, its acts are unauthoritative, void, and of no force; that to this compact each state acceded as a state, and is an integral party, its co-States forming, as to itself, the other party; that this government, created by this compact, was not made the exclusive or final judge of the extent of the powers delegated to itself, since that would have made its discretion, and not the Constitution, the measure of its powers; but that, as in all other cases of compact among powers having no common judge, each party has an equal right to judge for itself, as well of infractions as of the mode and measure of redress.

—*Kentucky Resolution,* 1798

22. The Kentucky Resolution was a response to which of the following?

A. The Alien and Sedition Acts

B. The Virginia Resolution

C. The issue of slavery

D. The creation of a Constitution

23. The argument in the passage was reflective of which of the following amendments?

A. The First Amendment

B. The Second Amendment

C. The Sixth Amendment

D. The Tenth Amendment

24. According to the passage, what created the Union?

A. The states

B. The people

C. The Constitution

D. The amendments

Questions 25–27 are based on the information below.

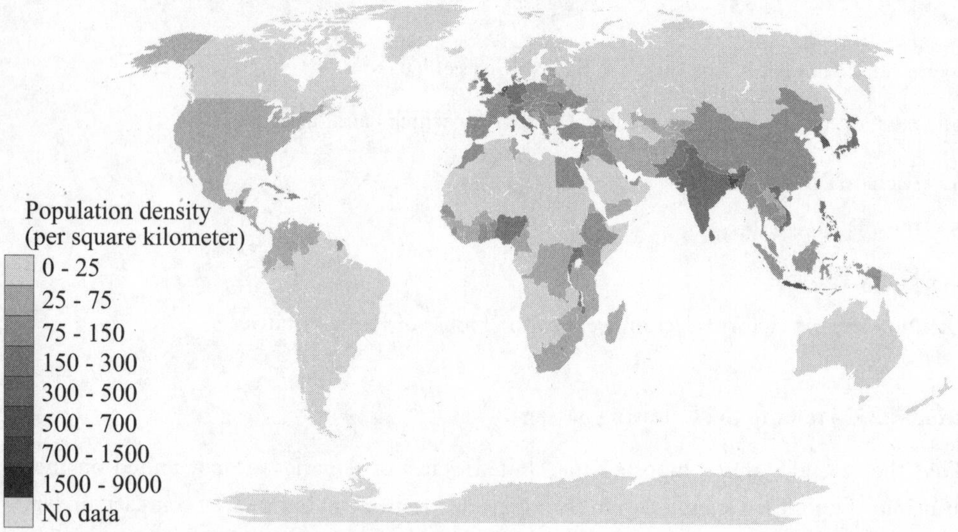

Source: https://commons.wikimedia.org/wiki/File:Population_density_countries_2017_world_map,_people_per_sq_km.svg

25. Countries that have a relatively low population density (0–25) include all of the following EXCEPT:

A. Canada

B. China

C. Most countries in South America

D. Saudi Arabia

26. Which of the following countries has the **most** people per square kilometer?

A. The United States

B. Canada

C. India

D. Brazil

27. Select the location in the Eastern Hemisphere that is below the equator with the highest population density. (Enter your answer on the answer sheet.)

Questions 28–30 refer to the following chart.

	Articles of Confederation	US Constitution
Levying taxes	Congress may request states to pay taxes	Congress has the right to levy taxes on individuals
Federal courts	No federal court system	Issues between states and citizens to be regulated by federal court system and Supreme Court
Regulation of trade	No provision for regulation of interstate trade	Congress has the right to regulate trade between states
Raising an army	Congress may not draft troops; states contribute militia	Congress may raise an army

28. According to the chart, the Articles of Confederation and US Constitution share which of the following powers?

A. The power to tax

B. The power to regulate trade

C. The power to raise a militia

D. They share no powers.

29. According to the chart, the US Constitution attempted to address the growing debt of the federal government by ☐.

30. For which of the following reasons was the Articles of Confederation replaced?

A. It lacked adequate power to enforce laws or raise funds, creating a federal government that was too weak to survive.

B. It gave the federal government too much power, which created a wide range of fear among citizens that had just broke from the monarchy of Great Britain.

C. It was the first true government for the new nation, and the intent was always to revise and replace it after the Revolutionary War.

D. Too much power was divided between the three branches of government, creating a government that was unable to govern effectively.

Question 31 refers to the following information.

The 2008–2009 Great Recession hit the United States economy hard. According to the Bureau of Labor Statistics (BLS), the number of unemployed Americans rose from 6.8 million in May 2007 to 15.4 million in October 2009. During that time, the US Census Bureau estimated that approximately 170,000 small businesses closed. Mass layoffs peaked in February 2009 when employers gave 326,392 workers notice. Productivity and output fell as well. Job losses, declining home values, declining incomes, and uncertainty about the future caused consumption expenditures to decrease. According to the BLS, household spending dropped by 7.8%.

Home foreclosures and the meltdown in US financial markets called for immediate action by Congress, the President, and the Federal Reserve Bank. For example, the government implemented programs such as the American Restoration and Recovery Act to help millions of people by providing tax credits for homebuyers, paying "cash for clunkers," and extending unemployment benefits. From cutting back on spending, filing for unemployment, and losing homes, millions of people were affected by the recession.

31. According to the passage, which of the following was NOT a cause of the recession?

A. Lack of Congressional action

B. Unemployment

C. Diminishing income

D. Decrease in consumer spending

Questions 32 and 33 refer to the following passage.

UNITED STATES v. NIXON, PRESIDENT OF THE UNITED STATES, ET AL.

Following indictment alleging violation of federal statutes by certain staff members of the White House and political supporters of the President, the Special Prosecutor filed a motion under Fed. Rule Crim. Proc. 17 (c) for a subpoena duces tecum for the production before trial of certain tapes and documents relating to precisely identified conversations and meetings between the President and others. The President, claiming executive privilege, filed a motion to quash the subpoena. The District Court, after treating the subpoenaed material as presumptively privileged, concluded that the Special Prosecutor had made a sufficient showing to rebut the presumption and that the requirements of Rule 17 (c) had been satisfied. The court thereafter issued an order for an in camera examination of the subpoenaed material, having rejected the President's contentions (a) that the dispute between him and the Special Prosecutor was nonjusticiable as an "intra-executive" conflict and (b) that the judiciary lacked authority to review the President's assertion of executive privilege. The court stayed its order pending appellate review, which the President then sought in the Court of Appeals. The Special Prosecutor then filed in this Court a petition for a writ of certiorari before judgment (No. 73-1766) and the President filed a cross-petition for such a writ challenging the grand-jury action (No. 73-1834). The Court granted both petitions.

32. Which of the following event was the **most likely** context for the statement above?
  A. The Red Scare
  B. The 1960 election
  C. The Vietnam War
  D. The Watergate scandal

33. The original source of the passage is **most likely** which of the following?
  A. The Supreme Court
  B. The Executive Branch
  C. A local newspaper
  D. A history textbook

Question 34 refers to the table below.

Federal Spending (Annual Average % GDP)	
Carter (1979–1981)	20.62
Reagan (1982–1989)	21.63
Bush, George H.W. (1990–1993)	21.27
Clinton (1994–2001)	18.79
Obama (2010–2017)	21.53

34. Which of the following is the **most likely** cause of higher levels of federal spending under President Reagan?
  A. Increased funding for defense spending
  B. Increased funding for environmental programs
  C. Increases in taxes
  D. Increases in government regulation

Question 35 refers to the passage below.

You've heard a lot about Obamacare, as it's come to be known. You heard a lot about it in the six and a half years since I signed it into law. And some of the things you heard might even be true. But one thing I want to start with is just reminding people why it is that we fought for health reform in the first place. Because it was one of the key motivators in my campaign.

—Barack Obama, October 2016

35. The term "Obamacare" became synonymous with the passing of the [ ] and was used as a negative connotation by President Obama's detractors.

ANSWER KEYS AND EXPLANATIONS

Reasoning Through Language Arts

Part I

1. D
2. B
3. A
4. B
5. B
6. A
7. C
8. A
9. B
10. Please consider my application for your open administrative assistant position at Anderson Consulting. (B)
11. My former colleague Vanessa Smith, who works in your Marketing department, (C).
12. over that time, I have developed strong organizational and administrative skills. (A)
13. daily job duties and achievements (B).
14. whether that's working with internal teams, interacting with clients, or handling vendors. (D)
15. With my experience at a busy medium-sized company, (B)
16. role (C).
17. I can meet and exceed (D)
18. Answering phones, customer service, and coordinating schedules

Part II

See explanation

Part III

19. B
20. C
21. A
22. D
23. Ireland, Germany, Turkey
24. A
25. B
26. A
27. B
28. D
29. B
30. A
31. A
32. D
33. C
34. D
35. A
36. C
37. B
38. D
39. A
40. Appropriate clothing: D; Inappropriate clothing: A, B, C
41. It was so nice to meet you at Andrew's party the other day! (B)
42. My designers are creative and innovative, and they know how to meet your highest standards. (C)
43. both digital and print (D)
44. strong and work (C)
45. ok
46. to
47. right
48. its

Part I

1. **The correct answer is D.** It turns out that the cat has a difficult personality, so Susan's mistrust of the cat is well-founded. There is not enough information given about Susan herself to conclude that she is mistrustful of more than just the cat (choice A). Because her dislike is described only in terms of Doc, there is not enough information to tell whether she dislikes all cats just as much (choice B). Nothing in the passage indicates Susan is unhappy with her employment (choice C).

2. **The correct answer is B.** Mrs. Blythe is skeptical of Susan's dislike about Doc. In lines 35–36, it's revealed Mrs. Blythe repeatedly asks Susan why she feels the way she

does, suggesting that Mrs. Blythe does not agree with Susan (choice A) and does not necessarily want to get rid of the cat (choice D). There is also not enough information about Mrs. Blythe's own personal feelings about the cat for the reader to know if she fully disagrees with Susan (choice C), or if Mrs. Blythe just wants to know more about why Susan feels this way.

3. **The correct answer is A.** The last paragraph details how the cat's Mr. Hyde personality "scared her stiff," so *frightened* is the correct answer.

4. **The correct answer is B.** In lines 86–89, the cat in his "Dr. Jekyll" mood is described as a "drowsy, affectionate, domestic, cushion-loving puss," but in his "Mr. Hyde" (choice C) mood, he is described as "a wild thing" with "a savage snarl." Dr. Blythe (choice A) is a member of the (human) family, and Jack Frost (choice D) is the cat who gave birth to Doc.

5. **The correct answer is B.** Individuals exhibiting violent and erratic behavior often have their behavior attributed to demonic possession, so to describe a cat with Jekyll-and-Hyde personality swings as "possessed by the devil" is the best choice here. Comparing the cat to an Egyptian sphinx (choice A) describes the cat in his calm mode but does not describe how his personality changes. "Cassandra-like croakings" (choice C) describe Susan's statements about the cat, not the cat itself. Saying the cat has "an unearthly beauty about him" (choice D) describes the cat's physical appearance, not his personality.

6. **The correct answer is A.** Lines 25–29 describe Rilla's original cat, Jack Frost. Susan (choice B) lives in the house, but does not seem to like the cats. Miss Cornelia (choice C) is a visitor, but does not seem to have anything specific to do with any of the cats. Walter (choice D) helps name Jack Frost's kitten, but he does not appear to be a direct owner of the cat.

7. **The correct answer is C.** Although *vouchsafe* is most likely an unfamiliar word, based on the context, *offer* is the best option. There is no indication of the tone of Susan's words, so *scream* (choice A) is not an appropriate choice. Both *refuse* (choice B) and *silence* (choice D) don't fit, because Susan is speaking the words.

8. **The correct answer is A.** The word *electrified* (line 72) is used to describe the visitors' reaction, and of the given options, *surprised* is the word closest in meaning. While the visitors might have felt happiness (choice B) or amusement (choice D), neither word has the same connotation as *electrified.* To feel anger (choice C) about the kitten's arrival would not be logical.

9. **The correct answer is B.** There are enough details given about Doc's changing behavior and personality to suggest that Dr. Blythe's statement is inaccurate and does not illustrate Doc's true personality (choice C). Susan does not see Doc as "contented" animal, so choice A is not an accurate conclusion. The sentence also does not compare Doc specifically with any other cats, so choice D is incorrect as well.

10. **The correct answer is *Please consider my application for your open administrative assistant position at Anderson Consulting.* (B).** The opening sentence should be clear and to the point, and choice B is the best, most straightforward option. Choice A is too brief, and doesn't explain what the writer is applying for. Choice C also is not clear on what job the writer is applying for, and it is also redundant, given that the reader already knows she works at Anderson Consulting. Choice D has too many adjectives.

11. **The correct answer is *My former colleague Vanessa Smith, who works in your Marketing department,* (C).** An appositive phrase (like "who works in your marketing department") should be set off with commas. Choice A is missing all punctuation and is a run-on sentence. Choice B incorrectly uses semicolons instead of commas. Choice D uses parentheses instead of commas, but assumes a too-casual tone by using *she* instead of *who*.

12. **The correct answer is *over that time, I have developed strong organizational and administrative skills.* (A).** As written in choice A, the second half of this sentence completes the author's point and presents the information correctly and succinctly. Choice B is awkwardly phrased, with "over that time" inserted into the sentence in a way that's confusing. Choice C takes out necessary information and makes the sentence vague. In choice D there is a lack of parallel structure in the compound subject (*development* and *growing*), and the sentence changes to the passive voice.

13. **The correct answer is *daily job duties and achievements.* (B).** The listed nouns should agree, and in this case that means making both plural. Choice B does this correctly. Choice A turns *achieve* into a verb and makes it past tense. Choice C creates a redundant list, unnecessarily adding *my* several times into the sentence. Choice D incorrectly has the singular noun "achievement."

14. **The correct answer is *whether that's working with internal teams, interacting with clients, or handling vendors.* (D).** The important thing in this sentence is presenting the list items in a clear, concise way. Choice D does this by creating three clear, separate verb–noun phrases, in which all of the verb and nouns agree. Choice A confusingly creates two different lists, and it is unclear which terms are supposed to match up. Choice B uses the same verb phrase three times, which is redundant. Choice C moves back and forth between tenses.

15. **The correct answer is *With my experience at a busy medium-sized company,* (B).** Look out for misplaced modifiers. The writer is not a medium-sized company (which is suggested by choices A and C). Rather, she is trying to say that she currently works for a medium-sized company (choice B). Choice D gets around this by fleshing out the clause, but it creates a run-on sentence when joined to the second part.

16. **The correct answer is *role* (C).** *Roll* (choice A) and *role* are commonly confused words; given that Terry is talking about her current job, the synonym *role* is correct. *Route* (choice B) and *row* (choice D) do not make sense with the context of the sentence.

17. **The correct answer is *I can meet and exceed* (D).** There is actually no punctuation necessary here. The colon (choice A) incorrectly sets up the expectation of a list. The comma (choice B) incorrectly pauses the sentence. The ellipsis (choice C) suggests that there's either a pause in speaking or that text has been removed. Neither is the case in this sentence.

18. **The correct answers are answering phones, customer service, and coordinating schedules.** There is no mention in the passage of managing interns, designing presentations, or planning events.

Part II

Extended response. Answers will vary. You will find two sample analyses on pages 947–948.

Part III

19. **The correct answer is B.** Paragraph four (lines 62–71) gives the height of a Missis-

sippi mud mass as "two hundred and forty-one feet high." The depth of the river at the Ohio junction is 87 feet (choice A). The length (in miles) of the Mississippi River is 4,300 (choice C). Choice D (675) is the number of miles of land the river would cover if it had a straight path.

20. **The correct answer is C.** The repeated use of the word *remarkable* best supports that the author feels the river is awe-inspiring. *Remarkable* is the opposite of *ordinary* (choice A) and *boring* (choice B). There is not enough information given to suggest that the author fears the river (choice D).

21. **The correct answer is A.** In the previous part of the sentence, the author is talking about steamboats, so it is most likely that flats and keels are different kinds of boats, and not describing the geography of the riverbed (choice B), the flow of the water (choice C), or the narrowness of the river's mouth (choice D).

22. **The correct answer is D.** By comparing the amounts of water discharged by the different world rivers, the author is demonstrating just how much bigger the Mississippi River's drainage basin is. As the author shows how much bigger the Mississippi's water drainage is than other rivers, he illustrates its superiority, but he doesn't offer an opinion of the superiority or inferiority of American rivers (choice A). Although there is a contrast between the Mississippi and these other rivers, there is not enough information given to prove that no two rivers are alike (choice B). This paragraph does not mention how long the Mississippi River is (choice C).

23. **The correct answers are Ireland, Germany, and Turkey.** Mexico is mentioned only as part of the Gulf of Mexico, and Canada is not mentioned at all.

24. **The correct answer is A.** Almost all of the facts given about the Mississippi River show how "remarkable" it is, suggesting that the author is enthralled by it. Although there are no first-person opinions given in the passage, you can use the tone of the information to determine how the author feels about the subject matter. The other answer options do not match the tone of the passage.

25. **The correct answer is B.** The first sentence states that climate change is one of the most complex issues facing us today, so it would make sense that the main idea of the passage reflects that a complex problem will require complex solutions. Choice A incorrectly categorizes climate change as a problem with simple solutions, when the first paragraph states that it is a complex issue. Choice C contradicts the passage, which describes long-term actions. Choice D doesn't work because the passage states that "while climate change is a global issue, it is felt on a local scale."

26. **The correct answer is A.** The second paragraph (lines 20–32) describes how carbon dioxide levels have been "on a relentless rise," which means that carbon dioxide in the atmosphere is increasing, not decreasing (choice B) or staying the same (choice C). The article is about the importance of climate change, so choice D does not make sense.

27. **The correct answer is B.** The fifth paragraph (lines 60–71) describes the process of adaptation, which includes adapting to different climates. Mitigation involves reducing greenhouse gases, eliminating choices A and D. While drought is listed as an example of climate change, it is not one of the author's approaches to addressing climate change.

28. **The correct answer is D.** Because most of the passage involves the author describing the options and plans in place for fighting climate change, you can infer that the author believes that change is possible. In the first paragraph (lines 1–19), stopping greenhouse gases is used as an example of what *could* happen, but there is no indication that the author believes that stopping all emissions is possible (choice A). In the second sentence of the second paragraph (lines 20–23), the author mentions how people can affect the amount of climate change, so choice B does not fit the context. The first paragraph states that climate change involves many different disciplines, so it is unlikely that he believes that economists (choice C) can solve the issue alone.

29. **The correct answer is B.** In lines 75–82, the author describes the climate throughout history, and reveals that the climate was stable for 12,000 years.

30. **The correct answer is A.** By illustrating how climate change has affected historical civilizations and showing that the climate has become less stable, the description gives the reader the sense that something needs to be done soon, creating a sense of urgency and a call to action. The opposite of choice B is true. The description is not humorous, so choice C is incorrect. The passage provides information supporting that climate change is real, so choice D cannot be correct.

31. **The correct answer is A.** In the seventh paragraph (lines 88–100), planning for heatwaves (choices B), dealing with stormwater (choice C), and improving water storage (choice D) are all included as ways cities and local governments are adapting to climate change. The passage does not discuss creating large-scale policies.

32. **The correct answer is D.** Choices A and B are too limited, given that the author talks about a "two-pronged approach" that includes both "mitigation" and "adaptation." Choice C suggests that the passage is only about the history of climate changes, when one of the main ideas is how to prepare for the future.

33. **The correct answer is C.** Paragraph 7 states that the department head decides when employees can dress casually. There is no specific timing mentioned, so choice A is incorrect. Paragraph 6 states that casual dress is allowed only in "special" circumstances, so choice B is incorrect. Office social events or offsite activities (choice D) may count as "special circumstances," but there is not enough information given to make this conclusion.

34. **The correct answer is D.** Paragraph 2 explains that Universal Inc. is trying to convey a specific, professional image with its dress code policy. Employees are allowed to dress how they want (within the general guidelines), so choice A doesn't fit. Although the passage does include information about punishments for breaking the dress code, it is not a main idea of the passage, so choice B is incorrect. There is no information in the passage to suggest that the policy is meant to create a special feeling for employees, so choice C is incorrect as well.

35. **The correct answer is A.** The sentence lets the employees know what *might* happen if they break the dress code more than once. "Up to and including termination" suggests that there are consequences that may escalate to getting fired, if the violations happen several times. Choice B oversimplifies the sentence; the original sentence suggests that punishments get more severe as the number of violations increases. Choice C is incorrect because the sentence shows that there are

consequences to breaking the rules. Choice D is incorrect because the sentence mentions that employees who "repeatedly" violate the rules will face increasingly harsh punishments.

36. **The correct answer is C.** According to the bulleted list in Paragraph 8, company logo shirts are always appropriate. However, open-toed sandals like flip-flops (choice A) and sleeveless shirts (choice D) are considered workplace-inappropriate. Paragraph 11 specifically mentions cologne (choice B) as a potential violation of the dress code.

37. **The correct answer is B.** The introductory paragraphs explain that the company "strives" to create a specific corporate image using its employees' appearance. There is no requirement that employees be attractive (choice D), just that they dress neatly and professionally. The policy describes how casual dress is allowed only in certain circumstances, so that tone is at odds with choice A. The maintenance of work areas (choice C) is mentioned as an example of how appearances are valuable to the company, but it is not the focus of the passage.

38. **The correct answer is D.** *Conforming* is used as an adjective here to describe clothes that follow the dress code guidelines; in other words, clothes that are suitable. *Inappropriate* (choice A) and *original* (choice C) have meanings that are the opposite of *conforming*. *Business* (choice B) might be tempting because the policy describes formal business attire, but *business* does not mean the same as *conforming*.

39. **The correct answer is A.** Only choice A describes an attire-related rule. The others would be irrelevant to the dress code and would not support the information in the passage.

40. **Appropriate clothing: blazer. Inappropriate clothing: yoga pants, sneakers, cargo shorts.** Based on the bulleted list in the "Casual Attire" section, athletic clothes, such as yoga pants (choice A) and casual shoes such as sneakers (choice B) are not appropriate work clothing. Shorts (choice C) of any type are not allowed.

41. **The correct answer is *It was so nice to meet you at Andrew's party the other day!* (B).** Choice A awkwardly breaks up this greeting into two clauses, when it could be much cleaner. Choice B does this by making it one clear, succinct sentence. Choice C uses *me* as a subject, when *I* should be the subject. Choice D leaves out important information (that Jeffrey enjoyed meeting Miriam).

42. **The correct answer is *strong and work* (C).** Choice C uses the conjunction *and* to connect the fragment by connecting the subject *we* (the pronoun part of the contraction *we're*) to the compound predicate *are* (the verb part of the contraction *we're*) and *work*. Compound predicates do not require commas (choice A), so the comma is correctly omitted. Adding a semicolon (choice B) creates a run-on sentence. Starting a new sentence with *and* (choice D) creates a sentence fragment.

43. **The correct answer is *both digital and print* (D).** In this sentence, you're looking for correct parallelism with the correlatives (*both…and*, *either…or*, *neither…nor*). Choice A incorrectly uses *both* with *or*. Choice B correctly uses *either* with *or*, but this is actually the opposite meaning of what the author intends. He's trying to show that his team does print *and* digital design, so choice B is incorrect overall. Choice C incorrectly uses *either* with *and*.

44. **The correct answer is *My designers are creative and innovative, and they know how to meet your highest standards.* (C).** Choice C creates a clear sentence in which the reader knows that the designers are creative and innovative, and that they will meet the customer's standards. Choice A contains a misplaced modifier. "Innovative and creative" describes the designers, not the standards. Choice B solves this issue but creates a redundant sentence by using "highest standards" twice. Choice D is awkwardly structured, which results in the adjectives *innovative* and *creative* being used improperly.

45. **The correct answer is ok.** The possessive pronoun *your* is the correct word to use in the sentence. Its homonym, *you're*, is the contraction for "you are," which would not make sense in the context of the sentence.

46. **The correct answer is *to*.** The adjective *too*, meaning "also," used here does not fit in the context of the sentence. The word *to*, which is part of the sentence's verb in its infinitive form (to think) is the proper word choice.

47. **The correct answer is *right*.** The verb *write* is not the correct word choice for the sentence. The adjective *right*, meaning "correct," properly fits the context of the sentence.

48. **The correct answer is *its*.** The contraction *it's*, meaning "it is," does not fit into the context of the sentence. The possessive pronoun *its* is the correct word choice here.

Extended Response: Sample Essays

High-Scoring Analysis

Although both passages make valid points about the minimum wage and what it means to employees, employers, and the economy, I found the argument in Passage 1 to be more persuasive. Passage 1 effectively demonstrates that addressing the minimum wage, even with a drastic increase, is something that needs to happen sooner than later.

Passage 1's most compelling argument is the timeline of minimum wage increases throughout American history. By describing the origins, and emphasizing that the minimum wage has actually increased very little over the past 100+ years, the writer shows how the minimum wage has failed the American worker. This gap between the original intentions and how it works, in reality, for American workers, was thought-provoking. I thought it was a very strong argument for forcing the minimum wage to catch up with modern times.

I do agree somewhat with Passage 2's point that we have to be careful about making sudden changes to a large part of the American working economy. However, I felt that the writer did not do enough to explain why the $15 minimum wage wouldn't work. For example, if you warn people about something bad coming but don't provide enough details, how can they prepare? Passage 2 just doesn't provide enough evidence to sway the reader away from a higher minimum wage. To make an informed decision to support Passage 2, I would want to know how many jobs are lost when the wages are higher, as well as how much profit companies are losing by paying their employees more. The supporting details were too lacking.

Secondly, based on the information in Passage 1 about the history of the minimum wage in the US, the information in Passage 2 seems to create a mismatch in priorities. Passage 2 is concerned with the needs of the employers, while passage 1 focuses on the employees. I found the employees to be a more compelling focus, especially since the author of Passage 1 showed how many gaps there are in the system, creating injustice. In particular, the stat that "there isn't a single county in the US where a family of four can be supported on a single minimum-wage income" was eye-opening, and was an excellent point to make.

Similarly, first passage does a good job of explaining why action is needed now. It has a more urgent tone that the second passage does not have. This felt like more of a call to action, and not just a case of "let's think about it more until things get worse." The writer of Passage 1 knows that change is necessary no matter what, and uses better facts and statistics to show why the change in the minimum wage is valid. This urgency is effective, highly effective, and makes me want to learn more about how to get the minimum wage changed on the federal level.

Explanation

This response is a high-scoring analysis because it shows understanding of the arguments made in both passages. The response writer has chosen one over the other because of the supporting details and points made in the passage. The response writer also explains what kind of information he or she would *like* to see to make Passage 2 be a better argument, which demonstrates analysis and organizational skills. There are a few grammatical errors throughout the response, but overall the writer shows a strong grasp of standard English conventions.

Low-Scoring Analysis

In Passage 1, the writer argues that the minimum wage exists for American workers, and provides specific details about how much the minimum wage has been throughout American history.

In Passage 2, the writer argues that although change may be necessary, we should think twice about the damage done to the economy and to employers.

So which one is right? Both have valid answers. I like the second passage best. My aunt owns a small business and why should she pay her employees more just because they think they deserve more? If you want to make $15 an hour, you can look for a second job or go back to school to learn better work skills. There's no magic paycheck.

Explanation

This is a low-scoring response because the writer does very little to come up with a detailed analysis of either passage. The response is too short, and its first two paragraphs are merely restatements of the original passages. There's no discussion of the nuances of either passage, or an examination of how either passage supports its writer's points. Although the response writer does try to use a personal anecdote to take a stance on the issue, it has little to do with either passage. It also describes the writer's own personal opinions without tying them to the information presented in the passages. The extended response should be a detailed analysis of the information presented, not just a summary of the passage(s) and a statement of personal opinion.

Mathematical Reasoning

1. \$1,040	**17.** C	**33.** (−0.25, 0)
2. C	**18.** B	**34.** 1
3. C	**19.** B	**35.** A
4. D	**20.** A	**36.** B
5. C	**21.** 6.28×10^7	**37.** D
6. $x = 0$ and $x = \frac{3}{2}$	**22.** C	**38.** B
7. B	**23.** 1,400	**39.** C
8. $\frac{8}{45}$	**24.** B	**40.** D
9. −10	**25.** B	**41.** 725
10. A	**26.** B	**42.** $\frac{750,000}{4,500} = \frac{1,100,000}{p}$
11. D	**27.** D	**43.** 18 inches
12. C	**28.** C	**44.** C
13. $3z < \frac{1}{z} < -z < z^2$	**29.** $\frac{4}{49}$	**45.** C
14. A	**30.** D	**46.** \$276
15. B	**31.** A	
16. 28	**32.** C	

1. **The correct answer is \$1,040.** 160% of \$400 is 1.6(\$400) = \$640. Based on this information, the final sale price is \$400 + \$640 = \$1,040.

2. **The correct answer is C.** Use the order of operations to compute:

$$\begin{aligned} &-1-[3(4-7)-(-3)(-2)] \\ &= -1-[3(-3)-(-3)(-2)] \\ &= -1-[-9-6] \\ &= -1-[-15] \\ &= -1+15 \\ &= 14 \end{aligned}$$

Choice A represents the value of the expression inside the square brackets. Choice B is the result of a sign error in the last step. Choice D is the result of an arithmetic error.

3. **The correct answer is C.** Substitute $x = \frac{1}{2}$ and $y = -2$ into $\left(\frac{x}{y} - \frac{y}{x}\right)^{-1}$ and simplify:

$$\begin{aligned} \left(\frac{\frac{1}{2}}{-2} - \frac{-2}{\frac{1}{2}}\right)^{-1} &= \left(-\frac{1}{4} + 4\right)^{-1} \\ &= \left(\frac{-1+4(4)}{4}\right)^{-1} \\ &= \left(\frac{15}{4}\right)^{-1} \\ &= \frac{4}{15} \end{aligned}$$

Choice A has the wrong sign. Choice B is the reciprocal of the correct answer, which is a result of not handling the outer exponent −1 correctly. Choice D has the wrong sign, and the outer exponent −1 was not handled correctly.

4. **The correct answer is D.** To subtract rational expressions with unlike denominators, first find the least common denominator (LCD), which is $(x + 2)(2x + 1)$. Rewrite the fraction using the LCD.

$$\frac{2x-1}{x+2} - \frac{2x}{2x+1}$$
$$= \frac{(2x-1)(2x+1)}{(x+2)(2x+1)} - \frac{(2x)(x+2)}{(x+2)(2x+1)}$$
$$= \frac{(2x-1)(2x+1)-(2x)(x+2)}{(x+2)(2x+1)}$$

Then, subtract and simplify as shown:

$$\frac{(2x-1)(2x+1)-(2x)(x+2)}{(x+2)(2x+1)}$$
$$= \frac{4x^2-1-2x^2-4x}{(x+2)(2x+1)}$$
$$= \frac{2x^2-4x-1}{2x^2+5x+2}$$

Choice A is the result of incorrectly canceling the term $2x^2$ in the top and bottom of the rational expression $\frac{2x^2-4x-1}{2x^2+5x+2}$. Choice B is the result of incorrectly canceling terms rather than fractions in the rational expressions, and then incorrectly adding the numerators and denominators. Choice C is incorrect because you cannot subtract fractions by subtracting their numerators and denominators; you must find a common denominator and then subtract the numerators.

5. **The correct answer is C.** The interest earned on the 3% account is $750(0.03) = $22.50, and the interest earned on the 2.5% account is $500(0.025) = $12.50. So the total interest earned is $35.00. Choice A represents the interest earned on the 2.5% account. Choice B represents the interest earned on the 3% account. Choice D is the result of adding the two percentages to get 5.5%, and then computing that percentage of the total $1,250.

6. **The correct answer is $x = 0$ and $x = \frac{3}{2}$, plotted below.**

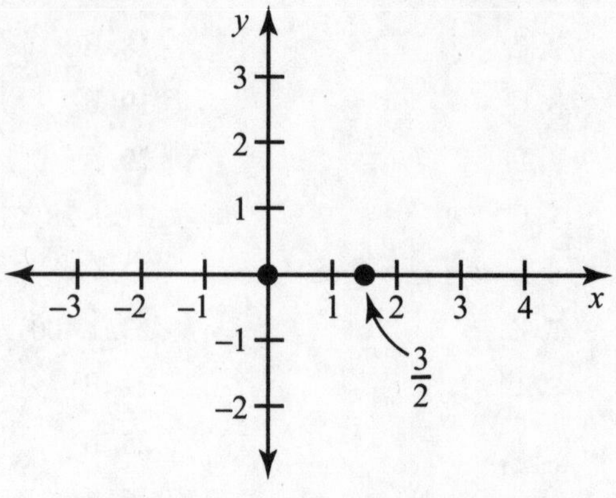

To find the x-intercepts, set $f(x) = 0$ and solve for x:

$$6x^2 - 9x = 0$$
$$3x(2x - 3) = 0$$
$$x = 0, \frac{3}{2}$$

7. **The correct answer is B.** Let h be the height of the cylinder. Using the volume formula $V = \pi r^2 h$ with $r = \sqrt{2}$ and $V = 8\pi$ cubic meters, we see the following:

$$8\pi = \pi\left(\sqrt{2}\right)^2(h)$$
$$8\pi = 2\pi h$$
$$h = 4$$

Next, since the cylinder is closed, the surface area formula is $SA = 2\pi r^2 + 2\pi rh$. Evaluate this when $r = \sqrt{2}$ and $h = 4$ yields

$$SA = 2\pi\left(\sqrt{2}\right)^2 + 2\pi\sqrt{2}\cdot 4$$
$$= 4\pi + 8\sqrt{2}\pi$$
$$= 4\pi\left(1 + 2\sqrt{2}\right) \text{ square meters.}$$

Choice A is the result of computing the height incorrectly. Choice C is part of the surface area formula—the lateral surface area. Choice D is the result of incorrect factoring.

8. **The correct answer is $\frac{8}{45}$.** Multiply the three fractions to get the desired proportion:

$$\frac{2}{3}\cdot\frac{3}{5}\cdot\frac{4}{9}=\frac{8}{45}$$

9. **The correct answer is –10.** A line parallel to the line with the equation $0.4(1.1 - 0.2y) = 0.8x$ must have the same slope. Write this equation in slope-intercept form to identify the slope:

$$\begin{aligned}0.4(1.1\quad 0.2y) &= 0.8x\\ 0.44 - 0.08y &= 0.8x\\ 0.08y &= -0.8x + 0.44\\ y &= -\frac{0.8}{0.08}x + \frac{0.44}{0.08}\end{aligned}$$

The slope is $-\frac{0.8}{0.08} = -10$.

10. **The correct answer is A.** For a linear system of two equations to have no solution, the lines must be parallel. So the slopes of the two lines must be equal AND the y-intercepts must be different. To determine the value of A, write both equations in slope-intercept form:

$$\begin{aligned}x &= -\frac{1}{2}y + 1\\ x - 1 &= -\frac{1}{2}y\\ y &= -2x + 2\end{aligned}$$

$$\begin{aligned}Ay - \frac{1}{2}x &= -1\\ Ay &= \frac{1}{2}x - 1\\ y &= \frac{1}{2A}x - \frac{1}{A}\end{aligned}$$

Equate the slopes and solve for A: $-2 = \frac{1}{2A}$ so that $A = -\frac{1}{4}$. Since this value of A does not result in the two lines having the same y-intercepts, the system has no solution. Choice B represents the value of $\frac{1}{A}$. Choice C represents the value of $\frac{1}{2A}$. Choice D is incorrect because there is a value of A for which the two lines forming this system have the same slope.

11. **The correct answer is D.** If the sixth score is 16, then the ordered list of scores would be 11, 15, 16, 16, 16, 18. The median is the average of the third and fourth scores, namely 16. For all the other choices, the median would remain 15.5.

12. **The correct answer is C.** If $x > 2$, then $2 - x$ must be negative. It will be an integer as long as x is an integer, for example $x = 3$. Choice A will be negative, but it cannot be an integer because the denominator is larger than the numerator, meaning it will be a fraction between –1 and 0. Choice B cannot be negative because the numerator and denominator are both positive for any choice of $x > 2$. Choice D is incorrect because $2x$ is positive for any choice of $x > 2$.

13. **The correct answer is $3z < \frac{1}{z} < -z < z^2$.** The smallest of these expressions is the one whose value is the most negative. Only $3z$ and $\frac{1}{z}$ are negative. Of these two expressions, $3z$ is more negative because $-1 < \frac{1}{z} < 0$, since z is a negative integer less than –1. Next, both $-z$ and z^2 are positive. Since $z < -1$, it follows that $-z < z^2$.

14. **The correct answer is A.** The area of the rectangle is (5)(8) = 40 square feet. To find the area of the right triangle portion, you need the third side; for this example, we'll call it h. Using the Pythagorean theorem yields $2^2 + h^2 = 5^2$, so that $h = \sqrt{21}$. So the area of the triangle is $\frac{1}{2}(2)(\sqrt{21}) = \sqrt{21}$ square feet. Thus, the area of the shaded region is $(40 + \sqrt{21})$ square feet. Choice B represents the area of the rectangle. Choice C represents the perimeter of the rectangle. The value in choice D uses the perimeter of the rectangle instead of the area.

15. **The correct answer is B.** In 1 hour, Kyle completes $\frac{1}{3}$ of the job and Tom completes $\frac{1}{\frac{5}{2}} = \frac{2}{5}$ of the job. If they work together, then in 1 hour, they complete $\frac{1}{x}$ of the job. This must equal $\frac{1}{3} + \frac{2}{5}$. Choice A is incorrect because each of the three quantities (3, 2.5, and x) should be replaced by their reciprocals. Choice C is incorrect because this statement is equivalent to the equation $3 + 2.5 = x$, and in this equation each of the three quantities (3, 2.5, and x) should be replaced by their reciprocals. Choice D is incorrect because the right side of the equation should be $\frac{1}{x}$.

16. **The correct answer is 28.** Substitute $x = -1$ into the expression and simplify using the order of operations:

$$\begin{aligned} f(-1) &= 1 - [(-1)(1 - 2(-1))]^3 \\ &= 1 - [-(1 + 2)]^3 \\ &= 1 - [-3]^3 \\ &= 1 - (-27) \\ &= 1 + 27 \\ &= 28 \end{aligned}$$

17. **The correct answer is C.** The radius, r, is one-half the diameter, namely 200 feet. So the surface area is $S = 4\pi(200)^2 = 160{,}000\,\pi$ square feet. So the cost for the entire job is $\$25(160{,}000\,\pi) = \$4{,}000{,}000\pi$. Choice A represents the surface area, not the cost for the job. The value in choice B would be the surface area, not the cost of the job, if you incorrectly used the diameter instead of the radius in the computation. Choice D is the result of incorrectly using the diameter instead of the radius when computing the surface area.

18. **The correct answer is B.** The length of the rectangle is $4\left(\frac{3}{4}\right) = 3$ inches and the width is $\frac{3}{4}$ inch. So the area of the rectangle is $3\left(\frac{3}{4}\right) = \frac{9}{4}$ square inches. Since the radius of a disc is $\frac{3}{8}$ inch, the area of one disc is $\pi\left(\frac{3}{8}\right)^2 = \frac{9}{64}\pi$ square inches. Since there are four discs inside the rectangle, the area of the shaded region is

$$\begin{aligned} \frac{9}{4} - 4\left(\frac{9}{64}\pi\right) &= \frac{9}{4} - \frac{9}{16}\pi \\ &= \frac{9}{4}\left(1 - \frac{\pi}{4}\right) \text{ square inches.} \end{aligned}$$

Choice A is the result of using the wrong radius of the disc. Choice C is the result of computing 8^2 as 16, not 64. Choice D is the result of incorrectly subtracting the area of one disc, not four.

19. **The correct answer is B.** Let r be the radius of the circle. Using the circumference gives the equation $2\pi r = \pi\sqrt{2}$, so that $r = \frac{\sqrt{2}}{2}$ meters. So the area is $\pi\left(\frac{\sqrt{2}}{2}\right)^2 = \frac{\pi}{2}$ square meters. Choice A is the result of incorrectly identifying the radius. Choice C is the result of multiplying the base and exponent when simplifying $\left(\frac{\sqrt{2}}{2}\right)^2$. Choice D is incorrect because the radius was not squared when the area was computed.

20. **The correct answer is A.** The amount spent on household items is $\frac{2}{5}(\$450) = \$180$. The amount that remains after this expense is $\$450 - \$180 = \$270$. Sixty percent of \$270 is $\frac{3}{5}(\$270) = \$162$. The amount that remains is $\$270 - \$162 = \$108$. Choice B represents 60% of \$270. Choice C represents the amount that remains after the household items expense. Choice D is the result of identifying 60% as 60 and subtracting it from \$450.

21. The correct answer is 6.28×10^7. Subtract the two quantities:

$$\begin{aligned}&\left(7.1\times10^7\right)-\left(8.2\times10^6\right)\\&=\left(71\times10^6\right)-\left(8.2\times10^6\right)\\&=(71-8.2)\times10^6\\&=62.8\times10^6\\&=6.28\times10^7\end{aligned}$$

22. The correct answer is C. The volume is $2.5m^2 = 5.625$. So $m^2 = 2.25$ and $m = 1.5$ feet. Therefore, the area of the top of the deck box is $(1.5)(2.5) = 3.75$ square feet. Choice A represents the value of m, and choice B represents the value of m^2. Choice D is the result of computing the area of the top of the box by adding the width and length, instead of multiplying them.

23. The correct answer is 1,400. First, find the fraction of items that corresponds to personalized stickers:

$$1-\left(\frac{3}{8}+\frac{3}{32}+\frac{1}{16}+\frac{1}{4}\right)=1-\frac{25}{32}=\frac{7}{32}$$

So the number of stickers is $\frac{7}{32}(6,400)=1,400$.

24. The correct answer is B. Since there are three 6-sided dice, the number of total outcomes is $6^3 = 216$. Of these outcomes, there are six ways that all three dice will come to rest on the same number. Therefore, the probability is $\frac{6}{216}=\frac{1}{36}$. Choice A represents the probability of any single outcome. Choice C represents the probability of any outcome for one die, not three. Choice D is the result of incorrectly multiplying the base and the exponent $(6 \times 3 = 18)$ and then computing the probability as $\frac{6}{18}=\frac{1}{3}$.

25. The correct answer is B. Combine the radicands using the exponent rules, then simplify:

$$\begin{aligned}&\sqrt[4]{27z^2w^5}\cdot\sqrt[4]{3z^6w^2}\\&=\sqrt[4]{\left(27z^2w^5\right)\cdot\left(3z^6w^2\right)}\\&=\sqrt[4]{81z^8w^7}\\&=3z^2w\cdot\sqrt[4]{w^3}\end{aligned}$$

The value in choice A has the expressions outside the radical and inside the radical reversed. Choices C and D are the result of incorrectly computing the fourth root of a power. Since it is a fourth root, you must take groups of variables raised to the fourth power out of the radical. For example, $w^7 = w^4 \cdot w^3$. One group of 4 came out of the radical, and w^3 stayed under the radical.

26. The correct answer is B. Solve for x:

$$\begin{aligned}\frac{1}{3}\left(\frac{5}{2}x-2\right)&\geq\frac{1}{6}+x\\\frac{5}{6}x-\frac{2}{3}&\geq\frac{1}{6}+x\\5x-4&\geq1+6x\\-5&\geq x\end{aligned}$$

Choices A and D are the result of not canceling the terms correctly in the last step of the inequality. You must add the opposite of a number or expression to both sides of an inequality to cancel it on one side. The expression in choice C uses the wrong inequality sign.

27. The correct answer is D. The y-intercept is 2,000 and the slope is –40 since she is descending (the height is getting smaller). Therefore, the height above the ground after s seconds is $2,000 - 40s$. Choice A represents an increase in height, not a decrease. Choice B is incorrect because you should not multiply the initial height by 40. Choice C represents the distance the bungee jumper descended after s seconds.

28. **The correct answer is C.** The expression $(6+3x)(x^2-1)$ is not equivalent to $6(1-x^2)+3x(x^2-1)$ because it is missing a factor of −1. For all the other choices, if you multiply them out and compare to the original, you will see they are equivalent.

29. **The correct answer is $\frac{4}{49}$.** Substitute $x=-\frac{2}{3}$ into $\left(\frac{x}{3x-\frac{1}{3}}\right)^2$ to get:

$$\left(\frac{-\frac{2}{3}}{3\left(-\frac{2}{3}\right)-\frac{1}{3}}\right)^2=\left(\frac{-\frac{2}{3}}{-2-\frac{1}{3}}\right)^2$$
$$=\left(\frac{-\frac{2}{3}}{-\frac{7}{3}}\right)^2$$
$$=\left(\frac{2}{7}\right)^2$$
$$=\frac{4}{49}$$

30. **The correct answer is D.** Solve the inequality for *y*:

$$x\le\frac{1}{2}y+1$$
$$x-1\le\frac{1}{2}y$$
$$2x-2\le y$$

The line's *y*-intercept is -2, and its slope is 2, so it rises from left to right. Also, the region above the line should be shaded.

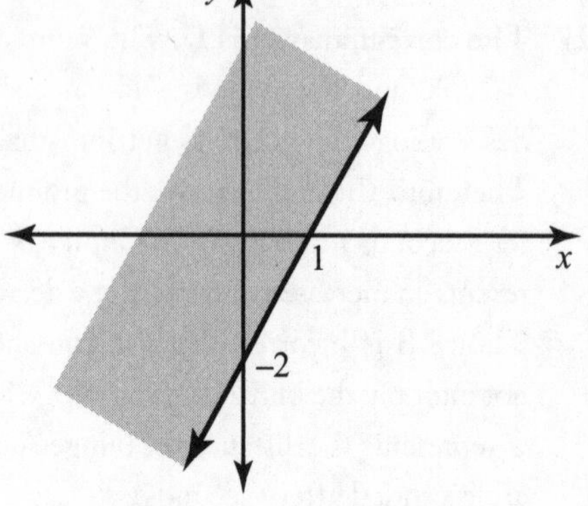

The line in choice A does not rise from left to right, and it is shaded below. The line in choice B does not rise from left to right. The line in choice C is correct, but it is shaded below, not above.

31. **The correct answer is A.** The portion of the job that the less powerful space heater completes in *h* hours is $\frac{1}{3}h$; the more powerful one completes $\frac{1}{2}h$ of the job in *h* hours. Summing these should give 1. So the equation that can be used to solve for *h* is $\frac{1}{3}h+\frac{1}{2}h=1$.

Choice B is incorrect because you should be dividing *h* by 3 and *h* by 2 instead of multiplying them before adding them. Choice C is incorrect because the *h* should be in the numerator of the fractions on the left side. Choice D is incorrect because each of the two expressions on the left side of the equation should be replaced by its reciprocal.

32. **The correct answer is C.** The length, *l*, is $\frac{1}{2}+2w$, which means the area is $w\left(\frac{1}{2}+2w\right)=\frac{1}{2}w+2w^2$. Since the area must be between 6 and 8 square feet, we have the inequality:

$$6\le\frac{1}{2}w+2w^2\le 8$$
$$12\le w+4w^2\le 16$$

Choice A is missing a term in the area formula. Choice B is the result of using the perimeter of the window instead of its area. Choice D is the result of computing the area of the rectangle as if the width, *w*, were 2.

33. **The correct answer is (−0.25, 0).** Set the function equal to 0 and solve for *x*:

$$0.5(1.3-2.8x)-1=0$$
$$0.5(1.3-2.8x)=1$$
$$1.30-2.8x=2$$
$$-2.8x=0.7$$
$$x=-\frac{0.7}{2.8}$$
$$x=-0.25$$

34. The correct answer is 1. Complete the square to find the vertex of the graph of this quadratic function; then, the y-value is the maximum value.

The vertex is (–3, 1) and so therefore the maximum value is 1.

$$\begin{aligned} f(x) &= -2x^2 - 12x - 17 \\ &= -2\left(x^2 + 6x\right) - 17 \\ &= -2\left(x^2 + 6x + 9\right) - 17 + 18 \\ &= -2(x+3)^2 + 1 \end{aligned}$$

35. The correct answer is A. The domain of a rational function is the set of all real numbers that do not make the denominator equal to 0. The only real number that makes the denominator 0 is 5. So the domain is the set of all real numbers except 5. Choice B is incorrect because –3 and 3 do not make the denominator 0, and therefore they should not be excluded from the domain. Choice C is incorrect because –3, –2, and 3 do not make the denominator 0, and therefore they should not be excluded from the domain. Choice D is also incorrect because 0 does not make the denominator 0, and therefore it should not be excluded from the domain.

36. The correct answer is B. The average value of f on [1, 4] is:

$$\frac{f(4)-f(1)}{4-1} = \frac{\frac{4}{5}-\frac{1}{2}}{3} = \frac{\frac{3}{10}}{3} = \frac{1}{10}$$

Choice A is the result of dropping the denominator in the final computation. Choice C is incorrect because the value needs to be divided by the length of the interval. Choice D represents the length of the interval.

37. The correct answer is D. This graph does not pass the vertical line test (meaning there is at least one vertical line that intersects the graph in more than one point), so it is not a function.

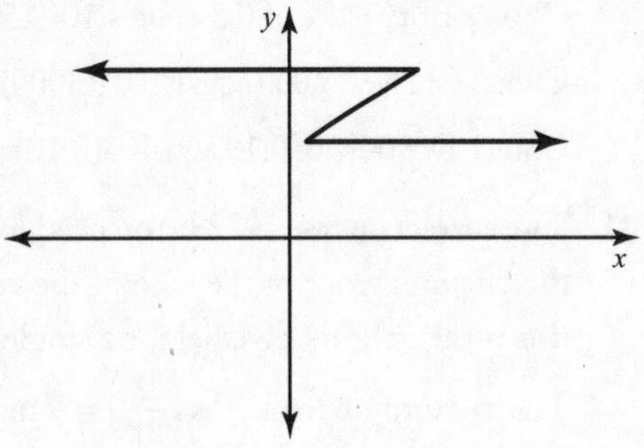

All the other representations match each x-value to exactly one y-value, which means they are functions.

38. The correct answer is B. Let x be the amount of sodium in $2\frac{3}{8}$ cups of soup. Set up and solve the following proportion:

$$\begin{aligned} \frac{\frac{1}{2}}{15} &= \frac{2\frac{3}{8}}{x} \\ \frac{1}{2}x &= \left(2\frac{3}{8}\right)(15) \\ x &= 2 \times \left(2\frac{3}{8}\right) \times (15) \end{aligned}$$

Choice A is incorrect because you should multiply by $\left(2\frac{3}{8}\right)$, not divide by it. Choice C is incorrect because you should multiply by 15, not divide by it. Choice D is incorrect because you should multiply by 2, not divide by it.

39. The correct answer is C. Observe that $\frac{y}{0.1} = 10y$. Since $y > 10$, multiply both sides of this inequality by 10 to get $10y > 100$. Choice A can be less than 100 if $y = 20$, for instance. Choice B can never be larger than 100 because you are dividing 100 by a number larger than 1. Choice D is incorrect because $0.1y = \frac{y}{10}$, and since $10 < y < 100$, this will be less than 10 for all choices of y.

40. The correct answer is D. To solve, compute all four quantities and choose the smallest.

Choice A: 0.5% of 10,000 equals 0.005(10,000) = 50

Choice B: 1,000% of 0.5 equals $10(0.5) = 5$

Choice C: 1% of 5,000 equals $0.01(5000) = 50$

Choice D: 500% of 0.10 equals $5(0.10) = 0.5$

41. The correct answer is 725. You need to find the circumference of the base of the can—this is the length of a label for a single can. The circumference is $2\pi\left(\frac{9}{2\pi}\right) = 9$ inches. Based on this information, the number of cans that can be labeled with a single roll is $\frac{6,525}{9} = 725$.

42. The correct answer is $\frac{\mathbf{750,000}}{\mathbf{4,500}} = \frac{\mathbf{1,100,000}}{\boldsymbol{p}}$. Since p is in the denominator, the numerator of the fraction on the left-side is 750,000 and the denominator is 4,500. Similarly, the numerator of the fraction on the right-side is 1,100,000.

43. The correct answer is 18 inches. Since 1 year is 12 months, it follows that 3 years is $12(3) = 36$ months. Multiply by 0.5 inch to get the length of the hair, which is $36(0.5) = 18$ inches.

44. The correct answer is C. Let x be the number of yards rushed by the running back who rushed for fewer yards. Then, the number of yards rushed by the other, y, is $3x$. So one of the equations of the system is $y = 3x$. Since together the two running backs rushed for a total of 1,728 yards, the other equation is $x + y = 1,728$. This gives the system shown in choice C. Choice A is incorrect because the terms on the left side of the first equation should be added, not multiplied, and the $3x$ should be on the right side of the second equation. Choice B is incorrect because the $3x$ should be on the right side of the second equation. Choice D is incorrect because the $3y$ in the first equation should be replaced by just y.

45. The correct answer is C. The yo-yo travels 18 inches in one second. So in 4 seconds, it travels $4(18) = 72$ inches. Choice A represents the distance it travels in one second. Choice B represents the distance it travels in two seconds. Choice D represents the distance it travels in five seconds.

46. The correct answer is $276. The walkway is shown below:

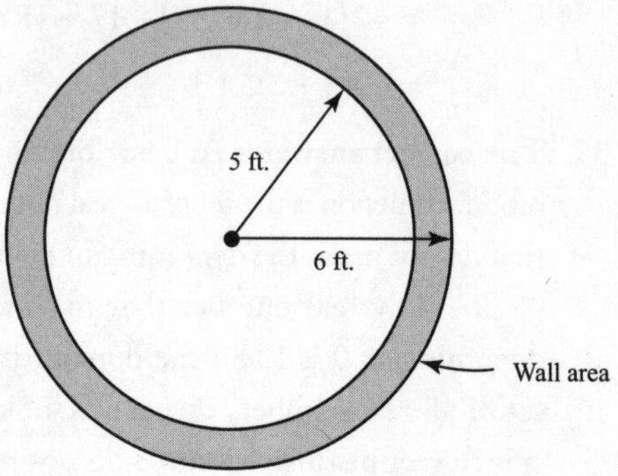

The area of the walkway is $\pi(6)^2 - \pi(5)^2 = 11\pi$ square feet. The cost is $\$8(11\pi)$, which is about $276.

Science

1. B	**11.** C	**21.** B	**31.** B
2. D	**12.** C	**22.** C	**32.** C
3. C	**13.** B	**23.** B	**33.** B
4. D	**14.** D	**24.** C	**34.** D
5. B	**15.** inertia (A)	**25.** B	**35.** H_2SO_4 is a Brønsted-Lowry acid and HSO_4^- is its conjugate base.
6. 6 kg	**16.** C	**26.** A	
7. B	**17.** C	**27.** D	
8. A	**18.** D	**28.** A	
9. B	**19.** C	**29.** D	
10. A	**20.** A	**30.** B	

1. **The correct answer is B.** The passage states that igneous rocks are formed when molten rock, or magma, cools into its solid form. While it is true that the passage also states that magma (choice D), which is found only beneath the earth's surface, can reach the earth's surface through a volcanic eruption, this is not the best answer because a month after an eruption, the molten rock (lava) will have had time to cool down into igneous rock. A month is not enough time for sedimentary rock (choice A) to form. The passage states that metamorphic rock (choice C) typically forms deep within the earth.

2. **The correct answer is D.** Compare the structures and functions of the large and small intestines. The large intestine is shorter than the small intestine, and there is no mention of a complex interior structure in the large intestine. As most of the water is absorbed in the small intestine, and the main difference between the small and large intestines is the length and complexity of the small intestine, it stands to reason that its inner surface (covered with villi and microvilli) helps to absorb water and nutrients. The villi in the small intestine are described as soft and stationary, ill-suited to physically break down material, so choice A is incorrect. Since chyme moves through the large intestine without any help from villi, choice B is not the best answer. It also makes little sense to have an extra long small intestine just to help chyme move through it. The large intestine does not have villi, yet reverse movement into the small intestine is not discussed as a problem, so preventing chyme from moving backward into the stomach (choice C) is not the purpose of the villi.

3. **The correct answer is C.** Bears are apex organisms and can eat almost anything else in the web if they want to. Bears can eat other consumers, but they can also feed down across every level of consumer to eat berries, which come from plants. Even if the sun were considered part of the food web, the sun connects directly to producers with nothing in between, so choice A is incorrect. Choice B is incorrect for the same reason; there are no levels between decomposers and other consumers. Choice D crosses many levels, all the way from apex predators to primary consumers, but bears can feed even farther down the food web than owls.

4. **The correct answer is D.** The blood–brain barrier (BBB) blocks harmful molecules and particles, especially pathogens, while allowing in substances necessary for the brain's survival. The drawback is that antibodies

and immune cells cannot cross the barrier to fight any infection or disease that gets into the brain, which can result in serious problems. Since there is transport of some gases and other substances across the BBB, complete separation of the brain and the circulatory system (choice A) does not occur. Runaway immune responses are less likely to affect the brain since immune products can't cross the BBB, but the prevention of autoimmune disease in the brain (choice B) is not the BBB's primary purpose. The passage states that hormones pass freely into the brain through diffusion, so controlling their flow (choice C) is not the purpose of the BBB.

5. **The correct answer is B.** The passage describes how endothelial cells line the inside of blood vessels throughout the body. Endothelial cells form a key component of the blood–brain barrier but are also found in other blood vessels, not exclusively in the barrier (choice C). The passage states that endothelial cells line blood vessels throughout the body, not in all tissues throughout the body (choice A). While endothelial cells are found inside blood vessels that serve the central nervous system, such as in the brain, they are found in all blood vessels in all systems, not exclusively the central nervous system (choice D).

6. **The correct answer is 6 kg.** Force $F = 24$ N and acceleration $a = 4$ m/s^2. Putting those numbers into $F = ma$, you get:

$$24 \text{ N} = m(4 \text{ m/s}^2)$$

To solve for m, divide F by a:

$$m = \frac{F}{a} = \frac{24}{4} = 6 \text{ kg}$$

7. **The correct answer is B.** A week after treatment, only group A, all of whom still have their appendix, had a healthy microbiome, suggesting that the good bacteria are connected to the appendix in some way. This evidence doesn't completely confirm the conclusion, but it is the best option among those provided. A specific immune response that defends the appendix (choice A) implies that the appendix is important to the body, but it gives no indication of the function of the appendix or if that function is related to restoring gut bacteria. Choice C implies that there may be some health benefit to the appendix but does not link it specifically to the microbiome. Choice D does not support the researchers' conclusion; the microbiome is affected by diet and birth, but the passage does not say if these factors are similar in both groups, so there is no way to link any differences to the appendix.

8. **The correct answer is A.** To maximize mechanical advantage, the ratio of L_e to L_r must be as large as possible, giving the lever a longer handle. Position A is about as close to the load as it is possible to be, so L_e is as long as possible and L_r is as short as possible, giving the maximum possible value of *IMA* in the equation $\text{IMA} = \frac{L_e}{L_r}$.

Moving the fulcrum to position B (choice B) places the fulcrum right next to the force, so L_r becomes much longer than L_e and IMA is less than one. Moving the load to position B (choice C) places the load right next to the force, so there is no mechanical advantage at all. Moving the force to position D (choice D) places the force right on top of the fulcrum, so the value of L_e becomes zero, making IMA zero as well.

9. **The correct answer is B.** The passage states that light speed, *c*, must be measured in a vacuum so that its speed is unaffected by matter or any other aspect of the medium it is passing through. Measuring light through glass or air might change the results, so light speed is measured in a vacuum to ensure that *c* is constant. Choice A is incorrect since certain other types of radiation and particles can also travel at the speed of

light. The passage states that matter can never travel at the speed of light without infinite energy and it is impossible to achieve infinite energy, so choice C is incorrect. Choice D is incorrect since it is not certain whether tachyons actually exist. Furthermore, since nobody has ever observed a tachyon, its properties cannot be confirmed, including the speed at which it travels.

10. **The correct answer is A.** Time slows down at light speed relative to a stationary object, no matter how far the object is traveling. To an observer traveling at light speed for 4.3 years (the clock is the observer in this case), only a few minutes will pass. It will always be a very short amount of time that passes at light speed; 2.3 years (choice B) might be accurate for a clock traveling roughly half of light speed. Choice C is incorrect because 4.3 years is the amount of time that will pass on the stationary clock relative to the clock moving at light speed. Choice D is incorrect as 186,000 miles/second is the speed of light or the speed of the clock in this case, not a measured amount of time.

11. **The correct answer is C.** As long as the Punnett square is properly filled in, it is easy to determine the possible outcomes for every possible combination of the parents' alleles. As shown in the square that was initially filled in, match each of the father's alleles with each of the mother's alleles, like this:

	R	*r*
R	*RR*	*Rr*
r	*Rr*	*rr*

Three out of four of the squares have at least one *R* allele, and according to the description of dominance, any combination including at least one *R* allele will have red eyes. The fourth possibility, which should occur one out of four times, has only *r* alleles and will be white-eyed. The other answer choices are incorrect proportions based on the genotypes being crossed.

12. **The correct answer is C.** The player will transform potential energy into kinetic energy as soon as he swings the bat, but it is his tensed arm muscles that actually hold the potential energy. It is his arms that will actually bring the bat into motion. The incoming ball (choice A), is in motion and has kinetic energy. The bat (choice B) is functioning merely as an extension of the arms. The bat itself holds no energy until the arms swing it. Home plate (choice D) has no kinetic or potential energy in this situation. It is not going to move.

13. **The correct answer is B.** The passage states that iron(III) hydroxide is a bright yellow-orange color, so it must be present if the Rio Tinto is bright orange. In addition, the passage mentions that AMD is often diluted when it flows into natural water sources (like a river), and it is then that its pH drops enough for iron(III) hydroxide to form. Choices A and C are incorrect because dissolved iron(II) and iron(III) ions are not bright orange; it is insoluble (solid) iron(III) oxide that is bright orange. While sulfuric acid in AMD is present in the river in a diluted form, choice D is incorrect because sulfuric acid is colorless and not responsible for the bright orange color of the river.

14. **The correct answer is D.** The amount of movement can be determined by measuring how much the distance between a set of markers on each side of the boundary grows over time. By measuring the movements between markers along the boundary at different locations, a researcher can learn about the rate of movement along the entire rift in case it is not spreading apart at the exact same rate in each spot. One measurement (choice A) is not enough to determine the rate of movement, and the exact locations of the valley edges might be impacted

by other forces, such as erosion. Since different divergent boundaries may move at different rates, using their measurements (choice B) will not provide accurate results. Using only one set of markers (choice C) will measure the rate of movement at only one particular spot. Measuring at different spots along the rift will provide more accurate results.

15. **The correct answer is *inertia* (A).** Inertia is the tendency of an object in motion to stay on course unless its motion is altered by some other force. Once the train drops, inertia keeps the train moving forward, while the track guides its direction. Inertia allows the train to keep moving along the track. Gravity (choice A) is the force that gets the train moving but does not affect the path of the train once it has begun moving. Momentum (choice C) affects how the train moves. It determines whether the train will be able to keep moving against friction, air resistance, and gravity on the uphill portions but does not affect the motion of the train itself. Velocity (choice D) is a component of momentum. Inertia will move an object at the same velocity unless disrupted, but the velocity does not determine where the object is moving.

16. **The correct answer is C.** The passage states that ammonia (along with hydrogen peroxide and ammonium persulfate) opens the outer cells of the hair strand, which allows the dye to get into and stay inside the hair strand, permanently coloring the hair. Choices A and D are incorrect because couplers, not ammonia, link the dye monomers together into larger intermediate dye molecules (polymers). Choice B is incorrect because oxidizers, not ammonia, react with the polymers to create the final dye color.

17. **The correct answer is C.** According to the geologic time scale, the Pennsylvanian Period began 320 million years ago (Ma) and ended around 286 Ma. A date of 316 Ma falls squarely inside the Pennsylvanian Period. The Permian Period (choice A) began 286 Ma, which is later than 316 Ma. The Mesozoic Era (choice B) began 245 Ma, which is later than 316 Ma. The Mississippian Period (choice D) ended 320 Ma, which is earlier than 316 Ma.

18. **The correct answer is D.** The passage notes that stars are massive objects, and further notes that it takes a massive object (Neptune) to alter the movements of another massive object (Uranus). Only a planet with a large mass can be detected through wobble; small planets do not have enough mass to have a measurable impact on a star. Choices A and B are incorrect since small planets will not have enough mass to impact a star, and a planet's brightness is not relevant to this method. Choice C is incorrect, as the diameter of the planet is less important than its mass, and again the brightness is irrelevant. Any planet massive enough to impact a star can be detected through wobble regardless of its brightness.

19. **The correct answer is C.** The passage states that stars are so bright that they obscure any nearby, dimmer objects, such as orbiting planets. If it were possible to block the star's glare (think of using your hand to block the glare of the sun in the sky), then dimmer objects may become visible. In this case, it would be a direct observation of the planet, not an indirect observation of the planet's influence on nearby objects. A few planets have been discovered and observed by this method. Choices A and B are both observations of a planet's influence on a star, not direct observations of the planet itself. Choice D is not possible; the beginning of the passage states that exoplanets are so far away that they cannot be directly observed.

20. **The correct answer is A.** Looking at the data in the table, when [Fe^{2+}] goes from 2.0

$\times 10^{-5}$ mol/L to 3.0×10^{-5} mol/L as $[Ce^{4+}]$ is held constant, rate goes from 2.0×10^{-7} mol/L·s to 3.0×10^{-7} mol/L·s. In other words, as $[Fe^{2+}]$ increases 1.5 times, rate also increases 1.5 times. Therefore, rate increases by the same factor that $[Fe^{2+}]$ increases by when $[Ce^{4+}]$ is held constant. Choice B is incorrect because rate also increases by the same factor that $[Ce^{4+}]$ increases by when $[Fe^{2+}]$ is held constant. When $[Ce^{4+}]$ triples from 1.0×10^{-5} mol/L to 3.0×10^{-5} mol/L, rate also triples from 3.0×10^{-7} mol/L·s to 9.0×10^{-7} mol/L·s. Choice C is incorrect because we've already seen that rate is affected by changes in concentration of the two reactants. Choice D is incorrect because we've seen that rate increases, not decreases, by the same factor that $[Fe^{2+}]$ increases by when $[Ce^{4+}]$ is held constant.

21. **The correct answer is B.** By 9 months, the population has flattened out at a level just below *K* in graph B, which shows the logistic growth model. If *K* is 5,000, at 9 months this population is around 4,900. Choice A is roughly the population level at 5 months. Choice C is incorrect since the dashed line represents *K*, and the population levels off below *K*. Choice D is incorrect, as 10,000 is about what the population in graph A, not graph B, would be if growth continued exponentially.

22. **The correct answer is C.** The beginning part of this growth curve looks like exponential growth, since the population increases at an ever-growing rate. Around 6 months, the population surpasses *K*, meaning the population is too high for the environment to support. The population then declines to a level that can be supported, just below *K*. At this point the population levels off, as in logistic growth. Choices A and B are incorrect, as the growth shown does not directly conform to either exponential (graph A) or logistic (graph B) growth. Choice D at first glance seems plausible, since growth rapidly exceeds available resources. However, while the population corrects to a manageable level, it does not completely collapse and go to zero.

23. **The correct answer is B.** The original double-stranded molecule separates, and then each of the strands serves as a template for a new strand. Therefore, the process results in 4 strands: 2 originals and 2 copies. Since each original makes one copy, each resulting double-stranded molecule contains one original strand from the original cell and one copy. Choices A and D are incorrect since each daughter cell needs to have a complete set of DNA. Since DNA is double-stranded, if either daughter cell received only single, unconnected strands, it would not have a complete genetic blueprint. Choice C is incorrect since each original serves as a template for a new copy, pairing up with that copy.

24. **The correct answer is C.** At altitudes above 20 km, the temperature increases about 17 degrees with each 5 km increase in altitude. If that trend continues, the next temperature value in the series (31 miles, or 50 km) should be around 30°F. While the temperature holds steady around −75°F until an altitude of 20 km is reached, above 20 km the temperature begins to steadily increase, so choice A is incorrect. Choice B is incorrect because −39°F is the temperature at 31 km, not 31 miles. Choice D represents a much larger jump in temperature than the steady increase seen between 20 and 45 km.

25. **The correct answer is B.** The passage states that symbiosis is dependent on close physical proximity between organisms, while it defines mutualism as any relationship between organisms where both organisms benefit. It does not say that a symbiotic relationship cannot also be mutualistic, nor

answers practice test 3

does it say that all mutualisms need to take place in close proximity. Since a symbiotic relationship can also be mutualistic, as in the case of the zooxanthellae, choice A is incorrect. The passage does not state that symbioses are only marine (choice C). Choice D contradicts the information in the passage, which states the difference between mutualism and symbiosis.

26. **The correct answer is A.** The passage states that rapid temperature increase can kill the zooxanthellae. If the zooxanthellae are killed, their red or yellow pigments are no longer present, leaving only the diminished coral organisms and the plain, limestone skeleton. This situation is called coral "bleaching" and can have serious consequences for coral reefs. Red and yellow (choice B) are the pigment colors of live zooxanthellae, but the zooxanthellae are killed by sharp temperature increases. Even if the zooxanthellae die, the limestone skeleton is still present, and stone does not shrink (choice C). Zooxanthellae provide most, but not all the host's nutrients. Without replacing the zooxanthellae, the host will eventually die (choice D), but it will not die immediately.

27. **The correct answer is D.** Density is the mass of a substance divided by its volume. To illustrate, consider that 1 gram (g) of water that takes up 1 milliliter (mL) of volume when it is a liquid has a density of 1 g/mL. When the water freezes, it will have a greater volume. Even if you don't know the actual ice volume, the same mass divided by a bigger number will give you a smaller density. (In reality, its frozen volume will be 1.1 mL, which means the density of ice = 1 g ÷ 1.1 mL = 0.9 g/mL). Ice is less dense than liquid water, which means it will float to the surface as it freezes. Less dense materials float in denser materials, while denser materials sink. Based on this information, choices A, B, and C are incorrect.

28. **The correct answer is A.** Na_2SO_4 breaks down into 3 ions in water: 2 Na^+ ions and 1 SO_4^{2-} ion. So a 1 M Na_2SO_4 solution has 3 moles of ions per liter of solution. Of the choices given, only $CaCl_2$ also breaks down into 3 ions: 1 Ca^{2+} ion and 2 Cl^- ions. Since this solution is also a 1 M solution, it also has 3 moles of ions per liter of solution. And because it is also in water, it will have the same freezing point as a 1 M Na_2SO_4 solution in water. Even though choice B is the same solute, it is not the same concentration so it will not have the same freezing point. Choice C is incorrect because $MgSO_4$ breaks down into 2 ions in water: 1 Mg^{2+} ion and 1 SO_4^{2-} ion. Therefore, it will not have the same concentration of ions and will not freeze at the same temperature. Even though the concentration of solute in choice D is the same, the solvent is different. The passage states that the solvent *does* matter for colligative properties. Water is H_2O; H_2O_2 is hydrogen peroxide.

29. **The correct answer is D.** The question requires you to take a quick look at the graph and compare lifespans and relative weights of the four answer choices. Humans (choice A) have the longest lifespan and lowest weight of the four possibilities and so clearly have the longest lifespan relative to body size. Zebras (choice B) weigh a lot less than bison but have longer lifespans, so we can conclude that zebras also do not have the shortest lifespan relative to body size. Comparing bison (choice C) to elephants reveals that elephants live about three times as long as bison but weigh five times as much. That means that, while elephants have a long lifespan, their much higher weight gives them the shortest lifespan by weight.

30. **The correct answer is B.** The passage states that more than one type of photoreceptor must be activated for color vision. In low light, only rods are activated, so humans can

see only in black and white under these conditions. While it's true that only a few photons activate the photoreceptors in low light (choice A), this fact does not explain why humans see only in black and white at low light levels. The passage indicates that the types of photoreceptors that are activated are responsible for color vision, not the number of photons activating the photoreceptors. It is also true that the ratio of activated rods to cones is higher in low light (choice D), but it is the fact that only rods are active in low light that prohibits color vision under low-light conditions. Choice C is not true; humans possess photoreceptors to see color, but they are not activated in low light.

31. **The correct answer is B.** The passage states that transparent (clear) and flexible plastics tend to be amorphous. Plastic sandwich bags are clear and flexible, so their material is amorphous. Similarly, contact lenses are clear and flexible, so their material is amorphous, not crystalline (choice A). A toy car is rigid, so its material is more crystalline and orderly, not random (choice C). A clear seat cover is flexible, so it will have a random amorphous structure, not an orderly structure (choice D).

32. **The correct answer is C.** Ethylene has two carbon atoms that are double bonded to each other, and each carbon atom is also bonded to two hydrogen atoms. When ethylene molecules are linked together to form polyethylene, the double bond between the two carbon atoms becomes a single bond. Each carbon atom is still bonded to two hydrogen atoms, so choices A and B are incorrect. Each carbon atom is bonded to two carbon atoms and two hydrogen atoms in the polyethylene polymer molecule, so choice D is incorrect.

33. **The correct answer is B.** Differences in density, caused by temperature, create and sustain the convection currents in the outer core. As denser material sinks, lighter material rises, and their combined motion creates the electrical currents that generate the magnetic fields that form the earth's overall magnetic field. The inner core is not directly involved in creating the currents in the outer core, nor does the inner core rotate (choice A). The rotation of the earth (choice C) mainly helps align the magnetic field, while convection in the outer core is the primary generator. Since all that matters are that the outer core is hot enough to be liquid at ambient pressure and that there are temperature gradients present, the outer core's exact temperature (choice D) is unimportant so long as those conditions are met.

34. **The correct answer is D.** In order to test if citrus fruits could heal sailors afflicted with scurvy, Lind compared the effects of eating citrus with other, noncitrus treatments. Since Lind kept other aspects of the sailors' lives constant, the only variable is the treatment assigned to each group. If all other conditions are kept constant, the noncitrus groups can be used to see if the citrus fruit is the variable that benefits the sailors. The problem with Lind's setup is that every group received some type of intervention, so he would not know what would have happened if he left the sailors alone. A true control group would leave diet constant but give the sailors in the group no treatment of any kind. A group ingesting less citrus (choice C) is too similar to the experimental group 5 to truly count as a control.

35. **The correct answer is H_2SO_4 is a Brønsted-Lowry acid and HSO_4^- is its conjugate base.** H_2SO_4 donates hydrogen ions to OH^-, forming its conjugate base, HSO_4^-. H_2O is the conjugate acid of OH^-. Thus, H_2SO_4 is a Brønsted-Lowry acid and HSO_4^- is its conjugate base. OH^- is a Brønsted-Lowry base and H_2O is its conjugate acid.

Social Studies

1. D	**11.** B	**21.** B	**32.** D
2. C	**12.** A	**22.** A	**33.** A
3. D	**13.** December 2005	**23.** D	**34.** A
4. populist	**14.** June 2008	**24.** A	**35.** Affordable Care Act (or Patient Protection and Affordable Care Act)
5. C	**15.** June 2008	**25.** B	
6. A	**16.** December 2005	**26.** C	
7. D	**17.** C	**27.** Java, Indonesia	
8. B	**18.** A	**28.** D	
9. A	**19.** C	**29.** Levying taxes	
10. Secretary of State	**20.** Republican (or Conservative)	**30.** A	
		31. A	

1. **The correct answer is D.** State residency is not a requirement to be President; therefore, it is not shared between all elected offices. Age (choice A), citizenship (choice B), and US residency (choice C) are shared requirements.

2. **The correct answer is C.** Maine was not one of the original British colonies and cannot be found labeled on the map. Massachusetts (choice A), Virginia (choice B), and Pennsylvania (choice D) can all be found labeled on the map as original British colonies.

3. **The correct answer is D.** The creation of a post office is not mentioned in the passage; therefore, it was not a concern of the party. Railroads (choice A), banking (choice B), and distribution of wealth (choice C) are all addressed in the passage.

4. **The correct answer is populist.** The People's Party became known as the Populist Party during the 1890s as a result of their willingness to accept many different groups, such as those with agrarian interests, in their fight against monopolies and the gold standard.

5. **The correct answer is C.** Jefferson discusses the need for the majority to be mindful of creating oppressive rule, while the minority need to understand the will of the majority is to be followed. Choice A is incorrect because Jefferson believes party should not divide the country. Jefferson relates that the will of the majority should prevail, but that will must be rightful, reasonable, and lawful, (implying if it is not, then it cannot always be followed), so choice B is incorrect. Jefferson believes the majority, not the minority, must be mindful of the oppression it can create (choice D).

6. **The correct answer is A.** Jefferson believed the strife created between Federalists and Democratic Republicans was dividing the nation and caused considerable tension over issues such as the National Bank, taxes, and foreign policy. Jefferson does not address debt (choice B) in his speech. Foreign invasion (choice C) is not an issue Jefferson alluded to in his speech. Any problems with the Articles of Confederation (choice D) were no longer an issue, as the Articles had long been replaced by the time of Jefferson's speech.

7. **The correct answer is D.** Jefferson's election was a virtual tie with Aaron Burr and had to be settled in the House of Representatives,

meaning when Jefferson took over as President, a large part of the nation did not directly support him. Although Jefferson alludes to a dissolving Union (choice A), he does so only in theory and does not believe it is an actual threat. Jefferson does not believe the minority is lacking rights (choice B), only that the majority need to be mindful of those rights. Jefferson does not give any support that a rebellion is on the horizon (choice C) and believes his speech is reflective of the need to understand all sides.

8. **The correct answer is B.** The image, especially the use of the flower, reflects the conflict between protesters and soldiers during the Vietnam War. There are no connections in the image to events during the early 50s (choice A), specifically no evidence of the Korean conflict. The type of war protest pictured is specific to the Vietnam area and not to any conflict during the late 80s (choice C) or early 90s (choice D).

9. **The correct answer is A.** The image shows protestors using symbols of peace standing across from soldiers whose job it is to fight in an unpopular war. There is no evidence of oppression (choice B), as the soldiers are holding their position but not encroaching on the protest. The image does not portray a transition of power (choice C) or of any other kind. While there are symbols of peace and a lack of violence, the context of the image does not suggest forgiveness (choice D), only a willingness to come to a peaceful solution.

10. **The correct answer is *Secretary of State*.** Following the path of progression, the Secretary of State follows the President pro tempore of the Senate.

11. **The correct answer is B.** The ruling stated that slavery could extend to any part of the country; therefore, the Missouri Compromise (which restricted slavery to below the 36° 30' line) was no longer valid. Slavery was already legal (choice A); it was strengthened in a sense because it could extend throughout the country. Choice C is incorrect because the ruling used the Constitution as support for slavery. Choice D is incorrect because the ruling claimed slavery was legal to move to any territory in the nation.

12. **The correct answer is A.** The willingness of members of Congress to use violence when debating slavery was reflective of the growing intensity over the debate. At the time this drawing was created, the South had yet to leave the Union (choice B). There was no election (choice C) taking place in the image, only violence over slavery. There is no support for choice D that one party was a minority compared to the other; knowing the context of the image lends support to the claim the issue was over slavery.

13. **The correct answer is December 2005.** This is the point at which the lowest number of Months to Sell inventory was accompanied by the lowest inventory, making it ideal to sell a home. Home sales were at their second highest on the entire chart, but because of the short selling time and (lack of) inventory, it was best to sell at this time for top dollar and a quick sale.

14. **The correct answer is June 2008.** This is the point at which it would take the longest to sell a home, according to the months in inventory. Coupled with the amount of inventory being almost equal to the amount of sales, this factor would make it a buyers' market and difficult for a seller to quickly sell their home for top dollar.

15. **The correct answer is June 2008.** Buyers have the most power when the Months to Sell value is high and inventory is also high. In June 2008, both of these values were at their highest. At this point, buyers had their

pick of the market, and sellers had to compete within a crowded market.

16. **The correct answer is December 2005.** At this point in the graph, sales were high, inventory was low, and Months to Sell inventory was at its lowest. Therefore, because of a small number of options and the fact that sellers were able to offload stock quickly, buyers would have to compete for available stock, meaning sellers could increase their fees.

17. **The correct answer is C.** Russia had the greatest number of migrants according to the legend, as the country is found in the upper region of Asia, in the Eastern Hemisphere (top right corner) and has the darkest shading of the choices. Neither Brazil (choice A), Egypt (choice B), nor Canada (choice D) are shaded as dark as or darker than Russia, as indicated by the key.

18. **The correct answer is A.** India is located in Asia and has the darkest shading of the choices, so you could conclude that it is the destination for the most migrants. China (choice B), Vietnam (choice C), and Japan (choice D) are not shaded as dark as India, meaning that fewer migrants are found in these countries than in India.

19. **The correct answer is C.** The judicial branch, or the Supreme Court, may use judicial review to overturn laws. The legislative branch (choice A) can pass another bill to remove the law, but it would not be overturning it using the Constitution. The executive branch (choice B) and states (choice D) cannot overturn laws and must take their case to the Supreme Court.

20. **The correct answer is *Republican (or Conservative)*.** The descriptions provided in the question are reflective of a conservative Republican found on the right side of the political spectrum.

21. **The correct answer is B.** Kennedy won more electoral votes (303) and states even though he narrowly won the popular vote, making him the elected President. Nixon (choice A) won 219 electoral votes, and Byrd (choice C) won 15 electoral votes. Because Kennedy met the criteria of winning the most electoral votes (over 270), he became the US President without a House of Representatives election (choice D).

22. **The correct answer is A.** The passage of the Alien and Sedition Acts in 1798 by President Adams invoked a response of nullification by both Virginia and Kentucky. The Virginia Resolution (choice B) supported the Kentucky Resolution in rejecting the Acts. Slavery (choice C) was not mentioned in the passage, only abuses of power. The Constitution was written in 1789 (choice D) and was being used as support for Kentucky's claims.

23. **The correct answer is D.** The Tenth Amendment affords the powers not granted to the federal government to the states, and Kentucky is arguing that federal power is created only through the compact (or joining) of the states. Freedom of speech (choice A) is not at the heart of the matter in this specific passage, although it was an issue with the Sedition Act. The right to bear arms (choice B) is not mentioned in the passage. The right to a fair trial (choice C) is not mentioned in the passage.

24. **The correct answer is A.** According to the passage, the compact (or joining together) of the states by signing the Constitution is what formed the Union. The people (choice B), the Constitution (choice C), and its amendments (choice D) are components that help to govern the United States, but it was the willingness of the states, representing the people, to sign the Constitution that formed the Union.

25. **The correct answer is B.** Of the choices given, only China has a population density greater than 0–25 per square kilometer. Canada (choice A), most countries in South America (choice C), and Saudi Arabia (choice D) are shaded the lightest, which represents low population density.

26. **The correct answer is C.** India is shaded the darkest, making it the most densely populated according to the key. The United States (choice A), Canada (choice B), and Brazil (choice D) are not shaded as darkly as India.

27. **The correct answer is *Java, Indonesia*.** According to the map, the region of Java, Indonesia, is the most densely populated; its shading represents a population of between 700 and 1,000 people per square kilometer.

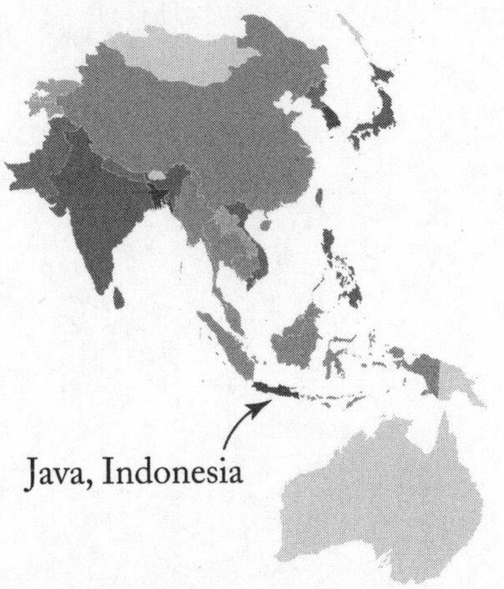

28. **The correct answer is D.** The two documents share no similar powers, according to the chart. The Constitution was written to address the issues with the Articles, including all those mentioned in the chart.

29. **The correct answer is *levying taxes*.** The federal government under the Constitution was granted the power to tax to increase revenue instead of having to request it from states under the Articles.

30. **The correct answer is A.** The Articles struggled to provide a competent government for the United States, placing it into debt with little respect from foreign powers or ability to regulate interstate trade or a militia. After Shays' Rebellion, The Articles of Confederation were replaced with a Constitution that had a strong executive branch, checks and balances, and a federal government with the power to tax. Under the Articles, the federal government had little to no power because of a fear it would become Great Britain, so choice B is incorrect. Choice C is incorrect because the government was not originally intended to fail, and there were calls only to revise the document, not replace it, during the Constitutional Convention. Choice D is incorrect because there was only one branch of government, the Legislative, under the Articles.

31. **The correct answer is A.** Congress did act after the recession hit, but the passage lays no blame on the legislative branch for a lack of action prior to the recession. Unemployment (choice B), diminishing income (choice C), and decreased consumer spending (choice D) were all economic causes for the recession.

32. **The correct answer is D.** President Nixon's unwillingness to provide recordings of his involvement in the Watergate scandal is referred to in the passage. There is no reference in the passage to the Red Scare (choice A), the 1960 election (choice B), or the Vietnam War (choice C), and the context of the case make all of them inappropriate choices.

33. **The correct answer is A.** The source is a typical citation for a court case and the information provided within the passage, including numeric references to legal precedents, give more support to this answer. Choice B is incorrect because the President is referred to in third person and would not be referencing his own case in this fashion.

A newspaper (choice C) would not be written in this tone or use numeric references to legal precedents as are found in the passage. A history textbook (choice D) would not be written in this tone and, although the passage could be found within a history textbook, it would not be the original, but a secondary, source.

34. **The correct answer is A.** A return to high tensions at the end of the Cold War during the Reagan Presidency resulted in an increase of defense spending and military budgets, and drove the overall federal spending up. Reagan decreased funding for environmental programs (choice B), and he decreased taxes (choice C) and government regulation (choice D).

35. **The correct answer is the *Affordable Care Act (or Patient Protection and Affordable Care Act).*** President Obama made it a primary goal to pass the Affordable Care Act during his administration, which also increased the amount of debt in the federal government during his second term. It was seen very negatively by his opponents and labeled "Obamacare" in order to directly attach him to the program.

ARE YOU READY TO TAKE THE GED® TEST?

Now that you have spent a great deal of time and effort studying for the GED® test and taking this Practice Test, hopefully you are well-prepared to take the GED® test. But, it's best to make sure that you are completely ready. Check your scores from this Practice Test on the table below to see where you stand.

	All Set—Well-Prepared	Possibly Ready	Need More Preparation
Reasoning Through Language Arts	37–49	25–36	0–24
Mathematical Reasoning	34–36	23–33	0–22
Science	26–33	18–25	0–17
Social Studies	26–35	18–25	0–17

If your scores are in the "All Set—Well-Prepared" column, you are probably ready to take the actual GED® test, and you should apply to take the test soon. If some of your scores are in the "Possibly Ready" column, you should focus your study on those areas where you need to improve most. "Possibly Ready" means that you are probably ready enough to earn a GED® diploma, but it's not a bad idea to spend a little more time brushing up and improving your chances to pass the actual GED® test.

If any of your scores fell in the lowest category, take more time to review the pertinent chapters in this book—and in any high school text books, if necessary. Good luck!

PART VIII

APPENDIX

Word List

A

abbreviate (verb) to make briefer, to shorten. *Because time was running out, the speaker had to abbreviate his remarks.* **abbreviation** (noun).

abrasive (adjective) irritating, grinding, rough. *The manager's rude, abrasive way of criticizing the workers was bad for morale.* **abrasion** (noun).

abridge (verb) to shorten, to reduce. *The Bill of Rights is designed to prevent Congress from abridging the rights of Americans.* **abridgment** (noun).

absolve (verb) to free from guilt, to exonerate. *The criminal jury absolved Mr. Callahan of the murder of his neighbor.* **absolution** (noun).

abstain (verb) to refrain, to hold back. *After his heart attack, William was warned by his doctor to abstain from smoking, drinking, and overeating.* **abstinence** (noun), **abstemious** (adjective).

accentuate (verb) to emphasize, to stress. *The overcast skies and chill winds only accentuate our gloomy mood.* **accentuation** (noun).

acrimonious (adjective) biting, harsh, caustic. *The election campaign became acrimonious, as the candidates traded insults and accusations.* **acrimony** (noun).

adaptable (adjective) able to be changed to be suitable for a new purpose. *Some scientists say that the mammals outlived the dinosaurs because they were more adaptable to a changing climate.* **adapt** (verb), **adaptation** (noun).

adulation (noun) extreme admiration. *The young actress received great adulation from critics and fans following her performance in the Broadway play.* **adulate** (verb), **adulatory** (adjective).

adversary (noun) an enemy or opponent. *When the former Soviet Union became an American ally, the United States lost a major adversary.* **adversarial** (adjective).

adversity (noun) misfortune. *It's easy to be patient and generous when things are going well; a person's true character is revealed under adversity.* **adverse** (adjective).

aesthetic (adjective) relating to art or beauty. *Mapplethorpe's photos may be attacked on moral grounds, but no one questions their aesthetic value—they are beautiful.* **aestheticism** (noun).

affected (adjective) false, artificial. *At one time, Japanese women were taught to speak in an affected high-pitched voice, which was thought girlishly attractive.* **affect** (verb), **affectation** (noun).

aggressive (adjective) forceful, energetic, and attacking. *Some believe that a football player needs a more aggressive style of play than a soccer player.* **aggression** (noun).

alacrity (noun) promptness, speed. *Thrilled with the job offer, he accepted with alacrity—"Before they can change their minds!" he thought.* **alacritous** (adjective).

allege (verb) to state without proof. *Some have alleged that Foster was murdered, but* *all the evidence points to suicide.* **allegation** (noun).

alleviate (verb) to make lighter or more bearable. *Although no cure for AIDS has been found, doctors are able to alleviate the suffering of those with the disease.* **alleviation** (noun).

ambiguous (adjective) having two or more possible meanings. *The phrase, "Let's table that discussion" is ambiguous; some think it means, "Let's discuss it now," while others think it means, "Let's save it for later."* **ambiguity** (noun).

ambivalent (adjective) having two or more contradictory feelings or attitudes; uncertain. *She was ambivalent toward her impending marriage; at times she was eager to go ahead, while at other times she wanted to call it off.* **ambivalence** (noun).

amiable (adjective) likable, agreeable, friendly. *He was an amiable lab partner, always smiling, on time, and ready to work.* **amiability** (noun).

amicable (adjective) friendly, peaceable. *Although they agreed to divorce, their settlement was amicable and they remained friends afterward.*

amplify (verb) to enlarge, expand, or increase. *Uncertain as to whether they understood, the students asked the teacher to amplify his explanation.* **amplification** (noun).

anachronistic (adjective) out of the proper time. *The reference, in Shakespeare's* Julius Caesar *to "the clock striking twelve" is anachronistic, since there were no striking timepieces in ancient Rome.* **anachronism** (noun).

anarchy (noun) absence of law or order. *For several months after the Nazi government was destroyed, there was no effective government in parts of Germany, and anarchy ruled.* **anarchic** (adjective).

anomaly (noun) something different or irregular. *Tiny Pluto, orbiting next to the giants Jupiter, Saturn, and Neptune, had long appeared to be an anomaly.* **anomalous** (adjective).

antagonism (noun) hostility, conflict, opposition. *As more and more reporters investigated the Watergate scandal, antagonism between Nixon and the press increased.* **antagonistic** (adjective), **antagonize** (verb).

antiseptic (adjective) fighting infection; extremely clean. *A wound should be washed with an antiseptic solution. The all-white offices were bare and almost antiseptic in their starkness.*

apathy (noun) lack of interest, concern, or emotion. *Tom's apathy toward his job could be seen in his lateness, his sloppy work, and his overall poor attitude.* **apathetic** (adjective).

arable (adjective) able to be cultivated for growing crops. *Rocky New England has relatively little arable farmland.*

arbiter (noun) someone able to settle disputes; a judge or referee. *The public is the ultimate arbiter of commercial value; it decides what sells and what doesn't.*

arbitrary (adjective) based on random or merely personal preference. *Both computers cost the same and had the same features, so in the end I made an arbitrary decision about which one to buy.*

arcane (adjective) little-known, mysterious, obscure. *Eliot's* Waste Land *is filled with arcane lore, including quotations in Latin, Greek, French, German, and Sanskrit.* **arcana** (noun, plural).

ardor (noun) a strong feeling of passion, energy, or zeal. *The young revolutionary proclaimed his convictions with an ardor that excited the crowd.* **ardent** (adjective).

arid (adjective) very dry; boring and meaningless. *The arid climate of Arizona makes farming difficult. Some find the law a fascinating topic, but for me it is an arid discipline.* **aridity** (noun).

ascetic (adjective) practicing strict self-discipline for moral or spiritual reasons. *The so-called Desert Fathers were hermits who lived an* *ascetic life of fasting, study, and prayer.* **asceticism** (verb).

assiduous (adjective) working with care, attention, and diligence. *Although Karen is not a naturally gifted math student, by assiduous study she managed to earn an A in trigonometry.* **assiduity** (noun).

astute (adjective) observant, intelligent, and shrewd. *The reporter's years of experience in Washington and his personal acquaintance with many political insiders made him an astute commentator on politics.*

atypical (adjective) not typical; unusual. *In* Hyde Park on Hudson, *Bill Murray, best known as a comic actor, gave an atypical dramatic performance.*

audacious (adjective) bold, daring, adventurous. *Her plan to cross the Atlantic single-handed in a 12-foot sailboat was audacious, if not reckless.* **audacity** (noun).

audible (adjective) able to be heard. *Although she whispered, her voice was picked up by the microphone, and her words were audible throughout the theater.* **audibility** (noun).

auspicious (adjective) promising good fortune; propitious. *The news that a team of British climbers had reached the summit of Everest seemed an auspicious sign for the reign of newly crowned Queen Elizabeth II.*

authoritarian (adjective) favoring or demanding blind obedience to leaders. *Despite Americans' belief in democracy, the American government has supported authoritarian regimes in other countries.* **authoritarianism** (noun).

B

belated (adjective) delayed past the proper time. *She called her mother on January 5th to offer her a belated "Happy New Year."*

belie (verb) to present a false or contradictory appearance. *Lena Horne's youthful appearance belied her long, distinguished career in show business.*

benevolent (adjective) wishing or doing good. *In old age, Carnegie used his wealth for benevolent purposes, donating large sums to found libraries and schools.* **benevolence** (noun).

berate (verb) to scold or criticize harshly. *The judge angrily berated the two lawyers for their unprofessional behavior.*

bereft (adjective) lacking or deprived of something. *Bereft of parental love, orphans sometimes grow up to be insecure.*

bombastic (adjective) inflated or pompous in style. *Old-fashioned bombastic political speeches don't work on television, which demands a more intimate style of communication.* **bombast** (noun).

bourgeois (adjective) middle class or reflecting middle-class values. *The Dadaists of the 1920s produced art deliberately designed to offend bourgeois art collectors, with their taste for respectable, refined, uncontroversial pictures.* **bourgeois** (noun).

buttress (noun) something that supports or strengthens; a projecting structure of masrony or wood. *The endorsement of the American Medical Association is a powerful buttress for the claims made about this new medicine. The buttress on the south wall of the medieval castle was beginning to crumble.* **buttress** (verb).

camaraderie (noun) a spirit of friendship. *Spending long days and nights together on the road, the members of a traveling theater group develop a strong sense of camaraderie.*

candor (noun) openness, honesty, frankness. *In his memoir about the Vietnam War, former defense secretary McNamara described his mistakes with remarkable candor.* **candid** (adjective).

capricious (adjective) unpredictable, whimsical. *The pop star Madonna has changed her image so many times that each new transformation* *now appears capricious rather than purposeful.* **caprice** (noun).

carnivorous (adjective) meat-eating. *The long, dagger-like teeth of the Tyrannosaurus make it obvious that this was a carnivorous dinosaur.* **carnivore** (noun).

carping (adjective) unfairly or excessively critical; querulous. *New York is famous for its demanding critics, but none is harder to please than the carping John Simon, said to have single-handedly destroyed many acting careers.* **carp** (verb).

catalytic (adjective) bringing about, causing, or producing some result. *The conditions for revolution existed in America by 1765; the disputes about taxation that arose later were the catalytic events that sparked the rebellion.* **catalyze** (verb).

caustic (adjective) burning, corrosive. *No one was safe when the satirist H. L. Mencken unleashed his caustic wit.*

censure (noun) blame, condemnation. *The news that the senator had harassed several women brought censure from many feminists.* **censure** (verb).

chaos (noun) disorder, confusion, chance. *The first few moments after the explosion were pure chaos: no one was sure what had happened, and the area was filled with people running and yelling.* **chaotic** (adjective).

circuitous (adjective) winding or indirect. *We drove to the cottage by a circuitous route so we could see as much of the surrounding countryside as possible.*

circumlocution (noun) speaking in a roundabout way; wordiness. *Legal documents often contain circumlocutions that make them difficult to understand.*

circumscribe (verb) to define by a limit or boundary. *Originally, the role of the executive branch of government was clearly circumscribed, but that role has greatly expanded over time.* **circumscription** (noun).

circumvent (verb) to get around. *When James was caught speeding, he tried to circumvent the law by offering the police officer a bribe.*

clandestine (adjective) secret, surreptitious. *As a member of the underground, Balas took part in clandestine meetings to discuss ways of sabotaging the Nazi forces.*

cloying (adjective) overly sweet or sentimental. *The deathbed scenes in the novels of Dickens are famously cloying: as Oscar Wilde said, "One would need a heart of stone to read the death of Little Nell without dissolving into tears . . . of laughter."*

cogent (adjective) forceful and convincing. *The committee members were won over to the project by the cogent arguments of the chairman.* **cogency** (noun).

cognizant (adjective) aware, mindful. *Cognizant of the fact that it was getting late, the master of ceremonies cut short the last speech.* **cognizance** (noun).

cohesive (adjective) sticking together, unified. *An effective military unit must be a cohesive team, all its members working together for a common goal.* **cohere** (verb), **cohesion** (noun).

collaborate (verb) to work together. *To create a truly successful movie, the director, writers, actors, and many others must collaborate closely.* **collaboration** (noun), **collaborative** (adjective).

colloquial (adjective) informal in language; conversational. *Some expressions from Shakespeare, such as the use of thou and thee, sound formal today but were colloquial English in Shakespeare's time.*

competent (adjective) having the skill and knowledge needed for a particular task; capable. *Any competent lawyer can draw up a will.* **competence** (noun).

complacent (adjective) smug, self-satisfied. *Until recently, American auto makers were complacent, believing that they would continue* *to be successful with little effort.* **complacency** (noun).

composure (noun) calm, self-assurance. *The company's president managed to keep his composure during his speech even when the teleprompter broke down, leaving him without a script.* **composed** (adjective).

conciliatory (adjective) seeking agreement, compromise, or reconciliation. *As a conciliatory gesture, the union leaders agreed to postpone a strike and to continue negotiations with management.* **conciliate** (verb), **conciliation** (noun).

concise (adjective) expressed briefly and simply; succinct. *Less than a page long, the Bill of Rights is a concise statement of the freedoms enjoyed by all Americans.* **concision** (noun).

condescending (adjective) having an attitude of superiority toward another; patronizing. *"What a cute little car!" she remarked in a condescending style. "I suppose it's the nicest one someone like you could afford!"* **condescension** (noun).

condolence (noun) pity for someone else's sorrow or loss; sympathy. *After the sudden death of Princess Diana, thousands of messages of condolence were sent to her family.* **condole** (verb).

confidant (noun) someone entrusted with another's secrets. *No one knew about Jane's engagement except Sarah, her confidant.* **confide** (verb), **confidential** (adjective).

conformity (noun) agreement with or adherence to custom or rule. *In my high school, conformity was the rule: everyone dressed the same, talked the same, and listened to the same music.* **conform** (verb), **conformist** (noun, adjective).

consensus (noun) general agreement among a group. *Among Quakers, voting traditionally is not used; instead, discussion continues until the entire group forms a consensus.*

consolation (noun) relief or comfort in sorrow or suffering. *Although we miss our dog very much, it is a consolation to know that she died quickly, without suffering.* **console** (verb).

consternation (noun) shock, amazement, dismay. *When a voice in the back of the church shouted out, "I know why they should not be married!" the entire gathering was thrown into consternation.*

consummate (verb) to complete, finish, or perfect. *The deal was consummated with a handshake and the payment of the agreed-upon fee.* **consummate** (adjective), **consummation** (noun).

contaminate (verb) to make impure. *Chemicals dumped in a nearby forest had seeped into the soil and contaminated the local water supply.* **contamination** (noun).

contemporary (adjective) modern, current; from the same time. *I prefer old-fashioned furniture rather than contemporary styles. The composer Vivaldi was roughly contemporary with Bach.* **contemporary** (noun).

contrite (adjective) sorry for past misdeeds. *The public is often willing to forgive celebrities who are involved in some scandal, as long as they appear contrite.* **contrition** (noun).

conundrum (noun) a riddle, puzzle, or problem. *The question of why an all-powerful, all-loving God allows evil to exist is a conundrum many philosophers have pondered.*

convergence (noun) the act of coming together in unity or similarity. *A remarkable example of evolutionary convergence can be seen in the shark and the dolphin, two sea creatures that developed from different origins to become very similar in form.* **converge** (verb).

convoluted (adjective) twisting, complicated, intricate. *Tax law has become so convoluted that it's easy for people to accidentally violate it.* **convolute** (verb), **convolution** (noun).

corroborating (adjective) supporting with evidence; confirming. *A passerby who had* *witnessed the crime gave corroborating testimony about the presence of the accused person.* **corroborate** (verb), **corroboration** (noun).

corrosive (adjective) eating away, gnawing, or destroying. *Years of poverty and hard work had a corrosive effect on her beauty.* **corrode** (verb), **corrosion** (noun).

credulity (noun) willingness to believe, even with little evidence. *Con artists fool people by taking advantage of their credulity.* **credulous** (adjective).

criterion (noun) a standard of measurement or judgment. *In choosing a design for the new taxicabs, reliability will be our main criterion.* **criteria** (plural).

critique (noun) a critical evaluation. *The editor gave a detailed critique of the manuscript, explaining its strengths and its weaknesses.* **critique** (verb).

culpable (adjective) deserving blame, guilty. *Although he committed the crime, because he was mentally ill he should not be considered culpable for his actions.* **culpability** (noun).

cumulative (adjective) made up of successive additions. *Smallpox was eliminated only through the cumulative efforts of several generations of doctors and scientists.* **accumulation** (noun), **accumulate** (verb).

curtail (verb) to shorten. *The opening round of the golf tournament was curtailed by the severe thunderstorm.*

D

debased (adjective) lowered in quality, character, or esteem. *The quality of TV journalism has been debased by the many new tabloid-style talk shows.* **debase** (verb).

debunk (verb) to expose as false or worthless. *Magician James Randi loves to debunk psychics, mediums, clairvoyants, and others who claim supernatural powers.*

decorous (adjective) having good taste; proper, appropriate. *Prior to her visit to Buckingham Palace, the young woman was instructed to demonstrate the most decorous behavior.* **decorum** (noun).

decry (verb) to criticize or condemn. *The workers continued to decry the lack of safety in their factory.*

deduction (noun) a logical conclusion, especially a specific conclusion based on general principles. *Based on what is known about the effects of greenhouse gases on atmospheric temperature, scientists have made several deductions about the likelihood of global warming.* **deduce** (verb).

delegate (verb) to give authority or responsibility. *The president delegated the vice president to represent the administration at the peace talks.* **delegate** (noun).

deleterious (adjective) harmful. *About 30 years ago, scientists proved that working with asbestos could be deleterious to one's health, producing cancer and other diseases.*

delineate (verb) to outline or describe. *Naturalists had long suspected the fact of evolution, but Darwin was the first to delineate a process—natural selection—through which evolution could occur.* **delineation** (noun)

demagogue (noun) a leader who plays dishonestly on the prejudices and emotions of his followers. *Senator Joseph McCarthy was a demagogue who used the paranoia of the anti-Communist 1950s as a way of seizing fame and power in Washington.* **demagoguery** (noun).

demure (adjective) modest or shy. *The demure heroines of Victorian fiction have given way to today's stronger, more opinionated, and more independent female characters.*

denigrate (verb) to criticize or belittle. *The firm's new president tried to explain his plans for improving the company without appearing to* *denigrate the work of his predecessor.* **denigration** (noun).

depose (verb) to remove from office, especially from a throne. *Iran was once ruled by a monarch called the Shah, who was deposed in 1979.*

derelict (adjective) neglecting one's duty. *The train crash was blamed on a switchman who was derelict, having fallen asleep while on duty.* **dereliction** (noun).

derivative (adjective) taken from a particular source. *When a person first writes poetry, her poems are apt to be derivative of whatever poetry she most enjoys reading.* **derivation** (noun), **derive** (verb).

desolate (adjective) empty, lifeless, and deserted; hopeless, gloomy. *Robinson Crusoe was shipwrecked and had to learn to survive alone on a desolate island. The murder of her husband left Mary Lincoln desolate.* **desolation** (noun).

destitute (adjective) very poor. *Years of rule by a dictator who stole the wealth of the country had left the people of the Philippines destitute.* **destitution** (noun).

deter (verb) to discourage from acting. *The best way to deter crime is to ensure that criminals will receive swift and certain punishment.* **deterrence** (noun), **deterrent** (adjective).

detractor (noun) someone who belittles or disparages. *The famous singer has many detractors who consider his music boring, inane, and sentimental.* **detract** (verb).

deviate (verb) to depart from a standard or norm. *Having agreed upon a spending budget for the company, we mustn't deviate from it; if we do, we may run out of money soon.* **deviation** (noun).

devious (adjective) tricky, deceptive. *The CEO's devious financial tactics were designed to enrich his firm while confusing or misleading government regulators.*

didactic (adjective) intended to teach, instructive. *The children's TV show* Sesame Street *is designed to be both entertaining and didactic.*

diffident (adjective) hesitant, reserved, shy. *Someone with a diffident personality should pursue a career that involves little public contact.* **diffidence** (noun).

diffuse (verb) to spread out, to scatter. *The red dye quickly became diffused through the water, turning it a very pale pink.* **diffusion** (noun).

digress (verb) to wander from the main path or the main topic. *My high school biology teacher loved to digress from science into personal anecdotes about his college adventures.* **digression** (noun), **digressive** (adjective).

dilatory (adjective) delaying, procrastinating. *The lawyer used various dilatory tactics, hoping that his opponent would get tired of waiting for a trial and drop the case.*

diligent (adjective) working hard and steadily. *Through diligent efforts, the townspeople were able to clear away the debris from the flood in a matter of days.* **diligence** (noun).

diminutive (adjective) unusually small, tiny. *Children are fond of Shetland ponies because their diminutive size makes them easy to ride.* **diminution** (noun).

discern (verb) to detect, notice, or observe. *I could discern the shape of a whale off the starboard bow, but it was too far away to determine its size or species.* **discernment** (noun).

disclose (verb) to make known; to reveal. *Election laws require candidates to disclose the names of those who contribute large sums of money to their campaigns.* **disclosure** (noun).

discomfit (verb) to frustrate, thwart, or embarrass. *Discomfited by the interviewer's unexpected question, Peter could only stammer in reply.* **discomfiture** (noun).

disconcert (verb) to confuse or embarrass. *When the hallway bells began to ring halfway* *through her lecture, the speaker was disconcerted and didn't know what to do.*

discredit (verb) to cause disbelief in the accuracy of some statement or the reliability of a person. *Although many people still believe in UFOs, among scientists the reports of "alien encounters" have been thoroughly discredited.*

discreet (adjective) showing good judgment in speech and behavior. *Be discreet when discussing confidential business matters—don't talk among strangers on the elevator, for example.* **discretion** (noun).

discrepancy (noun) a difference or variance between two or more things. *The discrepancies between the two witnesses' stories show that one of them must be lying.* **discrepant** (adjective).

disdain (noun) contempt, scorn. *The professor could not hide his disdain for those students who were perpetually late to his class.* **disdain** (verb), **disdainful** (adjective).

disingenuous (adjective) pretending to be candid, simple, and frank. *When Texas billionaire H. Ross Perot ran for president, many considered his "jest plain folks" style disingenuous.*

disparage (verb) to speak disrespectfully about, to belittle. *Many political ads today both praise their own candidate and disparage his or her opponent.* **disparagement** (noun), **disparaging** (adjective).

disparity (noun) difference in quality or kind. *There is often a disparity between the kind of high-quality television people say they want and the low-brow programs they actually watch.* **disparate** (adjective).

disregard (verb) to ignore, to neglect. *If you don't write a will, when you die, your survivors may disregard your wishes about how your property should be handled.* **disregard** (noun).

disruptive (adjective) causing disorder, interrupting. *When the senator spoke at our college, angry demonstrators picketed, heckled, and engaged in other disruptive activities.* **disrupt** (verb), **disruption** (noun).

dissemble (verb) to pretend, to simulate. *When the police questioned her about the crime, she dissembled, acting as if she were unfamiliar with the victim..*

dissipate (verb) to spread out or scatter. *The windows and doors were opened, allowing the smoke that had filled the room to dissipate.* **dissipation** (noun).

dissonance (noun) lack of music harmony; lack of agreement between ideas. *Most modern music is characterized by dissonance, which many listeners find hard to enjoy. There is a noticeable dissonance between two common beliefs of most conservatives: their faith in unfettered free markets and their preference for traditional social values.* **dissonant** (adjective).

diverge (verb) to move in different directions. *Frost's poem* The Road Less Traveled *tells of the choice he made when "Two roads diverged in a yellow wood."* **divergence** (noun), **divergent** (adjective).

diversion (noun) a distraction or pastime. *During the two hours he spent in the doctor's waiting room, the game on his cell phone was a welcome diversion.* **divert** (verb).

divination (noun) the art of predicting the future. *In ancient Greece, people wanting to know their fate would visit the priests at Delphi, supposedly skilled at divination.* **divine** (verb).

divisive (adjective) causing disagreement or disunity. *Throughout history, race has been the most divisive issue in American society.*

divulge (verb) to reveal. *The people who count the votes for the Oscar awards are under strict orders not to divulge the names of the winners.*

dogmatic (adjective) holding firmly to a particular set of beliefs with little or no basis. *Believers in autocratic doctrine tend to be* *dogmatic, ignoring evidence that contradicts their beliefs.* **dogmatism** (noun).

dominant (adjective) greatest in importance or power. *Turner's* Frontier Thesis *suggests that the existence of the frontier had a dominant influence on American culture.* **dominate** (verb), **domination** (noun).

dubious (adjective) doubtful, uncertain. *Despite the chairman's attempts to convince the committee members that his plan would succeed, most of them remained dubious.* **dubiety** (noun).

durable (adjective) long lasting. *Denim is a popular material for work clothes because it is strong and durable.*

duress (noun) compulsion or restraint. *Fearing that the police might beat him, he confessed to the crime, not willingly but under duress.*

E

eclectic (adjective) drawn from many sources; varied, heterogeneous. *The Mellon family art collection is an eclectic one, including works ranging from ancient Greek sculptures to modern paintings.* **eclecticism** (noun).

efficacious (adjective) able to produce a desired effect. *Though thousands of people today are taking herbal supplements to treat depression, researchers have not yet proved them efficacious.* **efficacy** (noun).

effrontery (noun) shameless boldness. *The sports world was shocked when a professional basketball player had the effrontery to choke his head coach during a practice session.*

effusive (adjective) pouring forth one's emotions very freely. *Having won the Oscar for Best Actress, Sally Field gave an effusive acceptance speech in which she marveled, "You like me! You really like me!"* **effusion** (noun).

egotism (noun) excessive concern with oneself; conceit. *Robert's egotism was so great that all he could talk about was the importance—and the brilliance—of his own opinions.* **egotistic** (adjective).

egregious (adjective) obvious, conspicuous, flagrant. *It's hard to imagine how the editor could allow such an egregious error to appear.*

elated (adjective) excited and happy; exultant. *When the Washington Redskins' last, desperate pass was intercepted, the elated fans of the Philadelphia Eagles began to celebrate.* **elate** (verb), **elation** (noun).

elliptical (adjective) very terse or concise in writing or speech; difficult to understand. *Rather than speak plainly, she hinted at her meaning through a series of nods, gestures, and elliptical half sentences.*

elusive (adjective) hard to capture, grasp, or understand. *Though everyone thinks they know what "justice" is, when you try to define the concept precisely, it proves to be quite elusive.*

embezzle (verb) to steal money or property that has been entrusted to your care. *The church treasurer was found to have embezzled thousands of dollars by writing phony checks on the church bank account.* **embezzlement** (noun).

emend (verb) to correct. *Before the letter is mailed, please emend the two spelling errors.* **emendation** (noun).

emigrate (verb) to leave one place or country to settle elsewhere. *Millions of Irish emigrated to the New World in the wake of the great Irish famines of the 1840s.* **emigrant** (noun), **emigration** (noun).

eminent (adjective) noteworthy, famous. *Vaclav Havel was an eminent author before he was elected president of the Czech Republic.* **eminence** (noun).

emissary (noun) someone who represents another. *In an effort to avoid a military showdown, former President Jimmy Carter was sent as an emissary to Korea to negotiate a settlement.*

emollient (noun) something that softens or soothes. *She used a hand cream as an emollient on her dry, work-roughened hands.* **emollient** (adjective).

empathy (noun) imaginative sharing of the feelings, thoughts, or experiences of another. *It's easy for a parent to have empathy for the sorrow of another parent whose child has died.* **empathetic** (adjective).

empirical (adjective) based on experience or personal observation. *Although many people believe in ESP, scientists have found no empirical evidence of its existence.* **empiricism** (noun).

emulate (verb) to imitate or copy. *The British band Oasis admitted their desire to emulate their idols, the Beatles.* **emulation** (noun).

encroach (verb) to go beyond acceptable limits; to trespass. *By quietly seizing more and more authority, Robert Moses continually encroached on the powers of other government leaders.* **encroachment** (noun).

enervate (verb) to reduce the energy or strength of someone or something. *The extended exposure to the sun along with dehydration enervated the shipwrecked crew, leaving them almost too weak to spot the passing vessel.*

engender (verb) to produce, to cause. *Countless disagreements over the proper use of national forests have engendered feelings of hostility between ranchers and environmentalists.*

enhance (verb) to improve in value or quality. *New kitchen appliances will enhance your house and increase the amount of money you'll make when you sell it.* **enhancement** (noun).

enmity (noun) hatred, hostility, ill will. *Long-standing enmity, like that between the Protestants and Catholics in Northern Ireland, is difficult to overcome.*

enthrall (verb) to enchant or charm. *The Swedish singer Jenny Lind enthralled American audiences in the nineteenth century with her beauty and talent.*

ephemeral (adjective) quickly disappearing; transient. *Stardom in pop music is ephemeral; many of the top acts of ten years ago are forgotten today.*

equanimity (noun) calmness of mind, especially under stress. *FDR had the gift of facing the great crises of his presidency—the Depression and the Second World War—with equanimity and even humor.*

eradicate (verb) to destroy completely. *American society has failed to eradicate racism, although some of its worst effects have been mitigated.*

espouse (verb) to take up as a cause; to adopt. *No politician in America today will openly espouse racism, although some behave and speak in racially prejudiced ways.*

euphoric (adjective) a feeling of extreme happiness and well-being; elation. *One often feels euphoric during the earliest days of a new love affair.* **euphoria** (noun).

evanescent (adjective) vanishing like a vapor; fragile and transient. *As she walked by, the evanescent fragrance of her perfume reached me for just an instant.*

exacerbate (verb) to make worse or more severe. *The roads in our town already have too much traffic; building a new shopping mall will exacerbate the problem.*

exasperate (verb) to irritate or annoy. *Because she was trying to study, Sharon was exasperated by the yelling of her neighbors' children.*

exculpate (verb) to free from blame or guilt. *When someone else confessed to the crime, the previous suspect was exculpated.* **exculpation** (noun), **exculpatory** (adjective).

exemplary (adjective) worthy to serve as a model. *The Baldrige Award is given to a company with exemplary standards of excellence in products and service.* **exemplar** (noun), **exemplify** (verb).

exonerate (verb) to free from blame. *Although the truck driver was suspected at first of being involved in the bombing, later evidence* *exonerated him.* **exoneration** (noun), **exonerative** (adjective).

expansive (adjective) broad and large; speaking openly and freely. *The LBJ Ranch is located on an expansive tract of land in Texas. Over dinner, she became expansive in describing her dreams for the future.*

expedite (verb) to carry out promptly. *As the flood waters rose, the governor ordered state agencies to expedite their rescue efforts.*

expertise (noun) skill, mastery. *The software company was eager to hire new graduates with programming expertise.*

expiate (verb) to atone for. *The president's apology to the survivors of the notorious Tuskegee experiments was his attempt to expiate the nation's guilt over their mistreatment.* **expiation** (noun).

expropriate (verb) to seize ownership of. *When the Communists came to power in China, they expropriated most businesses and turned them over to government-appointed managers.* **expropriation** (noun).

extant (adjective) currently in existence. *Of the seven ancient* Wonders of the World, *only the pyramids of Egypt are still extant.*

extenuate (verb) to make less serious. *Jeanine's guilt is extenuated by the fact that she was only 12 when she committed the theft.* **extenuating** (adjective), **extenuation** (noun).

extol (verb) to greatly praise. *At the party convention, speaker after speaker rose to extol their candidate for the presidency.*

extricate (verb) to free from a difficult or complicated situation. *Much of the humor in the TV show* I Love Lucy *comes in watching Lucy try to extricate herself from the problems she creates by fibbing or trickery.* **extricable** (adjective).

extrinsic (adjective) not an innate part or aspect of something; external. *The high price of old baseball cards is due to extrinsic factors, such as the nostalgia felt by baseball fans for the stars of their youth, rather than the inherent beauty or value of the cards themselves.*

exuberant (adjective) wildly joyous and enthusiastic. *As the final seconds of the game ticked away, the fans of the winning team began an exuberant celebration.* **exuberance** (noun).

F

facile (adjective) easy; shallow or superficial. *The one-minute political commercial favors a candidate with facile opinions rather than serious, thoughtful solutions.* **facilitate** (verb), **facility** (noun).

fallacy (noun) an error in fact or logic. *It's a fallacy to think that "natural" means "healthful"; after all, the deadly poison arsenic is completely natural.* **fallacious** (adjective).

felicitous (adjective) pleasing, fortunate, apt. *The sudden blossoming of the dogwood trees on the morning of Matt's wedding seemed a felicitous sign of good luck.* **felicity** (noun).

feral (adjective) wild. *The garbage dump was inhabited by a pack of feral dogs that had escaped from their owners and become completely wild.*

fervent (adjective) full of intense feeling; ardent, zealous. *In the days just after his religious conversion, his piety was at its most fervent.* **fervid** (adjective), **fervor** (noun).

flagrant (adjective) obviously wrong; offensive. *Nixon was forced to resign the presidency after a series of flagrant crimes against the U.S. Constitution.* **flagrancy** (noun).

flamboyant (adjective) very colorful, showy, or elaborate. *At Mardi Gras, partygoers compete to show off the most wild and flamboyant outfits.*

florid (adjective) flowery, fancy; reddish. *The grand ballroom was decorated in a florid style. Years of heavy drinking had given him a florid complexion.*

foppish (adjective) describing a man who is foolishly vain about his dress or appearance. *The foppish character of the 1890s wore bright-colored spats and a top hat; in the 1980s, he wore fancy suspenders and a shirt with a contrasting collar.* **fop** (noun).

formidable (adjective) awesome, impressive, or frightening. *According to his plaque in the Baseball Hall of Fame, pitcher Tom Seaver turned the New York Mets "from lovable losers into formidable foes."*

fortuitous (adjective) lucky, fortunate. *Although the mayor claimed credit for the falling crime rate, it was really caused by several fortuitous trends.*

fractious (adjective) troublesome, unruly. *Members of the British Parliament are often fractious, shouting insults and sarcastic questions during debates.*

fragility (noun) the quality of being easy to break; delicacy, weakness. *Because of their fragility, few stained-glass windows from the early Middle Ages have survived.* **fragile** (adjective).

fraternize (verb) to associate with on friendly terms. *Although baseball players aren't supposed to fraternize with their opponents, players from opposing teams often chat before games.* **fraternization** (noun).

frenetic (adjective) chaotic, frantic. *The floor of the stock exchange, filled with traders shouting and gesturing, is a scene of frenetic activity.*

frivolity (noun) lack of seriousness; levity. *The frivolity of the Mardi Gras carnival is in contrast to the seriousness of the religious season of Lent that follows.* **frivolous** (adjective).

frugal (adjective) spending little. *With our last few dollars, we bought a frugal dinner: a loaf of bread and a piece of cheese.* **frugality** (noun).

fugitive (noun) someone trying to escape. *When two prisoners broke out of the local jail, police were warned to keep an eye out for the fugitives.* **fugitive** (adjective).

G

gargantuan (adjective) huge, colossal. *The building of the Great Wall of China was one of the most gargantuan projects ever undertaken.*

genial (adjective) friendly, gracious. *A good host welcomes all visitors in a warm and genial fashion.*

grandiose (adjective) overly large, pretentious, or showy. *Among Hitler's grandiose plans for Berlin was a gigantic building with a dome several times larger than any ever built.* **grandiosity** (noun).

gratuitous (adjective) given freely or without cause. *Since her opinion was not requested, her harsh criticism of his singing seemed a gratuitous insult.*

gregarious (adjective) enjoying the company of others; sociable. *Naturally gregarious, Emily is a popular member of several clubs and a sought-after lunch companion.*

guileless (adjective) without cunning; innocent. *Deborah's guileless personality and complete honesty make it hard for her to survive in the harsh world of politics.*

gullible (adjective) easily fooled. *When the sweepstakes entry form arrived bearing the message, "You may be a winner!" my gullible neighbor tried to claim a prize.* **gullibility** (noun).

H

hackneyed (adjective) without originality, trite. *When someone invented the phrase, "No pain, no gain," it was clever, but now it is so commonly heard that it seems hackneyed.*

haughty (adjective) overly-proud. *The fashion model strode down the runway, her hips thrust forward and a haughty expression, like a sneer, on her face.* **haughtiness** (noun).

hedonist (noun) someone who lives mainly to pursue pleasure. *Having inherited great wealth, he chose to live the life of a hedonist, traveling the world in luxury.* **hedonism** (noun), **hedonistic** (adjective).

heinous (adjective) very evil, hateful. *The massacre by Pol Pot of more than a million Cambodians is one of the twentieth century's most heinous crimes.*

hierarchy (noun) a ranking of people, things, or ideas from highest to lowest. *A cabinet secretary ranks just below the president and vice president in the hierarchy of the executive branch.* **hierarchical** (adjective).

hypocrisy (noun) a false pretense of virtue. *When the sexual misconduct of the television preacher was exposed, his followers were shocked at his hypocrisy.* **hypocritical** (adjective).

I

iconoclast (noun) someone who attacks traditional beliefs or institutions. *Comedian Stephen Colbert enjoys his reputation as an iconoclast, though people in power often resent his satirical jabs.* **iconoclasm** (noun), **iconoclastic** (adjective).

idiosyncratic (adjective) peculiar to an individual; eccentric. *She sings pop music in an idiosyncratic style, mingling high-pitched whoops and squeals with throaty gurgles.* **idiosyncrasy** (noun).

idolatry (noun) the worship of a person, thing, or institution as a god. *In Communist China, Chairman Mao was the subject of idolatry; his picture was displayed everywhere, and millions of Chinese memorized his sayings.* **idolatrous** (adjective).

impartial (adjective) fair, equal, unbiased. *If a judge is not impartial, then all of her rulings are questionable.* **impartiality** (noun).

impeccable (adjective) flawless. *The crooks printed impeccable copies of the Super Bowl tickets, making it impossible to distinguish them from the real ones.*

impetuous (adjective) acting hastily or impulsively. *Stuart's resignation was an impetuous act; he did it without thinking, and he soon regretted it.* **impetuosity** (noun).

impinge (verb) to encroach upon, touch, or affect. *You have a right to do whatever you want, so long as your actions don't impinge on the rights of others.*

implicit (adjective) understood without being openly expressed; implied. *Although most clubs had no rules excluding minorities, many had an implicit understanding that no member of a minority group would be allowed to join.*

impute (verb) to credit or give responsibility to; to attribute. *Although Helena's comments embarrassed me, I don't impute any ill will to her; I think she didn't realize what she was saying.* **imputation** (noun).

inarticulate (adjective) unable to speak or express oneself clearly and understandably. *A skilled athlete may be an inarticulate public speaker, as demonstrated by many post-game interviews.*

incisive (adjective) clear and direct expression. *Franklin settled the debate with a few incisive remarks that summed up the issue perfectly.*

incompatible (adjective) unable to exist together; conflicting. *Many people hold seemingly incompatible beliefs: for example, supporting the death penalty while believing in the sacredness of human life.* **incompatibility** (noun).

inconsequential (adjective) of little importance. *When the flat screen TV was delivered, it was a different shade of gray than I expected, but the difference was inconsequential.*

incontrovertible (adjective) impossible to question. *The fact that Alexandra's fingerprints were the only ones on the murder weapon made her guilt seem incontrovertible.*

incorrigible (adjective) impossible to manage or reform. *Lou is an incorrigible trickster, constantly playing practical jokes no matter how much his friends complain.*

incremental (adjective) increasing gradually by small amounts. *Although the initial cost of the Medicare program was small, the incremental expenses have grown to be very large.* **increment** (noun).

incriminate (verb) to give evidence of guilt. *The fifth amendment to the Constitution says that no one is required to reveal information that would incriminate him or her in a crime.* **incriminating** (adjective).

incumbent (noun) someone who occupies an office or position. *It is often difficult for a challenger to win a seat in Congress from the incumbent.* **incumbency** (noun), **incumbent** (adjective).

indeterminate (adjective) not definitely known. *The college plans to enroll an indeterminate number of students; the size of the class will depend on the number of applicants and how many accept offers of admission.* **determine** (verb).

indifferent (adjective) unconcerned, apathetic. *The mayor's small proposed budget for education suggests that he is indifferent to the needs of our schools.* **indifference** (noun).

indistinct (adjective) unclear, uncertain. *We could see boats on the water, but in the thick morning fog their shapes were indistinct.*

indomitable (adjective) unable to be conquered or controlled. *The world admired the indomitable spirit of Nelson Mandela; he remained courageous despite years of imprisonment.*

induce (verb) to cause. *The doctor prescribed a medicine that was supposed to induce a lowering of the blood pressure.* **induction** (noun).

ineffable (adjective) difficult to describe or express. *He gazed in silence at the sunrise over the Taj Mahal, his eyes reflecting an ineffable sense of wonder.*

inevitable (adjective) unable to be avoided. *Once the Japanese attacked Pearl Harbor, American involvement in World War II was inevitable.* **inevitability** (noun).

inexorable (adjective) unable to be deterred; relentless. *It's difficult to imagine how the mythic character of Oedipus could have avoided his evil destiny; his fate appears inexorable.*

ingenious (adjective) showing cleverness and originality. *The Post-it™ note is an ingenious solution to a common problem—how to mark papers without spoiling them.* **ingenuity** (noun).

inherent (adjective) naturally part of something. *Compromise is inherent in democracy, since everyone cannot get his or her way.* **inhere** (verb), **inherence** (noun).

innate (adjective) inborn, native. *Not everyone who takes piano lessons becomes a fine musician, which shows that music requires innate talent as well as training.*

innocuous (adjective) harmless, inoffensive. *I was surprised that Melissa took offense at such an innocuous joke.*

inoculate (verb) to prevent a disease by infusing with a disease-causing organism. *Pasteur found he could prevent rabies by inoculating patients with the virus that causes the disease.* **inoculation** (noun).

insipid (adjective) flavorless, uninteresting. *Some TV shows are so insipid that you can watch them while reading without missing a thing.* **insipidity** (noun).

insolence (noun) an attitude or behavior that is bold and disrespectful. *Some feel that news reporters who shout questions at the president are behaving with insolence.* **insolent** (adjective).

insular (adjective) narrow or isolated in attitude or viewpoint. *Americans are famous for their insular attitudes; they seem to think that nothing important has ever happened outside of their country.* **insularity** (noun).

insurgency (noun) uprising, rebellion. *The angry townspeople had begun an insurgency bordering on downright revolution; they were collecting arms, holding secret meetings, and refusing to pay certain taxes.* **insurgent** (adjective).

integrity (noun) honesty, uprightness; soundness, completeness. *"Honest Abe" Lincoln is considered a model of political integrity. Inspectors examined the building's support beams and foundation and found no reason to doubt its structural integrity.*

interlocutor (noun) someone taking part in a dialogue or conversation. *Annoyed by the constant questions from someone in the crowd, the speaker challenged his interlocutor to offer a better plan.* **interlocutory** (adjective).

interlude (noun) an interrupting period or performance. *The two most dramatic scenes in* King Lear *are separated, strangely, by a comic interlude starring the king's jester.*

interminable (adjective) endless or seemingly endless. *Addressing the United Nations, Castro announced, "We will be brief"—then delivered an interminable 4-hour speech.*

intransigent (adjective) unwilling to compromise. *Despite the mediator's attempts to suggest a fair solution, the two parties were intransigent, forcing a showdown.* **intransigence** (noun).

intrepid (adjective) fearless and resolute. *Only an intrepid adventurer is willing to undertake the long and dangerous trip by sled to the South Pole.* **intrepidity** (noun).

intrusive (adjective) forcing a way in without being welcome. *The legal requirement of a search warrant is supposed to protect Americans from intrusive searches by the police.* **intrude** (verb), **intrusion** (noun).

intuitive (adjective) known directly, without apparent thought or effort. *An experienced chess player sometimes has an intuitive sense of the best move to make, even if she can't explain it.* **intuit** (verb), **intuition** (noun).

inundate (verb) to flood; to overwhelm. *As soon as the playoff tickets went on sale, eager fans inundated the box office with orders.*

invariable (adjective) unchanging, constant. *When writing a book, it was her invariable habit to rise at 6 a.m. and work at her desk from 7 to 12.* **invariability** (noun).

inversion (noun) a turning backwards, inside-out, or upside-down; a reversal. *Latin poetry often features inversion of word order; for example, the first line of Virgil's* Aeneid: *"Arms and the man I sing."* **invert** (verb), **inverted** (adjective).

inveterate (adjective) persistent, habitual. *It's very difficult for an inveterate gambler to give up the pastime.* **inveteracy** (noun).

invigorate (verb) to give energy to, to stimulate. *As her car climbed the mountain road, Lucinda felt invigorated by the clear air and the cool breezes.*

invincible (adjective) impossible to conquer or overcome. *For three years at the height of his career, boxer Mike Tyson seemed invincible.*

inviolable (adjective) impossible to attack or trespass upon. *In the president's remote hideaway at Camp David, guarded by the Secret Service, his privacy is, for once, inviolable.*

irrational (adjective) unreasonable. *Richard knew that his fear of insects was irrational, but he was unable to overcome it.* **irrationality** (noun).

irresolute (adjective) uncertain how to act, indecisive. *The line in the ice cream shop grew as the irresolute child wavered between her two favorite ice cream flavors before finally choosing one.* **irresolution** (noun).

J

jeopardize (verb) to put in danger. *Terrorist attacks jeopardize the fragile peace in the Middle East.* **jeopardy** (noun).

juxtapose (verb) to put side by side. *Juxtaposing the two editorials revealed the enormous differences in the writers' opinions.* **juxtaposition** (noun).

L

languid (adjective) without energy; slow, sluggish, listless. *The hot, humid weather of late August can make anyone feel languid.* **languish** (verb), **languor** (noun).

latent (adjective) not currently obvious or active; hidden. *Although he had committed only a single act of violence, the examining psychiatrist said it's likely he always had a latent tendency toward violence.* **latency** (noun).

laudatory (adjective) giving praise. *The ads for the movie are filled with laudatory comments from critics.*

lenient (adjective) mild, soothing, or forgiving. *The judge was known for his lenient disposition; he rarely imposed long jail sentences on criminals.* **leniency** (noun).

lethargic (adjective) lacking energy; sluggish. *Visitors to the zoo are surprised that the lions appear so lethargic, but, in the wild, lions sleep up to 18 hours a day.* **lethargy** (noun).

liability (noun) an obligation or debt; a weakness or drawback. *The insurance company had a liability of millions of dollars after the town was destroyed by a tornado. Slowness afoot is a serious liability in an aspiring basketball player.* **liable** (adjective).

lithe (adjective) flexible and graceful. *The ballet dancer was almost as lithe as a cat.*

longevity (noun) length of life; durability. *The reduction in early deaths from infectious diseases is responsible for most of the increase in human longevity over the past two centuries.*

lucid (adjective) clear and understandable. *Hawking's* A Short History of the Universe *is a lucid explanation of modern scientific theories about the origin of the universe.* **lucidity** (noun).

lurid (adjective) shocking, gruesome. *While the serial killer was on the loose, the newspapers were filled with lurid stories about his crimes.*

M

malediction (noun) curse. *In the fairy tale "Sleeping Beauty," the princess is trapped in a death-like sleep because of the malediction uttered by an angry witch.*

malevolence (noun) hatred, ill will. *Critics say that Iago, the villain in Shakespeare's* Othello, *seems to exhibit malevolence with no real cause.* **malevolent** (adjective).

malinger (verb) to pretend incapacity or illness to avoid a duty or work. *During the labor dispute, hundreds of employees malingered, forcing the company to slow production and costing it millions in profits.*

malleable (adjective) able to be changed, shaped, or formed by outside pressures. *Gold is a very useful metal because it is so malleable.* **malleability** (noun).

mandate (noun) order, command. *The new policy of using only organic produce in the restaurant went into effect as soon as the manager issued his mandate about it.* **mandate** (verb), **mandatory** (adjective).

maturation (noun) the process of becoming fully grown or developed. *Free markets in the former communist nations are likely to operate smoothly only after a long period of maturation.* **mature** (adjective and verb), **maturity** (noun).

mediate (verb) to act to reconcile differences between two parties. *During the baseball strike, both the players and the club owners* *were willing to have the president mediate the dispute.* **mediation** (noun).

mediocrity (noun) the state of being middling or poor in quality. *The New York Mets finished in ninth place in 1968 but won the world's championship in 1969, going from horrible to great in a single year and skipping mediocrity.* **mediocre** (adjective).

mercurial (adjective) changing quickly and unpredictably. *The mercurial personality of Robin Williams, with his many voices and styles, made him perfect for the role of the ever-changing genie in* Aladdin.

meticulous (adjective) very careful with details. *Repairing watches calls for a craftsperson who is patient and meticulous.*

mimicry (noun) imitation, aping. *The continued popularity of Elvis Presley has given rise to a class of entertainers who make a living through mimicry of "The King."* **mimic** (noun and verb).

misconception (noun) a mistaken idea. *Columbus sailed west with the misconception that he would reach the shores of Asia.* **misconceive** (verb).

mitigate (verb) to make less severe; to relieve. *Wallace certainly committed the assault, but the verbal abuse he'd received helps to explain his behavior and somewhat mitigates his guilt.* **mitigation** (noun).

modicum (noun) a small amount. *The plan for your new business is well designed; with a modicum of luck, you should be successful.*

mollify (verb) to soothe or calm; to appease. *Samantha tried to mollify the angry customer by promising him a full refund.*

morose (adjective) gloomy, sullen. *After Chuck's girlfriend dumped him, he lay around the house for a couple of days, feeling morose.*

mundane (adjective) everyday, ordinary, commonplace. *Moviegoers in the 1930s liked the glamorous films of Fred Astaire because they provided an escape from the mundane problems of life during the Great Depression.*

munificent (adjective) very generous; lavish. *Ted Turner's billion-dollar donation to the United Nations was one of the most munificent acts of charity in history.* **munificence** (noun).

mutable (adjective) likely to change. *A politician's reputation can be highly mutable, as seen in the case of Harry Truman—mocked during his lifetime, revered afterward.*

N

narcissistic (adjective) showing excessive love for oneself; egoistic. *Andre's room, decorated with photos of himself and the sports trophies he has won, suggests a narcissistic personality.* **narcissism** (noun).

nocturnal (adjective) of the night; active at night. *Travelers on the Underground Railroad escaped from slavery to the North by a series of nocturnal flights. The eyes of nocturnal animals must be sensitive in dim light.*

nonchalant (adjective) appearing to be unconcerned. *Unlike the other players on the football team who pumped their fists when their names were announced, John ran on the field with a nonchalant wave.* **nonchalance** (noun).

nondescript (adjective) without distinctive qualities; drab. *The bank robber's clothes were nondescript; none of the witnesses could remember their color or style.*

notorious (adjective) famous, especially for evil actions or qualities. *Warner Brothers produced a series of movies about notorious gangsters such as John Dillinger and Al Capone.* **notoriety** (noun).

novice (noun) beginner. *Lifting your head before you finish your swing is a typical mistake committed by the novice at golf.*

nuance (noun) a subtle difference or quality. *At first glance, Monet's paintings of water lilies all look much alike, but the more you study them,* *the more you appreciate the nuances of color and shading that distinguish them.*

nurture (verb) to nourish or help to grow. *The money given by the National Endowment for the Arts helps nurture local arts organizations throughout the country.* **nurture** (noun).

O

obdurate (adjective) unwilling to change; stubborn, inflexible. *Despite the many pleas he received, the governor was obdurate in his refusal to grant clemency to the convicted murderer.*

objective (adjective) dealing with observable facts rather than opinions, interpretations, or emotions. *When a legal case involves a shocking crime, it may be hard for a judge to remain objective in his rulings.*

oblivious (adjective) unaware, unconscious. *Karen practiced her oboe with complete concentration, oblivious to the noise and activity around her.* **oblivion** (noun), **obliviousness** (noun).

obscure (adjective) little known; hard to understand. *Mendel was an obscure monk until decades after his death when his scientific work was finally discovered. Most people find the writings of James Joyce obscure; hence the popularity of books that explain his books.* **obscure** (verb), **obscurity** (noun).

obsessive (adjective) haunted or preoccupied by an idea or feeling. *His concern with cleanliness became so obsessive that he washed his hands 20 times every day.* **obsess** (verb), **obsession** (noun).

obsolete (adjective) no longer current; old-fashioned. *W. H. Auden said that his ideal landscape would include water wheels, wooden grain mills, and other forms of obsolete machinery.* **obsolescence** (noun).

obstinate (adjective) stubborn, unyielding. *Despite years of effort, the problem of drug abuse remains obstinate.* **obstinacy** (noun).

obtrusive (adjective) overly prominent. *Philip should sing more softly; his bass is so obtrusive that the other singers can barely be heard.* **obtrude** (verb), **obtrusion** (noun).

ominous (adjective) foretelling evil. *Ominous black clouds gathered on the horizon, for a violent storm was fast approaching.* **omen** (noun).

onerous (adjective) heavy, burdensome. *The hero Hercules was ordered to clean the Augean Stables, one of several onerous tasks known as "the labors of Hercules."* **onus** (noun).

opportunistic (adjective) eagerly seizing chances as they arise. *When Princess Diana died suddenly, opportunistic publishers quickly released books about her life and death.* **opportunism** (noun).

opulent (adjective) rich, lavish. *The mansion of newspaper tycoon Hearst is famous for its opulent decor.* **opulence** (noun).

ornate (adjective) highly decorated, elaborate. *Baroque architecture is often highly ornate, featuring surfaces covered with carving, sinuous curves, and painted scenes.*

ostentatious (adjective) overly showy, pretentious. *To show off his wealth, the millionaire threw an ostentatious party featuring a full orchestra, a famous singer, and tens of thousands of dollars' worth of food.*

ostracize (verb) to exclude from a group. *In Biblical times, those who suffered from the disease of leprosy were ostracized and forced to live alone.* **ostracism** (noun).

P

pallid (adjective) pale; dull. *Working all day in the coal mine had given him a pallid complexion. The new musical offers only pallid entertainment: the music is lifeless, the acting dull, the story absurd.*

parched (adjective) very dry; thirsty. *After two months without rain, the crops were shriveled and parched by the sun.* **parch** (verb).

pariah (noun) outcast. *Accused of robbery, he became a pariah; his neighbors stopped talking to him, and people he'd considered friends no longer called.*

partisan (adjective) reflecting strong allegiance to a particular party or cause. *The vote on the president's budget was strictly partisan: every member of the president's party voted yes, and all others voted no.* **partisan** (noun).

pathology (noun) disease or the study of disease; extreme abnormality. *Some people believe that high rates of crime are symptoms of an underlying social pathology.* **pathological** (adjective).

pellucid (adjective) very clear; transparent; easy to understand. *The water in the mountain stream was cold and pellucid. Thanks to the professor's pellucid explanation, I finally understand relativity theory.*

penitent (adjective) feeling sorry for past crimes or sins. *Having grown penitent, he wrote a long letter of apology, asking forgiveness.*

penurious (adjective) extremely frugal; stingy. *Haunted by memories of poverty, he lived in penurious fashion, driving an old car and wearing only the cheapest clothes.* **penury** (noun).

perceptive (adjective) quick to notice, observant. *With his perceptive intelligence, Holmes was the first to notice the importance of this clue.* **perceptible** (adjective), **perception** (noun).

perfidious (adjective) disloyal, treacherous. *Although he was one of the most talented generals of the American Revolution, Benedict Arnold is remembered today as a perfidious betrayer of his country.* **perfidy** (noun).

perfunctory (adjective) unenthusiastic, routine, or mechanical. *When the play opened, the actors sparkled, but by the thousandth night their performance had become perfunctory.*

permeate (verb) to spread through or penetrate. *Little by little, the smell of gas from the broken pipe permeated the house.*

persevere (adjective) to continue despite difficulties. *Although several of her teammates dropped out of the marathon, Gail persevered.* **perseverance** (noun).

perspicacity (noun) keenness of observation or understanding. *Journalist Murray Kempton was famous for the perspicacity of his comments on social and political issues.* **perspicacious** (adjective).

peruse (verb) to examine or study. *Caroline perused the contract carefully before she signed it.* **perusal** (noun).

pervasive (adjective) spreading throughout. *As news of the disaster reached the town, a pervasive sense of gloom could be felt.* **pervade** (verb).

phlegmatic (adjective) sluggish and unemotional in temperament. *It was surprising to see Tom, who is normally so phlegmatic, acting excited.*

placate (verb) to soothe or appease. *The waiter tried to placate the angry customer with the offer of a free dessert.* **placatory** (adjective).

plastic (adjective) able to be molded or reshaped. *Because it is highly plastic, clay is an easy material for beginning sculptors to use.*

plausible (adjective) apparently believable. *According to the judge, the defense attorney's argument was both powerful and plausible.* **plausibility** (noun).

polarize (verb) to separate into opposing groups or forces. *For years, the abortion debate has polarized the American people, with many people voicing extreme views and few trying to find a middle ground.* **polarization** (noun).

portend (verb) to indicate a future event; to forebode. *According to folklore, a red sky at dawn portends a day of stormy weather.*

potentate (noun) a powerful ruler. *The Tsar of Russia was one of the last hereditary potentates of Europe.*

pragmatism (noun) a belief in approaching problems through practical rather than theoretical means. *Roosevelt's approach to the Great Depression was based on pragmatism: "Try something," he said. "If it doesn't work, try something else."* **pragmatic** (adjective).

preamble (noun) an introductory statement. *The preamble to the Constitution begins with the famous words, "We the people of the United States of America..."*

precocious (adjective) mature at an unusually early age. *Picasso was so precocious as an artist that, at nine, he is said to have painted far better pictures than his teacher.* **precocity** (noun).

predatory (adjective) living by killing and eating other animals; exploiting others for personal gain. *The tiger is the largest predatory animal native to Asia. Microsoft has been accused of predatory business practices that prevent other software companies from competing with it.* **predation** (noun), **predator** (noun).

predilection (noun) a liking or preference. *To relax from his presidential duties, Kennedy had a predilection for spy novels featuring James Bond.*

predominant (adjective) greatest in numbers or influence. *Although hundreds of religions are practiced in India, the predominant faith is Hinduism.* **predominance** (noun), **predominate** (verb).

prepossessing (adjective) attractive. *Smart, lovely, and talented, she has all the prepossessing qualities that mark a potential movie star.*

presumptuous (adjective) going beyond the limits of courtesy or appropriateness. *The senator winced when the presumptuous young staffer addressed him as "Chuck."* **presume** (verb), **presumption** (noun).

pretentious (adjective) claiming excessive value or importance. *For a shoe salesman to call himself a "Personal Foot Apparel Consultant" seems awfully pretentious.* **pretension** (noun).

procrastinate (verb) to put off, to delay. *If you habitually procrastinate, try this technique: never touch a piece of paper without either filing it, responding to it, or throwing it out.* **procrastination** (noun).

profane (adjective) impure, unholy. *It is inappropriate and rude to use profane language in a church.* **profane** (verb), **profanity** (noun).

proficient (adjective) skillful, adept. *A proficient artist, Louise quickly and accurately sketched the scene.* **proficiency** (noun).

proliferate (verb) to increase or multiply. *Over the past 25 years, high-tech companies have proliferated in northern California, Massachusetts, and Seattle.* **proliferation** (noun).

prolific (adjective) producing many offspring or creations. *With more than 300 books to his credit, Isaac Asimov was one of the most prolific writers of all time.*

prominence (noun) the quality of standing out; fame. *Barack Obama rose to political prominence after his keynote address to the 2004 Democratic National Convention.* **prominent** (adjective).

promulgate (verb) to make public, to declare. *Lincoln signed the proclamation that freed the slaves in 1862, but he waited several months to promulgate it.*

propagate (verb) to cause to grow; to foster. *John Smithson's will left his fortune for the founding of an institution to propagate knowledge, without saying whether that meant a university, a library, or a museum.* **propagation** (noun).

propriety (noun) appropriateness. *The principal questioned the propriety of the discussion the teacher had with her students about another instructor's gambling addiction.*

prosaic (adjective) everyday, ordinary, dull. *"Paul's Case" tells the story of a boy who longs to escape from the prosaic life of a clerk into a world of wealth, glamour, and beauty.*

protagonist (noun) the main character in a story or play; the main supporter of an idea. *Leopold Bloom is the protagonist of James Joyce's great novel* Ulysses.

provocative (adjective) likely to stimulate emotions, ideas, or controversy. *The demonstrators began chanting obscenities, a provocative act that they hoped would cause the police to lose control.* **provoke** (verb), **provocation** (noun).

proximity (noun) closeness, nearness. *Neighborhood residents were angry over the proximity of the sewage plant to the local school.* **proximate** (adjective).

prudent (adjective) wise, cautious, and practical. *A prudent investor will avoid putting all of her money into any single investment.* **prudence** (noun), **prudential** (adjective).

pugnacious (adjective) combative, bellicose, truculent; ready to fight. *The slugger, a pugnacious outfielder for the Detroit Tigers, got into more than his fair share of brawls, both on and off the field.* **pugnacity** (noun).

punctilious (adjective) very concerned about proper forms of behavior and manners. *A punctilious dresser like James would rather skip the party altogether than wear the wrong color tie.* **punctilio** (noun).

pundit (noun) someone who offers opinions in an authoritative style. *The Sunday morning talk shows are filled with pundits, each with his or her own theory about the week's political news.*

punitive (adjective) inflicting punishment. *The jury awarded the plaintiff one million dollars in punitive damages, hoping to teach the defendant a lesson.*

purify (verb) to make pure, clean, or perfect. *The new plant is supposed to purify the drinking water provided to everyone in the nearby towns.* **purification** (noun).

Q

quell (verb) to quiet, to suppress. *It took a huge number of police officers to quell the rioting.*

querulous (adjective) complaining, whining. *The nursing home attendant needed a lot of patience to care for the three querulous, unpleasant residents on his floor.*

R

rancorous (adjective) expressing bitter hostility. *Many Americans are disgusted by recent political campaigns, which seem more rancorous than ever before.* **rancor** (noun).

rationale (noun) an underlying reason or explanation. *Looking at the sad faces of his employees, it was hard for the company president to explain the rationale for closing the business.*

raze (verb) to completely destroy; demolish. *The old Coliseum building will soon be razed to make room for a new hotel.*

reciprocate (verb) to give and take mutually. *If you'll watch my children tonight, I'll reciprocate by taking care of yours tomorrow.* **reciprocity** (noun).

reclusive (adjective) withdrawn from society. *During the last years of her life, actress Greta Garbo led a reclusive existence, rarely appearing in public.* **recluse** (noun).

reconcile (verb) to make consistent or harmonious. *FDR's greatness as a leader can be seen in his ability to reconcile the demands and values of the varied groups that supported him.* **reconciliation** (noun).

recrimination (noun) a retaliatory accusation. *After the governor called his opponent unethical, his opponent angrily replied with recriminations that the governor was a hypocrite.* **recriminate** (verb), **recriminatory** (adjective).

recuperate (verb) to regain health after an illness. *Although Marie left the hospital two days after her operation, it took her a few weeks to fully recuperate.* **recuperation** (noun), **recuperative** (adjective).

redoubtable (adjective) inspiring respect, awe, or fear. *Johnson's knowledge, experience, and personal clout made him a redoubtable political opponent.*

refurbish (verb) to fix up; renovate. *It took three days' work by a team of carpenters, painters, and decorators to completely refurbish the apartment.*

refute (verb) to prove false. *The company invited reporters to visit their plant in an effort to refute the charges of unsafe working conditions.* **refutation** (noun).

relevance (noun) connection to the matter at hand; pertinence. *Testimony in a criminal trial may be admitted only if it has clear relevance to the question of guilt or innocence.* **relevant** (adjective).

remedial (adjective) serving to remedy, cure, or correct some condition. *Affirmative action can be justified as a remedial step to help minority members overcome the effects of past discrimination.* **remediation** (noun), **remedy** (verb).

remorse (noun) a painful sense of guilt over wrongdoing. *In Poe's story* The Tell-Tale Heart, *a murderer is driven insane by remorse over his crime.* **remorseful** (adjective).

remuneration (noun) pay. *In a civil lawsuit, the attorney often receives part of the financial settlement as his or her remuneration.* **remunerate** (verb), **remunerative** (adjective).

renovate (verb) to renew by repairing or rebuilding. *The television program* This Old House *shows how skilled craftspeople renovate houses.* **renovation** (noun).

renunciation (noun) the act of rejecting or refusing something. *King Edward VII's renunciation of the British throne was caused by his desire to marry an American divorcee, something he couldn't do as king.* **renounce** (verb).

replete (adjective) filled abundantly. *Graham's book is replete with wonderful stories about the famous people she has known.*

reprehensible (adjective) deserving criticism or censure. *Although Pete Rose's misdeeds were reprehensible, not all fans agree that he deserves to be excluded from the Baseball Hall of Fame.* **reprehend** (verb), **reprehension** (noun).

repudiate (verb) to reject, to renounce. *After it became known that Duke had been a leader of the Ku Klux Klan, most Republican leaders repudiated him.* **repudiation** (noun).

reputable (adjective) having a good reputation; respected. *Find a reputable auto mechanic by asking your friends for recommendations based on their own experiences.* **reputation** (noun), **repute** (noun).

resilient (adjective) able to recover from difficulty. *A professional athlete must be resilient, able to lose a game one day and come back the next with confidence and enthusiasm.* **resilience** (noun).

resplendent (adjective) glowing, shining. *In late December, midtown New York is resplendent with holiday lights and decorations.* **resplendence** (noun).

responsive (adjective) reacting quickly and appropriately. *The new director of the Internal Revenue Service has promised to make the agency more responsive to public complaints.* **respond** (verb), **response** (noun).

restitution (noun) return of something to its original owner; repayment. *Some Native American leaders are demanding that the U.S. government make restitution for the lands taken from them.*

revere (verb) to admire deeply, to honor. *Millions of people around the world revered Mother Teresa for her saintly generosity.* **reverence** (noun), **reverent** (adjective).

rhapsodize (verb) to praise in a wildly emotional way. *That critic is such a huge fan of Toni Morrison that she will surely rhapsodize over the writer's next novel.* **rhapsodic** (adjective).

S

sagacious (adjective) discerning, wise. *Only a leader as sagacious as Nelson Mandela could have united South Africa so successfully and peacefully.* **sagacity** (noun).

salvage (verb) to save from wreck or ruin. *After the hurricane destroyed her home, she was able to salvage only a few of her belongings.* **salvage** (noun), **salvageable** (adjective).

sanctimonious (adjective) showing false or excessive piety. *The sanctimonious prayers of the TV preacher were interspersed with requests that the viewers send him money.* **sanctimony** (noun).

scapegoat (noun) someone who bears the blame for others' acts; someone hated for no apparent reason. *Although Buckner's error was only one reason the Red Sox lost, many fans made him the scapegoat, booing him mercilessly.*

scrupulous (adjective) acting with extreme care; painstaking. *Disney theme parks are famous for their scrupulous attention to small details.* **scruple** (noun).

scrutinize (verb) to study closely. *The lawyer scrutinized the contract, searching for any sentence that could pose a risk for her client.* **scrutiny** (noun).

secrete (verb) to emit; to hide. *Glands in the mouth secrete saliva, a liquid that helps in digestion. The jewel thieves secreted the necklace in a tin box buried underground.*

sedentary (adjective) requiring much sitting. *When Officer Samson was given a desk job, she had trouble getting used to sedentary work after years on the street.*

sequential (adjective) arranged in an order or series. *The courses for the chemistry major are sequential; you must take them in order, since each course builds on the previous ones.* **sequence** (noun).

serendipity (noun) the act of lucky, accidental discoveries. *Great inventions sometimes come about through deliberate research and hard work, sometimes through pure serendipity.* **serendipitous** (adjective).

servile (adjective) like a slave or servant; submissive. *The tycoon demanded that his underlings behave in a servile manner, agreeing quickly with everything he said.* **servility** (noun).

simulated (adjective) imitating something else; artificial. *High-quality simulated gems must be examined under a magnifying glass to be distinguished from real ones.* **simulate** (verb), **simulation** (noun).

solace (verb) to comfort or console. *There was little the rabbi could say to solace the husband after his wife's death.* **solace** (noun).

spontaneous (adjective) happening without plan. *When the news of Kennedy's assassination broke, people everywhere gathered in a spontaneous effort to share their shock and grief.* **spontaneity** (noun).

spurious (adjective) false, fake. *The so-called Piltdown Man, supposed to be the fossil of a primitive human, turned out to be spurious, although who created the hoax is still uncertain.*

squander (verb) to use up carelessly, to waste. *Those who had made donations to the charity were outraged to learn that its director had squandered millions on fancy dinners and first-class travel.*

stagnate (verb) to become stale through lack of movement or change. *Having had no contact with the outside world for generations, Japan's culture gradually stagnated.* **stagnant** (adjective), **stagnation** (noun).

staid (adjective) sedate, serious, and grave. *This college is definitely not a "party school"; the students all work hard, and the campus has a reputation for being staid.*

stimulus (noun) something that excites a response or provokes an action. *The arrival of merchants and missionaries from the West provided a stimulus for change in Japanese society.* **stimulate** (verb).

stoic (adjective) showing little feeling, even in response to pain or sorrow. *A soldier must respond to the death of his comrades in stoic fashion, since the fighting will not stop for his grief.* **stoicism** (noun).

strenuous (adjective) requiring energy and strength. *Hiking in the foothills of the Rockies is fairly easy, but climbing the higher peaks can be strenuous.*

submissive (adjective) accepting the will of others; humble, compliant. *At the end of Ibsen's play* A Doll's House, *Nora leaves her husband and abandons the role of submissive housewife.*

substantiate (verb) verify or support by evidence. *The charge that Nixon had helped to cover up crimes was substantiated by his comments about it on a series of audio tapes.* **substantiated** (adjective), **substantiation** (noun).

sully (verb) to soil, stain, or defile. *Nixon's misdeeds as president did much to sully the reputation of the American government.*

superficial (adjective) on the surface only; without depth or substance. *Her wound was superficial and required only a light bandage. His superficial attractiveness hides the fact that his personality is lifeless and his mind is dull.* **superficiality** (noun).

superfluous (adjective) more than is needed, excessive. *Once you've won the debate, don't keep talking; superfluous arguments will only bore and annoy the audience.*

suppress (verb) to put down or restrain. *As soon as the unrest began, thousands of helmeted police were sent into the streets to suppress the riots.* **suppression** (noun).

surfeit (noun) an excess. *Most American families have a surfeit of food and drink on Thanksgiving Day.* **surfeit** (verb).

surreptitious (adjective) done in secret. *Because Iraq avoided weapons inspections, many believed it had a surreptitious weapons development program.*

surrogate (noun) a substitute. *When the congressman died in office, his wife was named to serve the rest of his term as a surrogate.* **surrogate** (adjective).

sustain (verb) to keep up, to continue; to support. *Because of fatigue, he was unable to sustain the effort needed to finish the marathon.*

T

tactile (adjective) relating to the sense of touch. *The thick brush strokes and gobs of color give the paintings of van Gogh a strongly tactile quality.* **tactility** (noun).

talisman (noun) an object supposed to have magical effects or qualities. *Superstitious people sometimes carry a rabbit's foot, a lucky coin, or some other talisman.*

tangential (adjective) touching lightly; only slightly connected or related. *Having enrolled in a class on African-American history, the students found the teacher's stories about his travels in South America of only tangential interest.* **tangent** (noun).

tedium (noun) boredom. *For most people, watching the Weather Channel for 24 hours would be sheer tedium.* **tedious** (adjective).

temerity (noun) boldness, rashness, excessive daring. *Only someone who didn't understand the danger would have the temerity to try to climb Everest without a guide.* **temerarious** (adjective).

temperance (noun) moderation or restraint in feelings and behavior. *Most professional athletes practice temperance in their personal habits; too much eating or drinking, they know, can harm their performance.* **temperate** (adjective).

tenacious (adjective) clinging, sticky, or persistent. *Tenacious in pursuit of her goal, she applied for the grant unsuccessfully four times before it was finally approved.* **tenacity** (noun).

tentative (adjective) subject to change; uncertain. *A firm schedule has not been established, but the 2020 Super Bowl has been given the tentative date of February 3.*

terminate (verb) to end, to close. *The Olympic Games terminate with a grand ceremony attended by athletes from every participating country.* **terminal** (noun), **termination** (noun).

terrestrial (adjective) of the earth. *The movie* Close Encounters of the Third Kind *tells the story of the first contact between beings from outer space and terrestrial humans.*

therapeutic (adjective) curing or helping to cure. *Hot-water spas were popular in the nineteenth century among the sickly, who believed that soaking in the water had therapeutic effects.* **therapy** (noun).

timorous (adjective) fearful, timid. *The cowardly lion approached the throne of the wizard with a timorous look on his face.*

toady (noun) someone who flatters a superior in hopes of gaining favor; a sycophant. *"I can't stand a toady!" declared the movie mogul. "Give me someone who'll tell me the truth—even if it costs him his job!"* **toady** (verb).

tolerant (adjective) accepting, enduring. *San Franciscans have a tolerant attitude about lifestyles: "Live and let live" seems to be their motto.* **tolerate** (verb), **toleration** (noun).

toxin (noun) poison. *DDT is a powerful toxin once used to kill insects but now banned in the United States because of the risk it poses to human life.* **toxic** (adjective).

tranquility (noun) freedom from disturbance or turmoil; calm. *She moved from New York City to rural Vermont seeking the tranquility of country life.* **tranquil** (adjective).

transgress (verb) to go past limits; to violate. *No one could fathom why the honor student transgressed by shoplifting hundreds of dollars in merchandise from his favorite clothing store.* **transgression** (noun).

transient (adjective) passing quickly. *Long-term visitors to this hotel pay a different rate than transient guests who stay for just a day or two.* **transience** (noun).

transitory (adjective) quickly passing. *Public moods tend to be transitory; people may be anxious and angry one month but relatively content and optimistic the next.* **transition** (noun).

translucent (adjective) letting some light pass through. *Panels of translucent glass let daylight into the room while maintaining privacy.*

transmute (verb) to change in form or substance. *In the Middle Ages, the alchemists tried to discover ways to transmute metals such as iron into gold.* **transmutation** (noun).

treacherous (adjective) untrustworthy or disloyal; dangerous or unreliable. *Nazi Germany proved to be a treacherous ally, first signing a peace pact with the Soviet Union, then invading. Be careful crossing the rope bridge; parts are badly frayed and treacherous.* **treachery** (noun).

tremulous (adjective) trembling or shaking; timid or fearful. *Never having spoken in public before, he began his speech in a tremulous, hesitant voice.*

trite (adjective) boring because of over-familiarity; hackneyed. *Her letters were filled with trite expressions, like "All's well that ends well" and "So far so good."*

truculent (adjective) aggressive, hostile, belligerent. *Hitler's truculent behavior in demanding more territory for Germany made it clear that war was inevitable.* **truculence** (noun).

truncate (verb) to cut off. *The poor copying job truncated the playwright's manuscript: the last page ended in the middle of a scene, halfway through the first act.*

turbulent (adjective) agitated or disturbed. *The night before the championship match, Serena Williams was unable to sleep, her mind turbulent with fears and hopes.* **turbulence** (noun).

U

unheralded (adjective) little known, unexpected. *In a year of big-budget, much-hyped, mega-movies, this unheralded foreign film has surprised everyone with its popularity.*

unpalatable (adjective) distasteful, unpleasant. *Although I agree with the candidate on many issues, I can't vote for her because I find her position on capital punishment unpalatable.*

unparalleled (adjective) with no equal; unique. *His victory in the golf tournament by a full 12 strokes was an unparalleled accomplishment.*

unstinting (adjective) giving freely and generously. *Eleanor Roosevelt was much admired for her unstinting efforts on behalf of the poor.*

untenable (adjective) impossible to defend. *The theory that this painting is a genuine van Gogh became untenable when the artist who actually painted it came forth.*

untimely (adjective) out of the natural or proper time. *The untimely death of a youthful Princess Diana seemed far more tragic than Mother Teresa's death of old age.*

unyielding (adjective) firm, resolute, obdurate. *Despite criticism, Mario Cuomo was unyielding in his opposition to capital punishment; he vetoed several death penalty bills as governor.*

usurper (noun) someone who takes a place or possession without the right to do so. *Kennedy's most devoted followers tended to regard later presidents as usurpers, holding the office they felt he or his brothers should have held.* **usurp** (verb), **usurpation** (noun).

utilitarian (adjective) purely of practical benefit. *The design of the Model T car was simple and utilitarian, lacking the luxuries found in later models.*

utopia (noun) an imaginary, perfect society. *Those who founded the Oneida community dreamed that it could be a kind of utopia—a prosperous state with complete freedom and harmony.* **utopian** (adjective).

V

validate (verb) to officially approve or confirm. *The election of the president is validated when the members of the Electoral College meet to confirm the choice of the voters.* **valid** (adjective), **validity** (noun).

variegated (adjective) spotted with different colors. *The brilliant, variegated appearance of butterflies makes them popular among collectors.* **variegation** (noun).

venerate (verb) to admire or honor. *In Communist China, Chairman Mao Zedong was venerated as an almost god-like figure.* **venerable** (adjective), **veneration** (noun).

verdant (adjective) green with plant life. *Southern England is famous for its verdant countryside filled with gardens and small farms.* **verdancy** (noun).

vestige (noun) a trace or remainder. *Today's tiny Sherwood Forest is the last vestige of a woodland that once covered most of England.* **vestigial** (adjective).

vex (verb) to irritate, annoy, or trouble. *It vexes me that she never helps with any chores around the house.* **vexation** (noun).

vicarious (adjective) experienced through someone else's actions by way of the imagination. *Great literature broadens our minds by giving us vicarious participation in the lives of other people.*

vindicate (verb) to confirm, justify, or defend. *Lincoln's Gettysburg Address was intended to vindicate the objectives of the Union in the Civil War.*

virtuoso (noun) someone very skilled, especially in an art. *Vladimir Horowitz was one of the great piano virtuosos of the twentieth century.* **virtuosity** (noun).

vivacious (adjective) lively, sprightly. *The role of Maria in* The Sound of Music *is usually played by a charming, vivacious young actress.* **vivacity** (noun).

volatile (adjective) quickly changing; fleeting, transitory; prone to violence. *Public opinion is notoriously volatile; a politician who is very popular one month may be voted out of office the next.* **volatility** (noun).

W

whimsical (adjective) based on a capricious, carefree, or sudden impulse or idea; fanciful, playful. *Dave Barry's* Book of Bad Songs *is filled with the kind of goofy jokes that are typical of his whimsical sense of humor.* **whim** (noun).

Z

zealous (adjective) filled with eagerness, fervor, or passion. *A crowd of the candidate's most zealous supporters greeted her at the airport with banners, signs, and a marching band.* **zeal** (noun), **zealot** (noun), **zealotry** (noun).

Mathematics Formula Sheet

Appendix B

The GED Mathematical Reasoning Test contains a formula sheet, which displays formulas relating to geometric measurement and certain algebra concepts. Formulas are provided to test takers so that they may focus on *application*, rather than the *memorization*, of formulas.

Mathematics Formula Sheet

The GED Mathematical Reasoning Test contains a formula sheet, which displays formulas relating to geometric measurement and certain algebra concepts. Formulas are provided to test takers so that they may focus on *application*, rather than the *memorization*, of formulas.

Area of a:		
parallelogram	$A = bh$	
trapezoid	$A = \frac{1}{2}h(b_1 + b_2)$	
Surface Area and Volume of a:		
rectangular/right prism	$SA = ph + 2B$	$V = Bh$
cylinder	$SA = 2\pi rh + 2\pi r^2$	$V = \pi r^2 h$
pyramid	$SA = \frac{1}{2}ps + B$	$V = \frac{1}{3}Bh$
cone	$SA = \pi rs + \pi r^2$	$V = \frac{1}{3}\pi r^2 h$
sphere	$SA = 4\pi r^2$	$V = \frac{4}{3}\pi r^3$
	(p = perimeter of base B; $\pi \approx 3.14$)	
Algebra		
slope of a line	$m = \frac{y_2 - y_1}{x_2 - x_1}$	
slope-intercept form of the equation of a line	$y = mx + \text{b}$	
point-slope form of the equation of a line	$y - y_1 = m(x - x_1)$	
standard form of a quadratic equation	$y = ax^2 + bx + c$	
quadratic formula	$x = \frac{-b \pm \sqrt{b^2 - 4ac}}{2a}$	
Pythagorean theorem	$a^2 + b^2 = c^2$	
simple interest	$I = prt$	
	(I = interest, p = principal, r = rate, t = time)	

NOTES

NOTES

NOTES

NOTES

NOTES

NOTES

NOTES

NOTES

NOTES

NOTES

NOTES

NOTES